CHORAL REPERTOIRE

CHORAL REPERTOIRE

DENNIS SHROCK

OXFORD

UNIVERSITY PRESS

2009

OXFORD
UNIVERSITY PRESS

Oxford University Press, Inc., publishes works that further
Oxford University's objective of excellence
in research, scholarship, and education.

Oxford   New York
Auckland   Cape Town   Dar es Salaam   Hong Kong   Karachi
Kuala Lumpur   Madrid   Melbourne   Mexico City   Nairobi
New Delhi   Shanghai   Taipei   Toronto

With offices in
Argentina   Austria   Brazil   Chile   Czech Republic   France   Greece
Guatemala   Hungary   Italy   Japan   Poland   Portugal   Singapore
South Korea   Switzerland   Thailand   Turkey   Ukraine   Vietnam

Published by Oxford University Press, Inc.
198 Madison Avenue, New York, New York 10016

www.oup.com

Oxford is a registered trademark of Oxford University Press

Library of Congress Cataloging-in-Publication Data
Shrock, Dennis.
Choral repertoire / Dennis Shrock
p.   cm.
Includes index
ISBN 978-0-19-532778-6
1. Choruses—bibliography   I. Title
ML128.C48 S57 2009
782.5 22   2008014351

15

Printed in the United States of America
on acid-free paper

PREFACE

The purpose of this book is to present and discuss the choral music of the most significant composers from the Western Hemisphere throughout recorded history. The selection of composers has been determined by their impact on the development of choral music as an art form, and the selection of repertoire has been determined by the relative merit of compositions as reflected by critical acclaim, popularity and frequency of performance, and availability in academic and commercial publications. In other words, composers have been chosen on the basis of their historical significance, and compositions have been identified on the basis of their being acknowledged as artistically superior works of art, on their presence in programs of credited ensembles, and on their existence in scholarly editions. The selection process, therefore, has focused on representative composers and compositions, not on an unqualified and all-inclusive coverage of composers and their music. By being selective, it is hoped that masterpieces of Western choral music will be brought to light, comprehended, and performed more frequently, and that students, practitioners, and enthusiasts of choral music will be guided through the maze of a large and complex array of repertoire. As an aid in this process, composers and repertoire are presented according to their relative importance. The most prominent composers are given separate entries, with performance annotations of their most noteworthy compositions; the composers of lesser prominence are also given separate entries, but with discussion of their repertoire contained in narrative form; and composers of least prominence are discussed in the beginning material of appropriate countries. All composers discussed in the book are listed in the composers' index; the first page indication following a composer's name, generally in bold typeface, is the primary entry. The following pages are in regular typeface and indicate secondary references, with specific composer names in parentheses. Most lists of composers in the narrative introductions to eras and countries are in chronological order.

In the process of choosing composers and compositions, decisions have been made regarding the relative status of a composer as a producer of original compositions and the relative originality of those compositions. Composers whose choral output consists mostly of or who are known primarily for their arrangements of preexisting material (i.e., folk songs or spirituals) are generally excluded, as are the arranged compositions themselves. Arrangements are included, however, if they are a part of a composer's output of original repertoire or if they are substantially original in design. For instance, Renaissance masses that incorporate Gregorian chants or that parody previously composed motets are essentially original compositions, while harmonizations of folk songs and hymns are not.

The compositions that are discussed and annotated are considered choral if they were composed for an ensemble of voices—generally soprano, alto, tenor, and bass (SATB). This criterion includes music composed specifically for ensembles of solo voices as well as music composed for ensembles comprised of multiple singers per voice part. Reasoning for such an inclusive definition of choral music acknowledges and is based on performance practices in existence during the era of composition as well as in subsequent years. For example, madrigals and chansons that were composed during the Renaissance era, while conceived as solo vocal compositions, were frequently performed (with the approval of the composers) by multiple voices and instruments per part. Also, vocal chamber works of the nineteenth century (Brahms quartets, for example) have a long and continuous history of being performed by choral as well by solo ensembles. Indeed, madrigals, chansons, and other vocal chamber works have been and are on the whole performed more by choral ensembles than by soloists.

The material in the book is organized and presented in three categories—historical era, countries within the era, and composers within the country or group of countries. The eras are arranged consecutively in order of time, the countries are arranged according to their relative importance in initiating the era and influencing other countries, and the composers are listed chronologically according to their birthdates (either documented or assumed). Each era begins with a discussion of its time frame and scope and also with an overview of general stylistic traits, and each country or group of countries begins with a listing of representative composers, genres, and musical characteristics. Genres are identified according to broad categories of definition, structure, usage, and style. For instance, requiems are included as masses, passions are included as oratorios, and the various subcategories of motets (e.g., offertories, graduals, and antiphons) are all grouped together.

Composers have been placed in eras based on the overall or most salient characteristics of their choral music, their influence in history, and/or their traditional classification by scholars. These are particularly important considerations regarding transitional composers—those who lived and worked in times of change and who wrote music in both old and new styles. Thus Guillaume Dufay, Gilles de Bins Binchois, Jean de Ockeghem, and Antoine Busnois are classified as Renaissance composers because their most significant choral output exhibits traits that would become standard during the Renaissance era; Heinrich Schütz, who lived well into the Baroque era and who subscribed to *prima prattica* ideals throughout most of his life, and Claudio Monteverdi, whose early music is Renaissance in style, are both identified as Baroque because their mature and most recognized repertoire is infused with Baroque traits (in addition, Monteverdi was one of the chief proponents of the *seconda prattica*); Franz Schubert composed a considerable amount of music that scholars classify as Romantic in nature, although he is included with Classical era composers since his choral output (especially that which is sacred) is similar in most ways to other Classical era compositions; on the other hand, while Ludwig van Beethoven composed a considerable amount of music that scholars classify as Classical in nature, his most important choral works and his historical impact are Romantic.

Each composer entry includes the following information: a brief discussion of his or her life with regard to professional activity, especially that involving choral music; an accounting by genre of choral compositions; and a description of the individual genres, with commentary about specific compositions. As is mentioned above, the entries of major composers (those who have made the most significant impact on the development of choral music or who have composed the most significant repertoire) also include performance annotations of important works, listed either according to familiarity (i.e., with the most familiar, frequently performed, or highly acclaimed works listed first) or in chronological order according to the date of composition (therefore identifying the works relative to the composer's development).

The annotations include: (1) the original title, with subtitle, alternate titles, and textual source or translation (if critical to the understanding of the work); (2) opus or catalogue numbers as they exist or are helpful to the identification of the particular work; (3) date of composition if known; (4) specific scoring, including use of the term *chorus* for compositions intended for multiple singers per part and *voices* for compositions intended for single voices per part, the listing of vocal divisions beyond general distributions (e.g., SSAATTBB), and identification of orchestral instruments or requirements beyond those for standard or large orchestra; (5) approximate timings in minutes (rounded to quarter portions); and (6) commentary that elucidates aspects of performance. Regarding titles, works that are polytextual (i.e., works with two or more separate texts that occur simultaneously) are listed with a slash between the individual text sources (e.g., the medieval motet *Nuper rosarum flores / Terribilis est locus iste* by Guillaume Dufay). Works that are multimovement (i.e., works comprised of separate texts that occur successively) are listed with a dash between the individual text sources (e.g., the Renaissance motet *Tu es Petrus - Quodcumque ligaveris* by G. P. da Palestrina). Regarding sources, all Psalms are identified according to the modern listing. Regarding scoring, the requirements for soloists are listed as S for soprano or high mezzo-soprano, A for low mezzo-soprano or contralto, T for tenor, and B for baritone or bass. A slash between voice parts, either for solo voices (e.g., S/S) or choruses (e.g., SATB/SATB), indicates distribution of the voices or choruses in separate ensembles. The term *orchestra* implies scoring for double winds (two flutes, two oboes, two clarinets, and two bassoons), four horns, two trumpets, three trombones, timpani, and strings (violins in two sections, violas, cellos, and string basses). The term *large orchestra* implies scoring for triple winds, extra brass, and percussion instruments in addition to timpani. Scoring for instruments beyond these categories is generally indicated in parentheses.

Original spellings have been preserved as much as possible, and thus the reader will find variant versions of the same word. For example, the Latin word for *heaven* will appear variously as *celi, caeli,* and *coeli.* Original capitalizations of titles, both of compositions and of other publications, have also been preserved. However, references to works and certain words have been standardized. For instance, words referring to religious deities such as *he, father,* and *son* always appear in lower case. Also, archaic usage of words such as *thou* and *thy* have been avoided and changed to *you* and *your.* Consistent with modern usage, all abbreviations of the word *saint* appear without a period (i.e., the abbreviation is *St* instead of *St.*).

Definitions of most foreign terms as well as of genres and frequently cited musical words or phrases are found in the glossary and also occasionally in the text narrative. The definitions are only cursory and not meant to be a full explication of etymology, usage, development, or interpretation. Consequently, the reader may wish to refer to standard music dictionaries. Titles in foreign languages are translated in the text only as the translations provide meaningful elucidation to the substance of the composition. Standard Latin titles (e.g., *Ave Maria*) and Psalms (e.g., *Laudate Dominum*) are not translated. However, biblical references are provided for the Psalms.

It is hoped that this book will be of use to a wide and diverse readership, including the practicing choral conductor, teacher of choral conducting or choral literature courses, student of choral music, choral enthusiast, and choral scholar. It is further hoped that the encyclopedic organization of material as well as the nature of the material itself will accommodate the differing needs, interests, and experiences of readers. In accommodating those readers who will search for specific data as well as those who will peruse or study material more comprehensively, certain pieces of information are occasionally duplicated (e.g., titles and dates of compositions appear in both the discussion of works and annotations). However, duplication of information is minimal and thus the reader is encouraged to access both the narrative and annotated portions of material in order to be fully informed about a particular composer, subject, or work.

ACKNOWLEDGMENTS

I wish to express sincere and heartfelt thanks to the following people:

Barbara Reynolds, my dearest and most cherished friend, who faithfully and enthusiastically researched every source and reference, verified every spelling, made helpful suggestions regarding grammar and syntax, and read the entirety of every page of every draft for clarity and continuity. She was my teammate in the writing of the book, and her expertise, devotion, and positive spirit were more helpful to me than I can ever adequately express.

H. Scott Raab, canon musician at St Paul's Episcopal Cathedral in Oklahoma City, who was of considerable help with sacred repertoire and who aided me in the editorial process.

Vladimir Morosan, president of *Musica Russica,* who reviewed the Russian material and advised me on matters of comprehensiveness and accuracy.

D. Jason Bishop, director of choral activities at Penn State University–Erie campus, who assisted me with Latin translations.

My Santa Fe family Linda and Bob Ging, Rich DePippo and Doug Howe, and Dorothy Massey, who cared for me and kept me sane during my many months of solitary writing.

And my graduate students, who inspired me with their hunger for knowledge, spurred me on with their commitment to professional growth, and motivated me with their high expectations.

CONTENTS

CHORAL REPERTOIRE

1

THE MEDIEVAL ERA

The Medieval era spans the time from approximately 900 to 1500, or from the beginning of musical notation in a format that indicated pitches and rhythms on a staff to the end of polyphonic music treated as a series of unrelated or nonintegrated separate voice parts. Before 900 musical notation was limited to neumes and other symbols that indicated only general pitch and rhythm; there were no means to convey the essential components of music so that it could be reliably transmitted from written characters to aural sounds or from composer to performer. But during the early part of the tenth century treatises such as *Musica enchiriadis* and manuscripts such as the *St Gall cantatorium* and *St Martial troper* indicated either syllables of text or neumatic symbols on staves to fix pitches relative to each other, and during the latter part of the tenth century treatises and manuscripts indicated both pitches and rhythms. By the eleventh century a relatively standardized system of notation had been developed, and at the beginning of the twelfth century distinct genres and individual composers began to emerge and be identified.

Medieval genres consisted of monophonic chants, laude, and songs during the earlier years of the era, and polyphonic mass movements, mass cycles, motets, and secular songs during the later years. The sacred genres (chants, laude, mass movements and cycles, and motets) were generally sung by solo voices in combination with each other or by multiple voices per part. The secular genres (songs by the troubadours and trouvères, and the ballades, rondeaux, and virelais of the *formes fixes*) were performed by unaccompanied single solo voices (the monophonic songs), by single solo voices accompanied by instruments (the polyphonic compositions with only one texted voice part), or by multiple solo voices with or without instrumental participation (the multitexted polyphonic compositions).

Chant (often called plainchant or plainsong) is the monophonic liturgical music of the Christian Church. It is generally divided into various categories that reflect historical time frame, geographical location, or sectarian usage: *Old Roman* is the category of liturgical chant composed between the seventh and ninth centuries; *Mozarabic* refers to the chant repertoire composed during the same time period but specifically sung by Christians in Spain under Muslim rule; *Gallican* refers to those chants composed in Gaul before the tenth century; *Ambrosian*, named after St Ambrose (ca.340–397), is the chant repertoire centered in Milan during the twelfth and thirteenth centuries and known for several hymn texts, presumably written by St Ambrose himself (including "Deus Creator omnium," "Veni redemptor gentium," and "Illuxit orbi"); *Gregorian* is the label given to the liturgical chant repertoire officially sanctioned by the Roman Catholic Church and customarily used throughout Europe from the tenth century onward; and finally, *Sarum* is the term used for Gregorian chants that were modified and used throughout the British Isles between the thirteenth and sixteenth centuries, especially at Salisbury Cathedral.

Gregorian chant most likely began in the late seventh century with Pope Gregory (590–604), who called for a common liturgy as a part of his efforts to consolidate different factions of the Catholic Church throughout Italy and Spain. Pope Leo IV (847–855) termed the sung portions of the liturgy in use during his time *Gregoriana carmina* (Gregorian songs), and Pope John VIII (872–882) credited Gregory with composing many of the chants. While Gregory may in fact have had a role in the origination of chant, the music was not circulated in manuscripts until the tenth century, and most of the chants that became standardized were either notated or composed in the eleventh and twelfth centuries. Even at this time and after, standardization was still relative. Variations of chants occurred as copyists made mistakes or as modifications were made as a result of oral transfers. Thus composers living during the Medieval and Renaissance eras might have known different versions, albeit slight, of the same chant. Complete unification of Gregorian chant did not occur until the publication of the *Liber usualis,* which was ordered by Pope Pius X in a *motu proprio* of 1903 and prepared by the Benedictine monks of Solesmes, France.

The total body of Gregorian chant, which includes music for all the Ordinary and Proper services as well as for the Offices, is vast and complex. However, the number of chants that have become popular and that are performed separately (apart from liturgical services) is somewhat limited. The best known of these, listed here alphabetically and with page numbers in parentheses where the chants can be found in the 1956 edition, number 801, of the *Liber usualis* (chants with two page numbers refer to simple and solemn forms, respectively), are *Ave Maria* (1679), *Cantate Domino* (826), *Dies irae* (1810), *Hodie Christus natus est* (413), *Magnificat anima mea* (207–212), *O magnum mysterium* (382), *Pange lingua* (957), *Salve regina* (279 and 276), and *Victimae paschali laudes* (780). Other familiar chants include *Alma redemptoris mater* (277 and 273), *Angelus Domini* (787), *Ave maris stella* (1259), *Ave regina caelorum* (278 and 274), *Christus factus est* (655), *De profundis* (499), *Deus in adjutorium* (1027), *Haec dies* (783), *Jubilate Deo omnis terra* (480), *Justorum anime* (1547), *Lauda sion* (945), *Laudate Dominum* (562), *Laudate Dominum* (1275), *Miserere mei Deus* (526), *Nunc dimittis* (271), *O sacrum convivium* (959), *O vos omnes* (767), *Puer natus est* (408), *Regina caeli* (278 and 275), *Stabat mater* (1634), *Tristis est anima mea* (630), *Tu es Petrus* (1332), *Ubi caritas* (675), *Veni creator spiritus* (885), *Veni sancte spiritus* (880), *Veni sponsu Christi* (1217), and *Venite adoremus* (1052).

Most of these chants are syllabic, with occasional melismatic passages (*Haec dies,* which is predominantly melismatic, is an exception). Most of the chants are also through-composed, although there are notable examples of musical structures that correspond to textual patterns. For instance, in the solemn version of *Salve regina* (often called "The Great Salve"), the opening two parallel phrases of text—"Salve, regina, mater misericordiae" (Hail, queen, mother of mercy) and "Vita, dulcedo, et spes nostra, salve" (Life, sweetness, and our hope, hail)—are matched by nearly identical musical phrases. Likewise, the following two phrases that begin "Ad te clamamus" (To you we cry) and "Ad te suspiramus" (To you we sigh) are also musically similar. In the solemn version of *Ave regina caelorum*, the first two phrases begin identically, and in *Ubi caritas*, the five phrases of text result in a musical structure of AAABB.

Nonliturgical monophonic compositions include laude composed for use in private devotionals, and church dramas composed as theatrical productions within sacred services. The laude are mainly simple syllabic chants set in verse/refrain format to Italian texts. *Gloria in cielo e pace in terra* from the fourteenth-century *Florence Laudario* is an example. The church dramas (often called liturgical dramas because of their association with liturgical feasts) are biblical stories set to monophonic melodies for soloists and chorus and are performed with costumes, scenery, and staging. Famous examples include *The Play of Daniel, The Play of Herod, The Play of Mary, The Stranger,* and *The Bridegroom*.

Monophonic compositions derived from Gregorian chant and polyphonic mass movements and motets are divided into four separate periods—St Martial (1100–1180), Notre Dame (1180–1260), Ars Antiqua (1260–1320), and Ars Nova (1320–1500). The St Martial period, so named because of a large collection of manuscripts housed in the Benedictine monastery of St Martial in Limoges, is characterized by monophonic *tropes* and *sequences*, and two-voiced compositions in *discant* and *organum* styles. The *organum* style was especially important to the development of polyphony, for it contained compositional elements that were to be incorporated into most compositions for the remainder of the era. The lower part was a portion of a chant melody with its original Latin text that was set to very slow-moving rhythms, while the upper part, with a different Latin text, was a freely composed melody set to considerably faster-moving rhythms. The titles of these bitextual compositions, such as *Vox nostra resonet / Benedicamus domino,* consist of the first words of each text, beginning with the top voice part.

The Notre Dame period is known for a large body of repertoire that was written for liturgical services at Notre Dame Cathedral in Paris. Two composers are closely associated with this period—Léonin, who was active between about 1180 and 1190, and Pérotin, who was active around the year 1200. Léonin is credited with writing the *Magnus liber organi de gradali et antifonario* (Great book of organum for the gradual and antiphoner), which is a collection of mostly two-voiced pieces with elaborate melismatic upper parts over very slow-moving lower parts. Pérotin supposedly revised the *Magnus liber* and added pieces for three and four voice parts. Examples include the four-part *Viderunt omnes* and *Sederunt principes,* each of which is set to one text, with the upper parts in a rhythmically active *discant* style over a slow-moving fragment of chant.

The Ars Antiqua compositions continued the convention of rhythmically active upper parts set to their own texts over a slower-moving, chant-based lower part. However, the upper parts were often set to French texts, and each part had individual rhythmic characteristics (one was usually faster moving than the other or others). The lower parts were taken from chant or secular song repertoire. An example, which comes from the *Montpellier Codex* (one of the richest sources of music from the Ars Antiqua) is *Celui en qui / La belle estoile / La belle, en qui / Johanne.* In this motet the top voice part is a secular text that extols the virtues of Lady Marion, the second voice part praises the Virgin Mary, the third part is a secular love poem, and the bottom part is the middle syllable of the name Johannes (St John).

The Ars Nova, which took its name from the treatise *Ars nova* written in about 1322 by Philippe de Vitry, is distinguished by music organized according to isorhythmic techniques (i.e., at least one of the voice parts—usually the lowest—was divided into several identical rhythmic phrases called *talea,* or identical rhythmic and melodic phrases called *color*). The upper parts, frequently of similar rhythmic values, shared short musical motifs. While isorhythm was a characteristic throughout the Ars Nova, the relative rhythmic activity between the parts changed. The mass movements and motets at the beginning of the period by such composers as Philippe de Vitry, Guillaume de Machaut, and Johannes Ciconia continued to have fast-moving upper parts against a slower-moving lower part. Music composed at the end of the era by Leonel Power and John Dunstable had parts that were more rhythmically similar. By the time of the early-Renaissance composers Gilles de Bins Binchois, Jean de Ockeghem, and Antoine Busnois, compositions for four voices became the norm, with melodic and rhythmic material integrated among the parts.

Almost all of the compositional activity during the early and middle years of the Medieval era was centered in Italy and France. Monophony developed in Italy, polyphony developed in France, and most composers spent their lives in one country or the other. By the latter years of the era compositional activity included England and Burgundy (the area now occupied by northern France and the Netherlands).

The major Medieval-era composers are Hildegard von Bingen, who was an innovator in the composition of monophonic plainsong separate from Gregorian liturgical chant; Machaut and Ciconia, the poet-composers whose works were mainly polytextual; and Power and Dunstable, who infused the continental style with British characteristics.

HILDEGARD VON BINGEN 1098–1179

Hildegard (the name used in all reference sources) was born in Bermerscheim, near Mainz, Germany. She began having mystical visions at age five, and at eight her parents sent her to a convent associated with the Benedictine monastery of St Disibod near Bingen. She remained at the convent for approximately forty years, leading a completely ascetic life for the first half of this time, with contact to the outside world only through letters, and becoming *magistra* when her superior died in 1126. During the next two decades she became famous locally for her prophecies and miracles, and in 1147 she founded her own convent in the nearby town of Rupertsberg. The convent flourished, and in 1152 it was officially recognized by the Archbishop of Mainz. During the 1140s and 1150s Hildegard compiled a book of her visions, notated in poetry and music and entitled *Scivias,* an abbreviation of the phrase "Scito vias Domini" (Know the ways of the Lord). Two other books of her visions followed before 1160—*Liber vite meritorum* (Book of the merits of life) and *Liber divinorum operum* (Book of divine works), which together with *Scivias* form a trilogy that in modern times has been called *Symphonia armonie celestium revelationum* (Symphony of the harmony of celestial revelations). Hildegard also wrote two medical treatises during the 1150s—*Physica*, about herbal cures, and *Cause et curae*, about compound medicine. In addition, she wrote what is believed to be the first sacred musical drama—*Ordo vir-*

tutum (Rite of the virtues). Between 1160 and 1170 she made numerous preaching and missionary visits to cities throughout Germany, and in September 1179 she died at her convent in Rupertsberg at age eighty-one.

There are a total of seventy-seven monophonic chants in the three volumes of *Symphonia armonie*. Hildegard's poetry for the chants focuses on women, particularly the Virgin Mary and St Ursula, and is replete with exotic imagery. For example, Mary is described as the "viridissima virga" (greenest branch), whose "calor solis in te sudavit sicut odor balsami" (scent was like balsam distilled in the sun), and the "flos quem hyems de flatu serpentis numquam lesit" (flower that the winter of the serpent's breath has never hurt). St Ursula—the martyred princess of the fourth century who supposedly traveled with eleven thousand virgins before her death by the Huns in Cologne, Germany—is described as a "favus distillans" (dripping honeycomb) with "mel et lac sub lingua eius" (milk and honey under her tongue). The music of the chants is idiosyncratic, with unusual melodic contours set in unconventional modal contexts. While certain melodic motifs occur with frequency, the music seems to have no formal organization. The writing in *Ordo virtutum* is less irregular; it consists mostly of syllabic settings of narration that relate a morality story about the soul (called "Anima") struggling with sixteen virtues and the devil.

CHANTS
SELECTED AND LISTED ACCORDING TO FAMILIARITY

O viridissima virga (in praise of Mary) – 4:15 minutes.

Columba aspexit per cancellos fenestre (in praise of St Maximin) – 7:30 minutes.

O clarissima mater sancta medicine (in praise of Mary) – 7:30 minutes.

O presul vere civitatis (in praise of St Disibod) – 7:45 minutes.

O Jerusalem, aurea civitas (in praise of St Rupert) – 10:30 minutes.

O virtus sapientiae (in praise of wisdom) – 1:45 minutes.

O dulcissimi amator (in praise of Jesus) – 9:15 minutes.

Spiritui sancto honor sit (in praise of St Ursula) – 6:45 minutes.

Favus distillans Ursula virgo fuit (in praise of St Ursula) – 6:30 minutes.

O Ecclesia, oculi tui similes saphiro sunt (in praise of St Ursula) – 10 minutes.

O rubor sanguinis (in praise of Mary) – 1:30 minutes.

O virga ac diadema purpure regis (in praise of Mary) – 6:30 minutes.

ADAM DE LA HALLE B.1245–1250

Little information exists about the birth and death dates of Adam de la Halle (who is referenced under Adam, not Halle). There is conjecture that he died in Naples between 1285 and 1288. However, he may have died in England sometime after 1306. The former conclusion seems most logical, given that Adam spent most of his life in Italy and that the report of his death is in a document written by his nephew. From commentary in Adam's two plays—*Le jeu de Robin et de Marion* and *Le jeu d'Adam ou de la feuillie*—it is known that he studied in Paris and that he worked in Italy at the courts of Charles of Anjou and Robert II, Count of Artois.

In addition to approximately sixty monophonic songs, Adam composed five motets and six-teen polyphonic rondeaux. The motets are early examples of the genre's form and style that would become popular during the later years of the Medieval era: they are polytextual, with two freely composed rhythmically active upper voice parts in French over a rhythmically inactive lower part that is often a fragment of Gregorian chant. This lower part is often untexted, although it is given the Latin name of its derivation in the title of the motet. Examples include *De ma dame vient / Diex, comment porroie / Omnes* and *J'os bien a m'amie parler / Je n'os a m'amie aler / Seculum*. The rondeaux, also scored for three voices, are homophonic, with all voices texted and with structures of refrains and verses. Fourteen of the rondeaux are in the *formes fixes* that would be-come popular later in the era.

PHILIPPE DE VITRY 1291–1361

Vitry was perhaps born in the Champagne region of France, and he may have studied at the Sor-bonne and received a degree in music, though there is no proof of either his birthplace or mu-sical studies. What is known is that he was a canon at Notre Dame in Clermont-en-Beauvais be-ginning in 1322; that he served in a secretarial capacity to the French kings Charles IV (Charles IV le bel, 1322–1328), Philip VI (Philippe VI de Valois, 1328–1350), and John II (Jean II de France, 1350–1364); and that he was appointed Bishop of Meaux in 1351. He was a noted intel-lectual, poet, philosopher, mathematician, historian, and musician, and he received praise from many notable people of his day, including the poet Petrarch (Francesco Petrarca, 1304–1374), who called Vitry "the great philosopher of our age" and "an unparalleled poet of France."

Although Vitry most certainly wrote numerous poems, treatises on various subjects, and musical compositions, all that have survived are two poems (*Le chapel des trois fleurs de lis* and *Le dit du franc Gontier*), one treatise (*Ars nova*), and approximately twelve motets. The poems, about political circumstances of the time, were popular and were circulated throughout France. The treatise (ca.1322) is undoubtedly one of the most important musical discourses in history; it pre-sented new concepts of rhythm and notation, and its title became the reference for all music composed until approximately 1500. The motets, which manifest the principles set forth in *Ars nova*, followed the model initiated by Adam de la Halle of two rhythmically active upper voices above a slower-moving lower part. However, Vitry gave the motet an isorhythmic structural or-ganization that would be emulated by later composers of the fourteenth century. That is, most of the parts were constructed in repeated rhythmic patterns (*talea*).

Six of the motets can conclusively be ascribed to Vitry, another six have a high degree of probable authenticity, and several more are assumed to be by Vitry based on stylistic grounds. Many of the texts, like the poems, deal with political circumstances of the time, and several of the motets are contained in *Roman de Fauvel*, a collection of pieces by numerous composers that were integrated into a poem by Gervais de Bus. *O canenda / Rex quem / Rex regum* praises the crusade leader Robert, King of Sicily and Jerusalem, and *Petre clemens / Lugentium siccentur / Non est inventus* is about the controversial seat of the papacy (Avignon or Rome). Other notable motets are *Garrit Gallus / In nova fert / N[euma]* for AAT voices, *Tuba sacre fidei / In arboris / Virgo sum* also for AAT voices, and *Vos quid admiramini / Gratissima virginis / Gaude gloriosa* for ATTT voices. In this last-named motet, the lowest voice (which is based on the text phrase "Gaude gloriosa" from the chant antiphon *Ave regina caelorum*) has a ninety-measure *color* that is divided into six *talea,* and the upper voices contain numerous rhythmic repetitions.

JACOPO DA BOLOGNA FL.1340–1360

Jacopo (referenced under Jacopo, not Bologna) may have been born in Bologna. However, he spent the majority of his life in Milan and Verona—at the court of Luchino Visconti in Milan from 1339 until the death of Visconti in 1349, at the court of Mastino II and Alberto della Scala in Verona from 1349 until the death of Alberto in 1352, and back in Milan thereafter. As with most composer-poets of the Medieval era, his presence in the courts is known not from any documentary evidence, but rather from textual references in his musical compositions and from references in the music of contemporary composers. For instance, Jacopo's madrigal *Lo lume vostro* and motet *Lux purpurata* both praise Visconti, and the madrigal *O in Italia* refers to twin sons born to Visconti on August 4, 1346. Jacopo's presence in Milan is confirmed by references in the madrigals of Giovanni de Cascia and Piero (no known other name), who both worked for Mastino II in Verona. Also, Jacopo's madrigal *Non al suo amante,* set to a poem by Petrarch (the only known musical setting of Petrarch's poetry during the poet's life), was no doubt composed in Milan, where Petrarch was in residence after 1347. Finally, the late three-voiced madrigal *Aquila altera / Creatura gentile / Uccel di Dio* was most likely composed in 1355 for the coronation of Charles IV, whose crest was depicted with an eagle. The superius (soprano) text speaks of a lofty eagle with a valiant eye; the contratenor (alto) text refers to the eagle as a noble creature, worthy to ascend on high; and the tenor text compares the eagle to the bird of God, who triumphs with great deeds on earth.

Jacopo composed one motet, one lauda, and thirty-two madrigals. In addition, he wrote a treatise, *L'arte del biscanto misurato* (The art of measured polyphony), and numerous poems. The motet *Lux purpurata,* which is considered to be Jacopo's most beautiful composition, is for three voices (SAT), two of which (SA) are texted. Twenty-five of the madrigals are for two voices, and seven are for three voices. All voices are texted and were presumably sung by soloists. Many of the madrigals were quite popular during the latter half of the fourteenth century; they existed throughout Italy in multiple manuscripts and in varying versions (i.e., some of the madrigals are scored for both two and three voices). The best known of these are *Aquila altera / Creatura gentile / Uccel di Dio* and *Si come al canto* for TTB voices, *Fenice fu'* and *Non al suo amante* for AB voices, and *O cieco mondo* for ST voices.

GUILLAUME DE MACHAUT CA.1300–1377

Machaut was likely born in or near Reims (formerly spelled Rheims), where he spent the major part of his life. Like most other composers of the time, he was a poet as well as a musician, and his poems contain commentary on major contemporary events as well as laudatory tributes to himself and to the lives of notable people he met. The poems are particularly personal in that he describes his amorous feelings and praises his own music. For example, in his most famous poem, *Loange des dames,* which was written when he was an old man, he confesses his love for the nineteen-year-old Péronne d'Armentières, and in another poem he states that he finds pleasure in listening to his rondeau *Dix et sept, cinc, trese* and ballade *Quant Theseus / Ne quier veoir.* There is little biographical information in the poetry, however, and as a consequence, all that is known about Machaut's professional activities are the mere facts of his position as secretary to Jean de Luxembourg, King of Bohemia, from 1323 to the king's death in 1346, and as a canon at Reims Cathedral beginning in 1340. While in the employ of the king, Machaut traveled widely and became famous for his poems and compositions, and while serving at Reims Cathedral, he was visited by numerous dignitaries, including Charles II, King of Navarre; Jean, Duke of Berry; and Philip the Bold, Duke of Burgundy. Late in his life Machaut reproduced some of his manuscripts for important patrons, and he collected and organized his entire output of poetry and music.

Machaut composed one mass cycle, twenty-three motets, one hocket, forty-two ballades, twenty-two rondeaux, thirty-three virelais, and nineteen lais. In addition, he wrote approximately three hundred poems. All his music is in the Ars Nova style as described and exhibited by Philippe de Vitry; all but three of the motets, the *Hoquetus David,* and four of the mass movements are isometric; and all the works are polyphonic except for the lais, most of the virelais, and one of the ballades.

The mass cycle *Messe de nostre dame* is unquestionably the most famous composition of the Medieval era. Probably composed in the 1360s for Saturday celebrations of the Lady Mass at Reims Cathedral, it is the first-known cycle of the five portions of the Roman Catholic Mass Ordinary. The Kyrie, Sanctus, and Agnus Dei (plus the Ite missa est, which is not part of the Ordinary but which Machaut added at the end of the mass) are isometric and based on the Gregorian chant *Kyrie cunctipotens genitor.* The Gloria and Credo are free in melodic material and constructed according to non-isorhythmic techniques. The isometric procedures are complex and imaginative. In the Christe portion of the Kyrie, for instance, all four voice parts are divided into three *talea,* and in addition, the rhythms of two of the parts are mirrored. Specifically, the triplum (soprano) and motetus (alto) each have *talea* that begin and end simultaneously; the tenor and contratenor are also paired with *talea,* although they do not line up with the triplum and motetus; and the tenor and contratenor rhythms, apart from the *talea,* are grouped in two-measure segments that mirror each other as seen from the beginning and end of the movement. Furthermore, the triplum and motetus *talea* are somewhat deceptive in that they are separated by measures of independent rhythm. The non-isorhythmic construction techniques are also worthy of note, especially regarding the modern nature of the material's organization. As an example, the Gloria begins with a four-measure introduction, proceeds with four large sections that are divided into repeated patterns (A, B, and C), and ends with a short coda-like section. Additionally, there is a motif of seven notes that pervades the entire movement.

All of the motets are polytextual. Furthermore, all but two have three simultaneous texts, seventeen are in a combination of French and Latin, and four are only in Latin. As was mentioned above, most of the writing is isorhythmic, with both *color* and *talea,* and in ten of the motets the final *talea* is in rhythmic diminution. A few of the motets contain texts that glorify particular people or that comment on political situations of the time. *Bone pastor Guillerme /*

Bone pastor qui pastores, for example, was composed in 1324 for Guillaume de Trie, Archbishop of Reims, and *Plange, regni respublica / Tu qui gregem / Apprehende arma et scutum et exurge* refers to the conquests of Charles, Duke of Normandy. The majority of the motets, however, combine French texts about the anguishes of love with fragments of Gregorian chant. In *De souspirant cuer dolent / Tous corps qui de bien amer / Suspiro,* the first text includes the phrase "Puis que n'a de pité point dou mal que j'endure, qui me fait en desirant languir" (She has no pity for the ills I suffer, and makes me languish in desire); the second text ends with the phrase "Ou merci procheinnement de ma dame debonnaire, ou morir en languissant" (I must soon receive from love my sweet lady's grace or else die languishing); and the bottom chant fragment is set to the word "suspiro" (I sigh).

While most of the ballades, rondeaux, and virelais are polyphonic, they have only one voice that is texted. That is, they were intended to be performed as solo songs with instrumental accompaniment. Machaut even commented on performance by organ, bagpipes, and other instruments. The three pieces that have multiple texts, including *Quant Theseus / Ne quier veoir* (a four-part ballade with two texted parts), have become well known. The rondeau *Ma fin est mon commencement* (My end is my beginning) is famous for its namesake canonic structure: the lower voice part states the same music twice, first forward and then backward, while the two upper parts do likewise, interchanging music at the middle of the rondeau.

MASS

Messe de nostre dame – SATB voices – 27 minutes.

MOTETS
SELECTED AND LISTED IN THE ORDER MACHAUT INDICATED IN HIS COMPLETE WORKS

*De souspirant cuer dolent / Tous corps qui de bien amer /
Suspiro* – ATT voices – 3:30 minutes.

Puis que la douce rousée / De bon espoir / Speravi – AAT voices – 4 minutes.

Ha! Fortune / Qui es promesses de fortune / Et non est qui adjuvet –
ATB voices – 2:30 minutes.

Helas! Où sera pris confors / Hareu! Hareu le feu / Obediens usque ad mortem –
SAT voices – 2:15 minutes.

Fins cuers doulz / Dame, je sui cilz – TTT voices – 3 minutes.

Biauté parée de valour / Trop plus est bele / Je ne sui mie certeins –
TTB voices – 2:30 minutes.

Veni creator spiritus / Christe, qui lux es / Tribulatio proxima est –
SATT voices – 5 minutes.

*Plange, regni respublica / Tu qui gregem / Apprehende arma et scutum et
exurge* – ATBB voices – 4 minutes.

Inviolata genitrix / Felix virgo / Ad te suspiramus – ATBB voices –
4:30 minutes.

JOHANNES CICONIA CA.1370–1412

There is conjecture that Ciconia was born in about 1335 and that as a young adult he was em-ployed in Avignon. However, historical documents citing his presence in Italy, stylistic analysis of his music, and comparison of references in his music to historical events reasonably place his birth at about 1370 in Liège and his employment in Italy. A letter from Pope Boniface IX in 1391 mentions Ciconia's association with Cardinal Philippe d'Alençon at S Maria in Trastevere, Rome; Ciconia's madrigal *Una panthera* was composed later in the decade for the visit of digni-taries to the court of Giangeleazzo Visconti in Pavia; and after 1401 Ciconia composed four motets praising bishops of Padua Cathedral, including *O felix templum jubila* for Stefano Carrara, *Albane, misse celitus / Albane, doctor maxime* for Albane Michel, and *Petrum Marcello Venetum / O Petre, antistes inclite* for Pietro Marcello. In addition, two motets— *Ut te per omnes celitus / Ingens alumnus Padue* and *Doctorum principem / Melodia suavissima / Vir mitis*—praise Francesco Zaba-rella, Archpriest of Padua Cathedral and the person responsible for appointing Ciconia *cantor et custos* (musical leader and tutor) of the cathedral in 1403. Other compositions include references to Francesco Carrara, Lord of Padua, in the madrigal *Per quella strada lacteal del cielo,* and Michele Steno, Doge of Venice from 1400 to 1413, in the motet *Venecie, mundi splendor / Michael, qui stena domus / Italie mundicie.*

Like most other notable composers of the Medieval era, Ciconia was a poet who wrote texts that included not only the names of important people of the time, but also his own name. Un-like these other composers, however, Ciconia often elaborated on his name. These references occur frequently in the motets. For example, *O felix templum jubila* ends with a plea to bishop Stefano Carrara "to receive me, Ciconia, although I am unworthy of such an honor"; the tenor part of *Venecie, mundi splendor / Michael, qui stena domus / Italie mundicie* ends with the signa-ture "Johannes Ciconia," which corresponds to the "Amen" at the end of the other texts; and the duplum text of *Petrum Marcello Venetum / O Petre, antistes inclite* ends with the statement "Help your Ciconia who brought this song into being."

The most significant and distinguishing characteristic in Ciconia's music is *hocket.* Long pas-sages in most of the motets consist of very short two- or three-note motifs that are passed back and forth from voice to voice with considerable rhythmic activity. Notable examples occur at the ends of *Venecie, mundi splendor / Michael, qui stena domus / Italie mundicie* and the Gloria *Et in terra pax / Spiritus et alme,* as well as throughout *Doctorum principem / Melodia suavissima / Vir mitis.*

Ciconia composed eleven mass movements, ten motets, fifteen ballatas, four madrigals, three virelais, and two canons. He also wrote a treatise on music—*Nova musica.* The mass move-ments, which are settings of the Gloria and Credo portions of the Ordinary, include four Glorias and three Credos for three voices, and three Glorias and one Credo for four voices. Most of the settings are like motets in that they have text in only the top two voice parts. However, two of the settings have text in only one voice part, and two have text in all voice parts. These latter two settings—a Gloria and Credo paired because of similar melodic material—are unique in that all three voice parts of each setting are of comparable rhythmic density and imitative texture.

Most of the motets are scored for three voice parts. The top two (triplum and duplum), with different texts in Latin, are characterized by fast-moving rhythmic activity, similar ranges, shared melodic material, and extensive passages of *hocket.* The lower voice part (tenor) is un-texted and characterized by slower-moving rhythms. The texts are frequently celebratory in nature and, as is mentioned above, allude to specific people, places, or events. In addition to the citations of this sort already mentioned, *O Padua, sidus preclarum* praises the city of Padua, and *Venecie, mundi splendor / Michael, qui Stena domus / Italie, mundicie* describes Venice as being the splendor of the world and the pride of Italy.

The secular music, all for solo voices, is in French (the virelais), Italian (the madrigals and ballatas), and Latin (the canons). The ballatas, which combine stylistic features of Jacopo da Bologna and Philippe de Vitry, are mostly for two and three voices, with the tenor of the three-voiced pieces generally untexted (although one ballata, *Deduto sey*, has text in all three voice parts). Three of the madrigals are for two voices, while the fourth is for three voices, all texted. One of the virelais, *Aler m'en veus en strangne partie*, a farewell to France, is for two voices, while the other two virelais and both canons are for three voices.

MASS MOVEMENTS
SELECTED AND LISTED ACCORDING TO FAMILIARITY

Gloria and *Credo* (listed as numbers 1 and 2 in the complete works) – SST voices (all texted) – 9:30 minutes.

Gloria and *Credo* (listed as numbers 3 and 4 in the complete works) – SS voices texted and TT parts untexted – 8 minutes.

Gloria (listed as number 5 in the complete works and subtitled "Spiritus et alme") – SS texted and T untexted – 4:30 minutes.

MOTETS
SELECTED AND LISTED ACCORDING TO FAMILIARITY

Venecie, mundi splendor / Michael, qui Stena domus / Italie, mundicie – SAT voices (all texted) – 5 minutes.

Doctorum principem / Melodia suavissima / Vir mitis – SS voices texted and TT parts untexted – 2:30 minutes.

Ut te per omnes celitus / Ingens alumnus Padue – SS voices texted and TT parts untexted – 2:30 minutes.

O Padua, sidus preclarum – SA voices texted and T part untexted – 3 minutes.

O felix templum jubila – SA voices texted and TT parts untexted – 3:30 minutes.

Albane, misse celitus / Albane, doctor maxime – SS voices texted and TT parts untexted – 3 minutes.

LEONEL POWER CA.1370S–1445

Nothing is known about Power's date or place of birth, although it is assumed from stylistic characteristics of his music that he was born between 1370 and 1380. There is also no information about his musical training or youth and little information about his activities as an adult.

He instructed the choristers in the London chapel of Thomas, Duke of Clarence, sometime before 1421, and from 1423 until his death he was associated with Canterbury Cathedral, most likely as a choirmaster.

He composed seven complete or partial mass cycles, nineteen individual mass movements, and eighteen motets. Of these works, six are attributed to John Dunstable as well as to Power. Two of the mass cycles contain all five portions of the Ordinary, one cycle contains all portions except the Kyrie, two have only Gloria and Credo portions, and two have only the Sanctus and Agnus Dei. All of the cycles are unified by melodic material—a relatively innovative procedure during Power's lifetime. The first of the complete cycles is based on the Gregorian chant *Rex seculorum,* and the second is based on an unknown source and is therefore referred to as *Sine nomine* (without name). The almost complete cycle, Power's most famous, is based on the Gregorian chant *Alma redemptoris mater.* Two of the remaining partial cycles and many of the individual mass movements are based on Sarum chants.

Most of the motets are also based on chant (generally, but not always, the chant corresponding to the motet's name). In some of the motets, such as *Beata progenies* and the three-voiced setting of *Ave regina celorum,* the chant is stated completely in one voice. In other motets the chant is either paraphrased in one voice (as in *Gloriose virginis*) or treated freely throughout all voices (as in the four-voiced setting of *Ave regina celorum*). Three of the motets—*Beata progenies,* the three-voiced setting of *Ave regina celorum,* and *Beata viscera*—are in discant style, while most of the other motets are characterized by rhythmically active and independent voice parts. A majority of the motets have only one texted voice part. However, three motets—*Alma redemptoris mater,* the four-voiced setting of *Ave regina celorum,* and *Gloriose virginis*—have two texted voice parts, and four motets—*Anima mea, Ibo michi ad montem, Quam pulchra es,* and *Salve sancta parens*—have all voice parts texted. *Ave regina celorum* is unique in that the texted voice parts (SA) are similar in their rhythmically active texture while the other voice parts (TT) are similarly inactive. This setting of *Ave regina celorum* is also unique in having passages of *hocket.*

MOTETS

COMPLETE AND LISTED ALPHABETICALLY

Alma redemptoris mater – ATT voices (A texted) – 5 minutes. This motet is also attributed to Dunstable.

Alma redemptoris mater – STT voices (S and the first T texted) – 4 minutes. This motet is also attributed to Dunstable.

Anima mea – AT voices (A texted) – 3 minutes.

Anima mea – STT voices (all texted) – 3:30 minutes.

Ave regina celorum – ATB voices (B texted) – 1:30 minutes.

Ave regina celorum – SATT voices (SA texted) – 3 minutes.

Beata progenies – ATB voices (B texted) – 1:30 minutes.

Beata viscera – ATB voices (T texted) – 1:15 minutes.

Gloriose virginis – AABB voices (AA texted) – 1:30 minutes.

Ibo michi ad montem – STT voices (all texted) – 3 minutes.

Mater ora filium – STT voices (S texted) – 1:30 minutes.

Quam pulchra es – TBB voices (all texted) – 4 minutes.

Regina celi letare – ATT voices (A texted) – 3:30 minutes.

Salve mater salvatoris – STT voices (S texted) – 3:30 minutes. This motet is
    also attributed to Dunstable.

Salve regina – ATB voices (A texted) – 4 minutes.

Salve regina – ATT voices (A texted) – 5:30 minutes.

Salve sancta parens – STT voices (all texted) – 1:30 minutes.

JOHN DUNSTABLE CA.1390–1453

As with Leonel Power, there is no documentation of Dunstable's date or place of birth, and very little information about his life. He was an astronomer, mathematician, and musician, and he was in the service of John, Duke of Bedford, and Humfrey, Duke of Glouster. He also was associated with the parish church of St Stephen Walbrook, where he was buried. The sparsity of biographical detail about Dunstable's life is surprising, considering that he was one of the most famous musicians of the age and praised by numerous authors, including the well-known theorists Johannes Tinctoris and Franchinus Gaffurius. Dunstable was also credited with originating a new sound called *contenance angloise* (English countenance), which featured more triadic harmonies and smoother-moving melodies than had been the norm in earlier works by English composers and which was in contrast to mainland European works.

Dunstable's extant compositional output includes five mass cycles, fourteen individual mass movements, thirty-nine motets, and five secular pieces. Some of these works are also attributed to Leonel Power and Guillaume Dufay, and there is speculation that Dunstable composed a second Magnificat, the ballade *Je languis,* and the Christmas carol *I pray you all.* The mass cycles include two complete settings of the Ordinary (*Missa Rex seculorum* and *Missa Sine nomine*), one complete cycle except for an Agnus Dei (*Missa Da gaudiorum premia*), and two cycles that contain only Glorias and Credos (*Jesu Christe fili Dei* and a work based on an unknown and unnamed source). The individual mass movements include two Kyries, five Glorias, three Credos, three Sanctuses, and one Agnus Dei. Almost all of the movements, whether in cycles or not, follow the model of masses and motets written by previous composers. However, Dunstable's masses are more modern in that the lowest part is frequently texted, and the rhythmic activity of this part approaches that of the upper parts.

Approximately half the motets are similar to the mass movements in scoring and texture, and half follow the traditional model of slow-moving and untexted tenor parts. About a third of all the motets are isorhythmic, two-thirds are without rhythmic organization, and several (e.g., the well-known *Quam pulchra es*) are in *discant* style. Several motets also feature the new compositional technique of paraphrasing a chant melody in the top voice. These motets include *Ave regina celorum, Regina celi letare,* and one of Dunstable's most famous isorhythmic motets, *Veni sancte spiritus / Veni creator spiritus,* which was copied in five major manuscripts of the time. The lowest voice part of the motet, precisely the "mentes tuorum visita, imple superna gra-" portion of the *Veni creator* Gregorian chant, has three *color* in successively diminished rhythmic values (the ratio proportion being 3:2:1), each composed of two *talea*. Two different *talea* comprise each third of the top voice of the motet, which is a paraphrase of the *Veni creator* chant. The first two *talea* of this top voice paraphrase the first four phrases of the chant ("Veni creator spiritus," "Mentes tuorum visita," "Imple superna gratia," and "Quae tu creasti pectora"), and the last two *talea* repeat the first and second phrases, thus imparting an ABA melodic structure to the top voice part.

MASS CYCLES AND MASS MOVEMENTS
SELECTED AND LISTED ACCORDING TO FAMILIARITY

Missa Rex seculorum – ATT voices (A and the first T texted) – 28 minutes.

Missa Da gaudiorum premia – ATB voices (AT with mass text and B with chant text) – 21 minutes.

Gloria and *Credo* (*Jesu Christe fili Dei*) – TBB voices (T and the first B with mass text, and second B with chant text) – 13:30 minutes.

Gloria and *Credo* (numbers 11 and 12 in the historical collection *Musica Britannica*) – SSTT voices (SS and the first T texted) – 15 minutes.

MOTETS
SELECTED AND LISTED ACCORDING TO FAMILIARITY

Quam pulchra es – ATB voices (all texted) – 2:30 minutes.

Veni sancte spiritus / Veni creator spiritus – SATT voices (all texted) – 6 minutes.

Speciosa facta es – STT voices (S texted) – 2 minutes.

Ave regina celorum – ATT voices (all texted) – 5:30 minutes.

Sub tuam protectionem – ATB voices (A texted) – 4:15 minutes.

Beata mater – ATB voices (A texted) – 2:30 minutes.

Regina celi letare – STT voices (all texted) – 5 minutes.

Ave maris stella – STT voices (S texted) – 3:45 minutes.

Salve scema sanctitatis / Salve salus / Cantant celi – ATBB voices (AT texted) – 7 minutes.

2

THE RENAISSANCE ERA

For convenience, historians generally list the beginning and ending dates of the Renaissance era at century markers—1500 and 1600, respectively. More accurately, the era began during the final decades of the fifteenth century and ended, for the most part, by the third decade of the seventeenth century. The attributes that would define and generally characterize the initial years of the Renaissance—single texts, standard scoring for SATB ensembles, integrated musical material (i.e., motivic material distributed throughout all voice parts), and imitative textures—began appearing as early as the 1470s in the music of such composers as Guillaume Dufay and Jean de Ockeghem. These composers also wrote in Medieval styles (e.g., isorhythmic configurations in sacred music and *formes fixes* structures in secular music), and thus the end of the fifteenth century was transitional, with relatively consistent application of Renaissance styles not being evidenced until the beginning of the sixteenth century in the music of Loyset Compère, Alexander Agricola, and Josquin Desprez. The change to new styles was not complete during the early years of the sixteenth century, however. A few Medieval compositional styles continued to be found—such as the combination of original Gregorian cantus firmus textual phrases along with other texts and long and prolix poems or prose narratives. Similarly, the styles of the Renaissance existed side by side with the new styles of the Baroque era during the first two decades of the seventeenth century. Fixing one date for both the ending of the Renaissance and the beginning of the Baroque is particularly troublesome, for the Baroque began in 1600 but the Renaissance did not end until the deaths of Jan Pieterszoon Sweelinck in 1621 and William Byrd in 1623. A few composers even carried the Renaissance style much later (e.g., Melchior Franck, who died in 1639, and Gregorio Allegri, who died in 1652).

At the beginning of the Renaissance, styles were mainly characterized by long phrases of text and incipient forms of imitative polyphony (e.g., imitation being confined to duets or imitation not prevalent in all voice parts). By the middle of the era, texts often consisted of only several short phrases, and textures were generally unified by pervasive imitation. At the end of the era, compositional traits were varied: sacred works to Latin texts were generally structured of alternating passages of imitative polyphony and homophony; chorales, Psalm settings, and anthems that were composed for the Protestant Reformation sects as well as lighthearted madrigals, chansons, and other related forms were often homophonic; and serious Italian madrigals consisted of continuous phrases of imitative polyphony. The only unifying characteristics of late Renaissance compositions were short fragments of text (i.e., single words or phrases consisting of only several words) that were set to equally short musical motifs, and varied rhythms that reflected the expressive implications of specific words or short phrases. These word-oriented characteristics were the result of a desire—initiated by the Council of Trent and begun in 1542 by Pope Paul III to reform Catholic liturgies—to effectuate clarity of text in performance.

Almost all the early Renaissance composers were born and educated in the area of Europe that at the time was called Flanders or northwest Burgundy and that now is occupied by Belgium and northwestern France. These composers—such as Dufay, Agricola, and Desprez—held appointments throughout France and Italy, where they served in various royal or princely courts and where they developed the style of imitative polyphony. By the middle of the era, the majority of recognized and significant composers—including Adrian Willaert, G. P. da Palestrina, and Andrea Gabrieli—were born and employed in Italy and were known for their works in a pervasive imitative style (called point of imitation). By the end of the era, there was no single center of compositional activity; composers came from and worked throughout Europe—for instance, Tomás Luis de Victoria in Spain; Hans Leo Hassler and Melchior Franck in Germany; and William Byrd and Thomas Morley in England. England was last in manifesting Renaissance styles because native composers did not study abroad, and it was not until the middle of the sixteenth century that foreign repertoire was available for performance.

The Renaissance era was especially important for the creation of genres that either would continue throughout the remaining historical eras or would disappear during the seventeenth through nineteenth centuries and then reappear in the twentieth century. The enduring genres, those newly created during the Renaissance, include the sacred forms developed as a result of the Protestant Reformation—the French Calvinist Psalm setting, German Lutheran chorale and chorale motet, and English anthem. The genres that were created and that flourished during the Renaissance but that did not experience a continuous history are the madrigal (both Italian and English) and chanson. Genres that were created during the Medieval era—the mass (including Requiem), motet, and related sacred genres such as the Magnificat—continued to be popular throughout the Renaissance and all successive eras. Masses during the Renaissance, which were almost always polyphonic and imitative compositions based on preexisting material (chants, other masses, motets, chansons, and madrigals), utilized a variety of interesting construction techniques. The most common technique employed a preexisting tune as a cantus firmus, usually placed in the tenor voice and scored in longer note values than the other voice parts. The tune was generally presented without modification or elaboration; however, it was frequently inverted (upside down), retrograde (backwards), and retrograde inverted (upside down and backwards), as well as in its original form. Further common construction techniques were paraphrase (a modification and elaboration of a preexisting tune), parody (the insertion of a polyphonic section of a preexisting composition into the mass texture), *soggetto cavato* (a cantus firmus built from pitches derived from the vowels of a person's name), and *quodlibet* (the employment of multiple secular preexisting tunes). Motets at the beginning of the era occasionally employed Gregorian chant phrases as a cantus firmus, whereas motets during the middle years of the era often employed chant material as a basis for point-of-imitation phrases (e.g., Palestrina's *Veni sponsa Christi* uses the four phrases of the Gregorian chant as the organizing material for the four phrases of the motet). By the end of the era, motets were by and large free in both melodic content and structure. Magnificats, on the other hand, were most often based on chant and composed in *alternatim* style throughout the era (i.e., phrases of Gregorian chant alternated with passages of imitative polyphony).

Virtually all the Renaissance genres were composed for voices without specified instrumental accompaniment. Scoring for specific instruments was one of the main traits of the Baroque. However, instrumental participation during the Renaissance was common, especially during the latter half of the era. The serpent (a bassoon-like instrument) often played along with bass voices in masses and motets, and it also accompanied Gregorian chants (even following the singers when they processed). In addition, the organ was frequently used to support the a cappella textures of sacred genres. Most cathedrals, chapels, and courts had several organs for this purpose, often with an organ in each performance location. For example, St Mark's Basilica had an organ in each of its four balconies. For festival occasions or for institutions with elaborate musical programs, consorts of instruments (families of recorders, viols, or sackbuts) would play with the SATB vocal parts *colla parte*. That is, a family or consort of instruments (all recorders or all viols, for instance) would accompany a specific vocal scoring—either throughout the piece of music or throughout a complete autonomous section of it. Another family or consort of instruments would be used for another piece or for another section of music, the decision being determined by the expressive characteristics of the music or by the instrumental resources available.

ᘒ FRANCE ᘒ

While almost all of the composers who were considered French during the Renaissance worked in France, a number of the composers were born and employed in the region of northwestern Europe that today comprises western Belgium, the southwestern portion of the Netherlands, and northern France. In order to include this area with all of France and properly identify the total territory of musical activity, historians use the term *Franco-Flemish*. More precisely, however, the term refers to composers and their repertoire from the area of northwestern Europe no farther north than Ghent in Belgium and no farther south than Chartres in France. Eleven composers—Guillaume Dufay, Gilles de Bins Binchois, Jean de Ockeghem, Antoine Busnois, Loyset Compère, Alexander Agricola, Josquin Desprez, Pierre de La Rue, Jacob Obrecht, Nicolas Gombert, and Jacobus Clemens non Papa—were born in this area; six composers—Pierre Passereau, Claudin de Sermisy, Pierre Certon, Claude Goudimel, Claude Le Jeune, and Guillaume Costeley—were born in Paris; and four composers—Jean Mouton, Antoine Brumel, Clément Janequin, and Loys Bourgeois—were born in other cities in northern France. Only two composers at the very end of the era were born elsewhere: Jan Pieterszoon Sweelinck was born in the Netherlands and Peter Philips was born in London. Of particular note, the first nine composers of the era were from the Franco-Flemish region, and the last five composers (excluding Sweelinck and Philips) were from Paris.

Approximately half of the French composers had appointments in the royal court, where they served kings from Louis XI (1461–1483) to Henri IV (1589–1610). Three of these composers also served in the court of the Sforza family in Milan, and two served in Ferrara. All the significant composers born in the fifteenth century wrote sacred music exclusively for the Catholic Church, while all but two (Bourgeois and Philips) born in the sixteenth century wrote sacred music for both the Catholic and Protestant churches. Bourgeois composed only Calvinist Psalm settings and a few chansons, and Philips composed only Latin motets and Italian madrigals. It should be noted that François I, who reigned from 1515 to 1547 and who was called Le Père et Restaurateur des Lettres (the father and restorer of letters), is considered to be the first truly Renaissance monarch in France. Dedicated to art and literature, he brought Leonardo da Vinci to France in the last years of the artist's life, and he greatly increased the holdings of the royal library. Both Henri II (1547–1559) and Charles IX (1560–1574) persecuted the Huguenots (Protestants who were advocates of the precepts of John Calvin) and thus created an atmosphere that limited the composition of Protestant church music. Henri IV, the only Protestant king of France during the Renaissance era, enacted religious liberties that allowed Protestant church music to flourish.

The composers not working for French kings were generally employed at major cathedrals, chapels, churches, and courts throughout France and the Netherlands. Dufay, Binchois, and Busnois had positions at the Burgundian court; La Rue served at the Habsburg-Burgundian court; Brumel spent several years at Notre Dame Cathedral in Paris; Janequin's career was at Angers and Auch cathedrals and also at the court of the Duke of Guise; Clemens non Papa was succentor for two years at St Donaas in Bruges; Bourgeois was a singer and *maître des enfants* at St Pierre and St Gervais cathedrals in Geneva; Certon had appointments as a clerk and *maître des enfants* at Sainte-Chapelle in Paris; Philips was organist at the court of Archduke Albert in Brussels; and Sweelinck served his entire life at the Oude Kirk in Amsterdam.

The sacred genres for Catholic liturgies consisted of mass cycles (including Requiems), separate mass movements, Latin motets, and Magnificats; the sacred music for use by Protestants was limited to Psalm settings and sacred chansons; and the secular music was almost exclusively devoted to chansons. Virtually all the masses were based on preexisting melodies, used as a cantus firmus in the tenor voice part early in the era or as material for pervasive imitation in all voice parts during the end of the era. Gregorian chants were the most common sources of preexisting material, although chansons were popular sources with composers early in the era, and Dufay, Ockeghem, Busnois, Compère, Desprez, La Rue, Obrecht, Mouton, and Brumel all set masses based on the L'homme armé tune. Motets were the freest of the genres in terms of musical content and structure: those composed early in the era often incorporated Gregorian chant and exhibited structural techniques such as canon, those in the middle of the era occasionally employed chant as a basis for point-of-imitation phrases, and those at the end of the era utilized text phrases or single words as the basis for imitation or free expression. Magnificats, which were composed by most of the composers in the early and middle years of the era, generally consisted of alternating passages of polyphony and Gregorian chant (called *alternatim* style).

Settings of Psalms followed the publication of various psalters for use by the Huguenots;

Bourgeois is credited with composing a number of tunes and four-part hymn-like settings, and Goudimel followed with more homophonic settings and with some elaborated arrangements. Later composers frequently set the psalter tunes in one of three styles—hymn-like, with the tune often in the tenor part; slightly adorned, with the tune in the soprano part and imitative phrases in the other parts; and motet-like, with imitative phrases in all parts.

The chansons have a particularly interesting history. Those by the early composers Dufay, Binchois, Ockeghem, Busnois, Compère, Agricola, and La Rue, and the early pieces of Josquin, are mainly in the *formes fixes*. Later composers such as Obrecht, Mouton, and Brumel composed chansons in the imitative style of motets at the time. By the middle of the sixteenth century, however, a new homophonic style emerged, one popularized by the famous Parisian publisher Pierre Attaingnant. From the late 1520s until his death in about 1551, Attaingnant published approximately thirty-six volumes of chansons, most of them in the new so-called "Parisian" style. Other publishers followed Attaingnant, including Adrian Le Roy and Robert Ballard in Paris, and Jacques Moderne in Lyons. Chansons became so fashionable that composers such as Passereau, Janequin, Sermisy, Certon, Le Jeune, and Costeley devoted their compositional output to, and became known mainly for, contributions to the genre. The Parisian and imitative styles were prevalent throughout the latter half of the sixteenth century, and other styles emerged as well. Janequin wrote chansons in the "programmatic" style (narrative works that featured onomatopoeic sounds), and Le Jeune wrote pieces governed by the rhythmic principles of *musique mesurée* (long and short rhythms that corresponded to accented and unaccented speech syllables).

In addition to the composers cited above and discussed further in this section of the Renaissance era, mention should be made of Antoine de Févin (ca.1470–1512), Jean Richafort (ca. 1480–ca.1548), and Pierre Sandrin (ca.1490–ca.1561). Févin and Richafort composed masses, motets, Magnificats, and chansons in the styles of their day, and several of their works were frequently parodied by later composers; Sandrin composed only chansons, one of which— *Doulce mémoire*—became quite famous. Three other composers—Adrian Willaert (ca.1490– 1562), Jacques Arcadelt (ca.1505–1568), and Orlando di Lasso (ca.1532–1594)—were born in Flanders and are occasionally listed with other Franco-Flemish composers. They had no employment in France or Belgium, however, and their music does not reflect Franco-Flemish styles. Consequently, they are discussed under the countries that best represent them—Italy in the case of Willaert and Arcadelt, and Germany in the case of Lasso.

GUILLAUME DUFAY (DU FAY) CA.1397–1474

Dufay, whose name was spelled Du Fay and pronounced in three syllables during his lifetime (Du-fa-y), was thought for many years of the twentieth century to have been born in about 1400. However, evidence from contemporary documents and musical references place the date more plausibly at about 1397. He was most likely born in Cambrai, where he was a chorister at the local cathedral from 1409 to 1412 and a subdeacon from 1418 to 1420. During the subsequent years he traveled frequently between northwestern Burgundy, Savoy (in southeastern France), and cities in Italy, composing music for his patrons and, like Johannes Ciconia and others, often mentioning their names in the texts. The ballade *Resvelliés vous* was composed for the wedding of Carlo Malatesta while Dufay was at his court in Rimini from 1420 to 1424, and the motets *Rite maiorem Jacobum* and *Apostolo glorioso* were composed for Cardinal Louis Aleman while Dufay was at his court in Bologna from 1426 to 1428.

Dufay entered the service of the papal chapel in Rome in 1428 and departed in 1433 because the chapel was in disarray. He then served as *maistre de chapelle* for Duke Amédée VIII of Savoy for two years, and in 1435 he returned to the papal chapel, which had moved to Florence. While in Florence, he composed his famous isorhythmic motet *Nuper rosarum flores / Terribilis est locus iste* for the consecration of S Maria del Fiore (the Duomo) by Pope Eugenius IV on May 25, 1436. Political situations necessitated Dufay's return to Savoy in 1437, although the conflict between Pope Eugenius IV, who was deposed in 1439, and Dufay's former patron Duke Amédée, who became Pope Felix V, made it impossible for Dufay to work at either the papal chapel or Savoy. Therefore, in 1439 he went to the Burgundian court of Philip the Good, who ruled over one of the most lavish musical establishments in Europe from 1419 to 1467. Many important musicians of the time visited the court, including Johannes Tinctoris in 1460 and Jean de Ockeghem in 1463. Dufay remained in the service of the Burgundian court, although he also served as a canon and *maître des petits vicaires* (master of the children) at the Cambrai Cathedral from 1458 until the end of his life. He was acknowledged by his contemporaries to be the leading composer of his age, and his music served as an important catalyst of compositional techniques during the Renaissance era.

Dufay composed six complete mass cycles (a seventh, *Missa Caput*, is probably by another, unknown composer), seven partial mass cycles, nineteen individual mass movements, approximately ninety motets, four Magnificats, and eighty chansons. Two of the complete masses— *Missa Resvelliés vous* (formerly listed as *Missa Sine nomine*) and *Missa S Jacobi*—were composed early in Dufay's career and reflect late Medieval styles. The other four masses—*Missa L'homme armé, Missa Se la face ay pale, Missa Ecce ancilla Domini,* and *Missa Ave regina celorum*—were composed later and exhibit styles that were to become standard during the Renaissance. These later masses are all scored for four texted voices (SATB), they are all based upon preexisting material, and they all employ a tenor cantus firmus. Basing the mass on secular music was especially modern; Dufay's *Missa L'homme armé* may have been the first of the dozens of masses set to this tune, and the use of his own chansons as material for *Missa Resvelliés vous* and *Missa Se la face ay pale* was certainly unprecedented. This latter mass is notable for several reasons: the cantus firmus is heard nine times throughout the mass (once in the Kyrie, Sanctus, and Agnus Dei, and three times each in the Gloria and Credo); each movement begins with identical melodic material (a head motif) stated in the soprano voice; and the Gloria and Credo movements end with the full texture of the chanson's distinctive triadic harmonies. The incomplete mass cycles, individual mass movements (mostly for three voices,) and Magnificats (each on a different Gregorian chant tone) also have chant paraphrases in the soprano voice. The famous *Gloria ad modum tube* is scored for two texted voices (SS or TT) that form a strict canon and two untexted parts that imitate a two-note trumpet call and increasingly diminish in rhythmic values.

The motets are of two types—polyphonic and discant. Most of the polyphonic motets are modeled after the older continental style of Ciconia, with multiple texts, rhythmically active upper parts that exchange motivic material, and independent rhythmically inactive lower parts. Thirteen of these motets are isorhythmic, including Dufay's single five-voiced work, *Ecclesie militantis / Sanctorum arbitrio / Bella canunt gentes / Gabriel / Ecce nomen Domini*, composed for the coronation of Pope Eugenius IV in 1431, and *Nuper rosarum flores,* mentioned above in reference to the consecration of the Florence Duomo. The isorhythmic structure of this latter motet features *talea* that are repeated in the rhythmic proportions 6:4:2:3, which supposedly mirror the architectural proportions of the cathedral's famous dome by Filippo Brunelleschi. Other notable polyphonic motets are the three-voiced *Flos florum,* which has an unusually florid upper part, and the four-voiced *Ave regina celorum,* which Dufay composed at the end of his life and which he requested be sung at his deathbed. The discant motets, mostly for three voices, are in the English *contenance angloise* style of Dunstable, with homophonic textures in a style referred to as *fauxbourdon:* the lower two voices follow the general shape of the top voice, which is often a paraphrase of a chant melody. The resulting effect is one of parallel motion chords. Examples are *Jesu corona virginum; Vos, qui secuti;* and the three-voiced setting of *Ave regina celorum.*

The secular pieces, generally scored for one texted voice and intended for soloists, are mostly in the *formes fixes.* Noteworthy examples include the ballade *C'est bien raison* and the rondeaux *Donnés l'assault* and *Adieu ces bons vins de Lannoys.* Well-known secular pieces with two texted voices include the ballade *La belle se siet* and the virelai *Helas mon dueil.* The rondeau *Ce moys de may* is scored for three texted voices, and Dufay's best-known secular piece, *Vergine belle,* is scored for one texted voice (set to an Italian text by Petrarch) and is in a free form.

MASS CYCLES AND MASS MOVEMENTS
SELECTED AND LISTED ACCORDING TO FAMILIARITY

Missa Se la face ay pale – SATB chorus – 35 minutes.

Missa L'homme armé – SATB chorus – 39 minutes.

Missa Ecce ancilla Domini – SATB chorus – 37 minutes.

Missa Ave regina celorum – SATB chorus – 43 minutes.

Missa Resvelliés vous – ATB chorus – 20 minutes.

Gloria ad modum tube – SATB chorus – 2:30 minutes.

MOTETS
SELECTED AND LISTED ACCORDING TO FAMILIARITY

Ave regina celorum – SATB chorus – 8 minutes.

Ave regina celorum – ATT chorus – 3 minutes.

Flos florum – SAT chorus – 4 minutes.

Nuper rosarum flores / Terribilis est locus iste – SATB chorus – 6:30 minutes.

O gemma, lux et speculum / Sacer pastor Barensium / Beatus Nicolaus adhuc –
    SATB chorus – 5 minutes.

O sancta Sebastiane / O martyr Sebastiane / O quam mira / Gloria et honore –
    SATB chorus – 4:30 minutes.

Inclita stella maris – SATB chorus – 3:30 minutes.

Salve flos Tusce gentis / Vos nunc, Etruscorum iubar / Viri mendaces – SATB chorus – 6 minutes.

GILLES DE BINS BINCHOIS CA.1400–1460

Binchois was probably born in Mons, France, where he received his musical education at the local court and at the church of St Germain. He was an organist at the nearby church of Ste Waudru beginning in 1419, and sometime in the 1420s he joined the Burgundian court, remaining there for approximately three decades. From 1452 until his death he served as provost of the church of St Vincent in Soignies. He was held in high esteem during the early years of the Renaissance—his compositions were copied in more than fifty manuscripts during the latter decades of the fifteenth century, and many of his motets and chansons were parodied by other composers. He was often associated with Guillaume Dufay, his probable colleague at the Burgundian court, with whom he is depicted in the famous 1451 illumination entitled *Le champion des dames* by Martin le Franc.

Binchois composed thirty-four mass movements, twenty-eight motets, six Magnificats, one Te Deum, forty-nine rondeaux, and eight ballades. The mass movements, which include three Gloria/Credo and five Sanctus/Agnus Dei pairs, are based on various Ordinary chants of the mass. For example, the Kyrie "Angelorum" paraphrases the Kyrie from Mass VIII (page 37 in the *Liber usualis*), the Kyrie "Orbis factor" paraphrases the Kyrie from Mass IX (page 46), and the Kyrie "Cunctipotens" paraphrases the Kyrie from Mass IV (page 25). The motets and most of the Magnificats are in a simple *discant* or *fauxbourdon* style, and most are also characterized by cross-relations and repeated use of a four-note rhythmic figure. Only one motet is isorhythmic—*Nove cantum melodie / Tanti gaude germinis / . . . enixa meritis,* composed for the baptism of Prince Anthoine of Burgundy in 1431. This motet is of particular interest in that the text names all nineteen chapel singers at the time, including Binchois himself. The secular songs, unlike those of Dufay, generally conform to older practices of scoring for three parts, only one of which is texted. An exception is the well-known *Filles à marier* for SATB voices, all texted.

JEAN DE (JOHANNES) OCKEGHEM CA.1410–1497

Ockeghem was most likely born in Saint Ghislain, near Mons and the family town of Okegem in East Flanders. He was also most likely a chorister with Gilles Binchois at the church of St Germain in Mons. In 1443 or 1444 Ockeghem became a *vicaire-chanteur* (lay singer) at the Cathedral of Our Lady in Antwerp, and from 1446 to 1448 he held a similar position at the Moulins court of Charles I, Duke of Bourbon. During this time he also had contact with Guillaume Dufay at the Burgundian court under Philip the Good, whose sister was the wife of Charles I. In 1451 Ockeghem joined the royal chapel under Charles VII (Charles le Victorieux, 1422–1461), and in 1454 he was named *premier chapelain* (first chaplain singer). He remained at the royal court under Louis XI (Louis le Prudent, 1461–1483) and Charles VIII (Charles l'Affable, 1483–1498), becoming *maistre de chapelle de chant du roy* in 1464. He was highly respected by his contemporaries, including the theorist Johannes Tinctoris, who called Ockeghem the leading composer of the age, and by his fellow composers Josquin Desprez, Pierre de La Rue, Antoine Brumel, and Loyset Compère, each of whom composed a lament on Ockeghem's death.

Ockeghem composed ten complete mass cycles, three partial mass cycles, one Requiem, five motets, and twenty-one chansons. The predominance of mass cycles in his sacred output is indicative of a practice that would become common throughout the early years of the Renaissance. Also indicative of more modern practices is the scoring of most masses for SATB voices (all texted) and the parodying of preexisting material. *Missa Ecce ancilla Domini* is based on a Gregorian chant (Ockeghem's only mass to use a sacred melody), *Missa Au travail suis* is based on the cantus firmus of a rondeau generally ascribed to Ockeghem, *Missa Caput* is based on the cantus firmus of a previously composed *Missa Caput* (formerly ascribed to Dufay), and *Missa L'homme armé* is based on the popular secular song of the time. Ockeghem's three most famous masses are not based on preexisting material and are representative of the composer's penchant for mathematical complexities. *Missa prolationum* (prolation or mensuration mass), so called because of its simultaneous use of all four of the prolations (time signatures) prescribed by Philippe de Vitry in his treatise *Ars nova,* consists of double canons that begin in unison and progress through all intervals until the octave; *Missa cuiusvis toni* (in whatever mode) is designed to be sung in any of the existing modes or key signatures; and *Missa Mi-mi* uses only a two-note interval as a head motif and unifying factor throughout the mass. The *Requiem* is the earliest extant polyphonic setting of the mass for the dead. It is divided into five sections (Introitus, Kyrie, Graduale, Tractus, and Offertorium), each of which is based on the Gregorian chant corresponding to its text (notated in the soprano voice part in a slightly ornamented manner). While its overall scoring is for SATB, many sections are scored for two and three voices.

Two of the motets are based on Gregorian chants: *Salve regina* employs the chant in the bass part (not uncommon for Ockeghem), and *Alma redemptoris mater* paraphrases the chant in the tenor part. The other three motets—*Ut heremita solus, Intemerata Dei mater,* and *Ave Maria*—are freely composed. *Intemerata Dei mater* is interesting in that it is divided into sections, some of which are scored for two and three voices, and all of which have different meters.

All of the secular compositions are scored for three voices and structured in the traditional *formes fixes. Prenez sur moi* is a triple canon, and *Mort tu as navré de ton dart / Miserere,* a lament on the death of Binchois, is in ballade form but with both French and Latin texts—the top voice part has ten verses of a French text, while the two middle parts have the text which begins "Miserere pie."

MASSES
SELECTED AND LISTED ACCORDING TO FAMILIARITY

Missa prolationum – SATB chorus – 32 minutes.

Missa cuiusvis toni – SATB chorus – 27 minutes.

Missa Mi-mi – SATB chorus – 30 minutes.

Missa Caput – SATB chorus – 35 minutes.

Missa L'homme armé – SATB chorus – 30 minutes.

Missa De plus en plus – SATB chorus – 36 minutes.

Requiem – SATB chorus – 30 minutes.

MOTETS
COMPLETE AND LISTED ACCORDING TO FAMILIARITY

Ut heremita solus – SATB chorus – 7 minutes.

Intemerata Dei mater – SATTB chorus – 7:30 minutes.

Salve regina – SATB chorus – 8:30 minutes.

Alma redemptoris mater – SATB chorus – 5 minutes.

Ave Maria – SATB chorus – 3 minutes.

SECULAR WORKS
SELECTED ACCORDING TO VOCAL PARTICIPATION

Mort tu as navré de ton dart / Miserere – SATB chorus – 9:30 minutes.

Prenez sur moi – three-voiced canon – 2 to 5 minutes depending upon
   repetitions.

ANTOINE BUSNOIS (BUSNOYS) CA.1430–CA.1492

Busnois was born in Busnes (a version of his name) near Pas-de-Calais in northeastern France. Little is known of his childhood and musical training, although from references in four of his chansons it is probable that he studied in Paris. In 1465 he held a clerical position at the church of St Martin in Tours, and later that year he held a similar position at the church of St Hilaire-le-Grand in Poitiers. In 1467 he became a singer at the court of Charles the Bold, Duke of Burgundy, and from 1477 until 1482 he served Charles's daughter and successor, Mary of Burgundy. For the final decade of his life Busnois was a cantor at the church of St Sauveur. He was well known and esteemed during his lifetime. The famous theoretician Johannes Tinctoris dedicated one of his treatises to both Jean de Ockeghem and Busnois, Ockeghem composed a lament on his death, and the early Renaissance composer Loyset Compère often praised him. In addition, several of his chansons were parodied by composers in the early years of the sixteenth century: *Je ne demande* was used as the basis of masses by Jacob Obrecht and Alexander Agricola, and *Fortuna desperata* was used in masses by Obrecht and Josquin Desprez.

Busnois composed two mass cycles, ten motets, one Magnificat, and sixty-one secular pieces (fifty-eight chansons, two Italian madrigals, and one Flemish song). The sacred works are like those of Ockeghem in that they feature mensuration puzzles and canons. The masses—*Missa L'homme armé* and *Missa O crux lignum*—are both scored for SATB chorus, with slightly ornamented versions of the tunes on which they are based used as a cantus firmus in the tenor part, and with head motifs that begin each movement. Several of the motets (e.g., *Victimae paschali laudes, Gaude caelestis domina,* and both settings of *Regina coeli*) are based on Gregorian chants. Others are freely composed. *Anthoni usque limina,* a motet in honor of St Anthony Abbot, contains a puzzle indicated by the picture of a bell, and *In hydraulis,* composed in 1467 as a tribute to Ockeghem (who Busnois compared to Pythagoras), contains an ostinato on the word "vale" (farewell). Busnois includes his own name in both motets.

The secular works, most of which are in the older *formes fixes,* include the chansons *Je ne demande* for SATB, *Fortuna desperata* in two versions (one for ATB and one for SATB), *A une damme j'ay fait veu* for ATB, and *Vostre beauté / Vous marchez du bout du pié* for SATB.

LOYSET COMPÈRE CA.1445–1518

Compère was born in Hainaut, Burgundy (now Belgium). Nothing is known about his youth, musical training, or professional activity before 1474, when he became a singer in the cappella of Galeazzo Maria Sforza in Milan. Compère was probably sent to Milan by Ockeghem, who, because of close ties between the Sforzas and Louis XI of France, was asked to provide singers for the Milanese court. With the death of Galeazzo in 1477 and the reduction of the cappella, Compère returned to France and entered the royal court. In 1486 he was appointed a *chantre ordinaire* under Charles VIII, and in 1494 he was promoted to *chappelain ordinaire et chantre de nostre chappelle.* After the death of Charles, Compère served as dean of the church of St Géry in Cambrai until 1500 and as provost of the church of St Pierre in Douai until 1504. The last years of his life were spent at the church of St Quentin.

Compère composed two mass cycles, several separate mass movements, forty motets, six Magnificats, and approximately fifty chansons. The two mass cycles are based on preexisting material: *Missa L'homme armé* employs the popular tune as a cantus firmus, and *Missa Alles regrets* parodies Hayne van Ghizeghem's famous chanson. The motets include three groups of *motetti missales* (works that substituted for portions of the Mass Ordinary in the Milanese rite) and sixteen individual motets. Three of the individual motets warrant mention—*Omnium bonorum plena* (a parody of Ghizeghem's *De tous biens plaine*), *Officium de cruce* (an example of expressive word painting), and *Ave Maria, gratia plena* (one of the most famous motets of the early sixteenth century). *O bone Jesu,* previously ascribed to Compère, was probably composed by Francisco de Peñalosa. The Magnificats consist of settings on six of the Gregorian chant tones—tone one for four voices, tone four for two voices, two settings of tone six for four voices, tone seven for four voices, and tone eight for three voices.

The chansons, Compère's most popular compositions, include five pieces that are polytextual, with both French and Latin texts (e.g., *Male bouche / Circumdederunt* and *Royne de ciel / Regina celi*) and approximately forty pieces in the *formes fixes* (e.g., *Venés, regretz* for three voices and *L'aultre jour* for four voices). Fourteen of the chansons were published by Ottaviano Petrucci in Venice.

ALEXANDER AGRICOLA CA.1446–1506

Agricola may have been born in Ghent, Belgium, where he was most likely a chorister at the church of St Nicholas. From 1471 to 1474 he sang in and composed for the cappella at the court of Galeazzo Maria Sforza in Milan—one of the first of several Belgian musicians to do so—and from 1474 to 1476 he served in a similar capacity at the court of Lorenzo de' Medici in Florence. Beginning in 1476 Agricola was employed as a singer at Cambrai Cathedral in northern France, sometime in the late 1480s he joined the French royal court of Charles VIII, he returned to Italy in 1491 to sing at the Florence Cathedral, and for unknown reasons he went back to the French royal chapel in 1492. In 1500 he was engaged as a singer and composer at the court of Philip the Fair, Duke of Burgundy and King of Castile, and during a visit of the court to Spain in 1506 he died of the plague. His death is confirmed in the elegy *Epitaphion Alexandri symphonistae regis Castiliae,* which may have been composed by Heinrich Isaac and which notes that Agricola died at the age of sixty while traveling with his master. Agricola worked with Isaac in Florence and with Pierre de La Rue in Burgundy, and he was noted as having one of the most beautiful singing voices of the age. The style of his music exhibits characteristics of Ockeghem and Obrecht, with long melodic phrases, sequences, ostinatos, and parallel tenths. However, Agricola's phrases are often constructed of short motifs, and the long flow of polyphonic lines is interrupted by frequent cadences.

Agricola composed eight complete mass cycles, five separate mass movements (four Credos and one Sanctus), eighteen motets (including two settings of Salve regina), two sets of Lamentations, three Magnificats, and approximately fifty polyphonic secular songs. Most of the masses are scored for four voices and are structured around cantus firmi of preexisting secular compositions. *Missa Je ne demande* uses a chanson by Antoine Busnois, *Missa In myne zin* uses a polyphonic Flemish song by Agricola himself, and *Missa Le serviteur* and *Missa Malheur me bat* are most likely based on chansons by Dufay and Ockeghem, respectively. The other masses as well as the Lamentations and Magnificats are all based on Gregorian chants.

The motets exhibit a variety of construction techniques. *Si dedero* is based on chant, the second of the *Salve regina* settings employs chant plus the tenor of Walter Frye's motet *Ave regina celorum,* and the first of the *Salve regina* settings is structured on a complex canon at the interval of the second with the rubric "facie ad faciem" (meaning that the second voice of the canon is to be sung inverted). *Transit Anna timor,* Agricola's only secular motet, is a lengthy work in two movements that describes the fortitude of Queen Anne of France during an illness of Louis XII. *Nobis sancte spiritus,* perhaps Agricola's most famous motet, is in a freely imitative style.

Most of the secular pieces are scored for three voices and are in the *formes fixes.* Examples include *En actendant, Allez regretz,* and *Vostre hault bruit.* Agricola's popular chanson *Je n'ay dueil* is for four voices.

JOSQUIN DESPREZ (DES PREZ) CA.1450–1521

The spelling "Desprez," based on an early-sixteenth-century letter, has been standard for many years, although "des Prez" is used in recent studies because Josquin himself wrote his name in three words as an acrostic—IOSQVIN PREZ DES—in the motet *Illibata Dei virgo nutrix,* and also because there is conjecture that he was born in the village of Prez in northern France. There are also two ways of referring to the composer—by his first name Josquin, and by his surname Desprez (or des Prez). He was generally called by his first name during and after his lifetime, and thus some historical studies and reference sources (such as *The New Grove Dictionary of Music and Musicians*) list his name under *J.* However, because the sixteenth-century letter mentioned above and other contemporaneous documents confirm his surname as Desprez, other attributions (such as those found in libraries) are catalogued under *D.* In addition to these two spelling and reference issues, there are two customary beliefs with respect to Josquin's date of birth—in about 1440 (which was the generally accepted opinion until recently), and in about 1450 (which current research supports).

He was most likely born in Burgundy, near the present-day region of Hainaut in Belgium (the location of the village Prez), and he probably was a chorister at the church of St Quentin (where Loyset Compère spent the final years of his life). It is also probable that he studied with or knew of Ockeghem. Josquin's *Missa D'ung aultre amer* and the motets *Tu solus qui facis mirabilia* and *Victimae paschali laudes* are all early works based on Ockeghem's chanson *D'ung aultre amer,* and *Alma redemptoris mater / Ave regina celorum,* one of Josquin's few polytextual motets, quotes the beginning of Ockeghem's *Alma redemptoris mater.* In addition, Josquin and Ockeghem are praised together in Compère's 1472 motet *Omnium bonorum plena,* and Josquin composed an elegy on the death of Ockeghem—*Nymphes des bois* (also called *La déploration de Johan. Ockeghem*), which employs the "Requiem aeternam" Gregorian chant as a cantus firmus. In this elegy, considered to be one of the most profound of its kind, Josquin calls upon the "nymphes des bois" (nymphs of the woods) and "chantres experts de toutes nations" (expert singers of all nations) to mourn their dead master, "le vrai trésoir de musique" (the truest treasure of music). Josquin even included his own name as well as those of Brumel and Compère.

From 1477 to 1480 Josquin was a singer in the court of René, Duke of Anjou, in Aix-en-Provence, and from 1481 to 1484 he was a singer in the French royal chapel of Louis XI. Between 1484 and 1489 he served in the court of Cardinal Ascanio Sforza in Milan, and between 1489 and 1498 he sang in the papal chapel. Because of political turmoil in Rome, he returned to the Sforza court in 1498 and then to the French court in about 1500, and in 1503 he went back to Italy for a one-year appointment as *maestro di cappella* at the court of Ercole I d'Este in Ferrara. The last years of his life were spent as provost at the church of Notre Dame in Condé-sur-l'Escaut, where he was buried. He bequeathed his estate to the church, with the request that his motets *Pater noster, qui es in celis - Ave Maria, gratia plena* and *Ave Maria . . . virgo serena* be sung in front of his house during all liturgical processions.

Josquin was, and is, considered to be the finest composer of the early Renaissance. Several sixteenth-century composers, including Nicolas Gombert, wrote laments on his death, and numerous authors of musical treatises, including Heinrich Glarean and Adrianus Petit Coclico, praised him above all other composers. Ottaviano Petrucci, who never published more than one book each of any composer's music, devoted three books to Josquin, and Pierre Attaingnant published many of Josquin's chansons. Today Josquin is considered to be the most important composer in the development of imitative polyphony. He is especially noted for duet-like pairing of voices (usually soprano with alto and tenor with bass) and for the use of ostinatos.

His compositional output includes eighteen mass cycles, 109 motets, and seventy-eight chansons and frottolas. All the early works exhibit traits of construction techniques that were prevalent in the late years of the Medieval era. The masses and motets are based upon cantus firmi that are either mathematically organized or formed from a notational puzzle, and the chansons are in the style of *formes fixes* pieces by composers such as Guillaume Dufay. Of the early masses, *Missa di dadi* utilizes notational puzzles based on the numbers of dots that appear on the faces of dice; *Missa Hercules dux Ferrarie* is a *soggetto cavato* mass with a cantus firmus constructed of the solmization pitches (*re ut re ut re fa mi re*) that correspond to the vowels in the mass's title; and the cantus firmus of *Missa L'homme armé super voces musicales* (the first of two masses on the popular song) is structured of successive steps of a hexachord presented in various mensuration canons. In addition, the cantus firmus of *Missa Fortuna desperata* is formed from all three voice parts of an anonymous preexisting chanson, and *Missa Mater patris* is a parody of two voices from a motet by Antoine Brumel.

Of the early motets, two are based upon entire melodies from preexisting chants and chansons. *Victimae paschali laudes - Dic nobis, Maria* uses the Gregorian chant in the alto and tenor voice parts as well as two chansons—Ockeghem's *D'ung aultre amer* and Ghizeghem's *De tous bien plaine*—in the soprano voice, and *Stabat mater - Eya mater, fons amoris* uses the tenor of Binchois' chanson *Comme femme desconfortée* as a cantus firmus in long notes. Other early motets utilize fragments of preexisting material. *Illibata Dei virgo nutrix - Ave virginum decus hominum* has a three-note cantus firmus ostinato, set to the solmization syllables *la mi la*, that is telescoped proportionally as in motets by Dufay and Dunstable; *Miserere mei, Deus* has a cantus firmus built from a short fragment of chant that is repeated as an ostinato on descending and ascending pitch levels; and the five-voiced *Salve regina - Eya ergo, advocata nostro* has a cantus firmus that consists of the four-note opening of the chant melody on two pitch levels. The cantus firmus treatments in the latter two of these motets are particularly noteworthy. In *Miserere mei, Deus* an eight-note phrase, each note corresponding to a syllable of the text's first three words, is placed in the second tenor part (which has no other music) and stated at the end of twenty-one sections of music; the first eight statements begin on pitches that successively descend a scale, the second eight statements begin on pitches that ascend the same scale, and the last five statements descend halfway through the scale. In *Salve regina - Eya ergo, advocata nostro* only the opening two four-note motifs are notated, followed by the rubric "Qui perserveraverit salvus erit" (He who persists will be saved). To realize the cantus firmus (the alto voice part, called quinta pars), one must interpret the meaning of "persists" as "multiple repetitions" and simply repeat the two four-note motifs throughout the entire motet. Doing so results in twenty-four statements of the motif—twelve in the first third of the motet, six in the second third, and six in the final third.

Of the early chansons, *Cela sans plus* is in the form of a rondeau; *Parfons regretz* is constructed on a cantus firmus in the middle voice part, with motifs that are treated imitatively in the other parts; *Adieu mes amours* features two independent voice parts over a double canon; and *Petite camusette* is entirely canonic.

The later masses, motets, and chansons dispense with notational puzzles, preexisting material limited to one cantus firmus voice part, and the *formes fixes,* and instead, they present musical material freely and in a texture that is unified by statements of motifs or phrases that pervade all voice parts. For example, the L'homme armé tune is stated in all voice parts of *Missa L'homme armé sexti toni,* the solmization motif *la sol fa re me* is presented hundreds of times throughout the fabric of *Missa La sol fa re mi,* and the chant "Pange lingua" is paraphrased, imitated, and used as a head motif to unify the entire texture of *Missa Pange lingua.* Similarly, imitative techniques permeate and integrate the voice parts in the motets *Praeter rerum seriem, De profundis,* and *In principio erat verbum.* In *Pater noster, qui es in celis - Ave Maria, gratia plena* Josquin artfully combines a two-voice canon derived from two Gregorian chants (one in each movement) with polyphony based on the chants to form a cohesive imitative texture. Two motets—*Gaude virgo mater Christi* and *Memor esto verbi tui - Portio mea, Domini*—exhibit the voice pairing technique that was such an important characteristic of Josquin's late writing. Each motet is also in an ABA-like structure: motifs used at the end of the motet are drawn from the motet's beginning phrase. *Memor esto verbi tui - Portio mea* is particularly interesting in that it almost entirely consists of duet passages, including very short motif-like phrases that are in dialogue between the upper and lower voices. This dialogue effect is noteworthy because the motifs are melodically and rhythmically almost identical. In *Ave Maria . . . virgo serena*, Josquin's most celebrated motet in the new imitative style, the six verses of the motet's text are set in six different imitative styles, from pure canon at the unison and octave in verse one, to varieties of imitative duets in verses two through four, to a disguised canon in a homophonic texture in verse five, to pervasive imitation in verse six. Also new and unique, Josquin closes the motet with a homophonic coda in the form of a personal plea—"O mater Dei, memento mei, Amen" (O mother of God, remember me, Amen). The *Missa de beata virgine*, Josquin's most popular mass during the sixteenth century, is also in an imitative style. However, because each movement is based on a different Gregorian chant and the movements have varied scoring, it may be a compilation of movements rather than a unified work.

MASSES
SELECTED AND LISTED ACCORDING TO FAMILIARITY

Missa Pange lingua – SATB chorus – 30 minutes.

Missa de beata virgine – SATB chorus for the Kyrie and Gloria, and SATTB chorus for the Credo, Sanctus, and Agnus Dei – 35 minutes.

Missa La sol fa re mi – SATB chorus – 29 minutes.

Missa Hercules dux Ferrarie – SATB chorus – 27 minutes.

Missa L'homme armé sexti toni – SATB chorus – 32:30 minutes.

Missa Ave maris stella – SATB chorus – 24 minutes.

Missa Faisant regretz – SATB chorus – 22 minutes.

MOTETS
SELECTED AND LISTED ACCORDING TO FAMILIARITY

Ave Maria . . . virgo serena – SATB chorus – 5:30 minutes.

Pater noster, qui es in celis - Ave Maria, gratia plena – SSATTB chorus – 9 minutes.

Salve regina - Eya ergo, advocata nostro – SATTB chorus – 6:30 minutes.

Miserere mei, Deus (Psalm 51) – SATTB chorus – 16 minutes.

Illibata dei virgo nutrix - Ave virginum decus hominum – SATTB chorus – 4:30 minutes.

Absalon, fili mi – TBBB chorus – 4 minutes.

De profundis (Psalm 130) – SATBB chorus – 4 minutes.

Gaude virgo mater Christi – SATB chorus – 3:15 minutes.

Memor esto verbi tui - Portio mea, Domine (Psalm 119:49–64) – SATB chorus – 5 minutes.

Alma redemptoris mater / Ave regina celorum – SATB chorus – 6 minutes.

Inviolata, integra et casta es – SATTB chorus – 5:30 minutes.

Vultum tuum deprecabuntur omnes divites plebes – SATB chorus – 18 minutes.

Domine, ne in furore (Psalm 38) – SATB chorus – 5 minutes.

Praeter rerum seriem – SSATBB chorus – 5 minutes.

O Domine Jesu Christe – SATB chorus – 12 minutes.

Victimae paschali laudes - Dic nobis, Maria – SATB chorus – 3 minutes.

CHANSONS AND FROTTOLAS
SELECTED AND LISTED ACCORDING TO FAMILIARITY

Nymphes des bois – SATTB chorus – 5:30 minutes.

Parfons regretz – SAATB voices – 3 minutes.

Allégez moy – SSATTB voices – 4 minutes.

Petite camusette – SATTB voices – 1:30 minutes.

Se congié prens – SATTB voices – 3 minutes.

Baisez moy, ma doulce amye – SATB voices – 1:30 minutes.

El grillo – SATB voices – 1:30 minutes.

Scaramella va alla guerra – SATB voices – 2 minutes.

Mille regretz – SATB voices – 2 minutes.

PIERRE DE LA RUE CA.1452–1518

La Rue was born in Tournai, the oldest city in Belgium, where he received his musical training as a chorister at the local cathedral. As a young adult he sang in churches in Brussels and Ghent, and from the early 1490s until his death he was employed at the Habsburg-Burgundian court under Maximilian and his son Philip the Fair. During this service he traveled frequently throughout France and Germany, meeting and collaborating with such composers as Heinrich Isaac and Josquin Desprez.

La Rue composed thirty mass cycles, one Requiem, six separate mass movements (one Kyrie and five Credos), twenty-four motets, eight Magnificats (one on each chant tone), and twenty-four chansons. He most likely did not compose the Lamentations of Jeremiah previously ascribed to him. The sacred repertoire exhibits both conservative styles (such as canons and cantus firmi in one voice based on preexisting material) and more modern styles (such as voice pairings and imitative polyphony). The secular music includes only three chansons in the *formes fixes*—*A vous non autre, Ce n'est pas jeu,* and *De l'oeil de la fille du roy.* All the other chansons, free in structure, presage the type of freely imitative and homophonic writing common in the later Parisian chansons.

Several masses are based on secular material, including *Missa L'homme armé* and *Missa Incessament* (based on his own chanson *Incessament mon pauvre cueur lamente*). However, unlike his contemporaries, who based most of their masses on secular songs of the day, La Rue based most of his on chant melodies. In addition, La Rue occasionally employed multiple chant melodies—as in *Missa de beata virgine* and *Missa de septem doloribus*—and he frequently quoted preexisting material extraneous to the chants. For instance, the chant *O dulcis amica Dei* is added to the final Agnus Dei of *Missa Ave sanctissima Maria,* the L'homme armé melody is incorporated into the texture of *Missa Sancta dei genitrix,* and the soprano part in the last phrase of Josquin's motet *Ave Maria . . . virgo serena* is quoted in *Missa de septem doloribus.* Two masses— *Missa O salutaris hostia* and *Missa Ave sanctissima Maria*—are completely canonic, and two masses—*Missa Cum iocunditate* and *Missa Sancta dei genitrix*—feature ostinatos. Canons and ostinatos are also prominent features of the motets and chansons. For example, the chanson *En espoir vis* and the motets *Ave sanctissima Maria, Da pacem Domine,* and the first of the *Salve regina* settings are completely canonic; *Cent mille regretz* and *Fors seulement* are partially so.

The *Missa pro fidelibus defunctis* (Requiem) is La Rue's most famous work. Like the Requiem of Ockeghem, it features low bass parts, and as in the music of Josquin, the scoring contains extensive passages for two voices. La Rue's Requiem is divided into seven movements—Introitus, Kyrie, Psalmus ("Sicut cervus"), Offertorium, Sanctus, Agnus Dei, and Communio—that vary in scoring from ATBB to ATBBB to SATB to SATBB. Most of the movements are based on the Gregorian chants that correspond to their texts, and most of the movements also begin with or contain a short chant incipit.

MASSES
SELECTED AND LISTED ACCORDING TO FAMILIARITY

Missa pro fidelibus defunctis (Requiem) – SATBBB chorus – 27 minutes.

Missa Assumpta est Maria – SATB chorus – 31 minutes.

Missa L'homme armé – SATB chorus – 27 minutes.

Missa Incessament – SATBB chorus – 42 minutes.

MOTETS
SELECTED AND LISTED ACCORDING TO FAMILIARITY

O salutaris hostia – SATB chorus – 4 minutes.

Pater de caelis Deus – SATTBB chorus – 10:30 minutes.

Lauda anima mea Dominum (Psalm 146) – SATB chorus – 4:30 minutes.

Ave regina caelorum – ATTB chorus – 2 minutes.

JACOB OBRECHT CA.1457–1505

Obrecht was probably born in Ghent, Belgium, where his father was a trumpeter, and he most likely received his musical training as a chorister under Antoine Busnois at the Burgundian court. From 1480 to 1485 he held positions in Bergen op Zoom, Netherlands, and Cambrai, France, and from 1485 to 1504 he went back and forth between appointments in Bruges and

Antwerp. During the last year of his life he served as *maestro di cappella* at the court of Ercole I d'Este in Ferrara, Italy. It is interesting to note that Josquin Desprez served a one-year appointment in Ercole's court the year before Obrecht served. Josquin left Ferrara because of the plague, but Obrecht stayed and died from it.

The two composers were often compared, although not because of their similarities. Josquin was thought to have composed slowly and when it suited him, while Obrecht composed quickly (a mass in a single day, according to one account) and in compliance with his professional responsibilities. In addition, Josquin's compositions were considered archaic in that they were filled with canons and notational puzzles, while Obrecht's compositions were considered modern, accessible, and euphonious (the noted theorist Johannes Tinctoris referred to them as sweet-sounding). These estimations of Obrecht's music were undoubtedly the result of the many parallel thirds, sixths, and tenths in his masses and motets.

Obrecht composed thirty mass cycles that can be ascribed to him with certainty (plus another five that can be attributed to him on stylistic grounds), approximately thirty motets (including three settings of Salve regina), one Magnificat, and thirty secular pieces. It is unlikely that he composed the St Matthew Passion that is occasionally attributed to him. Most of the masses are based on preexisting material used as unadorned cantus firmi in the tenor voice part. *Missa Beata viscera* and *Missa Sub tuum presidium* utilize BVM (Blessed Virgin Mary) chants; *Missa de tous biens playne* and *Missa Fors seulement* parody chansons by Ghizeghem and Ockeghem, respectively; and *Missa Fortuna desperata*, *Missa Je ne demande*, and *Missa L'homme armé* all replicate tenor cantus firmi from compositions by Busnois. In *Missa L'homme armé*, for instance, Obrecht arranged the notes of the L'homme armé melody exactly as Busnois had arranged them in his *Missa L'homme armé* with one exception: whereas Busnois set the melody in inversion (upside down) in the Agnus Dei, Obrecht set it in retrograde inversion (upside down and backwards). To further pay tribute to Busnois, Obrecht followed the latter's division of text, mensuration signs, voice distributions, and overall length. Obrecht even used motifs of the tune in other voice parts as Busnois had done. However, Obrecht's use of other unifying motifs, duets in exact imitation, sequential patterns, and parallel thirds, sixths, and tenths clearly identify his mass as Renaissance and not Medieval.

The motets are similarly based on preexisting material, although more on sacred than on secular models. *Ave regina celorum* uses the tenor cantus firmus of Walter Frye's motet; *Mille quingentis / Requiem aeternam* (an elegy to Obrecht's father) incorporates the Introit from the Requiem mass; and *Factor orbis / Canite tuba*, *Mater patris / Sancta Dei genitrix*, and *O beate Basili / O beate pater* are all based on Gregorian chants.

The secular repertoire, which is divided between chansons and polyphonic songs with Dutch texts, consists of many pieces that are imitative and do not adhere to *formes fixes* structures. Many are also textless or have only identifying text incipits, thus indicating instrumental rather than vocal performance.

JEAN MOUTON CA.1459–1522

All that is known about Mouton's youth is that he was born near Samer in northern France. In 1477 he was a singer at the church of Notre Dame in Nesle (also in northern France), and in 1483 he was appointed *maître de chapelle* there. In 1500 he was named *maître des enfants* at Amiens

Cathedral, and the following year he assumed the same position at the church of St André in Grenoble. Several years later he entered the court of Queen Anne of Brittany, serving her as a singer and composer. With her death in 1514 Brittany came under French rule, and Mouton served Louis XII and François I until 1518, at which time he succeeded Loyset Compère at the church of St Quentin. Mouton was a highly respected composer during his lifetime. Heinrich Glarean praised his writing as "facili fluentem filio cantum" (melody flowing in a supple thread), and he also included several of Mouton's motets in his famous treatise *Dodecachordon*.

Mouton composed fifteen mass cycles, one hundred motets, nine Magnificats, and twenty-five chansons. Most of the masses and motets, like those of his contemporaries, are based on preexisting material. Examples include the masses *Missa Alma redemptoris mater* and *Missa Benedictus Dominus Deus,* and the motets *Noli flere, Maria* and *Regem confessorum Dominum.* Many works in all the genres are also canonic, including the chansons *En venant de Lyon* and *Qui ne regrettroit* (a lament on the death of Antoine de Févin), and Mouton's most famous motet, *Nesciens mater virgo virum* (which consists of a quadruple canon). Several of the motets were composed for ceremonies in the royal court: *Quis dabit oculis* was written for Queen Anne's death, *Domine salvum fac regem* was written for the coronation of François I, *Exalta regina Galliae* was written to celebrate François's victory at the battle of Marignano, and *Exsultet conjubilando Deo* was written for a visit between François and Pope Leo X. Other notable motets (e.g., *Ave Maria . . . virgo serena, Ave sanctissima Maria,* and *Ave Maria gemma virginum*) are set to texts in praise of the Virgin Mary. While Mouton based many of his compositions on preexisting material and while he employed canons as a structural device, he did not limit his borrowed material to a cantus firmus in one voice part, and the canons were not derived from notational puzzles. The textures of his music appear as and sound like integrated polyphony.

ANTOINE BRUMEL CA.1460–CA.1512

Brumel was born near Chartres and likely sang as a chorister at Chartres Cathedral before singing there as an adult beginning in 1483. In 1486 he was appointed *maître des enfants* at the church of St Pierre in Geneva, France, and in 1498 he accepted the same position at Notre Dame Cathedral in Paris. Because of a dispute with officials at Notre Dame, he left the cathedral in 1501 and joined the choir at the ducal court in Chambéry. In 1506 he was named *maestro di cappella* at the court of Alfonso I d'Este in Ferrara, Italy, following Josquin Desprez, who had held the position in 1503 and 1504, and Jacob Obrecht, who had held the position in 1505. When the court chapel was disbanded in 1510, Brumel became a priest in Mantua, where he presumably died. He is noted for the sonorous character of his music, which some scholars believe is the result of studies with Josquin, and for linearly smooth vocal lines, which foreshadow the later writing of Palestrina.

Brumel composed fifteen mass cycles, seven separate mass movements, thirty-one motets, three Magnificats, and five chansons. The early masses are based on preexisting material such as the cantus firmus works of Obrecht. In *Missa Berzerette savoyenne* (based on the chanson by Josquin) the entire melody is presented in the soprano voice of the Kyrie and then in the tenor voice of the other movements. The melody is stated once in the Agnus Dei followed by the rubric "Ut jacet primo cante per duplum post retroverte," signifying that the melody is to be sung first as stated and then in retrograde. In *Missa Ut re mi fa sol la* the hexachord serves as a cantus firmus in the tenor voice as well as motivic material for the other voice parts. In *Missa L'homme armé* and *Missa Victimae paschali laudes* the song and chant melodies are treated in traditional manners. Later masses are either canonic or free in construction. *Missa A l'ombre d'ung buissonet*, based on Josquin's chanson, is entirely constructed of canons, and *Missa Et ecce terra motus*, based on the first seven notes of the Gregorian Easter antiphon, features a three-part canon set in distinctly long rhythmic values. This latter mass became famous for its scoring: it is one of the first works of the Renaissance era to be composed for twelve voice parts (SSSAAATTTBBB). Brumel's other famous masses are *Missa de beata virgine* (a late work that paraphrases various Gregorian Mass Ordinary chants) and *Missa pro defunctis* (the first polyphonic setting of the mass for the dead that includes the Dies irae).

A few of the motets are based on a cantus firmus in the tenor voice. An example is *Lauda Sion salvatorem*, a lengthy work that alternates polyphony with chant. Most of the motets, however, incorporate preexisting material into the overall vocal texture. Examples include *Haec dies*, *Regina caeli laetare*, and *Sub tuum praesidium*. Other well-known motets are *Laudate Dominum de caelis*, *Mater patris et filia*, *O Domine Jesu Christe*, and *Heth - Cogitavit Dominus* (a setting of the fifth letter of the Hebrew alphabet from Lamentations 2:8, 11).

Two of the chansons are popular—*Tous les regretz* and *Du tout plongiet / Fors seulement*. The first is mostly homophonic and in a style similar to the Parisian chansons of the mid-sixteenth century. The second incorporates the soprano voice of Ockeghem's chanson in the tenor voice.

PIERRE PASSEREAU FL.1509–1547

Nothing is known about Passereau's life except that he was a singer for the Count of Angoulême (who became François I) from 1509 throughout the king's reign between 1515 and 1547. In addition, nothing is known about Passereau's music except that he composed twenty-five chansons and one motet. The paucity of biographical and musically related information is unfortunate given the fact that Passereau was the first composer to be recognized exclusively for his secular repertoire and that his *Il est bel et bon* not only became one of the most popular chansons of the sixteenth century, but remains so today. This piece exhibits many of the compositional features (e.g., pervasive imitative polyphony, voice pairings, integrated refrain phrases, and modern tonality) that would define the Parisian chanson and that would characterize the genre throughout the remainder of the sixteenth century. Also, with its humorous text and onomatopoeic sounds (the clucking of hens), it helped popularize the chanson and contribute to its success as a fashionable genre.

CLÉMENT JANEQUIN (JANNEQUIN) CA.1485–CA.1558

Janequin was born in Châtellerault (south of Tours, France), where he most likely sang in the local church choir and where he was trained as a priest. From 1505 to 1523 he served in a secretarial capacity to Lancelot Du Fau in Bordeaux, and from 1523 to 1529 he similarly served Jean de Foix, Bishop of Bordeaux. Janequin was *maître des enfants* at Auch Cathedral from 1531 to 1534, *maître de chapelle* at Angers Cathedral from 1534 to 1537, and from the early 1550s until his death he served the Duke of Guise, first as *chantre ordinaire* and then as *compositeur ordinaire*.

Janequin composed two masses, one surviving motet, and more than 250 chansons. Both masses—*Missa super L'aveuglé dieu* and *Missa super La bataille*—are based on his own chansons, and his motet *Congregati sunt* is based on a Gregorian chant. Most of the chansons (e.g., *Au joli jeu*) are of the Parisian type like *Il est bel et bon* by Pierre Passereau, with short imitative phrases, paired voices, repeated sections that serve as refrains, and modern tonalities. However, Janequin is best known for his programmatic works, which are longer pieces set to narrative texts that prominently feature onomatopoeic sounds. *Le chant des oiseaux* (The song of the birds), for instance, contains lengthy passages of bird-like calls (many on single notes that imitate chirps) that are framed by the refrain "Réveillez vous, coeurs endormis, le dieu d'amour vous sonne" (Wake up, sleepy hearts, the god of love is calling you). In *La bataille* (The battle)—also called *La Guerre* and *La bataille de Marignan*—sounds of drums and fifes are intermingled in a depiction of the 1515 Battle of Marignano: men are called to battle, the fleur de lys is carried as a banner, drums and other instruments accompany the fight, the French soldiers kill their enemies, and victory comes to the French king—"Victoire au noble roy Francoys." Other lesser-known programmatic chansons are *L'alouette, La chasse,* and *Les cris de Paris*.

CHANSONS
SELECTED AND LISTED ACCORDING TO FAMILIARITY

Le chant des oiseaux – SATB voices – 4 minutes.

La bataille – SATB voices – 6 minutes.

Au joli jeu – SATB voices – 2 minutes.

Pourquoi tournés vous vos yeux – SATB voices – 2 minutes.

CLAUDIN DE SERMISY CA.1490–1562

Like Josquin Desprez, Claudin de Sermisy was and is often referred to by his first name. However, unlike Josquin, Claudin is always referenced by his surname, Sermisy. The locations of his birth and childhood years are unknown, although it is believed that he was associated with Sainte-Chapelle in Paris as a young adult. In 1510 he was a singer in the chapel of Queen Anne of Brittany, and after her death in 1514 when Brittany came under French rule, he sang in the courts of Louis XII (who died in 1515) and François I (who ruled from 1515 to 1547). With his colleague Jean Mouton, Sermisy is known to have sung at the funeral of Louis XII, at a meeting between Pope Leo X and François I in 1515, and at meetings between Henry VIII of England and François I in 1520 and 1532. Sermisy's motet *Da pacem Domine* was performed during this latter meeting. In 1533 he was named *sous-maître* of the royal court, and during the final decade of his life he also maintained an association with Sainte-Chapelle, where he was buried. He was well regarded during and after his life; many of his chansons were transcribed for performance by lute, and upon his death a lament was composed by Pierre Certon.

Sermisy composed thirteen mass cycles, several separate mass movements, one Requiem, seventy-eight motets, ten Magnificats, one Passion, one set of Lamentations, and 175 chansons. Most of the masses, like those of his predecessors and contemporaries, are based on preexisting material. *Missa Domine quis habitabit, Missa Domini est terra, Missa Quare fremuerunt gentes,* and *Missa Tota pulchra es* are based on his own motets, and *Missa plurium motetorum* is based on a combination of motets by Josquin, Févin, Sermisy himself, and others. One of three masses based on Gregorian chants—*Missa Novem lectionum*—was sung frequently at Sainte-Chapelle during the sixteenth century. The Requiem, Magnificats (which include a setting on each of the Gregorian chant tones), Passion (a setting of text from St Matthew), and Lamentations are also based on chant. However, these works are in *alternatim* style. All of the masses and other sacred works mentioned above are scored for four voices (SATB) except *Missa Quare fremuerunt gentes,* which is scored for five voices (SATTB). In addition, all of the masses are characterized by syllabic settings of text, short phrases of imitative polyphony, and occasional passages of homophony.

The motets were very popular during Sermisy's lifetime and were often included in liturgical services sung for the kings. Most are similar to the masses in style and scoring, although a few are scored for other voicings. *Deus misereatur nostri* is for five voices, and *Salve regina* is for six voices. Other notable motets, all for four voices, are *Benedic anima mea Domino; Resurrexi, et adhuc tecum sum; Exurge, quare obdormis, Domine;* and *Noe, noe, magnificatus est.*

The chansons—with their lighthearted subjects, syllabic text settings, basically homophonic textures, and repeated sections of music—best exemplify the Parisian chanson. Well-known examples include *Jouyssance vous donneray* and *Tant que vivrai* (both about the constancy and joys of love); *Martin menoit son porceau* (about the follies of casual sexual encounters); and *Hau, hau, hau le boys* and *La, la maistre Pierre* (about the pleasures of wine). Chansons with more serious texts include the exceptionally sonorous *Pour ung plaisir* and *Languir me fais.*

NICOLAS GOMBERT CA.1495–CA.1560

Gombert was most likely born in Belgium, close to the birthplaces of Loyset Compère, Josquin Desprez, Pierre de La Rue, and Jacob Obrecht. Nothing is known about Gombert's youth, although there is reason to believe that he studied with Josquin in Condé-sur-l'Escaut. In 1526 he became a singer in the court of Charles V (Ruler of Burgundy, Archduke of Austria, and King of Spain, Naples, and Sicily at the time), in 1529 he was appointed *maître des enfants,* and the final several years of his life were spent at the church of Notre Dame in Tournai. He was one of the most respected composers in Europe at the time of his death. Hermann Finck wrote in his 1556 treatise *Practica Musica,* "Gombert, pupil of Josquin of fond memory, shows all musicians the path, nay more, the exact way to refinement and the requisite imitative style." In addition, many of Gombert's works were published in France and Italy, and numerous composers of the late sixteenth century (including Orlando di Lasso, Clemens non Papa, Cristóbal de Morales, and Claudio Monteverdi) based their masses on his motets and chansons.

Gombert composed nine surviving mass cycles, more than 160 motets, eight Magnificats, and approximately seventy chansons. Most of the masses are based on motets and chansons of the time. *Missa Beati omnes* and *Missa Media vita* parody his own motets, and *Missa Je suis desheritée* and *Missa Sur tous regretz* use material from chansons by Pierre Cadéac and Jean Richafort, respectively. The preexisting material is never used in a strict fashion (i.e., as a cantus firmus) but is loosely paraphrased in all the voice parts. For instance, each movement in *Missa Media vita* begins with clearly identifiable material from the motet model, while the remaining portions of the movements often consist of newly created melodies and rhythms. In addition, the voice parts are characterized by continuous imitative polyphony. This style of linked points of imitation, which would become the norm for the generation of composers after Gombert, was relatively new. Paired voices, varied rhythms, and changing meters gave way to a consistently unified texture. Finck commented on this style in *Practica Musica,* writing that Gombert "composes music altogether different from what went on before, for he avoids pauses and his work is rich with full harmonies and imitative polyphony." Also new for the time was the expansion of scoring from four to five (three masses) and six voices (two masses), with a further increase of voices in Agnus Dei movements. For example, the Agnus Dei of the six-voiced *Missa Tempore paschali* is for twelve voices.

A few of the motets are in older styles and were composed for ceremonial occasions. *Musae Jovis,* Gombert's extraordinary elegy on the death of Josquin, uses the chant *Circumdederunt me* as a cantus firmus in statements of reduced rhythmic proportion, and *Felix Austriae domus* was composed for the coronation of Ferdinand I in 1531. Most of the motets, however, are in the new style described above. Notable examples are *Tulerunt Dominum meum* for eight voices, two of the three settings of *Regina caeli* (those for four and twelve voices), *In te Domine speravi* and *Media vita* for six voices, and *Anima mea liquefacta est* for five voices. There is no evidence that Gombert composed *Lugebat David,* formerly ascribed to him. The Magnificats—one on each of the eight Gregorian chant tones—are considered to be Gombert's finest works. They are all for four voices, with expansion in the final sections as noted above in the masses, and they are also all in *alternatim* style.

A few of the chansons (e.g., *Amours vous me faictes* and *Quant je suis au prez de mamye*) are of the Parisian type composed by Claudin de Sermisy, and a few are of the programmatic type composed by Clément Janequin. *Or escoutez* has sounds that suggest the chasing of a rabbit, and *Resveillez vous* is an arrangement of Janequin's *Le chant des oiseaux.* Most of the chansons are in the imitative style that characterizes the majority of the masses and motets. Examples include *Mille regretz* and *Changeons propos* for six voices; *Ayme qui vouldra* for five voices; and *C'est à grand tort, En aultre avoir,* and *Vous estes trop jeune* for four voices.

JACOBUS (JACOB) CLEMENS (CLEMENT) NON PAPA
CA.1510–CA.1556

It is presumed that Clemens non Papa was born in Belgium and educated in Paris; there are references to the Clement family in Belgium at the time, and several of his chansons were published in Paris in the 1530s by Pierre Attaignant. In 1544 and 1545 Clemens was succentor at St Donaas Cathedral in Bruges, and thereafter he composed without official appointment for various Flemish dignitaries and organizations, including Charles V, a Marian brotherhood, and St Pieterskerk in Leiden. His original name was Jacob Clement, but he was called Clemens non Papa, probably in jest, to distinguish him from Pope Clemens VII.

He composed fourteen mass cycles, one Requiem, two separate mass movements (a Kyrie and a Credo), two complete Magnificat cycles, 233 motets, 150 settings of the Psalms in Dutch, approximately ninety chansons, and eight polyphonic Dutch songs. The masses, excluding the Requiem, are all parodies of motets and chansons. Two masses—*Missa Ecce quam bonum* and *Missa Pastores quidnam vidistis*—are based on his own motets, and three masses are parodies of chansons by well-known composers of the time—Adrian Willaert (*Missa A la fontaine*), Nicolas Gombert (*Missa En espoir*), and Claudin de Sermisy (*Languir me fais*). Like Gombert, Clemens composed in a pervasively imitative style and expanded voicing in the Agnus Dei portions of the mass. The Requiem (*Missa defunctorum*) is based on Gregorian chant. Most of the motets are for four voices and are in the imitative style of the masses. Only two motets—*Circumdederunt me* and *Si diligis me*—employ cantus firmus technique. Three are unique in being set to texts in praise of music; an example is *Musica dei donum optimi* (Music, God's greatest gift). The Dutch Psalm settings, called *souterliedekens* and *lofzangen,* are all three-voiced settings of familiar tunes (not the same as those used in Calvinist psalters), with the tune stated clearly in either the soprano or tenor voice.

The four-voiced chansons are in the homophonic and syllabic style of Sermisy, while the five- and six-voiced chansons are in the imitative style of Gombert. The secular Dutch pieces are imitative, but in a style that is simpler than the imitative chansons.

MASSES AND MOTETS
SELECTED AND LISTED ACCORDING TO FAMILIARITY

Pastores quidnam vidistis – SATTB chorus – 4:45 minutes.

Missa Pastores quidnam vidistis – SATTB chorus – 28 minutes.

Missa defunctorum – SATB chorus – 20 minutes.

Ego flos campi – SAATTBB chorus – 4:15 minutes.

Musica dei donum optimi – SATB chorus – 4 minutes.

Vox in Rama audita est – SATB chorus – 3:15 minutes.

Ave Maria – SSATB chorus – 2:30 minutes.

Crux fidelis – SATB chorus – 3 minutes.

Tribulationes civitatum – SATB chorus – 5:15 minutes.

Pater peccavi – SATB chorus – 8:30 minutes.

LOYS BOURGEOIS CA.1510–CA.1560

There is no information or speculation about the childhood or musical training of Bourgeois, and there is very little information about his later life or musical activities. All that is known are general facts about his employment and publications: three of his total output of four chansons (*Ce moys de may, Si par faveur d'amour,* and *Ung soir bien tard*) were published by Jacques Moderne in 1539; he was a singer and *maître des enfants* at the churches of St Pierre and St Gervais in Geneva from 1545 until 1552; two volumes of his Psalm settings—*Pseaulmes de David* and *Le premier livre des pseaulmes*—were published by the Beringen brothers of Lyons in 1547; he wrote a treatise (*Le droict chemin de musique*) on sight-singing in 1550; and a revised and augmented version of the 1547 *Pseaulmes de David* was issued in 1554. The superficiality of these biographical details is surprising and regrettable, since Bourgeois was the first important contributor of music for the Calvinist Church. He composed some and organized all of the melodies that were set to translations of the Psalms by Clément Marot and Théodore de Bèze and were used in the first Calvinist Psalter, and he composed four-voiced settings of these and other melodies for use in church and private devotional services. A number of the melodies that are contained in present-day Protestant hymnals are attributed to Bourgeois, including *Old Hundredth* (the Doxology), *Rendez à Dieu,* and *Geneva 42* ("As the hart with eager yearning," Psalm 42). The first of the 1547 volumes, *Pseaulmes de David,* contains simple four-voiced homophonic settings of all 150 Psalms. The second volume, *Le premier livre des pseaulmes,* contains twenty-four settings in which the voice parts are slightly independent and imitative. *Mon Dieu me paist* (Psalm 23), *Pourquoy font bruit* (Psalm 2), *Las, en ta fureur aigue* (Psalm 38), and *Du fond de ma pensee* (Psalm 130) are structured mostly in points of imitation. Others, such as *L'Omnipotent a mon Seigneur* (Psalm 110) and *A Toy, mon Dieu, mon cueur monte* (Psalm 25), have only a few short imitative phrases.

PIERRE CERTON CA.1510–1572

According to existing data, Certon's life was spent entirely in Paris. From 1529 to 1532 he was a clerk at Notre Dame Cathedral, from 1532 to 1536 he held a similar position at Sainte-Chapelle, and from 1536 until his death he was *maître des enfants* at Sainte-Chapelle. In addition, he was appointed *chantre de la chapelle du Roy* and *compositeur de musique de la chapelle du Roy* in the 1560s. He was friends with Sermisy, for whom he composed an elegy similar to that composed by Josquin for Ockeghem.

Certon composed eight extant mass cycles, three separate mass movements, one Requiem, forty-four motets, one Magnificat, four volumes of Calvinist Psalm settings and spiritual chansons, and one hundred secular chansons. The Requiem (*Missa pro defunctis*) and one of the masses (*Missa Sus le pont d'Avignon*) paraphrase preexisting melodies. The other masses are parodies of motets or chansons. All the masses are structured with successive points of imitation separated occasionally by brief passages of homophony, and all are scored overall for four voices, with sections of movements for two or three voices. In *Missa Sus le pont d'Avignon,* for instance, at least one section of each movement is scored for reduced voices, including SAT for the Christe, TB for the Crucifixus and Et resurrexit, and SA for the Benedictus.

Most of the motets are similar to the masses in style, but with more varied scoring. *Ave Maria* and *Da pacem* are for three voices; *Asperges me, Sub tuum praesidium,* and one of three settings of *Regina caeli* are for four voices; *O crux splendidior* and *Quam dilecta* are for five voices; and *Ave virgo gloriosa* and the final setting of *Regina caeli* are for six voices. Two motets feature archaic construction techniques: *Inviolata integra* is built of canons, and *Deus in nomine tuo* contains numerous ostinatos.

The secular chansons are basically of two types—imitative like the masses and motets, and homophonic like the popular Parisian chansons. Examples of the imitative type are *Que n'est elle auprès de moi* (a commentary on love's deception), *Je suis déshéritée* (a lament on unrequited love), and *C'est trop parlé de Bacchus* (a drinking song). Examples of the Parisian style of chanson are *J'espère et crains* (a poignant expression of the duplicity of life) and Certon's most famous chanson, *La, la, la, je ne l'ose dire* (a tale about an adulterous wife).

CLAUDE GOUDIMEL CA.1514–1572

It is likely that Goudimel had musical training and was employed as a singer or composer in a church or court sometime during his life; his composition of masses, motets, and Magnificats suggests this possibility. However, no records of musical activity exist. He was a student at the University of Paris from 1549 to 1551, from 1551 to 1557 he was employed by the publisher Nicolas Du Chemin (becoming Chemin's partner in 1552), and from 1557 until his death during the St Bartholomew's Day Massacre in 1572 he lived in the Huguenot city of Metz.

Goudimel composed five mass cycles, ten motets, three Magnificats, 299 Calvinist Psalm settings, and approximately seventy chansons. The masses, represented by *Missa Il ne se treuve en amitié* and *Missa Le bien que j'ay,* are based on chansons of the time and are in the continuous imitative style of Nicolas Gombert. The motets are also constructed similarly. *Gabriel angelus apparuit*, composed for the feast of John the Baptist, and *Videntes stellam*, composed for Epiphany, consist entirely of points of imitation, often with repeated phrases of text and musical material within each point. In addition, both motets are lengthy and divided into two parts, each part concluding with the same text and music.

The Calvinist Psalm settings are in the three styles fashionable during the day—those that are completely homophonic and hymn-like; those with alto, tenor, and bass parts slightly varied from the soprano melody; and those that are in the imitative motet style. Goudimel composed eighty-two settings in the first style, 150 settings in the second style, and sixty-seven settings in the third style. Many of the homophonic settings are harmonizations of tunes that were composed by Loys Bourgeois and that are contained in Protestant hymnals of today. Examples include *Old Hundredth* (the Doxology), *Geneva 42* ("As the hart with eager yearning," Psalm 42), and *Geneva 124* (Old 124th). Numerous other Psalm tune harmonizations appeared in psalters of the seventeenth century such as the Ainsworth Psalter of 1612. An example is the setting of *Psalm 65* ("O God, praise waits for thee in Sion"), the tune of which was also used for Psalms 57, 60, 67, 113, and 145.

The chansons, like those of Pierre Certon, are divided between imitative and Parisian types. The imitative chansons do not consist completely of points of imitation; there are passages of homophony and sections of music that are freely composed. However, some of the chansons in this style (e.g., *Amour me tue*) consist of phrases that are imitated with inverted melodies. The Parisian type is represented by *Qui renforcera ma voix,* an elegy on the death of Marguerite de Navarre.

CLAUDE (CLAUDIN) LE JEUNE CA.1528–1600

Le Jeune may have spent his youth in or near Valenciennes (close to Cambrai) in northern France. However, he lived most of his life in Paris, where he was a member of the Académie de Poésie et de Musique beginning in 1570; *maître des enfants* at the court of François, Duke of

Anjou and brother of Henri III, from 1582 to the mid-1590s; and *maître compositeur ordinaire de la musique de nostre chambre* under King Henri IV for the last four years of his life.

His compositional output consists of one mass cycle, eleven motets, one Magnificat, 348 Calvinist Psalm settings, forty-two sacred chansons, sixty-five secular chansons, forty-three Italian canzonettas, and 133 airs. The mass, motets, and Magnificat are presumably early works in that they were composed in the conservative imitative style of Gombert. The Calvinist Psalm settings span Le Jeune's adult life and are in a variety of styles. The first Psalms coincide with the three styles exhibited by Goudimel—four-voiced settings in simple hymn-like homophony; four-voiced settings with some imitation in the alto, tenor, and bass voices; and expanded settings with imitative polyphony in all four voices. Later settings, especially those published under the title *Dodécacorde* in 1598, are lengthy works that are based on the standard Geneva tunes and that consist of stanzas for a variety of voicings—mainly two to seven. The final Psalms, those from the posthumous publication *Pseaumes en vers mesurez* of 1606, are settings of Jean-Antoine de Baïf and Agrippa d'Aubigné translations in the *musique mesurée* style.

The *musique mesurée* style (also called *vers mesurée*), of which Le Jeune was the chief musical proponent, is characterized by rhythmic values that correspond to the accented and unaccented syllables of text. Accented syllables were set to long note values (usually half notes), while unaccented syllables were set to shorter note values (usually quarter notes). The result was a metrically free but patterned composition. The style was initiated by Baïf, who formed the Académie de Poésie et de Musique in order to revive humanist ideals and recapture the supposed essence of Greek music, with simple, syllabic musical settings that emulated natural speech rhythms and that contained no artificial construction techniques such as canon or imitation. The Académie, with ultrastrict rules, did not captivate the imaginations of composers other than Le Jeune and did not last beyond the death of King Charles IX in 1574. It was replaced by the Académie du Palais, which subscribed to much freer views about musical composition.

The sacred chansons represent a synthesis of the imitative and word-oriented styles of the Psalm settings. For instance, the thirty-six works in the *Octonaires de la vanité et inconstance du monde* (Reflections on the vanity and inconstancy of the world) are constructed of short imitative phrases, homophonic passages, syllabic text settings, and occasional word painting. The short phrases, whether imitative or homophonic, are especially notable in that they signal the *prima prattica* style of the early Baroque era.

The secular chansons parallel the development of the Psalm settings: the early pieces are in conservative imitative styles, while the later pieces are constructed according to the principles of *musique mesurée.* The seven-voiced (SSATTBB) *Susanne ung jour* is based on the popular tune, which is used as a cantus firmus in the first tenor voice and which is treated as an inverted canon in the second soprano voice. Le Jeune set the tune completely and ended the chanson by repeating its first and final phrases. In addition, the tune is used as imitative material in other voice parts. *Revoici venir du printemps,* Le Jeune's most famous composition in any genre, demonstrates the *rechant* (refrain) format of most pieces in the *musique mesurée* style. The chanson begins with the short refrain "Revoici venir du printemps, l'amoureuse et belle saison" (Springtime returns once again, the season of love and beauty). Two-, three-, four-, and five-voiced *chants* (verses) then follow in succession, each separated by repetitions of the refrain. The entire chanson is completely set to long and short note values that correspond to the accented and unaccented syllables of text, with occasional melismas that fill in the long notes. Other pieces in the *musique mesurée* style are *Ce n'est que fiel* and *Amour cruel que pense tu* (both scored for SATBB), and *Fiere cruelle* (scored for SATB).

CHANSONS
SELECTED AND LISTED ACCORDING TO FAMILIARITY

Revoici venir du printemps – SSATB voices – 3:30 minutes.

Amour cruel que pense tu – SATBB voices – 3 minutes.

Susanne ung jour – SSATTTB voices – 2:30 minutes.

D'une coline – SATTB voices – 3 minutes.

Ce n'est que fiel – SATTB voices – 3 minutes.

Si dessus voz levres de roses – SATB voices – 2:45 minutes.

Le feu, l'air, l'eau, la terre (from *Octonaires de la vanité . . .*) – SATB voices – 8 minutes.

Quel monstre voyje (from *Octonaires de la vanité . . .*) – SATB voices – 8:30 minutes.

GUILLAUME COSTELEY CA.1530–1606

Like Claude Le Jeune, Costeley spent the majority of his life in Paris, where he was also a member of the Académie de Poésie et de Musique and a musician at the French royal court. Unlike Le Jeune, however, Costeley composed very few works in the *musique mesurée* style promoted by the Académie, and his service at the royal court was under the reigns of Charles IX (1560–1574) and Henri III (1574–1589). Very little else is known about Costeley except that the firm Le Roy & Ballard published one hundred of his chansons and three motets in 1570 under the title *Musique de Guillaume Costeley,* and that the pronunciation of his name can be determined from phonetic spellings—Cotelay and Cautelay—in several sixteenth-century sources.

His total output of vocal music consists of the works published by Le Roy & Ballard plus twenty airs. The motets—*Audite caeli quae loguor, Domine salvum fac regem,* and *Eructavit cor meum verbum bonum*—are all in the imitative style of Costeley's contemporaries. The second of the motets is notable in that it was one of the first works to set the text that would be used in liturgical services for Louis XIV and thus would be set by many composers of the Baroque era. Most of the chansons are divided between those in imitative and those in Parisian styles. Examples of the imitative pieces include *En ce beau moys* for SSATB; *Mignonne, allons voir si la roze* for SAT verses and SATB refrain; and *Arreste un peu mon coeur* for SATTB. All are in the style of Le Jeune's sacred chansons, with syllabic settings of text, short points of imitation interspersed with occasional passages of homophony, and a few examples of word painting. The popular Christmas chanson *Allon, gay bergeres* for SATB voices is structured of the homophonic refrain "Allon, gay bergeres, soyez legeres, suyvez moy" (Come, gay shepherds, be joyful, follow me) separated by brief imitative verses. Examples of the Parisian chansons include *Je voy des glissantes eaux* and *Las, je n'eusse jamais pensé,* both for SATB. Costeley composed several programmatic chansons in the style of *La bataille* by Clément Janequin. An example is *Hardis François* (You fearless French), sometimes called *La prise de Calais* (The taking of Calais), a representation of the French victory at Calais in January 1558. Costeley's few pieces in the *musique mesurée* style include the airs *Il n'est trespass plus glorieux* and *Heureux qui d'un soc laboureur.*

PETER PHILIPS CA.1560–1628

Philips was most likely born in London, where he was a chorister at St Paul's Cathedral. After his voice changed, he studied with William Byrd, who was a Gentleman of the Chapel Royal beginning in 1572, and in 1582, at the age of about twenty-two, Philips left England and went to the English College in Rome, where he could freely practice his Catholicism and where he served as organist. In 1585 he met Lord Thomas Paget, also an English Catholic refugee, who was visiting in Rome and who engaged Philips as his organist. Philips traveled with Paget and his household to Genoa, Madrid, Paris, Antwerp, and eventually Brussels, and when Paget died in 1590, Philips returned to Antwerp, where, in his own words, he "mainteyned him self by teaching of children of the virginals." In 1593 he traveled to Amsterdam to study briefly with Sweelinck, and in 1597 he was appointed organist at the court of Archduke Albert in Brussels, where he worked with John Bull (who had fled England and joined the court in 1613) and where he remained until the archduke's death in 1621.

Philips composed approximately three hundred Latin motets, one set of Litanies, and fifty Italian madrigals. The motets initially appeared in the anthology *Hortus musicalis* of 1609, which contained three motets by Philips—one, *Vulnera manuum,* being a translation of his madrigal *Ditemi, O diva mia.* Other motets were published in volumes devoted exclusively to Philips. The first of these, *Cantiones sacrae, pro praecipuis festis totius anni et communi sanctorum* (Sacred songs, for special feasts of the whole year and the Common of the Saints) published in 1612, is a collection of sixty-nine five-voiced motets in a variety of styles. A few of the motets, such as *Pater noster,* are conservatively polyphonic, with cantus firmus and canons. Most, however, including the well-known *O beatum et sacrosanctum diem* and *Ascendit Deus,* are mainly homophonic, with polychoral effects and expressive word painting. In *O beatum et sacrosanctem diem,* for instance, the text fragment "in sono tubae" (to the sound of the trumpet) is set as a triad that emulates a trumpet fanfare and that is passed back and forth between voices in dialogue. A similar effect is seen at the text phrase "in voce tubae" (to the call of the trumpet) in *Ascendit Deus.* A second volume of *Cantiones sacrae,* containing thirty eight-voiced double choir motets, was published in 1613. The motets in this second volume, such as *Hodie nobis de caelo* and *Ave Jesu Christe,* are like the motets of Sweelinck, with short phrases of text in dialogue between groups of voices. The next three publications of motets—*Gemmulae sacrae* of 1613, *Deliciae sacrae* of 1616, and *Paradisus sacris cantionibus consitus* of 1628—contain vocal concertos for one to three voices and basso continuo in the *seconda prattica* style. The 1628 publication, consisting of 106 vocal concertos, was highly successful and reprinted several times. The set of Litanies, *Litaniae Beatae Mariae Virginis,* consists of nine motets for four to nine voices and basso continuo.

Like the motets, the madrigals first appeared in an anthology—*Melodia olympica,* edited by Philips and published by Pierre Phalèse in 1591. Revealing Philips's knowledge of the Italian madrigal repertoire, it contains five works by Luca Marenzio, four by Giovanni Maria Nanino, three by Palestrina, three by the Antwerp composer Cornelius Verdonck, and four by Philips himself. The first book of madrigals devoted entirely to his own compositions, *Il primo libro de madrigali,* appeared in 1596; his second, *Madrigali,* was published in 1598; and his third, *Il secondo libro de madrigali,* was issued in 1603. The first and third of these books contain six-voiced madrigals, while the middle book contains pieces for eight voices. All the madrigals are in a late-Renaissance Italian style, with varied rhythms in a generally point-of-imitation texture. An example is the *note nere* madrigal *Nero manto vi cinge* in the 1603 collection. Unlike in the motets, there is very little word painting.

MOTETS
SELECTED AND LISTED ACCORDING TO FAMILIARITY

Ascendit Deus – SSATB chorus – 3:30 minutes.

O beatum et sacrosanctum diem – SSATB chorus – 3 minutes.

Ave Jesu Christe – SATB/SATB chorus – 5 minutes.

Hodie nobis de caelo – SATB/SATB chorus – 5 minutes.

Tibi laus, tibi Gloria – SSATB chorus – 3 minutes.

Ave regina caelorum – SATB/SATB chorus – 4 minutes.

Surgens Jesus – SSATB chorus – 2 minutes.

MADRIGALS
SELECTED AND LISTED ACCORDING TO FAMILIARITY

Nero manto vi cinge – SSATTB voices – 3 minutes.

Ditemi, O diva mia – SSAATTBB voices – 3:30 minutes.

Hor che dal sonna vinta – SSAATTBB voices – 3:30 minutes.

Io son ferito – SSATTB voices – 3:30 minutes.

JAN PIETERSZOON SWEELINCK CA.1562–1621

Sweelinck was born in Deventer in the eastern area of the Netherlands, and from childhood until his death he lived in Amsterdam. As a result, he does not follow in the line of composers from Belgium and France, but rather stands alone as a unique figure in the history of music during the Renaissance era. He most likely received his earliest musical education from his father, who was an organist at the Oude Kirk in Amsterdam and who died in 1573, and he succeeded his father perhaps as early as 1577 (at age fifteen). He remained in this position his entire life, leaving Amsterdam only for very brief periods to assess organs in nearby cities, and he passed his position on to his son, who held it until 1652. Despite his duties at Amsterdam's most important church (which included providing music for two daily services), virtually all of his choral music was composed for use in private devotionals. Also, despite his confinement to a city not known for its musical culture, he was well known throughout Europe, and he attracted many students, including Samuel Scheidt. Sweelinck was called the Orpheus of Amsterdam and was buried in the Oude Kirk.

He composed thirty-nine motets, 153 Calvinist Psalm settings, thirty-three secular chansons, and nineteen Italian madrigals, in addition to seventy keyboard works. The motets, all but two of which were published in 1619 as *Cantiones sacrae,* are in a pervasive imitative style. They are distinctive, however, and unlike imitative motets by Franco-Flemish Renaissance composers in that the points of imitation consist of numerous melodic/rhythmic repetitions of short phrases. In *Gaudete omnes,* for example, the title phrase occurs seventeen times in the space of seven measures. The second phrase, "et laetamini," occurs twenty-six times in just six measures (seven of these times are in the bass voice). In *Angelus ad pastores ait* the phrase "gaudium magnum" occurs twenty-nine times in three and a half measures. Other features of Sweelinck's motets are distinctive as well, including basso seguente parts, coda-like sections on the word "Alleluia" in fourteen of the motets, and refrain-like phrases that separate points of imitation. These latter two characteristics are prominent in *Hodie Christus natus est,* Sweelinck's most familiar motet.

The Calvinist Psalm settings, all with French texts by Clément Marot and Théodore de Bèze, were published in four volumes, beginning in 1604 and ending in 1621. Most of the settings are based on standard Geneva tunes and are in a style that combines imitative phrases with passages of homophony. But unlike the works of other composers in this style, Sweelinck's settings are frequently scored for five, six, or eight voices and are often divided into two or more sections or movements. *Or soit loué l'Eternel* (Psalm 150), for instance, is scored for eight voices and is divided into three sections, each consisting of two verses of text, and *Vous tous les habitans des cieux* (Psalm 148) is scored for seven voices and is divided into seven sections. *Or soit loué l'Eternel* also has echo effects and numerous examples of word painting. The Psalm settings were quite popular during their day, circulating throughout Europe, where two volumes were reprinted in Berlin under German titles.

The secular chansons and madrigals were published in *Rimes françoises et italiennes* in 1612. The chansons, most of them for five voices, are in a style similar to that of the Psalm settings— imitative polyphony is alternated with homophony. The madrigals, most of them for two or three voices, are more complex, especially in terms of varied rhythms that characterize expressive changes in the text.

CALVINIST PSALM SETTINGS
SELECTED AND LISTED ACCORDING TO FAMILIARITY

Or soit loué l'Eternel (Psalm 150) – 1614 – SSAATTBB chorus – 7:15 minutes.

Chantez á Dieu chanson nouvelle (Psalm 96) – 1621 – SATB chorus – 6 minutes.

Or sus, serviteurs du Seigneur (Psalm 134) – 1614 – SATB chorus – 3 minutes. The tune *Old Hundredth* (the Doxology) is quoted as a cantus firmus in the bass voice of the first part of the motet.

Or sus, serviteurs du Seigneur (Psalm 134) – 1604 – SSATBB chorus –
  3 minutes. The tune *Old Hundredth* (the Doxology) is paraphrased in
  the soprano parts.

Vous tous les habitans des cieux (Psalm 148) – 1614 – SSAATTB – 11:30 minutes.

D'ou vient, Seigneur, que tu nous as espars (Psalm 74) – 1614 – SATB chorus –
  5 minutes.

Vous tous qui la terre habitez (Psalm 100) – 1614 – SSATB chorus – 4 minutes.

Revenge moy, pren la querelle (Psalm 43) – 1614 – SSAATTBB chorus – 3 minutes.

MOTETS
SELECTED AND LISTED ACCORDING TO FAMILIARITY

Hodie Christus natus est (for Christmas) – 1619 – SSATB chorus and basso
  continuo – 3 minutes.

Ab oriente venerunt Magi (for Epiphany) – 1619 – SSATB chorus and basso
  continuo – 4 minutes.

De profundis clamavi (Psalm 130:1–8) – 1619 – SATTB chorus and basso
  continuo – 5 minutes.

Cantate Domino canticum novum (Psalm 96:1–3) – 1619 – SSATB chorus
  and basso continuo – 3 minutes.

Laudate Dominum omnes gentes (Psalm 117:1–2) – 1619 – SSATB and basso
  continuo – 3 minutes.

Gaudete omnes et laetamini – 1619 – SSATB and basso continuo – 3 minutes.

Venite, exultemus Domino (Psalm 95:1–3) – 1619 – SSATB chorus and basso
  continuo – 3 minutes.

Angelus ad pastores ait (for Christmas) – 1619 – SSATB chorus and basso
  continuo – 2:30 minutes.

O sacrum convivium (for Communion) – 1619 – SATTB chorus and basso
  continuo – 3:30 minutes.

Qui vult venire post me (Matthew 16:24) – 1619 – SATTB – 3:15 minutes.

ॐ ITALY ॐ

The first generation of so-called Renaissance Italian composers—Philippe Verdelot, Adrian Willaert, Jacques Arcadelt, Cipriano de Rore, Philippe de Monte, and Giaches de Wert—were born in present-day Belgium and northern France but spent the majority of their lives working in Italy and developing Italian styles of composition. All the later composers were native Italians, most of whom remained in Italy their entire lives. Only five composers were born in Italy but employed in other countries: Arcadelt spent the final years of his life in France; Monte worked at the court of Maximilian II in Vienna; Alfonso Ferrabosco served Queen Elizabeth I in England; and Luca Marenzio and Giovanni Francesco Anerio spent a brief period of time at the court of Polish King Sigismund III in Warsaw.

The major centers of composition were Venice and Rome, with Ferrara and Mantua being specialized centers of activity for madrigals. Of the thirty-three most notable composers of the era, twenty-two held significant positions in these four cities, and seventeen composers were associated with either St Mark's Basilica in Venice or the papal choir in Rome. Those employed at St Mark's include Willaert, Rore, and Giovanni Croce as *maestri di cappella* and Andrea Gabrieli, Claudio Merulo, and Giovanni Gabrieli as organists; Nicola Vicentino and Costanzo Porta were students. The singers in the papal choir were Costanzo Festa, Arcadelt, Domenico Maria Ferrabosco, Rore, Palestrina, Giovanni Maria Nanino, Felice Anerio, and Gregorio Allegri. Five composers—Vicentino, Rore, Alessandro Striggio, Luzzasco Luzzaschi, and Carlo Gesualdo—served at the court in Ferrara, and four others—Wert, Giovanni Giacomo Gastoldi, Lodovico Viadana, and Sigismondo d'India—all had positions in Mantua.

The main compositional genres were masses, motets, and madrigals, with canzonets, villanellas, and ballettos achieving a degree of popularity at the end of the era. The masses began in the style of the early sixteenth-century Franco-Flemish composers, with a prevalence of tenor cantus firmi, notational puzzles, canons, and other structural devices such as *soggetto cavato*. In addition, the early masses were based on preexisting material—usually chants, chansons, and motets. Later masses continued to be based on preexisting material, including madrigals, but the structural devices gave way to pervasive imitation. Finally, the masses at the end of the sixteenth century exhibited characteristics dictated by the Council of Trent, which was initiated by Pope Paul III in 1542 and which met intermittently until 1563. As a part of the Counter-Reformation, the Council of Trent mandated intelligibility of text in all sacred music and thus promoted the composition of declamatory and syllabic musical settings. Other text-oriented characteristics followed, including expressive word painting and the alternation of brief sections of imitative polyphony based on short motif-like subjects with passages of homophony.

The motets were similar in their development from archaic construction techniques to more modern text-oriented textures. In addition, the motets were frequently composed in cycles for the liturgical year or in two separately titled movements. The cycles for special feast days consisted of individual motets, each to be sung at its specific occasion. The two-movement motets—which are frequently listed, published, and performed separately—were conceived as a single entity, however, and often composed with an ABCB structure (i.e., each movement of the motet ends with the same music, although the first B generally ends in the dominant key and the second B ends in the tonic). Many motets are also scored for multiple choirs (specified by the terms *polychoral* or *cori spezzati*) and for forces of eight or more voices.

The madrigal was the chief secular genre of the Italian Renaissance. Every composer discussed in this section of the era but Allegri composed madrigals, and many composers wrote more than one hundred. Arcadelt composed 200, Wert composed more than 225, Marenzio composed more than 425, and Monte composed approximately 1,100. The madrigal began and was basically understood as a serious art form, one that had compositional traits closely resembling the motet and that therefore had imitative polyphony as its normal characteristic of texture.

Madrigal composition went through three periods of development in Italy during the Renaissance. In the first period, composers generally set the serious poetry of Petrarch (Francesco Petrarca, 1304–1374) and other humanist poets such as Giovanni Boccaccio (1313–1375). Scoring was mostly for four voices, textures consisted of uncomplicated polyphony and homophony, and rhythmic values had little variation. Representative composers are Verdelot, Costanzo Festa, Willaert, Sebastiano Festa, and Arcadelt. The first printed appearance of the term *madrigal* was in the title of the publication *Madrigali de diversi musici: libro primo de la Serena*, which was issued in Rome in 1530 and which contained eight madrigals by Verdelot and two by Costanzo Festa.

The second period of madrigals is characterized by numerous traits: (1) a variety of rhythmic values that expanded the notation from the conventional use of half and whole notes (white notation) to include shorter note values such as eighths and quarters (black notation—called during the time *note nere*); (2) expanded textures to a standard of five and six voices, with not infrequent writing for seven and eight voices; (3) fewer settings of poetry by Petrarch and more settings of contemporary poets and of less serious subject matter; (4) a greater amount of homophony and corresponding lesser amount of polyphony; (5) short motifs as opposed to long phrases; (6) occasional use of chromaticism for expressive purposes; and (7) melodic passages that depict specific textual characteristics (referred to as word painting, madrigalism, or *musica reservata*). Major representative composers exhibiting these traits include Andrea Gabrieli, Rore, Monte, Palestrina, Wert (the early madrigals), and Alfonso Ferrabosco. Other composers of this period who contributed substantially to either the madrigal repertoire or to its development are Vincenzo Ruffo, Vicentino, Porta, and Striggio.

The third and final style period is characterized by a focus on texts set in an expressive and declamatory manner. At the end of the sixteenth century, ideals of expression resulted in greater degrees of varied rhythms within a polyphonic texture, and mid-century developments of expression and word painting were heightened and magnified: rhythmic variety became disjunct, expression became emotional, and word painting became mannered. These characteristics are evidenced in the late madrigals of Wert, all the madrigals of Marenzio and Gesualdo, and the early madrigals of Claudio Monteverdi. Other lesser-known composers—such as Nanino, Luzzaschi, and Salamone Rossi—also wrote in this style. At the beginning of the seventeenth century, ideals of declamation resulted in elements of monody, including recitative and independent instrumental accompaniment of solos, duets, and trios.

The lighter forms of secular music during the end of the sixteenth and beginning of the seventeenth century were mainly homophonic and generally comedic. Three forms were most popular—the villanella, canzonet, and balletto. The villanella, which was a counterpart to the madrigal, was generally for three voices and written for play-like entertainments. In addition, it often poked fun at the madrigal by joking about serious subjects or madrigal trends, and also by purposely breaking, in a humorous way, some of the basic rules of traditional harmony. The canzonet, generally set to pastoral poetry, was similar to the villanella, although less rustic. The ballettos were, as the name implies, dance songs. They were often composed for five voices and are repetitive in structure (AABB), with *fa la la* refrains. Many of these lighter forms were composed in sets for costumed entertainments, and although the sets may not have consisted of a preponderance of madrigals, they are called madrigal comedies. Composers of these lighter forms include Orazio Vecchi, Gastoldi, and Adriano Banchieri.

Most of the madrigals, villanellas, canzonets, and ballettos were published in books devoted to single composers. However, many madrigals also appeared in collections such as *Madrigali de diversi musici: libro primo de la Serena,* mentioned earlier. A particularly famous collection is *Il trionfo di Dori,* published in Venice in 1592 by Angelo Gardano and consisting of twenty-nine six-part madrigals composed by twenty-nine of the most famous composers of the time, including (in order of appearance in the collection) Vecchi, Giovanni Gabrieli, Marenzio, Giammateo Asola, Monte, Croce, Striggio, Felice Anerio, Gastoldi, Porta, and Palestrina. Distinctively, each madrigal ends with a setting of the phrase "Viva la bella Dori" (Long live fair Dori).

Composers who are not discussed in this section of the Renaisssance era, but who made noteworthy contributions to the development of the madrigal and other genres in Italy, are Gioseffo Zarlino (ca.1517–1590), Baldassare Donato (ca.1525–1603), Giovanni Battista Mosto (ca. 1550–1596), and Giovanni Bassano (ca.1560–1617). Zarlino, who studied with Willaert in Venice and succeeded Rore as *maestro di cappella* of St Mark's, composed forty motets and thirteen madrigals. The motets include the first polyphonic cycle of texts from the Song of Songs, and the madrigals include settings of popular Petrarch poems such as *I'vo piangendo.* Zarlino is best known, however, for his 1558 theoretical treatise *Le istitutioni harmoniche,* which discusses rules for counterpoint. Donato was a singer at St Mark's in Venice and then *maestro di cappella* after Zarlino. He is known for his villanellas, first published in 1550 and subsequently reprinted several times, and also for two ballettos—*Chi la gagliarda* and *Viva sempre in ogni etade.* His most popular villanella is *O dolce vita mia* for SATB voices. Mosto, who was *maestro di cappella* at Padua Cathedral for ten years, composed madrigals that were popular in England. Finally, Bassano was a cornet player and director of instrumental ensembles at St Mark's in Venice and was known for his polychoral motets (e.g., *Dic, Maria, nobis*) and canzonets, and for his 1585 treatise on ornamentation, *Ricercate, passaggi et cadentie.*

PHILIPPE VERDELOT CA.1480–CA.1550

Although there is no conclusive evidence, various circumstances suggest that Verdelot was born in France or Flanders: his name is of French derivation; he twice parodied a motet by the relatively unknown Franco-Flemish composer Jean Richafort (ca.1480–ca.1548); and he composed several chansons early in his career. There is also no evidence that he moved to Italy as a young man, although the textual content and style of several madrigals suggest that he was in Venice and Bologna between 1510 and 1520. From 1522 to 1527 he held positions at the Florence Cathedral, first as *maestro di cappella* at the baptistery and then as *maestro di cappella* at the cathedral itself. There is no knowledge of his activity or whereabouts from 1527 until his death.

Verdelot composed two masses, fifty-eight motets, one Magnificat, four chansons, and approximately 130 madrigals. Both masses are based on Richafort's *Philomena praevia.* In the first mass, *Missa Philomena,* a head motif is constructed from the motet's opening phrase, and in the second mass, which is unnamed, several motifs are drawn from phrases in the motet's second part. Verdelot's early motets are based on notational puzzles and canons. *Tanto tempore vobiscum sum,* for instance, is constructed around the pitches *re, re, sol* (the vowels in Verdelot's name), and *Ave sanctissima Maria* is a three-part canon. Later motets such as *Ad Dominum cum tribularer* and *Gaudent in celis* are more text oriented and declamatory. This declamatory style was quite popular, and many of Verdelot's motets were parodied by notable composers throughout Europe, including Arcadelt, Palestrina, Gombert, Lasso, and Morales. Verdelot's *Si bona suscepimus* was so popular that it was printed in six anthologies of the time and parodied by five composers, including Lasso and Morales.

Verdelot is best known today for his madrigals, which exhibit the style of expressive declamation, homophony alternating with imitative polyphony, and tonal harmonies that would be adopted by the majority of Italian composers during the second half of the Renaissance era. *Italia mia,* one of the most admired madrigals of the entire sixteenth century, is an example. Petrarch's poem about the destruction of Italy's landscape by war, specifically the sack of Rome in 1527, is given a predominantly syllabic setting, with almost no repetition of text to impede the comprehension or dramatic impact of the text's message. Moreover, Verdelot balances homophony with imitation to take advantage of expressive communication. Thus phrases such as "le piaghe mortali che nel bel corpo tu si spesse veggio" (the many mortal wounds that I see in your beautiful body [Italy]) and "dove doglioso e grave or seggio" (where sorrowful and sad I now sit) achieve poignant accentuation. To further aid the poetry, Verdelot demarcates the ends of poetic lines with cadences, and he matches the five sections of poetic text with five corresponding sections of music. Two other madrigals set to texts about the social unrest of the time are *Italia, Italia, ch'hai si longamente* and *Trista Amarilli mia.* Several madrigals, including *Amor, io sento l'alma* and *Quanto sia lieto il giorno,* are set to texts by the famous Italian politician and author Niccolò Machiavelli (1469–1527).

MADRIGALS
SELECTED AND LISTED ACCORDING TO FAMILIARITY

Italia mia – SATBB voices – 5 minutes.

Madonna'l tuo bel viso – SATB voices – 3 minutes.

Dormend' un giorno – ATBBB voices – 2 minutes.

I vostr' acuti dardi – SATB voices – 2 minutes.

Donna, se fera stella – ATTBB voices – 3 minutes.

Amor, io sento l'alma – SATB voices – 2 minutes.

Quanto sia lieto il giorno – SATB voices – 3 minutes.

COSTANZO FESTA CA.1485–1545

Born near Turin, Costanzo Festa is considered to be the first native Italian composer of the Renaissance era. For several years before 1517 he served at the court of Costanza d'Avalos, Duchess of Francavilla, on the island of Ischia in the Bay of Naples, and from 1517 until his death he was a singer in the papal chapel, where he served under the Medici popes Leo X and Clement VII and where he worked with Arcadelt and Morales.

Festa composed four masses, ninety motets (including thirty hymns for Vespers services), twelve Magnificats, eight sets of Lamentations, and approximately one hundred madrigals. Typical of the time, all the masses are based on preexisting material; two use Gregorian chants and two use chanson melodies. *Missa Carminum* (also called *Missa diversorum tenorum*) is a quodlibet mass that employs five of the most popular chanson melodies of the time—L'homme armé, J'ay pris amours, Petite camusette, Adieu mes amours, and De tous biens pleine. Some of the motets are similar to the masses in being based on preexisting material. For example, the two-part, five-voiced *Dominator caelorum* uses the Gregorian chant *Da pacem Domine* as a strict cantus firmus in the tenor voice. Other motets, such as the eight-voiced *Inviolata, integra et casta Maria*, are canonic. However, most of the motets are generally more modern in that they use rhythmic values, melodic contours, and imitative textures to highlight texts. Examples include the four-voiced Vespers hymn *Petrus beatus catenarum laqueos* and the five-voiced *Super flumina Babylonis*. This latter motet includes chant from the Gregorian Requiem Mass to heighten the sad nature of the text "Super flumina Babylonis illic sedimus et flevimus" (By the waters of Babylon we sat down and wept). The Magnificats, which are the first settings in the Renaissance to be fully polyphonic (earlier settings combined chant with polyphony in *alternatim* style), include a complete set on each of the eight Gregorian chant tones.

Like Verdelot, Festa is known today mostly for his madrigals. In addition, the madrigals of the two composers are similarly syllabic, with alternating passages of homophony and polyphony. *Donna non fu ne fia* and *Qual' anima ignorante* are examples. Festa's madrigals are less declamatory, however, and more varied in texture. *Così suav'e'l foco* and *Dur' è'l partito*, for instance, both begin with duet passages. As was mentioned in the introduction to this chapter, the first publication of madrigals, the title of which contained the first use of the term *madrigal* (*Madrigali de diversi musici: libro primo de la Serena*), included eight madrigals by Verdelot and two by Festa.

SEBASTIANO FESTA CA.1490–1524

Sebastiano Festa was probably the brother of Costanzo, and he also probably lived in Rome for most of his life. However, he did not distinguish himself as either a composer or a performer, and all that is known about him is his connection with the Rome court of Ottobono Fieschi, Bishop of Mondovì, sometime in the 1520s. Festa's compositional output, no doubt limited by his death at an early age, includes only four motets and twelve madrigals, all scored for SATB voices and all with alternating passages of imitative polyphony and homophony in a manner typical of the time. Examples include the motet *Angele Dei* and the madrigals *Vergine sacra* and *O passi sparsi*. This latter piece, set to a Petrarch sonnet, was popular during the latter half of the sixteenth century.

ADRIAN WILLAERT CA.1490–1562

Willaert was born in Belgium and received his musical education from Jean Mouton at the French royal court. In 1514 or 1515 Willaert became a singer at the court of Cardinal Ippolito I d'Este in Ferrara, and in 1527 he was appointed *maestro di cappella* at St Mark's Basilica in Venice. He was an important figure in the development of Venice as one of the main cultural centers of Europe during the mid-sixteenth century: he established the practice of *cori spezzati* (broken or divided choirs), which became a prominent feature of music at St Mark's; he helped foster the music publishing industry, especially the companies established by Antonio Gardano and Girolamo Scotto; and he taught many important composers, including Gioseffo Zarlino, Cipriano de Rore, Nicola Vicentino, and perhaps Andrea Gabrieli. Many composers and theorists of the seventeenth century claimed that Willaert's music represented the pinnacle of *prima prattica* writing, and many historians today consider Willaert to be the most important composer between Josquin Desprez and G. P. da Palestrina.

Willaert composed nine masses, more than two hundred motets, two Magnificats, sixty-four chansons, approximately seventy madrigals, and thirteen villanellas. Most of the masses were composed early in Willaert's career and thus exhibit traits of the beginning years of the Renaissance era. Three masses—*Missa Gaude Barbara, Missa Laudate Deum,* and *Missa Queramus cum pastoribus*—are based on motets by Mouton; *Missa Mente tota* is based on a motet by Josquin; and *Missa ut mi sol* is a *soggetto cavato* mass. Willaert's single late mass, *Missa Mittit ad virginem,* is based on his own motet. The motets include polyphonic hymn settings, Psalms for the office of Vespers, and separate works for no particular liturgical function. The hymn settings were composed as a cycle for important celebrations during the liturgical year. Most are canonic and are based on the Gregorian chant that corresponds to the liturgical festival, and most alternate sections of original chant with polyphony for various groupings of voices (from two to six). The Psalms for Vespers range from settings that alternate chant with four-voiced polyphony to large-scale works for double chorus that became very popular at St Mark's and that also became the model for many double chorus works throughout the late years of the Renaissance and the beginning years of the Baroque. The remaining motets are varied in style, although they exhibit mostly the pervasive imitative textures that were admired during the middle and latter decades of the sixteenth century. They are varied in scoring as well: one is for three voices, seventy-eight are for four voices, fifty-one are for five voices, thirty-eight are for six voices, and five are for seven voices.

The chansons were composed for the Ferrara court, which was French speaking. Some are canonic while others are in the popular homophonic Parisian style. The madrigals, which are often settings of Petrarch sonnets divided into two large sections or movements, are like contemporaneous motets, with consistently imitative polyphony. *Amor mi fa morire,* set to a text about the fashionable subject of unrequited love, became one of the dozen or so most popular madrigals of the sixteenth century. The villanellas, published in a well-known collection entitled *Canzone villanesche alla napolitana,* which contained twenty pieces by Willaert and others, are homophonic and strophic, with a single refrain at the end of each verse. Most are set to light-hearted texts in Neopolitan dialects. An example is *Cingari simo venit'a giocare donn' alla coriolla de bon core* (We are gypsies come to play the game called Queen of Hearts).

MOTETS

SELECTED AND LISTED ACCORDING TO FAMILIARITY

Christi virgo - Quoniam peccatorum mole – SATB chorus – 5:30 minutes.

O magnum mysterium – SATB chorus – 2:30 minutes.

O Thoma, laus et gloria – SATB chorus – 2 minutes.

Veni sancte spiritus – SATB chorus – 8 minutes.

Sacro fonte regenerata – SATTB chorus – 7:30 minutes.

Laus tibi, sacra rubens – SATTB chorus – 7 minutes.

MADRIGALS
SELECTED AND LISTED ACCORDING TO FAMILIARITY

Amor mi fa morire – SAAT voices – 2:30 minutes.

Qual più diversa e nova cosa fu mai – SATB voices – 2:30 minutes.

Cantai, hor piango – a two-madrigal cycle – SAATTB voices – 5:30 minutes.

Grat'e benigna donna – a two-madrigal cycle – SATB voices – 4 minutes.

Quanto più m'arde – a two-madrigal cycle – SATTB voices – 4:15 minutes.

Passa la nave mia – a two-madrigal cycle – SSATTB voices – 7 minutes.

Qual dolcezza giamai – a two-madrigal cycle – SATTB voices – 6:30 minutes.

JACQUES (JACOB OR JAKOB) ARCADELT CA.1505–1568

It is likely that Arcadelt was born in France, where he received his musical education. He moved to Florence sometime in the 1520s and began composing madrigals for the Medici court (examples of which are *Deh dimm' amor se l'alma* and *Io dico che fra voi,* both set to texts by Michelangelo, and *Vero inferno è il mio petto,* set to a text by Lorenzino de' Medici), and in the 1530s he was employed by Alessandro de' Medici. In 1537, when Alessandro was murdered by Lorenzino, Arcadelt moved to Rome, entering the papal chapel as a singer two years later, and in 1551 he returned to France, entering the royal court and serving Charles of Lorraine, brother of the Duke of Guise, as well as kings Henri II and Charles IX. Although Arcadelt began and ended his life in France and although he composed a large number of works to French texts, he is considered an Italian composer, in large part because of his status as the archetypal Italian madrigalist during its first period of development.

His compositional output consists of three masses, twenty-four motets (plus two spiritual chansons), one Magnificat, three sets of Lamentations, 125 secular chansons, and more than two hundred madrigals. The masses are typically works that paraphrase preexisting material. For example, his most famous mass, the six-voiced *Missa Noe, noe,* is based on a motet by Jean Mouton. The other sacred works—including the three motets *O pulcherrima mulierum, Filiae Jerusalem,* and *Haec dies*—combine points of imitation with occasional passages of homophony.

The chansons range in style from those that are canonic and pervasively imitative to those that are basically syllabic. The chansons in the latter style, similar to the Parisian chansons published by Pierre Attaingnant from the 1520s until his death in about 1551 and by Jacques Moderne thereafter, were the most popular. Forty-four of them were given sacred texts by Claude Goudimel and published in about 1566 as *L'excellence des chansons.*

The madrigals, characterized by syllabic settings of texts and alternating phrases of imitative polyphony and homophony, are similar to those of Philippe Verdelot and Costanzo Festa, although Arcadelt's polyphony is generally less complicated and therefore accessible, and the

texture of his madrigals balances homophony and imitative polyphony in a manner that elucidates the expressive qualities of text. *Il bianco e dolce cigno,* without a doubt the most popular
madrigal of the sixteenth century, is an example. The first and third phrases of text are homophonic, while the second and fourth are imitative. In the homophonic sections the declamatory
setting enhances the natural accentuation and emotion of text, with especially poignant expression of such words as "piangendo" (weeping) and "morire" (dying). The imitative sections seem
to follow inevitably and to underscore the text's building intensity—especially with the many
repetitions of the madrigal's final phrase, "di mille morte il dì sarei contento" (with a thousand
deaths a day I would be content).

In addition to establishing the style of madrigal composition in the early Renaissance, Arcadelt also established the style of madrigal publication, a style that issued madrigals in successively numbered books (i.e., *Il primo libro di madrigali, Il secundo libro, Il terzo libro,* etc.) and that
would be followed for more than a hundred years. Also, Arcadelt began the composition of
madrigal cycles (i.e., madrigals in three, four, or more movements). For example, *Chiare fresch'
e dolce acque,* a setting of a complete Petrarch canzone, is a cycle in five movements. Arcadelt's
madrigal books were so popular that they were reprinted numerous times. *Il primo libro,* for instance, which contained *Il bianco e dolce cigno,* was reprinted at least fifty-eight times between
1539 and 1654.

MADRIGALS
SELECTED AND LISTED ACCORDING TO FAMILIARITY

Il bianco e dolce cigno – SATB voices – 3 minutes.

Io dico che fra voi – SATB voices – 3 minutes.

Deh dimm' amor se l'alma – SATB voices – 2:30 minutes.

S'infinita bellezza – SATTB voices – 3 minutes.

O felic' occhi miei – SATB voices – 2 minutes.

Sostenette quei di fugaci e rei – SATB voices – 2 minutes.

Voi ve n'andat' al cielo – SATB voices – 2:30 minutes.

Da bei rami scendea – SATB voices – 3 minutes.

Qual'hor m'assal' amore – a two-madrigal cycle – SATTB voices – 2:30 minutes.

Se'l chiar' almo splendore – SATTB voices – 3 minutes.

Dormendo un giorno a Baia – SAT voices – 2 minutes.

CHANSONS
SELECTED AND LISTED ACCORDING TO FAMILIARITY

Margot labourez les vignes – SATB voices – 1 minute.

Sa grand beauté – SATB voices – 2:30 minutes.

Quand je vous ayme ardentement – SATB voices – 2 minutes.

Du temps que j'estois amoureux – SATB voices – 2:15 minutes.

En ce mois délicieux – SATB voices – 2:30 minutes.

VINCENZO RUFFO CA.1508–1587

Ruffo was born in Verona, where he sang as a chorister and then adult singer at the Verona Cathedral from 1520 to 1534. In 1542 he was appointed *maestro di cappella* at Savonna Cathedral, and the following year he entered the court of Alfonso d'Avalos, Governor-General of Milan, remaining there until Alfonso's death in 1546. Ruffo then returned to Verona and was appointed *maestro di cappella* at the Accademia Filarmonica in 1551 and *maestro di cappella* at the cathedral in 1554, holding both positions simultaneously. During the 1550s he taught Giammateo Asola and perhaps Andrea Gabrieli and Marc'Antonio Ingegneri, and from 1563 to 1572 he served as *maestro di cappella* at the Milan Cathedral under Archbishop Carlo Borromeo, one of the important leaders of the Counter-Reformation, who insisted that sacred musical texts be intelligible. From 1573 until his death Ruffo worked in small churches in Pistoia and Sacite.

He composed five books of masses, seven books of motets, two Magnificats, and approximately 260 madrigals. The masses and motets trace the stylistic development from densely imitative works based on cantus firmus to homophonic declamatory compositions that adhere to the edicts of the Counter-Reformation. The early masses include *Missa Alma redemptoris mater* for four equal voices, which is believed to be the first printed polyphonic mass by a native Italian composer, and *Missa Quem dicunt homines* for SATTB chorus, based on a motet by Jean Richafort. The late masses are represented by *Missa Sanctissimae trinitatis* for SATTBB chorus and *Missa de de* [sic] *profundis* for SATTB chorus. The texture of both late masses is mainly homophonic (the Gloria and Credo of the *Missa de de profundis* almost entirely so), and in the preface of the publication in which *Missa Sanctissimae trinitatis* is contained (*Quarto libro di messe a sei voci* of 1574) Ruffo acknowledges that he had attempted to make the text as intelligible as possible.

The madrigals include several for SATTB voices set to spiritual texts by Petrarch (e.g., *Vergine santa, Vergine sol'al mondo,* and *I'vo piangendo i miei passati tempi*) and the popular secular pieces *Non rumor di tamburi* for SATB voices and *L'aquila è gita al ciel* for SATTB voices.

NICOLA VICENTINO 1511–CA.1576

Vicentino was born in Vicenza, near Venice, and he claimed to have studied with Adrian Willaert at St Mark's Basilica. Vicentino worked in the court of Cardinal Ippolito II d'Este in Ferrara during the 1540s and 1550s, and in 1563 he was appointed *maestro di cappella* at the cathedral in his hometown of Vicenza. Circumstances were not favorable for him there, however, and the following year he resigned his position and traveled to Milan, where he died of the plague. He is known mostly for his treatise *L'antica musica ridotta alla moderna prattica* (Ancient music adapted to modern practice), which discusses tuning systems and explains that the arrangement of pitches in music can be chromatic and enharmonic as well as diatonic. As a demonstration of his views, he invented an *arcicembalo,* a harpsichord that had two keys for each half step (one for flats and one for sharps).

Although Vicentino composed four books of motets and five books of madrigals, most of these have been lost, and only two motets— *Heu mihi Domine* and *Infelix ego omnium*—and two madrigals— *Solo e pensoso* and *Passa la nave mia*—are in the repertory today. The latter work, a two-madrigal cycle for six voices (SSATTB) set to a Petrarch poem, was a model for the serious motet-like textures that would be emulated by many composers in the middle decades of the sixteenth century.

DOMENICO MARIA FERRABOSCO 1513–1574

Domenico Maria, father of Alfonso, was born in Bologna, where he was a singer at the church of S Petronio during the late 1530s and early 1540s and *maestro di cappella* beginning in 1547. He also served as director of public performances and palace musicians for the city of Bologna beginning in 1540. In 1550 he moved to Rome and sang in the papal chapel with Palestrina until 1555, when Pope Paul IV adhered to strict Vatican policy and dismissed all married personnel (which included Palestrina and another married singer). Ferrabosco was then appointed *maestro di cappella* at the church of S Lorenzo in Damaso. After just a year in this position he went to France and worked at the court of Charles de Guise, Cardinal of Lorraine, and he most likely returned to Bologna sometime during the last years of his life, though it is only known that he died there.

Ferrabosco composed two motets and approximately fifty madrigals. The motets— *Ascendens Christus* and *Usquequo Domine*—are in the imitative style of the day, and the madrigals alternate imitative phrases and homophonic passages in the style of Verdelot, Costanzo Festa, and Arcadelt. All of Ferrabosco's works as well as the composer himself would probably be completely unknown today were it not for the success of one madrigal, *Io mi son giovinetta*, which was printed in at least forty-six anthologies and sixteen manuscripts during the 1540s and which is comparable to *Italia mia* by Verdelot and *Il bianco e dolce cigno* by Arcadelt in being one of the most popular madrigals of the sixteenth century.

CIPRIANO DE RORE CA.1515–1565

Rore was born in a small town west of Brussels in Belgium. There is no documentation about his youth or musical training, although from references in the prefaces of several Venetian publications it can be assumed that he studied with Adrian Willaert. It is also probable that Rore remained in Venice until the mid-1540s, since it is known that he was commissioned to compose music for several noblemen living there at the time. In 1546 he was appointed *maestro di cappella* at the court of Duke Ercole II d'Este of Ferrara, and when the duke died in 1559, Rore joined the musical forces at the Farnese court in Parma. He succeeded Willaert as *maestro di cappella* at St Mark's Basilica in 1562 but served in this capacity for only two years, returning to Parma for the final year of his life.

Rore composed four masses, fifty-one extant motets, two Magnificats, 107 madrigals, and four chansons. It is doubtful that he composed the Passion setting based on the Gospel of St John that has been ascribed to him. The masses include two that were composed for Duke

Ercole II while Rore was in Ferrara: *Missa Praeter rerum seriem* is based on the same-named motet by Josquin Desprez, who had been *maestro di cappella* at the Ferrara court under Duke Ercole I, and *Missa Vivat felix Hercules,* which utilizes the *soggetto cavato* technique and is based on the vowels of the duke's name, follows the model of Josquin's similar mass for Ercole I. Of the other two Rore masses, *Missa Doulce mémoire* is based on a chanson by Pierre Sandrin, and *Missa a note negre* is based on his own chanson *Tout ce qu'on peut en elle voir.* It should be noted that the title of this latter mass, which translates as "Mass in black notes," refers to the new practice of writing in short rhythmic values such as quarter and eighth notes (with black note heads) instead of the normal longer rhythmic values of half and whole notes (with white note heads).

The motets range in style from early works that are purely imitative and that emulate Willaert (e.g., the large-scale canonic *Descendi in ortum meum* and *Ave regina caelorum*) to later works that combine imitative polyphony with homophony and that vary rhythmic values for expressive nuance (e.g., *Hodie Christus natus est* and *Quem vidistis pastores*). The incorporation of shorter *note nere* rhythms in the motets is of significance in that composers wrote in a similar manner throughout the remainder of the sixteenth century. The Magnificats are both based on Gregorian chant tones (*primi toni* and *sexti toni*) and are in *alternatim* style.

Like almost all of the early-sixteenth-century Italian composers, Rore became famous for his madrigals, and just as Willaert, Arcadelt, and Domenico Maria Ferrabosco each had one madrigal that was especially popular, Rore was known for *Ancor che col partire.* This madrigal, published by Perissone Cambio and Alessandro Gardane in *Primo libro di madrigali a quatro voci* of 1547, is an example of the ABB structure of madrigals that was becoming popular at the time. Most of Rore's other madrigals were published in seven books—five for five voices and two for four voices. The early books contain numerous settings of Petrarch poems in the imitative style of Willaert (e.g., *Per mezz'i boschi, Alla dolce ombra,* and the eleven-madrigal cycle *Vergine bella*). The later books contain fewer settings of Petrarch poetry and more of poetry by contemporaries such as Bartolomeo Ferrino, Giovanni della Casa, Luigi Tansillo, Torquato Tasso, and Ludovico Ariosto. Portions of Ariosto's 1532 *Orlando furioso,* a parody of medieval romances and commentary on Italian Renaissance court society, were especially popular. The contemporary poetry was less serious than that of Petrarch and more varied in emotional content. Thus Rore and other composers had material for more rhythmic variety, and the incorporation of *note nere* rhythms became more and more commonplace. Because Rore was the first significant composer to use a wide range of rhythmic values in his madrigals, he is considered the de facto leader of the second generation of madrigal composers.

MASSES AND MOTETS

SELECTED AND LISTED ACCORDING TO FAMILIARITY

Missa Praeter rerum seriem – SSATTBB chorus – 30 minutes.

Missa Vivat felix Hercules – SATTB chorus – 22 minutes.

Infelix ego – SSATTB chorus – 12:15 minutes.

Ave regina caelorum – SSATTBB chorus – 6 minutes.

Descendi in ortum meum – SSATTBB chorus – 5:30 minutes.

MADRIGALS
SELECTED AND LISTED ACCORDING TO FAMILIARITY

Ancor che col partire – SATB voices – 2:30 minutes.

O morte, eterno fin – SATTB voices – 3:30 minutes.

Strane ruppi – a two-madrigal cycle – SATTB voices – 5 minutes.

Dal le belle contrade d'oriente – SATTB voices – 3:30 minutes.

Sfrondate, o sacre dive – SATTB voices – 3 minutes.

Non è ch'il duol – a two-madrigal cycle – SATB voices – 3:30 minutes.

Mia benigna fortuna – a two-madrigal cycle – SATB voices – 3:30 minutes.

L'alto signor – a two-madrigal cycle – SSATTB voices – 4 minutes.

O sonno, o della queta – a two-madrigal cycle – SATB voices – 2:30 minutes.

Alla dolce ombra – SSATB voices – 8:30 minutes.

PHILIPPE DE MONTE 1521–1603

Monte was born in Mechelen, Belgium, near Brussels, where he presumably was a chorister at St Rombouts Cathedral. In the early 1550s he taught music to the children of banker Domenico Pinelli in Naples; between 1554 and 1555 he was in England as a singer in the chapel of Philip II of Spain, who was consort to Queen Mary Tudor; and in 1556 he became a member of the choir at Cambrai Cathedral in northern France. For the next several years Monte traveled to various cities in Italy, including Venice, Florence, and Naples, and in 1568 he was appointed *Kapellmeister* at the court of Maximilian II in Vienna. While in Vienna he met and worked with many notable musicians, including Orlando di Lasso, who was at the court of Duke Albrecht V of Bavaria at the time. From about 1580 until his death Monte lived in Prague, where the court had been relocated under Maximilian's successor, Rudolf II, and where he was buried at the church of St Jakub.

Monte composed approximately forty masses (including a Requiem), 260 motets, fifty chansons, and eleven hundred madrigals. The masses, which follow the tradition of early-sixteenth-century Franco-Flemish composers in being parodies, are based on his own madrigals and chansons (e.g., *Missa La dolce vista*) as well as on works by composers such as Josquin, Verdelot, Rore, Palestrina, Lasso, and Wert. Some of the motets, including the canonic *Gaudent in caelis* and *Ad te, Domine, levavi anima meam,* follow earlier traditions. However, most of them are in the freely imitative style of the mid-sixteenth century. Unique to Monte are numerous structural repetitions of text, with restatements of phrases within points of imitation and also with restatements of entire sections of music. Of the ten books of motets published during Monte's life, seven are scored for five voices, two for six voices, and only one for four voices. In addition, there are several motets scored for larger forces (e.g., *Benedictio et claritas* for twelve voices arranged in three choirs—SATB/SATB/SATB).

Monte is the most prolific composer of madrigals in the history of music. His secular madrigals were published in thirty-four books—nineteen for five voices, nine for six voices, four for four voices, and one each for three and seven voices. His sacred or spiritual madrigals were issued in five books for five to seven voices and in a collection of five-part works entitled *Eccellenze di Maria vergine* and devoted exclusively to texts about the Virgin Mary. The early secular madrigals are generally settings of Petrarch poems in the style of Willaert, while the later madrigals are settings of contemporary pastoral poetry, with short motifs, *note nere* rhythms, chromaticism, large sections of homophony, and word painting. *Ahi, chi mi rompe il sonno*, published in book three of 1570, was one of the most popular madrigals of its day, appearing in numerous manuscript copies and madrigal collections. Other notable madrigals are *Scipio, l'acerbo caso;* the five-madrigal cycle *La dolce vista; Lungo le chiare linfe,* which was published in *Il trionfo di Dori* in 1592; and the eight-madrigal cycle *Già havea l'eterna man,* set to portions of Ariosto's *Orlando furioso.*

MOTETS
SELECTED AND LISTED ACCORDING TO FAMILIARITY

O suavitas et dulcedo – SSATTBB – 4:30 minutes.

Peccantem me quotidie – SSATB – 2 minutes.

Parce mihi, Domine – SSATTB – 7 minutes.

Factum est silentium – SSATTB – 2:30 minutes.

MADRIGALS
SELECTED AND LISTED ACCORDING TO FAMILIARITY

Ahi, chi mi rompe il sonno – SSATB – 5 minutes.

Scipio, l'acerbo caso – SATTB – 3 minutes.

Leggiadre ninfe – SSATTB – 3 minutes.

Verament' in amore – SSATB – 2 minutes.

Fa ch'io riveggia – SSAT – 2 minutes.

Lungo le chiare linfe – SSATTB – 1:30 minutes.

Dolorosi martir' – SATB voices – 2:30 minutes.

Amorosi pensieri – SSATTB voices – 2 minutes.

Vergine pura – SSATTB voices – 3:30 minutes.

La dolce vista – SSATTB voices – 2:15 minutes.

GIOVANNI PIERLUIGI DA PALESTRINA CA.1525–1594

Palestrina is both the name that Giovanni Pierluigi was called during his life and after (although he referred to himself as Giovanni Petraloysio), and also the name of a town near Rome where he was probably born. He received his musical training as a chorister at S Maria Maggiore in

Rome beginning in about 1537, and in 1544 he was appointed organist at S Agapito Cathedral in Palestrina. In 1551 he began singing in the Cappella Giulia (the Vatican chapel for the training of Italian musicians) and in 1555, with the election of Cardinal Giovanni del Monte of Palestrina as Pope Julius III, Palestrina became a singer in the Cappella Sistina (the papal chapel). Julius III died after only three months as pope and was succeeded by Marcellus II, who died after only three weeks. The next pope, Paul IV, adhered to strict Vatican policy regarding membership in the papal chapel and dismissed Palestrina and two other married singers, one of whom was Domenico Maria Ferrabosco. Palestrina was then appointed *maestro di cappella* at San Giovanni in Laterano, succeeding Orlando di Lasso, and in 1561 he was appointed to the same position at S Maria Maggiore. In 1566 he became *maestro* at the Seminario Romano, and the following year, while maintaining the position at the Seminario, he began service at the court of Ippolito II d'Este in Tivoli. In 1571 Palestrina returned to the Cappella Giulia as *maestro di cappella,* remaining in this position until his death at age sixty-eight.

Palestrina's influence and reputation during the latter half of the sixteenth century were extraordinary. Not only did he hold leading musical positions in Rome's most notable sacred institutions, but he also served during the Council of Trent and was considered to be its musical figurehead and the musical leader of the Counter-Reformation. Indeed, Palestrina was thought to be the savior of Catholic church music. Today he is the best-known and most critically acclaimed composer of the Renaissance era.

He composed 104 masses, 529 motets, thirty-five Magnificats, eleven Litanies, four sets of Lamentations, and approximately 140 madrigals. His large output of masses (more than that of any composer before him) no doubt reflects his long tenure in the major churches of Rome and also his perceived position as leader of Catholic church music. Half the masses are parodies of preexisting polyphonic compositions, about a third are paraphrases of preexisting melodies, and the remainder are freely composed. One might expect that the masses based on preexisting material would utilize traditional construction techniques. However, this is not so. Only seven masses use a cantus firmus (e.g., *Missa Ave Maria, Missa Ecce sacerdos magnus* composed for Pope Julius III, and the five-voiced *Missa L'homme armé*), and only one mass, *Missa Ut re mi fa sol la,* uses the *soggetto cavato* technique.

Of the parody masses, thirty-one are based on works by other composers and twenty-two are based on his own works, most of which are motets. It is interesting to note that many of these motets, which were obviously well liked by Palestrina, include works that are popular today (e.g., *Assumpta est Maria,* the four-voiced *Dies sanctificatus,* the eight-voiced *Hodie Christus natus est,* the six-voiced *Tu es Petrus,* and *Veni sponsa Christi*). Three of his madrigals used as models are also popular—*Già fu chi' m'ebbe cara, Io son ferito* (used in the *Missa Petra sancta*), and *Vestiva i colli* (one of the most published works of the sixteenth century). The parodies of works by other composers include *Missa Benedicta es,* based on a motet by Josquin Desprez; *Missa O sacrum convivium,* based on a motet by Cristóbal de Morales; *Missa Gabriel archangelus,* based on a motet by Philippe Verdelot; and *Missa Qual è il più grand' amore* and *Missa Quando lieta sperai,* based on madrigals by Cipriano de Rore.

Of the paraphrase masses, most are based on Gregorian chants; sixteen use chants from liturgical mass cycles, one (the *Missa pro defunctis*) uses chants from the Requiem Mass, and many others use familiar chants from important liturgical feasts or celebrations (e.g., the antiphons *Alma redemptoris mater* and *Regina coeli,* and the hymn *Iste confessor*). Only a few secular tunes are used as models, including two masses based on L'homme armé.

Of the freely composed masses, the *Missa Papae Marcelli* is the most famous and by far the most celebrated mass of the Renaissance. Published in 1567, it was likely composed shortly after the death of Pope Marcellus II in 1555 and in response to the pope's desire for music that met the mandates of the Council of Trent. On the third day of his papacy, which happened to be Good Friday, Pope Marcellus II met with the musicians of the papal chapel and encouraged them to compose music that reflected the solemnity of its purpose and that allowed text to be intelligible to worshippers. Palestrina's *Missa Papae Marcelli* not only satisfied these requirements with its vertically oriented polyphony (as opposed to the traditional linear polyphony, which diffused text), it also became the exemplar of new music for the church and a model for other composers.

Most of the masses have sections scored for both smaller and larger forces than the indicated vocal scoring. For instance, in *Missa Vestiva i colli* (SATTB) the Christe is scored for SATT, the Crucifixus and Benedictus are scored for SSAT, and the final Agnus Dei for SSATTB; in *Missa Dies sanctificatus* (SATB) the Crucifixus is scored for SSAA and the Benedictus for SSAT; and in *Missa Assumpta est Maria* (SSATTB) the Christe is scored for ATTB, the Crucifixus for SSAA, and the Benedictus for SSAT.

The motets include sixty-five hymns for four to six voices in *alternatim* style composed as a cycle for the liturgical year, and sixty-eight offertories for five voices in imitative motet style, also composed as a cycle for the liturgical year. The offertories, individually and collectively, are considered to be masterpieces. The motets also include multiple settings of the same text. For instance, there are four settings each of Alma redemptoris mater and Regina coeli, five each of Ave Maria and Ave regina coelorum, six of Miserere mei, and seven of Benedictus Dominus.

The style of the motets represents imitative polyphony in its most idealized state, with balanced melodic shapes, consistently prepared and resolved dissonances, and structural symmetry. Melodies and rhythms are not varied for expressive purposes as in the motets by Rore, and textures do not alternate phrases of imitative polyphony with passages of homophony as in the motets of Andrea Gabrieli, although a number of motets open with homophonic passages. Palestrina's motets are modeled after the pervasive point-of-imitation style as practiced by Adrian Willaert and other Franco-Flemish masters. In particular, melodies are characterized by wide melodic intervals, with stepwise motion in the opposite direction following any leap of a third or a fourth; rhythms are within a narrow range of durational values, with a preponderance of half and quarter notes (in present-day transcriptions); and harmonies are logically ordered, with buildup of tension followed by inevitable resolution. Moreover, phrase structures are well balanced. As is seen in *Veni sponsa Christi,* a motet for the ordination of nuns, the text is divided into four short phrases—"Veni sponsa Christi" (Come, bride of Christ), "accipe coronam" (receive the crown), "quam tibi Dominus" (that for you the Lord), and "praeparavit in aeternam" (has prepared in eternity)—each given equal treatment imitatively. The first and second points of imitation, as well as the third and fourth points, are overlapped slightly, while there is a clear textural demarcation between points two and three. Many other motets are constructed similarly, including *Sicut cervus, Super flumina Babylonis,* and *Dies sanctificatus.* The two-movement motets *Canite tuba - Rorate coeli* and *Tu es Petrus - Quodcumque ligaveris,* also in the point-of-imitation style described above, are structured in ABCB format. The B sections in the first movements of the motets (*Canite tuba* and *Tu es Petrus*) end in dominant keys, whereas the B sections in the second movements (*Rorate coeli* and *Quodcumque ligaveris*) end in the tonic.

The madrigals, similar in style and structure to the motets, are overshadowed by the sacred works. However, many of the madrigals were quite popular during the latter half of the sixteenth century. *Io son ferito* and *Vestiva i colli,* for instance, were two of the most popular madrigals of the era, reprinted numerous times and parodied by such composers as Orazio Vecchi and Adriano Banchieri in their madrigal comedies. The six-voiced *Quando dal terzo cielo* was selected for inclusion in *Il trionfo di Dori*.

MASSES
SELECTED AND LISTED ACCORDING TO FAMILIARITY

Missa Papae Marcelli – SATTBB chorus – 31:30 minutes.

Missa Tu es Petrus – SSATBB chorus – 28 minutes.

Missa Hodie Christus natus est – SSAB/ATTB chorus – 31 minutes.

Missa Dies sanctificatus – SATB chorus – 26 minutes.

Missa Veni sponsa Christi – SATB chorus – 27 minutes.

Missa Viri Galilaei – SAATTB chorus – 34 minutes.

Missa O rex gloriae – SATB chorus – 24 minutes.

Missa pro defunctis – SATTB chorus – 22 minutes.

Missa Vestiva i colli – SATTB chorus – 25 minutes.

Missa Aeterna Christi munera – SATB chorus – 20 minutes.

Missa L'homme armé – SATTB chorus – 22 minutes.

Missa Lauda Sion – SATB chorus – 27 minutes.

Missa Iste confessor – SATB chorus – 23 minutes.

Missa O admirabile commercium – SATTB chorus – 21 minutes.

Missa Memor esto – SATTB chorus – 22 minutes.

Missa Assumpta est Maria – SSATTB chorus – 20 minutes.

MOTETS
SELECTED AND LISTED ACCORDING TO FAMILIARITY

Sicut cervus – SATB chorus – 4 minutes.

Super flumina Babylonis – SATB chorus – 3:30 minutes.

Dies sanctificatus – SATB chorus – 3 minutes.

Canite tuba - Rorate coeli – SSATB – 5:30 minutes.

O magnum mysterium – SSAATB chorus – 3:30 minutes.

Tu es Petrus - Quodcumque ligaveris – SSATTB chorus – 5:30 minutes.

Hodie Christus natus est – SATB/SATB chorus – 4 minutes.

Veni sponsa Christi – SATB chorus – 3:30 minutes.

Exsultate Deo – SAATB chorus – 4 minutes.

Alma redemptoris mater – SATB – 3 minutes.

Ego sum panis vivus – SATB chorus – 3 minutes.

Stabat mater – SATB/SATB chorus – 8:30 minutes.

Jubilate Deo – SATB chorus – 4 minutes.

Ave Maria – SSATB – 3:30 minutes.

Ave Maria – SATB chorus – 3 minutes.

O rex gloriae – SATB chorus – 4 minutes.

Christe, qui lux es et dies – SATTB chorus – 5 minutes.

Lucis creator optime – SATTB chorus – 5:30 minutes.

MADRIGALS
SELECTED AND LISTED ACCORDING TO FAMILIARITY

Vestiva i colli – a two-madrigal cycle – SATTB voices – 4 minutes.

Io son ferito – SSAAT voices – 3 minutes.

Già fu chi m'ebbe cara – SATB voices – 2:45 minutes.

Alla riva del Tebro – SATB voices – 2:30 minutes.

Vergine bella – SATTB voices – 4 minutes.

COSTANZO PORTA CA.1528–1601

Porta was born in Cremona, where he received his musical instruction at the convent of Porta S Luca. In 1549 he moved to Venice and studied (along with Claudio Merulo and Gioseffo Zarlino) under Adrian Willaert, *maestro di cappella* at St Mark's Basilica, and in 1552 he was appointed *maestro di cappella* at Osimo Cathedral. In 1565 he was appointed to the same position at the Cappella Antoniana in Padua, and from 1567 to 1589 he served at the Basilica in Ravenna, making short visits during his time there to Ferrara, where he became acquainted with Luzzasco Luzzaschi, and to Mantua, where he met Giaches de Wert. Porta was appointed *maestro di cappella* at the Padua Cathedral in 1589, and in 1595 he returned to the Cappella Antoniana. He was highly respected during his time, and was praised in treatises by Giovanni Maria Artusi and Lodovico Zacconi for his polyphonic expertise.

Porta composed fifteen masses (including one Requiem), more than three hundred motets, and approximately 150 madrigals. Most of the masses are parodies of motets and madrigals by notable composers of the time. *Missa secundi toni* is based on Palestrina's famous madrigal *Ves-*

tiva i colli, *Missa tertii toni* is based on Rore's madrigal *Come havran fin*, and *Missa Audi filia* is based on the same-named motet by Nicolas Gombert. Most of the masses are also in ultraconservative styles, with numerous cantus firmi and canons. Examples include the thirteen-voiced *Missa Ducalis* and the eight-voiced *Missa Da pacem*, both of which have cantus firmi with separate texts. The motets are similarly in styles of earlier times, in particular those exhibited by Gombert and Willaert. Examples include *Regina coeli*, *Hodie Christus natus est*, *Ego sum pastor bonus*, and *Voce mea*, all of which are constructed of continuous points of imitation. *Diffusa est gratia* and *Vidi speciosam* are well-known works that employ canons, and the forty-six hymn settings are in *alternatim* style.

The madrigals are also mainly imitative, although they frequently contain varied rhythms that are used for expressive purposes. For instance, *Da lo spuntar de matutini albori* (one of the madrigals in *Il trionfo di Dori*) has *note nere* rhythms that paint the phrase "fù risonar tra l'onde e faggi e fiori" (resounding amid the waves, beech trees, and flowers), and parallel thirds that depict "cantando" (singing).

ANDREA GABRIELI CA.1532–1585

Andrea Gabrieli, uncle of Giovanni Gabrieli, was born in Venice. No documentation exists about his youth or musical training, although it is assumed that he studied with Adrian Willaert, who was *maestro di cappella* at St Mark's Basilica from 1527 until his death in 1562. The publication circumstances of two early Gabrieli madrigals—*Piangete occhi miei* and *Giovane donna sott'un verde lauro*—suggest that he was in Verona in the early 1550s, but from 1555 to 1557 he was back in Venice serving as organist at the church of S Geremia. Between 1557 and 1566 he lived in Milan and traveled to Prague and cities in Germany with the court of Albrecht V, Duke of Bavaria. Orlando di Lasso was also with the court at this time, and the two composers became close associates. In 1566 Gabrieli was appointed main organist at St Mark's Basilica, a position he would keep for the remainder of his life. While at St Mark's he taught his nephew Giovanni, the theorist Lodovico Zacconi, and the German composers Gregor Aichinger and Hans Leo Hassler.

Gabrieli composed six masses, approximately 120 motets, one Magnificat, and more than 180 madrigals. Four of the masses (all those scored for six voices) are parodies of Italian motets and madrigals and are in the imitative style of early-sixteenth-century composers. The other two masses (those scored for four voices) are in a more modern style, with a predominance of syllabically set texts, short motivic phrases, and homophonic textures. Most of the motets are also in this modern style, one that was in keeping with the ideals of the Council of Trent, and most are scored for one choral ensemble of five or six voices. It should not be assumed, therefore, that Andrea Gabrieli, like his nephew Giovanni, composed mainly polychoral motets. Only about a dozen of Andrea's motets are scored for multiple ensembles of eight to twelve voices. Examples are the eight-voiced *Lucida ceu fulgida* and *Quem vidistis pastores*, the ten-voiced *Exsultate justi in Domino* and *Laudate Dominum in sanctis eius*, and the twelve-voiced *Deus misereatur nostri* and *Benedicam Dominum*.

Like many of his contemporaries, Gabrieli is best known for his madrigals. They are in the style of the day, with varied rhythms, syllabically set texts, short phrases, and textures that alternate between imitative polyphony and homophony. However, there are very few instances of word painting. Gabrieli's most famous madrigal, *Sonno diletto e caro,* rivaled Willaert's *Amor mi fa morire,* Arcadelt's *Il bianco e dolce cigno,* Rore's *Ancor che col partire,* and Palestrina's *Vestiva i colli* in being one of the most popular madrigals of the sixteenth century.

MOTETS
SELECTED AND LISTED ACCORDING TO FAMILIARITY

Jubilate Deo omnis terra – SSAT/ATTB chorus – 3:30 minutes.

De profundis – SSATTB chorus – 6:30 minutes.

Angelus ad pastores – SATB chorus – 4 minutes.

Diligam te, Domine – SATB chorus – 3:30 minutes.

Quem vidistis pastores – SSAATTBB chorus – 2:30 minutes.

MADRIGALS
SELECTED AND LISTED ACCORDING TO FAMILIARITY

Sonno diletto e caro – SSATTB voices – 3 minutes.

O beltà rara – SATTB voices – 2 minutes.

Caro dolce ben mio – SATTB voices – 3 minutes.

Occhi sereni – SATB voices – 2:15 minutes.

Ecco l'aurora con l'aurata fronte – SATTB voices – 2:30 minutes.

Due rose fresche – SATTB voices – 2:15 minutes.

Tirsi morir volea – SSATTTB voices – 3:30 minutes.

Quand' io ero giovinetto – a two-cycle madrigal – SSATB voices – 5 minutes.

Felici d'Adria – SSAATTBB voices – 4 minutes.

Cantiam di Dio – SATB/SATB/SATB voices – 5 minutes.

GIAMMATEO ASOLA CA.1532–1609

Asola was born in Verona, where he most likely studied music with Vincenzo Ruffo. He also studied for the priesthood and held clerical positions at the churches of S Stefano and S Maria in Organo, both in Verona. In 1577 he was appointed *maestro di cappella* at Treviso Cathedral, the following year he was appointed to the same position at Vicenza Cathedral, and from 1582 until his death he served as a priest at the church of S Severo in Venice.

Asola composed five books of masses (which contain two Requiems), fifteen books of motets, one Passion (based on passages from all four Gospels), one set of Lamentations, two books of sacred or spiritual madrigals, and two books of secular madrigals. Many of the works in all the genres are scored for equal voices, including *Missa Octavi toni* for four equal parts and the *Madrigali accomodati da cantar in fuga* for two voices in canon. Many other works are scored for men's voices, including *Missa Sexti toni* and the motets *Tantum ergo* and *Quem vidistis pastores*. Yet a sizable number of works are scored for three voices, including one of the Requiems, the motets *Deus canticum novum* and *O vos omnes*, and the two books of spiritual madrigals entitled *Le vergini a tre voci*. The first of these books consists of eleven madrigals, each beginning with the word "Vergine" (e.g., *Vergine belle, Vergine saggia*, and *Vergine pura*). The most popular of Asola's works, however, are not in any of the voicings described above (i.e., equal, men's, or three-part): *Missa Regina coeli* is a polychoral work scored for SATB/SATB chorus, and *In una verde piaggia*, one of the madrigals in *Il trionfo di Dori*, is scored for SSATTB voices.

CLAUDIO MERULO 1533–1604

Merulo was born in Correggio, north of Florence, and in his youth probably went to Venice to study with Adrian Willaert, *maestro di cappella* of St Mark's Basilica from 1527 to 1562. In 1556 Merulo was appointed organist at Brescia Cathedral, and the following year he was appointed second organist at St Mark's. He remained in this latter position for twenty-seven years, often taking over the responsibilities of main organist and developing a reputation as one of the most knowledgeable organ builders of the time. In 1584 he moved to the Farnese court in Parma, and in 1587 he added the position of organist at both the church of the Madonna della Steccata and the Parma Cathedral, where he was buried. Although he composed and was respected for his numerous vocal works, he was known mostly for his organ masses and toccatas as well as instrumental ricercars and canzonas.

Merulo composed ten masses, approximately one hundred motets, four Magnificats, and over ninety madrigals. Most of the masses, scored for five voices, are parodies—not of motets and madrigals, as was typical of the time, but of motets and chansons (e.g., the two chanson-based works *Missa Susanne un giour* and *Missa Oncques amour*). Other masses are polychoral works such as *Missa Benedicam Dominum* for twelve voices. Several of the motets (e.g., the eight-voiced *Ave gratia plena*) are also polychoral. However, most are scored for four, five, and six voices and are in the modern style of the day, with short phrases, basically syllabic text settings, and alternating passages of polyphony and homophony. An example is the six-voiced *Peccantem me quotidie*.

The majority of the madrigals, similar to the motets in textures of alternating polyphony and homophony, were issued in four books—one for three voices, one for four voices, and two for five voices. The five-voiced *Quand' io penso al matire* is well known.

GIACHES DE WERT 1535–1596

Wert was born in Flanders, possibly Ghent, and thus was the last notable composer of the Renaissance to have been born in the Franco-Flemish area of Europe and to have spent his life in Italy. He most likely went to Naples as a chorister at the court of Maria di Cardova, Marchesa of Padulla, and in about 1550 he was at the court of Count Alfonso Gonzaga in the small town of

Novellara. During the late 1550s Wert traveled to Mantua and Ferrara, where he was exposed to the madrigals of Cipriano de Rore, and sometime in the early 1560s he was appointed *maestro di cappella* at the governor's court in Milan. From 1565 to 1592 he served as *maestro di cappella* at the ducal chapel of S Barbara in Mantua, and from 1592 until his death he continued to compose for the Mantuan court, although its musical direction had passed to Giovanni Gastoldi. While employed in Mantua, Wert made frequent visits to the d'Este court in Ferrara (the two courts, less than fifty miles apart, had close connections), and he composed music for the court's famous female vocal ensemble, the Concerto delle donne.

Wert composed seven masses, one Requiem (of questionable authenticity), approximately 170 motets, five Magnificats, and more than 225 madrigals. Most of the masses and all of the Magnificats are based on Gregorian chants and are in *alternatim* style. The *Missa Dominicalis*, for instance, alternates newly composed polyphony with the chant *Kyrie orbis factor*. The motets include 127 hymns composed as a cycle for important liturgical celebrations at S Barbara. Like the masses and Magnificats, many are in *alternatim* style, with Wert's polyphony characterized by simplicity of presentation reflective of the ideals promoted by the Council of Trent. The other motets are similar in terms of text declamation; however, some (e.g., *Ascendente Jesu in naviculam*) contain modern elements of rhythmic variety for textual expression.

Most of the madrigals were published in sixteen books between 1558 and 1595. Fourteen of these books are for five voices, with only one for four voices and one for four to seven voices. In addition, there is a book of canzonets and villanellas for five voices. The early madrigals are conservative, with settings of serious poetry, alternating passages of homophony and imitative polyphony, and rhythmic values that vary only slightly for expressive purposes. Examples include *Amor, io fallo* and *Di pensier in pensier,* both settings of Petrarch poems. The later madrigals are settings of contemporary poems in a more declamatory style, with a preponderance of homophony and with textures that vary for expressive purposes. *Giunto a la tomba,* a two-madrigal cycle set to a poem by Torquato Tasso, begins with declamatory homophony similar to the choral recitative employed by Claudio Monteverdi in the madrigals from his middle period. In addition, the madrigal features melismatic word painting to the text "A fin sgorgando un lagrimoso rivo" (A tearful stream at length gushing). *Vezzosi augelli,* also set to a poem by Tasso, has numerous instances of word painting, including long melismas in parallel thirds to the word "cantan" (sing). Wert's most famous madrigal, *D'un si bel foco,* was not published in one of the books devoted exclusively to his works but was contained in the anthology *Musica di XIII autori illustri a cinque voci,* published by Antonio Gardane in 1576.

MADRIGALS

SELECTED AND LISTED IN CHRONOLOGICAL ORDER OF PUBLICATION

D'un si bel foco – a two-madrigal cycle – SATTB voices – 4 minutes.

Chi salirà per me madonn'in cielo – SATB voices – 2:30 minutes.

Amor, io fallo – a two-madrigal cycle – SATTB voices – 5 minutes.

Giunto a la tomba – a two-madrigal cycle – SATTB voices – 6 minutes.

Solo e pensoso – a two-madrigal cycle – SSATB voices – 3 minutes.

Forsennata gridava – SSATB voices – 2 minutes.

Vezzosi augelli – SSATB voices – 3 minutes.

Valle, che di' lamenti miei – a two-madrigal cycle – SATTB voices – 6:30 minutes.

Mia benigna fortuna – a two-madrigal cycle – SATTB voices – 4 minutes.

Donna, tu sei si bella – SSATTB voices – 2 minutes.

Ah dolente partita – SSATB voices – 3 minutes.

MARC'ANTONIO INGEGNERI CA.1536–1592

Ingegneri was born in Verona, where he was a chorister at the cathedral and likely sang under Vincenzo Ruffo, who was appointed *maestro di cappella* in 1554. During the late 1550s Ingegneri presumably lived in Padua and Venice, there is some evidence that during the early 1560s he was acquainted with Cipriano de Rore in Parma, and in 1566 he was employed at the monastery of S Abbondio in Cremona. In 1576 he was appointed *maestro di cappella* at the Cremona Cathedral and, while serving in this position, he taught Claudio Monteverdi.

Ingegneri composed two books of masses, six books of motets, one set of Lamentations, and nine books of madrigals. The early masses and motets generally exhibit construction techniques such as cantus firmus, paraphrasing of Gregorian chants, and canon. The masses *Gustate ed videte, Susanne un jour,* and *Laudate pueri Dominum* are all parodies, and the motet *Noe noe* is a double canon. The later masses and motets are more modern and freely composed, with syllabic text settings and homophonic textures. The four-voiced motet *In monte Oliveti,* for example, is almost entirely homophonic. The *Responsoria hebdomadae sanctae* (Responsories for Holy Week), previously ascribed to Monteverdi, are Ingegneri's best-known works. They are all scored for four voices (except for several three-voiced sections), their textures are basically homophonic, and their formal structures are often ABCB. Other frequently performed motets are *Ecce quomodo moritum* and *O bone Jesu.*

The madrigals are in the style of Rore, with varied rhythms used to express particular sentiments of text phrases and with settings of the most famous poets of the Renaissance. *Due rose fresch'e* and *Non vede un simil par d'amanti il sole* are settings by Petrarch, *Ardi e gela a tua voglia* and *Mentre io mirava fiso* are by Tasso, and *La verginella è simil alla rosa* is by Ariosto.

ALESSANDRO STRIGGIO CA.1537–1592

Striggio was born in Mantua to an aristocratic family that was in high standing at the Gonzaga court. Nothing is known about his youth or musical training except that he developed into a virtuoso player of viols and lutes. His son Alessandro (ca.1573–1630) was also an accomplished viol player as well as a librettist who wrote the texts for Monteverdi's opera *Orfeo* and ballo *Tirsi e Clori.* In 1559 the elder Striggio entered the court of Cosimi I de' Medici in Florence, where he remained until the final years of his life. During the 1570s he became acquainted with Orlando di Lasso during several trips to the Bavarian court in Munich, and during the 1580s he composed madrigals for the famous female vocal ensemble, the Concerto delle donne, during time spent at the court of Alfonso II d'Este in Ferrara.

Striggio composed one mass, one motet, and approximately 150 madrigals, plus several works for intermedii and theater presentations. The mass, *Missa in dominicis diebus,* is based on Gregorian chant and is in *alternatim* style. The motet, *Ecce beatam lucem,* is one of the several sacred works of the late sixteenth century scored for forty voices (distributed into four ensembles of eight, ten, sixteen, and six voices each, with two of the ensembles meant for instruments). Most of the madrigals were published in seven books—five for five voices and two for six voices—and are mainly homophonic, with brief motif-like passages in imitation and with rhythms that vary little from one another. In addition, the texts are set syllabically. Examples include *O ben felice a pieno* for five voices (SATTB) and *Partirò dunque* and *Non rumor di tamburi* for six voices (SSATTB). Two other six-voiced madrigals were popular during their day: *Eran le ninfe e pastori* was included in the collection *Il trionfo di Dori,* and *Nasce la pena mia* was parodied by Philippe de Monte. Other madrigals became popular in England: *Non rumor di tamburi,* translated as *Love hath proclaimed war by trumpet sounded,* was included in Thomas Watson's 1590 publication *The first sett of Italian Madrigalls Englished.*

ALFONSO FERRABOSCO 1543–1588

Alfonso, son of Domenico Maria, was born in Bologna, where the elder Ferrabosco was a singer at the church of S Petronio and director of public performances and palace musicians for the city. Alfonso was exposed to the musicians at the papal chapel while his father was a singer there between 1550 and 1555, and he studied with his father in France thereafter. In 1562 Alfonso was appointed a musician at the court of Queen Elizabeth I of England, where he remained for almost twenty years, and between the early 1580s and his death at age forty-five he served at the court of Carlo Emanuele I, Duke of Savoy. Ferrabosco was one of the first Italian musicians and the first Italian madrigalist to be employed in England. As such, he was influential in the development of the English madrigal. He had a close association with William Byrd, and fourteen of his works (twelve madrigals and two chansons in English translation) were included in the first collection of madrigals in England, *Musica transalpina,* published by Nicholas Yonge in 1588. Thomas Morley included five Ferrabosco madrigals in the 1598 edition of *Musica transalpina.*

Ferrabosco's choral output includes forty-two motets, four sets of Lamentations, one English anthem, sixty-four Italian madrigals, and five French chansons. The motets include several lengthy, multimovement works such as *Benedic anima mea Domino* (Psalm 104) for three to six voices in eleven movements and *Inclina Domine aurem tuam* (Psalm 86) for three to seven voices in six movements. Most of the motets, however, are scored for single ensembles in one movement. Examples include a second setting of Psalm 104 for five voices and three settings of *Da pacem* (two for six voices and one for five voices). Only one of the motets, the five-voiced *Da pacem,* uses a cantus firmus; the others are in the imitative style of Orlando di Lasso.

The madrigals also include several lengthy, multimovement works: *A la dolc' ombra* and *Mentre ti fui si grato* are cycles of six madrigals, and *Vergine bella,* like the identically titled work by Cipriano de Rore, is an eleven-madrigal cycle. The style of these and most of the other madrigals is conservative, with imitative textures and with rhythms that vary only slightly to portray shifting moods of text. *Poi ch'io non poss' amore,* for instance, is almost completely imitative, and there is only one phrase with rhythmic characterization—"Fa l'ali tu al mio cor acciò che vole intorno al car' adore" (Give wings to my heart so that it may fly around the beloved heart). The chansons include settings of three texts also set by Lasso—*Las, voulez vous; Le rossignol;* and *Susanne un jour.*

GIOVANNI MARIA NANINO CA.1543–1607

Nanino was born in Rome and sang as a chorister at the cathedral in the nearby town of Vallerano. He also may have sung under Palestrina at S Maria Maggiore in the early 1560s. In 1567 Nanino succeeded Palestrina as *maestro di cappella* at S Maria Maggiore, in 1575 he was appointed *maestro di cappella* at S Luigi dei Francesi, and in 1577 he was admitted as a singer to the papal choir. He remained with the papal choir until his death, serving as *maestro di cappella* several times after 1586 (the position of *maestro di cappella* at the papal choir was a rotating one at the time). He had many students during his career, including Felice Anerio, and he was considered to be second only to Palestrina as a composer. His brother Giovanni Bernardino Nanino (ca.1560–1623) was also a composer who had several significant *maestro di cappella* positions in Rome; however, none of his compositions are known today.

Giovanni Maria Nanino composed several masses, approximately twenty-four motets, five sets of Lamentations, three books of madrigals, and one book of canzonets. Only one of the masses has been published—*Missa Vestiva i colli,* based on Palestrina's famous madrigal. The motets, mostly for four and five voices, are in a conservative style that alternates passages of imitative polyphony with homophony. Examples are *Hodie Christus natus est, Diffusa est gratia,* and *Adoramus te Christe.*

Like most Italian composers in the latter part of the sixteenth century, Nanino was known for his madrigals. Indeed, he was perhaps the most represented composer in madrigal collections between 1555 and 1620, and books devoted entirely to his madrigals were reprinted often during his lifetime. The music ranges in style from imitative (represented in *Dolorosi martir* and *Le strani voci,* both set to serious texts) to homophonic (represented by *Morir non può'l mio core,* which is a setting of a lighthearted text such as was beginning to be popular at the time). This latter madrigal was published in Thomas Watson's 1590 edition of *Italian madrigals englished* under the title *All ye that joy in wailing.*

LUZZASCO LUZZASCHI CA.1545–1607

Luzzaschi was born in Ferrara, where he was exposed to the madrigals of Cipriano de Rore, *maestro di cappella* at the Este court until 1559. In 1561 Luzzaschi was appointed second organist at the court, in 1564 he was promoted to first organist (with responsibilities for playing all keyboard instruments and for composing), and in approximately 1570 he became director of the court's *musica da camera,* which included performances by the famous female vocal ensemble, the Concerto delle donne. He also served as organist at the Ferrara Cathedral and at the Accademia della Morte. Numerous musicians of the time praised his work: Adriano Banchieri called him one of the greatest virtuoso keyboardists of the time, Carlo Gesualdo admired his expressive writing, and Girolamo Frescobaldi acknowledged his excellent pedagogical skills.

Luzzaschi composed one book of motets and eight books of madrigals—seven books for five voices and one book (*Madrigali per cantare et sonare a uno, e doi, e tre soprani*) composed specifically for the Concerto delle donne. The motets are not known today. However, a number of the madrigals are recognized for their exceptional expressive qualities and for their manifestation of the textual ideals of the *seconda prattica*. Luzzaschi described these ideals in the preface to his sixth book of madrigals, published in 1596: "Since poetry was the first to be born, music reveres and honors her as his lady, so much so that music, having become virtually a shadow of poetry, does not dare move its foot where its superior has not gone before. From this it follows that if the verse . . . weeps, laughs, runs, stops, implores, denies, screams, falls silent, lives, and dies, these effects should be vividly expressed in music." To manifest these expressive ideals, Luzzaschi's madrigals exhibit such features as abrupt changes of texture, momentary chromaticism, and word painting that underscores textual meaning. In *Il vedervi e lasciarvi*, for example, the phrase "Ahi lasso" (Ah alas) is suddenly set to much slower rhythms than the surrounding phrases; in *Qui'vi sospiri, pianti* the single words "sospiri" (sighing), "pianti" (weeping), and "lagrimai" (tearful) are given chromatic treatment; and in *Itene mie querele*, perhaps Luzzaschi's most famed madrigal, the phrase "Itene mie querele precipitose a volo" (Go, my laments, hastily in flight) is divided into two very different fragments, the first completely homophonic and declamatory, and the second melismatic and descriptive.

ORAZIO VECCHI 1550–1605

Vecchi was born in Modena and received his education from the Benedictine monks of S Pietro. He was ordained a priest in the 1570s but did not serve in that capacity until late in his life. As a young adult he traveled throughout Italy, becoming acquainted with Andrea Gabrieli and Claudio Merulo and collaborating with them both on the composition of a theatrical work for the marriage celebration of Francesco de' Medici. In 1581 Vecchi was appointed *maestro di cappella* at Salò Cathedral, and in 1583 he accepted the same position at Modena Cathedral. He discontinued his musical career in 1586, becoming a canon at Correggio Cathedral and later an archdeacon. However, he returned to music and to his position as *maestro di cappella* at Modena Cathedral in 1593. During the 1590s he also worked at the court of Duke Cesare d'Este in Modena, where he was appointed *maestro di corte* in 1598.

Vecchi composed one book of masses and a separate mass entitled *Missa Julia*, four books of motets, one set of Lamentations, one Magnificat, two books of madrigals, six books of canzonets, several books and individual works of varied secular forms, and the madrigal comedy *L'Amfiparnaso*. The masses are conservative, characterized by pervasive polyphony and cantus firmus construction. The motets, which include a cycle of hymns for the liturgical year, are more modern, with alternating textures of imitative polyphony and homophony, varied rhythms, word painting, and polychoral effects.

The madrigals, generally set to serious poetry, are similar in style to the motets. *Leggiadretto Clorino* has varied rhythmic patterns and alternating passages of imitative polyphony and homophony; *Hor ch'ogni vento tace*, one of the madrigals in the collection *Il trionfo di Dori*, has instances of word painting, including melismas on the words "aura" (breeze), "l'onde" (the waves), and "cantiam" (let us sing); and *Il bianco e dolce cigno,* an elaborated paraphrase of Arcadelt's famous madrigal of the same name, has ornamental figures on the words "cantando" (singing) and "gioia" (joy).

The canzonets—published in one book for three voices, four books for four voices, and one book for six voices—are mostly homophonic pieces set to humorous or lighthearted texts. *Fa una canzona senza note nere* (Sing me a song without black notes) pokes fun at the serious madrigal style of Marenzio; *Fammi una canzonetta* and *Gioite tutti* are set to texts about the merriment of singing; and *So ben, mi, c'ha bon tempo* has *fa la la* refrains. Many of the canzonets are also strophic, including the four-versed *Caro dolce mio bene* and the five-versed *So ben, mi, c'ha bon tempo.*

The books of varied secular forms—*Selva di varia ricreatione* of 1590, *Il convito musicale* of 1597, and *Le veglie di Siena* of 1604—contain serious madrigals such as *Fummo felici un tempo* and *Chi è fermato,* and lighthearted pieces such as *Diversi linguaggi* (Diverse languages), which fuses five voice parts of a Marenzio madrigal with four newly composed voice parts—all in different languages or dialects. A cycle of sixteen madrigals entitled *L'humore musicale* (The musical humors) concludes *Le veglie di Siena.* The first madrigal is in the form of a prologue that invites listeners to enjoy "gli humori della musica moderna" (the humors of modern music), and the final madrigal is in the form of a finale that praises the "cigni cantori" (singing swans) for their "dolci e vari umori" (sweet and varied moods). In between, each madrigal expresses a different mood, from *L'humor grave* (The serious mood) to *L'humor balzano* (The dancing mood).

Two separately published works are of particular interest. The first, *Battaglia d'Amor e Dispetto* (Battle of Love and Scorn), is a four-madrigal, double chorus work composed for the wedding of Clelia Farnese to Marco Pio di Savoia in 1587 and scored for ten voices (SATB/SSATTB). The text, which begins "Accingeter' amanti a l'alta impresa, e stat'a la difesa" (Make yourselves ready, lovers, for a great battle, and stand on guard), has onomatopoeic battle sounds and includes the names of the wedding couple. The second work, *Mascherata della Malinconia et Allegrezza* (Masquerade of Melancholy and Cheerfulness), is a three-madrigal, double chorus work composed for the wedding of Duke Cesare d'Este's daughter Laura in 1604 and also scored for ten voices (SATTB/SSATB). The first madrigal of the cycle consists of a dialogue between the two choruses (one representing melancholy and the other cheerfulness), the middle madrigal is a balletto of four verses with the refrain "Viva l'amore" (Long live love), and the final madrigal brings the two choruses together with the text "O ben felice e fortunato Amore, che in un moment' alegra e attrist' il core" (O happy and fortunate love, that at the same time both saddens and cheers our hearts).

Vecchi is best known for his madrigal comedy *L'Amfiparnaso,* a work consisting of thirteen scenes that comment on the life of the times through commedia dell'arte characters such as the old man Pantalone, the bumbling doctor Graziano, the courtesan Hortensia, and the young lovers Lucio and Isabella. The title *L'Amfiparnaso* refers to the two slopes of Parnassus—comedy and tragedy—and each of the scenes consists of a short, spoken summary of the dialogue followed by a five-voiced madrigal (or in one case, a four-voiced parody of Rore's *Ancor che col partire*). The texts of the madrigals read as a narrative between the various characters. However, no individual roles are assigned; the dialogue is all sung by the vocal ensemble. While the work appears to be theatrical, Vecchi said that it was not to be staged.

MADRIGAL COMEDY

L'Amfiparnaso – SSATB voices – 56 minutes.

MADRIGALS
SELECTED AND LISTED ACCORDING TO FAMILIARITY

Il bianco e dolce cigno – SSATB voices – 3:30 minutes.

Hor ch'ogni vento tace – SSATTB voices – 3:15 minutes.

Fummo felici un tempo – SSATB voices – 3:30 minutes.

Io soffrirò cor mio – SATB voices – 3 minutes.

Dolcissimo ben mio – SATB voices – 2:30 minutes.

Leggiadretto Clorino – SSATB voices – 3 minutes.

CANZONETS
SELECTED AND LISTED ACCORDING TO FAMILIARITY

Fa una canzona – SATB voices – 2 minutes.

Fammi una canzonetta – SATB voices – 2:30 minutes.

Gioite tutti – SSATB voices – 2:30 minutes.

Il cocodrillo geme – SATB voices – 5 minutes.

So ben, mi, c'ha bon tempo – SATB voices – 4 minutes.

S'udia un pastor l'altr' hieri – SST voices – 4:15 minutes.

Caro dolce mio bene – SSAT voices – 4 minutes.

LUCA MARENZIO CA.1553–1599

Marenzio was born near Brescia in northern Italy, where he probably was a chorister at Brescia Cathedral. It is also probable that he spent time at the Gonzaga court in Mantua during the late 1560s. During the early 1570s he was in the service of Cardinal Cristoforo Madruzzo in Rome, and from 1578 to 1586 he was a singer and lutenist at the court of Cardinal Luigi d'Este, also in Rome. After Luigi d'Este's death in 1587, Marenzio served Cardinal Ferdinando de' Medici for several years and then Cardinal Cinzio Aldobrandini, in 1595 he was appointed *maestro di cappella* at the court of Polish King Sigismund III in Warsaw, and in 1598 he returned to Italy, where he worked independently in Venice and Rome. He was considered by many Renaissance musicians to be the finest composer of the late sixteenth century and the chief exemplar of the expressive style that was popular during this time. In particular, his standing among his contemporaries designated him as the de facto leader of the late Renaissance madrigal style.

Marenzio composed four masses that can be ascribed with certainty, approximately seventy motets, two Magnificats, and more than 425 madrigals, canzonets, and villanellas. The masses and Magnificats are in the typical conservative style of the time: they are parodies of preexisting motets (e.g., *Missa Ego sum panis, Missa Jubilate Deo,* and *Missa Laudate Dominum*), and they are characterized by consistent textures of imitative polyphony. The early motets are similarly imitative. However, the later motets consist of short melodic fragments and varied rhythms and textures that highlight specific words. In *Tribus miraculis,* for example, three voices open the motet with melismas on the words "Tribus miraculis" (Three miracles), and later similar melismas ornament the words "vinum" (wine) and "Jordane" (Jordan) as they follow homophonic statements of "hodie" (today). In like manner, melismas decorate the words "apparuit" (appeared) and "canunt" (sing) as they follow simple statements of "hodie" in *Hodie Christus natus est.*

The madrigals were issued in twenty-four books between 1580 and 1599—ten books for five voices, six books for six voices, five books for three voices, two books for four voices, and one book for four to six voices—averaging more than one book per year. The books were not distributed equally throughout these nineteen years, however; there were four books in 1584, five in 1585, and three in 1587. In addition, there were two books in both 1581 and 1595. This total represents more books (and more madrigals) than all the combined publications of the English madrigalists. Marenzio's early madrigals are generally in the imitative, polyphonic style fashionable during the middle years of the sixteenth century, with settings of serious poetry, often by Petrarch. The later madrigals are frequently settings of less serious subject matter by contemporary poets and have word painting as their distinguishing characteristic. Beyond this, the later madrigals feature instances of eye music (i.e., rhythmic notation that visually depicts words or phrases). As an example, Marenzio notates two whole notes to represent his beloved's eyes in *Occhi lucenti* (clear eyes). Also included in the later madrigals is melodic flamboyance (i.e., florid passages), written to show off the virtuosic vocal skills of singers such as those in the Concerto delle donne. *Rivi fontane e fiumi* is an example. Other notable madrigals include *Fiere Silvestre,* the two-madrigal cycle *Solo e pensoso,* and *Leggiadre ninfe e pastorelli amanti,* which was included in *Il trionfo di Dori* and many other late-sixteenth-century collections. The canzonets and villanellas, which are not well known today, were published in five books, all for three voices.

MADRIGALS
SELECTED AND LISTED ACCORDING TO FAMILIARITY

Solo e pensoso – a two-madrigal cycle – SATTB voices – 5 minutes.

Leggiadre ninfe e pastorelli amanti – SSATTB voices – 3:30 minutes.

Fiere Silvestre – SATTB voices – 2 minutes.

I' piango – SATTB voices – 3 minutes.

O fere stelle – SSATTB voices – 3:30 minutes.

Rivi fontane e fiumi – SSATB voices – 3 minutes.

Crudele acerba – SSATB voices – 4 minutes.

Dolorosi martir – SATTB voices – 3:30 minutes.

Vezzosi augelli – SATB voices – 2:15 minutes.

Scendi dal paradiso – SSATB voices – 3:30 minutes.

Crudel perché mi fuggi – SSATTB voices – 3 minutes.

Fuggito è 'il sonno – SATTB voices – 3:15 minutes.

Dissi a l'amata mia – SATB voices – 3 minutes.

Ahime, tal fu d'Amore – SATTBB voices – 4 minutes.

Chi vuol' udir' – SATB voices – 4:30 minutes.

Ov'è condotto il mio amoroso stile – SATB voices – 2:30 minutes.

GIOVANNI GIACOMO GASTOLDI CA.1554–1609

Nothing is known about Gastoldi's early life except that he was born in the town of Caravaggio, near Cremona. In 1572 he was named a subdeacon at the ducal chapel of S Barbara in Mantua, and throughout the remainder of his life other positions followed there, including teacher of counterpoint from 1579 to 1587, singer beginning in 1581, substitute *maestro di cappella* for the ailing Giaches de Wert in 1585 and 1586, and successor to Wert in 1588. Gastoldi remained *maestro di cappella* at S Barbara until his death.

He composed seventeen books of sacred music and ten books of secular vocal music. Most of the sacred books contain a combination of masses and motets, while the secular books are divided between traditional madrigals and lighter forms such as the canzonet and balletto. The masses are mainly for eight voices and are in the conservative polyphonic style of the time. The motets, especially settings of Psalms for Vespers services, are simpler and more direct, exhibiting the Council of Trent ideals of textual clarity and the new declamatory style of writing that was in vogue at the end of the sixteenth century. The book entitled *Psalmi ad vesperas in totius anni solemnitatibus* of 1588 (a cycle of four-voiced settings for the liturgical year) was quite popular and was reprinted five times. Another book, *Integra omnium solemnitatum vespertina psalmodia*, was also popular and went through several reprintings.

Of the secular music—five books of madrigals, three books of canzonets, and two books of ballettos—the ballettos were the pieces that were reprinted the most (the five-voiced book was reprinted thirty times) and also were the pieces that made Gastoldi famous. They are generally constructed of two sections, each repeated and each ending in a *fa la la* refrain, and their textures are almost entirely homophonic. Most of the ballettos were given titles—for example, *Amor vittorioso* (Victorious love), *Il bell' umore* (Good humor), and *Il premiato* (The prize winner)—although these titles have nothing to do with either the balletto's poetry or musical content. The ballettos were also intended for dancing, which Gastoldi confirms in the preface to the books by stating that the pieces are to be sung, played, and danced. The madrigals combine short phrases of imitative polyphony with passages of homophony, and the rhythmic patterns vary to highlight textual content. An example is the six-voiced *Al mormorar de liquidi cristalli,* which was included in the collection *Il trionfo di Dori.*

BALLETTOS
SELECTED AND LISTED ACCORDING TO FAMILIARITY

Amor vittorioso (Victorious love) – SSATB voices – 2 minutes.

Il bell' umore (Good humor) – SSATB voices – 2 minutes.

Il premiato (The prize winner) – SSATB voices – 2 minutes.

Caccia d'amore (Love goes hunting) – SSATB voices – 2 minutes.

La belleza (The beauty) – SSATB voices – 2 minutes.

La sirena (The siren) – SSATB voices – 2 minutes.

L'ardito (The brave) – SSATB voices – 2 minutes.

Il piacere (The pleasures) – SSATB voices – 2 minutes.

Il ballerino (The dancer) – SSB voices – 1:30 minutes.

GIOVANNI GABRIELI CA.1555–1612

Giovanni Gabrieli, nephew of Andrea Gabrieli, was born in Venice, where he most likely studied under his uncle, who from 1566 to 1585 was *maestro di cappella* of St Mark's Basilica. In the 1570s Giovanni followed in Andrea's footsteps by spending time with Orlando di Lasso at the court of Duke Albrecht V in Munich, then returning to Venice to work at St Mark's. In 1584 Giovanni substituted for organist Claudio Merulo, who had moved to Parma, and in 1585 he officially took over Merulo's position. In 1585 Giovanni also was appointed organist at the Scuola Grande di S Rocco, a position he held along with that at St Mark's until his death. He was recognized as an important teacher, especially of musicians from Denmark and Germany, including Heinrich Schütz. Today he is recognized as the most important sixteenth-century composer of polychoral motets.

Gabrieli composed seven mass movements (two Kyries, one Gloria, and two Sanctus/Benedictus cycles), ninety-four motets, seven Magnificats, thirty-two madrigals and related secular vocal genres, and numerous instrumental canzonas, ricercars, toccatas, and fugues. Although the composition of masses had clearly declined in popularity by the end of the sixteenth century, it is peculiar that Gabrieli composed no complete mass cycles, especially cycles based on existing motets and madrigals, but instead resumed the Medieval-era practice of composing separate mass movements. It is also noteworthy that all his mass movements as well as the Magnificats are polychoral works scored for a large number of voice parts: each of the mass movements is scored for twelve parts, and the Magnificats are scored for eight to thirty-three parts.

The motets, for which Gabrieli is best known, range from small-scale works for SATB choir to large-scale polychoral works for up to nineteen voice parts. Many of the smaller works were composed early in Gabrieli's career, both while he was in Munich and during his first years at St Mark's. The larger works were frequently composed for festival celebrations. For example, the ten-voiced *Deus, qui beatum Marcum* was composed for the feast of St Mark, and the fourteen-voiced *In ecclesiis* was composed for the feast of the Ascension. Most of the motets scored for eight or more voice parts are polychoral; that is, they are scored for groups of voices in choirs that often sing independently of each other and that also often echo each other. Not all the voice parts of the polychoral works were sung, however; some parts were specifically intended for instruments. For instance, the second choir of *Suscipe, clementissime Deus,* which accounts for six of the motet's thirteen parts, and the third choir of *In ecclesiis,* which accounts for six of the motet's fourteen parts, are completely untexted. Moreover, it was common for singers to be accompanied or replaced by instruments—from ensembles of recorders and gambas to cornets, zinks, and sackbuts. It was most common to have each choir accompanied by an organ (there was an organ in each of St Mark's four balconies).

Gabrieli is not known today for his madrigals, although several were famous during his lifetime. These include *Se cantano gl'augelli,* which was in the collection *Il trionfo di Dori,* and *Lieto godea,* which was reprinted in several late-sixteenth-century anthologies.

MOTETS
SELECTED AND LISTED ACCORDING TO FAMILIARITY

O magnum mysterium – SATB/SATB chorus and instruments – 4 minutes.

Hodie Christus natus est – SATB/SATB chorus and instruments – 3:30 minutes.

Jubilate Deo – SSAATTBB chorus and instruments – 5 minutes.

Jubilate Deo – SSAATTTTBB chorus and instruments – 4 minutes.

O Jesu mi dulcissime – SATB/SATB chorus and instruments (first setting) – 5 minutes.

Angelus ad pastores – SSAATB/ATTBBB chorus and instruments – 3:30 minutes.

In ecclesiis – SATT/SATB/SSSATB chorus – 4:30 minutes.

Plaudite omnes terra – SAAT/SATB/ATBB chorus and instruments – 4 minutes.

Beata es, virgo Maria – SSATBB chorus and instruments – 3:30 minutes.

Omnes gentes plaudite manibus – SSAT/ATBB/ATBB/SATB chorus and instruments – 4 minutes.

Buccinate in neomenia tuba – SSATB/SATBB/SATB/TBBBB chorus and instruments – 4 minutes.

Exaudi Domine – SSAATB chorus and instruments – 3:30 minutes.

Domine, exaudi orationem meam – SSAB/TBBB chorus and instruments – 3 minutes.

Timor et tremor – SATTBB chorus and instruments – 3:30 minutes.

Suscipe, clementissime Deus – SATTBB/TTBBBB chorus and instruments – 5 minutes.

MADRIGALS
SELECTED AND LISTED ACCORDING TO FAMILIARITY

Se cantano gl'augelli – SSATTB voices – 3 minutes.

Lieto godea – SATB/SATB voices – 3 minutes.

Quand'io ero giovinetto – SSATB voices – 3:30 minutes.

Donna leggiadra e bella – SAATB voices – 2 minutes.

Dolci care parole – SATTB voices – 2 minutes.

GIOVANNI CROCE CA.1557–1609

Croce was born in a small town on the outskirts of Venice and received his musical education from Gioseffo Zarlino, who was *maestro di cappella* at St Mark's Basilica from 1565 to 1590. Croce was also trained as a cleric, and during the 1580s he served as a singer and lay priest at the church of S Maria Formosa. In the early 1590s he was appointed *Vice-maestro di cappella* at St Mark's, and in 1603 he was promoted to *maestro di cappella.*

He composed three books of masses, six books of motets, one Magnificat, one set of Lamentations, four books of madrigals, two books of canzonets, and two madrigal comedies. Most of the masses are either parodies or paraphrases of preexisting material. The parodies include *Missa Decantabat, Missa Percussit Saul mille,* and a mass based on Clément Janequin's chanson *La guerre.* The paraphrases include *Missa Sexti toni, Missa Tertii toni,* and *Missa Octavi toni*—all based on Gregorian chant masses. The motets range from simple four-part pieces in a pervasive imitative style (e.g., *O sacrum convivium, Cantate Domino,* and *In monte Oliveti*) to elaborate polychoral compositions and cantata-like works with sections of music scored for soloists. These latter works were some of the first compositions to be written with a basso continuo part (called *basso per l'organo,* it was actually a basso seguente part).

The madrigals and canzonets were popular in England, especially with Thomas Morley, who supposedly emulated Croce's style. Moreover, it is believed that Croce's *Ove tra l'herbe e i fiori* in the collection *Il trionfo di Dori* inspired Morley to compile *The Triumphs of Oriana.* Croce's six-voiced, two-madrigal cycle *Valli profonde* was popular in Italy. The madrigal comedies are *Triaca musicale,* which consists of vignettes of Venetian life, and *Mascarate piacevoli et ridicolose,* a depiction of the various characters in a carnival entertainment.

FELICE ANERIO CA.1560–1614

Felice Anerio, older brother of Giovanni Francesco Anerio, was born and spent his entire life in Rome. From 1568 to 1574 he was a chorister at S Maria Maggiore under *maestro di cappella* Giovanni Maria Nanino, and from 1575 to 1579 he was a singer at the Cappella Giulia. He served as a singer at the church of S Luigi dei Francesi for one year beginning in 1579; however, his activities during the next four years are unknown. In 1584 he was appointed *maestro di cappella* at the Collegio degli Inglesi, and in 1594 he succeeded Palestrina as composer of the papal choir.

Anerio composed four masses, two books of motets, two books of sacred or spiritual madrigals, approximately twelve sacred or spiritual canzonets, five books of secular madrigals, and one book of secular canzonets. The masses are parodies of preexisting works (e.g., *Missa Vestiva i colli*, based on Palestrina's famous madrigal) and are in a conservative style characterized by successive points of imitation. The motets are also mainly imitative, although the vertical nature and tonal orientation of the imitation, combined with passages of homophony, make the music seem more homophonic than polyphonic. Representative motets include *Vidi speciosam, Ad te levavi, Christe redemptor omnium,* and the very well-known *Christus factus est.*

The secular works were (and are) not nearly as well known as the motets. However, the madrigal *Sotto l'ombroso speco* became famous because of its inclusion in the collection *It trionfo di Dori.*

GIOVANNI FRANCESCO ANERIO CA.1567–1630

Giovanni Francesco Anerio, younger brother of Felice Anerio, was born in Rome. Like Felice, Giovanni Francesco may have sung as a chorister at S Maria Maggiore, but there is no documentation to support this assumption. In the 1580s and 1590s he was affiliated with the oratories established by Filippo Neri, serving as organist at both Ss Crocifisso and S Marcello, and in 1600 he was employed at San Giovanni in Laterano (his precise position is unknown). Beginning in 1603 he served as *maestro di cappella* at several churches in Rome, including S Spirito in Sassia and S Maria dei Monti, and in about 1625 he was appointed *maestro di cappella* at the court of Polish King Sigismund III in Warsaw.

Anerio composed approximately twelve masses (including one Requiem), one hundred motets in eighteen published books, three Passions, four books of madrigals, and three books of lighter secular vocal pieces. The masses, most of which were issued with nonindependent basso continuo parts, range from imitative works in the style of the Franco-Flemish composers of the early sixteenth century to polychoral and syllabic works of the late sixteenth century. Masses in the earlier style include the canonic *Missa Surge illuminare* and the cantus firmus based *Missa pro defunctis;* polychoral works include *Missa Constantia* for three SATB choirs and *Missa Pulchra es* for two SATB choirs; and syllabic and homophonic masses include Anerio's four-voiced arrangement of Palestrina's *Missa Papae Marcelli* and the four-voiced *Missa La battaglia.* The Gloria and Credo movements of this latter mass are almost entirely homophonic. The Requiem (*Missa pro defunctis*) is divided into nine movements (Introitus, Kyrie, Dies irae, Domine Jesu Christe, Sanctus, Agnus Dei, Lux aeterna, Libera me, and Kyrie in absolutione), many of which alternate passages of homophony with Gregorian chant.

The motets are also in varied styles. The early works (e.g., *Cantate Domino, O salutaris hostia,* and *Ave verum corpus*) are generally similar to the motets of Giovanni Francesco's brother Felice, with vertically conceived imitative polyphony alternating with passages of homophony. *Ego sum panis vivus* of 1607 is scored for SATB/SATB chorus and basso continuo and is in the polychoral style of Giovanni Gabrieli. The later motets (e.g., *Spiritus sanctus replevit* and *Jesu decus angelorum*) are soloistic, with extended ornamental melodic passages and scoring for an independent basso continuo part. The motets from *Selva armonica* of 1617 are illustrative. The publication contains twenty-seven devotional works for one to four voices and basso continuo, twenty-one of which are in Italian and six of which are in Latin. *Ecco vien fuor la* is scored for SST voices, *Dio ti salvi, Maria, madre divina* is scored for SSAB voices, and *O del gran redentor madre alma e bella* is scored for SATB voices.

Anerio is best known for his madrigal book of 1619 entitled *Teatro armonico spirituale di madrigale,* which contains ninety-four dramatic sacred compositions for use during the Vespers services in the oratory at S Girolamo della Carità. Many of the compositions are characteristic of oratorios composed in the Baroque era by Giacomo Carissimi. For instance, Anerio's *Dialogo del figliuol prodigo,* which relates the story of the Prodigal Son, is about fifteen minutes in duration, has solo roles for the Son (soprano) and the Father (bass), and has ensemble parts for the servants and the narration. The instrumental scoring is large and specific for the time—two violins, cornetto, and basso continuo consisting of theorbo, lute, and organ. Another work, *Dialogo di David* (the story of David and Goliath), is a bit longer (approximately eighteen minutes) and has solo roles for Goliath (bass) and David (soprano) and ensemble parts for the Israelites and the narration. Instrumental scoring is for basso continuo only. Yet another work (perhaps the most oratorio-like of Anerio's compositions) is *Dialogo della Conversione di San Paolo,* which is approximately twenty minutes in duration and has solo roles for Saul (tenor), Jesus (bass), and Ananias (tenor) and ensembles representing the Israelites, soldiers and angels, and most of the narration. In addition, a double chorus that reflects on the action of the story closes the work. Instrumental scoring is identical to that of *Dialogo del figliuol prodigo.*

LODOVICO (DA) VIADANA CA.1560–1627

Viadana was born in the city of Viadana, near Parma. In 1594 he was appointed *maestro di cappella* at Mantua Cathedral, at the turn of the century he lived in Padua and Rome, and from 1602 to 1614 he served as *maestro di cappella* at several religious institutions in northern Italy, including the convent of S Luca in Cremona, Concordia Cathedral near Venice, and Fano Cathedral east of Florence. From 1614 to the end of his life he served as a cleric in Bologna, Busetto, and Gualtieri.

His compositional output consists of one book of masses plus several masses published separately, one Requiem, twenty-two books of motets, a set of Lamentations, and two books of canzonets. The early sacred music—that composed and published in the sixteenth century—includes the book of masses, the Requiem (*Missa pro defunctis*), and the first four books of motets. All the music is scored for four or five voices and optional basso continuo and can be represented by Viadana's most famous composition, *Exsultate justi* for SATB chorus. This motet begins and ends with a homophonic section of music in triple meter, and its center section consists of short phrases of imitative polyphony.

The sacred music composed in the seventeenth century, all scored for one to four voices and obligatory basso continuo, includes the first publication of small-scale sacred pieces composed for few numbers of voices with accompaniment. Entitled *Il Cento Concerti Ecclesiastici a una, a due, a tre, & a quattro voci conn il Basso Continuo per sonar nell'Organa* (One hundred sacred concertos for one, two, three, and four voices, with basso continuo for organ), this publication was seminal in that it signaled the beginning of a new genre (vocal concerto) and style of writing (for solo voices and basso continuo) that would be prevalent throughout the Baroque era. As was explained by Viadana in the preface of the publication, "I saw that singers wishing to sing with organ, either with three voices, or two, or a single one by itself, were forced by the lack of compositions suitable to their purpose to take one, two, or three parts from motets in five, six, seven, or even eight [parts]. . . . [The result] is a lack of melody, and little continuity or meaning." Viadana went on to specify that the organ part is indispensable. The publication was quite popular, perhaps in part because the pieces could be performed with few resources. As a result, Viadana went on to compose two more books, one in 1607 that contained the uniquely scored *Missa dominicalis* for one voice and basso continuo, and another book in 1609.

CARLO GESUALDO CA.1561–1613

Gesualdo, sometimes referred to as the Prince of Venosa, was born about the same time that his family was invested with the principality of Venosa in southern Italy by King Philip II of Spain (who also ruled Naples and Sicily). In 1586 Gesualdo married his cousin Maria d'Avalos, and in 1590 he killed her and her lover Fabrizio Carafa (Duke of Andria) when they were supposedly caught "in flagrante delicto di fragrante peccato." Without any legal action being taken against him because of his princely status, Gesualdo then retired to his estate and focused on music, especially the composition and performance of madrigals. He often visited Ferrara, the center of madrigal composition at the time, and in 1594 he married Leonora d'Este, niece of Alfonso II, Duke of Ferrara. While at Ferrara, Gesualdo frequently played the lute and *arcicembalo* (the chromatic keyboard instrument invented by Nicola Vicentino), and he attended performances of and composed madrigals for the famed female vocal ensemble Concerto delle donne. He also made brief visits to Naples, Padua, and Venice. During the last two decades of his life he suffered from melancholy and became a recluse at his estate, devoting much of his time to composing madrigals.

His compositions include seventy motets and approximately 120 madrigals. The motets were published in three collections—one for five voices in 1603, one for six and seven voices also in 1603, and one for six voices in 1611. The 1603 collection for five voices includes the famous *O vos omnes*, and the 1611 collection consists of twenty-seven motets for the Tenebrae services of Holy Week. The 1603 collection for six and seven voices includes three unfinished motets—*Da pacem, Assumpta est Maria,* and *Illumina nos misericordiarum*—that were recomposed and completed in the twentieth century by Igor Stravinsky under the title *Tres sacrae cantiones.* The style of all Gesualdo's motets is conservative in texture, with phrases of imitative polyphony that alternate with passages of homophony, but they are progressive in harmonic language, with sudden shifts of chords and unexpected harmonic progressions and resolutions. The repetition of complete sections of music is also a modern element of the motets. In *O vos omnes* and *In monte Oliveti* (the first of the Responsory motets) the repetition results in an ABCB structure.

The madrigals were published in seven books—six for five voices and one for six voices. The first two books for five voices, both of 1594, were published under the pseudonym Gioseppe Pilonij and contain madrigals in the style of Luca Marenzio's later works, with only occasional variations in rhythmic texture and with a traditional harmonic language. The third and fourth books, of 1595 and 1596, respectively, contain madrigals in the style of Luzzasco Luzzaschi, with abrupt changes in texture, chromaticism, and unexpected harmonic shifts. Many of the madrigals in books one through four are plagiarisms. For instance, Gesualdo's *Itene, o miei sospiri* is almost a direct reproduction of Luzzaschi's *Itene mie querele*, and *Mercè, grido piangendo* is strikingly similar to the setting of the same text by Pomponio Nenna. Parodies of other composers' music was quite common and considered a tribute. However, most composers substantially reworked other composers' music, while Gesualdo basically copied it. The madrigals in the fifth and sixth books, both of 1611, take the elements found in books four and five to an extreme level, one that is idiosyncratic and mannered. Each verbal image is treated separately and often set off by rests, the chromaticism is extensive and unusual, and the harmonic language is so beyond the general expectations of the time that the resulting effect is one of surprise and shock.

MOTETS
SELECTED AND LISTED ACCORDING TO FAMILIARITY

O vos omnes – 1603 – SATTB chorus – 3:45 minutes.

In monte Oliveti – 1611 – SSATTB chorus – 4:30 minutes.

Tristis est anima mea – 1611 – SSATTB chorus – 4:30 minutes.

Ecce vidimus eum – 1611 – SSATTB chorus – 7 minutes.

Tenebrae factae sunt – 1611 – SSATTB chorus – 4:30 minutes.

Ave, dulcissima Maria – 1603 – SATTB chorus – 6:30 minutes.

Benedictus Dominus Deus Israel – 1611 – SSATTB chorus – 5 minutes.

Miserere mei, Deus – 1611 – SSATTB chorus – 9 minutes.

MADRIGALS
SELECTED AND LISTED IN REVERSE CHRONOLOGICAL ORDER
ACCORDING TO PUBLICATION

Moro, lasso – book six of 1611 – SSATB voices – 3:30 minutes.

Resta di darmi noia – book six of 1611 – SSATB voices – 3:15 minutes.

Itene, o miei sospiri – book five of 1611 – SSATB voices – 4 minutes.

Correte, amanti – book five of 1611 – SSATB voices – 3 minutes.

Mercè, grido piangendo – book five of 1611 – SSATB voices – 4 minutes.

Dolcissima mia vita – book five of 1611 – SSATB voices – 3:30 minutes.

Cor mio, deh, non piangete – book four of 1596 – SSATB voices – 3:15 minutes.

Luci serene e chiare – book four of 1596 – SSATB voices – 3 minutes.

Ecco, morirò dunque – a two-madrigal cycle in book four of 1596 – SSATB voices – 3:30 minutes.

Se chiudete nel core – book four of 1596 – SSATB voices – 3:30 minutes.

Languisco e moro – book three of 1595 – SSATB voices – 3 minutes.

Deh, se già fu crudele – book three of 1595 – SSATB voices – 3:30 minutes.

Crudelissima doglia – book three of 1595 – SATTB voices – 3 minutes.

ADRIANO BANCHIERI 1568–1634

Banchieri was born in Bologna, where he entered the Olivetan order of Benedictine monks and where he presumably learned to play the organ. In 1592 he entered the monastery of SS Bartolomeo e Ponziano in Luca, and for the next seventeen years he served in numerous churches and monasteries, including S Benedetto in Siena (1593), S Michele in Bosco (1594), S Elena in Venice (1605), and S Maria in Organo in Verona (1606). In 1609 he returned to S Michele in Bosco, where he remained until shortly before his death.

He composed twelve masses that are extant, approximately 150 motets and works in other small sacred forms, and more than two hundred secular pieces. In addition, he wrote twelve treatises and letters on musical subjects. All the masses consist of large sections of homophony with syllabic settings of text, and all but three of the masses substitute a motet for the Benedictus. As was common at the turn of the century, when traditional imitative *prima prattica* motets were giving way to various *seconda prattica* forms, Banchieri's smaller sacred works were called by a variety of terms. For instance, the titles of various publications range from *Concerti ecclesiastici* of 1595 to *Sacra armonia* of 1613. Only one publication used a traditional title—*Primo libro delle messe e motetti* of 1620. In general, the early motets (e.g., *Jubilate Deo*) are characterized by a traditional imitative texture and are scored for four to eight voices and optional basso continuo. The later motets are for one to three voices and obligatory basso continuo. An example is the two-voiced *Exultate justi in Domino* of 1622.

Two large-scale choral works, one secular and the other sacred, and both scored for SATB/SATB, are included at the end of the publication *Canzoni alla francese* of 1596, which consists mainly of instrumental canzonas. *La Battaglia* depicts a battle, with onomatopoeic sounds of trumpets and drums, and *Magnificat supra Lieto godea* is a parody of Giovanni Gabrieli's popular madrigal.

The secular compositions include six books of canzonets for three voices, each book containing twenty or so pieces that are related in terms of plot or dramatic story and that are similar to the madrigal comedies by Banchieri's contemporary, Orazio Vecchi. *La pazzia senile* of 1598, based on the commedia dell'arte character Pantaloon, was Banchieri's most famous of these works. Others were *Il metamorfosi* of 1601 and *Prudenza giovenile* of 1607. Additional publications of secular works include six books of pieces in a variety of forms for five voices. These books also contain cycles of madrigals that create madrigal comedy-like works. *Festino nella sera del giovedi grasso* (Entertainment on the evening of Carnival Thursday) of 1608 is the best known of these; it contains a variety of madrigals, villanellas, canzonets, and morescas, including *Contrapunto bestiale alla mente* (Counterpoint improvised by the animals), which is a presentation of bird, cat, and dog sounds over the ramblings of a drunken bass, all in the form of a *fa la la* balletto.

Banchieri's treatises include three that are notable—*L'organo suonarino* of 1605, which gives instructions for realizing figured bass numerals and for accompanying chant; *Conclusioni nel suono dell'organo* of 1609, which discusses modal theory; and *Cartella musicale* of 1615, which analyzes Psalm tones and vocal ornaments.

SIGISMONDO D'INDIA CA.1582–1629

D'India was born in Palermo, Sicily, into an aristocratic family. As a young adult he traveled to various Italian cities, including Florence in 1600, Mantua in 1606, Rome in 1608, and Parma in 1610, and from 1611 to 1623 he served at the court of Carlo Emanuele I in Turin. In 1623 d'India entered the Este court in Mantua, the following year he moved to Rome to work for Cardinal Maurizio of Savoy, and the year after that he returned to Mantua, where he remained until his death. He was a highly respected composer during the first half of the seventeenth century, recognized for his five-voiced madrigals and secular monodies.

D'India composed one mass, sixty-six motets, approximately two hundred madrigals for five voices in eight books, and more than one hundred solo songs and duets. The mass, *Missa Domine, clamavi ad te,* was composed for Pope Urban VIII in 1626 and performed in the Cappella Giulia. Unfortunately, it was then lost. The motets range from four- to six-part imitative works to two- and three-part pieces with basso continuo. The madrigals also range from traditional pieces in the a cappella styles of Luca Marenzio and Carlo Gesualdo to modern pieces with solo and duet passages accompanied by basso continuo. Book three contains representative pieces in both styles. The first ten madrigals alternate short imitative phrases with passages of homophony and are full-textured throughout. In addition, the texts are set syllabically and in a parlando fashion, and their basso continuo parts are nonindependent and therefore optional. These qualities are especially evident in the two-madrigal cycle *È partito il mio bene,* the very brief *Perchè non mi mirate,* and *Mercè grido piangendo,* which closely emulates Gesualdo's madrigal of the same name. The remaining ten madrigals in book three have solo and duet passages, virtuosic melismas, and independent basso continuo parts. In *Quel augellin che canta,* for example, there are solo lines and duet melismas on the word "canta" (sings); in *Io mi son giovinetta* there are extended duet passages accompanied by basso continuo; and in *Chi vuol haver felice* there are isolated examples of fast passage work (*passaggi*) and other melodically challenging passages, some with leaps of an octave.

GREGORIO ALLEGRI 1582–1652

Allegri was born in Rome, where he was a chorister at the church of S Luigi dei Francesi from 1591 to 1596 and a tenor from 1601 to 1604. It is assumed that he studied with Giovanni Maria Nanino, who was a member of the papal choir from 1577 until his death in 1607. From 1607 to 1621 Allegri was a singer at the cathedrals in Fermo and Tivoli, and in 1628 he was appointed *maestro di cappella* at S Spirito in Sassia, Rome. The following year he was admitted to the papal choir under Pope Urban VIII, and in the jubilee year of 1650 he was elected *maestro di cappella.*

Allegri composed five masses, thirty motets, two sets of Lamentations, one Te Deum, and two books of small sacred pieces entitled *Concertini.* All the works except for the concertini are in the full-textured vocal style of the late sixteenth century. The masses are based on preexisting material (e.g., *Missa Vidi turbam magnam,* which is a parody of Allegri's own motet), and most of the other compositions alternate phrases of imitative polyphony with passages of homophony. While these compositions are scored for basso continuo, the basso continuo parts are not independent. The concertini pieces (e.g., *De ore predentis* for ATB voices and basso continuo, and *Cantate Domino* for four voices and basso continuo) are scored for two to five voices and an independent basso continuo part.

Allegri is best known for his *alternatim* motet *Miserere,* a setting of Psalm 50 scored for SATTB/SSAB that became one of the most famous choral works in the late Renaissance style. It was composed in 1638 for performance during the Tenebrae Offices of Holy Week. The papal choir had a tradition of guarding its repertoire, and thus no scores were allowed to leave the premises; in addition, scores of the *Miserere* were not used by the choir because Tenebrae services were sung in total darkness. Furthermore, it was the custom of the time to ornament vocal music, and certain embellishments became so popular that they were repeated year after year. The *Miserere* became more and more famous and mysterious. Mozart attended a Tenebrae service in the 1780s and transcribed the *Miserere* from memory. Others did likewise, including Felix Mendelssohn. Various versions of the music began to appear until a particular one—with seven high Cs—came to be recognized as standard. It is this version that was performed by the papal choir until 1870, when the chapel forces were reduced and the choir no longer sang Tenebrae services. It is also this version that has achieved widespread popular appeal with choirs and audiences today.

❦ Spain and the New World ❦

Spain was unlike other countries during the Renaissance era in a number of respects. Most notably, almost all the significant Spanish composers were actually born in Spain. These include the major composers Cristóbal de Morales, Francisco Guerrero, and Tomás Luis de Victoria, as well as the less prominent composers Juan del Encina, Francisco de Peñalosa, Juan Vásquez, Matheo Flecha, Hernando Franco, and Juan Barahona Esquivel. One composer, Pedro de Escobar, was born in Portugal but for most of his life was employed in Spain. All the composers, unlike their counterparts in other European countries, were not confined to only a few major geographical areas. Instead, they were employed throughout Spain—from Salamanca and Ciudad Rodrigo in the northwest to Seville and Málaga in the southwest. Furthermore, major Spanish cities were not the hubs of activity, as Paris was in France, Rome and Venice were in Italy, and London was in England. Only Victoria worked in Madrid (at a small convent, not the cathedral), and no composers were active in Barcelona or Valencia. Four composers—Escobar, Peñalosa, Vásquez, and Guerrero—worked in Seville, and many of the other composers were employed in cities near Madrid, such as Palencia, Salamanca, Segovia, Avila, and Toledo. Finally, distinguishing Spain from the other European countries is the fact that Spanish composers held few leadership positions at royal or major noble courts. Only Peñalosa served a king (Ferdinand V), and Encina a well-known nobleman (the Duke of Alba); Victoria was in the service of King Philip II's sister, Dowager Empress María.

Although most of the significant Spanish composers were born and employed in Spain, four composers either studied or worked for a period of time in Rome: Encina, Peñalosa, and Morales sang in papal choirs, and Victoria held a number of positions at the Collegio Germanico. In addition, Guerrero made frequent visits to Rome, where he was well known. Escobar returned to his native Portugal at the end of his life, Franco studied in Spain but worked in Mexico, and Flecha spent the final years of his life working in Austria.

The musical genres were basically limited to Latin masses, motets, and Magnificats, and Spanish villancicos (both sacred and secular). Many composers, as was typical of the time, composed in most of these genres. However, Franco, Victoria, and Esquivel composed only sacred music, and Encina and Flecha composed only secular villancicos. The masses paralleled developments in Italy: works early in the era were constructed of cantus firmi and canons, whereas works later in the era were structured according to imitative techniques. Also, most of the masses were based on preexisting material—Gregorian chants, secular tunes, and motets of the time. For example, Peñalosa, Morales, and Guerrero all set masses to the L'homme armé tune, and Guerrero, Victoria, and Esquivel all composed masses that parodied Janequin's famous chanson *La bataille*. Peñalosa, Guerrero, and Palestrina were the most popular composers of motets used for parodies.

The Spanish motets were composed either in the point-of-imitation style of Roman composers such as Palestrina or in the polychoral dialogue style fashionable in Venice. Spanish composers did not embrace either the mandates of the Council of Trent or the *seconda prattica*. Consequently, there is little homophony in Spanish motets and no use of basso continuo except for accompaniment of villancicos at the end of the era. The Magnificats, generally in *alternatim* style, are equally conservative.

Just as the chanson was the chief and distinctive secular genre in France and the madrigal occupied the attention of Italian composers, the villancico was the secular genre of choice in Spain. It began in the early years of the sixteenth century as a lighthearted secular form but was quickly adopted (maintaining its lighthearted character) for special sacred celebrations, especially Christmas. Its texture is basically homophonic, and its form strophic, with verses (*coplas*) and a refrain (*estribillo*)—the verses occasionally scored for soloists and accompanied by basso continuo in the later years of the Renaissance.

PEDRO DE ESCOBAR CA.1465–1535

Escobar was born in Porto, Portugal, but spent most of his life in Spain. From 1489 to 1499 he was a singer in the chapel choir of Queen Isabella I, and from 1507 to 1514 he was *magiste puerorum* (master of the choristers) at Seville Cathedral. He returned to Portugal in 1521 to serve as *mestre da capela* at the court of Cardinal Dom Affonso, son of King Manuel I, although he took several extended leaves of absence during the last decades of his life to return to Spain.

Escobar composed two masses (including one Requiem), one mass movement, twenty-one motets, one Magnificat, and eighteen villancicos. The Requiem (*Missa pro defunctis*) is based on the Gregorian chant from the Mass for the Dead and is in a pervasively imitative texture. The mass movement is a Kyrie that was included in a complete mass cycle written by a number of composers, including Francisco de Peñalosa. The motets, in a polyphonic texture like the masses, include *Clamabat autem mulier Cananera, Regina caeli laetare, In nativitate Domine,* and *Ave maris stella.*

The villancicos, all homophonic and strophic, include *Virgen bendita sin par, Secaróme los pe-sares, Mis penas madre,* and the relatively well-known *Ora, sus, pues que ansí es.*

JUAN DEL ENCINA 1468–CA.1529

Encina was born in Salamanca, northwest of Madrid, and was likely taught by his brother Diego, who was a professor of music at Salamanca University. Juan sang at Salamanca Cathedral beginning in 1484; between 1492 and 1495 he served at the court of Don Fadrique de Toledo, Duke of Alba; and from 1500 to 1508 he lived in Rome, first serving Pope Alexander VI until the pope's death in 1503 and then employed at the court of Cardinal Francisco Loriz. In 1508 Encina moved to Málaga, where he worked as a cleric and administrator at the cathedral. In addition to music, he wrote plays, called *eglogas,* which were sacred dramas for Christmas, Shrove Tuesday, Holy Week, and Easter that interspersed villancicos with spoken dialogue. Representative works in this genre include *Egloga representada la misma noche de navidad* for Christmas Eve 1492, *Representacion a la muy bendita passion y muerte de nuestro precioso redentor* for Holy Week 1493, and *Egloga representada en la noche postrera de carnal* for Shrove Tuesday 1494.

Encina composed approximately eighty separate villancicos. Most are homophonic and strophic, with a single refrain at the end of each verse, and most are set to humorous or lighthearted texts. For example, *Hoy comamos y bebamos* from *Egloga representada la mesma noche de antruejo* for Shrove Tuesday is a drinking song, and *Cucú, cucú* is about the dangers of being a henpecked husband.

VILLANCICOS
SELECTED AND LISTED ACCORDING TO FAMILIARITY

Si abrá en este baldrés – SATB voices – 3 minutes.

Fatal la parte – SATB voices – 2 minutes.

Cucú, cucú – SATB voices – 1:45 minutes.

Antonilla es desposada – ATB voices – 2 minutes.

Más vale trocar – SATB voices – 2:30 minutes.

Una sañosa porfía – SATB voices – 4:30 minutes.

Mi libertad es sosiego – SATB voices – 2:30 minutes.

Amor con fortuna – SATB voices – 2:30 minutes.

Levanta Pascual, levanta – ATB voices – 2:30 minutes.

Triste España sin ventura – SATB voices – 3 minutes.

FRANCISCO DE PEÑALOSA CA.1470–1528

Peñalosa was born in Talavera de la Reina, just southwest of Madrid. In 1498 he became a singer in the chapel choir of King Ferdinand V, and in 1512 he was appointed *maestro de capilla* to Ferdinand's grandson, also named Ferdinand, whose residence was in S Pedro de Cardéna, near Burgos. In 1517 Peñalosa was admitted to the papal choir of Leo X in Rome, and in 1521 he went to Seville, where he held a variety of clerical and minor musical positions. He is noted as being the first native Spanish composer of masses and motets in an imitative style.

Peñalosa composed seven masses, sixteen motets, seven Magnificats, and nine villancicos. The masses follow the model of those written by the early Renaissance Franco-Flemish and Italian composers: they are parodies of motets and chansons (e.g., *Missa Adieu mes amours*) or paraphrases of Gregorian chants and popular secular tunes (e.g., *Missa de beata virgine* and *Missa L'homme armé*). In addition, they employ cantus firmus techniques in notational complexities. For instance, *Missa Ave Maria peregrina* is based on the Salve regina chant in its original form and the tenor of Hayne van Ghizeghem's chanson *De tous biens plaine* in retrograde. The motets are in a pervasively imitative style and include *Versa est in luctum* and *Sancta mater istud agas*, the latter of which was formerly attributed to Josquin Desprez. Both motets are scored for SATB.

CRISTÓBAL DE MORALES CA.1500–1553

Morales was born in Seville, where he probably sang as a chorister at the cathedral and where he was appointed cathedral organist in 1522. In 1526 he became *maestro de capilla* at Avila Cathedral, and in 1532 he left that position and traveled to Naples and Rome, serving Fernando de Silva in 1534 and singing in the papal chapel from 1535 to 1545. During the following years he held various *maestro de capilla* positions at major Spanish cathedrals and courts, including Toledo Cathedral from 1545 to 1547, the court of the Duke of Arcos in Marchena from 1548 to 1551, and Málaga Cathedral from 1551 until shortly before his death. He was (and is) considered the most important composer of Catholic church music between Josquin Desprez and Palestrina. His music was widely circulated in manuscripts throughout Europe and the New World, and numerous composers, including Guerrero and Victoria, parodied his motets. In addition, he was the most represented composer at the Sistine Chapel until the eighteenth century.

Morales composed twenty-three masses, eighty-eight motets, sixteen Magnificats, one set of Lamentations, six villancicos, and two madrigals. Most of the masses are parodies of preexisting motets and chansons or paraphrases of popular tunes. The parodies include *Missa Aspice Domine* on a motet by Nicolas Gombert, *Missa Benedicta es caelorum regina* on a Josquin motet, *Missa Mille regretz* on a Josquin chanson, *Missa Quaeramus cum pastoribus* on a motet by Jean Mouton, *Missa Quem dicunt homines* on a motet by Jean Richafort, and *Missa Si bona suscepimus* on a motet by Philippe Verdelot. The paraphrases include two settings of the Beata Virgine chant and two settings of the L'homme armé tune. Two masses are based on solfège syllables (*Missa Fa re ut fa sol la* and *Missa Ut re mi fa sol la*) and two masses are settings of the Requiem. All of the masses include sections scored for either (or both) smaller and larger forces than those specified for the work as a whole—in *Missa de beata virgine* for SATB chorus, the Sanctus and final Agnus Dei expand to SSATB; in *Missa L'homme armé* for SAATB chorus, there are sections for AAB, SAAB, and SAATBB; in *Missa Mille regretz* for SSAATB chorus, there are sections for SAT, SAB, and SAA; and in *Missa Ave maris stella* for SATTB chorus, there are reduced sections for STB, ST, and SAB and an expanded final Agnus Dei for SSATTB.

The motets have some traits of the early Renaissance. For instance, *Emendemus in melius,* the five-voiced *Andreas Christi famulus,* and the six-voiced *Veni domine* each have a cantus firmus with a text different from the surrounding voices. Most of the motets, however, are in the style fashionable during the middle years of the sixteenth century and typified by the compositions of Gombert: freely composed imitative polyphony is pervasive except for short sections of homophony. The Magnificats were among Morales's most popular compositions. They were composed in two cycles, each consisting of settings on the eight Gregorian chant tones (*primi toni, secundi toni, tertii toni,* etc.), and they are all for four voices, although different sections of the settings are frequently scored for textures of two or three voices. In addition, the Magnificats are consistently polyphonic (not in *alternatim* style, as was customary at the time). The villancicos include *Si n'os uviera mirado* and *Juicio fuerte sera dado.* The madrigals are *Ditimi o si o no* and *Quando lieta sperai.*

MASSES
SELECTED AND LISTED ACCORDING TO FAMILIARITY

Missa Mille regretz – SSAATB chorus – 29 minutes.

Missa Si bona suscepimus – SSAATB chorus – 4 minutes.

Missa Quaeramus cum pastoribus – SSATB chorus – 29 minutes.

Missa pro defunctis – SAATB chorus – 56 minutes.

Missa de beata virgine – SATB chorus – 17 minutes.

Missa L'homme armé – SATB chorus – 20 minutes.

Missa L'homme armé – SAATB chorus – 22 minutes.

Missa Ave maris stella – SATTB chorus – 24 minutes.

MOTETS
SELECTED AND LISTED ACCORDING TO FAMILIARITY

Emendemus in melius – SAATB chorus – 6 minutes.

Vidi aquam egredientem – SATB chorus – 4:15 minutes.

O sacrum convivium – SSATB chorus – 5 minutes.

Ecce sic benedicetur – SSAATB chorus – 4 minutes.

Manus tuae Domine – SSATB chorus – 3:30 minutes.

Veni Domine – SSAATB chorus – 2:30 minutes.

Regina caeli, laetare – SSAATB chorus – 3:45 minutes.

  Andreas Christi famulus - Dilexit Andream Dominus – SSAATTBB chorus – 6:15 minutes.

  Tu es Petrus - Quodcumque ligaveris – SSATB chorus – 5:30 minutes.

  Salve regina – SATB chorus – 5 minutes.

  At ille dixerunt – ATB chorus – 3:30 minutes.

  In die tribulationis – ATB chorus – 3 minutes.

JUAN VÁSQUEZ CA.1500–CA.1560

Vásquez was born in Badajoz, close to the border of Portugal in southwest Spain. In 1511 he was admitted as a singer at Plasencia Cathedral, and in 1530 he became a singer and teacher of the choristers at the cathedral in his hometown of Badajoz. He was a singer at Palencia Cathedral beginning in 1539, in 1545 he returned to Badajoz Cathedral as *maestro de capilla,* and in 1551 he left Badajoz and began service at the court of Don Antonio de Zuñiga in Seville.

  He composed one book each of sacred and secular music. The sacred collection, entitled *Agenda defunctorum,* contains motets for the office of Matins and Lauds and a setting of the Requiem. The secular collection, *Villancicos i canciones,* contains fifty villancicos for four and five voices and seventeen pieces in a variety of Italian forms. The villancicos, for which Vásquez is best known, generally have alternating textures of imitative polyphony and homophony. Examples include *Determinado amor a dar contento, Gentil señora mía,* and *Hermosíssima María,* all scored for SATTB voices. The four-voiced villancicos are more homophonic and frequently have repeated structures. *Si el pastorcico es nuevo,* for instance, is in an AAB form, while *Descendid al valle, la niña* is ABA. One of the most popular villancicos, *De los álamos vengo,* is imitative and through-composed.

FRANCISCO GUERRERO 1528–1599

Guerrero was born in Seville, where he studied with his older brother Pedro and where he became a singer at the cathedral in 1542. It is likely that he also studied with Morales, who was *maestro de capilla* at nearby Toledo Cathedral from 1545 to 1547. In 1546, at age seventeen, Guerrero was appointed *maestro de capilla* at Jaén Cathedral, but in 1549 he returned to Seville Cathedral to be assistant to *maestro de capilla* Pedro Fernández—with the stipulation that he succeed Fernández, who was sixty-four at the time. Fernández lived another twenty-five years, and although Guerrero assumed many of the primary musical responsibilities of the cathedral, it was not until the death of Fernández in 1574 that Guerrero was appointed *maestro de capilla.* He became exceptionally famous, traveling to Toledo, Córdoba, Segovia, Rome, and Venice to promote his music, and his compositions were circulated widely throughout Europe and the New World. His five-voiced motet *Ave virgo sanctissima,* published in 1566, was one of the most popular sacred compositions in Spain, and his music was performed more frequently in the New World than that of any other composer, including Morales and Victoria. In 1588, at the age of sixty, he made a pilgrimage to Jerusalem, Bethlehem, and Damascus, and he subsequently wrote a widely read autobiographical account of his journey to the Holy Land entitled *Viage de Hierusalem.*

Guerrero composed eighteen masses, approximately one hundred motets, sixteen Magnificats, one Passion, fifty villancicos, and five miscellaneous secular pieces. The masses are like pre-Council of Trent works in both structure and style. Gregorian chants (e.g., Beata virgine) and popular secular tunes (e.g., L'homme armé) were used for paraphrases, and motets such as Guerrero's own *Ave virgo sanctissima* and chansons such as Janequin's *La bataille* were used for parodies. In addition, Guerrero occasionally utilized cantus firmus technique, and portions of each mass vary in scoring. For instance, *Missa L'homme armé* and both settings of *Missa de beata virgine* employ cantus firmus, and *Missa de la batalla escoutez,* scored overall for SSATB, has sections for SSA, SAB, SSAT, and SSAATTBB. In terms of style, the textures of the masses are characterized by pervasive imitation, with only brief portions of homophony.

The early motets are like the masses in texture, whereas the later motets are more varied and feature word painting as an expressive device. In *Duo seraphim,* for example, only two of the twelve voices state the opening phrase "Duo seraphim clamabant alter ad alterum" (Two seraphim proclaimed one to the other), three voices state "Tres sunt qui testimonium dant in caelo" (There are three who give testimony in heaven), and all voices simultaneously announce "Plena est omnis terra gloria ejus" (The whole earth is full of his glory). Furthermore, the three choirs represent the Trinity.

The villancicos are often settings of humorous or folk-like texts for feasts such as Christmas, Epiphany, or Corpus Christi, and they are characterized by homophonic textures. A small number of the villancicos are through-composed (e.g., *En tanto que de rosa* and *Sanctíssima María*). However, most (e.g., *Vamos al portal* and *A un niño llorando*) are in an ABA format.

MASSES
SELECTED AND LISTED ACCORDING TO FAMILIARITY

Missa de la batalla escoutez – SSATB chorus – 29 minutes.

Missa Surge, propera amica mea – SSAATB chorus – 31 minutes.

Missa Ave virgo sanctissima – SSAATTB chorus – 30 minutes.

Missa Sancta et immaculata – SSATB chorus – 30 minutes.

Missa pro defunctis – ATTB chorus – 32 minutes.

Missa Congratulamini mihi – SSATB chorus – 30 minutes.

Missa Simile est regnum – SATB chorus – 25 minutes.

MOTETS
SELECTED AND LISTED ACCORDING TO FAMILIARITY

Ave virgo sanctissima – SSATB chorus – 4 minutes.

Canite tuba - Rorate caeli – SATB chorus – 4:30 minutes.

Duo seraphim – SSAT/SATB/SATB chorus – 4:15 minutes.

Pastores loquebantur - Videntes autem – SSATBB chorus – 5:30 minutes.

Ave Maria – SATB/SATB chorus – 4:15 minutes.

Usquequo, Domine – SSATTB chorus – 5:30 minutes.

Alma redemptoris mater – SATB chorus – 3:30 minutes.

Salve regina – SATB chorus – 8:30 minutes.

Gloriose confessor – SATB chorus – 2:30 minutes.

Quasi cedrus - Tota pulchra es – SATB chorus – 6:30 minutes.

VILLANCICOS
SELECTED AND LISTED ACCORDING TO FAMILIARITY

A un niño llorando – SSATB voices – 3 minutes.

Vamos al portal – SSATB voices – 3:30 minutes.

Virgen sancta – SSATB voices – 3 minutes.

Pastores, si nos queries – SSATB voices – 2:30 minutes.

Niño Dios d'amor herido – SATB voices – 2:30 minutes.

En tanto que de rosa – SSATB voices – 2:30 minutes.

La gracia y los ojos bellos – SSATB voices – 2:30 minutes.

Sanctíssima María – SSAT voices – 2 minutes.

Oy, Joseph, se os dán el suelo – SATB voices – 2:30 minutes.

Los reyes siquen la'strella – SATB voices – 2:30 minutes.

MATHEO FLECHA CA.1530–1604

Flecha was born in Prades, south of Barcelona, the nephew of Matheo Flecha (ca.1481–ca.1553), who was also a composer and who is credited with composing the famous villancico *Riu, riu chiu*. The elder Flecha was also *maestro de capilla* at Lérida Cathedral and composer of the familiar villancico *La bomba*. The younger Flecha was a chorister in the chapel choir of María and Juana, daughters of King Charles V, and from 1568 until his death he served in the court of Empress Isabella in Austria.

He composed two collections of secular music—one book containing mostly madrigals and one book mostly of villancicos. He also composed a mass and a book of motets, but these were lost. The madrigals include *Dal superbo furor de l'onde audaci* and *Deh porgi mano a l'affannat' ingegno*, and the villancicos include *La justa, Teresita hermana,* and *Ay que bino en tierra estrana*—this latter piece scored for SSATB voices that alternate between homophony and imitative polyphony.

HERNANDO FRANCO 1532–1585

Franco was born in Garrovillas, southwest of Madrid near the border of Portugal, and he is known to have been a chorister at Segovia Cathedral from 1542 to 1549. Nothing is known about his life for the next twenty-four years, although it is likely that he went to Mexico City in the early

1550s. He was appointed *maestro de capilla* at Guatemala Cathedral in 1573 and at Mexico City Cathedral in 1575, and for the following decade music in Mexico City flourished under Franco's leadership.

He composed only sacred music—twenty-two motets, sixteen Magnificats, and one set of Lamentations. The motets are in the polyphonic style of the mid-sixteenth century in Spain, with textures of pervasive imitation alternating with brief passages of homophony. *Salve regina* for five voices (there are three other settings of the same text, all for four voices) and *Memento mei Deus* for four voices are well known today. The Magnificats include two sets for four voices on each of the Gregorian chant tones; both sets use the chant melody as a cantus firmus and are in *alternatim* style, one set with polyphony on the odd-numbered verses and the other set with polyphony on the even-numbered verses. Both sets also contain sections for three and six voices. It should be noted that the popular hymn set in the Nahuatl language, *Dios itlazo nantzine*, was not composed by Hernando Franco, but by a Native American composer who took the name Don Hernando Franco (also Hernando don Franco) and who lived from about 1522 to 1580.

TOMÁS LUIS DE VICTORIA 1548–1611

Victoria was born in Avila, in central Spain, where he was a chorister at Avila Cathedral and a student at the Jesuit school of S Gil. At age fifteen or sixteen, when his voice changed, he entered the Jesuit Collegio Germanico in Rome, serving there as a singer and teacher and *maestro di cappella* beginning in 1573. He was also a singer and organist at S Maria di Monserrato from 1569 to approximately 1574. In 1575 he took minor orders for the priesthood, and in 1577 he became a chaplain at the church of S Girolamo della Carità. In 1583, in the dedication of his *Missarum libri duo* to King Philip II of Spain, Victoria expressed his desire to return to Spain and serve as a priest. Philip appointed Victoria chaplain to his sister, the Dowager Empress María, who resided at the Monasterio de las Descalzes de S Clara in Madrid. Victoria maintained this position, along with that of *maestro* of the convent choir, until María's death in 1603. From 1603 until his own death he served only as organist. The convent had one of the finest musical establishments in Spain, with a choir of four boys and twelve priests and instruments for special occasions.

Although Victoria led a quiet life, remaining out of the public eye, he was known to other composers of the time, and his music circulated widely and was highly respected. He was most certainly acquainted with Palestrina, with whom he may have studied, and he was friends with Guerrero, who was employed in Spain but who visited Rome frequently. In addition, his *Missa pro victoria* was popular with King Philip III, and *Missa Ave regina coelorum* and *Missa Alma redemptoris mater* were the best-known and most frequently performed masses in the New World.

Victoria composed only sacred music to Latin texts, including twenty masses, approximately 140 motets, eighteen Magnificats, nine sets of Lamentations, and two Passions. All of the works are characterized by pervasive imitation juxtaposed with brief portions of homophony, which was the common style in Rome and all of Spain during the latter decades of the sixteenth century. Many of the works are also for multiple choirs, a typical compositional feature in Spain. Victoria's music is unique, however, in its simplicity. Imitative polyphony is clear in texture, harmonies are tonal and logically ordered, and phrases are relatively short and well balanced. In addition, melodic and rhythmic patterns are often subtly expressive.

Most of the masses, including seven that are based on Victoria's own motets, are parodies (e.g., *Missa O magnum mysterium, Missa O quam gloriosum, Missa Dum complerentur,* and *Missa Vidi speciosam*). Three masses are parodies of motets by the most notable composers of the time: *Missa simile est regnum coelorum* and *Missa Surge propera* are based on the same-named works by Guerrero and Palestrina, respectively, and *Missa Gaudeamus* is based on *Jubilate Deo* by Morales. Victoria's most popular mass, *Missa pro victoria,* is based on Janequin's famous chanson *La bataille.* Typical of the time, the parody masses have movements or sections of movements that are scored for either reduced or increased forces. In the four-voiced (SATB) *Missa O magnum mysterium,* the Benedictus is for SAT and the Agnus Dei is for SSATB; in the five-voiced (SATTB) *Missa de beata Maria virgine,* several sections are for SATB and the final Agnus Dei is for SSAATTB; and in the six-voiced (SSAATB) *Missa Gaudeamus,* there are sections for ATB, SSAA, AATB, and SSAATTB. Four masses—*Missa Ave maris stella, Missa de beata Maria virgine, Missa pro defunctis,* and *Missa Officium defunctorum*—are based on Gregorian chant. The *Missa pro defunctis* (Mass for the Dead) is scored for four voices and was composed in 1583, while the *Missa Officium defunctorum* (Mass for the Office of the Dead) is scored for six voices and was composed in 1603 upon the death of Empress María. Both Requiems alternate brief passages of Gregorian chant with imitative polyphony, and both Requiems contain basically the same traditional movements (Introitus, Kyrie eleison, Offertorium, Sanctus, Agnus Dei, and Communio). However, the *Missa Officium defunctorum* also contains the Gradual, the Lectio II ad matutinum *Taedet animam meam,* and the highly acclaimed motet *Versa est in luctum.* While both Requiems are frequently given the same title (either "Requiem" or "Missa pro defunctis"), it is the 1603 work that is considered Victoria's masterpiece and the finest Requiem composed during the Renaissance.

The motets include four settings of the *Salve regina* (two for five voices, one for six voices, and one for eight voices) and two settings each (one for five and one for eight voices) of *Alma redemptoris mater, Ave regina coelorum,* and *Regina coeli.* All the *Salve regina* settings are based upon the Gregorian chant generally referred to as "The Great Salve" (page 276 in the *Liber usualis*). In the eight-voiced setting the motet begins with the first four notes of the chant (the notes that have served as a motto for many composers throughout history) and then continues with imitative polyphony divided into numerous sections that parallel the chant's phrases. Victoria alternates these sections between two SATB choirs and interpolates two sections for the choirs together in polychoral dialogue fashion. In total, the motet is divided into seven sections—three for choir one, two for choir two, and two for the choirs together. The other eight-voiced motets, such as *Ave regina coelorum,* are only in the traditional polychoral dialogue style. The four-voiced motets—those such as *Vere languores, Ave Maria, O magnum mysterium,* and *O quam gloriosum* that are famous today—are the most economical of Victoria's works in terms of length and texture, and also the most effective in terms of subtle expressiveness. *Vere languores* and *Ave Maria,* for instance, are almost entirely homophonic and syllabic, and *O magnum mysterium* and *O quam gloriosum* use sections of homophony and polyphony for expressive purposes (e.g., the homophony at "O beata virgo" in *O magnum mysterium* and the melismas on the word "gaudent" in *O quam gloriosum*).

The Magnificats include two complete cycles for four voices on each of the eight Gregorian chant tones and two individual polychoral settings (one on the first tone for SATB/SATB and one on the sixth tone for SATB/SATB/SATB). The four-voiced Magnificats are in *alternatim* style, with one eight-tone cycle being set to polyphony on the odd-numbered verses (beginning with the text "Anima mea Dominum") and the other cycle being set to polyphony on the even-numbered verses (beginning with the text "Et exsultavit spiritus meus"). Like the parody masses, the four-voiced Magnificats have sections for reduced and increased scoring. For example, the *Magnificat secundi toni* in the cycle with even-versed polyphony has sections for ATB, SSAT, and SAATBB. The Passions—*Passio secundum Joannem* and *Passio secundum Matthaeum*—as well as the Lamentations and a variety of motets for Holy Week, were published in 1585 under the title *Officium Hebdomadae.*

MOTETS
SELECTED AND LISTED ACCORDING TO FAMILIARITY

Vere languores – SATB chorus – 3 minutes.

O magnum mysterium – SATB chorus – 4 minutes.

O quam gloriosum – SATB chorus – 3:30 minutes.

Ave Maria – SATB chorus – 2:30 minutes.

O vos omnes – SATB chorus – 2:45 minutes.

Ave Maria – SATB/SATB chorus – 3:45 minutes.

Duo seraphim - Tres sunt – SSAA chorus – 3 minutes.

Regina coeli – SATB/SATB chorus – 3:30 minutes.

Ave regina coelorum – SATB/SATB chorus – 3:30 minutes.

Salve regina – SSAT/SATB chorus – 7 minutes.

Pueri Hebraeorum – SATB chorus – 2:30 minutes.

O Domine Jesu Christe – SSAATB chorus – 2:30 minutes.

Gaude Maria virgo – SSATB chorus – 2:30 minutes.

Vidi speciosam - Quae est ista – SSATTB chorus – 5 minutes.

Dum complerentur – SSATB chorus – 4 minutes.

Ne timeas Maria – SATB chorus – 3:45 minutes.

O sacrum convivium - Mens impletur gratias – SSSA chorus – 3 minutes.

MASSES
SELECTED AND LISTED ACCORDING TO FAMILIARITY

Missa Officium defunctorum – SSATTB chorus – 43 minutes.

Missa pro Victoria – SSATB/SATB chorus – 20 minutes.

Missa O magnum mysterium – SATB chorus – 22 minutes.

Missa O quam gloriosum – SATB chorus – 21 minutes.

Missa de beata Maria virgine – SATTB chorus – 23 minutes.

Missa Dum complerentur – SAATTB chorus – 29 minutes.

Missa Vidi speciosam – SSATTB chorus – 20 minutes.

Missa Gaudeamus – SSAATB chorus – 33 minutes.

Missa Ave maris stella – SATB chorus – 31 minutes.

Missa pro defunctis – SATB chorus – 18 minutes.

JUAN (DE) BARAHONA ESQUIVEL CA.1563–CA.1613

Esquivel was born in Ciudad Rodrigo in the Salamanca Province of western Spain, where he sang at the local cathedral. From 1581 to 1585 he served as *maestro di capilla* at Oviedo Cathedral in northwestern Spain, and from 1585 to 1591 he held the same position at Calahorra Cathedral in northcentral Spain. In 1591 he returned to his hometown of Ciudad Rodrigo, serving there as *maestro di capilla* at the cathedral until his death.

He composed one book each of masses and motets, each scored for four, five, six, and eight voices. The masses range in style from ultraconservative works utilizing compositional structures such as cantus firmus and canon to more modern, freely composed works with alternating sections of homophony and imitative polyphony. Most of the masses are parodies and include at least five works based on motets by Guerrero (one of which is *Missa Quasi cedrus*) and one based on Janequin's famous chanson *La bataille*. The masses also include two Requiems, one scored for SATB chorus and the other for SSATB, and works such as the *Missa Ignancia* based on the Gregorian chant sequence *Quodcumque ligaveris*. The motets are mostly in a pervasive point-of-imitation style. Examples include *Ego sum panis vivus* for SATB, *Repleti sunt omnes* for SSATB, and *Duo seraphim* for SSAATB.

⚘ GERMANY AND AUSTRIA ⚘

The significant composers of the Renaissance era who spent the majority of their lives working in Germany and Austria—unlike the composers in France, Italy, Spain, and England—were born in one of several countries, including present-day Belgium, the Czech Republic, Slovenia, Switzerland, Poland, and Italy, as well as Germany and Austria. In addition, composers born in Germany and Austria were not from limited geographical areas: nine composers were from cities scattered throughout northern Germany, four were from central or southern Germany, and two were born in different cities in Austria. Also unique to Germany and Austria during the Renaissance era, the several composers who were born in the same geographical region were not of the same or close to the same generation. For instance, the four composers born in or very near Belgium include Heinrich Isaac and Orlando di Lasso, who were separated by more than eighty years, and the two composers born in Nuremberg—Heinrich Finck and Hans Leo Hassler—were separated by more than a hundred years.

Places of employment also varied. Five composers served at the Imperial court in Vienna, two held positions at the major courts in Dresden and Munich, and most of the other composers held appointments in cities such as Innsbruck, Salzburg, Stuttgart, Augsburg, Berlin, Hamburg, Nuremberg, Freiburg, Weimar, Wolfenbüttel, and Coburg. Three composers worked for a period of time in the Czech Republic, and one worked in Hungary (these countries are included with Germany and Austria because their music is entirely representative of German/Austrian characteristics).

The genres of composition, as varied as the composers' places of birth and employment, include Latin mass cycles and mass movements, Magnificats, Passions and historiae, Latin and German motets, chorale settings, sacred and secular lieder, and chansons, madrigals, ballettos, canzonets, and polyphonic Dutch songs. Most composers wrote in a wide variety of these genres, including those that were sacred and secular and those set to both Latin and German texts. Only two composers in the era, Martin Luther and Philipp Nicolai, wrote no sacred music to Latin texts, and only Luther and his followers Balthasar Resinarius, Johann Walter, Hieronymus Praetorius, and Melchior Vulpius wrote no secular music of any kind. One composer, Paul Hofhaimer, wrote only secular music.

The genres basically divide into three categories—sacred works in Latin for the Catholic Church, sacred works in Latin and German for the Lutheran Church, and secular works for court and public entertainments in German, Italian, Latin, French, and Dutch. The genres for the Catholic Church—mass cycles and mass movements, Magnificats, and motets—were similar to those genres in Italy. Mass cycles and mass movements were almost entirely in a conservative point-of-imitation style and based on preexisting material such as Gregorian chants, motets, and chansons at the beginning of the era and generally only motets thereafter. The Magnificats, also mostly parodies, were composed in *alternatim* style and on the Gregorian chant tones. Motets in the early years were mostly polyphonic, with long phrases of text divided into points of imitation. In the middle years the imitative phrases alternated with passages of homophony, and the motets were frequently divided into separate movements or distinct sections, with scoring for larger vocal forces and with the different movements or sections of the motets scored for varied groupings of voices, including groups that were both smaller and larger than the overall scoring. The motets in the later years of the era were characterized by syllabic settings of text, exchanges of short motifs, and instances of expressive word painting. In addition, many late-era motets were in a polychoral dialogue style.

The genres for the Lutheran Church consisted of chorales, chorale motets, and sacred lieder in German; Latin motets; Latin Passions and German historiae; and Magnificats containing some movements in Latin and others in German. The chorales were the single most distinguishing genre of the Lutheran church. Created to serve the reform ideals of Martin Luther, who called for accessible music in the vernacular, the chorales were the counterparts of the French Psalms set and published in Calvinist psalters. In their most basic form, chorales were monophonic tunes, either newly composed or taken from the secular repertory and given sacred texts. Several composers, including Luther himself, wrote or adapted these tunes, which were then set in a two-part hymn-like form (homophonic and strophic, with the tune in the soprano voice part). The *stollen*, which comprised the first half of the chorale, was customarily repeated with new text; the *abgesang*, which ordinarily equaled the *stollen* in length, closed the chorale. Both portions consisted of two or three phrases of text, each marked with a fermata at its end (although the fermata was to be observed only if the oratory of the phrase warranted a pause or cadential demarcation). With its repeated structural parts, the form of the chorale was AAB (called bar form). The chorale tunes became so widespread and well known that composers used them as bases for motets, virtually identical to the Latin motets in structure and style, with the chorale tune featured prominently as a cantus firmus in the soprano voice part or with the tune used pervasively throughout all voice parts.

Of the remaining sacred genres, the lieder, commonly used for private devotionals, were similar to the hymn-like chorale settings, although the main melody was in the tenor instead of the soprano voice part, and the textures were characterized by homophony and passages of simple imitative polyphony. Portions of the early Lutheran liturgy maintained Latin segments of traditional Catholic services, and as a consequence Latin motets continued to be of interest to composers writing for the Lutheran Church. The Passions and historiae were almost identical genres, the general distinction being that Passions are settings in Latin to texts from the four Gospels about the death of Jesus, while the historiae contain original poetry that for the most part focuses on the resurrection. This distinction was not formalized or without exceptions, however, for a few of the Passion works contain text about the resurrection, and a few of the Passions are also in German. Two styles were prevalent in the Passions and historiae—polyphonic, with no solo roles, and responsorial, with the roles of the narrator (evangelist) and major individual characters set to recitation tones or monody and the role of the crowd (*turba*) set polyphonically. The Magnificats that were composed for Lutheran services often have German chorales interpolated into the traditional Latin text.

The lied, which was the most common genre of secular music in the era, was usually strophic and set to verses of a folk-like love poem, with a homophonic texture and a structure of repeated sections. Other secular genres were popular as well. Isaac, Jacobus Vaet, and Lasso composed French chansons; Ludwig Senfl, Lasso, and Hassler composed Italian madrigals; and Antonio Scandello, Jacob Regnart, and Gregor Aichinger composed Italian canzonets and ballettos.

Most of the genres were in a *prima prattica* style well into the beginning of the seventeenth century. Few composers were influenced by *seconda prattica* developments, and thus there were few vocal concertos and scorings for an independent basso continuo part. Indeed, few German and Austrian composers even bothered to include a basso continuo part that was not independent. Instrumental participation in the vocal genres was, however, popular. Most composers, especially late in the era, specifically commented in the prefaces to their publications that the vocal works were to be accompanied by instruments *colla parte* as the instruments were available. Michael Praetorius wrote extensively about this practice in his treatise *Syntagma musicum* of 1619, recommending many different instrumental combinations.

The most significant composers of the era are Heinrich Finck and Heinrich Isaac representing the early sixteenth century; Ludwig Senfl representing the middle years; Orlando di Lasso and Jacob Handl representing the end of the century; and Hans Leo Hassler, Michael Praetorius, and Melchior Franck representing the early years of the seventeenth century. All were prolific and all contributed to a variety of genres except for Praetorius, who composed almost exclusively for Lutheran liturgies. Other composers whose work was focused on Lutheran genres are Martin Luther, Balthasar Resinarius, Johann Walter, Caspar Othmayr, Johannes Eccard, Philipp Nicolai, Hieronymus Praetorius, Christoph Demantius, and Melchior Vulpius. Lesser-known composers who wrote in a variety of genres for both the Catholic and Lutheran liturgies are Thomas Stoltzer, Antonio Scandello, Jacobus Vaet, Jacob Regnart, Leonhard Lechner, Gregor Aichinger, and Nikolaus Zangius. As was mentioned above, Paul Hofhaimer composed only secular music to German texts.

HEINRICH FINCK CA.1444–1527

Finck was born in Bamberg, north of Nuremberg. Nothing is known of his youth or musical training, although it is presumed from commentary in the treatise *Practica musica* by his great uncle Hermann Finck that he was a chorister in Kraków, Poland. In 1482, when Heinrich was in his late thirties, he studied at the University of Leipzig, and in his early forties he traveled throughout Germany and Poland. In 1498 he was appointed *Kapellmeister* to Prince Alexander of Lithuania, who resided in Vilnius, and in 1501 he went to the royal court in Kraków when the prince became king of Poland. While in Kraków, Finck most likely taught Thomas Stoltzer, who was a chorister at the royal court. Finck left Poland in 1510 to serve as *Singemeister* at the ducal kapelle in Stuttgart, and when the kapelle disbanded in 1514, it is likely, though not certain, that he served Emperor Maximilian I of Austria. From 1519 to 1526 he held various positions at the cathedral in Salzburg, Austria, and in 1527, just months before his death, he was appointed *Kapellmeister* at the Vienna court of Ferdinand I.

Finck composed four masses that are extant plus several mass movements that are lost, seventy motets, two Magnificats, two sacred German lieder, and twenty-six secular lieder. The masses—*Missa Dominicalis* for four voices, *Missa super Ave praeclara* for five voices, *Missa in Summis* for six voices, and an untitled work for three voices—are all characterized by continuous imitative polyphony, with head motifs unifying the movements in *Missa super Ave praeclara* and chant elaborations in the soprano and tenor voices in the Kyrie, Sanctus, and Agnus Dei movements of *Missa in Summis;* the Gloria and Credo seem to be freely composed. The motets include several large-scale works composed for Mass Propers, a collection of hymns based on Gregorian chants, and independent works beginning with a chant incipit. Examples of the first type are *Rorate caeli, Puer natus est nobis,* and *Ecce advenit*—each consisting of six to ten movements entitled "versus," "sequence," and "alleluia." Examples of the second type are *Iste confessor, Veni creator spiritus,* and *Genitori genitoque*—each structured around a cantus firmus in the tenor voice and occasionally the soprano voice as well. The third type of motet is represented by *Veni sancte spiritus.* The two Magnificats are based on the seventh and eighth Gregorian chant tones and are in *alternatim* style.

The two sacred German pieces, *Christ ist erstanden* and *In Gottes Namen fahren wir,* are both based on cantus firmi and are imitative in texture. Examples of the German secular pieces—*Auf gut Gelück, O schönes Weib, Mein herzigs G,* and *Ach herzigs Herz*—are also imitative, but strophic. Most have three verses and are in an AAB form.

SACRED WORKS
SELECTED AND LISTED ACCORDING TO FAMILIARITY

Missa Dominicalis – SATB chorus – 28 minutes.

Missa super Ave praeclara – SATTB chorus – 24 minutes.

Missa in Summis – SATTBB chorus – 23 minutes.

O Domine Jesu Christe – SATB chorus – 8:30 minutes. (1) The motet is
divided into seven movements, each beginning with the same text
phrase; (2) the final movement is scored for SATTBB.

Christus resurgens - Quod enim vivit – SATTB chorus – 6 minutes.

Veni sancte spiritus – SAATTBB chorus – 3 minutes.

Iste confessor – SATB chorus – 2:15 minutes.

Veni creator spiritus – SATB chorus – 2:15 minutes.

Genitori genitoque – SATB chorus – 2:30 minutes.

Christ ist erstanden – SATTB chorus – 3 minutes.

In Gottes namen fahren wir – SATB chorus – 2:30 minutes.

SECULAR WORKS
SELECTED AND LISTED ACCORDING TO FAMILIARITY

Auf gut Gelück – SATB voices – 2:30 minutes.

O schönes Weib – SATB voices – 2:45 minutes.

Hab's je getan – SATB voices – 3 minutes.

Mein herzigs G – SATB voices – 3:15 minutes.

Ach herzigs Herz – SATB voices – 2:30 minutes.

HEINRICH ISAAC CA.1450–1517

Isaac was born in Belgium, as were his compatriots Alexander Agricola, Josquin Desprez, Pierre
de La Rue, and Jacob Obrecht—all of whom spent the majority of their lives in France. There is
no information about Isaac's life until his early thirties, when he was a musician at the court of
Duke Sigismund of Tyrol in Innsbruck. From 1485 until 1492 Isaac was a singer at both the baptistery and cathedral in Florence, and he was also teacher to Piero and Giovanni de' Medici, the
children of Lorenzo. After the death of Lorenzo in 1492 and the subsequent reduction of the
court's musical resources, Isaac traveled, eventually settling in Vienna, where in 1496 he was
appointed court composer to Emperor Maximilian I. While in Vienna, he taught Balthasar
Resinarius and Ludwig Senfl, and he became acquainted with Paul Hofhaimer. His position
with Maximilian allowed him to travel frequently, and he returned to Innsbruck and Florence
numerous times. In 1502 he vied with Josquin for the position of *maestro di cappella* at the court
of Ercole I d'Este in Ferrara (Josquin received the appointment), and in 1514 Pope Leo X
(who was Isaac's former pupil Giovanni de' Medici) honored him with a pension. Isaac then returned to Florence, where he died and was buried. He is often compared to Josquin for several
reasons—the similarity of their writing for paired voices, comparable textures of pervasive imitation, and the consistent high quality of their compositions. Also, there is speculation that
Isaac was Josquin's student. The two composers were leaders in the development of polyphony

away from strict usage of cantus firmus in the tenor voice and toward preexisting material that was infused into the entire vocal texture.

Isaac composed thirty-six extant mass cycles, thirteen Credo movements, approximately 250 motets, and 150 lieder, chansons, and frottolas. The masses are based on a wide variety of preexisting material, including Gregorian chants, motets, polyphonic chansons and chanson tunes, Dutch songs and song settings, and German lieder. Representative masses based on Gregorian chants include three settings of *Missa de Apostolis* (for four, five, and six voices), four settings of *Missa de beata virgine* (one for four, two for five, and one for six voices), and four settings of *Missa Paschalis* (two for four, and one each for five and six voices). Masses based on Gregorian Psalms and antiphons are *Missa Misericordias Domini, Missa Salva nos,* and *Missa Virgo prudentissima.* Other mass types include *Missa La mi la sol,* based on Isaac's motet *O praeclara; Missa Chargé de deul* and *Missa Et trop penser,* based on chanson tunes; *Missa Comme femme desconfortée* and *Missa Quant j'ay au cueur,* based on polyphonic chansons by Gilles de Bins Binchois and Antoine Busnois, respectively; *Missa Een vrolic wesen,* based on an anonymous Dutch song; and *Missa T'meiskin was jonck,* based on a Dutch setting by Jacob Obrecht. Finally, Isaac's most famous mass, *Missa Carminum,* is based on the combination of numerous German lieder. The Ordinary-based masses are composed in *alternatim* style and have no Credo movements, while the other masses are fully polyphonic and include all five portions of the Mass Ordinary. Many of the masses feature construction techniques such as cantus firmus in retrograde (e.g., *Missa Argentum et aurem* and *Missa T'meiskin was jonck*) and canon (e.g., *Missa Comme femme desconfortée* and *Missa Comment poit avoir joie*), and most of the writing is characterized by ostinatos and sequences such as in masses composed by Obrecht.

The motets are divided between those composed for Mass Propers and those that are independent. The two hundred motets for Mass Propers were organized in cycles for the liturgical year and published after Isaac's death in three monumental collections entitled *Choralis constantinus.* Most of these motets, like the masses based on Gregorian Mass Ordinary chants, are in *alternatim* style. The remaining fifty motets are fully polyphonic. Many of the motets in both styles are based on Gregorian chants that are set off by slightly longer rhythmic values than the non-Gregorian melodies and that move from voice part to voice part. Examples are *Tota pulchra es* and *Regina caeli laetare.* Many of the motets are also in two movements—one movement set to an Introit text and the other to a Psalm. Examples include *Puer natus est nobis - Cantate Domino canticum novum* for the feast of the Nativity, *Ecce advenit dominator Dominus - Deus, judicium tuum regi da* for Epiphany, and *Resurrexi, et adhuc tecum sum - Domine probastime, et cognovisti me* for Easter. Numerous motets (e.g., *Gustate et videte* and *Jerusalem surge*) begin with chant incipits but are otherwise in a pervasively imitative style without cantus firmus, and a few of the motets are grand works composed for ceremonial occasions. The polytextual *Optime divino date munere pastor ovili / Da pacem / Sacerdos et pontifex* was written for a meeting between the chancellor to Maximilian I and Pope Leo X in 1513, and *Virgo prudentissima* was composed in about 1507 for the impending coronation of Maximilian I as Holy Roman Emperor. A third ceremonial motet, *Quis dabit capiti meo aquam,* was composed for the funeral of Maximilian I.

The secular pieces, most of which are derivatives of the polyphonic tenor lied, generally feature a cantus firmus-like melody in the tenor voice. However, unlike the sacred compositions in which the tenor melody is in slightly longer note values than the other voices, all voice parts in the secular pieces are of similar rhythmic values. Isaac's most famous secular composition, and perhaps the most famous German secular piece of the Renaissance, is *Innsbruck* [originally spelled *Isbruck*], *ich muss dich lassen* (Innsbruck, I must leave you), which is set to a text that expresses sorrow at having to journey to a foreign land. The musical texture is basically homophonic, and the formal structure is strophic, with three verses. The melody, which may not have been composed by Isaac (i.e., Isaac may have arranged the preexisting tune), became famous as a contrafactum, with the sacred text "O Welt, ich muss dich lassen" (O world, I must leave you) used frequently as a chorale by German Baroque composers. J. S. Bach used a version of the chorale two times, to two different texts, in his *Passio secundum Mattaeum* BWV244—"Ich bins, ich sollte büßen" (It is I, I should atone) and "Wer hat dich so geschlagen" (Who has so tortured you).

MASSES
SELECTED AND LISTED ACCORDING TO FAMILIARITY

Missa Carminum – SATB chorus – 23 minutes.

Missa Virgo prudentissima – SSATTB chorus – 33:30 minutes.

Missa de apostolis – SSATTB chorus – 29 minutes.

Missa Paschalis – SSATTB chorus – 22 minutes.

MOTETS
SELECTED AND LISTED ACCORDING TO FAMILIARITY

Ecce virgo concipies – SATB chorus – 2 minutes.

O Maria, mater Christi - Ave domina - O jucunda - Ave sanctissima – SATB chorus – 7 minutes.

Tota pulchra es - Flores apparuerunt – SATB chorus – 4 minutes.

Ave sanctissima Maria - Tu es singularis - Ora pro nobis Jesum – SATB chorus – 7:30 minutes.

Optime divino . . . / Da pacem / Sacerdos et pontifex – SSATTB chorus – 9:30 minutes.

Gustate et videte – SATB chorus – 2 minutes.

Jerusalem surge – SATB chorus – 2 minutes.

Regina caeli laetare – SSATTB chorus – 6 minutes.

Virgo prudentissima – SSATTB chorus – 12 minutes.

Quis dabit pacem populo timenti – SATB chorus – 4:30 minutes.

Quis dabit capiti meo aquam – SATB chorus – 8:15 minutes.

Puer natus est nobis - Cantate Domino canticum novum – SSATTB chorus – 3:30 minutes.

Ecce advenit dominator Dominus - Deus, judicium tuum regi da – SSATTB chorus – 2:30 minutes.

Rorate caeli - Caeli enarrant gloriam Dei – SSATTB chorus – 2:30 minutes.

Viri Galilaei - Omnes gentes plaudite manibus – SSATTB chorus – 4:30 minutes.

PAUL HOFHAIMER 1459–1537

Hofhaimer was born in Radstadt, near Salzburg, and it is assumed (without documentation) that he received his musical education in Vienna at the court of Emperor Frederick V (also known as Emperor Frederick III of the Holy Roman Empire). In 1478 Hofhaimer began playing the organ at the court of Duke Sigismund of Tyrol in Innsbruck, and in 1489 he was named organist for life. He maintained this position while also serving as organist to Frederick's successor, Maximilian I, and in addition, he played on special occasions in Passau and at the Bavarian court in Munich. In 1515 he was made a knight and nobleman by Maximilian, and in 1519 when the emperor died, Hofhaimer was appointed organist at Salzburg Cathedral, serving the archbishop of Salzburg, Cardinal Matthäus Lang. Hofhaimer was considered to be the finest organist of his time, especially acclaimed for his improvisations, and he was a noted teacher of organists who held positions at St Mark's Basilica in Venice, St Stephen's Cathedral in Vienna, and cathedrals in Speyer and Passau, Germany.

Hofhaimer's extant compositional output comprises only twenty-six German lieder, all strophic (mainly consisting of three verses) and scored for SATB voices. Many, such as *Nach willen dein, Mein Traurens ist, Mein eynigs A,* and *Einr Jungfraw zart,* are in an AAB form. Others, such as *Ade mit Leid,* are through-composed. The textures vary from strictly homophonic to alternating passages of imitative polyphony and homophony.

THOMAS STOLTZER CA.1480–1526

Stoltzer was born in Schweidnitz, Silesia, now Poland, and he most likely studied with Heinrich Finck, *Kapellmeister* to the king of Poland from 1498 to 1510. Stoltzer is documented as being a priest in Breslau in 1519, and in 1522 he was appointed *magister capellae* at the Hungarian court of Ludwig II in Buda. While at the Hungarian court, Stoltzer composed the Latin motet *Beati omnes* for Ludwig's wedding as well as his four famous German motets set to translations of Psalms by Martin Luther.

Stoltzer's total compositional output includes four masses, 113 Latin motets, the four German motets mentioned above, five Magnificats, four sacred lieder, and ten secular lieder. All of the masses are based on German chorales and are scored for four voices (SATB). However, none contain all five portions of the Ordinary. *Missa duplex per totum annum* and *Missa Kyrie summum* have no Credos, *Missa Paschalis* (sometimes called the *Ostermesse*) has no Credo or Agnus Dei, and *Missa Kyrie angelicum* has no Credo, Sanctus, or Agnus Dei. The Latin motets are divided between those that utilize archaic construction techniques such as cantus firmus on long notes and notational puzzles (e.g., *Inter natos mulierum*), and those that feature newer styles of pervasive imitative polyphony and polychoral effects (e.g., *Anima mea liquefacta est*). Some of the motets also consist of numerous movements (a practice common in Germany at the time).

Benedicam Dominum, for instance, has four movements, the second and third of which are scored for fewer forces (two and three) than the first and fourth (for five voices). Stoltzer's best-known Latin motet, *O admirabile commercium,* is for five voices.

The four German motets are *Hilf, Herr, die Heiligen haben abgenommen* (Psalm 12) for six voices; *Herr, wie lang willst du mein so gar vergessen* (Psalm 13) for five voices; *Erzürne dich nicht über die Bösen* (Psalm 37) for six voices; and *Herr, neige deine Ohren* (Psalm 86) for six voices. Like the large-scale Latin motets, they are divided into several movements and their scoring varies. For example, *Erzürne dich nicht über die Bösen* for SATTBB chorus has seven movements—the third scored for SAB, the fourth for TTB, and the seventh expanded to SSATTBB.

The sacred lieder are represented by *Ich bin bei Gott in Gnaden* for SATB voices, and the secular lieder, mostly scored for four voices and in an imitative style, include *Entlaubet ist der Walde, Erst wird erfreut mein traurigs Herz,* and *Heimlich bin ich in Treuen dein.*

MARTIN LUTHER 1483–1546

Luther was born in Eisleben, near Leipzig, and was educated at schools in Mansfeld, Magdeburg, and Eisenach. In the early 1500s he studied law at the University of Erfurt, graduating with both bachelor's and master's degrees. However, he did not pursue a career in law but instead entered an Augustinian monastery in 1505, and in 1507 he was ordained a Catholic priest. During a trip to Rome in 1510 on behalf of the Augustinians he was deeply troubled by many church practices, especially indulgences. Nonetheless, he returned to Germany, received a doctorate in Roman Catholic theology, and became a professor at the University of Wittenberg in 1512. During the next several years he developed ideas for the reformation of church practices, and in 1517 he nailed his famous ninety-five theses to the door of Wittenberg's Schlosskirche. Because of this action and his outspoken criticisms of the Catholic Church, he was excommunicated in 1521. He retreated to Wartburg Castle, near Eisenach, where he translated the New Testament into German and further developed his theories of church reformation, and in 1529 he published the *Deudsch Catechismus.* Shortly thereafter he translated the Old Testament into the German vernacular, and for the remainder of his life he traveled throughout Germany preaching and giving lectures. Although he did not study music formally, Luther was a skilled musician; he played the lute and apparently had a fine singing voice. Furthermore, he was acquainted with the music of Josquin Desprez and Ludwig Senfl, and he worked closely with Johann Walter, who taught music to Luther's sons and who, under Luther's supervision, published the first book of music for the reformed German church—*Geystliche Gesangk Buchleyn,* issued in Wittenberg in 1524.

There has been considerable debate by music historians as to the authenticity of the hymn tunes (generally referred to as chorales) ascribed to Luther. There is no documentary evidence that he was actually the composer of the tunes, although there is considerable reason, including sixteenth-century commentary, to assume that he was. General opinion is that Luther is indeed the composer or first arranger of approximately thirty chorale melodies, including the newly composed *Aus tiefer Not schrei ich zu dir* (adapted from Psalm 80), *Ein feste Burg ist unser Gott* (from Psalm 46), and *Vom Himmel hoch da komm ich her* (from Luke 2). Well-known chorale melodies arranged from Gregorian chants include *Der du bist drei in Einigkeit* (from *O lux beata trinitas*), *Komm Gott, Schöpfer, Heiliger Geist* (from *Veni Creator Spiritus*), *Nun komm der Heiden Heiland* (from *Veni Redemptor*), and *Verleih uns Frieden gnädiglich* (from *Da pace Domine*). Other famous chorales, ones that Luther adapted from older German songs, are *Christ lag in Todesbanden* and *Komm heiliger Geist*.

BALTHASAR RESINARIUS CA.1485–1544

Resinarius was born in Tetschen, Bohemia (now Decin, Czech Republic), and received his musical education as a chorister at the chapel of Maximilian I in Vienna under Heinrich Isaac. In 1515 he entered the University of Leipzig, and in 1523 he returned to Tetschen to serve as a Catholic priest. He later became affiliated with the Lutheran Church and was made Bishop of Leipa. He was considered an important composer during his life, and much of his music was published by Georg Rhau in two collections—*Responsorium numero octoginta de tempore et festis iuxta seriem totius anni*, which contains eighty Latin motets for the church year and a Passion based on the Gospel of St John, and *Newe deudsche geistliche Gesenge*, which contains thirty chorale settings.

Resinarius's compositional output, all for the Lutheran Church, includes ninety Latin motets, one Passion, and thirty chorale settings. The Latin motets and German chorale settings are for the most part scored for SATB chorus and constructed of a cantus firmus in the tenor part, with imitative and mainly syllabic textures in the other parts. Sample motets are *Deus misericordiam, Factum est autem*, and *In principis erat verbum*. Chorale settings are based on many of the most common texts used by the Lutheran Church at the time, including *Verleih uns Frieden gnädiglich; Nun komm, der Heiden Heiland; Mit Fried und Freud ich fahr dahin; Wir glauben all an einen Gott;* and *Vater unser*—all also for SATB. The Passion, entitled *Summa Passionis secundum Joahannem*, is scored for SATB chorus in five movements and is entirely polyphonic. Most of the writing is imitative, although there are occasional alto and bass duet passages and also alternating passages between high (SA) and low (TB) voice parts.

LUDWIG SENFL CA.1486–1543

Senfl was born in Basel, Switzerland, but moved to Zurich with his family in 1488. In 1496 he became a chorister at the Hofkapelle of Emperor Maximilian I in Vienna, where he studied under Heinrich Isaac, and in about 1504, when his voice changed, he took a clerical position at Basel Cathedral. He remained associated with the Viennese Hofkapelle, however, copying motets by Isaac that would eventually be included in the *Choralis constantinus*. Senfl traveled with Isaac to Florence in 1508 and succeeded him at the Hofkapelle in Vienna in 1513, and with the death of Maximilian I in 1519 and the subsequent dissolution of the kapelle, he sought other employment, eventually being appointed *Komponist* at the Munich court of Duke Wilhelm of Bavaria in 1523. For the next twenty years Senfl composed numerous motets, which he added to those by Isaac for a compilation entitled *En opus musicum festorum dierum;* these motets would serve as

Roman Catholic Propers for the complete liturgical year. A few motets were also composed for the Lutheran Church, including two—*Non moriar, sed vivam* and *In pace idipsum*—presented as gifts to Martin Luther. Senfl was considered to be the most accomplished composer of his time. He was praised in treatises by Heinrich Glarean, Sebald Heyden, and Lodovico Zacconi, and his music was performed widely throughout Germany and Austria.

Senfl's compositional output consists of seven masses, approximately 420 motets, eight Magnificats, 250 lieder, two madrigals, one chanson, and three Latin secular polyphonic songs. These works do not include the motet *Quis dabit oculis nostris*, which was performed at the funeral services for Maximilian I and ascribed to Senfl; this motet was composed by Costanzo Festa. Senfl's masses are all based on Gregorian chants, generally featured as cantus firmi in the tenor voice. In *Missa Paschalis* the chant appears in short phrases in other voice parts as well as in long notes in the tenor; in *Missa super Nisi Dominus* and *Missa super Per signum crucis* the chants are used as head motifs at the beginnings of the five portions of the Ordinary; and in *Missa Dominicalis* (subtitled "L'homme armé"), the chant appears as a cantus firmus in long notes in the soprano voice, and the L'homme armé tune appears similarly in the tenor voice.

Approximately half of the motets were composed for Proper feast celebrations and divided into multiple movements. In the motet for the celebration entitled "In nativitate Domini ad tertiam Missam," the first movement is the Introit *Puer natus est*, the second and fourth are the Verses *Cantate Domino canticum novum* and *Dies sanctificatus*, the fifth through tenth consist of the Sequence *Per quem fit machina*, and the final movement is the Communion *Viderunt omnes*. Each movement (or each motet, since they are all listed and published separately) begins with a chant incipit followed by points of imitation matching phrases of text, and while the group of motets as a whole is scored for SATB chorus, there are sections for TTB and SATTB. The seven motets for "In Epiphania Domini" are similar and include the Introit *Ecce advenit*, the Verses *Deus, judicium tuum* and *Vidimus stellam ejus*, and the Sequence *Quae miris sunt modis*. The six motets for "In Festo SS Apostolorum Petri et Pauli" include the Sequence *Ecclesiam vestris doctrinis* and the Communion *Tu es Petrus*.

A large number of the motets not composed for Proper Offices are also in cycles of two or more movements. These include *Verbum caro factum est - Plenum gratiae - In principio erat verbum, Miserere mei Deus - Asperges me - Domine labia mea*, and *Omnes gentes - Ascendit Deus*. Many of the motets feature cantus firmi used in interesting ways. In *Non moriar, sed vivam*, for instance, identical statements of the cantus firmus migrate through the four voice parts, starting with the soprano and ending with the bass. Senfl's most celebrated motet, *Ave Maria - Ave vera humilitates*, which is a six-voiced parody of Josquin Desprez's famous four-voiced setting of *Ave Maria . . . virgo serena*, is based on the first six notes of Josquin's work and uses these notes as a cantus firmus that is stated in the tenor voice fifteen times. Senfl also expands and develops each of Josquin's points of imitation.

The lieder are mostly settings of secular texts, although a few are sacred. For example, *Vom Himmel kam der Engel Schar* is a chorale arrangement for SSATBB chorus with the chorale tune in the soprano voice, and *Gottes Gewalt, Kraft und auch Macht* is a motet-like work for SATTB chorus with a cantus firmus in canon between the two tenor voices. The secular works include *Lust hab ich ghabt zur Musica*, which contains an acrostic of the composer's name, and *Das Gläut zu Speyer* (also called *Gling glang*), which contains numerous onomatopoeic sounds of bells as from the cathedral bell tower in the city of Speyer.

MASSES
SELECTED AND LISTED ACCORDING TO FAMILIARITY

Missa Dominicalis (subtitled "L'homme armé") – SATB chorus – 25 minutes.

Missa Paschalis – SSATB chorus – 21 minutes.

Missa super Nisi Dominus – SATB chorus – 21 minutes.

Missa super Per signum crucis – SATB chorus – 22 minutes.

MOTETS
SELECTED AND LISTED ACCORDING TO FAMILIARITY

Ave Maria - Ave verum humilitas – SSATTB chorus – 8 minutes.

Veni creator spiritus – SSAATTBB chorus – 7 minutes.

Non moriar, sed vivam – SATB chorus – 3:15 minutes.

Omnes gentes - Ascendit Deus – SATTB chorus – 5:30 minutes.

De profundis - A custodia matutina – SATTB chorus – 4 minutes.

Miserere mei Deus - Asperges me - Domine labia mea – SATTB chorus – 9 minutes.

Verbum caro factum est - Plenum gratiae – In principio erat verbum – SAATTB chorus – 6:30 minutes.

PART SONGS
SELECTED AND LISTED ACCORDING TO FAMILIARITY

Das Gläut zu Speyer (Gling glang) – SSATTB voices – 3 minutes.

Ach Elslein, liebes Elselein – SATB voices – 2 minutes.

Ich weiss nit, was er ihr verheiss – SATB voices – 2 minutes.

Die Bruennelein, die da fliessen – SATB voices – 2 minutes.

Nun wöllt ihr hören neue Mär – SATB voices – 2 minutes.

JOHANN WALTER (WALTHER) 1496–1570

Walter was born in Kahla, southwest of Leipzig, and received his earliest musical education as a chorister there and in nearby Rochlitz. From 1521 to 1525 he was a singer in the Hofkapelle of Friedrich the Wise, Elector of Saxony, and in 1525 he traveled to Wittenberg, where he became acquainted with Martin Luther. After a brief period beginning in 1529 as a student at the University of Leipzig, Walter moved to Torgau, where he taught the choristers at the local cathedral and directed a *kantorei*. From 1548 to 1554 he was *Kapellmeister* at the Hofkapelle in Dresden, and from 1554 until his death he lived in retirement in Torgau. He is best known for aiding

Luther in the organization of music for reformed liturgical services, and for his collection of thirty-eight German chorale settings and five Latin motets entitled collectively *Geystliches gesangk Buchleyn,* published in Wittenberg in 1524. He is sometimes confused with his son, also named Johann, who lived from 1527 until 1578 and who was a minor composer known for three works—*A solis ortus cardine, Spes mea Christus,* and a Te Deum.

Walter composed seventeen Latin motets, nine Magnificats, two Passions, and approximately fifty German chorale settings. In addition, he wrote two treatises on musical subjects— *Lob und Preis der löblichen Kunst Musica* of 1538 and *Lob und Preis der himmlischen Kunst Musica* of 1564. The Latin motets, such as the four-voiced *Verbum caro factum est,* are in a pervasive point-of-imitation style, with long melismatic phrases and with a structure based on a cantus firmus in the tenor voice part that is in longer note values than the other voices. A few of the motets, such as *Lumen ad revelationem gentium* (Nunc dimittis), are in a chordal, Psalm-tone style, with antiphon sections that are somewhat polyphonic and Psalm verse sections that are completely homophonic and syllabic. The Magnificats include a complete set on each of the chant tones in *alternatim* style, and the Passions, which are responsorial (monody from soloists representing the various characters of the Passion story alternate with syllabic and homophonic choral passages), include settings of the Gospels according to St Matthew and St John (*Passio secundum Matthaeum* and *Passio secundum Johannem*).

Most of the German chorale settings are arrangements of chorale tunes that serve as a cantus firmus in one voice part. Examples include the four-voiced setting of *Christ lag in Todes Banden,* the four-voiced setting of *Komm, Heiliger Geist,* both the three- and four-voiced settings of *Christ ist erstanden,* the five-voiced setting of *Nun bitten wir den heiligen Geist* (in which the cantus firmus is in canon between the alto and second tenor voices), and the six-voiced setting of *Gib unserm fürsten und aller Obrigkeit.* An arrangement of the chorale tune "Wachet auf, ruft uns die stimme" is set as a strophic tenor lied entitled *Wach auf, wach auf, du deutsches Land, du hast genug geschlafen* (Wake up, wake up, Germany, you have slept enough). Other sacred German compositions, those not based on chorale tunes, are in a style similar to the Latin motets, with no cantus firmus. Examples of these include the four-voiced (SATB) *O wie selig ist der Tod,* the five-voiced (SATTB) *Vater unser,* and the six-voiced (SSATTB) *Verleih uns Frieden gnädiglich.* Only a few of the German motets (e.g., *Wohl dem, der nicht wandelt*) are in two movements.

CASPAR OTHMAYR 1515–1553

Othmayr was born in Amberg, near Heidelberg, and received his musical education in the Kapelle of Elector Friedrich II in Neumarkt and Amberg. In 1533 Othmayr entered the University of Heidelberg, receiving a bachelor's degree the following year and a master's degree in 1536, and from 1543 until his death he was an administrator at the Latin school of Heilsbronn monastery. He was acquainted with Johann Walter and Martin Luther, for whom he composed two elegies—*D. Martini Lutheri Symbolum* and *Epitaphium D. Martini Lutheri*—and he was an important contributor to the chorale repertoire of the early Lutheran Church.

Othmayr's compositional output includes approximately fifty Latin motets, one hundred German chorale settings, and fifty secular German lieder. The Latin motets are principally in the imitative style of the time, with few distinguishing characteristics. The German chorale settings are distinctive, however, in being largely set for two and three voices (there are forty duets and fifty trios). All are based on familiar Lutheran chorales, which appear as a cantus firmus in one of the voice parts. Examples of the duets include *Vom Himmel hoch da komm ich her* for TT, *Mit Fried und Freud ich fahr dahin* for AT, *Christ lag in Todes Banden* for AT, and *Ich freue mich* for SS. Examples of chorale settings for larger forces include *Mein himmlischer Vater* for SATTB, *O Mensch, bewein dein Sünde gross* for SATB, and *Verleih uns Frieden* for SATB.

The secular pieces are typically settings of folk or love poetry, with syllabic and somewhat imitative textures. Many of the pieces are also strophic and in an AAB form. *Es liegt ein Schloss in Österreich* for ATBB voices is syllabic and imitative; *Der Winter kalt is vor dem Haus* for SATB voices is strophic, with point-of-imitation phrases; *Entlaubet ist der Walde* for SATB voices is imitative and in an AAB structure; and *Ich armes Maidlein klag mich sehr* for ATTB voices is strophic, imitative, and in an AAB structure.

ANTONIO SCANDELLO 1517–1580

Scandello was born in Bergamo in northern Italy, where his father and brothers were trumpeters and where he was employed as a trumpeter himself in 1530. In 1547 he entered the court of Cardinal Madruzzi in Trent, and in 1549 he joined five other Italian musicians at the court of Elector Moritz of Saxony in Dresden. In 1562 he converted to the Protestant faith and was made a citizen of Dresden, in 1566 he was appointed *Vice-Kapellmeister* of the court, and in 1568 he was promoted to *Hofkapellmeister*. The Dresden court flourished under Scandello's leadership and was recognized as second only to the Munich court under Orlando di Lasso in terms of its musical stature.

Scandello composed eight masses, twelve motets, one Passion, one historia, three collections of sacred and secular lieder, and one collection of Italian secular music entitled *Il primo libro delle canzoni napolitane*. The masses are mostly Italian-styled parody works, exemplified by *Missa sex vocum super epitaphium illustrissimi principis Mauritii*, which is based on Scandello's motet *Mauritius cedidit* and composed as an elegy for Count Moritz, who died in battle in 1553. The motets—for example, *Beati omnes qui timet Dominum* and *Christus vere languores*, the latter of which Scandello called his "Cygnea cantio" (swan song)—are also in the imitative style of Italian compositions of the time. The Passion and historia are in a mixture of Italian and German styles and were notably influential in the development of works set to the Passion story throughout the remainder of the Renaissance era. In the responsorial historia entitled *Gaudii paschalis Jesu Christi* (also called the *Auferstehungshistorie*), the role of the Evangelist is set to recitation tones, while the remainder of the story is set polyphonically. This structure was especially significant, for Heinrich Schütz modeled his *Historia der frölichen und siegreichen Aufferstehung . . . Jesu Christi* (Easter Oratorio) on Scandello's historia, using the exact same text and dividing the compositional styles between recitation tones and polyphony.

Scandello was most recognized during his lifetime for his collections of German lieder— *Newe teutsche Liedlein* of 1568, *Newe und lustige weltliche deudsche Liedlein* of 1570, and *Newe schöne auserlesene geistliche deudsche Lieder* of 1575. The publication of 1570—which included the four-part lied *Ein Hennlein weiss* (The little white hen) with onomatopoeic sounds of cackles—was especially popular. The Italian pieces include the balletto *Bonzorno, Madonna* and the canzonet *Vorria che tu cantass'* with a refrain sung to the solfege syllables *fa mi la mi sol la.*

JACOBUS VAET CA.1529–1567

Vaet was born in either Kortrijk or Harelbeke, Belgium, and was a chorister at Onze Lieve Vrouwkerk in Kortrijk. In 1546 he entered the University of Leuven, and in 1550 he became a singer at the Vienna court of Emperor Charles V. He remained at the court for the duration of his life, in 1554 becoming *Kapellmeister* to Charles's nephew Archduke Maximilian II. While few details of Vaet's life and professional activity exist, it is known from commentary and compositions of the sixteenth century that he was a highly respected composer. Jacob Regnart composed an elegy on his death—*Defunctorum charites Vaetem*—and composers such as Jacob Handl parodied his works.

Vaet composed nine masses, three books of motets, eight Magnificats, and three chansons. The masses are all based on preexisting material, mostly motets by noteworthy Franco-Flemish composers, including Jean Mouton (whose motet was used in *Missa Confitemini*), Cipriano de Rore (*Missa Dissimulare*), Clemens non Papa (*Missa Ego flos campi*), and Orlando di Lasso (*Missa Tityre, tu patulae*). This latter mass is also based on Vaet's motet *Vitam quae faciunt,* which itself is a parody of Lasso's same-named motet. Other masses employing Vaet's own motets include *Missa J'ai mis mon Coeur* (on his *Salve regina*), *Missa Miser qui amat,* and *Missa Vitam quae faciunt beatiorum* (the motet of which, as was mentioned above, is based on Lasso's motet *Tityre, tu patulae*). The two remaining masses are *Missa pro defunctis,* based on Gregorian chant, and *Missa Quodlibetica,* based on a variety of German folk songs.

The motets are generally in an imitative texture similar to the works of the mid-sixteenth century Franco-Flemish composers. Examples include *De extremo judicio* and *O quam gloriosum est regnum,* scored for SATB, and *In tenebris* for SSATTB. Motets in two movements are also prevalent, for example *Laetatus sum - Rogate quae ad pacem sunt* for SATB and *Miserere mei - Ecce enim in iniquitatibus* for SATTB. Seventeen of the motets are set to serious secular texts such as "Musica Dei donum optimi, trahit homines, trahit Deos" (Music, God's greatest gift, draws men, draws God).

ORLANDO (ROLAND) DI LASSO (DE LASSUS) 1532–1594

Lasso was born in Mons, Belgium, south of Brussels, close to the birthplaces of such significant composers as Heinrich Isaac, Josquin Desprez, Nicolas Gombert, Jacobus Clemens non Papa, Adrian Willaert, Cipriano de Rore, and Philippe de Monte. Nothing is known about Lasso's early musical training, although there is speculation that he was a chorister at the church of St Nicholas in Ghent and that he had an extraordinarily beautiful singing voice. At age twelve he joined the court of Ferrante Gonzaga in Mantua, which was in Belgium during the summer of 1544 and in Mantua and Sicily thereafter, and in 1549 he entered the court of Constantino Castrioto in Naples. Two years later Lasso moved to Rome, where he was a singer in the court of Antonio Altoviti, and in 1553, at the age of twenty-one, he was appointed *maestro di capella* at one of the oldest and most important churches in Italy—San Giovanni in Laterano, the Cathedral of Rome. After only a little more than a year in this position he returned to Belgium to attend to his ailing parents, being succeeded at San Giovanni in Laterano by Palestrina. Lasso remained in Belgium for about a year, even though his parents had died before he arrived, and in 1556 he became a singer at the court of Duke Albrecht V of Bavaria in Munich. Seven years later he was appointed *Hofkapellmeister,* a position he held until his death thirty years later and a position he passed on to his sons Ferdinand (ca.1560–1609) and Rudolf (ca.1563–1625). Under Lasso's leadership, the musical resources at the court rivaled any in Europe, including courts and cathedrals in Italy. According to Massimo Troiano, a singer at the Munich court, and Michael Praetorius in his treatise *Syntagma Musicum,* the court had approximately sixty singers, including sixteen boys, five to six castratos, thirteen altos (countertenors), fifteen tenors, and twelve basses.

Lasso was an esteemed composer throughout his adult life. In 1555, at age twenty-three, the Belgian publisher Tylman Susato printed a book of his madrigals, chansons, and motets, and in the same year the Venetian publisher Antonio Gardane issued a book of his madrigals. The following year Susato published a book of motets. Publications continued, Lasso became recognized internationally, and he attracted numerous student composers to Munich, including both Andrea and Giovanni Gabrieli. In addition, Lasso garnered numerous honors: Emperor Maximilian II designated him a nobleman in 1570, King Charles IX of France hosted him in 1573 and 1574, and Pope Gregory XIII bestowed on him the title Knight of the Golden Spur in 1574. Today Lasso is recognized as the greatest composer of the Renaissance era in Germany, and one of the greatest composers in the history of Western music. He is especially recognized for his prolific output and for his cosmopolitanism—his contributions (in Latin, Italian, French, and German) to virtually all the European genres of the late sixteenth century.

His compositional output includes at least sixty masses, almost six hundred motets, 101 Magnificats, thirteen settings of Nunc dimittis, eighteen sets of Lamentations, four Passions, approximately two hundred madrigals and pieces in other Italian genres, 150 chansons, and ninety lieder. Most of the masses are parodies of his own motets, madrigals, and chansons, and also those of other notable Franco-Flemish and Italian composers of the early and middle years of the sixteenth century. Twenty of the masses are based on his motets, examples of which are *Credidi propter, Deus in adjutorium, Ecce Maria, Locutus sum, Osculetur me, Surge propera,* and *Vinum bonum;* one mass parodies his chanson *Susanne un jour.* Another twenty masses parody madrigals and chansons by other composers, especially those from Belgium. Included are eight works based on madrigals (three by Rore, two by Willaert, and one each by Palestrina, Sebastiano Festa, and Arcadelt) and twelve works based on chansons (three by Gombert, three by Claudin de Sermisy, two each by Pierre Certon and Clemens non Papa, and one each by Monte and Pierre Sandrin). Notable among this list are those based on some of the most renowned madrigals and chansons of the sixteenth century—Palestrina's *Io son ferito ahi lasso,* Rore's *Ite rime dolenti,* Festa's *O passi sparsi,* Willaert's *Rompi de l'empio core,* Sandrin's *Doulce mémoire,* Gombert's *Tous les regretz,* Clemens non Papa's *Entre vous filles,* and Certon's *Frère Thibault.* Most of the remaining masses are based on Gregorian chant. The famous *Missa pro defunctis* for five voices is an example.

The masses range in style from those that are mainly polyphonic, with continuous point-of-imitation sections, to those that are mainly homophonic, with brief sections of imitative polyphony. An example of the former is Lasso's most famous mass, *Missa Susanne un jour*, which, as was mentioned above, is based on his own chanson. An example of the homophonic style of writing is *Missa Doulce mémoire*, based on Sandrin's chanson.

The Magnificat and Nunc dimittis settings are, like the masses, based on preexisting material. Forty of the Magnificats are parodies of motets, madrigals, and chansons and are also in the traditional modes corresponding to Gregorian chant tones and in *alternatim* style, with polyphony for the even-numbered verses. Five of the Magnificats are based on Lasso's own motets—*Omnis enim homo* (*primi toni*), *Memor esto* (*secundi toni*), *Deus in adjutorium* (*septimi toni*), *Recordare Jesu pie* (*septimi toni*), and *Aurora lucis rutilat* (*octavi toni*); nine—examples of which are *Dessus le marché d'Arras* (*primi toni*), *Mais qui pourroit* (*secundi toni*), *Si vous estes m'amie* (*sexti toni*), and *Margot labouréz les vignes* (*septimi toni*)—are based on Lasso's chansons; and twenty-two are based on motets, madrigals, and chansons by other composers. As with the masses, Lasso chose for his models many highly reputed works by the most famous composers of the sixteenth century, including *Vergine bella* by Rore (*primi toni*), *Ultimi miei sospiri* by Verdelot (*secundi toni*), *Praeter rerum seriem* by Josquin (*secundi toni*), *Mort et fortune* by Gombert (*tertii toni*), *Ancor che col partire* by Rore (*quarti toni*), *Omnis homo primum bonum vinum ponit* by Wert (*sexti toni*), and *Benedicta es caelorum regina* by Josquin (*octavi toni*). Forty additional Magnificats are in five cycles based solely on the Gregorian chant tones. Eight of the Nunc dimittis settings are parodies, including one on Lasso's chanson *Susanne un jour*, one on his madrigal *Io son si stanco*, and one on his motet *Oculi mei semper*. Five are based on Gregorian chant.

The Passions, one on each of the four Gospel accounts, are all in responsorial style. The five-voiced St Matthew and St John settings (*Passio Domini nostri Jesu Christi secundum Mattheum* and *Passio . . . secundum Johannem*) alternate duets and trios for the texts of solo characters, with full-textured polyphonic sections for the crowd (*turba*). The four-voiced St Mark and St Luke settings (*Passio . . . secundum Marcum* and *Passio . . . secundum Lucam*) alternate chant-like monody for the solo characters, with full-textured polyphonic sections for the *turba*. The Lamentations include nine settings each for four and five voices, and the Litanies include twelve settings entitled *Litaniae beatae Mariae virginis* (two for four voices, five for five voices, two for nine voices, and one each for six, eight, and ten voices), three settings entitled *Litaniae omnium sanctorum* (one each for four, five, and seven voices), and the *Litaniae deiparae beatae Mariae virginis* for four voices.

The motets, unlike the masses, Magnificats, and other large-scale sacred works, are in a wide variety of styles. The four-voiced *Jubilate Deo* is constructed of four balanced points of imitation in the style of Palestrina, with overlaps between the first and last two phrases and with a cadential demarcation between the second and third phrase; the six-voiced two-movement *Timor et tremor* is mostly homophonic, with short phrases set to varied rhythms; the six-voiced *In hora ultima* contains numerous instances of word painting, with expressive settings of "tuba" (trumpet), "cithara" (cither), "jocus" (joking), "risus" (laughter), "saltus" (leaping), and "cantus" (singing); the twenty-four pedagogical *bicinia* (duets), published in 1577, demonstrate the various polyphonic techniques of the day; the thirteen four-voiced motets that comprise the cycle *Prophetiae Sibyllarum* are homophonic and highly chromatic, with varied *note nere* rhythms reflective of Rore; the seven multimovement motets of *Psalmi Davidis poenitentiales* alternate sections of imitative polyphony with passages of homophony; and the eight-voiced *Vinum bonum* is polychoral, as in the Venetian *cori spezzati* works of Giovanni Gabrieli.

The motets also vary in terms of textual content and purpose. Several motets are set to Latin poems in praise of wine. *Vinum bonum* is indicative, with a text that begins "Vinum bonum et suave, nunquam bibi vinum tale, vinum cor laetificat" (Wine good and sweet, never have I drunk such wine, wine rejoices the heart) and ends "Ergo Christum invocemus quod laetantes hic bibemus tale vinum porrigat. Fiat, fiat, fiat" (Therefore let us pray to Christ that we can happily drink the wine he provides. So be it, so be it, so be it). Other motets are set to Classical secular Latin texts. The two-movement *Dulces exuviae - Urbem praeclaram* is a setting of Dido's Lament, and the *Prophetiae Sibyllarum* is a setting of sixteenth-century anonymous verses about the ancient Greek sibyls. Yet other motets have texts for specific ceremonial occasions: *Multarum hic resonat* celebrated the name day of Wilhelm V in 1571, the three-voiced *Haec quae ter triplici* was for an occasion in 1575 that honored Duke Albrecht's three sons, and *Sponsa quid agis* was composed for Lasso's own wedding in 1558. Finally, a few of the texts deal with a variety of unrelated secular subjects, the most famous being *Musica Dei donum optimi*, a poem about the power of music that Lasso sets in an ABACADD form (the A consists of imitative statements of the word "Musica").

The two large-scale motet cycles mentioned above warrant further discussion. The *Prophetiae Sibyllarum*, most likely composed about 1550, when Lasso was a very young man living in Naples, consists of an introduction or prologue followed by the prophecies of twelve sibyls, each indicated by name (e.g., Sibylla Persica, Sibylla Libyca, Sibylla Delphica, Sibylla Cimmeria, etc.). The text of the introduction explains the nature of both the cycle's musical style and content: "Carmina chromatico, quae audis modulata tenore, haed sunt illa, quibus nostrae olim arcane salutis bis senae intrepido, cecinerung ore sibyllae" (Chromatic songs, which you hear in a modulatory manner, these are they in which the secrets of our salvation were sung with undaunted voices by the twelve sibyls). The *Psalmi Davidis poenitentiales*, composed for Duke Albrecht in the early 1560s, consists of seven Psalm settings, each divided into multiple movements that vary in scoring. The first setting, *Domine, ne in furore tuo arguas me . . . miserere* (Psalm 6), is divided into twelve movements, with scoring for SATTB, SAT, ATTB, TB, SATT, and SSATTB. The other settings, all with similar scoring, are *Beati quorum remissae sunt iniquitates* (Psalm 31) in sixteen movements, *Domine, ne in furore tuo . . . quoniam* (Psalm 37) in twenty-five movements, *Miserere mei Deus, secundum magnam* (Psalm 50) in twenty-two movements, *Domine exaudi orationem meam: et clamor* (Psalm 101) in thirty-one movements, *De profundis clamavi ad te Domine* (Psalm 129) in ten movements, and *Domine exaudi orationem meam . . . auribus percipe* (Psalm 142) in sixteen movements.

Lasso set most motet texts only once, unlike many other composers such as Palestrina. However, the Marian texts are an exception. Lasso composed four settings of *Alma redemptoris mater* (one for five, two for six, and one for eight voices), five settings of *Ave regina coelorum* (one each for three, four, and five voices, and two for six voices), and seven settings of *Regina coeli laetare* (one for four, three for five, two for six, and one for seven voices).

The madrigals, chansons, lieder, and related secular genres by and large parallel the styles of each genre during the time. The madrigals are settings of serious poetry by Petrarch, Tasso,

Ariosto, and other poets esteemed by composers during the sixteenth century. Lasso's first and last books of madrigals are indicative. *Il primo libro di madrigali*, published in 1555, which was so popular it was reprinted a dozen times in thirty years, contains such pieces as *Occhi piangete, Mia benigna fortun'e*, the two-madrigal cycle *Cantai, hor piango*, and the six-madrigal cycle *Del freddo Rheno*—all characterized by imitative polyphony and varied rhythms that express textual content. Lasso's most popular madrigal and one of the most printed madrigals of the sixteenth century, *S'io esca vivo*, was first published in 1579. *Madrigali novamente composti* of 1587, the last madrigal publication, contains sacred or spiritual madrigals, including the six-madrigal cycle *Per aspro mar* and one of Lasso's most acclaimed madrigals, *Deh, lascia, anima*. Other spiritual madrigals were composed just six weeks before Lasso's death. They form a collection of twenty madrigals and a Latin motet, entitled *Lagrime di San Pietro* (Tears of St Peter), that relate different stages of St Peter's remorse for having denied Jesus.

The other secular pieces in Italian—the ones set to lighthearted poetry and best known today—are not madrigals but rather villanellas, canzonets, and morescas. These include *Matona mia cara, O occhi manza mia, Tutto'l dì, Chi chilichi, O bella fusa, Hai Lucia*, and *Zanni piasi patro*.

The chansons are divided between those, such as *Susanne un jour, La nuict froide et sombre*, and *La terre les eaux va beauvant*, that are basically imitative and in motet style, and those, such as *Bon jour mon coeur* and *Quand mon mary*, that are basically homophonic and in the Parisian style. Finally, the lieder include motet-like works set to sacred texts and folk-like pieces set to secular texts. Examples of the former are *Christ ist erstanden, Gross ist der Herr im heiligen Thron, Vater unser im Himmelreich*, and the five-movement *Ich ruf zu dir mein Herr und Gott*. Examples of the latter are *Audite nova der Bawr von Eselsskirchen* and *Ich weiss nur ein hübsches Meidlein*.

MASSES AND MAGNIFICATS
SELECTED AND LISTED ACCORDING TO FAMILIARITY

Missa Susanne un jour – SATTB chorus – 19 minutes.

Missa Osculetur me – SATB/SATB chorus – 21 minutes.

Missa pro defunctis – SATB chorus – 27 minutes.

Missa pro defunctis – SATTB chorus – 34 minutes.

Missa Bell' Amfitrit'altera – SATB/SATB chorus – 24 minutes.

Missa Quand'io pens'al martire – SATB chorus – 21 minutes.

Missa Qual donna attende à gloriosa fama – SATTB chorus – 21 minutes.

Missa Ite rime dolenti – SATTB chorus – 20 minutes.

Missa Doulce mémoire – SATB chorus – 18 minutes.

Missa Credidi propter – SATTB chorus – 19 minutes.

Missa Frère Thibault – SATB chorus – 16 minutes.

Magnificat Praeter rerum seriem (secundi toni) – SSATTB chorus – 13:30 minutes.

Magnificat Dessus le marché d'Arras (primi toni) – SSATTB chorus – 12 minutes.

Magnificat Vergine bella (primi toni) – SATTB chorus – 14 minutes.

Magnificat Ancor che col partire (quarti toni) – SATTB chorus – 13 minutes.

MOTETS
SELECTED AND LISTED ACCORDING TO FAMILIARITY

Timor et tremor - Exaudi Deus – SAATTB chorus – 5:30 minutes.

Musica Dei donum optimi – SSATTB chorus – 4:30 minutes.

Ave verum corpus – SSATTB chorus – 3 minutes.

Domine, ne in furore tuo arguas me . . . miserere (Psalm 6) – a twelve-movement work – SATTB chorus – 10 minutes.

Jubilate Deo – SATB chorus – 2:30 minutes.

In hora ultima – SSATTB chorus – 4 minutes.

Resonet in laudibus – SATTB chorus – 4 minutes.

Surrexit pastor bonus – SSATB chorus – 2:30 minutes.

Alma redemptoris mater – SSATB chorus – 2:30 minutes.

Vinum bonum – SATB/SATB chorus – 3 minutes.

Omnes de saba venient – SATB/SATB chorus – 2:30 minutes.

Prophetiae Sibyllarum – a thirteen-movement work – SATB chorus – 31 minutes.

Proba me Deus – SATB chorus – 3 minutes.

Justorum animae – SSATB chorus – 2:30 minutes.

Lauda Sion salvatorem - Dies enim - Quod non capis - Ecce panis angelorum – SSATTB chorus – 13:30 minutes.

Salve regina – SSATTB chorus – 2:30 minutes.

Domine, labia mea aperies – SATB chorus – 2:30 minutes.

Surgens Jesus – SSATB chorus – 3 minutes.

Domine, Dominus noster – SSATTB chorus – 2:30 minutes.

In me transierunt – SATTB chorus – 2:30 minutes.

Heroum soboles, amor orbis – SSATTB chorus – 3 minutes.

Improperium exspectavit cor meum – SATB chorus – 2:30 minutes.

MADRIGALS AND POLYPHONIC CHANSONS
SELECTED AND LISTED ACCORDING TO FAMILIARITY

S'io esca vivo – SSATTB voices – 4 minutes.

Occhi piangete – SATB voices – 2 minutes.

Deh lascia anima – SATB voices – 3 minutes.

Mia benigna fortun'e – SATTB voices – 4 minutes.

Cantai, hor piango – a two-madrigal cycle – SATTB voices – 4 minutes.

Lagrime di San Pietro – a twenty-madrigal plus one-motet cycle – SSAATTB voices – 54 minutes.

Sol'e pensoso – a two-madrigal cycle – SATTB voices – 3:30 minutes.

Io son sì stanco sotto il grave peso – a two-madrigal cycle – SATTB voices – 3:30 minutes.

Per aspro mar – a six-madrigal cycle – SATB voices – 11 minutes.

Del freddo Rheno – a six-madrigal cycle – SATB voices – 10 minutes.

Susanne un jour – SATTB voices – 3 minutes.

La nuict froide et sombre – SATB voices – 2:30 minutes.

La terre les eaux va beauvant – SSATB voices – 3 minutes.

O faible esprit – a two-chanson cycle – SATTB voices – 4:30 minutes.

Gallans qui par terre et par mer – SATB voices – 2:30 minutes.

Dessus le marché d'Arras – SSATTB voices – 3 minutes.

Ardo, si, ma non t'amo – SATTB voices – 2 minutes.

VILLANELLAS, CANZONETS, HOMOPHONIC CHANSONS, AND LIEDER
SELECTED AND LISTED ACCORDING TO FAMILIARITY

Matona mia cara – SATB voices – 2:30 minutes.

O occhi manza mia – SATB voices – 2 minutes.

O la, o che bon eccho – SATB/SATB voices – 2:30 minutes.

Tutto'l dì – SATB voices – 2 minutes.

Hai Lucia buona cosa – SATB voices – 2:15 minutes.

Chi chilichi – SSATTB voices – 2:30 minutes.

O bella fusa – SATB voices – 2 minutes.

Bon jour mon coeur – SATB voices – 1:15 minutes.

Quand mon mary vient – SATB voices – 2 minutes.

O vin en vigne – SATB voices – 2 minutes.

Im Mayen – SATTB voices – 3 minutes.

Audite nova der Bawr von Eselsskirchen – SATB voices – 2:30 minutes.

Ich weiss nur ein hübsches Meidlein – SATB voices – 2 minutes.

Ein guten Raht - In Glück und Frewd – SSATTB voices – 3:30 minutes.

JACOB REGNART CA.1540–1599

Regnart was most likely born in Douai, north of Cambrai and close to Belgium. The circumstances of his youth are unknown. However, by 1557 he was a singer in the Hofkapelle of Archduke Maximilian under Jacobus Vaet, first in Prague and then in Vienna when Maximilian was crowned Emperor Maximilian II. From 1568 to 1570 Regnart traveled in Italy to learn the Italian style, and in 1570 he returned to the Viennese Hofkapelle to serve as teacher of the choristers. In 1579 Maximilian's successor Rudolf V (who was also Rudolf II of the Holy Roman Empire) appointed Regnart *Vice-Kapellmeister* at the Hofkapelle, which had moved to Prague, and in 1582 Regnart accepted the same position at the court of Archduke Ferdinand in Innsbruck, being promoted to *Kapellmeister* in 1579. The Innsbruck Kapelle was disbanded in 1596, and Regnart returned to his former position as *Vice-Kapellmeister* in Prague, then under *Kapellmeister* Philippe de Monte. Regnart was a popular and respected composer during his lifetime. Orlando di Lasso recommended him to succeed Antonio Scandello at the Saxon court in Dresden (Regnart declined), Archduke Ferdinand designated him a nobleman, and his three books of three-voiced lieder—*Teutsche Lieder* of 1574, 1577, and 1579—were reprinted many times.

Regnart composed four books of masses, five books of motets, a cycle of eight Magnificats, two books of Italian canzonets, and seven books of German lieder. The masses and motets are in a conservative style of imitative polyphony. Many of the motets (e.g., *Angelus ad pastoris ait, O admirabile commercium*, and *Ave regina caelorum*) are scored for SATTB chorus, and a significant number of others are in two or more movements. *Pater noster* for SATB chorus is in two movements, and *Benedic, anima mea*, also for SATB chorus, is in three movements (the middle movement scored for SAT).

The three-voiced lieder mentioned above are strophic, often structured in repeat forms such as AABB or AABBCC, scored for ATB voices, and in textures that alternate sections of imitative polyphony and homophony. Examples are *Ohn dich muss ich; Mein Mund der singt; Merkt alle die in Liebes Orden; Venus, du und dein Kind;* and *Ach Gott, ein grossen Pein.*

JACOB (JACOBUS) HANDL (GALLUS) 1550–1591

Handl was born in Ribnica, Slovenia, with the family surname Petelin (which translates as "rooster" in Slovenian, "Handl" in German, and "Gallus" in Latin). He studied at a Cistercian monastery in the Lower Carniola region of Slovenia, and in about 1564 he entered the Benedictine abbey at Melk in Austria. In the mid-1570s he traveled to cities in Moravia, Bohemia, and Silesia (now the Czech Republic and southern Poland), and he may have been a singer for a short period of time at the Prague court of Emperor Rudolf V under *Kapellmeister* Philippe de Monte. Handl was appointed choirmaster to the Bishop of Olomouc in about 1579, and from 1586 until his death he served as cantor at the church of St Jan na Brzehu in Prague. He was relatively unknown outside the geographic area in which he worked. However, he was held in high esteem by those who knew his music, and he was admired for his prolific output during his short life.

He composed twenty masses, three Passions, 374 motets, and one hundred secular pieces.

Most of the masses are parodies of his own motets and those by Clemens non Papa, Vaet, Verdelot, and Lasso. Other masses parody chansons (e.g., the four-voiced *Missa Un gay bergier*) and madrigals (e.g., the six-voiced *Missa Apri la fenestra*). The double-chorus *Missa Canonica,* as its name suggests, is structured of canons: in the outer two sections of the Kyrie the second chorus echoes the first at successively shorter intervals; the Christe is a double canon scored for SA/SA; the Gloria is similarly structured and divided into three sections, with the middle section scored for TB/TB; the structure of the Credo is identical to that of the Kyrie; the Sanctus has a middle section scored for SAT/SAT; and the Agnus Dei is entirely for double chorus. The three Passions have identical texts assembled from all four Gospels.

The motets were organized according to the liturgical year and published in four books entitled *Opus musicum.* The first three books have works for Proper feast days and the fourth book has the three Passions and works for saints and Marian festivals. The style of these motets is like that of the masses, largely based on preexisting material and canonically structured. Many of the motets, including Handl's most familiar works, are also polychoral, with the two choruses juxtaposed in dialogue and with frequent echoes of phrases and exchanges of short motifs. Examples are the famous *Pater noster,* which juxtaposes upper voices against lower voices, and *Ave verum corpus.* Handl's most renowned motet, *Ecce quomodo moritur justus,* is a homophonic four-voiced funeral work.

Most of the secular repertoire was composed during the final years of Handl's life and was published in three volumes collectively entitled *Harmonie morales.* The texts of the individual pieces are mainly about moral and ethical subjects in Latin by poets such as Ovid, Virgil, Catullus, and Horace, and in the preface to the collection Handl comments that "Moralia" is a substitute for "Madrigalia" and that the pieces are "so called, [because] they shun even the shadow of indecency." Representative texts include "Si tibi gratia, si sapientia formaque detur, solo superbia destruit omnia, si comitetur" (If you have grace, if also wisdom and beauty, only pride will destroy them all) and "Quod licet, ingratum est, quod non licet, acrius urit" (What is allowed has no appeal, what is not allowed is what is most attractive). Several of the texts, such as "Quam gallina suum parit ovum" (When the hen lays her egg) and "Heroes, pugnate viri fortissimi" (Heroes, fight strongly in battle), are less serious and include onomatopoeic sounds (e.g., clucking and battle noises).

MOTETS

SELECTED AND LISTED ACCORDING TO FAMILIARITY

Pater noster – SSAA/TTBB chorus – 5 minutes.

Ecce quomodo moritur justus – SATB chorus – 3:30 minutes.

Canite tuba – TTBB chorus – 2 minutes.

Mirabile mysterium – SATTB chorus – 3:45 minutes.

O magnum mysterium – TTBB/TTBB chorus – 2:15 minutes.

Ave verum corpus – SATB/SATB chorus – 3:30 minutes.

Resonet in laudibus – SATB/SATB chorus – 2:30 minutes.

Laetentur caeli – SSA/TTB chorus – 3 minutes.

Jesu, dulcis memoria – SAA/TBB chorus – 3:30 minutes.

Duo seraphim – SATB/SATB chorus – 2:30 minutes.

Omnes de Saba venient – SATTB chorus – 2:30 minutes.

Rorate caeli – SSA/TBB chorus – 2 minutes.

Confirma hoc, Deus – TTBB chorus – 3 minutes.

Veni sancte spiritus – SATB chorus – 3:30 minutes.

Ecce concipies – SATB chorus – 2:45 minutes.

Halleluja, in deiner Auferstehung – SATB/SATB chorus – 2:15 minutes.

LEONHARD LECHNER CA.1553–1606

Lechner was born in the Tirolean area of western Austria, and it is likely that, beginning in 1563, he was a chorister under Orlando di Lasso, *Hofkapellmeister* at the court of Duke Albrecht V in Munich. In about 1570, when his voice changed, Lechner went to the court of Prince Wilhelm in Landshut, Bavaria, which was disbanded shortly after he arrived. He then traveled to cities in Bavaria and Italy, settling in Nuremberg in 1575, where he accepted a position as an assistant teacher at the grammar school of St Lorenz. In 1583 he was appointed *Kapellmeister* at the Catholic court of Count Eitelfriedrich IV in Hechingen, near Stuttgart, but he fled the court in 1585 because, as a devout Lutheran, he feared for his safety. He found refuge in Stuttgart at the court of Duke Ludwig of Württemberg, who appointed Lechner *Vice-Kapellmeister* in 1586 and *Hofkapellmeister* in 1594. The Stuttgart court flourished under Lechner's leadership, growing to a musical complement of twenty-four singers and an equal number of instrumentalists.

Lechner composed four surviving masses, one Passion, approximately fifty Latin motets, and 250 sacred and secular works in German. The masses, in the imitative style of Lasso, are all parodies: *Missa Omnia quae fecisti* and *Missa Domine Dominus noster* are based on Lasso motets, and *Missa Non e lasso martire* and *Missa Non fu mai cervo* are based on madrigals by Cipriano de Rore and Luca Marenzio, respectively. The Passion, *Historia der Passion und Leidens unsers einigen Erlösers und Seligmachers Jesu Christi,* is based on the Gospel account of St John and is completely in a through-composed polyphonic texture without solos. The Latin motets, stylistically like the masses, were all composed and published early in Lechner's life (beginning in 1575).

The German works, whether set to sacred or secular texts, are generally serious in character, polyphonic in texture, and divided into multiple movements. They are also characterized by varied rhythms such as those heard in the serious madrigals of Rore and Marenzio, which Lechner no doubt became acquainted with during his travels in Italy. In his publication *Newe Teutsche Lieder* of 1577, for instance, there are numerous madrigalistic traits: the seven-movement *Christ, der du bist der helle Tag* has frequent melismas of eighth and sixteenth notes that contrast with the general syllabic texture of half and quarter notes; the very brief single movement *Ei, wie so gar freundlich* has repetitions and exchanges of single words and notes that contrast with a prevailing imitative texture; and the three-movement *Halt hart, Herz, höchster Hort* is distinguished by phrases that are distinctly different in rhythmic character. Lechner's final and most esteemed work, composed in 1606 very shortly before his death, is a fifteen-movement cycle entitled *Deutsche Sprüche von Leben und Tod*. Like Lasso's *Lagrime di San Pietro*, which was perhaps Lechner's model (being composed at the very end of Lasso's life and in twenty movements), it is a masterful summation of expressive compositional techniques.

JOHANNES ECCARD 1553–1611

Eccard was born in Mühlhausen, southwest of Leipzig, where he studied at the local Latein-schule. In 1569 he entered the court in Weimar as a chorister, and in 1571 he transferred to the Munich court, singing under *Hofkapellmeister* Orlando di Lasso. In 1577 Eccard entered the service of the wealthy weaver and merchant Jakob Fugger in Augsburg, and in 1580 he moved to Königsberg, beginning his service as a singer in the court of Margrave Georg Friedrich of Brandenburg-Ansbach and continuing with promotions to *Vice-Kapellmeister* in 1586 and *Kapellmeister* in 1604 under Georg Friedrich's successor, Elector Joachim Friedrich. From 1608 until his death Eccard served as *Kapellmeister* at the elector's primary residence in Berlin.

His compositions include one mass, two volumes of German motets, two volumes of Lutheran chorale settings, two volumes of sacred and secular lieder, and several madrigals. The mass, composed in 1579 and dedicated to Jakob Fugger and his brothers Hans and Marcus, is a five-voiced (SSATB) parody of the well-known anonymous chanson *Mon coeur se recommende à vous*, set in the point-of-imitation style prevalent in masses and Latin motets at the time. The two volumes of chorale settings—successive publications entitled *Newe christliche Gesäng* (New Christian songs)—are settings of poetry by the theologian Ludwig Helmbold (1532–1598). The two volumes of chorale settings—*Geistlicher Lieder auf den Choral oder gemeine Kirchen Melodey durchauss gerichtet* (Sacred songs on chorale or other church melodies thoroughly approved)—contain pieces in the simple and homophonic style, with the chorale tune in the soprano voice part as a cantus firmus, and pieces in the elaborate motet style, with the chorale treated imitatively in all the voice parts and with varied rhythms as in the style of Lasso. Eccard's familiar SATTB setting of *Christ lag in Todesbanden* is in the former style, and *Übers Gebirg Maria geht* and *Der Heilig Geist vom Himmel kam* are in the latter style.

The two volumes of sacred and secular lieder—*Newe deutsche Lieder gantz lieblich zu singen, und auff allerley musicalischen Instrumenten zu gebrauchen* (New German songs completely delightful for singing, and also for the use of all sorts of instruments)—contain motet-like sacred pieces such as the five-voiced *O Herr, durch deinen bittern Todt* and *Christ ist erstanden,* and SATB secular pieces in varied polyphonic and homophonic textures. Two of the secular pieces—*A Gut Singer und ein Organist* and *Der Music Feind seind Ignoranten*—have texts about music and musicians: "A Gut Singer und ein Organist gehören wol zusammen, zu voraus wo man frölich ist" (A good singer and an organist belong together, especially where people are happy) and "Der Music Feind seind Ignoranten, wil mans recht nennen so heissens Bachanten" (The enemies of music are ignorant fools who rightly should be called drunken revelers).

Of the madrigals, *Zanni et Magnifico* is a madrigal comedy in the style of Orazio Vecchi and Adriano Banchieri, with the voices portraying specific roles—Zanni (S and A), Il Magnifico (T), La Franceschina (T), and Tedesco (B). All of Eccard's compositions are scored for voices alone; the instruments mentioned in the title of the sacred and secular lieder are to be employed *si placet,* either playing with or without voices as resources are available.

PHILIPP NICOLAI 1556–1608

Nicolai was born near Kassel, and his academic and musical education was in Mühlhausen with poet and theologian Ludwig Helmbold and the organist at St Blasius, Joachim à Burck. Between 1574 and 1579 Nicolai studied theology in Wittenberg, and in 1583 he received his first appointment as a pastor. Other clerical positions followed, concluding with his becoming pastor at the church of St Katharinen in Hamburg.

He wrote several theological treatises and assembled one volume of music—*Der Freudenspiegel des ewigen Lebens*—which was reprinted numerous times during the first decades of the seventeenth century. This volume of music contains two of the most famous Lutheran chorale tunes—*Wie schön leuchtet der Morgenstern* and *Wachet auf, ruft uns die Stimme*. The melodies of both these tunes were most likely preexisting folk melodies to which Nicolai provided sacred texts. *Wie schön leuchtet der Morgenstern* is commonly translated as "How brightly shines the morning star" and is occasionally listed as the tune *Frankfurt* in hymnals today. *Wachet auf, ruft uns die Stimme* is translated as "Wake, awake, for night is flying" or "Sleepers wake, a voice is calling" and is listed in hymnals as either *Wachet auf* or *Sleepers, wake*.

HIERONYMUS PRAETORIUS 1560–1629

Hieronymus Praetorius, no direct relation to Michael Praetorius, was born in Hamburg, where he studied with his father, Jacob (ca.1530–1586), who was the organist at the church of St Jacobi. In 1580 Hieronymus was appointed organist for the city of Erfurt, and in 1582 he returned to Hamburg to assist his father at St Jacobi. He succeeded his father in 1568 and retained the position of main organist until his own death forty-three years later. He is noted for his large output of Latin works and for his part in compiling the collection of Lutheran chorales entitled *Melodeyen Gesangbuch,* which was published in 1604 and which contained eighty-eight four-voiced settings (twenty-one of his own) for use in Hamburg's four main Lutheran churches.

Praetorius composed six masses, nine Magnificats, ninety-six Latin motets, six German motets, and twenty-one German chorales. The masses are all parodies of motets: four—*Missa Angelus ad pastores, Missa Benedicam Dominum, Missa Factum est silentium,* and *Missa Tulerunt Dominum meum*—are on his own motets, while the other two—*Missa Non auferetur sceptrum* and *Missa Paratum cor meum*—are based on motets by Jacob Meiland and Stefano Felis, respectively. Eight of the Magnificats, all for eight voices and in *alternatim* style, form a cycle, with each setting on one of the eight Gregorian chant tones. The other Magnificat, on the fifth tone, includes the Lutheran Christmas chorales *Joseph, lieber Joseph mein* and *In dulci jubilo*. The Latin motets are mostly imitative, although approximately half of them are also polychoral and contain a basso seguente part. Examples include *Angelus ad pastores* for twelve voices (there is another setting for eight voices), *Decantabat populus Israel* for twenty voices, *Exultate justi* for sixteen voices, and *Factum est silentium* for eight voices. *Gaudete omnes* for six voices and *Musica est divinum donum* for five voices are entirely constructed of point-of-imitation phrases, without polychoral effects.

Two of the German motets—*Ein Kindelein so löbelich* for eight voices and *Herr Gott dich loben wir* (the German Te Deum) for sixteen voices—are based on Lutheran chorales, with poly-choral textures. The other German motets, including *Also hat Gott die Welt geliebt* for six voices, are freely composed and purely imitative.

HANS LEO HASSLER 1564–1612

Hassler was born in Nuremberg, where he and his two brothers, Kaspar and Jakob, studied with their father, organist at the Spitalkirche from 1558 until his death in 1591, and where he may also have studied with Leonhard Lechner, who taught at the school of St Lorenz from 1575 to 1583. Hassler developed into a virtuoso organist, and in 1584 he went to Venice to improve his skills and study with Andrea Gabrieli, who had been the main organist at St Mark's Basilica begin-ning in 1566. While in Venice, Hassler also became acquainted with Gioseffo Zarlino, Claudio Merulo, and fellow student Giovanni Gabrieli. With the death of Andrea Gabrieli in 1585, Hass-ler moved to Augsburg and became *Cammerorganist* (chamber organist) to the wealthy mer-chant Octavian Fugger II, and also *stadtpfeifer* (town piper) and director of music for the city. Fugger died in 1600, and in 1601 Hassler returned to Nuremberg to serve as organist at the Frauenkirche and at the court of Rudolf II, and also as the city's director of music. His final ap-pointment, from 1608 until his death of tuberculosis at age forty-seven, was as organist and *Kapellmeister* at the Dresden court of Elector Christian II of Saxony.

Hassler is considered to be one of the two finest German composers of the Renaissance (Or-lando di Lasso is the other), and he is often compared to Lasso in terms of cosmopolitanism and overall quality of repertoire. Both composers were fluent in multiple languages, and both com-posed in a large variety of genres prevalent in Europe during the latter part of the seventeenth century. Hassler is also compared to Palestrina in composing melodic lines that are fluid in shape, and in constructing balanced formal structures, with textures that unfold in logically sat-isfying harmonic designs.

His compositions include nine masses, 120 Latin motets, ninety-five German motets, twenty-five Italian madrigals, twenty-five Italian canzonets and ballettos, and sixty German lieder. Five of the masses are parodies named for the motets and madrigals upon which they are based (e.g., *Missa super Verba mea* and *Missa Come fuggir*), while four of the masses are un-named, with no identified model. Of the parody masses, *Missa super Dixit Maria,* based on Has-sler's own motet, is the most famous. It is a relatively brief work, with a texture of alternating imitative polyphony and homophony, and with scoring for SATB voices except the Crucifixus (SA), Et resurrexit (SAT), and Et iterum venturus est cum gloria (TB). In addition, the text is set syllabically, with very few repetitions in the Gloria and Credo movements. The mass that is scored for eight voices, often titled *Missa octo vocum,* is representative of the works that are un-named (two others are scored for four-voiced chorus and one for twelve-voiced chorus). It is a polychoral work similar to the masses of Jacob Handl: the second chorus often echoes the first, the phrases of the two choruses usually shorten as each movement progresses, there are occa-sional exchanges of short motifs, and the two choruses are unified at the end of the movements. Hassler's mass is less strict, however, than those of Handl. In the closing Kyrie of Hassler's mass, for instance, the second chorus has several independent phrases.

The Latin motets, like the masses, are divided between imitative works for four to six voices and polychoral works in Venetian dialogue style for six or more voices. A number of the imitative works, those that have achieved the greatest popularity, have repeated sections of music that result in structures such as ABB. In *Dixit Maria,* for example, the point-of-imitation phrase "Dixit Maria ad angelum" (Mary said to the angel) is followed by two nearly identical sections of music set to the text "Ecce ancilla Domini, fiat mihi secundum verbum tuum" (Behold the handmaid of the Lord, be it done to me according to your word). Similarly, the first phrase in *Tu es Petrus,* "Tu es Petrus, et super hanc petram aedificabo ecclesiam meam" (You are Peter, and on this rock I will build my church), is followed by repeated sections of music to the text "et portae inferi non praevalebunt adversus eam" (and the gates of hell shall not prevail against it). Some of the polychoral motets also have repeated sections of music. In *Verbum caro factum est,* also one of Hassler's popular motets, the structure is AAB, with the first phrase of text, "Verbum caro factum est et habitavit in nobis" (The word was made flesh and dwelt among us), repeated in almost identical sections before the motet concludes. All the small-scale motets artfully combine polyphony and homophony, with occasional duet sections and changes of meter, while the polychoral motets alternate both long and short phrases. Like Palestrina, Hassler often set the same Latin texts more than once. For instance, there are seven settings of Jubilate Deo—one each for four, five, six, twelve, and fifteen voices, and two settings for eight voices.

The German motets are also in two styles—imitative works like the Latin motets (which Hassler called "fugweiss componiert") and homophonic settings. Both styles are generally based on Lutheran chorale melodies; in the imitative works the melodies pervade all the voice parts in an almost exclusively point-of-imitation texture, and in the homophonic pieces the chorale is in the soprano voice part as a cantus firmus. The imitative works, like their Latin counterparts, often have repeated sections, although the German motets are structured in this way because of the typical AAB arrangement of chorales: the *stolen* (A) is stated twice, with different text phrases, prior to the statement of the *abgesang* (B). Examples include *Ein feste Burg ist unser Gott* and *O Mensch, bewein dein Sünde gross,* both from Hassler's 1607 publication *Psalmen und Christliche Gesäng.* The final work in this publication is *Vater unser in Himmelreich,* a setting in ten movements, each of which exhibits a different compositional technique.

The secular pieces, consisting of serious and lighthearted settings in both Italian and German, are naturally in a variety of styles. Italian madrigals such as the six-voiced *Musica è lo mio core* and the seven-voiced *Anchor che la partita* emulate styles of Marenzio, although Hassler's textures are less dense and not as rhythmically varied. The Italian canzonets, all for four voices, also emulate styles of Italian composers. Most of the German lieder, such as *Nun fanget an ein guts Liedlein* (Now let us begin a nice little song) and *Ihr musici* (You musicians), alternate lengthy passages of imitative polyphony with short passages of homophony. Other lieder, such as *Tanzen und Springen, Singen und Klingen* (Dance and leap, sing and chime), are homophonic ballettos with *fa la la* refrains. *Mein G'müth ist mir verwirret* (My soul has perplexed me) has a particularly interesting history. Its soprano part was taken by an unknown composer and set to the text "Herzlich thut mich verlangen" (My desire is willing), which was then adapted by Johannes Crüger to "O Haupt voll Blut und Wunden" (generally translated as "O sacred head now wounded"), one of the most frequently arranged Lutheran chorale melodies during the Baroque era and one of the best-known hymns of the modern era.

MASSES
SELECTED AND LISTED ACCORDING TO FAMILIARITY

Missa super Dixit Maria – SATB chorus – 18 minutes.

Missa octo vocum – SATB/SATB chorus – 22 minutes.

LATIN MOTETS
SELECTED AND LISTED ACCORDING TO FAMILIARITY

Dixit Maria (Luke 1:38) – SATB chorus – 3:15 minutes.

Verbum caro factum est (1 John:14) – SSATTB chorus – 3 minutes.

Tu es Petrus (Matthew 16:18) – SATB chorus – 3 minutes.

Cantate Domino (Psalm 96:1–3) – SATB chorus – 3 minutes.

Cantate Domino (Psalm 96:1–3) – SSATB chorus – 3 minutes.

Angelus ad pastores ait (Luke 2:8–11) – SATB chorus – 3 minutes.

Ave maris stella – SATB chorus – 2:30 minutes.

Jubilate Deo (Psalm 100) – SATB/SATB chorus – 2:30 minutes.

GERMAN MOTETS
SELECTED AND LISTED ACCORDING TO FAMILIARITY

O Mensch, bewein dein Sünde gross – SATB chorus – 5 minutes.

Aus tieffer Noth – SATB chorus – 4 minutes.

Ein feste Burg ist unser Gott – SATB chorus – 4:30 minutes.

LIEDER
SELECTED AND LISTED ACCORDING TO FAMILIARITY

Tanzen und Springen, Singen und Klingen – SSATB voices – 2 minutes.

Ihr musici – SSATTB voices – 2:30 minutes.

O Jungfrau, dein' Gestalt – SATB voices – 2:30 minutes.

Ach, weh des Leiden – SSATB voices – 2 minutes.

Nun fanget an ein guts Liedlein – SATB voices – 2:15 minutes.

GREGOR AICHINGER CA.1564–1628

Aichinger was born in Regensburg, northeast of Munich. Nothing is known about his youth or musical training, although it is likely that he sang as a chorister under Orlando di Lasso at the court of Albrecht V in Munich. In 1578 he enrolled as a student at the University of Ingolstadt, where he met and became friends with Jakob Fugger (1567–1626), and in 1584 he was appointed organist to Fugger's uncle, also named Jakob (1542–1598), in Augsburg. Aichinger held this position for the remainder of his life, while also making frequent trips to Italy to study both music and theology: in 1584 he studied with Giovanni Gabrieli in Venice, in 1586 he was a student at the University of Siena, and in 1599 he was a student at the University of Perugia.

His choral works were published in twenty-four books of Latin sacred music, two books of German sacred music, and one book of Italian secular music. The early Latin works are mostly in the imitative style of Lasso, with occasional passages of homophony, exchanges of short motifs between voices, and *note nere* rhythms. The two-movement SSATB motet *Noe, noe, noe - Attollite portas,* for instance, has extended points of imitation, duet passages, brief homophonic sections, and polychoral-like exchanges of very short phrases; *Factus est repente - Confirma hoc Deus* (SATB) combines conservative point-of-imitation phrases with motivic repetitions and widely varying rhythmic values; *Ave regina coelorum* (SATB) is mostly homophonic, with only an opening imitative phrase; and *Ubi est Abel* (SAB) alternates imitative phrases with very short repetitive motifs.

The later Latin works, which include six Magnificat settings, are similar in style to the early works. However, most of them are scored for three voices and an accompanying basso continuo part that is not independent. Examples from the publication *Cantiones ecclesiasticae* of 1607, all with basso continuo, include *Exsurgens Maria* for SST, *Ave gratia plena* for ATB, *Tres sunt qui testimonium* for ATB, and the Magnificats *Primi toni* for SST, *Secundi toni* for ATB, *Quarti toni* for SSB, *Sexti toni* for SAB, and *Octavi toni* for SAT. In addition, there is a parody Magnificat, *Ascendit Deus,* for SST. Aichinger also composed vocal concertos (i.e., soloistic works in the *seconda prattica* style and with an independent basso continuo part). Representative examples are *Angelus Domini* (SB), *Adoro te supplex* (TT), *Duo seraphim* (SSA), and *Salve regina* (TTB). A few of the vocal concertos (e.g., *Angelus Domini descendit* and *Paratum cor meum*) have violin parts as well.

CHRISTOPH DEMANTIUS 1567–1643

Demantius was born in Reichenberg, Bohemia (now Liberec, Czech Republic), where he most likely studied at the local Lateinschule. It is possible that he also studied at the school of St Lorenz in Bautzen. He enrolled at the University of Wittenberg in 1593, and in 1594 or 1595 he transferred to the University of Leipzig. In 1597 he was appointed to two positions in the city of Zittau—*Kantor* of the Johanneskirche, where Melchior Franck was a chorister, and director of the Singechor of the Johanneum Gymnasium—and in 1604 he was appointed *Kantor* at Freiburg Cathedral, where he remained for thirty-nine years.

Demantius composed approximately five books of Latin masses, Magnificats, and motets; two books of German motets and chorale settings; one Passion; and nine books of secular music. In addition, he wrote a treatise—*Isagoge artis musicae . . . kurtze Anleitung, recht und leicht singen zu lernen* (A short course of instruction on how to learn to sing correctly and easily)—that was very popular and went through ten printings between 1607 and 1671. Its final two printings contained an alphabetical dictionary of 175 musical terms, the first of its kind in Germany.

All of the sacred music composed by Demantius is in a conservative a cappella *prima prattica* style. There are no vocal concertos, and only one publication, *Triades Sioniae* of 1619, contains a basso continuo part (which is not independent but only supportive of the polyphonic vocal parts). It is unusual that a composer who lived well into the seventeenth century (his birth and death dates are identical to those of Claudio Monteverdi) did not embrace *seconda prattica* styles. However, he felt that the new styles were artistically inferior; in the preface to *Triades Sioniae* he expressed his opinion that the "concertante" style was a whim of fashion and basically worthless.

The sacred Latin works can be represented by the publication *Trias precum vespertinarum* of 1602, a collection of the Vespers Psalms *Deus in adiutorium* (Psalm 70) for five voices, and *Dixit Dominus* (Psalm 110), *Lauda Jerusalem* (Psalm 148), *Laudate Dominum* (Psalm 117), and *Laudate pueri* (Psalm 113) for six voices, followed by a Magnificat for three and five voices and a setting of the benediction *Benedicamus Domino* (Bless we the Lord, we give thanks to the Lord) for six voices. The Psalms are mostly homophonic, with syllabic settings of text, chant incipits, and some polychoral effects between high and low voices. The Magnificat is in *alternatim* style. The end of the publication's title states that the voices should be accompanied by "quibusvis instrumentorum musicorum generibus communi" (whatever kind of common musical instruments); this was the practice of instrumental "Unterstützung des Singechor" (support for the choir) endorsed by the municipal council of Zittau and widely practiced throughout Germany during the Renaissance era.

The most extensive of the sacred German publications is *Corona harmonica,* a collection of sixty-nine motets and a Te Deum published in 1610. The motets are characterized by short phrases of text set imitatively and by expressive word painting. In *Denn wer sich selbst erhöret* (Luke 18:14), for example, the words "erhöret" (exalts) and "erniedrigt" (humbles) are set to ascending and descending scalar passages, and in *Und wie Moses in der Wüsten* (John 3:14–15) the word "Schlang" (serpent) is set to a melismatic passage. Other motets from this collection include *Steh auf und nimm das Kindelein* (Matthew 2:20) and *Es ward eine Stille in dem Himmel* (Revelation 12:7–10). Two additional German motets not in *Corona harmonica* merit mention— *Das ist mir lieb* (Psalm 116) and *Weissagung des Leidens und Sterbens Jesu Christi* (Isaiah 53). Both are masterful works of Renaissance polyphony comparable to the late notable works of Heinrich Schütz. *Das ist mir lieb* is one of sixteen settings of Psalm 116 commissioned by the wealthy merchant Burckhard Grossmann in the year 1616 and published under the title *Angst der Hellen und Friede der Seelen* (Fear of hell and peace of the soul). Four other settings in this publication are by Michael Praetorius, Melchior Franck, Schütz, and Johann Hermann Schein. Demantius's lengthy setting (lasting approximately twelve minutes) is scored for five voices (SSATB) and is divided into four movements. *Weissagung des Leidens und Sterbens Jesu Christi* (Prophecy of the suffering and death of Jesus Christ) is a three-movement work of approximately eleven minutes' duration scored for six voices.

The Passion—*Deutsche Passion, nach dem Evangelisten S Johanne*—is the last entirely polyphonic Passion to be composed during the Renaissance era. It is scored for SSATTB voices and is in three movements, the first of which begins with an introduction to the Passion story similar to the "Introitus" or "Eingang" choruses that introduce the historiae of Schütz—"Höret das Leiden unseres Herren Jesu Christi aus dem Evangelisten Johanne" (Hear the suffering of our Lord Jesus Christ from the Gospel of St John). Similarly, the Passion ends with the text "Wir glauben, lieber Herr, mehre unsern Glauben. Amen" (We believe, dear Lord, increase our belief. Amen).

MELCHIOR VULPIUS CA.1570–1615

Vulpius was born in Wasungen, between Frankfurt and Leipzig, where he studied at the local Lateinschule. In 1588 he continued his studies at the Lateinschule in Speyer, in 1589 he was appointed *Kantor* at the Lateinschule in Schleusingen, and from 1596 until his death he held the same position at the Lateinschule in Weimar.

He composed approximately two hundred Latin and German motets, one Passion, and four hundred chorale settings, all for the Lutheran Church and all in a conservative *prima prattica* style without basso continuo accompaniment. Like his contemporary Christoph Demantius, Vulpius was not interested in the new soloistic developments of the seventeenth century. The Latin works were published in three books of *Cantionum sacrarum* (1602, 1603, and 1610) and one book entitled *Canticum Beatissimae Virginis Mariae* (1605). Most of the motets in these publications are scored for six or more voices, including *Factum est* and *De profundis* for six voices, *Exaltabo te, Domine* for eight voices, and *Gloria laus et honor* for twelve voices. The voice parts in this latter motet are distributed into three choruses (SSAT/SATB/ATBB) and the texture alternates between long imitative phrases and short passages in dialogue. In addition, there are varied rhythms that highlight expressive characteristics of the text. The German motets were also published in three collections—two of *Deutscher sontäglicher evangelischer Sprüche* (1612 and 1614) and one entitled *Kirchen Geseng und geistliche Lieder* (1604). The 1612 and 1614 publications are complementary in that the first volume contains works "von Advent bis auff Trinitatis" (from Advent to Trinity Sunday), and the other contains works "von Trinitatis bis auff Advent" (from Trinity Sunday to Advent). Examples from the 1612 publication, almost all for four voices (SATB), include *Jesus sprach zu dem Blinden* (Luke 18:41–43), *Herr, ich bin nicht wert* (Matthew 8:18), *Entsetzt euch nicht* (Mark 16:6–7), *Aber das Kind wuchs* (Luke 2:40), and *Es kommt aber die Zeit* (John 16:2–3). All these motets are simpler than the Latin works in both scoring and texture; scoring is typically for four voice parts, and textures include more numerous and lengthier passages of homophony.

The Passion—*Das Leiden und Sterben . . . Jesu Christi aus dem heiligen Evangelisten Matthäo*—is responsorial, with solo parts for an evangelist and important characters, and choral parts of four to six voices for *turba* and framing choruses. The chorale settings, for which Vulpius is best known, include several newly composed tunes that became standard in the Lutheran Church and that are included in many modern-day Protestant hymnals. *Christus der ist mein Leben* (Christ who is my life), which is the most popular, is sometimes listed as *Mein Leben* or *Bremen* and set to texts as varied as "Another year is dawning," "I worship thee, Lord Jesus," "Abide, O dearest Jesus," and "God is my strong salvation." Other chorale tunes include *Gelobet sei Gott*, which is sometimes listed as *O filii et filiae* (O sons and daughters), and *Das neugeborne Kindelein* (sometimes set to "Come, holy spirit").

NIKOLAUS ZANGIUS CA.1570–1618

Zangius was born in Königs Wusterhausen, southeast of Berlin. Nothing is known of his youth, musical training, or professional activity until 1597, when he was appointed *Kapellmeister* to Prince Bishop Philipp Sigismund in Iburg, which lies approximately halfway between Hamburg and Frankfurt. In 1599 he began service at the Marienkirche in Danzig, first as *Vice-Kapellmeister* and shortly thereafter as *Kapellmeister*, and in 1612 he succeeded Johannes Eccard as *Kapellmeister* to the Elector of Brandenburg in Berlin.

Zangius composed five books of Latin and German motets, one Magnificat, and one book of secular German lieder. Two of the motet books—*Harmonia votiva pro felici fato* (1602) and *Cantiones sacrae* (1611)—contain mostly works in Latin, while the other motet books—*Schöne newe ausserlesene geistliche und weltliche Lieder* (1594), *Etliche schöne teutsche geistliche und weltliche Lieder* (1597), and *Kurtz weilige newe teutsche weltliche Lieder* (1603)—contain works set to German texts. The works in all the books are in a *prima prattica* imitative style, with notable rhythmic variety, occasional polychoral effects, and frequent instances of word painting. An example is the macaronic motet (in Latin and German) *Congratulamini nunc omnes in Deo salutari nostro* from the 1611 publication. Scored for SSATTB chorus, the motet is in three movements. The first is a short section of imitative polyphony devoted to the text's title, "We all now rejoice in God our salvation"; the second, in German, is lengthier and alternates sections of imitative polyphony to the text "Maria, du zarte Jungfrau fein, hast uns geboren ein feines Kindelein" (Mary, you sweet virgin, have borne us a dainty little child) with polychoral-like homophony to the text "Jesus ist der Name sein" (Jesus is his name); the third movement, also in German, is a dialogue—single voices address Joseph with the questions "Was da? " (What is it?) and "Wo ist das neugeborne Kindelein?" (Where is the newborn little child?), while the entire ensemble answers with "Zu Bethlehem da ligt es in ein Krippelein" (In Bethlehem he lies in a little crib). This entire movement is basically homophonic and syllabic, with the exception of a melisma that expresses the verb "wiegen" (cradle).

MICHAEL PRAETORIUS 1571–1621

Michael Praetorius, no direct relation to Hieronymus Praetorius, was born in Creuzburg an der Werra, near Eisenach. He received his initial musical education from his father, a Lutheran pastor and an amateur musician, who early in Michael's life moved the family to Torgau. In 1582 Michael entered the gymnasium in Zerbst, in 1583 he continued his studies at the University of Frankfurt, and in 1587, at the age of sixteen, he was appointed organist at the church of St Marien. He relocated to Wolfenbüttel in about 1592, without a position, and in 1595 he became organist to Duke Heinrich Julius. He was promoted to court *Kapellmeister* in 1604 and retained this position until his death, although he traveled extensively and took several temporary positions in cities around Germany. In 1613 he served as temporary *Vice-Kapellmeister* at the electoral court in Prague, in 1614 he held the position of *Kapellmeister* to the Bishop of Magdeburg, in 1616 he worked at the court of Margrave Christian Wilhelm of Brandenburg in Halle with court organist Samuel Scheidt, in 1618 he went with Scheidt and Heinrich Schütz to reorganize the kapelle at Magdeburg Cathedral, and in 1619 the three composer/organists dedicated a new organ for the Margrave in Bayreuth.

Praetorius composed approximately fifteen hundred sacred vocal works published in twenty-two volumes during his lifetime. Nine of the volumes, issued from 1605 to 1610, are part of a series entitled *Musae Sioniae,* which is devoted to chorale and Lutheran liturgy settings in a variety of styles and scorings. Volumes one through four consist mostly of double chorus chorale settings, with texts exclusively in German and textures characterized by dialogue of short phrases between the two choruses. Examples include *In dulci jubilo, Christ lag in Todesbanden, Ein feste Burg ist unser Gott,* and *Von Himmel hoch,* the latter of which is strophic and divided into three movements. In addition to double chorus motets, volume two contains several compositions in the same style for three choruses, including *Ich ruf zu dir Herr Jesu Christ,* and volume three contains one work for nine voices (SATB/SATTB), *Nimm von uns Herr Gott.* Volume five consists of simple and short liturgy settings (German *missae,* Vespers hymns, and pieces for Advent and Christmas) scored for two to seven voices, and volume six consists of short, homophonic, and strophic four-voiced settings of chorales and freely composed pieces, including the famous *Es ist ein Ros entsprungen* (Lo, how a rose e'er blooming) and *Psallite unigenito,* a brief macaronic piece that alternates the Latin phrase "Psallite unigenito Christo Dei filio, psallite redemptori Domino, puerulo jacenti in praesepio" (Sing to Christ the only-begotten Son of God, sing to the redeemer Lord, the child lying in the manger) with the German text "Ein kleines Kindelein liegt in dem Krippelein; alle liebe Engelein dienen dem Kindelein und singen ihm fein" (A tiny child lies in the little crib; all the lovely angels serve the little child and sing sweetly to him). Volumes seven and eight are similar to volume six, and volume nine has multiple settings of several of the most familiar Lutheran chorales, each scored for two and three voices, with several scored for SATB.

Other volumes of sacred vocal works, each titled and published separately and each in the same styles as *Musae Sioniae,* include *Missodia Sionia* of 1611, which contains Kyrie and Gloria movements in Greek and Latin; *Hymnodia Sionia* of 1611, which contains short imitative motets set to Latin texts for two to eight voices; and *Eulogodia Sionia* of 1611, which contains Latin motets for special occasions during the liturgical year, including *Salve rex noster, Regina coeli,* and *Salve regina.* The 1611 publication *Megalynodia Sionia* contains Magnificat settings in *alternatim* style. Three of these settings—*Magnificat super Angelus ad Pastores ait, Magnificat super Ecce Maria et Sydus ex claro,* and *Magnificat Surrexit pastor bonus*—are parodies of preexisting motets (*Magnificat super Ecce Maria et Sydus ex claro* is based on two motets by Orlando di Lasso—*Ecce Maria* and *Sydus ex claro*), and all three settings have chorales interpolated into the Latin Magnificat text (i.e., each verse of newly composed polyphony is followed by a chorale). In the *Magnificat super Angelus ad pastores ait,* the chorale "Puer natus in Bethlehem" follows the verse "Et exultavit spiritus meus," and "In natili Domini" follows "Quia respexit humilitatem." The other chorales are "Herz, Sinn und unser G'müte," "Heut' lobt die werte Christenheit," "Vom Himmel kömmt," and "Parvulus nobis nascitur." *Urania* of 1613 contains more settings of chorales. Some, such as the SATB setting of *Christ lag in Todesbanden,* are strophic and in a typical AAB (*stolen* and *abgesang*) format. Others, such as *Allein Gott in der Höh sei Ehr,* are for double chorus, and yet others, for example *Meine Seele erhebt den Herrn,* are for triple chorus.

Praetorius's final publications contain works in *seconda prattica* styles—vocal concertos scored for soloists, with figured bass parts for basso continuo and with separate instrumental parts. Motets in *Polyhymnia Caduceatrix et Panegyrica* of 1619 include *Ein feste Burg ist unser Gott,* for two tenors and two basses with basso continuo; *Wenn wir in höchsten Nöten sein,* for two sopranos and two tenors plus four unspecified instrumental parts and basso continuo; *In dulci jubilo,* for four SATB choruses, four-part unspecified instrumental ensemble, and basso continuo; and *Wachet auf, ruft uns die Stimme,* for three sopranos, two altos, two tenors, and one bass, with basso continuo and specific scoring for string and brass instruments. This latter motet has some Monteverdi-like figural scoring for the instruments. The publication *Polyhymnia Exercitatrix* of 1620 also consists of vocal concertos, including *Ach Gott vom Himmel sieh darein,* for two sopranos, two basses, four unspecified instruments, and basso continuo. All four soloists and two of the instruments have fast passage work (*passaggi*) and exchanges of short motifs as in the motets by Schütz. Finally, the publication *Puericinium* of 1621 contains selected chorale settings for the liturgical year, each lengthy and elaborately scored. *Wie schön leuchtet der Morgenstern,* for instance, is in two movements and scored for triple chorus—the first for four-part instruments, the second for four sopranos and *colla parte* instruments, and the third for AATTB chorus and basso continuo.

A notable work not contained in the publications described above is *Das ist mir lieb,* a setting of Psalm 116 for SSATB that was commissioned by Burckhard Grossmann, a wealthy merchant from Jena, for a collection published in the year 1616 as *Angst der Hellen und Friede der Seelen.* Other contributing composers to the collection include Christoph Demantius, Melchior Franck, Heinrich Schütz, and Johann Hermann Schein.

While Praetorius is known for his numerous compositions, several of which are among the most widely performed of the German Renaissance repertoire, he is most famous for his treatise *Syntagma musicum,* a three-volume study of church music and performance practice. The first volume, written in Latin, is in two parts—the history of sacred music (beginning with that of Jewish, Greek, and Roman cultures) and the history of secular music (with quotes from Homer, Plato, and Sophocles). Also included is a description of ancient instruments. The second volume, written in German and subtitled "De organographia," is a thorough presentation of all known instruments of the time, with discussion of tunings, ranges, and timbres. A later supplement to this volume contains forty-two woodcuts of instruments. The third volume, also in German, discusses all the sacred and secular vocal genres of the time, musical theory and notation, and performance practice. This third volume also contains a dictionary of musical terms and an instructional guide for the realization of basso continuo parts.

SACRED WORKS
SELECTED AND LISTED ACCORDING TO FAMILIARITY

Es ist ein Ros entsprungen – SATB chorus – 3 minutes.

Psallite unigenito – SATB chorus – 1:15 minutes.

Resonet in laudibus – SSATTB chorus – 3 minutes.

In dulci jubilo – SATB/SATB chorus – 3 minutes.

In dulci jubilo – SSAT/ATBB chorus – 3 minutes.

Allein Gott in der Höh sei Ehr – SATTB chorus – 3 minutes.

Nun bitten wir den heiligen Geist – SATB/SATB chorus – 3 minutes.

Gott der Vater wohn uns bei – SATB/SATB chorus – 3:30 minutes.

Allein Gott in der Höh sei Ehr – SATB/SATB chorus – 2:30 minutes.

Aus tiefer Not schrei ich zu dir – SATB/SATB chorus – 4 minutes.

Komm heiliger Geist, Herre Gott – SATB/SATB chorus – 4 minutes.

Christ lag in Todesbanden – SATB/SATB chorus – 3:45 minutes.

Ein feste Burg ist unser Gott – SATB/SATB chorus – 3 minutes.

Von Himmel hoch – SATB/SATB chorus – 8 minutes.

Cantate Domino – SSAT/ATBB chorus – 4 minutes.

Pater noster, qui es in coelis – ATTB/ATTB chorus – 4:30 minutes.

Omnis mundis jocundeter – SATB chorus – 2 minutes.

Salve rex noster – SATB chorus – 4 minutes.

MELCHIOR FRANCK CA.1579–1639

Franck was born in Zittau on the eastern border of Germany near Dresden, where he likely encountered Christoph Demantius, *Kapellmeister* of the Johanneskirche and director of the Johanneum Gymnasium Singechor from 1597 until 1604. In 1600 Franck became a singer at the church of St Anna in Augsburg, and the following year he moved to Nuremberg to teach at the Egidienkirche. While in both Augsburg and Nuremberg it is probable that he came into contact with Hans Leo Hassler, who held positions in Augsburg from 1585 to 1601 and in Nuremberg thereafter. From 1602 or 1603 until his death approximately thirty-six years later Franck served as *Kapellmeister* to Duke Johann Casimir and his successor, Johann Ernst in Coburg.

Franck composed more than twelve hundred works, including one mass, thirty-three Magnificats, 560 motets, and numerous chorale settings, vocal concertos, and lieder. The motets, published in forty collections between 1601 and 1636 (more than one collection per year), are Franck's most significant works. A majority are in a *prima prattica* style and in German, although the motets in four collections have basso continuo parts, and the Latin compositions have German translations. The collection entitled *Contrapuncti compositi deutscher Psalmen und anderer geistlichen Kirchengesäng* of 1602 contains twenty-four four-voiced motets (Franck composed twenty-two of them and Christoph Buel composed two) that are characterized by point-of-imitation phrases and occasional word painting. An example of the strict point-of-imitation technique is *Vater Unser im Himmelreich,* which incorporates the Lutheran chorale into the soprano voice part. Examples of the imitative technique with word painting include the four-voice setting of *Aus tiefer Not schrei ich zu dir,* in which the lower voices express the phrase "Herr Gott, erhör mein Rufen" (Lord God, hear my call) as if calling to God in heaven from earth below, and *Ich ruf zu dir, Herr Jesu Christ* (I call to you, Lord Jesus Christ), which has an extended melisma on the word "klagen" (bewail). The collection *Gemmulae evangeliorum musicae* of 1623 contains short, homophonic settings of biblical texts and Lutheran chorales meant for small, inexperienced choirs, churches with depleted forces because of the Thirty Years War, and home devotional use. An example is *Also hat Gott die Welt geliebt* (John 2:16). The collection *Geistliche Gesäng und Melodeyen* (1608) contains some of Franck's most notable motets, including numerous settings of texts from the Song of Solomon. Three of these have become popular—*Du bist aller Dinge schön* (4:7–11), *Meine Schwester, liebe Braut* (4:12–16), and *Ich sucht des Nachts* (3:1–4). The scoring of all three motets is for SSATTB chorus, text settings are mainly syllabic, and textures are basically imitative, with occasional passages of homophony, polychoral effects, exchanges of short motifs, and word painting. Three other notable motets set to texts from the Song of Solomon, all scored for SATB/SATB, are *Steh auf, meine Freundin* (2:10–14), *Ich schlafe, aber mein Herz* (5:2–6), and *Was ist dein Freund für andern Freunden* (5:9–16).

Apart from the published collections mentioned above, Franck was one of sixteen composers who composed a setting of *Das ist mir lieb* (Psalm 116) for the 1616 publication *Angst der Hellen und Friede der Seelen,* commissioned by the wealthy merchant from Jena, Burckhard Grossmann. Christoph Demantius, Michael Praetorius, Heinrich Schütz, and Johann Hermann Schein also contributed to this publication.

The secular music, published in thirteen collections between 1602 and 1623, consists mostly of homophonic, strophic, and syllabic settings of folk-like texts. Examples from *Musik-alischer Bergkreyen* of 1602 include *Das Bergwerk wolln wir preisen, So wünsch ich ihr, Wie möcht ich frölich werden,* and *Ach schönes Jungfräulein.* All begin with a solo tenor phrase and continue with scoring for SATB voices. In addition, all have three verses and are in an AAB structure. A few secular pieces are motet-like, with scoring for larger forces, alternating sections of imitative polyphony and homophony, and occasional word painting. Examples include *O dass ich dich, mein Bruder* for SSATB and *Fahet uns die Füchse* for SSATTB, this latter piece containing expressive melismas on the word "Hirsch" (stag). Finally, Franck composed eleven quodlibets, most published in 1622. Examples, all for SATB voices, include *Compania, Nun fanget an,* and *Lasst uns fröhlich singen.* The latter two pieces have solfege and *fa la la* syllables intermixed with the narrative texts.

SACRED WORKS
SELECTED AND LISTED ACCORDING TO FAMILIARITY

Vater unser im Himmelreich – SATB chorus – 5 minutes.

Du bist aller Dinge schön – SSATB chorus – 3:15 minutes.

Meine Schwester, liebe Braut – SSATTB chorus – 3 minutes.

Ich sucht des Nachts – SSATTB chorus – 2:45 minutes.

Steh auf, meine Freundin – SATB/SATB chorus – 4 minutes.

Ich schlafe, aber mein Herz – SATB/SATB chorus – 4 minutes.

Was ist dein Freund für andern Freunden – SATB/SATB chorus –
     3:45 minutes.

Aus tiefer Not schrei ich zu dir – SATB chorus – 3 minutes. There is another
     setting of this text for SATTB chorus.

Ich ruf zu dir, Herr Jesu Christ – SATB chorus – 3 minutes.

Also hat Gott die Welt geliebt – SATB chorus – 2 minutes.

Der Herr ist mein getreuer Hirt – SATB chorus – 2:30 minutes.

Herr, nun lässest du deinen Diener – SSAB/ATTB chorus – 3 minutes.

Meine Seele erhebt (German Magnificat) – SATB chorus – 3 minutes.

SECULAR WORKS
SELECTED AND LISTED ACCORDING TO FAMILIARITY

Das Bergwerk wolln wir preisen – SATB voices – 2:30 minutes.

So wünsch ich ihr – SATB voices – 2:30 minutes.

Wie möcht ich frölich werden – SATB voices – 2:30 minutes.

Nun fanget an – SATB voices – 3 minutes.

Lasst uns fröhlich singen – SATB voices – 3 minutes.

⚮ ENGLAND ⚮

The Renaissance era in England was significantly different from the era in other countries because of the simple fact that England had little foreign influence. English Renaissance composers, except for one (Richard Dering), did not study abroad, and only one foreign composer of any distinction (Alfonso Ferrabosco) was employed in England. Some musical scores from other countries were imported, but these were basically limited to Italian madrigals at the end of the sixteenth century. The insular nature of England's musical climate resulted in a relatively late beginning and a very late end to the era. At the beginning of the sixteenth century, English composers such as Robert Fayrfax, William Cornysh, and John Taverner were still writing in Medieval styles, and during the first several decades of the seventeenth century, composers were either ignorant of or uninterested in *seconda prattica* developments. Consequently, while foreign composers such as Josquin Desprez and Pierre de la Rue were initiating the Renaissance era with new imitative textures during the 1520s, and Claudio Monteverdi and Heinrich Schütz were embracing new Baroque era forms and genres during the early years of the seventeenth century, English composers were adhering to such older forms and structures as Medieval polyphony at the beginning of the Renaissance and *prima prattica* styles and structures at the beginning of the Baroque. The Renaissance did not begin in England until the latter years of King Henry VIII's turbulent reign (which ended in 1547), and the era did not come to a complete end until the death of Thomas Tomkins in the 1650s.

Renaissance England was also unique in a number of other ways. For one, there was little effort to notate composers' biographical information, including birth dates and places and musical training. This kind of information was insignificant to people of the time, even for composers such as Christopher Tye and Thomas Tallis, who both became important members of the royal court and therefore whose activities during their childhood could have been recorded for historical record. On the other hand, English composers were interested in formal academic education. Of the forty-one composers who wrote significant works during the era and who are discussed in this section of the Renaissance, twenty-one of them received degrees from either Oxford or Cambridge universities (eleven from Oxford and ten from Cambridge). One composer, Thomas Bateson, received a degree from Trinity College, Dublin.

England was like France in having a center of musical activity at the royal court. Thirteen English composers were singers and/or organists at the Chapel Royal, and a number of other composers were instrumentalists for the kings and queens and their children. Interestingly, the designation for a singer of the Chapel Royal was "Gentleman," which was one of the highest musical ranks one could attain. England was like both France and Germany in dealing with the conflicting musical and religious circumstances of Roman Catholicism and the new Protestant faith. In England, Henry VII (1485–1509) was Catholic; Henry VIII (1509–1547), while in name a Protestant, still favored Catholic church music; Edward VI (1547–1553) was decidedly Anglican and supported the musical reforms of Oliver Cromwell and Thomas Cranmer; Mary Tudor (1553–1558) was Catholic and returned the court to traditional Latin genres; Elizabeth I (1558–1603) was an Anglican who encouraged the composition of both English anthems and Latin motets, both in simple and complex styles; and James I (1603–1625) and Charles I (1625–1649) were both Anglicans who supported only English church music.

The sacred Catholic genres consisted mainly of the mass, Magnificat, and motet. Hymn-like Psalm settings for Anglican psalters were also composed, but not in significant quantities by notable composers. The masses were composed without Kyries (which were occasionally written separately), the Magnificats were almost exclusively in *alternatim* style, and the motets were generally long polyphonic votive antiphons early in the era and shorter imitative works thereafter. The sacred Anglican genres consisted of the Service and the anthem. Most of the Services, like the masses in that they were musical settings of regular liturgical texts, were given Latin titles but were set to English texts. The Te Deum was sung to "We praise thee, O God," the Benedictus to "Blessed be the Lord God of Israel," the Creed to "I believe in one God," the Magnificat to "My soul doth magnify the Lord," and the Nunc dimittis to "Lord, now lettest thou thy servant depart in peace." Other settings of Service music included the Venite sung to "O come, let us sing unto the Lord," Jubilate to "Be joyful in the Lord, all ye lands," Kyrie to "Lord, have mercy upon us," Sanctus to "Holy, holy, holy, Lord God of hosts," and Gloria to "Glory be to God on high." The anthems were in two formats—full and verse. The full anthems were scored for chorus alone and were either small-scale basically homophonic pieces for four- or five-part chorus, or large-scale motet-like works with overlapping points of imitation. The verse anthems were scored for soloists, chorus, and either organ or ensemble of viols.

The scoring for much of the sacred music, both in Latin and English, was for SSATB chorus, with the various voice parts called treble, mean, contratenor, tenor, and bass. The treble signified a part for boys' voices, or choristers, with a high range or tessitura; the mean was a part for choristers that was a bit lower or average in range (common); the contratenor part was for male altos; and the tenor and bass parts were in traditional ranges for men. The singers were divided into two ensembles that faced each other in the area of the church, called the choir, located between the nave and the high altar; the ensemble on the right side of the choir was called *decani* (the dean's side of the altar), while the ensemble on the left side was called *cantoris* (the cantor's side of the altar). Composers often indicated in the scores of anthems and Services that one or the other side was to sing alone (signified by the abbreviation *dec.* or *can.*) or that both sides were to sing together (signified by the term *full*). Soloists in both anthems and Services were members of and sang from the chorus, and organ accompaniment was common, whether specifically scored or not. Organists played from vocal bass parts and improvised chords from the harmonies produced by the upper parts, or they wrote out reductions of the vocal parts in scores. Examples of these reductions exist in the famous *Batten Organbook*.

The secular genres consisted of the part song, madrigal, canzonet, ballett, and air (generally spelled "ayer" at that time). The part song—which was a short, homophonic, and strophic piece with verses and a refrain (called a burden)—existed early in the era, whereas the other genres were predominant from the 1580s until the 1650s. The madrigal, canzonet, and ballett were modeled on Italian counterparts that were imported to England and published in collections such as *Musica transalpina* (Music across the Alps) in 1588 and *Italian Madrigalls Englished* in 1590. *Musica transalpina,* edited by Nicholas Yonge, a collector of Italian madrigal books, contained English translations of five-voiced madrigals by Alfonso Ferrabosco and Marenzio and a number of four-voiced madrigals by Palestrina. *Italian Madrigalls Englished,* edited by Thomas Watson, a leader of the British elite, contained English translations of more five-voiced madrigals by Marenzio. A second volume of *Musica transalpina* followed in 1597 along with Thomas Morley's *Canzonets or Little Short Songs to Foure Voyces: celected out of the Best and Approved Italian Authors.* This latter collection featured canzonets and ballettos by Orazio Vecchi, Giovanni Croce, and Felice Anerio. A similar collection, *Madrigals to Five Voyces: celected out of the Best Approved Italian Authors,* followed the next year, and in 1601 Morley published *The Triumphes of Oriana*—a book of English madrigals by native composers based directly on the Italian collection *Il Trionfo di Dori* published in 1592. Both publications contain a similar number of six-voiced madrigals, canzonets, and ballettos or balletts by representative composers of the time, and all the pieces in both collections end with a similar text phrase—"Viva la bella Dori" (Long live fair Dori) in the Italian collection, and "Long live fair Oriana" in the English collection.

The English madrigal was like its Italian counterpart in being characterized by imitative polyphony, with word painting being a significant feature in the late years of the era. There were some striking differences, however. The English madrigal was more tonal and less rhythmically diverse, with word painting that was more obvious. The ballett, which was the most popular secular form in England, was like the Italian ballettos by Gastoldi, with homophonic textures, repeated musical passages, dance-like rhythms, and *fa la la* refrains. The canzonet was also homophonic, but unlike the ballett, it was more song-like (i.e., the topmost voice part was melodically prominent and the lower voice parts were accompanimental in nature, often with brief portions of imitation). The madrigals, canzonets, and balletts were scored for voices alone but were published with the expectation that performance would involve an ensemble of viols, either with singers *colla parte* or in place of singers. Indeed, the titles of virtually all publications contained the phrase "apt for both voices and viols." The air, which was a development of the canzonet, was first a song for solo voice with lute accompaniment (called a lute song) and later a vocal ensemble piece with all voice parts texted. Composers of airs generally set them both in solo and ensemble formats.

Two features of notation in England are particularly important and relevant to performance. The first, called "voice exchange," relates to the frequent practice of scoring two voice parts in the same range or tessitura, with melodic material exchanged imitatively between the two at the same pitch level. This practice of notation, which was most common in two soprano parts, was intended to produce an interchange of identical or similar timbres. Thus the two parts were sung by voices compatible in vocal quality, not by voices of differing qualities. That is, one part was not sung by sopranos (boy choristers) and the other by altos (male contratenors), nor was one sung by high sopranos (trebles) and the other by lower sopranos (mean). Instead, both parts were sung by voices of the same tessitura and vocal quality, either treble or mean, or a mixture of both on each part. The compatibility of vocal timbres between two parts participating in voice exchange is especially critical in the performance of pieces such as the famous *O pray for the peace of Jerusalem* by Thomas Tomkins, which is scored for SSTB, not SATB as is frequently indicated in present-day publications.

The second important notational feature in England during the Renaissance, called "cross relation" or "false relation," is the dissonance that occurs with the simultaneous or near simultaneous sounding of two notes a half step apart from each other. This dissonance is generally caused when a note in one voice part is the lowered seventh degree of the scale (approached melodically from below), while a note in another voice part is the raised seventh degree of the scale (approached melodically from above). Both notes are generally the same pitch, the one approached from below marked with a flat sign and the one approached from above not marked (or marked with a natural sign), or the lower one not marked and the higher one marked with a sharp sign. The effect caused by the cross relation, comparable to that caused by *musica ficta* and *musica recta* in music by continental composers, was not particularly dissonant to the ear, because the tuning during the Renaissance was more varied than today; during the Renaissance the raised pitch was slightly higher and the lowered pitch was slightly lower than those pitches would sound in today's equal-tempered tuning system.

The major composers of the era, those generally noted for both their sacred and secular music, are Robert Fayrfax, William Cornysh, John Taverner, Christopher Tye, Thomas Tallis, John Sheppard, William Byrd, Thomas Morley, Thomas Tomkins, Thomas Weelkes, Richard Dering, and Orlando Gibbons. Composers of lesser significance who wrote and were noted mostly for their sacred music are Robert Johnson, John Marbeck, Richard Farrant, William Mundy, Robert Parsons, Robert White, Nathaniel Giles, John Bull, Adrian Batten, Robert Ramsey, and John Hilton. Composers whose relative fame came mostly from their secular music are Henry VIII, Thomas Greaves, Michael Cavendish, George Kirbye, John Bennet, Thomas Vautor, John Farmer, Thomas Bateson, Francis Pilkington, Michael East, John Ward, and Thomas Ravenscroft. In addition, John Dowland, Thomas Campion, Robert Jones, and Thomas Ford were significant composers of airs, and John Wilbye was one of the major composers of madrigals. Finally, Giles Farnaby was a minor composer recognized for both his sacred and secular music.

Not all noteworthy choral repertoire of the English Renaissance is identified with a known composer. The authorship of several popular and frequently performed anthems, for instance, is unknown. These include the sixteenth-century *Rejoice in the Lord alway,* with text from Philippians 4:4–7; *O Lord, the maker of all thing* of about 1548, with text from the 1545 edition of the *King's Primer;* and the Easter Gradual *This is the day which the Lord hath made* of about 1600, with text from Psalm 118:24.

ROBERT FAYRFAX 1464–1521

Fayrfax was born in the village of Deeping Gate, in Lincolnshire County on the northeast coast of England. Nothing is known of his youth, musical training, or professional activity until he entered the Chapel Royal in 1497 as a lay clerk (a paid adult singer) under Henry VII. He received a bachelor of music degree from Cambridge University in 1501, and doctoral degrees from Cambridge in 1504 and Oxford University in 1511. In 1509 he sang for the coronation of Henry VIII, and he remained in the service of the Chapel Royal until his death, although there is speculation that he also served in some capacity at St Albans Abbey, where several of his manuscripts are housed and where he was buried.

Fayrfax composed five surviving mass cycles (another cycle, entitled *Missa Sponsus amat sponsam,* is incomplete), two Magnificats, eight complete motets (two others, *Gaude flore virginali* and *O bone Jesu,* have only one voice part each that is extant), and seven part songs (an eighth, *Myn hartys lust,* exists with only a bass part). The scoring for the majority of the sacred works, typical of the time, is for SSATB (treble, mean, contratenor, tenor, and bass). The masses all consist of only four movements of the Ordinary—Gloria, Credo, Sanctus, and Agnus Dei—and each movement begins with a head motif. In addition, all the masses but one are based on a Gregorian chant, used as a cantus firmus in the tenor voice part and scored in rhythmic values only slightly longer than the other voice parts. Also, most of the masses have sections of music that are varied in scoring. In the Gloria of *Missa O bone Jesu,* for instance, "Laudamus te" is for SAT, "Domini fili unigenite" for TTB, "Qui tollis peccata mundi" for SATB, and "Qui sedes ad dexteram patris" for TB. The textures of the masses are mostly polyphonic, although not imitative except for occasional passages between two voices, and some movements (e.g., the Sanctus in *Missa O bone Jesu*) have sparse text underlays.

The Magnificats are in *alternatim* style and vary in scoring as in the masses. In the *Magnificat super Regali ex progenie,* for example, each verse is scored for different forces than either the verse before or the verse after. Also like the masses, the Magnificats have some imitative writing for two voices.

The motets, all of which are votive antiphons, are more complex than the masses and Magnificats. Many of the motets have multiple meter changes, dense polyphonic textures, short homophonic passages or chords with fermatas at the ends of major sections of music, and ostinatos as in the motets of Josquin Desprez. Notable motets with these characteristics are *Ave lumen gratiae, Salve regina,* and *Ave Dei patris filia.*

The part songs are mainly settings of poetry about unrequited love scored for two or three solo voices and characterized by triple rhythms within simple duple meters, textures that are polyphonic but not imitative, and lengthy melismatic passages at the ends of phrases.

MASSES, MAGNIFICATS, AND MOTETS
COMPLETE

Missa O bone Jesu – ATTBB chorus – 41 minutes.

Missa O quam glorifica – SSATB chorus – 48 minutes.

Missa Regali ex progenie – SSATB chorus – 40 minutes.

Missa Tecum principium – SSATB chorus – 50 minutes.

Missa Albanus – SSATB chorus – 38 minutes.

Magnificat super Regali ex progenie – SSATB chorus – 15 minutes.

Magnificat super O bone Jesu – SSATB chorus – 14:30 minutes.

Aeternae laudis lilium – SSATB chorus – 11:30 minutes.

Ave Dei patris filia – SSATB chorus – 11:45 minutes.

Lauda vivi alpha – SSATB chorus – 16 minutes.

Maria plena virtute – SSATB chorus – 13 minutes.

O Maria Deo grata – SSATB chorus – 15:30 minutes. The tenor part of this motet is lost.

Salve regina – SSATB chorus – 12:30 minutes.

PART SONGS
COMPLETE

Alas for lak – ATB voices – 2 minutes.

I love, loved – ATB voices – 2:30 minutes.

Most clere of colour – ATB voices – 2:15 minutes.

Sumwhat musing – ATB voices – 3:30 minutes. This part song exists in two versions that are almost identical.

That was my woo – TB voices – 3 minutes.

To complayne me – ATB voices – 3:30 minutes.

Benedicite! What dremyd I – ATB voices – 3 minutes.

WILLIAM CORNYSH D.1523

No information exists about the birth or life of Cornysh before his presence at the royal court in 1493. It is known that at that time he acted in a number of dramatic productions or pageants. Several years later he entered the Chapel Royal under Henry VII as a Gentleman, and in 1509, with the death of Henry VII and the coronation of Henry VIII, he was appointed Master of the Children. He retained this position for the remainder of his life, while also directing court entertainments for important state occasions, including visits of the court to France in 1513 and 1520 and the visit of Austrian Emperor Charles V to England in 1522. Given his experience with court entertainment, it is not surprising that Cornysh is best known for his secular music.

His compositions include five surviving motets, one Magnificat, and sixteen part songs. The motets are like those of Robert Fayrfax, with whom Cornysh most certainly interacted; they have dense polyphonic textures and brief homophonic passages or chords with fermatas at the ends of major sections of music. In addition, like the masses of Fayrfax, they have extended phrases for two and three voices, and the text underlay is sparse. Two of Corynsh's motets, *Salve regina* and *Stabat mater*, are also long votive antiphons scored for five voices (treble, mean, contratenor, tenor, and bass). Two other motets, *Ave Maria mater Dei* and *Gaude virgo mater Christi*, are short and scored for four voices. The fifth motet, *Gaude flore virginali*, is a fragment scored for six voices. The *Magnificat* is almost identical in structure and style to those of Fayrfax; it is in *alternatim* style and scored overall for five voices, with large sections of the work for a variety of forces, including SSA, ATB, SSTT, and TTB. Cornysh's *Magnificat* is notable for virtuoso melodic writing at the closing text "sicut erat in principio."

Most of the part songs (e.g., *Blow thi horne hunter*) are short, homophonic, strophic, scored for three voices, and structured of verses and a refrain. *My love sche morneth* and *Ah robyn, gentle robyn*, Cornysh's most famous part song, are slightly different in that two voices repeat a phrase (burden) canonically while the third voice sings two verses over it. *Woefully arrayed* is different in that it is scored for four voices and is motet-like in length and texture. Its text is also sacred, although not liturgical.

SACRED WORKS
SELECTED AND LISTED ACCORDING TO FAMILIARITY

Ave Maria, mater Dei – SATB chorus – 3:30 minutes.

Salve regina – SSATB chorus – 14 minutes.

Stabat mater – SSATB chorus – 16:30 minutes.

Gaude virgo mater Christi – SATB chorus – 5:30 minutes.

Magnificat – SSATB chorus – 14 minutes.

SECULAR WORKS
SELECTED AND LISTED ACCORDING TO FAMILIARITY

Ah robyn, gentle robyn – ATB voices – 2:30 minutes.

Blow thi horne hunter – ATB voices – 3 minutes.

Woefully arrayed – SATB voices – 8:30 minutes.

Yow and I and Amyas – ATB voices – 2:30 minutes.

My love sche morneth – ATB voices – 2:30 minutes.

JOHN TAVERNER CA.1490–1545

Taverner was born near Boston in Lincolnshire County, close to the birthplace of Robert Fayrfax. There is speculation that Taverner was a chorister at the collegiate church in Tattershall, but no documentation about his life exists before his employment as a lay clerk there beginning in 1524. In 1526 he was appointed Master of the Choristers at the newly formed Cardinal College (now Christ Church) of Oxford University, and in 1530 he returned to Lincolnshire to serve as a lay clerk and Master of the Choristers at the parish church of St Botolph. This church had a large musical establishment comparable to those at major cathedrals and courts, with eight to ten choristers and ten to twelve lay clerks.

Taverner composed eight mass cycles, nine separate mass movements, three Magnificats, one Te Deum, and two part songs (two other secular pieces are solo songs). The mass cycles, typical of the time, include all portions of the Ordinary except the Kyrie and are generally based on chants from either the Gregorian repertory or the Sarum rite. The chants, employed as a cantus firmus, appear mainly in the top voice part, not the tenor as was routine in continental masses of the time, although in two of Taverner's masses—*Missa Corona spinea* and *Missa O Michael*—the cantus firmi do appear in the tenor voice parts. The chants as cantus firmi were also generally notated three times in each movement, with each statement set in successively shorter note values, a technique similar to that utilized by John Dunstable in his isorhythmic motets. This technique is evident in Taverner's early *Missa Gloria tibi trinitas,* based on the first antiphon of first Vespers for Trinity Sunday in the Sarum rite and characterized by a head motif at the beginning of each movement. This mass became famous for its setting of the "In nomine" portion of the Benedictus that many later composers, most notably Henry Purcell, parodied in instrumental consort music. Similar to *Missa Gloria tibi trinitas* in the distribution of the cantus firmi are *Missa Corona spinea,* which has a cantus firmus of unknown origin but was composed for the feast of the Holy Crown of Thorns, and *Missa O Michael,* which is based on two chants—those for the feast of St Michael in Monte Tumba and the feast of the Apparition of St Michael. Taverner's most famous mass, called *The Western Wynde* (or *Wind*), is the first English mass to be based on a secular melody. As is the case with its continental counterpart L'homme armé, the origin of the Western Wynde melody is unknown, although it probably was a favorite in King Henry VIII's court, since Christopher Tye and John Sheppard also composed masses based on it. Taverner's setting states the tune thirty-six times throughout the four movements of the mass; twenty-one of these statements are in the top voice part (the mean), ten are in the tenor voice, and five are in the bass.

The mass cycles scored for five and six voices were generally notated in clefs that indicated treble, mean, contratenor, tenor (or two tenors), and bass, although the pitch level was low and most modern editions notate the parts for soprano, alto, two tenors, and one or two basses. These larger-scaled masses were also composed in a more florid style than the four-part works, with occasional long melismas or passages with sparse text underlay. Whether scored for four, five, or six voices, the textures of the masses consist of continuous polyphony with little imitation, frequent ostinatos, and varied scoring. In *Missa Gloria tibi trinitas* the opening of the Credo is scored for SSATTB, the "Et in unum Dominum Jesum Christum" for SB, the "Et incarnatus est" for ATTB, and the "Crucifixus" for SSB. The SB duet is particularly noteworthy for its long melisma notated in continuous triple rhythms within a duple meter, and the SSB trio is exceptional for its fast and scalar passage work. The *Western Wynde* mass is also scored for varying vocal forces and has occasional virtuosic vocal passages (e.g., the SAB trio and TB duet in the Agnus Dei).

The separate mass movements include two Kyries, three Christes, and one Sanctus, Hosanna, Benedictus, and Agnus Dei. Of the two Kyries, one is entitled *Leroy* in reference to the king. The Magnificats—one each for four, five, and six voices—are unique in that they use the Gregorian Magnificat chant as a cantus firmus. Otherwise, Taverner's Magnificats are similar to other settings of the early English Renaissance: they are in *alternatim* style, with the even-numbered verses set polyphonically; they have long melismas at the ends of verses; and they vary in scoring. The *Te Deum* is similarly in *alternatim* style, although it is not varied in scoring and, being generally syllabic, has few melismas.

The motets, also based on chants, include twelve long votive antiphons in the style of Fayrfax and William Cornysh. Works such as *Ave Dei patris filia* and *Gaude plurimum,* Taverner's most popular motet during the sixteenth century, have long sections of free (i.e., nonimitative) polyphony, with occasional duet and trio passages, and with fermatas at the ends of major sections of music. Other motets, generally shorter, have phrases that are more imitative and syllabic. Examples are *O splendor gloriae* and *Ave Maria.*

The part songs include one (*In women is rest peas and pacience*) scored for ST voices characterized by long virtuosic melismas, and one (*The Bella*) that is homophonic and scored for SSTT voices.

MASS CYCLES AND MASS MOVEMENTS
SELECTED AND LISTED ACCORDING TO FAMILIARITY

Western Wynde Mass – SATB chorus – 32 minutes.

Missa Gloria tibi trinitas – SSATTB chorus – 35 minutes.

Missa Corona spinea – SSATTB chorus – 39 minutes.

Missa Christi Jesu, pastor bone (also called *Missa Sancti Wilhelme, pastor bone* after the twelfth-century St William of York, and *Small Devotion Mass*) – SATTB chorus – 25:30 minutes. The mass is a parody of Taverner's motet *Christe Jesu, pastor bone,* which was originally sung to the text "Sancti Wilhelme, pastor bone" at Cardinal College but was changed to "Christe Jesu, pastor bone" after Cardinal Wolsey, founder of Cardinal College and Archbishop of York, lost favor with King Henry VIII.

Missa Mater Christi – SATTB chorus – 34 minutes.

Missa O Michael – SSATTB chorus – 37 minutes.

Mean Mass – SATB chorus – 24 minutes.

Kyrie Leroy – SATB chorus – 3:45 minutes.

OTHER SACRED WORKS
SELECTED AND LISTED ACCORDING TO FAMILIARITY

Magnificat (called *Magnificat Nesciens mater*) – AATB chorus – 11:30 minutes.

Magnificat – SSATB chorus – 12 minutes.

Te Deum – SATTB chorus – 13 minutes.

Dum transisset sabbatum (version one) – SSATB chorus – 7 minutes.

In pace in idipsum – SATB chorus – 6 minutes.

Christe Jesu, pastor bone (also called *Sancti Wilhelme, pastor bone*) – SATTB chorus – 3:30 minutes.

Gaude plurimum – SSATB chorus – 13:15 minutes.

Ave Dei patris filia – SSATB chorus – 13 minutes.

O splendor gloriae – SSATB chorus – 10 minutes.

Ave Maria – SSATB chorus – 2 minutes.

HENRY VIII 1491–1547

King Henry VIII, son of King Henry VII, was born in Greenwich and educated in both liturgical and musical studies. From the time that he was crowned in 1509 at age eighteen until his death thirty-eight years later, music was an important part of the royal court. He increased the musical resources substantially, he sang and danced in musical entertainments, and he played the organ, lute, and virginal.

In addition, he composed thirty-four vocal and instrumental works, including two masses (both of which are lost), one surviving motet (*Quam pulchra es* for three voices), and twenty part songs. Two of these part songs—*Withowt dyscord* and *O my hart*—not only were popular during Henry's life but also continued to be popular throughout the sixteenth century. *Withowt dyscord* is scored for ATB voices and is in discant style (i.e., the upper part is melodically more important and more decorated than the lower parts); it is also strophic, with five verses. *O my hart* is also for ATB voices but is entirely homophonic. Other part songs include *Pastyme with good companye* and *Alac, alac what shall I do,* both for ATB voices, and *Alas, what shall I do for love* for SATB.

ROBERT JOHNSON CA.1500–1560

Robert Johnson, not to be confused with the lutenist of the same name who lived from about 1583 to 1633, was born in Duns, Scotland, where he became a Catholic priest. It is likely, though not certain, that he converted to the Protestant faith and fled to York, England, in the early 1530s. It is also likely that he spent the final years of his life in Windsor, just outside London. No documentation exists about these assumptions or about his employment, however, and the only evidence of his life comes from notes in the late-sixteenth-century St Andrews Psalter and from manuscripts of his compositions.

He composed ten motets, portions of two Anglican Services, two English anthems, and eight part songs. The motets are divided between long votive antiphons and shorter works set to a variety of biblical texts. The votive antiphons, such as *Ave Dei patris filia* and the five-voiced setting of *Dum transisset sabbatum,* are comparable to similar works by Robert Fayrfax, William Cornysh, and John Taverner, with multiple sections of music, lengthy melismas (or insufficient text underlay) at the ends of these sections, varied scoring, and textures of thick polyphony. The shorter works include a four-voiced setting of *Dum transisset sabbatum,* which is imitative except for a tenor cantus firmus based on the Gregorian chant; *Gaude Maria virgo,* also scored for four voices and in an imitative texture; and two Psalm settings. *Gaude Maria virgo* is interesting in that it has extended two-voiced passages that are similar in style to the late motets of Josquin Desprez. The Psalm settings—*Deus misereatur nostri* (Psalm 47) for four voices, and two settings of *Domine in virtute tua* (Psalm 11), both for five voices—are also imitative, although with fewer melismas than the other motets. Two additional Latin motets—*Dicant nunc Judei* and *Laudes*

Deo—are scored for only two voices. The Anglican Services include a homophonic and syllabic setting of the Te Deum, Benedictus, Creed, Magnificat, and Nunc dimittis. Of the anthems, it is assumed that *O eternal God* for four voices is the first extant setting of a sacred text in English for use in the new Anglican Church. Like many other later anthems, it is short, simple in style, mainly homophonic, and syllabic. Johnson's other anthem, similar in style, is *I geve you a new commaundement.* The part songs include *Defyled is my name,* supposedly composed for Anne Boleyn, and *Ty the mare tomboy.*

CHRISTOPHER TYE CA.1505–1573

Tye was most likely born in the vicinity of Cambridge and Ely, where the family name was common at the beginning of the sixteenth century. Nothing is known of his youth or training before his completion of a bachelor's degree in music from Cambridge University in 1536. In 1537 he became a lay clerk at King's College, and in about 1541 he was appointed *Magister choristarum* (Master of the Choristers) and organist at Ely Cathedral. This was at the time when Richard Cox (ca.1500–1581), one of the chief proponents of religious reform, was named Archdeacon of the cathedral. In 1545 Tye received a doctorate in music from Cambridge, and during the next several years, while maintaining his positions at Ely Cathedral, he likely had a significant presence at the royal court; this is assumed to be the case because Cox was tutor to Prince Edward, who wrote a poem about Tye and who regularly referred to Tye as "our music's lecturer." Furthermore, in the preface to his *The Actes of the Apostles,* dedicated to Prince Edward (i.e., King Edward VI in 1553 when *The Actes* were published), Tye called himself one of the "Gentylmen of hys grace's most honourable chappell." Tye was also listed as one of the "gentylmen of our chapel" at Mary Tudor's coronation in 1553. In the late 1550s he took holy orders, and in 1560 he was ordained a priest. He resigned his positions at Ely Cathedral in 1561 and was succeeded by Robert White, and for the remainder of his life he served as a cleric at Doddington-cum-Marche in the Isle of Ely.

Tye composed three mass cycles, one mass movement, two Magnificats and a Te Deum that survive in only one voice part, fourteen Latin motets (nine of which are complete), one Anglican Service, and sixteen anthems plus the collection of pieces entitled *The Actes of the Apostles.* The mass cycles are typical of the time in having no Kyrie and in being based on preexisting material. *Missa Euge bone* is most likely based on a lost chant antiphon of the same name, used as cantus firmus material in the soprano voice part and as a head motif at the beginning of the Gloria, Credo, Sanctus, and Agnus Dei. The mass also incorporates a phrase from Tye's motet *Quaesumus omnipotens:* music for the motet phrase "militamus miseri" is quoted exactly at the "Jesu Christe" segment of the mass phrase "Domine fili unigenite, Jesu Christe." This mass is also distinctive in having six successive fermatas over the opening six chords of the Sanctus—one each for the six syllables of "Sanctus, sanctus, sanctus." The *Mean Mass* (also called the *Peterhouse Mass* because the partbooks of the mass are housed in Peterhouse College at Cambridge University) has no identifiable cantus firmus model, but it is assumed that one is used in the highest voice part (the mean) of the mass. The *Western Wynd* is Tye's best-known mass and is comparable in scoring (four voices) and style (short imitative duet and trio passages within an overall nonimitative polyphonic texture) to the masses set to the same tune by John Taverner and John Sheppard. Tye pays homage to Taverner by emulating Taverner's downward scalar passages at the beginning of the Sanctus and by inserting a virtuosic passage in the tenor part of the Benedictus. Otherwise, Tye quotes the tune only in the mean voice part, quoting it there twenty-nine times, while Taverner quoted it thirty-six times in the mean, tenor, and bass parts. The one separate mass movement is a Kyrie based on the chant *Orbis factor.*

The motets include several settings of Psalms, which during the reign of Mary Tudor replaced the votive antiphons of her father Henry VIII and brother Edward VI. *Miserere mei Deus* (Psalm 51) is a long work with varied scoring (e.g., a central section for ATB) and an imitative texture; *Cantate Domino* (Psalm 96) is also a long imitative work but without varied scoring (it is SAATTB throughout); and *Omnes gentes plaudite manibus* (Psalm 47) is shorter and more syllabic. Other notable motets are *Gloria, laus et honor,* which is relatively syllabic except for a short melismatic and virtuosic contratenor passage, and *Peccavimus cum patribus,* which, with fermatas at the ends of major sections of music, resembles the votive antiphons of Taverner.

The anthems are divided between large-scale works that resemble motets and small-scale pieces that are syllabic and homophonic. The former style is represented by *Christ rising again from the dead; Give alms of thy goods; To father, son, and holy ghost; From the depth I called to thee;* and *I will exalt thee, O Lord.* This latter anthem is divided into two major sections, each of which consists of imitative phrases that alternate with brief passages of homophony. Examples of the homophonic style are seen in *Blessed are all they that fear the Lord, O Lord of hosts* and in the fourteen anthems contained in the collection *The Actes of the Apostles.* This collection contains syllabic, strophic (from ten to twenty verses), and mostly homophonic settings of metrical poetry derived from the first fourteen chapters of the New Testament. The settings were meant for private devotional use, and, as was described by Tye in the collection's preface, they were "to synge and also to play upon the Lute, very necessarye for studentes after theyr studye . . . and also for all Christians that cannot synge, to read the good and Godlye Storyes of the lyves of Christ hys Appostles." The comment regarding the lute most likely indicated accompaniment of one or more voices singing only the top voice part or accompaniment *colla parte* with voices on multiple parts.

MASSES AND MOTETS
SELECTED AND LISTED ACCORDING TO FAMILIARITY

Western Wynd Mass – SATB chorus – 27 minutes.

Missa Euge bone – SSAATB chorus – 26 minutes.

Mean Mass (also called *Peterhouse Mass*) – SAATB chorus – 26 minutes. The tenor part of the mass was lost and has been reconstructed by modern-day editors.

Kyrie Orbis factor – SATB chorus – 3:30 minutes.

Gloria, laus et honor – SSAT chorus – 3 minutes.

Miserere mei Deus – SATTB chorus – 9 minutes.

Quaesumus omnipotens – SSAATB chorus – 6:30 minutes.

Omnes gentes plaudite manibus – SSATB chorus – 4 minutes.

Peccavimus cum patribus – SAATTBB chorus – 9 minutes.

In pace in idipsum – SATB chorus – 4:30 minutes.

Cantate Domino – SAATBB chorus – 8 minutes.

Ad te clamamus exules (Salve regina) – ATTBB chorus – 3 minutes.

ANTHEMS
SELECTED AND LISTED ACCORDING TO FAMILIARITY

The Actes of the Apostles – SATB voices – 1 to 7 or 8 minutes per anthem, depending upon the number of verses sung.

Give alms of thy goods – SATB chorus – 2 minutes.

Blessed are all they that fear the Lord – SATB chorus – 3:30 minutes.

Deliver us, good Lord – SATB chorus – 3:30 minutes.

To Father, Son, and Holy Ghost – SSATB chorus – 3 minutes.

I will exalt thee, O Lord – SATB chorus – 6 minutes.

Christ rising again from the dead – SATTBB chorus – 4:30 minutes.

From the depth I called to thee – SATB chorus – 5:30 minutes.

O God, be merciful unto us – SATB chorus – 2 minutes.

My trust, O Lord, in thee is grounded – SSATB chorus – 4 minutes.

THOMAS TALLIS CA.1505–1585

Tallis was probably born in Kent, the region of his family ancestors, and he also probably received his early musical training there. His first employment was as organist at the Benedictine priory in Dover beginning in 1530 and as organist and singer at the church of St Mary-at-Hill in London beginning in 1537. From 1538 to 1540 he served as a singer at Waltham Abbey in Essex, and for the next three years he was a singer at Canterbury Cathedral. Then in 1543 he entered the Chapel Royal as a Gentleman, where he served as singer, organist, and composer for the remainder of his long life. This service was under the final four years of Henry VIII's reign, the entire reigns of Edward VI and Mary Tudor, and a little more than half the forty-five-year reign of Elizabeth I. While the length of this service is notable, his success at meeting the expectations of the royalty's fluctuating religious affiliations and musical desires is impressive. Tallis was also successful in achieving the first-ever exclusive license in England to print and publish music. This was granted in 1575 by Elizabeth I to the partnership of Tallis and William Byrd, who together soon thereafter published an anthology of thirty-four Latin motets (seventeen by each composer) entitled *Cantiones, quae ab argumento sacrae vocantur* (Songs which are called sacred on account of their texts), generally referred to simply as *Cantiones sacrae*.

Tallis composed two masses, one Magnificat, two sets of Lamentations, forty Latin motets, three Anglican Services (plus portions of other Services), twenty-four English anthems, and four part songs. The masses represent the two major styles of composition during the middle years of the sixteenth century. *Missa Puer natus est nobis* for seven voices, composed in 1554 for Mary Tudor, is in the mold of older Latin works. It is based on a Gregorian chant that is used as a cantus firmus in long notes, and the cantus firmus is set forth in rhythmic values according to a notational puzzle and is scored as a canon in the Agnus Dei. The particular chant, the Introit for Christmas Day from Isaiah 9:6—"Puer natus est nobis, et filius datus est nobis cujus imperium super humerum ejus" (A boy is born to us, and a son is given whose government is upon his shoulder)—was most likely chosen because Mary Tudor was believed to be pregnant at the time of the mass's composition. The other mass, an untitled work for four voices, is syllabic, homophonic, and freely composed (i.e., it is not based on preexisting material).

The Magnificat, like the larger of the two masses, is in a traditional Catholic style—*alternatim*, with polyphony set to the even-numbered verses. It is unique in being scored only for men's voices (TTBB). The Lamentations are also scored for men's voices and, following traditional practice, are settings of the lessons for Maundy Thursday at Matins that include the Hebrew letters of the alphabet. The first set begins with a section of music to the text "Incipit lamentatio Jeremiae prophetae" (Here begins the lamentation of Jeremiah the prophet), followed by sections set to Aleph (verse one), Beth (verse two), and the closing text, "Jerusalem, Jerusalem, convertere ad Dominum Deum tuum" (Jerusalem, Jerusalem, return to the Lord your God). All of the six sections of music are basically imitative statements of the single words or phrases of text, with the verses receiving extended treatment and containing passages of homophony. The second set of Lamentations, similar in style, begins with the text "De lamentatione Jeremiae prophetae" (The lamentation of Jeremiah the prophet) and continues with sections of music devoted to Ghimel (verse three), Daleth (verse four), He (verse five), and the closing text from the first set. The two sets of Lamentations, while consecutive in terms of verses, are separate works and in different tonalities.

The Latin motets, which span Tallis's entire career, are in a variety of styles. The very early works such as *Ave Dei patris* and *Salve intemerata* are votive antiphons like those of Robert Fayrfax, William Cornysh, and John Taverner: they are in two movements and scored overall for five voices, with sections of music for varying forces and with long polyphonic phrases. The motets composed under Mary Tudor's reign, such as *Loquebantur variis linguis* and *Gaude gloriosa Dei mater,* are large-scale multimovement works based on Gregorian chant and characterized by continuous imitative polyphony. *Gaude gloriosa Dei mater,* Tallis's most famous motet from the Mary Tudor period, is divided into three large sections—the first devoted to verses one and two of text, the second to verses three and four, and the third to verses five through nine. Most of the verses are scored for a different grouping of voices (only verses three and four are the same), and the final verse is the only one that begins with all six voice parts simultaneously. *Te lucis ante terminum* is in *alternatim* style, with the even-numbered verses of text set homophonically. The later motets, those composed for Elizabeth I and published in *Cantiones sacrae* of 1575, are generally shorter and are characterized by varying degrees of syllabic or melismatic text setting and also varying degrees of imitative polyphony or homophony. *Salvator mundi,* the first motet in the publication, is almost entirely imitative and is divided between melismatic and syllabic textures; *In manus tuas* is more vertically conceived and is almost entirely syllabic; *In ieiunio et fletu* begins homophonically and syllabically but ends with imitative and melismatic phrases; and *O nata lux de lumine* is entirely homophonic and syllabic. Later motets also include large-scale settings of Psalms such as *Laudate Dominum* (Psalm 117) and *Domine quis habitabit* (Psalm 15)—both characterized by lengthy points of imitation.

Tallis's most famous motet, his forty-voiced *Spem in alium,* was apparently inspired by Alessandro Striggio's forty-voiced motet *Ecce beatam lucem,* performed during Striggio's visit to the royal court in 1567. According to an apparent eyewitness, Thomas Wateridge, "it was wondered whether none of our Englishmen coud sett as good a song. Tallice beinge very skilful was felt to try ye Matter, wch he did and made one of forty partes wch was songe in the longe gallery at Arundell house." This account is most likely true, since the court of Arundell had a rich musical establishment at the time and since a manuscript copy of *Spem in alium* is in the Arundell library. Moreover, the balconies at Arundell lend themselves to Tallis's arrangement of forty voices distributed into eight five-voiced choirs and to the likelihood that the singers encircled the audience. The particular nature of the motet's structure, with points of imitation moving from the first to last of the eight choirs, followed by the same procedure in reverse and then *cori spezzati* effects, makes performance in the round probable or at least credible. The manuscript parts of the motet include a basso continuo part (which may not have been prepared by Tallis) that is designated "for ye organ" and that is in the form of a melodic bass line with figures underneath indicating chords to be realized.

Of the three Anglican Services, the most comprehensive and best known is called the *Dorian Service* or the *Short Service.* Its constituent sections, all scored for SATB and a basso continuo part with figures, include the Venite, Te Deum, Benedictus, Responses, Creed, Offertory, Sanctus, Agnus Dei, Gloria, Magnificat, and Nunc dimittis. Most of the sections are homophonic, with indications for *cantoris* and *decani* performance, and several of the sections (the Te Deum, Creed, and the Gloria) begin with a chant incipit.

A few of the anthems (e.g., *Blessed are those that be undefiled*) are motet-like, with somewhat lengthy phrases of imitative polyphony offset by brief passages of homophony. However, most of the anthems are small-scale pieces with polyphony and homophony reversed in priority (i.e., the homophony prevails). These shorter anthems, composed according to the ideals of text clarity, are also often in an AAB or ABB format. Examples include *If ye love me; O Lord, give thy holy spirit; Hear the voice and prayer;* and *Purge me, O Lord.* Other anthems such as *O Lord, in thee is all my trust* and *Verily, verily, I say unto you* are entirely homophonic and through-composed.

SACRED WORKS IN LATIN
SELECTED AND LISTED ACCORDING TO FAMILIARITY

O nata lux de lumine – SSATB chorus – 1:30 minutes.

Spem in alium – eight SATTB choruses – 9:30 minutes.

Gaude gloriosa Dei mater – SATTBB chorus – 16 minutes.

Lamentacio Jeremiae (Lamentations of Jeremiah) First Lectio – ATTB
    chorus – 8 minutes.

Lamentacione Jeremiae (Lamentations of Jeremiah) Second Lectio – ATTB
    chorus – 13 minutes.

Loquebantur variis linguis – SSAATBB chorus – 4 minutes.

Salvator mundi – SAATB chorus – 4 minutes.

Derelinquit impius – SATTB chorus – 4:30 minutes.

In manus tuas – SATTB chorus – 2:30 minutes.

Te lucis ante terminum – SAATB chorus – 2 minutes.

O sacrum convivium – SAATB chorus – 4:30 minutes.

Euge caeli porta – SATB chorus – 1:30 minutes.

SACRED WORKS IN ENGLISH
SELECTED AND LISTED ACCORDING TO FAMILIARITY

If ye love me – ATTB chorus – 2 minutes.

O Lord, give thy holy spirit – SATB chorus – 2 minutes.

Hear the voice and prayer – AATB chorus – 3 minutes.

Verily, verily I say unto you – SATB chorus – 1:30 minutes.

Purge me, O Lord – SATB chorus – 1:45 minutes.

A new commandment – TTBB chorus – 2 minutes. The lowest bass part was
  lost and has been reconstructed by modern-day editors.

Blessed are those that be undefiled – SAATB chorus – 5 minutes.

O Lord, in thee is all my trust – SATB chorus – 3 minutes.

JOHN MARBECK (MERBECKE) CA.1505–CA.1585

Nothing certain is known about Marbeck's birthplace or musical education, although in the preface to his biblical concordance, published in 1550 and dedicated to King Edward VI, he stated that he was "brought up in your highness' college at Windsor, in the study of music and playing of organs." The first listing of him as a musician at St George's Chapel of Windsor Castle, however, was not until 1531, and he was not cited as an organist and lay clerk until 1541. Records at St George's confirm that he continued to sing and play the organ there for the remainder of his life. He authored the first concordance of the English Bible sometime in the early 1540s, but it was destroyed in 1543 after he was arrested for heresy and sentenced to death. The sentence was reprieved by a royal pardon from Henry VIII, and Marbeck rewrote the concordance, which, as has been mentioned, was published in 1550. Also in 1550 he published his most important musical work, *The Books of Common Praier Noted,* a complete collection of Service music for use with the first issuance of *The Book of Common Prayer* in 1549.

In addition to this Service music, Marbeck composed one mass, two Latin motets, and one anthem. The mass, *Missa Per arma justiciae* for five voices, which contains no Kyrie and which has an abbreviated Credo text, is based on the antiphon of the same name for the Office of None on Mondays during Lent. The motets—*Ave Dei patris filia* and *Domine Jesu Christe*—are both scored for five voices and are in the polyphonic style of John Taverner. The anthem, *A virgin and mother,* is for three voices and in the syllabic and simple imitative style of most anthems of the time.

The music in *The Books of Common Praier Noted* includes adaptations of Sarum chants and newly composed melodies. The Responses for Holy Communion are contained in a number of modern-day Protestant hymnals and are still sung regularly. These include the Kyrie, Sanctus, Agnus Dei, and Gloria Deo. The Great Litany (O God the father, creator of heaven and earth, have mercy upon us) and Sursum Corda (Lift up your hearts. We lift them up unto thee) are also included in some hymnals.

JOHN SHEPPARD CA.1515–1558

As with so many of the early Renaissance English composers, nothing is known about Sheppard's birthplace or musical training. There is speculation that he was a chorister at St Paul's Cathedral, but there are no supporting documents to verify this. In 1543 he became instructor of the choristers at Magdalen College, Oxford, and from about 1548 until his death he was a Gentleman of the Chapel Royal, serving with Thomas Tallis and probably meeting Christopher Tye. He studied at Oxford for a doctorate in music, but the degree was never granted.

Sheppard composed five masses (all with no Kyries), two Latin Magnificats, sixty-six Latin motets, three Anglican Services plus several separate parts of Services, and fifteen anthems. The masses include one large-scale work, *Cantate,* scored for six voices and in the style of early-sixteenth-century votive antiphons, with long polyphonic and melismatic phrases. The other masses are smaller-scale works scored for four voices and with more syllabic and less melismatic textures. All are most likely based on preexisting material used as a cantus firmus. However, except for one mass, the sources of the cantus firmi have not been discovered. *The Frences Mass* was probably named for François I, King of France, and composed for his visit to London in November 1535; the mass *Be not afraide* is probably from a chant or motet set to the text phrase "Ne timeas Maria" (Be not afraid, Maria) from Luke 1:30; and the *Playnsong masse for a mene* (sometimes simply called the *Mean Mass*) is comparable to the continental *Sine nomine* (without name) masses and the simple English masses with an unknown cantus firmus in the soprano (mean) voice part. The *Western Wynde Mass* is based on the same popular secular tune as that used by John Taverner and Christopher Tye. Sheppard's mass is the shortest of the three (about half the length of Taverner's), and it also has the fewest repetitions of the tune (there are thirty-six statements in Taverner's mass, twenty-nine in Tye's, and twenty-four in Sheppard's). Sheppard's mass also has the most deletions of text in the Gloria and Credo.

The Latin Magnificats, like the masses, are in both older and more modern styles. The *Magnificat septimi toni* for six voices has sections of music for varied vocal forces and long phrases of melismatic polyphony. The *Magnificat primi toni* for four voices is full-textured throughout and more syllabic. Both Magnificats are in *alternatim* style and based on Gregorian chant. The Latin motets, most of which were composed during the reign of Mary Tudor, include numerous settings of Responses for specific celebrations of the Mass or Offices. These motets, like the Magnificats, are based on chant and in *alternatim* style. Examples include *Alleluia, Confitemini Domino* for Vigils of Resurrection and Pentecost; *Alleluia, per te, Dei genitrix* for Lady Mass at Eastertide; *In manus tuas* for Compline on Palm Sunday to Maundy Thursday; *In pace, in idipsum* for Compline between Quadragesima and Palm Sunday; and *Verbum caro factum est* for Matins at Christmas. The Mass Responses are scored for men's voices (TTBB), while the Office Responses have varied scorings for mixed voices.

Two of the Services—generally referred to as the *First Service* and *Second Service*—contain the Venite, Te Deum, Benedictus, Creed, Magnificat, and Nunc dimittis. Both Services, one scored for four voices and the other for five, have indications for *decani* and *cantoris* performance, and both are basically syllabic and homophonic, with only brief passages of imitative polyphony. The other Service, referred to as *e la mi*, contains settings of the Te Deum, Magnificat, and Nunc dimittis.

The anthems were composed during the reign of Edward VI and are in the style of the small-scale pieces by Thomas Tallis. For example, *Rejoice in the Lord always* is characterized by passages of homophony that alternate with relatively short and simple phrases of imitative polyphony. *Submit yourselves to one another* and *I give you a new commandment*, both similar in style, are in ABB format.

SACRED WORKS IN LATIN
SELECTED AND LISTED ACCORDING TO FAMILIARITY

Western Wynde Mass – SATB chorus – 20:30 minutes.

Frences Mass – SATB chorus – 12 minutes.

Be not afraide Mass – ATTB chorus – 11 minutes.

Playnsong masse for a mene – SATB chorus – 10 minutes.

Magnificat primi toni – SATB chorus – 7 minutes.

Magnificat septimi toni – SSATTB chorus – 10 minutes.

Verbum caro factum est – SSAATB chorus – 3 minutes.

In pace, in idipsum – SAAT chorus – 3 minutes.

In manus tuas – SATB chorus – 2:30 minutes.

SACRED WORKS IN ENGLISH
SELECTED AND LISTED ACCORDING TO FAMILIARITY

Christ rising again from the dead - Christ rising again, the first fruits – AATB chorus – 3:30 minutes.

Rejoice in the Lord always – SATB chorus – 2:30 minutes.

Submit yourselves to one another – AATB chorus – 2:30 minutes.

I give you a new commandment – AATB chorus – 2:30 minutes.

RICHARD FARRANT CA.1525–1580

Nothing is known about Farrant before his appointment as a Gentleman of the Chapel Royal in 1552. In 1564 he became Master of the Choristers and one of the organists at St George's Chapel, Windsor, and in 1569, while maintaining his positions at St George's, he returned to the Chapel

Royal as Master of the Choristers. He was known during his life as a dramatist who wrote for and directed the Chapel Royal choristers in plays with songs. None of these plays has survived, however, and only two songs are extant.

Farrant composed one Anglican Service and three anthems. The Service, for four voices and in the full-textured syllabic style (with *decani* and *cantoris* designations), consists of a Te Deum, Benedictus, Kyrie, Creed, Magnificat, and Nunc dimittis. The anthems include *Call to remembrance,* which alternates short phrases of imitative polyphony with passages of homophony, and *Hide not thou thy face,* which is entirely homophonic. Both, among the most popular Renaissance anthems in modern times, are scored for SATB chorus and are in the style of small-scale pieces by Thomas Tallis. Farrant's third anthem, *When as we sat in Babylon,* is one of the earliest examples in the verse style. It is strophic and scored for soprano (mean) solo, SATB chorus, four viols, and organ. The text, from the first seven verses of Psalm 137, is divided into four verses of music, each sung by the soloist accompanied by the viols and organ, with the SATB chorus and instruments repeating the last line of the verse. The final two verses of the Psalm are then alternated between soloists and chorus, ending in a brief "Amen." The familiar anthem *Lord, for thy tender mercy's sake* is attributed to both Farrant and John Hilton, although there is no evidence that it was written by either composer.

WILLIAM MUNDY CA.1528–CA.1591

Mundy was probably born in London, where he was a chorister at Westminster Abbey. In 1547, after his voice changed, he held a nonmusical position at St Martin Ludgate, and between 1548 and 1558 he served in an administrative capacity at St Mary-at-Hill, where his father was a sexton and where Thomas Tallis had been a singer and organist in 1537. In 1559 Mundy became a lay vicar (singer) at St Paul's Cathedral, and in 1564 he entered the Chapel Royal as a Gentleman. He is acknowledged for his motets and anthems but is also known as the father of John Mundy (ca.1555–1630), successor to Farrant as organist at St George's Chapel, Windsor, and composer of six motets (including a setting of *Dum transisset* for six voices) and the publication *Songs and Psalmes* of 1594.

William Mundy composed two masses (both for four voices and both titled *Mass upon the Square*), one Kyrie, twenty-two Latin motets, six Anglican Services, and thirteen anthems. The motets include several multisectional votive antiphons for six voices (e.g., *Vox patris caelestis* and *Maria virgo sanctissima*) in the style of the early sixteenth century, with varied scoring and long polyphonic phrases. In addition, Mundy composed numerous six-voiced syllabic and point-of-imitation Psalm settings, including *Miserere mei Deus* (Psalm 51), *Adolescentulus sum ego* (Psalm 119:141–144), *Domine, non est exaltatum* (Psalm 131), *Domine, quis habitabit* (Psalm 15), and *In aeternum* (Psalm 119:93–94, 96). Another Psalm setting for six voices, *Deus misereatur* (Psalm 67), is ascribed to both Mundy and Robert White.

The Services are all similar to those composed by Mundy's compatriots and predecessors at the Chapel Royal, with the exception that two—one for three voices and one for four voices—are scored exclusively for TTBB. An additional separate Te Deum is scored for five men's voices. The anthems are in a variety of styles. *A new commandment* (scored for AATB) and Mundy's most famous work, *O Lord, the maker of all things* (scored for SATB), are in an ABB form similar to that of the small-scale pieces by Tallis; *O Lord, I bow the knees of my heart* (for SAATB) is longer and consists of continuous phrases of imitative polyphony; *Ah, helpless wretch* is a verse anthem scored for alto solo, SSATB chorus, and organ; and *Prepare you, time weareth away* (for SATB) is a carol.

ROBERT PARSONS CA.1535–CA.1571

As with Richard Farrant, nothing is known about Parsons before his appointment in about 1563 as a Gentleman of the Chapel Royal. Parsons and Farrant most likely worked together on dramatic productions in the early 1560s, and Parsons may have been associated with the chapel during the final several years of Mary Tudor's reign, which ended in 1558. He remained at the chapel, composing both Latin and English church music, until his unfortunate death in a drowning accident in the River Trent. During his short life he gained considerable acclaim, and the eulogy at his funeral bemoans the fact that he did not live longer: "Qui tantus primo Parsone in flore fuisti, quantus in autumno in morere flores" (You who were so great, Parsons, in life's springtime, how great you would have been in autumn had not death intervened).

His choral works include nine Latin motets, one Latin Magnificat, two Anglican Services, two anthems, and five part songs. Most of the motets are large-scale works scored for five to seven voices. *O bone Jesu* is a lengthy multimovement work in the style of early-sixteenth-century votive antiphons, with varied scoring and long polyphonic phrases, and *Ave Maria,* which is undoubtedly one of the most beautiful motets of the entire English Renaissance, combines a cantus firmus with syllabic and melismatic text setting in a continuous point-of-imitation style. The cantus firmus treatment in *Ave Maria* is particularly noteworthy in its scalar and repeat structure: each of the soprano voice part's six phrases in the first half of the motet begins on successively ascending pitches, and the final two phrases of text (excluding the Amen) are identical to each other. In addition, the concluding lengthy Amen section (which covers sixteen measures) employs melodic material in the soprano voice that is presented at successively higher pitch levels. Other motets include *Credo quod Redemptor* and *Domine quis habitabit,* both for six voices. The Magnificat, probably composed during the reign of Mary Tudor, is one of the first settings of the English Renaissance not to be in *alternatim* style but to be composed with each verse set in imitative polyphony.

The first Service, variously scored for four to seven voices and often called *The Great Service,* contains settings of the Venite, Te Deum, Benedictus, Kyrie, Creed, Magnificat, and Nunc dimittis. The anthems are generally like the small-scale works that were in favor during the early reign of Elizabeth I, with scoring for larger vocal forces. *Holy Lord God almighty* is for five voices, and *Deliver me from mine enemies* is for six voices.

ROBERT WHITE (WHYTE) CA.1538–1574

White was probably born in the Holborn district of London. From shortly before 1555 until the early 1560s he was a chorister and then an adult singer at Trinity College, Cambridge, where in 1560 he received a bachelor's degree in music. In 1562 he was appointed Master of the Choristers at Ely Cathedral, succeeding his father-in-law, Christopher Tye, who had been Master of the Choristers and organist from about 1541 until 1561. In 1567 White became Master of the Choristers at Chester Cathedral, and in 1569 he was appointed to the same position at Westminster Abbey. He died of the plague when he was approximately thirty-six.

White composed seventeen Latin motets, one Latin Magnificat, two sets of Lamentations, and eight anthems. Many of the motets are settings of Psalms, including *Ad te levavi* (Psalm 123) for six voices; *Exaudiat te, Dominus* (Psalm 20) for five voices, which was arranged by White as *Cantate Domino* (Psalm 98) for three voices; three settings of *Domine, quis habitabit* (Psalm 15), all for six voices; and *Miserere mei, Deus* (Psalm 51) for five voices. Another Psalm setting, *Deus misereatur* (Psalm 67) for six voices, is also attributed to William Mundy. The style of these motets (e.g., *Ad te levavi*) is characterized by continuous points of imitation, with the beginnings of each phrase set syllabically and the final word or important syllable of the phrase treated to a simple melisma. Other motets include four settings—all for five voices—of verses two, four, and six of the Compline hymn "Christe qui lux es." White titled each motet *Precamur, sancta Domine* (the beginning text of verse two). One setting is basically homophonic, with the chant used as a cantus firmus in the soprano voice part for verses two and four and in the alto part for verse six, another setting employs the tune as a cantus firmus in the tenor voice part throughout, and in the remaining two settings the chant is used as a long-note cantus firmus in the soprano, with the other voices in imitative phrases of shorter rhythms. Both the Magnificat and the sets of Lamentations are traditional in form and texture. The Magnificat, set to the first tone of the Gregorian chant, is in *alternatim* style, with long polyphonic phrases, and the Lamentations, one for five voices and one for six, contain brief polyphonic sections of the initial letters of the Hebrew alphabet.

Of the anthems, *O how glorious art thou* is attributed to both White and William Byrd, and *The Lord bless us and keep us* is attributed to both Robert and William White (ca.1585–1667). Several other anthems are arrangements: *I will wash my hands* and *Let thy merciful ears* are taken from *O how glorious art thou,* and *O Lord, deliver me* is from Robert White's motet *Manus tuae fecerunt me.* Only one anthem, *Lord, who shall dwell in thy tabernacle,* has no connection to another piece.

WILLIAM BYRD CA.1540–1623

Byrd, who is considered the greatest composer of the English Renaissance, was born in London. He was a chorister at the Chapel Royal, where he sang under Thomas Tallis and became acquainted with John Sheppard, and after his voice changed he served as assistant to Tallis. In 1563, at approximately twenty-three years of age, Byrd was appointed Master of the Choristers and organist at Lincoln Cathedral, and in 1572 he returned to London, where he took the place of Robert Parsons as a Gentleman of the Chapel Royal. Byrd also served as organist of the Chapel Royal along with Tallis. In 1575, shortly after Queen Elizabeth I granted Byrd and Tallis the first-ever exclusive license in England to print and publish music, the two composers published an anthology of thirty-four Latin motets (seventeen by each composer) entitled *Cantiones, quae ab argumento sacrae vocantur* (Songs which are called sacred on account of their texts), but generally referred to simply as *Cantiones sacrae.* The anthology did not sell well, in part because of the newness of publications for purchase in England at the time and partly because the publication contained no anthems. Tallis died in 1585, and in 1588 Byrd, who then held the publication license alone and who had become well known throughout England, published *Psalmes, Sonets and Songs*—a collection of sacred and secular music set to English texts consisting of ten strophic Psalm settings, eighteen madrigal-like pieces described by Byrd as "Sonets and Pastorals," seven adaptations of previously composed consort songs entitled collectively "Songs of Sadnes and Pietie," and two "Funeral songs of Sir Philip Sidney." Unlike the *Cantiones sacrae* of thirteen years earlier, *Psalmes, Sonets and Songs* was successful and was reprinted twice within the year. Two of the Sonets and Pastorals—*Though Amaryllis dance in green* and *I thought that love had been a boy*—were especially popular, and *Lullaby, my sweet little baby*, which was one of the consort songs originally scored for solo voice and viols and arranged for five voices, became so well known that the entire publication was referred to as "Byrd's Lullabyes."

Quick to take advantage of his success, Byrd in 1589 published a collection of forty-seven intermingled sacred and secular pieces to English texts, entitled *Songs of Sundrie Natures, some of gravitie, and others of myrth, fit for all companies and voices*. Scored for three to six voices, this collection contained a few arrangements of previously composed consort songs and numerous newly composed pieces, including the anthem *Christ rising again*. In addition, sometime during the late 1580s he composed, but did not publish, his *Great Service*, which was added to three other Services and separate Responses composed earlier. He also contributed the madrigal *The fair young virgin* to the first issuance of *Musica transalpina* in 1588, and two settings (one for four voices and one for six) of *This sweet and merry month of May* to Thomas Watson's initial publication of *Italian Madrigals Englished* in 1590.

In 1593 Byrd curtailed his activity in London and moved to Essex, where he had contact with private groups of Roman Catholics. Previously, during the 1570s and early 1580s, he had maintained close relationships with several notable Catholics in London, including the earls of Oxford and Northumberland, and he also maintained a relatively comfortable balance between serving the Anglican Church under Queen Elizabeth I and observing his Catholic faith privately. However, during the later 1580s he was frequently fined and cited for recusancy (refusing to attend Anglican services), and finding the public persecution of Catholics intolerable, he felt committed to serve the Catholic Church as best he could. Consequently, two collections of Latin motets were published in 1589 and 1591—*Liber primus sacrarum cantionum* for five voices and *Liber secundus sacrarum cantionum* for five and six voices. These collections contain many of Byrd's most celebrated works in the point-of-imitation style, including *Haec dies quam fecit Dominus; Laetentur coeli - Orientur in diebus; Miserere mei, Deus;* and *O quam gloriosum est regnum - Benedictio et claritas*. In 1605 and 1607 he published two collections of Latin Propers for major Catholic feast days—*Gradualia ac cantiones sacrae* for three to five voices and *Gradualia seu cantionum sacrarum, liber saecundus* for four to six voices. The style of these motets, accessible to Catholics practicing privately and without accomplished musical forces, is characterized by textures of relative simple homophony. The famous *Ave verum corpus* and *Justorum animae* are examples. Byrd also composed, but did not publish, three masses for use in these private Catholic services.

Byrd's exclusive license to print and publish music, which had expired in 1596, was taken over by Thomas Morley, who had been Byrd's student and who was almost entirely committed to music set to English texts, especially secular. Perhaps because of their relationship and Morley's focus on English music, Byrd returned to varied popular English genres in his final publication, *Psalmes, Songs and Sonnets: some solemne, others joyfull . . . fit for Voyces or Viols of 3, 4, 5, and 6 Parts* of 1611.

In total, Byrd's compositional output numbers approximately 185 sacred works set to Latin texts and two hundred sacred and secular English works. The early Latin motets, those in the 1575 publication shared with Tallis, were influenced by Alfonso Ferrabosco, who served at the royal court from 1562 until the early 1580s. An especially Italian feature is the alternation of long points of imitation to short phrases of text, and very brief passages of homophony. In *Aspice Domine, quia facta est,* for example, the first phrase, "Aspice Domine, quia facta est desolata civitas" (Consider, Lord, how the city has become desolate), is a point of imitation thirty-eight measures long; the second phrase, "plena divitiis" (once so wealthy), is a homophonic section of only twelve measures; the third phrase, "sedet in tristitia" (she sits in sadness), consists of twenty-one measures of imitation; the fourth phrase, "non est consoletur" (no one can console her), is a four-measure passage of homophony; and finally, the fifth phrase, "nisi tu, Deus noster" (except you, our God), is a twenty-eight measure point of imitation. Other motets in the publication include *Emendemus in melius - Adiuva nos,* which is mainly homophonic; *Domine, secundum actum meum,* which is based on Ferrabosco's *Domine, secundum peccata mea;* and the three-movement *O lux, beata trinitas.*

The motets in the two volumes published in 1589 and 1591 are generally characterized by exchanges of short motif-like phrase fragments and brief point-of-imitation phrases that alternate with equally brief passages of homophony. This characteristic is especially apparent in *Haec dies quam fecit Dominus,* with a polychoral-like effect created between the exchanges of the text fragment "et laetemur" (and be glad). The two-movement motet *Laetentur coeli - Orientur in diebus* incorporates these same features into an ABBCB format (the first movement is ABB and the second movement is CB); *O quam gloriosum est regnum - Benedictio et claritas* and *Domine, secundum multitudinem* are entirely imitative, with no passages of homophony; and *Miserere mei, Deus* balances equal portions of imitative polyphony and homophony. *Laudibus in sanctis - Magnificum Domini,* the first motet in the 1591 publication, has notable examples of chromaticism.

As was mentioned earlier, the compositions in Byrd's final publications of Latin motets—the *Gradualia* of 1605 and 1607—contain works that are mainly homophonic and in a simple style for private Catholic gatherings or services without professional singers. The famous *Ave verum corpus,* which is in an AAB format with a very short Amen section after the final B, has only two brief sections of imitation—at the text "O Jesu fili Mariae" (O Jesus, son of Mary) and "miserere mei" (have mercy on me). This latter text fragment is also characterized by cross-relations: the pitch with a sharp sign on the syllable "me" of "mei" occurs in close proximity to the same pitch with a natural sign on the syllable "se" of "miserere." *O magnum misterium* is more consistently imitative. However, the imitative entrances are close together and some phrases occur as duets. In addition, this motet is in an ABCB format: the verse section "Ave Maria, gratia plena, Dominus tecum" (Hail Mary, full of grace, the Lord is with you), which is C, is interpolated between the text "Beata virgo, cujus viscera portare Dominum Christum" (Blessed virgin, whose womb carried the Lord Christ), which is B. The *Gradualia* publications also contain a number of motets scored for three voices, including the short three-movement *Memento salutis auctor - Maria, mater gratiae - Gloria tibi, Domine* for STB voices.

It is not certain when Byrd's three masses were composed, although it is assumed that the *Mass for four voices* was first (ca.1592), the *Mass for three voices* followed in about 1593, and the *Mass for five voices* was written in about 1595. All three masses are characterized by alternating homophony and polyphony, with very little imitation in the polyphonic sections. Byrd's only unifying device is a head motif at the beginning of most of the mass movements. All three masses have separate Benedictus movements, and all three are full-textured throughout (i.e., there are no sections for reduced or expanded scoring, although the masses for four and five voices have very brief duet and trio passages).

The three publications of music to English texts, while containing a number of sacred settings, have no anthems (i.e., no compositions meant for the Anglican liturgy and no settings in the familiar ABB format so common with Byrd's predecessors and compatriots). The sacred settings are what might be called spiritual madrigals or motets with English texts. The exquisite and popular *Lullaby, my sweet little baby* from the 1588 *Psalms, Sonets and Songs,* for instance, is in every way typical of the Italian madrigals by Alfonso Ferrabosco and other contemporary Italian madrigalists, except for its text about the birth of Jesus; *O Lord, my God* and *Lord in thy rage* from the 1589 *Songs of Sundrie natures* are both motet-like, with continuous points of imitation; and *Arise, Lord, into thy rest* and *Praise our Lord, all ye gentiles* from the 1611 *Psalmes, Songs and Sonnets* have varied rhythms, short imitative fragments of text, and vertical textures similar to the Italian madrigals contained in *Musica transalpina.* One of the most madrigal-like of Byrd's sacred settings, also contained in the 1611 publication, is *This day Christ was born,* subtitled "A Carroll for Christmas Day." Several other sacred English settings, including actual anthems, were not published during Byrd's lifetime, although they existed in numerous manuscripts. Examples are the well-known madrigal-like setting of *Sing joyfully,* the verse anthem *Teach me, O Lord,* and the vertically-textured *Prevent us, O Lord.*

Byrd's music specifically composed for Anglican liturgies consists of the *Short Service, Second Service, Third Service, Great Service,* and various selected Responses and Psalm settings. The *Short* and *Great* services both contain the Venite, Te Deum, Benedictus, Kyrie, Creed, Magnificat, and Nunc dimittis. The *Short Service* is so-called because it is modestly scored and brief in duration. The *Great Service,* which is considered one of Byrd's most accomplished compositions, is so-called because of its elaborate scoring and texture. The second and third Services contain only the Magnificat and Nunc dimittis.

The secular music consists mostly of arrangements of consort songs (e.g., *Lullaby, my sweet little baby*) and pieces modeled after the madrigals contained in the two volumes of *Musica transalpina* (1588 and 1597) and *Italian Madrigalls Englished* (1590). *Though Amaryllis dance in green* is a strophic and relatively homophonic ballett in the style of Orazio Vecchi; *Is love a boy - Boy, pity me* is a totally imitative work, with varied rhythms as in the madrigals of Luca Marenzio; *Come, woeful Orpheus* is characterized by chromaticism; and *This sweet and merry month of May,* Byrd's best-known secular piece, combines imitative polyphony of short phrases, homophony, and varied rhythms.

SACRED WORKS IN LATIN
SELECTED AND LISTED ACCORDING TO FAMILIARITY

Ave verum corpus – SATB chorus – 4 minutes.

Haec dies quam fecit Dominus – SSATTB chorus – 2:45 minutes.

Sacerdotes Domini – SATB chorus – 2 minutes.

O magnum misterium – SATB chorus – 4 minutes.

Justorum animae – SSATB chorus – 2:30 minutes.

Miserere mei, Deus – SATBB chorus – 3 minutes.

Emendemus in melius - Adiuva nos – SATTB chorus – 3 minutes.

O quam gloriosum est regnum - Benedictio et claritas – SSATB chorus –
     5:30 minutes.

Laetentur coeli - Orientur in diebus – SATTB chorus – 3:45 minutes.

Ne irascaris, Domine - Civitas sancti tui – SATTB chorus – 4:30 minutes.

Ego sum panis vivus – SATB chorus – 2:30 minutes.

Cibavit eos - Exultate Deo adjutori nostro – SATB chorus – 3 minutes.

Mass for four voices – SATB chorus – 21:30 minutes.

Mass for five voices – SATTB chorus – 21 minutes.

Mass for three voices – ATB chorus – 17 minutes.

SACRED WORKS IN ENGLISH
SELECTED AND LISTED ACCORDING TO FAMILIARITY

Sing joyfully – SSAATB chorus – 2:30 minutes.

Teach me, O Lord – SSAATB chorus – 3 minutes.

Lullaby, my sweet little baby – SAATB voices – 5 minutes.

Prevent us, O Lord – SAATB chorus – 2:30 minutes.

This day Christ was born – SSAATB chorus – 3 minutes.

Praise our Lord, all ye gentiles – SSATBB chorus – 3:30 minutes.

O Lord, my God – SATB chorus – 4 minutes.

Arise, Lord, into thy rest – SSATB chorus – 3 minutes.

Lord in thy rage – SAT chorus – 3 minutes.

Look down, O Lord – SSTB chorus – 2 minutes.

Christ rising again – SSATTB chorus – 3:30 minutes.

Great Service – SSAATTBB chorus – 30 minutes. The two alto parts occa-
     sionally divide, one each for *cantoris* and *decani*.

SECULAR WORKS
SELECTED AND LISTED ACCORDING TO FAMILIARITY

This sweet and merry month of May – SSATTB voices – 2:30 minutes.

This sweet and merry month of May – SATB voices – 2:30 minutes.

Though Amaryllis dance in green – SSATB voices – 2:15 minutes.

Is love a boy - Boy, pity me – SATB voices – 8 minutes.

Come, woeful Orpheus – SSATB voices – 3:30 minutes.

I thought that love had been a boy – SSATB voices – 3 minutes.

Wounded I am – Yet of us twain – SATB voices – 4 minutes.

THOMAS MORLEY CA.1557–1602

Morley was born in Norwich, where he was a chorister at the cathedral there. When his voice changed in about 1572, he most likely went to London to study with William Byrd, although there is no verification of this move except Morley's testimony, and sometime during the late 1570s he returned to his hometown, where in 1583 he was appointed Master of the Choristers and organist at Norwich Cathedral. He resigned the positions in 1587 and matriculated at Oxford University, receiving a bachelor's degree in music in 1588. The following year he became one of the organists at St Paul's Cathedral in London, and in 1592 he entered the Chapel Royal as a Gentleman. He worked alongside Byrd at the chapel, and when Byrd's license to print and publish music expired in 1596, Morley supervised the publication license for two years and then took it over. While Byrd had issued mostly sacred music and while Byrd and all English composers before him were known for their sacred compositions, Morley issued and became known mainly for his secular music.

As publisher, he issued several notable secular anthologies—*Canzonets or Little Short Songs to Foure Voyces: Celected out of the Best and Approved Italian Authors* in 1597; *Madrigals to Five Voyces: Celected out of the Best Approved Italian Authors* in 1598; and the famous *The Triumphes of Oriana* in 1601. The first two anthologies contain lighthearted madrigals, canzonets, and balletts by such Italian composers as Orazio Vecchi, Giovanni Croce, and Felice Anerio, and *The Triumphes of Oriana* contains madrigals by a variety of English composers, including John Wilbye, Michael East, Michael Cavendish, John Bennet, John Farmer, Thomas Tomkins, and Thomas Weelkes (see below for a fuller discussion of this publication). As composer, Morley was also interested mainly in secular music, publishing five collections of pieces in various forms between 1593 and 1597. Only one of these collections, *Madrigalls to Foure Voyces* (1594), was devoted to madrigals. The other collections—*Canzonets, or Little Short Songs to Three Voyces* (1593), *The First Booke of Canzonets to Two Voyces* (1595), *The First Book of Balletts to Five Voyces* (1595), and *Canzonets or Little Short Aers to Five and Sixe Voices* (1597)—consisted either of canzonets or balletts. Morley's publications were all successful; they fused elements of the Italian madrigal, canzonet, and balletto—which the English public had gotten to know through publications such as Nicolas Yonge's *Musica transalpina* and Thomas Watson's *Italian Madrigalls Englished*—with the English love of diatonic harmonies and vertical textures. Morley's publications also initiated the beginning of a long and fruitful generation of secular music in England, with numerous composers devoted to secular forms and with numerous compositions contributing to what would later be termed a golden age.

Morley composed nine Latin motets, three traditional Anglican Services plus music for the Burial Service and separate Responses and Psalms, five anthems, and approximately one hundred madrigals, canzonets, and balletts. The Latin motets are for the most part relatively short works in the style of Byrd's *Gradualia*. For instance, *Agnus Dei* and *Domine fac mecum* are only thirty-six and fifty-two measures in length, respectively, and they both consist entirely of brief imitative phrases, some of which include duets. The lengthy *Laboravi in gemitu*, which is often ascribed to Morley, may have been composed by Philippe Rogier and arranged by Morley, and similarly, *Gaude Maria virgo - Virgo prudentissima* may have been composed by Peter Philips. Morley's *Nolo mortem peccatoris* is not a Latin motet but rather an English anthem with a macaronic text (only the title phrase is in Latin).

Of the traditional Anglican Services, the *First Service* (also called the *Verse Service*) is the most comprehensive, consisting of the Venite, Te Deum, Benedictus, Kyrie, Creed, Magnificat, and Nunc dimittis. The Venite, Kyrie, and Creed sections are scored for the full complement of five voices throughout, the Te Deum and Benedictus have some solo sections, and the Magnificat and Nunc dimittis are scored as verse anthems. The *Second Service* (also for five voices) and the *Short Service* (for four voices) consist only of a Magnificat and Nunc dimittis. The *Burial Service* consists of seven short full anthems—*I am the resurrection; I know that my redeemer liveth; We brought nothing into this world; Man that is born of a woman; In the midst of life; Thou knowest, Lord, the secrets of our hearts;* and *I heard a voice from heaven saying.*

The anthems—those pieces that are separate from the Services, Psalms, and Responses— are in both full and verse formats. *O Jesu meek* and *Out of the deep* (which is an English version of De profundis) are both verse anthems scored for soloists, five-voiced chorus, and organ. *Teach me thy way, O Lord* (for five voices), *Nolo mortem peccatoris* (for four voices), and a different setting of *Out of the deep* (for six voices) are full anthems. As was mentioned above, most of *Nolo mortem peccatoris* is set to English words and is sometimes called by the first line of English text, "Father, I am thine only son."

Morley's madrigals represent the smallest number and least known of his secular compositions. In addition, they are unlike Italian madrigals of the late sixteenth century and English madrigals of the early seventeenth century. Instead, Morley's madrigals are more like his motets (modeled after works in Byrd's *Gradualia*), with brief imitative phrases, some of which include duets, alternating with large passages of homophony. *Aprill is in my mistris face,* his only popular madrigal today, is an example. Morley's main contribution to the madrigal repertoire is *The Triumphes of Oriana* (a collection of twenty-five madrigals, all ending with the words "Long live fair Oriana"), which was directly based on the Italian *Il Trionfo di Dori* (a collection of twenty-nine madrigals, all ending with the words "Viva la bella Dori"). Morley contributed two madrigals to this collection—*Arise, awake* and *Hard by a cristall fountaine*. Interestingly, *Arise, awake* is an arrangement of his own *Adiew, adiew* from the canzonets of 1597, and *Hard by a cristall fountaine* is a parody of Croce's *Ove tra l'herbe e i fiori*, which itself is one of the madrigals in *Il Trionfo di Dori*.

The balletts, which are the best known of Morley's compositions today, were modeled directly on Italian ballettos. For example, Morley's entire collection of *The First Book of Balletts to Five Voyces* (1595) is a copy of Giovanni Giacomo Gastoldi's *Balletti* of 1591, not only with an identical number and layout of pieces, but also with identical formal structures of the pieces (AABB with *fa la la* refrains) and with virtual translations of eight of Gastoldi's poems, including *Sing wee and chaunt it* (from *A lieta vita*), *Shoot, false love, I care not* (from *Viver lieto voglio*), and *My bonny lasse shee smyleth* (from *Questa dolce sirena*). Other familiar balletts in Morley's publication, also based on Italian ballettos, are *Fyer, fyer; I love, alas, I love; Leave, alas, this tormenting;* and *Now is the month of maying.* The balletts and their original models were so popular that Morley issued his entire collection in an Italian version entitled *Il primo libro delle ballete*. Thus many of the pieces went from texts in Italian to English and then back to Italian.

The canzonets were Morley's favorite genre (as can be deduced from his three personal publications and one anthology). The three-voiced canzonets in the publication of 1593 include pieces that are imitative like the madrigals (e.g., *Cease, myne eyes*) or homophonic and strophic with *fa la la* refrains (e.g., *Though Philomela lost hir love*); the two-voiced collection of 1595 contains imitative miniatures such as *I goe before, my darling* and *Goe yee, my canzonets*; and the five- and six-voiced canzonets of 1597 (e.g., *Sayd I that Amarillis was fairer* and *Lady you thinke you spite me*) are basically homophonic but with occasional short passages of simple imitative polyphony and with a structure of ABB. This latter collection was published with a lute part, which, as Morley explained in the preface to the collection, could be used for accompaniment of a solo voice singing the soprano part, for multiple voices singing all the parts, or for purely instrumental performance.

SACRED WORKS
SELECTED AND LISTED ACCORDING TO FAMILIARITY

Nolo mortem peccatoris – SATB chorus – 3:30 minutes.

Agnus Dei – SATB chorus – 2:30 minutes.

Out of the deep – A solo, SAATB chorus, and organ – 3:30 minutes.

Burial Service – SATB chorus – 25 minutes for all seven anthems.

MADRIGALS
SELECTED AND LISTED ACCORDING TO FAMILIARITY

Aprill is in my mistris face – SATB voices – 2 minutes.

Hard by a cristall fountaine – SSATTB voices – 3:15 minutes.

Arise, awake – SATTB voices – 2 minutes.

Now is the gentle season - The fields abroad – SATB voices – 5 minutes.

BALLETTS
SELECTED AND LISTED ACCORDING TO FAMILIARITY

Fyer, fyer – SSATB voices – two verses, each 2 minutes.

My bonny lasse shee smyleth – SATTB voices – two verses, each 2 minutes.

Now is the month of maying – SATTB voices – three verses, each 45 seconds.

Sing wee and chaunt it – SSATB voices – two verses, each 1 minute.

Shoot, false love, I care not – SSATB voices – two verses, each 1 minute.

I love, alas, I love – SATTB voices – 2:30 minutes.

Leave, alas, this tormenting – SATTB voices – 2:30 minutes.

CANZONETS
SELECTED AND LISTED ACCORDING TO FAMILIARITY

I goe before, my darling – SS or TT voices – 1:30 minutes.

Goe yee, my canzonets – SS or TT voices – 2 minutes.

Though Philomela lost hir love – SAT voices – 1:30 minutes.

Cease, myne eyes – SAT voices – 2 minutes.

THOMAS GREAVES FL.1604

All that is known about Greaves is that he was lutenist to Sir Henry Pierrepont of Notting-hamshire and that he compiled one volume of secular music in 1604 entitled *Songes of Sundrie Kindes: First, Aires to be Sung to the Lute and Base Violl; Next, Songes of Sadnesse for the Viols and Voyce; and Lastly, Madrigalles for Five Voyces*. The four madrigals in the collection (the other pieces are consort songs) include *England receive the rightful king*, composed for the coronation of James I in 1603; *Sweet nimphes that trippe along*, perhaps composed for Anne of Denmark, wife of James I; *Lady, the melting christall*, characterized by expressive text setting; and the relatively well known *Come away sweet love*, a ballett that has alternating sections of homophony and imitative passages set to *fa la la*. All the madrigals are scored for SSATB voices.

NATHANIEL GILES CA.1558–1634

Nathaniel Giles, not related to Thomas Giles who was a singer at St Paul's Cathedral in London, was born in or near Worcester. Nathaniel was a chorister at Worcester Cathedral beginning in 1569, and in 1581 he became Master of the Choristers. In 1585 he was appointed Master of the Choristers and organist at St George's Chapel, Windsor, and he also received a bachelor's degree in music from Oxford University. In 1597, while maintaining his positions at St George's Chapel, he began service as a Gentleman and Master of the Choristers at the Chapel Royal, and in 1622 he was granted a doctorate in music from Oxford.

Giles composed three Anglican Services, nineteen anthems (three full and sixteen verse), six motets (only three of which have text), and two madrigals. The Services include two complete settings (each containing a Te Deum, Jubilate, Kyrie, Creed, Magnificat, and Nunc dimittis) scored for soloists, chorus, and organ, and one setting (called the *Short Service*) containing only a Te Deum, Jubilate, Kyrie, and Creed. The three full anthems, generally in textures of overlapping points of imitation, are *Out of the deep - My soul flyeth to the Lord* for SAT, *O give thanks unto the Lord* for SAATB, and Giles's most famous work, *He that hath my commandments* for AATBB. The verse anthems include *Everlasting God* (for Michaelmas Day) and *Out of the deep have I called to thee,* both for SAATB solos, SAATB chorus, and organ. *What child was he,* scored for the same forces, is strophic.

JOHN BULL CA.1562–1628

Bull was born in Radnorshire, Wales, and began his musical education in 1573 as a chorister at nearby Hereford Cathedral in England. He transferred to the Chapel Royal the following year, and in 1578, when his voice changed, he became an apprentice to the Earl of Sussex. In 1582 he returned to Hereford Cathedral as organist, and the following year he added the position Master of the Choristers. He apparently was negligent in his duties, spending too much time in London, and thus was dismissed from his positions in Hereford in 1585. In 1586 he was admitted as a Gentleman of the Chapel Royal, and in that same year he received a bachelor's degree in music from Oxford University; in 1589 he received his doctorate from King's College, Cambridge. From 1597 to 1607 he taught at Gresham College in London while maintaining his position at the Chapel Royal, but in 1613 he fled to Brussels to avoid prosecution for adultery (although he claimed his departure from England was to avoid persecution for his Catholic religious views). He found immediate employment at the court of Archduke Albert, where he worked alongside Peter Philips. However, the archduke was persuaded by King James I of England to dismiss Bull, which he did in 1614, and in 1615 Bull was appointed assistant organist at Antwerp Cathedral, being promoted to principal organist in 1617.

Bull's compositional output was devoted mainly to keyboard works; he composed only seven extant anthems and spiritual songs, including the relatively well-known verse anthem *Almighty God, which by the leading star* (sometimes called the *Starre anthem*) for SSATB solos, SSAATB chorus, and organ. The full anthems include *Attend unto my tears, O Lord,* which exists in settings for both four and five voices, and *In the departure of the Lord* for four voices.

JOHN DOWLAND 1563–1626

Nothing is known about Dowland's birthplace and music education, although it is assumed that he spent his youth in London. Between 1579 and 1583 he served as lutenist in the household of Sir Henry Cobham, an English nobleman living in Paris, and in the late 1580s he studied at Christ Church, Oxford, where he received a bachelor's degree in 1588. During most of the 1590s he held temporary appointments in Germany and also traveled to Italy to study with Giovanni Croce and Luca Marenzio, and beginning in 1598 he was the principal lutenist at the court of Christian IV in Denmark. He returned to London in 1609 to serve as lutenist for Lord Walden, and from 1612 until his death, a period during which he was held in high regard as a performer and composer, he earned his living by playing concerts.

Dowland composed fourteen Psalms and spiritual songs, eighty-four lute songs (or airs), and more than one hundred pieces for the lute alone. The Psalms are settings of tunes and metrical texts from the English Psalter by Thomas Sternhold and John Hopkins, first published by John Day in 1562. All of Dowland's settings are hymn-like and strophic, with three to ten verses. In all the Psalms with English title and text—*Put me not to rebuke O Lord* (Psalm 38), both settings of *All people that on earth do dwell* (Psalm 100), *My soul praise the Lord, speak good of his name* (Psalm 104), *Lord to thee I make my moan* (Psalm 130), and *Behold and have regard, ye servants of the Lord* (Psalm 134)—the tune is in the tenor voice part. In the Psalm settings with Latin titles and English texts—including *Domine ne in furore* (Psalm 6), *Miserere mei Deus* (Psalm 51), *De profundis* (Psalm 130), and *Domine exaudi* (Psalm 143)—the tune is in the treble voice part. The spiritual songs, while also strophic, have more rhythmic variety. Examples include *Lamentatio Henrici noel* (O Lord turn not away thy face from him that lieth prostrate) and two settings of *The humble suit of a sinner* (O Lord of whom I do depend).

Most of the lute songs (called airs or ayers) were published in three collections—*The Firste Booke of Songes or Ayres of Fowre Partes with Tableture for the Lute* in 1597, which became immediately popular and went through at least four reprintings in the following decade; *The Second Booke of Songs or Ayres of 2, 4, and 5 parts: With Tableture for the Lute or Orpherian, with the Violl de Gamba* in 1600; and *The Third and Last Booke of Songs or Aiers . . .* in 1603. Virtually all of the songs were published in two forms, one for solo voice with lute accompaniment and one for three (ATB) or four (SATB) voices alone. In addition, many of the pieces had a separate part for bass viol, and lute accompaniment *si placet* was commonplace in performances of the three- and four-part settings. The songs scored for multiple voices are in a wide variety of forms, from simple strophic settings (such as most of the airs in the first book of 1597) to polyphonic settings resembling madrigals of the time.

LUTE SONGS
SELECTED AND LISTED ACCORDING TO FAMILIARITY

Come againe sweet love doth now envite – 1597 – SATB voices – 2 minutes.

What if I never speede – 1603 – SATB voices – 2 minutes.

Now, o now I needs must part – 1597 – SATB voices – 2 minutes.

Come heavy sleepe – 1597 – SATB voices – 3 minutes.

Fine knacks for ladies – 1600 – SATB voices – 2 minutes.

Go christall teares – 1597 – SATB voices – 2:30 minutes.

Deare, if you change Ile never chuse againe – 1597 – SATB voices – 2 minutes.

Come away, come sweet love – 1597 – SATB voices – 2:30 minutes.

Tosse not my soule – 1600 – SATB voices – 2:30 minutes.

GILES FARNABY CA.1563–1640

From the little information that exists about Farnaby, it seems that his life was similar to that of John Dowland. Both composers were probably born in London, studied at Oxford University, published books of Psalm settings and secular music, and spent their careers as instrumentalists, although Farnaby was a maker of virginals by trade. In 1592 he received a bachelor's degree in music from Oxford, in that same year nine of his Psalm settings were published in Thomas

East's *Whole Booke of Psalmes,* and in 1598 he published his one book of secular music, *Canzonets to Fowre Voyces with a Song of eight parts.* This latter collection contains nineteen four-voiced canzonets (half through-composed and half in an AAB format), one four-voiced madrigal (*Love shooting among many - Love shooting at another*), and the eight-voiced *Witness, ye heavens.* The Psalm settings are like those of Dowland, with homophonic textures, multiple verses, and the tune in the tenor voice part. The canzonets are like the four-voiced madrigals of Thomas Morley published in 1594: they alternate phrases of imitative polyphony and brief passages of homophony with occasional short duets and trios. However, Farnaby's pieces, most of which begin with a point of imitation, are predominantly polyphonic. Examples include *Ay me, poor heart,* which is an adaptation of a consort song for solo voice and viols and which Farnaby also arranged for keyboard; *Sometime she would, and sometime not; The curtain drawn;* and Farnaby's most famous piece, *Consture my meaning* (the first word in the title often spelled "Construe," although the spelling was "Consture" during Farnaby's lifetime).

MICHAEL CAVENDISH CA.1565–1628

Cavendish was probably born in Suffolk County, where his family was noted for its musical patronage. He was only an amateur musician and did not have a distinguished career (he was a servant to Prince Charles, son of King James I), although he was apparently recognized as a respectable composer, for he—along with such notables as John Wilbye, Thomas Tomkins, William Byrd, and Thomas Weelkes—was chosen by Thomas Morley to contribute a madrigal to *The Triumphes of Oriana.* Also, like many other amateur composers of the early seventeenth century (i.e., those without professional musical appointments, such as Giles Farnaby, John Farmer, and John Bennet), he was caught up in the wave of enthusiasm for the madrigals and related genres that were published in *Musica transalpina* and similar anthologies, and he composed one book himself. Published in 1598, the main title of this book is missing; however, the subtitle survives and fully explains the contents as well as performance practice conventions of the time—"14 Ayres in Tabletorie to the Lute expressed with Two Voyces and the Base Violl or the Voice and Lute only, 6 more to 4 Voyces and in Tabletorie, and 8 Madrigalles to 5 Voyces." Most of the four- and five-voiced settings are, like those of John Dowland, recastings of his lute songs (or ayres). Examples are *Wandring in this place* and *Everie bush new springing.* Unlike Dowland's, several of the five-voiced settings borrow music from other composers. *Zephyrus brings the time that sweetly scenteth* and *In flowre of Aprill springing* are based on Alfonso Ferrabosco's settings of these same texts contained in the 1597 edition of *Musica transalpina,* and similarly, *Come gentle swains* is based on Giovanni Croce's *Hard by a crystal fountain.* Cavendish made a different setting of *Come gentle swains,* his most famous composition, for *The Triumphes of Oriana.*

GEORGE KIRBYE CA.1565–1634

Nothing is known about the life of Kirbye except that he was employed as a musician at Rushbrooke Hall near Bury St Edmunds and that he was the first English composer to write madrigals in the serious Italian style. While other composers before him were aware of the serious Italian madrigal style through publications such as *Musica transalpina* and through numerous manuscripts and separate printings of madrigals by Alfonso Ferrabosco, Giovanni Croce, and Giovanni Francesco Anerio, these earlier English Renaissance composers chose pastoral or light-hearted poetry and set these texts in complementary simple manners. In contrast, Kirbye, who was followed by such notable composers of serious madrigals as John Wilbye and Thomas Weelkes, chose texts with weighty subjects and set them in the serious motet-like point-of-imitation style. The basic textures of both the lighthearted and more serious styles were similar, with phrases of imitative polyphony alternating with passages of homophony. However, the serious style was more varied, with each phrase treated expressively and with word painting as a common feature.

Kirbye composed two Latin motets, several anthems and spiritual part songs, nineteen Psalm settings, and twenty-five madrigals. The motets—*Quare tristis es · Convertere, anima mea* for four voices and *Vox in rama* for six voices—are examples of Kirbye's serious compositional style and are reflective of the madrigal textures described above. The anthems and spiritual part songs, which include *All my belief* and *O Jesu, looke*, are arrangements of consort songs and are in the style of the "Songes of Sadnes and Pietie" composed by William Byrd and published in his *Psalmes, Sonets and Songs* of 1588. The Psalm settings, all of which are homophonic and strophic, were published along with those of Giles Farnaby in Thomas East's *Whole Booke of Psalmes* (1592). In addition to these sacred compositions, Kirbye added sacred texts to three of his four-voiced madrigals: *Sleep now my muse* became *Sleepe, restles thoughtes; Farewell my love* became *Vayne worlde adiew;* and *Woe am I, my hart dies* was changed to *Woe is me, my strength fayles*.

Twenty-one of the madrigals (six for four voices, ten for five voices, and five for six voices) were published in Kirbye's single volume of 1597, entitled *The First Set of English Madrigalls to 4, 5, and 6 Voyces*. All of the madrigals are in a minor mode, and many (e.g., *See what a maze of error*) feature word painting. In addition, as was mentioned above, all the texts of these madrigals are serious. An example is *Sound out, my voice*, which is a translation of Palestrina's *Vestiva i colli* published in the 1597 edition of *Musica transalpina*. Kirbye's other madrigal, *With angels face and brightness*, is included in *The Triumphes of Oriana*.

THOMAS CAMPION 1567–1620

Campion, who was born in London, studied music at Peterhouse College, Cambridge, from 1581 to 1584, and law and the arts at Gray's Inn from 1586 to 1589. While at Gray's Inn, he wrote poetry and participated in the plays and masques that were a prominent feature of the institution and that were frequently performed for Queen Elizabeth I. By the early 1590s Campion had established himself as a poet, and in 1595 he published a collection of Latin poems entitled *Thomae Campiani poemata*. During the latter half of the 1590s he began setting his poems as lute songs, and in 1601 twenty-one of these songs were included in Philip Rosseter's *A Book of Ayers*. Campion studied medicine during the first years of the seventeenth century, receiving a doctorate in 1605 from the University of Caen, France, and referring to himself later as "Doctor of Physick." For the remainder of his life he composed and published collections of his lute songs, and he collaborated on elaborate masques that were performed for King James I. In addition, he wrote a treatise about poetry entitled *Observations in the Art of English Poesie* and a treatise on musical theory entitled *A New Way of making Fowre Parts in Counter-point, by a most Familiar, and Infallible Rule*.

The lute songs were published in two collections of two books each—*Two Bookes of Ayres, the First containing Divine and Morall Songs, and the Second Light Conceits of Lovers* in about 1613, and *The Third and Fourth Booke of Ayres* in about 1617 (the publications are undated). The lute songs in the first two books, like those of John Dowland, appear in two forms—one for solo voice and lute accompaniment and the other for multiple voices. About half of the ensemble settings are for three voices—including *Harden now thy hart with more than flinty rage, Jack and Jone they thinke no ill,* and *Sweet exclude me not nor be divided*—and the other half for four voices— including *As by the streames of Babilon, Lift up to heaven sad wretch thy heavy spright,* and *Sing a song of joy.* Campion's most famous lute song, also set for four voices, is *Tune thy musicke to thy hart.* The songs in *The Third and Fourth Booke of Ayres* exist only in settings for solo voice and lute. The masques, which contain a number of lute songs from the collections mentioned above, include *The Lords Maske* and *The Masque of Squires.*

ROBERT JONES FL.1597–1615

Jones apparently did not have a significant musical position during his life, and thus very little is known about him, including the places and dates of his birth and death. What is known is that he graduated with a bachelor's degree in music from Oxford University in 1597 and that he published five books of lute songs and one book of madrigals. In addition, he contributed a madrigal to *The Triumphes of Oriana.* The lute songs, like those of John Dowland and Thomas Campion, are generally scored twice, once for solo voice or voices and lute accompaniment and once for an ensemble of voices without lute. However, performance practices were not limited to only those choices, and Jones was especially helpful in this regard by specifying various options in the titles of his books. For instance, the title of his first book, published in 1600—*The First Booke of Songs or Ayres of Foure Parts with Tableture for the Lute, so made that all parts together, or either of them separately, may be sung to the lute, orpherian or viol de gambo*—suggests that any one or combination of voice parts may be sung, not just the soprano or all four voice parts together, and that accompaniment can be with lute, orpharion (a lute-like instrument), or viola da gamba (probably playing from the bass part, as a sort of basso continuo). Similarly, the book of madrigals published in 1607 and entitled *The first Set of Madrigals of 3, 4, 5, 6, 7, and 8 parts, for Viols and Voices, or for Voices alone, or as you please,* contains five madrigals scored for three voices, four for four voices, two for five voices, and one each for six, seven, and eight voices. The three-voiced pieces, all for SSA, include *Thine eyes so bright,* which is like the madrigals of Thomas Morley, with alternating phrases of imitative polyphony and homophony; *When I behold her eyes - But let her look in mine,* each movement of which is in an AAB format; and *Love, if a God thou art,* which is characterized by a dialogue of short motifs (e.g., the text fragment "if a God" at the beginning of the madrigal is tossed back and forth between the soprano and the other voices). *I come, sweet birds* for four voices and *Sweet, when thou singest* for five voices both feature word painting. Jones's contribution to *The Triumphes of Oriana* is *Fair Oriana seeming to wink at folly* scored for SSAATB.

JOHN BENNET FL.1599–1614

From the dedication to his book of madrigals, it is assumed that Bennet was born in the northwest of England between approximately 1575 and 1580. He composed one anthem, four Psalm settings, and eighteen madrigals. In addition, he contributed six secular pieces to Thomas

Ravenscroft's theoretical treatise, *A briefe Discorse of the True (but Neglected) Use of Charact'ring the Degrees.* The anthem, *O God of Gods - To the almighty trinity,* is in verse format and scored for solo voices, chorus, and viols; the Psalms settings, which are strophic and homophonic (like those of John Dowland), were included in *Barley's Psalter;* and the secular pieces in Ravenscroft's treatise include the canzonet *The elves dance.* All but one of the madrigals were published in Bennet's *Madrigalls to Foure Voyces* of 1599. Most of these pieces, like those mentioned above, are unknown today. However, one of the madrigals, *Weepe, O mine eyes,* not only is known today, it is perhaps the most popular and frequently performed Renaissance English madrigal in modern times. It is scored for SATB voices in an ABB format, with the A consisting of two points of imitation and the B consisting of duet imitation between the upper and lower voices. Other notable SATB madrigals in the 1599 publication are *O sleep, fond fancy* and *Ye restless thoughts.* While all of the madrigals are scored for four voices, they are not all for SATB. *Sing out, ye nymphes* is for SSTT, and *Weepe, silly soul disdained* and *I wander up and down* are for SSSA. These latter three madrigals, and all madrigals scored for two soprano parts, feature voice exchange (i.e., the two parts have an identical or almost identical range, and they share musical material at the same pitch or in the same tessitura). Bennet's one madrigal that was not published in the 1599 collection is *All creatures now are merry, merry minded,* which is perhaps the most famous madrigal in *The Triumphes of Oriana.*

THOMAS VAUTOR FL.1600–1620

Vautor, one of the minor madrigal composers whose works were popular at the beginning of the seventeenth century, received a bachelor's degree in music from Lincoln College, Oxford, in 1616. Later in his life he was employed by Sir George Villiers, a nobleman and father of the first Duke of Buckingham, who was reputedly the favorite lover of King James I. Vautor, like Michael Cavendish and John Bennet, published only one book of madrigals. Entitled *The First Set* [of Madrigals], *beeing Songs of divers Ayres and Natures of Five and Sixe parts, apt for Vyols and Voyces* and published in 1619, it contains thirteen pieces for five voices (one being in two movements) and five pieces for six voices. One of the five-voiced pieces, *Weepe, weepe, mine eyes,* is "an Elegie on the death of his right worshipfull Master, Sir Thomas Beaumont" (who died in 1614), scored for two soprano voices and five viols (two of the viols double the soprano parts). Similarly, *Melpomene, bewail thy sisters' loss - Whilst fatal sisters held the bloody knife,* an elegy composed for the death of Prince Henry in 1612, is scored mainly for two soprano voices and six viols (the top two viols doubling the soprano voices), although the second movement ends with text underlay in all six parts. The remaining pieces in the madrigal publication include the five-voiced *Mira cano, sol occubuit,* the six-voiced *Dainty sweet bird,* and Vautor's two most famous works—*Mother, I will have a husband* and *Sweet Suffolke owle.* The Latin madrigal, with long imitative phrases, is set to the text "Mira cano, sol occubuit, nox nulla secuta est" (I sing in wonder that the sun has died and no night has followed); *Dainty sweet bird,* scored for SSATTB voices, is characterized by rhythmic variety, voice pairings, and word painting (especially on "sing"); and *Mother I will have a husband* is mainly homophonic, scored for SSATB voices and in an ABA format. It is interesting to note that when the opening musical material of *Mother I will have a husband* returns, the two soprano parts are exchanged; that is, the second soprano becomes the first soprano and vice versa. *Sweet Suffolke owle,* also scored for SSATB voices and also featuring voice exchange between the two soprano parts, alternates phrases of imitative polyphony and homophony. In addition, the madrigal has notable examples of word painting: there are imitations of bird sounds with the text "te whit, te whoo," a long melisma is set to "rolls" in the phrase "thy note that forth so freely rolls," and the text "and sings a dirge for dying souls" is offset by longer rhythmic values and a slower meter.

JOHN FARMER FL.1591–1601

From remarks in the preface to Farmer's canons of 1591, it is assumed that he was born about 1570. During his youth he was under the patronage of Edward de Vere, Earl of Oxford, and from 1595 to 1599 he was Master of the Choristers and organist at Christ Church Cathedral in Dublin. For the last years of his life he lived in London. He composed forty canons, twenty settings of Psalms and Responses, and sixteen madrigals. The canons, all for two voices and all set to the same tune or cantus firmus, were published in 1591 as *Divers and Sundry Waies of Two Parts in One, to the Number of Fortie, upon One Playne Song*. The Psalms and Responses were contained in Thomas East's *English Psalter* of 1592, and the madrigals were in Farmer's *Madrigals to Foure Voyces* of 1599 and *The Triumphes of Oriana* of 1601. While the canons and Psalm settings are masterful examples of their genres, Farmer is best known for his madrigals, especially *Faire Phyllis*, which, along with John Bennet's *Weepe, O mine eyes*, is one of the most frequently performed madrigals in modern times. It is in an AABCC format, with notable examples of word painting: the opening phrase "Fair Phyllis I saw sitting all alone" is sung by only one voice, the phrase "but after her lover Amyntas hied" is begun with imitative entrances only one beat apart, and scalar passages depict the phrase "up and down he wandered." Two other madrigals are also well known—*Faire nymphs* and *A little pretty bonny lass*. The first, for SSATTB voices and published in *The Triumphes of Oriana*, is through composed, and the second, for SATB voices and published in Farmer's collection of 1599, is in ABB format. Several additional madrigals warrant mention: the eight-voiced *You blessed bowers* (which is the final madrigal in the 1599 collection), the four-voiced *Take time while time doth last* (which is thoroughly imitative), and *O stay sweet love - I thought my love* (both movements of which are ABB in structure).

THOMAS BATESON FL.1610–1630

Bateson was born in Cheshire County near Wales, most likely between 1570 and 1575. In 1599 he was appointed organist at Chester Cathedral, and in 1609 he became a singer and organist at Christ Church Cathedral in Dublin. He received a bachelor's degree in music from Trinity College, Dublin, in 1612 or 1615, and in 1622 he received a master of arts degree. Bateson composed one anthem (*Holie, Lord God allmightie* for seven voices) and fifty-three madrigals. The madrigals were published in two collections—*The first set of English Madrigales to 3, 4, 5, and 6 voices* in 1604, and *The Second Set of Madrigales to 3, 4, 5, and 6 Parts, apt for Viols and Voyces* in 1618. The first collection, for SSATTB voices, begins with *When Oriana walked* and has the subtitle inscription, "This song should have bene printed in the set of Orianaes" (i.e., *The Triumpes of Oriana*). It was not included because it was submitted too late for publication. Other madrigals in the first collection include *Come follow me, fair nymphs,* scored for SST voices in an imitative and rhythmically active texture, with dialogue of short motifs among the voices and with voice exchange between the two soprano parts, and the mainly homophonic *Your shining eyes,* scored for SAT voices. The four-voiced madrigals include *Whither so fast* and *If love be blind* for SATB, and *Adieu, sweet love* for SSAB (this latter madrigal featuring voice exchange between the two soprano voices). The five-voiced madrigals are represented by *Alas, where is my love* and Bateson's most popular work, *Those sweet delightful lilies.* Both are scored for SSATB, with characteristics of word painting and voice exchange. Popular madrigals in the second collection of madrigals are *Live not, poor bloom* for SATB, *The nightingale in silent night* for SSAT, and *Sadness, sit down* for SSATB.

FRANCIS PILKINGTON CA.1570–1638

Pilkington was born in Lancashire County in northern England, and in his youth he was under the patronage of the Earl of Derby. In 1595 he received a bachelor's degree in music from Lincoln College, Oxford, and from 1602 until the end of his life he served in a variety of musical and clerical capacities, including singer, precentor, and minister at Chester Cathedral, where he most certainly worked with Thomas Bateson. He composed one book of lute songs and two books of madrigals. The lute songs, published in *The First Booke of Songs or Ayres for 4 Voyces, apt for Lute, Orpharion, and Bass Violl* (1605), are, like those of John Dowland and Thomas Campion, scored so that they may be sung by a solo voice or by voices in ensemble, with various accompanimental options. Four notable songs in the collection are *Diaphenia, Rest sweet nimphes, Down a down thus Phillis sung,* and *Beautie sate bathing.* The first book of madrigals, entitled *The First Set of Madrigals and Pastorals for 3, 4, and 5 Voyces* and published in 1613, contains such pieces as *Sing we, dance on the green* for SSATB (a canzonet-like piece in AAB format); *Amyntas with his Phyllis fair* for SATB (a Morley-like madrigal, with alternating sections of imitative polyphony and homophony, and with descending scalar sequences depicting "down, dillie down"); and *What though her frowns and hard entreaties kill,* which is mostly homophonic. The second collection— *The Second Set of Madrigals and Pastorals of 3, 4, 5, and 6 Parts, apt for Violls and Voyces* of 1624— is represented by *Wake, sleepy Thyrsis* and *Sovereign of my delight* for SST (with voice exchanges between the two soprano parts); the mostly imitative *You gentle nymphs* for SSAB and *Palaemon and his Sylvia* for SATB; *Weepe, sad Urania,* an elegy on the death of Thomas Purcell (no known relation to Henry Purcell), scored mostly for two sopranos and five viols (with all parts texted at the end of the setting); and *O gracious God,* an anthem also called *O praise the Lord* for SSATB.

THOMAS TOMKINS 1572–1656

Tomkins was born in Pembroke, Wales, where his father, also named Thomas, became a singer at St David's Cathedral in 1576 and Master of the Choristers and organist in 1577. The younger Thomas was a chorister at the cathedral and then a student of William Byrd, to whom he dedicated his ballett *Too much I once lamented* with the inscription "To my ancient & much reverenced Master, William Byrd." In 1596 Tomkins was appointed organist at Worcester Cathedral, and in 1607 he received a bachelor's degree in music from Oxford University. He was made a Gentleman of the Chapel Royal in 1620, serving under Master of the Choristers Nathaniel Giles, and in 1621 he joined Orlando Gibbons as one of the chapel's organists.

Tomkins composed five Anglican Services plus a group of Responses and Psalms, 121 anthems, and thirty madrigals. Almost all of the sacred music was published posthumously in *Musica Deo sacra et ecclesiae anglicanae* of 1668 (generally referred to as *Musica Deo sacra*). The secular works and a few settings of sacred texts were published in *Songs of 3, 4, 5, & 6 parts* in 1622. The *First Service* (sometimes called the *Short Service*) and the *Second Service* are both full and are scored for four voices. In addition, both contain the same basic components: the *First Service* has the Venite, Te Deum, Benedictus, Kyrie, Creed, Magnificat, and Nunc dimittis, while the *Second Service* replaces the Benedictus with the Jubilate. The *Third Service* (also called the *Great Service*) is a verse setting of the Te Deum, Jubilate, Magnificat, and Nunc dimittis scored overall for eight voices, but with divisions for up to ten voices. The *Fourth Service* is a verse setting of the Te Deum, Magnificat, and Nunc dimittis for six voices, and the *Fifth Service*, also in verse format, consists of the Te Deum, Jubilate, Magnificat, and Nunc dimittis for five voices. All the Services have an organ part that is basically a reduction of the vocal parts.

The anthems are also divided between full and verse formats. The full anthems, almost all in an imitative style, include nineteen works scored for three voices. Most of these, such as *O Lord, rebuke me not* and *Out of the deep*, are for ATB. However, some are for other vocal distributions: *O Lord, open thou our lips* is for SAT, *Hear my prayer, O Lord, and consider* is for AAB, *Whom have I in heaven but thee* is for SAB, and *O Lord, how glorious are thy works* is for SST. The four-voiced full anthems are also variously scored. *Almighty and everlasting God which hatest nothing* and *I am the resurrection - I heard a voice from heaven saying* are for SATB; *Give ear unto my words - My voice shalt thou hear* and *The heavens declare* are for AATB (all men); and Tomkins's most popular anthem, *O pray for the peace of Jerusalem*, is for SSTB—the voice parts called by Tomkins, medius cantoris (mean on the *cantoris* side of the choir), medius decani (mean on the *decani* side of the choir), tenor, and bass. This scoring for two soprano voices has important performance practice implications, for not only are the two parts in the same vocal range, but they also exchange musical material. Full anthems scored for more than four voices include *Then David mourned with this lamentation* for SSATB, *O sing unto the Lord a new song* for SSAATBB, and *O praise the Lord, all ye heathen* for SSSAAATTTBBB.

The adroit balancing of imitative phrases in the full anthems, somewhat like that in Palestrina's motets, distinguishes Tomkins's anthems and significantly contributes to their high artistic status. *Then David mourned,* for instance, is divided into two overlapping points of imitation—one set to the text phrase "Then David mourned with this lamentation," and the other to "over Saul and over Jonathan his son." *O sing unto the Lord a new song* is divided into two sections of three text phrases each. The first section consists of the imitative "Sing unto the Lord a new song," the homophonic "Let the congregation of saints," and the imitative "sing praise unto him." The three phrases in the second section—"Let Israel rejoice in him that made him," "and let the children of Sion forever sing," and "Alleluia"—are all imitative. *O praise the Lord, all ye heathen* consists of imitative phrases except for the dramatic homophonic statement "and the truth of the Lord" in the center of the anthem.

The verse anthems are all scored for solo voices, chorus, and organ. Most of the anthems begin with a brief organ introduction followed by a solo and then alternating sections of music for chorus and varying solo combinations. *Behold, I bring you glad tidings* is unique in being scored for soprano solo only, SSAAAATTBB chorus, and organ. Similarly, *O Lord, let me know mine end* consists of long alto (contratenor) solos, SAATB chorus, and organ. *My beloved spake unto me* alternates various groupings of four solo voices in ensemble with SATB chorus, and *Above the stars* features the alto as soloist but also has solo parts for SSAABB in ensemble. *Above the stars* was set in a version for voices and viols as well as in a version for voices and organ.

Most of the pieces in *Songs of 3, 4, 5, & 6 parts* are settings of secular texts. Approximately half are madrigals characterized by word painting and alternating sections of imitative polyphony and homophony, and half are balletts, with repeated sections of music and *fa la la* refrains. Examples of the madrigals are *Adue, ye citty prisoning towers* (with descriptive melismas on the word "singing" and with short motifs exchanged between the voices), *Musicke devine* (with considerable rhythmic variety), and *O yes, has any found a lad* (with melismas on the word "flieth"). Examples of the balletts, all with *fa la la* refrains, are *See, see the shepheards queene; Too much I once lamented; Come, shepheards sing with me;* and *To the shady woods.* Four other pieces in the collection have sacred texts and were reprinted and included in *Musica Deo sacra.* The most famous of these, and probably the most famous composition by Tomkins, is *When David heard that Absolon was slain.* Its text and imitative texture are like his anthems. However, the texture is more vertically conceived, and unlike the anthems, the scoring was initially without a keyboard part. The work is properly, therefore, a spiritual madrigal. It is especially not, as it is frequently called in modern-day publications, a Tudor anthem, since the House of Tudor ended with Elizabeth I in 1603 (James I, who ruled from 1603 to 1625, and Charles I, who ruled from 1625 to 1649, were of the House of Stuart), and since it is unlike the anthems composed during the Tudor period.

SACRED WORKS
SELECTED AND LISTED ACCORDING TO FAMILIARITY

O pray for the peace of Jerusalem – SSTB chorus – 2 minutes.

I heard a voice from heaven saying – SATB chorus – 2:30 minutes.

Above the stars – SSAABB solos, SSATBB chorus, and organ – 4 minutes.

Then David mourned with his lamentation – SSATB chorus – 3:30 minutes.

Christ rising again from the dead (subtitled "for Easter Day") – SATB solos, SATB chorus, and organ – 3:30 minutes.

Almighty and everlasting God, which hatest nothing – SATB chorus – 3 minutes.

O sing unto the Lord a new song – SSAATBB chorus – 3:30 minutes.

The heavens declare – AATB chorus – 3 minutes.

O praise the Lord, all ye heathen – SSSAAATTTBBB chorus – 4:30 minutes.

Third (Great) Service – SSAATTBB solos, SSAAAATTBB chorus, and organ – 30 minutes.

My shepherd is the living Lord – SA solos, SATB chorus, and organ – 3:30 minutes.

I am the resurrection · I heard a voice from heaven saying – SATB chorus –
   4 minutes.

O Lord, grant the king a long life (subtitled "The Coronation Anthem") – SAB
   solos, SAATB chorus, and organ – 3:30 minutes.

God, who as at this time (subtitled "The Collect for Whitsunday," also called
   God, which as on this day) – SSATB solos, SAATB chorus, and organ –
   3:30 minutes.

Almighty God, which hast knit together (subtitled "The Collect for All Saints'
   Day") – SSAATTBB solos, SSAATTBB chorus, and organ – 4:30 minutes.

Behold, I bring you glad tidings – S solo, SSAAAATTBB chorus, and organ –
   3 minutes.

O Lord, let me know mine end – A solo, SAATB chorus, and organ – 5:30 minutes.

MADRIGALS AND BALLETTS
SELECTED AND LISTED ACCORDING TO FAMILIARITY

When David heard that Absolon was slain – SAATB voices – 4:30 minutes.

Adue, ye citty prisoning towers – SSATB voices – 3 minutes.

Too much I once lamented – SSATB voices – 5 minutes.

Musicke devine – SSATTB voices – 3 minutes.

O yes, has any found a lad – SATB voices – 2 minutes.

Come, shepheards, sing with me – SSATB voices – 3:30 minutes.

To the shady woods – SSATB voices – 2 minutes.

The fauns and satyrs tripping – SSATB voices – 4:30 minutes.

JOHN WILBYE 1574–1638

Wilbye was born in Suffolk County, northeast of London, and was employed for most of his life by the Kytson family, who lived in Hengrave Hall near Bury St Edmonds. The Kytsons were patrons of music who retained a relatively large number of musicians in their home until 1628, when Lady Elizabeth Kytson died and the musical establishment was disassembled. At that time Wilbye followed one of the remaining Kytsons to Colchester, where he stayed for the remainder of his life.

He composed three anthems, one Latin motet, and fifty-eight madrigals and canzonets. Two of the anthems—*I am quite tired* for four voices and *O God, the rocke of my whole strength* for five voices—were composed for William Leighton's *The Teares or Lamentacions of a Sorrowfull Soule* published in 1614. The third anthem, *O who shall ease me* for six voices, exists only in manuscript. The motet *Homo natus de muliere* (Job 14:1–2) is for six voices (SSAATB) and was also not published during Wilbye's lifetime. It is mainly imitative, with melismatic word painting and dramatic scoring that increases from two to five voices at the phrase "et fugit velut umbra" (he flees as it were a shadow).

The madrigals and canzonets were published in two collections—*The First Set of English Madrigals* in 1598 and *The Second Set of Madrigales, apt both for Voyals and Voyces* in 1609. In addition, Wilbye's madrigal *The lady Oriana* holds the distinction of being the first piece in *The Triumphes of Oriana* published in 1601. The six three-voiced pieces in the 1598 collection are like the canzonets of Thomas Morley, with short imitative phrases and repeated sections of music. *Fly love aloft to heaven, Weepe O mine eyes,* and *Yee restlesse thoughts* are examples. The mainly homophonic five-voiced *Flora gave mee fairest flowers,* one of Wilbye's most popular pieces, is also a canzonet like those of Morley. The other pieces are more in the serious madrigal style of George Kirbye, who was employed at nearby Rushbrooke Hall and who Wilbye most certainly knew. *Adew, sweet Amarillis,* another of Wilbye's most popular madrigals, has varied rhythms for expressive effect, exchanges of short motifs, and overlapping imitative phrases that alternate with homophonic (or mostly homophonic) passages. *Lady, when I beehold* for four voices (there is another setting for six voices) is similar, although there are notable duet passages and the homophony is more frequent.

The collection of 1609 is similar in content, scope, and style, although there are more examples of word painting. In the three-voiced *O what shall I doe,* for example, there are very long melismas in all three voices simultaneously on the word "swell" of the phrase "for tears being stopped will swell for scope"; *Weepe, mine eyes* for five voices has alternating phrases of varied rhythmic values (i.e., phrases scored for white note values alternate with phrases scored for black note values) and a dramatic homophonic parlando exclamation to the text "ah cruel fortune"; and *Sweet hony sucking bees - Yet sweet take heed* has several examples of word painting, including sequences of downward scalar passages on the text "ah, then you die." Wilbye's most acclaimed madrigal from the 1609 collection, and one of the most admired English madrigals of the entire Renaissance era, is *Draw on sweet night.* Structured of five points of imitation that coincide with the five sentences of the text (the first and last two of which are divided into overlapping subphrases), it is a masterpiece of balanced proportions.

SECULAR WORKS
SELECTED AND LISTED ACCORDING TO FAMILIARITY

Flora gave mee fairest flowers – SSATB voices – 1:30 minutes.

Adew, sweet Amarillis – SATB voices – 3 minutes.

Weepe, mine eyes – SSATB voices – 4:30 minutes.

Draw on sweet night – SSATTB voices – 5 minutes.

Sweet hony sucking bees – *Yet sweet take heed* – SSATB voices – 6 minutes.

Lady, when I beehold – SATB voices – 2:30 minutes.

The lady Oriana – SSATTB voices – 2:30 minutes.

O what shall I doe – SSB voices – 3 minutes.

Oft have I vowde – SSATB voices – 3:30 minutes.

THOMAS WEELKES 1576–1623

Weelkes was born in West Sussex, where his father was rector at the church of St Paul and where he most likely received his first musical education. He was appointed organist of Winchester College in 1598, he became a singer and organist at Chichester Cathedral in about 1601, and in 1602 he received a bachelor's degree in music from New College, Oxford. Weelkes claimed to have entered the Chapel Royal as a Gentleman sometime around 1602, but there are no records to support this claim, and at this time he was still employed at Chichester Cathedral. During the second decade of the seventeenth century he was repeatedly cited for public drunkenness, and in 1617 he was dismissed from his positions at the cathedral, although he returned temporarily in the early 1620s. However, most of the final years of his life were spent in London, where he died at age forty-seven.

Weelkes composed ten Anglican Services, approximately fifty anthems, and one hundred madrigals, balletts, and canzonets. Six of the Services are in verse format (for soloists, chorus, and organ) and the other four in full format (for chorus alone). Although none of the Services were published during the Renaissance and all the surviving manuscripts are incomplete, a number of portions from various Services have been published in modern times, including the Magnificat and Nunc dimittis from the *Sixth Service* (scored for SSAATB soloists, SAATB chorus, and organ); the Magnificat and Nunc dimittis from the *Service for Trebles* (for SSTBB solos, SSATB chorus, and organ); the Te Deum from the *Eighth Service* (for SSAATTB soloists, SAATTB chorus, and organ); and the Jubilate from the *First Service* (for SS soloists, SAATB chorus, and organ). The anthems, except for two in William Leighton's *The Teares or Lamentacions of a Sorrowfull Soule* of 1614, were also unpublished during the Renaissance. However, most of them survive in multiple manuscripts and have been issued in numerous modern-day publications. The full anthems are mainly imitative, although varied in treatment. *O Lord, arise*, for instance, is entirely constructed of medium-length phrases set to overlapping points of imitation; *Lord, to thee I make my moan* has a mixture of imitative phrase lengths, some of which are fragments of only two words; and *O how amiable are thy dwellings* and *All people clap your hands* have several homophonic passages that offset the imitative phrases. Weelkes's two most famous full anthems—*Hosanna to the son of David* and *Alleluia, I heard a voice*—are distinctive in having soloistic phrases that are texturally prominent. In the initial homophonic phrase of *Hosanna to the son of David*, for example, the tenor voice is rhythmically active while the other voices are not, and in *Alleluia, I heard a voice* the first bass declaims the text "I heard a voice as of strong thund'rings," with a virtuosic melisma on the word "thund'rings." This passage may have been meant for a soloist, but if so, it is the only solo passage in the anthem.

The majority of the madrigals, balletts, and canzonets were published in four collections. The first, *Madrigals to 3, 4, 5, & 6 Voyces* of 1597, contains mostly lighthearted pieces of little distinction. Exceptions are the chromatic *Cease sorrowes now* and the imitative *Three virgin nimphes*. The second collection, *Balletts and Madrigals to Five Voyces, with One to 6 Voyces* of 1598, contains a balance of both serious and nonserious pieces and was so popular that it was reprinted a decade after its initial publication. Two notable balletts, both with *fa la la* refrains, are *Harke all ye lovely saints above* and *Sing wee at pleasure*. The third collection, *Madrigals of 5 and 6 Parts, apt for the Viols and Voices* of 1600, contains two of Weelkes's most celebrated secular madrigals, both constructed of two movements. *O care, thou wilt dispatch mee - Hence, care, thou art too cruel* has elements of the ballett style (a mainly homophonic texture, with *fa la la* passages) fused with the serious imitative polyphony of madrigals, and *Thule, the period of cosmographie - The Andalusian merchant* is like the madrigals of Thomas Tomkins, with alternating sections of imitative polyphony and homophony, dramatic word painting, and rhythmic variety. The final collection of secular music, *Ayers or Phantasticke Spirites for Three Voices* of 1608, contains canzonets, mostly set to humorous texts. Examples include *Come sirrah Jacke hoe, fill some tobacco; Since Robin Hood, Maid Marion, and Little John are gone-a; Fowre armes, two neckes, one wreathing; The ape, the monkey, and baboon did meet;* and *Though my carriage be but carelesse.* Oddly, the 1608 collection also contains the serious and imitative madrigal elegy *Death hath deprived me of my dearest friend,* subtitled "A remembrance of my friend M. Thomas Morley."

Weelkes's famous secular madrigal *As Vesta was from Latmos hill descending* from *The Triumphes of Oriana* is one of the best-known English madrigals of the Renaissance, distinguished by striking instances of word painting, including upward scalar passages on the word "ascending," downward scalar passages to the text "came running down amain," two voices to the phrase "first two by two," three voices to "then three by three," only one voice to "all alone," and imitative entrances on the phrase "and mingling with the shepherds of her train." In addition, the madrigal ends with augmented statements of the phrase "Long live fair Oriana" in the bass part.

Two spiritual madrigals were not published in any of the collections mentioned above. *O Jonathan, woe is me for thee,* set to a poetic paraphrase of 2 Samuel 1:25–26, is mainly imitative, with several brief strategically placed homophonic passages that provide for poignant emotive expression. *When David heard that Absalom was slain,* set to the same text as that used by Tomkins (2 Samuel 18:33), is considered one of the great masterpieces of Renaissance polyphony. It is especially noted for the point-of-imitation phrase "would God I had died for thee" that builds to a climax of two cross-relations, both between the top soprano and tenor voices and both only two beats apart.

ANTHEMS
SELECTED AND LISTED ACCORDING TO FAMILIARITY

Hosanna to the son of David – SSATBB chorus – 3 minutes.

Alleluia, I heard a voice – SSATB chorus – 3:30 minutes.

O Lord, arise – SSAATBB chorus – 2:30 minutes.

All people clap your hands – SAATB chorus – 2:30 minutes.

Gloria in excelsis Deo (with continuing text "Sing my soul to God the Lord") – SSAATB chorus – 3:30 minutes.

Lord to thee I make my moan – SAATB chorus – 3 minutes.

O how amiable are thy dwellings – SAATB chorus – 3:30 minutes.

Give ear, O Lord – SSAATB solos, SAATB chorus, and organ – 4: 30 minutes.

In thee, O Lord – B solo, SATB chorus, and organ – 3 minutes.

MADRIGALS, BALLETTS, AND CANZONETS
SELECTED AND LISTED ACCORDING TO FAMILIARITY

When David heard that Absalom was slain – SSAATB voices – 4:45 minutes.

O Jonathan, woe is me for thee – SSAATB voices – 2:30 minutes.

As Vesta was from Latmos hill descending – SSATTB voices – 4 minutes.

Thule, the period of cosmographie - The Andalusian merchant – SSATTB voices – 6 minutes.

Harke all ye lovely saints above – SSATB voices – 3 minutes.

Sing wee at pleasure – SSATB voices – 3 minutes.

O care, thou wilt dispatch mee - Hence, care, thou art too cruel – SATTB voices – 6 minutes.

Like two proud armies – SSATTB voices – 4 minutes.

Death hath deprived me of my dearest friend – SSATTB voices – 5 minutes.

Come sirrah Jacke hoe, fill some tobacco – SST voices – 2 minutes.

Strike it up tabor – SST voices – 2 minutes.

Since Robin Hood, Maid Marian, and Little John are gone-a – SST voices – 2 minutes.

Fowre armes, two neckes, one wreathing – SSA voices – 2 minutes.

The nightingale, the organ of delight – SSA voices – 2 minutes.

Tan ta ra ran tan tant, cryes Mars – SSA voices – 2 minutes.

RICHARD DERING (DEERING) CA.1580–1630

Dering was born in London, where he most likely spent his youth and received his musical education. In about 1600 he enrolled at Oxford University, and in 1610 he received a bachelor's degree from Christ Church. In 1612 he went to Italy, first to Venice and then to Rome, where he converted from the Anglican faith to Catholicism, and in 1617 he went to Brussels, where he was appointed organist at the Benedictine convent of English nuns. While in Brussels he most certainly became acquainted with Peter Philips and John Bull. In 1625 he returned to England as Musician for the Lutes and Voices to King Charles I and organist to Queen Henrietta Maria, who was Catholic and was allowed to openly observe her faith even though the king was Anglican.

Dering composed sixty-three Latin motets, three anthems, fifty-five Italian madrigals and canzonets, and two English madrigals. The motets were published in three collections—*Cantiones sacrae quinque vocum, cum basso continuo ad organum* in 1617, *Cantica sacra senis vocibus cum basso continuo ad organum* in 1618, and *Cantica sacra* (posthumously) in 1662. Notable motets from the first collection include *Ave verum corpus; Jesu, dulcis memoria;* and *O bone Jesu.* Most of the well-known and critically acclaimed motets, however, are in the second collection. Examples include *Cantate Domino,* which is constructed of alternating sections of imitative polyphony and homophony, including dialogue of very short motifs (e.g., three notes to the syllables of "cantate"); *Jubilate Deo universa terra,* which has considerable rhythmic variety; *Quem vidistis pastores,* which features the upper and lower voices in dialogue; and Dering's most famous motet, *Factum est silentium*, which has all the characteristics listed above and which is a dramatic setting of the text for Lauds on Michaelmas Day, "Factum est silentium in coelo dum committeret bellum draco cum Michaele archangelo. Audita est vox milia milium, dicentium: salus, honor, et virtus omnipotenti Deo, alleluia" (There was silence in heaven while the dragon joined battle with the archangel Michael. A thousand cries were heard, saying: salvation, honor, and power be to almighty God, alleluia). While all the motets in the 1617 and 1618 collections are scored for organ, the organ parts are merely reductions of the vocal parts. The 1662 collection, however, contains vocal concertos scored for two and three voices and independent organ parts. An example is *Miserere mei, Deus* for SB and organ. It is interesting to note that many of the motets in all three collections are settings of the same texts used by Philips, including *Factum est silentium, Ave verum corpus, O quam suavis, Gaudent in coelis, O bone Jesu,* and *O crux ave spes unica.* The anthems are *And the king was moved* (in full format for five voices throughout), and *Almighty God, who through thy only begotten son* and *Unto thee, O Lord* (both in verse format for soloists, chorus, and organ).

The secular music includes two collections of Italian canzonets—*Canzonette a tre voce* published in 1620 and *Canzonette a quatro voce* published in 1620—and a group of eighteen Italian and two English madrigals that were not published until modern times. The canzonets are in the *prima prattica* style of Orazio Vecchi and Giovanni Croce, and the Italian madrigals are scored for one to three voices and are in the *seconda prattica* style of Claudio Monteverdi. In addition to compositions in these genres, Dering composed two works for single solo voice and an ensemble of viols that were also not published but that were quite popular during the seventeenth century—the quodlibets *The City Cries* and *The Country Cries.*

LATIN MOTETS
SELECTED AND LISTED ACCORDING TO FAMILIARITY

Factum est silentium – SSATTB chorus – 3 minutes.

Quem vidistis pastores – SSATTB chorus – 3:30 minutes.

Jubilate Deo universa terra – SSAATB chorus – 2:30 minutes.

Cantate Domino – SSATTB chorus – 3 minutes.

Ave verum corpus – SATTB chorus – 3:45 minutes.

Jesu, dulcis memoria – SATTB chorus – 3:30 minutes.

O bone Jesu – SATTB chorus – 3 minutes.

Ave virgo gratiosa (or *gloriosa*) – SSATB chorus – 2 minutes.

MICHAEL EAST CA.1580–1648

Michael East was probably the nephew of Thomas East (ca.1540–1608), the printer of many notable music collections, including *The Triumphes of Oriana,* both editions of *Musica transalpina,* and the metrical psalter *The Whole Booke of Psalmes, with their Wonted Tunes.* In 1606 Michael received a bachelor's degree in music from Cambridge University, and in 1609 he became a lay clerk at Ely Cathedral. He served in this capacity off and on for most of the next decade, and in 1618 he was appointed Master of the Choristers at Lichfield Cathedral, where he remained for thirty years.

Almost all of East's compositions were published in seven collections (a Magnificat and Nunc dimittis and a Burial Service exist only in manuscript). The first collection, *Madrigales to 3, 4, and 5 parts, apt for Viols and Voices* of 1604, contains seven pieces for three voices (one in two movements), eight pieces for four voices, and six pieces for five voices (two in two movements). Most of these pieces, such as the SSATB *All yee that joy in wayling*, have textures of alternating imitative polyphony and homophony, and a few of the pieces, such as the SSA *O doe not run away*, contain striking examples of word painting (e.g., a complete downward scale to the text "thou hast cast me down to the ground"). The second collection, *The Second Set of Madrigales to 3, 4, and 5 parts, apt for Viols and Voices* of 1606, is similar to the first in content and vocal distribution. *In dolorus complaining - Since tears would not obtain* for SSAT is characterized by rhythmic variety and voice exchange between the two soprano parts, and *O metaphysical tobacco*, one of East's most popular madrigals, is in ABB format. The third collection, *The Third Set of Bookes, wherein are Pastorals, Anthemes, Neopolitanes, Fancies, and Madrigales to 5 and 6 parts, apt both for Viols and Voyces* of 1610, consists of three mainly homophonic pieces in the style of Italian ballettos (the "Neopolitanes"), including *Come life, come death* for SSATB and *Poor is the life* for SSATTB—both in ABB format; four madrigals, including *Now must I part*; one pastorale in three movements scored for SS solos and three viols that alternate with SSATB chorus; two verse anthems—*When Israel came out of Egypt - What aileth thee* and *Turn thy face from my wickednesse*; and eight purely instrumental fantasies. The fourth collection, *The Fourth Set of Bookes, wherein are Anthemes for Versus and Chorus, Madrigals, and Songs of other Kindes to 4, 5, & 6 parts, apt for Viols and Voyces* of 1618, is similar to the third collection of 1610 and includes *Quicke, quicke, away dispatch - No haste but good* and *When David heard that Absalom was slaine*, which borrows musical material from Thomas Weelkes's setting of the same text. The fifth collection, *The Fift Set of Bookes, wherein are Songs full of Spirit and Delight, so composed that they are as apt for Vyols as Voyces* of 1618, contains only three-voiced pieces for viols; none have texts. The sixth collection, *The Sixt Set of Bookes, wherein are Anthemes for Versus and Chorus, apt for Violls and Voyces* of 1624, contains settings of sacred texts, including the full anthem *Awake and stand up*. Finally, the seventh collection, *The Seventh Set of Bookes, wherein are duos for Two Base Viols* of 1638, contains only instrumental pieces.

THOMAS FORD CA.1580–1648

Ford, who was one of the instrumental musicians in the royal court under King Charles I, composed approximately twenty anthems and forty secular pieces, most of which are unknown. The several compositions that are known, however, are quite familiar to modern-day choral musicians. These include the two anthems in William Leighton's *The Teares or Lamentacions of a Sorrowfull Soule* published in 1614—*Almighty God which hast me brought* for four voices (SATB) and *Not unto us but to thy name* for five voices (SSATB). Even better known are several of his lute songs, which, like those of John Dowland, were set for both solo voice with lute accompaniment and for SATB voices (with or without lute *colla parte*). Of particular fame are *What then is love;*

There is a ladie, sweet and kind; and *Since first I saw your face.* All were published in *Musicke of Sundrie Kindes* in 1607, and all are basically homophonic, strophic (with three to six verses), and in an ABB format.

ORLANDO GIBBONS 1583–1625

Gibbons was born in Oxford, and from 1596 to 1599 he was a chorister at King's College, Cambridge, where his brother Edward was Master of the Choristers. Orlando's younger brother Ellis, also a musician, contributed two madrigals to *The Triumphes of Oriana* in 1601. In 1603 Orlando entered the Chapel Royal as a Gentleman, and in 1606 he received a bachelor's degree in music from Cambridge. He held a number of important positions at the Chapel Royal, including senior organist and chamber musician to the king, and beginning in 1623 he also served as organist at Westminster Abbey. It is presumed, though not verified, that he received a doctorate from Oxford University in 1622.

He composed two Anglican Services plus a small number of Responses and Psalms, forty anthems, thirteen English madrigals (two of which are in two movements and one of which is in four movements), and two consort songs. The *First Service* (called the *Short Service* because of its syllabic texture and scoring for four voices) contains the Venite, Te Deum, Benedictus, Kyrie, Creed, Magnificat, and Nunc dimittis. The *Second Service* is scored for soloists, chorus, and organ and contains only the Te Deum, Jubilate, Magnificat, and Nunc dimittis.

The anthems include twenty-five works for chorus alone (full anthems) and fifteen works for soloists, chorus, and organ (verse anthems). The full anthems are structured of continuous and overlapping points of imitation, with little rhythmic variety and almost no passages of homophony. The smaller-scale full anthems are characterized by pervasive imitation and balanced phrases in the style of Palestrina motets or anthems by Thomas Tomkins. For example, the famous *Almighty and everlasting God* is divided into two sections, each of which consists of two relatively equal points of imitation and a short closing coda. The larger-scale full anthems are characterized by exchanges of musical material between *decani* and *cantoris* ensembles and also by imitative phrases of varying lengths. In *Hosanna to the son of David* there is frequent voice exchange at the same pitch level between the *decani* and *cantoris* parts, and in *O clap your hands together* the phrases vary from the lengthy "God is gone up with a merry noise, and the Lord with the sound of the trumpet" to the brief "O sing praises."

The verse anthems include six works scored for soloists, chorus, and organ, and nine works for soloists, chorus, and ensemble of viols. In general, those scored with organ accompaniment have multiple solo parts that are imitative (e.g., the SAATB solos in *Behold, I bring you glad tidings* and the SSA and SS solos in *If ye be risen again with Christ*). The anthems with viol accompaniment are more often for single solos, with the viol parts in an imitative texture (e.g., *Behold, thou hast made my days* and *This is the record of John*). This latter anthem, undoubtedly Gibbons's most famous composition, is particularly noteworthy for the narrative quality of the text from John 1:19 and the repetition of solo text phrases by the chorus.

The madrigals, all published in the collection entitled *The First Set of Madrigals and Mottets, apt for Viols and Voyces* of 1612, are generally like the full anthems in being constructed of overlapping points of imitation. The large-scale works such as *O that the learned poets of this time* and *Trust not too much, faire youth* are especially so. The four-movement *I waigh not fortunes frowne* -

I tremble not at noyse of warre · I see ambition never pleasde · I faine not friendship is also largely imitative; with its semisacred text, it is the only work in the collection that could be called a motet. The smaller-scale pieces are more vertically conceived, with less dense polyphony and with occasional passages that are homophonic in spirit (i.e., not all, but most voices at any one time are homophonic). Examples include *Daintie fine bird; Ah, deere hart;* and Gibbons's most famous secular piece, *The silver swanne.* The consort songs, scored for five solo voices and a consort of five viols, are *Do not repine, fair sun* and *The Cryes of London.* This latter work, which was quite popular during the seventeenth century, is divided into two movements, both of which consist of numerous brief vocal solo passages that depict street vendors selling their wares (e.g., "new mussels, new lily-white mussels" and "oysters, three-pence a peck"). The viols play in full textures throughout the work, while the solo passages are isolated and scattered except for the ending of the first movement, when the voices come together to sing "And so we make an end," and at the conclusion of the work's second movement, when they sing "and so goodnight."

ANTHEMS
SELECTED AND LISTED ACCORDING TO FAMILIARITY

This is the record of John – A solo, SAATB chorus, five viols, and organ – 4:15 minutes.

Almighty and everlasting God – SATB chorus – 2:30 minutes.

Hosanna to the son of David – SSAATTB chorus – 2:45 minutes.

O clap your hands together – SSAATTBB chorus – 5:45 minutes.

O Lord, in thy wrath – SSAATB chorus – 3:45 minutes.

O Lord, increase my faith – SATB chorus – 2:15 minutes.

Why art thou heavy, O my soul – SATB chorus – 2:30 minutes. The anthem is also ascribed to Henry Loosemore.

Behold, I bring you glad tidings – SAATB solos, SAATB chorus, and organ – 4:15 minutes.

Behold, thou hast made my days – A solo, SAATB chorus, five viols, and organ – 4:30 minutes.

Great Lord of Lords (also called *Great King of Gods*) – AAB solos, SAATB chorus, five viols, and organ – 4 minutes.

If ye be risen again with Christ – SSA solos, SSATB chorus, and organ – 4:30 minutes.

MADRIGALS
SELECTED AND LISTED ACCORDING TO FAMILIARITY

The silver swanne – SATTB voices – 2 minutes.

Daintie fine bird – SSATB voices – 2 minutes.

Ah, deere hart – SATTB voices – 2:30 minutes.

O that the learned poets of this time – SSATB voices – 3 minutes.

Trust not too much, faire youth – SSATB voices – 3:45 minutes.

What is our life – SSATB voices – 4 minutes.

JOHN WARD CA.1589–1638

Ward was born in Canterbury, where he was a chorister at Canterbury Cathedral between 1597 and 1604 and a choral scholar during the several years thereafter. In 1607 he entered the London household of arts patron Sir Henry Fanshawe, and in 1616, with Sir Henry's death and the subsequent reduction of musical activity by his son Sir Thomas, Ward supplemented his income as an attorney.

He composed two partial Anglican Services, twenty anthems, and approximately twenty-five madrigals. The Services—the *First Service* and the *Second Service*—both contain only Magnificat and Nunc dimittis settings. Both are also in verse format (scored for soloists, chorus, and organ). The anthems are mostly settings of Psalms, including *Praise the Lord, O my soul* (Psalm 103), *How long wilt thou forget me* (Psalm 13), *Let God arise* (Psalm 68), and *Have mercy on me* (Psalm 51). Several anthems were composed for ceremonial occasions—*No object dearer* for the death of Prince Henry in 1612; *This is a joyful, happy, holy day* for the investiture of Charles as Prince of Wales in 1616; and *If heaven's just wrath* for the death of Sir Henry Fanshawe.

Ward is best known for his madrigals published in 1613 in a collection entitled *The First Set of English Madrigals to 3, 4, 5, & 6 parts, apt both for Viols and Voyces, with a Mourning Song in memory of Prince Henry*. Most of the madrigals are imitative, like the serious works of John Wilbye, Thomas Weelkes, and Orlando Gibbons, and most are scored for two soprano voice parts that frequently participate in voice exchange. Examples are *My true love hath my heart - His heart his wound received* for SSA; *Sweet pity, wake* for SSAT; *Sweet Philomel - Ye sylvan nymphs* and *Upon a bank* for SSATB; and Ward's most famous madrigal, *Come, sable night* for SSATTB, which features voice exchange between the two tenor voices as well.

ADRIAN BATTEN 1591–1637

Batten was born in Salisbury and was a chorister at nearby Winchester Cathedral. In 1615 he became a singer at Westminster Abbey, where he was also a copyist of scores by such notable composers as Thomas Tallis, Thomas Weelkes, and Thomas Tomkins, and where he probably copied the collection of organ accompaniments named for him—the *Batten Organbook*. In 1626 he left Westminster Abbey and became a singer at St Paul's Cathedral.

He composed eight Anglican Services and approximately fifty anthems. The Services include the *Full Service* (which is scored for soloists, chorus, and organ, and which contains a Te Deum, Jubilate, Kyrie, Creed, Magnificat, and Nunc dimittis) and the *Short Service* (which is scored for four-part chorus and includes a Venite, Te Deum, Jubilate, Benedictus, Kyrie, Creed, Sanctus, Gloria, Magnificat, and Nunc dimittis). The anthems include several in verse format, such as *Hear my prayer O Lord, Out of the deep,* and *O Lord thou hast searched me out.* Batten is best known, however, for his small-scale mostly homophonic full anthems scored for SATB chorus. Some of the most popular of these are *O sing joyfully; When the Lord turned again the captivity of Sion; Let my complaint come before thee O Lord; Deliver us, O Lord our God;* and *O Praise the Lord all ye heathen.*

THOMAS RAVENSCROFT CA.1592–CA.1635

Ravenscroft was a chorister at St Paul's Cathedral in London and a student at Gresham College after his voice changed. In 1605 he received a bachelor's degree in music from Cambridge University, and from 1618 to 1622 he was Master of Music at Christ's Hospital. He composed sixteen anthems, three motets, six canzonets, and more than one hundred catches and rounds. In addition, he authored the treatise *A Briefe Discourse of the True (but Neglected) Use of Charact'ring the Degrees by their Perfection* (1614) and published the collection *The Whole Booke of Psalmes* (1621). Most of the anthems are in verse format for soloists, chorus, and ensemble of viols. Representatives are *Ah, helpless wretch; All laud and praise;* and his most famous anthem, *O let me hear thy loving kindness.* The canzonets, all scored for SATB voices in a homophonic texture, include *Toss the pot* and *By a bank as I lay.* The catches and rounds, for which he is most known, were published in 1609 in two collections—*Pammelia,* which contains one hundred secular and sacred pieces for three to ten voices and which is the earliest printed collection of its kind, and *Deuteromelia,* which contains fourteen songs and seventeen catches. Representative of the sacred rounds are *O Lord turne not away thy face* and *Remember O thou man* (subtitled "A Christmas Carroll"), both for four voices. The secular rounds include *Oken leaves* and *Wee be three poore mariners* for three voices, *Blow thy horne thou jolly hunter* for four voices, *Sing you now after me* for five voices, *Hey ho, what shall I do* for nine voices, and *Sing we now merrily* for ten voices.

ROBERT RAMSEY D.1644

Beginning in 1615 Ramsey was Master of the Choristers and organist at Trinity College, Cambridge, and in 1616 he received a bachelor's degree in music from the university. He composed two settings of the Te Deum and Jubilate in Latin, one Litany, four surviving Latin motets, one Anglican Service, eight complete anthems, eight madrigals, and several consort songs. The Latin church music was probably composed for Peterhouse College, Cambridge, where Latin was regularly sung during the early decades of the seventeenth century. One of the Te Deum/Jubilate works is scored for SATB chorus, with alternating sections for *decani* and *cantoris* ensembles. The other Te Deum/Jubilate is scored for SATTB solos (usually SAT together) and SATTB chorus. The motets, all of which alternate sections of imitative polyphony and homophony, are *O sapientia* for SSATB, *In monte Oliveti* and *O vos omnes* for SSATTB, and *Inclina Domine aurem tuam* for SSAATTBB. The Anglican Service, scored for SATB *decani* and *cantoris* choruses in a homophonic texture, has settings of the Te Deum, Jubilate, Kyrie, Litany, Creed, Magnificat, and Nunc dimittis. The seven full anthems include four for SSATB chorus (*Almighty and everlasting God, we humbly beseech; Almighty and everlasting God, which hast given; God, which as upon this day;* and *Grant, we beseech thee, Almighty God*), one for SATTB chorus (*O come, let us sing unto the Lord*), one for SSATTB chorus (*How are the mighty fallen*), and one for SSATBB chorus (*When

David heard that Absalon was slain). The verse anthem, *My song shall be alway*, is scored for B solo, SATB chorus, and organ.

The madrigals and consort songs include two pieces composed upon the death of Prince Henry—the famous *Sleep, fleshly birth* for SSATTB voices, and *Dialogues of Sorrow upon the death of the late Prince Henrie* for six voices and ensemble of six viols.

JOHN HILTON 1599–1657

John Hilton was the son of John Hilton (d.1609), who was an organist at Trinity College, Cambridge, and the composer of the madrigal *Fair Oriana, beauty's queen* in *The Triumphes of Oriana*. The younger Hilton received a bachelor's degree from Trinity College in 1626, and in 1628 he became organist at St Margaret's Church in Westminster. He composed four Anglican Services, seventeen anthems (five full and twelve verse), forty-two catches and rounds, and several canzonets. The Services include the *Whole Service* for four voices, which contains settings of the Te Deum, Jubilate, Kyrie, Magnificat, and Nunc dimittis. The anthems, many of which are ascribed to both Hiltons, include the famous *Call to remembrance* for SATB chorus. The catches and rounds were published in a popular collection entitled *Catch that Catch Can* (1652), and the canzonets, all for three voices, were published in *Ayers or Fa La's* (1627). Examples of the three-voiced rounds are *If you will drink for pleasure; March bravely on, boys; Pretty Nan;* and *Arm, arm, arm*.

3

THE BAROQUE ERA

The Baroque era began in the early years of the seventeenth century as a result of four circumstances: (1) a reaction against the overly dense textures of Renaissance polyphony, (2) a desire to emulate perceived attributes of Greek monody, (3) a shift from textures that were melodically linear and imitative to textures that were harmonically vertical and homophonic, and (4) an independent status of instruments in vocal music. None of these circumstances occurred suddenly, and all of them had their beginnings prior to the year 1600. For instance, leaders of the Protestant Reformation during the latter half of the sixteenth century desired music that was simple, direct, and accessible to the general uncultivated public, and the proponents of the Counter-Reformation leveled harsh criticism against Renaissance polyphony following the Council of Trent (1545–1563). Furthermore, interest in monody began in the 1580s with a group of Italian noblemen called the Florentine Camerata, vertical and homophonic textures became prevalent at the end of the sixteenth century as composers sought to write music that was uncluttered texturally, and the accompaniment of vocal works with keyboard instruments became a necessity with the composition of vocal solos and with the increasing performance of music by solo ensembles. By the beginning of the seventeenth century these circumstances—criticisms, interests, and practices—became pervasive, and the combination of vertically conceived harmonies and independent instrumental writing created a new style of composition.

This does not mean that the older style of the Renaissance era ceased to exist after 1600. Since the liturgies of the Catholic Church remained unchanged, most of the genres continued as they were, and since there were many conservative views among Church clerics, the new musical styles were often criticized and poorly received. Moreover, since the musical education of composers during the early seventeenth century continued to be based on the rudiments and principles of Renaissance compositional practices, virtually all composers of roughly the first seventy-five years of the seventeenth century wrote in both old and new styles. In addition, the old style continued to be venerated and emulated by a number of notable composers during the final years of the Baroque era.

The old style was referred to as *stile antico* (old style) or *prima prattica* (first practice), while the new style was called *stile moderno* (modern style) or *seconda prattica* (second practice), with other names such as *stile concertato* (contrasted style) and *stile rappresentativo* (representative style) used to denote specific characteristics of the new music. The old style composed in the seventeenth century was not, however, the same style previously composed in the sixteenth century, no matter how much composers of the Baroque era desired to emulate compositional techniques of the past. Significant characteristics of the old style had changed: the long imitative phrases of text had become short motif-like groups of words; textures of nondifferentiated rhythms had become varied rhythmic patterns that were used for expressive purposes; and modal-based polyphony that was horizontally conceived had become vertically conceived homophony or counterpoint. There were clear differences between actual sixteenth-century polyphonic compositions and seventeenth-century works that were patterned after them.

Whether old or new, the music of the seventeenth century almost always had instrumental participation in the form of basso continuo. That is, one or more melodic bass instruments (e.g., cello, violone, or bassoon) played from a specifically notated part while one or more chord-producing instruments (e.g., harpsichord, organ, theorbo, or lute) realized harmonies from the bass part. The notated bass part generally, but not exclusively, followed the vocal bass part in *prima prattica* compositions and outlined fundamental harmonies in *seconda prattica* works. The chords were not notated by the composer, but instead were improvised—or realized—by the performer. Simultaneous or interchangeable performance by multiple melodic and chord-producing instruments was common, especially in large-scale dramatic works such as oratorios. For example, the bassoon and harpsichord might have been used for one movement of a work, the violone and lute for another movement, and all instruments combined for yet other movements. It was not unusual for a basso continuo ensemble to consist of a harpsichord and an organ and for performers to use these two instruments in various combinations (Bach and Handel used both organs and harpsichords for performances of their Passions and oratorios). Genre, availability of instruments, texture of scoring, and character of drama determined usage.

Given that the Baroque era began with an idealization of monody, much of the early-seventeenth-century music in the *seconda prattica* style was scored for solo voices and basso continuo accompaniment. This was not only the case in new genres such as the cantata and opera, but also in old genres such as the motet and madrigal. As the era progressed and the *seconda prattica* gradually assumed a more prominent role, the music expanded in scoring. The basso continuo part became augmented by two independent violin parts; an ensemble of strings that included violas; obbligato instruments such as oboes, flutes, or horns; trumpets and timpani for festival works; and eventually a complete orchestra of flutes, oboes, bassoons, horns, trumpets, timpani, strings, and basso continuo. The textures of the music followed the scoring; music early in the era was more homophonic, whereas music at the end of the era was contrapuntal.

Other than opera, the most common vocal genres during the era were mass (including Requiem and separate mass movements), oratorio (including settings of the Passion), motet and related sacred settings such as the Magnificat and Te Deum, anthem and other Protestant Reformation forms such as the Calvinist Psalm setting and the German Lutheran chorale, cantata, ode, and madrigal. The mass remained the only genre that consistently involved choral forces throughout the era. The oratorio and cantata usually involved chorus during the middle and latter portions of the era, but in the early years they were often exclusively for soloists. The motet was scored for choral forces in its *prima prattica* form, but commonly for solo voices (often only one or two voices and basso continuo) in its *seconda prattica* form. The anthem and related genres, as well as multimovement works such as odes and most Magnificat settings, were often scored for a combination of soloists and chorus. Finally, the madrigal remained a genre intended only for soloists, either singly or in groups.

The Baroque era began in Italy and then spread to other countries as composers who had studied in Italy took positions in prominent courts, cathedrals, and venues throughout Europe and beyond. France, whose royal court was almost exclusively staffed by Italian musicians, adopted the new Baroque styles in the early years of the seventeenth century. Germany, which was predominantly Lutheran, followed somewhat later, and England did not embrace the new styles until the Restoration (i.e., in 1660 when Charles II returned from exile in France and began his reign). Spain, whose music was taken to the New World, remained attached to the Renaissance and manifested Baroque styles only in the villancico.

⊗ ITALY ⊗

The focus on monody and its transformation into opera was a natural development from the very popular late-sixteenth-century dramatic forms such as *intermedii* and *pastorales*. Furthermore, the social trappings of opera were intrinsically fashionable in Italian society. Courts mounted lavish productions that reflected wealth and status, the public reveled in operatic drama and worshipped star singers, and composers vied with each other for recognition and popular appeal. However, given that all major cities had cathedrals and that all courts had chapels, there was a need for sacred vocal music as well as opera. Also, given that most composers could not sustain themselves financially from the composition of operas alone, appointments to cathedral or court positions, with responsibilities for composing sacred music, were a necessity. Most composers therefore wrote music for both the operatic stage and the Church.

The primary sacred genres—those that were important in Italy as well as in other countries during the Baroque era—were the oratorio and Psalm setting. The oratorio began as a musical component of spiritual exercises or services that were a part of the Congregazione dell' Oratorio (Congregation of the Oratory), founded in Rome by St Philip Neri (1515–1595) in the mid-sixteenth century and officially recognized as a religious order by Pope Gregory XIII in 1575. Neri's services met in prayer halls, called *oratories* (the Latin for prayer is *oratio*), the most famous of which were those attached to the churches of S Girolamo della Caritá, Chiesa Nuova, and San Marcello, and the separate structure, Oratorio del Ss Crocifisso. The music for the oratory services generally consisted of a multisectional or multimovement setting of a sacred dramatic or moral allegorical text scored for soloists, chorus, and a small number of instruments. The most common texts were about Old Testament characters such as Jephtha, Jonah, or Zedekiah; the soloists often included a part for narrator or evangelist (called *testo* or *historicus*); and the most common instrumental scoring during the early years of the Baroque was for either a small group of basso continuo instruments (including cello, violone, bassoon, harpsichord, organ, lute, and theorbo) or for two violins and basso continuo. Two basic types of oratorio developed in Italy during the Baroque era—the *oratorio latino* and the *oratorio volgare*. As the nomenclatures indicate, the *latino* oratorios were settings of Latin texts, while the *volgare* oratorios were settings of Italian texts. The Latin oratorios, which had texts mostly in prose, were short-lived and confined to services in the Oratorio del Ss Crocifisso. The Italian oratorios, being in the language of the people and having poetic texts, were much more popular and thus long-lived. Many of the early oratorios were called by a variety of names, including *historicus, actus musicus, dialogus* or *dialogo, dramma sacro,* and *madrigale spirituale.* The term *oratorio* was not used consistently until the second half of the seventeenth century. As the oratorio gained in popularity, it began to be composed for and performed in court and public theaters.

Psalm settings were ordinarily extended single-movement works scored for chorus, two violins, and basso continuo during the early years of the era, and longer multimovement works scored for soloists, string ensemble with obbligato instruments, and basso continuo during the later years of the era. The Psalm texts set were almost always those used in Vespers services, and the texts always ended with a statement of the Gloria Patri—"Gloria Patri, et Filio, et Spiritui Sancto. Sicut erat in principio, et nunc, et semper, et in saecula saeculorum. Amen" (Glory be to the father, and to the son, and to the holy spirit. As it was in the beginning, is now, and ever shall be. Amen).

Other than opera, the primary secular genre was the cantata, which was almost always scored for solo voices. Madrigals, which were generally in the *prima prattica* style, continued to be composed throughout the era, although not in great numbers or by a large number of composers.

The major composers (and many minor ones as well) were attracted primarily to Rome, Venice, and Naples. Other cities such as Ferrara, Mantua, and Bologna were of lesser importance, although these cities also maintained active musical establishments that employed notable Baroque composers. Oratorios were especially popular in Rome, where public performances of opera were frowned upon throughout the Baroque era and completely prohibited during the reign of Pope Innocent XI. In addition, oratorios were in demand as the followers of St Philip Neri increased in number and as more and more oratories were built. Also, oratorios in Rome were greatly favored by private patrons of the arts such as Queen Christina of Sweden (who maintained a palace in Rome), cardinals Pietro Ottoboni and Benedetto Pamphilj (who wrote oratorio librettos), and Prince Francesco Maria Ruspoli (who employed a number of composers and who mounted a number of notable oratorio performances). Venice, one of two great centers of opera, also had the very important and famous Basilica di San Marco (St Mark's) as well as four well-known orphanages for girls that specialized in musical training. Musical positions at St Mark's were highly esteemed and sought after, and performances at the orphanages were social highlights that attracted Venice's cultural elite. Naples, the other great center of opera, had no outstanding cathedral, although it had the opulent court of the Spanish ambassador to the Vatican. Naples was also populated by numerous noblemen and arts patrons who supported both sacred and secular music.

The major Italian composers of the Baroque era—those who are discussed at length in this section—are Claudio Monteverdi, Giacomo Carissimi, Giovanni Legrenzi, Alessandro Stradella, Alessandro Scarlatti, Antonio Lotti, Antonio Caldara, Antonio Vivaldi, Padre Giovanni Battista

Martini, Baldassare Galuppi, and Giovanni Battista Pergolesi. Of these composers, Carissimi, Stradella, Scarlatti, and Caldara spent most of their time in Rome; Monteverdi, Legrenzi, Lotti, and Galuppi all served as *maestro di cappella* at St Mark's; and Legrenzi, Lotti, Vivaldi, and Galuppi all served at one of Venice's orphanages. Pergolesi was known for his work in Naples, while Martini spent his entire career in Bologna.

Other composers who made an impact on the development of choral music or who contributed significant choral works to the repertoire, also discussed here, are Giovanni Francesco Anerio, Girolamo Frescobaldi, Alessandro Grandi, Pietro Della Valle, Francesco Cavalli, Orazio Benevoli, Barbara Strozzi, Antonio Draghi, Giuseppe Ottavio Pitoni, Francesco Durante, Domenico Scarlatti, Benedetto Giacomo Marcello, Nicola Porpora, Leonardo Leo, and Quirino Gasparini.

CLAUDIO MONTEVERDI 1567–1643

Monteverdi was born in Cremona, where he studied with Marc'Antonio Ingegneri, *maestro di cappella* at the cathedral there. Monteverdi developed rapidly as an accomplished player of the viola da braccio and as a composer: during his teenage years he was engaged to play in various court ensembles in Verona and Milan; in 1582, when he was only fifteen, the Venetian publisher Antonio Gardane issued his first book of motets; and a book of his madrigals was published the following year. In 1590 he was appointed *suonatore di vivuola* (player of the viola) at the court of Duke Vincenzo Gonzaga in Mantua, a center of madrigal composition under the musical leadership of one of the most significant madrigal composers of the time, Giaches de Wert, and after a little more than ten years he was appointed *maestro della musica,* with responsibilities for teaching voice, composing madrigals and theater music, and conducting a female vocal ensemble modeled after the famous Concerto delle donne in Ferrara. When the duke died in 1612, Monteverdi was dismissed from the court along with most of the musical staff, and in 1613 he was appointed *maestro di cappella* at St Mark's Basilica in Venice, one of the most prestigious positions in Italy. His duties there included composing music for Holy Week, Easter, and Christmas services, as well as for numerous special feast days and state visits. Over the years, as he became increasingly famous, he assumed a significant leadership role in Venice and was active in welcoming musical guests, including Heinrich Schütz in 1628. Venice was hard hit by the plague of 1630, which killed approximately 50,000 residents, and Monteverdi became reclusive, taking religious orders in 1631 and entering the priesthood in 1632. For the next decade he focused his compositional activity on opera while his personal life was focused on family concerns, and after a brief trip to Mantua in 1643 to settle some financial matters, he died at the age of seventy-six.

Monteverdi's early compositions are in the Renaissance *prima prattica* style characterized by linear imitative vocal polyphony, whereas the later compositions are in the new Baroque *seconda prattica* style characterized by vertical sonorities, solo vocal melodies, and basso continuo accompaniment. It is important to note that Monteverdi not only composed in these different styles but was also significantly involved in the polemics regarding their differences. The prominent theorist Giovanni Maria Artusi (ca.1540–1613) wrote a treatise entitled *L'Artusi, overo Delle imperfettioni della moderna musica* (Artusi, or, Of the imperfections of modern music), which criticized Monteverdi for breaking the rules of counterpoint and usage of dissonance as established in the Renaissance by Gioseffo Zarlino (1517–1590), with whom Artusi had studied. Monteverdi replied to Artusi's criticism in the preface to his fifth book of madrigals with a defense of modern writing. A further defense came from Monteverdi's brother, Giulio Cesare, who wrote the preface to Claudio's *Scherzi musicali* of 1607. In this preface the term *prima prattica* was introduced to refer to music of the Renaissance, which held counterpoint (i.e., polyphony) to be more important than text. The term *seconda prattica* was introduced to refer to modern (Baroque) music, which subordinated melody and rhythm to text.

Monteverdi composed approximately fifty sacred vocal works, 270 madrigals and canzonets, and twenty stage works. Most of the sacred works are contained in three publications—*Sacrae cantiunculae* (1582), *Sanctissimae virgini missa senis vocibus ad ecclesiarum choros ac Vespere pluribus decantandae* (1610), and *Selva morale e spirituale* (1640). In addition, a mass and a few Psalm settings were published in 1650, after Monteverdi's death. The 1582 publication represents Monteverdi in his adolescence (he was fifteen); it contains motets, all for three voices, that are simple works in the *prima prattica* style of his teacher Ingegneri. The 1610 publication, often referred to simply as *Vespers,* represents Monteverdi at his compositional peak, with demonstrations of music both in *prima* and *seconda prattica* styles and in many different vocal and instrumental combinations and textures. The complete publication—which contains a mass, five Psalm settings and one hymn, five motets, and two Magnificats—appears to be an intentional compendium of early-seventeenth-century compositional styles, both old and new. The mass, entitled *Missa in illo tempore,* is a parody of a motet by Nicolas Gombert and is written in a conservative polyphonic style. The Psalm settings—*Dixit Dominus* (Psalm 110), *Laudate pueri Dominum* (Psalm 113), *Laetatus sum in his quae dicta sunt mihi* (Psalm 122), *Nisi Dominus aedificaverit domum* (Psalm 127), and *Lauda Jerusalem Dominum* (Psalm 148)—are for six to eight voices and six *colla parte* instruments and are generally in the style of madrigals at that time, with considerable rhythmic variety and word painting and with occasional choral recitative. The hymn—*Ave maris stella*—consists of an opening SATB/SATB verse followed by SATB and solo verses that alternate with instrumental ritornellos. Most of the motets, which are interspersed between the Psalm settings, are concertos for solo voices and basso continuo that feature *fioritura* (fast passage work). *Duo seraphim,* for three tenors, is especially virtuosic. Both Magnificats are multimovement works. One of them is for seven voices and six instruments and in the *seconda prattica* style, while the other is for six voices and basso continuo and in the *prima prattica* style. Performances today usually omit the mass and the simpler of the Magnificats and present what is called the *Vespro della Beata Vergine* portion of the complete publication.

Selva morale e spirituale of 1640 is similarly a collection of sacred works, generally of Psalm settings scored for six voices, two violins, and basso continuo. Interestingly, none of these works is in the *cori spezzati,* or polychoral, style that was a hallmark of St Mark's during the mid-sixteenth century. Instead, Monteverdi's writing is generally in a lightly textured *concertato* style, with small groups of voices and instruments that exchange motifs.

The madrigals, canzonets, and secular vocal concertos span Monteverdi's entire life and also represent both *prima* and *seconda prattica* styles. The canzonets and vocal concertos were published in three books—*Canzonette a tre voci* (1584) and two books entitled *Scherzi musicali* (1607 and 1632). The canzonets of 1584 are three-voiced pieces similar in style to the villanellas of Luca Marenzio. They are strophic, with numerous examples of word painting and high tessituras. The first of the *Scherzi musicali* books is similar, with simple homophonic three-voiced pieces. The second book, however, contains strophic solos and duets with basso continuo.

The madrigals were published in eight books during Monteverdi's lifetime and one book posthumously. The first four books consist mainly of *prima prattica* pieces, while the next four books represent the *seconda prattica*. Books one (1587) and two (1590), both for five voices, contain settings of pastoral poetry in the style of Wert's middle-period madrigals, with mildly varying textures and rhythms and a predilection for word painting. Examples are the three-madrigal cycle *Ardo, sì, ma non t'amo* from book one and *Ecco mormorar l'onde* from book two. This latter madrigal, with melismas on the word "cantar" (sing) and exchanges of motifs between high and low voices, is one of Monteverdi's best-known and most frequently performed works. The third and fourth books (1592 and 1603), also for five voices, show a development toward greater rhythmic freedom, texts set in a declamatory manner (with some choral recitative), and dissonances used for expressive nuance. Notable examples in book three are the two madrigal cycles— *Vattene pur crudel* and *Vivrò fra i miei tormenti*—based on texts from Torquato Tasso's poem *La Gerusalemme liberata*. Book four contains some of Monteverdi's most evocative and dramatic works, including *Sfogava con le stelle,* which contains seven instances of text phrases that are given no rhythms and that are to be sung freely, as recitative; *Si ch'io vorrei morire,* which has harmonic progressions of striking dissonance and which expresses its text in a highly erotic manner; *Luci serene e chiare,* which begins with the word painting of two whole notes that depict a lover's "clear and bright eyes"; and *Ohimè, se tanto amate,* which begins and ends with highly expressive statements of the word "Alas."

The fifth book of madrigals (1605) also contains many examples of expressive and dramatic music. Its most famous madrigal, *Cruda Amarilli,* became the focus of the controversy between *prima* and *seconda prattica* styles. In addition, the fifth book was published with an optional basso continuo part (in reality, a basso seguente part), thus showing the move toward more soloistic writing with accompaniment. The sixth book, published almost a decade later (1614), contains two large and important cycles—*Lamento d'Arianna* and *Lagrime d'amante al sepolcro dell'amata*—both composed shortly after the deaths of Monteverdi's wife in 1607 and alleged mistress Caterina Martinelli in 1608. *Lamento d'Arianna* begins with the madrigal *Lasciatemi morire,* which was originally composed as a solo aria in Monteverdi's opera *Arianna.* The aria, with opening text "Lasciatemi morire, e chi volete voi che mi conforte in così dura sorte" (Let me die, and who will it be that comforts me in such great martyrdom), was so popular that Monteverdi was persuaded to set it in madrigal form and to include the other three parts of Ottavio Rinuccini's poem (*O Teseo; Dove, dove è la fede;* and *Ahi, che non pur risponde*). To further underscore the importance of *Lasciatemi morire,* Monteverdi quoted it in the fifth madrigal (*O chiome d'or*) of *Lagrime d'amante al sepolcro dell'amata,* a cycle of six madrigals composed to a sestina (a poem of six six-line verses, each line of which ends with the same words arranged in varying order) about the emotions of a lover standing over the tomb of his beloved. Considered to be Monteverdi's most masterful setting of text, the cycle was commissioned by Duke Vincenzo Gonzaga, who is represented by the shepherd Glauco in the poem.

The seventh book of madrigals, entitled *Concerto settimo libro de madrigali con altri generi de canti* and published in 1619, moves even further toward solo writing by consisting mainly of duets with basso continuo. An example is the final work in the collection, *Tirsi e Clori,* for soprano and tenor duet and five-part vocal ensemble. Subtitled "Dialogo e Ballo" (dialogue and dance), it is structured of alternating solos sung by the two lovers Tirsi and Clori followed by a duet and a closing ensemble that relates dance to the movement of animals (specifically goats), stars, clouds, waves, and flowers. The eighth book was not published until 1638, almost two decades after book seven. Entitled *Madrigali guerrieri et amorosi,* book eight contains ten pieces set to poetry about war and thirteen to poetry about love. All are in varied textures with basso continuo; some, including the famous *Hor ch'el ciel e la terra,* have independent violin parts as well. The ninth book (1651), which seems to be a collection of music written during Monteverdi's early life, contains simple two- and three-voiced pieces.

Among Monteverdi's stage works are four important operas—*L'Orfeo* (1607), *Arianna* (1608), *Il ritorno d'Ulisse in patria* (1639–1640), and *L'incoronazione di Poppea* (1642–1643). *L'Orfeo* is generally considered to be the earliest opera that still receives contemporary performance. It consists of a combination of genres that existed at the time, including monody, ballet, and instrumental *intermedii. Arianna* was extremely popular during Monteverdi's time, but no performance materials survive except for the libretto and several versions of the lament "Lasciatemi morire." The final two operas were models for many later operas, with recitatives, arias, and choruses.

SACRED WORKS
SELECTED AND LISTED ACCORDING TO FAMILIARITY

Vespro della Beata Vergine – 1610 – SSAATTTTBB voices, two flutes (*fifare*), two recorders (*flauti*), four trumpets (*cornetti*), four trombones (*tromboni*), two violins (*violini da brazzo*), three violas (*viole da brazzo*), one double bass (*contrabasso da gamba*), and basso continuo consisting of organs, bass lutes (*chitarroni*), and harpsichords – 95 minutes. (1) The text is from Psalms 69:2, 109, 112, 121, 126, and 147:12–20, plus passages from Song of Solomon and Isaiah, and the traditional Magnificat; (2) the vocal scoring, which ranges from solo T to SATTB/SATTB, has frequent passages of *fioritura* and seems intended for soloists throughout; (3) present-day performances usually employ chorus for the Psalm settings and other thickly scored movements, and soloists for the remaining movements.

Gloria – 1640 – SSATTBB voices, two violins, and basso continuo – 12 minutes.

Beatus vir primo (Psalm 111) – 1640 – SSATTB voices, two violins, and basso continuo – 7 minutes. (1) This is a contrafactum of the canzonetta *Chiome d'oro* of 1619; (2) Monteverdi recommended additional scoring *colla parte,* if desired, for three *viole da brazzo* or three *tromboni.*

Laudate Dominum omnes gentes – also known as *Laudate Dominum Primo* (Psalm 117) – 1640 – SSTTB solos, SSAATTBB chorus, two violins, and basso continuo – 4:30 minutes. (1) The solo parts are integrated into the overall texture; (2) Monteverdi recommended additional scoring *colla parte,* if desired, for four *viole o tromboni.*

Beatus (Psalm 111) – 1640 – SSAATTB voices, two violins, and basso continuo – 9 minutes.

Laudate Dominum secondo (Psalm 117) – 1640 – SSAATTBB voices, two violins, and basso continuo – 3:15 minutes.

Laudate pueri primo (Psalm 112) – 1640 – SSATB voices, two violins, and basso continuo – 7:15 minutes.

Laudate pueri secondo (Psalm 112) – 1650 – SSATB voices and basso continuo – 7:30 minutes.

Dixit Dominus secondo (Psalm 110) – 1640 – SSAATTBB voices, two violins, and basso continuo – 8:15 minutes.

Adoramus te, Christe – 1620 – SSATTB voices and basso continuo – 3:30 minutes.

MADRIGALS
SELECTED AND LISTED IN CHRONOLOGICAL ORDER
ACCORDING TO DATE OF COMPOSITION

Se nel partir da voi – from book one, 1587 – SSATB voices – 2:30 minutes.

Ardo, sì, ma non t'amo – from book one, 1587 – SSATB voices – 2 minutes.

Ecco mormorar l'onde – from book two, 1590 – SSATB voices – 4 minutes.

Crudel, perché mi fuggi – from book two, 1590 – SSATB voices – 2:30 minutes.

Vattene pur crudel – a three-madrigal cycle from book three, 1592 – SSATB voices – 7 minutes.

Vivrò fra i miei tormenti – a three-madrigal cycle from book three, 1592 – SSATB voices – 9 minutes.

O primavera – from book three, 1592 – SSATB voices – 3 minutes.

Io mi son giovinetta – from book four, 1603 – SSATB voices – 2:30 minutes.

Quel augellin che canta – from book four, 1603 – SSATB voices – 2 minutes.

Sfogava con le stelle – from book four, 1603 – SSATB voices – 3:30 minutes.

Si ch'io vorrei morire – from book four, 1603 – SSATB voices – 3:30 minutes.

Luci serene e chiare – from book four, 1603 – SSATB voices – 3:30 minutes.

Ohimè, se tanto amate – from book four, 1603 – SSATB voices – 3 minutes.

Cruda Amarilli – from book five, 1605 – SATTB voices and optional basso continuo – 3 minutes.

T'amo, mia vita – from book five, 1605 – SATTB voices and optional basso continuo – 2:30 minutes.

O Mirtillo – from book five, 1605 – SATTB voices and optional basso continuo – 2:30 minutes.

Zefiro torna – from book six, 1614 – SSATB voices and optional basso continuo – 3:30 minutes.

Lamento d'Arianna – a four-madrigal cycle from book six, 1614 – SSATB voices and optional basso continuo – 13 minutes.

Lagrime d'amante al sepolcro dell'amata – a six-madrigal cycle from book six, 1614 – SSATB voices and optional basso continuo – 18 minutes.

Eccomi pronta ai baci – from book seven, 1619 – TTB solos and basso continuo – 2 minutes.

Tirsi e Clori – from book seven, 1619 – ST solos, SSATB chorus, and basso continuo – 13 minutes.

Combattimento di Tancredi e Clorinda – from book eight, 1638 – SST solos, two violins, viola, and basso continuo – 20 minutes.

Altri canti di Marte – from book eight, 1638 – SSATTB voices, two violins, two violas, viola da gamba, and basso continuo – 8 minutes.

Hor ch'el ciel e la terra – from book eight, 1638 – SSATTB voices, two violins, and basso continuo – 9 minutes.

GIROLAMO ALESSANDRO FRESCOBALDI 1583–1643

Frescobaldi was born and spent his youth in Ferrara, where he met and heard the madrigals of Luzzasco Luzzaschi and Carlo Gesualdo, and where he served as organist of the Accademia della Morte beginning at age fourteen. At about twenty he went to Rome, becoming known there as a virtuoso organist and serving as organist at St Peter's for approximately thirty-five years. He was and is known today mainly as a composer of keyboard works, published in ten books of toccatas, canzonas, ricercars, and other related genres. Extremely popular during the seventeenth and eighteenth centuries, many of the individual works went through multiple printings, and selected publications, especially *Fiori Musicali* of 1635, were praised and studied by notable late Baroque composers, including J. S. Bach.

Frescobaldi composed one book of madrigals, approximately thirty-five motets, two masses, and one Magnificat. The madrigals, which are representative of Frescobaldi's style, were composed in 1607 and 1608 during a trip to Brussels. Fifteen of the nineteen pieces are scored for SSATB voices a cappella, and the remaining four are scored for SAATB. All were composed as single works except for *Giunt'e pur Lidia il mio*, which is a cycle of three madrigals. The texture of each of the madrigals is similar to the textures found in pieces by Luzzaschi and Gesualdo: short imitative phrases and varied rhythms depict the direct meaning or emotion of the text phrase. However, Frescobaldi's harmonies are more conservative, with negligible use of dissonance and chromaticism.

ALESSANDRO GRANDI CA.1580–1630

There were two composers named Alessandro Grandi during the Baroque era—one discussed here and one born in 1638 who became *maestro di cappella* at Rimini Cathedral. The date of the earlier Grandi's birth is sometimes listed as between 1575 and 1586 and sometimes specifically as 1586. This latter date, or a date close to it, is unreasonable in that Grandi began serving as *maestro di cappella* at the Accademia della Morte in Ferrara between 1597 and 1600 and thus would have been only eleven to fourteen years of age. On the other end of the spectrum, it is un-likely that Grandi was born as early as 1575, since a birth in this year would have made him forty-two (relatively old) when he began as a singer at St Mark's Basilica under Monteverdi. The most likely year of birth, therefore, seems to be about 1580. The place of Grandi's birth is also un-known, although it was presumably in or near Ferrara, where he served as *maestro di cappella* at the Accademia dello Spirito Santo and the cathedral, as well as at the Accademia della Morte. Grandi became Monteverdi's deputy at St Mark's Basilica in 1620, and in 1627 he was appointed *maestro di cappella* at S Maria Maggiore in Bergamo.

Grandi composed several masses, approximately 250 motets, and eighty madrigals. Most of the masses are scored for three or four voices and basso continuo. An untitled work for ATTB chorus published in *Il primo libro de moteti con una messa* in 1610 is in the style of Giovanni Gabrieli, with short contrasting motifs and expressive word painting. Later masses, those pub-lished in 1630, feature solo passages and scoring for specific instruments. Most of the early motets are scored for two to four voices and basso continuo, while the later motets, which in-clude numerous settings of Psalms for Vespers services, are scored for eight voices. Grandi in-dicated that the eight-part scoring should be distributed between soloists and chorus or for soloists alone, with the chorus ad lib. The madrigals range from *prima prattica* pieces, with phrases characterized by varied rhythms, to *seconda prattica* pieces (e.g., *Mirar fuggir le stele*) that contain solo passages accompanied by basso continuo.

PIETRO DELLA VALLE 1586–1652

Della Valle is not known for his compositions, which consist of only three oratorios, but rather for his leadership of and commentary on musical life in Rome, and also for his experiments with different tuning systems. He was born in Rome to a noble family, and in his youth he stud-ied a variety of cultural disciplines, including music (harpsichord, viola da gamba, theorbo, and counterpoint), dance, and writing. His writings include several oratorio librettos and a defense of modern music entitled *Della musica dell'età nostra*. His only surviving oratorio, *Per la festa della santissimi purificatione,* is scored for five voices and basso continuo and is composed in five different modes (Dorian, Phrygian, Aeolian, Lydian, and Hypolydian). The basso continuo is in-tended for two specific instruments—a triharmonic harpsichord and a panharmonic violone—both of which could be tuned to varied modes.

FRANCESCO CAVALLI 1602–1676

Cavalli spent the majority of his life in Venice. He was a boy soprano and later a tenor at St Mark's Basilica while Monteverdi was *maestro di cappella,* and as an adult he served as second organist beginning in 1639 and as first organist in 1665 (although he assumed the role of first organist well before the title was bestowed on him). Cavalli's talents as both a singer and an organist were exceptional, and he was frequently praised for his abilities. However, he achieved fame as a com-poser of operas; his thirty-three works in that genre helped establish opera as a major musical force in Italy throughout the Baroque era. He also composed music for the Church, including several masses, three settings of the Magnificat, and approximately fifty motets. All these sacred compositions are in the *prima prattica* style, and many of them are also characteristic of the double chorus style established at St Mark's by Giovanni Gabrieli. Such is the case with Cavalli's *Messa concertata* (for SATB solos, SATB/SATB chorus, two trumpets, three trombones, strings, and basso continuo), in which the soloists are a part of and alternate with the first of the two choruses. Other notable works include the *Magnificat* for six voices, which was contained in the 1650 publication *Messa a 4 voci et salmi* of Monteverdi works, and which Cavalli no doubt edited, and the motet *Salve regina*, which most clearly represents Cavalli's style. *Salve regina* is scored for four voices (ATTB) and a basso continuo part that merely supports the voices and outlines the harmonies; the basic texture is one of very short imitative figures, often involving only single words such as "Salve" or "regina" (the "Salve" motif is based on the first four notes of the Gregorian chant found on page 276 in the *Liber usualis*); the texture becomes homophonic at major cadences; there are tempo changes that serve to characterize the changing moods of text; the harmonies, which are occasionally chromatic, are vertically conceived; and the composition is multisectional and approximately eight minutes in duration.

GIACOMO CARISSIMI 1605–1674

Nothing is known about Carissimi's youth and musical training except that he was born in Marino, a small town near Rome, and that at age eighteen he became a member of the Tivoli Cathedral choir and later the cathedral organist. At twenty-eight he moved to Assisi to become *maestro di cappella* at the Cathedral of S Rufino, and at twenty-nine he relocated to Rome to serve as *maestro di cappella* at the Collegio Germanico, the Vatican institution for the training of German priests and one of the most prestigious musical positions in all of Rome (it was once held by Tomás Luis de Victoria). Carissimi held the position for forty years, declining an invitation to succeed Claudio Monteverdi at St Mark's Basilica in Venice, but accepting other positions in Rome, which he held while continuing to serve at the Collegio Germanico: he was *maestro di cappella del concerto di camera* at the Rome court of Queen Christina of Sweden, for whom he composed a number of his cantatas, and *maestro di cappella* at the Oratorio del Ss Crocifisso, the institution for which he composed the majority of his oratorios—the works that ultimately brought him fame.

Carissimi was held in high regard during his lifetime. He taught and influenced a great number of composers, including Marc-Antoine Charpentier, and he can rightly be credited with initiating and shaping the development of the oratorio throughout Europe during the Baroque era. He composed at least eleven oratorios (nine in Latin and two in Italian), 160 cantatas, one hundred motets, and one mass. The precise dates and number of oratorios are unknown because they were not published during Carissimi's lifetime and the original scores have been lost. In addition, the authorship of some of the works that circulated during the seventeenth century in manuscript with Carissimi's name is uncertain. Furthermore, the categorization of some works as oratorios is difficult because the genre was just being developed and also because the term *oratorio* was not used consistently. That having been said, it is relatively certain that Carissimi's Latin oratorios include *Historia di Abraham et Isaac; Baltazar; Diluvium universale; Dives malus; Ezechias; Jephte; Jonas; Judicium extremum;* and *Judicium Salomonis.* The Italian oratorios include *Oratorio della Santissima Vergine* and *Daniele.* Two other oratorios—*Dialogo del Gigante*

Golia and *Regina Hester*—have recently been discovered and are thought to be by Carissimi, and two oratorios previously ascribed to Carissimi—*Job* and *Cain*—are now thought to be spurious. All his oratorios were probably composed between the late 1640s and approximately 1660, the period during which Carissimi was associated with Ss Crocifisso.

The Latin oratorios are all relatively similar in scope and scoring: their duration is from fifteen to thirty minutes; texts relate stories of biblical characters; most dialogue is transmitted through recitative accompanied by basso continuo; there are very few set pieces such as arias; and instrumentation is for basso continuo alone or for two violins and basso continuo. Most of the oratorios have character roles scored for specific and consistent solo parts (e.g., the part of Jephte is sung by the same tenor throughout the oratorio). However, the role of the narrator (called *historicus*) is generally scored for a variety of solos, duets, trios, and even choruses. The chorus also takes part in and comments on the action, and all the oratorios have a closing choral movement that summarizes or reflects on the moral of the story.

Jephte, Carissimi's most famous oratorio and undoubtedly the best-known Latin oratorio of the Baroque era, relates the biblical story of Jephtha, who vows to God to sacrifice the first person who greets him if he returns home victorious after war with the Ammonites and who, having triumphed in battle, is greeted by his daughter. The oratorio's choral writing is dramatic and colorful in the portrayal of war and victory—"Fugite, cedite, impii, corruite, et in furore gladii dissipamini" (Flee, yield, impious and corrupt, and fall from our swords) and "Cantemus omnes Domino, laudemus belli principem qui dedit nobis gloriam et Israel victoriam" (Let us all sing unto the Lord, and praise the mighty king who gives us the glory and Israel the victory). Also, the oratorio ends with an expressive lament for the impending death of Jephtha's daughter— "Plorate, filii Israel, plorate, omnes virginis" (Weep, children of Israel, weep all virgins).

Jonas, which relates the biblical story of Jonah and the whale, is much less known, even though its choral music is perhaps more dramatic, colorful, and expressive than that in *Jephte.* Notable examples are the storm at sea—"Et proeliabantur venti" (And the winds joined battle); the vomiting of the whale—"Et imperavit Dominus pisci, et evomuit Jonam" (And the Lord commanded the fish, and it spewed out Jonah); and the oratorio's final chorus—"Peccavimus, Domine, peccavimus" (We have sinned, Lord, we have sinned).

Ezechias relates the biblical story of King Hezekiah of Israel, who was told of his imminent death by Isaiah but who prayed to God and was granted fifteen more years of life and deliverance from the King of Assyria. The oratorio is noted for Hezekiah's prayer, set by Carissimi as a lengthy recitative with violin interludes over a ground bass.

Judicium extremum, based on the Gospel text for the Monday in the first week of Lent, does not tell a narrative story but instead portrays visions of the Last Judgment. Two choral sections are especially graphic—"Tunc, horribili sonitu, tubae clangentes vocabunt gentes, et a sepulcris excitabunt Angeli" (Then, with a terrible noise, resounding trumpets will call forth the peoples, and the Angels will awake them from their tombs) and "Quam magna, quam amara, quam terribilis erit dies novissima, cum advenerit Dominus ad judicandum nos" (How great, how bitter, how terrible will be the last day, when the Lord comes to judge us).

The majority of the cantatas, typical of the time, have secular texts and are scored for solo voices and basso continuo. Similarly, most of the motets, all of which have sacred texts, are scored for solo voices and basso continuo, although a few are scored for solos, chorus, and two violins with basso continuo. The Christmas motet *O anima festina* is an example. Alto and bass recitatives are scored for only basso continuo accompaniment, an extended soprano and alto duet (melodically in thirds) is accompanied by two violins and basso continuo, and the SATB chorus is scored for basso continuo accompaniment alone except for very short violin ritornellos. Many of the motets are for two and three sopranos with basso continuo.

Carissimi was formerly credited with having composed three masses, and there is some conjecture that he composed a fourth. However, it is now known that he did not compose either the *Missa septimi toni* (Kyrie, Gloria, and Credo only) or the *Missa a quinque et a novem cum selectis quibusdam cantionibus,* and there is no proof that he composed the *Missa Ut queant laxis,* which is a work in the *prima prattica* style based on the hexachord *ut, re, mi, fa, sol, la.* The only mass that is ascribed to Carissimi with certainty is the *Missa sciolto havean dall'alte sponde,* a work in a *prima prattica* polyphonic style.

ORATORIOS
SELECTED AND LISTED ACCORDING TO FAMILIARITY

Jephte – 1650s – SSSATB solos, SSATB chorus, and basso continuo – 24 minutes. (1) Solo roles are for a Narrator (variously sung by S, S, A, and B), Jephte (T), Jephte's daughter (S), an Israelite (B), and Echoes (SS or SA); (2) the solo writing consists mostly of recitative, with a few arioso-like pieces; (3) the music for the Echoes is brief and can easily and effectively be sung by members of the chorus; (4) the choral writing is SATB except for the final choral movement, "Plorate, filii Israel," which is SSATB and which is often extracted and performed separately.

Jonas – 1650s – SATTBB solos, SATB/SATB chorus, two violins, and basso continuo – 20 minutes. (1) Solo roles are for a Narrator (variously sung by S, S, A, T, B, and chorus), Jonah (T), God (B), the Helmsman of the ship (A), and Sailors (ATB, SAB, and BB); (2) there is one double chorus (the storm scene), one SSATTB chorus (the final chorus, "Peccavimus, Domine"), and one SATB chorus; (3) the violins generally double the chorus parts and are independent only in a short sinfonia that opens the oratorio and in several ritornellos between solo vocal phrases.

Ezechias – 1650s – SSATB solos, SSATB chorus, and basso continuo – 15:15 minutes. (1) Solo roles are for God (low B), Hezekiah (T), two Angels (SS), and Isaiah (A); (2) there is only one choral movement, which closes the oratorio; (3) the violin parts pervade the oratorio, especially in Hezekiah's solo "Dextera Domini."

Judicium extremum – 1650s – SSTBB solos, SSATB/ATB/ATB chorus, and basso continuo – 12:45 minutes. (1) Solo roles are for Christ (low B), a Prophet (B), two Angels (SS), and a Narrator (T); (2) there is also one brief passage for Cantus 1 and 2 (SS), and brief trios for the Righteous People (ATB) and Sinners (ATB); (3) there are a number of concerted solos in the triple chorus movements; (4) the two ATB choruses often echo the main SSATB chorus in the triple chorus movements; (5) the violins are scored for an opening sinfonia, several ritornellos between solo vocal phrases, and *colla parte* with the choral parts.

Baltazar – 1650s – SSSTB solos, SSSTB chorus, and basso continuo – 54 minutes. (1) Solo roles are for Baltazar (B), Daniel (S), a Narrator, (T), and Cantus 1 and 2 (SS); (2) there are a number of additional concerted solo passages in the choral movements; (3) the violins are scored for an opening sinfonia, numerous ritornellos between solo vocal phrases, and *colla parte* with the chorus parts.

Dives malus – 1650s – SSSTTB solos, SSTB/SATB chorus, and basso continuo – 20 minutes. (1) The oratorio is subtitled "Historia divitis" (History of the Wealthy) or "Storia del Ricco" (Story of the Rich Man); (2) the text is from Luke 16:19–31; (3) solo roles are for a Narrator (variously sung by S and T), the Rich Man (T), Abraham (B), and Cantus 1 and 2 (SS); (4) the oratorio consists mostly of choral movements that contain numerous concerted solos.

Historia di Abraham et Isaac – 1650s – SATTB solos, SATTB chorus, and basso continuo – 16 minutes. (1) The text is from Genesis 22:1–18; (2) solo roles are for a Narrator (T), God (B), Isaac (S), Abraham (T), and an Angel (A); (3) the oratorio has one choral movement.

Judicium Salomonis – 1650s – SSTB solos, two violins, and basso continuo – 12:30 minutes. (1) The text is from 1 Kings 3:16–28; (2) solo roles are for a Narrator (T), King Solomon (B), and Two Women (SS); (3) the oratorio comprises solo recitatives, a few SS duets and instrumental interludes, and a closing chorus (SSTB) that celebrates Solomon's judgment.

OTHER SACRED WORKS
SELECTED AND LISTED ACCORDING TO FAMILIARITY

Beatus vir (Psalm 112) – SSATB voices and basso continuo – 3:45 minutes.

Parce heu parce iam ô Jesu mi – SATB voices and basso continuo – 5 minutes.

O anima festina – AB recitatives, SA duet, SATB chorus, two violins, and basso continuo – 8 minutes. The motet, which some scholars believe is not by Carissimi, is for Christmas.

Lauda sion – SAB voices and basso continuo – 9:30 minutes. (1) The text is from the sequence by St Thomas Aquinas used for the celebration of Corpus Christi; (2) the motet consists of thirteen sections, including five trios, two duets (SA and SB), and six solos.

Desiderata nobis – ATB voices and basso continuo – 4 minutes. The text is for Christmas.

In te Domine speravi (Psalm 30) – ATB voices, two violins, and basso continuo – 9 minutes.

Benedictus Deus et Pater – SSS voices and basso continuo – 4:30 minutes.

Exulta, gaude, filia Sion – SS voices and basso continuo – 5 minutes. The text is for Christmas.

Surrexit pastor bonus – SSS voices and basso continuo – 2:30 minutes. The text is for Easter.

Missa sciolto havean dall'alte sponde – SSATB chorus and basso continuo – 50 minutes.

ORAZIO BENEVOLI 1605–1672

Benevoli, who was born and died in Rome, held several important church positions there during his lifetime, including *maestro di cappella* at S Maria in Trastevere, Santo Spirito in Sassia
(where Giovanni Francesco Anerio had served), S Luigi dei Francesi, and S Maria Maggiore. His
most prestigious appointment, however, was as *maestro di cappella* of the Cappella Giulia at St
Peter's, which he held for twenty-six years (from 1646 until his death). He composed approximately seven masses and thirty-four motets. The masses are in a Venetian polychoral style and
generally lavishly scored for twelve or more voice parts. Examples are the *Missa Angelus Domini*
of 1643 for twelve voices (SATB/SATB/SATB), the *Missa in angustia* of 1656 for sixteen voices
(SATB/SATB/SATB/SATB), and the *Missa Tu es Petrus* of 1666 to 1667 for sixteen voices (SATB/
SATB/SATB/SATB). He was formerly credited with composing the *Missa Salisburgensis* for fifty-
three voices, which was supposedly performed at the dedication of the Salzburg Cathedral in
1628. It is believed, however, that this mass was composed by Heinrich Ignaz Franz von Biber
and was not performed in Salzburg until 1682. Benevoli's motets are much smaller in scale,
scored for one to four voices, and are in a combination of *prima* and *seconda prattica* styles.

BARBARA STROZZI 1619–1677

Barbara Strozzi, also called Barbara Valle, was born in Venice and is unique among the composers of the Baroque era in being a woman and in composing only one piece of church music.
She was the adopted daughter of librettist Giulio Strozzi (1583–1652), who wrote the text for two
Monteverdi operas (the music of which is lost) and for most of Barbara's compositions, and she
was often the featured singer at concerts of the literary academy Accademia degli Unisoni,
which was founded by Giulio and which met in his home. Barbara studied singing with
Francesco Cavalli and composed eight books of vocal pieces that emulated his compositional
style of short motifs. *Il primo libro de madrigali* of 1644 contains madrigals for two to five voices
with basso continuo accompaniment, and all of the other publications contain cantatas and arias
for solo voices. For example, *Cantate, ariette e duetti* of 1651 consists of pieces scored for one to
two voices and basso continuo. *Cantate e ariette* of 1654 contains several pieces for three voices,
including *Desideri vani* (Vain desires) for SAB and basso continuo, as well as *La tre grazie* (The
three graces) for SSA voices and basso continuo. The single sacred piece, *Quis dabit mihi pennas
sicut columbe* (Oh that I had wings like a dove) from Psalm 55:6, is scored for three voices and
basso continuo and was published in Bartolomeo Marcesso's *Sacra corona, motetti a due e tre voci
di diversi eccelentissimi autori moderni* of 1656.

GIOVANNI LEGRENZI 1626–1690

Legrenzi was born in Clusone, a small town in northern Italy, where his father, Giovanni Maria,
was a composer and violinist at the local parish church. Nothing is known about young Giovanni's life before his appointment as organist at S Maria Maggiore in Bergamo in 1645 and his
subsequent appointment as *maestro di cappella* at the Accademia dello Spirito Santo in Ferrara

ten years later. He gained fame as a virtuoso organist and composer of operas and oratorios, and in 1665 he resigned his position in Ferrara to seek more prestigious and lucrative employment. He was offered, but declined the positions of *maestro di cappella* at the Modena Cathedral and S Maria Maggiore, where he had previously served as organist, and he applied but was not chosen for the position of *maestro di cappella* at the Milan Cathedral. He accepted two minor positions in Venice, one as *maestro di musica* at the Ospedale dei Dereletti in 1670 and the other as *maestro di coro* at the Congregazione dei Filippini at S Maria della Fava in 1671. In 1681 he was appointed *vice-maestro* at St Mark's Basilica, and four years later he became *maestro*. Legrenzi's time at St Mark's was short (he became ill in 1687 and had to limit his activity). However, his impact was significant. He taught Antonio Lotti and Antonio Caldara, and the Basilica's musical forces reached their zenith during his time there. The choir numbered six sopranos, seven altos, thirteen tenors, and ten basses, and the orchestra consisted of two cornets, three trombones, eight violins, eleven violas, two cellos, three violones (string basses), and a basso continuo group of four theorbos and one bassoon, in addition to the several organists always on hand.

Legrenzi composed seven oratorios, eleven collections of motets, two masses, and five collections of secular music, plus eighteen operas. Unfortunately, many of the works have not survived and many others have not been published. Most of the published works were originally issued in *Harmonia d'affetti devoti* op. 3 of 1655, *Salmi a 5* op. 5 of 1657, and *Sacri e festivi concenti, messa e psalmi a due chori* op. 9 of 1667.

Only three of the seven oratorios survive—*Il Sedecia, La vendita del core humano,* and *La morte de cor penitente*—and only *Il Sedecia* and *La vendita* have been published. Both of these oratorios are typical in their scoring for soloists and basso continuo and in their portrayal of text. *Il Sedecia* is based on the biblical story of Zedekiah, the last King of Judah, who unsuccessfully battles Nebuchadnezzar of Babylon and is taken captive and held in chains until his death. *La vendita del core humano* (The sale of the human heart) is an allegorical story about characters representing sacred and secular aspects of life, written by Pier Matteo Petrucci, a priest from the Congregazione dell' Oratorio di Jesu; the oratorio was quite popular during the latter part of the seventeenth century, being performed in Venice (1673, 1674, and 1696), Ferrara (1676), and Vienna (1692).

The motets and masses are in a variety of subgenres and styles, including solo works for one to three voices with basso continuo; larger, multisectional works in a *concertato* style scored for solos, chorus, and strings; polychoral works in the Venetian style popularized at St Mark's by Giovanni Gabrieli; and works in the Renaissance *prima prattica* style. Most of the published motets are in the latter style, with a basso continuo part that is nonindependent, and with numerous tempo changes and varied rhythmic patterns that express nuances of text.

ORATORIOS
SELECTED AND LISTED ACCORDING TO FAMILIARITY

Il Sedecia – 1676 – SSATB solos and basso continuo – 20 minutes. (1) Solo roles are for Zedekiah (T), Zedekiah's First Son (S), Zedekiah's Second Son (S), Nebuchadnezzar (B), and a Narrator (A); (2) there are two ensemble movements, one at the end of each part of the oratorio and both sung by the soloists.

La vendita del core humano (also called *Il cuor umano all'incanto*) – 1673 –
SATB solos and basso continuo – 60 minutes. (1) Solo roles are for the
Human Heart (S), a Guardian Angel (A), Vain Pleasure (T), Christ (T),
the World (B), and the Devil (B); (2) since Vain Pleasure and the World
are limited to the first half of the oratorio and the other roles are limited
to the second half, Legrenzi specified that Vain Pleasure and Christ be
sung by the same tenor, and similarly, the World and the Devil be sung
by the same bass; (3) there are two ensemble movements, one at the end
of each part of the oratorio and both sung by the soloists.

OTHER SACRED WORKS
SELECTED AND LISTED ACCORDING TO FAMILIARITY

Adoramus te, sanctissima crucem – 1655 – SATB voices and basso continuo –
4 minutes.

Dixit Dominus (Psalm 110) – 1654 – SATB voices, two violins, and basso continuo – 5 minutes.

Venite omnes – 1655 – SATB voices and basso continuo – 4 minutes.

Humili voce – 1655 – SSB voices and basso continuo – 3:30 minutes.

Exultate justi – 1665 – ATB voices and basso continuo – 3:30 minutes. The
motet contains a brief melodic passage for solo tenor.

Magnificat – 1657 – STB voices, two violins, and basso continuo – 7 minutes. The motet contains brief melodic passages for each of the vocalists.

Magnificat – 1667 – SATB/SATB chorus, strings, and basso continuo –
10:30 minutes. The strings divide into two violin and two viola parts.

Messa à due chori – SATB/SATB chorus, strings, and basso continuo –
20 minutes. The strings divide into two violin and three viola parts.

ANTONIO DRAGHI CA.1635–1700

Draghi was born in Rimini and probably educated in Mantua and Venice. At age twenty-three he
went to Vienna, where he was first a singer, then *Vice-Kapellmeister*, and finally *Kapellmeister* for the
dowager Empress Eleonora, the widow of Ferdinand III. In 1682 he left the dowager's court to become *Kapellmeister* to Leopold I at the imperial court, a position he kept until his death.

Draghi composed mostly dramatic music, including over one hundred operas and forty-one
oratorios. The oratorios are divided between those, such as *Il figlio prodigo* and *Jephte*, that were
composed to traditional texts about Old Testament characters, and *sepolcri*, such as *La sette do-
lori di Maria Vergine* and *La virtù della croce*, that were composed to texts dealing with the Passion story. The oratorios set to Old Testament stories are modern in style, with scoring that includes coloratura writing for soloists, two violins, and basso continuo. The *sepolcri* are somewhat
archaic, with simpler vocal scoring and accompaniment of violas or gambas and basso continuo.
In addition to the dramatic music, Draghi composed several masses, including the *Missa* in G
major of 1684 scored for SSATB solos, SSATB chorus, two violins, two violas, and basso con-

tinuo, and the *Missa assumptionis,* also of 1684, scored for SSATB solos, SSATB chorus, two trumpets, four trombones, two violins, four violas, and basso continuo.

ALESSANDRO STRADELLA CA.1639–1682

The precise location and year of Stradella's birth are uncertain. He was most likely born in Vignola, a small town near Modena, where his father, Marc' Antonio, was a military officer, and there is some conjecture that he was born in 1644. This date is improbable, however, given the later circumstances of his life. He lived in Rome beginning in 1653, and in 1655 he became a singer at S Marcello del Crocifisso, where he would have become acquainted with the oratorios of Giacomo Carissimi, Alessandro Scarlatti, and other notable composers of the time. Stradella came to the attention of Queen Christina of Sweden, who had a lavish and musically active court in Rome and who in 1663 commissioned him to compose the motet *Chare Jesu suavissime*—his first known composition. Other commissions quickly followed, including one for a cantata from Queen Christina the following year, and soon after that he composed motets, cantatas, serenatas, operas, and oratorios for many distinguished patrons throughout Italy. Stradella was apparently wealthy—a *gentiluomo* in Italian society—and he therefore moved easily among the Italian nobility and did not require a position such as *maestro di cappella* at a cathedral or court. He was also apparently a disreputable and rakish figure. In 1669 he was forced to flee from Rome for a short period of time because of his involvement in a plot to embezzle money from the Vatican, and in 1677 he was forced to leave Rome again (this time permanently) because of a public dispute with an important cardinal. He settled briefly in Venice (where he became intimate with the wife of a prominent Venetian nobleman), then Turin (where he took residence with the nobleman's wife), and finally Genoa (where he was murdered because of an indiscretion with another married woman). His personal life was the subject of numerous novels and stage works, including the opera *Alessandro Stradella* by Friedrich Flotow (1812–1883). However, his personal reputation did not seem to affect his compositional career. He continued to receive commissions throughout the later years of his life, and his compositions were acclaimed and performed frequently, especially in Genoa and Modena.

Stradella composed six oratorios, four motets for chorus, three sacred cantatas for chorus, and eight madrigals, in addition to more than one hundred cantatas and motets for solo voices. Many of the sacred works were the first of their kind to be scored for two groups of instruments—a *concerto grosso* group and a *concertino* group.

The oratorios include *S Editta, vergine e monaca; Ester, liberatrice del popolo ebreo; San Giovanni Battista; Susanna; S Giovanni Chrisostomo;* and *S Pelagia.* They are all typical of the time both in their subject matter and style of composition. The texts either are about important biblical figures (*Ester* and *Susanna*) or are moral allegories (*S Editta* and *S Pelagia*), and the scoring is for solos (SSATB) and basso continuo or for strings and basso continuo. In *Ester* the five soloists (Esther, Ahasuerus, Haman, Mordecai, and Celestial Hope) relate the biblical story of Queen Esther and her efforts to save the Israelites from annihilation by Haman and Ahasuerus, and in *S Editta* the soloists (Nobility, Beauty, Humility, Greatness, and the Senses) vie for moral alignment with Saint Edith. Both oratorios are scored for the soloists and basso continuo, and they consist mostly of recitatives and arias, with occasional ensemble pieces sung by the soloists.

The motets and cantatas are mainly scored for solo voices and basso continuo (e.g., more than one hundred of the cantatas are scored for soprano solo and basso continuo). Only a few are scored for either multiple voices (such as SSB, SAB, or SATB) or solo voices and chorus, and these are also scored for two violins and basso continuo or for two groups of strings that are in a *concerto grosso* relationship.

The madrigals, with texts about unrequited love, are all in a polyphonic *prima prattica* style characterized by points of imitation, rhythms that vary slightly to portray textual moods, and conservative diatonic harmonies. Although they are in the *prima prattica* style, some of the madrigals have a basso continuo part (which is only occasionally independent from the vocal bass part).

ORATORIOS
SELECTED AND LISTED ACCORDING TO FAMILIARITY

San Giovanni Battista – 1675 – SSATB solos, strings, and basso continuo – 80 minutes. (1) Solo roles are for St John (A), Herod (B), a Counselor (T), Herodias (S), and Herodias's daughter Salome (S); (2) there are four *tutti* ensemble movements, all in the first half of the oratorio and all for the soloists; (3) the strings are divided into two groups—a *concerto grosso* group of two violins, two violas, and basso continuo, and a *concertino* group of two violins and basso continuo.

Susanna – 1681 – SSATB solos, two violins, and basso continuo – 60 minutes. (1) Solo roles are for Susanna (S), Daniele (S), a Narrator (A), the First Elder (B), and the Second Elder (T); (2) the Narrator has arias as well as recitatives; (3) the ensemble movements, for the soloists, are scored for SSB, ATB, and SSATB; (4) most of the oratorio is scored for soloists and basso continuo alone (the violins consist mostly of ritornellos within the arias).

MOTETS
SELECTED AND LISTED ACCORDING TO FAMILIARITY

Convocamini, congregamini – SS solos, SATB chorus, two violins, and basso continuo – 4 minutes.

In tribulationibus, in angustiis – SSATB voices, two violins, and basso continuo – 3:30 minutes.

Pugna, certamen, militia est vita – 1675 – SATB voices and *concerto grosso* strings – 5:30 minutes.

SACRED CANTATAS
SELECTED AND LISTED ACCORDING TO FAMILIARITY

Esule dale sfere – *Per l'anime del Purg'rio* (for the Souls of Purgatory) – SB solos, SATB chorus, two violins, and basso continuo – 35 minutes. (1) Solo roles are for a Soul (S) and Lucifer (B); (2) the cantata is in thirty-two movements, nine of which are for chorus.

Ah! Troppo è ver – *Cantata per il Santissimo Natale* (cantata for the holy birth) – ca.1675 – SSSATB solos, SSATB chorus, strings, and basso continuo – 34 minutes. (1) Solo roles are for an Angel (S), Mary (S), the First Shepherd (S), Joseph (A), the Second Shepherd (T), and the Devil (B); (2) there are two choral movements—one for SSAT and one (called a *madrigal*) for SSATB; (3) both choral movements are scored for voices and basso continuo only; (4) the strings are divided into two groups—a *concertino* group of two violins and basso continuo and a *concerto grosso* group for violin, two violas, and basso continuo.

Si apra al riso ogni babro – *Per la notte del Santissimo Natale* (for the night of the holy birth) – 1670s – SAB solos, two violins, and basso continuo – 25 minutes. (1) There are no solo roles, although the text portrays the three soloists as shepherds who have visited the manger and have seen the Christ Child; (2) there are three trios (all called *madrigale*)—two are scored for voices and basso continuo, and one is scored for voices a cappella.

MADRIGALS
SELECTED AND LISTED ACCORDING TO FAMILIARITY

Tirsi un giorno piangea – SSATB voices a cappella – 7 minutes.

Pupilette amorose – SSATB voices a cappella – 6 minutes.

Piangette occhi dolenti – SSATB voices and basso continuo – 7 minutes.

Clori son fido amante – SSATB voices and basso continuo – 5:30 minutes.

GIUSEPPE OTTAVIO PITONI 1657–1743

Pitoni, who was born near and spent most of his life in Rome, held a number of important church positions during his long life (one month short of eighty-seven years). He was *maestro di cappella* at S Marco in the Palazzo Venezia from 1677 until his death sixty-six years later, he directed much of the music at the Collegio Germanico from 1686 until his death, he oversaw performances by Cardinal Pietro Ottoboni from approximately 1692 to 1731, and he was *maestro di cappella* at the Cappella Giulia at St Peter's. Given the breadth of activity that each of these positions must have required, and given the length of time that the positions were directed by Pitoni, it must be assumed that he heavily influenced church music in Rome during the last four or five decades of the Baroque era. This seems even more the case in that Pitoni was a prolific composer (approximately 270 masses and 235 motets). While some of the compositions were in a *seconda prattica* style, with scoring for solos, chorus, and instruments, most of the music, especially that composed before 1720, was in a very conservative *prima prattica* style that emulated the music of Palestrina, which Pitoni had studied in his youth. Like all *prima prattica* music of the Baroque era, Pitoni's music has a texture that is more homophonic than polyphonic or contrapuntal, and it also has a scoring that includes basso continuo. However, Pitoni's compositions seem to belong to the late sixteenth century rather than to the early eighteenth century, and the basso continuo parts are clearly optional. Perhaps the disparity between the music's style and era of composition explains why so little of the music is known today. Only a few of the motets are published and performed, including *Cantate Domine* (Psalm 96), *Vias tuas Domine* (Psalm 24:4), and *Christus factus est* (for Maundy Thursday, from Philippians 2:8–9). Each is scored for SATB chorus and optional basso continuo.

ALESSANDRO SCARLATTI 1660–1725

Alessandro Scarlatti—father of Domenico Scarlatti, the famous harpsichord composer and performer—was born in Palermo. Nothing is known about his youth except that he moved to Rome with his family when he was twelve. He was influenced by the rich cultural activity in Rome at the time, and he developed considerable musical ability. In 1678, when just eighteen, he was appointed *maestro di cappella* at S Giacomo degli Incurabili, and the following year, when he was nineteen, he composed an opera and an oratorio—both performed to high acclaim. He continued his swift rise to fame with appointments to two *maestro di cappella* positions the following year (1680)—one at the court of Queen Christina of Sweden, who had a palace in Rome, and the other at the church of Girolamo della Carità—and he also continued composing operas and oratorios. However, being more interested in opera, which was limited to private performance in Rome because of the strict edicts of Pope Innocent XI, he moved to Naples, where opera was flourishing and where he was appointed *maestro di cappella* at the court of the Spanish Ambassador to the Vatican. Scarlatti remained in Naples for eighteen years, composing forty operas, nine oratorios, sixty-five cantatas, and a small number of other miscellaneous works, and in 1702, to relieve himself of court pressures, he returned to Rome, where he was appointed assistant to the *maestro di cappella* of the Congregazione dell'Oratorio di S Filippo Neri at the Chiesa Nuova. Feeling that the demands of this position were too great, he quickly resigned and became assistant *maestro di cappella* at S Maria Maggiore. This latter position allowed him time to travel to other cities, such as Venice, to oversee production of his operas. In 1707 he was promoted to *maestro di cappella* at S Maria Maggiore, but the following year he was convinced to return to his previous position in Naples, where he remained until his death.

Scarlatti composed thirty-eight oratorios (twenty-three of which survive today), ten masses, 110 motets and other sacred works, more than six hundred secular cantatas (all for solo voices), and eight madrigals. Most of the oratorios are scored for soloists, strings, and basso continuo and consist of a series of recitatives and arias with a few duets and *tutti* ensemble movements. For example, *Sedecia, re di Gerusalemme,* Scarlatti's most famous oratorio, has twenty-seven recitatives, twenty-three arias, two duets, and only one *tutti* ensemble movement. As was typical of the time, no chorus was involved; the *tutti* movements were sung by the soloists (although one edition of *Sedecia* has fifteen measures scored for chorus in dialogue with the soloists). *Cain overo il primo omicidio* has several duets and no *tutti* ensemble movements. An exception to this scoring is *Davidis, pugna et Victoria,* which is Scarlatti's only extant oratorio in Latin (excluding the Passion) and which is scored for SSATB solos and a separate double chorus that sings in four extended movements.

The early oratorios, such as *Agar et Ismaele esiliati* and *La Giuditta,* were composed between 1683 and 1695 and consist of *secco* recitatives and short arias, with scoring for a small ensemble of strings. The late oratorios, including *Sedecia re di Gerusalemme* and *Cain,* were composed between 1700 and 1717 and consist of a few accompanied recitatives, *da capo* arias, and occasional scoring for *concertino solo* and *concerto grosso* groups of strings. The texts of the oratorios, conforming to general practices and expectations of the time, are about notable biblical characters such as David and Goliath (*Davidis, pugna et Victoria*) or are allegorical stories such as *Santissima Trinità,* which is a debate about the nature of the Holy Trinity between soloists representing Faith, Divine Love, Theology, Infidelity, and Time.

Sedecia, re di Gerusalemme was premiered in Rome in 1705 and was subsequently given multiple performances in many European cities, including Vienna and Florence. The success of the oratorio was no doubt due in part to the militaristic character of the oratorio's story and scoring as well as its obvious allusion to the political events of the time: the biblical story of Zedekiah from Jeremiah 39:1–10 was seen as relevant to the War of the Spanish Succession, which in 1705 was threatening Rome. Other notable oratorios are the Passion oratorio, *Passio D. N. Jesu Christi secundum Joannem* (ca.1680); *La Giuditta* (1693); *Abramo il tuo sembiante* (ca.1705), subtitled "Cantata per la Notte di Natale" (Cantata for the Night of the Nativity); and *La vergine addolorata* (1717). *La vergine addolorata,* Scarlatti's final oratorio, is sometimes called *Il Dolore di Maria Vergine.* The title discrepancy occurs because the cover of the original and only existing score of the oratorio is partly obliterated and all that remains is *Orat . . . di Maria Vergine.* The several oratorios without choral involvement that are annotated below are included because of their familiarity and artistic quality, and also because Scarlatti is considered to be the second-most important composer of oratorios (after Giacomo Carissimi) in Italy during the Baroque era.

The masses include *Messa di S Cecilia* (1720), *Messa per il Santissimo Natale* (1707), *Missa ad usum cappellae pontificiae* (1721), and two works entitled *Missa Clementina* (1705 and 1716). The early masses, including the two works composed for Pope Clement XI, are in the polyphonic *prima prattica* style of Palestrina; Scarlatti himself referred to this style as "alla Palestrina." The later masses, including the famous *Messa di S Cecilia,* are in the *seconda prattica* style and are scored for soloists, chorus, strings, and basso continuo.

The remaining sacred works include two Magnificats, four settings of Dixit Dominus (the most commonly set Psalm in Vespers services), and a setting each of Responsories and Lamentations. Like the masses, the motets are in both *prima* and *seconda prattica* styles. The *prima prattica* motets are often scored for SSATB chorus and supporting basso continuo. Several—notably *Tu es Petrus* and *O magnum mysterium*—are scored for double choir. The *seconda prattica* motets are scored for one to five voices and instrumental accompaniment of strings and basso continuo.

The madrigals are generally scored for SSATB voices a cappella and are in the expressive *prima prattica* style of Marenzio. *Mori, mi dici* is an excellent example. One madrigal—*Cor mio, deh, non languire*—is scored for SSSSA and was therefore undoubtedly composed for an ensemble such as the Concerto delle donne.

ORATORIOS
SELECTED AND LISTED ACCORDING TO FAMILIARITY

Sedecia, re di Gerusalemme – 1705 – SSATB solos, oboe, two trumpets, timpani, strings, and basso continuo – 90 minutes. (1) Solo roles are for Zedekiah (A), Zedekiah's wife Anna (S), Zedekiah's son Ismaele (S), Zedekiah's confidant Nadabbe (T), and Nebuchadnezzar (B); (2) only Zedekiah and

Nebuchadnezzar are biblical characters, the others are fictional and reflect the political message of the oratorio; (3) the oratorio comprises two
orchestral sinfoniae, two duets, and a final *tutti* ensemble movement.

La Giuditta – 1693 – SSATB solos, two flutes, trumpet, two trombones,
strings, and basso continuo – 94 minutes. (1) Major solo roles are for
Judith (S), Ozias (S), and a Priest (B); (2) minor solo roles are for Holofernes (A) and the Captain of the Ammonites (T); (3) there is only one
tutti ensemble movement, which closes the oratorio; (4) the strings are
divided into *concertino solo* and *concerto grosso* groups.

Davidis, pugna et Victoria – 1700 – SSATB solos, SATB/SATB chorus,
strings, and basso continuo – 85 minutes. (1) Solo roles are for David
(S), Jonathan (S), Saul (A), a Narrator (T), and Goliath (B); (2) there are
four choral movements, all for SATB/SATB; (3) the strings briefly divide
into a *concertino* solo group of two violins and a *concerto grosso* group of
two violins, viola, cello, and bass.

Passio D. N. Jesu Christi secundum Joannem – ca.1680 – SAATTB solos,
SATB chorus, strings, and basso continuo – 50 minutes. (1) Solo roles
are for a Narrator (A), Christ (B), Pilate (A), Peter (T), a Servant (S), and
a Jew (T); (2) the work is in one continuous movement, consisting mostly
of recitatives and arioso-like passages; (3) the chorus parts consist mostly
of short *turba* passages.

La vergine addolorata – 1717 – SSAT solos, flute, oboe, trumpet, strings, and
basso continuo – 150 minutes. (1) Solo roles are for Mary the mother of
Jesus (S), St John (S), Nicodemo (A), and Onìa (T); (2) there are no *tutti*
ensemble movements; (3) this was Scarlatti's final oratorio.

La Santissima Trinità – 1715 – SSATB solos, strings, and basso continuo –
67 minutes. (1) Solo roles are for Faith (S), Divine Love (S), Theology (A),
Infidelity (T), and Time (B); (2) there is only one *tutti* ensemble movement,
which closes the oratorio; (3) the text is similar to Cavalieri's *Rappresentatione
di Anima, et di Corpo* (Representation of the soul and the body) and Handel's *Il trionfo del Tempo e del Disinganno* (The triumph of time and truth).

MASSES

SELECTED AND LISTED ACCORDING TO FAMILIARITY

Messa di S Cecilia – 1720 – SSATB solos, SSATB chorus, strings, and basso
continuo – 52 minutes. (1) The solo parts always alternate with the choral
parts; (2) the mass was composed for St Cecilia celebrations at the
church of Santa Cecilia in Trastevere, Rome.

Messa per il Santissimo Natale – 1707 – SSATB/SATB chorus, two violins, and
basso continuo – 28 minutes. (1) The mass is for the celebration of
Christmas; (2) no original score exists, but the mass was constructed
from performance parts in Scarlatti's hand; (3) there are presumed solo
parts, which alternate with the choral parts.

Messe breve, e concertata a cinque voci – SSATB solos, SSATB chorus, and
basso continuo – 20 minutes. (1) The soloists are scored as a *concertino*

group, while the chorus is scored as a *concerto grosso* group; (2) the solo writing consists mostly of ensembles for all the singers (there are very few solo melodic passages); (3) the chorus always sings in conjunction with the soloists; (4) the basso continuo includes an organ, cello, and bass for the soloists and for the chorus.

Missa ad usum cappellae pontificiae – 1721 – SATB chorus and basso continuo – 31 minutes.

MOTETS AND OTHER SACRED WORKS
SELECTED AND LISTED ACCORDING TO FAMILIARITY

Exultate Deo (Psalm 81) – SATB chorus a cappella – 2:30 minutes.

Dixit Dominus (Psalm 110) – ca.1715 – SAB solos, SATB chorus, strings, and basso continuo – 22 minutes. (1) Each of the soloists has a separate aria, and there is a duet for soprano and alto; (2) there are also numerous solo passages within the four choral movements; (3) the strings are divided into three violin parts, without viola.

Tu es Petrus (Matthew 16) – ca.1707 – SATB/SATB chorus and basso continuo – 20 minutes.

O magnum mysterium – 1707 – SATB/SATB chorus and basso continuo – 6:15 minutes.

Ad te Domine levavi (Psalm 25) – ca.1708 – SATB chorus a cappella – 3:30 minutes.

Te Deum – SSATB solos, SSATB chorus, two oboes, two violins, and basso continuo – 10 minutes. The solo parts, which are brief, alternate with the choral parts.

Salvum fac populum (from the Te Deum) – SATB a cappella – 3:30 minutes.

MADRIGALS
COMPLETE AND LISTED ACCORDING TO FAMILIARITY

Mori, mi dici – SSATB voices a cappella – 5:30 minutes.

O selce, o tigre, o ninfa – SSATB voices a cappella – 4:30 minutes.

Arsi un tempo e l'ardore – SSATB voices a cappella – 3 minutes.

Intenerite voi, lacrime mie – SATTB voices a cappella – 4 minutes.

O morte, agli altri fosca – SSATB voices a cappella – 5 minutes.

Or che da te, mio bene – SATB voices and basso continuo ad lib. – 6:30 minutes.

Sdegno la fiamma estinse – SSATB voices a cappella – 4 minutes.

Cor mio, deh, non languire – SSSSA voices and basso continuo ad lib. – 5:15 minutes.

ANTONIO LOTTI CA.1667–1740

Lotti was most likely born in Hanover, Germany, where his father, Matteau, was *Kapellmeister* at the ducal chapel. In approximately 1683 Antonio moved to Venice, where he studied with and sang under Giovanni Legrenzi, *maestro di cappella* at St Mark's Basilica, and he remained at St Mark's except for a two-year appointment (1717–1718) at the Dresden court of Friedrich August II, advancing at the Basilica and holding several organ positions until he became *maestro di cappella* in 1736. He was also associated for most of his life with the Ospedale degli Incurabili, the most famous of the four Venetian orphanages for girls that specialized in musical training. Lotti was highly regarded during his lifetime, and manuscripts of his music circulated throughout Europe. Jan Dismas Zelenka and J. S. Bach are reported to have made copies of his *Missa sapientiae.*

Lotti's compositional output includes seven oratorios, ten complete masses plus numerous separate mass movements, approximately thirty motets, more than fifty secular cantatas (all composed for solo voices), and several collections of secular duets, trios, and madrigals. All of the oratorios except two—*Il voto crudele* (1712) and *L'umiltà coronata in Esther* (ca.1714)—have been lost, and only *L'umiltà coronata in Esther* has been published. Similar to the oratorios of Alessandro Stradella and Alessandro Scarlatti, it consists mostly of arias and recitatives and is scored for strings and basso continuo, with the strings divided into *concertino* and *concerto grosso* groups.

The masses include two notable works, *Missa Sapientiae* and *Missa pro defunctis,* the former of which is similar to the Neapolitan masses of the time: it consists only of the Kyrie and Gloria portions of the Mass Ordinary, and these are divided into multiple movements. The *Missa pro defunctis* is in four movements that are divided into smaller, clearly defined sections, most only a minute or two in length. The Dies irae, for instance, is in nineteen sections. The style of the writing represents most compositional features of the time, including short motivic fragments imitated in fugal fashion, concerted sections, and musical affects that paint the action or mood of text. All of the other masses, including the *Missa a 3 ad aequalis* (Mass for three equal voices), are in a *prima prattica* style, with alternating textures of imitative polyphony and homophony. Most of these masses are scored for SATB voices a cappella (one, in A minor, is scored for TTB) and contain all portions of the Ordinary. All the masses are characterized by harmonies that are typical of Lotti's penchant for suspensions—a hallmark of the popular *Crucifixus* for SSAATTBB chorus and strings *colla parte,* which is undoubtedly Lotti's most famous piece of music. The separate mass movements include the *Credo* in F major—a work in five distinct and separate sections, the second of which is the *Crucifixus* mentioned above. Lotti made other settings of the Crucifixus text, including one for six voices and another for ten voices, both annotated below.

Motets at the time were generally scored for solo voices and basso continuo, and Lotti composed a few of these. However, most of his motets are for chorus and are in the *prima prattica* style. An example is the famous *Miserere,* scored for SATB chorus and basso continuo and performed at St Mark's during Lauds every Thursday of Holy Week from 1733 until the beginning of the nineteenth century. The long text is segmented into simple points of imitation with frequent phrases of homophony, and each sentence of text is clearly delineated by a cadence and is given expressive treatment.

Most of the secular duets, trios, and madrigals were published in *Duetti, terzetti e madrigali a più voci* op.1 of 1705. The publication consists of twelve duets, four trios, and two madrigals, including the strikingly beautiful *Querèla amorosa* for two sopranos and continuo. The madrigals are in the *prima prattica* style of Marenzio, with varied rhythms and tempos that are expressive of textual moods, and all have basso continuo parts that are rarely independent of the vocal lines. *Spirto di Dio ch'essendo il mondo,* extremely popular during the eighteenth century, is the only secular work contained in the library of St Mark's Basilica.

MASSES AND MASS MOVEMENTS
SELECTED AND LISTED ACCORDING TO FAMILIARITY

Crucifixus – SSAATTBB chorus, strings *colla parte,* and basso continuo – 3:30 minutes. (1) This is the second movement of the *Credo* in F major; (2) it is often performed alone as a separate piece, a cappella.

Crucifixus – SSATTB chorus and basso continuo – 2:30 minutes.

Crucifixus – SSSAATTTBB chorus and basso continuo – 3:30 minutes.

Missa Sapientiae (Kyrie and Gloria) – SATB solos, SSATTB chorus, strings, and basso continuo – 32 minutes. (1) The solo writing consists mainly of passages for duet and quartet (there are very few solos and no arias); (2) the mass is often heard in an arrangement by Jan Dismas Zelenka (1679–1745) that adds parts for trumpet, flute, and two oboes.

Missa pro defunctis (Requiem) in F major – SSATB solos, SSATB chorus, two oboes, bassoon, trumpet, strings, and basso continuo – 48 minutes. (1) The solo writing consists mostly of ensembles for quartet; (2) most of the choral scoring is for SATB.

Missa a 3 ad aequalis (A minor) – SSA or TTB chorus a cappella – 11 minutes.

Credo – SATB chorus, strings, and basso continuo – 12 minutes. The work is divided into five movements, all for SATB chorus except movement two (*Crucifixus*), which is scored for SSAATTBB.

In terra pax – SSAAAATTTTBBBB, strings, and basso continuo – 4 minutes.

MOTETS
SELECTED AND LISTED ACCORDING TO FAMILIARITY

Miserere (Psalm 51) – SATB voices and basso continuo – 9 minutes.

Vere languores (Isaiah 53:4) – SATB voices a cappella – 2:30 minutes.

Vere languores (Isaiah 53:4) – SSA voices a cappella – 2:30 minutes.

Adoramus te – SATB voices a cappella – 1:30 minutes.

Ad Dominum cum tribularer (Psalm 120) – SATB voices and basso continuo – 3:30 minutes.

Ave regina coelorum – SATB voices a cappella – 3:30 minutes.

MADRIGALS AND DUETS
SELECTED AND LISTED ACCORDING TO FAMILIARITY

Spirto di Dio ch'essendo il mondo – 1736 – SATB voices a cappella – 4:30 minutes.

La vita caduca – 1705 – SSATB voices and basso continuo – 7:30 minutes.

Moralità d'una perla – 1705 – SATB voices and basso continuo – 5:30 minutes.

Inganni dell'umanità – 1705 – ATB voices and basso continuo – 4 minutes.

Lamento di tre amanti – 1705 – SSB voices and basso continuo – 6 minutes.
    The voice parts have extended melodic passages accompanied by an in-
    dependent basso continuo part.

Querèla amorosa – SS voices and basso continuo – 9:30 minutes.

ANTONIO CALDARA CA.1671–1736

Caldara was born in Venice, where he most certainly received his early musical education from his father, Giuseppe, who was a violinist, and from Giovanni Legrenzi, who was *maestro di cappella* at St Mark's Basilica from 1681 until his death in 1690. The young Caldara was an alto in the choir at St Mark's (along with Antonio Lotti, who was four years his senior), and he also played cello in the *cappella*. In addition, he developed as a composer, and during his twenties he was recognized for his operas and oratorios as well as for his liturgical and instrumental music. In 1699 he was appointed *maestro di cappella da chiesa e del teatro* at the court of the Duke of Mantua, a position held at the beginning of the Baroque era by Claudio Monteverdi. The court, which was famous for its lavish opera productions, experienced financial difficulties soon after Caldara arrived, and in addition, the duke was forced to flee from Mantua for political reasons. Consequently, Caldara went to Rome in 1707, and in 1709 he was appointed *maestro di cappella* at the court of Prince Francesco Maria Ruspoli. During Caldara's seven years at Ruspoli's court he composed approximately one hundred solo cantatas, fifty duets, seven trios, four operas, and nine oratorios, plus other miscellaneous compositions for occasions outside the court. In 1716 he was appointed *Vice-Kapellmeister* at the Imperial Court of Charles VI in Vienna (a prestigious appointment that he had sought for a number of years), and while at the Viennese court he composed thirty-four operas, twenty-three oratorios, more than one hundred masses, numerous motets, and various works for celebratory royal occasions. In total, therefore, Caldara composed more than three thousand works, including forty-two oratorios, more than one hundred masses and mass movements, two hundred motets and other miscellaneous sacred pieces, two hundred cantatas, and a number of secular vocal pieces (including approximately five hundred canons).

    The oratorios consist mostly of recitatives and arias. Except for occasional duets, the few movements for multiple voices are ensemble pieces to be sung by the soloists. The early oratorios—including the famous *Maddalena ai piedi di Cristo* of about 1698—were composed during the same time period as and exhibit similar characteristics of Alessandro Scarlatti's later oratorios: the recitatives are *secco*, and the arias, generally scored for a full ensemble of strings, are *da capo*. The later oratorios—including *Il martirio di S Caterina* of 1708, *S Flavia Domitilla* of 1713, *Il rè del dolore* of 1722, and *Joaz* (also spelled *Gioaz*) of 1726—are in the new *gallant* style characterized by thinner textures and reduced instrumentation. Caldara's only Passion oratorio—*La*

Passione di Gesù Cristo of 1730—is much like the other oratorios in being scored mainly for soloists (there are only three choral movements). However, the text is not biblical but allegorical, relating hypothetical conversations about the expected resurrection of Jesus after his crucifixion.

The masses are of three types—*solemne* (large-scale works with full orchestral accompaniment, composed in the *seconda prattica* style for festival occasions), *ordinariae* (small-scale works with string accompaniment, also composed in the *seconda prattica* style), and *da capella* (small-scale works with instruments doubling the vocal parts, composed in the *prima prattica* style). The *Missa Laetare* and *Missa in spei Resurrectionis* are examples of the *solemne* type, the *Missa Dolorosa* in E minor and *Missa Sancti Josephi* in B major are of the *ordinariae* type, and the *Missa* in F major is composed in the *da capella* style.

The *Magnificat* in C major is best known for the copy of it made by J. S. Bach. This copy was the only known existing source of the work until a manuscript signed by Caldara was discovered in the Österreichische Nationalbibliothek in Vienna at the end of the twentieth century. Bach's copy and Caldara's original are very similar but not identical; numerous rhythmic, pitch, text underlay, and articulation markings are in conflict. The work is typical of Caldara's general style, which represents aspects of both the conservative *prima prattica* that was commonplace in liturgical works of the time and the more modern *seconda prattica* that was evident in oratorios, operas, and other non-liturgical works. The third movement of the *Magnificat,* for instance, is imitative and reflective of Renaissance motets, while the first and final movements are homophonic, with independent instrumental material that is figural in character. In addition, the second movement is a short aria.

The motets are in both the *prima* and *seconda prattica* styles. Caldara's most famous motet—and perhaps his most famous work of any type—is his *Crucifixus* for sixteen voices. It is in the *prima prattica* style, consisting of long strings of imitative polyphony. Other motets, such as *Confitebor tibi Domini* and *Laudate pueri,* are multimovement works scored for soloists, chorus, and full orchestra.

As was typical of the time, most of the cantatas are for solo voice and basso continuo or for solo voice with strings and basso continuo. However, cantatas for liturgical festivals are generally for multiple voices. *Vaticini di Pace,* a Christmas cantata, is an example.

The madrigals are in the style of Marenzio, with varied rhythmic patterns that express different moods and characteristics of text, although Caldara adds tempo changes to further the expression. The madrigals are set to Italian secular poetry and scored for SATB or SSATB voices, with a basso continuo part that is not independent.

Caldara was highly regarded during his lifetime and afterwards: Georg Philipp Telemann claimed that he was a great influence to composers of the late Baroque era; Joseph Haydn sang his music and owned copies of two of his masses; Charles Burney, the famed British diarist and musical commentator, said that he was one of the greatest Italian composers of music for both the church and the stage; and, as was mentioned above, Bach copied one of his Magnificats.

ORATORIOS
SELECTED AND LISTED ACCORDING TO FAMILIARITY

Maddalena ai piedi di Cristo – ca.1698 – SSAATB solos, strings, and basso continuo – 120 minutes. (1) Solo roles are for Mary Magdalene (S), Martha (S), Earthly Love (A), Celestial Love (A), Christ (B), and a Pharisee (T); (2) there are no ensemble movements.

S Flavia Domitilla – 1713 – SSAT solos, two violins, and basso continuo –
   90 minutes. (1) Solo roles are for Flavia Domitilla (S), Achilleo (S), Nereo
   (A), and Aureliano (T); (2) there are four duets and no other ensemble
   movements.

La Passione di Gesù Cristo – 1730 – SSAB solos, SATB chorus, one trombone,
   strings, and basso continuo – 80 minutes. (1) Solo roles are for St John
   (S), Mary Magdalene (S), Peter (A), and Joseph of Arimathea (B); (2) the
   text relates hypothetical conversations about the expected resurrection of
   Jesus after his crucifixion; (3) the oratorio consists mostly of arias—there
   are only three choral movements; (4) the trombone is scored as an obbligato in one aria.

MASSES
SELECTED AND LISTED ACCORDING TO FAMILIARITY

Missa Dolorosa in E minor – 1735 – SATB solos, SATB chorus, strings, and
   basso continuo – 32:30 minutes. (1) The solos consist mostly of text
   phrases sung by the soloists in ensemble; (2) the basso continuo contains a bassoon, which has an obbligato part in the Gloria.

Missa Sancti Josephi in B major – SATB solos, SATB chorus, two violins, and
   basso continuo – 20 minutes. The solo writing is mostly for quartet,
   with a few solo melodic passages.

Missa in F major – SATB chorus a cappella – 12 minutes. The mass contains
   all the portions of the Ordinary, including a separate Benedictus movement, and is in an imitative *prima prattica* style.

MOTETS AND OTHER SACRED WORKS
SELECTED AND LISTED ACCORDING TO FAMILIARITY

Crucifixus – SSSSAAAATTTTBBBB chorus and basso continuo – 5 minutes.
   There are four short phrases of text, each treated imitatively and all intertwined.

Magnificat in C major – A solo, SATB chorus, four trumpets, timpani,
   strings, and basso continuo – 7 minutes. The motet is divided into four
   movements, three of which are choral.

Te Deum in C major – 1724 – SATB solos, SATB/SATB chorus, four trumpets, timpani, strings, and basso continuo – 12 minutes. (1) The work is
   sometimes referred to as the "Prague" *Te Deum,* although there is no evidence that it was composed for or performed in that city; (2) the solo
   writing consists of brief melodic passages and scoring for quartet; (3) the
   choral writing is basically in the Venetian polychoral style; (4) the violas
   are divided into two parts.

Te Deum in D major – ca.1711 – SATB/SATB chorus a cappella – 4 minutes.
   The motet is in the Venetian polychoral style.

Stabat Mater – after 1716 – SSATB solos, SATB chorus, two trombones, strings, and basso continuo – 25 minutes. (1) The work is divided into twelve very short movements that mostly alternate between solo ensemble and chorus; (2) all choral movements are in the *prima prattica* style; (3) the instrumental writing is mostly *colla parte,* with only a brief section for solo trombone in movement five and for independent strings in movement nine.

Dies irae – SSATB solos, SSATB chorus, strings, and basso continuo – 32 minutes. (1) The work is in nineteen movements—ten for chorus and nine for soloists; (2) movement five is scored for BB duet, and movement eight is scored for TTB trio; (3) the string writing alternates between *concertino* and *concerto grosso* groups.

Confitebor tibi (Psalm 111) – 1709–1716 – S solo, SATB chorus, two oboes, two violins, and basso continuo – 22 minutes. There are extensive soprano solos.

Si consistant adversum me (Psalm 26:3) – SATB chorus and basso continuo – 3 minutes. (1) The motet is in the *prima prattica* style and is divided into two main sections—largo and allegro; (2) the basso continuo is not independent.

Regina coeli (Queen of heaven) – SATB voices and basso continuo – 5:30 minutes.

Laudate pueri (Psalm 113) – 1716 – S solo, SATB chorus, two violins, and basso continuo – 10 minutes. The motet is divided into eight short and connected sections, some solo and some choral.

Miserere mei, Domine (Psalm 51) – SAB voices and basso continuo – 3 minutes.

Laboravi in gemitu meo – ATB voices and basso continuo – 2 minutes.

O sacrum convivium – SSB voices and basso continuo – 3:30 minutes.

MADRIGALS
SELECTED AND LISTED ACCORDING TO FAMILIARITY

Vola il tempo qual vento – SATB voices and basso continuo – 7 minutes.

Fra pioggie nevie gelo – SSATB voices and basso continuo – 8:30 minutes.

Di piaceri foriera giunge – SSATB voices and basso continuo – 6 minutes.

La speranza – SATB voices and basso continuo – 5:30 minutes.

ANTONIO VIVALDI 1678–1741

Vivaldi was born in Venice, where his father, Giovanni Battista, was a violinist at St Mark's Basilica. Antonio was not trained to be a musician, although he most certainly studied violin, since he occasionally substituted for his father at St Mark's. Instead, he studied for the priesthood and was ordained in March 1703; because of his red hair, he was nicknamed "il prete rosso" (the red priest). In September 1703 he was appointed *maestro di violono* at the Ospedale della Pietà, one of four Venetian orphanages for girls devoted to musical training and performance, and over the ensuing years he was promoted to successively higher ranks: in 1716 he was named *maestro de' concerti,* and in 1735 he was appointed *maestro di cappella,* the highest musical position he could attain there. Despite his advancement, his appointments were interrupted several times—once from 1709 to 1711 when the Pietà apparently had insufficient funds to retain him, and other times to accommodate his extended absences. From 1718 to 1720 he was in Mantua composing and attending to his operas, in 1723 and 1724 he was in Rome (also busy with his operas), and sometime between 1729 and 1733 he made protracted visits to Vienna and Prague. In 1737 he left the priesthood because the Church censured him for unbecoming conduct (the precise circumstances or reasons are unknown), and in 1738 the governing officials of the Pietà became intolerant of his lengthy absences and released him from his position. He then returned to Vienna, where he died in July 1741.

Vivaldi was and is most famous for his numerous instrumental compositions. He wrote more than five hundred sonatas and concertos, including the famous *Four Seasons,* and in addition, he composed forty operas (of which only twenty-one survive) and approximately forty cantatas and motets for solo voices, including the *Stabat Mater* RV621 for alto and strings. His choral output consists of three oratorios, one complete mass, several mass movements, approximately thirty Psalm settings, and one Magnificat. Only a single oratorio, generally referred to by its shortened title, *Juditha triumphans,* has survived. Its full title—*Juditha triumphans devicta Holofernes barbarie: sacrum militare oratorium hisce belli temporibus a psalentium virginum choro in Templo Pietatis canendum* (Judith Triumphant, Conqueror of the Barbaric Holofernes: A Sacred Military Oratorio Performed in Times of War by the Chorus of Virgin Singers, to Be Sung in the Church of the Pietà)—explains some important factors about the oratorio's text and performance circumstances. The story is based on the biblical account of Judith, who slays Holofernes. However, much of the oratorio's libretto refers to the seven-year war between Venice and Turkey that ended in 1716 (the year the oratorio was composed), and the characters in the oratorio are allegorical: Judith symbolizes Venice and Holofernes symbolizes the Sultan of Turkey. In addition, it is clear that the oratorio was composed for performance by the girls at the orphanage, since all the solo roles are for female voices.

The mass and a number of the other choral works were probably composed sometime around 1715, when the Pietà awarded special payment to Vivaldi for an entire mass, a Vespers service, an oratorio, and over thirty motets and other works. The mass is lost, although it is believed that the second of the *Gloria* settings (RV588) was one of its movements. The oratorio— probably *Moyses Deus Pharaonis*—is also lost.

The mass movements include two settings of the Gloria, as was mentioned above, and one setting each of the Kyrie and Credo. The two Gloria works are almost identical. Indeed, it seems as if the second of the two (RV588) is an arrangement of the first (RV589), which is the setting that is most popular today and which was undoubtedly Vivaldi's earliest sacred vocal composition. Furthermore, the Kyrie and Credo settings (as well as many of the Psalm settings) share what might be termed "stock" compositional features, including movements for unison chorus that feature scalar passages (as seen in "Deposuit potentes" from the *Magnificat* RV610a) and movements for homophonic chorus with figural string accompaniment (as seen in "Fecit potentiam" from the same Magnificat setting).

The Psalm settings include smaller works in one movement for SATB chorus and a few instruments (such as *Laetatus sum, Laudate Dominum,* and *In exitu Israel*) and larger multimovement works for double choir and a full complement of strings, with the occasional addition of other instruments such as oboes and trumpets. All of these larger works, including the Magnificats, were part of Vespers services at the time.

ORATORIO

Juditha triumphans RV645 – 1716 – SSAAA solos, SATB chorus, two flutes, two oboes, two trumpets, timpani, strings, and basso continuo – 125 minutes. (1) Solo roles are for Judith (A), Holofernes (A), Judith's handmaid Abra (S), Ozias (A), and Holofernes' aide Vagans (S); (2) there are five choral movements; (3) the flutes are used in only one aria, and the trumpets and timpani are used in only two of the choral movements.

MASS MOVEMENTS
SELECTED AND LISTED ACCORDING TO FAMILIARITY

Gloria RV589 – 1713 – SA solos, SATB chorus, oboe, trumpet, strings, and basso continuo – 27:30 minutes. (1) There are twelve movements, all short except for movement two, "Et in terra pax"; (2) solo movements are for soprano and alto, with an additional duet for two sopranos, and alto solo passages with chorus; (3) there are eight separate choral movements; (4) this work is one of the best-known and most popular choral works of the Baroque era.

Gloria RV588 – SSAT solos, SATB chorus, two oboes, trumpet, strings, and basso continuo – 30 minutes. There are eleven movements—four arias (A, T, and two S), one duet (SS), one trio (SAT), and five choruses.

Kyrie RV587 – SA/SA solos, SATB/SATB chorus, strings, and basso continuo – 8:30 minutes. The strings are divided into two groups, one for each choral ensemble.

Credo RV591 – SATB chorus, strings, and basso continuo – 10 minutes. The work is divided into four movements, all of which are choral.

OTHER SACRED WORKS
SELECTED AND LISTED ACCORDING TO FAMILIARITY

Beatus vir RV597 (Psalm 112) – SSATBB solos, SATB/SATB chorus, two oboes, strings, and basso continuo – 32 minutes. (1) The work is in nine movements—four double choruses, two duets (BB and SS), two arias (S and T), and one trio (ATB); (2) all solo movements end with an antiphon of ten measures scored for chorus; (3) the strings are divided into two groups, one for each choral ensemble; (4) the oboes are in the first group.

Beatus vir RV598 (Psalm 112) – SSA solos, SATB chorus, strings, and basso continuo – 7:15 minutes. The work has the same structure stated four times—A solo, SS duet, and SATB chorus.

Dixit Dominus RV594 (Psalm 110) – SSATB solos, SATB/SATB chorus, two oboes, two trumpets, strings, and basso continuo – 23 minutes. (1) The work is in ten movements—six for double chorus, two duets (SS and TB), and two arias (A and S); (2) the strings are divided into two groups, one for each choral ensemble; (3) the oboes and trumpets are in the first group.

Lauda Jerusalem RV609 (Psalm 148) – S/S solos, SATB/SATB chorus, strings, and basso continuo – 7:15 minutes. (1) The work consists of SS duets that alternate with the double choruses; (2) the strings are divided into two groups, one for each choral ensemble.

Laetatus sum RV607 (Psalm 122) – SATB chorus, strings, and basso continuo – 3:15 minutes.

Laudate Dominum RV606 (Psalm 117) – SATB chorus, strings, and basso continuo – 2 minutes.

In exitu Israel RV604 (Psalm 114) – SATB chorus, strings, and basso continuo – 3:30 minutes.

Credidi propter RV605 (Psalm 116) – SATTB chorus, strings, and basso continuo – 7 minutes. The strings, divided into two violin and two viola parts, are *colla parte* with the voices.

Confitebor RV596 (Psalm 111) – ATB solos, two oboes, strings, and basso continuo – 13 minutes. The work is divided into six movements, all comprising trios for the soloists (there are only brief solo melodic passages).

Magnificat RV610a – SSAT solos, SATB/SATB chorus, two oboes, strings, and basso continuo – 14 minutes. (1) Most of the choral movements are scored for SATB (only movement two is scored for SATB/SATB, and both of these SATB ensembles are identical); (2) the work is divided into nine movements—seven are choral, one is a duet (SS), and one is a trio (SAB); (3) the strings are divided into two groups, one for each choral ensemble; (4) the oboes are in the first group.

Magnificat RV610b – SSSAA solos, SATB chorus, two oboes, strings, and basso continuo – 20 minutes. (1) The solo movements are scored for specific girls at the Pietà (Apollonia, la Bolognesa, Chiaretta, Ambrosina, and Albetta) and replace the double chorus movement as well as the duet and trio of RV610a; (2) this *Magnificat* has eleven movements—six choruses and five arias.

Francesco Durante 1684–1755

Durante most likely studied with his father, Gaetano, who was a singer and who died when Francesco was fifteen, and with his uncle Don Angelo, who was *primo maestro* at S Onofrio a Capuano, one of four conservatories in Naples. It is assumed that after his studies with his uncle ended, Francesco studied with Giuseppe Ottavio Pitoni in Rome; several letters and related references support this supposition, although there is no documentation of proof. Nothing specific is known about Durante's life until 1728, when he was appointed *primo maestro* at Poveri di Gesù Cristo, one of the other conservatories in Naples. He held this appointment for ten years, during which time one of his students was Giovanni Battista Pergolesi, and in 1738 he was appointed *primo maestro* at yet another of the conservatories—S Maria di Loreto. He held this latter position until his death, while also serving at S Onofrio (succeeding Leonardo Leo) beginning in 1745.

Durante composed a few oratorios, twenty-eight masses (including three Requiems), and fifty motets (twenty of which are settings of Vespers Psalms). The only extant oratorio is *S Antonio di Padova,* which was composed in 1754, the year before his death, and was performed at the Oratorio della Congregazione di S Filippo Neri in Rome. The masses, most of them in a *prima prattica* style, include *Missa S Ildefonsi* for solos, chorus, strings, and basso continuo; *Missa in Palestrina* for SATB chorus a cappella; *Missa brevis* in C major for TTB chorus and basso continuo; *Messa in pastorale* for SATB chorus, strings, and basso continuo; and *Messa de' morti* in C minor for SATB/SATB chorus, strings, and basso continuo. The motets are in a variety of styles. Perhaps the best known is *Misericordias Domini* in C minor (a setting of Psalm 89 for SATB/SATB chorus in a Venetian polychoral style that features dialogue between the two choruses and tempo changes that reflect varying textual moods). Other motets include *Miserere mei, Deus* (a setting of Psalm 51 for SSATB chorus and basso continuo); *Laudate pueri* (a setting of Psalm 113 for SATB chorus, strings, and basso continuo); and *Christus factus est* (a setting of Philippians 2:8–9 for SAB chorus and basso continuo). In addition, Durante is credited with composing the *Magnificat a quattro voci* in B-flat major that was previously attributed to Pergolesi. This work is based on the first Gregorian chant tone as a cantus firmus and is scored for SATB solos, SATB chorus, two violins, and basso continuo.

DOMENICO SCARLATTI 1685–1757

Domenico Scarlatti, son of Alessandro Scarlatti, was born in Naples during the time that Alessandro was *maestro di cappella* at the court of the Spanish Ambassador to the Vatican. Given Alessandro's status and his son's quick development as a musical prodigy, especially as a harpsichord player, it is surprising that nothing is known about Domenico's musical training and that very little concern was given to the documentation of his adult life. Only general facts about his employment and travels are known. He was appointed organist and *clavicembalista di camera* (court keyboardist) at the Cappella Reale in Naples when he was fifteen, and from ages twenty to twenty-nine he was a freelance performer in Venice. Then in 1709 he was appointed *maestro di cappella* to Maria Casimira, former Queen of Poland, who had a court in Rome and who commissioned from Scarlatti six operas, one cantata, and one oratorio. In 1713 he was appointed *maestro di cappella* at the Cappella Guila in Rome, where he met and was involved professionally with George Frideric Handel, and from 1719 until his death he served as *mestre de capela* at the Royal Chapel in Lisbon, Portugal, where his responsibilities consisted of teaching the Infanta Maria Barbara and the king's younger brother, Don Antonio. While in Lisbon, he worked with the famous castrato Farinelli, although no details exist about Scarlatti's relationship with Farinelli or with Handel in Rome.

Scarlatti is known for his virtuosity at the keyboard and for his keyboard compositions, which include more than five hundred sonatas. His choral output is quite limited, consisting of several lost oratorios, three masses, approximately twenty motets, and five cantatas for solo voice. The masses include *Missa quatuor vocum* in G minor for SATB chorus a cappella; *Missa la stella* in A minor for SSATB solos, SATB chorus, and basso continuo; and a mass in D major for SATB/SATB chorus, two oboes, two horns, two trumpets, timpani, two violins, and basso continuo. The motets include *Cibavit nos Dominus* and *Te gloriosus,* both scored for SATB chorus and basso continuo, and both in a *prima prattica* style. The ten-movement *Stabat mater,* scored for SSSSAATTBB chorus and basso continuo, was probably composed by Scarlatti while he was serving at the Cappella Guila in Rome. The cantatas include Scarlatti's most famous composition—the *Stabat mater* for soprano solo, strings, and basso continuo, which he composed at the end of his life.

BENEDETTO GIACOMO MARCELLO 1686–1739

Marcello was born in Venice, where his father, Agostino, was a senator. The social status of the family allowed Benedetto and his older brother, Alessandro (1684–1750), both of whom studied literature and law, to pursue music as an avocation. Consequently, the Marcello brothers, like Alessandro Stradella, were noble dilettantes who had no formal training in music and who held no church or court musical positions. Benedetto's professional career was in public service: he held a number of important governor and magistrate positions. However, he was also a prolific and highly respected composer, with an output of four oratorios, nine masses, thirty motets, and five madrigals, plus 380 cantatas for solo voice, eighty-one duets, and seven trios.

The oratorios are *La Giuditta* (1709), *Joaz* (ca.1726), *Il pianto e il riso delle quattro stagioni dell'anno per la morte* (1731), and *Il trionfo della poesia* (1733). The first two works are settings of Old Testament stories, while the latter two oratorios are settings of stories about the Assumption of the Virgin Mary. *Joaz* is scored for SSATBB solos, SATB chorus, strings, and basso continuo. *Il pianto . . .* is scored for SATB solos, SATB chorus, strings, and basso continuo, with solo roles for Spring (S), Summer (A), Autumn (T), and Winter (B). The text, which is allegorical and reflective, relates the relationship each season had in the life of Mary. Her birth was in autumn, her death in summer, her annunciation in spring, and her immaculate conception in winter.

The masses, including a Requiem and the *Missa Clementina* for SATB chorus, are illustrative of Marcello's desire to restore composition to the purity of Renaissance polyphony and are thus in an imitative and *prima prattica* style. The motets include Marcello's most famous compositions, which were published in eight volumes between 1724 and 1726 as *Estro poetico-armonico; paragrasi sopri primi venticinque salmi.* These settings of the first fifty Psalms were known throughout Europe and praised by many composers, including Johann Mattheson and Georg Philipp Telemann. As is indicated in the title of the publication, the settings are paraphrases of the Psalms, in Italian, with added poetic passages. Most of the settings are multimovement or multisectional works scored for two to three voices and basso continuo; four of the settings are also scored for strings. Only one setting, *Psalm 10* (Mentro io tutta ripongo), is scored for four voices (SATB chorus, with short solo passages for alto and bass). This work is approximately nine minutes in duration and is divided into numerous sections that are delineated by tempo changes and that are characterized by varied madrigalistic rhythmic patterns. For instance, the text phrase "fuggi rapido e al monte vola" (fly swiftly to the mountains) has upward-rising melodic patterns in an allegro tempo, while the phrase "e'l bujo attendono" (they await patiently) is depicted with staccato notes at a soft volume. Other notable Psalm settings include *Psalm 40* (O beato chi pietoso) in D minor for ATB voices and basso continuo; *Psalm 3* (O Dio perchè) in G minor for SA voices and basso continuo; *Psalm 47* (Questa che al ciel s'innalza) in D major for STB voices and basso continuo; and *Psalm 44* (Dal cor ripieno) in D major for ATB voices and basso continuo.

NICOLA PORPORA 1686–1768

Porpora was born in Naples, where he received his early musical education at the Conservatorio dei Poveri di Gesù Cristo and where Alessandro Scarlatti was active composing and producing operas. Porpora became a part of the operatic milieu soon after his departure from the Conservatorio: he composed his first opera at age twenty-two, he received numerous commissions thereafter from various Neapolitan noblemen, and he became known as a teacher of singing (two of his students were the castrato Farinelli and the composer Johann Adolf Hasse). Porpora also served as *maestro di cappella* at the Conservatorio di S Onofrio and accepted commissions for operas in Rome (one of which was composed with Domenico Scarlatti). As he gained fame, he moved around Europe and took various positions, including *maestro di cappella* at three of the female orphanages in Venice (Ospedale degli Incurabili, Ospedale della Pietà, and the Ospedale dell'Ospedaletto); codirector of the Opera of Nobility in London, a company that was in competition with the Italian opera company under the direction of George Frideric Handel; *maestro di cappella* at the Conservatorio di S Maria di Loreto in Naples; and teacher of singing at the Imperial courts in Dresden and Vienna.

Porpora's main compositional focus was opera (he wrote a total of forty-four). However, he also composed eleven oratorios, five masses, several mass movements, and approximately forty motets, in addition to numerous cantatas for solo voices. The oratorios include the *Oratorio per la nascita di Gesù Cristo* and *Il Gedeone*. This latter work (scored for SATB solos, SATB chorus, two flutes, two horns, strings, and basso continuo) is also called *Il verbo in carne, oratorio per la natività di Gesù Cristo*. The masses are all identified by their keys: A major for five voices; A minor for four voices and basso continuo; C major for four voices and strings; and D major and G major for four voices and orchestra. The motets include two well-known works—*Laude Jerusalem* (Psalm 148) and *Laetatus sum* (Psalm 122)—both composed in 1745 for the girls at the Ospedaletto in Venice and both scored for SSAA chorus, strings, and basso continuo. In the first of these motets the chorus is homophonic and the strings are figural. In the second motet there is an alto solo that is somewhat melismatic.

LEONARDO LEO 1694–1744

Leo paralleled Nicola Porpora in many respects. He received his early musical education at one of the conservatories in Naples (S Maria della Pietà); he composed an opera at an early age and then received numerous commissions; he traveled to many European cities supervising the productions of his operas; he was a respected teacher (Niccolò Jommelli was one of his students);

he held *maestro di cappella* positions at two of the Naples conservatories; and he was associated with Alessandro Scarlatti, succeeding him as first organist at the court of the Spanish Ambassador to the Vatican and then as *maestro di cappella*.

Also like Porpora, Leo composed approximately fifty operas and was interested in maintaining the conservative *prima prattica* tradition of church music. In addition, Leo composed a comparable number of sacred compositions—twelve oratorios (including works titled sacred dramas), six masses, and approximately fifty motets and related genres. The oratorios include two works that were quite popular during Leo's lifetime—*S Elena al Calvario* (1734) and *La morte di Abelle* (1738). Both, consisting of recitatives and arias without choruses, are similar to the oratorios of Scarlatti. The masses, all Neapolitan in that they are settings of only the Kyrie and Gloria, are scored for SATB chorus and a nonindependent basso continuo (one mass), SATB chorus and instruments (one mass), and SSATB chorus and instruments (four masses). Of the other sacred works, the *Miserere* (for SATB/SATB chorus and basso continuo) and *Magnificat* (for SATB solos, SATB chorus, two violins, and basso continuo) are considered to be significant. The *Magnificat* is in one movement that is characterized by several tempo changes and a texture of soloists in ensemble alternating with the chorus.

Padre Giovanni Battista Martini 1706–1784

Martini (called Padre Martini) was born and spent his entire life in Bologna, where he received his first musical instruction from his father, a violinist and cellist. At age fifteen he began studying for the priesthood, at sixteen he began playing the organ at S Francesco, and at nineteen he was appointed *maestro di cappella* (a position he kept until the last years of his life). At twenty-three he was ordained a priest. He became well known throughout Europe and attracted numerous students, including J. Christian Bach, Niccolò Jommelli, and W. A. Mozart. Charles Burney, the British diarist, praised Martini for his personal geniality, and Mozart revered him as a teacher. Martini was honored with membership in important academies, including the Accademia dei Filarmonici di Bologna, and he was offered prestigious positions in Rome and Padua. However, except for several short visits to cities such as Florence and Rome, he remained in Bologna and devoted himself to his church duties, teaching, composition, and writing. He collected portraits of famous musicians, including J. C. Bach, and his library is estimated to have contained approximately seventeen thousand books. At the end of his life he was referred to as "Dio della musica de' nostri tempi" (God of music of our time).

Martini's compositional output includes approximately thirty masses for voices (there are many more masses scored for organ alone), seventeen mass movements, three extant oratorios, twenty-five Magnificats, fifty motets, and numerous secular canons, cantatas, and duets. Since Martini was known for his strict teaching of counterpoint, one would expect his compositions to reflect this style. However, all the works are in a modern, pre-Classical style characterized by vocal homophony and figural instrumental textures.

The masses are generally scored for either four or eight voices (about half of each) and accompaniment of organ alone or strings and organ. The oratorios include *L'assunzione di Salomone al trono d'Israello* of 1734 and *S Pietro* of 1739. The motets are divided between pieces for SATB chorus a cappella and for SATB solos, chorus, strings, and basso continuo. An example of the latter type is the famous *Domine, ad adjuvandum me festina*.

MASSES
SELECTED AND LISTED ACCORDING TO FAMILIARITY

Requiem – SATB voices and basso continuo – 30:30 minutes.

Missa solemnis – SATB voices and basso continuo – 21:30 minutes

MOTETS AND MAGNIFICATS
SELECTED AND LISTED ACCORDING TO FAMILIARITY

Domine, ad adjuvandum me festina (Psalm 70) – 1729 – SATB solos, SATB chorus, strings, and basso continuo – 6 minutes. The solo writing consists of a short duet for ST, a trio passage for STB, and an extended melodic passage for A.

Beatus vir (Psalm 112) – 1749 – SATB chorus, strings, and basso continuo – 4 minutes.

Nisi Dominus (Psalm 127) – 1746 – SAB voices, strings, and basso continuo – 7 minutes. Solo melodic passages alternate with passages for trio.

O salutaris hostia – SSTB voices a cappella – 3 minutes.

In monte Oliveti – SSA voices a cappella – 3:30 minutes.

Tristis est anima mea – SSA voices a cappella – 3:30 minutes.

BALDASSARE GALUPPI 1706–1785

Galuppi was born on the island of Burano, near Venice, and received his earliest musical instruction from his father, a violinist. He may also have studied with Antonio Lotti, organist at St Mark's Basilica at the time. Like many Italian composers of the Baroque era, Galuppi developed an intense interest in opera: he played the cembalo in Venetian opera houses when he was a teenager and he composed operas during his twenties. He also composed oratorios, including *Tobia il giovane* (1734). In 1740 he was appointed *maestro di musica* at the Ospedale dei Mendicanti, and while serving in this position for the next decade he made extended trips to supervise productions of his operas. For instance, he was in London for eighteen months between 1741 and 1743, and in the late 1740s he spent long periods of time in Milan, Rome, and Vienna. Despite his absences and his operatic focus, Venetian church authorities sought his services. In 1748 he was appointed *vice-maestro di cappella* at St Mark's, and he maintained his position at the Mendicanti until 1751. In 1762 he was promoted to *maestro di coro* at St Mark's and also *maestro di coro* at the Ospedale degli Incurabili, the most famous of the four Venetian orphanages for girls and the orphanage where Antonio Lotti had been employed. In 1764 Galuppi resigned the

Incurabili position and obtained a leave of absence from St Mark's (on the condition that he compose a certain number of works for Vespers services and a mass for Christmas), in order to serve as composer at the court of Catherine the Great in St Petersburg. He returned to St Mark's and was reappointed to his former position at the Incurabili in 1768, retaining these positions and composing sacred music almost exclusively for the remainder of his life.

Galuppi composed approximately twenty-seven oratorios (only two of which are extant) and two hundred Latin sacred works. The oratorios include *Adamo ed Eva* and *Tres pueri hebraei in captivitate Babylonis,* the latter of which was extremely popular and performed more than one hundred times during the late eighteenth century. The Latin sacred works include numerous mass movements and multimovement motets. Two of the mass movements, a *Gloria* and *Credo,* were composed to fulfill his obligations to provide music for Christmas services at St Mark's while he was in Russia. The *Gloria* consists of ten movements—several of the movements for soloists and the others for chorus. The *Credo* is divided into three movements.

ORATORIO

Adamo ed Eva (also called *Adamo caduto*) – 1747 – SSAT solos and basso continuo – 125 minutes. (1) Solo roles are for Adam (T), Eve (S), an Angel of Justice (A), and an Angel of Mercy (S); (2) the oratorio consists of twelve arias, two duets, and one *tutti* ensemble.

OTHER SACRED WORKS
SELECTED AND LISTED ACCORDING TO FAMILIARITY

Lauda Jerusalem (Psalm 148) – SAB solos, SATB chorus, strings, and basso continuo – 10:30 minutes. The motet is divided into four choral movements and three arias (S, A, and B).

Confitebor tibi, Domine (Psalm 111) – 1733 – SAB solos, two flutes, strings, and basso continuo – 35 minutes. (1) The motet is divided into twelve movements—five for SAB, two duets (SA), and five arias (two S, two B, and one A); (2) the flutes are notated only in movement eleven, although they may have doubled the violins in other movements.

Kyrie in E-flat major – SSATT solos, SATB chorus, two oboes, two horns, strings, and basso continuo – 12 minutes. The solo writing is characterized by duets in parallel thirds for SS and TT.

Gloria – 1766 – SATB solos, SATB chorus, two flutes, two oboes, two horns, two trumpets, strings, and basso continuo – 34 minutes. (1) The solos consist of three arias (S, S, and T), one concerted solo (A) with chorus, and two duets (SA and AB); (2) the chorus participates in six movements; (3) the flutes are used in only one movement and the trumpets in only two.

Credo – 1766 – AA solos, SATB chorus, two oboes, two horns, two trumpets, strings, and basso continuo – 8:15 minutes. The AA solos consist of one duet.

Laetatus sum (Psalm 122) – SSATB solos, SATB chorus, strings, and basso continuo – 10 minutes. (1) The motet is divided into four movements—

two for chorus, one duet (SS), and one aria (A); (2) there are also brief ATB solos in the first choral movement.

Nisi Dominus (Psalm 127) – SSA solos, SATB chorus, strings, and basso continuo – 24 minutes. (1) The motet is divided into seven movements—two for chorus, two duets (SA and SS), and three arias (two S and one A); (2) the chorus is also briefly involved in the SA duet.

Dixit Dominus (Psalm 110) – SATB chorus, two oboes, two horns, strings, and basso continuo – 10 minutes. This is an arrangement of Galuppi's 1775 work for SSAA and strings.

Beatus vir (Psalm 112) – SA solos, SATB chorus, two oboes, two horns, strings, and basso continuo – 17 minutes. Five of the motet's seven movements are for chorus.

GIOVANNI BATTISTA PERGOLESI 1710–1736

Pergolesi was born in Iesi, a small town near Florence, close to the eastern coast of Italy. He began his musical studies in Iesi, quickly developing into a virtuoso violinist, and in the early 1720s he moved to Naples to study composition. He supported himself for several years singing and playing violin in local theatrical productions, and in 1731, at the age of twenty-one, he received his first commission to compose an opera. He continued composing operas over subsequent years, becoming well known for his comic works such as *La serva padrona*. However, like many Italian composers of the Baroque era, he took appointments that also required the composition of sacred works. In 1732 he was appointed *maestro di cappella* at the court of Prince Ferdinando Colonna Stigliano; in 1734 he moved to Rome to supervise performances of music he had composed to celebrate the restoration of Italian rule in Naples; and in 1736, because of poor health, he moved to a Franciscan monastery near Naples. While at Stigliano's court, Pergolesi composed a mass and numerous Vespers motets for services in honor of St Emidius (protector against earthquakes) to commemorate the severe earthquakes Naples had suffered in 1733, and while at the Franciscan monastery he composed his two most famous works—*Stabat mater* and *Salve regina;* the former became immediately popular all over Europe and was reprinted more than any other musical work in the eighteenth century. The *Magnificat* in B-flat major that has traditionally been attributed to Pergolesi is in actuality by Francesco Durante.

Pergolesi composed two oratorios, two masses, and approximately ten motets. The oratorios are annotated below. The two masses consist of only Kyries and Glorias, as was the custom in Naples at the time, with both portions of the Ordinary divided into multiple sections. The masses were originally scored for soprano and alto solos, SSATB choir, and full orchestra. Subsequently, Pergolesi made polychoral arrangements. The *Missa* in D major, for instance, was arranged for two SSATB choirs and two orchestras, and the *Missa* in F major was arranged for three soloists, four SSATB choirs, and two orchestras. There are four other masses that were previously attributed to Pergolesi but that are now known not to have been composed by him—*Messe solenne* in C major, *Messe estense* in D major, the *Requiem* in B-flat major, and *Messe* in F major.

The Vespers Psalm settings are similar to the original structure and scoring of the masses:

texts are sectioned into separate movements for soloists and chorus, and accompaniment is for strings or larger orchestra. Both the *Stabat mater* and *Salve regina* are scored for only soloists—the *Stabat mater* for soprano and alto with strings and basso continuo, and the *Salve regina* for soprano with strings and basso continuo.

ORATORIOS
COMPLETE

La prodigi della divina grazia nella conversione e morte di San Guglielmo duca d'Aquitania – 1731 – ST solos and basso continuo – 26 minutes. (1) Solo roles are for San Bernardo (T) and Guglielmo (S); (2) the oratorio consists of an instrumental introduction followed by two arias (T and S) and a closing duet.

La morte di S Giuseppe (also called *La fenice sul rogo, ovvero La morte di S Giuseppe*) – ca.1731 – SSAT solos, two oboes, two horns, strings, and basso continuo – 30 minutes. (1) Solo roles are for the Archangel Michael (S), Divine Love (S), the Virgin Mary (A), and Joseph (T); (2) the oratorio consists of fourteen arias, two duets, and one quartet.

MASSES
COMPLETE AND LISTED IN CHRONOLOGICAL ORDER
ACCORDING TO DATE OF COMPOSITION

Missa in D major – 1731 – SA solos, SSATB chorus, two oboes, two horns, strings, and basso continuo – 32 minutes.

Missa in F major (called the *Missa Romana*) – 1732 – SATB solos, SSATB/SSATB chorus, two oboes, two horns, strings, and basso continuo – 30 minutes. (1) The strings are divided into two groups, one each for the two choral ensembles; (2) the oboes and horns are only in the first group.

MOTETS
SELECTED AND LISTED ACCORDING TO FAMILIARITY

Dixit Dominus in D major (Psalm 110) – 1732 – SSATB/SSATB chorus, two oboes, two horns, two trumpets, strings, and basso continuo – 24 minutes. (1) The solo writing consists of two short arias (both S), one SAB/SAB double trio, and brief SATB quartet passages that alternate with choral passages; (2) the strings are divided into two groups, one each for the two choral ensembles; (3) the oboes, horns, and trumpets are only in the first group; (4) there are two other settings of *Dixit Dominus*—one in 1730 (D major) and one in 1733 (C major).

Laudate pueri (Psalm 113) – S solo, SABB chorus, two oboes, trumpet, strings, and basso continuo – 20:30 minutes. (1) The solo writing consists of two arias and interchanges with the chorus; (2) the chorus sings in five of the work's seven movements.

Confitebor tibi (Psalm III) – 1731 – S solo, SSATB chorus, strings, and basso continuo – 20 minutes.

QUIRINO GASPARINI (1721–1778)

Gasparini was born in Gandino, near Bergamo, and studied composition first with the *maestro di cappella* of Milan Cathedral (G. A. Fioroni) and then with Padre Giovanni Battista Martini in Bologna. After holding minor positions in Brescia, Venice, and Bologna, where he was accepted as a member of the Accademia Filarmonica in 1751, Gasparini became director of music for Count D'Aziano of Vercelli in 1758 and *maestro di cappella* at Turin Cathedral in 1760, a position he retained until his death. He is sometimes confused with Francesco Gasparini (1668–1727), who taught Domenico Scarlatti and Benedetto Giacomo Marcello and who was *maestro di cappella* at the Ospedale della Pietà in Venice. The two Gasparinis were not related and probably did not know of each other. Quirino composed fourteen masses (including three Requiems), one Passion (*Passio secundum Marcum*), nine Litanies, three Magnificats, and approximately thirty-five motets, one of which, *Adoramus te,* was formerly thought to be composed by W. A. Mozart and was catalogued as K327. Another motet, *Plangam dolorem meum,* is also well known.

✿ FRANCE ✿

Music in France during the entire first half of the seventeenth century was influenced by and centered at the royal court. Furthermore, the music at the court was strongly influenced by Italian musicians and styles. This was especially so during the reigns of Henri IV (1589–1610) and Louis XIII (1610–1643), which were culturally dominated by Henri IV's Italian wife Marie de' Medici, and during the regency of Louis XIV's mother (1643–1661), which was under the control of its musical minister, the papal emissary to the Vatican, Giulio Mazarini (also known as Cardinal Mazarin). From 1661 (when Mazarini died and Louis XIV became eighteen and assumed full monarchal power) until his death more than fifty years later in 1715, the king determined much of the styles and genres of music in France. For example, his passion for dancing was responsible for the development of ballet music, and his preference for attending the *messe basse solennelle* (low mass) stimulated the composition of motets instead of masses. Furthermore, the influence of Louis XIV was pervasive, since most notable composers of the Baroque era in France, including all but two of the composers discussed in this section, were employed at the royal court.

Music for the *messe basse solennelle* included three kinds of motet: a *grand motet,* which is a large-scale work for soloists, chorus, strings, and basso continuo; a *petit motet,* which is a small-scale work for soloists and basso continuo; and a short setting of the text "Domine, salvum fac regem" (O Lord, grant the king a long life). The *grands motets* were typically scored for SSATB soloists, SATBB chorus, strings, and basso continuo, with the soloists and chorus arranged in a double chorus format: the soloists' chorus, called the *petit choeur,* consisted of brief solos (*récits*), duets, trios, and full ensemble passages for all five voices, while the second chorus, called the *grand choeur,* was notated separately and consisted mostly of passages for all the voices together. The strings were divided into six parts (two violins, three violas, and bass) and often played alone in *simphonie* and *ritournelle* movements. The *petits motets,* including the settings of the "Domine, salvum" text, were generally scored for one to three soloists, with duets or duet passages for two sopranos frequently singing together at the interval of a third.

The nomenclature of the voice parts was specific and unique. For female voices, the term *premier dessus* or *haut-dessus* indicated the first soprano part, *second dessus* indicated second soprano, and *bass-dessus* indicated alto. For male voices, the term *haute-contre* designated the alto part, *taille* indicated tenor, and *basse* indicated bass. In general, male altos sang in music scored for mixed voices (SATB), while female altos sang in music scored only for treble voices (SSA).

Perhaps because most sacred music consisted only of *grands* and *petits motets* of the types sung at the royal chapel, the choral output of French Baroque composers was limited, especially in comparison with the many hundreds of works written by Italian Baroque composers. Jean-Baptiste Lully, for instance, wrote a total of twenty-four motets, and Jean-Philippe Rameau wrote only four. Of the major French Baroque composers, only Marc-Antoine Charpentier wrote in excess of one hundred works. Masses and other compositions for liturgical services were needed by the many cathedrals and chapels across France, including those at Rouen, Chartres, Tours, Notre Dame, and Sainte-Chapelle. However, most music for these sacred institutions was written by minor composers, including Henry Du Mont and André Campra. The major composers were generally not attracted to religious institutions outside the royal court except for several convents in the vicinity of Paris that were noted for their commitment to musical excellence.

Two other factors contributed to the limited sacred output of composers. One was the system of music publication and performance in France, which until the end of the Baroque era was governed by royal privilege and was strictly regulated by individuals appointed by the king. Lully, for example, had complete control of French music publication and performance for most of his life. Also, notable performances outside the royal court and a few convents and private chateaux did not occur until after the death of Louis XIV. Of particular importance was the creation of the Concert spirituel, a public concert society formed in 1725 that began with performances of *grands motets* but that by the late 1730s featured oratorios and other large-scale choral works. The second factor limiting the composition of sacred music was its basic restriction to Catholic liturgies when many people in France were Calvinist Protestants. Although Henry IV, called *le bon roi Henry* (Good King Henry), granted religious liberties to Protestants in the Edict of Nantes, Louis XIII, with the aid of Cardinal Richelieu, retracted the liberties, and Louis XIV fought to keep the country Catholic. Only with the reign of Louis XV (1715–1774), whose liberal policies allowed the Protestant Reformation to have a cultural impact, did significant composers begin to write music set to French texts for Calvinist liturgical services or for private devotionals.

The most notable French Baroque composers of choral music are Jean-Baptiste Lully, Marc-Antoine Charpentier, Michel-Richard de Lalande, François Couperin, and Jean-Philippe Rameau, all of whom except Charpentier served under Louis XIV and thus wrote motets exclusively. Charpentier, who was the only composer to study abroad, wrote music in other genres, particularly the oratorio. Composers of lesser stature who made substantial or significant contributions to choral music are Henry Du Mont, Guillaume-Gabriel Nivers, André Campra, Nicolas Bernier, Jean Gilles, Louis-Nicolas Clérambault, Henri Madin, and Jean-Joseph Cassanéa de Mondonville. Most of these composers served in major churches as well as in the royal chapel, and thus their output includes masses and other liturgical music in addition to *grands* and *petits motets*.

HENRY DU MONT 1610–1684

Du Mont was born in Belgium near Liège and given the name Henry de Thier. At age eleven he became a chorister at the nearby Maastricht Cathedral, and for most of his twenties he served as organist there. At age twenty-eight he moved to Paris and changed his last name to Du Mont, the French equivalent of de Thier. While in Paris, he served as organist at a number of churches, including St Paul, and he also entered the service of the royal court. From 1652 to 1660 he was organist and harpsichordist for the Duke of Anjou, the king's brother, and beginning in 1660 he was the harpsichordist for Queen Marie-Thérèse. In 1663 he was appointed *sou-maître* for two quarters of the royal chapel, and in 1672 he was named *compositeur de musique de la Chapelle Royal*.

Du Mont composed approximately 150 motets, five masses, one Magnificat, and twenty-one chansons. Most of the motets were published in five books—*Cantica sacra . . . liber primus* (1652), *Meslanges . . . livre second* (1657), *Motets* (1668), *Motets* (1671), and *Motets pour la chapelle du roy* (posthumously in 1686). The earliest of the books is a collection of thirty-five motets scored for one to four voices and basso continuo, with nine of the motets having additional obbligato violin parts. The publication is credited with being the first in France to include an independent basso continuo part and to be composed for a small number of solo voices. As such, the motets are the first *petits motets* in France. A number of these *petits motets* are hybrid forms. *Cantate Domino,* for instance, is scored for SATB solos that alternate with SATB chorus and is thus characteristic of the *grands motets* that would be written by many French composers in the latter years of the Baroque era. Du Mont's later motets, those composed specifically for the royal chapel, clearly define the *grand motet*. They are scored for a *petit choeur* of SATTB soloists, a *grand choeur* of SATTB or SATBB voices, and an instrumental ensemble of five-part strings and basso continuo. Representative examples include *Nisi Dominus* (Psalm 127), *Benedicam Dominum* (Psalm 34), and *Beati omnes qui timet* (Psalm 128).

The masses, published as *Cinq messes en plain-chant* in 1669, are typical of works composed for provincial churches. They are scored for unison voices and are in a chant-like style but without actual Gregorian themes.

JEAN-BAPTISTE LULLY 1632–1687

Lully, born in Florence and given the name Giovanni Battista Lulli, did not study music in his youth. Instead, he was sent to Paris at age fourteen to be one of the *garçons de chambre* for Mlle de Montpensier, called the "Grande Mademoiselle," who was cousin to King Louis XIV and who lived at the Palais des Tuileries. Lully was exposed to a great deal of high-caliber music and dance at the Palais, and during the six years he served there he became an accomplished dancer and violinist. Since Louis XIV was also an accomplished dancer and since he was especially fond of music for strings, Lully had opportunity to interact with the king, to compose a number of instrumental works referred to as *ballets de cour,* and to conduct the *petits violons*—the king's small chamber ensemble, also called the *petite bande* (differentiated from the *Vingt-quatre violons du Roi,* called the *grande bande*). In 1653 he was named *compositeur de la musique instrumentale du Roi,* and in 1661 he was promoted to *surintendant de la musique et compositeur de la musique de la chambre.* He also became a naturalized citizen of France in 1661, at which time he changed his name to Jean-Baptiste Lully. The following year he advanced to *maître de la musique de la famille royale,* and a decade later he was granted a royal privilege that gave him control of all music publication and public performance in France. Meanwhile, throughout the 1660s he became fascinated with Italian opera, which was then produced in Paris by Francesco Cavalli, and he composed a number of incidental sacred works for royal celebrations, including *Miserere mei Deus* and *Te Deum.* After Cavalli departed France, Lully began composing operas (called *tragédies lyriques*), an example of which is *Alcest,* written in 1674. He did not return to the composition of sacred music until after 1683, when the king married Madame de Maintenon, and music for the royal chapel became more important than music for the royal stage.

In January 1687 while Lully was conducting a performance of his *Te Deum,* his conducting baton (a long narrow staff, held upright in the hand, that periodically was struck against the floor to keep time) hit and injured one of his toes. According to Le Cerf de la Viéville (one of Lully's contemporaries and a notable author, poet, and musical commentator), "In the heat of the moment [Lully] hit his toe with the sharp point of the cane with which he was beating time. An abscess developed, and gangrene spread rapidly because he refused to let his physician remove the toe. Although in the greatest physical distress, he put his financial affairs in order and made his peace with the church before dying on the morning of 22 March 1687."

Lully composed ten *grands motets* and fourteen *petits motets.* The *grands motets* adhered to the general structure and style of the time—large-scale multimovement works for soloists, chorus, strings, and basso continuo, structured in a double chorus format, with the strings divided into six parts. The most famous of the *grands motets* are *Miserere mei Deus, Te Deum, Dies irae,* and *Plaude laetare*—this latter work composed for the baptism of Louis XIV's son, the grand dauphin. The *petits motets* are scored for a small ensemble of soloists and basso continuo and were most likely composed for the convent of the Filles de l'Assomption on rue Saint-Honoré, which was well known for its high-quality musical performances. Seven of these motets are scored for three sopranos and basso continuo. The texts of the *grands motets* are generally from the Psalms, while the texts of the *petits motets* are by unknown seventeenth-century authors and generally deal with the Holy Sacrament (e.g., *Ave coeli, Anima Christi, O sapientia,* and *O dulcissime*) or the Holy Virgin (e.g., *Salve regina* and *Regina coeli*).

GRANDS MOTETS
SELECTED AND LISTED ACCORDING TO FAMILIARITY

Miserere mei Deus (Psalm 51) – 1663 – SSATB solos, SATBB chorus, strings, and basso continuo – 22 minutes. The soloists, who sing in ensemble throughout the motet, are reinforced by frequent passages for chorus.

Quare fremuerunt gentes (Psalm 2) – 1685 – SATTB solos, SATTB chorus, strings, and basso continuo – 9 minutes.

Plaude laetare – 1668 – ATB solos, SSATB/SATBB chorus, strings, and basso continuo – 7:15 minutes.

Te Deum – 1677 – SSATTB solos, SATB/SATBB chorus, two trumpets, strings, and basso continuo – 29 minutes.

De profundis (Psalm 130) – 1683 – SSATB solos, SATBB chorus, strings, and basso continuo – 16:30 minutes.

Dies irae – 1683 – SATB solos, SATB/SATBB chorus, strings, and basso continuo – 16 minutes.

Domine salvum – date unknown – SATB solos, SATTB chorus, strings, and basso continuo – 3 minutes.

Notus in Judaea Deus (Psalm 76) – date unknown – SATTB solos, SATTB chorus, strings, and basso continuo – 7:30 minutes.

PETITS MOTETS
SELECTED AND LISTED IN ALPHABETICAL ORDER

Anima Christi – SSS voices and basso continuo – 5:45 minutes.

Ave coeli – ATB voices and basso continuo – 3:30 minutes.

Dixit Dominus (Psalm 110) – SSS voices and basso continuo – 7 minutes.

Domine salvum – SSS voices and basso continuo – 2 minutes.

Exaudi Deus – ATB voices and basso continuo – 5 minutes.

Laudate pueri (Psalm 112) – SSS voices and basso continuo – 7:30 minutes.

O dulcissime – SSS voices and basso continuo – 6:30 minutes.

O sapientia – SAB voices and basso continuo – 4:30 minutes.

Omnes gentes – SAB voices and basso continuo – 9 minutes.

Regina coeli – SSS voices and basso continuo – 4 minutes.

Salve regina – SSS voices and basso continuo – 8 minutes.

GUILLAUME-GABRIEL NIVERS CA.1632–1714

Nivers was born in Paris and became known as an organist and theorist as well as a composer. From the early 1650s until his death he was organist at St Sulpice, and from 1678 until his death he was also one of the four *sous-maîtres* at the royal chapel. In addition, he replaced Henry Du Mont in 1681 as harpsichordist to the queen, and he was the first organist at Maison Royale de Saint-Louis at Saint-Cyr, the orphanage for girls of noble birth founded in 1686 by Louis XIV's second wife, Madame de Maintenon. Nivers' theoretical publications include one on the subject of composition (*Traité de la composition de musique* of 1667), two on Gregorian chant (*Disserta-*

tion sur le chant grégorien of 1683 and *Méthode certaine pour apprendre le plein-chant de l'eglise* of 1698), and one on basso continuo (*L'art d'accompagner sur la basse continue* of 1689). He was considered the leading authority of his day on Gregorian chant (although his transcriptions of chant were metered and melodically altered), and his treatise on composition was known throughout Europe.

He composed three books of organ works, two books of motets, one mass, and a cantata in honor of Madame de Maintenon. All the motets are for one or two voice parts and basso continuo, including *Quam pulchra es* (Song of Songs 4:1 and Luke 1:48), *Domine, ante te omne* (Psalm 38:9 and 40:10), and *O sacramentum sacramentorum* (text by an unknown author)—all scored for SA solos, SA chorus, and basso continuo.

MARC-ANTOINE CHARPENTIER 1643–1704

Very little is known about Charpentier's youth except that he was born in Paris and that he went to Italy in his early twenties to study with Giacomo Carissimi. Charpentier returned to Paris in 1670 and became *maître de musique* to Marie de Lorraine, the Duchess of Guise, who was a notable patron of the arts and who sponsored many musical performances in her home, including those in which Charpentier sang *haute-contre* (countertenor or male alto). In addition, he presented Italian motets and Carissimi oratorios at Marie de Lorraine's concerts, and he collaborated with Molière and the Comédie Française, writing incidental music for plays. Charpentier maintained his position with the Duchess until her death in 1688, although beginning in the early 1680s he also served as *maître de musique* at the court of the grand dauphin (which was separate from the king's court) and at St Paul-St Louis, the Jesuit church in Paris. Furthermore, King Louis XIV awarded him a pension, and in 1683 he was chosen to be one of the *sous-maîtres* at the royal chapel, a position he could not accept because of poor health. From 1698 until his death he was *maître de musique* at Sainte-Chapelle, one of the most important church positions in all of France.

Charpentier composed twelve masses (including three Requiems), twenty-two oratorios, eight cantatas, and approximately 430 motets and other miscellaneous sacred works. The masses vary considerably in terms of scoring and texture. For example, the *Messe pour le Port Royal* H5, composed for the nuns of the convent at Port-Royal, is scored for only female voices and consists mainly of solo melodies accompanied by basso continuo. Also, the mass contains Introit, Gradual, Offertory, and Communion movements as well as the traditional portions of the Ordinary. In contrast, the *Messe à quatre choeurs* H4, scored, as the title suggests, for four choruses, is in the late-Renaissance Italian polychoral style. The *Messe de minuit pour Noël* H9, Charpentier's most familiar mass and undoubtedly the most popular French mass of the Baroque era, is a parody work that is based on ten French Christmas carols (*noëls*), including "Joseph est bien marié," "Une jeune pucelle," "Or nous dite Marie," and "Les bourgeois de chastre." Charpentier incorporated the melodies of the *noëls* into the fabric of the mass and also noted at the end of several movements the instruction "icy l'orgue joüe le mesme noël" (here the organ plays the same *noël*). In addition, Charpentier noted that the violins should play the *noël* "Laissez paitre vos beste" at the Offertory of the Mass. The *Missa Assumpta est Maria* H11, Charpentier's final mass, is a large-scale celebratory work that may have been composed for the feast of the Assumption on

August 15, 1699, and performed at Sainte-Chapelle. However, it is more likely that it was composed for the opening day of Parlement in 1699, November 12, since an article in the *Mercure Galant* of November states that the Parlement "ceremony started with a solemn mass . . . by Marc-Antoine Charpentier."

The earliest of the Requiem masses, *Messe pour les trépassés à 8* H2, was composed in the 1670s, perhaps for the funeral service of an important member of the Guise family (the Duke of Guise, Louis-Joseph de Lorraine, died in 1671, and the dowager duchess of Orléans, Marguerite de Lorraine, died in 1672). The composition is the most lavish of the Requiems in scoring (see below), but it contains the fewest number of movements (only a Kyrie, Sanctus, Pie Jesu, Benedictus, and Agnus Dei). The *Messe des morts à 4* H7, which is noted for its inclusion of the motet *De profundis* (Psalm 130) and for its scoring of the Pie Jesu for SS duet, is written for more modest resources (eight soloists, four-part chorus, and only basso continuo accompaniment). The final Requiem, *Messe des morts à 4 et symphonie* H10, includes a setting of the Dies irae along with the Kyrie, Sanctus, Pie Jesu, and Agnus Dei.

Most of the oratorios are in the style of Carissimi: texts in Latin are based on Old Testament characters or allegorical messages, and the music is scored for soloists and chorus accompanied by basso continuo alone or with obbligato instruments (generally flutes, which were as common to Charpentier as oboes were to Handel) and basso continuo. Charpentier did not use the term *oratorio* for these dramatic works; instead he used a variety of terms, including *historia sacrée* (which was most frequent), *pastorale* (which was reserved for works on the Christmas story), *dialogus, canticum, meditation,* and *motet.*

The most familiar of the oratorios are *Judith sive Bethulia liberata* H391, *Mors Saülis et Jonathae* H403, *Judicium Salomonis* H422, and *In nativitatem Domini canticum* H416. Other notable oratorios include *Le reniement de St Pierre* H424, *Sacrificium Abrahae* H402, *Dialogus inter angelos et pastores Judeae in nativitatem Domini* H420, and *Filius prodigus* H399. It should be noted that Charpentier composed seven works on the Christmas story (H393, 414, 416, 420, 421, 482, and 483) and that many of these works—such as *In nativitatem Domini nostri Jesus Christi canticum* H414 and *In nativitatem Domini canticum* H314 and H416—have similar titles. Charpentier also composed three oratorios with identical titles on the life of St Cecilia, the patron saint of music—*Caecilia, virgo et martyr* H397, 413, and 415.

Judith sive Bethulia liberata was most likely composed shortly after Charpentier's return to France from Italy. Its text, from the Apocrypha book of Judith, relates the story of the Israelites held in captivity in the city of Bethulia by Holofernes, the leader of the Assyrians. Judith leaves the Israelite camp, which is under the leadership of Ozias, and goes to the Assyrian camp, where she seduces Holofernes and beheads him. The music consists mostly of *secco* recitatives, although it is known mainly for the instrumental interlude "Nuit," which depicts Judith's journey from one camp to the other.

Judicium Salomonis H422 was composed for the convening of Parlement on November 11, 1702. The biblical story of the oratorio correlates to this occasion by implicitly comparing King Louis XIV to King Solomon and by directly addressing the assembled political leaders of Parlement, whose judicial actions would be judged by God.

In nativitatem Domini canticum H416 was probably composed in the late 1680s for performance in the church of St Paul-St Louis. The oratorio's text is in two parts: the first, from Psalm 12:1, is a plea for salvation, and the second, from Luke 2:10–12, is the angel's announcement to the shepherds that Jesus has been born. The instrumental scoring is substantial and indicative of Charpentier's writing in other oratorios. Most notably, there are three separate instrumental movements—an opening "Prélude," a four-minute "Nuit" (Night) that separates parts one and two of the oratorio, and a "Marche des Bergers" (March of the Shepherds), which occurs before the final choruses. "Nuit" is an exquisite atmospheric interlude that depicts the calm of night before the angel appears to the shepherds, and the "Marche des Bergers" depicts the shepherds' journey to see the Christ Child. In addition to these separate instrumental movements, there are ritornellos in the three main choruses.

Le reniement de St Pierre H424, which relates the story of Peter's denial of Christ, is close in structure and style to the oratorios of Carissimi, especially *Jephte*. The instrumental scoring is for basso continuo alone; the solo writing is in the form of recitative except for occasional arioso-like passages; the chorus delivers some of the narration as well as commentary on the story; and the final chorus bears a striking similarity to "Plorate filii Israel" from *Jephte*, with an especially moving conclusion on the words "flevit amare" (wept bitterly).

The miscellaneous sacred works—including ten Magnificats, nine settings of the Litany of Loreto, fifty-four lessons and responsories for Tenebrae, four Te Deums, and forty-eight éléva-tion motets—most exemplify Charpentier's range of forms and variety of styles. A significant number of these works are scored for female voices (a preference of the Duchess of Guise) and composed for the nuns at the Cistercian convent of the Abbaye-aux-Bois and the convent of Port-Royal de Paris. Included among these works are the *Magnificat* H75, Litany setting H86, and two smaller works—*Alma redemptoris mater* H21 and *Regina coeli* H32. Most of the motets set to Psalm texts are scored for *dessus* (S), *haute-contre* (A), *taille* (T), and *basse* (B) solos and chorus, with solo, duet, trio, and full solo ensemble passages that alternate with passages for chorus. The *Te Deum* H146 is perhaps Charpentier's most elaborate sacred work, and the *Litanies de la vierge à 6 voix et dessus de violes* H83, known for a ritornello on the words "ora pro nobis," is his most popular motet.

MASSES
SELECTED AND LISTED ACCORDING TO FAMILIARITY

Messe de Minuit pour Noël H9 – ca.1694 – SSATB solos, SATB chorus, two flutes, strings, and basso continuo – 30 minutes. The solo writing consists of several SS and ATB passages that alternate with the chorus (marked *tous*).

Missa Assumpta est Maria H11 – 1702 – SSATTB solos, SSATTB chorus, two flutes, strings, and basso continuo – 32 minutes. (1) The mass includes the normal five movements of the Ordinary plus an opening orchestral *simphonie* and a closing motet, "Domine, salvum fac regem"; (2) the Christe portion of the Kyrie is a trio for ATB soloists; (3) all soloists interact with the chorus in the Kyrie, Gloria, and Credo, and the chorus is alone in the Sanctus, Agnus Dei, and motet.

Messe pour le Port Royal H5 – ca.1687 – SSS solos, S chorus, and basso continuo – 20 minutes.

Messe à quatre choeurs H4 – ca.1672 – SSSSAATTBBBB solos, SATB/SATB/SATB/SATB chorus, strings, and basso continuo – 30 minutes. The strings are divided into four, four-part ensembles, and the basso continuo scoring is for four organs.

Messe à 8 voix et 8 violons et flûtes H3 – 1670s – SSAATTBB solos, SSAATTBB chorus, two flutes, strings, and basso continuo – 50 minutes.

Messe des morts à 4 et simphonie H10 – 1690s – SATB solos, SATB chorus, two flutes, two oboes, strings, and basso continuo – 18 minutes. Solo, duet, trio, and quartet passages alternate with passages for chorus.

Messe pour les trépassés à 8 H2 – early 1670s – SSATB/SATB solos, SATB/SATB chorus, two flutes, strings, and basso continuo – 17 minutes. The strings are divided into two, four-part ensembles.

ORATORIOS (NOT ON THE CHRISTMAS STORY)
SELECTED AND LISTED ACCORDING TO FAMILIARITY

Judith sive Bethulia liberata H391 – 1674–1676 – SSATTBB solos, SATB chorus, two flutes, two violins, and basso continuo – 44 minutes. (1) Major solo roles are for Judith (S), Ozias (T), and Holofernes (B); (2) other soloists sing narration.

Mors Saülis et Jonathae H403 – early 1680s – SAAATBB solos, SSAATTBB chorus, two flutes, strings, and basso continuo – 37 minutes. (1) Major solo roles are for Saul (B), the Witch of Endor (A), Saul's father Samuel (B), David (T), and a Soldier (A); (2) the narration is relayed by ST duet, SA duet, ATB trio, and chorus; (3) the chorus is also scored in two other movements, one of which is a commentary on the bitter fate of war, characterized by striking dissonances and cross-relations, and the other of which is a commentary on the story as a whole; (4) there are several short instrumental preludes, including one entitled "rumor bellicus" (noise of war) that begins the oratorio.

Judicium Salomonis H422 – 1702 – SATB solos, SATB chorus, two flutes, two oboes, strings, and basso continuo – 38 minutes. (1) Solo roles are for Solomon (T), God (B), the True Mother (S), and the False Mother (A); (2) the narration is relayed by B and T solos; (3) there are four large and substantial choral movements; (4) the oboes are never independent—they mostly double the flutes in the choruses; (5) there are two orchestral preludes.

Sacrificium Abrahae H402 – 1680–1681 – SSSSATB solos, SSAATTBB chorus, two flutes, strings, and basso continuo – 19 minutes. (1) Major solo roles are for Abraham (T), God (B), and Isaac (A); (2) minor solo roles are for Abraham's wife Sara (S), two Servants (SS), and an Angel (S); (3) the narration is relayed by T solo, chorus, ATB trio, and SA duet; (4) the writing for flutes and strings is minimal.

Le reniement de St Pierre H424 – date unknown – SSATB solos, SSATB chorus, and basso continuo – 12 minutes. (1) Major solo roles are for Jesus (T), Peter (A), and a Narrator (B); (2) minor solo roles are for a Doorkeeper (S), a Maid (S), and a Kinsman of Malchus (T); (3) the chorus participates in narration as well as commentary on the story.

Caecilia, virgo et martyr H415 – 1686 – SSSAATB solos, two violins, and basso continuo – 25:30 minutes. (1) Major solo roles are for Caecilia (S), Caecilia's husband Valerianus (T), Valerianus's father Tiburtius (A), and a tyrant Almachus (B); (2) minor solo roles are for a Narrator (S) and two Angels (SA); (3) there are several SSAATB ensemble movements that are indicated as *tutti* and that are thus to be sung by the soloists; (4) the violin parts are minimal and occur mostly at cadences between major vocal phrases.

Filius prodigus H399 – 1680 – SATTBB solos, SATB chorus, two violins, and basso continuo – 26 minutes. (1) Major solo roles are for the Prodigal Son (A) and his Father (B); (2) minor solo roles are for the Prodigal Son's Older Brother (T) and a Narrator (STB); (3) there are three choral movements.

Caedes Sanctorum Innocentium (*Le Massacre des Innocents*) H411 – 1683–1685 – ATB solos, SSATTB chorus, two flutes, two violins, and basso continuo – 16 minutes. (1) Solo roles are for an Angel (A), Herod (B), and a Narrator (T); (2) most of the oratorio consists of choruses, some entitled "Chorus Matrum" and scored for SSA, and others entitled "Chorus Satellites" and "Chorus Fidelium" and scored for SSATTB.

PASTORALES (ORATORIOS ON THE CHRISTMAS STORY)
SELECTED AND LISTED ACCORDING TO FAMILIARITY

In nativitatem Domini canticum H416 – late 1680s – AATTB solos, SATB chorus, two flutes, strings, and basso continuo – 30 minutes. (1) Solos are for a Narrator (T), God (B), an Angel (A), a Shepherd (T), and two unspecified characters in the final chorus (AT); (2) all solos are brief and are intermixed with choruses; (3) there are four main choruses—*Choeur des Justes* (Chorus of the Righteous), *Choeur des Bergers* (Chorus of the Shepherds), *Choeur des Anges* (Chorus of the Angels), and *Tous* (All or Everyone); (4) the first half of the oratorio is scored for strings and basso continuo and the second half adds flutes.

Pastorale sur la naissance de notre Seigneur Jésus Christ H483 – 1683–1685 – SSATB solos, SATB chorus, two flutes, two violins, and basso continuo – 41 minutes. Solo roles are for two Angels (SA), two Shepherds (ST), and an Elder (B).

In nativitate Domini nostri Jesu Christi canticum H421 – 1698–1699 – SA solos, SSA chorus (all female), and basso continuo – 9 minutes. (1) Solo roles are for a Narrator (A) and an Angel (S); (2) the chorus parts are labeled "Chorus Pastorum" (Shepherd's Chorus).

Sur la naissance de notre Seigneur Jésus Christ H482 – 1683–1685 – SSSATBB solos, two violins, and basso continuo – 19 minutes. (1) The story is about two shepherds, Silvie and Tircis, who visit the manger in Bethlehem and who return to the hills of Judea to tell other shepherds of Jesus' birth; (2) major solo roles are for Silvie (S) and Tircis (A); (3) minor solo roles, most of which are scored in ensemble, are for five other shepherds (SSTBB); (4) the instrumental dances and ritornellos are notable.

In nativitatem Domini nostri Jesus Christi canticum H414 – 1683–1685 – SSSB solos, SSSATB chorus, two violins, and basso continuo – 15 minutes.

In nativitatem Domini canticum H314 – 1670s – SATB solos, SATB chorus, two flutes, two violins, and basso continuo – 4 minutes.

Dialogus inter angelos et pastores Judeae in nativitatem Domini H420 – 1690s – SATTBB solos, SATB chorus, two flutes, strings, and basso continuo – 12 minutes. Solo, duet, trio, and full ensemble passages alternate with passages for chorus.

MOTETS AND MISCELLANEOUS SACRED WORKS
SELECTED AND LISTED ACCORDING TO FAMILIARITY

Litanies de la vierge H83 – ca.1680–1683 – SSAATB solo ensemble, two violins, and basso continuo – 17 minutes. (1) This is perhaps Charpentier's best-known motet; (2) the six vocal parts were originally scored for six specific singers whom Charpentier named in the score, including himself as *haute-contre* (A).

Te Deum H146 – early 1690s – SSAATTBB solos, SATB chorus, two flutes, two trumpets, timpani, strings, and basso continuo – 24 minutes. There are ten movements—two arias (SB), one duet (SB), two trios, four choruses with solos, and an orchestral prelude.

Te Deum H145 – ca.1672 – SSAATTBB solos, SSAATTBB chorus, two flutes, strings, and basso continuo – 30 minutes.

Exsurgat Deus H215 (Psalm 68) – 1690s – SATB solos, two flutes, strings, and basso continuo – 4:30 minutes. Word painting is noteworthy throughout the motet.

Beatus vir H221 (Psalm 112) – 1690s – SATB solos and basso continuo – 8:30 minutes.

De profundis H189 (Psalm 130) – 1683 – SSSATB solos, SATB/SATB chorus, and double orchestra of flutes, strings, and basso continuo – 23 minutes. (1) This motet was composed for the burial of Queen Marie-Thérèse, the first wife of Louis XIV; (2) it is one of seven settings Charpentier made of this text.

Quatre antiennes à la vierge (Four antiphons to the virgin): *Alma Redemptoris* H44, *Ave regina coelorum* H45, *Regina coeli* H46, and *Salve regina* H47 – early 1690s – ATB solos, SATB chorus, two violins, and basso continuo – 4:30, 3:15, 3:30, and 5:15 minutes.

Magnificat H75 – 1683–1685 – SSA (all female) and basso continuo – 8:30 minutes.

Magnificat H73 – 1670s – ATB solos, two flutes, two violins, and basso continuo – 8:30 minutes.

Litanies de la vierge H86 – 1690s – SSA (all female) and basso continuo – 9:15 minutes.

Alma redemptoris mater H21 – 1670s – SA (both female) and basso continuo – 3 minutes.

Regina coeli H32 – 1680s – SA (both female) and basso continuo – 2:30 minutes.

Nisi Dominus H160 (Psalm 127) – 1670s – SATB solos, SATB chorus, two violins, and basso continuo – 5 minutes.

Exaudiat te Dominus H180 (Psalm 19) – 1681–1682 – SATB solos, SATB chorus, two violins, and basso continuo – 4 minutes.

Credidi propter H209 (Psalm 115) – 1690s – SATB solos, SATB chorus, two violins, and basso continuo – 4:30 minutes.

Confitebor tibi H220 (Psalm 111) – 1690s – SATB solos, SATB chorus, two violins, and basso continuo – 4:30 minutes.

MICHEL-RICHARD DE LALANDE 1657–1726

Lalande (also spelled La Lande and Delalande) was born in Paris, where he was a chorister at St Germain-l'Auxerrois from age nine to fifteen. Nothing else is known about his childhood except that he was given numerous solos because of his exceptional voice and that he learned to play the harpsichord and organ. He must have developed into a capable musician, for during his young adulthood he held positions in four Parisian churches—St Louis, Petit St Antoine, St Gervais, and St Jean-en-Grève. In 1683, at the age of twenty-six, King Louis XIV appointed him to one of the four *sous-maîtres* positions at the royal chapel, and in 1685 the king expanded Lalande's musical responsibilities at the court by naming him *compositeur de la musique de la chambre*—a position once held by Jean-Baptiste Lully. Lalande followed further in Lully's footsteps by being promoted to *surintendant de la musique de la chambre* in 1689 and *maître de musique de la chambre* in 1695. Additionally, Lalande took over two quarters of the chapel in 1693, three quarters in 1704, and in 1714 he was solely responsible for all chapel music. After the death of Louis XIV in 1715, Lalande began reducing his court activities, gradually eliminating his quarters of leadership at the royal chapel and turning over other responsibilities to his students. He died of pneumonia in 1726 and was buried at Notre Dame de Versailles.

Lalande was unlike Lully in compositional focus. While Lully composed mostly operas but only a few motets, Lalande composed mostly motets (over seventy, although only sixty-four are extant) but just a few operas and other secular works. Almost all of Lalande's motets are of the *grand* type (the several *petits motets* are adaptations or arrangements of portions of his larger works) and were composed for the royal chapel. However, their popularity was so great that they were performed by concert societies in Lyons, Aix-en-Provence, and Lille, and when the Concert spirituel was formed in Paris in 1725, the first performance was almost completely devoted to the motets of Lalande. Furthermore, they continued to be featured throughout the sixty-six years of the Concert spirituel's existence; accounts list more than six hundred performances of Lalande's motets, with *Cantate Domino* being the most popular.

The early *grands motets* are characterized by connected sections of music that are varied in scoring, meter, and tempo; short melodic passages (*récits*) for soloists; a concentration of homophonic textures; and instrumentation that is often *colla parte* with the voices. The late *grands motets* are divided into separate movements; the solo passages are in distinct movements; the textures are predominantly contrapuntal; the instrumental scoring is more independent; and the strings are often divided into five or six parts. Both early and late motets consist of solo, duet, and trio passages or movements that alternate with passages or movements for chorus. Many of the motets throughout Lalande's career feature Gregorian melodies that are treated as a cantus firmus.

Lalande revised many of his motets, rescoring and expanding them in later years to suit his newer style. Interestingly, Louis XIV objected to this revisionary practice, saying that the simple grace of the early compositions should be preserved and that the work on revisions took time away from new compositions.

GRANDS MOTETS
SELECTED AND LISTED ACCORDING TO FAMILIARITY

Te Deum – 1684 – SSATBB solos, SSATBB chorus, two oboes, two trumpets, timpani, strings, and basso continuo – 25 minutes. The motet is divided into nineteen sections, beginning with an instrumental *simphonie*.

Cantate Domino (Psalm 98) – 1707 – SSAB solos, SATBB chorus, two oboes, strings, and basso continuo – 24 minutes.

De profundis (Psalm 130 and two lines from the Requiem aeternam) – 1689 – SSATB solos, SATBB chorus, flute, oboe, strings, and basso continuo – 24 minutes. (1) The motet, which is in thirteen sections, was revised in 1715; (2) the flute and oboe are used sparingly as obbligato instruments.

Venite exultemus (Psalm 95) – 1700 – SATBB solos, SATBB chorus, two oboes, strings, and basso continuo – 26:30 minutes.

Confitebor tibi Domine in consilio (Psalm 111) – 1699 – SSATB solos, SATBB chorus, strings, and basso continuo – 30 minutes. The motet is in ten sections (five solos, one duet, one trio with chorus, one solo quartet, and two choruses).

Deus noster refugium (Psalm 45) – 1699 – SATBB solos, SATBB chorus – 21 minutes. The motet consists of sixteen movements, including the famous duet for two basses, "Propterea non timebimus."

Regina coeli – 1698 – STB solos, SATBB chorus, two flutes, strings, and basso continuo – 9 minutes.

Cantemus Domino (Exodus 15:1–18) – 1687 – SATBB solos, SATBB chorus, two flutes, two oboes, strings, and basso continuo – 22 minutes.

Jubilate Deo (Psalm 100) – 1689 – SSAATTB solos, SSATBB chorus, two flutes, two oboes, strings, and basso continuo – 14 minutes. The motet is divided into four movements—the first and last have solos that alternate with chorus, the second is a solo (T), and the third is a trio (SST).

Quare fremuerunt gentes (Psalm 2) – date unknown – SSB solos, SATB/SATB chorus, two flutes, two oboes, strings, and basso continuo – 25 minutes. Of the motet's seven movements, two are for SATBB chorus, and only one is for SATB/SATB chorus.

ANDRÉ CAMPRA 1660–1744

Campra was born in Aix-en-Provence, where he spent seven years at St-Sauveur: at age fourteen he became a chorister, at eighteen he began ecclesiastical studies, and at twenty-one he was made a chaplain. From 1681 to 1683 he was *maître de chapelle* at St Trophime in Arles, from 1683 to 1694 he was *maître de musique* at St Etienne in Toulouse, and from 1694 to 1700 he was *maître de musique* at Notre Dame Cathedral in Paris. With predilections for operatic rather than church music, however, he left his position at Notre Dame in 1700 to pursue a theatrical career. He had already composed a very successful opera-ballet (*L'Europe galante*) and divertissement (*Vénus, feste galante*) under an assumed name, and he had received support from significant Parisian patrons. His appointment in 1700 as *conducteur* at the Paris Opéra, the publication in 1708 of the first of his three books of cantatas for solo voice and basso continuo, and a pension in 1718 from King Louis XV in recognition of his talents as a composer of stage works confirmed his status and secured his future in secular music. Despite his activities composing secular music, Campra maintained an interest in church music, and in 1723 he took one of the *sous-maîtres* positions at the royal chapel relinquished by Michel-Richard de Lalande. In 1726, with Lalande's death, Campra assumed two quarters. He kept this position at the royal chapel and continued to compose opera-ballet works until his health failed in 1735.

His choral output consists of three masses (*Missa Ad majorem Dei gloriam* in 1699 for SATB chorus a cappella, *Messe de requiem* of about 1722, and a plainsong mass) and approximately one hundred motets, fifty-six of which were published in five books during his lifetime. Most of the motets are of the *petit* type, with scoring for one to three solo voices and basso continuo and the occasional addition of obbligato instruments. Representative works include the solo motets for soprano and basso continuo *O dulcis amor* from book three of 1703, *Salve regina* and *O sacrum convivium* from book one of 1695, and *Jubilate Deo* from book two of 1699. Only a few of the motets from the five books are scored for chorus. These include the well-known *In convertendo Dominus* (Psalm 126) from book two (scored for SATB solos, SSATBB chorus, strings, and basso continuo) and a *Te Deum*. Two additional books of motets, entitled *Pseaumes mis en musique à grand choeur*, were published in 1737 and 1738. Each of these books contains only two works, one of which is *Notus in Judea Deus*. Most of the motets not published during Campra's lifetime are of the *grand* type and include *De profundis* (Psalm 130) and *Deus noster refugium* (Psalm 46), both scored for SATB solos, SATBB chorus, two flutes, two oboes, strings, and basso continuo.

NICOLAS BERNIER 1665–1734

Bernier was born in Mantes-la-Jolie, a suburb of Paris. He most likely spent his youth there before studying in Italy, though there is no proof of this. In 1694 he was appointed *maître* at Chartres Cathedral, and in 1698 he was appointed *maître de musique* at St Germain l'Auxerrois in Paris, where Michel-Richard de Lalande had been a chorister from 1666 to 1672. In 1704 Bernier succeeded Marc-Antoine Charpentier as *maître de musique* at Sainte-Chapelle, and in

1723, while still at Sainte-Chapelle, he was appointed to one of the four *sous-maître* positions at the royal chapel (André Campra was appointed to one of the other positions at the same time). Three years later Bernier left Sainte-Chapelle and assumed an additional *sous-maître* position at the royal chapel.

Unlike most French Baroque composers, Bernier wrote no operas or ballets. However, like François Couperin, Jean-Philippe Rameau, Guillaume-Gabriel Nivers, and Henri Madin, he was a noted teacher, and he wrote an important treatise (*Principes de composition*). His compositional output includes forty-four *petits motets* for one to three voices, basso continuo, and obbligato instruments; eleven *grands motets* for SATB solos, SATB chorus, strings, and basso continuo; and approximately thirty-eight secular cantatas for one to two voices and basso continuo. Bernier's choral repertoire also included a mass and a Te Deum that have been lost. The *grands motets* include *Laudate Dominum* (Psalm 147), *Miserere mei Deus* (Psalm 57), *Confitebor tibi* (Psalm 111), and *Venite exultemus* (Psalm 95).

JEAN GILLES 1668–1705

Gilles, born near Avignon, was enrolled in the choir school of St-Sauveur in nearby Aix-en-Provence when he was eleven years old. Like André Campra, who was also enrolled in the choir school at this time, Gilles stayed at St-Sauveur. He became *sous-maître* and organist at age twenty, and *maître de musique* at age twenty-five. In 1695, at twenty-seven, he became *maître de musique* at the cathedral in Agda (a town close to Aix-en-Provence), and two years later he took the same position at St Etienne in Toulouse (the position Campra had left in 1694). Gilles remained at St Etienne until his death, even though he also worked for a short period of time at Notre Dame des Doms in Avignon.

Gilles composed two masses, fourteen *grands motets*, and eighteen *petits motets*. The masses include the *Messe en D* for SATBB voices and basso continuo, and the *Messe des morts* (Requiem) for SSATTB solos, SATBB chorus, two flutes, strings, and basso continuo. The *Messe des morts*, which, like the motets, has passages for soloists that alternate with chorus, became one of the best-known and respected vocal works in France. It was performed at the funerals of both Jean-Baptiste Lully in 1764 and King Louis XV in 1774. In addition, the Concert spirituel performed it frequently and Johann Mattheson (1681–1764), the German composer and theorist, called it one of the most beautiful works he had heard.

The *grands motets* include two works that were also performed frequently by the Concert spirituel—*Diligam te, Domine* and *Beatus quem elegisti*. The first of these is scored for SSATBB solos, SSATBB chorus, strings, and basso continuo and is divided into seven movements—four for soloists and three for soloists and chorus. Other *grands motets* include *Paratum cor meum deus* (Psalm 108) for SATTB solos, SATTB chorus, and basso continuo; *Laudate nomen Domini* (Psalm 135) for SATB solos, SATTB chorus, and basso continuo; and *Laetatus sum* (Psalm 122) for TTB solos, SATTB chorus, and basso continuo. Most of the *petits motets* are adaptations of movements from the *grands motets*.

FRANÇOIS COUPERIN 1668–1733

Couperin is often given the sobriquet "le grand" to distinguish him from his uncle, also named François (ca.1631–ca.1708), and to designate him as the most eminent of the many seventeenth- and eighteenth-century musicians in the Couperin family. He was born in Paris, where his father, Charles, was organist at St Gervais. François most likely demonstrated advanced musical skills in his youth and showed great promise, for at age ten, when his father died, St Gervais officials decided to hold the position of organist for him until his eighteenth birthday. Michel-Richard de Lalande was appointed organist in the interim. François fulfilled this expectation, and in addition to his appointment at St Gervais as planned, he was appointed one of the four organists at the royal chapel in 1693 (the same year that Lalande assumed two quarters as *sous-maître*). Couperin also taught harpsichord to the Duke of Burgundy and to other members of the royal family, and during the late years of the seventeenth century he composed a small number of motets. However, by the early eighteenth century most of his compositional focus was on keyboard music. In 1713 and 1717 he published his famous volumes entitled *Pieces de clavecin* (which became known throughout France, Italy, England, and Germany), and in 1717 he published his keyboard treatise *L'art de toucher le clavecin* (also known throughout Europe). In addition, he was appointed *ordinaire de la musique de la chambre du roi pour le clavecin* in 1717. Unlike Lully and Lalande, Couperin did not receive further appointments or advancements in the royal court, even though—during his lifetime and afterwards—he was clearly considered the greatest French composer of the Baroque era.

Couperin composed twelve *grands motets* and approximately thirty *petits motets*. Unfortunately, all of the *grands motets* and approximately half of the *petits motets* have been lost. The motets that survive were composed either for the *élévation* portion of the *messe basse solennelle* (the low solemn mass) that King Louis XIV attended or for Holy Week services at the Abbey de Lonchampt, which was very near Paris and which was known for the high quality of its musical presentations. The motets for the royal chapel include three works specifically ordered by the king ("composé de l'ordre du Roy") and about a dozen others. Those for the Abbey de Lonchampt include the *Trois Leçons de Ténèbres*, the third of which is unquestionably Couperin's most famous vocal composition.

All the *petits motets* are scored for one to three soloists and basso continuo or a small ensemble of instruments. Many of them—such as *Respice in me, Salve regina,* and the first two of the *Trois Leçons de Ténèbres*—are scored for a single solo voice and basso continuo. Others—such as *Tantum ergo, Lauda sion, Regina coeli laetare,* and the third of the *Leçons*—are scored for two sopranos and basso continuo. Only a few—*Tantum ergo* and the *versets* for the king—are scored for three voices and an instrumental ensemble. Most of the solos were composed for specific singers (such as Couperin's cousin Marguerite-Louise), whose names are noted in the music. All the motets are divided into sections that generally correspond to verses of biblical text and that are scored for various solo and instrumental combinations. For instance, the first of the three motets ordered by Louis XIV (*Quatre versets* of 1703) is structured as follows: the first section (Psalm 118:11) is for two sopranos a cappella; the second section (verse twelve) is for soprano solo, two violins, and basso continuo; the third section (verse thirteen) is for the other soprano solo, two flutes, and violin; and the fourth section (verse fourteen) is for the two sopranos and violin.

PETITS MOTETS
SELECTED AND LISTED ACCORDING TO FAMILIARITY

Troisième Leçon à deux voix (The Lamentations of Jeremiah 1:10–14) – 1713–
1717 – SS solos and basso continuo – 10:30 minutes. The five verses of
text are linked by a ritornello, which is set to the Hebrew letters of the
biblical verses (Jod, Caph, Lamed, Mem, and Nun) and which is sung
before the actual text of the verses.

Veni sponsa Christi – ca.1703 – also called *Motet à Sainte Suzanne* – SAB
solos, two violins, and basso continuo – 17:30 minutes.

Laudate pueri Dominum (Psalm 113) – 1693–1697 – SSB solos, two violins,
and basso continuo – 12 minutes. The motet is in eight sections (verses
five and six of the Psalm are combined).

Quatre versets d'un motet composé de l'ordre du Roy (Psalm 118:11–14) – 1703 –
SS solos, two flutes, two violins, and basso continuo – 10 minutes.

Sept versets d'un motet composé de l'ordre du Roy (Psalm 84:4–8, 11–13) – 1704 –
SSATB solos, two flutes, two oboes, two violins, and basso continuo –
17:30 minutes.

Sept versets d'un motet composé de l'ordre du Roy (Psalm 79:1–3, 9–12, 15) –
1705 – SAB solos, two flutes, two oboes, two violins, and basso continuo –
15 minutes.

LOUIS-NICOLAS CLÉRAMBAULT 1676–1749

Clérambault was born in Paris, where his father, Dominique, was a violinist in King Louis XIV's
famous *Vingt-quatre violons du Roi*. Nothing is known about Louis-Nicolas until he was appointed
organist at the church of Grands Augustins in 1707. In 1715 he succeeded Guillaume-Gabriel
Nivers, who had died the year before, at both St Sulpice and the Maison Royal de Saint-Louis at
Saint-Cyr, and for the remainder of his life he was well known as one of France's most celebrated
organists.

He composed five books of secular cantatas, five books of sacred motets (which included
Magnificats and a Te Deum), and one oratorio. The cantatas are all scored for one or two solo
voices and basso continuo, with the occasional addition of strings. The motets are divided between smaller pieces written for the girls at the orphanage at Saint-Cyr and larger works scored
for soloists and mixed chorus. Examples of the former include *Hodie Christus natus est* and *O rex
gloriae*, both scored for SA solos, SA chorus, and basso continuo. Examples of the latter include
Afferte Domino (Psalm 28) for ATB solos, SATB chorus, two oboes, trumpet, timpani, strings,
and basso continuo; *Magnificat* for SATB solos, SATB/SATB chorus, two flutes, two oboes, strings,
and basso continuo; and *Te Deum* for SATB solos, SATB chorus, two flutes, trumpet, strings, and
basso continuo. All these latter works feature brief solo, duet, trio, and full ensemble passages
that alternate with passages for chorus.

The oratorio *L'Histoire de la femme adultère* is a setting of the story from John 8:1–11 about
Jesus and the woman accused of adultery. It is scored for SATBB solos, SATB chorus, two vio-

lins, and basso continuo; solo roles are for the Adulteress (S), Jesus (A), two Jews (T and B), and a Narrator (B).

JEAN-PHILIPPE RAMEAU 1683–1764

Rameau was born in Dijon, where his father was organist at St Etienne. When he was young, Jean-Philippe was sent to the Jesuit Collège des Godrans to receive a liberal education that would prepare him for a career in law, but he was interested in music, and at age eighteen he went to Italy to absorb the Italian style. He returned to France after only several months, and during the next twenty years he served as organist for numerous cathedrals and abbey churches, including those in Avignon, Clermont-Ferrand, Lyons, Montpellier, and St Etienne, where he succeeded his father. In 1723, realizing that his ambitions lay outside church music, he moved to Paris to write harpsichord pieces, operas (*tragédies lyriques*), and theoretical treatises. During the 1720s and 1730s he published two of his four books of harpsichord music, he composed his first opera (*Hippolyte et Aricie*), and he wrote the two most important of his theoretical treatises—*Traité de l'harmonie reduite à ses principes naturels* and *Nouveau système de musique théorique*. His compositions became known and respected, and in 1745 Louis XV appointed him *compositeur du cabinet du roy*. However, writing about music became his chief ambition, and for the remainder of his long life (he died shortly before his eighty-first birthday) he wrote approximately thirty more treatises, books, articles, and letters about the state of music in France.

Rameau composed six secular cantatas (five for solo voices and one a duet for soprano and bass) and five motets, four of which are extant. Of these, three are *grands motets* most likely composed for the concert hall (not the royal chapel), and one is an example of *prima prattica* writing in the polyphonic style that was published in his *Traité de l'harmonie*. The three *grands motets*— *Deus noster refugium*, *In convertendo*, and *Quam dilecta*—are typical of the time in being scored for soloists, chorus, and an ensemble of instruments. In addition, they are divided into multiple distinct and separate movements (i.e., fully developed arias, duets, and choruses). The motet in *prima prattica* style, *Laboravi clamans*, is scored only for chorus and basso continuo and is unique among the French Baroque sacred repertoire. It consists of four points of imitation, corresponding to the four phrases of the text, that pervade all voice parts and that are intertwined throughout the motet. The writing is masterful and compelling.

MOTETS
COMPLETE AND LISTED ACCORDING TO FAMILIARITY

Laboravi clamans (Psalm 69:3) – 1722 – SSATB chorus and basso continuo – 3:30 minutes.

In convertendo (Psalm 126) – ca.1718   SAB solos, SSATBB chorus, two flutes, oboe, strings, and basso continuo – 23 minutes.

Deus noster refugium (Psalm 46) – before 1716 – SSATTBB solos, SSATB chorus, two oboes, strings, and basso continuo – 26:30.

Quam dilecta (Psalm 84) – ca.1720 – SSATB solos, SSATBB chorus, two flutes, strings, and basso continuo – 20 minutes.

HENRI MADIN 1698–1748

Madin was born in a small town east of Paris. No information exists about him before his appointment as assistant to Sébastien de Brossard at Meaux Cathedral in 1719. In 1731 he became *maître de la chapelle* at Tours Cathedral, and in 1737 he took the same position at Rouen Cathedral. The following year he was appointed *sous-maître de musique de la chapelle royale,* and in 1742 he also became *maître des pages de la musique.*

Madin composed five masses, twenty-six *grands motets,* and six *petits motets.* His masses include the *Missa Dico ego opera mea regi* of 1743 and the *Missa brevis Velociter currit sermo ejus* of 1746, both for SATB chorus and basso continuo and both based on Psalter melodies. "Dico ego opera mea regi" comes from the second line of verse one of Psalm 45 (I speak of the things which I have made touch the king), and "Velociter currit sermo ejus" comes from verse 15 of Psalm 147 (His word runneth swiftly). Except for a brief introduction to the Kyries of each mass, the basso continuo parts in both masses only double the voice parts. In addition, the basso continuo parts are meant specifically for organ alone. The *Missa Dico ego opera mea regi* is in an imitative *prima prattica* style throughout, with occasional passages for two and three voices and with tempo and meter changes within the Gloria and Credo portions of the Ordinary that characterize textual drama. The *Missa brevis* has a basic homophonic and four-part texture throughout, with only brief sections of imitation and a few duet passages. The *Missa brevis* also includes the élévation text "O salutaris hostia."

The *grands motets* include titles common to most of the French Baroque composers: *Beatus vir; Cantate Domino; De profundis; Deus noster refugium; Diligam te, Domine;* and *Notus in Judea.* The *petits motets* were composed for the order of Les Filles de la Miséricorde (The Girls of Mercy). They are all scored for two sopranos and basso continuo, with the addition of violins in three of the motets. The final motet is the very beautiful *Motet pour l'assomption de la sainte vierge et pour le commun des vierges martyres* (Motet for the assumption of the holy virgin and for the common of the martyred virgins).

JEAN-JOSEPH CASSANÉA DE MONDONVILLE 1711–1772

Mondonville was born in Narbonne, in southern France, where his father was the organist at the local cathedral. The young Mondonville studied violin, in 1731 he moved to Paris and established himself as a soloist and composer of instrumental sonatas, and in 1734 he made his solo debut at the Concert spirituel. During the late 1730s he became known for his *grands motets,* which were being performed regularly at the Concert spirituel, and in 1739 he entered the service of King Louis XV as a *violon de la chamber et de la chapelle.* He was appointed to one of the *sous-maître* positions at the royal chapel in 1744, and in 1755 he became director of the Concert spirituel.

His choral output consists of nine extant *grands motets* and six *petits motets.* Typical of the genres as they had been composed from the beginning of the Baroque era in France, the *grands motets* are multimovement works set to Psalm texts and scored for soloists, chorus, and instruments, and the *petits motets* are settings of Psalm and other liturgical texts scored for soloists and basso continuo. Mondonville's *grands motets* are unique in treating the texts in expressive manners that would become standard at the end of the eighteenth century. For example, the phrase "elevaverunt flumina vocem suam" (the floods have lifted up their voice) from *Dominus regnavit* is painted by choral and instrumental scale passages and arpeggios. In addition, the movements of the motet are headed by expressive tempo terms such as "lent et mesuré" (slow and stately) and "gratieusement" (gracefully). Many of Mondonville's motets were extremely popular and received numerous performances. *Dominus regnavit* was performed at the Concert spirituel two to four times per year between 1735 and 1758; *De profundis,* composed for the funeral service of Henri Madin, was performed forty times between 1748 and 1762; and *In exitu Israel,* premiered for King Louis XV in 1753, had eight performances at the Concert spirituel in 1755.

MOTETS

SELECTED AND LISTED ACCORDING TO FAMILIARITY

Dominus regnavit (Psalm 93) – 1734 – SSATBB solos, SATBB chorus, strings, and basso continuo – 22 minutes.

De profundis (Psalm 130) – 1748 – SSAB solos, SATBB chorus, strings, and basso continuo – 23 minutes.

In exitu Israel (Psalm 114) – 1755 – SABB solos, SATBB chorus, strings, and basso continuo – 26 minutes.

❧ GERMANY ❧

As in France, the vocal/choral music in Germany during the Baroque era was almost entirely sacred. However, while the French repertoire was composed predominantly for the Catholic Church, the German repertoire was composed for the Lutheran Church. Only two notable German composers during the era wrote Catholic church music—Heinrich Schütz, who was employed for most of his life at the Catholic court in Dresden, and Johann Christian Bach, who converted to Catholicism after trips to Italy. Two minor composers—Heinrich Ignaz Franz von Biber and Johann Joseph Fux—were actually Austrian, not German, and worked most of their lives in Catholic Austrian courts. They are discussed here because their music, while set exclusively to Latin texts, generally reflects German characteristics. Another minor composer—Jan Dismas Zelenka—worked in Dresden and, like Schütz, composed Catholic church music.

Most of the German composers were born and employed in the small geographical area that became East Germany, an area that, at 41,000 square miles, is approximately the size of the island of Cuba or the state of Ohio. Only three minor composers were born outside this region. Andreas Hammerschmidt and Biber were born in Bohemia (now the Czech Republic), and Fux was born in Austria. In addition, almost all the German composers were virtuoso organists who achieved fame during their lifetimes for their performances, not their compositions.

The genres of German Baroque music conformed to the Lutheran liturgy and reflected the relative importance of its constituent components. For instance, chorales, cantatas, and motets were important, but masses were not. Chorales were the most significant musical component of the Lutheran liturgy; to engage the congregation as Martin Luther idealized, they were almost exclusively set to German texts (the vernacular), they were composed to simple melodies (called chorale tunes), and they were strophic (multiple verses of text were sung to the same music). Many composers made arrangements of popular chorale tunes written by Martin Luther, Johann Walther, and other Renaissance-era Germans, and many composers employed chorale tunes, often as a cantus firmus, in their motets, cantatas, and masses. Cantatas, also set almost exclusively to German texts and often employing chorale tunes as a cantus firmus or chorale arrangements in hymn form, were the most distinctive genre of the era. During the early and mid years of the seventeenth century they were similar to Italian vocal concertos—small-scale works in multiple sections scored for solo voices, a few obbligato instruments (generally two violins), and basso continuo. Later in the era they were large-scale works divided into separate movements and scored for soloists, chorus, strings, and instruments befitting the occasion of the work (e.g., oboes, horns, and trombones for somber occasions, and trumpets and timpani for festival occasions).

Motets, settings of both Latin and German texts that were often sung at funerals and other special services, were customarily in the style of Venetian polychoral dialogue works of the late Renaissance. Masses (called *missae* or *missae brevis*) consisted only of the Kyrie and Gloria portions of the Ordinary and continued to be sung in Latin. Other genres reflected the importance of local traditions. Passion oratorios, sung during Holy Week, were important in many of the major court and church cities, and Magnificats and Te Deums were composed for special celebratory functions.

In terms of performance, it should be noted that many compositions of the early Baroque era were scored for unspecified instruments *si placet*. Composers expected that instruments would be utilized as resources were available, with trumpets or oboes substituting for violins, or with any variety and number of instruments doubling vocal parts *colla parte*. In numerous instances, mostly in motets, composers indicated in their scores that instruments should or could be substituted or added. In other instances, no mention of instrumentation was indicated, although the *si placet* practice was so pervasive that it was expected.

No discussion of the Baroque era in Germany would be complete without considerable mention of the Bach family, which produced more than seventy-five organists/composers over the course of seven generations. While the most famed of the Bachs was Johann Sebastian, nine of his predecessors, two of his contemporaries, and four of his sons also composed significant repertoire. For ease of comprehension, the important family members from five of the generations are listed and discussed here in chronological order. The first of these five generations is represented by Johann (ca.1550–1626), also called Johannes Hans. The second generation includes four of his sons—Johann (1604–1673), like his father, also called Johannes Hans; Christoph (1613–1661); Heinrich (1615–1692); and Wendell (ca.1629–1682). In the third generation are two sons of Christoph—Georg Christoph (1642–1697) and Johann Ambrosius (1645–1695)—and two sons of Heinrich—Johann Christoph (1642–1703) and Johann Michael (1648–1694). The fourth generation includes Johann Sebastian (1685–1750), who was the son of Johann Ambrosius; Johann Nicolaus (1669–1753), who was the son of Johann Christoph; and Johann Ludwig (1677–1731), who was the grandson of Wendell. Finally, the fifth generation includes Johann Ernst (1732–1777), who was the great-grandson of Johann (1604–1673), and four sons of Johann Sebastian—Wilhelm Friedemann (1710–1784), Carl Philipp Emanuel (1714–1788), Johann Christoph Friedrich (1732–1795), and Johann Christian (1735–1782). The birth and death dates of all these family members are repeated below for clarity of identification.

Johann (ca.1550–1626), by trade a baker and carpetmaker, was the first of the family to become a professional musician. He was a *spielmann* (minstrel or fiddler) in Wechmar, the town of his birth, and he traveled as a *stadtpfeifer* (town piper) to cities such as Gotha, Arnstadt, Erfurt, and Eisenach.

Johann (1604–1673) was the first to compose vocal music that survives today. He was born in Wechmar but spent most of his life in Erfurt, where he was a *stadtpfeifer* and organist at the Predigerkirche. Three of his compositions survive and are included in the *Alt-Bachisches Archiv*. The first, *Unser leben ist ein Schatten,* is a motet in a typical double chorus dialogue style for SSATTB/ATB voices and basso continuo. The second, *Sei nun wieder zufrieden* (Psalm 116:7–10), is a motet for SSAT/ATTB voices and basso continuo that features extended sections of music for each of the ensembles alone. The third, *Weint nicht um meinen,* is a homophonic chorale setting of nine verses for SATB voices.

Christoph (1613–1661), Heinrich (1615–1692), and Wendell (ca.1629–1682) are basically known only as the fathers of more important members of the family, although all three pursued musical careers. Christoph was an instrumentalist in Weimar, Erfurt, and Arnstadt. Heinrich was a town musician in Schweinfurt and Erfurt and organist of the Liebfrauenkirche in Arnstadt. His one surviving vocal composition, *Ich danke dir, Gott,* is a short cantata (vocal concerto) for SSATB soloists (*favoriti chor*), SATB *ripieno chor,* two violins, two violas, and basso continuo. Little is known about the life of Wendell, and no compositions of his survive.

Georg Christoph (1642–1697), born in Erfurt, became *Kantor* in the town of Themar in 1668 and *Kantor* in Schweinfurt in 1684. He is known today by one surviving composition—*Siehe, wie fein und lieblich ist es* for TTB and basso continuo.

Johann Ambrosius (1645–1695), like his father and brother, began his musical career as a *stadtpfeifer*. However, he later took positions as a violinist in Erfurt and as a court trumpeter and *Hausmann* (director of town music) in Eisenach. He was highly respected and is credited with establishing Eisenach as a center of musical excellence.

Johann Christoph (1642–1703) and his brother, Johann Michael (1648–1694), were the first family members to compose a significant amount of music that survives today. Both composers are discussed at length later in this section of the Baroque era.

Johann Sebastian (1685–1750) and Johann Ludwig (1677–1731) also receive individual discussions below. Johann Nicolaus (1669–1753), cousin of Johann Sebastian and Johann Ludwig, was organist at the two main churches in Jena—the town church and the university church (Kollegienkirche)—and leader of the university collegium musicum. In addition, he was a builder of harpsichords. He is known today for his one extant composition—*Missa sopra cantilena Allein Gott in der Höh,* a setting of the Kyrie and Gloria based on the Lutheran chorale mentioned in the mass title. Scoring is for SA solos, SATB chorus, two violins, two violas, and basso continuo, with occasional ensemble passages for SATB soloists and with a separate *ripieno* part in the Gloria for the chorale melody.

Johann Ernst (1732–1777) studied at the Thomasschule in Leipzig under his uncle, Johann Sebastian. In 1742 he assisted his father, Johann Bernhard (1676–1749), who was town organist in Eisenach, in 1749 he succeeded his father, and in 1756 he was appointed *Hofkapellmeister.*

He composed five cantatas, one Magnificat, one mass, one motet, and one Passion oratorio—*O Seele, deren Sehnen* of 1764, which is modeled after Carl Heinrich Graun's *Der Tod Jesu*.

Of Johann Sebastian's six sons who became musicians, Wilhelm Friedemann (1710–1784), Carl Philipp Emanuel (1714–1788), Johann Christoph Friedrich (1732–1795), and Johann Christian (1735–1782) achieved fame and are discussed individually below. They, as well as other composers who lived after the death of Johann Sebastian Bach in 1750, composed in a style generally referred to as *empfindsamer Stil* (sentimental style), which was more homophonic and syllabic than the contrapuntal style of Johann Sebastian or other late Baroque composers. While the older and newer styles were texturally different, the new style maintained numerous characteristics that related it more to the Baroque than to the Rococo style seen in the late works of Georg Philipp Telemann or to the Classical styles of W. A. Mozart and Joseph Haydn.

In summary, the most important members in the three most significant generations of the Bach family are Johann Christoph (1642–1703) and Johann Michael (1648–1694) in the third generation, Johann Ludwig (1677–1731) and Johann Sebastian (1685–1750) in the fourth generation, and Carl Philipp Emanuel (1714–1788), Johann Christoph Friedrich (1732–1795), and Johann Christian (1735–1782) in the fifth generation.

Major composers outside the Bach family, all from northern Germany, are Heinrich Schütz, Johann Hermann Schein, Samuel Scheidt, Dietrich Buxtehude, Johann Pachelbel, Johann Kuhnau, Georg Philipp Telemann, Christoph (Johann) Graupner, and Gottfried August Homilius. Composers of lesser significance, including those who worked in both Germany and Austria, are Johannes Crüger, Thomas Selle, Andreas Hammerschmidt, Franz Tunder, Heinrich Ignaz Franz von Biber, Johann Schelle, Johann Joseph Fux, Friedrich Wilhelm Zachow, Jan Dismas Zelenka, Johann Mattheson, Johann Gottfried Walther, and Carl Heinrich Graun.

HEINRICH SCHÜTZ (HENRICUS SAGITARIUS) 1585–1672

Schütz was born in the small town of Köstritz (now Bad Köstritz) near Dresden and probably received his first musical training in Weissenfels, where his family had moved when he was five years old. When he was thirteen he went to Kassel to sing as a chorister in the Kapelle of Landgrave Moritz, a noted patron of the arts, and in 1609, after a brief period of law studies at the University of Marburg, he went to Venice, supported by Moritz, to study with Giovanni Gabrieli. Schütz excelled and completely absorbed the Italian style, as is exhibited in his Italian madrigals, and he brought his newly acquired skills back to Kassel after Gabrieli's death in 1612. In 1615 Schütz moved to the court of Johann Georg, Elector of Saxony, who was of a higher noble and political status than Moritz and who also had one of the most extravagant musical courts in Germany at the time. Schütz was appointed *Kapellmeister* to Johann Georg and remained in his service for forty-one years (i.e., until the elector's death in 1656). For many of these years Schütz composed large-scale works for the court, such as the Psalms of David in 1619, and he also served as the court's musical ambassador. In 1617, for instance, he went to Gera to help reorganize music at the court of Prince Heinrich Posthumus von Reuss; in 1618 he went to Magdeburg, along with Michael Praetorius and Samuel Scheidt, to help reorganize the music at the Kapelle there; and in 1619 he joined Praetorius and Scheidt in inaugurating a new organ in Bayreuth.

The Dresden court began to suffer economically in the 1620s as a result of the Thirty Years War, and the music program declined dramatically. Many musicians left the court, and those who remained received no salary for years. Schütz found relief from these circumstances in 1628 and 1629 by studying again in Venice, this time with Claudio Monteverdi, and by serving as temporary *Kapellmeister* in 1634 to Crown Prince Christian of Denmark. Schütz also served as temporary *Kapellmeister* in 1639 and 1640 for Georg of Calenberg in Hanover, and as *Kapellmeister* again in Denmark during the years 1642 to 1644. For the other years during the war Schütz served the Dresden Court by composing small-scale pieces for limited resources such as are contained in the two volumes of *Kleiner geistlichen Concerten*. In 1645, when he was sixty years of age, he took regular long vacations to Weissenfels, the town of his youth, and in 1656, when he was seventy-one, Johann Georg died and his successor, Johann Georg II, appointed Schütz the equivalent of *Kapellmeister* emeritus, allowing him to retire from regular duties. The court's musical resources improved gradually, and Schütz composed works for a variety of forces, concluding with two of his most monumental works—the *Teutsch Magnificat* (German Magnificat) and his *Schwanengesang* (Psalm 119). He suffered a stroke on the morning of November 6, 1672, and died later that afternoon at age eighty-seven.

Like Monteverdi, Schütz was a transitional composer. His early works are in the Renaissance style of the final decades of the sixteenth century in Italy, while his late works are in the Italian Baroque *prima* and *seconda prattica* styles. Unlike Monteverdi, however, Schütz did not convert completely to Baroque sensibilities. He maintained a keen interest in both Renaissance and Baroque styles throughout his life, showing himself to be a consummate master of each. He is considered to be the greatest German composer of the early Baroque era as well as one of the greatest composers of all time.

Schütz composed approximately five hundred works that survive, including nineteen madrigals, six oratorios, one Requiem-like work, 360 motets and vocal concertos, and over one hundred chorale-like settings. Almost all of these compositions were published in volumes that were devoted to a specific genre and that contained only his music, although several compositions were published in volumes containing the music of other composers. One such composition— a setting of Psalm 116, *Das ist mir lieb* (SWV51)—was composed for a collection of sixteen settings of this Psalm by sixteen composers and published in the year 1616. Other composers contributing to the collection, published under the title *Angst der Hellen und Friede der Seelen,* include Christoph Demantius, Michael Praetorius, Melchior Franck, and Johann Hermann Schein.

The madrigals were Schütz's first compositions, written during his trip to Venice to study with Gabrieli and published in 1611 in a collection entitled *Il primo libro de madrigali*. All the madrigals in the collection are scored for SSATB voices a cappella, and all are modeled after and convincingly representative of the pervasive point-of-imitation Italian madrigals in favor at the time, with skillful rhythmic variety and expressive word painting.

The six oratorios include one setting for Easter (SWV50), one setting for Christmas (SWV435), one setting of the seven last words of Jesus on the cross (SWV478), and three Passions (SWV 479, 480, and 481). The Easter oratorio was composed in 1623. According to Schütz, it was to be sung for spiritual Christian reflection during Vespers on Easter Day or during private devotions at Eastertime. Its style of composition is a combination of the Renaissance German *historiae* as composed by Leonhard Lechner and Antonio Scandello, and Baroque oratorios as composed by Giacomo Carissimi. The text, which is an assemblage of passages from the four

Gospels, is identical to the text used by Scandello in his Easter historia. The music consists mostly of recitative (the Baroque influence), with the distinction that the part of the Evangelist is set to traditional recitation tones (the Renaissance influence). The only set pieces are three choral movements—two that traditionally begin and end the work (the *Introitus* or *Eingang* and the *Beschluss*) and one that is a part of the drama and sung by a crowd (*turba*).

The Christmas oratorio was composed in 1664, more than forty years after the Easter oratorio. Both works similarly begin and end with *Eingang* and *Beschluss* choruses, and both deliver most of the story through recitative. However, the Christmas oratorio contains eight set solo pieces, each of which Schütz labeled *Intermedium*. These alternate with the Evangelist's narration and consist of arias, trios, and quartets sung by angels, shepherds, the three wise men, and priests.

The setting of the seven last words of Jesus on the cross (*Die sieben Wortte*) was composed in 1645, halfway between the Easter and Christmas oratorios. Like the other works, it begins and ends with opening and closing choruses, although unlike the other works, the three main dramatic roles in *Die sieben Wortte*—Jesus and the Two Criminals—are set as solo recitatives, and in addition, the Evangelist's narration is set partly for a soloist and partly for chorus (similar to the oratorios of Carissimi). Also unique is the accompaniment of the words of Jesus by strings (such as would be done more than eighty years later by J. S. Bach in his *Passio secundum Mattaeum* BWV244).

The three Passions—Matthew, Luke, and John—were composed in 1665 and 1666 toward the end of Schütz's life. They all relate the Passion story in an older, pre-Baroque style, with the parts of the Evangelist and other characters scored in nonrhythmic recitation tones (i.e., text phrases are written under single long notes, similar to Psalm tones in Gregorian chant), and with the chorus scored for opening and closing movements and numerous *turba* passages. Most unusual for works in the middle of the Baroque era, all three Passions are completely a cappella; there are no instruments involved, not even basso continuo. In spite of this, the Passions are highly expressive, with a flow of solos and *turba* choruses that creates compelling dramatic action.

The Requiem-like work of 1636—*Musicalische Exequien* (Musical obsequies or funeral rites)—was commissioned by Prince von Reuss for performance at his burial service. Schütz set the texts chosen by Reuss in three motets, or as Schütz called them, "concerted works." The first is in the form of a German *missa* (i.e., the texts correspond to the portions of the Kyrie and Gloria), with alternating sections of music for various solo combinations and chorus; the second motet is characteristic of Venetian polychoral works by Gabrieli, with phrases of text in dialogue between the two choral groups; and the third motet is also polychoral. This final motet is distinctive, however, in that the two choral ensembles have different texts. The first sings the Song of Simeon or Nunc dimittis, "Herr, nun lässest du deinen Diener" (Lord, now let thy servant depart in peace), while the second sings "Selig sind die Toten" (Blessed are the dead). The combination of the three motets, sometimes referred to as Schütz's German Requiem, is considered one of the great masterpieces of choral repertoire.

Most of the individual motets are contained in three publications—*Psalmen Davids* (Psalms of David), *Cantiones sacrae* (Sacred songs), and *Geistliche Chor-Music* (Sacred choral music). The Psalms of David, published in 1619 as *Psalmen Davids sampt etlichen Moteten und Concerten*, were the first works Schütz composed for the Dresden court. As such, they were meant to take advantage of the court's extensive vocal and instrumental resources and also to demonstrate the grand Venetian music Schütz had experienced at St Mark's Basilica. The entire publication consists of twenty polychoral Psalm settings in Latin and six settings of other biblical verses that Schütz variously called *motetto, canzon,* or *concert.* These latter settings are vocal concertos scored for solos, chorus, and instruments. The Psalms, scored for two to four choirs and unspecified instruments *colla parte,* are similar in style to the polychoral motets of Gabrieli, although unlike Gabrieli, Schütz set the texts in a declamatory manner, which he referred to as the new *style recitativo.* This declamatory manner, which would become a hallmark of all his compositions and would distinguish and elevate him above other composers, was a fusion of late Renaissance ideals of text clarity and early Baroque ideals of speech declamation; musical rhythms closely mirrored natural speech patterns.

Cantiones sacrae, published in 1625, is a collection of motets set to Latin texts (mostly Psalms) in a *prima prattica* point-of-imitation style. Several features of the imitative technique are distinctive, including treatment of short motifs, repetition of musical material, and word painting with Italian Baroque musical figures. For instance, in *Cantate Domino,* the most famous motet from the collection, Schütz builds an imitative structure from single words (e.g., "cantate" and "tympano"), he repeats entire phrases, and he word-paints "canticum" in the typical manner of many early Baroque Italian composers—a melismatic passage sung by two voices at the interval of a third. The publication contains twenty-two motets, approximately half of which consist of two or three movements (an exception is the motet that begins *Quid commisisti,* which is in five movements). The motets were composed a cappella, and many editions present them this way. However, Schütz added basso continuo parts to the publication because the purely a cappella style was no longer fashionable.

Geistliche Chor-Music was published in 1648 as a set of instructive motets in the *prima prattica* style. As Schütz wrote in the preface of the publication, "I have composed a few slight works without basso continuo so that budding German composers, before they proceed to the 'concertato' style, may first [compose music] wherein the only true basis of good counterpoint is to be found." In spite of this message, Schütz provided a basso continuo part so that organists could accompany the chorus if needed, or so that the organist could transcribe the motets for organ alone. The motets are scored for five to seven voice parts and are arranged according to the liturgical year.

Other motets were published separately, including the two great masterpieces—the *Teutsch* or *Deutsches Magnificat* and the monumental setting of Psalm 119. Both works were composed in 1671, the year before Schütz died, and both are scored for SATB/SATB chorus and basso continuo. The *Magnificat* is in the Venetian dialogue style that Schütz favored throughout his life. The setting of Psalm 119, composed for his funeral, is divided into eleven movements or separate motets, each of which consists of sixteen verses of the Psalm text (each verse beginning with a letter of the Hebrew alphabet), and each of which begins with a chant incipit and ends with the Doxology. Schütz chose Psalm 119 because according to German tradition it is a summary of all the other Psalms, which in turn were believed to be a summary of the entire theological content of the Bible. Of special significance is verse 54, the central verse of Psalm 119, which Schütz chose as the text that would be the main topic of his funeral sermon: "Thy statutes have been my songs in the house of my pilgrimage."

The vocal concertos were published in two volumes of *Kleiner geistlichen Concerten* (Small sacred concertos) and three volumes of *Symphoniae sacrae* (also called *Symphoniarum sacrarum*). All the volumes contain music in the Baroque *seconda prattica* style scored for solo voices, obbligato instruments, and basso continuo. The two volumes of *Kleiner geistlichen Concerten* were published in 1636 and 1639, respectively, to meet the then-limited vocal and financial resources at the Dresden court. Consisting of small-scale pieces for solo voices with only basso continuo accompaniment, each book begins with solos, which are then followed by duets, trios, quartets, and quintets. The first collection contains four solos, eleven duets (four for two sopranos), four trios (including one for three basses), four quartets (two for SATB, one for SSTB, and one for SSBB), and one quintet (SSATB). The second collection contains five solos, ten duets, five trios, seven quartets (four for SATB, two for SSTT, and one for SSSB), and five quintets (three for SSATB and two for SATTB). The music represents Schütz at the height of his abilities to convey expressive qualities of text through effective musical motifs.

The first volume of *Symphoniae sacrae,* published in Venice in 1629 during the time that Schütz was studying with Monteverdi, contains fifteen settings of Latin texts—eight solos, four duets, and three trios. The second and third volumes, containing a total of forty-eight settings of German texts, were published in Dresden in 1647 and 1650, respectively. The second volume consists mostly of solos and duets for sopranos or tenors with accompaniment of two violins and basso continuo. The third volume is scored for larger groups of soloists, including some in double chorus format, with two violins, basso continuo, and additional unspecified instruments *si placet*. The style of writing in all three volumes is reminiscent of Monteverdi's music in his *Selva morale e spirituale* of 1640.

The chorale-like settings were published in two collections of 1628 and 1640 entitled *Psalmen Davids . . . durch D. Cornelium Beckern* (called the Becker Psalter), and one volume of *Zwölff geistliche Gesänge* (Twelve sacred songs) in 1657. The Becker Psalter, so-called because the texts of the Psalms are rhymed settings in German by the Leipzig theologian Cornelius Becker, contains simple, homophonic, chorale-like settings of almost all the 150 Psalms, composed for the morning and evening devotions of the choirboys. The *Zwölff geistliche Gesänge* consists of German settings of liturgical Lutheran texts, including the Missa and Litany, specifically composed in a simple manner for small church choirs.

The following collections and individual works are listed in chronological order of publication. While all of the multimovement works such as the first two madrigals are titled separately in the *Sämtliche Werke* (Complete Works edition) and given independent SWV numbers, it should be noted that these are single, unified compositions.

MADRIGALS – 1611
SELECTED AND LISTED IN ORDER OF SWV NUMBER

O primavera - O dolcezze amarissime d'amore SWV1 and 2 – SSATB voices
a cappella – 3 and 2:30 minutes.

Ride la primavera SWV7 – SSATB voices a cappella – 3 minutes.

Io moro, ecco ch'io moro SWV13 – SSATB voices a cappella – 3 minutes.

Vasto mar, nel cui seno SWV19 – SSATB voices a cappella – 3:30 minutes.

PSALMS OF DAVID – 1619
SELECTED AND LISTED IN ORDER OF SWV NUMBER

Warum toben die Heiden SWV23 (Psalm 2) – SATB/SATB/SATB/SATB chorus and basso continuo – 4 minutes. Although all four SATB ensembles are texted, two are titled *Coro Favorito* and specifically meant to be sung, and two are titled *Coro Capella* and have indication for unspecified instruments *colla parte*.

Ach Herr, straf mich nicht SWV24 (Psalm 6) – SATB/SATB chorus and basso continuo – 4:30 minutes.

Aus der Tiefe ruf ich, Herr, zu dir SWV25 (Psalm 130) – SATB/SATB chorus and basso continuo – 3:45 minutes.

Wie lieblich sind deine Wohnungen SWV29 (Psalm 84) – SSAT/TTBB chorus and basso continuo – 6 minutes.

Der Herr ist mein Hirt SWV33 (Psalm 23) – SSAT/SATB chorus and basso continuo – 4 minutes.

Singet dem Herrn ein neues Lied SWV35 (Psalm 98) – SATB/SATB chorus and basso continuo – 5 minutes.

Jauchzet dem Herrn, alle Welt SWV36 (Psalm 100) – SATB/SATB chorus and basso continuo – 4 minutes. This Psalm setting is often referred to as the "Echo Psalm," since the second chorus is an exact repetition of and is noted several beats after the first chorus.

Alleluja, lobet den Herren SWV38 (Psalm 150) – SATB solos, SATB/SATB chorus, and basso continuo – 7:30 minutes.

EASTER ORATORIO – 1623

Historia der frölichen und siegreichen Aufferstehung unsers einigen Erlösers und Seligmachers Jesu Christi SWV50 (History of the joyful and victorious resurrection of our unique redeemer and savior Jesus Christ) – SSSSAATTTBB solos, SATB chorus, four gambas, and basso continuo – 40 minutes. (1) Major solo roles are for the Evangelist (T) and Jesus (A); (2) minor solo roles are for Mary Magdalene (S), Three Women at the Sepulchre (SSS), a Young Man at the Sepulchre (A), Two Men at the Sepulchre (TT), Two Angels (TT), Two Disciples (TT), and Three Chief Priests (TBB); (3) the roles of the Two Men at the Sepulchre, Two Angels, and Two Disciples may be sung by the same tenors.

CANTIONES SACRAE – 1625
SELECTED AND LISTED IN ORDER OF SWV NUMBER

O bone, o dulcis, o benigne Jesu - Et ne despicias humilites SWV53 and 54 – SATB chorus and basso continuo – 5:30 minutes total.

Deus, misereatur nostri SWV55 (Psalm 67:2) – SATB chorus and basso continuo – 2:15 minutes.

Verba mea auribus percipe - Quoniam ad te clamabo SWV61 and 62 (Psalm 5:1–3) – SATB chorus and basso continuo – 5 minutes total.

Heu mihi, Domine SWV65 (Psalm 31:2) – SATB chorus and basso continuo – 4 minutes.

In te Domine, speravi SWV66 (Psalm 31:2–3) – SATB chorus and basso continuo – 2:30 minutes.

Sicut Moses serpentem in deserto SWV68 (John 3:14–15) – SATB chorus and basso continuo – 2:30 minutes.

Ad Dominum cum tribularer - Quid detur tibi SWV71 and 72 (Psalm 120:1–4) – SATB chorus and basso continuo – 6 minutes total.

Supereminet omnem scientiam - Pro hoc magno mysterio SWV76 and 77 – SSATB chorus and basso continuo – 6:30 minutes.

Cantate Domino canticum novum SWV81 (Psalm 149:1–3) – SATB chorus and basso continuo – 2:30 minutes.

Domine, ne in furore tuo - Quoniam non est in morte - Discedite a me SWV85, 86, and 87 (Psalm 6) – SATB chorus and basso continuo – 7:15 minutes total.

BECKER PSALTER – 1628 AND 1640

Psalmen Davids, hiebevorn in teutzsche Reimen gebracht, durch D. Cornelium Beckern SWV97–256 (The Psalms of David, hitherto set in German rhyme by Cornelius Becker) – SATB voices a cappella – each Psalm is from 30 seconds to 2 minutes, depending on the number of verses sung.

SYMPHONIAE SACRAE, BOOK ONE – 1629
SELECTED AND LISTED IN ORDER OF SWV NUMBER

O quam tu pulchra es, amica mea / Veni de Libano SWV265 and 266 (Song of Solomon) – TB solos, two violins, and basso continuo – 9 minutes.

Fili mi, Absolon SWV269 – B solo, four trombones, and basso continuo – 5 minutes.

Jubilate Deo in chordis et organo SWV276 – TTB solos, trumpet, and basso continuo – 5:30 minutes.

MUSICALISCHE EXEQUIEN – 1636
COMPLETE

Nacket bin ich vom Mutterliebe kommen SWV279 (text assembled from numerous biblical passages and Lutheran chorales) – SSATTBB solos, SSATTB chorus, and basso continuo – 23 minutes. In the preface to the motet Schütz states that the solo parts can be sung by six voices (SSATTB), with the alto substituting for the second bass.

Herr, wenn ich nur dich habe SWV280 (Psalm 73:25–26) – SATB/SATB chorus and basso continuo – 3:30 minutes.

Herr, nun lässest du deinen Diener SWV281 (Luke 2:29–32, Revelation 14:13, and the Wisdom of Solomon 3:1) – SATTB/SSB chorus and basso continuo – 4:30 minutes. Schütz states that the SSB ensemble is an attempt "to convey something of the joy of the blessed disembodied Soul in Heaven. . . . The SATTB chorus is to be placed in close proximity to the organ, but the SSB chorus is to be set up at a distance." Schütz also recommends having multiple SSB ensembles placed "at different places around the church."

KLEINER GEISTLICHEN CONCERTEN – 1636 AND 1639
SELECTED AND LISTED IN ORDER OF SWV NUMBER

Erhöre mich, wenn ich rufe SWV289 (Psalm 86:1) – SS solos and basso continuo – 2:30 minutes.

Nun komm, der Heiden Heiland SWV301 – SSBB solos and basso continuo – 3 minutes.

Ein Kind ist uns geboren SWV302 (Isaiah 9:1–6) – SATB voices and basso continuo – 3:30 minutes.

Verbum caro factum est SWV314 (John 1:14) – SS solos and basso continuo – 3:30 minutes.

Hodie Christus natus est SWV315 – ST solos and basso continuo – 4 minutes.

Ich bin jung gewesen SWV320 (Psalm 37:25) – BB solos and basso continuo – 2:30 minutes.

Herr, wann ich nur dich habe SWV321 (Psalm 73:25–26) – SST solos and basso continuo – 3 minutes.

Die Seele Christi heilige mich SWV325 – ATB solos and basso continuo – 4 minutes.

Ich ruf zu dir, Herr Jesu Christ SWV326 – SSSB solos and basso continuo – 2:15 minutes.

Ist Gott für uns SWV329 (Romans 8:31) – SATB solos and basso continuo – 2:45 minutes.

Die Stimm des Herren SWV331 (Psalm 29:4) – SATB solos and basso continuo – 4:30 minutes.

Jubilate Deo omnis terra SWV332 (Psalm 100) – SATB solos and basso continuo – 5:30 minutes.

Sei gegrüsset, Maria SWV333 (Luke 1:28–38) – SA solos, SSATB chorus, and optional five-part unspecified instruments – 6 minutes. (1) The solos, accompanied by basso continuo, consist of a dialogue between the angel Gabriel (A) and the Virgin Mary (S); (2) the chorus is scored for one short movement that closes the work; (3) the instruments are scored for a brief opening *symphonia;* (4) identical music is used for *Ave Maria* SWV334.

Was betrübst du dich SWV335 – SSATB solos and basso continuo – 3:30 minutes.

THE SEVEN LAST WORDS – 1645

Die sieben Wortte unsers lieben Erlösers und Seeligmachers Jesu Christi: so er am Stamm des Heiligen Creutzes gesprochen SWV478 (The seven words of our blessed savior and redeemer Jesus Christ: which he spoke on the trunk of the holy cross) – SAATTB solos, SATTB chorus, five gambas, and basso continuo – 20 minutes. (1) Solo roles are for the Evangelist (S, A, and T), Jesus (T), and Left and Right Criminals (A and B); (2) the chorus sings opening (*Introitus*) and closing (*Conclusio*) movements in addition to several short *turba* passages; (3) the gambas accompany the words of Jesus, play two interludes, and accompany the chorus *colla parte.*

SYMPHONIAE SACRAE, BOOK TWO – 1647
SELECTED AND LISTED IN ORDER OF SWV NUMBER

Von Gott will ich nicht lassen SWV366 – SSB solos, two violins, and basso continuo – 8:15 minutes.

Freuet euch des Herren, ihr Gerechten SWV367 – ATB solos, two violins, and basso continuo – 7 minutes.

GEISTLICHE CHOR-MUSIC – 1648
SELECTED AND LISTED IN ORDER OF SWV NUMBER

Es wird das Szepter von Juda SWV369 (Genesis 49:10–11) – SATTB chorus and optional basso continuo – 3:30 minutes.

Es ist erschienen die heilsame Gande Gottes SWV371 (Titus 2:11–14) – SSATB chorus and optional basso continuo – 4 minutes.

Die mit Tränen säen SWV378 (Psalm 126:5–6) – SSATB chorus and optional basso continuo – 3:15 minutes.

Also hat Gott die Welt geliebt SWV380 (John 3:16) – SATTB chorus and optional basso continuo – 3 minutes.

Ich bin eine rufende Stimme SWV383 (John 1:23, 26–27) – SSATTB chorus and optional basso continuo – 4 minutes.

Ein Kind ist uns geboren SWV384 (Isaiah 9:5–6) – SSATTB chorus and optional basso continuo – 2:30 minutes.

Die Himmel erzählen die Ehre Gottes SWV386 (Psalm 19:2–7) – SSATTB chorus and optional basso continuo – 5 minutes.

Selig sind die Toten SWV391 (Psalm 126:5–6) – SSATB chorus and optional basso continuo – 4:15 minutes.

SYMPHONIAE SACRAE, BOOK THREE – 1650
SELECTED AND LISTED IN ORDER OF SWV NUMBER

Wo der Herr nicht das Haus bauet SWV400 (Psalm 127) – SSB solos, two violins, and basso continuo – 7 minutes.

Mein Sohn, warum hast du uns das getan SWV401 (Luke 2:48–49 and Psalm 84:1–4) – SAB solos, SATB chorus, two violins, two violas, and basso continuo – 7:30 minutes. (1) Solo roles are for the Boy Jesus (S), Mary (A), and Joseph (B); (2) the instruments accompany the chorus *colla parte* except for a short opening *symphonia.*

O Herr hilf, o Herr lass wohl gelingen SWV402 (Psalm 118:25 and Matthew 21:9) – SSB solos, two violins, and basso continuo – 3 minutes.

Siehe, es erschien der Engel des Herren SWV403 (Matthew 2:13–15) – STTB solos, SATB chorus, two violins, and basso continuo – 4:45 minutes.

Vater unser, der du bist im Himmel SWV411 (Matthew 6:9–13) – T solo, SATTB/SATB chorus, and basso continuo – 5:30 minutes. (1) The T solo is brief; (2) the second chorus (SATB), also brief, occurs at the end of the motet.

Saul, Saul, was verfolgst du mich SWV415 (Acts 9:4–5) – SSATBB/SATB/SATB voices, two violins, and basso continuo – 3 minutes.

Nun danket alle Gott SWV418 – SSATTB/SATB voices, two violins, and basso continuo – 5:30 minutes.

ZWÖLFF GEISTLICHE GESÄNGE – 1657
SELECTED AND LISTED IN ORDER OF SWV NUMBER

Kyrie, Gott Vater in Ewigkeit SWV420 – SATB voices and optional basso continuo – 7 minutes.

Unser Herr Jesus Christus in der Nacht SWV423 (1 Corinthians 11:23–25 and Matthew 26:26–28) – SATB voices and optional basso continuo – 5 minutes.

Aller Augen warten auf dich SWV429 (Psalm 145:15–16 and Matthew 6:9–13) – SATB voices and optional basso continuo – 4 minutes. The motet is a blessing before eating.

CHRISTMAS ORATORIO – 1664

Historia, der freuden- und gnadenreichen Geburth Gottes und Marien Sohnes, Jesu Christi SWV435 (History of the joyful and miraculous birth of God and Mary, Jesus Christ) – STB solos, SATB chorus, two recorders, two trombones, two trumpets, bassoon, four gambas, and basso continuo – 50 minutes. (1) Major solo roles are for an Angel (S), the Evangelist (T), and Herod (B); (2) minor solo roles are for three Shepherds (AAA), three Kings (TTT), four High Priests (BBBB), and a chorus of Angels (SSATTB); (3) the SATB chorus sings opening (*Eingang*) and closing (*Beschluss*) movements; (4) various combinations of instruments pervade the oratorio.

PASSIONS – 1665–1666
SELECTED

Historie des Leidens und Sterbens unsers Herrn und Heylandes Jesu Christi: nach dem Evangelisten St Johannem SWV481 (History of the suffering and death of our Lord and Redeemer Jesus Christ: as told by St John) – STTTBB solos and SATB chorus – 40 minutes. (1) Major solo roles are for the Evangelist (T), Jesus (B), and Pilate (T); (2) minor solo roles are for a Maid (S), Peter (T), and a High Priest (B); (3) the chorus sings opening (*Exordium*) and closing (*Beschluss*) movements in addition to numerous *turba* passages.

GERMAN MAGNIFICAT – 1671

Meine Seele erhebt den Herren SWV494 – SATB/SATB chorus and basso continuo – 8 minutes.

PSALM 119 – 1671

Königs und Propheten Davids hundert und neunzehender Psalm SWV482–492 (Psalm 119) – SATB/SATB chorus and basso continuo – 75 minutes.

JOHANN HERMANN SCHEIN 1586–1630

Schein was born near Dresden and received his musical training at the Dresden Hofkapellen and the University of Leipzig. In 1613 he was employed to teach the children of a noble family in Weissenfels, and in 1615 he was appointed *Kapellmeister* to Duke Johann Ernst the Younger in Weimar. A year later he took the prestigious position of *Kantor* at Leipzig's two main Lutheran churches, the Thomaskirche and the Nikolaikirche, a position he held for the remainder of his life and the same position J. S. Bach would hold a little more than a century later. In addition to his duties at the Leipzig churches, Schein had the opportunity to compose occasional music for weddings, burials, and town council elections. He was a respected composer and was often linked to his contemporaries with like-sounding names, Heinrich Schütz (born a year before Schein) and Samuel Scheidt (born a year after Schein). The German theorist and historian Wolfgang Capsar Printz referred to the three composers in his 1690 publication *Historische Beschreibung der edelen Sing- und Kling-Kunst* (Historical Description of the Noble Art of Singing and Playing) as the great S's. Schein was a prolific composer of both sacred and secular vocal music, and all of his music emulated the late Renaissance madrigalistic style. This style is especially notable in the sacred repertoire, which Schein specifically intended to be secular in treatment of text. For instance, the collection entitled *Fontana d'Israel* contains twenty-six madrigals set to German religious poetry that Schein stated were "auf . . . Italian-Madrigalische Manier" (in the Italian madrigal style).

Schein composed 353 sacred and ninety-seven secular works, most of which were issued in eight publications—four sacred and four secular. This vast output is impressive given the fact that Schein suffered from a variety of illnesses (including tuberculosis, gout, and scurvy) and that he died at the young age of forty-four.

The sacred publications—*Cymbalum Sionium* (1615), *Opella nova* (1618 and 1626), *Fontana d'Israel* or *Israelis Brünnlein* (1623), and *Cantional* (1627)—are similar to those of Samuel Scheidt: the first volume contains Latin and German motets scored for multiple choruses a cappella; the middle volumes contain many motets based on Lutheran chorales scored for a variety of voices and basso continuo; and the final volume is a collection of strophic chorales—some arrangements of existing tunes and some new compositions. In addition, the publications are stylistically similar to those of Scheidt: the early motets are in a Venetian dialogue style (e.g., *Alleluia! Ich danke dem Herren*); the middle motets are characterized by varying rhythmic patterns that highlight textual expression (e.g., the famous *Die mit Tränen säen*); and the final works are hymn-like pieces for both liturgical and private devotional usage (e.g., *Nun komm, der Heiden Heiland*, which appears in two settings at the beginning of *Cantional*). Also like Scheidt, Schein often composed multiple settings of the same text. An example is *Christ lag in Todesbanden*, scored for three voices in *Opella nova* and for both four and five voices in *Cantional*.

The secular publications—*Venus Kräntzlein* (1609), *Musica boscareccia* (1621, 1626, and 1628), *Diletti pastorali* (1624), and *Studenten-Schmauss* (1626)—are unique in that Schein was one of the few German composers of the Baroque era to have a serious interest in secular music and to write his own texts. *Venus Kräntzlein* contains homophonic pieces that have a folk song quality and that are generally scored for SSATB voices a cappella. The three *Musica boscareccia* (also called *Wald-Liederlein*) volumes contain pieces set to texts that are reminiscent of the Italian pastoral poetry of the 1570s and that are scored for SSB (the bass part has both text and figures and can therefore be sung and also played as a basso continuo). The music was quite popular; all three volumes were reprinted numerous times, including a publication entitled *Musica boscareccia sacra* that substituted sacred texts for the original secular poetry. *Diletti pastorali* contains madrigal-like pieces scored for SSATB voices and basso continuo, and *Studenten-Schmauss* contains five drinking songs for SSATB voices, the bass part of which also has figures for basso continuo.

The compositions for special events in Leipzig are often more elaborate in both scoring and style than the compositions contained in the above-mentioned publications. Examples include the funeral motets *Herr, wie lange* and *Ich will schweigen*, the celebratory motet *Freuet euch des Herren*, and the setting of Psalm 116, *Das ist mir lieb*, composed for a wealthy merchant who commissioned sixteen composers (including Christoph Demantius, Michael Praetorius, Melchior Franck, and Heinrich Schütz) to set Psalm 116 in the year 1616 and who published the collection under the title *Angst der Hellen und Friede der Seelen*. Schein's setting is the first in the collection.

SACRED MOTETS
SELECTED AND LISTED IN ORDER OF PUBLICATION

Lobet den Herrn in seinem Heiligtum – 1615 – SSATB voices a cappella – 5:30 minutes.

Verbum caro factum est – 1615 – SSATTB voices a cappella – 6 minutes.

O Domine Jesu Christe – 1615 – SSATTB voices a cappella – 5 minutes.

Ich will schweigen (Psalm 39:10–12) – 1617 – SSATTB voices a cappella – 4:45 minutes.

Christ lag in Todesbanden – 1618 – SSB voices and basso continuo – 6 minutes.

Gelobet seist du, Jesu Christ – 1618 – SSB voices and basso continuo – 2:30 minutes.

Vater unser im Himmelreich – 1618 – SSB voices and basso continuo – 3 minutes.

Aus tiefer Not – 1618 – SSB voices and basso continuo – 2:30 minutes.

Ich ruf zu dir – 1618 – SSB voices and basso continuo – 3 minutes.

Die mit Tränen säen (Psalm 126:5–6) – 1623 – SSATB voices and basso continuo – 3 minutes.

Ist nicht Ephraim mein teurer Sohn – 1623 – SSATB voices and basso continuo – 5 minutes.

Siehe, nach Trost war mir sehr bange (Isaiah 38:17–19) – 1623 – SSATB voices and basso continuo – 5 minutes.

Das ist mir lieb (Psalm 116) – 1623 – SSATB voices and instruments *colla parte* – 7:30 minutes.

Nun danket alle Gott – 1623 – SSATTB voices and basso continuo – 4:30 minutes.

Ich freue mich im Herren – 1623 – SSATB voices and basso continuo – 3:15 minutes.

Wende dich, Herr (Psalm 25:16–18) – 1623 – SSATB voices and basso continuo – 4 minutes.

Herr, lass meine Klage (Psalm 119:169–171) – 1623 – SSATB voices and basso continuo – 3 minutes.

Herr, wie lange (Psalm 13:2–4) – 1627 – SSATB voices and basso continuo – 6 minutes.

Nun komm, der Heiden Heiland – 1627 – two settings for SATB voices and basso continuo – 2 minutes (chorale with eight verses) and 45 seconds (motet with one verse).

Von [sic] *Himmel hoch da komm ich her* – 1627 – two settings for SATB voices and basso continuo – 3 minutes (chorale with 15 verses) and 45 seconds (motet with one verse).

Komm, heiliger Geist – 1627 – two settings for SATB voices and basso continuo – 2 minutes (chorale with three verses) and 2 minutes (motet with one verse).

Zion spricht, der Herr hat (Isaiah 49:14–16) – 1629 – SSATB voices and basso continuo – 4:30 minutes.

SECULAR PART SONGS
SELECTED AND LISTED ACCORDING TO FAMILIARITY

Mein Schifflein lief im wilden Meer – 1624 – SSATB voices and basso continuo – 4 minutes.

O Amarilla zart – 1624 – SSATB voices and basso continuo – 2:45 minutes.

Aurora schön mit ihrem Haar – 1624 – SSATB voices and basso continuo – 3 minutes.

Die Vöglein singen – 1624 – SSATB voices and basso continuo – 2 minutes.

Ihr Brüder, lieben Brüder mein – 1626 – SSATB voices and basso continuo – 3 minutes.

SAMUEL SCHEIDT 1587–1654

Scheidt was born in Halle, northwest of Leipzig, where he studied at the local gymnasium. At age sixteen he was appointed organist at the Moritzkirche in Halle, at twenty he went to Amsterdam to study with Jan Pieterszoon Sweelinck, and at twenty-two he returned to Halle to serve as court organist to Margrave Christian Wilhelm of Brandenburg. His duties at the court included composing and playing both organ and harpsichord music, as well as working with notable guests such as Michael Praetorius (who visited the court in 1616) and Heinrich Schütz (who visited in 1618). Scheidt also traveled with Praetorius and Schütz to the courts in Magdeburg in 1618 and Bayreuth in 1619. In 1619 Scheidt was officially appointed *Kapellmeister*, the duties of which he added to those of organist, and for the next six years he led a flourishing and highly regarded musical establishment. Unfortunately, the Margrave joined the Thirty Years War in 1625, and the court's musical resources were reduced dramatically; most of the singers and instrumentalists left Halle, and Scheidt, who remained, received no salary. He earned his living for several years by teaching and composing for various patrons in other cities, and in 1628 he was appointed *director musices* for the city of Halle, a position that included directing music for civic occasions and serving as *Kapellmeister* at Halle's main church, the Marktkirche. The court returned to its former splendor in 1638 under the leadership of Duke August of Saxony, and Scheidt was able to resume his role as *Kapellmeister* and lead a once-again successful musical establishment until his death on Good Friday in 1654.

His choral output consists of two masses, fourteen Magnificats, twenty-eight Latin motets, 147 German motets, and 113 chorales. The works in all the genres except chorales were generally composed in a *prima prattica* style that was common to most German composers during the early years of the Baroque era. The vocal texture consists of short fragments of text, often consisting of only one or two words, that are given a point-of-imitation treatment; rhythmic patterns are varied for expressive purposes, with occasional examples of word painting; and scoring is for voices with basso continuo that is mainly a replication of the vocal bass part. The few compositions with accompaniment beyond basso continuo are scored for unspecified instruments *colla parte*.

The masses—*Missa super Herr unser Herrscher* and *Missa super Nun danket alle Gott*—are both settings of the Kyrie and Gloria in the *prima prattica* style described above and are based on Lutheran chorale melodies. Eight of the Magnificats form a cycle (each cycle consisting of one Magnificat on each of the eight Gregorian chant tones); the other six are for important liturgical feasts and contain Lutheran chorales interpolated into the Latin text. The *Magnificat* SSWV299 alternates six verses of the traditional Latin text with six chorales for Christmas, including "Vom Himmel hoch," "Das Kindelein in dem Krippelein," "Psallite unigenito," and "Joseph, lieber, Joseph mein." Likewise, the *Magnificat* SSWV309 alternates six verses of the Latin text with six chorales for Easter, including "Jesus Christus, unser Heiland," "Ich bin die

Auferstehung," and "Erstanden ist der Herre Christ." The Latin verses and the chorales in these two settings, along with a setting for Whitsunday, are scored for a variety of voices, including duets and trios.

Most of the motets are contained in six publications—*Cantiones sacrae octo vocem* (1620), *Concertuum sacrorum* (1622), and four books of *Geistliche Concerten* (1631, 1634, 1635, and 1640). The 1620 publication contains Latin and German motets for double chorus a cappella, the 1622 publication contains motets for a variety of voice combinations and instruments (mostly *colla parte*), and the remaining publications contain works for a variety of voice combinations— generally few in number—and basso continuo. In addition, these later books are arranged according to the liturgical year, with settings of texts for the major feast days grouped together. Scheidt set many of the most common Latin and German texts used in the Lutheran Church, and of these he made multiple settings of the more popular texts. The longer motets are divided into multiple sections, each scored for different voice combinations. For example, *Cantate Domino* SSWV73 is in five sections, one each for TT, AT, TTB, SATB, and SATTB. The motets that are most popular today are *Surrexit pastor bonus* SSWV23, *Angelus ad pastores* SSWV13, *In dulci jubilo* SSWV15, and *Duo Seraphim* SSWV10—this latter motet distinguished by its word painting: the phrase "Duo Seraphim clamabant alter ad altcrum: sanctus, sanctus, sanctus, Dominus Deus sabaoth" (Two Seraphim proclaimed one to another, holy, holy, holy, Lord God of hosts) is sung by two soloists, and "Plena est omnis terra gloria ejus" (The whole earth is full of his glory) is sung by all vocal forces. Also popular are the Magnificat settings SSWV299 and 309.

MASS AND MAGNIFICATS
SELECTED AND LISTED IN ORDER OF SSWV NUMBERS

Magnificat SSWV74 – SATB/SATB voices and unspecified *colla parte* instruments – 5:30 minutes.

Missa super Herr unser Herrscher SSWV83 – SATB/SATB voices and unspecified *colla parte* instruments – 8:30 minutes. (1) The Mass includes only the Kyrie and Gloria; (2) portions of the mass are scored for SS, T, and STB.

Magnificat SSWV299 – SSATTB voices and basso continuo – 16 minutes. This setting incorporates chorales for Christmas.

Magnificat SSWV309 – SSATB voices and basso continuo – 17 minutes. This setting incorporates chorales for Easter.

Deutsches Magnificat SSWV331 – SATB voices and basso continuo – 7:30 minutes.

MOTETS
SELECTED AND LISTED IN ORDER OF SSWV NUMBERS

Komm, heiliger Geist SSWV8 – SATB/SATB voices a cappella – 4 minutes.

Duo Seraphim SSWV10 (Isaiah 6:1–3) – SS solos and SSAT/ATBB voices a cappella – 4 minutes.

Angelus ad pastores SSWV13 (Luke 2:10–11) – SATB/SATB voices a cappella – 3:45 minutes.

In dulci jubilo SSWV15 – SATB/SATB voices and two trumpets (*clarini*) – 3:30 minutes.

Ein feste Burg ist unser Gott SSWV16 – SATB/SATB voices a cappella – 4:30 minutes.

Surrexit pastor bonus SSWV23 – SATB/SATB voices a cappella – 4 minutes.

Nun danket alle Gott SSWV30 – SATB/SATB voices a cappella – 3 minutes.

Cantate Domino SSWV73 (Psalm 96:1–6) – SATTB voices, trumpet (*cornet*), four violas (*viola bracci*), three trombones (*tromboni*), four bassoons, and basso continuo – 6:30 minutes.

Angelus ad pastores SSWV77 (Luke 2:10–11) – SATB/SATB voices and unspecified *colla parte* instruments – 5:30 minutes.

Wir glauben all an einen Gott SSWV182 – STB voices and basso continuo – 7 minutes.

Vater unser im Himmelreich SSWV184 – STB voices and basso continuo – 5 minutes.

Wie schön leuchtet der Morgenstern SSWV185 – STTB voices and basso continuo – 7:30 minutes. The motet is in three sections—the first scored for STB, the second for TTB, and the third for TTB or SSB.

Danket dem Herren SSWV196 (Psalm 136) – STB voices and basso continuo – 9 minutes. Melodic passages marked "vox sola" alternate with choral passages.

An Wasser flüssen Babylon SSWV203 (Psalm 137) – STB voices and basso continuo – 6 minutes.

Ein feste Burg ist unser Gott SSWV206 – SSTB voices and basso continuo – 7 minutes. The motet is in two sections—the first scored for STB and the second for SS or TT.

Herr, unser Herrscher SSWV217 (Psalm 8:1–4) – SSTB voices and basso continuo – 7:30 minutes. Distinctive features of the motet include choral recitative, echo effects, and word painting.

Miserere mei Deus SSWV223 (Psalm 50:3) – SATBBB voices, four violas da gamba *colla parte,* and basso continuo – 5:30 minutes.

Lobet, ihr Himmel, den Herren SSWV225 (Psalm 48:1–6) – SSATTB voices and basso continuo – 7 minutes. (1) The motet is in three sections—the first and last scored for SSATTB and the middle for TT; (2) distinctive features of the motet include echo effects, forceful homophonic passages, and word painting.

Jauchzet Gott, alle Land SSWV249 (Psalm 66:1–9) – SSATB voices and basso continuo – 6 minutes.

Nun komm, der Heiden Heiland SSWV279 – ATB voices and basso continuo – 8 minutes.

Resonet in laudibus SSWV286 – SSTB voices and basso continuo – 5 minutes.

Ein Kind geborn zu Bethlehem SSWV292 – SSATTB voices and basso continuo – 6:30 minutes.

Ein Kindelein so löbelich SSWV297 – SATB voices and basso continuo – 5 minutes.

Christ lag in Todesbanden SSWV303 – STB voices and basso continuo – 3:30 minutes.

Lobet den Herren, alle Heiden SSWV332 – SSATTB voices and basso continuo – 4 minutes.

JOHANNES CRÜGER 1598–1662

Crüger was born and educated in Guben, a city near Berlin on the border between Germany and Poland. During his teenage years he traveled extensively throughout northern Germany, Austria, and Hungary, and eventually he settled for a period in Wittenberg, where he studied theology. From 1615 to 1622 he served as a tutor to the children of a noble family in Berlin, and from 1622 to the end of his life he served as *Kantor* at the Nikolaikirche.

Crüger is best known for his chorale settings, and he is acknowledged to be the first person in Germany to set chorales to a figured bass (some scored for only melody and figured bass and some scored for four voices and figured bass). His settings, published in five collections during his life, include more than five hundred arrangements of preexisting melodies and approximately twenty original compositions. The most popular of the collections—*Praxis pietatis melica*—went through several revisions and more than forty reprints. The original publication in 1647 contained simple, homophonic settings for four voices and basso continuo. A revision in 1649, entitled *Geistliche Kirchen-Melodien,* included settings for four voices, two optional obbligato instruments (either violin or trumpet), and basso continuo. A second revision in 1658, entitled *Psalmodia sacra,* included settings for four voices, three unspecified instruments, and basso continuo. The settings with obbligato instruments were in effect vocal concertos, very similar to those by Claudio Monteverdi and Heinrich Schütz, although Crüger's compositions were unique in that they involved chorale melodies. Many of Crüger's original chorale melodies are some of the most well known chorales of today, including "Herzliebster Jesu," "Jesu, meine Freude," and "Schmücke dich, o liebe Seele."

THOMAS SELLE 1599–1663

Selle was born in Bitterfeld, near Leipzig. Nothing certain is known about his life before his enrollment at the University of Leipzig, although it is probable that during his youth he studied at the Thomasschule under Sethus Calvisius (1556–1615). From approximately 1624 to 1641 he held *Kantor* positions in Heide and Itzehoe, and from 1641 until his death he served as *Kantor* at the Johanneum in Hamburg.

He composed two oratorio Passions, including a *Johannespassion* that was considered to be one of the finest Passion settings of the seventeenth century, 282 motets (eighty-nine set to Latin texts and 193 to German texts), and two masses. The *Johannespassion* is scored for SSATTB solos, SSATTB chorus, two trumpets, trombone, three violins, two bassoons, and basso continuo, with major solo roles for an Evangelist (T), Jesus (B), and Pilate (A), and minor solo roles for a Maid (S), Peter (T), and a Servant (S). Each of the solos is scored for a different combination of instruments (e.g., two bassoons and basso continuo for the Evangelist, and two violins and basso continuo for Jesus). The Passion was one of the first of its kind to be scored for independent instruments and to have instrumental interludes. The motets are in the style of Johann Hermann Schein, who was *Kantor* at the Thomasschule before Calvisius; text phrases are treated with varying rhythmic patterns, and textures are characterized by vocal concerto-like effects. The masses are both settings of the Kyrie and Gloria—the *Missa à 8* scored for SATB/SATB chorus and basso continuo in a dialogue style, and the *Missa super Sey mir gnädig* scored for SATTB chorus and basso continuo.

Andreas Hammerschmidt CA.1611–1675

Hammerschmidt was born in Brüx, Bohemia (now the Czech Republic), where he most likely received his early musical education. At age eighteen he moved with his family to Freiberg, Germany, and at twenty-two he was appointed organist at the court of Count Rudolf von Brünau in Weesenstein. The following year he became organist at the church of St Petri in Freiberg, and five years later he assumed the same position at St Johannis in Zittau, where he remained until his death. He was a highly respected organist and composer, invited to cities in northern Germany to inspect and concertize on organs, and he received numerous laudatory comments from notable composers of the time, including Heinrich Schütz. At the time of his death he was called the Orpheus of Zittau.

Hammerschmidt composed approximately 420 sacred works (motets, cantatas, vocal concertos, and arias) and sixty-eight secular part songs. Most of the motets, with texts in Latin and German, are in a traditional imitative *prima prattica* style, scored for voices and optional basso continuo and modeled after the compositions in Schütz's *Geistliche Chor-Music*. The cantatas, vocal concertos, and arias, with texts only in German, are in the *seconda prattica* style of *concertato* works scored for soloists, chorus, various obbligato instruments, and basso continuo. Both motets and cantatas, all composed for the Lutheran Church, are characterized by madrigalistic word painting (Hammerschmidt even called a number of the pieces sacred madrigals). Examples of the motets include *Singet dem Herrn ein neues Lied* (Psalm 96:1–3) for SATB solos, SATB chorus that alternates in *concertato* fashion with the soloists, and optional basso continuo; *Schaffe in mir, Gott, ein reines Herz* (Psalm 51:12–14) for SSATBB chorus and optional basso continuo; *Meine Seele erhebet den Herrn* (The German Magnificat) for SS solos, SSATB chorus, two violins, two violas, and basso continuo; and *Wie lieblich sind deine Wohnungen* (Psalm 84:2–3) for SSATB chorus and optional basso continuo. Examples of the cantatas include *O ihr lieben Hirten*, a Christmas work scored for SATB solos, SATB chorus, two unspecified obbligato instruments, and basso continuo; *Darum wachet, denn ihr wisset weder Tag* (Matthew 25:13 and the last stanza of "Wie schön leuchtet der Morgenstern") for SSATB chorus, two violins, and basso continuo; *Wo ist der neugeborne König der Juden* (Matthew 2:2, 5 and "Ein Kind geboren zu Bethlehem"), a work for Epiphany scored for SSATB chorus, two violins, and basso continuo; and *Heilig ist der Herr,* a work for Trinity Sunday scored for SSATB chorus, two unspecified obbligato instruments, and basso continuo.

The secular pieces, published in three volumes of *Weltliche Oden* (1642, 1643, and 1649), are settings of common German poems of the time scored as solos, duets, and trios, with violin obbligato and basso continuo accompaniment.

FRANZ TUNDER 1614–1667

Tunder was born in Bannesdorf, north of Hamburg, where he most likely studied with his father and the *Kantor* of a church in the nearby town of Burg. At age eighteen he was appointed court organist in Gottorf, and at twenty-seven he became organist at the Marienkirche in Lübeck, where he would remain until his death. In addition to his regular duties at the church, he organized evening concerts, called *Abendmusiken,* modeled after similar concerts in the Netherlands. These evening concerts, which Tunder's successor Dietrich Buxtehude would make famous, featured organ and vocal works by a variety of German and Italian composers.

Since many of Tunder's vocal compositions were not published, his complete output is unknown. All that exist today are seventeen vocal concertos and motets. Examples of the vocal concertos, all characteristic of church cantatas written by later German Baroque composers, are *Helft mir Gottes Güte preisen* for SSATB voices, strings, and basso continuo; *Wend' ab deinen Zorn* for SSATTB voices, strings, and basso continuo; and *Ein' feste Burg* for SATB voices, strings, and basso continuo. Each of these works is based on a Lutheran chorale melody used as a cantus firmus, and each is divided into sections of music based on verses of the chorale text. The motets—including *Salve coelestis pater, O Jesu dulcissime,* and *Hosianna dem Sohne Davids*—are similar to works by Heinrich Schütz, with numerous examples of word painting and with musical motifs that mirror spoken speech inflections.

DIETRICH BUXTEHUDE CA.1637–1707

The precise location of Buxtehude's birth is unknown. He claimed to have been born in Denmark, but there are no records of this, and knowledge of his family's location does not begin until approximately 1638, when his father, Johannes (ca.1601–1674), was appointed organist at St Maria Kyrka in Helsingborg, Denmark. Dietrich presumably studied with his father, whose career he paralleled closely. In 1657 he became organist at St Maria Kyrka in Helsingborg, and in 1660 he was appointed organist at the Marienkirche in Elsinore (a church close to St Olai Kirke, where his father was organist at the time). In 1668 he succeeded Franz Tunder as organist at the Marienkirche in Lübeck, Germany. This was one of the most prestigious sacred musical positions in northern Germany, one that Buxtehude would hold and one whose reputation would be maintained for forty years. Numerous musical dignitaries, including George Frideric Handel in 1703 and J. S. Bach in 1705, visited Buxtehude to hear his famous Abendmusik concerts—performances presented each year on the five Sunday evenings before Christmas.

It should be noted that the organist at the Marienkirche and other relatively small churches was in effect the *Kapellmeister,* with responsibilities for composing, leading the music program, and performing at the keyboard. It should also be noted that Buxtehude was best known as an organ virtuoso, acclaimed for his improvisations, and it was probably for this reason that luminaries such as Handel and Bach, both keyboard virtuosos themselves, traveled to Lübeck.

Buxtehude composed 128 surviving works, all but eight of them sacred, and almost all of them small-scale compositions written for the liturgical services at the Marienkirche. These works exhibit the characteristics of Baroque *seconda prattica* vocal concertos as composed by Claudio Monteverdi and Heinrich Schütz: they are scored for one to three voices, two violins, and basso continuo, and they are characterized by varied rhythms and expressive word painting. However, the works were called cantatas, not vocal concertos, probably because Buxtehude was not a cosmopolitan traveler like most of his colleagues (he left Lübeck only once—to visit Hamburg in 1687 to examine a new organ there) and was therefore not aware of the cantata as a secular genre. Moreover, he had almost no exposure to secular music. Whether or not this lack of knowledge was the cause for the shift in terminology, the cantata as named by Buxtehude would lose its secular connotation over time and become a sacred genre associated with Protestant services for all future historical eras.

The structure of the typical cantata, as illustrated by *Jesu, meine Freude* BuxWV60, consists of an opening instrumental prelude followed by sections of music (delineated by biblical or poetic verses) scored for various solos, duets, and trios, with frequent and intermittent instrumental ritornellos. This is also the structure of Buxtehude's extraordinary work *Membra Jesu nostri* BuxWV75, which is a collection of seven cantatas set to the Latin poem *Rythmica Oratio* by the medieval French theologian and mystic Bernard de Clairvaux (1090–1153). Buxtehude's seven cantatas follow the seven sections of the poem, each one of which is addressed to a part of Jesus' body—"Ad pedes" (to the feet); "Ad genua" (to the knees); "Ad manus" (to the hands); "Ad latus" (to the side); "Ad pectus" (to the breast); "Ad cor" (to the heart); and "Ad faciem" (to the face).

CANTATAS

SELECTED AND LISTED IN ORDER OF BUXWV NUMBER (ALSO ALPHABETICAL BY TITLE)

Afferte Domino gloriam, honorem BuxWV2 (Psalm 28:3) – SSB voices and basso continuo – 6 minutes.

Aperite mihi portas justitiae BuxWV7 (Psalm 118:19–20, 24–26) – ATB voices, two violins, and basso continuo – 5 minutes.

Befiehl dem Engel, dass er komm BuxWV10 – SATB voices, two violins, and basso continuo – 6 minutes. The cantata is for Michaelmas and is based on the chorale "Christe, du bist der helle Tag."

Cantate Domino canticum novum BuxWV12 (Psalm 96) – SSB voices and basso continuo – 8 minutes.

Das neugebor'ne Kindelein BuxWV13 – SATB voices, three violins, and basso continuo – 6:30 minutes. The cantata is for New Year's services.

Der Herr ist mit mir BuxWV15 (Psalm 118:6–7) – SATB voices, two violins, and basso continuo – 5:15 minutes.

Du Frieden-Fürst, Herr Jesu Christ BuxWV21 – SSB voices, two violins, two violas, bassoon, and basso continuo – 11 minutes.

Erfreue dich, Erde, der Himmel erschall BuxWV26 – SSAB voices, two trumpets, timpani, two violins, and basso continuo – 5:30 minutes.

Erhalt uns, Herr, bei deinem Wort BuxWV27 – SATB voices, two violins, and basso continuo – 5 minutes.

Herzlich lieb, hab ich dich o Herr BuxWV41 – SSATB voices, two violins, two violas, and basso continuo – 9:30 minutes.

In dulci jubilo BuxWV52 – SSB voices, two violins, and basso continuo – 7 minutes. The cantata is for Christmas.

Jesu dulcis memoria BuxWV56 – SS voices, two violins, and basso continuo – 9:30 minutes.

Jesu dulcis memoria BuxWV57 – ATB voices, two violins, and basso continuo – 7:15 minutes.

Jesu, komm, mein Trost und Lachen BuxWV58 – ATB voices, two violins, viola, and basso continuo – 9 minutes.

Jesu, meine Freude BuxWV60 – SSB voices, two violins, and basso continuo – 6:30 minutes.

Nichts soll uns scheiden von der Liebe Gottes BuxWV77 (Romans 8:39) – SAB voices, two violins, and basso continuo – 10:30 minutes.

Nun danket alle Gott BuxWV79 – SSATB voices, four trumpets, two violins, viola, and basso continuo – 13 minutes.

Pange lingua gloriosi corporis mysterium BuxWV91 – SSAB voices, two violins, two violas, and basso continuo – 5 minutes. The cantata is for communion services.

Surrexit Christus hodie BuxWV99 – SSB voices, three violins, and basso continuo – 5:45 minutes. The cantata is for Easter.

Wachet auf, ruft uns die Stimme BuxWV100 – SSB voices, three violins, viola, and basso continuo – 7 minutes.

Walts Gott mein Werk ich lasse BuxWV103 – SATB voices, two violins, and basso continuo – 6:30 minutes.

OTHER SACRED WORKS
SELECTED AND LISTED ACCORDING TO FAMILIARITY

Membra Jesu nostri BuxWV75 (The limbs of Christ) – SSATB voices, two violins, five violas, and basso continuo – 58 minutes. The violas are used in only the sixth movement.

Benedicam Dominum BuxWV113 (Psalm 34) – SSATB solos, SATB chorus, bassoon, two cornettos, four trumpets, five trombones, two violins, and basso continuo – 7:30 minutes.

Missa brevis BuxWV114 – SSATB and basso continuo – 9 minutes. This work, which some scholars believe is not by Buxtehude, is a setting of the Kyrie and Gloria.

JOHANN CHRISTOPH BACH 1642–1703

Johann Christoph Bach, uncle of Johann Sebastian (1685–1750) and brother of Johann Michael (1648–1694), is considered the most important member of the Bach family in the generations before his nephew. He was born in Arnstadt, the city in which many of the Bachs lived and worked, and he studied with his father, Heinrich, who was town musician and organist at the Liebfrauenkirche. In 1663 Johann Christoph was appointed organist at the Arnstadt Castle chapel, and in 1665 he moved to the nearby town of Eisenach, where he remained until his death at age sixty-one and where he held a number of positions, including organist of the Georgenkirche, civic organist, and harpsichordist and composer for the Duke of Eisenach. While in Eisenach he also worked closely with his cousin, the trumpeter Johann Ambrosius Bach (1645–1695), who was Johann Sebastian's father. Johann Christoph was highly regarded during his time; Johann Sebastian, who performed many of his motets and cantatas during his first years as *Kantor* at the Thomaskirche in Leipzig, referred to his works as profound.

Johann Christoph Bach composed thirteen motets, three choral cantatas, and one work called a *dialogus* for an ensemble of soloists. Most of these works were collected in the *Alt-Bachisches Archiv*. The motets are in the style typical of the time: they are scored for chorus with basso continuo accompaniment (which generally replicates the vocal parts and is therefore rarely independent); the chorus parts usually divide into two SATB ensembles that participate in a dialogue of short motifs as in the motets of Heinrich Schütz; the texts often combine biblical passages and pietistic poetry; the inclusion of Lutheran chorales is common, with a statement of the chorale tune as a cantus firmus at the end of the motet; the texts frequently deal with funereal themes or festival occasions such as Christmas; and there are tempo and meter changes that characterize the various portions of text. Bach's most famous motet, *Ich lasse dich nicht,* is an example. It is in two parts, the first of which consists of a dialogue between two SATB choruses and the second of which consists of the two choruses joined into one. The second part also contains the chorale tune "Warum betrübst du dich, mein Herz" and is in a different meter and tempo.

The cantatas, sometimes called vocal concertos, are also typical of the time: they are scored for solo voices, chorus, and orchestra of strings and basso continuo; the parts for soloists are brief; the texts consist of pietistic poetry derived from biblical stories; and the music is divided into short sections that are varied in tempo and meter similar to the early cantatas of J. S. Bach. The twenty-two-movement cantata *Es erhub sich ein Streit* was especially popular during its day. The *dialogus,* entitled *Herr, wende dich und sei mir gnädig,* is in one movement and is scored for SATB solos (without chorus), strings, and basso continuo.

MOTETS

COMPLETE AND LISTED ACCORDING TO FAMILIARITY

Ich lasse dich nicht (Genesis 32:26 and a verse of the chorale "Warum betrübst du dich, mein Herz" by Hans Sachs) – SATB/SATB chorus and basso continuo – 4 minutes. The motet is sometimes attributed to J. S. Bach, although it was most likely composed by Johann Christoph.

Fürchte dich nicht (Isaiah 43:1, Luke 23:43, and a verse of the chorale "O Traurigkeit, o Herzeleid" by Friedrich von Spee) – SATTB chorus and basso
continuo – 5 minutes. The chorale melody is in the soprano part as a
simple cantus firmus.

Der Mensch, vom Weibe geboren (Job 14:1–2 and a verse of the chorale "Ach
wie nichtig, ach wie flüchtig" by Michael Franck) – SSATB chorus and
basso continuo – 3:30 minutes. The motet is in two sections, the first
characterized by echo effects and the second by a simple homophonic
statement of the chorale.

Unsers Herzens Freude hat ein Ende (Jeremiah 5) – SATB/SATB chorus and
basso continuo – 7:30 minutes. The rhythmic activity between the two
choruses is especially dramatic.

Merk auf, mein Herz und sieh dorthin (seven verses of Martin Luther's Christmas chorale "Vom Himmel hoch, da komm ich her") – SATB/SATB
chorus and basso continuo – 12 minutes. (1) The motet is divided into
several sections that vary in tempo and meter; (2) the chorale tune appears as a cantus firmus. in the soprano parts at the end of the motet.

Lieber Herr, Gott, wecke uns auf (a translation by Martin Luther of the Collect
for Advent "Excita Domine corda nostra") – 1672 – SATB/SATB chorus
and basso continuo – 4 minutes. The motet, in one movement, is characterized by multiple meter and tempo changes.

Der Gerechte, ob er gleich zu zeitlich stirbt (Song of Solomon) – 1676 – SATTB
chorus and basso continuo – 5 minutes.

Herr, nun lässest du deinen Diener (Luke 2:29–32) – SATB/SATB chorus and
basso continuo – 7 minutes.

Herr, wenn ich nur dich habe (Psalm 73:25–26) – SATB/SATB chorus and
basso continuo – 7 minutes.

Was kein Aug gesehen hat (1 Corinthians 2 and the chorale "Ach, was ist doch
unser Leb'n") – SATB/SATB chorus and basso continuo – 6 minutes.

Sei getreu bis in den Tod – SSATB chorus and basso continuo – 3 minutes.

Es ist nun aus mit meinem Leben – SATB chorus – 5:30 minutes. The motet
consists of seven homophonic verses of the chorale.

Mit Weinen hebt sichs an – SATB chorus – 3 minutes. The motet consists of
three homophonic verses of the chorale.

CANTATAS
COMPLETE AND LISTED ACCORDING TO FAMILIARITY

Es erhub sich ein Streit (Revelation 12:7–12) – TTB solos, SATBB/SATTB chorus, four trumpets, timpani, strings, and basso continuo – 7:30 minutes.
(1) The cantata was composed for the feast of St Michael; (2) the strings
divide into three violin and three viola parts; (3) the cantata has two instrumental movements—an opening sonata and an internal sinfonia.

Meine Freundin, du bist schön (Song of Solomon) – SATB solos, SATB chorus, strings, and basso continuo – 24 minutes. (1) The cantata was composed for a wedding celebration; (2) the solo writing consists of one solo (S), one duet (SB), one trio (SAT), and several passages for quartet; (3) the chorus parts divide occasionally; (4) the string scoring includes a solo violin part; (5) the violas divide into three parts (although the top part can be played by a violin); (6) there are descriptive texts before several sections of the music (e.g., "A lover is strolling along, all on his own, but unexpectedly he encounters his beloved").

Die Furcht des Herren – SAATB solos, SATTB chorus, strings, and basso continuo – 7:30 minutes. (1) The cantata was composed for the election of the Eisenach town council; (2) solo roles are for Wisdom (S), Junior Treasurer (A), Junior Burgomaster (A), Senior Treasurer (T), and Senior Burgomaster (B); (3) the chorus portrays the Plenary Council; (4) the strings divide into two violin and two viola parts.

HEINRICH IGNAZ FRANZ VON BIBER 1644–1704

Biber was born near Reichenberg, Bohemia (now Liberec, Czech Republic). Nothing is known about his education or whereabouts before the 1660s, when he was employed as a violinist at the court of Prince-Bishop Karl in Olomouc. In 1670 he moved to Salzburg, where he variously held the positions of violinist in the Kapelle, *Vice-Kapellmeister,* and *Hofkapellmeister* in the archbishop's court. He was a virtuoso violinist, and most of his compositions were for that instrument, including programmatic works such as *Battalia,* a suite for strings and basso continuo that depicts various sights and sounds of battle, and *Sonata violino solo representativa,* a sonata for solo violin and basso continuo that depicts the sounds of birds and animals.

Biber's few vocal works, all sacred and all composed late in his life, include two Requiems, three masses, and music for three Vespers services. Some of the works, such as the *Missa à 4 voci in contrapuncto,* are in a strict *prima prattica* a cappella style that was typical of much liturgical Catholic music outside Italy during the Baroque era. Other works, such as the *Requiem* in F minor and the *Missa Sancti Henrici,* are in a conservative Baroque *concertato* style, with brief solos, duets, and trios that alternate with choral passages, and with scoring for instruments, especially trombones, that are mostly *colla parte* with the vocalists. Most of Biber's sacred music, however, is grand in scope, with scoring for large forces that took advantage of performing spaces in Salzburg's cathedral. Like St Mark's Basilica in Venice, the Salzburg cathedral had four musician balconies, each with its own organ. Examples of the grand works include the *Requiem à 15 in Concerto* in A major scored for SSATBB solos and chorus, two oboes, two bass trumpets, timpani, three trombones, strings, and basso continuo, and the *Vesperae à 32* (sometimes referred to by its complete title, *Ad majorem Dei Gloriam, Beatae Mariae Virginis Assumptae*) scored for two vocal ensembles (eight-part soloists and eight-part chorus), three instrumental ensembles (four trumpets and timpani, strings, and trombones), and basso continuo that includes four organs. Biber also may have composed the fifty-three-part mass entitled *Missa Salisburgensis,* which was formerly attributed to Orazio Benevoli.

JOHANN MICHAEL BACH 1648–1694

Johann Michael Bach—brother of Johann Christoph (1642–1703) as well as first cousin of Johann Sebastian's father, Johann Ambrosius (1645–1695), and the father of Johann Sebastian's first wife, Maria Barbara—was born in Arnstadt, where many of the Bach family members lived and worked and where he succeeded his elder brother Johann Christoph as organist at the castle chapel. Johann Michael moved to the town of Gehren in 1673 and spent the remainder of his life there as civic organist, town clerk, and builder of clavichords and violins.

Eighteen of Johann Michael Bach's vocal works have survived, including fourteen motets and four choral cantatas. Eleven of the motets, some of which were performed by Johann Sebastian in his first years as *Kantor* at the Thomaskirche in Leipzig, are contained in the *Alt-Bachisches Archiv.*

The motets by Johann Michael are similar to those composed by his brother Johann Christoph: they are all scored for chorus (or double chorus) and basso continuo, the texts generally combine biblical passages and pietistic poetry, and Lutheran chorales are often included. *Ehre sei Gott in der Höhe* is a typical example. It is scored for double chorus and basso continuo, its text combines passages from Luke and the Lutheran chorale "Vom Himmel hoch," and it includes a statement of the chorale tune. Furthermore, the motet is divided into two sections. In the first, the double chorus participates in a dialogue of short biblical text phrases, and in the second, the two ensembles combine, the sopranos singing the chorale tune as a cantus firmus and the other voices continuing with the biblical text.

The cantatas, sometimes called vocal concertos, are varied in textual content and format, although they are otherwise like the cantatas of Johann Christoph and other Lutheran composers of the time. They are of relatively short duration; they are scored for soloists, chorus, and instruments, with few extended passages for solo voices; and they are divided into sections that are characterized by tempo and meter changes.

MOTETS
SELECTED AND LISTED ACCORDING TO FAMILIARITY

Halt, was du hast (Revelation 3:11 and verses of the chorale "Jesu, meine Freude") – SATB/ATTB chorus and basso continuo – 5:15 minutes. The motet is in two parts—the chorale is sung simultaneously with the biblical passages in the first part, and both choruses sing the chorale in the second part.

Ehre sei Gott in der Höhe (Luke 2:14 and the final verse of the Lutheran chorale "Vom Himmel hoch") – SATB/SATB chorus and basso continuo – 4 minutes. The chorale tune is sung by the sopranos as a cantus firmus at the end of the motet.

Nun hab' ich überwunden – SATB/SATB chorus and basso continuo – 3 minutes. The voices combine into one SATB ensemble for the final portion of the motet, with the chorale tune "Christus, der ist mein Leben" sung by the sopranos as a cantus firmus.

Das Blut Jesu Christi – SATTB chorus and basso continuo – 4 minutes. A chorale tune of unknown origin is sung by the sopranos as a cantus firmus at the end of the motet.

Herr, wenn ich nur dich habe (Psalm 73:25–26 and verses of the chorale "Ach Gott, wie manches Herzelied") – SATTB chorus and basso continuo – 5 minutes. (1) The motet was composed for the funeral of Friedrich Ernst; (2) the chorale tune "O Jesu Christ, mein's Lebens Licht" is sung four times by the sopranos as a cantus firmus.

Fürchtet euch nicht (Luke 2:10) – SATB/SATB chorus and basso continuo – 3:30 minutes. The two choruses join into one SATB ensemble for the final portion of the motet, with the sopranos singing the chorale "Gelobet seist du, Jesu Christ" as a cantus firmus.

Sei, lieber Tag, willkommen – SSATTB chorus and basso continuo – 3:15 minutes. (1) The source of the text, for New Year's Day, is unknown; (2) the motet is characterized by frequent dialogue between the upper and lower voices.

Nun treten wir ins neue Jahr – SATB/SATB chorus and basso continuo – 4 minutes.

CANTATAS
COMPLETE AND LISTED ACCORDING TO FAMILIARITY

Ach bleib bei uns, Herr Jesu Christ – SATB chorus, two violins, and basso continuo – 6 minutes. (1) The text, for an evening service or a funeral, is by Philipp Melanchthon and Nikolaus Selnecker; (2) the cantata begins with an opening sonata that features the two violins in fast Monteverdi-like scalar passages.

Liebster Jesu, hör mein Flehen (Matthew 15:21–28) – SATTB solos, strings, and basso continuo – 7 minutes. (1) The text is for the second Sunday in Lent; (2) the solos represent the roles of a Canaanite (S), Christ (B), and three Disciples (ATT); (3) the cantata opens with a short instrumental symphonia and closes with the chorale "Nun lob' mein Seel' den Herren"; (4) the strings divide into two violin and two viola parts.

Herr, der König freuet sich (Psalm 21:2–7) – SSATB solos, SSATB chorus, strings, and basso continuo – 6 minutes. (1) There are brief solo ATB passages in the style of Monteverdi, but otherwise the soloists sing in ensemble; (2) the violas divide into two parts.

Herr, komm hinab (John 4:47–54) – STB solos, SATB chorus, strings, and basso continuo – 6 minutes. (1) The text is for the twenty-first Sunday after Trinity; (2) solos consist of one TB duet and one S aria; (3) there is one choral movement; (4) the strings divide into two violin and two viola parts.

JOHANN SCHELLE 1648–1701

Schelle was born in Geising, where his father was a church musician and schoolmaster. From ages seven to seventeen (when his voice changed) he was a chorister at the electoral chapel in Dresden under Heinrich Schütz, and from seventeen to twenty-two he was a student at the

Thomasschule and University of Leipzig. For the next seven years he served as *Kantor* at a church in nearby Eilenburg, and from age twenty-nine until his death he served as *Kantor* of the Thomaskirche in Leipzig. While at the Thomaskirche, he revised the liturgy by replacing Latin motets with German chorale cantatas.

Schelle composed approximately fifty surviving works, including *Christus ist das Gesetzes Ende* (Romans 10:4) for SSAT/ATTB solos, SSAT/ATTB chorus, and optional basso continuo (his only work published during his life); *Aus der Tiefen rufe ich, Herr* for SATB chorus, two violins, two violas, and basso continuo; *Barmherzig und gnädig ist der Herr* for SSATB chorus, two violins, two violas, and basso continuo; *Christus, der ist mein Leben* for SSATB solos, SSATB chorus, four violins, four violas, and basso continuo; *Heut' triumphieret Gottes sohn* for SSATB solos, SSATB chorus, two violins, two violas, and basso continuo; *Nun danket alle Gott* for SSATB solos, SATB chorus, two trumpets, two violins, and basso continuo; and *Vom Himmel kam der Engel Schar* for SSATB solos, SSATB chorus, two horns, two trumpets, two trombones, timpani, two violins, three violas, and basso continuo.

JOHANN PACHELBEL 1653–1706

Johann Pachelbel, father of Wilhelm Hieronymus Pachelbel (1686–1764) and Charles Theodore Pachelbel (1690–1750), was born in Nuremberg, where he received his musical education from several relatively unknown local teachers. At age sixteen he was appointed organist at the Lorenz-kirche, at nineteen he was selected to be deputy organist at St Stephen's Cathedral in Vienna, and at twenty-four he was appointed court organist, under *Kapellmeister* Daniel Eberlin, to Prince Johann Georg in the city of Eisenach. When musical circumstances at the court became unsat-isfactory soon after Pachelbel arrived, he moved to Erfurt and served there as organist at the Predigerkirche for twelve years. While in Erfurt he became acquainted with Johann Ambrosius Bach (1645–1695), father of Johann Sebastian, and with Johann Christoph (1642–1703), Johann Sebastian's uncle. At Ambrosius's request, Pachelbel taught Johann Christoph and became god-father to his sister, Johanna Juditha. In 1690 Pachelbel moved to Württemberg, serving there as organist at the court of Duchess Magdalene Sibylla, and two years later he took the position of town organist in the city of Gotha. In 1695 he returned to his hometown of Nuremberg, where he was appointed organist at St Sebald. Like many of the north and central German church mu-sicians of the late-sixteenth and early-seventeenth centuries, including Dietrich Buxtehude and J. S. Bach, Pachelbel excelled as an organist, achieving fame through his organ performances and compositions.

In addition to more than two hundred works for organ, Pachelbel composed nineteen arias (four of which involve chorus), eleven motets, eleven cantatas, twelve Ingressus settings, thir-teen Magnificats, and two masses. Pachelbel's arias were the equivalent of Italian cantatas; they were generally composed for special occasions such as weddings, funerals, and birthdays, and they were scored for soloists, several obbligato instruments, and basso continuo. Two of the arias—*So ist denn dies der Tag* and *So ist denn nur die Treu*—are for solo voices, four-part chorus, and strings, and two of the arias—*Voller Wonder, voller Kunst* and *Wohl euch, die ihr in Gott verliebt*—are for four-part chorus and basso continuo.

Typical of the time, most of the motets are scored for double chorus with a basso continuo part that basically doubles the voices. Only one motet, the smallest of the three settings of *Der Herr ist König,* is for five voices and independent basso continuo. Most of the motets are also settings of German texts (only two are in Latin) that are taken from either the Psalms or Lutheran chorales. The style is similar to that of the dialogue motets composed by Heinrich Schütz, Johann Hermann Schein, and Samuel Scheidt.

The cantatas are all large-scale works scored for soloists, chorus, strings, and basso continuo, with the occasional addition of trumpets and timpani. As with the motets, the texts of the cantatas are taken from Psalms and Lutheran chorales. The musical structures usually consist of an opening instrumental movement followed by sections of music that correspond to biblical or chorale verses, the musical sections consisting of solos that alternate with duets, trios, and choruses. A number of the cantatas feature a chorale melody sung by the soprano voices as a cantus firmus. An example is *Christ lag in Todesbanden:* verse one is for chorus, with the sopranos singing the chorale tune; verse two is a soprano and tenor duet; verse three is a bass solo; verse four is a solo for tenor followed by a solo for alto; verse five is for chorus, with the chorale tune in the tenor part; verse six is a soprano and tenor duet; and verse seven is for chorus.

The Ingressus motets and Magnificats were composed as parts of Vespers services, the Ingressus motets being set to the combined antiphon texts "Deus in adjutorium meum intende" and "Domine, ad adjuvandum me festina" with the Gloria Patri and a closing Alleluia. They are all scored for four- or five-part chorus, strings, and basso continuo, except for the setting in C major, which adds trumpets and timpani. The Magnificats are all scored for chorus and varying instrumental combinations. Only one setting (in E-flat major) involves soloists.

MOTETS
SELECTED AND LISTED ACCORDING TO FAMILIARITY

Jauchzet dem Herrn (Psalm 100) – SATB/SATB chorus and basso continuo – 7 minutes.

Der Herr ist König (Psalm 99) – SATB/SATB chorus and basso continuo – 4 minutes.

Der Herr ist König (Psalm 99) – SSATB chorus and basso continuo – 4 minutes.

Nun danket alle Gott – SATB/SATB chorus and basso continuo – 5 minutes.

CANTATAS
SELECTED AND LISTED ACCORDING TO FAMILIARITY

Was Gott tut, das ist wohlgetan – SATB voices, two violins, two violas, and basso continuo – 12 minutes.

Jauchzet dem Herrn (Psalm 100) – SSATB solos, SSATB chorus, two oboes, two violins, two violas, and basso continuo – 14:30 minutes.

Christ lag in Todesbanden – SATB solos, SATB chorus, two violins, three violas, bassoon, and basso continuo – 13 minutes.

Halleluja! Lobet den Herrn (Psalm 150) – SSATB solos, SSATB chorus, two oboes, five trumpets, timpani, trombone, two violins, three violas, and basso continuo – 13:30 minutes.

INGRESSUS AND MAGNIFICAT SETTINGS
SELECTED AND LISTED ACCORDING TO FAMILIARITY

Deus in adjutorium (Psalm 70:2) – SSATB solos, SSATB chorus, four trumpets, timpani, two violins, three violas, and basso continuo – 10:15 minutes.

Magnificat in C major – SSATB solos, SSATB chorus, four trumpets, timpani, two violins, three violas, and basso continuo – 18:15 minutes.

Magnificat in D major – SATB chorus and basso continuo – 7 minutes. Pachelbel notes that four string instruments can be added ad lib.

Magnificat in G major – SATB chorus, two violins, and basso continuo – 7 minutes.

Magnificat in B-flat major – SSATB solos, SSATB chorus, two oboes, two violins, three violas, and basso continuo – 11 minutes.

Missa brevis in D major – SATB chorus and basso continuo – 10 minutes. The mass includes only Kyrie and Gloria movements.

JOHANN KUHNAU 1660–1722

Kuhnau was born in Geising, near Dresden, and was given the Bohemian name of his family's ancestry, Cuno Kuhn. At age ten he studied with the organist at the Dresden court, and a year later he became a chorister at the Dresden Kreuzkirche. At twenty he began a liberal education at the Johannem Gymnasium in Zittau, and two years later he matriculated as a law student at the University of Leipzig. He combined law studies with musical activity, mostly substituting as organist at area churches, and at twenty-four, after graduation, he opened a law practice and was also appointed organist at the Thomaskirche. It was at this time that he changed his name to Johann Kuhnau, although he often called himself by his original first name Cuno. For the next seventeen years his law practice flourished, and he also became known for his keyboard performances and compositions. His two books of *Neue Clavier-Übung* (published in 1689 and 1692) and his *Biblische Historien* (published in 1700) brought him considerable fame. The six sonatas in the *Biblische Historien,* each composed to represent a story from the Old Testament (e.g., the fight between David and Goliath), were especially popular. In 1701, with the death of Johann Schelle, he was appointed *Kantor* at the Thomaskirche, a position he would hold for the remainder of his life and that would be given to J. S. Bach after his death. While much of his keyboard music was published during his lifetime and performed throughout Germany, none of his vocal music was published, and approximately half of this output has been lost.

Kuhnau's repertoire for voices includes twenty-three surviving cantatas, one Magnificat, and five motets. The cantatas generally consist of an opening instrumental movement followed by recitatives, arias, and choruses—a structure that was a new development in the sacred cantata (i.e., before Kuhnau, cantatas had consisted only of sections of music, not separate movements, for solo voices). An example of the new structure is his most famous work, *Uns ist ein Kind geboren,* which was formerly attributed to J. S. Bach and was catalogued as BWV142. Its seven movements consist of an overture, chorus, brief bass aria, chorus, tenor aria, alto recitative and aria, and chorale. The *Magnificat* is constructed of five arias, two duets, and five choral movements. The motets are all in the *prima prattica* imitative style of the late Renaissance. *Tristis est anima mea,* another of Kuhnau's famous compositions and one of the most finely wrought and effective *prima prattica* motets of the Baroque era, is representative. It was performed frequently during the eighteenth century, and a parody of it, most likely by J. S. Bach, was included as a movement in the pastiche Passion cantata *Ein Lämmlein geht und trägt die Schuld* by Carl Heinrich Graun.

CANTATAS
SELECTED AND LISTED ACCORDING TO FAMILIARITY

Uns ist ein Kind geboren (Isaiah 9:5–6) – ATB solos, SATB chorus, two flutes, two oboes, strings, and basso continuo – 17 minutes.

Wie schön leuchtet der Morgenstern – SST solos, SATB chorus, two horns, two violins, two violas, and basso continuo – 13:30 minutes. (1) The solos for the two sopranos are brief, while the solos for tenor (a recitative and *da capo* aria) are lengthy; (2) the cantata ends with a homophonic chorale setting for the chorus.

Christ lag in Todesbanden – SATB solos, SATB chorus, two trumpets, two violins, two violas, and basso continuo – 16 minutes.

Gott, sei mir gnädig (Psalm 51:3–10) – SATB solos, SATB chorus, two violins, two violas, and basso continuo – 12 minutes. The cantata is in one multi-sectional movement that consists of alternating solos and choral passages.

Lobe den Herren, meine Seele (Psalm 103) – STB solos, SSATB chorus, two trumpets, three trombones, two violins, two violas, and basso continuo – 14 minutes.

Wenn ihr fröhlich seid an euren Festen – SSATB solos, SSATB chorus, three trumpets, timpani, two violins, two violas, bassoon, and basso continuo – 20 minutes.

Ich freue mich im Herrn (Isaiah 61:10) – SATB solos, SATB chorus, two violins, viola, and basso continuo – 14:30 minutes.

OTHER SACRED WORKS
SELECTED AND LISTED ACCORDING TO FAMILIARITY

Tristis est anima mea (Matthew 26:38) – SSATB voices and basso continuo – 5 minutes.

Magnificat – SATB solos, SSATB chorus, two oboes, three trumpets, timpani, two violins, two violas, and basso continuo – 20:30 minutes.

JOHANN JOSEPH FUX 1660–1741

Fux was born in southeast Austria and most likely received his initial musical education in Graz. In 1680 he entered the University of Graz, and in 1683 he studied at the university in Ingolstadt, Germany, and also served there as organist at the church of St Moritz. In 1688 he traveled to Italy, and several years later he settled in Vienna, where he was appointed organist at the Schottenkirche and where he presented the manuscripts of several masses to Emperor Leopold I. The emperor was apparently impressed, for in 1698 he appointed Fux *Hofkapellmeister*. Fux retained this position, with different titles, under Leopold's successors, Joseph I and Charles VI, and he also served as *Vice-Kapellmeister* and then *Kapellmeister* at St Stephen's Cathedral.

Fux composed a large amount of sacred music. However, he is known today only for his treatise *Gradus ad Parnassum,* which is considered to be one of the most important studies of counterpoint ever written. His choral output includes approximately eighty masses (including three Requiems), fifty motets, thirteen surviving oratorios, and one Te Deum. Since Fux idealized the music of Palestrina (as is evident in *Gradus ad Parnassum*) and since most liturgical music for the Catholic Church in Vienna during the Baroque era was conservative, many of the masses and motets are in a strict *prima prattica* a cappella style. Fux even referred to this style as "stylus a cappella." The two masses catalogued as K7 and K29 are examples. Other masses are in a conservative *concertato* style that Fux called "stylus mixtus." These works—represented by masses catalogued as K5, K10, K28, and K43—are scored for soloists, chorus, and instruments—the soloists alternating solos, duets, and trios with choral passages, and the instruments scored independently. For example, *Missa Velociter currit* K43 is scored for SATB solos, SATB chorus, two violins, and basso continuo, with three trombones doubling the alto, tenor, and bass choral parts. Most of the solos are written for quartet, the choral texture is imitative, and the violins are almost always together.

The motets are all in the "stylus a cappella." Representative examples include *Ad te, Domine levavi animam meam* K153 for the first Sunday in Advent and *Tollite portas* K152 for Christmas. Both are scored for SATB chorus a cappella. The oratorios follow in the tradition of those composed by Antonio Caldara and thus consist of recitatives, arias, and choruses accompanied mostly by strings and basso continuo. Fux's most famous oratorio, *La fede sacrilega nella morte del precursor San Giovanni Battista* K291 of 1714, is about the execution of St John the Baptist as demanded by Herod's wife (Herodias) and daughter (Oletria, generally known as Salome). Scoring is for SSATB soloists, SSATB chorus (which sings several *turba* passages), chalumeau, and basso continuo.

FRIEDRICH WILHELM ZACHOW 1663–1712

Zachow was born in Leipzig and received his musical education from his father, a *stadtpfeifer,* and from faculty at the Thomasschule. In 1667 he moved with his family to Eilenberg, where he likely studied at the Nikolaischule, and in 1684 he was appointed organist at the Marienkirche in Halle, a position he retained until his death. His compositions include twenty-eight cantatas, one mass, and two motets. The cantatas are all typical of the time: texts are in German;

scoring for soloists consists of recitatives and arias; the choral movements are mostly in a *concertato* style; and instruments include strings and oboes, with the occasional addition of flutes and horns and with trumpets and timpani for festival works. Examples are *Herr, wenn ich nur dich habe* for SATB solos, SATB chorus, strings, and basso continuo; *Uns ist ein Kind geboren* for SATB solos, SATB chorus, oboe, strings, and basso continuo; *Herzlich tut mich verlangen* for SSATB solos, SATB chorus, three oboes, strings, and basso continuo; *Lobe den Herrn, meine Seele* for SSATB solos, SSATB chorus, two oboes, two horns, strings, and basso continuo; and *Triumph, victoria* for SSATTB solos, SATB chorus, two trumpets, two trombones, timpani, strings, and basso continuo. The mass, for SATB chorus and basso continuo, is entitled *Missa super Christ lag in Todesbanden.*

JOHANN LUDWIG BACH 1677–1731

Johann Ludwig Bach, third cousin of Johann Sebastian (1685–1750) and the only other Bach of his generation to achieve fame, was born in Thal, near Eisenach. He presumably studied with his father, the organist Johann Jacob (1655–1718), who was of the same generation as, but not directly related to, Johann Christoph (1642–1703) and Johann Michael (1648–1694). From age eleven to sixteen Johann Ludwig attended the Gotha Gymnasium, from sixteen to nineteen he studied theology, and at twenty-two he began the first of several musical appointments in the town of Meiningen (just south of Eisenach and Gotha)—court musician in 1699, *Kantor* of the Schlosskirche in 1703, and court *Kapellmeister* in 1711. He is sometimes referred to as the "Meiningen Bach" because of his long tenure in that city.

The extant complete compositions of Johann Ludwig Bach include twenty cantatas, eleven motets, two masses, one Magnificat, one oratorio, and funeral music for Duke Ernst Ludwig. The cantatas were the best known and most respected of his compositions throughout the eighteenth and nineteenth centuries. C. P. E. Bach commented on the quality of the choruses; Carl Friedrich Zelter, director of the Berlin Singakademie, included several of them on programs he conducted; and J. S. Bach performed eighteen of them during his third year in Leipzig. One of the cantatas, *Denn du wirst meine Seele nicht in der Hölle lassen,* was mistakenly attributed to J. S. Bach and catalogued as BWV15. All the cantatas use texts that combine biblical passages and pietistic poetry, and all are scored for soloists, chorus, and a small group of instruments, generally strings.

The motets are Johann Ludwig's most popular compositions today. Like those of his predecessors, most are scored for double chorus and basso continuo, and they contain a combination of biblical passages and pietistic poetry suitable for funerals or special liturgical services such as Christmas. Most also include a Lutheran chorale. Unlike the motets of Johann Christoph and Johann Michael, those of Johann Ludwig feature word painting (e.g., melismas on the word "Freude" in *Das ist meine Freude*) and short motifs that are passed between two sets of voices (usually two SATB choruses) in quick succession. Both *Das ist meine Freude* and *Uns ist ein Kind geboren* begin distinctively with repeated statements of the text's first word, separated by rests and sung alternately by the two choruses. Other features unique to Johann Ludwig include notably expressive sections of music (e.g., the middle section of *Sei nun wieder zufrieden* and the beginning section of *Unsere Trübsal*) and occasional solo movements (e.g., the middle portion of *Die richtig für sich gewandelt haben*). One motet—*Gott sei uns gnädig*—is for solo bass, and two motets—*Ich habe dich ein klein Augenblick verlassen* and *Gedenke meiner, mein Gott*—have extended duet passages.

The most famous mass, *Missa sopra Allein Gott in der Höh' sei Ehr'*, is a German *missa* (containing only Kyrie and Gloria movements) and, as the title implies, is based on a Lutheran chorale. The melody of this chorale is incorporated as a *ripieno* cantus firmus in the three middle portions of the Gloria movement, and, coincidentally, the text of the chorale is a translation of the Latin "Gloria in excelsis Deo."

CANTATAS
SELECTED AND LISTED ACCORDING TO FAMILIARITY

Der Herr wird ein Neues im Lande erschaffen (Jeremiah 31:22) – SATB solos, SATB chorus, two oboes, strings, and basso continuo – 19 minutes. (1) The text is for the Visitation of our Lady; (2) of the cantata's seven movements, two are for chorus, two are arias, two are recitatives, and one is an arioso; (3) the final chorus is an elaboration of the chorale "Nun lob' mein Seel' den Herren."

Ja, mir hast du Arbeit gemacht (Isaiah 43:24–25, Luke 18:31–33, and the chorale "Herzliebster Jesu") – SATB solos, SATB chorus, strings, and basso continuo – 19 minutes. (1) The text is for the Sunday before Ash Wednesday (called Quinquagesima or Esto mihi); (2) of the cantata's eight movements, one is a chorus, four are arias, two are recitatives, and one is a duet; (3) the chorus movement consists of two verses of the chorale.

Die Weisheit kömmt nicht in eine boshafte Seele (Book of Wisdom, which is one of the deutero-canonical books of the Old Testament, and the chorale "O du allersüß'ste Freude") – SATB solos, SATB chorus, two oboes, strings, and basso continuo – 15 minutes. (1) The text is for the fourth Sunday after Easter; (2) of the cantata's seven movements, two are for chorus, two are recitatives, two are arias, and one is an arioso; (3) the final choral movement is a simple harmonization of the chorale, with orchestral elaboration.

Denn du wirst meine Seele nicht in der Hölle lassen – SATB solos, SATB chorus, three trumpets, timpani, strings, and basso continuo – 21 minutes. (1) The cantata is for Easter; (2) there are three short arias (STB), three duets (two for SA and one for TB), two recitatives (S and TB), and one choral movement; (3) the cantata was previously thought to be composed by J. S. Bach and was catalogued as BWV15.

Die mit Tränen säen (Psalm 126:5–6, Romans 8:18, and the chorale "Kommt her zu mir") – SATB solos, SATB chorus, strings, and basso continuo – 20 minutes. (1) The text is for the third Sunday after Easter; (2) of the cantata's seven movements, two are for chorus (one of these is a chorale), two are recitatives (SA), two are arias (SA), and one is a duet (TB).

MOTETS
COMPLETE AND LISTED ACCORDING TO FAMILIARITY

Das ist meine Freude (Psalm 73:28) – SATB/SATB chorus and basso continuo – 4:30 minutes. (1) The choral writing features madrigalisms and echo effects; (2) the motet is in one movement and is unified in tempo and melodic material.

Sei nun wieder zufrieden (Psalm 116:7–9) – SATB/SATB chorus and basso continuo – 8:45 minutes. (1) The motet is in three distinct sections—fast, slow, fast—each of which features the two choruses in dialogue; (2) the slow section is especially sonorous.

Unsere Trübsal (2 Corinthians 4:17–18) – SSATTB chorus and basso continuo – 4:30 minutes. (1) The motet is in three sections, each with a different meter and tempo; (2) the two soprano voice parts, often singing together at the interval of a third, are juxtaposed against the lower voice parts.

Uns ist ein Kind geboren (Isaiah 9:5–6) – SATB/SATB chorus and basso continuo – 7:30 minutes. (1) The text is for Christmas; (2) the motet is in four sections—the first (as described above) is characterized by repetitions of a single word and dialogue of short motifs between the two choruses, the second is characterized by Psalm tones as cantus firmus statements, the third is Venetian-like with dialogue of longer text phrases between the two choruses, and the fourth is a fugue.

Wir wissen, so unser irdisches Haus (2 Corinthians 5:1–2 and verses six and seven of the chorale "Alle Menschen müssen sterben") – SATB/SATB chorus and basso continuo – 7 minutes. The motet is characterized by melismas, hocket-like settings of words, and dialogue of short phrases between the two choruses.

Das Blut Jesu Christi (1 John 1:7 and the chorale "Jesu, du hast weggenommen") – SATB/SATB chorus and basso continuo – 5:45 minutes. The motet is in two sections—the first consists of short motifs in dialogue between the two choruses, and the second is a simple homophonic statement of the chorale.

Ich habe dich ein klein Augenblick verlassen (Isaiah 54:7–8 and poetry of unknown authorship) – SATB/TB/ST chorus and basso continuo – 9:15 minutes. The first chorus presents the biblical text, after which the second and third choruses (labeled "Parens" and "Defunctus") present seven verses of the poetry.

Gott sei uns gnädig (Psalm 67) – SATBB/SATB chorus and basso continuo – 5:30 minutes. The second bass part of the first chorus is unique and separate from the other voice parts—it has scalar passages and pedal tones as well as long melismas.

Gedenke meiner, mein Gott (Nehemiah 5:19 and a chorale by Benjamin Schmolck) – SATB/SATB chorus and basso continuo – 12 minutes. The motet is in three parts—the opening and closing parts for the two choruses in dialogue and the middle part for TB duet.

Ich will auf den Herren schauen (Micah 7:7 and a chorale of unknown authorship) – SATB/SATB chorus and basso continuo – 8 minutes. The motet is in three sections—the opening and closing for the two choruses in dialogue and the middle for the second chorus alone.

Die richtig für sich gewandelt haben (Isaiah 57:2 and a chorale of unknown authorship) – SATB/SATB/SATB chorus and basso continuo – 7:30 minutes. Most of the motet is a dialogue between the first and second choruses (the third chorus consists only of duet passages for SA and TB).

MASS

Missa sopra Allein Gott in der Höh' sei Ehr' – 1716 – SATB solos, SATB chorus, strings, and basso continuo – 16 minutes. (1) The text consists of the traditional Kyrie and Gloria portions of the Mass Ordinary plus three verses of the chorale "Allein Gott"; (2) the solo work is mostly for SA; (3) the chorus is featured in all eight movements of the mass; (4) the chorale, in German, is scored for a second soprano part in the three middle portions of the Gloria.

JAN DISMAS ZELENKA 1679–1745

Zelenka was born in Lounovice, Bohemia (now the Czech Republic), and studied with his father, an organist. In his early twenties he attended Clementinum College in Prague, and at age thirty-one he became a bass player in the Dresden royal orchestra. In 1715 he traveled to Vienna, where he became acquainted with Johann Joseph Fux and Antonio Lotti, and in 1720 he returned to Dresden, where he was given the title *Kirchen-compositeur* (church composer) at the royal court. He is noted for his harmonic individuality characterized by chromaticism, surprising chord progressions, and contrapuntal complexity.

Zelenka's choral output consists of three oratorios, ten masses, two Magnificats, seven Litanies, and approximately sixty motets. The masses include three large-scale works in cantata format (i.e., the Gloria and Credo are divided into separate and distinct movements, some of which are solo arias)—*Missa Gratias agimus tibi* of 1730 (also called *Missa Brevis* in D major) scored for SSAATB solos and chorus, two flutes, two oboes, four trumpets, timpani, strings, and basso continuo; *Missa Sanctissimae Trinitatis* in A minor of 1736 for SATB solos and chorus, two oboes, strings, and basso continuo; and *Missa Omnium sanctorum* in A minor of 1741 for the same forces as *Missa Sanctissimae Trinitatis*. The Litanies are represented by *Litaniae Laurentanae "Salus infirmorum"* and *Litaniae Laurentanae "Consolatrix afflictorum,"* both scored for SATB solos and chorus, two oboes, strings, and basso continuo.

Most of the motets consist of short SATB and optional basso continuo settings for Matins services celebrated during Holy Week. *Responsoria pro hebdomada sancta* of 1723, for example, consists of nine motets for Maundy Thursday (including *In monte Oliveti* and *Tristis est anima mea*), nine for Good Friday (including *Vinea mea electa* and *Tenebrae factae sunt*), and nine for Holy Saturday (including *O vos omnes* and *Sepulto Domino*). The other motets are larger-scale works in two or three movements, each of which is divided into sections that are varied in meter and tempo. Representative examples are *Beatus vir* (Psalm 112) for STB solos, SATB chorus, two oboes ad lib., two violins, two violas, and basso continuo; *Dixit Dominus* (Psalm 110) for SATB solos, SATB chorus, two trumpets and timpani ad lib., strings, and basso continuo; *Laudate pueri Dominum* (Psalm 113) for SSAB chorus, two violins, viola ad lib., and basso continuo; and *In exitu Israel* (Psalm 114) for SATB solos, SATB chorus, two oboes, strings, and basso continuo.

JOHANN MATTHESON 1681–1764

Matteson was born in Hamburg, where he remained his entire life and where his broad education incorporated the subjects of music, dance, art, mathematics, law, languages, and literature. The disciplines of music, languages, and literature prevailed and were intertwined throughout his life. Excelling as a singer from a young age, he was given solos in Hamburg churches and was a treble chorister in Hamburg opera productions. He also sang solo operatic roles as a child and was a prominent tenor as an adult. Several of his operatic experiences were with George Frideric Handel, who in 1703 played harpsichord for a performance of Mattheson's opera *Cleopatra* (which featured the composer in one of the leading roles). In addition, in 1705 Mattheson sang leading roles in Handel's *Almira* and *Nero,* and the two composers later traveled together to Lübeck, where they each explored and eventually dismissed the possibility of succeeding Dietrich Buxtehude as organist at the Marienkirche.

In 1704 Mattheson's career focused on languages when he became tutor to Cyrill Wich, the son of the English ambassador to Hamburg Sir John Wich, and then became Sir John's secretary in 1706. While serving in these positions, Mattheson learned English law and politics and translated a number of books from German into English. In 1715, while maintaining his position with Sir John, Mattheson became *Kapellmeister* at the Hamburg cathedral, with responsibilities for composing and conducting Passion oratorios each Lenten season. He set the Brockes Passion text in 1718, and in 1719 he conducted Handel's Brockes Passion one day and Telemann's setting of the same text the following day. During the next decade Mattheson composed more than twenty-four oratorios. Unfortunately, because of the bombing of Hamburg during World War II, only one of these oratorios survives—*Das Lied des Lammes.* Mattheson called the work a spiritual opera and expressed the opinion that it, as well as all sacred music, should elicit the same emotions as operatic music. In 1728 he resigned his position at the cathedral as a result of increasing deafness (he became completely deaf in 1735), and he turned his attention to the writing of articles and treatises. The most important of these are *Grosse General-Bass-Schule* of 1731 (a tutorial on playing from a figured bass), *Der vollkommene Capellmeister* of 1739 (a comprehensive guide for the church musician), and *Grundlage einer Ehren-Pforte* of 1740 (a compilation of biographies of 149 musicians, including himself).

GEORG PHILIPP TELEMANN 1681–1767

Telemann was born in the small city of Magdeburg, southwest of Berlin, where in his youth he learned to play the violin, flute, harpsichord, and organ. At age twelve he composed his first work, an opera, and at thirteen, while studying in the town of Zellerfeld, he composed one motet each week for the local church choir. At sixteen he attended the Gymnasium Andreanum in Hildeschein, composing music for school dramas and cantatas for the monastery chapel of

St Godehard, and at twenty he entered the University of Leipzig to study law. His numerous musical activities soon overshadowed his academic pursuits, however, and a year after he arrived in Leipzig, he founded and conducted a student collegium musicum. In addition, the mayor of the city engaged him to compose music for the city's two main churches (the Thomaskirche and Nikolaikirche), which were under the musical leadership of *Kantor* Johann Kuhnau and of organist Christoph Graupner. During the same year Telemann also became music director of the Opernhaus auf dem Brühl, for which he composed several operas, and two years later he added the position of organist at the Neue Kirche.

At twenty-four, recognizing his musical potential, needing to remove himself from inevitable conflicts with Kuhnau, and desiring to lead his own musical establishment, he accepted the position of *Kapellmeister* at the court of Count Erdmann II of Promnitz in Sorau (now Zary, Poland). The count favored French repertoire and the court's musical resources were substantial, and therefore Telemann had exposure to the works of composers such as Jean-Baptiste Lully and André Campra and had opportunity to compose numerous instrumental works in the French Baroque style. Telemann also became acquainted with Erdmann Neumeister, the court's chaplain at the time and the poet and librettist of many sacred Lutheran cantatas. Three years later, at age twenty-seven, Telemann was appointed *Konzertmeister* and then *Kapellmeister* to Duke Johann Wilhelm in Eisenach, where his responsibilities included composing numerous cantatas for services in the duke's court chapel. In Eisenach Telemann also became close friends with J. S. Bach, who chose him to be godfather to Bach's son, Carl Philipp Emanuel.

Continuing his move up the musical ladder, Telemann became director of music for the city of Frankfurt at age thirty-one and music director of Hamburg's five main Lutheran churches at forty. The Frankfurt position required him to direct and compose music for the two main Lutheran churches (the Barfüsserkirche and Katharinenkirche), conduct and compose for the local collegium musicum, and lead and compose music for civic occasions. The Hamburg position, which was one of the most prestigious musical posts in Germany, required two cantatas each Sunday, one Passion oratorio each year, and numerous compositions for civic occasions and for the local collegium musicum. In addition to his church duties, Telemann also became music director of the Hamburg Opera, for which he composed more than a dozen operas. With the death of Kuhnau in 1722, Telemann was offered the post of *Kantor* in Leipzig. However, Hamburg officials made counteroffers that Telemann felt he could not refuse. The Leipzig post was then offered to Graupner, who was at the time in Darmstadt and, encountering circumstances similar to Telemann, also declined. The post then went to J. S. Bach. Telemann remained an active composer for the entire duration of his long life (he died at the age of eighty-six), and he was considered the greatest German Baroque composer after J. S. Bach.

Telemann's compositional output consists of more than one thousand sacred cantatas, dozens of secular cantatas, approximately fifty Passion oratorios, eight other oratorios, twelve masses, and approximately fifty miscellaneous motets. The cantatas range from small-scale pieces for soloists and a few instruments to large-scale works scored for soloists, chorus, and instruments, including trumpets and timpani. Examples of the small-scale pieces include those in the *Harmonischer Gottesdienst*—a cycle of cantatas for the liturgical year, each scored for a single solo voice and each consisting of two arias separated by a recitative. Composed in 1725, these cantatas were meant for private devotional services as well as for churches with limited musical forces. Examples of the large-scale works include those composed for festival occasions. *Heilig,*

heilig, heilig ist Gott, for instance, which was written for the consecration of the Dreieinigkeits-kirche (Church of the Holy Trinity) in 1747, consists of twenty-six movements (four choruses, six chorales, eight recitatives, and eight arias). In addition, as is specified below, its instrumentation reaches orchestral proportions.

The early oratorios—those composed while Telemann was in Frankfurt—include *Der für die Sünden der Welt gemarterte und Sterbende Jesus* (a setting of the libretto by Barthold Heinrich Brockes also composed by Handel and Mattheson) and a collection of five works called the David Oratorios. The Brockes Passion (1716) was the first oratorio presented in Frankfurt, and the David Oratorios (1718)—entitled *Der königliche Prophete David, als ein Fürbild unseres Heylandes Jesu, in fünff verschiedenen Oratorien* (The Kingly Prophet David, as a prefiguration of our savior Jesus, in five different oratorios)—were written for the local collegium musicum. The remaining oratorios, including twenty-three settings of the Passion story composed while Telemann was in Hamburg, are settings of librettos that combine biblical passages with reflective poetry—poetry written to place the contemporary believer as both a witness of and a responsible party for the actions of the Passion events. In the St Luke Passion of 1728, for example, the oratorio's five sections are each introduced by a passage from the Old Testament that prepares the listener (worshipper) for the Passion drama. Gospel passages then follow. Arias with reflective poetry are attached to the Old Testament texts, whereas Lutheran chorales are attached to the Gospel passages. Telemann's most popular oratorio, *Seliges Erwägen des Leidens und Sterbens Jesu Christi,* is entirely set to reflective poetry (there are no biblical passages), and *Der Tag des Gerichts,* composed when Telemann was eighty, is set to four "Contemplations," each of which presents conflicts between those who believe in Jesus and those who do not. Twelve solo roles (including Religion, Reason, Mockery, and Disbelief) relate the various conflicts.

CANTATAS

SELECTED AND LISTED ACCORDING TO FAMILIARITY

Heilig, heilig, heilig ist Gott TWV2:6 – 1747 – SATB solos, SATB chorus, oboe, chalumeau, bassoon, two horns, three trumpets, timpani, strings, and basso continuo – 77 minutes. The text consists of various biblical passages and reflective poetry.

Die Tageszeiten TWV20:39 – 1757 – SATB solos, SATB chorus, two flutes, two oboes, bassoon, trumpet, strings, and basso continuo – 53 minutes. (1) The work consists of four separate cantatas: *Der Morgen* (Morning), *Der Mittag* (Noon), *Der Abend* (Evening), and *Die Nacht* (Night); (2) each cantata features different vocal and instrumental solos: soprano and trumpet, alto and viola da gamba, tenor and flutes, and bass and oboes and bassoon.

Das ist je gewisslich wahr TWVI:181 – 1717 – ATB solos, SATB chorus, two oboes, strings, and basso continuo – 8 minutes. This work was formerly attributed to J. S. Bach and was catalogued as BWV141.

Nun komm der Heiden Heiland TWVI:1177 – ca.1711 – ATB solos, SATB chorus, two oboes, strings, and basso continuo – 11 minutes.

Uns ist ein Kind geboren TWVı:1451 – 1718 – SSAB solos, SATB chorus, three trumpets, timpani, two oboes, strings, and basso continuo – 10 minutes. The cantata is for the Christmas season.

Gelobet seist du, Jesu Christ TWVı:612 – 1719 – ATB solos, SATB chorus, two oboes, strings, and basso continuo – 12 minutes.

Machet die Tore weit TWVı:1074 – 1719 – SATB solos, SATB chorus, two oboes, strings, and basso continuo – 25 minutes. The cantata is for the Advent season.

Ehre sei Gott in der Höhe TWVı:411 – 1756 – SATB solos, SATB chorus, three trumpets, timpani, strings, and basso continuo – 20 minutes. The cantata is for the Christmas season.

In dulci jubilo TWVı:939 – 1719 – SATB solos, SATB chorus, two horns, strings, and basso continuo – 15 minutes. The cantata is for the Christmas season.

Daran ist erschienen die Liebe Gottes TWVı:165 – 1717 – SATB solos, SATB chorus, recorder, strings, and basso continuo – 16:30 minutes. (1) The cantata is for Whitsuntide; (2) the recorder is featured prominently; (3) the cantata consists of three arias, one duet, one recitative, one chorus, and one chorale.

Jesu, meine Zuversicht TWVı:984 – 1754 – SATB solos, SATB chorus, flute, recorder, oboe, two horns, two trumpets, strings, and basso continuo – 15 minutes. The cantata is for Easter.

Nun danket alle Gott TWVı:1166 – SATB solos, SATB chorus, flute, two trumpets, timpani, strings, and basso continuo – 15 minutes.

Hosianna dem Sohne David TWVı:809 – 1720 – SS solos, SSB chorus, two violins and basso continuo – 18 minutes. The cantata is for the Advent season.

Du, o schönes Weltgebäude TWVı:394 – 1754 – SATB solos, SATB chorus, two flutes, two oboes, strings, and basso continuo – 16:30 minutes.

Christus, der ist mein Leben TWVı:138 – 1754 – SATB solos, SATB chorus, two flutes, two oboes, bassoon, strings, and basso continuo – 11 minutes.

Jesu, meine Freude TWVı:965 – 1719 – SATB solos, SATB chorus, two oboes, two bassoons, strings, and basso continuo – 16 minutes.

Ich bin, ja, Herr, in deiner Macht TWVı:822 – 1754 – SATB solos, SATB chorus, two flutes, two oboes, horn, trumpet, strings, and basso continuo – 14 minutes.

ORATORIOS
SELECTED AND LISTED ACCORDING TO FAMILIARITY

Seliges Erwägen des Leidens und Sterbens Jesu Christi TWV5:12 (Holy reflections on the life and death of Jesus Christ) – 1722 – SSTTBB solos, SATB chorus, two flutes (doubling two piccolos and two recorders), two oboes (doubling two chalumeaux), two bassoons, two horns, strings, and basso continuo – 112 minutes. (1) Solo roles are for the Daughter of Zion (S), a Believer (S), a Devout One (T), Peter (T), Jesus (B), and Caiaphas (B); (2) there are eleven chorales and no other choruses.

Der Tag des Gerichts TWV6:8 (The day of judgment) – 1762 – SSSAATTBBB solos, SATB chorus, two oboes, two horns, two trumpets, timpani, strings, and basso continuo – 100 minutes. (1) Major solo roles are for the Religious One (S), the Reasonable One (A), the Mocker (T), and the Disbeliever (B); (2) minor solo roles are for an Archangel (S), three Blessed Ones (S, A, and T), Jesus (B), and St John (B); (3) the oratorio contains eleven short choruses.

Die Auferstehung und Himmelfahrt Jesu TWV6:6 (The resurrection and ascension of Jesus) – 1760 – SSATBB solos, SATB chorus, two flutes, two oboes, two horns, three trumpets, timpani, strings, and basso continuo – 32 minutes. Solo roles, consisting of brief recitatives, are for Mary Magdalene (S), Jesus (B), an Evangelist (T), and Thomas (T).

Der Tod Jesu TWV5:6 (The death of Jesus) – 1755 – SAATBB solos, SATB chorus, two flutes, two oboes, horn, strings, and basso continuo – 40 minutes. (1) There are no solo roles; (2) the choral movements consist of six chorales and four *turba*-like passages.

Die Hirten bei der Krippe zu Bethlehem TWV1:797 (The shepherds by the manger in Bethlehem) – 1759 – SATBB solos, SATB chorus, two flutes (doubling two recorders), two oboes, bassoon, two horns, three trumpets, timpani, strings, and basso continuo – 50 minutes. There are two choruses and four chorales.

Johannespassion TWV5:30 (St John Passion) – 1745 – STTTBBB solos, SATB chorus, two flutes, two oboes, bassoon, trumpet, strings, and basso continuo – 90 minutes. Solo roles are for Mary Magdalene (S), an Evangelist (T), Peter (T), Pilate (T), Jesus (B), and two Servants (B and B).

Markuspassion TWV5:44 (St Mark Passion) – 1759 – SATBB solos, SATB chorus, two flutes, two oboes, strings, and basso continuo – 108 minutes.

MOTETS AND OTHER SACRED WORKS
SELECTED AND LISTED ACCORDING TO FAMILIARITY

Laudate Jehovam, omnes gentes TWV7:25 (Psalm 117) – 1758 – SATB chorus, two violins, and basso continuo – 5:30 minutes.

Ich habe Lust abzuschieden TWVdeest (Philippians 1:23 and the chorale "Herzlich tut mich verlangen") – SATB chorus and basso continuo – 2:30 minutes.

Ich will schauen dein Antlitz in Gerechtigkeit TWVdeest (Psalm 17:15) – SATB chorus and basso continuo – 3:15 minutes.

Der Gott unsers Herrn Jesu Christi TWV8:4 (Ephesians 1:17–18) – SATB chorus and basso continuo – 2:15 minutes.

Meine Seele erhebt den Herrn TWV1:1104 (Luke 1:46–47) – 1717 – SS solos, SSB chorus, strings ad lib., and basso continuo – 2:30 minutes.

Lobet den Herrn, alle Heiden TWV7:28 (Psalm 117) – date unknown – SS solos, SAB chorus, strings ad lib., and basso continuo – 2 minutes.

Selig sind die Toten TWV:8:13 (Revelation 14:13) – SATB chorus and basso continuo – 5:15 minutes.

Meine Seele erhebt den Herrn TWV9:18 (German Magnificat) – date unknown – SATB solos, SATB chorus, two flutes, two oboes, strings, and basso continuo – 20 minutes.

Magnificat TWV9:17 – ca.1705 – SATB solos, SATB chorus, two oboes, two trumpets, strings, and basso continuo – 20 minutes. The text is in Latin.

Serenata eroica – In dunkler Angst, bestürzt und bange TWV4:7 (In dark fear, dismayed and anxious) – 1733 – SSTTBB solos, SATB chorus, two recorders, two flutes, two oboes, oboe d'amore, chalumeau, two bassoons, two horns, six trumpets, timpani, strings, and basso continuo – 84 minutes. Composed for the funeral of Friedrich August of Saxony, the soloists represent Saxony (S), Wisdom (S), Time (T), Majesty (T), Heroism (B), and Magnanimity (B).

CHRISTOPH (JOHANN) GRAUPNER 1683–1760

Graupner, also called Johann Christoph Graupner, was born in Kirchberg, near Dresden, where he received his early musical education from local church musicians. From age thirteen to twenty-one he studied at the Thomasschule in Leipzig with Johann Schelle (*Kantor* from 1677 until his death in 1701) and Johann Kuhnau (organist from 1684 to 1701 and then *Kantor*). From age twenty-one to twenty-four he studied law at the University of Leipzig, as Kuhnau had done twenty years earlier and as Georg Philipp Telemann had also done several years before Graupner. Telemann and Graupner became friends, and Graupner no doubt heard performances of the university collegium musicum, which Telemann was directing at the time. After his three years in Leipzig, Graupner moved to Hamburg to become harpsichordist of the Oper-am-Gänsemarkt, and two years later he was appointed *Vice-Kapellmeister* at the court of Ernst Ludwig, Landgrave of Hessen-Darmstadt. Three years later he was promoted to *Kapellmeister*. In 1722, with the death of Kuhnau, Graupner was selected as the next *Kantor* of the Thomaskirche. However, Landgrave Ernst Ludwig refused to release him from his position at the Darmstadt court, and additionally he made conditions for Graupner too favorable for him to leave. The Thomaskirche position subsequently went to J. S. Bach, and Graupner remained in Darmstadt for the rest of his life.

During the years 1707 through 1719 Graupner composed ten operas and no other vocal music. However, when the Darmstadt's court opera company disbanded in 1719 for economic reasons, Graupner composed no more operas, and for the next thirty years he composed cantatas (approximately 1,400 of which are sacred and two dozen of which are secular). Like almost all other composers during the Baroque era in Germany, he also composed keyboard pieces, a number of which had programmatic subtitles. The sacred cantatas were similar to those of his teacher Kuhnau, with a structure of recitatives, arias, duets, and choruses and with the frequent addition of chorales. The early works had minimal instrumental accompaniment, whereas the later ones had instrumental forces that were symphonic in nature.

CANTATAS
SELECTED AND LISTED ACCORDING TO FAMILIARITY

Herr, deine Augen sehen nach dem Glauben – 1740 – SATB solos, SATB chorus, two oboes, strings, and basso continuo – 16 minutes. The cantata is for Palm Sunday.

Ihr Pharisäer dieser Zeit – 1740 – STB solos, SATB chorus, two oboes, strings, and basso continuo – 13 minutes. (1) The cantata is for Maundy Thursday; (2) the chorus is scored only for a simple homophonic chorale at the end of the cantata.

Wo gehet Jesus hin – SATB solos, SATB chorus, strings, and basso continuo – 9:30 minutes. The cantata is for *Esto mihi*.

Mein Gott, warum hast du mich verlassen – 1712 – SSATB solos, SSATB chorus, strings, and basso continuo – 14 minutes.

Ach wie nichtig, ach wie flüchtig – 1728 – SATB solos, SATB chorus, strings, and basso continuo – 10 minutes.

Der Heiland ruft auf Flut und Wellen – 1743 – SATB solos, SATB chorus, strings, and basso continuo – 11 minutes. The cantata is for Epiphany.

Aus der Tiefen rufen wir (Psalm 130) – 1723 – SATB solos, SATB chorus, two oboes, three trumpets, timpani, strings, and basso continuo – 13:30 minutes.

Machet die Tore weit – SAT solos, SATB chorus, two flutes, oboe, strings, and basso continuo – 18 minutes.

Also hat Gott die Welt geliebt (John 3:16) – SB solos, SATB chorus, strings, and basso continuo – 16 minutes.

Wir haben nicht mit Fleisch und Blut zu kämpfen – TB solos, SATB chorus, strings, and basso continuo – 15 minutes.

JOHANN GOTTFRIED WALTHER 1684–1748

Walther was born in Erfurt, where he received his musical education from Johann Bernhard Bach, distant cousin of Johann Sebastian Bach and organist at the Kaufmannskirche. In 1702 Walther was appointed organist at the church of St Thomas in Erfurt, and in 1707 he was appointed organist at the church of St Peter and St Paul in Weimar, where he would remain until his death. While in Weimar, Walther worked with J. S. Bach, who was organist at the court of the Duke of Weimar from 1708 until 1717 and who was godfather to Walther's eldest son.

Like Johann Joseph Fux, Walther is basically remembered today for writing an important treatise—*Musicalisches Lexicon,* which was the first major music dictionary in German and the first music dictionary to include definitions of musical terms and biographies of major musicians. His compositional output supposedly numbered ninety-two vocal works. However, only one work survives—the mass movement *Kyrie, Christe, Kyrie eleison über Wo Gott zum Haus nicht giebt sein Gunst.*

JOHANN SEBASTIAN BACH 1685–1750

Bach was born in Eisenach, a small town northeast of Frankfurt, where his father, Johann Ambrosius (1645–1695), was a trumpeter in the local court orchestra and director of music for the town. It is presumed that Johann Sebastian received his musical education from his father, who died when Johann Sebastian was ten, and for the next five years from his older brother, Johann Christoph (1671–1721). Studying with family members had been a tradition in the Bach family since the late sixteenth century. At age fifteen Johann Sebastian secured a position as chorister, violinist, and organist in Lüneberg, a town on the outskirts of Hamburg, and for the next several years he made several trips to Hamburg to hear and play the organs there and, no doubt, to experience other forms of music, since Hamburg was at that time one of the most important musical centers in Germany. Bach quickly became known as an organ virtuoso and was often engaged to play concerts on new or restored instruments in northern Germany. In 1703, when he was just eighteen, he was offered the position of organist at the Neukirche in Arnstadt after playing a recital there. Bach accepted the position, but—as would be typical of him for the remainder of his life—he yearned for advancement and greater prestige. In 1707 he was appointed organist at the church of St Blasius in Mühlhausen, the following year he moved to Weimar as court organist, and in 1717 he became *Kapellmeister* to the Duke of Cöthen (now Köthen).

In 1722, with the death of Johann Kuhnau, one of the most prestigious positions in all of northern Germany became open—*Kantor* at the Thomaskirche in Leipzig. Numerous famous musicians applied for the position, including Georg Philipp Telemann, but for various reasons, most of these musicians withdrew from consideration, and Bach was appointed in 1723. As *Kantor*, he was responsible for providing music in Leipzig's four main Lutheran churches and also for special events of the town council and weddings and funerals of notable civic residents. Upon arrival in Leipzig, Bach immediately began composing a cycle of cantatas for the church year and other works for special events. These included the motet *Jesu, meine Freude* BWV227 for the funeral of the postmaster's wife in July, Cantata BWV119 (*Preise, Jerusalem, den Herrn*) for the elections of the city council in August, the first version of the *Magnificat* BWV243a for Christmas Day, and the *Passio secundum Johannen* BWV245 for Good Friday 1724. Bach continued this pace of compositional activity, eventually composing five complete cycles of sacred cantatas (about three hundred total), four more Passion settings, and five masses. In addition, he conducted works of his sons and contemporaries such as Telemann, Handel, and Graun; he continued to travel, especially to Dresden, and to play organ recitals; he conducted the local collegium musicum; and he sought, unsuccessfully, more prestigious employment at the court of Friedrich August II in Dresden. In the late 1740s Bach developed cataracts, and in March and April of 1750 he underwent two eye operations (interestingly, performed by the same doctor who operated on Handel). Bach's operations were unsuccessful and traumatic, and he died of a stroke on July 28 at age sixty-five.

Bach's compositional output of choral music consists of two hundred surviving cantatas (approximately another hundred have been lost), twenty-eight extant secular cantatas (from a total of thirty), five masses, one Magnificat (that survives in two versions), five oratorios (including two Passions that survive), seven motets, and numerous chorale arrangements.

The early sacred cantatas (those composed during Bach's years at Arnstadt and Mühlhausen) are characterized by a predominance of texts taken directly from the Bible, multisectionalized movements, frequent examples of word painting, short arioso sections for soloists, and accompaniment of strings and basso continuo. Cantata BWV150 (*Nach dir, Herr, verlanget mich*), believed to be composed before 1707 and Bach's earliest surviving cantata, is an example. The first movement, which is just three minutes in duration, has six tempo changes, each of which corresponds to variations in textual content. The second movement is a one-and-a-half-minute arioso, and the third movement paints the path to righteousness with a scalar passage that ascends from the basses to the violins. The early cantatas are also predominantly choral; there are few solo passages, and these are fairly short. Examples are BWV4 (*Christ lag in Todesbanden*), BWV131 (*Aus der Tiefe rufe ich, Herr, zu dir*), BWV106 (*Gottes Zeit ist die allerbeste Zeit*), and BWV196 (*Der Herr denket an uns*).

Later sacred cantatas—those composed during Bach's years at Weimar and Leipzig—are characterized by texts of pietistic poetry or a combination of biblical passages and pietistic poetry, chorale movements, extended movements all in one tempo and all based on a single compositional idea, less frequent and more subtle word painting, lengthy *da capo* arias, and accompaniment that involves obbligato wind instruments. These cantatas are also less choral; most begin with a chorus and end with a chorale. Examples are BWV1 (*Wie schön leuchtet der Morgenstern*), BWV78 (*Jesu, der du meine Seele*), BWV80 (*Ein feste Burg ist unser Gott*), and BWV140 (*Wachet auf, ruft uns die Stimme*). Bach also wrote a number of solo cantatas, including BWV51 (*Jauchzet Gott in allen Landen*) for soprano and BWV82 (*Ich habe genug*) for bass.

The secular cantatas were composed for special civic occasions, weddings, funerals, and performances by the collegium musicum. They generally feature a string of recitatives and arias, with only two choruses (opening and closing). Some of the secular cantatas, such as *Schweigt stille, plaudert nicht* BWV211 (the Coffee Cantata), *Mer hahn en neue Oberkeet* BWV212 (the Peasant Cantata), and *Weichet nur, betrübte Schatten* BWV202 (the Wedding Cantata), have no choral writing at all. Representative cantatas with chorus are *Lass, Fürstin, lass noch einen Strahl* BWV198, composed in 1727 for the funeral of Christiane Eberhardine, Electress of Saxony and former Queen of Poland; *Geschwinde, ihr wirbelnden Winde* BWV201, subtitled "Der Streit zwischen Phoebus und Pan" (The Contest between Phoebus and Pan) and composed in 1729 for the celebration of Michaelmas; and *Auf, schmetternde Töne der muntern Trompeten* BWV207a, composed in 1735 for the name day of August III, Elector of Saxony.

The masses include four *missae* and the collection of movements referred to as the *B minor Mass* BWV232. The *missae* were composed between 1735 and 1744 for unknown circumstances, although it is assumed that they were used in festival services, since the Catholic Kyrie and Gloria were parts of the Lutheran liturgy in university cities such as Leipzig. Each of the *missae* consists of a choral Kyrie and a Gloria divided into five movements (three arias framed by two choruses). The work known as the *B minor Mass* consists of all the Ordinary portions of the Catholic mass. However, these portions were composed over a long period of time, and Bach did not conceive of them as a unified entity. He merely assembled the portions, without a title, at the end of his life. The Sanctus was composed for and performed on Christmas Day 1724. The *missa* (Kyrie and Gloria) was composed in 1733 and dedicated to August II, Elector of Saxony, in the hope of securing a position at the Dresden court. The Credo (Symbolum Nicenum) and the remainder of the mass (Osanna, Benedictus, Agnus Dei, and Dona nobis pacem) were composed between 1747 and 1749 for unspecified reasons. No performances of the complete work were given or planned during Bach's life, and the separate portions of the mass were not reworked and adapted to a new unified composition such as Bach had done with so many other works. In addition, the complete mass is quite disparate in performing forces. For instance, the Kyrie and Gloria are scored for SSATB chorus, most of the Credo is for SATB, the Sanctus is for SSATTB, and the Osanna for SATB/SATB. Furthermore, the Sanctus is the only movement scored for three oboes.

The most logical assumption for the assembly of a Catholic mass is that Bach felt that a completed work would further his chances of employment at the Dresden court. It is also possible, however, that Bach merely wanted to demonstrate his skill at writing in diverse styles, or that he was inclined (as he demonstrated in numerous other instances) to complete a major work. The collection of movements does, in fact, show Bach's extraordinary skill in composing in the *prima prattica* styles familiar to Catholic composers and also in the various *seconda prattica* styles prevalent throughout Europe. For example, seven movements of the work are in the imitative motet style of the Renaissance, and of these, the beginning of the Credo is based on the opening notes of the Gregorian chant, which is treated in augmentation during the imitative process, and in the Confiteor portion of the Credo, chant fragments are presented in augmentation as a cantus firmus. *Seconda prattica* styles include ritornello arias, *concertato* expositions, and fugues.

The *Magnificat* exists in two versions. The first (BWV243a), composed in 1723 and performed during Bach's initial Christmas season in Leipzig, is in the key of E-flat major and includes four chorale movements (listed and annotated below) that are interpolated into the traditional Latin text from Luke 1:46–55. For the second version (BWV243), composed between 1728 and 1731, Bach changed the key to D major, made minor alterations to the music and orchestration, and removed the four chorales. It is this second version that is popular today. Another setting of the Magnificat text exists in German as Cantata BWV10, *Meine Seele erhebet den Herrn*, composed in 1724.

The oratorios consist of two extant Passions and one work each for Christmas, Easter, and Ascension. All are traditional in both textual content and musical form: the texts consist of biblical passages interspersed with reflective pietistic poetry, and the music incorporates framing choruses, short *turba* passages, recitatives, arias, and chorales. The two Passion settings are the *Passio secundum Johannen* (St John Passion) BWV245 and the *Passio secundum Mattaeum* (St Matthew Passion) BWV244. The setting based on St John, composed in 1724, is economical in length and scoring, while the setting based on St Matthew is monumental. The other three oratorios are the *Oratorium tempore Nativitatis Christi* (Christmas Oratorio) BWV248, *Oratorium Festo Paschatos* (Easter Oratorio) BWV249, and *Oratorium auf Himmelfahrt* (Ascension Oratorio) BWV11. The Christmas work consists of six separate cantata-like compositions, meant for performance on the six Sundays of the Christmas season (1734–1735). Most of the separate sections have framing choruses, and all have *turba* choruses and chorales. The oratorios for Easter and Ascension are of standard length.

The motets have traditionally included six works, catalogued BWV225 through 230. However, it is believed that Bach did not compose *Lobet den Herrn alle Heiden* BWV230 but that he may have composed *Der Gerechte kommt um* BWVdeest, which is a parody of *Tristis est anima mea* by Johann Kuhnau. This latter work, which exists only as a movement in the pastiche Passion cantata *Ein Lämmlein geht und trägt die Schuld* by Carl Heinrich Graun, bears all the stylistic markings of Bach and should be counted among his motets. A listing of Bach motets should also include *O Jesu Christ, mein Lebens Licht,* which was catalogued as cantata BWV118 but which Bach entitled a motet and which is motet-like in construction and style. Two other Bach works— *Sei lob und Preis mit Ehren* BWV231 and *Nun ist das Heil und die Kraft* BWV50—are occasionally referred to as motets but are in actuality movements from cantatas (BWV231 is a movement from BWV28, and BWV50 is probably a surviving movement from a cantata that has been lost).

The motets are generally scored for double chorus, and they are in two or three movements, the final movement often being a chorale. *Singet dem Herrn ein neues Lied* BWV225 is famous for its contrapuntal complexity, and *Jesu, meine Freude* BWV227 is famous for its mirror construction (i.e., its first and final movements are identical chorale settings, the second and penultimate movements are almost identical, movements that approach the middle of the motet are characterized by trios and chorales, and the center movement is a fugue). The motets were composed not for church services but rather for funerals or celebratory occasions that were nonliturgical (motets that were performed during the Lutheran services of the time came from a collection called the *Florilegium Portense* that consisted of approximately 270 pieces assembled between 1603 and 1621). Most of Bach's motets were composed for funerals—*Der Geist hilft unser Schwachheit auf* BWV226 for Johann Heinrich Ernesti (October 20, 1729); *Jesu, meine Freude* BWV227, as mentioned above, for the wife of Leipzig's postmaster (July 18, 1723); and *Fürchte dich nicht* BWV228 for the wife of a city official (February 4, 1726). *Singet dem Herrn ein neues Lied* BWV225 was probably composed for the birthday of the Elector Friedrich August I of Saxony (May 12, 1727).

In addition to the original compositions described above, Bach harmonized approximately four hundred chorale melodies. Most of these are included in the cantatas, oratorios, and motets. However, some stand alone. The best known of these independent chorales include "Aus tiefer Not schrei ich zu dir," "Brich an, o schönes Morgenlicht," "Christ lag in Todesbanden," "Ein feste Burg ist unser Gott," "Es ist das Heil uns kommen her," "Jesu, meine Freude," "Nun danket alle Gott," "O Haupt voll Blut und Wunden," and "Wie schön leuchtet der Morgenstern."

EARLY SACRED CANTATAS
SELECTED AND LISTED ACCORDING TO FAMILIARITY

Nach dir, Herr, verlanget mich BWV150 (Psalm 25) – ca.1707 – SATB solos, SATB chorus, two violins, and basso continuo – 15 minutes. (1) There are four choral movements, one aria (S), one trio (ATB), and a sinfonia; (2) the basso continuo group includes bassoon, which has a specific obbligato part in movement five.

Aus der Tiefe rufe ich, Herr, zu dir BWV131 (Psalm 130) – 1707 – SATB solos, SATB chorus, oboe, strings, and basso continuo – 25 minutes. (1) There are three choral movements and two duets (SB and AT); (2) the strings are divided into one violin and two viola parts.

Christ lag in Todesbanden BWV4 (Christ lay in death's bonds) – 1707 – SATB solos, SATB chorus, strings, and basso continuo – 19 minutes. (1) The text, for a Lenten service, is by Martin Luther; (2) there are three choral movements, two duets (SA and ST), two arias (T and B), and a sinfonia;

(3) the strings are divided into two violin and two viola parts; (4) the original chorus parts have indications for *colla parte* instrumental doublings of cornetto (S) and trombones (ATB).

Gottes Zeit ist die allerbeste Zeit BWV106 (God's time is the very best time) – 1707 – SATB solos, SATB chorus, two recorders (*blockflöten*), two violas da gamba, and basso continuo – 20 minutes. (1) The text, entitled "Actus tragicus," is from various biblical and Lutheran chorale sources; (2) there are two choral movements, one aria (A), and a sinfonia; (3) both choral movements have solo passages.

Der Herr denket an uns BWV196 (Psalm 115:12–15) – 1708 – STB solos, SATB chorus, strings, and basso continuo – 11 minutes. (1) The cantata was probably written for a wedding; (2) there are two choral movements, one aria (S), one duet (TB), and a sinfonia.

Gott ist mein König BWV71 (God is my king) – 1708 – SATB solos, SATB chorus, two recorders (*blockflöten*), two oboes, three trumpets, timpani, strings, and basso continuo – 18 minutes. (1) The text is from various biblical and Lutheran chorale sources; (2) the cantata was composed for the election of the Mühlhausen town council; (3) there are four extended choral movements, two arias (A and B), and one duet (ST).

Ich hatte viel Bekümmernis BWV21 (I have great distress in my heart) – ca.1714 – SATB solos, SATB chorus, oboe, three trumpets, timpani, strings, and basso continuo – 37 minutes. (1) The text is from various biblical and Lutheran chorale sources; (2) the cantata was first performed on the third Sunday after Trinity, although Bach indicated that it was suitable "per ogni tempo" (for any time of the liturgical year); (3) there are four extensive choral movements, two arias (S and T), one recitative/duet (SB), and one recitative/aria (T).

Nun komm, der Heiden Heiland BWV61 (Now come, savior of the heathen) – 1714 – STB solos, SATB chorus, strings, and basso continuo – 15 minutes. (1) The text is by Martin Luther; (2) BWV62 of 1724 is set to the same text; (3) the cantata was first performed on the first Sunday in Advent; (4) there are two choral movements, two recitatives (T and B), and two arias (S and T); (5) the strings are divided into two violin and two viola parts.

LATE SACRED CANTATAS
SELECTED AND LISTED ACCORDING TO FAMILIARITY

Wie schön leuchtet der Morgenstern BWV1 (How beautifully shines the morning star) – 1725 – STB solos, SATB chorus, two oboes, two horns, strings, and basso continuo – 25 minutes. (1) The text is by Philipp Nicolai; (2) the cantata was first performed for the feast of the Annunciation (March 25, 1725); (3) there are two choral movements, two recitatives (T and B), and two arias (S and T); (4) the violins are divided into *violino concertante* one and two, and *violino ripieno* one and two; (5) the oboes are oboes da caccia.

Wachet auf, ruft uns die Stimme BWV140 (Awake, the voice calls to us) – 1731 – STB solos, SATB chorus, horn (*corno* or *zink*), two oboes and oboe da caccia, strings, and basso continuo – 29 minutes. (1) The text is by Philipp Nicolai; (2) the cantata was first performed on the twenty-seventh Sunday after Trinity; (3) there are two choral movements, two duets (both SB), two recitatives (T and B), and one aria (T); (4) the violins call for a *violino piccolo,* which is featured in a virtuoso solo in movement three.

Ein feste Burg ist unser Gott BWV80 (A mighty fortress is our God) – 1735 – SATB solos, SATB chorus, two oboes, strings, and basso continuo – 23 minutes. (1) The text is by Salomon Franck and Martin Luther; (2) the cantata was composed for the feast of the Reformation; (3) there are three choral movements (a lengthy motet expostulation of the chorale melody, a unison statement of the chorale with instrumental elaboration, and a straightforward chorale setting), two duets (SB and AT), two recitatives (T and B), and one aria (S); (4) Bach's son, Wilhelm Friedemann, added trumpets and timpani to movements one and five; (5) movement five calls for two oboes d'amore plus taille (oboe da caccia); (6) movement seven calls for two oboes da caccia playing in unison.

Herz und Mund und Tat und Leben BWV147 (Heart and mouth and deed and life) – 1723 – SATB solos, SATB chorus, two oboes, oboe d'amore, trumpet, strings, and basso continuo – 32 minutes. (1) The cantata, which is in two parts and was composed for the feast of the Visitation of Mary, consists of an opening choral movement, two chorales, three recitatives (A, T, and B), and four arias (S, A, T, and B); (2) the chorales are settings of the famous music referred to as "Jesu, joy of man's desiring."

Wir danken dir BWV29 (Psalm 75 and the chorale "Nun lob' mein Seel' den Herren") – 1731 – SATB solos, SATB chorus, two oboes, three trumpets, timpani, strings, and basso continuo – 24 minutes. (1) The cantata was composed for Leipzig town council elections; (2) there are two choral movements, three arias (S, A, and T), two recitatives (A and B), and a sinfonia; (3) the opening choral movement is the original music for the Gratias agimus tibi/Dona nobis pacem of the *B minor Mass;* (4) there are organ obbligatos in movements one and seven (movement one is a transcription of the Partita for solo violin BWV1006); (5) Bach considered this cantata one of his favorites.

Nun ist das Heil und die Kraft BWV50 (Now is salvation and strength) – ca.1740 – SATB/SATB chorus, two oboes and oboe da caccia, three trumpets, timpani, strings, and basso continuo – 3:30 minutes. (1) The text is for the feast of St Michael; (2) the cantata consists of only one movement (probably the first of a lost cantata).

Jesu, der du meine Seele BWV78 (Jesus, you of my soul) – 1724 – SATB solos, SATB chorus, flute (*traverso*), two oboes, horn, strings, and basso continuo – 21 minutes. (1) The text, by Johann Rist, is for the fourteenth Sunday after Trinity; (2) there are two choral movements, one duet ("Wir eilen mit schwachen" for SA), and two recitatives/arias (T and B).

Nun danket alle Gott BWV192 (Now thank we all our God) – 1730 – SB solos, SATB chorus, two flutes (*traverso*), two oboes, strings, and basso continuo – 12 minutes. (1) The text, by Martin Rinckart, is for a marriage ceremony; (2) there are two choruses and one duet (SB).

SECULAR CANTATAS
SELECTED AND LISTED ACCORDING TO FAMILIARITY

Lass, Fürstin, lass noch einen Strahl BWV198 (Princess, let one more ray) – 1727 – SATB solos, SATB chorus, two flutes (*traverso*), two oboes, strings, and basso continuo – 38 minutes. There are three choral movements, four recitatives (S, A, T, and B), and three arias (S, A, and T).

Auf, schmetternde Töne der muntern Trompeten BWV207a (Up, resounding sounds of the cheerful trumpets) – 1735 – SATB solos, SATB chorus, two flutes (*traverso*), two oboes plus oboe d'amore and oboe da caccia, three trumpets, timpani, strings, and basso continuo – 28 minutes. (1) There are two choral movements, four recitatives (S, A, T, and B), two arias (A and T), and one duet (SB); (2) movement one is the original music for the first movement of the Christmas Oratorio.

MASSES
COMPLETE AND LISTED ACCORDING TO FAMILIARITY

B minor Mass BWV232 – assembled between 1747 and 1749 – SSATB solos, SSAATTBB chorus, two flutes, three oboes, two bassoons, horn, three trumpets, timpani, strings, and basso continuo – 107 minutes. (1) The text consists of the complete traditional Roman Mass Ordinary; (2) there are eighteen choral movements (scored for SATB, SSATB, SSATTB, and SATB/SATB), six solos (S, A, A, T, B, and B), and three duets (SS, ST, and SA); (3) two movements—Gratias agimus tibi and Dona nobis pacem—have the same music.

Missa in G minor BWV235 – 1735–1744 – ATB solos, SATB chorus, two oboes, strings, and basso continuo – 30 minutes. (1) The text consists of the traditional Kyrie and Gloria; (2) there are three extended choral movements and three arias (A, T, and B).

Missa in A major BWV234 – 1735–1744 – SAB solos, SATB chorus, two flutes, strings, and basso continuo – 38 minutes. (1) The text consists of the traditional Kyrie and Gloria; (2) there are three extended choral movements, three arias (S, A, and B), and brief SATB solo passages within the choruses.

Missa in F major BWV233 – 1735–1744 – SAB solos, SATB chorus, two horns, two oboes, strings, and basso continuo – 25 minutes. (1) The text consists of the traditional Kyrie and Gloria; (2) there are three extended choral movements and three arias (S, A, and B).

Missa in G major BWV236 – 1735–1744 – SATB solos, SATB chorus, two oboes, strings, and basso continuo – 30 minutes. (1) The text consists of the traditional Kyrie and Gloria; (2) there are three extended choral movements, two arias (T and B), and one duet (SA).

MAGNIFICATS
COMPLETE AND LISTED ACCORDING TO FAMILIARITY

Magnificat in D major BWV243 – 1728–1731 – SSATB solos, SSATB chorus, two flutes, two oboes, three trumpets, timpani, strings, and basso continuo – 27 minutes. (1) This is a revision of the Magnificat composed in 1723 and consists only of the Latin text from Luke 1:46–55; (2) there are five choruses, five short arias (S, S, A, T, and B), one trio (SSA), and one duet (AT); (3) Bach specified that the basso continuo should consist of organ, cello, bass, and bassoon, all of which are to play in each movement except number ten, "Suscepit Israel."

Magnificat in E-flat major BWV243a – 1723 – SSATB solos, SSATB chorus, and two recorders (*blockflöten*), two oboes, three trumpets, timpani, strings, and basso continuo – 35 minutes. (1) Four chorale movements (two in German—"Vom Himmel hoch" for SATB and "Freut euch und jubiliert" for SATB—and two in Latin—"Gloria in excelsis Deo" for SSATB and "Virga Jesse floruit" for SB duet) are interpolated into the traditional Latin Magnificat text; (2) choral and solo movements are as in the revision in D major BWV243.

ORATORIOS
COMPLETE AND LISTED ACCORDING TO FAMILIARITY

Passio secundum Johannen BWV245 – 1724 – SATTBB solos, SATB chorus, two flutes (*traverso*), two oboes, strings, and basso continuo – 110 minutes. (1) The text, in German, consists of biblical passages and pietistic poetry; (2) major character roles are for the Evangelist (T), Jesus (B), and Pilate (B); (3) minor character roles are for Peter (B), a Maid (S), and a Servant (T); (4) the choral writing consists of numerous *turba* sections, opening and closing framing choruses, and eleven chorales; (5) the instrumentation includes two oboes d'amore, two oboes da caccia (no more than two oboes play at any one time), two violas d'amore, viola da gamba, and lute.

Passio secundum Mattaeum BWV244 – 1727 and 1729 – SSAATTBB solos, SATB/SATB chorus, four flutes (*traverso*), four oboes, strings, and basso continuo – 170 minutes. (1) The text, in German, consists of biblical passages and pietistic poetry; (2) Bach divided the performing forces into two groups—two sets of soloists, chorus, and orchestra—and clearly indicated the group from which each musical number was to be performed; (3) there are nine recitatives and arias of pietistic poetry for the soloists from the first group, and five recitatives and arias of pietistic poetry for the soloists from the second group; (4) major character roles are for the Evangelist (T) and Jesus (B); (5) minor character roles are for Judas (B), Pilate (B), Pilate's Wife (S), First and Second Maids (SS), First and Second Witnesses (AT), two High Priests (TB), and Peter (B); (6) Jesus' text is accompanied by strings; (7) the chorus, which is divided into two SATB ensembles, has numerous *turba* sections, framing choruses, and thirteen chorales; (8) the opening chorus, "Kommt, ihr Töchter," has a *ripieno* chorale melody in addition to parts for the SATB/SATB chorus—this *ripieno* melody is texted but was performed by a gallery organ during Bach's time; (9) the two groups of the orchestra are each scored for two flutes (*traverso*), two oboes, strings, and basso continuo; (10) the instrumentation includes two recorders, two oboes d'amore, two oboes da caccia, and viola da gamba; (11) Bach used two organs, one for each group.

Oratorium tempore Nativitatis Christi BWV248 (often called the *Weihnachtsoratorium*) – 1734 – SSATTBB solos, SATB chorus, two flutes (*traverso*) doubling two recorders (*blockflöten*), two oboes doubling two oboes d'amore and two oboes da caccia, two horns, three trumpets, timpani, strings, and basso continuo – 140 minutes. (1) The text, in German, consists of biblical passages and pietistic poetry; (2) character roles are for the Evangelist (T), an Angel (S), and Herod (B)—the Evangelist, which is a major role, sings in all parts of the oratorio, the Angel sings only in part two, and Herod only in part six; (3) the choral writing consists of numerous *turba* sections, framing choruses, and fifteen chorales; (4) each of the six parts of the oratorio is from twenty-one to twenty-seven minutes in duration.

Oratorium Festo Paschatos (Oster-Oratorium) BWV249 – 1725 – SATB solos, SATB chorus, two flutes (*traverso*) doubling two recorders (*blockflöten*), two oboes doubling two oboes d'amore, three trumpets, timpani, strings, and basso continuo – 41 minutes. (1) The text, in German, consists of biblical passages and pietistic poetry; (2) there are solo recitatives for S, A, T, and B, but only arias for S, A, and T; (3) there are two framing choruses.

Oratorium auf Himmelfahrt BWV11 (Ascension Oratorio "Lobet Gott in seinen Reichen") – 1734–1735 – SATB solos, SATB chorus, two flutes, two oboes, three trumpets, timpani, strings, and basso continuo – 29 minutes. (1) The text, in German, consists of biblical passages and pietistic poetry; (2) there are two extended framing choruses and one chorale setting; (3) movement four, "Ach, bleibe doch," is the original music for the Agnus Dei from the *B minor Mass*.

MOTETS

SELECTED AND LISTED IN CHRONOLOGICAL ORDER OF BWV NUMBER

O Jesu Christ, mein Lebens Licht BWV118 (Oh Jesus Christ, my life's light) – ca.1736 – SATB chorus, two *litui* (ancient trumpets), cornetto, and three trombones – 9 minutes. (1) The text is from a funeral hymn by Martin Behm; (2) the motet is in one movement.

Singet dem Herrn ein neues Lied BWV225 (Psalm 149 and a chorale of unknown authorship) – ca.1727 – SATB/SATB chorus – 13 minutes. (1) The motet is divided into three movements (the first and second for SATB/SATB and the third for SATB); (2) the choral writing is highly contrapuntal; (3) basso continuo participation is presumed, and instruments *colla parte* would have been likely during Bach's time.

Der Geist hilft unser Schwachheit auf BWV226 (Romans 8 and a chorale by Martin Luther) – ca.1729 – SATB/SATB chorus, unspecified instrumental parts *colla parte,* and basso continuo – 7:30 minutes. (1) The instrumental parts are original; (2) the motet is divided into three movements—the first for SATB/SATB and the second and third for SATB (the third, a traditional chorale setting).

Jesu, meine Freude BWV227 (Jesus, my joy) – 1723 – SSATB chorus – 20 minutes. (1) The motet is divided into eleven movements—five (all arrangements of the chorale) for SATB, four for SSATB, one for SSA, and one for ATB; (2) basso continuo participation is presumed, and instruments *colla parte* would have been likely during Bach's time.

Fürchte dich nicht BWV228 (Isaiah 41 and 43, and a chorale by Paul Gerhardt) – ca.1726 – SATB/SATB chorus – 8 minutes. (1) The motet is divided into two movements—the first is a dialogue between the two SATB choruses, and the second features a chorale cantus firmus in the soprano with an elaborate ATB accompaniment; (2) basso continuo participation is presumed, and instruments *colla parte* would have been likely during Bach's time.

Komm, Jesu, komm BWV229 (Come, Jesus, come) – date unknown – SATB/SATB chorus – 8 minutes. (1) The text is by Paul Thymich; (2) the motet is divided into two movements—the first for SATB/SATB and the second, a traditional chorale setting; (3) basso continuo participation is presumed, and instruments *colla parte* would have been likely during Bach's time.

Der Gerechte kommt um BWVdeest (The righteous rise again) – SSATB chorus, two oboes, strings, and basso continuo – 7 minutes. (1) The text is from Isaiah 57:1–2; (2) Bach, or some other composer, added independent instrumental parts to Kuhnau's vocal parts (which have not been altered).

CARL HEINRICH GRAUN CA.1703–1759

Graun was born near Dresden and received his musical education at the Dresden Kreuzschule. Like Johann Mattheson, he had a particularly fine solo voice and frequently performed in operatic productions—in solo soprano roles as a child and tenor roles after his voice changed. Unlike Mattheson, however, Graun's interests were completely centered on opera. He studied scores assiduously, once transcribing an opera by Antonio Lotti after having heard it only three times, and he composed arias as a teenager and then complete operas in his twenties. In addition, he became acquainted with Crown Prince Frederick, who had a great love for opera, and who in 1740, when he acceded to the Prussian throne and became Frederick II (also known as Frederick the Great), appointed Graun royal *Kapellmeister.* In this position Graun became associated with C. P. E. Bach, a keyboardist at the court who often accompanied the king's flute playing, and with Johann Joachim Quantz, a flutist in the court orchestra who directed many of the instrumental performances.

While Graun's position as *Kapellmeister* was focused on stage works (he composed more than two dozen operas for Frederick the Great), there were occasions that required the composition of sacred vocal repertoire, including four masses, one oratorio, two Magnificats, one Te Deum, nine cantatas, and twelve motets. One of the cantatas, *Ein Lämmlein geht und trägt die Schuld,* is not an original work but a pastiche of music by other composers and contains a movement, "Der Gerechte kommt um," that is a parody of *Tristis est anima* by Johann Kuhnau and that is thought to have been composed by J. S. Bach. The oratorio *Der Tod Jesu* was much better known than any of Graun's operas. Composed in 1755 to a libretto written the previous year by noted philosopher and poet Karl Wilhelm Ramler, it was one of the most popular works of its time in Germany. Its libretto contained only reflective poetry, and Graun's music met the public's taste for theatrical and pictorial text setting. Almost all the recitatives are accompanied, with frequent changes of melodic and rhythmic design to highlight specific characteristics of text, and most of the arias are in an ABA form, with the A and B sections in different meters and tempos. The oratorio contains five choruses and six chorales and is scored for SSTB solos, SATB chorus, two flutes, two oboes, two bassoons, strings, and basso continuo.

WILHELM FRIEDEMANN BACH 1710–1784

Wilhelm Friedemann (W. F.) Bach was born in Weimar during the time that his father, Johann Sebastian (1685–1750), was court organist. Like his brothers, he received his musical education from his father, enrolling as a student at the Thomasschule in Leipzig. He also studied mathematics, philosophy, and law at the University of Leipzig. In 1733 he was appointed organist at the Sophienkirche in Dresden, and in 1746 he was appointed organist at the Liebfrauenkirche in Halle, resigning this latter position for unknown reasons in 1764. For the remainder of his life he earned a living by teaching privately and by selling his father's manuscripts. He composed twenty-one surviving church cantatas, including the Epiphany cantata *Wie schön leuchtet der Morgenstern* for SA solos, SATB chorus, strings, and basso continuo, and the Easter cantata *Erzittert und fallet* for SATB solos, SATB chorus, strings, and basso continuo.

GOTTFRIED AUGUST HOMILIUS 1714–1785

Homilius was born near Dresden, where he was educated and where he served as substitute organist at the Annenschule. In 1735 he attended the University of Leipzig as a law student and studied music with J. S. Bach, who was *Kantor* at the Thomaskirche. Homilius was also assistant organist at the Nikolaikirche. In 1742 he was appointed organist at the Frauenkirche in Dresden, and in 1755 he was promoted to *Kantor* at the Kreuzkirche, with responsibilities for directing the music programs at Dresden's three main Lutheran churches (the Kreuzkirche, Frauenkirche, and Sophienkirche) and for teaching music at the Kreuzschule. He was known for his motets and cantatas, which were reprinted frequently during the latter years of the seventeenth century.

Homilius composed eleven oratorios, two hundred cantatas, approximately sixty motets, and twelve Magnificats. The oratorios consist mostly of Passions composed for Holy Week services in Dresden. Three of them—those based on the Gospels of St John, St Mark, and St Matthew—are like the Passions of J. S. Bach in that they combine biblical accounts with Lutheran chorales and pietistic poetry. The *Johannespassion,* for instance, relates the Passion story through numerous *secco* recitatives for the evangelist, occasional *secco* recitatives for characters such as Jesus and Peter, and fourteen short *turba* passages for the chorus. Arias and chorales accompanied by obbligato instruments and strings draw parallels between the biblical events and Lutheran theological thought of the late seventeenth century. The other Passions, including the most famous, *Ein Lämmlein geht und trägt die Schuld*, are lyrical dramas comparable to those of Carl Heinrich Graun and Carl Phillip Emanuel Bach. They are devoid of biblical passages and characters and entirely devoted to reflective poetry. The biblical Passions are in the style of the late Baroque, with occasional melismatic passages for the vocalists and figural music for the instruments. The lyrical dramas are in the *empfindsamer Stil* (sentimental style), with syllabic settings of text and predominantly homophonic textures.

The cantatas are similar to the oratorios in both structure and style: recitatives are *secco*, arias are accompanied by obbligato instruments and strings, choral movements consist of both chorales and other choruses, and the style combines the figural qualities of late Baroque instrumental music with the syllabic and homophonic choral textures of the *empfindsamer Stil*. Most of the cantatas contain one or two choruses and a closing chorale; *Heilig ist unser Gott, der Herr Gott Zebaoth* is interesting in that it contains four choral movements, all set to different texts but the same music.

The motets are either settings of biblical passages with chorale texts or settings of biblical passages alone. Those that combine texts do so in a variety of ways. In *Da es nun Abend ward* and *Unser Leben währet siebenzig Jahr* the texts occur simultaneously, while in *So gehst du nun, mein Jesu, hin* and *Selig sind die Toten* the chorale is treated as a cantus firmus in the soprano voice. In *Sehet, welch eine Liebe* the chorale is a cantus firmus in the bass voice, and in *Siehe, das ist Gottes Lamm* the chorale appears homophonically in the second of the two choruses while the first chorus sings the biblical text. The motets that are devoted solely to biblical texts generally feature word painting, with tempo changes and melismatic passages. *Die mit Tränen säen* and *Machet die Tore weit* are examples. Most of the motets in both categories have textures that are basically homophonic and syllabic, although there are occasional imitative phrases (e.g., in *Die mit Tränen säen* and *Unser Vater in dem Himmel*). All the motets are scored for a cappella chorus (SATB or SATB/SATB), although participation of basso continuo would have been common during the Baroque era.

ORATORIOS
SELECTED AND LISTED ACCORDING TO FAMILIARITY

Ein Lämmlein geht und trägt die Schuld – SATB solos, SATB chorus, two flutes, two oboes, two bassoons, strings, and basso continuo – 100 minutes.

Johannespassion (also called by the first line of text, *Der Fromme stirbt*) – SSATB solos, SATB chorus, two flutes, two oboes, two bassoons, two horns, strings, and basso continuo – 120 minutes. (1) Major solo roles are for an Evangelist (T) and Jesus (B); (2) minor solo roles are for Pilate (B), two Servants (A and T), Peter (T), and a Maid (S); (3) arias are for SATB, with one duet for SS; (4) there are ten choral movements—nine chorales and one closing chorus, which is strophic and homophonic (chorale-like).

Weihnachtsoratorium (Christmas Oratorio, also called *Die Freude der Hirten über die Geburt Jesu*) – SATB solos, SATB chorus, two flutes, two oboes, two bassoons, three horns, three trumpets, timpani, strings, and basso continuo – 100 minutes.

CANTATAS
SELECTED AND LISTED ACCORDING TO FAMILIARITY

Heilig ist unser Gott, der Herr Gott Zebaoth – SAT solos, SATB chorus, two flutes, two oboes, strings, and basso continuo – 18:30 minutes. The cantata is for Trinity Sunday.

Der Herr ist Gott, der uns erleuchtet – SAT solos, SATB chorus, two oboes, two trumpets, timpani, strings, and basso continuo – 23:30 minutes. The cantata is for Whitsunday.

Selig seid ihr, wenn ihr geschmähet werdet – SATB solos, SATB chorus, two flutes, two oboes, strings, and basso continuo – 16:30 minutes. The cantata is for the Sunday after Ascension.

Gott fähret auf mit Jauchzen – SAB solos, SATB chorus, two horns, strings, and basso continuo – 14:30 minutes. The cantata is for the feast of the Ascension.

MOTETS
SELECTED AND LISTED ACCORDING TO FAMILIARITY

Unser Vater in dem Himmel (Matthew 6:9–13, the Lord's Prayer) – SATB chorus – 4:30 minutes.

Die mit Tränen säen (Psalm 126:5–6) – SATB chorus – 5:30 minutes.

Selig sind die Toten (Revelation 14:13 and the chorale "Selig, selig sind die Toten, die am Ende wohl Bestehn") – SATB chorus – 5:30 minutes.

Die richtig für sich gewandelt haben (Isaiah 57:2 and the chorale "Ach ich habe schon erblicket") – SATB chorus – 5 minutes.

So gehst du nun, mein Jesu, hin (John 11:16 and the chorale "So gehst du nun, mein Jesu, hin") – SATB chorus – 3 minutes.

Siehe, das ist Gottes Lamm (John 1:29 and the chorale "Christe, du Lamm Gottes") – SATB/SATB chorus – 4 minutes.

Sehet, welch eine Liebe (1 John 3:1 and the chorale "O Patris caritas") – SATB chorus – 3 minutes.

CARL PHILIPP EMANUEL BACH 1714–1788

Carl Philipp Emanuel (C. P. E.), second and most famous son of Johann Sebastian (1685–1750), is noted for his music in the pre-Classical style called *empfindsamer Stil* (sentimental style). He was born in Weimar during the time that his father was court organist to the Duke of Weimar, and he was nine when Johann Sebastian accepted the position as *Kantor* at the Thomaskirche in Leipzig. Like his older brothers, C. P. E. studied during his youth with his father, thus following a tradition that had been established for several generations. At age seventeen he began studying law at the University of Leipzig, and three years later he transferred to the University of Frankfurt, where in addition to his law studies he composed music for public festivals and civic events. Four years later, having become recognized as a virtuoso keyboardist, he moved to Berlin and accepted a position as harpsichordist to the future King Frederick II of Prussia. C. P. E. remained in this position for nearly thirty years, accompanying the king, who loved to play the flute, working with other composers such as Carl Heinrich Graun (Bach played the harpsichord in the first performance of Graun's *Der Tod Jesu*), and writing an important keyboard treatise, *Versuch über die wahre Art das Clavier zu spielen* (Essay on the True Art of Playing Keyboard Instruments). In 1768 C. P. E. succeeded his godfather, Georg Philipp Telemann, as Hamburg's *Musikdirektor der Hauptkirchen* (i.e., music director of Hamburg's five main Lutheran churches), a position that required him to conduct a large number of Passions, cantatas, motets, and other vocal compositions. Most of these works were compilations or pastiches (i.e., assembled movements from the works of other composers, not adaptations or reworkings such as was done by his father and Handel). This was the case with most of his twenty-one Passions, which cannot be considered original compositions. In addition, he conducted numerous performances of complete works by composers such as Graun, Hasse, Telemann, Handel, and, of course, his father. Bach continued his musical activities in Hamburg for twenty years, dying of a chest ailment at the age of seventy-four.

Carl Philipp Emmanuel Bach composed three original oratorios and approximately a dozen cantatas, motets, and other sacred works. The first oratorio—*Die Israeliten in der Wüste* of 1769—has a traditional libretto that tells a biblical story. The second and third oratorios—*Die letzten Leiden des Erlösers* of 1770 and *Die Auferstehung und Himmelfahrt Jesu* of 1777 to 1778—have librettos in a new style referred to as "lyrical drama." This style has no biblical quotes or dramatic action but instead, has reflective poetry that intends to place the contemporary person as witness to and responsible party for biblical events (especially the death and resurrection of Jesus). Johann Georg Sulzer wrote in his famous treatise on music of the time (*Allgemeine Theorie der schönen Künste*), "The designation 'lyrical drama' indicates that in this genre there is no gradually developing plot with machinations, intrigues, and intertwined actions, such as that found in theatrical drama. Instead, the oratorio features various persons who are strongly affected by a noble quality of religion." Sulzer further states that "each person quite emphatically expresses his sentiments about this, sometimes individually and sometimes jointly. The purpose of this drama is to penetrate the hearts of the listeners with similar sentiments." Karl Wilhelm Ramler, who lived in Berlin from 1745 until his death in 1798 and who was Bach's close friend, was the chief proponent and author of the new lyrical dramas. Ramler's two oratorio librettos—"Der Tod Jesu" of 1755 and "Die Auferstehung und Himmelfahrt Jesu" of 1760—were set by many composers, including Graun and Telemann. The music that corresponds to this lyrical drama is generally characterized by homophony, light textures, conspicuous word painting, and frequent use of accompanied recitative.

Bach was particularly fond of *Die Auferstehung*, commenting in a letter to his publisher, "I can, without any foolish egotism whatsoever, state that it is one of my finest masterpieces." Contemporary opinion was in agreement. A newspaper review of the March 1778 premiere (which also included Bach's motet *Heilig*) stated, "They [the oratorio and motet] would confer upon our Bach immortality as one of the greatest musical masters, they are so rich in novelty, dignity, and power." Furthermore, *Die Auferstehung* was popular throughout the eighteenth century; among many performances, three were presented in Vienna in 1788 by Gottfried van Swieten (who was responsible for the premiere of Haydn's *Die Schöpfung*) and conducted by W. A. Mozart.

The motets and cantatas include a sacred nonliturgical cantata and several cantatas and motets for festive liturgical occasions. The nonliturgical cantata, entitled *Klopstocks Morgengesang am Schöpfungsfeste* (Klopstock's Morning Song on the Celebration of Spring), was composed to a poem by the famous poet Friedrich Gottlieb Klopstock, who lived in Hamburg and who wrote works in the new lyric style that were religious in character but not theologically dogmatic. Bach's liturgical compositions include *Heilig, Anbetung dem Erbarmer, Auf schicke dich,* and a Magnificat. *Heilig* is one of Bach's best-known works and also one of his most favorite. He wrote to his publisher: "Here I displayed the greatest and boldest diligence for an exceptional work. . . . It shall be my swansong, and serve to ensure that I am not too quickly forgotten after my death."

ORATORIOS
COMPLETE AND LISTED IN CHRONOLOGICAL ORDER
ACCORDING TO DATE OF COMPOSITION

Die Israeliten in der Wüste – 1769 – SSTB solos, SATB chorus, two flutes, two oboes, bassoon, two horns, three trumpets, timpani, strings, and basso continuo – 80 minutes. (1) The libretto, about the Israelites in the desert, is by Daniel Schiebeler; (2) solo roles are for Moses (B), Aaron (T), and two Israelites (SS); (3) there is an additional solo for tenor that consists of one brief recitative that precedes the final chorus; (4) the oratorio is in twenty-nine movements, six of which are for chorus (one of these being a chorale).

Die letzten Leiden des Erlösers – 1770 – SSATB solos, SATB chorus, two flutes, two oboes, two bassoons, two horns, timpani, strings, and basso continuo – 120 minutes. (1) The libretto by L. Karsch is about the last sufferings of Jesus; (2) since the text is a lyrical drama, there are no solo roles; (3) the oratorio is in twenty-six movements, five of which are for chorus; (4) one of the choral movements consists of a chorale cantus firmus followed by a large double fugue, and one of the choral movements is a traditional homophonic chorale setting.

Die Auferstehung und Himmelfahrt Jesu – 1777–1778 – STB solos, SATB chorus, two flutes, two oboes, bassoon, two horns, three trumpets, timpani, strings, and basso continuo – 72 minutes. (1) The libretto by Karl Wilhelm Ramler is about the resurrection and ascension of Jesus; (2) since the text is a lyrical drama, there are no solo roles; (3) the oratorio is in twenty-two movements, six of which are for chorus; (4) three of the choruses have identical musical material; (5) the choruses that close the two halves of the oratorio are extended fugues; (6) the bass aria, "Ihr Tore Gottes, öffnet euch," is popular and often extracted and performed separately.

CANTATAS, MOTETS, AND OTHER SACRED WORKS
SELECTED AND LISTED ACCORDING TO FAMILIARITY

Klopstocks Morgengesang am Schöpfungsfeste – 1783 – SS solos, SATB chorus,
two flutes, strings, and basso continuo – 12 minutes. (1) The text is
from Klopstock's poem of the same name, which is about God in nature;
(2) the cantata is in nine movements, two of which are for chorus.

Heilig (Isaiah 6:3) – 1776 – A solo, SATB/SATB chorus, and double orchestra (two oboes, three trumpets, timpani, strings, and basso continuo in
each orchestra) – 7 minutes. (1) The motet is in two movements—a
brief solo (A) and an extended chorus; (2) Bach separated the choruses
in performance by placing one on a balcony.

Magnificat – ca.1749 – SATB solos, SATB chorus, two flutes, two oboes, two
horns, three trumpets, timpani, strings, and basso continuo – 41 minutes. (1) The text is in Latin; (2) there are four choral movements, four
arias (S, A, T, and B), and one duet (AT); (3) the final choral movement is
an extended fugue.

Anbetung dem Erbarmer (Psalm 86:8 and an unknown German source) –
1784 – SATB solos, SATB chorus, two flutes, two oboes, three trumpets,
timpani, strings, and basso continuo – 21 minutes. (1) The text is for
Easter; (2) there are three choral movements, one of which is a chorale; (3)
the cantata contains the famous bass aria "Ach, als in siebenfält'ge Nacht."

Auf schicke dich (John 3:16 and the chorale "Wir Christenleut hab'n jetzt und
Freud") – 1775 – SATB solos, SATB chorus, two flutes, two oboes, three
trumpets, timpani, strings, and basso continuo – 17 minutes. (1) The
text is for Christmas; (2) the cantata is in thirteen movements, five of
which are choral.

JOHANN CHRISTOPH FRIEDRICH BACH 1732–1795

Johann Christoph Friedrich (J. C. F.), second youngest son of Johann Sebastian (1685–1750),
was a composer of works in the pre-Classical Italianate style. He was born in Leipzig during the
time that his father was *Kantor* at the Thomaskirche, and, like his brothers, he studied music
with his father during his youth. He was close to his older brother, Carl Philipp Emanuel (1714–
1788), and the two visited each other and shared musical ideas throughout their lives. It is assumed that J. C. F. entered the University of Leipzig at age seventeen to study law, but there is
no record of this. With the death of his father in 1750 when J. C. F. was eighteen, he moved to
the small town of Bückeburg to play in the court orchestra of Count Wilhelm, and after nine
years he was promoted to *Konzertmeister*, a position he kept for the remainder of his life.

When J. C. F. arrived at the Bückeburg court—which had an active musical schedule, with
twice-weekly performances of oratorios, cantatas, symphonies, operas, and chamber music—it
was almost exclusively Italianate in musical style; both the *Konzertmeister*, Angelo Colonna, and
the court composer, Giovanni Battista Serini, were Italian, and Count Wilhelm had a particular
liking for Italian secular music. The Italianate style gave way to new German styles, however,
when the count married Marie Barbara Eleonore in 1765 and when the poet and theologian Johann Gottfried Herder became the court's clergyman in 1771. The count's wife favored Protes-

tant church music, and Herder became one of the most recognized authors of oratorio librettos in Germany.

J. C. F. composed seven oratorios, nine sacred cantatas, five motets, and two part songs. Of this output, only four of the oratorios, four of the cantatas, three of the motets, and the two part songs are extant. The relatively small number of choral works, especially in comparison with the prolific output of his father and older brother C. P. E., had not only to do with J. C. F.'s limited occasion to compose choral works for the Bückeburg court but also with his general practice of presenting other composers' works instead of writing new ones.

Bach's oratorios were composed to librettos, referred to as "lyrical dramas," that are in a reflective style, with no biblical quotes, generally no dramatic plots, and texts that involve the eighteenth-century listener in biblical situations. For further information about lyrical dramas, see the Johann Georg Sulzer quotes under the discussion of C. P. E. Bach's oratorios. The music set to these librettos was in the new *empfindsamer Stil* (sentimental style), which was characterized by homophony, light textures, word painting and pictorial orchestral effects, and numerous accompanied recitatives. This style was in contrast to late Baroque counterpoint, thick textures, periodic affects, and numerous arias.

Die Kindheit Jesu, J. C. F.'s most popular oratorio, reflects on mankind's redemption through the thoughts of three characters (or character groups) witnessing the birth of Christ—the shepherds, Mary, and Simeon, all of whom relate personal feelings about salvation. To specify that the oratorio is a lyrical drama—a reflective meditation instead of a dramatic story—it is subtitled "Ein biblisches Gemälde" (A biblical picture). Most of the characters' dialogue is delivered in accompanied recitative (there are only two arias—the Angel's announcement and Mary's lullaby), and special pictorial effects include three orchestral interludes at the beginning of the oratorio, each sharing musical material and each entitled "Himmlische Musik, fernher, ohne Worte" (Heavenly music, from afar, without words). *Die Pilgrime auf Golgotha* relates the feelings of pilgrims who take a journey to the Holy Land to see where Jesus suffered. When they arrive, they encounter a hermit watching over the Holy Tomb who tells them his sentiments about the Stations of the Cross. Most of the text is related through accompanied recitative that features pictorial orchestral effects. Both *Die Auferweckung Lazarus* and *Der Tod Jesu* relate traditional biblical stories—the raising of Lazarus from the dead and the death of Jesus—through poetry about the events; there are no direct biblical quotations.

The cantatas (all for solos, chorus, and small orchestra) are multimovement works that were written for special occasions such as Ascension, the feast of St Michael, or the birthday of a notable person in the Bückeburg court. The motets, similar to those works by J. C. F.'s ancestors, are generally scored for chorus with only basso continuo accompaniment; additionally, many contain a Lutheran chorale. However, they are in the new pre-Classical Italianate style characterized by the development of short motifs and by homophonic textures.

ORATORIOS

COMPLETE AND LISTED ACCORDING TO FAMILIARITY

Die Kindheit Jesu – 1773 – SATBB solos, SATB chorus, two flutes, two horns, strings, and basso continuo – 36 minutes. (1) The libretto, described above, is by Johann Gottfried Herder; (2) solo roles are for an Angel (S), Mary (A), two Shepherds (TB), and Simeon (B); (3) there are also brief S and A solos in the final choral movement; (4) the chorus "Holde, hohe Wundernacht" (Beautiful night of great wonder) is frequently extracted from the oratorio and performed alone; (5) the oratorio is divided into twelve movements, five of which are for chorus (two of these being chorales).

Die Pilgrime auf Golgotha – ca.1769 – SSAB solos, SATB chorus, two flutes, two oboes, two horns, strings, and basso continuo – 135 minutes. (1) The libretto, described above, is by F. W. Zachariä; (2) solo roles are for the First Pilgrim (S), an Angel (S), the Second Pilgrim (A), and a Hermit (B); (3) there are also brief S, A, and T solos in the choruses; (4) the oratorio is divided into twenty-eight movements, five of which are for chorus and three of which share musical material; (5) there is an obbligato harpsi-chord part.

Die Auferweckung Lazarus – 1773 – SATTTB solos, SATB chorus, two flutes, two oboes, two horns, strings, and basso continuo – 60 minutes. (1) The libretto, by Johann Gottfried Herder, is about the raising of Lazarus from the dead; (2) solo roles are for Martha (S), Mary (A), two Bystanders (TT), and Lazarus (T); (3) there are eight choruses, five of which are chorales.

CANTATAS
SELECTED ACCORDING TO FAMILIARITY

Miserere (Psalm 51) – ca.1770 – SATB solos, SATB chorus, strings, and basso continuo – 51 minutes. (1) The cantata is in twelve movements (four cho-ruses, two duets, one trio, and five arias); (2) the choruses are mostly ho-mophonic (in the *empfindsamer Stil*).

MOTETS
SELECTED ACCORDING TO FAMILIARITY

Wachet auf, ruft uns die Stimme (Awake, the voices call to us) – ca.1780 – SATB chorus and basso continuo – 16 minutes. (1) The text is by Philipp Nico-lai; (2) the traditional chorale tune is incorporated throughout the motet and used as motivic material, a cantus firmus, and a homophonic SATB setting.

JOHANN CHRISTIAN BACH 1735–1782

Johann Christian Bach was the youngest son of Johann Sebastian (1685–1750) and the brother of Carl Philipp Emanuel (1714–1788) and Johann Christoph Friedrich (1732–1795). Johann Christian was born in Leipzig and, following long-standing family tradition, received his musi-cal instruction from his father, who was *Kantor* at the Thomaskirche. At age fourteen, when his father died, he moved to Berlin and continued musical studies with his brother C. P. E. Five years later, in 1755, he set out on his own and went to Italy—first to Bologna, where he studied coun-terpoint with Padre Giovanni Battista Martini, and then to Milan, where he served as second or-ganist at the cathedral. He converted to Catholicism in 1757, and between 1757 and 1760 he composed a number of sacred Latin choral works. His interests turned to secular music with the composition of his first opera, *Artaserse,* in 1760, and he established himself as a recognized composer with his second opera, *Catone in Utica,* in 1761. Thereafter, he focused almost completely on opera and related vocal forms such as the solo cantata. Bach moved to London in 1762, fulfilling a commission from the King's Theatre to compose two operas, and he lived in London for the remainder of his life, although he made several significant visits to Mannheim (1772 and 1775) and Paris (1778) to oversee productions of operas he had composed for these cities.

Soon after his move to London he was appointed music master to Queen Charlotte, who was of German birth, and he began a public concert series with his childhood friend Carl Friedrich Abel, whose father had worked with Bach's father in Cöthen. Bach's duties for the queen included giving music lessons to the royal family, accompanying the king (who played flute), directing musical performances, and composing chamber music. The concert series, which took place from January to May except during Holy Week, featured vocal music, concertos, sonatas, and symphonies by Bach and Abel. Concerts on the series also featured the pianoforte, which Bach presumably first introduced to the public in 1768. The concert series was quite popular for a period of time: there were ten concerts in 1765 and fifteen each year from 1766 until 1781. In 1770 Bach initiated oratorio performances during Lent and composed *Gioas, rè di Giuda*—the libretto of which is about the grandson of Athalia, Gioas, who became King of the Jews. The oratorio concerts were not successful, however, and Bach composed no more works in this genre.

Bach was an important figure in the musical and social circles of London. He was friends with the writer Charles Burney and the artist Thomas Gainsborough (who painted two portraits of Bach, one of which was sent to Padre Martini as a gift), and he became acquainted with Leopold and Wolfgang Amadeus Mozart when they visited London in 1764. Bach and the young Mozart played harpsichord duets, and Mozart later wrote of his admiration for Bach. By 1781 Bach's health began to decline, and he died on New Year's Day 1781 at age forty-six.

Johann Christian Bach composed twenty Latin choral works, one oratorio, and one English anthem in addition to twelve operas, ten cantatas for solo voices, seventy songs and duets, approximately eighty symphonies and concertos, and more than one hundred instrumental chamber works and keyboard pieces. (Note that there are no Lutheran works or settings of German texts.) The Latin choral works include four mass movements, one partial Requiem, three Magnificats, two Te Deums, and ten motets. Almost all of these works are in multimovements and are scored for a quartet of soloists, chorus, and orchestra. They are also in a conservative Italian Baroque style, with choruses that are imitative and contrapuntal.

LATIN WORKS
SELECTED AND LISTED ACCORDING TO FAMILIARITY

Domine ad adjuvandum (Psalm 69) – 1758 – S solo, SATB chorus, two oboes, two horns, strings, and basso continuo – 11 minutes. (1) The motet is in three movements—choral, solo, and choral; (2) the choral texture is basically homophonic.

Credo in C major – 1758 – SATB chorus, two oboes, two horns, strings, and basso continuo – 20 minutes. (1) The work is in six movements; (2) the choral texture is basically homophonic.

Magnificat – 1760 – SATB solos, SATB chorus, two oboes, two horns, strings, and basso continuo – 10 minutes. (1) This is the last of Bach's three Magnificat settings, all in the key of C major; (2) the work is in five movements, all involving chorus.

Dixit Dominus (Psalm 110) – SATB solos, SATB chorus, two oboes, horn, strings, and basso continuo – 20 minutes. The work is in nine movements, five involving chorus.

Kyrie – ST solos, SATB chorus, two oboes, two horns, strings, and basso continuo – 6 minutes. The work is in three movements—the outer two choral and the center, Christe, a duet.

Gloria in D major – 1758 – SATB solos, SATB chorus, two oboes, two horns, strings, and basso continuo – 40 minutes. (1) This is the first of Bach's two settings (the second setting is in the key of G major); (2) it is in nine movements, two of which are choral.

Requiem aeternam (Introitus) and *Kyrie* – 1757 – SATB solos, SATB chorus, two oboes, two horns, strings, and basso continuo – 8 minutes. (1) The *Requiem aeternam* is in three sections—ABA—each beginning with a chant incipit; (2) the instruments are entirely *colla parte*.

ORATORIO

Gioas, rè di Giuda – 1770 – SSAATB solos, SATB chorus, two flutes, two oboes, two bassoons, two horns, two trumpets, timpani, strings, and basso continuo – 134 minutes. (1) Solo roles are for Sebia (S), Ismaele (S), Gioas (A), Athalia (A), Gioiada (T), and Matan (B); (2) the role of Athalia is meant for a countertenor and the role of Ismaele for a castrato; (3) there are additional solos for two boys (trebles); (4) the chorus portrays Hebrew Maidens, Levites, and followers of Athalia and Matan.

❧ ENGLAND ❧

England experienced a long period of cultural stability during the reign of Elizabeth I (1558–1603) in the Renaissance era. However, for approximately one hundred years after her death (the first hundred years of the Baroque era), the cultural life of the country was unsettled and protean. Dramatic changes occurred as the monarchy was abolished and then restored, as Parliament was variously ignored and heeded or dispensed with and then reinstated, and as the country's rulers adopted Anglican or Roman Catholic practices. James I (1603–1625), as an outsider from Scotland, faced increasing difficulties with Parliament; his son Charles I (1625–1649) polarized the country by ruling without Parliament for eleven years (the "Eleven Years Tyranny"), by marrying a Roman Catholic, and by appointing an archbishop who made unpopular reforms to the Anglican liturgy; Oliver Cromwell (1649–1658), who declared himself Lord Protector of the Commonwealth after the execution of Charles I for treason, disbanded the

Chapel Royal and other royal institutions and also suppressed most artistic endeavors; and Richard Cromwell (1658–1659), Oliver's son, abdicated. Charles II (1660–1685), who had been living in France during the Commonwealth, not only restored the monarchy and its royal institutions, but also brought to England some of the cultural elements he had witnessed at the courts of Louis XIV in Paris and Versailles. These included the establishment of the Royal Violins, which were modeled directly on the *Vingt-quatre violons du Roi,* and the expansion of the anthem to emulate the *grand motet.* However, like his father, Charles II polarized the country by dissolving Parliament. James II (1685–1688), a Roman Catholic who had been Duke of York, fled the country as a result of the Glorious Revolution; Mary II (1689–1694) ruled jointly with her husband, William III of Orange, until her death, at which time William ruled alone until his death in 1702; William strengthened the Church of England and during his reign Parliament enacted the Bill of Rights, which required that all future monarchs be Protestant; during the reign of William's successor, Anne (1702–1714), Parliament created the Act of Settlement and thus gave itself power to choose all future heirs to the throne; and William's cousin, Sophia, Electress of Hanover, was chosen after Anne's death, since none of Anne's children were living. However, Sophia died shortly after Anne, and the throne went to her son, the Elector of Hanover, who became George I (1714–1727) and who, along with his son George II (1727–1760), was able to reestablish a period of cultural stability for the final years of the Baroque era.

With such a state of change and disorder throughout the country for most of the Baroque era, there was little opportunity for the nurturing and development of composers. In addition, with cultural activity confined to London, the composers who did develop depended on the support the city provided. Consequently, only a few composers reached a significant status, and of those, most were trained and employed in a select few chapels and cathedrals. In terms of training, seven of the composers discussed here—Pelham Humfrey, Michael Wise, John Blow, Henry Purcell, Jeremiah Clarke, William Croft, and Maurice Green—were choristers at the Chapel Royal, and one composer, William Boyce, was a chorister at St Paul's Cathedral. Five composers, all of minor status, were choristers in cathedrals outside London—John Amner in Ely, Henry and William Lawes in Salisbury, William Child in Bristol, and Matthew Locke in Exeter. In addition, only one of the English native composers (Humfrey) ever ventured outside the country (he traveled to France and Italy for a brief period of study). In terms of employment, all the composers but one had positions at the Chapel Royal, and most of them also had positions at Westminster Abbey and St Paul's Cathedral. The most famous composer in England during the Baroque era—George Frideric Handel—was born in Germany and trained there and in Italy.

Because England was so isolated from foreign influences during the first sixty years of the seventeenth century, the new *seconda prattica* styles that were prevalent in Italy, France, and Germany were not adopted by English composers, who continued to write in the style of the late Renaissance. Some aspects of this late Renaissance style, such as homophonic textures and harmonic orientation, were indicators of the emerging Baroque, and some minor composers, such as John Amner and Henry Lawes, can be considered transitional composers. However, independent basso continuo parts, scoring for strings, and extended passages or movements for single soloists were not employed by English composers until the reign of Charles II. Consequently, it can be said that the Baroque era in England did not begin in essence until 1660. The seventeenth-century composers who wrote before this time—Amner, Henry and William Lawes, William Child, Locke, Humfrey, and Wise—are nonetheless considered a part of the Baroque era.

Most of the genres that were popular during the era were directly related to the Anglican Church and the royal court. The church music included anthems and Services, while the court music included odes and masques. Genres outside the church and court included oratorios, catches, and glees. The anthem was the most significant sacred genre; it was a part of every composer's output, and it represented most composers at their artistic peak. As in the Renaissance, the anthem continued to be of the full and verse types. However, during the Baroque era the full anthem had brief ensemble passages for soloists and the verse anthem had string accompaniment. In addition, the verse anthem developed into a large-scale form that was divided into separate movements for soloists, chorus, and instruments.

The Services did not capture the artistic imagination of the Baroque composers. Most of the chapels and cathedrals used Service music from the Renaissance that was collected into volumes such as John Barnard's *The First Book of Selected Church Musick,* and since most chapels and cathedrals favored short versions of Services, composers did not feel that they had opportunity for artistic expression. Composers who wrote Services generally set only the Te Deum and Jubilate of Morning Prayer and the Magnificat and Nunc dimittis of Evening Prayer. The other musical parts of Morning Prayer (Venite, Benedicite, and Benedictus) and Evening Prayer (Cantate Domino and Deus misereatur), and all the musical parts of Holy Communion (Kyrie, Creed, Sanctus, and Gloria in excelsis) received very few settings.

The arrangement of choral forces in Anglican churches continued the tradition begun in the Renaissance era: the singers were seated facing each other in the area of the church, called the choir, that is located between the nave and the high altar; the right side of the choir held an SATB ensemble called *decani* (the dean's side of the altar), while the left side of the choir held an SATB ensemble called *cantoris* (the cantor's side of the altar). Composers often indicated in the scores of anthems and Services that one or the other side was to sing alone (signified by the abbreviation *dec.* or *can.*) or that both sides were to sing together (signified by the term *full*). Soloists in both anthems and Services were members of and sang from the chorus.

The basso continuo part of all music sung in the church was limited to organ alone. Consequently, organ is listed in the annotated anthems and Services below instead of basso continuo. Odes and oratorios employed multiple chord-producing and melodic bass instruments (including organs, harpsichords, lutes, theorbos, string basses, and bassoons) and thus are given the general designation of basso continuo.

Of the secular genres, the ode was the most significant. It was the featured music at all royal birthdays, on occasions that welcomed dignitaries home from military victories or extended absences, on New Year's Day celebrations, and at observances of St Cecilia's Day. Poets such as John Dryden wrote poems specifically meant to be set as odes, and, with little restrictions as to length and scoring, composers embraced the ode as a genre compatible with their highest artistic ideals. The St Cecilia odes, with texts in praise of music, are especially noteworthy. Masques were also favored entertainments for royal occasions; however, generally being a part of a larger dramatic production, they often contain little choral music.

While Handel became famous for his numerous oratorios, the genre was not popular with other composers. The reason for this unpopularity no doubt corresponds to the professional circumstances of the composers; Handel served the public, who welcomed oratorios as substitutes for operas, while the other composers served the royalty, who had little interest in dramatic music.

JOHN AMNER 1579–1641

Amner was born in Ely, where he received his first musical instruction. In his twenties and early thirties he studied music at Oxford and Cambridge universities, receiving bachelor's degrees from both institutions, and for most of his adult life he held various positions at Ely Cathedral.

He composed forty-one anthems and six Services. The anthems range from simple four- and five-part pieces with optional organ accompaniment to extended works for soloists, chorus, and viols. Examples of the former type include *Lift up your heads* for SSATB chorus divided into *decani* and *cantoris* ensembles, *Blessed be the Lord God* for SATB chorus, *Remember not, Lord, our offences* for SAATB chorus, and *I will sing unto the Lord* (entitled by Amner "an alleluia, in memorie of the Gunpowder Day, 1605") for SAATB chorus. Examples of the lengthier anthems include *Consider, all ye passersby* for A solo, SAATB chorus, and viols or organ; *My Lord is hence removed* for T solo, SSATTB chorus, and viols; and Amner's most popular anthem, *O ye little flock,* for SSAT solos, SSAATB chorus, and organ or viols.

The Services include a Magnificat and Nunc dimittis from the *Cesar's Service*—both small-scale works in a homophonic texture and both scored for SSATB solos, SSATB chorus, and optional organ. Another familiar Magnificat and Nunc dimittis pair (also scored for SSATB solos, SSATB chorus, and organ) is from the *Second Service.*

HENRY LAWES 1596–1662

Henry Lawes, older brother of William Lawes, was born near Salisbury, where he most likely was a chorister in the Salisbury Cathedral choir. He tutored the children of the Earl of Bridgwater (the precise dates are unknown), and he served as a Gentleman of the Chapel Royal from 1626 until his death. Although few details are known about his life, it is obvious from contemporary commentary that he was highly respected. John Milton wrote a laudatory sonnet that prefaced a collection of Lawes's Psalms, and one of Lawes's anthems, *Zadok the priest,* was sung at the coronation of Charles II.

Lawes composed approximately fifty anthems and more than five hundred songs. The anthems consist mostly of three-voiced settings of metrical Psalm texts published in two collections—*A Paraphrase upon the Psalmes of David* and *Choice Psalmes put to Musick.* Examples from the second collection include *Who trusts in thee, With sighs and cries, Now the Lord his reign begins,* and *Lord to my prayers*—all scored for SSB and organ.

WILLIAM LAWES 1602–1645

William Lawes, younger brother of Henry Lawes, was born in Salisbury, where it is presumed that he sang in the cathedral choir. Nothing certain is known about his life before his appointment in 1635 as Musician in Ordinary for the Lutes and Voices under Charles I, although it is likely that he became acquainted with Charles I before this time. Lawes is known mostly for his extensive output of instrumental consort music. However, he also composed some significant vocal music, including forty anthems, ten canons, and approximately 250 secular songs, duets, and trios. The anthems include *Let God arise* for B solo, SATB chorus, and organ, and *The Lord is my light* for TTB solos, STTB chorus, and organ. In addition, like his brother's vocal output, a number of the anthems are simple settings of the Psalms. *All people that on earth do dwell* (Psalm 100) is his most famous of these simple settings. The secular vocal chamber music includes *What ho, we come to be merry* for ATB voices and basso continuo, and *Music, the master of thy art is dead* for SSB voices and basso continuo.

WILLIAM CHILD CA.1606–1697

Child was born in Bristol and probably studied with the organist at Bristol Cathedral. In his early twenties he was a music student at Oxford University, graduating with a bachelor's degree in 1631, and he became associated with St George's Chapel, Windsor, assuming the post of organist sometime around 1632. With the restoration of the monarchy at the end of the Commonwealth, he was appointed one of the organists at the Chapel Royal, where his duties included playing the organ at the coronations of Charles II in 1660, James II in 1685, and William and Mary in 1689. He continued his studies at Oxford, receiving a doctorate in music in 1663, and he also continued to play the organ at St George's Chapel, where he was buried near the entrance to the organ loft.

Child composed eighty anthems, eighteen Services, several motets, and three catches. The best-known anthems and motets are in a conservative, imitative, and a cappella style similar to that of Orlando Gibbons and other late Renaissance composers. Examples include *O Lord, grant the king a long life* for SATB chorus (composed for the coronation of George II and repeated for the coronation of James II), *O God, wherefore art thou absent from us* and *O bone Jesu* for SATB chorus, *Sing we merrily* for SSAATBB chorus (composed as an exercise for his bachelor's degree), and *O Lord God, the heathen are come into thine inheritance* for SAATB chorus. Other anthems—still conservative, but occasionally scored for soloists and chorus—include *Behold how good and joyful* for SATB solos, SATB chorus, and organ; *O pray for the peace of Jerusalem* for SATB solos, SATB chorus, and organ; and *Praise the Lord O my soul* for SATB chorus and organ.

The Service music includes a *Te Deum, Jubilate, Kyrie eleison, Nicene Creed, Magnificat,* and *Nunc dimittis* in E minor for SATB solos, SATB chorus, and optional organ. All six pieces were published as a set in William Boyce's *Cathedral Music,* although the *Magnificat* and *Nunc dimittis* are now published and performed separately.

MATTHEW LOCKE CA.1621–1677

Locke was probably born in or near Exeter, and he most likely lived in this vicinity until his late thirties, when he became associated with the Chapel Royal. All that is known with certainty is that he was a chorister at Exeter Cathedral and that he became acquainted with the future King Charles II, who lived in Exeter until his father's execution in 1649. During the Commonwealth (1649–1659), while Charles II was in France, Locke worked with several drama companies, writing and gaining fame for his theater music and becoming friends with John Playford and Samuel Pepys. When Charles II returned to England in 1660 as king, Locke was immediately appointed to several notable royal court positions, including private composer in ordinary to the king, organist to the queen, and leader of the Royal Violins. The position as organist to the queen was significant, for Locke, the queen, and the queen's mother were Roman Catholics, and Services at the queen's chapel (St James) and the queen mother's chapel (Somerset House) became well known throughout England. Locke's position as a respected composer of music for both the stage and the church was passed on to Henry Purcell, who, upon Locke's death, assumed leadership of the Royal Violins and who composed the ode *What hope for us remains now he is gone.*

Locke composed thirty-two anthems that are extant, fifteen Latin motets, two Services, six sacred Latin canons, and incidental music for twenty stage plays. Many of the anthems are of the verse type common in England at the time, with alternating solo and choral sections and accompaniment for organ alone. Examples include *How doth the city sit solitary, Turn thy face from my sins,* and *Lord, let me know mine end.* This latter anthem, one of Locke's best known, is in six movements—ATB trio, SS duet, AB duet, AT duet, SSAT quartet, and SATB chorus. Other anthems—English versions of the *grands motets* that Charles II heard during his exile in Paris and Versailles—are scored for SATB solos, SATB chorus, and strings, with instrumental introductions and ritornellos. An example is *O be joyful in the Lord, all ye lands.* One anthem—*Be thou exalted Lord,* subtitled "A Song of Thanksgiving for His Majestys Victory Over the Dutch on St James His Day" and performed for Charles II in August 1666—is uniquely scored for SATB/SATB/SATB chorus, five-part string ensemble, four-part viol ensemble, and organ. The motets are scored for soloists only, with accompaniment of two treble viols, bass viol, and organ. Examples are *Ad te levavi oculos meos* for SAB voices, *Audi, Domine, clamantes ad te* for SSATB voices, and *Super flumina Babylonis* for SATB voices.

PELHAM HUMFREY 1647–1674

Humfrey was presumably born in London, where he became a chorister at the Chapel Royal in 1660, the year that Charles II began his reign and the Chapel Royal was restored. From 1664 to 1666 he traveled to France and Italy, becoming acquainted with the music of Jean-Baptiste Lully and Giacomo Carissimi, and in 1666, upon his return to London, he was appointed a Musician for the Lute at the Chapel Royal. The following year he was made a Gentleman of the chapel, and in 1672 he became assistant organist to Matthew Locke and Master of the Children (one of the children being Henry Purcell). Humfrey died at age twenty-six and was buried in the cloisters of Westminster Abbey.

He composed nineteen anthems and two odes. The anthems are in the style of the *grands motets* that Humfrey would have heard in France and that were favored by Charles II, who also heard them while he was in exile in France during the Commonwealth. These anthems, similar to those by Matthew Locke, are scored for soloists, chorus, strings, and organ, with instrumental introductions and ritornellos. Examples are *O Lord my God, why hast thou forsaken me* for ATB solos, SATB chorus, strings, and organ; *O give thanks unto the Lord* for ATTB solos, SATB chorus, strings, and organ; and *Hear my crying, O God* for SATTB solos, SATB chorus, strings, and organ. The few anthems scored without strings include *Hear, O heav'ns* for ATB solos, SATB chorus, and organ, and the shorter of the two settings of *Have mercy upon me, O God* for ATB solos, SATB chorus, and organ. The two odes—*See, mighty sir* and *When from his throne*—were both composed for court celebrations in 1672.

MICHAEL WISE CA.1647–1687

Wise, whose place of birth is unknown, was a chorister along with Pelham Humfrey at the Chapel Royal in the days of its restoration after the Commonwealth. Wise was a lay clerk at St George's Chapel, Windsor, and at Eton College from 1666 to 1668, and in 1669 he began serving as one of the organists at Salisbury Cathedral. In 1676, while still serving at Salisbury, he rejoined the Chapel Royal as a Gentleman, and in 1687 he was appointed Master of the Choristers at St Paul's Cathedral. He was expected to resign his position at Salisbury but fatefully did not. One of the Salisbury staff engaged him in a fight and killed him.

His compositional output includes thirty anthems and four Services. The anthems are not in the style of Matthew Locke and Pelham Humfrey, with scoring for strings. Instead, they are in the older style of verse anthems by William Child and Jeremiah Clarke, with accompaniment for organ alone. Examples include *The ways of Sion do mourn* for SB solos, SATB chorus, and organ; *The Lord is my shepherd* for SS solos, SATB chorus, and organ; *Prepare ye the way* for SSAB solos, SATB chorus, and organ; and *I will sing a new song* for SATB solos, SATB chorus, and organ. The Services include a Morning and Evening Service in D minor, an Evening Service in E-flat major, a Communion Service in E major, and a Communion Service in F minor.

JOHN BLOW 1649–1708

Blow was born in Newark, near Nottingham, and received his musical education there and in London, where he was a chorister at the Chapel Royal. In 1668, at age nineteen, he was appointed organist at Westminster Abbey—the first of many prestigious positions, most of which he would hold simultaneously throughout the duration of his life. In 1674 he became a Gentleman of the Chapel Royal and also Master of the Children, in 1676 he began serving as one of the three organists at the Chapel Royal, in 1687 he added the position Master of the Choristers at St Paul's Cathedral, and in 1700 he was named Composer of the Chapel Royal. He worked with Henry Purcell and William Child, who were the other two organists at the Chapel Royal, and he composed music for Charles II, James II, and William and Mary. He was held in high regard throughout his lifetime and was buried near Purcell in the north aisle of Westminster Abbey.

Blow composed approximately one hundred anthems, ten Services, two Latin choral motets, thirty odes for royal celebrations, fifty secular song-like pieces, one opera, and fourteen catches. Most of the anthems include passages for adult male soloists—alto (countertenor), tenor, and bass. The large-scale anthems with accompaniment of strings and organ have extended solo passages or independent sections of music for soloists, while the small-scale anthems have very brief passages for soloists in ensemble. The Services consist of small-scale anthem-like settings scored for chorus and organ, with passages for soloists in ensemble and with alternation of *decani* and *cantoris* sides of the ensemble. Several Services (those in A major, G major, and E minor) were published in William Boyce's *Cathedral Music*. The most famous of the two motets and Blow's most famous composition in any genre is *Salvator mundi,* composed for unknown reasons and in the imitative *prima prattica* style typical of late Renaissance Italian motets.

Eighteen of the odes were composed for New Year's Day celebrations, six were written for the birthdays of kings and queens, and five were specifically meant for St Cecilia's Day observances. Most of the odes are multimovement works scored for soloists, chorus, strings, and organ. *Begin the song,* Blow's first and most popular ode to St Cecilia, is divided into nine movements—an overture, three movements for alto solo and chorus, two duets (AT and SB), two solos (T and B), and a concluding chorus. *The glorious day is come,* Blow's next most popular ode, is in one multisectional movement, with extended solos, duets, and choruses separated by instrumental ritornellos.

The song-like pieces, mostly scored for two or three voices and basso continuo, were published in a collection entitled *Amphion Anglicus* (1700). The final piece in the collection—*Sing, sing ye muses*—is scored for SATB chorus and is Blow's best-known secular work today. The opera *Venus and Adonis* is similar to Purcell's *Dido and Aeneas* in that both operas conclude with laments sung by the chorus, and both laments are often extracted and performed separately.

CORONATION ANTHEMS
SELECTED AND LISTED ACCORDING TO FAMILIARITY

God spake sometime in visions – 1685 – SSAATTBB solos, SSAATTBB chorus, strings, and organ – 12 minutes.

Let thy hand be strengthened – 1685 – SATB chorus and organ – 1:30 minutes.

Behold, O God our defender – 1685 – SSATB chorus and organ – 2 minutes.

The Lord is a sun and a shield – 1689 – ATB solos, SATB chorus, strings, and organ – 8 minutes.

Let my prayer come up – 1689 – SATB chorus and organ – 1 minute.

OTHER ANTHEMS (LARGE-SCALE)
SELECTED AND LISTED ACCORDING TO FAMILIARITY

And I heard a great voice – ATBB solos, SATBB chorus, strings, and organ – 5 minutes.

I beheld, and lo, a great multitude – ATBB solos, SATB chorus, strings, and organ – 9 minutes.

Blessed is the man that hath not walked – AABB solos, SATB chorus, strings, and organ – 8:30 minutes.

I said in the cutting off of my days – ATT solos, SATB chorus, strings, and organ – 10:30 minutes.

The Lord is my shepherd – ATBB solos, SATB chorus, strings, and organ – 11 minutes.

Lord, who shall dwell in thy tabernacle – ATBB solos, SATB chorus, three recorders, strings, and organ – 9:30 minutes.

O Lord, I have sinned – SATB solos, SATB chorus, and organ – 7 minutes.

O Lord, thou hast searched me out – BB solos, SATB chorus, and organ – 6 minutes.

OTHER ANTHEMS (SMALL-SCALE)
SELECTED AND LISTED ACCORDING TO FAMILIARITY

Turn thee unto me – SATB chorus and organ – 5:30 minutes.

O praise the Lord of heaven – SATB chorus and organ – 3:30 minutes.

Teach me thy way, O Lord – SATB chorus and organ – 3 minutes. There is a brief section of music for SSATBB solos.

Praise the Lord, O my soul – SATB chorus and organ – 4:30 minutes. There is a brief section of music for SSAATTBB solos.

My God, my God, look upon me – SATB chorus and organ – 4 minutes.

Lord, thou art become gracious – SATB chorus and organ – 3 minutes.

My days are gone like a shadow – SATB chorus and organ – 2:30 minutes.

MOTETS
COMPLETE

Salvator mundi – SSATB chorus and organ – 4 minutes.

Gloria patri, qui creavit nos – SSATB chorus and organ – 3:30 minutes.

SERVICES
SELECTED AND LISTED ACCORDING TO FAMILIARITY

Te Deum, Jubilate, Kyrie eleison, Nicene Creed, Cantate Domino, and *Deus misereator* in A major – SATB solos, SATB chorus and optional organ – 4, 2:30, 1, 3:30, 4, and 2:30 minutes.

Te Deum, Jubilate, Kyrie eleison, Nicene Creed, Magnificat, and *Nunc dimittis* in G major – same scorings and timings as the Service music in A major.

Te Deum, Jubilate, Kyrie eleison, Nicene Creed, Cantate Domino, and *Deus mis-ereator* in E minor – same scoring and timings as the Service music in A major.

ODES AND OTHER SECULAR WORKS
SELECTED AND LISTED ACCORDING TO FAMILIARITY

Begin the song (Ode for St Cecilia's Day 1684) – SATB solos, SATB chorus, strings, and organ – 22 minutes.

The glorious day is come (Ode for St Cecilia's Day 1691) – SATB solos, SATB chorus, two recorders, two oboes, English horn, two trumpets, timpani, strings, and organ – 30 minutes.

Sing, sing ye muses – 1700 – SATB chorus, two violins, and basso continuo – 3:30 minutes.

With solemn pomp let mourning cupids bear (from *Venus and Adonis*) – S solo, SATB chorus, strings, and basso continuo – 5 minutes. The solo role is sung by Venus.

HENRY PURCELL 1659–1695

Very little is known about the life of Purcell, including the place of his birth, circumstances of his musical education, or details related to his professional career. This is surprising considering he was recognized as a musical prodigy in his childhood and was highly respected and well known as an adult. Moreover, he composed a great deal of music during his short life, most of it performed to considerable acclaim. Roger North, the noted British author of musical textbooks, stated in 1726 that Purcell was the greatest British composer who had ever lived; George Frideric Handel commented in 1752 that Purcell's music was better than his own; and Charles Burney in 1776 credited Purcell as being superior to all his predecessors. Modern musical historians have compared Purcell to W. A. Mozart in that both were child prodigies and considered geniuses, both were known for setting texts that ranged from sacred to salacious, and both died in their mid-thirties.

What is known about Purcell's life is that he was a chorister at the Chapel Royal and that he began composing at age eight. At fourteen, when his voice changed, he became assistant to the keeper of the king's keyboard and wind instruments, and he began tuning the organ at Westminster Abbey when he was fifteen. At eighteen he succeeded Matthew Locke as composer-in-ordinary for the king's Royal Violins, at twenty he was appointed one of the organists at Westminster Abbey, succeeding John Blow, and at twenty-three he was appointed organist at the Chapel Royal, where he remained until his untimely death at age thirty-six.

Purcell composed approximately one hundred anthems, several Services, twenty-four odes, six operas, fifty catches, and more than three hundred solo songs, duets, and trios. The large-scale anthems (verse anthems) are multisectional works scored for soloists, chorus, and organ, with the frequent addition of strings. The sections of the anthems are delineated by solos, duets, trios, and larger solo ensembles, all of which alternate with passages for chorus and with instrumental ritornellos (e.g., two of Purcell's best-known anthems—*Rejoice in the Lord alway* and *Behold now, praise the Lord*).

The small-scale anthems (full anthems) are generally in one unified section and scored for chorus without extended solo passages, although brief passages for soloists are not uncommon. Purcell's most famous anthems are of this type. *Hear my prayer, O Lord* consists of a single point of imitation on the text "Hear my prayer, O Lord, and let my crying come unto thee" from the first verse of Psalm 102. The brevity of the text and music and the singularity of treatment suggest that the anthem was probably the first portion of a lengthier work that either was planned by Purcell but never completed or was composed and lost. *Remember not, Lord, our offences*, undoubtedly Purcell's most frequently performed anthem, consists of alternating homophonic and imitative passages for chorus. The *Funeral Sentences* have a few passages scored for soloists, but they are brief and are within an overall unified motet-like imitative texture. *I was glad* is scored for chorus throughout, with sections of text delineated by changing meters and tempos.

Of the twenty-four odes, four were composed for St Cecilia's Day observances, six were written for birthday celebrations of Queen Mary II, ten were intended for occasions that welcomed dignitaries home after victorious military battles or miscellaneous extended absences, and four were performed for various other celebrations. The first of the St Cecilia odes, *Welcome to all pleasures,* was composed in 1683 for the inaugural concert of the Musical Society. The text, by Christopher Fishburn, extols the virtues of music and makes direct reference to the "gentlemen lovers of musick" who had formed the society. One of the alto (countertenor) arias in the ode "Here the Dieties approve" became famous during Purcell's lifetime. The best known of the St Cecilia odes, *Hail! Bright Cecilia,* was composed for the Musical Society's annual meeting in 1692. The text, by Nicholas Brady, is similar to John Dryden's St Cecilia poem of 1687, with comparisons made between elements of nature and musical instruments. An alto solo in this ode also became famous; entitled "Tis nature's voice," it was sung at the first performance by Purcell himself. The most famous of the odes, *Come, ye sons of art,* was composed in 1694 for the thirty-third birthday celebration of Queen Mary II. It consists of seven movements, including the duet "Sound the trumpet" and the arias "Strike the viol" and "Bid the virtues."

The operas—*Dido and Aeneas, Dioclesian, The Fairy Queen, The Tempest, The Indian Queen,* and *King Arthur*—are included here for discussion because they often contain set pieces such as masques that are not integral to the dramatic action of the opera and that therefore may be extracted and performed separately. In addition, Purcell's operas are frequently performed today by choral ensembles in concert settings or in settings with minimal staging. Strictly speaking, *Dido and Aeneas* is Purcell's only true opera, since it is the only opera with a libretto completely set to music (the other works, often called "semi-operas," have some spoken dialogue). *Dido and Aeneas,* the most frequently performed of the dramatic works, was composed in 1689 and is famous for Dido's final aria, "Dido's Lament," as well as for the Witches' music in act two and the final chorus of act three, "With drooping wings ye Cupids come." *Dioclesian,* composed in 1690, closes with Purcell's most familiar masque, often referred to as *The Masque in Dioclesian.* A tribute to the power of love over war, it contains several highly effective duets (SS and BB), and it concludes with the famous trio "Triumph victorious Love, thou hast tam'd almighty Jove" and the chorus "Then all, rehearse in lofty verse the glory of almighty love."

The catches, which represent Purcell at his most clever and prurient, include the following, each cited with its complete text: (1) "If all be true that I do think, there are five reasons we should drink: good wine, a friend, or being dry, or lest we should be by and by, or any other reason why"; (2) "When V and I together meet, we make up 6 in house or street; yet I and V may meet once more, and then we 2 can make but 4; but when that V from I are gone, alas, poor I can make but I"; and (3) "Once, twice, thrice, I Julia tried, the scornful puss as oft denied; and since I can no better thrive, I'll cringe to ne'er a bitch alive; so kiss my arse disdainful sow, good claret is my mistress now."

ANTHEMS AND MOTETS
SELECTED AND LISTED ACCORDING TO FAMILIARITY

Remember not, Lord, our offences – ca.1679–1681 – SSATB chorus and optional organ – 3 minutes.

Hear my prayer, O Lord – ca.1685 – SSAATTBB chorus and optional organ – 2:30 minutes.

Funeral Sentences (called also *Burial Service* and consisting of the three movements "Man that is born of a woman," "In the midst of life," and "Thou knowest, Lord, the secrets of our hearts") – ca.1678 – SATB chorus and optional organ – 6:30 minutes.

Thou know'st, Lord, the secrets of our hearts (second setting) – 1695 – SATB chorus and optional organ – 1:30 minutes.

Rejoice in the Lord alway – ca.1683–1684 – ATB solos, SATB chorus, strings, and organ – 8 minutes. This anthem is often called the "Bell Anthem" because of descending, bell-like scalar motifs in the instrumental prelude.

I was glad – 1685 – SSATB chorus and optional organ – 4 minutes. The anthem, formerly attributed to John Blow, was composed for the coronation of James II and repeated for the coronation of William and Mary.

My heart is inditing – 1685 – SSAATTBB solos, SSAATTBB chorus, strings, and organ – 16 minutes. The anthem was composed for the coronation of James II.

Praise the Lord, O Jerusalem – 1689 – SSATB chorus, strings, and organ – 7 minutes. The anthem, composed for the coronation of William and Mary, contains brief passages for ATB solos.

Blow up the trumpet in Sion – ca.1677 – SSSAATTTBB solos, SSAATTBB chorus, and organ – 7 minutes.

It is a good thing to give thanks – 1680–1681 – ATB solos, SATB chorus, strings, and organ – 12 minutes.

O praise God in his holiness – 1680–1681 – ATBB solos, SATB chorus, strings, and organ – 8 minutes.

Lord, how long wilt thou be angry – ca.1683 – ATB solos, SSATB chorus, and organ – 4 minutes.

Thy word is a lantern – ca.1690–1694 – ATB solos, SATB chorus, and organ – 4:30 minutes.

O sing unto the Lord – 1688 – B solo, SATB chorus, strings, and organ – 12 minutes.

O praise the Lord, all ye heathen – ca.1679 – TT solos, SATB chorus, and organ – 3:30 minutes.

Let mine eyes run down with tears – ca.1682 – TB solos, SSATB chorus, and organ – 9 minutes.

O God, thou art my God – ca.1681–1682 – SATB chorus and organ – 5 minutes. The anthem contains brief solo ATB and SSA passages.

Behold now praise the Lord – ca.1678 – ATB solos, SATB chorus, strings, and organ – 6 minutes. The anthem ends with brief ATB trio and choral passages that are in a double chorus dialogue format.

Blessed is he whose unrighteousness is forgiv'n – ca.1679–1681 – SATB chorus and organ – 7 minutes. The anthem contains brief SSATTB solo passages.

Bow down thine ear – ca.1679–1681 – TB solos, SATB chorus, and organ – 6 minutes.

My beloved spake – by 1677 – ATBB solos, SATB chorus, strings, and organ – 9 minutes.

Jehova, quam multi sunt hostes (Psalm 3) – 1677–1678 – TB solos, SSATB chorus, and organ – 6:30 minutes.

Beati omnes qui timent Dominum (Psalm 128) – 1677–1678 – SB solos, SSAB chorus, and organ – 4:30 minutes.

SERVICES
SELECTED AND LISTED ACCORDING TO FAMILIARITY

Te Deum laudamus and *Jubilate Deo* in D major – 1694 – SSAATB solos, SSATB chorus, two trumpets, strings, and organ – 23 minutes.

Magnificat and *Nunc dimittis* in G minor – before 1682 – SSATB solos, SATB chorus, and organ – 8 minutes.

Magnificat and *Nunc dimittis* in B-flat major – before 1682 – SATB solos, SATB chorus, and organ – 7:30 minutes.

Te Deum laudamus and *Jubilate Deo* in B-flat major – before 1682 – SATB solos, SATB chorus, and organ – 8 minutes.

ODES
SELECTED AND LISTED ACCORDING TO FAMILIARITY

Come, ye sons of art – Ode for the birthday of Queen Mary II, 1694 – SAAB solos, SATB chorus, two oboes, two trumpets, strings, and organ – 25 minutes.

Hail! Bright Cecilia – Ode for St Cecilia's Day, 1692 – SAATBB solos, SSAATB chorus, three recorders, two oboes, two trumpets, timpani, strings, and organ – 53 minutes.

Now does the glorious day appear – Ode for the birthday of Queen Mary II, 1689 – SATBB solos, SATB chorus, strings, and organ – 23 minutes.

Arise, my muse – Ode for the birthday of Queen Mary II, 1690 – AATB solos, SATB chorus, two recorders, two oboes, two trumpets, strings, and organ – 21 minutes.

Welcome to all the pleasures – Ode for St Cecilia's Day, 1683 – SSATB solos, SATB chorus, strings, and organ – 17 minutes.

Welcome, welcome, glorious morn – Ode for the birthday of Queen Mary II, 1691 – SATBB solos, SATB chorus, two oboes, two trumpets, strings, and organ – 27 minutes.

Who can from joy refrain – Ode for the birthday of the Duke of Gloucester, 1695 – SSAATB solos, SSATB chorus, three oboes, trumpet, strings, and organ – 21 minutes.

Fly, bold rebellion – Welcome ode for King Charles II, 1683 – SSAATBB solos, SSAATBB chorus, strings, and organ – 19 minutes.

OPERAS
SELECTED AND LISTED ACCORDING TO FAMILIARITY

Dido and Aeneas – 1689 – SSSSSAATTB solos, SATB chorus, strings, and basso continuo – 53 minutes. (1) Major solo roles are for Dido (S), her sister Belinda (S), a Sorceress (A), and Aeneas (T); (2) minor solo roles are for the First and Second Witches (SS), a Sailor (T), a Second Woman (S), a Spirit (A), and an unnamed man (B).

The Masque in Dioclesian – 1690 – SSTBB solos, SATB chorus, two oboes, two trumpets, timpani, strings, and basso continuo – 40 minutes.

JEREMIAH CLARKE CA.1674–1707

Nothing is known about the early life of Clarke, including the place of his birth or the circumstances of his musical education, although it is presumed that he was born in or near London, since he was a chorister at the Chapel Royal at the time of the coronation of James II in 1685. From about 1692 to 1695 he was organist at Winchester College, and from 1699 to 1704 he was organist at St Paul's Cathedral. Shortly after his move to St Paul's he was appointed a Gentleman-extraordinary at the Chapel Royal along with his friend and fellow composer William Croft. Clarke was prone to melancholy throughout his adulthood and died at approximately age thirty-three from a self-inflicted gunshot. He is best known for his *Trumpet Voluntary*, which was originally scored for harpsichord and was arranged at the beginning of the twentieth century by Sir Henry Wood in today's most commonly known version for trumpet and organ.

Clarke composed twenty-one anthems, ten odes, a collection of Psalms and hymns, and several Services. Most of the anthems are of the verse type, with scorings for soloists, chorus, and organ. Examples include *I will love thee, O Lord my strength* and *How long wilt thou forget me, O Lord.* This latter anthem consists of a lengthy soprano solo followed by a short, homophonic closing for SATB chorus. *I will love thee, O Lord my strength* similarly ends with a short homophonic closing choral section, "He shall send down from on high," which is sometimes extracted and performed alone. One of Clarke's few full anthems—*Praise the Lord, O Jerusalem* for SATB chorus and organ—was a staple in Anglican services throughout the nineteenth century.

The odes include *Come, come along for a dance and a song,* composed on the occasion of Henry Purcell's death in 1695; *Let nature smile,* composed for a celebration of Queen Anne's birthday; and *O harmony, where's now thy power,* composed for New Year's Day festivities in 1706.

WILLIAM CROFT 1678–1727

Croft was born in Warwick, south of Birmingham, and received his musical education as a chorister at the Chapel Royal. In 1700 he was appointed organist at St Anne's Church in Soho and also a Gentleman-extraordinary at the Chapel Royal. While at the chapel, he shared the position of organist with Jeremiah Clarke until Clarke's death in 1707, and he served as the Master of the Children following the death of John Blow in 1708. He also served as one of the organists at Westminster Abbey, where he is buried close to Henry Purcell.

Croft composed seventy-five anthems, four Services, and two odes. The anthems, typical of the time, are divided between full and verse types. Examples of the full anthems include *O be joyful in the Lord, all ye lands,* scored for SATB chorus throughout and in an imitative texture, and *Hear my prayer, O Lord,* scored for SSAATTBB chorus and organ. The verse anthems, which represent most of Croft's output, range from those that are of modest length and structured in one multisectioned movement to those that are lengthy and divided into separate movements. Examples of the former type include *We will rejoice* for ATB solos, SATB chorus, and organ; *O Lord, rebuke me not* for ATB solos, SSATTB chorus, and organ; *O praise the Lord, all ye heathen* for ATB solos, SATB chorus, and organ; and *God is gone up with a merry noise* for SSAATB solos, SATB chorus, and organ. In all four of these anthems, the soloists are scored as an ensemble (trio or sextet) in the center of the anthem. *Rejoice in the Lord, O ye righteous,* an example of the longer verse anthem, is divided into five movements and is scored for AB solos, SATB chorus, oboe, strings, and organ.

The Anglican liturgical music includes a Morning and Communion Service in A major, a Morning and Communion Service in B minor, a Morning and Evening Service in E-flat major, and a Morning Service in D major. The first three of these are short and scored for SATB chorus. However, the *Te Deum* and *Jubilate* in the D major Service are large-scale works (45 and 12 minutes, respectively), scored for SATB solos, SATB chorus, two oboes, two trumpets, strings, and organ. In addition to the above Services, Croft composed a Burial Service. In four movements and scored for SATB chorus a cappella throughout, it is a tribute to Henry Purcell: the movement "Thou knowest, Lord, the secrets of our hearts" borrows one of Purcell's *Funeral Anthems* intact, and the other movements are in the style of Purcell.

Only one of the two odes is known today—*Prepare, ye sons of art,* composed for a birthday celebration of Queen Anne.

GEORGE FRIDERIC HANDEL 1685–1759

Handel was born in Halle, Germany, a small city north of Leipzig, where he spent his youth studying music theory, organ, harpsichord, and violin with Friedrich Wilhelm Zachow. At age seventeen Handel was appointed organist at the local Calvinist cathedral, and the following year he moved to Hamburg, where he served as a violinist and harpsichordist in the opera orchestra and where he became acquainted with Johann Mattheson, *Kapellmeister* of the Hamburg Cathedral and a proponent of sacred dramatic music. While in Hamburg, Handel also became acquainted with Barthold Heinrich Brockes, author of an important Passion oratorio libretto that was set by numerous composers, including Telemann in 1716, Handel in 1716 or 1717, and Mattheson in 1718.

At age twenty-one Handel went to Italy and began composing operas, oratorios, cantatas, and motets for many of the most important venues and arts patrons throughout the country. In 1710, having gained considerable fame, he was appointed *Kapellmeister* to the Elector of Hanover—an appointment that began with an eight-month visit to London. When Handel returned to Hanover to commence his duties for the Elector, he stayed only fifteen months before negotiating another visit to London, one that continued indefinitely and thus strained his relationship with the Elector. However, events transpired in Handel's favor when Queen Anne of England died in the summer of 1714 and was succeeded by none other than the Elector, who became King George I. Handel therefore remained in England without reprehension, becoming a British subject in 1727 and formally changing the spelling of his name from Georg Friedrich Händel to George Frideric Handel.

He held a number of positions while in England, including resident composer to the Earl of Carnarvon (later to be named the Duke of Chandos) in 1717 and 1718, music director of the Royal Academy of Music (a company devoted to the production of Italian operas) from 1719 to 1728, codirector of the King's Theatre (which also produced Italian operas) from 1729 to 1738, and composer at the Chapel Royal from 1732 to the end of his life. In addition, he composed numerous occasional works such as *Water Music* in 1717 and *Music for the Royal Fireworks* in 1749.

Handel began to lose sight in his left eye in 1751 during the composition of his final oratorio, *Jephtha*, a fact he noted precisely as he was composing the chorus "How dark, O Lord, are thy decrees." Several doctors tried to correct his eyesight, including John Taylor, who operated twice on J. S. Bach in 1750. But, as with Bach, Handel's operations were unsuccessful, and he went totally blind. Nevertheless, throughout the next eight years he composed several songs; performed organ recitals; participated in the revivals of his oratorios *Solomon, Susanna,* and *Messiah;* and oversaw the production of *The Triumph of Time and Truth.* He died in his home on April 14, 1759, and was buried in the south transept (Poet's Corner) of Westminster Abbey on April 20.

Handel's choral works include twenty-one oratorios, four Coronation Anthems, eleven Chandos Anthems, three Latin Psalm settings, approximately ten odes and other occasional works, one masque, and one Passion. There is some conjecture that he composed another Passion, *St John,* but this has not been substantiated.

Most of Handel's oratorios were composed late in his career, when English tastes had turned away from Italian opera—the genre that had interested and occupied Handel for most of his life. It was only with the cancellation of his opera season in 1738 because of a lack of subscribers that Handel began focusing his attention on oratorio. Prior to 1738 he had composed two oratorios—*Il Trionfo del Tempo e del Disinganno* (1707) and *La Resurrezione* (1708)—when he was in Rome and opera was forbidden, and he composed three oratorios—*Esther* (1732), *Deborah* (1733), and *Athalia* (1733)—during a brief two-year period when he was in London and his operas were declining in popularity. A preliminary version of *Esther* had been composed in 1718, when Handel was employed by the Earl of Carnarvon, and a successful revival of it in 1732 piqued his interest and he composed *Deborah* and *Athalia* the next year. The interest waned until 1738, when he composed *Saul* and *Israel in Egypt.* Then, in 1741 he began composing one or two oratorios each year until his blindness in 1752. These oratorios are *Messiah* (1741), *Samson* (1741), *Semele* (1743), *Joseph and His Brethren* (1743), *Hercules* (1744), *Belshazzar* (1744), *Occasional Oratorio* (1746), *Judas Maccabaeus* (1746), *Alexander Balus* (1747), *Joshua* (1747), *Solomon* (1748), *Susanna* (1748), *Theodora* (1749), and *Jephtha* (1751). An additional oratorio, *The Triumph of Time and Truth,* is a translation of the 1737 revision of *Il trionfo del Tempo e della Verità* and was performed in 1757.

The majority of the oratorios were composed during the summer and early fall seasons, and most were also completed within the span of one month (*Messiah* is not the only oratorio to hold this distinction). In addition, as was indicated above, Handel composed two oratorios each summer and fall for the years 1733, 1738, 1741, 1743, 1744, 1746, 1747, and 1748. The premieres of the oratorios generally occurred during the winter and spring of the years following composition.

Three oratorios—*Il Trionfo del Tempo e del Disinganno, Semele,* and *Hercules*—are on secular subjects. *Semele* and *Hercules* are not called oratorios by some scholars because oratorios in England were normally sacred. However, *Semele* was advertised as being "After the Manner of an Oratorio" and *Hercules* as "an Oratorio call'd *Hercules.*" Since both works bear all the characteristics of oratorios, especially those on allegorical subjects that were so familiar to Handel in Italy, they are included here under the oratorio category. All the other oratorios have biblical texts, relate stories of biblical characters, or address Christian circumstances. The three oratorios with texts taken directly from the Bible—*Messiah, Israel in Egypt,* and the *Occasional Oratorio*—are uncharacteristic of oratorio librettos and were not popular during Handel's time. *Messiah* only became popular in 1750, when it was presented for charity in the chapel of the Foundling Hospital in London. The most popular of the oratorios in the eighteenth century were *Samson* and *Judas Maccabaeus,* the latter being performed more frequently than any of Handel's other oratorios. *Joshua,* which impressed Joseph Haydn, was also frequently performed and highly acclaimed during the eighteenth century, and *Saul* was popular during the nineteenth century.

Handel often took movements from previously composed works and adapted them for his oratorios. He most frequently borrowed from himself, although he also borrowed from other composers of the Baroque era, and most of the borrowings were taken from works composed shortly before the oratorios. The original version of *Esther* (1718) borrowed nine movements from the *Brockes Passion* (1716 or 1717), and the revised version (1732) borrowed two movements from the Coronation Anthems (1727) and one from the *Ode for the Birthday of Queen Anne* (1713 or 1714). More than half of the music of *Deborah* was borrowed, without alteration, from earlier compositions, and the first large section of *Israel in Egypt* was taken intact from the Funeral Anthem for Queen Caroline (1737). *Israel in Egypt* (1738) also used material from other composers, including Dionigi Erba and Giacomo Carissimi. Of particular interest are four choruses from *Messiah* that Handel borrowed from secular Italian duets he composed just seven weeks before beginning the oratorio. "For unto us a child is born" and "All we like sheep" were taken from the two allegro portions of the cantata for two sopranos *No, di voi non vo' fidarmi,* and "His yoke is easy" and "And he shall purify" were taken from the cantata *Quel fior che all' alba ride.* The choruses and their original counterparts are strikingly similar. For instance, the first thirty measures of "For unto us" and "No, di voi" differ only slightly in rhythm. However, differences between the secular and sacred texts could not be more pronounced. "For unto us a child is born" replaces the original text "No, di voi non vo' fidarmi," which translates as "No, I do not want to trust you," a passage about blind love and cruel beauty.

In addition to borrowing previously composed works, Handel revised previously performed works for new performances. These revisions were almost always for circumstantial, not artistic, reasons; Handel would transpose arias or rewrite them for new singers, write entirely new arias for new singers, or delete or add movements to meet public expectations. There is not, therefore, an authentic version of this or that work, but merely this or that version of it as it was presented in this or that performance. For instance, for the second performance of *Israel in Egypt,* just one week after its premiere, Handel announced that there would be "Alterations and Additions" and that the oratorio would be "short'ned and Intermix'd with Songs." *Messiah* changes include a choral version in 1745 of "Their sound is gone out," revised versions in 1750 of the arias "But who may abide" and "Thou art gone up on high," and a rewriting and reduction (from ninety-six to forty-five bars) of the aria "Why do the nations." For a full discussion of

Messiah revisions, see *A Textual Companion to Handel's Messiah* by Watkins Shaw. In the case of one oratorio, revisions resulted in changes of its title. Handel added choral movements to *Il Trionfo del Tempo e del Disinganno* in 1737 and changed its title to *Il trionfo del Tempo e della Verità*. Then in 1757 he had the revised version of 1737 translated to English and called *The Triumph of Time and Truth*.

Il Trionfo del Tempo e del Disinganno (1707) and *La Resurrezione* (1708) were composed for Prince Ruspoli when Handel was in Italy. They are the only two of Handel's oratorios in Italian, and, modeled after oratorios by Giovanni Legrenzi, Alessandro Scarlatti, and Antonio Caldara, they consist mostly of recitatives and arias, with only a few ensemble pieces to be sung by the soloists. Both oratorios, although unstaged, were given elaborate performances, since oratorios in the early years of eighteenth-century Rome took the place of opera, which was forbidden by papal decree. *La Resurrezione,* performed on Easter Sunday and Monday of 1708, was especially grand. It was conducted by Arcangelo Corelli, and the performance space was decorated with the title of the oratorio above a proscenium and a painting behind and above the performers that depicted scenes from the oratorio.

Esther (sometimes called *Haman and Mordecai*) was Handel's first oratorio in English. It was composed and premiered in 1718 and given subsequent performances under the direction of a number of different people, including the Master of the Children of the Chapel Royal, who presented the oratorio to a private audience on Handel's birthday in 1732 (February 23). Pleased by the oratorio's reception, Handel planned a public performance. However, this was frowned upon by the Bishop of London, who was also the Dean of the Chapel Royal and who objected to Handel's plans on the grounds that it would be immoral to have the children of the Chapel Royal (who had sung in the private performance) appear in a public opera house. Consequently, Handel revised and expanded the oratorio and presented it in April with professional adult singers.

Deborah, which was composed in February and premiered in March 1733, was not successful. Audiences stayed away from the premiere because Handel had doubled the price of admission, and critics felt that the drama was weak. *Athalia,* on the other hand, premiered at the Sheldonian Theatre in Oxford on July 10, 1733, to what was reported to be an enthusiastic audience of 3,700.

Saul was composed from July 23 to September 27, 1738, and premiered in January 1739. It is considered Handel's first great oratorio and the work that begins his mature period; it is also one of his most dramatic oratorios, the drama being enhanced by stage directions (even though there was no actual staging) printed in the score and in the published libretto (called a wordbook), which audiences customarily followed as they were listening to the performance. Thus a listener could better envision dramatic actions such as Saul throwing his javelin at Jonathan. *Saul* is also more expansive than Handel's previous oratorios: it includes twelve choral movements and five separate and lengthy orchestral sinfonias, and it is scored for five major and seven minor solo roles and an orchestra consisting of a large number of specific basso continuo instruments and a carillon. According to *Saul's* librettist, Charles Jennens, the carillon produces a sound "like a set of Hammers Striking upon anvils. 'Tis play'd upon with Keys like a Harpsichord, and with this Cyclopean instrument [Handel] designs to make poor Saul stark mad." The orchestral sinfonias include the "Dead March," which is one of Handel's most effective instrumental compositions, and the choruses include the famous "How excellent Thy name, oh Lord" (entitled "An Epinicion or Song of Triumph for the victory over Goliath and the Philistines") and "Mourn, Israel, mourn thy beauty lost" (entitled "Elegy on the death of Saul and Jonathan"). The oratorio received numerous performances throughout Handel's life, and it went on to become the most frequently performed of Handel's oratorios in the nineteenth century (*Messiah* was more frequently performed only in the twentieth century).

Israel in Egypt was begun October 1, 1738, just five days after Handel completed *Saul*. The second part of the oratorio, entitled "Exodus," was composed first (from October 1 to 11); the third part, entitled "Moses' Song," was composed next (from October 15 to 20); and the first part, as was mentioned earlier, was taken from the Funeral Anthem for Queen Caroline, *The Ways of Zion Do Mourn,* which Handel had composed the previous December. The music of the anthem was unaltered; only the text was revised slightly, and the title of the anthem was changed to "The Lamentation of the Israelites for the Death of Joseph." *Israel in Egypt* is unique. It is not based on a character or characters, nor does it have a plot or a libretto that is a poetic adaptation of biblical accounts (instead, the libretto comes directly from the Bible). Furthermore, Handel scored most of the oratorio for the chorus (there are twenty-eight choral movements and only five arias and three duets). The public did not react favorably to these unique elements. Especially troublesome were the presentation of actual Bible verses in a public theater and the scant number of arias. To address these objections, Handel advertised that the second performance would have "Alterations and Additions" and would be "short'ned and Intermix'd with Songs." Handel also removed the entire first part of the oratorio and replaced it with an organ concerto ("The Cuckoo"). In spite of the public's reaction to the premiere and Handel's extensive revisions, the original version of *Israel in Egypt* is considered a masterpiece, one that shows Handel at his most creative. Especially noteworthy is the descriptive writing of the plagues—frogs, flies and lice, locusts, hailstones and fire, and darkness. Also, the double chorus, "I will sing unto the Lord, for he hath triumphed gloriously," which both begins and ends "Moses' Song," is believed by many to be Handel's most brilliant chorus.

Perhaps because of the poor reception of *Israel in Egypt,* Handel did not continue composing oratorios. Instead, he focused on the ode—*Ode for St Cecilia's Day* (1739) and *L'Allegro, il Penseroso ed il Moderato* (1740)—and opera—*Imeneo* (1740) and *Deidamia* (1741). In the summer of 1741, however, he received an invitation to present a series of benefit concerts in Dublin that would include both old and new oratorios. Handel accepted the invitation, planned revivals of *Esther* and *Saul,* and began composing a new oratorio—*Messiah.*

Messiah was begun on August 22 and finished on September 14 (a total of twenty-four days), and it premiered on April 13, 1742. The new oratorio was extremely well received. On April 10, three days before the premiere, a Dublin newspaper reported that "Yesterday Morning, at the Musick Hall . . . there was a publick Rehearsal of the *Messiah,* Mr. Handel's new sacred Oratorio, which in the opinion of the best Judges, far surpasses anything of that Nature which has been performed in this or any other Kingdom." A subsequent article after the premiere confirmed this sentiment by stating, "Words are wanting to express the exquisite Delight it afforded to the admiring crouded Audience. The Sublime, the Grand, and the Tender, adapted to the most elevated, majestick and moving Words, conspired to transport and charm the ravished Heart and Ear." The Dublin audiences apparently did not mind that *Messiah,* like *Israel in Egypt,* had a libretto drawn directly from the Bible, with no characters and no dramatic plot. Nonetheless, despite the acceptance in Dublin, Handel avoided putting the title of *Messiah* in advertisements for London performances, and London audiences were mixed in their reaction. Indeed, *Messiah* became popular in London only when Handel presented it in 1750 in the sacred venue of the chapel at the Foundling Hospital.

Samson was begun on September 29, 1741 (fifteen days after the completion of *Messiah*), and was finished exactly one month later on October 29. The premiere, which did not take place until February 18, 1743, was a great triumph for Handel. The public reacted so favorably that the premiere was immediately followed by seven more performances—the greatest number of consecutive performances for any of Handel's oratorios, either before or after *Samson*. Even newspaper reports acknowledged this phenomenon: "*Samson* has been performed . . . to more crouded Audiences than were ever seen; more People being turned away for Want of Room each Night than hath been seen at the Italian Opera." The oratorio marked a return by Handel to a traditional libretto based on a biblical character and to a balance of scoring for solo and choral forces. Of the eighteen choral movements, three are notable: "Awake the trumpet's lofty sound" from the beginning of the oratorio; "Let their celestial concerts all unite" from the end of the oratorio; and "O first created beam," a phrase of which ("Let there be light") Haydn virtually copied in his oratorio *Die Schöpfung* (The Creation).

Semele, Joseph and His Brethren, Hercules, and *Belshazzar* all followed in quick order. *Semele* and *Joseph and His Brethren* were composed during the summer of 1743 and premiered in 1744 within a month of each other (*Semele* on February 10 and *Joseph and His Brethren* on March 2). Similarly, *Hercules* and *Belshazzar* were composed during the late summer and early fall of 1744 and premiered in 1745 (*Hercules* on January 3 and *Belshazzar* on March 27). One of the works of each year was set to a secular text while the other work was a setting of a traditional sacred story. Both works of 1743 are considered weak; neither was particularly well received by audiences, and neither has been performed much since. However, both works of 1744 are considered strong, especially *Belshazzar,* which was one of Handel's favorite oratorios. It represents Handel at the height of his maturity and expressive powers, and it contains some of his most beautiful choruses, including "Sing, oh ye heavens" and "Recall, oh king, thy rash command" (which begins with an extended a cappella passage).

Occasional Oratorio, Judas Maccabaeus, Alexander Balus, and *Joshua* all have militaristic themes and musical characteristics, and all reflect the nationalistic mood of England following unsuccessful attempts to overthrow the Hanoverian monarchy during 1745 and the spring of 1746. The *Occasional Oratorio* was composed in January 1746 and first performed in February, with subsequent performances later that year and one in 1747. The text was assembled from various portions of the Bible, with some poetic paraphrases by John Milton and with no characters or attempt to relate a story. The public was immediately aware of the connection between the oratorio's libretto and the current events in England; an observer of a rehearsal a week before the oratorio's premiere commented that "the words . . . are expressive of the rebels' flight and our pursuit of them."

Judas Maccabaeus was composed from July 8 or 9 to August 11 of the same year (1746) and was performed six times during April and May 1747. It was also performed frequently in subsequent years (thirty-three times), thus making it the most performed of Handel's oratorios during the composer's lifetime. The libretto was intended to parallel the sentiments of the *Occasional Oratorio* and to directly connect biblical and contemporary English characters. It was clear to the audiences of the time that the role of Judas Maccabaeus represented the Duke of Cum-

berland, and, as related by the oratorio's librettist, Thomas Morell, the text was designed to glorify the duke upon his returning victorious in April 1746 from the battle of Culloden in Scotland. Several arias and choruses that are often extracted and performed alone testify to the oratorio's popularity. Included are Simon's aria with chorus from act one, "Arm, arm, ye brave / We
come"; Judas's aria with chorus from act two, "Sound an alarm / We hear"; and two choruses
from act three, "Sing unto God, and high affections raise" and "Hallelujah, Amen."

Alexander Balus and *Joshua* were both composed during the summer of 1747—*Alexander
Balus* between June 1 and July 4, and *Joshua* between July 19 and August 19—and both were premiered within two weeks of each other in March 1748. *Alexander Balus,* the libretto of which is
based on biblical passages that immediately follow the story of Judas Maccabaeus in 1 Maccabees 10–11, was obviously meant to be a sequel to *Judas Maccabaeus* and therefore yet another
oratorio to capitalize on the public's interest in current political events. Both the libretto and
music were considered weak, however, and the oratorio was not well received. It was performed
only five times during Handel's lifetime—three times in its initial season and twice in 1754.

Joshua fared better and was popular throughout the eighteenth century. Handel revived it
frequently, and it was performed throughout England after his death, including during four seasons (1759, 1769, 1773, and 1781) of the Three Choirs Festival. Its libretto is filled with highly
dramatic scenes, its orchestration is lavish and colorful, and it contains a large number of
engaging choral movements (fourteen in all), including "Glory to God the strong cemented
wall" from act two and "See the conqu'ring hero comes" from act three. Joseph Haydn is reported to have been extremely impressed with "Glory to God the strong cemented wall," and
Handel was so fond of "See the conqu'ring hero comes" that he inserted it intact in revivals of
Judas Maccabaeus.

Solomon, Handel's final oratorio to make a connection between biblical and eighteenth-
century British society, was composed between May 5 and June 13, 1748, with a premiere in
March 1749. No accounts of the premiere exist, and with only two performances during the
1750s and 1760s, it is probable that eighteenth-century public reaction was not strong. However,
with its numerous memorable choruses and large and lavish orchestration, *Solomon* is today
considered to be one of Handel's most masterful oratorios.

Susanna was begun in July 1748, one month after Handel finished *Solomon,* and it premiered in February 1749, one month before the premiere of *Solomon.* It seemed to audiences at
the time, and also to audiences since, that Handel had not fully committed himself to the new
oratorio. The libretto, by an unknown author, mixed humor (the two bumbling elders lusting
after Susanna) with serious biblical elements in a manner that had not been done before and
that Handel did not set convincingly. Also, the score has fewer choral movements than any other
Handel oratorio except *Alexander Balus.*

Theodora was composed between June 28 and July 31, 1749, and premiered in March 1750. As
with *Solomon* and *Susanna,* the public did not react favorably to the new oratorio. The nonbibli-
cal libretto, which is about the persecution of the Christians at the end of the Roman Empire, was
apparently inaccessible to the audiences, and the music did not engage their interests. However,
Handel allegedly liked *Theodora* more than his other oratorios. Thomas Morell, the oratorio's librettist, commented that Handel believed the chorus at the end of act two, "He saw the lonely
youth," to be superior to the "Hallelujah" chorus from *Messiah.*

Jephtha, Handel's final complete composition, was composed in spurts from January to August 1751 and premiered in February 1752. Handel's compositional process was interrupted by periods of poor health and temporary blindness. As was mentioned above, Handel noted the fact that he was losing sight in one of his eyes as he was composing the chorus that ends act two, "How dark, O Lord, are thy decrees! All hid from mortal sight!" After the first section of the chorus, Handel wrote, "Reached here on 13 Febr. 1751, unable to go on owing to weakening of the sight of my left eye." *Jephtha,* which shows no weakening of Handel's creative ability, was well received at its premiere and was performed seven times during Handel's lifetime.

The *Triumph of Time and Truth,* which is a translation by Thomas Morell of the 1737 version of *Il trionfo del Tempo e della Veritá,* was performed three times in March 1757 and twice more in 1758. The English version did not contain exactly the same music as the 1737 oratorio. For *The Triumph of Time and Truth,* Handel revised two arias from the original 1707 version of the Italian oratorio and added eight other movements—four for chorus—from his previous compositions.

The four Coronation Anthems were Handel's first royal commission as a naturalized British subject, composed for the coronation of George II and Caroline in Westminster Abbey on October 11, 1727. The order of the anthems in the autograph score is *Zadok the priest, Let thy hand be strengthened, The King shall rejoice,* and *My heart is inditing.* However, the order of the anthems in the actual coronation service was *The King shall rejoice* (performed during the part of the service referred to as the Recognition of the King), *Zadok the priest* (performed during the King's anointing), *Let thy hand be strengthened* (performed during the Inthronisation), and *My heart is inditing* (performed during the Queen's coronation). All the anthems are completely choral; there are no solos or separate instrumental movements.

The eleven Chandos Anthems were written in 1717 and 1718 while Handel was the resident composer at the Earl of Carnarvon's estate in Cannons, approximately twenty miles northwest of London. The anthems generally consist of six to eight movements, including an instrumental overture or sinfonia, solos, and choruses. The scoring of the first six of the anthems reflects the limited resources at the estate; there were no altos and no violas. The later anthems have alto parts but retain the string texture of two violins and basso continuo.

The three Latin Psalm settings—*Dixit Dominus, Laudate pueri Dominum,* and *Nisi Dominus*— are Handel's first choral compositions, composed in 1707 when he was twenty-two years old and had just arrived in Italy. *Dixit Dominus*—with its engaging musical figures, challenging melismas, and dramatic word painting—is especially popular today.

The odes include *Ode for the Birthday of Queen Anne* (1713 or 1714), *Alexander's Feast* (1736), *Ode for St Cecilia's Day* (1739), *L'Allegro, il Penseroso ed il Moderato* (1740), and *The Choice of Hercules* (1751). No records of the performance of Queen Anne's birthday ode exist, although it is assumed that it was written for and performed on February 6, 1713. It is sometimes referred to by the ode's first line of text, "Eternal source of light divine," which is a solo for alto with trumpet obbligato. *Alexander's Feast* (the full title of which is *Alexander's Feast, or the Power of Music*) and *Ode for St Cecilia's Day* were composed for festival performances, held annually on St Cecilia's observance day, November 22. The texts for both odes, which illustrate the wide-ranging power of music, were originally written by John Dryden and specifically meant for musical settings. The Concerto grosso in C major, subtitled "Alexander's Feast," was one of four added compositions for the first performance of *Alexander's Feast,* since the ode was deemed to be too short for an entire evening's entertainment. *L'Allegro, il Penseroso ed il Moderato,* with a libretto adapted by Charles Jennens from John Milton, was inspired by the successes of the two Dryden settings, while *The Choice of Hercules* was composed as an additional act to *Alexander's Feast.*

The occasional works include the *Utrecht Te Deum* and *Jubilate* (Handel's first compositions in English), composed for the Peace of Utrecht and performed at St Paul's Cathedral on July 7, 1713; the Funeral Anthem for Queen Caroline (*The Ways of Zion Do Mourn*), performed on December 12, 1737; the *Dettingen Te Deum,* composed to celebrate the British victory at Dettingen, Germany, and performed at the Chapel Royal on November 27, 1743; and the Foundling Hospital Anthem (*Blessed are they that considereth the poor*).

The Passion—entitled *Der für die Sünden der Welt gemarterte und sterbende Jesus* (Who for the Sins of the World Jesus Suffered and Died), but generally called the "Brockes Passion" (Barthold Heinrich Brockes wrote the text)—was composed in 1716 or 1717 for unknown reasons. It is in the form of German Lutheran Passions of the time: a series of recitatives, arias, and choruses (including Lutheran chorales) relate the story of the suffering and death of Jesus.

ORATORIOS
ORIGINAL STANDARD VERSIONS, COMPLETE AND LISTED IN CHRONOLOGICAL ORDER

Il Trionfo del Tempo e del Disinganno – 1707 – SSAT solos, two oboes, strings, and basso continuo – 150 minutes. (1) The text, by Cardinal Benedetto Pamphilj, is an allegory about the struggle between earthly and spiritual pleasures; (2) solo roles are for Beauty (S), Pleasure (S), Truth (A), and Time (T); (3) there are two quartets, both sung by the soloists.

La Resurrezione – 1708 – SSATB solos, two recorders, two flutes, two oboes, two trumpets, trombone, timpani, strings, and basso continuo – 116 minutes. (1) The libretto, by Carlo Sigismondo Capece, relates the biblical events from Good Friday to Easter Sunday and also the conflict between an Angel and Lucifer; (2) solo roles are for Mary Magdalene (S), an Angel (S), Mary Cleopha (A), St John (T), and Lucifer (B); (3) the part of Mary Magdalene was sung by a female for the first performance, but for all subsequent performances the part was sung by a castrato; (4) the only ensemble pieces are two duets and two choruses, all sung by the soloists.

Esther – 1718 – SSATTTTTTB solos, SATB chorus, two oboes, two bassoons, two horns, trumpet, harp, strings, and basso continuo – 97 minutes. (1) The libretto, by an unknown author, was adapted from the play *Esther, or Faith Triumphant* by Thomas Brereton and the biblical story in Esther 2–8; (2) major solo roles are for Esther (S), Ahasuerus (T), Mordecai (T), and Haman (B); (3) minor solo roles are for an Israelite Woman (S), three Israelites (ATT), Habdonah (T), and an Officer (T); (4) the roles of the second Israelite, Habdonah, and the Officer are sometimes sung by the same person; (5) there are seven choral movements—the final one briefly divides into two bass parts.

Deborah – 1733 – SSATTBBB solos, SATB/SATB chorus, two oboes, two bassoons, three horns, three trumpets, timpani, strings, and basso continuo – 138 minutes. (1) The libretto, by Samuel Humphreys, is based on the story of conflict between the Israelites and Canaanites as related in

Judges 4 and 5; (2) major solo roles are for Deborah (S), Jael (S), Barak (A), and Abinoam (B); (3) minor solo roles are for Sisara (T), the Chief Priests of the Israelites and Baal (BB), and a Herald (T); (4) Sisara can be sung by an alto; (5) there are fifteen choral movements, most of them short; (6) notable choruses are "See the proud chief" and "Doleful tidings."

Athalia – 1733 – SSAATB solos, SSSAATTBB chorus, two flutes, two oboes, two bassoons, two horns, two trumpets, timpani, strings, and basso continuo – 122 minutes. (1) The libretto, based on 2 Kings 11, is about Athalia, Queen of Judah and daughter of Jezebel, who has forsaken the God of Israel to worship Baal; (2) solo roles are for Athalia (S), Josabeth (S), Joas (A), Joad (A), Mathan (T), and Abner (B); (3) there are eleven choral movements, variously scored for sopranos in unison, three-part sopranos, ATB, SATB, and SATB/SATB.

Saul – 1738 – SSSATTTTTBBB solos, SATB chorus, two flutes, two oboes, two bassoons, two trumpets, timpani, three trombones, carillon (a bell keyboard instrument), harp, strings, and basso continuo (specifically consisting of theorbo, harpsichord, and two organs) – 135 minutes. (1) The libretto, by Charles Jennens, is based on biblical passages in 1 Samuel that relate the story of David's relationship with King Saul and his son Jonathan after David kills the giant Goliath; (2) major solo roles are for Saul (B), Jonathan (T), David (A), Merab (S), and Michal (S); (3) minor solo roles are for a High Priest (T), the Witch of Endor (T), an Amalekite (T), Abner (T), Doeg (B), Samuel (B), and an unnamed person (S); (4) the part of David was composed for a female singer, although Handel occasionally had it sung by a male; (5) there are twelve choral movements.

Israel in Egypt – 1738 – SSATBB solos, SATB/SATB chorus, two oboes, two bassoons, two trumpets, timpani, three trombones, strings, and basso continuo – 140 minutes for all three parts of the oratorio or 100 minutes if part one is deleted. (1) The libretto, which tells of the plagues and the crossing of the Red Sea, consists of Bible verses presumably assembled by Handel; (2) the scoring for soloists consists of four recitatives (T), five arias (SAAAT), and three duets (SS, AT, and BB); (3) approximately half of the twenty-eight choruses are scored for SATB/SATB, while the other half are scored for SATB.

Messiah – 1741 – SATB solos, SATB chorus, two trumpets, timpani, strings, and basso continuo – 140 minutes. (1) The libretto consists of Bible verses compiled by Charles Jennens; (2) the oratorio is in three large sections, unnamed, but generally referred to as "Christmas," "Easter," and "Resurrection"; (3) Handel frequently conducted performances with two or three soprano and alto soloists, always only one tenor, and almost always only one bass; (4) all choruses are scored for SATB except for "Lift up your heads," which is scored for SSATB; (5) the original orchestration was for strings and basso continuo, with trumpets and timpani in the "Hallelujah" and "Worthy Is the Lamb" choruses, trumpets—marked "da lontano e un poco piano" (from a distance and somewhat soft)—in "Glory to God," and one trumpet in the aria "The trumpet shall sound"; (6) two oboes plus one bassoon and one horn were added by Handel for later performances.

Samson – 1741 – SSSATTTBB solos, SATB chorus, two flutes, two oboes, two
bassoons, two horns, two trumpets, timpani, strings, and basso continuo –
145 minutes. (1) The libretto by Newburgh Hamilton, an adaptation of
John Milton's *Samson Agonistes,* relates the story of Samson's evolution
from a captive of the Philistines to their conqueror; (2) major solo roles
are for Samson (T), Manoah (B), Micah (A), Dalilah (S), and Harapha
(B); (3) minor solo roles, all with very little music, are for a Philistine
Man and Woman (ST), an Israelite Man (T), and a Virgin (S); (4) one
chorus divides into SSATTB; (5) the flutes play only in the "Dead March."

Semele – 1743 – SSAAATTBBB solos, SATB chorus, two oboes, two horns,
two trumpets, timpani, strings, and basso continuo – 150 minutes.
(1) The libretto, by an unknown author, is about the daughter of Cadmus, King of Thebes, who renounces her betrothed and is killed by the
blinding lightning of Zeus; (2) major solo roles are for Semele (S), Ino
(A), Jupiter (T), Cadmus (B), Athamas (A), Sommus (B), Juno (A), and
Iris (S); (3) minor solo roles, consisting of single recitatives, are for
Apollo (T) and a Priest (B); (4) the trumpets are used in only one chorus
and the horns in only two choruses; (5) there are ten choral movements,
all SATB.

Joseph and His Brethren – 1743 – SSSAAATTBB solos, SATB chorus, two flutes
(doubling two violins), two oboes, three trumpets, timpani, strings, and
basso continuo – 163 minutes. (1) The libretto, by James Miller, is based
on the story of Joseph's forgiveness of his brothers as related in Genesis
39–45; (2) major solo roles are for Joseph (A), Pharaoh (B), Simeon (T),
Judah (T), Benjamin (S), Asenath (S), and Phanor (A); (3) minor solo
roles are for Reuben (B), Potiphera (A), and a High Priest (S); (4) all
three trumpets are used in only one chorus; (5) there are ten choral
movements, all SATB.

Hercules – 1744 – SSATBB solos, SATB chorus, two oboes, two horns, two
trumpets, timpani, strings, and basso continuo – 180 minutes. (1) The
libretto, by Thomas Broughton, is an adaptation of Ovid's *Metamorphoses*
and Sophocles' *Trachinians:* the accidental death of Hercules caused by
the magical lures of his wife Dejanira; (2) major solo roles are for Hercules (B), Dejanira (S), Hyllus (T), Iöle (S), and Lichas (A); (3) minor solo
roles are for the Priest of Jupiter (B), an Oechalian (S), and a Trachinian
(B); (4) the horns play only in the final chorus.

Belshazzar – 1744 – SAATTBB solos, SSATTB chorus, two oboes, two trumpets, timpani, strings, and basso continuo – 175 minutes. (1) The libretto,
by Charles Jennens, is based upon both biblical and historical accounts
of the fall of Babylon under the reign of Belshazzar; (2) major solo roles
are for Belshazzar (T), Nitocris (S), Cyrus (A), Daniel (A), and Gobrias
(B); (3) minor solo roles are for Arioch (T) and a Messenger (B); (4) there
are fourteen choral movements—three for SSATTB and the others for
SATB.

Occasional Oratorio – 1746 – SSTB solos, SATB/SATB chorus, two oboes,
two bassoons, two horns, three trumpets, timpani, strings, and basso
continuo – 144 minutes. (1) The libretto, by an unknown author, consists of biblical passages and paraphrases that relate no story but rather

circumstances of war, desire for peace, and praise to God for victory;
(2) seven of the fourteen choral movements were taken directly from earlier works, including "God save the king" from the Coronation Anthem *Zadok the Priest* and "I will sing unto the Lord," "Who is like unto Thee," and "He gave them hailstones" from *Israel in Egypt;* (3) the trumpets and timpani are used frequently throughout the oratorio; (4) the two horns are used in only one chorus; (5) the chorus divides into eight parts in only four movements.

Judas Maccabaeus – 1746 – SSSATBB solos, SATB chorus, two flutes, two oboes, two horns, three trumpets, timpani, strings, and basso continuo – 180 minutes. (1) The libretto, by Thomas Morell, is based on 1 Maccabees 2–8, in which Judas Maccabaeus and his brother Simon defend Israel's right against the Syrians to worship their God instead of false idols; (2) major solo roles are for Judas Maccabaeus (T), Simon (B), and an Israelite Woman and Man (SS); (3) minor solo roles are for a Messenger (A), Eupolemus (B), and a Priest (S); (4) one chorus is for SSA and another for SS.

Alexander Balus – 1747 – SSATBB solos, SATB chorus, two oboes, two horns, two trumpets, timpani, strings, and basso continuo – 154 minutes. (1) The libretto, by Thomas Morell, follows that of Judas Maccabaeus in 1 Maccabees: the alliance between Alexander Balus, King of Syria, and Jonathan, chief of the Jews since the death of his brother Judas Maccabaeus, is threatened by Ptolomee, King of Egypt; (2) major solo roles are for Alexander Balus (A), Jonathan (T), Cleopatra (S), and Aspasia (S); (3) minor solo roles are for Ptolomee (B), a Courtier (B), and two Messengers (SB); (4) there are eight choral movements, all for SATB; (5) two flutes, harp, and mandolin are indicated in Cleopatra's aria "Hark, hark, hark."

Joshua – 1747 – SSATB solos, SATB chorus, two flutes, two oboes, two horns, three trumpets, timpani, strings, and basso continuo – 125 minutes. (1) The libretto, by Thomas Morell, is based on the story of the fall of Jericho and Debir as it is related in the biblical book of Joshua; (2) solo roles are for Joshua (T), Caleb (B), Othniel (A), Achsah (S), and an Angel (S); (3) there are thirteen choral movements, all SATB except for two (SSA and SS) borrowed intact from *Judas Maccabaeus.*

Solomon – 1748 – SSSSATB solos, SATB/SATB chorus, two flutes, two oboes, two bassoons, two horns, two trumpets, timpani, strings, and basso continuo – 135 minutes. (1) The libretto, by an unknown author, extols the many virtues of King Solomon; (2) major solo roles are for Solomon (A), Zadok (T), a Levite (B), Pharaoh's Daughter (S), Nicaule (S), and the First and Second Harlots (SS); (3) a minor solo role is for an Attendant (T); (4) Handel used two soloists to cover the four soprano roles; (5) there are thirteen choral movements—seven for SATB/SATB, five for SSATB, and one for SATB; (6) the choruses "May no rash intruder," "Music, spread thy voice around," and "Draw the tear from hopeless love" are especially popular today; (7) four successive choral movements in act three form a masque—an entertainment for the Queen of Sheba; (8) the string division calls for two viola parts throughout the oratorio.

Susanna – 1748 – SSSATTBB solos, SATB chorus, two oboes, two trumpets, strings, and basso continuo – 156 minutes. (1) The libretto, by an unknown author, is based on the apocryphal story of Susanna and the elders in Daniel 13; (2) major solo roles are for Susanna (S), an Attendant (S), Joacim (A), the Two Elders (TT), and Chelsias (B); (3) minor solo roles are for Daniel (S) and a Judge (B); (4) there are nine choral movements, all for SATB; (5) the trumpets are used in only the final two choruses.

Theodora – 1749 – SAATTB solos, SATB chorus, two oboes, two horns, two trumpets, timpani, strings, and basso continuo – 130 minutes. (1) The libretto, by Thomas Morell, is based on *The Martyrdom of Theodora and of Didymus,* a seventeenth-century novel by Robert Boyle: Theodora, a Christian virgin, and Didimus, a Roman officer, refuse to worship Jove and are sentenced to death by Valens, the prefect of Antioch; (2) major solo roles are for Theodora (S), Irene (A), Valens (B), Didimus (A), and Septimus (T); (3) a minor solo role is for a Messenger (T); (4) there are eleven choral movements, all for SATB; (5) notable choruses are "He saw the lonely youth," "Come, mighty Father," and "Blest be the hand"; (6) there are two flutes scored in one short instrumental interlude; (7) the horns, trumpets, and timpani are used only in several choruses.

Jephtha – 1751 – SSSATB solos, SATB chorus, two flutes, two oboes, two horns, two trumpets, strings, and basso continuo – 175 minutes. (1) The libretto, by Thomas Morell, is based on the story in Judges 11 of Jephtha's promise to sacrifice the first person who greets him after his victory in battle over the Ammonites (it will be his daughter, who in Morell's libretto is spared at the last moment); (2) major solo roles are for Jephtha (T), Zebul (B), Storgè (S), Iphis (S), and Hamor (A); (3) a minor solo role is for an Angel (S); (4) the part of Storgè is scored in the mezzo-soprano range; (5) the part of Hamor was sung by a countertenor and the part of the Angel by a boy soprano; (6) there are ten choral movements, all SATB except for one ("Chorus of Boys") for SS; (7) the two trumpets are used only in the final choral movement, the two horns are used in one movement, and the second flute doubles the first.

The Triumph of Time and Truth – 1757 – SSATB solos, SATB chorus, two oboes, two horns, two trumpets, timpani, strings, and basso continuo – 120 minutes. (1) The oratorio is a translation of the 1737 version of *Il trionfo del Tempo e della Verità;* (2) solo roles are for Beauty (S), Deceit (S), Counsel (A), Pleasure (T), and Time (B); (3) there are eleven choral movements, all for SATB except "Pleasure submits to pain," which is scored for SSSSAA solos and SSAATB chorus; (4) two flutes are indicated in one aria, "On the valleys, dark and cheerless."

CORONATION ANTHEMS
COMPLETE AND LISTED IN ORDER OF PUBLICATION

Zadok the priest – 1727 – SSAATTBB chorus, two oboes, two bassoons, three trumpets, timpani, strings, and basso continuo – 5:30 minutes. The violins are divided into three parts.

Let thy hand be strengthened – 1727 – SAATB chorus, two oboes, strings, and basso continuo – 8 minutes. The violins are divided into only two parts.

The King shall rejoice – 1727 – SAATBB chorus and instrumentation as in the first anthem – 11 minutes.

My heart is inditing – 1727 – SAATB chorus and instrumentation as in the first anthem – 12 minutes.

CHANDOS ANTHEMS
COMPLETE ORIGINAL VERSIONS, LISTED IN ORDER OF PUBLICATION

O be joyful in the Lord (Psalm 100) – 1717 – STB solos, STB chorus, oboe, two violins, and basso continuo – 20 minutes. The anthem has four choral movements and two duets (SB and ST).

In the Lord put I my trust (from Psalms 9, 11, 12, and 13) – 1717 – T solo, STB chorus, oboe, bassoon, two violins, and basso continuo – 21 minutes. The anthem has four choral movements and three short arias (all T).

Have mercy upon me (Psalm 51) – 1717 – ST solos, STB chorus, oboe, bassoon, two violins, and basso continuo – 20 minutes. The anthem has three choral movements, one duet (ST), and two short arias (T and S).

O sing unto the Lord a new song (Psalm 96) – 1717 – ST solos, STB chorus, two oboes, bassoon, two violins, and basso continuo – 14 minutes. The anthem has three choral movements, one duet (ST), and one aria (T).

I will magnify thee (Psalm 145) – 1717 – ST solos, STB chorus, oboe, bassoon, two violins, and basso continuo – 23 minutes. (1) The anthem has three choral movements and four arias (three T and one S); (2) a later version of the anthem borrows material from other Chandos anthems, including the duet from *O sing unto the Lord a new song* rescored for AB.

As pants the hart (Psalm 42) – 1717 – ST solos, STB chorus, oboe, bassoon, two violins, and basso continuo – 20 minutes. (1) The anthem has three choral movements, one duet (ST), and two arias (S and T); (2) two later versions exist—one expanded for the Chapel Royal.

My song shall be alway (Psalm 89) – 1717 – SATB solos, SATB chorus, oboe, bassoon, two violins, and basso continuo – 25 minutes. The anthem has three choral movements, one trio (STB), one duet (AB), and two solos (S and T).

O come let us sing unto the Lord (Psalm 95) – 1718 – STT solos, STTB chorus, two flutes, oboe, bassoon, two violins, and basso continuo – 26 minutes. (1) The anthem has three choral movements and four arias (two for T1 and one each for S and T2); (2) the flutes are used only in the opening sonata and in the first tenor aria.

O praise the Lord with one consent (Psalm 135) – 1718 – STB solos, STTB chorus, oboe, two violins, and basso continuo – 25 minutes. The anthem has three choral movements and four arias (STTB).

The Lord is my light (Psalm 27) – 1718 – ST solos, SATTB chorus, two flutes, oboe, two violins, and basso continuo – 25 minutes. (1) The anthem has four choral movements and four solos (three T and one S); (2) the first choral movement is the only one that divides into five parts (all other choral movements are for STTB); (3) the flutes are used in only one aria.

Let God arise (Psalm 68) – 1717 – ST solos, STB chorus, oboe, bassoon, two violins, and basso continuo – 20 minutes. (1) The anthem has three choral movements and two arias (S and T); (2) a later version of the anthem was expanded for the Chapel Royal.

LATIN PSALM SETTINGS
COMPLETE AND LISTED ACCORDING TO FAMILIARITY

Dixit Dominus (Psalm 110) – 1707 – SSATB solos, SSATB chorus, strings, and basso continuo – 33 minutes. (1) The solos are all ensemble pieces to be sung by members of the chorus; (2) the strings divide into two violin and two viola parts.

Laudate pueri Dominum in D major (Psalm 112) – 1707 – S solo, SATB chorus, two oboes, strings, and basso continuo – 19 minutes. The soprano solo is in dialogue with the chorus throughout.

Nisi Dominus (Psalm 126) – 1707 – ATB solos, SSATB chorus, strings, and basso continuo – 12 minutes. (1) The solos are all brief; (2) the strings divide into two violin and two viola parts.

ODES AND OCCASIONAL WORKS
SELECTED AND LISTED ACCORDING TO FAMILIARITY

Alexander's Feast – 1736 – STB solos, SSATTBB chorus, two flutes, two oboes, two bassoons, two horns, two trumpets, timpani, strings, and basso continuo – 84 minutes. (1) The timing does not include the Concerto grosso in C, subtitled "Alexander's Feast," which is 12:30 minutes and which is occasionally played before the second part of the ode; (2) there are eight choral movements—all SATB except for movement six (SSATTBB) and movement nine (ATB); (3) the violins are divided into three parts.

Ode for St Cecilia's Day – 1739 – ST solos, SATB chorus, two oboes, two trumpets, timpani, strings, and basso continuo – 50 minutes. There are three choral movements.

The Ways of Zion Do Mourn (Funeral Anthem for Queen Caroline) – 1737 – SSATB chorus, two oboes, bassoon, strings, and basso continuo – 45 minutes. (1) The anthem consists of an overture followed by twelve choral movements (some very short); (2) the text is entirely biblical, drawn mainly from Lamentations, Job, and Psalms.

Ode for the Birthday of Queen Anne – 1713 or 1714 – SAB solos, SATB/SATB chorus, two oboes, trumpet, strings, and basso continuo – 26 minutes.

(1) The chorus sings in seven of the nine movements—always with the same text ("The day that gave great Anna birth, who fix'd a lasting peace on earth") but with different music; (2) the choruses are all SATB except for the final movement, in which the second chorus echoes the first.

Dettingen Te Deum – 1743 – B solo, SSATB chorus, two oboes, two bassoons, three trumpets, timpani, strings, and basso continuo – 40 minutes. There are occasional solo ensemble pieces to be sung by members of the chorus.

Utrecht Te Deum – 1713 – SSAATB solos, SSAATTB chorus, flute, two oboes, bassoon, two trumpets, strings, and basso continuo – 18 minutes. (1) All solos are intermixed with the chorus in *concerto grosso* fashion; (2) most of the ten choruses are scored for SSATB; (3) movement seven is scored SST/AATB; (4) the violins are divided into three parts.

Utrecht Jubilate – 1713 – AAB solos, SSAATTB chorus, two oboes, two trumpets, strings, and basso continuo – 16:30 minutes. (1) The chorus is SATB and SSATB except for movement six; (2) the violins are divided into three parts.

Blessed are they that considereth the poor (Foundling Hospital Anthem) – 1749 – SSAT solos, SATB chorus, two oboes, two trumpets, timpani, strings, and basso continuo – 30 minutes. (1) The text is from Psalms 41, 72, and 112 plus passages from Ecclesiastes and Revelation; (2) the chorus sings in four of the seven movements; (3) the final chorus is the "Hallelujah" from *Messiah*.

The Choice of Hercules – 1751 – SSAT solos, SATB chorus, two flutes, two oboes, two bassoons, two trumpets, strings, and basso continuo – 45 minutes. (1) The text is from Joseph Spence's *Polymetis*; (2) solo roles are for Pleasure (S), Virtue (S), Hercules (A), and an Attendant (T); (3) there are five choral movements, all for SATB.

L'Allegro, il Penseroso ed il Moderato (Mirth, Melancholy, and Moderation) – 1740 – SATB solos, SATB chorus, two oboes, two bassoons, two trumpets, timpani, strings, and basso continuo – 138 minutes. (1) The text was adapted by Charles Jennens from John Milton's poem; (2) the violins divide into three parts occasionally, the flute is used in only one aria, and the horn is used in only one aria.

MASQUE

Acis and Galatea – 1718 – STTB solos, STTTB chorus, two oboes, two recorders (doubling the oboes), two violins, and basso continuo – 75 minutes. (1) The libretto is by John Gay (author of the *Beggar's Opera*) and Alexander Pope and is based on John Dryden's English adaptation of book thirteen from Ovid's poem *Metamorphoses*; (2) solo roles are for Galatea (S), Acis (T), Damon (T), and Polypheme (B); (3) portions of Damon's part are written in the tenor clef, although Damon was always sung by a boy soprano in performances that Handel conducted; (4) there are four choral movements.

PASSION

Der für die Sünden der Welt gemarterte und sterbende Jesus (Brockes Passion) –
    1716 or 1717 – SSAATTBB solos, SATB chorus, two oboes, strings, and
    basso continuo – 140 minutes. (1) The libretto is by Barthold Heinrich
    Brockes; (2) major solo roles are for an Evangelist (T), Jesus (B), the
    Daughter of Zion (S), and Peter (T); (3) minor solo roles are for Judas
    (A), a Believer (A), Pilate (B), and Mary (S), plus other brief incidental
    solos; (4) of 106 movements, there are eleven choruses and five chorales.

MAURICE GREENE 1696–1755

Greene was born in London, where his father was chaplain at the Chapel Royal and where he received his musical education as a chorister under Jeremiah Clarke and Charles King, and as an organ student at St Paul's Cathedral under Richard Brind. At age eighteen he was appointed organist at the London church of St Dunstan-in-the-West, and at twenty-two he moved to St Andrew's, Holborn. Several months after he began his service at St Andrew's, Brind died and Greene succeeded him as organist at St Paul's. He retained this position for almost a decade, becoming friends with George Frideric Handel and William Boyce. He also became involved in the establishment of several musical societies, including the Academy of Ancient Music. In 1727 he was appointed Master of the King's Musick at the Chapel Royal, one of the most prestigious positions in England. He is noted for amassing a sizable library of musical scores and for bequeathing the library to Boyce.

Greene composed sixty anthems, thirty-eight odes, eight settings of the Te Deum, three oratorios (two of which are extant), two masques, one Service, and a small collection of catches and canons for three and four voices. Only a limited amount of this output is known today. *Lord, let me know mine end*, a funeral anthem with a text from verses four through seven of Psalm 39, is Greene's best-known and most frequently performed anthem. Its imitative texture over a walking bass line and its duet for two sopranos (trebles) are notable accomplishments of masterful craftsmanship and engaging harmonic suspensions. *O clap your hands*, which is in a point-of-imitation texture throughout, is reminiscent of Orlando Gibbons's setting of the same text. *Arise, shine, O Zion* and *Behold, I bring you glad tidings* are both lengthy verse anthems, with extended passages for soloists alternating with equally extended passages for chorus. *Sing we merrily*, an anthem divided into distinct movements, is similar to the Chandos anthems of Handel. The remaining anthems have characteristics of the full and verse anthems described above, with frequent examples of duet passages for two sopranos.

ANTHEMS
SELECTED AND LISTED ACCORDING TO FAMILIARITY

Lord, let me know mine end – SS solos, SATB chorus, and organ – 6:30 minutes.

O clap your hands – SSATB chorus and organ – 3:30 minutes.

Arise, shine, O Zion – SATB solos, SATB chorus, and organ – 12 minutes.

Behold, I bring you glad tidings – SS solos, SATB chorus, and organ – 6:30 minutes.

Sing we merrily – SSAT solos, SSATB chorus, two flutes, two oboes, bassoon, trumpet, strings, and organ – 20 minutes. The anthem is in five movements—a duet for two sopranos with chorus, a tenor solo with chorus, a soprano and alto duet, an alto recitative and solo, and a closing movement for chorus.

My God, my God, look upon me – T solo, SSATB chorus, and organ – 7:30 minutes.

Let my complaint come before thee – SSATB chorus and organ – 3:15 minutes.

Hearken unto me, ye holy children – ATB solos, SATB chorus, two oboes, strings, and organ – 11 minutes.

Hear my prayer – ATB solos, SATB chorus, and organ – 5 minutes.

Bow down thine ear, O Lord – SSATBB chorus and organ – 3 minutes.

The king shall rejoice – SSATB solos, SSATB chorus, two oboes, two trumpets, strings, and organ – 11:30 minutes.

How long wilt thou forget me, O Lord – SS solos, SSAATTBB chorus, and organ – 7:30 minutes.

God is our hope and strength – SATB solos, SATB chorus, and organ – 8:30 minutes.

Acquaint thyself with God – A solo, SATB chorus, and organ – 5:30 minutes. The anthem consists of a lengthy alto solo (scored in the tenor range) followed by a brief choral closing.

O God of my righteousness – ST solos, SSATB chorus, and organ – 5:30 minutes. The anthem consists of soprano and tenor solos and duets followed by a choral closing.

OTHER WORKS
SELECTED AND LISTED ACCORDING TO FAMILIARITY

Ode on St Cecilia's Day – ATB solos, SATB chorus, two flutes, two oboes, bassoon, two trumpets, timpani ad lib., strings, and basso continuo – 20 minutes.

The song of Deborah and Barak – 1732 – ATB solos, SATB chorus, two oboes, two bassoons, two trumpets, timpani, strings, and basso continuo – 45 minutes.

WILLIAM BOYCE 1711–1779

Boyce was born in London, where he was a chorister at St Paul's Cathedral under Charles King and, after his voice changed, an organ student under Maurice Greene. In 1734 Boyce was appointed organist at the chapel of the Earl of Oxford, and in 1736 he became organist at St Michael's

Church in Cornhill. From 1736 to 1755 he served as a composer in ordinary to the Chapel Royal, studied at Cambridge University (receiving a doctorate in music in 1749), and composed numerous dramatic secular works. In 1755 he succeeded Greene as Master of the King's Musick, and three years later he was appointed one of the three organists at the Chapel Royal. His compositional focus changed with these new appointments, and for the final years of his life he composed anthems and odes exclusively. His output during the last two decades of his life is impressive, especially considering the fact that he was almost totally deaf and that he expended a great deal of energy compiling and publishing a large collection of sacred music by British composers of the seventeenth and eighteenth centuries. At the time of his death he was one of the most respected composers in England. The music for his funeral service was sung by the combined choirs of St Paul's Cathedral, Westminster Abbey, and the Chapel Royal, and he was buried in the great crossing of St Paul's.

Since Boyce was living during the first thirty or so years of the Classical era, it might be assumed that his music would represent that style. However, his deafness prevented him from hearing the new style, and his music reflected his interest in the styles of the past. Several of his anthems are a part of the general repertoire today, but he is known mostly for his three published volumes of music by various British composers, including John Blow, Henry Purcell, Pelham Humfrey, and Orlando Gibbons. These volumes—published in 1760, 1768, and 1773—are entitled collectively *Cathedral Music, being a Collection in Score of the Most Valuable and Useful Compositions for that Service by the Several English Masters of the Last Two Hundred Years.*

Boyce composed sixty-five anthems, five Services for the Anglican Church, fifty-eight odes, two sacred cantatas, one serenata, and several glees, catches, and rounds. Most of the anthems are of the *verse* type, with solos, duets, trios, and other solo ensemble passages alternating with passages for chorus. The structure of *The heavens declare the glory of God,* for example, consists of an extended ATB trio, a lengthy B solo, a short homophonic choral statement, an ATB trio, and a choral closing. Similarly, *O where shall wisdom be found* consists of an extended SSATB solo quintet, a short homophonic choral statement, an ATB trio, and a SSATB choral closing. The festival anthems scored for instruments are divided into separate movements. *The king shall rejoice,* composed for the coronation of George III in 1761, contains three solo movements (S, A, and T), one movement for AB duet and chorus, and one completely choral movement. *O sing unto the Lord a new song* is divided into four movements—two SB duets, one S solo, and one SB duet with chorus. The Service music is typically in a homophonic texture scored for chorus and organ, the chorus parts alternating between *decani* and *cantoris* sides of the ensemble, and the organ part optional.

The odes include *Pass but a few* (Pindar's Ode), composed for New Year's celebrations in 1774; *Strike, strike the lyre,* composed in about 1750 for the birthday of Frederick, Prince of Wales; and *Let grief subside* and *Another passing year is flown,* composed in 1751 and 1752, respectively, for birthday celebrations of George, Prince of Wales.

The serenata *Solomon* is oratorio-like in construction (scored for soloists, chorus, and orchestra) but not intent. The libretto, based on biblical accounts in the Song of Solomon, is a series of love poems that are exchanged throughout the various seasons of the year by a shepherd (simply referred to as He in the libretto) and his lover (referred to as She), with periodic commentary by a chorus. The work, approximately seventy-five minutes in duration, was popular during the latter half of the eighteenth century.

ANTHEMS AND SERVICES
SELECTED AND LISTED ACCORDING TO FAMILIARITY

The king shall rejoice – 1761 – AB solos, SSATB chorus, two oboes, two bassoons, two trumpets, timpani, strings, and organ – 7:30 minutes.

The souls of the righteous – 1760 – SSATB chorus, two flutes, two horns, two trumpets, timpani, strings, and organ – 17 minutes.

Lord, thou has been our refuge – 1755 – SSAT solos, SATB chorus, two recorders, three oboes, two trumpets, timpani, strings, and organ – 24 minutes. The third oboe is doubled by the viola.

O sing unto the Lord a new song – ca.1740 – SB solos, SATB chorus, and organ – 12 minutes.

O where shall wisdom be found – ca.1769 – SSATB solos, SSATB chorus, and organ – 8 minutes.

By the waters of Babylon – ca.1740 – SATB solos, SATB chorus, and organ – 7:30 minutes.

Save me, O God – ca.1735 – SATB chorus and organ – 4:30 minutes.

Turn thee unto me – ca.1749 – SA solos, SSATB chorus, and organ – 5 minutes.

Te Deum and *Jubilate* in C major – ca.1760 – SATB chorus and organ – 6 minutes.

❧ SPAIN AND THE NEW WORLD ❧

Spain did not embrace the Baroque era as did other countries. While Italy, France, Germany, and England adopted various traits of the *seconda prattica* and as a consequence developed new genres, Spain held on to the past. Sacred music, consisting of masses and motets for the Catholic Church, continued to be in the *prima prattica* styles of the Renaissance, and secular music, which was limited to the villancico (a popular form in Spain since the fifteenth century), exhibited only limited characteristics of the *seconda prattica*.

Spain also lacked the artistic support structures of the other countries. The monarchs of the era were weak and culturally indifferent, private patronage was virtually nonexistent, and church institutions relied on the accomplishments of Renaissance composers. The monarchy was especially negligent regarding artistic matters. Philip III (1598–1621) was considered to be ineffectual in all areas of leadership; Philip IV (1621–1665), who is held responsible for the military and cultural decline of the country, was interested in letters and art, but not music; Charles II (1665–1700), who, because of mental and physical limitations, was completely uneducated; and Philip V (1700–1746), the son of Louis, Grand Dauphin of France, suffered from depression and melancholy and was preoccupied with the War of Spanish Succession. Only Ferdinand VI (1746–1759) had a keen interest in music (he patronized the famous castrato Farinelli), although he also suffered from melancholy and was considered an ineffective leader. The consequences of monarchical weakness and musical apathy as well as the reliance on styles and genres of the past resulted in a climate in which composers had little incentive to develop or to write notable repertoire.

In a discussion of Spain during the Baroque era, mention should be made of Portugal, which was under the Spanish rule of Philip III and Philip IV in the early years of the seventeenth century but which regained its independence in 1640. At that time Portugal came under the rule of John IV, who not only had a keen interest in music but was a composer and author of texts about music. His two compositions are SATB a cappella motets in the *prima prattica* style—*Adjuva nos* and the well-known *Crux fidelis*. His two musical writings are on the subject of the music he loved—*prima prattica* compositions; one, prompted by a sixteenth-century letter, is a defense of polyphony, and the other is a defense of Palestrina's *Missa Panis quem ego dabo*.

Spain's influence during the Baroque era was manifested in the New World (Mexico and South America), where talented Spanish composers emigrated beginning in the sixteenth century and where music was utilized as a significant tool to colonize native populations and to convert the indigenous peoples to Christianity. The sacred masses and motets composed in the New World remained in antiquated styles of Cristóbal de Morales, Francisco Guerrero, and Tomás Luis de Victoria, whose works had been sent in large number for use in the new cathedrals. However, the villancicos were transformed; texts became sacred and styles developed into a unique genre. The secular poetry of the past was replaced by sacred verses (mostly for the Christmas season), and the purely vocal a cappella texture was supplanted by music for soloists, chorus, and basso continuo, with the occasional addition of other instruments.

Spain's few notable composers during the Baroque era—Juan Bautista Comes, Sebastián Durón, Francisco Pascual, and Antonio Soler—served in only several major cathedrals, most notably Lérida, Valencia, El Burgo de Osma, and Palencia. The New World composers—Gaspar Fernandes, Juan de Lienas, Juan Gutiérrez de Padilla, Francisco López Capillas, Juan de Araujo, Antonio de Salazar, Manuel de Zumaya, and Ignacio Jerusalem—mostly served in cathedrals in Puebla and Mexico City. Puebla, formally called Puebla de los Angeles (City of Angels) and located halfway between Veracruz and Mexico City, was one of the largest and most advanced cities in Mexico during the seventeenth century. Among its many cultural assets, it had nineteen printing presses and the first public library in the Americas. The Puebla Cathedral was the wealthiest and most prominent cathedral in the New World, especially under Bishop Palafox y Mendoza, who served from 1640 to 1655 and who supported a large and active musical program. The cathedral's chorus numbered fourteen boys and twenty-eight men, and numerous instrumentalists were employed to accompany festival services. The Mexico City Cathedral also had a large and active musical program, especially under *maestros de capilla* Salazar, Zumaya, and Jerusalem.

GASPAR FERNANDES CA.1570–1629

Fernandes was born in Portugal, where he became a singer and organist at the Évora Cathedral. He moved to the New World sometime during the end of the sixteenth century, and in 1599 he was engaged as organist at the Guatemala Cathedral. Shortly thereafter he was appointed *maestro de capilla,* and in 1606 he became the first composer of the Baroque era to serve as *maestro de capilla* at the Puebla Cathedral. He held this position until his death, although for the last seven years of his life he shared responsibilities with Juan Gutiérrez de Padilla, who succeeded him.

Fernandes composed two masses, three motets, one Magnificat, and more than two hundred villancicos. Given the fact that most of the music in the New World at the beginning of the seventeenth century consisted of *prima prattica* works from Spain, it is not surprising that Fernandes composed in this style. Two works are notable: *Elegit eum Dominus,* composed in 1612 "para la entrada del birrey" (for the entry of the viceroy [into Puebla]) and scored for SSATB a cappella chorus, is the earliest known Latin secular work composed in the New World; and *Eso rigor e repente,* for SAATB chorus with optional instruments *colla parte,* became one of the most popular Christmas villancicos of the seventeenth century.

JUAN BAUTISTA COMES CA.1582–1643

Comes was born in Valencia, Spain, where he received his musical education as a choirboy at the cathedral there. From 1605 to 1608 he was associated with the Lérida Cathedral, first as a singer and then as *maestro de capilla,* and from 1608 to 1613 he served as *vicemaestro de capilla* at the Real Colegio del Corpus Christi (the Patriarca) in Valencia. In 1613 he was appointed *maestro de capilla* at the Valencia Cathedral, in 1618 he became *vicemaestro* of the royal chapel in Madrid, and in 1628 he returned to the Real Colegio del Corpus Christi as *maestro.* Circumstances were not favorable for Comes as *maestro* at the Colegio, however, and he was reinstated as *maestro* at the Valencia Cathedral.

Comes composed six masses, approximately one hundred motets, one Magnificat, and one hundred villancicos. All of the masses are in the *prima prattica* imitative style prevalent during the late Renaissance in Italy. Examples are *Misa Exsultet caelum,* a paraphrase of a version of the Gregorian chant "Exultet orbis gaudis" for SATB chorus a cappella; *Misa Iste confessor,* a parody of Palestrina's mass of the same name for SSAT/SATB chorus a cappella; *Misa Ad instar praelii constructa* (Mass on the beginning of war), a parody of Victoria's *Missa pro Victoria* for SSAT/SATB/SATB chorus a cappella; *Misa qué fértil que es el año* (Mass on how fertile is the year) for SSAT/SATB chorus a cappella; and *Misa de tres contrabajos* (Mass with three basses) for SATB/SATB/SATB chorus a cappella. Most of the motets are in a Venetian polychoral dialogue style. Examples include *Beatus vir* for SSAT/SATB chorus a cappella and *Dixit Dominus* for SATB/SATB/SATB/SATB chorus and specific basso continuo instrumentation of harp for chorus one, organ for chorus two, organ and vihuelas for chorus three, and cornets, sackbuts, and bassoon for chorus four. The *Magnificat,* one of the composer's few published works and one of his best known, is polychoral and scored for SATB/SATB chorus a cappella. The villancicos are in the traditional verse/refrain (*copla/estribillo*) style common during the time. *A la sombra estáis* is an example.

JUAN DE LIENAS FL.1617–1654

Lienas was probably born in Spain, although there is no evidence to prove this. The only records of his life consist of a few comments made about him by presumed colleagues, and the only records of his music consist of manuscripts housed at the Encarnación Convent in

Mexico City. These manuscripts consist of two masses (one of which is a Requiem), eleven motets, three Magnificats, and two sets of Lamentations. All of the works are in a *prima prattica* imitative style. The *Missa super fa re ut fa sol la* is a *soggetto cavato* mass that emulates the style of the early Renaissance by basing cantus firmus material on solmization syllables. The motets include two works that are relatively well known today. The first, *Credidi* (Psalm 116:10–16), is a multisectional work scored for SATB/SATB chorus a cappella and characterized by frequent changes of meter and tempo. The second, the four-voiced setting of *Salve regina* (another setting is for eight voices) is a work for SATB chorus a cappella based on the Gregorian chant of the same name in *alternatim* style (i.e., verses of chant alternate with verses set to imitative polyphony). The Magnificats, all similar in scoring and characterization, include *Magnificat* for ten voices, *Magnificat primi toni* for eight voices, and *Magnificat tertii toni* for five voices.

JUAN GUTIÉRREZ DE PADILLA CA.1590–1664

Padilla was born in Málaga, Spain, where he was a choirboy at the cathedral under *maestro de capilla* Francisco Vásquez. At age twenty-three he was appointed *maestro de la colegiata* at Jerez de la Frontera, and at twenty-six he was appointed *maestro de capilla* at Cádiz Cathedral. Sometime shortly before 1622 he went to the Puebla Cathedral in Mexico, where he was to work for the remainder of his life. He was first a singer under Gaspar Fernandes and then *maestro de capilla* after Fernandes's death. During his forty-two years at Puebla he established himself as Mexico's leading composer.

Padilla composed five masses, approximately thirty-five motets, one Passion, two sets of Lamentations (one for four voices and one for six voices), and more than sixty villancicos. The masses and motets, many of which are for double choir, are settings of standard texts, including *Missa Ave regina* and four settings of *Dixit Dominus*. In addition, the masses and motets are all in the *prima prattica* style of the late Renaissance, with consistent textures of pervasive imitation and no independent instrumental parts. Padilla's particular style is characterized by chromaticism, cross-relations, and expressive word painting. The motet *Versa est in luctum*, for instance, has an inversion of the original melody to depict the text "my harp is turned to mourning," and *Circumdederunt me dolores* has downward chromatic lines that express "the sorrows of death have surrounded me and the perils of hell have found me."

MASSES
SELECTED AND LISTED ACCORDING TO FAMILIARITY

Missa Ave regina coelorum – SATB/SATB chorus – 17 minutes.

Missa Ego flos campi – SATB/SATB chorus – 21 minutes.

Missa Joseph fili David – SATB/SATB chorus – 18 minutes.

MOTETS AND LAMENTATIONS
SELECTED AND LISTED ACCORDING TO FAMILIARITY

Versa est in luctum – SSATB chorus – 3 minutes.

Circumdederunt me dolores – SSAATB chorus – 5 minutes.

Deus in adiutorium (Psalm 70:1) – SATB/SATB chorus – 2:45 minutes.

Mirabilia testimonia tua – SATB/SATB chorus – 10 minutes.

Transfigi, dulcissimi Domine – SSAB chorus – 4 minutes.

Exultate justi in Domino (Psalm 33:1–6) – SATB/SATB chorus – 3 minutes.

Salve regina – SATB/SATB chorus – 6 minutes.

Vidi turbam – SSAATB chorus – 2 minutes.

Hieremiae prophetae lamentationes – SSATTB chorus – 21:30 minutes.

VILLANCICOS
SELECTED AND LISTED ACCORDING TO FAMILIARITY

A siolo flasiquiyo – SATB solos, SSATTB chorus, and basso continuo – 4:30 minutes.

Las estreyas se rien – SAT/ATB solos, SAT/ATB chorus, and basso continuo – 4:30 minutes.

Albricias, pastores – SATB solos, SATB chorus, and basso continuo – 5 minutes.

A la xacara xacarilla – SATB solos, SATB chorus, and basso continuo – 4:30 minutes.

FRANCISCO LÓPEZ CAPILLAS CA.1605–1674

López Capillas was most likely born in Mexico, where he sang as a choirboy in the Mexico City Cathedral. In 1641 he was appointed bassoonist and second organist at the Puebla Cathedral under *maestro de capilla* Juan Gutiérrez de Padilla, and in 1645 he relinquished his duties as a bassoonist and assumed responsibilities as a singer. He was appointed main organist in 1647, but the following year a political situation caused his dismissal. His whereabouts for the next several years are unknown, although it is presumed that he sang in and composed works for the Mexico City Cathedral, where he was appointed main organist and *maestro de capilla* in 1654.

López Capillas composed eight masses, fifteen motets, eight Magnificats, and one Passion setting. All the works, typical of the time, are in a *prima prattica* imitative style scored for chorus a cappella. Most of the masses are parodies: *Missa Aufer a nobis* and *Missa super Alleluia* parody the composer's own motets; *Missa Benedicta sit Sancta Trinitas* and *Missa Quam pulchri sunt* parody Palestrina motets; and *Missa Batalla* parodies Janequin's famous programmatic chanson. Other masses (e.g., *Missa Pange lingua*) are based on Gregorian chant. The motets include *Gloria laus et honor, Aufer a nobis, Christus factus est*, and *Quicumque voluerit*. The Magnificats, all scored for SATB chorus in *alternatim* style, include settings on each of the eight Gregorian chant tones; those on the first and second tones are the best known. The Passion setting—*Passio Domini nostri Jesu Christi secundum Matthaeum*—also incorporates chant.

JUAN DE ARAUJO 1646–1712

Araujo was born in Villafranca de los Barros, a city in the area of western Spain called Extremadura. Nothing is known of his life before his enrollment in the 1660s as a student at the University of S Marcos in Lima, Peru, where he and his family had moved. He most likely traveled to Panama, although there is no certainty of this journey. In 1672 he began service as a priest in Lima, and from 1680 until his death he was *maestro de capilla* at La Plata Cathedral in Bolivia.

Araujo composed several motets, three sets of Lamentations, two Magnificats, and approximately two hundred villancicos. The Lamentations and motets are generally in a *prima prattica* a cappella style scored for multiple choruses and characterized by word painting. The Magnificats are scored for ten and eleven voices, respectively; the motet *Dixit Dominus* is for eleven voices; and the motet *Ut queant laxis* is for eight voices. The villancicos include *Los coflades de la estleya*, a Christmas negrito for SS solos, SATB chorus, and basso continuo; *Oigan, escuchen, atiendan*, a setting in honor of St Paola for T solo, SATB chorus, and basso continuo; and *Dime amor, que prodigio es aquéste* for ST solos, SATB chorus, and basso continuo. The negrito (or negrilla) was a popular form of villancico that was composed to a Christmas text about people with dark skin, mostly children, who worshipped at the manger and celebrated the birth of the Christ Child.

ANTONIO DE SALAZAR CA.1650–1715

Salazar was probably born in Spain, but there are no records to verify this assumption. There are also no records of his early life and training. He must have developed significant musical skills, for as an adult he held the two most important positions in the New World: in 1679 he was appointed *maestro de capilla* at the Puebla Cathedral, and in 1688 he was appointed to the same position at the Mexico City Cathedral. He was the only musician of the Baroque era to hold both these prestigious posts.

Salazar composed two masses (one of which is a Requiem), approximately twenty-four motets, two Magnificats, and twenty villancicos. The masses and motets are all in a conservative *prima prattica* style, with few examples of the word painting and chromaticism that were favored by most other New World composers. Some of the motets, such as *O sacrum convivium*, are scored for SATB/SATB chorus a cappella and emulate the Venetian dialogue style of the late Renaissance. Others, such as *Te Joseph Celebrent*, are pervasively imitative, and a few, such as *Aeterna Christi munera*, are basically homophonic. Several of the motets, including *Egregie Doctor*, were composed in conjunction with Salazar's student Manuel de Zumaya; Salazar wrote the first part of the motet, and Zumaya wrote the second part. The villancicos are all in a *seconda prattica* style, with scoring for solos, chorus, and basso continuo, or for solos and basso continuo without chorus. The duet *Tacara tacara qui yo soy Antoniyo* is an example of this latter type.

SEBASTIÁN DURÓN 1660–1716

Durón was born in Briheuga, a city in central Spain. At age twelve he began studying organ at the Saragossa Cathedral, and at nineteen he was appointed assistant organist. His musical abilities were soon recognized throughout Spain, and he was offered some of the most prestigious positions in the country, including second organist at the Seville Cathedral, *maestro de capilla* at the El Burgo de Osma Cathedral (1685) and the Palencia Cathedral (1686), organist at the royal chapel in Madrid, and finally *maestro de capilla* at the royal chapel.

Durón composed three masses, twenty motets, four sets of Lamentations, and fifteen villancicos. As was typical at the time, most of the sacred works with Latin texts were polychoral and in a *prima prattica* imitative style. Two of the masses—*Misa à 12* and *Misa de difuntos* (Requiem)—are scored for twelve-part chorus, while the other mass—*Missa Ave maris stella*—is scored for eight-part chorus. Also typical of the time, most of the villancicos are for Christmas. *Al dormir el sol en la cuna del alva* for SS solos, SATB chorus, and basso continuo is an example.

MANUEL DE ZUMAYA CA.1678–1755

Zumaya was born in Mexico City, where he studied organ at the cathedral under José de Ydiáquez and sang under *maestro de capilla* Antonio de Salazar. In 1708 Zumaya was appointed second organist at the cathedral, in 1714 he became the main organist, and in 1715 he succeeded Salazar as *maestro de capilla*. In 1738 Zumaya went to Oaxaca, where he assisted the archbishop, and in 1745 he was appointed *maestro de capilla* at the Oaxaca Cathedral. His last name is spelled with a Z (Zumaya) in all official documents; however, he generally spelled it with an S (Sumaya), which is frequently seen today.

He composed three masses, twenty-five motets, one set of Lamentations, approximately one hundred villancicos, and several operas (his opera *Partenope* was the first opera in the Western Hemisphere to be written by an American-born composer). Unlike most of his compatriots, his masses are in a *seconda prattica* style, with scoring for soloists, chorus, strings, and basso continuo. An example is the *Misa à 5*, which is scored for T solo, SATB chorus, strings, and basso continuo and which features the soloist and chorus in a *concerto grosso* relationship. The motets, several of which were composed jointly by Zumaya and his teacher Salazar (Salazar wrote the first part of the motet and Zumaya wrote the second part), are in a *prima prattica* style. An example is *Egregie Doctor*. The set of Lamentations—*Hieremiae Prophetae Lamentationes* (Lamentations of the prophet Jeremiah)—are also in a *prima prattica* style. The villancicos include *Celebren, publiquen* for SATB solos, SATB chorus, trumpet, strings, and basso continuo, and the famous *Sol-fa de Pedro*, which was composed as a test piece for Zumaya's audition as *maestro de capilla* at the Mexico City Cathedral and which is scored for SATB solos, SATB chorus, and basso continuo.

FRANCISCO PASCUAL 1683–1743

Pascual was born near Segovia. Nothing is known of his life before his appointment as an instrumentalist in 1711 at El Burgo de Osma Cathedral. In 1718 he was appointed *maestro de capilla* at the Valladolid Cathedral, the following year he assumed the same position at the Astorga Cathedral, and from 1723 until his death he served as *maestro de capilla* at the Palencia Cathedral.

Pascual composed two masses (one of which is a Requiem), twenty-five motets, twenty sets of Lamentations, and approximately 240 villancicos. The motets are predominantly polychoral works for a cappella chorus, while the Lamentations are scored for soloists, chorus, and optional basso continuo. The villancicos, most of which are for Christmas, are scored for soloists, chorus, two violins, and basso continuo.

IGNACIO JERUSALEM (Y STELLA) 1707–1769

Jerusalem was born in Lecce, Italy, where his father was a violinist at the local Jesuit church. Nothing is known about Ignacio's youth, musical training, or professional activity before 1743, when he began playing violin in the orchestra at the Antiguo Coliseo theater in Mexico City. Shortly after this time he became director of the theater orchestra, and in 1746 he began teaching at the Colegio de Infantes. He also was associated with the Mexico City Cathedral, where he was appointed *maestro de capilla* in 1750.

Jerusalem composed nine masses (including two Requiems), more than forty motets, five Magnificats, eleven sets of Matins responsories, and approximately fifty villancicos. The sacred repertoire is mainly in the *gallant* style, characterized by homophony and scored for soloists, chorus, horns, strings, and basso continuo. Many of the motets are large-scale multimovement works. *Dixit Dominus,* for example, is in five movements—chorus, ATB trio, chorus, B solo, and chorus. Most of the villancicos, on the other hand, are small-scale works scored for single soloists, strings, and basso continuo. Examples include *Cherubes y pastores* for alto and *Soy vaquero* for bass.

SACRED WORKS
SELECTED AND LISTED ACCORDING TO FAMILIARITY

Responsorio sequndo de SS José (Second responsory for St Joseph) – SATB chorus, two oboes, two horns, strings, and basso continuo – 2:45 minutes.

Matines para nuestra señora de Guadalupe (Matins for our lady of Guadalupe) – 1764 – SATB solos, SATB chorus, two oboes, two horns, two trumpets, timpani, strings, and basso continuo – 60 minutes.

Dixit Dominus (Psalm 110) – SAB solos, SATB chorus, two horns, strings, and basso continuo – 9 minutes.

Christus natus est nobis – SA solos, SATB chorus, two horns, strings, and basso continuo – 2 minutes.

Hodie nobis caelorum – AB solos, SATB chorus, two trumpets, strings, and basso continuo – 11 minutes.

O magnum mysterium – SATB solos, SATB chorus, two horns, strings, and basso continuo – 10:30 minutes.

Verbum caro factum est – AB solos, SATB chorus, two horns, strings, and basso continuo – 7:30 minutes.

Misa in D major – SATB solos, SATB/SATB chorus, two trumpets, timpani, strings, and basso continuo – 20 minutes. The authorship of this work is questionable.

ANTONIO SOLER (PADRE ANTONIO SOLER Y RAMOS)
1729–1783

Soler was born in Olot, Catalonia, where his father was a musician in the local military band. At age six Antonio was enrolled as a choirboy at Escolonía, the singing school of the Montserrat Monastery near Barcelona. At twenty-one he was appointed *maestro de capilla* at Seo de Urgel Cathedral, and at twenty-three he was ordained a subdeacon there. That same year he entered the monastery at El Escorial, where the royal family resided during the autumn months, and at twenty-eight he was appointed *maestro de capilla*. For the remainder of his life he divided his time between El Escorial and the royal palace in Madrid, becoming acquainted with notable musicians such as Domenico Scarlatti and Padre Giovanni Battista Martini, with whom he corresponded frequently. He is noted for his keyboard sonatas and concertos for two organs, and also for his treatise *Llave de la modulación* (Key to modulation), which demonstrates techniques for modulating from any key to another.

Soler composed thirteen masses (including four Requiems), approximately one hundred motets, twenty-eight sets of Lamentations, thirteen Magnificats, and 132 villancicos. Many of the motets are large-scale works that resemble German cantatas in scoring and in scope. They are multimovement compositions, with recitatives, arias, choruses, and accompaniment of strings and basso continuo. *Salve*, Soler's best-known motet, is divided into six movements—a brief instrumental introduction followed by a dialogue between soloist and chorus, an aria, an instrumental ritornello, a solo with choral interjections, another aria, and another dialogue between soloist and chorus. The villancicos are typically set to humorous texts for the Christmas season and are scored for one or two soloists, chorus, two violins, and basso continuo. *Congregante y festero* is an example: the text relates a story about a congregant of a church who discusses his preferences for a Christmas motet he would like the choirmaster to compose; in the process he bargains over payment, suggests a text ("Gloria in excelsis Deo"), and asks that the motet end in a fugue (which it does).

MOTET
SELECTED ACCORDING TO FAMILIARITY

Salve – 1753 – S solo, SATB chorus, strings, and basso continuo – 11 minutes. The text is the traditional Latin sequence "Salve regina, mater misericordiae."

VILLANCICOS
SELECTED AND LISTED ACCORDING TO FAMILIARITY

Congregante y festero (Congregant and feastmaster [choirmaster]) – 1761 – ST solos, SATB/SATB chorus, two violins, and basso continuo – 9 minutes.

Contradanza de colegio (Contradanza of the school) – 1773 – S solo, SATB chorus, two violins, and basso continuo – 8 minutes. A contradanza is a popular eighteenth-century dance.

Cielos! que opuestas voce (Heavens! What opulent voices) – 1765 – SSAT solos, SSAT/SATB chorus, two trumpets, two violins, and basso continuo – 15 minutes. Most of the solo writing is for two sopranos.

De un maestro de capilla (From a choirmaster) – 1763 – ST solos, SSAT chorus, two violins, and basso continuo – 11 minutes.

4

The Classical Era

The Classical era began in the second half of the eighteenth century as a reaction against the thick contrapuntal and ornamental textures of the Baroque, and it ended by the second decade of the nineteenth century, when formal structures were replaced by freer forms. Traditionally, the dates used to mark the beginning and end of the era are 1750 (the death of J. S. Bach) and 1820 (the relative emergence of new directions in the music of Berlioz and Beethoven). As with all eras, however, the dates are only convenient markers; styles began and ended over a period of time, and some genres adopted newer traits quickly while others held to older traditions. In general, the choral genres were conservative and slow to adopt new stylistic trends. Thus while opera, ballet, and instrumental forms began to change styles in the 1730s and 1740s, masses, motets, and oratorios did not evolve into genres with new characteristics until the 1770s and even later.

Three terms signaled the arrival of the Classical era and also defined its character—*rococo,* which was originally used to describe French architecture that had lightness and grace; *style gallant,* which referred to music that was refined and accessible as opposed to learned and academic; and *empfindsamer Stil* (sentimental style), which characterized music that was uncomplicated and direct in expression. The music of the Classical era was, therefore, light in texture, homophonic in orientation, and clear-cut in terms of structure. Contrapuntal writing was limited to fugal sections at a few specified points in masses (e.g., the ends of the Gloria and Credo movements) and other large-scale sacred works (e.g., the ends of Magnificats and Te Deums), and structures were organized according to the principles of formal symphonic designs such as sonata, rondo, and variation.

The structures of music during the Classical era did not, as many people suggest, preclude expressive considerations, and the ideals of structural clarity, refinement, order, and restraint (all of which the term *classicism* connotes) did not negate a desire for expressive communication. As verbalized by many Classical-era composers, including W. A. Mozart, and as clearly written by Johann Georg Sulzer in his *Allgemeine Theorie der schönen Künste* (General theory of the beautiful art) of 1771 to 1774, "The most important, if not the only function of a perfect musical composition is the accurate expression of sentiments and passions with all their particular shadings. . . . Every composition, whether it is vocal or instrumental, should possess a definite character and be able to arouse specific sentiments in the minds of listeners. . . . Expression is the soul of music."

Expression was aided by tempo terms, which conveyed more than rates of tempo. For instance, *allegro* meant cheerful as well as fast, *grave* meant solemn, and *vivace* meant lively and spirited (not *very fast,* as it is translated today). In addition, composers used terms such as *maestoso* (majestic) and *affetuoso* (affectionate) to aid in the communication of sentiments. Orchestral scoring also contributed to expressive communication. Percussion and brass instruments, techniques such as tremolo, and increased numbers of performing forces were all used to create dramatic effects. The size of performing forces was especially striking. A total of 525 performers (275 singers and 250 instrumentalists) participated in the 1784 Commemoration of Handel in Westminster Abbey, the number of performers increasing to 616 in 1785, 806 in 1787, and 1,068 in 1791. At a similar event in Berlin in 1786 there were 119 singers and 189 instrumentalists (including twelve flutes, twelve oboes, and ten bassoons).

Three other aspects of orchestration during the Classical era are notable: (1) all orchestral ensembles included at least one keyboard instrument (harpsichord, organ, or pianoforte) that was played by a person who read from a string bass part and realized appropriate chords (Joseph Haydn is documented as playing thusly in performances of his Paris and London symphonies in the 1790s); (2) wind parts were doubled or tripled according to the number of strings (doubled with more than twenty strings, and tripled with more than forty strings); and (3) the first and second violins were always positioned across from each other, with the first violins to the left and the second violins to the right of the conductor.

The ratio of orchestral players to choral singers was generally two to one (i.e., twice the number of instrumentalists as choristers). Haydn conducted performances of *The Creation* in March 1800 with sixty instrumentalists and a choir of twenty-four, and Salieri conducted performances in March 1808 with sixty instrumentalists and a choir of thirty-two. The famous Tonkünstler-Societät performances of *The Creation,* conducted by Haydn, consisted of an orchestra of 120 and a choir of sixty—the orchestra including tripled winds (i.e., three players on each of the flute, oboe, clarinet, bassoon, and horn parts to balance eighteen players on each of the string parts). The small number of singers in proportion to the large number of instrumentalists was, in part, satisfying in balance, because the singers were usually positioned in front of the orchestra. In performances such as the Handel festivals in Westminster Abbey in 1784, platforms were built to raise the orchestra above and behind the choir, and in most other choral/orchestral performances, the choir was positioned on the floor or on a slightly raised platform, with the orchestra behind the choir on a stage or a higher platform. This arrangement is depicted in a famous painting of a performance of Haydn's *The Creation* given at Old University in Vienna on March 27, 1808.

❧ AUSTRIA AND GERMANY ❧

The relative roles of Austria and Germany during the Baroque and Classical eras were reversed. Germany was clearly the more dominant country during the Baroque, with significantly greater musical activity and numbers of important composers, while Austria was manifestly preeminent during the Classical era. Ten of the fourteen notable Classical-era composers worked in Austria—Johann Ernst Eberlin, Leopold Mozart, Anton Cajetan Adlgasser, Michael Haydn, and Wolfgang Amadeus Mozart in Salzburg, and Florian Leopold Gassmann, Johann Georg Albrechtsberger, Carl Ditters von Dittersdorf, Antonio Salieri, and Franz Schubert in Vienna. In addition, two other composers—Joseph Haydn and Johann Nepomuk Hummel—were from and spent a great deal of time in or near Vienna (Haydn was in Eisenstadt, just across the Austrian border from Vienna, and Hummel, who spent the final years of his life in Weimar, Germany, spent most of his life in Vienna). Only the remaining two composers worked in Germany: Johann Adolf Hasse served at the court in Dresden (which was Catholic) and Christian Friedrich Gregor, who was Moravian, lived and worked in Herrnhut.

Three other German composers, the most famous sons of J. S. Bach—Carl Philipp Emanuel (1714–1788), Johann Christoph Friedrich (1732–1795), and Johann Christian (1735–1782)—lived and composed during the Classical era but are not included here, partly for stylistic considerations and partly for reasons of convenience. Their music, as well as the late music of Georg Philipp Telemann, is in a pre-Classical or Rococo style and is best understood in the context of late-Baroque German idioms. In like manner, the discussion of J. S. Bach's sons is most logical and comprehensible as a closure to the Baroque rather than a beginning to the Classical era. On the other hand, Franz Schubert, who is often considered to be a composer of the Romantic era, is discussed here because his choral music is much more Classical than Romantic in style; this is especially so regarding his church music, which conforms to the Classical structures used by Mozart and the Haydn brothers and which is conservative in harmonic language. Schubert's secular part songs, while occasionally Romantic in tonal juxtapositions, are also mainly Classical in their approach to text setting and in their scoring.

The shift of musical activity from Germany to Austria created a comparable shift in focus from genres such as chorales, chorale motets, and cantatas for Lutheran liturgies to masses, Magnificats, Te Deums, and Latin motets for Catholic services. In addition, almost all Classical-era composers wrote oratorios. The masses during the early years of the Classical era were structurally similar to those in the latter part of the Baroque, with the Gloria and Credo portions of the Ordinary divided into separate movements and with some of these movements scored for solos (i.e., arias). The masses during the later years of the era, composed in response to reform mandates by Emperor Joseph II of Austria and Archbishop Colloredo of Salzburg, were shorter in length and less florid in style; all portions of the Ordinary were in one movement, and writing for soloists was basically syllabic and was scored mostly for ensembles. The Magnificats and Te Deums were similar to the masses in structure and style, often with development of motifs and long fugal closing sections, and with scoring for soloists, chorus, and large instrumental ensemble. The motets were small-scale works that for the first time in history were not primarily imitative. Instead, they were written in two combined textures: the vocal parts were basically homophonic and inactive, while the instrumental writing was figural and rhythmically active.

The oratorios at the beginning of the era were generally set to Italian texts and composed for the Tonkünstler-Societät in Vienna or the court in Salzburg. The Tonkünstler-Societät, founded in 1772 by Gassmann, featured Italian oratorios by Hasse, Joseph Haydn, Albrechtsberger, Dittersdorf, Salieri, and Gassmann himself. Oratorios in Italian and German by Eberlin, Leopold Mozart, Adlgasser, and Michael Haydn were performed in Salzburg.

JOHANN ADOLF HASSE 1699–1783

Hasse was born in Bergedorf, Germany, and most likely received his musical education in nearby Hamburg. He joined the Hamburg Opera company as a tenor soloist in 1718, and the following year he became a member of the opera company at the court in Brunswick. In 1721 he went to Italy, first to Venice, Bologna, Florence, and Rome, and then to Naples, where he stayed for approximately six years—studying with Alessandro Scarlatti, working at the S Bartolomeo opera company, and composing operas for performances throughout Europe. He married the famous soprano Faustina Bordoni in 1730, and in 1731 he was appointed *Kapellmeister* at the electoral court of Friedrich Augustus II in Dresden. For the remainder of his life he combined his duties at the court with frequent visits to Austria, Venice, and Naples to oversee productions of his operas.

In addition to sixty-three operas, Hasse composed seventeen masses (including three Requiems), thirty-six separate mass movements, eleven oratorios, one Magnificat, five Te Deums, four sets of Lamentations, and seventy-seven motets. The masses are large-scale works for soloists, chorus, and orchestra, with the five portions of the Ordinary divided into separate movements. The Gloria of the *Messe* in D minor, for instance, has five movements—"Gloria in excelsis Deo" for solo quartet and chorus, "Domine Deus, Rex caelestis" for soprano solo, "Qui tollis peccata mundi" for tenor solo and chorus, and "Quoniam tu solus sanctus" and "Cum sancto spiritu," both for chorus. As in almost all masses of the Classical era, the Benedictus is also a separate movement.

Of the oratorios, the first, *Daniello,* was written for the Vienna court under Charles VI and premiered there in 1731. The second and third, *Serpentes ignei in deserto* and *S Petrus et S Maria Magdalena,* were written for the Ospedale degli Incurabili (one of four orphanages for girls in Venice that specialized in musical training), while the remaining eight oratorios were composed for the Dresden court. Most of these works were well received at their premieres and given numerous subsequent performances, including those presented by the Tonkünstler-Societät in Vienna. Hasse's final and most popular oratorio, *La conversione di Sant' Agonstino,* was composed in 1750 to a libretto by noted singer and poet Maria Antonia Walpurgis (1724–1780), daughter of Elector Karl Albert of Bavaria. The libretto, related mostly in *secco* recitatives and arias, is about the conversion of a sinner to sainthood. Solo roles are for St Augustine (A), Augustine's mother Monica (S), Augustine's brother Navigio (B), a friend named Alipio (A), a priest named Simpliciano (T), and an unnamed person (S). Two choral movements, both for SATB, conclude the two parts of the oratorio, and instrumental scoring is for two flutes, two oboes, two horns, strings, and basso continuo.

The Te Deum settings and many of the motets are large-scale works divided into separate movements and scored for woodwind, brass, and stringed instruments. *Regina caeli* in D major, composed in the early 1750s, and the *Te Deum* in D major, composed for the dedication of the new Dresden court chapel in 1751 and performed along with the *Messe* in D minor, are both in three movements—the first and last for solo quartet and chorus, and the middle for soprano solo. The *Miserere* in C minor, first composed for female voices in the early 1730s and later arranged by Hasse for mixed soloists and chorus, is in eight movements—"Miserere mei Deus" for chorus, "Tibi soli peccavi" for B solo, "Ecce enim in iniquitatibus" for SA and AT duet and chorus, "Libera me" for SA duet, "Quoniam si voluisses" for S solo, "Begigne fac, Domine" for chorus, "Gloria patri" for A solo, and "Sicut erat in principio" for chorus.

SACRED WORKS
SELECTED AND LISTED ACCORDING TO FAMILIARITY

Messe in D minor – SSATB solos, SATB chorus, two flutes, two oboes, two horns, two trumpets, timpani, strings, and basso continuo – 45 minutes.

Te Deum in D major – S solo, SATB chorus, two oboes, two horns, two trumpets, timpani, strings, and basso continuo – 18:30 minutes. The choral parts divide into brief SSAA passages that may be sung by soloists.

Miserere in C minor (Psalm 51) – SATB solos, SATB chorus, two flutes, two oboes, strings, and basso continuo – 25 minutes.

Regina caeli in D major – A solos, SATB chorus, two horns, two oboes, strings, and bass continuo – 12:30 minutes.

Beatus vir in A minor (Psalm 112) – SATB solos, SATB chorus, two oboes, strings, and basso continuo – 6 minutes.

Confitebor tibi in F major (Psalm 111) – SATB solos, SATB chorus, two oboes, strings, and basso continuo – 7 minutes.

Laudate coeli in D major (Psalms 148:1, 112:4, and 97:3) – B solo, SATB chorus, two oboes, two trumpets, timpani, strings, and basso continuo – 7 minutes.

Dixit Dominus in C major (Psalm 110) – SATB solos, SATB chorus, two oboes, two horns, strings, and basso continuo – 5 minutes.

Laudate pueri in A major (Psalm 113) – SSA solos, SATB chorus, two oboes, strings, and basso continuo – 25 minutes.

Venite pastores in D major – SAT solos, SATB chorus, two flutes, two oboes, two bassoons, two horns, strings, and basso continuo – 6 minutes.

JOHANN ERNST EBERLIN 1702–1762

Eberlin was born in a small town west of Munich and attended the Jesuit gymnasium of St Salvator in nearby Augsburg. From 1721 until 1723 he was a student at the Benedictine university in Salzburg, and in 1726 he became one of the organists at the Salzburg Cathedral. He advanced at the cathedral and in 1749 was appointed *Hofkapellmeister* as well as organist at the Salzburg court. His position in the development of the Classical era is important in that he was the first of a long line of significant composers in Salzburg (including Michael Haydn and W. A. Mozart) and therefore influenced the styles these composers later manifested and formalized.

Eberlin composed sixty-seven masses (including nine Requiems), thirteen oratorios (including three Passions), and approximately two hundred motets. Few of these works are known today, and many of them are stylistically transitional. For instance, the Passion oratorio *Der blutschwitzende Jesus* combines elements of traditional Baroque works containing biblical passages (i.e., characters such as Jesus, Peter, and an evangelist relate the crucifixion story) with elements of the *empfindsamer Stil* lyrical drama (i.e., characters such as the Daughter of Zion and the Believing Soul relate the story to eighteenth-century thought). In addition, most of the text is set to accompanied recitative; there is only one choral movement—the one that closes the oratorio. Other works have stylistic traits that would become common throughout the early years of the Classical era in Salzburg. The *Te Deum* in C major is in one movement divided into three sections and scored for SATB solos, SATB chorus, two trumpets, timpani, two violins, and basso continuo. Solo passages, which contain some melismatic writing, alternate with homophonic choral sections of music, and the work ends with an extended double fugue, the first subject set to the text phrase "In te Domine speravi" (In you Lord I have trusted) and the second subject to "non confundar in aeternam" (let me never be confounded). *Dixit Dominus*—scored for SATB solos, SATB chorus, four trumpets, timpani, two violins, and basso continuo—is distinctive in being divided into five sections: the first, third, and fifth are scored mostly for the chorus, and the second and fourth are scored for soloists with solo trumpet obbligato. The *Magnificat*—scored for SATB solos, SATB chorus, four trumpets, timpani, strings (including violas), and organ—is in one section, unified by a seven-measure ground bass stated fourteen times throughout the work.

LEOPOLD MOZART 1719–1787

Leopold Mozart, father of Wolfgang Amadeus Mozart, was born in Augsburg, Germany, where he attended the Augsburg Gymnasium between 1727 and 1735 and the Lyceum of St Salvator in 1735 and 1736. He continued his education at the Benedictine university in Salzburg, studying philosophy and law, and he received a bachelor's degree in philosophy in 1738. Having become proficient as an organist and violinist, he took a position as musician to Count Johann Baptist, and in 1743 he became a violinist in the court orchestra of Archbishop Leopold Anton Freiher von Firmian. In 1756, the year of his son's birth, he authored the violin treatise *Versuch einer gründlichen Violinschule,* and in 1763 he was appointed *Vice-Kapellmeister* at the Salzburg court, although at this point in his life and for the next decade he spent the majority of his time touring with and working to advance the career of his son. For the final years of his life Leopold continued to focus his energies on Wolfgang—editing, copying, and cataloguing his compositions and working to ameliorate conflicts between Wolfgang and Archbishop Colloredo.

Unfortunately, Leopold did not pay particular attention to the preservation of his own compositions. Nor did anyone else, and as a consequence most of them have been lost. All that survive are a few masses, oratorios, Litanies, motets, and German part songs. The masses are best represented by the *Missa solemnis* in C major, composed about 1764 and scored for SATB solos, SATB chorus, flute, two horns, two trumpets, timpani, strings, and basso continuo. Like many masses of the late eighteenth century, including those by Johann Adolf Hasse, each portion of the Ordinary is divided into separate movements. The Gloria, for example, is divided into five movements—"Gloria in excelsis Deo" for solo quartet and chorus, "Laudamus te" for soprano solo, "Gratias agimus tibi" for solo quartet and chorus, "Quoniam tu solus sanctus" for alto solo, and "Cum sancto spiritu" for chorus. Mozart's mass is further characterized by frequent tempo changes within the movements. Other works that have been published and that are occasionally performed today include the *Missa brevis* in A major (for SATB solos, SATB chorus, two violins, and basso continuo) and the motet *Beata es virgo Maria* in C major (for S solo, SATB chorus, two trumpets, timpani, two violins, and basso continuo).

CHRISTIAN FRIEDRICH GREGOR 1723–1801

Gregor was born in the Silesian area of Poland, where he was raised and educated by Count Pfeil. In 1742 he joined the Moravian community in Herrnhut, Germany, and in 1756 he was ordained a minister. He also served as an administrator of the Moravian church, visiting congregations in Germany, Holland, and North America, and in 1789 he was named a bishop. In 1778 Gregor compiled and edited the German Moravian hymnal, composing or arranging more than three hundred hymn tunes, and in 1784 he contributed music to the Moravian *Choral-Buch*. He also composed four-voiced chorales for the publication entitled *Die gewöhnlichsten Choral-Melodien der Brüdergemeinen* and several German anthems that were published separately. The anthems include the well-known *Hosianna* for SATB/SATB chorus, and two versions of *Und da alles vollendet war*, one in 1763 for chorus, flute, and strings, and one in 1780 for chorus, clarinet, and strings.

FLORIAN LEOPOLD GASSMANN 1729–1774

Gassmann was born northwest of Prague, Czech Republic, and was educated at the Jesuit gymnasium in nearby Chomutov. As a young adult he traveled to Italy, where he studied with Padre Giovanni Battista Martini in Bologna and composed operas for performance in Venice. In 1763 he succeeded Christoph Willibald Gluck as *Kapellmeister* at the imperial court in Vienna, from 1765 to 1766 he returned to Venice to supervise and conduct his opera *Achille in Sciro*, and in 1772 he was promoted to *Hofkapellmeister* of the Viennese court chapel. Meanwhile, in 1771 he founded Vienna's first musical organization devoted to public concerts, the Tonkünstler-Societät, which began by presenting Italian oratorios and symphonic works during Advent and Lent.

Gassmann composed five masses (including a Requiem), one oratorio, and approximately forty motets. The masses include the *Missa solemnis* in C major for SATB chorus, two oboes, four trumpets, timpani, strings, and basso continuo in addition to three trombones that, in the custom of the time, doubled the choral alto, tenor, and bass parts *colla parte*. Also following current customs, the portions of the Mass Ordinary were divided into separate movements (e.g., the Gloria and Credo are each divided into four movements). The *Requiem*—which is written in motet style and is incomplete (it contains only the Introit, Te decet hymnus, Requiem aeternam, and Kyrie)—is scored for SATB chorus, two oboes, two trumpets, two trombones, strings, and basso continuo; all the instruments double the voice parts *colla parte*. The oratorio *La betulia liberata* was composed for and first performed at the Tonkünstler-Societät's inaugural concert during Lent 1772. The motets include *Stabat mater* for SATB chorus and basso continuo; *O salutaris hostia* and *Regina caeli* for SATB chorus, two violins, and basso continuo; *Veni creator spiritus* for TB solos, SATB chorus, two oboes, strings, and basso continuo; and *Viderunt omnes* and *Tui sunt caeli*, both for SATB chorus, two oboes, two trumpets, timpani, strings, and basso continuo.

ANTON CAJETAN ADLGASSER 1729–1777

Adlgasser, born in Upper Bavaria, was a chorister at the court chapel in Salzburg beginning in 1744. In 1750 he was appointed court and cathedral organist under *Hofkapellmeister* Johann Ernst Eberlin (who had taken the position in 1749), and in 1760 he also became organist at the Dreifaltigkeitskirche in Salzburg. Except for a one-year leave of absence in 1674 to study with Padre Giovanni Battista Martini in Bologna, he remained in both positions until his untimely death at age forty-eight. W. A. Mozart succeeded him at the court and cathedral, and Michael Haydn succeeded him at the Dreifaltigkeitskirche.

Adlgasser composed six complete masses (including two Requiems), five surviving oratorios, fifteen Litanies, approximately eighty motets, and forty-four German hymns and songs. Most of this repertoire is unknown today. However, the oratorios were important during his lifetime and received numerous performances. They include *Christus am Ölberg* in 1754, *Die wirkende Gnade Gottes oder David in der Busse* in 1756, *Esther* in 1761, and *Ochus regans oder Samuel und Heli* in 1763. The *Litaniae de venerabili altaris sacramento* (scored for SATB solos, SATB chorus, two trumpets, timpani, two violins, and basso continuo) is also considered to be an important work.

JOSEPH HAYDN 1732–1809

Haydn was born in Rohrau, Austria, a small town southeast of Vienna, the second of twelve children born to parents who were amateur musicians. Haydn's brother Michael, who also became a noted composer, was sixth. Joseph was sent to school in the nearby town of Hainburg at about age six and began violin, organ, and harpsichord lessons there. From eight to approximately eighteen he sang as a chorister at St Stephen's Cathedral in Vienna and also further developed his violin and keyboard skills. After leaving the cathedral when his voice changed, he freelanced in Vienna as a teacher and performer, serving as accompanist for Nicola Porpora, the renowned voice teacher, and also composing several masses and motets. In 1759, at twenty-seven, Haydn took a position at the court of Count Morzin, and the following year he was appointed *Kapellmeister* to Prince Nikolaus Esterházy, whose lavish court was just across Austria's border in Eisenstadt, Hungary. Haydn continued in the service of the Esterházys the remainder of his life, serving Nikolaus for thirty years, his son Anton for four years, and Anton's son Nikolaus for fifteen years. The first Nikolaus had broad and substantial musical interests, and supported a large musical establishment. Anton did not share his father's love of music and dismissed most of the court's musicians, although he retained Haydn in a minimal capacity. With Anton's death in 1794, his son Nikolaus rebuilt the musical resources, returned the court to a state of musical splendor, and elevated Haydn again to a position of importance.

During the reign of the first Nikolaus, Haydn spent much of his time in Eisenstadt compos-ing operas, symphonies, and chamber music. However, with few responsibilities during Anton's reign, Haydn was free to travel. His first major trip was in 1791 to London, where the entrepre-neur Johann Peter Salomon had arranged for him to compose and conduct an opera, six sym-phonies, and a variety of other pieces. His compositions were all received enthusiastically by London audiences, he was granted an honorary doctorate from Oxford University, and in several years he became one of the best-known and most performed composers in all of Europe. While in London, Haydn also attended some of the Handel Commemoration concerts in Westminster Abbey, hearing *Messiah* and *Israel in Egypt* in addition to excerpts from *Esther, Saul, Judas Mac-cabaeus,* and *Deborah.* After one of these performances, Haydn asked a friend, the famous vio-linist and fellow composer Françoise-Hippolyte Barthélemon, to suggest an oratorio libretto subject that he might set. Barthélemon supposedly took a Bible and said, "Here, take this, and start at the beginning." Coincidentally, in 1795 during Haydn's second visit to London, Salomon presented him with an oratorio libretto, presumably written for Handel years earlier, based on Milton's *Paradise Lost.* Haydn gave the libretto to his friend and collaborator Baron Gottfried van Swieten, who translated it into German for Haydn to review and consider setting to music.

Meanwhile, Anton's son Nikolaus, who succeeded his father in 1794, desired Haydn's re-turn to the Esterházy court, although only to compose a new mass each year to celebrate the name day of Princess Maria. Haydn fulfilled this expectation beginning in 1796, and in 1798 he completed his *Paradise Lost* oratorio, which was called *Die Schöpfung* and which was immedi-ately retranslated back into English as *The Creation.* When the score was published in 1800, it contained both German and English texts. Its enormous success prompted Haydn to compose *Die Jahreszeiten,* the libretto of which was also translated into German from an original English text (a poem entitled *The Seasons* by James Thomson). *Die Jahreszeiten* was not as successful as *Die Schöpfung,* although both works became the most frequently performed Classical-era orato-rios throughout Europe during the nineteenth century.

In the final decade of his life Haydn composed six masses for the Esterházy court, a *Te Deum* for Empress Marie Therese, and a group of part songs and canons in addition to several opuses of string quartets. He also conducted until 1803 and attended performances of his works under the direction of other conductors, the final being *Die Schöpfung* in March 1808 conducted by An-tonio Salieri. Haydn's health declined after this, and he confined himself to his home on the out-skirts of Vienna, where he died on May 31, 1809, only one month after the city had been con-quered by Napoleon. A memorial service that included a performance of the Mozart *Requiem* was held at the Schottenkirche on June 15.

Haydn composed fourteen masses, three oratorios, several other large-scale sacred vocal works, a choral version of *Die sieben letzten Worte unseres Erlösers am Kreuze,* approximately a dozen small-scale sacred vocal works, one cantata, thirteen part songs, a madrigal, and over forty canons. Most accountings of the masses list only twelve, since two very early compositions were lost. However, the Haydn scholar H. C. Robbins Landon discovered one of the missing masses—*Missa Brevis alla capella* ("Rorate coeli desuper")—in 1957. The validity of the find is inconclusive, since Haydn's name does not appear on the manuscript, although most scholars believe that the mass is authentic. The twelve traditional masses fall into two periods—six between 1749 and 1782, and six between 1796 and 1802. During the fourteen-year interval separating these two periods, Haydn was busy composing in other genres, mostly instrumental. Moreover, he had little incentive to compose sacred music, for in 1783 Emperor Joseph II had instituted a reform of church music called *Gottesdienstordnung,* which, among other restrictions, required that there be no instruments with masses except on Sundays and special feast days.

Haydn's early masses are varied; some, such as the *Missa Sancti Nicolai* ("Nikolaimesse") and the *Missa brevis Sancti Joannis de Deo* ("Kleine Orgelmesse"), are of the *brevis* type (short), while others, such as the *Missa in honorem BVM* ("Missa Sancti Josephi" or "Grosse Orgelmesse") and the *Missa Cellenis* ("Mariazeller Messe"), are of the *solemnis* type (solemn or full, meant for festival occasions). The *brevis* masses are characterized by reduced orchestrations and short durations, with textual phrases in the Gloria and Credo movements often telescoped or overlapped (i.e., each of the four choral voice parts have different phrases of text simultaneously). The *solemnis* masses are characterized by fuller orchestrations and longer durations, with the Gloria and Credo movements often divided into three distinct sections (fast, slow, fast). The *Missa Cellenis in honorem BVM* ("Cäcilienmesse") is unique in being a cantata mass: the five portions of the Ordinary are divided into separate movements, with a structure of arias and choruses similar to cantatas of the Baroque era. The Gloria, for instance, is divided into seven separate movements, while the Credo is divided into four. The most popular of the early masses are the *Missa Sancti Nicolai* and the *Missa brevis Sancti Joannis de Deo,* both of which are especially accessible, elegant, and charming.

The late masses, which were composed, as is mentioned above, to celebrate the name day of Princess Maria of the Esterházy court, are different from the earlier masses although similar to each other. They are all symphonic in nature; that is, the movements are in symphonic forms such as sonata, variation, and rondo. In addition, they are all of the *solemnis* type, and the writing for soloists is in quartet format. The *Missa in tempore belli* ("Paukenmesse") and the *Missa in angustiis* ("Nelsonmesse"), known for their melodic beauty and structural balance, are the most popular of the late masses.

All the masses, whether early or late, have separate Benedictus movements, which were almost always set for soloists, and most of the masses were named by Haydn. Some of the names refer to circumstances of performance and some to salient expressive compositional characteristics. (See the comments under each mass listed below for specific details.)

The first oratorio, *Il ritorno di Tobia,* was composed for the 1775 Lenten concert series of the Tonkünstler-Societät, Vienna's first public concert society. It is in the Italianate style popular at the time, except for a large number of choruses. The choruses no doubt reflect Haydn's awareness of Handel oratorios, and they also probably account for the oratorio's success. A review of the premiere stated, "The choruses, above all, were lit by a fire otherwise only to be found in Handel; in short, the whole very large audience was delighted, and here too Haydn was the great artist whose works are in great favor all over Europe."

The second oratorio, *Die Schöpfung,* had its premiere in April 1798 by the Gesellschaft der Associierten, a private concert society founded by van Swieten. The oratorio was so successful that the Gesellschaft repeated it the following year, and it was also given a public performance by the Tonkünstler-Societät. It is completely in the Handelian mold—divided into three sections, infused with numerous examples of highly descriptive and effective word painting, and filled with choruses. The first two parts of the oratorio depict the first six days of creation; part three relates the thanks of Adam and Eve for the glories of creation and their love for one another. The word painting includes the representation of chaos in the orchestral prelude to the oratorio, the forceful setting of "und es ward Licht" (and there was light) in day one, the storms in day two, the rising of the sun and moon in day four, and the animals (including the creeping sinuous worm) in day five. Of the numerous remarkable choruses, several have been regularly extracted and have become staples of choral programming, especially *Die Himmel erzählen die Ehre Gottes* (The heavens are telling the glory of God) and *Vollendet ist das grosse Werk* (Achieved is the glorious work).

Haydn's final oratorio, *Die Jahreszeiten*, was also composed for and premiered (April 24, 1801, at Vienna's Palais Schwarzenberg) by van Swieten's Gesellschaft. Its text, as was mentioned above, comes from the English poem *The Seasons* by James Thomson, which was popular at the time, and each of its four major sections (the seasons) begins with an orchestral overture or introduction headed by a scenic description. Spring begins with "Die Einleitung stellt den Übergang vom Winter zum Frühling vor" (The introduction paints the passage of winter to spring); Summer with "Die Einleitung stellt die Morgendämmerung vor" (The introduction paints the dawn of day); Autumn with "Der Einleitung Gegenstand ist des Landmanns freudiges Gefühl über die reiche Ernte" (The introduction's subject is the countryman's feeling of joy over a good harvest); and Winter with "Die Einleitung schildert die dicken Nebel, womit der Winter anfängt" (The introduction depicts the thick fog at the approach of winter). Throughout the oratorio, a farmer, his daughter, a young peasant, and a chorus of country folk and hunters relate various attributes of the seasons. Haydn apparently found the text difficult to set. According to his biographer, Georg August Greisinger, "Haydn often complained bitterly over the unpoetic text of *The Seasons* and how hard it was for him to find inspiration to compose." Also, Giuseppe Carpini, who attended the premiere performance, quoted Haydn as saying, "I am pleased that the audience liked my music, but . . . the 'Seasons' is no second 'Creation'. The reason is simple: in one work the characters are angels and in the other they are peasants."

The large-scale sacred vocal works include two settings of the Te Deum and single settings of the Stabat mater and Salve regina. The first *Te Deum* (also attributed to Haydn's brother Michael) was composed in about 1764 for Nikolaus Esterházy and is believed to be one of Haydn's earliest sacred compositions. The second *Te Deum* was composed between 1798 and 1800 for Marie Therese, the second wife of Emperor Franz I and the presumed soprano soloist in Viennese performances of Haydn's oratorios. The motivation for the composition and the occasion of its premiere was a visit between the royal family and Lord Nelson in the autumn of 1800. The work, one of Haydn's most frequently performed choral compositions, is structured in one movement, divided into three sections (fast, slow, fast), and scored for chorus and orchestra without soloists.

The *Stabat mater*, composed for performance on Good Friday 1767, was Haydn's first major choral work for the Esterházy court. Haydn was so proud of it that he sent a manuscript copy to Johann Adolph Hasse, the famous composer and conductor, who mounted a performance in Vienna in 1771. The work, which is in the expressive *Sturm und Drang* style of composition popular at the time, then became quite popular (and remained one of Haydn's favorite compositions), being performed in 1779 in Leipzig and from 1781 to 1789 in Paris at the Concerts spirituels.

The *Salve Regina* was composed in 1771 specifically for solo quartet (the description "à Quattro voci ma soli" appears after the title), which sings in ensemble for most of the work (i.e., there are few solo melodic passages). Haydn's setting is divided into two movements, each of which is further divided into two sections that are varied in tempo, and it is scored for accompaniment of strings and organ, the organ part having significant obbligato solos.

Die sieben letzten Worte unseres Erlösers am Kreuze was first composed in 1785 for orchestra alone and for performance on Good Friday 1786 at the church of Santa Cueva in Cádiz, Andalusia. Haydn later arranged it for string quartet and put the "words" in the score before each corresponding musical movement. This version was performed on St Cecilia's Day 1787 at the Schlosskirche in Vienna. A third version came about after Haydn heard a performance of the work arranged for choir by Joseph Friebert, *Kapellmeister* of the Passau Cathedral, and edited by van Swieten. Haydn then made his own choral setting in about 1795 and had it published in 1801.

The small-scale sacred vocal works include six Psalm settings in English composed in approximately 1794 at the request of Haydn's friend William Dechair Tattersall, rector of an Anglican church in London, who was compiling a collection of accessible congregational music. Haydn's Psalms are scored for SAB chorus, and most are homophonic and strophic.

The part songs were written between 1796 and 1801 for no special reason. As Haydn stated, "These songs were composed purely *con amore*, in happy hours, and not on order." They are similar to pieces composed by his brother Michael for various civic singing groups in Salzburg, and also pieces that were popular in England at the time. Most are scored for SATB voices and piano; a few are for a trio of voices and piano. The texts are generally humorous, no doubt reflecting Haydn's "happy hours." *Die Harmonie in der Ehe* (Harmony in Marriage) is a spoof about amicability in marriage—the wife supposedly desires the same foolish pastime pleasures as the husband—and *Die Beredsamkeit* (Eloquence) is a tribute to the virtues of Rhine wine, which can make one loquacious. On the other hand, *Abendlied zu Gott* is a tender and sweet setting of a simple prayer. Both *Die Harmonie in der Ehe* and *Die Beredsamkeit* are popular with present-day high school, college, and community choirs.

The madrigal, entitled *The Storm,* was composed in 1792 and was Haydn's first composition to an English text. Unlike typical madrigals, which are generally short a cappella pieces, Haydn's madrigal is relatively lengthy and is scored for orchestral accompaniment. The madrigal genre classification, assigned by Haydn, no doubt reflects the music's many tempo changes and word painting of the phrases "wild uproar of the winds" and "bless'd calm, return again."

MASSES

COMPLETE AND LISTED IN CHRONOLOGICAL ORDER
ACCORDING TO DATE OF COMPOSITION

Missa brevis in F major – ca.1749 – SS solos, SATB chorus, two violins, and
    organ – 11 minutes. (1) The soloists, always in duet, alternate with the
    chorus in every movement except the Benedictus, which is for the
    soloists alone; (2) the music of the Kyrie is repeated in the "Dona nobis

pacem" portion of the Agnus Dei; (3) the Gloria and Credo movements end with the same music; (4) the Credo text is telescoped.

Missa Brevis alla capella ("Rorate coeli desuper") – before 1750 – SATB chorus, two violins, and basso continuo – 5 minutes. (1) The mass is in G major; (2) the Kyrie is based on the Gregorian chant *Rorate coeli desuper* (Isaiah 45:8), which is the Introit for the fourth Sunday in Advent; (3) the Gloria and Credo texts are telescoped.

Missa Cellenis in honorem BVM ("Cäcilienmesse") – 1766 – SATB solos, SATB chorus, two oboes, two bassoons, two horns, two trumpets, timpani, strings, and organ – 70 minutes. (1) The mass is in C major; (2) the title refers to the annual celebration on the name day of St Cecilia, November 22, by the Viennese Brotherhood of St Cecilia; (3) the BVM in the title stands for Beatissimae Virginis Mariae (Blessed Virgin Mary); (4) there are soprano and tenor solo movements, and extended solo passages for all the soloists.

Missa in honorem BVM ("Missa Sancti Josephi" or "Grosse Orgelmesse") – ca.1769 – SATB solos, SATB chorus, two English horns, two horns, two trumpets, timpani, strings, and organ – 40 minutes. (1) The mass is in E-flat major; (2) the original title refers to one of the feast days of the Virgin Mary; (3) Haydn later added the title "Sancti Josephi," probably because of a performance on St Joseph's Day, March 19, which was also Haydn's name day; (4) the third title refers to obbligato organ solos in the Kyrie, Gloria, Benedictus, and Agnus Dei; (5) except for a brief tenor solo in the Credo ("Et incarnatus est"), the solo scoring is for quartet; (6) the use of English horns reflects Haydn's preference for these instruments during the 1760s and 1770s.

Missa Sancti Nicolai ("Nikolaimesse") – 1772 – SATB solos, SATB chorus, two oboes, two horns, strings, and organ – 26 minutes. (1) The mass is in G major; (2) the title supposedly refers to performance on the name day, December 6, of Prince Nikolaus of Esterházy; (3) the solo scoring is for quartet except for a soprano solo in the Gloria ("Gratias agimus tibi") and a tenor solo in the Credo ("Et incarnatus est"); (4) the Benedictus is entirely for solo quartet; (5) the Credo text is telescoped; (6) the "Dona nobis pacem" portion of the Agnus Dei is set to the same music as the beginning of the Kyrie.

Missa brevis Sancti Joannis de Deo ("Kleine Orgelmesse") – ca.1775 – S solo, SATB chorus, two violins and organ – 15 minutes. (1) The mass is in B-flat major; (2) the original title refers to St John of God, the founder of the Brothers of Mercy in Eisenstadt, for whom the mass was composed; (3) the second title refers to an obbligato organ solo in the Benedictus; (4) the mass is entirely choral except for a soprano solo in the Benedictus; (5) the Gloria and Credo texts are telescoped; (6) the Gloria is extremely brief in duration (only thirty-one measures).

Missa Cellenis ("Mariazeller Messe") – 1782 – SATB solos, SATB chorus, two oboes, bassoon, two trumpets, timpani, strings, and organ – 33 minutes. (1) The mass is in C major; (2) the second title, given by Haydn, refers to Mary of Zell (Zell being a small pilgrimage town); (3) there is little writing for soloists.

Missa Sancti Bernardi von Offida ("Heiligmesse") – 1796 – SATB solos, SATB
chorus, and two oboes, two clarinets, two bassoons, two horns, two
trumpets, timpani, strings, and organ – 37 minutes. (1) The mass is in
B-flat major; (2) the original title refers to Bernard of Offida (1604–
1694), a Capuchin monk who cared for the poor; (3) the second title
refers to the German chorale "Heilig," which Haydn employs in the
Sanctus; (4) there is little solo writing in this mass, although the solo
scoring expands to SSATBB in the "Et incarnatus est" portion of the
Credo.

Missa in tempore belli ("Paukenmesse") – 1796 – SATB solos, SATB chorus,
two oboes, bassoon, two trumpets, timpani, strings, and organ – 40
minutes. (1) The mass is in C major; (2) the original title refers to the
time of war (tempore belli), during which the mass was composed;
(3) the second title refers to the timpani solo, which is a prominent feature in the Agnus Dei; (4) the first performance was on December 6,
1796, St Stephen's Day; (5) except for a bass solo accompanied by solo
cello in the Gloria ("Qui tollis"), the solo scoring is for quartet; (6) the
Benedictus is entirely for solo quartet; (7) for a later performance of the
mass, Haydn added a flute, two clarinets, and a horn to the instrumental
scoring.

Missa in angustiis ("Nelsonmesse") – 1798 – SATB solos, SATB chorus, three
trumpets, timpani, strings, and organ – 40 minutes. (1) The mass is in
D minor; (2) the original title, by Haydn, refers to the time of war during
which the mass was being composed; (3) the second title refers to Lord
Nelson, who had won a decisive battle in August 1798 and who had become Haydn's friend in 1800; (4) there are obbligato organ solos in the
Kyrie, Gloria, and Sanctus movements; (5) the first part of the Credo is
composed as a canon between the choral ST and AB voices; (6) Haydn
later added instrumental parts for flute, two oboes, and bassoon.

Theresienmesse – 1799 – SATB solos, SATB chorus, two clarinets, two trumpets, timpani, strings, and organ – 45 minutes. (1) The mass is in B-flat
major; (2) the title, not by Haydn, came about after a performance of the
mass for Empress Marie Therese, who had sung the soprano solos in
performances of *Die Schöpfung* and *Die Jahreszeiten;* (3) except for brief
passages in the Gloria and Benedictus, the solo scoring is for quartet;
(4) there is more scoring for solo quartet in this mass than in any of the
others.

Schöpfungsmesse – 1801 – SATB solos, SATB chorus, two oboes, two clarinets, two bassoons, two horns, two trumpets, timpani, strings, and
organ – 45 minutes. (1) The mass is in B-flat major; (2) the title refers to
Haydn's quote from his oratorio *Die Schöpfung* (a brief solo by Adam in
part three) in the "Qui tollis" portion of the Gloria; (3) the solo scoring is
mostly for quartet.

Harmoniemesse – 1802 – SATB solos, SATB chorus, two oboes, two clarinets,
two bassoons, two horns, two trumpets, timpani, strings, and organ –
40 minutes. (1) The mass is in B-flat major; (2) the title refers to the
prominent scoring for wind instruments; (3) except for brief passages
for each of the soloists, the solo scoring is for quartet.

ORATORIOS
COMPLETE AND LISTED ACCORDING TO FAMILIARITY

Die Schöpfung (*The Creation*) – 1796–1798 – STB solos, SATB chorus, three
flutes, two oboes, two clarinets, three bassoons, two horns, two trumpets, three trombones, timpani, strings, and basso continuo – 105 minutes. (1) Solo roles in parts one and two of the oratorio are for archangels
Gabriel (S), Uriel (T), and Raphael (B); (2) in part three the roles are for
Eve (S) and Adam (B), which are sung by the soprano and bass from
parts one and two; (3) the third flute is used only in movement twenty-
seven, the third bassoon is a contrabassoon, and the basso continuo keyboard can be played on either a harpsichord or a pianoforte; (4) documentation of late-eighteenth-century performances cite a chorus of
eighty singers and an orchestra composed of six flutes, six oboes, six
clarinets, six bassoons, four contrabassoons, six horns, four trumpets,
five trombones, two sets of timpani, thirty-six violins, eighteen violas,
eighteen cellos, and twelve basses, plus an additional cello and bass with
the pianoforte for the basso continuo.

Die Jahreszeiten (*The Seasons*) – 1799–1800 – STB solos, SATB chorus, two
flutes, two oboes, two clarinets, three bassoons, four horns, two trumpets, three trombones, timpani, triangle, tambourine, strings, and basso
continuo – 130 minutes. (1) Solo roles are for a farmer named Simon
(B), his daughter Jane (S), and Lucas, a young countryman who is in love
with Jane (T); (2) the chorus represents country peasants and hunters;
(3) the second flute doubles piccolo, the third bassoon is a contrabassoon, and the basso continuo keyboard can be played on either a harpsichord or a pianoforte; (4) the choruses are all SATB except for the final
one, which is SATB/SATB.

MISCELLANEOUS SACRED WORKS
SELECTED AND LISTED ACCORDING TO FAMILIARITY

Te Deum (subtitled "for Empress Marie Therese") – 1798–1800 – SATB chorus, flute, two oboes, two bassoons, three trumpets, timpani, strings, and
organ – 12 minutes. (1) The work is in one movement, divided into three
sections (Allegro, Adagio, and Allegro moderato); (2) the final section
ends with a long fugue.

Stabat mater – 1767 – SATB solos, SATB chorus, two oboes (doubling two
English horns), bassoon, strings, and organ – 60 minutes. The work is
in twelve movements—seven for soloists, four for soloists and chorus,
and one for chorus alone.

Die sieben letzten Worte unseres Erlösers am Kreuze – choral version ca.1795 –
SATB solos, SATB chorus, two flutes, two oboes, two clarinets, two
bassoons, contrabassoon, two horns, two trombones, two trumpets, timpani, strings, and organ – 63 minutes. (1) The text is in German; (2) the
work is divided into two sections, with five movements per section;
(3) the solo writing is entirely for quartet.

Te Deum (subtitled "for Prince Nikolaus Esterházy") – ca.1764 – SATB solos, SATB chorus, two oboes, two trumpets, timpani, strings, and organ – 8:30 minutes. (1) The solo writing consists of an extended tenor passage and a brief trio for alto, tenor, and bass; (2) the work is in one movement divided into three sections (Allegro moderato, Adagio, Allegro moderato).

PART SONGS
SELECTED AND LISTED ACCORDING TO FAMILIARITY

Die Harmonie in der Ehe – 1796–1801 – SATB chorus and pianoforte – 2:30 minutes.

Die Beredsamkeit – 1796–1801 – SATB chorus and pianoforte – 2:30 minutes.

Alles hat seine Zeit – 1796–1801 – SATB chorus and pianoforte – 2 minutes.

Abendlied zu Gott – 1796–1801 – SATB chorus and pianoforte – 5 minutes.

JOHANN GEORG ALBRECHTSBERGER 1736–1809

Albrechtsberger was born in Klosterneuburg, near Vienna, where he was a chorister at the local Augustinian church. From 1749 to 1754 he sang at Melk Abbey, and between 1754 and 1755 he studied at the Jesuit seminary in Vienna. He served as organist at churches in Raab (now Györ, Hungary) and Maria Taferl (near Melk) from 1755 until 1759, from 1759 until 1765 he was organist at Melk Abbey, in 1772 he was appointed organist and *Vice-Kapellmeister* at St Stephen's church in Vienna, and in 1793 he was promoted to *Kapellmeister*. Praised by W. A. Mozart and Joseph Haydn, Albrechtsberger was considered the finest organist of his time. He was also a noted teacher, who attracted students such as Ludwig van Beethoven, and he was the author of several important treatises, including *Gründliche Anweisung zur Composition . . . mit einem Anhange von der Beschaffenheit und Anwendung aller jetzt üblichen musikalischen Instrumente*, a study of composition published in 1790.

Albrechtsberger composed thirty-eight masses (including three Requiems), six oratorios, ten Vespers settings, sixteen Magnificats, two Te Deums, and approximately two hundred motets. Only a few of these works are known today, including the *Missa* in D major composed in 1783 and scored for SATB chorus and basso continuo; the oratorios *Oratorium de Passione Domini* of 1762, *Oratorium de nativitate Jesu* of 1772, and *Die Pilgrime auf Golgatha* of 1781 (which was one of the first German oratorios performed by the Tonkünstler-Societät); and the motet *Jubilemus salvatori* scored for SATB chorus, two trumpets, timpani, two violins, and basso continuo.

MICHAEL HAYDN 1737–1806

Like his older brother Joseph, Michael was born in Rohrau, Austria. At about age eight he joined Joseph as a chorister at St Stephen's Cathedral in Vienna, and at twelve he became a substitute organist. When his voice changed at sixteen he went to the local Jesuit seminary, where he most likely encountered fellow student Johann Georg Albrechtsberger and where he studied works of Johann Joseph Fux (including his treatise *Gradus ad Parnassum*), J. S. Bach, George Frideric Handel, Carl Heinrich Graun, and Johann Adolf Hasse. Haydn also freelanced as a teacher. In 1760 he was appointed *Kapellmeister* to the Bishop of Grosswardein in Hungary (now Oradea, Romania), in 1762 he succeeded Johann Ernst Eberlin as cathedral organist for Archbishop Sigismund Schrattenbach in Salzburg, and in 1777 he followed Anton Cajetan Adlgasser at the Dreifaltigkeitskirche in Salzburg. In 1782 Haydn took over for W. A. Mozart, who had resigned as court organist, and the following year he was asked to succeed his brother as *Kapellmeister* to Prince Nicolaus Esterházy. Michael did not accept the position, however, but instead remained in Salzburg—working there a total of forty-three years. He was highly regarded during his day. A monument was erected to him at the monastery church of St Peter in Salzburg, and the famous German author E. T. A. Hoffmann wrote: "All connoisseurs of music know, and have known for some time, that as a composer of sacred music Michael Haydn ranks among the finest artists of any age or nation. . . . In this field he is fully his brother's equal."

Haydn composed approximately thirty-five masses (including two Requiems), six oratorios, thirteen cantatas, five Te Deums, twelve Litanies, four hundred motets, eighty part songs, and eighty canons. Several of the early masses are in a *prima prattica* Renaissance style modeled on the "stylus a cappella" works of Fux (copies of which Haydn owned). *Missa Sanctae crucis* of 1762, for example, is scored for voices alone, the Kyrie and Agnus Dei are structured of overlapping points of imitation, and the Gloria and Credo are almost entirely homophonic. Other early masses, those composed before Haydn arrived in Salzburg, are in the prevalent style of the mid-eighteenth century, with extended melismatic passages for soloists that alternate with homophonic choral textures, and with instrumental scoring for two trumpets, two trombones that play *colla parte* from the alto and tenor chorus parts, timpani, two violins, and basso continuo. *Missa Beatissimae virginis Mariae* of 1758 is an example, with the exception that it has an obbligato trombone part in the "Et incarnatus est" portion of the Credo.

The masses composed in Salzburg conformed to the reformed ideals of brevity and simplification mandated by Emperor Joseph II and Archbishop Colloredo, who had succeeded Archbishop Schrattenbach in 1772. Haydn responded to the mandates by virtually eliminating all florid passages for soloists and by limiting the length of the Gloria and Credo movements (the two movements with long texts). In *Missa Sancti Joannis Nepomuceni* of 1772 and *Missa Sancti Ruperti* of 1782, for example, the Gloria is in one section, without divisions. The Benedictus remained long because it was performed during the portion of the mass referred to as the Elevation of the Host (the preparation of Communion elements), which took from four to five minutes. The masses that were longer and more elaborate were generally written for specific important occasions—the *Requiem* in C minor in 1771 for the death of Archbishop Schrattenbach; *Missa Sancti Joannis Nepomuceni,* named in honor of Bohemia's martyred saint Joanne Nepomuceni (1340–1393), in 1772 to celebrate the arrival of Schrattenbach's successor, Count Hieronymus Colloredo; *Missa Sancti Hieronymi* in honor of Archbishop Colloredo and performed at a special service on All Saints' Day, November 1, 1777; *Missa sotto il titulo de S Theresiae* in 1801 for Empress Marie Therese, who sang the soprano solos in the premiere performance; and *Missa sub titulo Sancti Francisci Seraphici* to celebrate the name day of Emperor Francis I in 1803.

The oratorios are almost completely unknown today. However, it is interesting to note that

Haydn's first contribution to this genre was a collaboration with Anton Cajetan Adlgasser and W. A. Mozart. Each of the three composers wrote a movement of *Die Schuldigkeit des ersten Gebots* in 1767 (only Mozart's movement has survived).

The Te Deums are for the most part scored for chorus and orchestra, while the Litanies are scored for soloists, chorus, and orchestra. The final two Te Deums were composed to accompany the masses written for Marie Therese in 1801 and Francis I in 1803. The 1803 Te Deum, which is popular today, is a single-movement work divided into the text sections "Te Deum Laudamus" (Vivace), "Te ergo quaesumus" (Largo), "Aeterna fac cum sanctis tuis" (Allegretto), and "In te Domine speravi" (Vivace). The *Litaniae de sanctissimi nominis Jesu* of 1768 is a five-movement work divided into the text sections "Kyrie" (for chorus alone), "Jesu, fili Dei" (for solo and chorus), "Jesu refugium nostrum" (for chorus), "Jesu thesaure" (for solo duets and quartet), and "Jesu, gaudium angelorum" (for solo quartet and chorus).

The motets, like the masses, are in both old and new styles. Representing the *prima prattica* motets, which were composed mainly for Advent and Lent, are *In monte Oliveti - Tristis est anima mea* and *Ecce vidimus eum* for Maundy Thursday, *Vinea mea electa* and *Caligaverunt oculi mei* for Good Friday, and *O vos omnes* and *Ecce quomodo moritur Justus* for Holy Saturday. Motets for other occasions during the liturgical year are generally scored for soloists, chorus, two violins, and basso continuo, with the occasional addition of horns or obbligato instruments such as oboes. Haydn's most famous motet, *Timete Dominum*, was composed as a companion piece to the *Missa Sancti Hieronymi* and is scored for soloists and chorus, with accompaniment of wind instruments.

MASSES
SELECTED AND LISTED IN CHRONOLOGICAL ORDER
ACCORDING TO DATE OF COMPOSITION

Missa Beatissimae virginis Mariae – 1758 – SATB solos, SATB chorus, two trumpets, two trombones, timpani, two violins, and basso continuo – 30 minutes.

Missa Sancti Gabrielis – between 1758 and 1760 – SATB solos, SATB chorus, two trumpets, timpani, two violins, and basso continuo – 15 minutes.

Missa Sanctae crucis – 1762 – SATB chorus a cappella – 18 minutes.

Requiem in C minor (also called *Missa pro defuncto Archiepiscopo Sigismundo*) – 1771 – SATB solos, SATB chorus, two oboes, two trumpets, three trombones, timpani, two violins, and basso continuo – 50 minutes.

Missa Sancti Joannis Nepomuceni – 1772 – SATB chorus, two oboes, two trumpets, timpani, three trombones, two violins, and basso continuo – 20 minutes.

Missa Sancti Hieronymi – 1777 – SATB solos, SATB chorus, two oboes, two bassoons, three trombones, and basso continuo – 34 minutes. (1) The instrumentation for wind instruments, called "harmonium," is unusual but not unique; (2) the trombone parts mostly, but not exclusively, double the alto, tenor, and bass choral parts.

Missa Sancti Ruperti (also called the "Jubiläumsmesse") – 1782 – SATB solos, SATB chorus, two oboes, two horns, two trumpets, three trombones, timpani, strings, and basso continuo – 35 minutes.

Missa Sanctae Ursulae (also called the "Chiemsee-Messe") – 1793 – SATB solos, SATB chorus, two trumpets, timpani, two violins, and basso continuo – 40 minutes.

Missa Sanctae Theresiae (also called the "Theresienmesse") – 1801 – SATB solos, SATB chorus, two oboes, two trumpets, timpani, two violins, and basso continuo – 40 minutes.

Missa sub titulo Sancti Francisci Seraphici – 1803 – SATB solos, SATB chorus, two trumpets, timpani, strings, and basso continuo – 45 minutes.

Missa sub titulo Sancti Leopoldi – 1805 – SSA solos, SSA chorus, two horns, two violins, and basso continuo – 20 minutes.

OTHER SACRED WORKS
SELECTED AND LISTED ACCORDING TO FAMILIARITY

Salve regina in A major – SATB chorus, two violins, and basso continuo – 3 minutes.

Timete Dominum – SATB solos, SATB chorus, two oboes, two bassoons, three trombones, and basso continuo – 8 minutes. An eighteenth-century scoring for two oboes and strings also exists, not by Haydn.

Ave Maria in F major – SATB chorus, two violins, and basso continuo – 5 minutes.

Ave Maria in A minor – SATB chorus, two trumpets, two violins, and basso continuo – 3 minutes.

Laudate populi in D major – SATB solos, SATB chorus, two trumpets, two violins, and basso continuo – 7 minutes.

Dixit Dominus in F major – SSA solos, SSA chorus, two violins, and basso continuo – 4 minutes.

Te Deum in D major – SATB chorus, two oboes, two trumpets, timpani, strings, and basso continuo – 13 minutes.

CARL DITTERS VON DITTERSDORF 1739–1799

Dittersdorf was born in Vienna and learned to play the violin as a child. When he was eleven he joined the Schottenkirche orchestra, and at twelve he held a position in the orchestra of Prince Joseph Friedrich von Sachsen-Hildburghausen. At twenty-two Dittersdorf moved to the Burgtheater orchestra, and at twenty-five he succeeded Michael Haydn as *Kapellmeister* to the Bishop of Grosswardein in Hungary (now Oradea, Romania). When the bishop's court was disassembled in 1769 Dittersdorf was appointed *Kapellmeister* for the Bishop of Breslau in Jauernig (now Javorník in northeast Czech Republic), a position he retained for the remainder of his life, although he made frequent extended trips to Vienna to conduct his oratorios, operas (Singspiels), and symphonies.

Dittersdorf composed thirteen masses (including one Requiem), three surviving oratorios, five Litanies, and approximately ten motets. The masses are in the style of those composed by the Haydn brothers, with similar scoring and structural elements. For instance, Dittersdorf's most famous mass, *Missa solemnis* in C major k326, is scored for SATB solos, SATB chorus, two oboes, two trumpets, timpani, two trombones that play *colla parte* from the alto and tenor chorus parts, two violins, and basso continuo. The scoring is distinguished by a solo violin part that was likely played by Dittersdorf himself. As for structure, the mass is divided into six movements (the Benedictus is set separately), and the Gloria and Credo are each divided into three sections.

Two of the oratorios were composed for performances by the Tonkünstler-Societät: *La liberatrice del popolo giudaico nella Persia, o sia l'Ester* (generally called simply *Esther*) was commissioned and conducted by Florian Leopold Gassmann in 1773, and *Giob* was conducted by Dittersdorf in 1786. The motets include *Regina caeli*, scored for SS solos, SATB chorus, two trumpets, timpani, two violins, and basso continuo and characterized by frequent long melismas in thirds for the soloists that contrast with a homophonic choral texture.

ANTONIO SALIERI 1750–1825

Salieri was born in Legnago, close to Milan, Italy, and as a child he studied the violin with his brother and organ with a local church musician. At age fifteen he went to Venice, where he met and became the student of Florian Leopold Gassmann, and when Gassmann returned to Vienna in 1766, Salieri followed him, continued his studies, and quickly developed into a reputable opera composer. He also gained the support of Emperor Joseph II, and when Gassmann died in 1774, the emperor appointed the twenty-four-year-old Salieri *Kammerkomponist* (court composer) and also music director of the Italian opera company in Vienna. For the next fourteen years he composed operas for theaters in Vienna, Milan, Venice, Rome, and Paris. In 1788 he was appointed the emperor's *Hofkapellmeister*, and from then until his retirement thirty-six years later, his compositional focus was on church music. He served as president and conductor of the Tonkünstler-Societät, and he also had numerous students, including Ludwig van Beethoven and Franz Schubert.

Salieri composed six masses (including one Requiem), one oratorio, three Te Deums, two Magnificats, and approximately eighty-five motets. His first mass, *Missa stylo a cappella,* was composed when he was seventeen and is in the imitative *prima prattica* style of Johann Joseph Fux and the very early works of Michael Haydn (although Salieri's mass has no Gloria and the text of the Credo is telescoped). The remaining four masses (excluding the Requiem) are in the full orchestral style of Joseph Haydn. Both the *Missa* in D major (composed about 1788) and the *Missa* in D minor (of 1805) have orchestral scoring for two oboes, two bassoons, four trumpets, two trombones, timpani, strings (including violas), and organ. In addition, the Gloria and Credo movements of both masses are divided into multiple sections (five in the Gloria of the *Missa* in D major). The masses are also characterized by tempo markings such as *Allegro spirituoso, Allegro maestoso, Allegretto,* and *Un poco adagio* that attempt to convey specific aspects of expression and speed. The *Missa* in B-flat major is similar in scoring (SATB solos, SATB chorus, two oboes, two bassoons, two trumpets, two trombones, timpani, strings, and organ), although unique in structure: the Gloria is in one undivided movement, the first and last of the Credo's three sections are entirely choral and mostly homophonic, and the middle section of the Credo features a soprano solo with solo oboe obbligato. The *Requiem* in C minor was composed in 1804 and is scored for SATB solos, SATB chorus, two oboes, English horn, two bassoons, two trumpets, three trombones, timpani, strings, and organ.

Salieri's oratorio *La passione di Gesù Cristo* was composed in 1776 and premiered at the Tonkünstler-Societät the following year. It is scored for SATB solos, SATB chorus, two flutes, two oboes, two bassoons, two horns, two trumpets, timpani, strings, and basso continuo. Other notable choral works include the *Krönungs Te Deum* for SATB chorus (without solos) and orchestra, and the motets *Populi timete, Liberasti nos Domine, Veni sancte spiritus,* and *Confirma hoc Deus.*

Wolfgang Amadeus Mozart 1756–1791

Mozart was born in Salzburg, the seventh and last child of Leopold Mozart. Wolfgang quickly exhibited extraordinary musical talents and became recognized as a child prodigy: he began composing and playing the harpsichord in public when he was five, and between the ages of six and fifteen he traveled across Europe with his father, presenting his compositions and performing in major royal courts. When he was six, for instance, he played in Munich for the Elector of Bavaria and in Vienna for Marie Therese, and when he was eight he played in Paris for King Louis XV and in London for King George III. Mozart composed his first symphony at eight, at ten he wrote the first part of the oratorio *Die Schuldigkeit des ersten Gebots* (the second and third parts, now lost, were composed by Michael Haydn and Anton Cajetan Adlgasser, respectively), and his first mass, motet, and opera were composed when he was twelve. Also at twelve he transcribed the famous *Miserere* by Gregorio Allegri after hearing it once during a Lenten service at the Sistine Chapel in Rome. At sixteen Mozart was appointed *Konzertmeister* at the Salzburg court under Archbishop Colloredo, at seventeen he composed the solo motet *Exsultate, jubilate,* and at twenty-one, feeling oppressed and underappreciated in Salzburg and desiring more lucrative employment, he requested and was granted release from his court position. He traveled to Mannheim and Paris but, unsuccessful in securing a position, he returned to Salzburg the following year to become court organist with a higher salary and with more time to travel. Mozart's relationship with the archbishop became even more strained than it had been before, however, and after barely a year he requested and was granted another release from his position. He then settled in Vienna, where he earned his living by teaching and presenting his compositions to interested supporters, one of whom was Baron Gottfried van Swieten (1733–1803), an important patron of music in Vienna at the time. In 1787, at age thirty-one, Mozart took the position of court *Kammermusicus* in Vienna and composed *Don Giovanni* K527. He continued to travel and compose operas (including *Così fan tutte* K588 in 1790 and *Die Zauberflöte* K620 in 1791) as well as orchestral and chamber music. After a brief illness during a trip to Prague, he died approximately two months before his thirty-sixth birthday.

Mozart composed eighteen masses (including one Requiem), several mass movements and an incomplete mass, eight miscellaneous large-scale sacred works (including four Litanies and two Vespers settings), approximately twenty motets, one complete oratorio, and seven cantatas.

The works are generally referred to by their catalogue numbers—the original *K* numbers (assigned by Ludwig von Köchel in *W.A. Mozarts Werke*) and the revised *K* numbers (found in *W.A. Mozart: Neue Ausgabe sämtlicher Werke*) in parentheses.

Most of the masses were composed while Mozart was quite young. Two—K139 (47a) and K49 (47d)—were composed when he was twelve, and two—K65 (61a) and K66 (66)—when he was thirteen. The next nine masses—K167 (167), K192 (186f), K194 (186h), K220 (196b), K262 (246a), K257 (257), K258 (258), K259 (259), and K275 (272b)—were composed when he was between the ages of seventeen and twenty-one and in his original position with Archbishop Colloredo, and two masses—K317 (317) and K337 (337)—were composed when he was twenty-three and twenty-four and in his second position with the archbishop. The final mass—K427 (417a)—which is incomplete, was composed when he was twenty-six and twenty-seven. The *Requiem* K626 (626), which is also incomplete, was composed in 1791, the year Mozart died at age thirty-five.

Approximately half the masses are of the *brevis* (short) type, with modest orchestral scorings and brief durations, although not with telescoped texts as found in some of Joseph Haydn's *missae brevis*. Mozart's other masses are of the *solemnis* type (solemn or full, meant for festival occasions), with fuller orchestrations and somewhat longer durations. All the masses composed for the Salzburg court under Archbishop Colloredo (a total of eleven) are relatively confined in duration because, as Mozart wrote to Padre Giovanni Battista Martini in 1776, "A mass, with the whole Kyrie, the Gloria, the Credo, the Epistle sonata, the Offertory or Motet, the Sanctus and the Agnus Dei, must last no more than three-quarters of an hour." In addition, all these masses are scored without violas. The very early masses usually have numerous brief sections of music with varied tempos that expressively portray phrases of text. The Credo of the *Missa brevis* K49 (47d), for instance, has eleven different tempos. The later masses generally have a basic structure and scoring typical of all masses composed during the Classical era: the entire work is divided into six movements (Kyrie, Gloria, Credo, Sanctus, Benedictus, and Agnus Dei), with the Gloria and Credo consisting of three connected sections; the Gloria and Credo end with fugues; the "Dona nobis pacem" portion of the Agnus Dei often reprises music from the Kyrie; a quartet of soloists interchanges material with the chorus; there are no arias or extended solo passages; the movements are often based upon symphonic forms, most frequently sonata and rondo; and three trombones generally play from the alto, tenor, and bass choral parts (in some instances, the trombones are scored with short independent material, but in most instances, they only double, *colla parte*, the choral parts).

The *Missa* K427 (417a), customarily referred to as the "Great Mass in C minor," is unique. It was begun shortly after Mozart's marriage to Constanze and was intended as a gift to her. In addition, it was composed in the Baroque "cantata mass" style, because Mozart wished to please his patron at the time, Baron van Swieten, who favored music from the Baroque era. (Mozart conducted a number of Baroque works in van Swieten's home, including Handel's *Acis and Galatea* and *Messiah*.) Reflecting the Baroque style, the six portions of the mass are divided into separate movements; the Gloria, for instance, is in eight movements, one of which is a soprano aria, one a duet for two sopranos, and one a trio for two sopranos and tenor. In addition, many of the textures and structures are Baroque in nature. Mozart completed only the Kyrie and Gloria, which were performed in Salzburg in October 1783 with Constanze singing one of the solo soprano parts. He sketched two portions of the Credo ("Credo in unum Deum" and "Et incarnatus est") plus the Sanctus and Benedictus, and these were orchestrated by a number of different people after his death. No one has attempted to construct the missing movements, however, so the mass exists only in abbreviated form.

The *Requiem* was a commission that was initiated secretively by Count Walsegg-Stuppach, an amateur composer who wished to claim the work as his own and present it as a memorial for his recently deceased wife. Mozart fully composed and orchestrated the first movement (Introitus) before he died, and in addition, he left sketches of the voice parts and a figured bass line for the second movement (Kyrie), most of the third movement (Dies Irae), and part of the fourth movement (Offertorium). This included music through the first eight measures of the "Lacrimosa" in the third movement and most of the "Hostias" in the fourth movement. Furthermore, Mozart apparently wrote some suggestions for orchestrations and told his wife that "the first fugue, as is customary, should be repeated in the last piece." Two of his students, Franz Jakob Freystädtler and Franz Xaver Süssmayr, completed the orchestration of the Kyrie and presented it with the Introitus at a memorial service for Mozart five days after his death. Mozart's wife then gave the score to Joseph Eybler, a friend and respected composer, who orchestrated most of the Dies Irae. Since Eybler had spent a great deal of time with Mozart just before his death, and since Eybler's orchestration was written directly into Mozart's score, it is possible that Mozart supervised the orchestration before he died. After Eybler returned the score to Constanze, she gave it to Süssmayr, who completed the work—claiming to have composed the remainder of the Offertorium, the beginning of the Communio, and all of the Sanctus, Benedictus, and Agnus Dei. The completed work was performed twice in 1793, once by Count Walsegg-Stuppach, who copied and presented it under his own name, and once by Baron van Swieten, who presented it under Mozart's name. Süssmayr's version of the *Requiem*—edited by Leopold Nowak in 1967 and published in the *Neue Mozart Ausgabe* (NMA)—then went on to become one of the most frequently performed choral works in history. Since that time several people have published alternative versions. Franz Beyer reworked the orchestration (published by Kunzelman in 1979); Richard Maunder omitted the Sanctus and Benedictus and added a fugal "Amen" from presumed Mozart sketches (Oxford, 1988); H. C. Robbins Landon made substantial alterations to the orchestration (Breitkopf, 1991); and Duncan Druce (Druce, 1984) and Robert Levin (Neuhausen/Stuttgart, 1993) composed entirely new movements.

Of the four Litanies, two use the ancient sacrament text—*Litaniae de venerabili altaris sacramento* K125 (125) and K243 (243)—and two the sixteenth-century text to the Blessed Virgin Mary established in the chapel of Loreto—*Litaniae Laurentanae BVM* K109 (74e) and K195 (186d). The settings of the sacrament text have nine movements, identical in both settings except for movement six, and each movement employs the response "miserere nobis" (have mercy on us) numerous times. In addition, both of these Litanies are similar in scoring and duration. The settings of the Loreto text have five identical movements, and each movement employs the response "ora pro nobis" (pray for us) numerous times. The earlier of these settings is scored lightly and is brief in duration, while the later setting is scored for additional instruments and is much longer. The *Litaniae* K109 (74e) was composed for performance at Archbishop Colloredo's summer residence in May 1771, and the *Litaniae* K243 (243) was performed at the Salzburg Cathedral on Palm Sunday 1776. Nothing is known about performances of the other two settings.

The two Vespers settings—*Vesperae de Dominica* K321 (321) and *Vesperae solennes de confessore* K339 (339)—both have six movements that are identical in text and scoring except for movement six, "Laudate Dominum," which is scored for soprano solo, orchestra, and obbligato organ in K321, and soprano solo with chorus and orchestra in K339. The two settings are remarkably similar in other respects as well. Both utilize a solo quartet in combination with the chorus in movements one through three and six, and both set movement four, "Laudate pueri," for chorus alone in Renaissance point-of-imitation style with instruments *colla parte*. Nothing is known about the performances of the works. However, it is unlikely that they were performed as sets, with the movements following each other. More likely, they were performed as the masses, with spoken portions of the liturgy separating the various movements. Of the two settings, the *Vesperae solennes de confessore* is more popular, and its "Laudate Dominum" movement, which is one of the best known of all Mozart works, is often extracted and performed alone.

The very early motets—such as *Miserere* K85 (73s), *Quaerite primum* K86 (73v), and *God is our refuge* K20 (20)—are a cappella and were written as composition exercises while Mozart was traveling. The later motets are generally scored for solo voices, mixed chorus, and instrumental ensemble similar to that used in the masses and other larger sacred works. All of the motets are short and in one movement, except for two settings of *Regina coeli*, K108 (74d) and K127 (127), which are in multiple movements. Mozart's final composition, *Ave verum* K618 (618), is his most familiar motet and undoubtedly his most frequently performed work.

The cantatas include *Grabmusik* K42 (35a) and *Davidde penitente* K469 (469). *Grabmusik* was composed for performance during Holy Week 1767 (when Mozart was eleven) and is a type of *sepolcro* oratorio that relates the Passion story, but without literary dramatic action. It was originally composed for two soloists who represent the Soul (B) and an Angel (S), and it was structured as a series of recitatives and arias. Mozart added a movement for chorus in 1775. *Davidde penitente* was composed in 1785 for performance by the Tonkünstler-Societät in the futile hope that the society would accept Mozart as a member. The work is basically a resetting of the Kyrie and Gloria of the *Missa* K427 (417a). This is to say, Mozart took the music of these two movements of the mass and merely changed the text. He also added a cadenza in the final movement and composed two additional arias, thus structuring the cantata as a ten-movement work, five of which are for chorus.

MASSES AND MASS MOVEMENTS
SELECTED AND LISTED ACCORDING TO FAMILIARITY

Requiem K626 (626) – 1791 – SATB solos, SATB chorus, two basset horns, two bassoons, two trumpets, three trombones, timpani, strings, and organ – 50 minutes. (1) The solo writing is mostly for quartet (the "Tuba mirum" and "Recordare" sections of the Dies irae and the Benedictus are entirely so), with very few solo passages; (2) the basset horns are a type of clarinet developed in the 1770s, with a dark tone and alto range; (3) the Kyrie and Communio share the same music—a brief soprano solo followed by an extended fugue.

Missa ("Krönungsmesse") K317 (317) – 1779 – SATB solos, SATB chorus, two oboes, two horns, two trumpets, timpani, two violins, cello, bass, and organ – 26 minutes. (1) The mass is in C major; (2) the title, not assigned by Mozart, was previously thought to reflect the ceremonial crowning of an image of the Virgin Mary in the church of Maria-Plain, which is north of Salzburg, although it is now believed that the title refers to the first performance of the mass at the coronation of Leopold II as King of Bohemia in August 1791; (3) identical music is used for the Kyrie and "Dona nobis pacem" portion of the Agnus Dei; (4) the Agnus Dei, which begins as a soprano solo, is reminiscent of the soprano aria "Dove sono" from *Le nozze di Figaro;* (5) the Benedictus is entirely for solo quartet; (6) the orchestration includes three trombones that double the alto, tenor, and bass choral parts *colla parte.*

Missa solemnis K337 (337) – 1780 – SATB solos, SATB chorus, two oboes, two bassoons, two trumpets, timpani, two violins, cello, bass, and organ – 22 minutes. (1) The mass is in C major; (2) the first performance was in 1780 for Easter services at the Salzburg Cathedral; (3) the Agnus Dei, which begins as a soprano solo with organ obbligato, is reminiscent of the soprano aria "Porgi, amor, qualche ristoro" (Hear my plea, God of love) from *Le nozze di Figaro;* (4) the Benedictus is choral, not solo; (5) the orchestration includes three trombones that double the alto, tenor, and bass choral parts *colla parte.*

Missa K427 (417a) – 1782–1783 – SSTB solos, SSAATTBB chorus, flute, two oboes, two bassoons, two horns, two trumpets, three trombones, timpani, strings, and organ – 55 minutes. (1) The mass is in C minor and is generally referred to as the "Grosse Messe in C-moll" (Great Mass in C minor); (2) it is incomplete, consisting only of the Kyrie, Gloria, two sections of the Credo ("Credo in unum Deum" and "Et incarnatus est"), and sketches for the Sanctus and Benedictus; (3) the chorus is divided into SATB/SATB for two movements (the "Qui tollis" of the Gloria and the Sanctus); (4) the Benedictus is for SSTB solo quartet; (5) the violas divide into two parts; (6) the flute plays only in the "Et incarnatus est."

Missa K257 (257) – 1776 – SATB solos, SATB chorus, two oboes, two trumpets, timpani, two violins, cello, bass, and organ – 25 minutes. (1) The mass is in C major; (2) it is sometimes referred to as the "Credo Mass" because of the four-note motif that pervades the Credo; (3) the first performance was in Salzburg in November 1776; (4) the Benedictus is entirely for solo quartet; (5) the orchestration includes three trombones that double the alto, tenor, and bass choral parts *colla parte.*

Missa solemnis ("Weisenhausmesse") K139 (47a) – ca.1768 – SATB solos, SATB chorus, two oboes, four trumpets, three trombones, timpani, strings, and organ – 43 minutes. (1) The mass is in C minor; (2) the title refers to the first performance of the mass in December 1768 for the consecration of the orphanage chapel in Vienna; (3) the solo writing consists of solos and duets as well as passages for solo quartet; (4) the violas divide into two parts; (5) the Gloria and Credo movements have numerous meter and tempo changes.

Missa ("Dominicusmesse") K66 (66) – 1769 – SATB solos, SATB chorus, two oboes, two horns, four trumpets, timpani, strings, and organ – 42 minutes. (1) The mass is in C major; (2) the title refers to Mozart's friend, Father Dominicus, for whom the mass was composed and first performed in October 1769; (3) the solo writing consists of solos and duets as well as passages for solo quartet; (4) the Gloria and Credo movements have numerous meter and tempo changes.

Missa brevis K192 (186f) – 1774 – SATB solos, SATB chorus, two violins, cello, bass and organ – 20 minutes. (1) The mass is in F major; (2) the mass is sometimes called the "Small Credo Mass" because of the four-note motto from the Gregorian chant "Lucis creator" used throughout the Credo; (3) the Benedictus is entirely for solo quartet; (4) the orchestration includes three trombones that double the alto, tenor, and bass choral parts *colla parte;* (5) Mozart later added two trumpets to the orchestration.

Kyrie K341 (368a) – 1780–1781 – SATB chorus, two flutes, two oboes, two clarinets, two bassoons, four horns, two trumpets, timpani, strings, and organ – 8 minutes.

Kyrie K33 (33) – 1766 – SATB chorus, strings, and organ – 9 minutes.

LITANIES
SELECTED AND LISTED ACCORDING TO FAMILIARITY

Litaniae de venerabili altaris sacramento K125 (125) – 1772 – SATB solos, SATB chorus, two oboes, two horns, two trumpets, strings, and organ – 35 minutes. (1) The work is in nine movements—two for soloists (S and T), three for SATB soloists and chorus, and four for chorus alone; (2) the orchestration includes three trombones that double the alto, tenor, and bass choral parts *colla parte.*

Litaniae de venerabili altaris sacramento K243 (243) – 1776 – SATB solos, SATB chorus, two oboes, two horns, strings, and organ – 35 minutes. (1) The work is in nine movements—three for soloists (S, S, and T), three for soloists (SATB) and chorus, and three for chorus alone; (2) two of the movements for soloists feature coloratura writing; (3) the first and final movements share musical material; (4) the orchestration includes three trombones that double the alto, tenor, and bass choral parts *colla parte.*

Litaniae laurentanae BMV K109 (74e) – 1771 – SATB solos, SATB chorus, two violins, cello, bass, and organ – 11 minutes. (1) The work is in five movements—one for solo quartet, two for solo quartet and chorus, and two for chorus alone; (2) the violas divide into two parts; (3) the orchestration includes three trombones that double the alto, tenor, and bass choral parts *colla parte.*

VESPERS SETTINGS
COMPLETE AND LISTED ACCORDING TO FAMILIARITY

Vesperae solennes de confessore K339 (339) – 1780 – SATB solos, SATB chorus, two trumpets, timpani, two violins, cello, bass, and organ – 26 minutes. (1) The work is in six movements—five for solo quartet and chorus, and one for chorus alone; (2) the orchestration includes three trombones that double the alto, tenor, and bass choral parts *colla parte.*

Vesperae de Dominica K321 (321) – 1779 – SATB solos, SATB chorus, two trumpets, timpani, two violins, cello, bass, and organ – 32 minutes.

(1) The work is in six movements—four for solo quartet and chorus, one for S solo with organ obbligato, and one for chorus alone; (2) the orchestration includes three trombones that double the alto, tenor, and bass choral parts *colla parte.*

MOTETS AND MISCELLANEOUS SACRED WORKS
SELECTED AND LISTED ACCORDING TO FAMILIARITY

Ave verum corpus K618 (618) – 1791 – SATB chorus, strings, and organ – 4 minutes.

Alma Dei creatoris K277 (277) – before 1781 – SATB solos, SATB chorus, two violins, cello, bass, and organ – 5:30 minutes. (1) The solo writing is mostly for quartet; (2) the orchestration includes three trombones that double the alto, tenor, and bass choral parts *colla parte.*

Regina coeli K276 (321b) – ca.1779 – SATB solos, SATB chorus, two oboes, two trumpets, timpani, two violins, cello, bass, and organ – 7 minutes. (1) This is the most popular of Mozart's three settings of this text; (2) the solo writing is mostly for quartet; (3) the final "Alleluia" is reminiscent of Handel's setting of "Hallelujah" in *Messiah.*

Sancta Maria, mater Dei K273 (273) – 1777 – SATB chorus, strings, and organ – 3:30 minutes.

Te Deum K141 (66b) – 1769 – SATB chorus, four trumpets, timpani, two violins, cello, bass, and organ – 7:30 minutes. The work is in one movement divided into several sections with varying tempos.

Veni sancte spiritus K47 (47) – 1768 – SATB solos, SATB chorus, two oboes, two horns, two trumpets, timpani, strings and organ – 4 minutes. The solo writing, which is minimal, is mostly for quartet.

Venite populi K260 (248a) – 1776 – SATB/SATB chorus, two violins, cello, bass, and organ – 5:30 minutes. (1) The choral writing is in Venetian dialogue style; (2) the orchestration includes three trombones that double the alto, tenor, and bass choral parts *colla parte.*

Davidde penitente K469 (469) – 1785 – SST solos, SATB chorus, two flutes, two oboes, two clarinets, two bassoons, two horns, three trombones, timpani, strings, and organ – 46 minutes.

Grabmusik K42 (35a) – 1767 – SB solos, SATB chorus, two oboes, two horns, strings, and organ – 23 minutes.

JOHANN NEPOMUK HUMMEL 1778–1837

Hummel was born in Pressburg (now Bratislava, Czech Republic) and studied with his father, who had been a violinist and music director at the Theatre auf der Wieden in Vienna since 1786. Like W. A. Mozart, with whom he studied and lived for a period of time, the young Hummel was a child prodigy, performing on the violin at age five and on the pianoforte at age six. Also like

Mozart, Hummel toured extensively with his father. For the four years between 1788 and 1792 they traveled to and performed in Prague, Dresden, Berlin, Hamburg, Copenhagen, Edinburgh, London, and numerous other European cities. In 1792, when Johann was fourteen, father and son returned to Vienna, and for the next several years Johann studied with Johann Georg Albrechtsberger, Antonio Salieri, and Joseph Haydn. In 1804 Hummel was appointed *Konzertmeister* at the court of Prince Nikolaus Esterházy in Eisenstadt, Hungary (where he worked alongside Haydn). However, he was dismissed from this position in 1811 for not attending to his duties. He then taught and toured for the remainder of his life while also serving as *Hofkapellmeister* in Stuttgart from 1816 until 1818 and as *Kapellmeister* in Weimar thereafter.

Hummel composed five masses, one Te Deum, twelve cantatas, and approximately twenty part songs. The masses were all composed while Hummel was employed by Prince Esterházy, and like the late Haydn masses, they were presumably performed on the name day of Princess Maria, one per year between 1804 and 1808. The most famous of these masses is in B-flat major (the others are in E-flat major, D major, D minor, and C major) and is scored for SATB chorus (without solos), two oboes, two bassoons, two trumpets, timpani, strings (with violas), and organ. Hummel also included parts for two clarinets, which he noted could replace the oboes ("Statt der Oboe kann es auf Clarinet zur Abwechslung gespielt werden").

FRANZ SCHUBERT 1797–1828

Schubert was born in Vienna and received his early musical education from his father, a schoolmaster who taught him violin, and from his brother, who taught him piano. Beginning at age nine or ten he studied organ, singing, and harmony at the parish church of Liechtental, and at eleven he became a chorister at the Imperial Court Chapel under *Kapellmeister* Antonio Salieri and organist Josef Eybler (the first person to attempt completion of W. A. Mozart's *Requiem* after the composer's death). When Schubert's voice changed at sixteen, he left the court chapel and entered a training program for elementary school teachers. The following year he began teaching in his father's school and also began composing actively and developing a close circle of friends who were instrumental in performing his music. During the next several years he composed an astonishingly large number of works, including his first four masses, hundreds of songs (145 were composed during 1815 alone), several symphonies, and numerous string quartets and piano sonatas. Notable among the songs are *Gretchen am Spinnrade* D118, composed in 1814 when Schubert was only seventeen, and *Erlkönig* D328, composed in 1815 when he was eighteen. These songs as well as part songs and instrumental chamber works were often performed in intimate concerts called *Schubertiade* ("Schubertiades" in English). Other concerts of Schubert's works included the "Abendunterhaltungen," which were presentations by the Vienna Gesellschaft der Musikfreunde on Thursday evenings. In 1819, at age twenty-two, Schubert left his position at his father's school in order to teach music to the children of Count Johann Esterházy; he continued in this position for several years while still maintaining an active schedule of composing and participating in performances throughout Vienna. In 1822 he became seriously ill, although he recovered enough after a year to resume composing actively. His illness returned in 1828, however, and he died in November of that year at age thirty-one.

Schubert composed six Latin masses, one German mass and one German Requiem, thirty motets (including six settings of Tantum ergo), seventy-one part songs, several cantatas, one unfinished oratorio, and nine canons. The works are catalogued by D numbers, assigned by the historian Otto Erich Deutsch and indicated in *F. Schubert: Neue Ausgabe sämtlicher Werke.*

The Latin masses are easily identified by their keys: F major D105, G major D167, B-flat major D324, C major D452, A-flat major D678, and E-flat major D950. All of the masses, typical of the time, are divided into six movements (Kyrie, Gloria, Credo, Sanctus, Benedictus, and Agnus Dei), and except for the G major mass, all are of the *solemnis* type (solemn or full, meant for festival occasions). In addition, these masses have large orchestrations, movements based on symphonic forms (e.g., sonata, variation, or ABA), scoring of the Benedictus generally for a quartet of solo voices (with few individual solo passages), and multisectional Gloria and Credo movements that begin nonliturgically (i.e., the opening text phrases "Gloria in excelsis Deo" and "Credo in unum Deum" are set musically rather than given to the liturgist to intone). The G major mass is of the *brevis* type (short) and is scored for only strings and organ, with the Gloria and Credo movements in one section and tempo.

Unique to Schubert, portions of the Gloria and Credo texts in all the masses are varied: individual words are repeated, the standard order of phrases is interchanged, and most striking, some words and phrases are deleted. The deletions—such as "Qui sedes ad dexteram Patris" (who sits at the right hand of the father) from the Gloria, and "Credo in unam, sanctam, catholicam et apostolicam Ecclesiam" (I believe in one, holy, catholic, and apostolic church) from the Credo—are intriguing and inexplicable. Scholars conjecture that they were oversights, local liturgical traditions, or reflections of Schubert's beliefs (or lack thereof). The first two suppositions are unlikely in that Schubert made textual deletions in all his masses, and no masses by other composers of the time delete any text. The idea that Schubert deleted certain phrases because he did not believe in them has merit; from numerous letters and accounts it is clear that he had a negative view of the Catholic Church. In addition, composers were beginning to express themselves more personally in the second decade of the nineteenth century, as the Romantic era began to emerge. Texts—even those as traditionally sacrosanct as the Latin mass—were subject to manipulation and personal interpretation.

The first Latin mass was composed for the 100th anniversary of the Liechtental church, where Schubert sang in his youth; the premiere was in October 1814. The second Latin mass, composed in six days during March 1815, was also written for and performed at the Liechtental church; it is undoubtedly Schubert's most famous and frequently performed sacred work. The composition and performance circumstances of the remaining four Latin masses (composed in 1815, 1816, 1819 to 1822, and 1828) and the *Deutsche Messe* (German mass) of 1827 are unknown.

The other sacred settings are similar to the masses in style and format. They are almost all scored for a quartet of soloists, mixed chorus, and orchestra and are in one movement divided into several connecting sections varied by tempo. A few of the sacred settings, such as the *Stabat mater* D175 of 1815, are scored for choir and orchestra alone and are in one continuous movement. Others, such as the *Stabat mater* D383 of 1816, are scored for soloists, chorus, and orchestra and are divided into multiple movements, with arias and duets as well as ensembles for the solo quartet. These examples are in the minority, however. Most of the sacred works are like the *Magnificat* D486 of 1815, which is scored for soloists, chorus, and orchestra and is in one movement divided into three sections.

The part songs are in three categories—those written for mixed voices, those for male voices, and those for female voices. The part songs for mixed voices were most likely composed for performance by Schubert's friends in the *Schubertiade* or in concerts by the Gesellschaft der Musikfreunde. *Des Tages Weihe* D763, for instance, with the opening text "Schicksalslenker, blicke nieder auf ein dankerfültes Herz" (Guider of destiny, look down on a heart filled with thanks), was composed for a friend who had returned to good health after a grave illness. As chamber pieces performed in homes or in other intimate surroundings, the part songs for mixed voices would have been performed by an ensemble of soloists rather than by a choral ensemble. Extended solo passages in pieces such as *Des Tages Weihe* and *Gebet* D815 support this assumption. The part songs for male voices, which are the most numerous, were written for the male singing societies called *Liedertafeln* that were popular throughout Austria and Germany. Some of these societies had purely musical agendas and thus sang more serious repertoire, such as *Gesang der Geister über den Wassern* D705 and *Sehnsucht* D656. Other societies were mainly social, combining singing with drinking, and thus they sang simpler repertoire with less serious texts, such as *Widerspruch* D865, *An den Frühling* D338, and five different drinking songs (*Trinklieder*). Most of the women's part songs were composed for a small female ensemble conducted by one of Schubert's close friends, Anna Fröhlich. Examples are *Der 23. Psalm* D706, which was written for Anna and her sisters, and *Ständchen* D920, which was written for the birthday of one of Anna's pupils. Schubert scored the solo part in *Ständchen* for the student but inadvertently set the choral parts for men. When this error of scoring was brought to his attention, he quickly rescored the choral parts for women. *Ständchen* exists, therefore, in two versions.

The majority of the part songs are either a cappella or accompanied by piano, and a few of the piano-accompanied pieces scored for men's voices have an indication for performance by guitar or piano. In addition, most of the texts are secular. A few of the pieces for men are strophic, and a few have notable word painting. An example of the latter effect can be seen in *Der Gondelfahrer* D809: the lower voices have a repetitive pattern that characterizes a gondola being rocked gently by the waves in the lagoons of Venice, and a succession of chords sounds the ringing of bells in St Mark's tower.

The cantatas were composed for special occasions such as name days, and they are brief and insubstantial. The oratorio *Lazarus oder Die Feier der Auferstehung* D689 (Lazarus, or the Celebration of the Resurrection) was intended to be a full-length, three-part work. However, Schubert composed only the first part and what appears to be half of the second part (approximately seventy-five total minutes of music). No sketches exist for the uncompleted music, and Schubert's writing in the second act merely stops, without cadence, in the middle of a solo passage. The oratorio is scored for SSATT solos, SATB chorus, and orchestra. The writing is through-composed for the most part, although there is extensive writing for solo voices. In addition, the chorus divides into SSAA and TTBB ensembles.

MASSES

COMPLETE AND LISTED ACCORDING TO FAMILIARITY

Missa D167 in G major – 1815 – STB solos, SATB chorus, strings, and organ – 22 minutes. (1) Solo passages consist of brief melodies for soprano in the Kyrie, for soprano and bass in the Gloria and Agnus Dei, and for the trio of soloists in the Benedictus; (2) the Credo is entirely choral.

Missa D950 in E-flat major – 1828 – SATB solos, SATB chorus, two oboes, two clarinets, two bassoons, two horns, two trumpets, three trombones, timpani, and strings – 55 minutes. (1) The solo writing, all for trio or quartet, is limited to the middle portion of the Credo, the Benedictus, and the Agnus Dei (the Kyrie, Gloria, and Sanctus are entirely choral); (2) the choral parts divide into SSATTBB in the Gloria and SSATTB in the Credo; (3) no organ part is specified in the score, although its participation would have been standard.

Missa D678 in A-flat major – 1819–1822 – SATB solos, SATB chorus, flute, two oboes, two clarinets, two bassoons, two horns, two trumpets, three trombones, timpani, strings, and organ – 46 minutes. The trombones mainly double the alto, tenor, and bass chorus parts *colla parte*.

Missa D324 in B-flat major – 1815 – SATB solos, SATB chorus, two oboes, two bassoons, two trumpets, timpani, strings, and organ – 28 minutes.

Missa D452 in C major – 1816 – SATB solos, SATB chorus, two violins, and basso continuo – 23 minutes. The mass is also scored for two oboes or two clarinets, two trumpets, and timpani ad lib.

Missa D105 in F major – 1814 – SSATTB solos, SATB chorus, two oboes, two clarinets, two bassoons, two horns, strings, and organ – 35 minutes. The mass has two versions of the "Dona nobis pacem" portion of the Agnus Dei—one of eighty-seven measures that is basically homophonic, and one of 142 measures that is mostly fugal.

Deutsche Messe D872 – 1827 – SATB chorus, two oboes, two clarinets, two bassoons, two horns, two trumpets, three trombones, timpani, organ, and string bass ad lib. – 12 minutes (if all verses are performed). (1) The work is also called *Gesänge zur Feier des heiligen Opfers der Messe* (Songs for the Celebration of the holy Offering of the Mass) and, in addition, the "Wind Mass" because of its scoring; (2) the work consists of eight movements, each in German and each corresponding to a Latin counterpart; (3) all the movements are homophonic, strophic, and of brief duration.

OTHER SACRED WORKS
SELECTED AND LISTED ACCORDING TO FAMILIARITY

Magnificat D486 – 1815 – SATB solos, SATB chorus, two bassoons, two trumpets, timpani, strings, and organ – 9:30 minutes. The solo writing, for quartet, occupies the entire middle section of the work.

Stabat mater D175 – 1815 – SATB chorus, two oboes, two clarinets, two bassoons, three trombones, strings, and organ – 7:30 minutes. (1) The work is in one movement; (2) the text is in Latin; (3) the texture is basically homophonic.

Stabat mater D383 – 1816 – STB solos, SATB chorus, two flutes, two oboes, two bassoons, contra bassoon, two horns, three trombones, and strings – 38 minutes. (1) The work is sometimes called the "Klopstock" *Stabat mater* because of its German text by F. G. Klopstock; (2) it is in twelve movements—three arias (for STB), one duet (ST), one trio (STB), one trio with chorus, and six choruses; (3) the chorus in movement five divides into SSAATTBB.

Tantum ergo D962 – 1828 – SATB solos, SATB chorus, two oboes, two clarinets, two bassoons, two horns, two trumpets, three trombones, timpani, and strings – 6 minutes. (1) This is the last of Schubert's setting of the Tantum ergo text; (2) the solo writing is for quartet; (3) the music is strophic, divided into two verses.

Tov lehodos D953 – 1828 – SATB solos and SATB chorus a cappella – 4:45 minutes. (1) The text, from Psalm 92:2–9, is in Hebrew; (2) the piece was composed for Schubert's friend Salomon Sulzer, cantor of the Seitenstettengasse Temple in Vienna, who asked leading composers of the day to compose music to standard Hebrew liturgical texts; (3) except for an extended baritone solo accompanied by the chorus, the solo writing is for quartet.

PART SONGS FOR MIXED VOICES
SELECTED AND LISTED ACCORDING TO FAMILIARITY

Der Tanz D826 – 1828 – SATB voices and piano – 1 minute.

Lebenslust D609 – 1818 – SATB voices and piano – 1 minute.

Des Tages Weihe D763 – 1822 – SATB voices and piano – 5 minutes. The opening consists of an extended solo for baritone.

Gebet D815 – 1824 – SATB voices and piano – 9:30 minutes. There are vocal solo melodies throughout the work.

An die Sonne D439 – 1816 – SATB voices and piano – 6:30 minutes.

PART SONGS FOR MEN'S VOICES
SELECTED AND LISTED ACCORDING TO FAMILIARITY

Widerspruch D865 – ca.1826 – TTBB voices and piano – 2:30 minutes.

Der Gondelfahrer D809 – 1824 – TTBB voices and piano – 3:30 minutes.

Nachthelle D892 – 1826 – T solo, TTBB voices, and piano – 5:45 minutes.

Gesang der Geister über den Wassern D714 – 1820 – TTTTBBBB voices and instrumental ensemble of two violas, two cellos, and string bass – 11:15 minutes. (1) The voices are sometimes together and sometimes in two choruses that dialogue with each other; (2) frequent changes of tempo dramatize the text.

Die Nacht D983c – ca.1822 – TTBB a cappella – 3 minutes. The piece is strophic, with four verses of text.

An den Frühling D338 – ca.1816 – TTBB a cappella – 3 minutes. The piece is strophic, with four verses of text.

Sehnsucht D656 – 1819 – TTBBB a cappella – 4:30 minutes. The text, Mignon's song from *Wilhelm Meister* by Goethe, begins "Nur wer die Sehnsucht kennt" (Only one who has felt longing).

Trinklied D847 – 1825 – TTBB a cappella – 2 minutes. (1) The full title of the piece is *Trinklied aus dem 16. Jahrhundert;* (2) the text is in Latin.

PART SONGS FOR WOMEN'S VOICES
SELECTED AND LISTED ACCORDING TO FAMILIARITY

Ständchen D920 – 1827 – A solo, SSAA voices, and piano – 5 minutes. This piece was also set by Schubert for A solo, TTBB voices, and piano; however, the setting for all female voices serves the original intent of the composition (see the discussion above).

Der 23. Psalm D706 – 1820 – SSAA voices and piano – 4:30 minutes.

Gott in der Natur D757 – 1822 – SSAA voices and piano – 6 minutes.

❧ ITALY AND FRANCE ❧

Both Italy and France, like Austria, were Catholic countries during the Classical era. Italy had been Catholic since the Medieval era, of course, and France had been Catholic except for a brief period of the Baroque era, during which there were several composers who wrote for the Protestant Calvinist Church. Sacred music did not, however, capture the creative imaginations of Italian and French Classical-era composers, whose main interests were in opera and purely instrumental forms. Of the seven composers discussed in this section, six of them (Niccolò Jommelli, François-Joseph Gossec, Henri-Joseph Rigel, Domenico Cimarosa, Luigi Cherubini, and Gioachino Rossini) achieved fame from their operas, and the other composer, Luigi Boccherini, was a cellist who wrote mainly string trios, quartets, quintets, and symphonies. Sacred music also did not have the widespread support of clerical administrators, who continued to be interested in works of the Renaissance and Baroque eras. Support for and interest in contemporary choral works came only from public organizations such as the Concert spirituel, and educational institutions such as the Conservatoire, both in Paris, and the Italian orphanages (e.g., the Ospedale degli Incurabili in Venice) and conservatories (e.g., the Conservatorio di S Onofrio in Naples). The Concert spirituel, a public concert series founded in 1725, began featuring newly composed oratorios and other large-scale sacred works in 1755; the orphanages were famous for their performances of sacred choral works; and the conservatories included choral works, both sacred and secular, as a major component of their educational mission.

The genres represented by these choral works were basically limited to masses (including Requiems), sacred oratorios, large-scale settings of Te Deums and Magnificats, motets, and secular cantatas composed in France beginning in the 1790s to texts dealing with revolutionary subjects. Most composers wrote settings of the Requiem as well as of the Mass Ordinary. The Ordinary settings were typically scored for soloists and chorus, with instrumental accompaniment of winds in pairs, trumpets, timpani, and strings. The Requiems, which became the most notable works of the era, often called for larger and more colorful instrumental forces. Gossec's *Messe des morts*, for example, is scored for a sizable complement of wind and brass instruments in addition to a regular orchestral ensemble, and Cherubini's *Requiem* in C minor includes a tam-tam. Many of the oratorios were considered to be exceptional during their time, especially those by Jommelli, Gossec, and Rigel. The Te Deums, Magnificats, and motets were not significant, however, except for a few large-scale works by Jommelli and Cimarosa.

Niccolò Jommelli 1714–1774

Jommelli was born in Aversa, Italy, where he received his first musical education as a chorister at the cathedral there. At age eleven he entered the Conservatorio di S Onofrio in Naples, and at fourteen he transferred to the Conservatorio Pietà dei Turchini. He was influenced, as he said later in life, by Johann Adolf Hasse and Carl Heinrich Graun, who were in Naples during the 1720s, and he developed an interest in opera, composing his first works in that genre during his early twenties. In 1741 he went to Bologna to supervise the production of one of his operas and to study with Padre Giovanni Battista Martini, and in about 1743 he was appointed *maestro di cappella* at the Ospedale degli Incurabili in Venice. He remained in Venice for approximately six years, composing oratorios and motets for the Ospedale, although he also continued to compose operas for and travel to other cities in northern Italy, including Bologna, Turin, Ferrara, and Padua. In 1749 he was elected to the post of *maestro coadiutore* (assistant musical director) of St Peter's in Rome, but when in 1750 he arrived in Rome to assume his duties, he was appointed *maestro di cappella*. In 1754 Duke Carl Eugen of Württemberg, who according to the musical diarist Christian Friedrich Daniel Schubart had one of the finest musical establishments in Europe, convinced Jommelli to be *Ober-Kapellmeister* at his court in Stuttgart, and in 1768, without having to appear in person, he was engaged to compose operas for the court of José I in Lisbon. Jommelli returned to Naples in 1769 to care for his ailing wife and to spend his final years in retirement.

He composed three masses (including a Requiem), three separate mass movements, four surviving oratorios, four Magnificats, two Te Deums, one set of Lamentations, and approximately fifty motets. His most famous mass, the *Missa* in D major composed in 1766, is scored for SATB solos, SATB chorus, two oboes, two horns, strings, and organ. It is distinguished by an instrumental sinfonia that separates the Gloria and Credo and by numerous brief motto-like statements of the word "Credo" interspersed throughout the first and last sections of the Credo movement. In addition, this movement has striking examples of word painting, including sequentially descending melodic patterns to the text "descendit de caelis" (came down from heaven) and a rising scalar passage to the text "et ascendit in coelum" (and he ascended to heaven). Furthermore, the Benedictus, which is not a separate movement as in so many masses of the Classical era, is a duet for soprano and alto characterized by extensive melismas. Sections of this mass were arranged and included in Jommelli's *Missa* in D major of 1769. The Requiem, entitled *Missa pro defunctis,* is in E-flat major and is scored for SATB solos, SATB chorus, strings, and organ. The mass movements, all with numerous soprano and alto solos composed for the students at the Ospedale degli Incurabili, include a Kyrie and Gloria pair in F major and a Credo in D major.

The oratorios *Isacco figura del redentore* and *La Betulia liberata* were composed in 1742 and 1743, respectively, for performance in the oratory of Santa Maria della Consolazione in Venice. *Gioas* was composed in 1745 for the students of the Ospedale degli Incurabili, and Jommelli's most famous oratorio, *La passione di Gesù Cristo,* was composed in 1749 for performance in Rome, with subsequent performances in Prague in 1765 and 1767, London in 1770, Copenhagen in 1775, and Lisbon in 1786. The libretto, by the poet Pietro Metastasio (1698–1782), relates the story of the crucifixion as told to Peter (T) on Holy Saturday by Mary Magdalene (S), John (A), and Joseph of Arimathea (B). Scoring is for the four solo roles, SATB chorus, two flutes, two oboes, two horns, strings, and basso continuo.

The *Te Deum* in D major, composed in 1763 to celebrate the birthday of Duke Carl Eugen, became one of the most popular eighteenth-century settings of this text. The music critic Johann Adam Hiller wrote about it in 1787: "In weighing this work against Handel's [*Utrecht Te Deum* of 1713] some could say that the scales would be exactly in balance, or even that the scales would tip in favor of Jommelli." The motets include *Tenebrae factae sunt, In monte Oliveti,* and *Vinea mea electa*—all three for Holy Week and scored for SATB chorus.

FRANÇOIS-JOSEPH GOSSEC 1734–1829

Gossec was born in southwest Belgium and was a chorister at several churches in the vicinity and at the Cathedral of Notre Dame in Antwerp. In 1751 he went to Paris, where he played violin and bass in the orchestra of Alexandre-Jean-Joseph Le Riche de la Pouplinière, and in 1762 he was appointed *directeur* of the private theater of the Prince of Condé in Chantilly. In 1769 he founded the Concert des Amateurs, a public concert society similar to the Concert spirituel, and in 1773 he began serving as codirector of the Concert spirituel. He was appointed *sous-directeur* of the Paris Opéra in 1780, and in 1784 he founded the Ecole Royale de Chant, renamed the Institut Nationale de Musique in 1793 and the Conservatoire Nationale Supérieur de Musique (commonly referred to simply as the Conservatoire) in 1795.

Gossec composed two masses (including a Requiem), one surviving oratorio, five surviving motets, and approximately fifty extant cantatas. The mass, *Dernière messe des vivants,* was composed in 1813 and was scored for soloists, chorus, and orchestra—with movements consisting of the regular five portions of the Ordinary plus the motets *O salutaris hostia* (placed between the Sanctus and Agnus Dei) and *Domine salvum fac* (placed after the Agnus Dei). The Requiem, *Messe des morts,* was composed in 1780 and also was scored for soloists, chorus, and orchestra—with the orchestration noted for its extra instruments and expressive deployment. Gossec wrote to a friend about the "Tuba mirum" (Wondrous trumpet) portion of the Dies irae: "The audience was alarmed by the dreadful and sinister effect of the three trombones together with four clarinets, four trumpets, four horns, and eight bassoons hidden in a distant and lofty part of the church to announce the last judgment, while the orchestra expressed terror with muted tremolos in all the strings."

The oratorio *La nativité* was composed for performance by the Concert spirituel on Christmas Eve 1774. Its libretto is a version of the traditional Christmas story about shepherds who see the Star of Bethlehem's bright light and are guided by it to the manger in Bethlehem. Solo roles are for a Shepherdess (S), Shepherd (A), Voice from Heaven (S), Narrator (T), and one of the Magi (B). Choral scoring is for a Chorus of Shepherds (SATB) and a Chorus of Angels (SSAT), both of which perform as a double chorus in the final movement of the oratorio (the Chorus of Angels is to be offstage and out of sight). Orchestral scoring is for two flutes, two oboes, two clarinets, two bassoons, four horns, timpani, and strings.

HENRI-JOSEPH RIGEL 1741–1799

Rigel was born in Wertheim, southeast of Frankfurt, Germany, and studied with Niccolò Jommelli in Stuttgart before moving to Paris in 1768 and establishing himself as a composer of piano pieces. By 1774 his symphonies were being performed by such organizations as the Concert spirituel, and by the late 1770s he achieved success with his operas. He was appointed *maître de solfège* at the Ecole Royale de Chant in 1783, and in 1785, when the school was renamed the Conservatoire, he became a professor of piano. In 1787 he was named *chef d'orchestre* of the Concert spirituel while maintaining his position at the Conservatoire.

Rigel composed four oratorios, two motets, and three revolutionary cantatas. His first oratorio, *La sortie d'Egypte,* was composed in 1774 and became one of the most popular oratorios of its time; it was performed by the Concert spirituel twenty-seven times between 1775 and 1786. Its libretto, based on Exodus 11–15, is the story of the Israelites's escape from the bondage of the Egyptians. Scoring is for Moses (B), an Israelite (T), a quartet of Israelites (SSTB), chorus (SATB), two oboes, two clarinets, two bassoons, two horns, two trumpets, timpani, and strings. The chorus represents the Israelites in one movement of the oratorio and the Egyptians in another movement. In the oratorio's final movement the sopranos and altos (on one side of the stage) represent the Israelites, while the tenors and basses (on the other side of the stage) represent the Egyptians.

LUIGI BOCCHERINI 1743–1805

Boccherini was born in Lucca, Italy, the son of singer and bass player Leopoldo Boccherini. From ages eight to ten Luigi was a chorister at the Seminario di S Martino in Lucca, and from ten to thirteen he studied cello in Rome with G. B. Costanzi. Boccherini returned to Lucca, where he performed and composed works for the cello and was called the "celebre suonatore di Violoncello" (famous player of the cello), and from ages fourteen to twenty-seven he toured with his father throughout Europe, often staying for months at a time in such cities as Venice, Florence, Vienna, and Paris. Leopoldo died in 1766, and in 1770 Luigi settled in Madrid, accepting the position *Compositore e virtuoso di camera* for Don Luis, the Spanish Infante and younger brother of King Charles III. In 1785 Boccherini was also appointed to the Real Capilla of Charles III. While maintaining these positions, others followed in later years, including *compositeur de notre chamber* to Crown Prince Wilhelm of Prussia (later Friedrich Wilhelm II), which he held without ever appearing in Prussia, and *director de orquesta y compositor* for María Josefa Alfonsa Pimental in Madrid. Boccherini, who during his life owned two Stradivarius cellos, died of tuberculosis in Madrid and was buried at S Justo y Pastor; his remains were moved in 1927 to the church of S Francesco in his hometown of Lucca.

Boccherini composed one mass (which is lost), three mass movements, two oratorios, and three large-scale motets. The mass movements—a *Kyrie* in B-flat major, *Gloria* in F major, and *Credo* in C major—are all scored for four-part chorus and instruments and are divided into several movements. The *Gloria,* for instance, is scored for two horns, strings, and organ and is divided into five movements—"Gloria in excelsis" for chorus, "Laudamus te" for soprano and tenor duet, "Qui tollis peccata mundi" for chorus, "Qui sedes ad dexteram patris" for bass solo, and "Cum sancto spiritu" for chorus. This last movement exists in two versions—an extended setting of 166 measures and a shorter setting of thirty-eight measures. The choral writing throughout the *Gloria* is mainly homophonic and syllabic, while the solo writing contains melismas.

DOMENICO CIMAROSA 1749–1801

Cimarosa, like Niccolò Jommelli, was born in Aversa, Italy, and schooled in Naples; Cimarosa was a chorister at the monastery of S Severino de' Padri Conventuali and the Conservatorio di S Maria di Loreto. Also like Jommelli, Cimarosa developed an interest in opera and achieved fame composing comic works in that genre. In 1779 he became one of the minor organists at the royal chapel in Naples, and in about 1782 he was appointed *maestro di cappella* at the Ospedale dell'Ospedaletto. He moved to a similar position in 1787 at the court of Catherine II in St Petersburg, Russia, and in 1791, when the court's musical resources were reduced, he relocated to Vienna to serve as *Kapellmeister* to Leopold II. Cimarosa returned to Naples in 1793, and in 1796 he was appointed the main organist at the royal chapel of King Ferdinand. However, in 1799 he was imprisoned for his allegiance to republican forces that opposed the king, and upon his release he fled to Venice, where his health deteriorated and he died at age fifty-one.

He composed ten masses (including one Requiem), five separate mass movements, six oratorios, approximately fifteen cantatas, one Magnificat, one Te Deum, and ten motets. The Requiem (*Missa pro defunctis*), the most famous of his masses, is in the key of G minor; it is scored for SATB solos, SATB chorus, two horns, strings, and organ and is divided into eighteen movements—five for soloists, eleven for chorus, and two for soloists and chorus. The *Magnificat* and *Te Deum* are also well-known works. The *Magnificat,* composed in 1769, is in the key of D major and is scored for SATB chorus (with no solos), two oboes, two trumpets, two violins (no violas), and basso continuo; it is in one movement divided into four sections. The *Te Deum,* composed in 1798, is in the key of C major and is scored for SAT solos, SSATB chorus, two horns, strings, and organ, with obbligato parts for oboe, clarinet, and trumpet. Like the *Magnificat,* it is in one movement divided into multiple sections.

LUIGI CHERUBINI 1760–1842

Cherubini was born in Florence, Italy, the son of Bartolomeo Cherubini, *maestro al cembalo* at the Teatro della Pergola. Luigi studied with his father and local musicians in Florence and began composing mass movements at age thirteen. At fourteen he composed the cantata *La pubblica felicità* for a celebration service in the Florence Cathedral in honor of Duke Leopold of Tuscany (later Emperor Leopold II), and between eighteen and twenty-one he studied in Bologna and Milan. He achieved considerable fame with operas composed for and presented in Florence, Rome, and Venice, and in 1784 he was appointed resident composer of the King's Theatre in London (the theater devoted to the production of Italian opera). In 1786 he relocated to Paris, where he fulfilled commissions for the Paris Opéra and the Théâtre de Monsieur, and in 1795 he began teaching at the newly founded Conservatoire Nationale de Musique. In 1816 he also became *Surintendant de la musique du roi,* a position appointed by Louis XVIII and shared with Jean-François Le Sueur. While holding the positions at the Conservatoire and royal chapel, Cherubini continued to compose and experience success with his operas, especially *Médée* in 1797. However, he also studied, composed, and conducted church music. For instance, he copied works by Palestrina, Handel, and Pergolesi; he composed a Requiem for the twenty-fourth anniversary of Louis XVI's execution as well as masses for the coronations of Louis XVIII and Charles X; and he conducted the first Parisian performance of Mozart's *Requiem.* In 1822 he was appointed *directeur* of the Conservatoire, and for the next two decades he worked diligently to improve the standards of students, to hire internationally famous teachers (including Gioachino Rossini in 1826), and to establish the institution as one of the finest music schools in Europe.

Cherubini composed twelve surviving masses (including two Requiems), two pairs of separate mass movements, approximately forty motets, twenty surviving cantatas, and sixty-three canons. The most famous of the masses, and one of the most famous works of the Classical era, is the *Requiem* in C minor, composed to commemorate the death of Louis XVI. A large-scale work for chorus and orchestra (there are no solos), with dramatic elements of expression that would become common during the Romantic era, it is divided into seven movements—Introitus and Kyrie; Graduale ("Requiem aeternam"); Sequentia ("Dies irae" and "Lacrimosa"); Offertorium ("Domine Jesu Christe," "Quam olim Abrahae," and "Hostias"); Sanctus and Benedictus; Pie Jesu; and Agnus Dei and Communio. In addition to an SATB chorus, the *Requiem* is scored for two oboes, two clarinets, two bassoons, two horns, two trumpets, three trombones, timpani, tam-tam (which plays once in the Dies irae), and strings. There is no indication for organ, although one would probably have been included, especially since the Requiem's premiere was at the church of St Denis in Paris. Cherubini's other Requiem was composed in 1836. To appease the Archbishop of Paris, who objected to performances of the *Requiem* in C minor with female singers, it was scored only for three-part male chorus and orchestra.

Additional important works include the *Missa solemnis* in D minor for SATB solos, SATB chorus, and orchestra composed in 1811; the motet *O salutaris hostia* of 1857 or 1858 for SSTB voices; and the madrigal *Ninfa crudel* for SSATB voices and basso continuo composed in 1783 while Cherubini was a student in Florence.

GIOACHINO ROSSINI 1792–1868

Rossini was born in Pesaro, Italy, where his father was a hornist and his mother a singer. Gioachino studied with his parents, learning to both sing and play the horn, and he toured with them to cities in northern Italy, including Bologna, where the family had moved when he was twelve and where he began singing and playing in local opera houses and also began composing arias for performance in local opera productions. At age fourteen, being recognized for his extraordinary singing ability, he was admitted into the prestigious Accademia Filarmonica, and between fourteen and eighteen he studied formally at the Liceo Musicale under Padre Giovanni Battista Martini's successor, Padre Stanislao Mattei—spending considerable time becoming acquainted with the music of Joseph Haydn and W. A. Mozart. When he was nineteen, he conducted Haydn's *Die Jahreszeiten* (The Seasons) at the Accademia dei Concordi in Bologna, and at the end of his life he called Mozart "the admiration of my youth, the desperation of my mature years, and the consolation of my old age."

Meanwhile, Rossini's first opera, a commission from the Teatro S Moisè in Venice, was composed when he was eighteen. Other operas followed in quick succession, and by the time he was forty he had composed forty operas, with three operas composed each year between 1811 and 1819. Both *L'Italiana in Algeri* and *Tancredi,* Rossini's first major successes, were composed in 1813 for Venice, and *Il barbiere di Siviglia* (originally called *Almaviva*) was composed in 1816 for Rome. Other well-known operas include *La cenerentola* of 1817, *Semiramide* of 1823, and his final opera, *Guillaume Tell,* of 1829. At that time Rossini was only thirty-seven.

For the remainder of his life, secure financially, he composed at his leisure a small amount of choral, vocal, and instrumental chamber works. These include the *Stabat mater, Petite messe solennelle,* several small-scale sacred pieces, and a collection of piano pieces, songs, and vocal ensemble works he referred to as *Péchés de vieillesse* (Sins of old age). Rossini also maintained his interest in great choral composers of the past, subscribing in 1857 to the complete works of J. S. Bach (which began publication in 1850, the 100th anniversary of Bach's death). The *Stabat mater* was begun in 1832, but Rossini set only six of ten movements and assigned the other four movements to a friend, Giovanni Tadolini. This composite work was performed on Good Friday 1833, but not published. Almost ten years later, with publication imminent, Rossini composed the movements previously given to Tadolini plus a concluding Amen, and the complete Rossini work was then performed in Paris (January 1842) and in a highly acknowledged Bologna performance (March 1842) conducted by Gaetano Donizetti.

The *Petite messe solennelle* was composed for the consecration of a patron's private chapel in March 1864 and was scored for twelve voices (including substantial SATB solos), two pianos, and a harmonium. Rossini orchestrated it several years later, fearing that if he did not, someone else would. He referred to the mass as "the last mortal sin of my old age," and he inscribed the following words at the end of the Agnus Dei: "Dear God. Here it is, finished, this poor little Mass. Have I written musique sacrée [sacred music] or sacrée musique [sacrilegious music]? I was born for *opera buffa,* you know it well! Little science, some heart, that's all. Be blessed, then, and grant me a place in Paradise." The work contains an instrumental "Preludio Religioso" between the Credo and Sanctus, and the soprano solo motet *O salutaris hostia* (a different setting of this text than that which Rossini composed in 1857) between the Sanctus and Agnus Dei.

The *Péchés de vieillesse* include only ten vocal ensemble works: *I gondolieri* and *La passeggiata* for vocal quartet and piano; *Toast pour le nouvel an* for vocal octet a cappella; *La nuit de Noël* for vocal octet, bass solo, piano, and harmonium; *Choeur de chasseurs démocrates* for male chorus, tam-tam, and two tambourines; *Quelques mesures de chant funèbre: à mon pauvre ami Meyerbeer* for male chorus and drum; *Ave Maria* for chorus and organ; *Preghiera* for eight male voices a cappella; *Cantemus Domino* for vocal octet a cappella, composed in a Renaissance imitative style in double choir format; and *Le Départ des promis* for SSAA choir (in actuality a duet since there is only one soprano and one alto part) and piano. The famous *Duetto buffo di due gatti* (Comic duet of two cats) for soprano and alto with piano accompaniment is ascribed to Rossini without any documentation.

In addition to the works listed and discussed above, Rossini composed the *Messa di Gloria* in 1820 (a setting of the Kyrie and Gloria) and *Mosè in Egitto* in 1818. This latter work contained the term "oratorio" in its original title and the phrase "azione tragico-sacra" (tragic sacred drama) in the original printed libretto. In addition, a newspaper article before the first performance stated, "Rossini is finishing writing the music of an *oratorio* for the Royal Theater of San Carlo." The premiere performance in 1818 at the Neapolitan Teatro San Carlo was staged, however, and late in life Rossini called the work an opera. It is scored for SSATTTBB solos, SATB chorus, and orchestra of two flutes (doubling two piccolos), two oboes, two clarinets, two bassoons, four horns, two trumpets, three trombones, serpent, timpani, bass drum, cymbals, triangle, harp, and strings.

SACRED WORKS
SELECTED AND LISTED ACCORDING TO FAMILIARITY

Stabat mater – begun in 1832 and revised and completed in 1842 – SATB solos, SATB chorus, and orchestra – 60 minutes. (1) The solo writing consists of extended operatic arias; (2) the solo alto part is in the mezzo-soprano range; (3) three of the work's ten movements are for chorus.

Petite messe solennelle – 1864 (revised in 1867) – original version for twelve voices, two pianos, and harmonium – revised version for SATB solos, SATB chorus, and full orchestra – 80 minutes. (1) The solo writing consists of extended operatic arias; (2) seven of the work's fourteen movements are for chorus.

Messe di gloria – 1820 – SATTB solos, SATB chorus, and full orchestra – 60 minutes.

O salutaris hostia – 1857 – SATB chorus a cappella – 2:30 minutes.

Trois choeurs religieux – 1844 – SSA chorus and piano (with added S solo in the last piece) – 11 minutes. (1) The three pieces are "La foi" (Faith), "L'espérance" (Hope), and "La charité" (Charity); (2) each piece is approximately 3:30 minutes in duration.

SECULAR WORKS
SELECTED AND LISTED ACCORDING TO FAMILIARITY

I gondolieri – date unknown – SATB voices and piano – 5 minutes.

La passeggiata – date unknown – SATB voices and piano – 5:15 minutes.

Toast pour le nouvel an – date unknown – SATB voices a cappella – 2:30 minutes.

La pastorelle – ca.1821 – SATB voices a cappella – 4:30 minutes.

☙ ENGLAND ❧

The musical climate in England during the Classical era was not conducive to new compo-sition but instead was almost completely focused on the continued performance of works by George Frideric Handel. This was especially so with the several London theaters, such as Covent Garden and Drury Lane, that developed concert series during the latter part of the eighteenth century. In 1775, for instance, only one new work was performed in the theaters of London—an oratorio by John Stanley. Otherwise, there were nineteen performances of seven Handel works, including three performances of *Samson,* four of *Judas Maccabaeus,* and six of *Messiah* (these three oratorios were the most popular Handel works during the Classical era). In 1785 the only composer to compete with Handel was Thomas Arne, whose oratorio *Judith* was performed in the Little Theatre in the Haymarket. Handel's music also dominated the many programs sponsored by organizations for the benefit of hospitals and other programs presented in newly organized festivals all across England. The Foundling Hospital, site of the first *Messiah* performance in 1750, continued annual performances of *Messiah* until 1777, and the Three Choirs Festival, begun in about 1713 and still in existence today, regularly featured a variety of Handel oratorios during the Classical era. The major focus on Handel was, of course, the com-memoration concerts in Westminster Abbey, which began in May and June 1784 and continued annually for most of the remaining years in the eighteenth century. The initial series of concerts, which were meant to mark the 100th anniversary of Handel's assumed birth date and the twenty-fifth anniversary of his burial, was epic. A gigantic gallery was erected to hold the 275 choristers and 250 instrumentalists, the existing organ was disassembled and a new one built for the occasion, and performances were attended by dignitaries from all over Europe.

The new British composers who managed to emerge during the Classical era and achieve some degree of popularity were often associated with Handel performances. For example, Arne worked with Handel and often followed in his footsteps, conducting his oratorios in the years following successful premieres; Stanley helped manage the Handel oratorio series in London theaters for twenty-six years and also conducted performances of *Messiah* in Dublin; and Samuel Arnold, who succeeded Stanley as director of the Lenten oratorio series at Drury Lane, was one of the supporters for the publication of Handel's complete works. It was only the composers born after Handel's death—Thomas Attwood and Samuel Wesley—who developed a degree of independence. Attwood composed no oratorios (the only composer of the era in England to not contribute to the genre) but rather Anglican Services, anthems, catches, glees, and musical comedies. Wesley, who did contribute to the oratorio and Anglican genres, was the only composer to write Latin masses, motets, and Magnificats. All the genres were conservative in style, with no traits or characteristics that could be considered new or modern except for an economy of scoring and a spareness of texture.

THOMAS ARNE 1710–1778

Arne was born in London and educated at Eton, where he became a proficient player of the recorder, spinet, and violin and where he began composing theater works. In 1732 he formed a small company at the Little Theatre in the Haymarket that began performing masques, including Handel's *Acis and Galatea,* and in about 1734 he became the house composer for the theater at Drury Lane. He founded the Society of Musicians (later called the Royal Society of Musicians) in 1738 along with Handel, William Boyce, and Johann Christoph Pepusch, and he began presenting oratorios in Dublin after Handel's success with *Messiah* in 1742. As a point of interest, Arne's sister Susanna Cibber was a famous soprano, who sang in the Dublin performances of *Messiah* and other oratorios under Handel's direction and who also was one of the leading artists at Covent Garden. After several years in Dublin, Arne returned to Drury Lane and then followed his sister to Covent Garden, conducting operas and masques in both companies during the next decade. He taught singing privately and composed short theatrical pieces for his students during the 1760s, and during the 1770s he produced some of his most successful works, including *Artaxerxes* and *The Fairy Prince.*

Arne was a prolific composer. However, many of his compositions have been lost, and of those that are extant, a considerable number are incomplete or exist only in partial scores. Complete and surviving works include one oratorio, approximately twenty masques and operas, and several odes. In addition, he wrote the hymn tune *Arlington,* which is variously sung in modern times to the text "O for a thousand tongues to sing," "O for a faith that will not shrink," or "Am I a soldier of the cross."

The oratorio *Judith* was composed for performance at Drury Lane during Lent 1761. It was well received at its premiere and subsequently was revived at Drury Lane in 1762, the King's Theatre in the Haymarket in 1765, the Three Choirs Festival in Gloucester in 1766, and Covent Garden in 1773. The libretto is based on the biblical story found in Judith 7–15: Judith beheads Holofernes and liberates the city of Bethulia from the Assyrians. Scoring is for Judith (S), her handmaiden Abra (S), Ozias (T), an elder named Charmis (B), Holofernes (T), two Israelites (T and S), an Assyrian Woman (S), chorus (SATB), two flutes, two oboes, two bassoons, two horns, two trumpets, timpani, harp, strings, and basso continuo. The chorus, representing both the Israelites and the Assyrians, sings in nine of the oratorio's twenty-eight movements; the parts of Ozias and Holofernes were sung in some performances an octave higher by the castrato Giusto Ferdinando Tenducci; the harp plays in only one movement; and the basso continuo calls for both harpsichord and organ.

The masques were basically spoken plays with interpolated songs and choruses (not designated to be sung by specific characters or groups of people). *Comus,* Arne's most famous masque, was first produced in 1738 at Drury Lane. It contains three choral movements and several songs that became popular throughout England. *Alfred* was originally produced in 1740 and was scored with one concluding choral movement, "Rule Brittania." It was revised in 1753 and retitled *Alfred the Great,* given additional songs and choruses, and advertised as being performed "in the manner of an oratorio." *The Judgment of Paris,* another popular masque, was produced in 1740 with five choral movements.

The odes include *God bless our noble king* of 1745 for ATB solos, ATB chorus, two oboes, two horns, strings, and basso continuo; *An ode upon dedicating a building to Shakespeare* of 1769 for speaker, SSSSTB solos, SATB chorus, two oboes, two horns, strings, and basso continuo; and *Whittington's Feast* (sometimes referred to as an oratorio) of 1776 for SSTB solos, SATB chorus, two flutes, two oboes, two bassoons, two horns, two trumpets, timpani, drum, strings, and basso continuo.

JOHN STANLEY 1712–1786

Stanley was born in London and at age two was blinded in an accident. He studied organ during his youth with Maurice Greene, who began serving as organist at St Paul's Cathedral in 1718, and at about age twelve he was appointed organist at the nearby church of All Hallows Bread Street. At fourteen he moved to St Andrew's, Holborn; at seventeen he received a bachelor's degree from Oxford University; and during his twenties, having become an accomplished violinist as well as organist, he led numerous orchestral concerts. During the 1750s he conducted Handel oratorios, and after Handel's death in 1759 he directed the Lenten oratorio series at Covent Garden. In addition, Stanley directed the Lenten oratorio series at Drury Lane beginning in 1770, and he conducted *Messiah* performances at the Foundling Hospital in Dublin between 1775 and 1777. He succeeded William Boyce as Master of the King's Musick in 1779, and for the remaining years of his life he composed New Year's Day and birthday odes for the royal court.

Stanley's output includes three oratorios, ten anthems, fifteen odes (most of which have been lost), and numerous cantatas for solo voice and instruments. The oratorios are *Jephtha* (ca.1751), *Zimri* (produced at Covent Garden in 1760 and 1761), and *The Fall of Egypt* (produced at Drury Lane in 1774 and 1775). This last oratorio, based on the biblical story found in Exodus 7–15, describes the plagues that fell upon the Egyptians and the escape of the Israelites across the Red Sea (act one of the oratorio is about the plague of darkness, act two depicts the parting of the Red Sea by Moses, and act three relates the destruction of the pursuing Egyptians). Solo roles representing the Egyptians are Pharaoh (T), his son Sephres (S), his sister Menytis (S), and Eunuch Officers (S and S); Israelite solo roles are Moses (B), two Elders (T and T), four Israelites (T, T, S, and S), and a Messenger (T). An SATB chorus that represents both Egyptians and Israelites is featured in seven of the oratorio's twenty-five movements (plus three movements with soloists). Instrumental scoring is for two flutes, two oboes, bassoon, two horns, two trumpets, timpani, strings, and basso continuo.

SAMUEL ARNOLD 1740–1802

Arnold was born in London and was a chorister at the Chapel Royal. In 1764 he became harpsichordist at Covent Garden, in 1769 he began producing his own theater pieces at Marylebone Garden, and in 1777 he was named principal composer and director of the Little Theatre in the Haymarket. He was appointed organist at the Chapel Royal in 1783, and in 1786 he succeeded

John Stanley as director of the Lenten oratorio series at Drury Lane. Beginning in 1789 he was also the principal conductor of the Academy of Ancient Music, and in 1793 he became organist at Westminster Abbey. In addition to his conducting responsibilities and composing activities, he maintained an interest in musicology, promoting the publication of the complete works of Handel and the continuation of William Boyce's *Cathedral Music,* and working with Thomas Busby on the publication of *The New Musical Magazine.* Arnold was a highly respected musician during his lifetime and was buried in Westminster Abbey.

He composed six original oratorios, six Anglican Services, seventeen anthems, and ten odes. The oratorios include *The Cure of Saul,* composed for the Three Choirs Festival in Hereford in 1771, and *The Prodigal Son,* composed for the installation of Chancellor Lord North at Oxford University in 1773. Arnold also assembled three pastiche oratorios—*Omnipotence, Redemption,* and *The Triumph of Truth*—consisting mostly of choruses from works by Handel. The Services—all homophonic and scored for SATB chorus (divided into *cantoris* and *decani* ensembles) and an organ part that basically doubles the choral voices—are identified by their keys (B-flat, C, D, F, G, and A). The anthems include *Who is this that cometh from Edom* (from Isaiah 63) for ATB solos, SATB chorus, and organ.

THOMAS ATTWOOD 1765–1838

Attwood was born in London and, like Samuel Arnold, was a chorister at the Chapel Royal. When his voice changed at age sixteen, he became a page to the Prince of Wales, who, recognizing his servant's musical talents, sent him abroad for study—to Naples and Vienna for two years each. In Vienna Attwood studied with W. A. Mozart, who reputedly said of his student, "He partakes more of my style than any scholar [student] I ever had, and I predict that he will prove a sound musician." Returning to London, Attwood taught the Duchess of York in 1791 and the Princess of Wales in 1795 and gained fame as an arranger of comic opera pastiches. In 1796 he was appointed organist at St Paul's Cathedral and also composer at the Chapel Royal, and in 1813 he was one of the founders of the Philharmonic Society. For the next decade he conducted many Mozart symphonies, and during the 1830s he became close friends with Felix Mendelssohn, who dedicated several organ pieces to his friend and who played organ concerts at St Paul's.

Attwood composed five Anglican Services, four Kyrie/Sanctus pairs, eighteen anthems, plus numerous catches and glees and musical comedies. Two of the anthems are large-scale works composed for coronations—*I was glad* for George IV (formerly Attwood's patron, the Prince of Wales) and *O Lord, grant the king a long life* for William IV. The other anthems are all small-scale pieces, generally scored in verse format for a single soloist, SATB chorus, and organ. Examples are the well-known *Come, holy ghost* and *Turn thy face from my sins.*

SAMUEL WESLEY 1766–1837

Wesley was born in Bristol, the son of Anglican clergyman and hymn writer Charles Wesley (1707–1788) and nephew of Methodism's founder John Wesley (1703–1791). Samuel was a child prodigy, who, according to his father, was able to play keyboard instruments at age three and who at age five "had all the recitatives and choruses of [Handel's] *Samson* and *Messiah,* both words and notes, by heart." William Boyce called Samuel the "English Mozart." At about age twelve Samuel developed a keen interest in Latin church music, emulating his father, who he said was "fond of the Old Masters Palestrina, Corelli, Geminiani, and Handel." In the 1770s the Wesley family moved to London, and from 1779 to 1787 Samuel and his elder brother Charles gave subscription concerts in their home. In 1784 Samuel converted to Catholicism and composed a mass (*Missa de spiritu sancto*), which he sent to Pope Pius VI. He retracted his conversion soon after it was made, although he continued his interest in Latin church music, attending services in Catholic embassies in London and composing numerous Latin motets. During the last decades of the century he gained recognition as a virtuoso organist, and for the remainder of his life he performed regularly throughout London: he played one of his organ concertos in a concert featuring Joseph Haydn's *The Creation* in 1800; he was organist for the Covent Garden oratorio concerts beginning in 1813; and he played a concert with Felix Mendelssohn at Christ Church, Newgate Street, in 1837.

Wesley composed five Latin masses (including a Requiem), sixty Latin motets, two Latin Magnificats, two oratorios, two Anglican Services, thirty-five anthems, one ode, approximately fifty hymns, and about fifty secular part songs. All of the Latin works, whether a cappella or accompanied, are based on styles of the past—generally chant-based or imitative in texture. Two of the masses, including the Requiem, are chant settings: the *Missa de spiritu sancto* mentioned earlier is in a point-of-imitation style scored for SSAATB voices, and *Missa pro angelis* is for SATB solos, SATB chorus, and organ. Several of the motets are scored for double chorus with strings and organ (e.g., *Deus majestatis intonuit*) or with organ accompaniment alone (e.g., *In exitu Israel*). *Tu es sacerdos* for four voices (there is another setting for six voices) and *Constitues eos principes* are both a cappella. *Exultate Deo* (published with an English translation and entitled *Sing aloud with gladness*) is probably Wesley's most familiar motet. It alternates imitative phrases with passages of homophony as in late-sixteenth-century *prima prattica* works, and it is scored for SSATB chorus, strings, and organ. The instruments double the choral parts except for a ten-measure closing at the end of the motet. Wesley's large-scale setting of *Confitebor tibi, Domine* (Psalm 111) is unique and the most modern of his Latin works. It is divided into fifteen movements—eight for soloists (five arias, one recitative, one duet, and one trio) and seven for chorus—and scored for SATB solos, SATB chorus, two flutes, two oboes, two bassoons, two trumpets, timpani, strings, and organ.

❧ THE UNITED STATES ❧

Before the latter half of the eighteenth century, choral music in the United States was for the main part limited to Psalm tunes in books that had come with the Pilgrims from Europe. *The Book of Psalmes: Englished both in Prose and Metre* by Henry Ainsworth (called the *Ainsworth Psalter*), which contained thirty-nine tunes, was the most popular and was used in the United States beginning in the 1620s. Thomas Ravenscroft's *Whole Book of Psalmes* of 1621, which contained simple four-part settings, and the ninth edition of the *Bay Psalm Book,* which contained thirteen tunes, were also sources of music. Singing treatises, such as John Tuft's *Introduction to the Art of Singing Psalm Tunes* and Thomas Walter's *The Grounds and Rules of Musick Explained or An Introduction to the Art of Singing by Note,* were published beginning in the 1720s, and by the 1760s American psalters began to appear. Examples include Josiah Flagg's *Collection of the Best Psalm Tunes* of 1764 and William Tans'ur's *Royal Melody Complete* of 1767. Concurrent with the publications of music were singing schools that existed to teach musical literacy, especially sight-reading.

Performances of European choral music began in the 1770s, and, as in England, works of George Frideric Handel dominated the programs. The first-known advertised public concerts consisted of excerpts from Handel's *Messiah* in New York City in 1770, with programs of excerpts performed frequently in succeeding years in numerous other cities, including Boston, Philadelphia, and Bethlehem (Pennsylvania). In addition, Handel commemoration concerts, modeled after the Westminster Abbey events and consisting of excerpts from a variety of oratorios, began occurring in both Boston and Philadelphia in 1786—only two years after the original English commemoration. The first complete performance of *Messiah* did not occur, however, until 1818 in Boston.

Music in the United States during the Classical era was also affected by Moravians, who fostered the composition of anthems for their worship services and who formed major communities in Bethlehem, Pennsylvania, and Salem (now Winston-Salem), North Carolina. Composers such as Christian Friedrich Gregor (discussed under Austria and Germany) visited the communities in the 1770s and encouraged the establishment of music programs in the churches. Other European composers stayed in the American communities and contributed to their cultural advancement. Conrad Beissel (1691–1768) settled at the Ephrata Cloister in Lancaster, Pennsylvania, and composed more than one thousand hymns; Johann Friedrich Peter (1746–1813) arrived in 1770 and traveled among all the established communities; Johannes Herbst (1735–1812) served the communities in Salem and in Lancaster and Lititz, Pennsylvania, beginning in 1786; David Moritz Michael (1751–1827) conducted the first American performance of Joseph Haydn's *The Creation* in Bethlehem in 1811; and Johann Christian Bechler (1784–1857) arrived in 1806 and served as pastor of the Salem congregation. Another Moravian, John Antes (discussed below) was born in America but spent his life as a missionary in Egypt and as an administrator in England.

Composers born in the United States and not connected with European movements include the Presbyterian minister James Lyon; Francis Hopkinson, one of the signers of the Declaration of Independence; Samuel Felsted, the composer of the first American oratorio; the iconoclast William Billings; Supply Belcher; and Daniel Read.

JAMES LYON 1735–1794

Lyon was born in Newark, New Jersey, and received his education at the College of New Jersey (now Princeton University). He taught singing in Philadelphia beginning in 1760; in 1764 he moved to Nova Scotia, where he served as a Presbyterian minister; and in 1772 he returned to the United States as a minister in Machias, Maine. He is known for his 1761 collection entitled *Urania, or a Choice Collection of Psalm-Tunes, Anthems, and Hymns, from the most approved Authors, with some Entirely New, in Two, Three, and Four Parts.* Most of the music in the collection was by European composers. However, six pieces were by Lyon, including the hymn *Whitefield* set to the text "Come, thou almighty king, help us thy name to sing." Other compositions include the SATB anthem *Friendship*, published in John Strickney's *Gentleman and Lady's Musical Companion* of 1774.

FRANCIS HOPKINSON 1737–1791

Hopkinson was born in Philadelphia, where he studied law at the College of Philadelphia (now the University of Pennsylvania). He learned to play the harpsichord as a teenager, and during his adult years he occasionally taught psalmody and served as organist at Christ Church, Philadelphia. Other musically related activities involved collecting manuscripts of choral music by British composers such as Handel and Thomas Arne, and compiling and publishing two collections of Psalm tunes for use in the church—*A Collection of Psalm tunes* in 1763 and *The Psalms of David . . . for the Use of the Reformed Protestant Dutch Church* in 1767. Although active in the church, serving as Secretary of the 1789 General Convention of the Episcopal Church that authorized the first American *Book of Common Prayer,* his career was in law: he became an attorney in 1761 and a judge in 1779. In addition, he was one of the signers of the Declaration of Independence in 1776 and was the first Secretary of the Navy.

Hopkinson composed three anthems, eight songs, and two odes. The anthems include *An Anthem from the 114th Psalm* ("What aileth thee, O thou sea"), composed in 1760 and believed to be the earliest dated anthem by a native-born American. The song *My days have been so wondrous free* was composed in 1759 and is similarly believed to be the first surviving secular song written in America. The other songs were published as a collection in 1788. One of the odes, *An Ode for the 4th of July, 1788,* contains text only. However, the other ode, *America Independent or The Temple of Minerva,* composed in 1781, is fully musical. Subtitled "An Oratorical Entertainment," its vocal scoring is for the Genius of France (S), the Genius of America (A), a High Priest (T), and the High Priest of Minerva (B). These characters portray the special natures (the meaning of genius) of America and France in arias, duets, trios, and a concluding quartet. The instrumental scoring is uncertain but probably consisted of two oboes, two horns, strings, and basso continuo.

JOHN ANTES 1740–1811

Antes was born near Bethlehem, Pennsylvania, where he studied at the Moravian boys' school. From ages sixteen to approximately twenty-four he was an instrument maker who built violins, violas, cellos, and pianos in Bethlehem, and in 1764 he joined the Moravian community in Herrnhut, Germany (which Christian Friedrich Gregor had joined in 1742). In 1769 Antes was ordained a Moravian minister, and from 1770 to 1781 he served as a missionary in Egypt. For the final years of his life he was the business manager of the Fulneck Moravian community in England.

Antes composed thirty-one anthems and sacred solo songs and fifty-nine hymn tunes. Only a few of his compositions were published, although most manuscripts survive and are housed in libraries in the Bethlehem and Herrnhut communities. The most famous of the anthems, *Go, congregation, go,* is scored for soprano or tenor solo, SATB chorus, and strings. It is constructed in verse format, with the soloist alone in the first half of the anthem and the chorus alone (singing the chorale "Surely he hath borne our griefs and carried our sorrows") in the second half. Other familiar anthems include *How beautiful upon the mountains; Sing and rejoice, O daughter of Zion;* and *My heart shall rejoice in his salvation.*

SAMUEL FELSTED CA.1743–1802

Little is known about the life of Felsted except that he was probably born in Philadelphia; he lived for a short time in New York City; he was organist at Saint Andrew's Parish in Kingston, Jamaica; and he composed the first oratorio in America—*Jonah.* It is a short work in twelve movements (five recitatives, four airs, two choruses, and an overture), scored for Jonah (T), a Narrator (T), SATB chorus, and unspecified instruments (the only surviving score has a keyboard reduction of the original instrumental parts). Early documented performances were in 1779 in Jamaica; 1788 at the German Church, Nassau Street, in New York City; and 1789 by the Musical Society of New York and at the Stone Chapel in Boston.

WILLIAM BILLINGS 1746–1800

Billings was born in Boston, where in his youth he was an apprentice to a tanner and in his adult years a worker in the leather trade. During most of his life he was also associated with the American revolutionary movement and some of its important Boston leaders, including Samuel Adams and Paul Revere. According to a contemporary account, he was "a singular man, of moderate size, short of one leg, with one eye, without an address, and with an uncommon negligence of person." It was also said that he had "a rasping voice that in singing became a bellow." He had no formal musical education but was probably self-taught, learning to read from Psalm books that were imported from England and that were available in most churches. He was, however, devoted to the musical education of others and spent many years teaching in the newly formed public singing schools and in local churches. He also wrote lengthy discourses on the philosophy of music, musical fundamentals, and performance practice. These discourses were in the prefaces to his six collections of music—*The New-England Psalm-Singer* published in 1770; *The Singing Master's Assistant, or Key to Practical Music* of 1778 (also known as *Billing's Best,* which was issued in four editions by 1789); *Music in Miniature* of 1779; *The Psalm-Singer's Amusement* of 1781; *The Suffolk Harmony* of 1786; and *The Continental Harmony* of 1794. The first of these publications contains an essay on the nature and properties of sound (probably written by Dr. Charles Stockbridge) and a discussion by Billings of matters such as vocal production, tempo, and meter. It also contains a dictionary of musical terms. In the second publication, Billings wrote a lengthy declaration of music's positive qualities, beginning with a defense of his personal enthusiasm: "That I am a Musical Enthusiast I readily grant, and I think it is impossible for any of its true Votaries to be otherwise; for when we consider the many wonderful effects which music has upon the animal spirits, and upon the nervous system, we are ready to cry out in a fit of enthusiasm!—Great art thou O MUSIC! and with thee there is no competitor."

The musical output of Billings consists of fifty-one fuguing tunes, fifty-two anthems, approximately 230 hymns, and four canons. The fuguing tunes are four-voiced a cappella pieces that begin with a brief homophonic and syllabic section and that end with an extended section of imitative counterpoint in fugal style. According to Billings, "There is more variety in one piece of fuguing music than in twenty pieces of plain song, for while the tones do most sweetly coincide and agree, the words are seemingly engaged in a musical warfare." He continues, describing the imitative texture: "While each part is mutually striving for mastery and sweetly contending for victory, the audience are most luxuriously entertained, and exceedingly delighted. . . . Now the solemn bass demands their attention, now the manly tenor, now the lofty counter, now the volatile treble, now here, now there, now here again." The anthems are similarly constructed, often with several alternating sections of homophony and imitative counterpoint, frequent solo melodic lines (meant for performance by an entire section of singers), changing meters, and varied rhythms.

The hymns, which generally have place names as titles (e.g., Nantucket, Hampshire, Concord, Sudbury, Suffolk, Cambridge, and Andover), are generally short, homophonic, and strophic settings of sacred texts (not associated with the place names of the hymn title), with the main tune in the tenor voice. *Kittery,* perhaps the most famous hymn composed by Billings, is set to a poetic adaptation of the Lord's Prayer. Billings apparently composed the tenor voice first, then added the bass, followed by the soprano and alto. In performance, the soprano and tenor parts were sung by both males and females. Billings stated that a piece "so sung (although it has but four parts) is in effect the same as six. Such a conjunction of masculine and feminine voices is beyond expression sweet and ravishing."

The canons include *Wake ev'ry breath,* subtitled "A Canon of 6 in One with a Ground" and published in the *The New-England Psalm-Singer.* To realize the canon, six voices sing the main tune while a seventh voice continuously repeats the ground bass (to the text "To bless the great redeemer king"). The canon is famous for its engraving by Paul Revere, printed on the front of the collection with the canon scored in a circle around the depiction of a group of singers gathered at a table. Billings's most familiar canon, and without a doubt his most familiar piece of music, is *When Jesus wept,* "A Canon of 4 in 1," from *The New-England Psalm-Singer.*

Two pieces not easily categorized in the above genres demonstrate Billings's humor. The thirteen-measure *Jargon*—set to the text "Let horrid Jargon split the air and rive the nerves asunder: Let hateful discord greet the ear as terrible as thunder"—consists completely of dissonant chords (there is not a consonance in the entire piece). In *Modern music* Billings pokes fun at various compositional procedures and the relationship between performers and audiences, concluding with the poetic lines, "And now we address you as friends to the cause, Performers are modest and write their own laws; Altho' we are sanguine and clap at the bars, 'Tis the part of the hearers to clap their applause."

CANONS AND MISCELLANEOUS WORKS

When Jesus wept – a canon for four voices – approximately 3 minutes.

Wake ev'ry breath – a canon for six voices over a ground bass – approximately 3 minutes.

Modern music – SATB voices a cappella – 3:15 minutes.

Jargon – SATB voices a cappella – 1 minute.

ANTHEMS

I am the rose of Sharon – SATB chorus a cappella – 3:30 minutes.

I am come into my garden – SATB voices a cappella – 4:30 minutes.

An Anthem, for Thanksgiving (Psalm 148 "O praise the Lord of heaven") – SATB voices a cappella – 4 minutes.

Lamentation over Boston – SATB voices a cappella – 6 minutes.

David's lamentation ("David, the king, was grieved and moved") – SATB chorus a cappella – 1 minute.

As the hart panteth – SATB chorus a cappella – 4 minutes.

Retrospect, an Anthem from Sundry Scriptures ("Was not the day dark and gloomy") – SATB voices a cappella – 5 minutes.

The Mariner's Anthem ("They that go down to the sea in ships") – SATB voices a cappella – 4 minutes.

Easter Anthem ("The Lord is ris'n indeed") – SATB voices a cappella – 3 minutes.

HYMNS

Kittery ("Our father, who in heaven art") – SATB chorus a cappella – 3 minutes.

Washington ("Lord, when thou did'st ascend on high") – SATB chorus a cappella – 2 minutes.

America ("To thee the tuneful anthem soars") – SATB chorus a cappella – 2 minutes.

Chester ("Let tyrants shake their iron rod") – SATB chorus a cappella – 2 minutes.

Charleston, An Hymn for Christmas ("While shepherds watch'd their flocks by night") – SATB chorus a cappella – 2 minutes.

Richmond ("My beloved, haste away") – SATB chorus a cappella – 3 minutes.

Corsica ("The Lord almighty is a God") – SATB chorus a cappella – 2 minutes.

SUPPLY BELCHER 1751–1836

Belcher was born in Stoughton (now Sharon), Massachusetts, the son of the town's first physician. The young Belcher was a merchant in Boston during the 1770s, where he sang under William Billings in public singing schools and became interested in the fuguing style of writing, and in 1778 he returned to his hometown and purchased an inn that he turned into a tavern and that became a favorite meeting place for singers. He composed approximately seventy-five choral pieces, most of which were collected in *The Harmony of Maine* published in 1794. Many of the pieces, both sacred and secular, are like hymns by Billings—homophonic and strophic, with the main melody in the tenor voice. Examples include *Cumberland* ("He reigns, the Lord, the savior"), *York* ("Set down that glass, for know ye not the anguish of a drinker's lot"), and *Omega* ("No brandy will we take, we'll rum and gin forsake"). Other pieces, including *Spring* ("The scatt'red clouds are fled at last") and *Advent* ("The Lord descended from above"), are longer and more complex works like Billings's anthems. The *Ordination Anthem* ("Hail, hail, hail, thou king of saints"), Belcher's most elaborate work, is scored for SSATB solos and SATB chorus, with a lengthy section for soprano duet. Its final section is reminiscent of Handel's "Hallelujah" chorus from *Messiah* and earned Belcher the nickname "The Handel of Maine."

DANIEL READ 1757–1836

Read was born in Attleborough, Massachusetts, near Providence, Rhode Island, and worked during his youth as a farmer. After service in the Continental Army, he settled in New Haven, Connecticut, where he operated a general store and made combs. Although a self-taught musician, he published two collections of music, authored a musical treatise (*An Introduction to Psalmody* of 1790), and coedited the first American musical periodical—*The American Musical Magazine*, which was issued in 1786 and 1787. His initial publication, *The American Singing Book* of 1785, was one of the earliest American collections of music devoted entirely to one composer, and his second publication, *The Columbian Harmonist*, was issued in three volumes and contained pieces by Read and other composers. Volume one, published in 1793, contains "new Psalm tunes"; volume two is a combination of popular American and English Psalm tunes; and volume three contains "anthems and set-pieces . . . chiefly new." All three volumes were reprinted in 1805, 1807, and 1810.

5

THE ROMANTIC ERA

The Romantic era began in the 1820s when ideals of elegance changed to those of grandiosity, conventional structures gave way to freer forms, and expressive individuality determined textual selection and treatment. Throughout most of the Classical era, adjectives such as sweet, refined, and graceful were used to characterize musical composition and performance, even when choral ensembles and orchestras were very large. Many primary-source quotations verify this view, including a comment by the French author Marie-Henri Beyle (1793–1842) in his 1817 book (published under the pseudonym César Bombet) about the lives of Mozart and Haydn. Beyle makes reference to an early-nineteenth-century Handel festival concert in Westminster Abbey, stating, "Although 377 stringed instruments accompanied a single voice, such was the lightness of the effect, they did not overpower or incommode it." Large numbers of performers did not necessarily presume loud volumes of sound. However, the majority of composers at the beginning of the Romantic era desired to create imposing and grandiose effects—such as is evident in Berlioz's *Grande messe des morts* and Beethoven's *Missa solemnis* and *Symphony #9*. Composers also desired to create overtly dramatic effects, and, as a result, the dynamic ranges of volume became extreme and the use of numerous expressive markings became commonplace. Indications for very loud volumes were contrasted with those for very soft volumes, and various symbols for articulation and emphasis were employed to vary the scope or compass of dramatic portrayal. In addition, more and more Italian terms were used to indicate precise tempo and expressive intent.

As a further means to manifest dramatic characterizations, composers began to expand upon traditional construction techniques such as sonata, fugue, and ABA configurations, or to forsake these altogether for new forms. The Gloria of Beethoven's *Missa solemnis*, for example, stretches the parameters and adds to the traditional sectional division of this portion of the Roman Mass Ordinary, and the final movement of *Symphony #9* has a coda that is multisectional and of significant proportion. New forms developed from the binding of recitative, aria, and chorus into interconnected and fluid sections of music (such as is exhibited in Robert Schumann's *Das Paradies und die Peri*), and motivic material designed to represent a specific emotion or character was employed throughout a work in the form of leitmotifs. Although Richard Wagner is identified with both the leitmotif term and its usage, he was not the first to employ the technique. Felix Mendelssohn made use of it in his oratorio *Elias,* and many composers such as Sir Edward Elgar used it to create free-formed works unified only by the use of recurring motivic material. New genres include the choral symphony (e.g., Beethoven's *Symphony #9* and Mendelssohn's *Lobgesang*), dramatic symphony (e.g., Berlioz's *Roméo et Juliette*), non-narrative poetic cantata (e.g., Schumann's *Manfred* and Brahms's *Rhapsodie, Schicksalslied,* and *Nänie*), and other unspecified genres such as Beethoven's *Meeresstille und glückliche Fahrt.* In addition, Romantic-era composers treated traditional genres in an entirely individualistic manner. Examples include Requiems by Schumann, Brahms, and Fauré.

The most significant attribute of Romantic-era choral music pertains to literary text used in a personal manner either to explain the musical content of a work or to conform to a composer's specific views about the text. Almost all the French composers of the Romantic era, for instance, wrote explanatory program notes in their choral music. For example, Jean-François Le Sueur fabricated stories and situational contexts for the Mass Ordinary, and Berlioz provided stage directions for his unstaged oratorios. Also, German composers either explained their large-scale symphonic works, as Mahler did in his symphonies, or created their own texts, as Brahms did in his *Ein deutsches Requiem.* Otherwise, it was not uncommon for Romantic-era composers to alter traditional sacred texts. Beethoven, for instance, changed the order of words in several mass movements and also repeated sections of text out of their traditional order, and Fauré used only selected portions of the standard Latin text for his *Requiem.*

While excessive dramatic expression initiated the Romantic era and was evident until the second decade of the twentieth century, many composers throughout the era remained committed to traditional structural forms and objective principles of expression. For example, a number of composers subscribed to the principles of the Cäcilienverein, a movement founded in 1867 by Franz X. Witt (1834–1888) to propagate a cappella works in the style of Palestrina and to limit the instrumental scoring of church music compositions to only organ accompaniment. Other Romantic-era composers looked to the works of Handel, Haydn, and Mozart as models. Thus most of the Romantic era was characterized by two very different aesthetic principles— one progressive and inventive, and the other conservative and backward-looking.

❧ FRANCE ❧

The Conservatoire de Paris served as the major center of compositional activity in France during the Romantic era. Originally founded in 1784 by François-Joseph Gossec as the Ecole Royale de Chant, it was renamed the Institut Nationale de Musique in 1783 and further renamed the Conservatoire Nationale Supérieur de Musique (its present full and official name) in

1795. Virtually all the musicians of the era studied at the Conservatoire, including the major composers Hector Berlioz, Charles Gounod, César Franck, Camille Saint-Saëns, and Gabriel Fauré, and the less significant choral composers Jean-François Le Sueur, Léo Delibes, Théodore Dubois, Georges Bizet, Jules Massenet, Charles-Marie Widor, Vincent d'Indy, and Louis Vierne. Many of these composers entered the Conservatoire when they were children (e.g., Delibes at age eleven and Massenet and Bizet at age nine), and many also went on to serve as professors there. The six students who returned to teach (Franck, Delibes, Dubois, Massenet, Fauré, and Widor) created a significant musical continuum in that generations overlapped and compositional styles and techniques were learned and then passed on.

Other educational institutions were also important. The Ecole Niedermeyer, where Saint-Saëns taught and Fauré studied, was founded in 1853 to train church musicians; the Société Nationale de Musique—which engaged Franck, Saint-Saëns, Dubois, Massenet, Fauré, and d'Indy—was founded in 1871 to promote new French music; and the Schola Cantorum, represented by d'Indy and Vierne, was founded in 1894 to focus on genres other than opera (which at the time predominated at the Conservatoire). In addition to these schools, amateur choral societies, collectively referred to as the Orphéon, were prevalent throughout France and were influential in either commissioning or encouraging works, especially for male voices. Catholic churches in Paris were influential as well. Franck and Dubois served at Ste Clotilde; Saint-Saëns, Dubois, and Fauré worked at La Madeleine; Widor, Fauré, and Vierne were associated with St Suplice; and Vierne was also organist at Notre Dame. Only Berlioz, Massenet, and d'Indy held no church positions.

A significant number of French Romantic composers were also authors. Berlioz and Widor wrote noteworthy orchestration books; Le Sueur, Saint-Saëns, and Dubois wrote philosophical treatises; and d'Indy wrote several biographies of famous composers. Furthermore, Berlioz, Saint-Saëns, and Fauré were music critics for Parisian newspapers or magazines.

The musical genres that were important to the French composers of the Romantic era included masses, motets, oratorios, cantatas, and part songs. The masses, which were composed by all but three of the composers discussed in this section (Bizet, Widor, and d'Indy), are varied in content and style. The liturgical works—those meant for performance as part of a Catholic mass—generally contain six portions of the traditional Ordinary (Kyrie, Gloria, Credo, Sanctus, Benedictus, and Agnus Dei) plus two motets—"O salutaris" and "Domine, salvum." A number of the liturgical masses are also in a neo-Renaissance imitative style, with simple accompaniment for organ. The concert masses are larger-scale works containing only five portions of the Ordinary (the Sanctus and Benedictus combined into one movement), with scoring for soloists, chorus, and orchestra. The Requiems, also concert works, are especially distinctive. Berlioz's *Grande messe des morts* is characteristically Romantic in its monumental orchestral scoring and dramatic expression; Saint-Saëns' *Messe de Requiem,* while orchestral in scoring, is conservative and reflective of past styles; and Fauré's *Requiem* is personal, subdued, and intimate. Le Sueur's masses are unique in that they contain verbal programmatic descriptions.

The oratorio was important during the early years of the era, but not during the later years. For instance, the first nine composers (chronologically) except for Delibes and Bizet composed multiple oratorios, whereas the last four composed none. Coincidentally, most of the composers of oratorios (e.g., Berlioz, Gounod, Saint-Saëns, and Massenet) also composed multiple and significant operas, while the majority of composers who wrote no oratorios also wrote no operas.

Nearly all of the oratorios were titled or called by untraditional terms or genre descriptions, including "trilogie sacrée" (sacred trilogy), "légende dramatique" (dramatic legend), "eglogue biblique" (biblical eclogue or pastoral dialogue), "poème-symphonie" (poetic symphony), and "scène biblique" (biblical scene). These oratorios were also given scenic descriptions and stage directions, although the works were performed with neither set designs nor staging.

The motets are generally simple works set to traditional Latin texts, with homophonic textures and scoring for mixed voices and organ accompaniment; the cantatas, which are mainly settings of revolutionary texts, are either unknown today or considered to be artistically insignificant; and the part songs, most of which were composed for the amateur male singers of the Orphéon societies, range from short uncomplicated pieces to lengthy works calling for virtuosic vocal skills.

JEAN-FRANÇOIS LE SUEUR 1760–1837

Le Sueur was born near Abbeville, northwest of Amiens, and was a chorister at churches in both cities. From ages sixteen to twenty-six he held the position *maître de musique* at various churches and cathedrals in northern and central France, including St Etienne in Dijon, St Julien in Le Mans, St Martin in Tours, and Holy Innocents and Notre Dame in Paris. He became known for his *grands motets,* which were performed frequently by the Concert spirituel between 1782 and 1786, and for his operas and revolutionary hymns, which were composed in the 1790s. From 1795 until 1802 he taught at the Paris Conservatoire, and from 1802 until it was closed in 1830 he was *maître de musique* at the Tuileries Chapel, sharing the position with Luigi Cherubini from 1816 to 1830. Le Sueur taught Hector Berlioz beginning in 1822, and he authored numerous historical and philosophical treatises, including the music history and theory text *Exposé d'une musique imitative et particulière à chaque solennité* in 1787.

Of particular significance was Le Sueur's belief that all music—sacred and secular, vocal and instrumental—should convey specific emotions. He especially felt that all liturgical music should be dramatic and represent or imitate human sentiments. To this end he inserted extensive program notes in his scores—theatrical descriptions of traditional liturgical passages, fictionalized representations of text sung by biblical characters, stage directions in unstaged works, and verbal guides to musical passages.

He composed and published seventeen volumes of church music (many of the volumes containing works in a mixture of genres) and approximately ten hymns on revolutionary poems and odes. The most significant of the sacred works are masses written for special feast days that are oratorio-like, with programmatic overtures, nonliturgical phrases added to the Ordinary, and descriptive program notes. Accompanying the masses for Christmas, Easter, Pentecost, and Assumption, Le Sueur wrote elaborate notes that provide situational contexts of the mass texts and that also assist the listener/worshipper in experiencing the emotions of the texts. In the mass for Christmas, for example, Le Sueur indicates that the passage "Gloria in excelsis Deo, et in terra pax hominibus bonae voluntatis" (Glory to God in the highest, and on earth peace to men of good will) is sung by an angel to shepherds. The shepherds then sing "Laudamus te, benedicimus te" (We praise you, we bless you) as they journey to Bethlehem, and "Adoramus te, glorificamus te" (We worship you, we glorify you) as they see Jesus in the manger. In the mass for Pentecost, the beginning Gloria text is supposedly sung by Jesus' disciples, who sing "Domine Deus, rex coelestis, Deus pater omnipotens" (Lord God, heavenly king, God the father almighty) as a promise to build the Christian Church. In the mass for the Assumption, the apostles, who are "motionless and seized with emotion, bow down while singing 'Adoramus te, glorificamus te.'" In the preface to the mass for the Assumption, Le Sueur explains his perceived connection between masses and oratorios: "My purpose is to force myself to produce the effect that results from an oratorio, which is a species of dramatic poetry."

The other works that Le Sueur variously called masses and oratorios are more oratorio-like. They are structured of recitatives, arias, and choruses, and they generally relate stories based on biblical characters. Examples include *Ruth et Noëmi* and *Ruth et Booz*, which were composed as a sort of cycle for performance on two consecutive Sundays. *Ruth et Noëmi*, based on the first chapter of Ruth, is the story of Naomi's journey with Ruth to Bethlehem from Moab. *Ruth et Booz*, based on the remaining chapters in Ruth plus passages from other Old Testament books, relates the story of Ruth's betrothal to Boaz. Solo roles in the first work are for Naomi (S) and Ruth (S), and in the second work for Ruth (S) and Boaz (T). Both works are scored for choruses that represent various groups of people (i.e., Israelites, shepherds, and harvesters), and both have instrumental accompaniment of two flutes, two oboes, two clarinets, two bassoons, two horns, and strings. Both works also have extensive stage directions, scenic descriptions, and program notes to aid the listener in the dramatic action of the story. Near the end of *Ruth et Noëmi*, for example, the Israelites greet Naomi "and render homage to this woman so beloved, so respected in their country. Naomi, by a courteous gesture, full of goodness, acknowledges their recognition." During the instrumental "March pastorale" in *Ruth et Booz*, "Boaz, in the presence of Naomi, swears by the God of Israel that he will take Ruth for his wife, for all the people of the city to know that she is a young woman filled with virtue."

HECTOR BERLIOZ 1803–1869

Berlioz was born in La Côte-Saint-André, northwest of Grenoble, and received a classical education from his father, a physician. Hector excelled in French and Latin literature and was especially attracted to the works of Virgil and the story of Dido and Aeneas. He did not study music formally, although he became proficient on the flute and guitar, and he learned the rudiments of music theory from reading Rameau's *Traité de l'harmonie*. At about age thirteen he began composing and contemplating a career in music. However, at seventeen he was sent to Paris to study medicine at the Ecole de Médecine. While in Paris he attended the Opéra, where he was impressed by Gluck's *Iphigénie en Tauride*, and he studied scores at the Conservatoire. He also began studying privately with Jean-François Le Sueur. Berlioz graduated with a baccalauréat de sciences physiques in 1824, but deciding against a medical career, he devoted his time to composition, and he earned a living by teaching a few music students, singing in the chorus of the Théâtre des Nouveautés, and writing articles for various newspapers and magazines. In 1826 he formally entered the Conservatoire, continuing his studies there with Le Sueur.

Berlioz's love of literature was rekindled in 1827 when he read Goethe's *Faust* in a French translation and when he attended a performance of Shakespeare's *Hamlet* at the Odéon theater and fell in love with the English actress Harriet Smithson, who played the part of Ophelia. About

Faust, he later wrote in his *Mémoires,* "This marvelous book fascinated me from the first. I could not put it down. I read it incessantly, at meals, at the theater, in the street, everywhere," and about *Hamlet* and Smithson he wrote, "The impression made on my heart and mind by her extraordinary talent, nay her dramatic genius, was equaled only by the havoc wrought in me by the poet she so nobly interpreted. . . . Shakespeare . . . struck me like a thunderbolt. . . . I recognized the meaning of grandeur, beauty, and dramatic truth." Berlioz developed an obsession for Smithson—an "idée fixe"—that was manifested as a recurring melodic motif throughout his most famous symphonic work, the *Symphonie fantastique,* composed in 1830 and subtitled "Épisode de la vie d'un artiste" (Episode in the life of an artist). Each of the symphony's five movements relates a form of Berlioz's obsession, and each movement is headed by a programmatic description. For example, the heading of the first movement, Rêveries – Passions (Musings – Desires), begins, "The artist sees, for the first time, a woman who embodies all his ideals"; the heading of the second movement, Un bal (A ball), includes the phrase "everywhere the beloved's image springs to mind and troubles him greatly"; in the third, Scène aux Champs (Scene in the country), "he reflects on his solitude and hopes that he will not be alone much longer"; in the fourth, Marche au supplice (March to the scaffold), "the artist, convinced that his love is spurned, takes opium, hallucinates, and believes that he has murdered his love and is watching his own execution"; and in the fifth, Songe d'une nuit du sabbat (Dream of a witches' sabbath), he "is surrounded by ghosts, sorcerers, and monsters, all gathered for his funeral." These programmatic descriptions are important to an understanding of the symphony's choral/orchestral sequel, *Lélio, ou le retour à la vie* (Lelio, or the return to life).

In 1828 Berlioz began presenting concerts of his works in Paris, and in 1830 he won the prestigious Prix de Rome, an award given to composition students at the Conservatoire, with the stipulation that they study for two years in Italy. Berlioz stayed in Italy for only fifteen months, living at the Villa Medici in Rome and traveling frequently to Florence. He returned to Paris in 1832, married Harriet Smithson in 1833, and resumed his efforts to gain recognition by presenting concerts of his own music, featuring himself as conductor after 1835. The Parisian audiences were not receptive to him, however, and he had to support his family by writing critiques of other composers' works and by continuing to write miscellaneous literary articles. He also wrote an orchestration treatise, *Grand traité d'instrumentation et d'orchestration modernes,* which was published in 1843. While he was not well received in Paris, his compositions became recognized and received positive critical acclaim in other European cities, and in 1842 he conducted concerts in Brussels, Frankfurt, Stuttgart, Weimar, Leipzig, and Dresden, among others. He met Robert Schumann and Richard Wagner and resumed a friendship with Felix Mendelssohn, whom he had met earlier in Italy, and he established himself as one of the leading composers and conductors of his time. In 1845 he toured throughout France, Austria, and Hungary, and in 1847 he conducted concerts in London. Berlioz finally achieved recognition in Paris during the 1850s with performances of his oratorio *L'enfance du Christ* and his opera *Les Troyens* (based on the Dido and Aeneas story he so loved from his youth), and his final years were spent conducting in Paris and continuing to tour throughout Europe. His life is documented in *Mémoires de Hector Berlioz,* a collection of his diary entries published the year after his death.

Berlioz composed twenty large-scale works for soloists, chorus, and orchestra, and ten works for chorus and piano or organ. In chronological order, the most famous of the large-scale works are *Messe solennelle* (1824), *Huit scènes de Faust* (1828–1829), *Lélio, ou le retour à la vie*

(1831–1832), *Grande messe des morts* (1837), *Roméo et Juliette* (1839), *La damnation de Faust* (1845–1846), *Te Deum* (1849), and *L'enfance du Christ* (1850–1854). Other choral/orchestral works include the revolutionary hymn *Marseillaise* (1845) scored for double chorus and orchestra, and *L'Impériale,* a cantata composed for Napoleon's birthday in 1854 but not performed until 1856.

The *Messe solennelle* was commissioned by the church of St Roch in Paris and first performed there in 1825. A subsequent performance occurred at St Eustache in 1827. Several years later Berlioz supposedly destroyed all copies of the work, along with other works of his youth that he considered inferior. However, a complete copy of the mass was found in 1992 in a church in Antwerp. The *Messe solennelle* is a setting of the five portions of the Roman Mass Ordinary plus three additions—a motet pour l'offertoire (Offertory motet) between the Credo and Sanctus set to the text from Exodus 15, "Quis similes tui, quis in fortibus, Domine" (Who is like unto thee, who compares in strength, Lord); "O salutaris hostia, quae coeli pandas ostium" (O redeeming sacrifice, who opens the gate of heaven) between the Sanctus and Agnus Dei; and "Domine, salvum fac regem nostrum" (O Lord, save our king) at the end of the mass. The last two of these additions were standard in masses composed during the Baroque and Classical eras in France. Themes from the mass are featured prominently in Berlioz's later orchestral works. Most notably, the theme from the Gratias was used in the slow movement of *Symphonie fantastique.*

The *Huit scènes de Faust,* composed shortly after Berlioz had read Goethe's *Faust,* is a collection of eight scenes from the book, each scored for a different combination of voices and instruments and each bearing an epigraph in English from either *Romeo and Juliet* or *Hamlet.* For example, the first scene, "Chants de la fête de Pâques" (Easter hymn), is headed by Ophelia's line from *Hamlet* "Heavenly powers, restore him" and is scored for a chorus of angels and a chorus of disciples. The second scene, "Il paysans sous les tilleuls" (The peasants under the linden trees), is headed by Capulet's line "Who'll now deny to dance? She that makes dainty, I'll swear hath corns" from *Romeo and Juliet* and is scored for soprano solo and a chorus of peasants. As in the case of the *Messe solennelle,* Berlioz gathered together as many copies of the *Huit scènes* he could and burned them. The work had been published in 1829, however, and numerous copies survived.

Lélio, ou le retour à la vie is a sequel or companion piece to *Symphonie fantastique,* designed to be performed directly after the symphony. Berlioz described this sequel as "a *Méloloque* that acts as a continuation of the 'Episode in the life of an artist' and that is to be performed after the symphony as a completion of a concert program." The work, composed between 1831 and 1832 and revised in 1855, features an actor (the artist from *Symphonie fantastique,* now named Lélio) who narrates dialogue in front of a closed curtain before and after each of the work's six movements. Before movement one, entitled "Le pêcheur" (The fisherman), Lélio enters, "feeble and staggering," surprised he is still alive. He wonders if his friend Horatio is aware of his torment, but Horatio is singing his favorite ballad, "Ballade de Goethe" (sung with piano accompaniment behind the curtain). Lélio then ruminates about Hamlet, after which a "Choeur d'ombres" (Chorus of phantoms), also behind the curtain, sings "Froid de la mort, nuit de la tombe, bruit eternal des pas du temps" (Chill of death, night of the tomb, unending sound of time's footsteps). Lélio exclaims his disgust for those who modernize the language of Shakespeare, and with "a brace of pistols, a belt, a carbine, and a sabre" he pretends to join a group of bandits, who sing the "Chanson de brigands" (Song of the brigands). Next, Lélio envisions himself serenading his beloved, and an imaginary voice behind the curtain, to the accompaniment of harp and ten-part strings, sings "O mon donheur, ma vie, mon être tout entire, mon Dieu, mon univers" (Oh my bliss, my life, my whole being, my god, my universe). However, Lélio is sad that he is not with "his Juliet, his Ophelia" (his Harriet), and a harp, with clarinet and strings, plays "La harpe éolienne – Souvenirs" (The Aeolian harp – Memories). Recovering from his sadness, Lélio determines to channel his love for Harriet through music and to compose a fantasy for chorus and orchestra on Shakespeare's *Tempest*. This is performed with the stage curtain open, thus revealing the chorus and orchestra for the first time. After the fantasy, Lélio compliments the performers, the curtain closes, and a solo violin plays the "idée fixe" motif from the *Symphonie fantastique*.

The *Grande messe des morts* (Requiem) was composed as a tribute to the men who died in the Revolution of 1830, but it was actually premiered at a ceremony in December 1837 that honored the death of General Damrémont, who had been killed earlier that year. It is famous for its epic scoring of the "Tuba mirum" (Wondrous trumpet) portion of the Dies Irae, which calls for a very large orchestra plus four brass choirs positioned at the four corners of the performance hall or church. Berlioz specified that each of the brass choirs should consist of four trumpets and four trombones, with the addition of two tubas in one of the choirs and four tubas in another. The main orchestra is scored for an unspecified number of strings plus four flutes, two oboes, two English horns, four clarinets, eight bassoons, twelve horns, four trumpets, four trombones, sixteen timpani, bass drum, four tam-tams, and ten cymbals. However, Berlioz wanted to have the number of players and instruments increased to 120 violins, forty violas, forty-five cellos, thirty-seven string basses, fourteen flutes, twelve oboes, five saxophones, fifteen clarinets, sixteen bassoons, sixteen horns, eighteen trumpets, twelve trombones, three ophicleides, two bass tubas, thirty harps, thirty pianos, and ten sets of timpani, plus the other percussion specified in the score. Balancing these orchestral forces was to be a choir of 360 adult singers and an additional forty children. The scoring for such large forces, including extra instruments at a distance from the main orchestra, was not new. François-Joseph Gossec scored the "Tuba mirum" portion of his Requiem of 1780 (which Berlioz would have known) for a separate ensemble of winds and brass. The grandiose scoring of both composers' Requiems is limited to the "Tuba mirum" and only a few other brief sections; the remaining portions of both works are modestly scored.

The composition of *Roméo et Juliette* was made possible by the famous violinist Niccolò Paganini, who had given Berlioz a large sum of money to support his compositional efforts. The work was conceived as "something splendid and on a grand and original plan, full of passion and imagination, worthy to be dedicated to the glorious artist [Paganini] to whom I owed so much." Berlioz called his composition a "symphonie dramatique" (dramatic symphony), and in the preface to the score he elaborated that it was "neither an opera in concert form nor a cantata, but a symphony with choruses." The choruses were to "prepare the audience for those scenes in which feelings and passions must be expressed by the orchestra" and "to explain the action." The work premiered in November 1839 at the Paris Conservatoire with Berlioz conducting, and attending the concert were many eminent musicians, including Richard Wagner, who said that Berlioz's music opened "a completely new world" for him. The symphony is divided into four major parts, with each part further divided into solo, orchestral, and choral/orchestral movements and with most of these movements headed by scenic descriptions. Part two, for instance, has three movements: "Romeo alone – Sadness – Distant noises of music and dancing – Great feast at the Capulets's"; "Love Scene: Serene night – The Capulets's garden silent and deserted – The young Capulets pass on their way from the ball, singing reminiscences of its music"; and "Scherzo: Queen Mab, or the fairy dream."

La damnation de Faust, composed while Berlioz was on tour during 1845 and 1846, premiered at the Opéra-Comique in Paris on December 6, 1846. The reaction of the audience was dispassionate, prompting Berlioz to note, "Nothing in all my artistic career ever wounded me so deeply as this unexpected indifference. It was a cruel discovery, but useful in the sense that . . . from that time forth I never risked so much as a twenty-franc piece on the popularity of my music with the Parisian public." The work subsequently received high praise in performances throughout Europe, however, with enthusiastic reception in cities such as Berlin, Dresden, Weimar, and Vienna. Berlioz originally called his composition an "opera de concert" (concert opera) but later changed it to "légende dramatique" (dramatic legend). He did not refer to it as an oratorio as he had done with *L'enfance du Christ,* even though it has all the attributes of an oratorio (i.e., a story told through recitatives, solos, and choruses) and is classified as such today. Like *L'enfance du Christ,* it is divided into four large parts, each of which is divided into scenes, although unlike *L'enfance du Christ,* the parts and scenes connect and unfold to create a continuous drama. Part one presents Faust as an old and unhappy man; part two introduces Mephistopheles, who shows Faust the joys of youthful revelry and love; part three brings Faust and his new love Marguerite together; and part four reveals that Mephistopheles has taken Faust away from Marguerite, who is condemned to death for killing her mother and who can be saved only if Faust agrees to serve Mephistopheles forever, which he does.

La damnation de Faust also has scenic descriptions. The beginning of part one, for instance, is on the "plaines de Hongrie" (plains of Hungary), with "Faust seul, dans les champs au lever du soleil" (Faust alone, in the fields at sunrise), and the beginning of part two is in "Nord de l'Allemagne" (North Germany), with "Faust seul dans son cabinet de travail" (Faust alone in his study). Many of the scenes are highly dramatic and atmospheric, including the "Choeur de gnomes et de sylphs" (Chorus of gnomes and sylphs), during which Faust, being lulled to sleep, first sees the image of Marguerite; the orchestral "Menuet des follets" (Dance of the wisps) that charms Marguerite into falling in love with Faust; the descent of Faust and Mephistopheles into hell during "La course à l'abîme" (The ride to the abyss); the chorus of the damned and devils in "Pandaemonium" (Pandemonium), which is set to a text in an imaginary, infernal language (example phrases of which are "Irimiru Karabrao" and "Tradioun Marexil fir Trudinxé burrudixé"); and the "Choeur d'esprits célestes" (Chorus of celestial spirits), during which Marguerite ascends into heaven. The oratorio represents Berlioz at the peak of his compositional powers and is considered to be one of the great masterpieces of the genre.

The *Te Deum* premiered at the church of St Eustache in Paris in April 1855. Like the Requiem, it is scored for large forces (Berlioz idealized twelve harps and six hundred children in addition to four flutes, two oboes, two clarinets, four bassoons, four horns, four trumpets, three trombones, ophicleide, tuba, timpani, extra percussion, and organ). As described by Berlioz, the organ "at one end of the church answers the orchestra and choirs at the other, [like the] pope and emperor speaking in dialogue from opposite ends of the nave." The entire work is divided into seven movements, the final of which is an orchestral "March pour la presentation de drapeaux" (March for the presentation of the colors). Berlioz subtitled the choral/vocal movements, giving the portions of text a genre heading: three movements (Te Deum laudamus, Tibi omnes angeli, and Christe rex gloriae) are called hymns, two (Dignare, Domine and Te ergo quaesumus) are called prayers, and Judex crederis is called a hymn and prayer.

L'enfance du Christ, subtitled a "trilogie sacrée" (sacred trilogy) but called an oratorio by Berlioz, was composed over a period of time. A short strophic choral piece entitled *L'adieu des bergers à Sainte Famille* (The farewell of the shepherds to the Holy Family) was written and performed in 1850. Later that year Berlioz added an overture and a piece entitled *Le repos de la Sainte Famille* (The resting of the Holy Family) and conducted the three-movement work at the Gewandhaus in Leipzig in 1853. The following year he framed the three-movement work with other pieces, called scènes, to complete the oratorio *L'enfance du Christ.* Derived from the original strophic choral piece, the entire work is about the massacre of the Holy Innocents by King Herod and the flight of the Holy Family to Egypt. It is divided into three parts—"Le songe d'Hérode" (Herod's dream), "La fuite en Egypt" (The flight to Egypt), and "L'arrivée à Saïs" (The arrival at Sais)—and each of these parts is headed by a scenic description (e.g., "The shepherds assemble before the manger of Bethlehem," "The shepherds bid farewell to the Holy Family," and "The Holy Family resting at the way-side"). Berlioz noted the following logistical comment in the preface to the work: "During the whole of the first part, the male choristers are to stand alone on one side of the stage in sight of the public, while the sopranos and altos stand behind the stage by an organ. At the beginning of the second part, they [sopranos and altos] are to take their places on the stage opposite the men, with the exception of four sopranos and four altos, who are to remain behind the stage to the end to sing the Amen," which occurs at the conclusion of the oratorio's final chorus, "O mon âme."

The well-known small-scale choral works, those with piano or organ accompaniment, include *Le ballet des ombres* (The dance of the ghosts) and *La mort d'Ophélie* (The death of Ophelia). *Le ballet des ombres* is subtitled "Ronde nocturne" (night roundelay or midnight revel) and was headed by the Shakespeare lines, "Tis now the very witching night, when churchyards yawn, and hell itself breathes out contagion to this world." The music is characterized by atmospheric portamentos in the choral parts and eerie-sounding melodic figures in the piano part. *La mort d'Ophélie,* subtitled "Ballade d'après Shakespeare" (Ballade after Shakespeare), also has an atmospheric piano part—one that depicts the rippling water that becomes Ophelia's grave.

CHORAL/ORCHESTRAL WORKS
SELECTED AND LISTED ACCORDING TO FAMILIARITY

La damnation de Faust – 1845–1846 – ATBB solos, SSATTBB chorus, and orchestra (including three piccolos that double three flutes, two English horns that double two oboes, bass clarinet, four bassoons, numerous percussion instruments, and eight to ten harps that play from one part) – 128 minutes. (1) Solo roles are for Faust (T), Mephistopheles (B), Marguerite (A), and Brander (B); (2) the full chorus represents peasants, Christians at Easter celebration, gnomes and sylphs, and celestial spirits; (3) the men of the chorus portray drunkards, soldiers and students, and demonic and damned souls; (4) Berlioz calls for a children's chorus ad lib. in the final movement.

Grande messe des morts (Requiem) – 1837 – T solo, SSTTBB chorus, and orchestra – 83 minutes. (1) The second soprano choral parts are generally sung by altos; (2) see the discussion above for a complete listing of instrumentation.

L'enfance du Christ – 1850–1854 – STTBBBB solos, SSAATTBB chorus, and orchestra – 95 minutes. (1) Solo roles are for a Narrator (T), Mary (S), Joseph (B), Herod (B), the commander of Herod's night patrol Polydorus (B), a Centurion (T), and the Father of an Ishmaelite family (B); (2) the chorus portrays Herod's Soothsayers (TTBB), Angels (SSAA), Shepherds (SATB), Romans (B), Egyptians (BB), and Ishmaelites (SATB); (3) the oratorio ends with an a cappella chorus, "O mon âme" (Oh my soul), which is often extracted and performed separately; (4) the oratorio's first-composed choral movement, "L'adieu des bergers à Sainte Famille" (The farewell of the shepherds to the Holy Family), is also frequently extracted and performed separately.

Te Deum – 1849 – T solo, SATB/SATB/SA chorus, and orchestra – 50 minutes. (1) The tenor soloist sings only briefly in one movement; (2) the SATB choruses are to consist of adult singers, while the SA chorus is to consist of children; (3) see the discussion above for details of orchestration.

Roméo et Juliette – 1839 – ATB solos, SSATTB chorus, and orchestra – 130 minutes. (1) The soloists do not portray roles but instead comment on dramatic action; (2) the second soprano choral parts are generally sung by altos; (3) the chorus divides into a semichorus (ATB), a double chorus of men (each scored for TBB), and a double chorus (each scored for STB) representing the Capulets and Montagues.

Messe solennelle – 1824 – STB solos, SATB chorus, and orchestra – 53 minutes. (1) The work begins with an orchestral prelude; (2) the Gloria is divided into three movements and the Credo into four; (3) the orchestration calls for tam-tam (which Berlioz himself played in the premiere performance), buccin (a military trombone), serpent (an instrument commonly used during the time to accompany chant in churches), and ophicleide (a predecessor of the tuba).

Lélio, ou le retour à la vie – 1831–1832 – speaker, TB solos, SATB chorus, and orchestra (including piccolo, English horn, four trumpets, harp, and piano four hands) – 50 minutes. (1) The soloists, chorus, and orchestra perform behind a closed curtain until the final movement of the work; (2) movement three is scored for TTBB chorus, and movement six for SSATT; (3) the orchestral strings divide into ten and eleven parts in movements four and five, respectively.

SMALL-SCALE WORKS
SELECTED AND LISTED ACCORDING TO FAMILIARITY

Le ballet des ombres – 1828 – SATB chorus and piano – 3 minutes.

La mort d'Ophélie – 1848 – SA chorus and piano – 3:30 minutes. The alto divides briefly into two parts.

Tantum ergo – date unknown – SSA solos, SSA chorus, and organ – 3 minutes.

Le chant des Bretons (version one) – 1835 – TTBB chorus and piano –
   2:30 minutes.

Chant guerrier – 1829 – T solo, TBB chorus, and piano – 3 minutes.

Chanson à boire – 1829 – T solo, TB chorus (with occasional divisions to
   TBB and TTB), and piano – 3 minutes.

L'apothéose ("Chant héroïque") – 1848 – S or T solo, SATTBB chorus, and
   piano – 3 minutes.

CHARLES-FRANÇOIS GOUNOD 1818–1893

Gounod was born in Paris, where his father, François-Louis, was a successful painter and en-
graver and his mother, Victoire, a pianist. Charles-François received a classical education and
did not become interested in or study music until he was a teenager; he attended his first opera
at age thirteen and began taking composition lessons privately from Antoine Reicha at sixteen.
With the death of Reicha in 1836, Gounod entered the Paris Conservatoire, studying with Fromental Halévy and Jean-François Le Sueur, among others, and winning the Prix de Rome with
his cantata *Fernand* in 1839. During his two years in Italy (a stipulation of the Prix de Rome) he
became acquainted with the music of Palestrina, which he admired greatly, and with Fanny
Hensel (sister of Felix Mendelssohn), who introduced him to the keyboard music of her brother
and J. S. Bach. During his year in Austria and Germany (another stipulation of the Prix de Rome)
he met and heard some of the orchestral music of Mendelssohn, and upon returning to Paris in
1843, he was appointed *maître de chapelle* at the church of the Séminaire des Missions Etrangères.
Gounod remained in this position until 1848, after which he composed independently for three
years, and in 1851 he was appointed director of vocal instruction for the public schools of Paris and
also director of the Paris Orphéon, the main amateur choral society in France at the time. During
the early 1850s he met Georges Bizet and Camille Saint-Saëns, whose careers he promoted, and
in 1859 he had his first operatic success with performances of *Faust* at the Paris Opéra. His next
successful opera, *Roméo et Juliette*, was produced by the Théâtre-Lyrique in 1867. Interestingly,
these two operas have librettos based on the favorite subjects of Hector Berlioz.

Gounod moved to London in 1870 to avoid the Franco-Prussian War, and after the successful performance of his motet *Gallia* for the opening of the International Exposition at Royal Albert Hall in 1871, he was appointed director of the newly formed Royal Albert Hall Choral Society. He returned to Paris in 1874 and composed more operas, and he revisited England in 1882
to conduct *La rédemption* and in 1885 to conduct *Mors et vita*—both oratorios commissioned by
the Birmingham Festival and both well received and highly acclaimed. After *La rédemption*, the
British public referred to Gounod as the successor to Handel and Mendelssohn, and after the
premiere of *Mors et vita*, Queen Victoria ordered a special performance held in Royal Albert Hall.
During the last years of his life Gounod returned to the composition of liturgical music reflective of the works by Palestrina that he had admired during his years in Italy. Of particular merit
are a Requiem and two masses based on Gregorian chants, all scored for chorus and organ
accompaniment.

Gounod composed twenty-one masses (including four Requiems), three oratorios, approximately seventy-five Latin motets, twenty-one small-scale sacred pieces in French and English, and twenty-six secular part songs. Most of the masses, especially those composed early and late in his life, are modest works scored for chorus a cappella or chorus and organ. The *Messe brève et salut,* composed in 1846 while Gounod was *maître de chapelle* at the church of the Séminaire des Missions Etrangères, is scored for men's voices a cappella, with a texture that is basically homophonic. It contains all five portions of the Ordinary, each set in a single movement, plus the motet "O salutaris hostia" between the Sanctus and Agnus Dei, and the standard closing to most French liturgical masses, "Domine, salvum." The mass was retitled *Messe #2* "aux sociétés" in 1862 and rescored with an organ part ad lib. (the part basically doubles the vocal parts). The *Messe brève #6,* subtitled "aux cathédrales," and the *Messe brève #7,* subtitled "aux chapelles," were both composed in about 1890. These latter masses contain the motet "O salutaris hostia." However, they have no Credo movements because the Credo was generally sung as a Gregorian chant during liturgical services.

The masses composed during the mid-part of Gounod's career are larger-scale works scored for soloists, chorus, and orchestra. The most famous is the *Messe solennelle de Sainte Cécile,* composed for the church of St Eustache in Paris and premiered there on St Cecilia's Day, November 22, 1855. Being a concert work, not intended to be sung during regular liturgical services, it contains no "O salutaris hostia" or "Domine, salvum." However, it does have an organ "Offertory" before the Sanctus. The five portions of the Ordinary plus the Benedictus are all set in single movements, with the Gloria and Credo divided into three sections (fast, slow, fast). The solo writing consists of brief melodic passages and trios, and the choral textures are almost exclusively homophonic. The *Messe du Sacré-Coeur de Jésus,* composed in 1876, is similar in scoring, structure, and texture, although it contains much less writing for the soloists, and the organ "Offertory" is replaced by an orchestral "La Communion."

The first oratorio, *Tobie,* was composed in 1865 and premiered in Lyons with Gounod conducting. The second and third oratorios, as is mentioned above, were commissioned and premiered by the Birmingham Festival in 1882 and 1885. Like Haydn's *Die Schöpfung,* the works were set to a libretto in the composer's native language and translated into English for performance and publication, and like *L'enfance du Christ* by Berlioz, the works were called sacred trilogies instead of oratorios. Other Haydn and Berlioz connections include an overture to *La rédemption* that Gounod calls "The Creation . . . descriptive of Chaos" (similar to the overture in Haydn's *Die Schöpfung*), and scenic descriptions at the beginnings of both oratorios' major sections and movements (similar to Berlioz's descriptions in *L'enfance du Christ* and other oratorios).

La rédemption is unique for the time in being structurally and musically unified: the work begins with a prologue that is divided into three sections; the main body of the work is divided into three large parts, each of which is further divided into six movements (three plus three); and a musical motif is heard three times in the prologue and three times each in part one and part two. As an explanation for the number *three* and as a description of the oratorio's three parts, Gounod comments, "This work is a lyrical setting of the three great facts on which depend the existence of the Christian Church: (1) The Passion and the Death of the Savior; (2) His glorious life on earth from His Resurrection to His Ascension; and (3) The spread of Christianity in the world through the mission of the Apostles." Gounod further describes the three sections of the prologue as "the Creation, the Fall of our first parents, and the promise of a Redeemer."

As examples of Gounod's scenic descriptions and other unifying organizational structures, the six movements of part one (which Gounod notes are "linked together so as to form a single musical series") carry the headings: "an instrumental march representing the brutality of the pagan force dragging Jesus to execution"; "a lamentation . . . representing Christian compassion," which is based on the Gregorian chant *Vexilla Regis prodeunt* (forth the royal banners go); a "resumption of the instrumental march"; a lamentation sung by the "Holy Women on seeing Jesus fall under the weight of the Cross"; "Words of Jesus to the Holy Women"; and the second "resumption of the instrumental march." The form of this first movement of part one is therefore ABABA.

Mors et vita, a sequel to *La rédemption,* is similarly structured. Musical motifs unify the entire work, and explanatory notes and scenic descriptions are provided in the oratorio's preface and libretto. In terms of explanation, Gounod states that "the essential features" of the work are "the tears which death causes us to shed here below; the hope of a better life; the solemn dread of unerring Justice; and the tender and filial trust in eternal Love." Descriptions are basically limited to titles such as "Requiem," "The Sleep of the Dead," and "The Vision of Saint John," which occur as headings of the oratorio's major parts.

Other miscellaneous sacred works include the motet *Gallia,* with text from Lamentations divided into four movements ("Quomodo sedet sola," "Viae Sion lugent," "O vos omnes," and "Vide, Domine, affictionem meam"); *Les sept paroles de N. S. Jésus-Christ sur la croix* (The seven last words of Jesus on the cross), composed in 1858 and set in one movement divided into seven sections; and a *Magnificat* composed in 1874 and modeled after English Renaissance settings in *alternatim* style (Gounod alternates verses for soprano solo with verses for the chorus).

MASSES
SELECTED AND LISTED ACCORDING TO FAMILIARITY

Messe solennelle de Sainte Cécile – STB solos, SATB chorus, and orchestra (including harp and organ) – 43 minutes. The choral parts occasionally divide into SATTBB.

Messe du Sacré-Coeur de Jésus – SATB solos, SATB chorus, and orchestra – 30 minutes. (1) The soloists, as a quartet, sing only in the Sanctus; (2) the choral parts occasionally divide into SATTBB.

Messe brève #6 in G major ("aux cathédrales") – SATB chorus and organ – 15 minutes.

Messe brève #7 in C major ("aux chapelles") – TB solos, SATB chorus, and organ – 14 minutes.

Messe brève #5 in C major ("aux séminaires") – TBB solos, TBB chorus, and organ – 16 minutes.

Messe brève #4 in C major ("à la Congrégation") – SA solos, SA chorus, and organ – 12 minutes.

Messe brève #2 in G major ("aux sociétés") – TTBB chorus and organ – 12 minutes.

ORATORIOS
SELECTED AND LISTED ACCORDING TO FAMILIARITY

La rédemption – SSSAATTTBBB solos, SATB chorus, and orchestra – 140 minutes. (1) Major solo roles are for Narrators (T and B) and Jesus (B); (2) minor solo roles are for Mary (S), the Impenitent Thief (B), the Penitent Thief (T), the Three Holy Women at the Sepulchre (SAA), an Angel (T), and a Voice from Heaven (S); (3) the chorus represents the Crowd (SATB), Priests (TB), Guards (TB), Priests of Sanhedrin (TT), Apostles (TB and SATB), Lamenting Women (S), and a Celestial Choir (SATB).

Mors et vita – SATB solos, SATB chorus, and orchestra – 150 minutes. (1) There is only one solo role, for Jesus (B); (2) other solo writing is for SATB quartet; (3) the chorus divides into SATB/SATB for one short movement, SSAATTBB for another short movement, and occasionally SSATTB in other movements.

MISCELLANEOUS SACRED WORKS
SELECTED AND LISTED ACCORDING TO FAMILIARITY

Gallia – S solo, SATB chorus, and orchestra – 15 minutes.

Les sept paroles de N. S. Jésus-Christ sur la croix – SATB solos and SATB chorus a cappella – 15 minutes.

Noël (subtitled "Chant des Religieuses") – SA solos, SSA chorus, and organ – 5 minutes.

Bethléem (subtitled "Pastorale sur un Noël du 18 siècle") – SATB chorus and organ – 4:15 minutes.

Pater noster – SATB chorus and organ – 4:30 minutes.

Magnificat – S solo, SATB chorus, and organ – 5 minutes.

Te Deum – SATB solos, SATB chorus, two harps, and organ – 21 minutes.

CÉSAR FRANCK 1822–1890

Franck was born in Liège, Belgium, where he began studies at the Liège Conservatoire at age eight. At thirteen he began to perform as a piano recitalist, at fifteen he enrolled at the Paris Conservatoire, and for the next eight years he composed instrumental pieces and continued touring as a virtuoso pianist—performing a concert in 1837 with Franz Liszt. In 1846 he taught privately and in the public schools of Paris, and during the next ten years he served as organist at several Parisian churches, including Notre Dame de Lorette in 1847, St Jean-St François in 1851, and Ste Clotilde in 1858. He held this latter position for the remainder of his life (thirty-two years) while also serving as the organ instructor at the Paris Conservatoire beginning in 1872. He was highly respected as both an organist and a composer and was awarded the Légion d'Honneur in 1885.

Franck composed one mass (another is scored for only bass solo and organ), five oratorios, four cantatas, and approximately twenty motets. The mass, *Messe à 3 voix* op.12 (sometimes called *Messe solennelle*), was composed in 1860. Like the concert masses of Gounod, it is scored mostly for chorus in a homophonic texture, and the Gloria and Credo are in single movements divided into three sections (fast, slow, fast).

The first oratorio, *Ruth,* was composed in 1845 and subtitled "églogue biblique" (biblical eclogue or pastoral dialogue). The premiere performance at the Paris Conservatoire in 1846 was unsuccessful, but a revised version performed in 1871 was well received by the Parisian public. Nothing is known about the second oratorio, *La tour de Babel,* subtitled a "petit oratorio" and composed in 1865. The third oratorio, *Rédemption,* was composed between 1871 and 1872 and premiered in 1873 by the newly formed Concert National. Subtitled a "poème-symphonie" (poetic symphony), it is divided into three parts in the manner of oratorios by Berlioz and Gounod. Part one deals with the contemplation of Christ's birth, part two is an orchestral representation of Christ's good deeds, and part three is a reflection on humankind's sins and the hope of redemption through prayer. The premiere performance was even less successful than that of *Ruth.* The performers were inadequately prepared and openly restive, and the conductor, Eduard Colonne, omitted the oratorio's second part. Two of Franck's students at the time, Henri Duparc and Vincent d'Indy, convinced the composer to revise the work, which he did in 1874, and it was subsequently performed to critical acclaim.

Franck's fourth oratorio, *Les béatitudes,* was composed over the ten-year span between 1869 and 1879 and first performed in Franck's apartment in February 1879 with piano accompaniment. The first performance with orchestra was in Dijon in June 1891, the year after Franck's death, and the first performance in Paris was in 1893. The oratorio consists of a prologue and eight movements—the prologue relating the generally sinful state of the world at the time of Christ, and the eight movements relating specific evils to their corresponding beatitudes from the Sermon on the Mount (Matthew 5:3–10). Each beatitude is quoted as a heading to its parallel movement (e.g., "Blessed are the poor in spirit, for theirs is the kingdom of Heaven" at the beginning of movement one), and each beatitude is sung in the movement by the Voice of Jesus, either as a direct biblical quote or as a paraphrase. In addition, all but one of the movements has a Celestial Chorus that either relates the sin or reiterates the beatitude. Like Gounod's *La rédemption,* Franck's oratorio is unified by musical motifs. An eight-measure melody represents Christ and is heard in total or in part in all the movements, and a shorter melody represents Satan and is heard in the final two movements. Nothing is known about the fifth oratorio, *Rébecca,* called a "scène biblique" and composed in 1881.

The cantata *Les sept paroles du Christ au croix* (The seven words of Christ on the cross) was composed in 1859 but never performed during Franck's lifetime. Furthermore, it remained unknown until 1955, when an autograph score was sold by a private owner to the University of Liège. Its structure is like that of *Les béatitudes,* with a prologue followed by movements that relate sayings of Jesus. However, *Les sept paroles* has no dramatic action and no interaction between soloists and chorus. Instead, the work is structured as a cantata, with some movements scored for soloists, some for chorus, and some for soloists and chorus. Each of the movements is unique in scoring and structure. For instance, the prologue, set to the text "O vos omnes," is for soprano solo alone; word one, "Pater, dimitte illis, non enim sciunt quid faciunt" (Father, forgive them, for they know not what they do), is for chorus alone; word two, "Hodie mecum eris in paradiso" (Today you will be with me in paradise), is for TT duet; word three, "Mulier, ecce filius tuus" (Woman, see your son), is for chorus and ST duet in ABA form; word four, "Deus meus, ut quid dereliquisti me" (My God, why have you forsaken me), is chorale-like for chorus alone; word five, "Sitio" (I thirst), is for bass solo and chorus in ABAB form; word six, "Consummatum est" (It is finished), is for chorus and tenor soloist in ABA form; and word seven, "Pater, in manus tuas commendo spiritum meum" (Father, into your hands I commend my spirit), is for tenor soloist with chorus. Most of the words are augmented by other sacred texts (e.g., passages from the Stabat mater with word three).

The most famous of the motets, *Panis angelicus,* was originally composed for solo tenor, with harp, cello, bass, and organ accompaniment but was arranged in the twentieth century for tenor and chorus with varying accompaniments. The text—"Panis angelicus, fit panis hominum, dat panis coelicus figures terminum. O res mirabilis manducat Dominum, pauper, servus, et humilis" (Bread of angels, becomes bread of men, the heavenly bread superseding that of men. O marvelous thing, that a poor man, a slave, and humble one can ingest the Lord)—comes from the sixth stanza of the hymn "Sacris solemnis" by St Thomas Aquinas.

Other motets include *Psaume CL* (Psalm 150) composed in 1883 for the dedication of a new organ at the Paris Institut des Jeunes Aveugles (Institute for the Young Blind), *Quare fremuerunt gentes* (Psalm 2) in 1871 for the feast of Ste Clotilde, and *Quae est ista* composed in 1871 for the feast of the Assumption.

SACRED WORKS
SELECTED AND LISTED ACCORDING TO FAMILIARITY

Les béatitudes – SSATBB solos, SATB chorus, and orchestra – 130 minutes. (1) There is only one major solo role, the Voice of Jesus (B); (2) minor solo roles are for an unnamed tenor in the prologue; a Mother (A), an Orphan (S), a Wife (S), and a Husband (T) in beatitude three; an unnamed tenor in beatitude four; the same tenor and an Angel of Mercy (S) in beatitude five; an Angel of Death in beatitude six; Satan (B) and a quintet of Peacemakers (SATBB) in beatitude seven; and Satan (B) and Mater Dolorosa (S) in beatitude eight; (3) the chorus portrays a Celestial Chorus in most of the beatitudes, plus Slaves, Thinkers, and Priests (TB), Pagan and Jewish Women (SA), and Tyrants (B); (4) the chorus "Le ciel est loin" (Heaven is far away) from movement two is well known and occasionally extracted and performed separately.

Les sept paroles du Christ au croix – STTB solos, SATB chorus, and orchestra – 45 minutes. The chorus divides into SAATB in movement one.

Messe à 3 voix – STB solos, STB chorus, and orchestra – 46 minutes. (1) The original orchestration was reduced to harp, cello, bass, and organ in an arrangement made by Franck in 1861; (2) most published editions of the mass include the solo motet *Panis angelicus* between the Sanctus and Agnus Dei.

Psaume CL (Psalm 150 "Halleluiah, louez le Dieu caché dans ses saints tabernacles") – SATB chorus and orchestra – 5 minutes.

Quare fremuerunt gentes (Psalm 2) – B solo, SATB chorus, strings, and organ – 4 minutes.

Quae est ista – SATB chorus, harp, cello, bass, and organ – 7 minutes.

CAMILLE SAINT-SAËNS 1835–1921

Saint-Saëns was born in Paris, where he began studying piano with an aunt at age three. At ten he made his formal public debut as a performer in a concert of the Beethoven *Piano Concerto* in C minor op.37 and the Mozart *Piano Concerto* in B-flat major K450, both of which he played from memory. At thirteen he enrolled at the Paris Conservatoire, studying composition with Fromental Halévy and analyzing the works of Bach, Handel, and Mozart, and during the next several years he became personally acquainted with some of the well-known composers living in Paris, including Rossini, Berlioz, Gounod, and Liszt. In 1853 he was appointed organist at the church of St Merry, and four years later he assumed the same post at La Madeleine. In 1861, while remaining at La Madeleine, he began teaching at the Ecole Niedermeyer, where one of his students was Gabriel Fauré, and in 1867 his cantata *Les noces de Prométhée* won first prize in a competition sponsored by the Grande Fête Internationale du Travail et de l'Industrie and judged by Berlioz, Gounod, Rossini, and Verdi. Saint-Saëns began championing the music of Liszt and Schumann, and in 1871 he and his friend Romain Bussine founded the Société Nationale de Musique, whose mission was to promote new music.

Saint-Saëns also wrote numerous articles for such publications as the *Gazette musicale* and *Revue bleue,* and he continued performing as a virtuoso pianist. In the 1880s and 1890s he toured cities in Europe, South America, Scandinavia, and Russia and was acclaimed as one of the greatest performers and composers of his time. In 1893, after conducting a concert performance (in the manner of an oratorio) of his opera *Samson et Dalila* at Covent Garden in London, he was awarded an honorary doctorate from Cambridge University (Oxford University awarded him an honorary doctorate in 1907). In 1900 he was made a Grand Officier of the Légion d'Honneur, and in 1901 he became president of the Académie des Beaux-Arts. He continued touring, giving concerts in Philadelphia, Chicago, and Washington, D.C., in 1906, and in New York City and San Francisco in 1915. During the final years of his life he concentrated on writing his memoirs and articles about the aesthetics of music. In *Ecole buissonnière: notes et souvenirs* of 1913 he wrote, "Music is something besides a source of sensuous pleasure and keen emotion. . . . He who does not derive absolute pleasure from a simple series of well-constructed chords, beautiful only in their arrangement, is not really fond of music."

Saint-Saëns composed two masses (one of which is a Requiem), four oratorios, approximately twenty motets for chorus, and forty secular cantatas and part songs. The *Messe à quatre voix* op.4 was composed in 1855 while Saint-Saëns was organist at the church of St Merry. Like most large-scale French masses of the time, it is scored for soloists, chorus, and orchestra (with harp and organ), and the Gloria and Credo are composed as a single movement. Unlike most concert or symphonic masses, however, it contains the motet "O salutaris hostia" between the Sanctus and Agnus Dei. Saint-Saëns's mass is distinctive also in several other respects: the choral writing contains imitative passages, especially in the Kyrie; there are occasional short recitative passages for both vocal and instrumental soloists; the Credo is in one tempo throughout; the Benedictus is entirely orchestral; and the mass closes with an extended orchestral postlude. The *Messe de Requiem* op.54, composed in 1878 and also scored for soloists, chorus, and orchestra, is divided into eight movements—Requiem and Kyrie, Dies irae, Rex tremendae, Oro supplex, Hostias, Sanctus, Benedictus, and Agnus Dei—all of which involve the chorus. The soloists are frequently scored as a quartet that is in double chorus-like dialogue with the chorus, and the text is frequently fragmented into short phrases separated by orchestral passages (this is especially so in the Dies irae). Although the vocal/choral writing contains some imitative passages, most of the choral textures are homophonic.

The most famous of the oratorios, *Oratorio de Noël* op.12, was composed in twelve days while Saint-Saëns was organist at La Madeleine, and it premiered there on Christmas Day 1858. The work, which is modeled on the second portion of J. S. Bach's *Oratorium tempore Nativitatis Christi* BWV248 (Christmas Oratorio), begins with an instrumental prelude subtitled "Dans le style de Séb. Bach" (In the style of Sebastian Bach) and continues with vocal/instrumental movements that are cantata-like in structure. Only the first movement—which begins with the biblical passage from Luke 2:8, "Et pastores errant in regione eadem vigilantes" (And in the same region there were shepherds keeping vigil) and ends with verse fourteen, "Gloria in altissimis Deo, et in terra pax hominibus bonae voluntatis" (Glory to God in the highest, and on earth peace to men of good will)—conveys a story through dramatic dialogue. The other movements are settings of biblical texts that reflect on the Christmas story—"Expectans expectavi Dominum" (I waited patiently for the Lord) from Psalm 40:1; "Domine, ego credidi, quia tu es Christus" (Lord, I have believed that you are the Christ) from John 11:27; "Benedictus qui venit in nomine Domini" (Blessed is he who comes in the name of the Lord) from Psalm 118:26–28; "Quare fremuerunt gentes et populi meditati sunt inania" (Why do the nations rage and the people think vain thoughts) from Psalm 2:1; "Tecum principium in die virtutis tuae, in splendoribus sanctorum" (With you is sovereignty in the splendor of holiness on the day of your birth) from Psalm 110:3; "Laudate coeli, et exulta terra" (Praise, heavens, and exult, earth) from Isaiah 49:13; Consurge, filia Sion" (Rise, daughter of Zion) from Lamentations 2:19; and "Tollite hostias, et adorate Dominum in atrio sancto ejus" (Bring offerings and worship the Lord in his holy habitation) from Psalm 96:9–13. In addition, like Gounod's *Les sept paroles du Christ au croix*, the movements are set numbers variously scored for soloists, chorus, or soloists and chorus; there are no recitatives.

The other oratorios are *Les Israëlites sur la montagne d'Oreb* composed in about 1848; *Le déluge* op.45 composed in 1875; and *The promised land* op.140 commissioned by the English publisher Vincent Novello and premiered in 1913 at the Three Choirs Festival in Gloucester Cathedral. This latter oratorio, originally set to an English text taken from Numbers, Deuteronomy, and Psalms, is scored for a Narrator (T and A), Moses (B), Aaron (T), unnamed soloists (SATB), chorus (SATB/SATB), and orchestra. The writing, especially for chorus, is reflective of Handel's *Israel in Egypt*.

Most of the motets are short simple pieces composed for the limited vocal resources at the churches of St Merry and La Madeleine, and most of the part songs were composed for the singers in one of the many choral societies of the Orphéon. The motet *Ave verum* in E-flat major, in an AABB format, is entirely homophonic except for a brief imitative Amen. The part song *Calme des nuits* op.68 no.1, considered by many to be one of the most beautiful secular settings of the Romantic era in France, is also mostly homophonic. The part songs for men's voices are generally substantial compositions that testify to the high level of amateur singing in France during the latter years of the Romantic era.

SACRED WORKS
SELECTED AND LISTED ACCORDING TO FAMILIARITY

Oratorio de Noël op.12 – (generally called the "Christmas Oratorio") – SSATB solos, SATB chorus, strings, harp, and organ – 40 minutes.

Messe à quatre voix op.4 – SATB solos, SATB chorus, and orchestra – 43 minutes.

Messe de Requiem op.54 – SATB solos, SATB chorus, and orchestra – 38 minutes. The choral parts occasionally divide into SSAATTBB.

Ave verum corpus in D major – SSAA chorus and organ – 3:30 minutes.

Ave verum corpus in E-flat major – SATB chorus and organ – 3 minutes.

Tantum ergo – SSAATTBB chorus and organ – 3 minutes.

Veni creator spiritus – TTBB chorus and organ – 3 minutes.

SECULAR WORKS
SELECTED AND LISTED ACCORDING TO FAMILIARITY

Calme des nuits op.68 no.1 – SATB chorus a cappella – 4 minutes.

Les fleurs et les arbres op.68 no.2 – SATB chorus a cappella – 2 minutes.

Saltarelle op.74 – TTBB chorus a cappella – 5:30 minutes.

Aux aviateurs op.134 – TTBB chorus a cappella – 8 minutes.

Aux mineurs op.137 – TTBB chorus a cappella – 8:30 minutes.

Sérénade d'hiver – TTBB chorus a cappella – 6:15 minutes.

Hymne au printemps – TTBB chorus a cappella – 8 minutes.

LÉO DELIBES 1836–1891

Delibes was born in St Germain du Val in western France, and received his earliest musical instruction from his mother and an uncle. At age eleven he began studying at the Paris Conservatoire and also began singing as a chorister at La Madeleine, and at thirteen he began singing as a chorister at the Paris Opéra. At seventeen he was appointed organist at the church of St Pierre-de-Chaillot and accompanist at the Théâtre Lyrique, and at twenty he wrote the first of his many comic operettas. During the 1860s he was chorusmaster at the Théâtre Lyrique, preparing vocal ensembles for such operas as Gounod's *Faust*, Bizet's *Les pêcheurs de perles*, and Berlioz's *Les Troyens*, and beginning in 1864 he was also chorusmaster at the Paris Opéra. His famous ballet *Coppélia* was composed in 1870 and his opera *Lakmé* in 1883. Meanwhile, in 1881 he was appointed composition professor at the Conservatoire.

Delibes composed one mass for children's voices and approximately twenty part songs for the singers in the Paris Orphéon. The mass, *Messe brève* for SA chorus and organ, is in the simple style of liturgical works by Gounod, and the part songs are similar to those composed by Saint-Saëns. Eight of the part songs are scored for male voices (TTBB) a cappella, including *La nuit de Noël, Pastorale, Les chants lorrains, Marche de soldats,* and *Chant de la paix.* Three—*Hymne de Noël, Avril,* and *C'est Dieu*—are scored for SATB voices a cappella; two—*Les Norwègiennes* and *Les nymphes des bois*—are for SA chorus and piano; and seven (e.g., *En avant, Noël,* and *Les pifferari*) are scored for three equal voices.

THÉODORE DUBOIS 1837–1924

Dubois was born near Reims and studied piano under the *maître de chapelle* of Reims Cathedral. At age seventeen he entered the Paris Conservatoire, where he excelled in piano, organ, and harmony, and in 1855 he was appointed organist at the church of St Louis-des-Invalides. In 1858 he moved to Ste Clotilde, serving there with César Franck, and in 1861 he won the Prix de Rome. During his stay in Italy he, like Charles-François Gounod before him, came to admire the music of Palestrina. On his return to Paris from Rome in 1863 he was appointed *maître de chapelle* at Ste Clotilde, a position he held until 1869. He was appointed professor of harmony at the Conservatoire in 1871, and in 1877, while maintaining his position at the Conservatoire, he replaced Camille Saint-Saëns as organist at La Madeleine. In 1891 Dubois became professor of composition at the Conservatoire, and in 1896 he was appointed its director. Like Saint-Saëns, he combined the roles of composer, performer, and teacher with that of author, publishing six pedagogical works during his lifetime, including *Traité de contrepoint et de fugue* in 1901, *Leçons de solfège* in 1905, and *Traité d'harmonie théorique et pratique* in 1921.

Dubois composed twelve masses (including one Requiem), five oratorios, seventy-one motets, ten cantatas and hymns, and eight part songs. Very few of the works are known or performed today, with the exception of one oratorio, the masses *Messe solennelle de Saint-Rémi* (scored for TB solos, SATB chorus, and orchestra) and *Messe pontificale* (for SATB solos, SATB chorus, and organ), and the motet *Tu es Petrus* (for B solo, SSTB chorus, and organ).

The oratorio *Les sept paroles du Christ,* composed in 1867, may be the best known and most frequently performed oratorio of the French Romantic era. It was premiered on Good Friday 1867 at Ste Clotilde and subsequently performed in Paris virtually every year after that until the second decade of the twentieth century. Originally scored for full orchestra, Dubois later arranged it for harp, timpani, and organ. The oratorio, modeled on Franck's work of the same name, has a Latin text, a prologue that begins with the phrase "O vos omnes" and ends with a passage from Ruth 1:20, and the "Stabat mater" included as a part of the third of the seven last words. Dubois's work is more dramatic than Franck's, however, and is distinguished by an orchestral passage that depicts the earthquake following the death of Jesus. The remaining oratorios are relatively unknown. *Le paradis perdu,* subtitled "drame-oratorio," is based on Milton's *Paradise Lost* (the story of Adam and Eve expelled from Paradise) and was first performed at the Salle du Châtelet in 1878; *Notre-Dame de la mer,* which is about miracles celebrated at the chapel of Notre-Dame de la mer located in southern France, received its premiere at the Cirque des Champs Elysées in 1897; *Le baptême de Clovis,* set to a Latin ode to France by Pope Leo XIII, was premiered at Reims Cathedral on Ascension Day 1899; and *La prière de France,* subtitled "poème-oratorio," is not a dramatic work but rather a reflection of the hymn text and chant "Adoro te supplex" that is contained in the work. It was composed in 1917 and scored for baritone solo, chorus, and piano.

GEORGES BIZET 1838–1875

Bizet was born in Paris to parents who were singers and who taught their son the rudiments of music. At age nine the young Bizet enrolled in piano and solfège classes at the Paris Conservatoire, and he so excelled in his studies that he won an award in solfège his first year and an award in piano at age twelve. He began studying organ when he was fourteen and composition the following year, and at seventeen he wrote his first orchestral work, *Symphony #1,* and opera, *La maison du docteur.* At nineteen he won the Prix de Rome for his cantata *Clovis et Clotilde,* and while in Rome he composed a Te Deum and an ode-symphony entitled *Vasco de Gama.* During the years following his return to Paris he composed mostly operas, including *Les pêcheurs de perles* in 1863, *L'arlésienne* in 1872, and *Carmen* in 1873 and 1874. His health declined in the mid-1870s, and he died of a heart attack at age thirty-six.

Bizet's compositional output includes nine completed and surviving choral/orchestral works (several other works either were begun and never finished or were lost). Of the existing works, two have entered the performing repertory— *Valse avec choeur* and *Te Deum.* The *Valse avec choeur* was composed in 1855 and is scored for SATB chorus and chamber orchestra of flute, two clarinets, two horns, two trumpets, trombone, and strings. Its text begins with the phrase "La valse légère doit plaire aux amants" (The light waltz gives pleasure to the lovers) and includes a lengthy section of *la, la, la*'s. The *Te Deum,* composed in 1858, is scored for ST solos, SATB chorus, and orchestra (including harp and organ ad lib.). The work is divided into four movements, and the text is rearranged to end with the phrase "Sanctus, Dominus, Deus Sabbaoth" (Holy, Lord, God of the Sabbath).

JULES MASSENET 1842–1912

Massenet was born near St Etienne in southeastern France and received his first musical instruction from his mother, a pianist. At age nine he began piano and solfège lessons at the Paris Conservatoire, at seventeen he won an award in piano, and at nineteen he received an award in counterpoint and fugue. He supported himself by teaching piano privately and by playing the timpani at the Théâtre Lyrique, where he was introduced to operas by Gounod, Gluck, Mozart, and Weber. Massenet won the Prix de Rome in 1863 with his cantata *David Rizzio* (now lost), and in Italy during 1864 and 1865 he met and became acquainted with the music of Franz Liszt. After his return to Paris in 1866 Massenet composed numerous operas, songs, and piano and orchestral works, and in 1877 he received his first major success with the opera *Le roi de Lahore.* He was appointed professor of composition at the Conservatoire and was elected to the Institute de France in 1878, and throughout the next two decades he wrote some of his most acclaimed operas, including *Hérodiade* in 1881, *Manon Lescaut* in 1884, *Le Cid* in 1885, *Werther* in 1892, *Thaïs* in 1894, and *Cendrillon* in 1899.

In addition to thirty-six operas, Massenet composed two masses (both lost), four oratorios, five surviving motets, and approximately twelve part songs. The first oratorio, *Marie-Magdeleine*, was composed between 1871 and 1872 and premiered at the Odéon by the Concert National on Good Friday 1873. It was extremely well received and subsequently performed six times during Lent the following year at the Opéra-Comique. A review by Saint-Saëns stated enthusiastically, "Let us begin by joyfully verifying the complete success of the most audacious attempt that a musician has made in Paris since Berlioz's *L'enfance du Christ.*" Saint-Saëns also compared Massenet's music to that of other composers: "It derives from Gounod, while barely giving that impression. . . . [It] is to Gounod as Schumann is to Mendelssohn." *Marie-Magdeleine,* like most of Massenet's operas and other oratorios, is about the life of a woman. Mary Magdalene, called Méryem in the oratorio, is represented in three acts: Méryem meeting Jesus at the well outside the city of Magdala; Jesus and Judas visiting Méryem at her home; and Méryem witnessing Jesus' crucifixion at Golgotha and later visiting his tomb and telling the disciples that he has risen from the dead. The oratorio is noted for its realistic dramatic portrayals and for its effective character developments. No doubt because of these characteristics, several performances during the 1870s and 1880s were staged.

The second oratorio, *Eve,* was composed in 1874 and premiered by the newly formed Société française de l'harmonie sacrée, which was modeled on London's Sacred Harmonic Society and which presented performances of Handel oratorios, including *Judas Maccabaeus* and *Messiah.* Like *Marie-Magdeleine, Eve* is divided into three major acts and contains highly dramatic effects. Act one of the oratorio depicts the beauties of paradise and the innocence of Eve; act two relates Eve's temptation in the Garden of Eden (a chorus of night voices and spirits from the abyss tempt Eve to eat from the Tree of Knowledge); and act three characterizes the curse of God, with music from the Gregorian chant *Dies irae* and with colorful scoring for a large orchestra that includes a thunder machine. The oratorio was not as successful as *Marie-Magdeleine,* probably because of the sensuous treatment of the biblical characters, who celebrate rather than lament their actions and lustful natures.

La vierge, Massenet's third oratorio, was composed in 1877 and 1878 and premiered in 1880 by the Concerts historiques de l'Opéra, with the composer conducting. It was not well received by Parisian audiences (the third of its scheduled premiere performances was cancelled because of insufficient ticket sales), perhaps because it lacked the overall dramatic effects of the earlier two oratorios. Massenet reflected on the experience as "a rather painful memory in my life. Its reception was cold and only one fragment seemed to satisfy the large audience. . . . They encored three times the passage that is still performed occasionally, the prelude to part four, 'Le dernier sommeil de la vierge.'" The oratorio presents four scenes from the life of the Virgin Mary—the Annunciation, the wedding at Cana, the crucifixion of Jesus on Good Friday, and the Assumption.

The final oratorio, *La terre promise,* was composed between 1897 and 1899 and premiered at the church of St Eustache in 1900. Like the previous oratorios, it is divided into large acts or parts. However, unlike the other works, the parts are not subdivided into scenes or movements. Each of the parts is titled and headed with a biblical quotation: part one is called "Moab" (The Alliance) and begins with Deuteronomy 4:1, "Keep the precepts of the Lord so that you might possess that excellent country which you will enter, just as God swore to your fathers"; part two, "Jericho" (The Victory), begins with Joshua 6:20, "The people having made a great shout, the walls of Jericho fell down to their foundations, and everyone entered the city"; and part three, "Canaan" (The Promised Land), is headed by Joshua 22:6, "He then sent the people away, each into his own land." The textual narrative is conveyed by a soloist called "La Voix" (the Voice), sung by a baritone in part one, a tenor in part two, and a soprano in part three. A chorus mostly represents Israelites. The orchestral scoring calls for eight French horns, eleven trumpets (seven of which are clarion trumpets that are positioned apart from the main orchestra and that signal the destruction of Jericho's walls), four bassoons (one of which is a contrabassoon), a contrabass saxophone, and at least two harps.

The part songs include the cycle *Chansons des bois d'Amaranthe* (Songs from the Amaranth Woods), composed in 1900 for vocal soloists with piano accompaniment. Two of the cycle's pieces—"O bon printemps" (Oh beautiful spring) and "O ruisseau" (Oh stream)—are for soprano, alto, and tenor, and two others—"Chères fleurs" (Dear flowers) and "Chantez" (Sing)—are for vocal quartet (SATB). The remaining piece, "Oiseau des bois" (Bird of the forest), is a duet for soprano and alto. The two quartets—"Chères fleurs" and "Chantez"—have been extracted from the cycle and are published separately.

CHARLES-MARIE WIDOR 1844–1937

Widor was born in Lyons, where he studied organ with his father, an organ builder and performer. Charles-Marie developed rapidly, and at age eleven was playing organ at the local grammar school. He later went to Brussels to study composition with François-Joseph Fétis, who was a specialist in Gregorian chant, and organ with Jacques Nicolas Lemmens, who introduced him to the organ works of J. S. Bach. At sixteen Widor returned to Lyons as organist at the church of St François, and later that year he was appointed organist at St Sulpice in Paris. During his twenties and thirties he became known for his virtuoso organ performances, especially his improvisations, and also for his multimovement organ symphonies and orchestral works such as the ballet *La korrigane*, which was successfully produced at the Paris Opéra in 1880. During the 1880s he served as a critic for *L'estafette* and conductor of the Concordia choral society, in 1890 he succeeded César Franck as organ professor at the Paris Conservatoire, and in 1896 he succeeded Théodore Dubois as professor of composition. Widor remained at the Conservatoire, where his students included Louis Vierne, Albert Schweitzer (with whom he edited five editions of J. S. Bach's organ works), Marcel Dupré, Arthur Honegger, and Darius Milhaud. Widor also remained at St Sulpice, serving there a total of sixty-four years. In 1904 he published *Technique de l'orchestre moderne*, a large orchestration treatise that was a supplement to Berlioz's work of 1843, and in 1910 he was elected to the Académie des Beaux-Arts.

In addition to ten organ symphonies and a number of other organ and orchestral works, Widor composed nine motets and four part songs. The motets, mostly small-scale pieces for chorus and organ, include *Quam dilecta tabernacula tua* (Psalm 84) for SATB chorus (divided occasionally into SATTBB) and *Tantum ergo* for baritone solo, SATTBB chorus, and organ.

GABRIEL FAURÉ 1845–1924

Fauré was born in Pamiers, near Toulouse in southern France, and as a child he frequently played the harmonium in the chapel of the Ecole Normale in nearby Montgauzy. At age nine he went to Paris, and for the next eleven years he studied at the newly formed Ecole de Musique

Classique et Religieuse (later called Ecole Niedermeyer after its founder and main teacher, Louis Niedermeyer). The school specialized in training church musicians, and its curriculum was generally limited to the study of ancient music, especially Gregorian chant and Renaissance polyphony. After Niedermeyer's death in 1861, Saint-Saëns began teaching composition at the school and introduced modern music into the curriculum, including works by Robert Schumann, Franz Liszt, and Richard Wagner (all of whom became important to Fauré in his later life). In 1866 Fauré was appointed organist at the church of St Sauveur in Rennes, and in 1870 he became assistant organist at Notre-Dame de Clignancourt in Paris, serving in this latter position only several months before enlisting as a soldier in the Franco-Prussian War. When the war ended in 1871, he served as organist at St Honoré d'Eylau and then as assistant organist at St Sulpice. He also formed the Société Nationale de Musique in 1871 with Vincent d'Indy, Henri Duparc, and Emmanuel Chabrier, and he met André Messager, who would become his close friend and travel companion as well as an esteemed composer and music director of the Opéra-comique in Paris and Covent Garden in London.

In 1874 Fauré began substituting for Saint-Saëns at La Madeleine, and in 1877, when Dubois became organist there, Fauré was appointed *maître de musique*. Fauré remained at La Madeleine, although he traveled whenever possible to Germany to hear the music of Liszt and Wagner (he attended several performances of the Ring cycle). In 1892 Fauré was appointed inspector of the national conservatories in the French provinces, and in 1896 he succeeded Dubois as main organist at La Madeleine. In addition, he succeeded Massenet as professor of composition at the Conservatoire, where his students included Maurice Ravel, Jean Roger-Ducasse, and Nadia Boulanger. Fauré began serving as music critic for *Le Figaro* in 1903, and in 1905 he succeeded Dubois as director of the Conservatoire. Fauré was an effective administrator, who instituted major reforms and elevated the Conservatoire's status, and he became recognized as one of France's most renowned composers. In 1920, the year he retired from the Conservatoire, he was awarded the Grand-Croix of the Légion d'Honneur, and in 1922 a national tribute concert of his music was given at the Sorbonne. He became increasingly deaf and weak during the last years of his life, and he died on November 4, 1924, at the age of seventy-nine.

Fauré composed two masses (including a Requiem), twelve choral motets and other sacred settings, and five secular pieces. Both the masses were composed over a period of about twenty years, and both masses exist in multiple versions. The *Messe basse* was originally written in 1881 as a combined effort between Fauré and his friend André Messager. Fauré composed the Gloria, Sanctus, and Agnus Dei movements, and Messager composed the Kyrie and O salutaris (there was no Credo). Scoring was for a three-part female chorus, solo violin, and harmonium (organ without pedals). Messager rescored the accompaniment for full orchestra the following year, and in 1907 Fauré composed his own Kyrie and a separate Benedictus, omitted the Gloria, and rescored the new work for soprano solo, two-part female chorus, and harmonium.

The *Requiem* was originally written in 1887 and first performed at La Madeleine on January 9, 1888. At this time the work consisted of five movements (Introit and Kyrie, Sanctus, Pie Jesu, Agnus Dei and Communion, and In paradisum), with scoring for solo soprano, mixed chorus, solo violin, divided parts for the violas and cellos, basses, harp, timpani, and organ. Fauré subsequently added horn and trumpet parts for a performance at La Madeleine in May 1888. Two additional movements—the Offertory and Libera me—were added sometime during the early 1890s; parts of the Offertory had been sketched in 1887, although the entire movement was probably not completed until 1890, and the Libera me was completed at the beginning of 1892 and performed as a separate movement in January by the Société Nationale de Musique at the church of St Gervais. The augmented work, which Fauré considered complete, was performed at La Madeleine on January 21, 1893, with three trombones added to the orchestration. The *Requiem* was not performed again or published, however, for another seven years (the vocal score appeared in 1900 and the orchestral score in 1901). Performances of this symphonic version took place in Lille on May 6, 1900; in Paris at the World Exhibition on July 12, 1900; and at the Paris Conservatoire on April 6, 1901. Orchestration at this time was for two flutes, two clarinets, two bassoons, four horns, two trumpets, three trombones, timpani, two harps, strings, and organ. This symphonic orchestration—which was likely done not by Fauré but by Roger-Ducasse—resulted from the publisher's desire for a work that would meet standard expectations, with forces appropriate for festivals and concert hall performances.

Despite Fauré's apparent approval of the large orchestration, he intended his *Requiem* to be intimate. In a January 1904 article in *Le Figaro* he wrote that he disliked the "large-scale dramatic effects" of Berlioz's *Requiem,* and in an interview with the author and biographer Louis Aguettant in July 1902 he stated, "It has been said that my *Requiem* . . . is a lullaby of death. It is thus that I see death: as a happy deliverance, an aspiration towards happiness above, rather than as a painful experience." Furthermore, in an August 1900 letter to the conductor Eugène Ysaÿe, who was preparing to lead the first performance of the *Requiem* in Brussels, Fauré commented that the *Requiem* "is as gentle as I am myself." Specific to his preference for the original chamber-like orchestration, he noted in an October 1900 letter to Ysaÿe, "You will see how angelic the violins are in the Sanctus after all those violas." Fauré also wrote to Ysaÿe that the baritone soloist should have a "soothing" voice, with the quality of a "precentor," and in a letter to the singer and voice teacher Claire Croiza in August 1922 he wrote that the Pie Jesu "was written for a boy's voice."

Fauré's selection of text for the *Requiem* also confirms his preference for gentle and intimate characteristics. He used only the final lines of the Dies irae—"Pie Jesu Domine, dona eis requiem" (Merciful Lord Jesus, grant them rest)—which he set as a separate movement for the first time in history, and he inserted two texts that are not part of the traditional Requiem Mass—the responsory of the burial rite, Libera me, which ends "Requiem aeternam dona eis, Domine, et lux perpetua luceat eis" (Eternal rest grant to them, Lord, and light perpetual shine upon them), and the antiphon, In paradisum, which begins "In paradisum deducant te angeli" (May the angels lead you into paradise).

Fauré's ideals of expression are aided by repetition of text and music. In the first part of the Introit, for instance, the word "luceat" in the phrase "et lux perpetua luceat eis" (and light perpetual shine upon them) is stated four times in succession; the Offertory begins and ends with numerous imitative statements of the opening phrase "O Domine Jesu Christe, rex gloriae, libera animas omnium fidelium" (O Lord Jesus Christ, king of glory, liberate the souls of all the faithful); the Pie Jesu, which similarly begins and ends with identical text and music, has six statements of the text "dona eis requiem" (grant them rest) set to similar melodic patterns; and in one of the most satisfying moments in sacred choral music, an orchestral recapitulation of the Agnus Dei occurs after the Communion text, which itself is repeated from the Introit. In all, five of the Requiem's seven movements are in some sort of ABA form.

In addition to the balanced forms of the movements, it should be noted that the *Requiem* as a whole has a symmetrical structure: movement four (Pie Jesu) for soprano solo stands in the center; movements two (Offertory) and six (Libera me) are in ABA form and are scored for bari-tone solo and chorus; movements one (Introit and Kyrie) and five (Agnus Dei and Communion) each contain two textual units; and movements three and seven are through-composed and for chorus alone.

The smaller-scale sacred settings are divided between motets set to traditional Latin texts (e.g., *Ave verum* and the three settings of *Tantum ergo*) and spiritual texts in French. The Latin motets are generally scored for chorus and organ without pedals (originally a harmonium), while the sacred settings in French are scored for chorus and piano. *Les djinns* is a setting of the lengthy poem by Victor Hugo (1802–1885) about the cacophony and malevolence of the super-natural creatures called the jinn.

Cantique de Jean Racine, which was a student work that won Fauré the premier prix in com-position, is one of the most frequently performed sacred pieces of the Romantic era. Its text, probably by the French dramatist Jean Racine (1639–1699), is based on a prayer from the Roman breviary.

Pavane was composed in 1887 for orchestra alone (the most frequent manner of perform-ance today) and premiered on November 25, 1888, at a concert conducted by Charles Lam-oureux. Fauré added parts for mixed chorus set to a poem by Robert de Montesquiou (the cousin of the work's dedicatee, Countess Élisabeth Greffulhe) for a performance three days later pre-sented by the Société Nationale de Musique. Subsequent performances during Fauré's life in-cluded dancers. *Madrigal,* composed in 1883 for solo quartet and piano, is set to a poem by Paul-Armand Silvestre (1837–1901) about the inconstancy of man's amorous affections.

SACRED WORKS
SELECTED AND LISTED ACCORDING TO FAMILIARITY

Requiem op.48 – SB solos, SATB chorus, and orchestra – 35 minutes. (1) The soprano soloist sings only in the Pie Jesu, and the baritone soloist sings in the Offertory and Libera me; (2) the choral parts occasionally divide into SATTBB; (3) see above for a discussion of orchestration.

Cantique de Jean Racine op.11 – SATB chorus and piano – 4:45 minutes.

Messe basse – S solo, SA chorus, and organ without pedals – 10 minutes. (1) The soprano soloist sings in the Kyrie and Benedictus; (2) the choral parts are frequently in unison.

Ave verum op.65 no.1 – SA chorus and organ (without pedals) – 2:30 minutes.

Tantum ergo op.65 no.2 – SSA solos, SSA chorus, and organ (without pedals) – 2:15 minutes.

Tantum ergo in G-flat major – S or T solo, SATB chorus, and organ (without pedals) – 1:45 minutes.

Tantum ergo op.55 in A major – T solo, SATBB chorus, harp, and organ (with pedals) – 2:45 minutes.

Maria, mater gratiae op.47 no.2 – SA or TB chorus and organ (without ped-als) – 2:30 minutes.

Ecce fidelis servus op.54 – STB chorus and organ (with pedals) – 2 minutes.

SECULAR WORKS

SELECTED AND LISTED ACCORDING TO FAMILIARITY

Pavane op.50 – orchestra and SATB chorus ad lib. – 6 minutes.

Madrigal op.35 – SATB chorus and piano – 4:15 minutes.

Les djinns op.12 – SATB chorus and piano – 4:15 minutes.

VINCENT D'INDY 1851–1931

D'Indy was born in Paris and studied piano and harmony privately in his youth. He was prodigious in his development, and as a child he played a recital for an audience that included Rossini and Gounod. At age eighteen d'Indy traveled to Italy, and at nineteen he enlisted as a soldier in the Franco-Prussian War. After the war he studied law at the Sorbonne and organ and composition at the Paris Conservatoire with César Franck, and he frequently attended recitals in the home of Saint-Saëns, where he met and heard the music of Bizet, Massenet, and Widor. In 1873 d'Indy traveled to Weimar to study piano with Liszt, and for the following several years he continued his studies in Paris and traveled to Dresden, Vienna, Munich, and Bayreuth to hear operas (including Wagner's Ring cycle). He also served as chorusmaster of the Concert Nationale (the orchestra founded by the violinist Edouard Colonne [1838–1910] and later renamed the Colonne Concerts), preparing vocal ensembles for such works as Beethoven's *Symphony #9* and Berlioz's *L'enfance du Christ*. In the 1880s d'Indy began a career as a conductor, in 1885 he won the Grand Prix de la Ville de Paris for his cantata *Le chant de la cloche,* and in 1887 he won acclaim for his *Symphonie sur un chant montagnard français,* an extended work for piano and orchestra. Along with Charles Bordes and Alexandre Guilmant, he founded the Schola Cantorum in 1894, and in 1904 he became its director. He wrote biographies of several composers, including Franck in 1906, Beethoven in 1911, and Emmanuel Chabrier and Paul Dukas in 1920, and he continued to teach and conduct until his death at age eighty.

D'Indy composed six Latin motets, several cantatas and part songs, and three sets of chansons based on French folk songs. The motets, generally in a neo-Renaissance imitative style, include *Cantate Domino* op.22 for STB solos, SATB chorus, and organ; *Ave regina coelorum* op.79 for SATB chorus a cappella; and *Deus Israel conjungat vos* op.41 for SATB voices a cappella. This latter motet is a setting of texts from the Roman Catholic Nuptial Mass and was composed for the marriage of d'Indy's daughter. The cantatas include settings of both sacred and secular texts. *Le chant de la cloche* op.18, sometimes called an oratorio, is a series of vignettes based on the moralistic story of a bellmaker by Friedrich von Schiller, with scoring for T solo, SATB/SATB chorus, and orchestra; *Sainte Marie-Magdeleine* op.23—scored for A solo, SSA chorus, organ, and piano—is a two-part work, part one of which tells the story of Jesus' anointing by Mary Magdalene and part two of which relates the story to contemporary commitment to the church and devotion to Christ; and *Cantate de fête pour l'inauguration d'une statue* op.37, composed for the dedication of a statue of dramatist Emile Augier in the city of Valence, is scored for B solo, TTBB chorus, and orchestra.

The part songs are varied in both textual content and scoring. *Sur la mer* op.32 is an extended work in ABA format for S solo, SSAA chorus, and piano; *L'art et le peuple* op.39, based on Victor Hugo's text about fraternity and liberty, is scored for TTBB chorus a cappella (with a later arrangement by d'Indy for male chorus and orchestra); *Le bouquet de printemps* op.93 and *Les trois fileuses* op.97 are small-scale works scored for SSA chorus a cappella; and *La vengeance du mari* op.105 is a dialogue between two soloists, L'amarit (S) and Le mari (B), with commentary by an SATB chorus and with original accompaniment of piano (later arranged for wind ensemble). The folk song settings, d'Indy's most celebrated works, include *Trois chansons populaires françaises* op.82, *Six chants populaires français* op.90, and *Six chants populaires français* op.100. All three sets are scored for a variety of solos and choral voicings a cappella.

LOUIS VIERNE 1870–1937

Vierne was born in Poitiers in southcentral France with a visual impairment that allowed him only partial sight. At age six he studied piano and solfège privately, and at ten, when his family moved to Paris, he continued his studies at the Institut des Jeunes Aveugles (Institute for the Young Blind). At eighteen he began studying harmony with César Franck, and at twenty he joined Franck's organ class at the Conservatoire. He continued at the Conservatoire, studying with Widor after Franck's death in 1890, and in 1892 he began substituting for Widor at St Sulpice. In 1900 he was appointed organist at Notre Dame Cathedral, and in 1912, while continuing at the cathedral, he was named a professor at the Schola Cantorum. Throughout the final decades of his life, recognized as one of the great organists of the time, he toured throughout France, England, and North America.

As a composer, Vierne is noted for his six organ symphonies, four volumes of organ pieces (collectively published as *24 Pièces de fantaisie* and issued as op.51 and 53 in 1926 and op.54 and 55 in 1927), and another volume of organ pieces (*24 pièces en style libre,* issued as op.31 in 1914) referred to as "Songs without words." His choral output consists of only two motets and one mass, cantata, and sacred French setting. The motets and mass are scored for mixed voices and organ. *Tantum ergo* op.2 and *Ave Maria* op.3, both composed in 1886, are in the style of Fauré, with homophonic vocal textures and accompaniment that doubles the voice parts except for brief interludes. The mass, *Messe solennelle* op.16, was composed in 1900 and is in a neo-Renaissance style, with alternating phrases of imitative polyphony and homophony.

◈ ITALY ◈

Interest in choral music by Italian composers during the Romantic era continued the decline that had occurred during the Classical era, while interest in opera continued to rise in popularity. Only three notable Italian composers of the nineteenth century—Gaetano Donizetti, Giuseppe Verdi, and Giacomo Puccini—wrote choral music of any significance, and these three composers are best known for their operas. Moreover, each of the composers wrote multiple operas that not only became standard works of the genre, but also became some of the most popular operas of all time. Fortunately, the choral works by these composers, almost all sacred and in Latin, are also noted for their artistic excellence and for their popularity.

GAETANO DONIZETTI 1797–1848

Donizetti was born in Bergamo, northeast of Milan, and at age nine began studying music at the Lezioni Caritatevoli, a training school for musicians founded by the *maestro di cappella* of the Bergamo Cathedral. Donizetti excelled as a singer and keyboardist, and at fourteen he was celebrated locally for his improvisation abilities (he apparently was able to compose a song instantly to a prescribed text while simultaneously improvising an unrelated keyboard waltz). At eighteen he entered the Liceo Filarmonico Comunale in Bologna, and at nineteen he composed his first musical drama, *Il pigmalione*. His first operatic commission, *Enrico di Borgogna* for S Luca in Venice, came when he was twenty, and by the time he was thirty he had composed twenty-one operas for opera houses in Mantua, Naples, Milan, Palermo, Rome, and Paris. In his early thirties he served as director of the royal opera theaters in Naples, and during his thirties and forties he composed his most famous operas—*Anna Bolena* in 1830, *L'elisir d'amore* in 1832, *Lucia di Lammermoor* and *Maria Stuarda* in 1835, *La fille du regiment* in 1840, and *Don Pasquale* in 1843. He became a noted conductor as well as composer and in 1842 was invited to conduct the Italian premiere of Rossini's *Stabat mater*. In 1842 he was also appointed *Hofkapellmeister* at the Habsburg court in Vienna. Symptoms of syphilis became apparent shortly after his arrival in Vienna, and in 1846 he had to be confined to an asylum. He was moved to a private home in 1847 and died the following year at age fifty.

Donizetti composed approximately 120 sacred works, including four Requiems and numerous motets and separate mass movements. The *Messa di Requiem*, one of three works he wrote in memory of the opera composer Vincenzo Bellini (who died September 23, 1835), is the most famous of the Requiems, although it is incomplete. Scored for SATBB solos, SATB chorus, and orchestra, the completed movements include "Introduzione" for orchestra, "Introito" (Requiem and Te decet hymnus) for a "quartettino" and chorus, "Kyrie" for chorus, "Antifona" (In memoria aeterna) for chorus, "Dies irae" for TB solos and chorus, "Tuba mirum" for TBB trio, "Judex ergo" for SB duet, "Rex tremendae majestatis" for SB solos and chorus, "Ingemisco" for T solo, "Praeces meae" for ATB trio, "Confutatis maledictis" for SATBB quintet and chorus, "Oro suplex" for B solo, "Lacrymosa" for chorus, "Offertorio" for B solo and TBB chorus, "Lux aeterna" for chorus, and "Libera me" for B solo, SATB quartet, and chorus.

Other choral works include *Magnificat* in D major composed in 1819, *Credo* in D major composed in 1824 for St Cecilia's Day celebrations, *Messa di Gloria e Credo* in C minor composed in 1837, *Ave Maria* in F major of 1842, and *Miserere* in G minor composed in 1843 for the Vienna court. In addition, choral movements such as the Chorus of Servants from *Don Pasquale* are occasionally excerpted from his operas.

GIUSEPPE VERDI 1813–1901

Verdi was born in a small town near Parma in northern Italy, and at age nine he began playing the organ at the church of S Michele in Busseto. At eleven he enrolled at the local *ginnasio* for classical studies, and at twelve he commenced musical studies with the *maestro di capella* of S Bartolomeo and also with the director of the local philharmonic society. At eighteen, being denied admission to the Milan conservatory (later named for him), he studied privately with the *maestro di concertatore* at La Scala, and at twenty he played continuo keyboard in a performance of Haydn's *The Creation*. Verdi returned to Busseto in 1836 to serve as *maestro di capella* at S Bartolomeo but went back to Milan three years later to embark on an operatic career. His first opera, *Oberto, conte di San Bonifacio,* was premiered at La Scala in 1839, and for the remainder of his life, like Donizetti before him and Puccini after him, Verdi composed and supervised productions of operas for cities throughout Europe. *Nabucco* was composed for Milan in 1842, *Ernani* for Venice in 1844, *Macbeth* for Florence in 1847, *Rigoletto* for Venice in 1851, *Il trovatore* for Rome and *La traviata* for Venice in 1853, *Les vêpres siciliennes* for Paris in 1855, *La forza del destino* for St Petersburg in 1862, *Aida* for Cairo in 1871, *Otello* for Milan in 1887, and his final opera, *Falstaff,* for Milan in 1893. During the final years of his life he devoted himself to the building of a hospital and a retirement home for musicians (Casa di Riposo), and on January 21, 1901, he suffered a stroke while in Milan. He died six days later at the age of eighty-seven, and although he specified in his will that he wanted a simple burial without ceremony, a memorial service concert conducted by Arturo Toscanini was followed by a procession of hundreds of thousands of mourners who sang the Chorus of Hebrew Slaves from *Nabucco*, "Va pensiero," through the streets of Milan.

Verdi's choral output consists of two masses (including one Requiem), two motets, a setting of the Lord's Prayer, and four sacred pieces collectively entitled "Quattro pezzi sacri." The first mass, *Messa di Gloria,* was composed between 1832 and 1834, with scoring for SATB solos, SATB chorus, and orchestra. The *Messa da Requiem* began as a project to honor Rossini, who was greatly admired by Verdi and who had died in November 1868. Four days after Rossini's death Verdi wrote to his publisher, Tito Ricordi, "To honor the memory of Rossini I would wish the most distinguished Italian composers to compose a Requiem Mass to be performed on the anniversary of his death." Verdi proposed several conditions, including participation by only Italian composers and performance in Bologna by both male and female choral singers (something not allowed in Italian churches at the time). He also suggested that following the premiere performance of the mass, "it should be sealed and placed in the archives of [Bologna], from which it should never be taken, except for anniversaries, if posterity should decide to celebrate them." Thirteen composers were selected (none except Verdi known today), with Verdi composing the final movement, Libera me. The mass was to be completed by May 18, 1869. There were troubles with virtually all aspects of the process, however, and the composite Requiem, titled *Messa per Rossini,* was not performed on schedule. Indeed, it was not performed until September 11, 1988 (in a performance at the Liederhalle in Stuttgart, Germany, conducted by Helmuth Rilling).

On May 22, 1873, Italy's beloved poet Alessandro Manzoni died, and within two weeks Verdi again wrote to Ricordi, this time proposing that he himself "compose a Mass for the Dead to be performed next year for the anniversary of [Manzoni's] death." The proposal was accepted and on March 7, 1874, Verdi completed his Requiem, which included a revised version of the Libera me composed for Rossini. The premiere took place as planned on May 22, 1874, at the Cathedral of San Marco in Milan with a chorus of 120 singers and an orchestra of one hundred instrumentalists. It is interesting to note that Verdi had fourteen days of rehearsal with the soloists and chorus, and for the performance the chorus and orchestra were placed side by side—the orchestra on the left and the chorus on the right. In addition, there was an intermission (which subsequently became standard) after the conclusion of the Dies irae. Later performances took place at La Scala on May 25 with 120 choral singers and 110 orchestral players; at the Opéra-Comique in Paris between June 9 and 22 (seven performances) with a total of two hundred performers; at St Ann's Church in New York City on October 25 with a chorus of twenty and organ accompaniment; at Royal Albert Hall in London in May 1875 with a chorus of 1,200 and an orchestra of 150; and at the Hofoperntheater in Vienna in June 1875 with a chorus of 150 and an orchestra of one hundred. For the 1875 performances Verdi replaced the fugue originally set to the "Liber scriptus" text with an alto solo.

The *Messa da Requiem* is divided into seven movements—Introit and Kyrie, Dies irae, Offertory, Sanctus, Agnus Dei, Lux aeterna, and Libera me—with each of the movements composed as a single entity except the Dies irae, which is subdivided into nine sections. Like several of the great Requiems of the Romantic era (including those composed by Gabriel Fauré and Johannes Brahms), Verdi's work has a mirror or balanced construction. Two of the movements at the beginning of the Requiem (Introit and Kyrie, and Dies irae) and two of the movements at the end (Agnus Dei and Libera me) are scored for soloists and chorus; two movements (the Offertory in the first half of the Requiem and the Lux aeterna in the second half) are scored for soloists without chorus; and the center movement (Sanctus), an expansive double fugue, is scored for chorus alone. Most of the movements have internal balanced structures as well: the Introit is ABA, with the "Te decet hymnus" text set as B; the nine movements of the Dies irae are organized into three groups of three sections each, with a clear division at the end of sections three and six; the Offertory begins with an orchestral introduction that is divided into three related phrases (the third of which is an inversion of the first two) and continues with vocal/orchestral sections organized in an ABCBA format; the Agnus Dei is divided into three near-identical sections; and the Lux aeterna is structured as ABABAB.

In addition to highly dramatic operatic solos, notable features of the *Messa da Requiem* include a bass drum part marked quadruple forte in the Dies irae, four offstage trumpets marked "in lontananza ed invisibili" (in the distance and invisible) in the "Rex tremendae" portion of the Dies irae, the choral double fugue in the Sanctus (mentioned above), writing in octaves for the soprano and alto soloists in the Agnus Dei, an a cappella section for soprano soloist and chorus in the Libera me, and chant-like phrases that both begin and end the Libera me.

The Quattro pezzi sacri consist of two a cappella and two choral/orchestral works, all composed around 1890 and published collectively in 1898. The *Ave Maria* is based on a newly invented scale that Verdi called "enigmatic" and was published as a puzzle in the magazine *Gazzetta musicale*. This scale—which is constructed of a half step followed by a minor third, three whole steps, and two half steps—is used as a cantus firmus in long notes, first ascending and then descending, in each voice part (the bass and alto at one pitch level, and the tenor and soprano a perfect fourth higher). Verdi's writing is so accomplished and seemingly inevitable that neither the unique organization of the scalar passages nor their use as a cantus firmus seems unusual. The *Laudi alla vergine Maria* is a setting of the first twenty-one lines from the final Canto (Canto thirty-three) of Dante's *Paradiso*. The *Stabat mater* is a through-composed setting (except for the theme that begins and ends the work) of the entire traditional Latin text. It is acknowledged for its expressive and sometimes graphic depiction of Mary's presence at the crucifixion of Jesus. The *Te Deum*, a setting of the complete traditional Latin text (with the omission of one word, "Domine," at the end of the work), is also through-composed and noted for its dramatic effects. It is especially noted for its opening, which is taken from Gregorian chant and which is scored for a cappella double male chorus and for the SSAATTBB a cappella setting of the text phrase "Salvum fac populum tuum, Domine, et benedic haereditati tuae" (Save your people, Lord, and bless your inheritance).

The least known and least performed of Verdi's choral works, *Pater noster,* is an elaborated setting of the Lord's Prayer in Italian, closely based on lines one through twenty-four in chapter eleven of Dante's *Purgatorio.* An example of the elaboration can be seen in lines one through three: "O Padre nostro, che ne' cieli stai, santificato sia sempre il tuo nome, e laude e grazia di ciò che ci fai" (Oh our father, who are in heaven, hallowed is your name always, and praise and thanks be for all that you do).

In addition to the choral works discussed above, choral movements from Verdi operas are frequently extracted and performed separately. The most notable of these is "Va pensiero," the Chorus of Hebrew Slaves from *Nabucco* mentioned above. This chorus, which reflects the yearnings of the slaves for their liberation and for their homeland, became a symbol of Italian nationalism during the latter part of the nineteenth century. Other popular opera choruses include the Triumphal Chorus from *Aida,* "Gloria all' Egitto"; the Anvil Chorus from *Il trovatore,* "Vedi, le fosche notturne"; the Gypsy Chorus from *La traviata,* "No siamo Zingarelle"; and the Chorus of Scottish Refugees from *Macbeth,* "Patria oppressa."

SACRED WORKS
SELECTED AND LISTED ACCORDING TO FAMILIARITY

Messa da Requiem – 1874 – SATB solos, SSAATTBB chorus, and orchestra (including piccolo, four bassoons [featured as a solo quartet in the Libera me], eight trumpets [four of which are offstage], and bass drum) – 85–90 minutes. (1) Verdi labeled the A solo "mezzo soprano," although he referred to it in correspondence as "contralto"; (2) the chorus is divided into SATB parts except for SSAATTBB in the Dies irae, TTT in the Rex tremendae, and SATB/SATB in the Sanctus; (3) Verdi specified the ideal choral distribution as twenty-four sopranos, twelve altos, thirty-two tenors, and thirty-two basses (for a total of thirty-six women and sixty-four men).

Ave Maria – ca.1890 – SATB chorus a cappella – 5 minutes.

Stabat mater – ca.1890 – SATB chorus and orchestra (including piccolo, four bassoons, bass drum, and harp) – 12 minutes. The choral parts divide briefly into SAATTBB.

Te Deum – ca.1890 – SATB/SATB chorus and orchestra (including piccolo, English horn, bass clarinet, four bassoons, and bass drum) – 15 minutes. (1) The choral parts occasionally divide into SSAATTBB/SSAAT-TBB; (2) there is a brief soprano solo (sung from the chorus) at the end of the work.

Laudi alla vergine Maria – ca.1890 – SSAA chorus a cappella – 5:30 minutes.

Pater noster – 1880 – SSATB chorus a cappella – 6 minutes.

GIACOMO PUCCINI 1858–1924

Puccini was born in Lucca to a family that had been church musicians and composers of dramatic works for many years. His great-great-grandfather, Giacomo (1712–1781), studied with Padre Giovanni Battista Martini in Bologna, served as organist of San Martino Cathedral in Lucca, and composed masses, motets, a Magnificat, and dramatic cantatas for city celebrations; his great-grandfather, Antonio (1747–1832), followed in his father's footsteps, studying in Bologna, becoming organist at San Martino and composing dramatic cantatas; his grandfather, Domenico (1772–1815), worked with Antonio at San Martino and would likely have succeeded him had he not died at an early age; and finally, his father, Michele (1813–1864), succeeded Antonio as organist at San Martino, taught piano at the Istituto femminile di S Ponziano, and composed eight masses and two operas. The young Giacomo, whose full name was Giacomo Antonio Domenico Michele Secondo Maria Puccini, was expected to follow in the line of his father and forefathers and become organist at San Martino. In fact, with Michele's death when Giacomo was only six, the position was filled temporarily, and the city council of Lucca issued a decree stating that Puccini would become organist when he reached maturity.

He did not demonstrate an interest in music during his youth. He received a classical education, and although he became organist at San Martino at age fourteen, he was sixteen before he began to study music formally (at the Istituto Musicale Pacini in Lucca). At twenty-two he transferred to the Conservatorio Giuseppe Verdi in Milan, and while in Milan he attended performances at La Scala and became interested in opera. His first opera, *Le villi,* was composed in 1883, and thereafter he devoted himself almost exclusively to the genre. Of his most famous operas, *Manon Lescaut* was composed in 1893, *La bohème* in 1896, *Tosca* in 1900, *Madama Butterfly* in 1904, and *Il trittico* in 1918. His last opera, *Turandot,* remained unfinished at his death and was not premiered until 1926.

Puccini's choral output consists of one mass, one separate mass movement (a Credo composed in 1874), one choral motet (*Plaudite populi,* also composed in 1874), and a single-movement Requiem. The mass was composed in 1880 as a student exercise and titled *Messa a quattro.* After its premiere that same year it was forgotten and not rediscovered until the 1950s, at which time it was retitled *Messa di Gloria.* It is scored for TB solos, mixed chorus, and orchestra and consists of the traditional five portions of the Mass Ordinary, each set as a single movement. The structural treatment of the movements is conventional (e.g., the Kyrie is in an ABA format, the Gloria and Credo are divided into multiple sections, and the Benedictus section of the Sanctus is a solo). However, there are some unique notable features: the Gloria is divided into ten sections, with musical material from the first section reappearing in the middle (section five) and at the end of the movement (section ten); this final section of the Gloria combines the fugue subject from section nine with the musical material from the beginning of the movement; the word "Laudamus" in the "Laudamus te" section of the Gloria (section three) is set as four syllables; and the Credo is unified by numerous repetitions of its opening motif. The *Requiem* was composed in 1905 for the fourth anniversary of Verdi's death and scored for chorus, solo viola, and organ. Its text consists only of the phrases "Requiem aeternam dona eis, Domine" (Rest eternal grant to them, Lord) and "et lux perpetua luceat eis" (and let perpetual light shine on them).

As with Verdi, choral movements or sections from Puccini operas are occasionally extracted and performed separately. Especially popular is the Invocation to the Moon from *Turandot*, "Perche tarda," and the Humming Chorus from *Madama Butterfly*.

❧ AUSTRIA AND GERMANY ❧

Austria and Germany produced a majority of the most significant composers of choral reper-toire during the Romantic era—composers such as Ludwig van Beethoven, Felix Mendels-sohn, Robert Schumann, Franz Liszt, Anton Bruckner, Johannes Brahms, Antonín Dvořák, and Gustav Mahler, whose names have become synonymous with musical fame and whose works head lists of artistic superiority and frequency of performance. (Beethoven is included here be-cause his musical temperament—his desire for grand effects, his proclivity for personal expres-sion, and his creative individualism—were Romantic. Dvořák is also included here because his music is Germanic in character and because his native land of Bohemia, like Liszt's native land of Hungary, had no widespread character of independence in art music during the nineteenth century.) Two other famous and important composers—Richard Wagner and Richard Strauss—are known for their operas, although these composers, like their Italian counterparts, composed some noteworthy choral music as well. Also, composers such as Peter Cornelius, Joseph Rhein-berger, and Max Reger, while not universally renowned, are credited with composing choral music of high artistic merit. Lesser-known but important Austrian and German Romantic-era composers are Carl Loewe, Fanny Hensel (sister of Felix Mendelssohn), Clara Schumann (wife of Robert Schumann), Max Bruch, Heinrich von Herzogenberg, Hugo Wolf, and Georg Schu-mann.

In addition to their fame as composers, Beethoven, Mendelssohn, and Liszt were among the most notable pianists of the Romantic era (if not of all time). Clara Schumann was also a famed pianist, who did not equal her male counterparts in preeminence as a composer but who certainly equaled them in celebrity as a performer. Mendelssohn, Mahler, and Strauss were renowned conductors, Loewe was a noted singer, and Bruckner and Reger were distinguished organists. Furthermore, like composers in France during the Romantic era, many Austrian and German composers had a keen interest in literature and served as critics or reviewers for news-papers and magazines. Robert Schumann founded the *Neue Leipziger Zeitschrift für Musik*, a pe-riodical (later to become the *Neue Zeitschrift für Musik*) that reviewed and presented related arti-cles about contemporary compositions; Wagner was well known for his published polemics about the direction of new music; Cornelius was a significant proponent of the New German School of composition (centered in Weimar and represented by the Neu-Weimar-Verein) and author of promotional material published in the *Neue Zeitschrift für Musik* and other periodicals; and Wolf, who became known for his criticisms of Brahms and his support for Wagner and Liszt, served as a critic for the Vienna *Salonblatt*.

Most of the Austrian and German composers were divided in their belief that music should look to the past and maintain or restore older styles and forms, or that music should look forward and forge new paths and create new genres. A number of those composers who modeled their works on past styles (e.g., Liszt) adhered to the precepts of the Cäcilienverein, a popular society of composers in the latter part of the nineteenth century whose mission was to return Catholic church music to the style of Palestrinian imitative polyphony. Other historically minded composers—such as Mendelssohn, Brahms, Herzogenberg, and Reger—were intensely interested in and influenced by the music of J. S. Bach. Yet other composers, including Bruch and Rheinberger, were merely against the seemingly radical views and practices of composers such as Robert Schumann and Wagner, who were advocates of the New German School and who were influential in originating a modern, seemingly structure-free type of composition.

The genres that most interested the conservative composers were motets and masses, both of which were generally based on traditional forms of the past. Motets were almost exclusively scored for a cappella chorus and set in an imitative texture, and masses were either Renaissance or Classical in structure and style (i.e., the a cappella masses were reflective of the Palestrina model, while the choral/orchestral masses were modeled on works by W. A. Mozart and Joseph Haydn). Only a few masses (e.g., those in D minor and F minor by Bruckner and the *Requiem* by Dvořák) were modern in that they were unified by recurring motifs. Even the Brahms *Requiem*, while Romantic in concept, is quite traditional in its formal structure.

Oratorios were both backward- and forward-looking. Most—including those by Loewe, Mendelssohn, Bruch, Rheinberger, Dvořák, Herzogenberg, and Georg Schumann—were modeled on works by Bach and Handel. Only those by Robert Schumann and Liszt were composed in a new manner, one that forsook traditional number forms and instead were structured in a fluid and through-composed fashion.

Cantatas and other choral/orchestral works were generally new in concept. Many of these works, beginning with Beethoven's *Fantasie für Klavier, Chor und Orchester c-moll* op.80 (the "Choral Fantasy") and *Meeresstille und glückliche Fahrt* op.112 (Calm Sea and Prosperous Voyage), have no genre classification or have a classification that might be termed a non-narrative poetic cantata. These works—especially popular with Robert Schumann, Bruckner, Brahms, Bruch, and Strauss—are simply settings of secular texts scored for chorus and orchestra, with their formal structures often free or based on textual organization. The choral symphony was also a new genre. Beethoven's *Symphony #9*, which was the first of this kind, was followed by Mendelssohn's *Symphony #2* (Lobgesang) and Mahler's second, third, and eighth symphonies.

The part songs were basically similar to those composed during the Classical era by the Haydn brothers and Schubert—small-scale pieces set to secular poetry and scored for a cappella chorus or chorus with piano accompaniment. Some composers—notably Cornelius, Wolf, and Georg Schumann—also set texts dealing with spiritual subjects, and other composers—including Brahms and Dvořák—set folk or nationalistic texts and also incorporated folk melodies or made choral arrangements of native folk tunes.

LUDWIG VAN BEETHOVEN 1770–1827

Beethoven was born in Bonn to a musical family. His grandfather had been *Kapellmeister* of the electoral chapel as well as an acclaimed singer, and his father had been a singer in the chapel and a teacher of piano and violin. The young Beethoven studied with his father and began performing in public at age eight, and several years later he continued his studies with court organist Christian Gottlob Neefe, who wrote, "Louis van Betthoven [sic], a boy of eleven years and of most promising talent, plays the piano very skillfully and with power, and reads at sight very well." Beethoven became Neefe's assistant at age eleven, and he also began playing harpsichord in the court orchestra. At twelve he wrote his first composition—nine variations for piano on a theme by Ernst Christoph Dressler (WoO63)—and for the next four years he composed piano and other instrumental chamber works for local performances. In addition, he played viola in the court orchestra and local theater and responded to a few special occasions with vocal works, including two cantatas—one for the death of Emperor Joseph II (*Cantate auf den Tod Kaiser Joseph des Zweiten* WoO87) and one for the accession of Leopold II (*Cantate auf die Erhebung Leopold des Zweiten zur Kaiserwürde* WoO88).

In December 1790 Joseph Haydn invited Beethoven to move to Vienna to be his student. With the trip arranged and paid for by the Elector of Bonn, Beethoven went to Vienna in November 1792 and studied with Haydn for a year, after which time Haydn wrote to the elector that Beethoven would "in time [become] one of Europe's greatest composers." Haydn left Vienna for London in 1793, and Beethoven began studies with Johann Georg Albrechtsberger, *Kapellmeister* at St Stephen's Cathedral, and Antonio Salieri, imperial *Kapellmeister*. Throughout the following years Beethoven composed some significant piano works, including the *Sonate pathétique* op.13 in 1799 and the "Moonlight" Sonata op.27 no.2 in 1801, and, being recognized as one of the finest pianists in all of Europe, he concertized in many cities, including Prague, Dresden, and Berlin. In 1801, at age thirty, he began to acknowledge his increasing deafness, writing to his close friend Franz Gerhard Wegeler, "For almost two years I have ceased to attend any social functions because I find it impossible to say to people: I am deaf. . . . You can scarcely believe what an empty, sad life I have had." In 1802, during a hoped-for therapeutic trip to the small town of Heiligenstadt, he came to terms with the severity of his deafness and wrote a declaration to that effect, known as the "Heiligenstadt Testament."

After returning to Vienna he engaged in a period of intense compositional activity, writing his oratorio *Christus am Oelberge* op.85 in two weeks, and in 1807 he received a commission from Haydn's employer, Prince Nikolaus Esterházy, to write a mass (*Missa* in C major op.86) in celebration of the prince's wife's name day and thus follow the tradition of Haydn, who had composed six masses for the princess between 1796 and 1802. Beethoven was honored by the commission, but, inexperienced in sacred vocal works and intimidated by the prospect of being compared with Haydn, he wrote to Nikolaus, "I shall deliver the mass to you with timidity since you, Serene Highness, are accustomed to having the inimitable masterpieces of the great Haydn performed for you." The performance did not go well, probably because Beethoven's deafness prevented him from adequately rehearsing the music. Nikolaus was displeased, and Beethoven was so upset he rededicated the score to his friend Prince Ferdinand Kinsky.

In 1808 Beethoven presented one of the first concerts devoted entirely to his works. Included on the program were the fifth and sixth symphonies, the fourth piano concerto, and a newly composed finale—the "Choral Fantasy." The following year he declined an offer to serve as *Kapellmeister* at the court in Kassel and accepted instead an annuity for life that was funded by three of his greatest supporters—Archduke Rudolf, Princess Lobkowitz, and Prince Kinsky. In 1819 Rudolf, to whom Beethoven taught piano and composition, was made a cardinal and also Archbishop of Olmütz in Moravia (now Olomouc in the Czech Republic). To celebrate the occasion, Beethoven planned a grand mass, writing to Rudolf, "The day on which a High Mass composed by me will be performed during the ceremonies solemnized for Your Imperial Highness will be the most glorious day of my life." Beethoven became involved with other compositions, however, including his ninth symphony, and did not complete the mass (which he called *Missa solemnis*) until 1822. The work was performed in St. Petersburg in April 1824, and shortly after three movements (Kyrie, Credo, and Agnus Dei—advertised as "Three Sacred Hymns") were performed on a concert program at the Kärntnertor-Theater in Vienna. The mass did not receive another performance until 1845 in Russia, eighteen years after Beethoven's death. Although the three movements of the *Missa solemnis* were well received in 1824, and although Beethoven considered the mass his greatest work, he wrote no more vocal compositions but instead concentrated on string quartets. In December 1826 he developed jaundice and cirrhosis of the liver, and he died in his home the following March at age fifty-six.

Beethoven composed two masses, one oratorio, ten cantatas, one choral symphony, two choral/orchestral works belonging to no specific genre, and one part song. The *Missa* in C major op.86, being a relatively early work and commissioned to follow Haydn's final mass by only five years, is conservative and in the mold of Haydn's late masses. It is divided into the customary six movements (Kyrie, Gloria, Credo, Sanctus, Benedictus, and Agnus Dei); the scoring is for solo quartet, SATB chorus, and standard orchestra; the movements are based on familiar symphonic forms; the Gloria and Credo movements end with fugues; the solo writing in the Benedictus is mostly for quartet; and the music of the Kyrie returns at the end of the Agnus Dei. However, Beethoven was more emotional in his text setting than was standard at the time, and he clearly set expressive performance as a priority. For instance, his tempo marking for the Kyrie contains ten words (unparalleled at the time)—"Andante con moto assai vivace quasi allegretto ma non troppo" (Walking with vivacious motion as in an allegretto, but not too much); dynamic markings that range from pianissimo to fortissimo are in abundance throughout the score; and words are isolated and repeated to create dramatic effect—for example "et" at the beginning of the phrase "et sepultus est" (and was buried). In addition, extension of the final Gloria and Credo sections, with numerous alternations between text phrases and the word "Amen," builds tension and increases dramatic impact.

The *Missa solemnis* op.123 is like Beethoven's earlier mass only in standard format. Otherwise, it stretches the limits of all compositional elements, more than any other mass before or since, to achieve an epic scope and grandeur. Every movement demonstrates Beethoven's commitment to extremes. The Kyrie (223 measures) is in three distinct sections, each of which is as long as most complete Classical-era Kyries. The Gloria (569 measures) is expanded from the normal three sections to five, with each of these sections further divided into subsections; the final section, a fugue of 210 measures (more than a third of the movement), is itself in three parts. The Credo (472 measures) is in six sections and also has a fugue in three parts that is a little more than a third of the entire movement (167 measures). The Sanctus (234 measures), which includes the Benedictus, is in six parts, with an orchestral Preludium before the Benedictus that depicts the host of the Eucharist through the sound of a solo flute, and with a violin solo in the Benedictus that approaches concerto proportions in both technical virtuosity and length. Finally, the Agnus Dei (434 measures) is in four parts, the second of which is headed by the phrase "Bitte um inneren und äußeren Frieden" (Plea for inner and outer peace), and the third of which features trumpets and timpani set to military-like motifs and solo recitatives marked "ängstlich" (apprehensive or fearful). Throughout the entire mass Beethoven emphasizes virtually every phrase of text, often with numerous repetitions and expressive markings to ensure dramatic portrayal. Beyond this, Beethoven heads the mass with the inscription "Von Herzen – Möge es wieder zu Herzen gehn" (From the heart – May it again go to the heart).

Christus am Oelberge op.85, Beethoven's only oratorio and his first dramatic vocal work, was composed in a burst of energy shortly after the Heiligenstadt Testament and was performed during Holy Week 1803. The work is divided into six movements, each consisting of a recitative, aria, and ensemble, and each depicting a scene from the biblical account of Jesus on the Mount of Olives. In movement one Jesus prays for strength; in movement two a solo angel and chorus of angels address mankind, hailing the redeemed and condemning the unredeemed; in three, a duet between Jesus and an angel, Jesus resigns himself to his fate; in four Jesus welcomes death as the soldiers enter the Garden of Gethsemane to arrest him; in five the confused disciples beg for mercy; and in six the oratorio concludes with a general song of praise. Reviews of the premiere were mixed, and Beethoven himself was not entirely satisfied. In 1804 he wrote to his publisher that because he had written the work in such a short period of time, "naturally some passages did not altogether satisfy me." In 1811, when the work was finally published, he again wrote, "It was my first work in that style and, moreover, an early work; it was written in a fortnight during all kinds of disturbances and other unpleasant and distressing events in my life." Despite the mixed reviews and Beethoven's misgivings, the oratorio was performed frequently in Germany and England during the nineteenth century.

The *Symphony #9* op.125 is unquestionably the best-known choral/orchestral work ever written. It is recurrently on concert programs across the world, and audiences invariably receive it with rapturous enthusiasm. The reason for its great popularity is not only its masterful music, but also its message, "Alle Menschen werden Brüder" (All men become brothers), which is a part of Friedrich von Schiller's celebrated poem *An die Freude* and which Beethoven set in the symphony's fourth movement. Like many of Beethoven's other late compositions, the *Symphony #9* is normative in overall format and structure but unique in design and structural relationships. For instance, it has four commonplace fast-fast-slow-fast movements (the second fast being a scherzo), but the first movement is approximately twice as long as first movements by Mozart and Haydn, and the fourth movement is as long as most entire Classical-era symphonies. Moreover, the huge theme-and-variation structure of the fourth movement bears no resemblance to anything previously written by Beethoven or any other composer. Of course, the most notable and innovative feature of Beethoven's symphony is the vocal writing in the fourth movement. This movement, which makes the symphony's message explicit and which restates motifs from previous movements and thus unifies the entire symphony, begins with strident and discordant chords that suggest strife and conflict. Recitatives that seem to ask for relief from the strife are played by the string basses, with brief excerpts from the symphony's first three movements stated as a presumed attempt to answer the string bass questions and mollify the strife. Finding no satisfactory answer, the string basses present something entirely new—a simple melody that is repeated three times and that builds with each repetition to a triumphant conclusion. Then Beethoven returns to the discordant chords of the movement's opening. However, the solo bass voice now takes over the role of the string basses, giving actual words and therefore clarity of meaning to the questions and answer of the simple melody—"Alle Menschen werden Brüder." Following this are more vocal and instrumental variations and a multi-sectioned coda that extends and increases the triumphant quality expressed previously.

Beethoven's other choral/orchestral works include two compositions that have become a part of the standard performing repertoire—*Fantasie für Klavier, Chor und Orchester c-moll* op.80 (called the "Choral Fantasy") and *Meeresstille und glückliche Fahrt* (Calm Sea and Prosperous Voyage) op.112. Both works are the first of their kind—secular compositions for chorus and orchestra that belong to no traditional genre. As was mentioned above, the *Fantasie* was composed in 1807 to be the finale of the first concert devoted entirely to Beethoven's works. It consists of an extended section for piano alone, which was played by Beethoven in the premiere performance, followed by a series of variations for piano and orchestra on a folk song-like melody. The soloists and chorus participate only in the final variation, the chorus singing a total of two and a half minutes. The text is similar to that of Schiller's *An die Freude,* praising peace and joy. *Meeresstille und glückliche Fahrt* was composed between 1814 and 1815 and first performed in Vienna in December 1815. It is a setting of two contrasting poems by Goethe, the first a slow hushed movement scored for chorus and strings beginning with the text "Tiefe Stille herrscht im Wasser, ohne Regung ruht das Meer" (Deepest calm lies on the water, motionless and peaceful is the sea), and the second a fast exuberant movement for chorus and full orchestra beginning with the phrase "Die Nebel zerreissen, der Himmel ist helle" (The mists begin to scatter, the sky grows bright).

Elegischer Gesang op.118 (Elegaic song) was composed in 1814 in memory of the deceased wife of one of Beethoven's close friends, Johann Freiherrn von Pasqualati. It represents Beethoven's one contribution to the secular part song genre made popular by Franz Schubert in Vienna in the early nineteenth century. As with most part songs of the time, performance was intimate (probably in a home), the vocal parts being sung by a quartet of soloists and the instrumental parts being played by a string quartet or piano.

SECULAR WORKS
SELECTED AND LISTED ACCORDING TO FAMILIARITY

Symphony #9 in D minor op.125 – 1822–1824 – SATB solos, SATB chorus, and orchestra – 60–70 minutes. (1) Except for brief tenor and bass solo passages, the solo writing is scored for quartet; (2) the orchestration includes piccolo, contrabassoon, triangle, cymbals, and bass drum; (3) the soloists, chorus, and extra instruments are used only in the final movement; (4) the duration (from 60–70 minutes) depends upon performance of tempo markings indicated by Beethoven on the newly invented metronome (considered by some scholars to be unreliable) or upon tempo markings indicated by the Italian tempo terms (which represent the traditional approach)—the metronome markings resulting in faster tempos and the Italian tempo terms resulting in slower tempos, especially in the third movement.

Fantasie für Klavier, Chor und Orchester c-moll (Choral Fantasy) op.80 – 1807 – SSATTB solos, SATB chorus, piano, and orchestra – 18 minutes. Except for brief SATB passages, the solo writing is scored for sextet.

Meeresstille und glückliche Fahrt op.112 – 1814–1815 – SATB solos, SATB chorus, and orchestra – 8 minutes. There are very brief SATB solo passages.

Elegischer Gesang op.118 – 1814 – SATB chorus and strings – 7:30 minutes.
(1) The piece was probably intended for four soloists; (2) the strings can
be replaced by piano accompaniment.

Die Ruinen von Athen op.113 – 1811 – SB solos, SATB chorus, and orchestra
(including piccolo, contrabassoon, triangle, cymbals, and bass drum in
the movement entitled "Marcia alla turca") – 38 minutes.

König Stephan op.117 – 1811 – SATB chorus and orchestra – 24 minutes.
(1) The male choral parts divide into TTTTB in one movement and
TTBB in another; (2) the work contains solo speaking parts.

SACRED WORKS
SELECTED AND LISTED ACCORDING TO FAMILIARITY

Missa solemnis op.123 – 1819–1823 – SATB solos, SATB chorus, and orchestra – 72–78 minutes. (1) Except for occasional solo melodies, the solo
writing is scored for quartet; (2) the choral writing is demanding both in
tessitura and in stamina; (3) there is an extended and challenging violin
solo in the Benedictus; (4) the trombones mostly double the alto, tenor,
and bass choral parts; (5) the orchestration includes contrabassoon.

Missa in C major op.86 – 1807 – SATB solos, SATB chorus, and orchestra –
48 minutes. (1) Except for brief passages in the Gloria and Credo, the
solo writing is scored for quartet; (2) the orchestration includes organ,
but only two horns and no trombones.

Christus am Oelberge – op.85 – 1803 – STB solos, SATB chorus, and orches-
tra – 48 minutes. (1) The solo roles are for an Angel (S), Christ (T), and
Peter (B); (2) the role of Peter is brief; (3) the chorus portrays soldiers
(TTB), disciples (TT), and angels (SATB and occasionally SATTB); (4)
Beethoven quotes the "Hallelujah" chorus from Handel's *Messiah* in the
final fugue of the work; (5) the orchestration includes only two horns.

Der glorreiche Augenblick op.136 – 1814 – STB solos, SATB chorus, and
orchestra – 34 minutes. The choral parts all divide briefly.

CARL LOEWE 1796–1869

Loewe was born near Halle and began musical studies with his father, a local church musician.
At age ten the young Loewe became a chorister at the court chapel in Cöthen, and at twelve he
joined the Stadtsingechor in Halle under the direction of Daniel Gottlob Türk. Loewe also studied privately with Türk, who in addition to his position with the Stadtsingechor, was organist at
the Marktkirche and professor of music at Halle University. In 1817 Loewe succeeded Türk as
organist at the Marktkirche and also began studies in theology and philology at the university.
He became known for his exceptional singing ability, and between 1819 and 1820 he toured
throughout Germany, giving vocal recitals in cities such as Dresden, Weimar, and Jena and

meeting and becoming acquainted with such notable people as Carl Maria von Weber, Johann Wolfgang Goethe, and Johann Nepomuk Hummel. After the tour he was appointed professor and *Kantor* at the gymnasium in Stettin and organist at the Jakobikirche. The following year he was promoted to music director of the city, and during the next several decades he conducted numerous major choral/orchestral works, including Bach's *Passio secundum Mattaeum* BWV244 in 1831 and *Passio secundum Johannen* BWV245 in 1841. He remained in Stettin, although he continued to tour—performing again throughout Germany in 1837, in London in 1847, in Sweden and Norway in 1851, and in France in 1857—until poor health forced his retirement in 1866.

While Loewe's compositional output consists mostly of solo songs (called *Balladen*), of which he wrote more than three hundred, he also composed fifteen completed oratorios, one Te Deum, four cantatas, nine motets, and approximately fifteen sets of part songs. The first oratorio, *Die Festzeiten* op.66, was composed between 1825 and 1836 and called by Loewe a "geistliches Oratorium" (sacred oratorio). It is actually, however, a series of cantatas like those written by Bach and collectively called the *Oratorium tempore Nativitatis Christi* BWV248 (Christmas Oratorio). Loewe's cantatas are grouped into three sets for the liturgical year—"Advent und Weihnachten" (Advent and Christmas), "Fasten, Charfreitag und Ostern" (Lent, Good Friday, and Easter), and "Himmelfahrt und Pfingsten mit Anschluss von Trinitatis" (Ascension and Pentecost to Trinity Sunday). The other oratorios, while completely separate works, can be grouped into homologous categories. Two—*Die eherne Schlange* op.40 of 1834 and *Die Apostel von Philippi* op.48 of 1835—are completely choral (i.e., without solo recitatives or arias) and scored for men's voices a cappella (although the first work calls for an optional trombone to accompany the chorales, and the second work has optional parts for two flutes, two oboes, three trombones, and timpani). Three oratorios—*Gutenberg* op.55 of 1836, *Palestrina* (without opus number) of 1841, and *Johann Hus* op.82 of 1842—deal with historical figures. *Gutenberg* was premiered on August 14, 1837, in Mainz to inaugurate a monument to the printer Johann Gutenberg; *Palestrina*, about the sixteenth-century composer, contains quotes from *Ave Maria* and the Sanctus, Benedictus, and Agnus Dei of the *Missa Papae Marcelli;* and *Johann Hus*, about the life of the late-fourteenth- and early-fifteenth-century Czech Christian reformer, includes a "Missa canonica" (a Kyrie scored as an a cappella four-voiced canon). Loewe's remaining oratorios deal primarily with religious subjects: *Die Zerstörung Jerusalems* op.30 of 1829 is about the destruction of Jerusalem by Emperor Titus; *Polus von Atella* of 1860 is about the third-century pagan actor Genesius, who converted to Christianity and was martyred; and *Die Auferwekkung des Lazarus* op.132 of 1863 is about the raising of Lazarus from the dead.

Loewe's most famous oratorio, his Passion *Das Sühnopfer des neuen Bundes* (The expiatory sacrifice of the new covenant), was composed in 1847 and scored for SATBB solos, mixed chorus, strings, and organ. The soloists do not have specific roles but sing narrative passages as well as biblical texts about the Passion story, which Loewe gathered from the four Gospels. The chorus, in the manner of Baroque Lutheran oratorios, sings crowd (*turba*) passages and chorales. The work is divided into three parts: the first depicts events in the life of Jesus from his time at the house of Lazarus in Bethany to the Last Supper; the second deals with Christ's betrayal; and the third describes the crucifixion and entombment.

Other notable choral works include the *Te Deum* scored for chorus and orchestra, the Easter cantata *Komm, Gott Schöpfer*, the motet *Salvum fac regem* for SATB chorus, and two part songs set to Goethe texts—*Die Walpurgisnacht* and *Gesang der Geister über den Wassern*, both scored for chorus with piano accompaniment.

FANNY (CÄCILIE) HENSEL (MENDELSSOHN-BARTHOLDY)
1805–1847

Hensel, the sister of Felix Mendelssohn, was born in Hamburg, where in her youth she was influenced by the intellectualism and sophisticated culture of her mother, a pianist, and her father, a prosperous banker. She studied piano with her mother and other notable artists in Hamburg, and composition with Carl Friedrich Zelter, director of the Berlin Singakademie and advocate for the music of J. S. Bach. Like her brother, Fanny excelled as a pianist and began composing at an early age. She supposedly was able to play all of Bach's *Das wohltemperirtes Clavier* (The well-tempered Clavier) from memory at age thirteen, and she wrote her first composition, a song for her father, when she was fourteen. Perhaps because of their proximity in age and similarity of talent and predisposition, Fanny and Felix were close friends. The two often advised each other on compositional matters and constructively criticized each other's work, and Fanny's only public performance (in 1838) was of Felix's first piano concerto. Fanny married the painter Wilhelm Hensel in 1829 (Felix did not marry until 1837) and accompanied him on two extended trips to Italy—one between 1839 and 1840 and the other in 1845. While there she became close friends with Charles-François Gounod and advised him on compositional matters, and she also composed some of her most important works, including the "Reise-Album" mentioned below. She died suddenly of a stroke at age forty-one, just six months before her brother, who was only thirty-eight.

Hensel composed approximately 250 solo songs, twenty-eight choral works, and twelve vocal trios. The choral works include three large-scale compositions—two cantatas, *Hiob* and *Lobgesang*, and one oratorio, *Oratorium nach den Bildern der Bibel*. The second of the cantatas, *Lobgesang*, was composed in 1831 for the birthday of her son Felix Ludwig Sebastian Hensel and subtitled "Meine Seele ist stille" (My soul is tranquil). It is scored for SA solos, SATB chorus, and orchestra and is divided into five movements—an introduction (Pastorale), chorus, alto recitative, soprano aria, and chorus.

The smaller-scale works include *Zum Fest der heiligen Cäcilia* for SATB chorus and piano; *Enleitung zu lebenden Bilder* for narrator, SATB chorus, and piano; *Schweigend sinkt die Nacht* for SATB/SATB chorus a cappella; and two vocal quartets—*Lass fahren hin* for TTBB and *Dämmernd liegt der Sommerabend* for SATB—composed in Italy during 1839 and 1840 and combined with sixteen other pieces (songs, duets, and piano works) plus paintings by her husband in a collection Hensel called her "Reise-Album" (Travel Album). Other part songs include several scored for SAB voices a cappella (e.g., *Wer will mir wehren zu singen, O Herbst*, and *Schweigt der Menschen laute Lust*).

Her most popular works are six part songs for SATB voices a cappella published as *Gartenlieder* op.3 in 1846. The set includes three settings of poetry by Joseph von Eichendorff ("Hörst du nicht die Bäume rauschen," "Schöne Fremde," and "Abendlich schon rauscht der Wald") and one setting each of poems by Hensel's husband, Wilhelm ("Morgengruss"), Ludwig Uhland

("Im herbst"), and Emanuel Geibel ("Im Wald"). Wilhelm Hensel also wrote the poetry for *Nachtreigen*, which was composed in 1829 and scored for a cappella double chorus.

FELIX MENDELSSOHN (MENDELSSOHN-BARTHOLDY)
1809–1847

Mendelssohn was born in Hamburg into an intellectual and cultured Jewish family. His grandfather, Moses, was a noted philosopher, and his father, Abraham, was a successful banker. Like his elder sister Fanny, Felix studied classical subjects such as mathematics and French with his father and the fine arts subjects of German literature and piano with his mother. Also like his sister, Felix was a child prodigy, playing his first piano recital at nine and composing his first piece, *Recitativo* for piano, at eleven. The family lived in Hamburg from 1804 to 1811 and then in Berlin, where the children were baptized Christian in 1816 and the name Bartholdy was added to the original surname Mendelssohn. In 1819, at age ten, Felix began studies in composition with Carl Friedrich Zelter, director of the Berlin Singakademie, who introduced the young Felix to Johann Wolfgang Goethe (a close friend later in life) and to the choral works of Bach and Handel. Felix was also introduced to the music of Palestrina and other Renaissance composers by Johann Nepomuk Schelble, conductor of the Cäcilienverein in Frankfurt-am-Main and a strong proponent of church music reform. Mendelssohn's first noteworthy composition, the overture to Shakespeare's *A Midsummer Night's Dream* op.21, was composed when he was seventeen and premiered by Carl Loewe in Stettin when Felix was eighteen. At twenty Mendelssohn conducted a revival of Bach's *Passio secundum Mattaeum* (St Matthew Passion) to celebrate the 100th anniversary of the work's composition.

During his early twenties Mendelssohn sang in the Berlin Singakademie and studied at the University of Berlin; in 1829 he performed his works in London and Edinburgh; and in 1830 he gave piano recitals and conducted orchestras in Munich, Salzburg, Vienna, Venice, Florence, and Rome. In 1833, as a result of a commission by the Philharmonic Society of London, he conducted the premiere of his *Italian Symphony* and was piano soloist in Mozart's *Piano Concerto in D minor* K466, and in that same year he conducted performances of Handel's *Israel in Egypt* at the Lower Rhine Music Festival in Düsseldorf. Mendelssohn was so well received in Düsseldorf he was appointed head of music for the city, and during the next three years he conducted numerous choral works there, including Beethoven's *Symphony #9*, Mozart's *Davidde penitente*, and Handel's *Messiah, Judas Maccabaeus, Solomon,* and *Alexander's Feast*. In May 1836 Mendelssohn conducted his own oratorio, *Paulus* (St Paul), and in the following several years he continued to be a featured conductor and composer in Düsseldorf and in other cities hosting the Lower Rhine Music Festival. Among the many choral/orchestral works he conducted were Handel's *Joshua* in 1838, Beethoven's *Mass in C* op.86 in 1839, and Haydn's *Die Schöpfung* in 1846.

Mendelssohn's second oratorio, *Elias* (Elijah), was commissioned by the Birmingham Festival in 1845 and premiered the following summer. Meanwhile, Mendelssohn had relinquished his directorship position in Düsseldorf in 1834 because of administrative difficulties, and in 1835 he was named conductor of the Leipzig Gewandhaus Orchestra. He retained this position for the remainder of his life, promoting the careers of pianists such as Clara Schumann, who performed with him twenty-one times, and of composers such as Robert Schumann and Franz

Liszt. Beginning in 1842 Mendelssohn also served as *Generalmusikdirektor* for church and sacred music at the Court of Friedrich Wilhelm IV in Berlin, and as head of the Leipzig Music Academy (now the Hochschule für Musik), which he founded in 1843. His health began deteriorating in the mid-1840s, and after the death of his sister in May 1847 he became seriously ill. He suffered a series of strokes in October and died on the fourth of November at age thirty-eight.

Mendelssohn composed two oratorios, eight secular cantatas, twenty-six sacred cantatas and other large sacred works, forty small sacred pieces, and sixty secular part songs. The oratorios are similar in many respects to the Bach and Handel works that Mendelssohn heard, studied, and conducted. Both *Paulus* and *Elias* are structured in two large parts, each of which is divided into recitatives, arias, choruses, and chorales, and the forms of the individual movements are Baroque in style. Mendelssohn was unapologetic about his practice of looking back to past repertoire: "No one can prohibit me from delighting in and continuing to develop what the great masters have bequeathed me, because not everyone should be expected to start from the beginning again. Composition is to me a continuation, to the best of my abilities, not a dead repetition of what already exists." This "continuation" consisted in part of unifying the oratorios with motifs and with musical connections of individual movements. For instance, the chorale "Wachet auf, ruft uns die Stimme" is used throughout *Paulus* (beginning as a cantus firmus in the overture), and there are several leitmotifs used in *Elias*. In addition, many of the movements of *Elias* are joined together to create dramatic scenes.

Paulus relates the story of Saul, who persecutes the Christians until his conversion on the road to Damascus, when he is blinded for three days. He then changes his name to Paul and becomes a Christian missionary. The oratorio was composed in German, but, like the works of Haydn, it was immediately translated into English. The premiere (in German) at the Lower Rhine Music Festival in Düsseldorf in May 1836, with a chorus of 356 and an orchestra of 172, was immediately followed by performances (in English) in Liverpool in October 1836, Boston in May 1837, and London and Birmingham during the summer of 1837. Many other performances followed, and the oratorio became one of Mendelssohn's most popular works and the most frequently performed oratorio during the nineteenth century. Several of the choruses are often extracted and performed as separate pieces. These include "Siehe! Wir preisen selig, die erduldet haben" (Behold! Blessed is the man who endureth temptation) and "Wie lieblich sind die Boten, die den Frieden verkündigen" (How beautiful are the messengers who preach the gospel of peace).

Mendelssohn began thinking about his second oratorio, which he wanted to be about the prophet Elijah, immediately after the premiere of *Paulus*. He worked with two librettists but could not convince them to provide texts that were dramatic enough. Mendelssohn wanted Elijah to be "a real prophet through and through: strong, zealous, and yes, even bad-tempered, angry, and brooding." It was not until 1845, when the Birmingham Festival commissioned Mendelssohn to "provide a new oratorio or other music," that he began composing. He set his own libretto in German, although he closely supervised a translation into English, which he wanted to correspond to the King James Version of the text (he even changed rhythms in the music to accommodate English). The premiere, in August 1846 in Birmingham Town Hall with Mendelssohn conducting, included a chorus of 271 singers—seventy-nine sopranos, sixty altos (all male), sixty tenors, and seventy-two basses—and an orchestra of 125 players (with doubled winds). Reviews of the performance were exceptionally laudatory. The *Times* noted: "The last note of *Elijah* was drowned in a long-continued unanimous volley of plaudits, vociferous and deafening. It was as though enthusiasm, long-checked, had suddenly burst its bonds, and filled the air with shouts of exaltation. Mendelssohn, evidently overpowered, bowed his acknowledgements, and quickly descended from the conductor's rostrum; but he was compelled to appear again, amidst renewed cheers and huzzas. Never was there a more complete triumph—never a more thorough and speedy recognition of a great work of art." Mendelssohn revised the oratorio during the next year ("I am right not to rest until such work is as good as it is in my power to make it") and conducted numerous performances in the years that followed. Interestingly, he never conducted a performance in German. As with *Paulus,* several of the choral movements from *Elias* are regularly extracted and performed as separate pieces. These include "Wohl dem, der den Herrn fürchtet" (Blessed are the men who hear him) and "Siehe, der Hüter Israels" (He watching over Israel).

Mendelssohn began a third oratorio, *Christus,* in the final year of his life but was able to complete only small portions of it. Fortunately, one of these portions is a choral movement similar to the great choruses of *Paulus* and *Elias.* The *Christus* chorus, "Es wird ein Stern aus Jacob aufgehn" (There shall a star from Jacob come forth), concludes with a statement of the chorale "Wie schön leuchtet der Morgenstern" (How brightly shines the morning star). Like the choruses from *Paulus* and *Elias,* it is published and performed separately.

The two best known of the secular cantatas are *Die erste Walpurgisnacht* (The First Walpurgis Night) op.60 and *Ein Sommernachtstraum* (A Midsummer Night's Dream) op.61. The first of these was composed in 1831 and 1832 (revised in 1843) to a ballad by Goethe that describes the pagan festival celebrated to greet spring: on Walpurgis Night, April 30, the eve of May Day, witches supposedly gather for a demonic orgy. Mendelssohn's teacher, Carl Zelter, had been given the text to set to music. However, Zelter couldn't "find the mood that imbues the piece," so the twenty-two-year-old Mendelssohn took over the composition. *Ein Sommernachtstraum*— commissioned by Friedrich Wilhelm IV, King of Prussia, as incidental music to Shakespeare's play—was first performed in October 1843 at the Neues Palais in Potsdam. The work consists of thirteen movements, including the overture Mendelssohn had composed in 1826 when he was seventeen and the famous "Hochzeitsmarsch" (Wedding March), which accompanies the marriage of Duke Theseus and Hippolyta as well as other pairs of lovers at the end of Shakespeare's act four. Only two of the movements are scored for vocal forces—the lullaby "Lied mit Chor," during which Oberon places a spell on Titania that makes her fall in love with the first creature she sees when she awakes, and the finale "Bei des Feuers mattem Flimmern, Geister, Elfen, stellt euch ein" (Through the fire's faint glimmer, stand in readiness you ghosts and elves).

The sacred cantatas and other large sacred works include the symphony-cantata *Lobgesang* and a number of multimovement Psalm settings. *Lobgesang* op.52 was commissioned by the city of Leipzig for the 400th anniversary of Gutenberg's invention of the printing press and was first performed at the Thomaskirche in Leipzig in June 1840. The work consists of a long orchestral sinfonia in three parts, which came from music that Mendelssohn had sketched for a proposed symphony several years earlier, plus nine vocal/choral movements: "Alles, was Odem hat, lobe den Herrn" (All that have breath, praise the Lord) for soprano solo and chorus; "Saget es, die ihr erlöst seid durch den Herrn" (Tell it, that you are redeemed through the Lord) for tenor solo; "Saget es, die ihr erlöset seid von dem Herrn aus aller Trübsal" (Tell it, that you are redeemed by the Lord of all affliction) for chorus; "Ich harrete des Herrn, und er neigte sich zu mir" (I waited on the Lord and he inclined unto me) for soprano duet and chorus; "Stricke des Todes hatten uns umfangen" (The bonds of death had closed around us) for tenor solo; "Die Nacht ist vergangen, der Tag aber herbeigekommen" (The night has departed, the day is at hand) for chorus; "Nun danket alle Gott" (Now thank we all our God) for chorus; "Drum sing' ich mit meinem Liede ewig dein Lob, du treuer Gott" (In my hymn I sing of your everlasting praise, you true God) for soprano and tenor duet; and "Ihr Völker bringet her dem Herrn Ehre und Macht" (You people, offer to the Lord glory and might) for chorus. Mendelssohn assembled the text from biblical verses and from the chorale "Nun danket alle Gott."

Most of the large-scale sacred works were not commissioned or composed for church performance. Mendelssohn wrote to one of his friends in 1831, "If I have written several pieces of sacred music, it is because it was a need of mine, the same need one sometimes has to read a certain book, the Bible, for example, or any other, and that book alone can satisfy you." Nevertheless, many of the large sacred works had specific occasions attached to them. *Der 42. Psalm* op.42 was composed on Mendelssohn's honeymoon; *Der 115. Psalm* op.31 was a birthday present to his sister Fanny; *Lauda Sion* was composed for the church of St Martin in Liège; and *Der 98. Psalm* op.91 was composed for the 1844 New Year's celebration of the Berlin Court. Many scholars and musicians consider the Psalms some of Mendelssohn's most inspired choral compositions.

The smaller sacred pieces were generally composed either for the Berlin Cathedral Choir, which Mendelssohn conducted as part of his duties as *Generalmusikdirektor* at the Berlin court of King Friedrich Wilhelm IV, or for some other specific choral ensemble. In addition, they were meant for liturgical performance. *Die deutsche Liturgie* and *Sechs Sprüche* op.79 (composed to favorite texts of the king) are examples.

The secular part songs were composed not for performance, either public or private, but for social entertainment or enrichment of singers. As Mendelssohn wrote to his friend Karl Klingemann in 1839, "I want to continue with the four-part songs and have thought a lot about what I can do with this art form. The most natural seems to me to be for four people who go walking together, being in the woods, or in a rowing-boat." Several collections of the part songs are even subtitled "To be sung in the open air." Approximately half the part songs are for mixed voices and half are for male voices. Most are a cappella, strophic (with several verses), and basically homophonic. The duets op.63 for female voices with piano accompaniment, which are considered to be artistically superior, are often included in Mendelssohn's part song repertoire and are frequently performed by ensembles of female voices.

ORATORIOS

COMPLETE AND LISTED ACCORDING TO FAMILIARITY

Elias (Elijah) op.70 – 1846 – SSAATTBBBB and treble solos, SATB chorus, and orchestra – 120 minutes. (1) Major solo roles are for Elijah (B), a Widow (S), an Angel (A), and Obadiah (T); (2) minor solo roles are for a Queen (A), Ahab (T), a Child (treble), and unnamed SBB; (3) there are also vocal ensemble movements for double quartet (SSAA/TTBB), trio (SSA), female quartet (SSAA), and mixed quartet (SATB); (4) the chorus expands to SSAATTBB in one movement; (5) although there is no part written for it, an organ was used in the premiere.

Paulus (St Paul) op.36 – 1834–1836 – SSTBBB solos, SATB chorus, and orchestra – 116 minutes. (1) Solo roles are for Saul/Paul (B), Stephen (T), Ananias (T), Barnabas (T), and two False Witnesses (BB), plus two unnamed sopranos and a tenor (one soprano and the tenor serve as narrators); (2) all the solo tenor roles are usually sung by one person; (3) the chorus divides into SSATB for two movements and SSAA for one.

SECULAR CANTATAS
SELECTED AND LISTED ACCORDING TO FAMILIARITY

Die erste Walpurgisnacht op.60 – 1831–1832 – ATTBB solos, SSAATTBB chorus, and orchestra – 36 minutes. (1) Solos are for a Druid (T), a person from the crowd of Druids (A), a Priest (B), a Druid Guard (B), and a very small part for a Christian Guard (T); (2) the chorus, which is featured predominantly throughout the work, portrays groups of Druids and Christian guards.

Ein Sommernachtstraum op.61 – 1826–1843 – SS solos, several speaking parts, SSAA chorus, and orchestra – 60–70 minutes (complete). (1) There are speaking parts for Titania and Oberon, plus a very brief part for Puck at the end of the cantata; (2) most performances include only eight movements: Overture; #1 (Scherzo); #3 (Lied mit Chor); #5 (Allegro appassionato); #7 (Con moto tranquillo); #9 (Hochzeitsmarsch); #11 (Ein Tanz von Rüpeln); and #13 (Finale).

LARGE-SCALE SACRED WORKS
SELECTED AND LISTED ACCORDING TO FAMILIARITY

Lobgesang (Hymn of Praise) op.52 – 1840 – SST solos, SATB chorus, and orchestra (including organ) – 60–70 minutes. (1) Mendelssohn called the work "eine Symphonie-Cantate" but it was labeled *Symphony #2* after his death; (2) two choral movements are SSAA and SATTBB and the chorale is SSATTB.

Der 42. Psalm (Wie der Hirsch schreit) op.42 – 1837 – S solo, SATB chorus, and orchestra (including organ) – 25 minutes. (1) The work is in seven movements, with the chorus participating in four of them; (2) movement three is scored for S solo and SSA chorus, and movement six is scored for S solo and TTBB quartet; (3) movements four and seven begin with the same text and music.

Der 114. Psalm (Da Israel aus Aegypten zog) op.51 – 1839 – SSAATTBB chorus and orchestra – 13 minutes. (1) This is Mendelssohn's only large work that is completely choral; (2) it is in one movement, divided into five sections; (3) the first section, an expansive homophonic chorale-like treatment of verses one and two of the Psalm, returns as section five.

Lauda Sion op.73 – 1846 – SATB solos, SATB chorus, and orchestra – 28 minutes. (1) The text is in Latin; (2) the work is in seven movements, with the chorus participating in five of them; (3) movement four is scored for solo quartet and orchestra.

Hymn (Lass', o Herr, mich Hülfe finden) op.96 – 1843 – A solo, SATB chorus, and orchestra of two flutes, two oboes, two clarinets, two bassoons, two horns, and strings – 14 minutes. The work is in three movements, all with A solo, chorus, and orchestra.

Hymn (Hör' mein Bitten) (Hear my prayer) – 1844 – S solo, SATB chorus, and orchestra of two oboes, two clarinets, two bassoons, two horns, timpani, and strings – 10 minutes. The work is in one movement, divided into several sections.

Der 115. Psalm (Nicht unserm Namen, Herr) op.31 – 1830 – STB solos, SATB chorus, and orchestra of two flutes, two oboes, two clarinets, two bassoons, two horns, and strings – 20 minutes. (1) The work is in four movements, with the chorus participating in three of them; (2) the chorus expands to SSAATTBB at the beginning of movement four, which is a cappella.

Der 95. Psalm (Kommt, lasst uns anbeten) op.46 – 1838 (revised in 1841) – SST solos, SATB chorus, and orchestra – 25 minutes. (1) The work is in five movements, with the chorus participating in four of them; (2) the tenor soloist is prominent (the soprano soloists, in duet, are only in movement three); (3) movement two ends distinctively in a vocal canon.

Der 98. Psalm (Singet dem Herrn ein neues Lied) op.91 – 1843 – SATB/SATB chorus and orchestra (including harp and organ) – 8 minutes. (1) The work is in three short movements; (2) movement one opens with a brief B solo, followed by the double chorus a cappella; (3) the first of the double choruses has brief solo quartet passages; (4) this is the only sacred work scored for harp.

SMALL-SCALE SACRED WORKS
SELECTED AND LISTED ACCORDING TO FAMILIARITY

Verleih' uns Frieden (Grant us thy peace) – 1831 – SATB chorus and orchestra of two flutes, two clarinets, two bassoons, strings, and organ – 5:30 minutes. The cellos divide into two parts.

Ave Maria op.23 no.2 – 1830 – T solos, SSAATTBB chorus, and orchestra of two clarinets, two bassoons, cello, bass, and organ – 7 minutes. (1) The tenor solos consist of brief incipits to the choral sections; (2) there are brief sections for solo octet.

Es wird ein Stern aus Jacob aufgehn (There shall a star from Jacob come forth) from the unfinished oratorio *Christus* op.97 – 1847 – SATB chorus and orchestra – 5 minutes. (1) The piece ends with a homophonic statement of the chorale "Wie schön leuchtet der Morgenstern" (How brightly shines the morning star), followed by a brief orchestral recapitulation of the work's opening vocal melody; (2) the main body of the piece is similar to "Siehe, der Hüter Israels schläft noch schlummert nicht" (He watching over Israel slumbers not nor sleeps) from *Elias*.

Der 43. Psalm (Richte mich, Gott) op.78 no.2 – 1844 – SSAATTBB chorus a cappella – 3:30 minutes. (1) The piece is in one movement, divided into three connected sections; (2) the music to the text phrase "Was betrübst du dich meine Seele," which also appears in Psalm 42, is identical to the music Mendelssohn wrote in *Der 42. Psalm.*

Die deutsche Liturgie – 1846 – SATB/SATB chorus a cappella – 8 minutes. (1) The work is in three movements—Kyrie eleison, Ehre sei Gott in der Höhe, and Sanctus; (2) movement three (often referred to as "Heilig") is very popular and often extracted and performed alone; (3) there are brief passages for solo quartet in movement two.

Sechs Sprüche op.79 – 1843–1846 – SSAATTBB chorus a cappella – 10 minutes. (1) The work consists of six pieces, each for a special day in the liturgical year—Weihnachten (Christmas), Am Neujahrstage (On New Year's Day), Am Himmelfahrtstage (On Ascension Day), In der Passionszeit (In Passion Week), Im Advent (In Advent), and Am Charfreitage (On Good Friday); (2) each of the pieces is from 1:30 to 2 minutes in duration, and each ends with the text "Hallelujah."

PART SONGS
SELECTED AND LISTED ACCORDING TO FAMILIARITY

Abschied vom Walde op.59 no.3 – 1843 – SATB voices a cappella – 2:30 minutes.

Die Nachtigall op.59 no.4 – 1843 – SATB voices a cappella – 1:30 minutes.

Sechs zweistimmige Lieder op.63 – 1844 – SS duet with piano accompaniment – 12 minutes.

ROBERT SCHUMANN 1810–1856

Schumann was born in Zwickau, a small town close to Dresden and Leipzig. His father was an author, book dealer, and lexicographer, who made a name for himself by translating the works of Sir Walter Scott and Lord Byron into German. Robert read many of the books in his father's shop and developed a keen interest in literature, which he maintained for his entire life and which greatly influenced his compositions. He began studying piano at age seven and performing in public at eleven, and his first two compositions, both choral, were written when he was twelve. During the next several years he wrote poems and short biographies of famous composers, and he formed a literary society (Literarischer Verein) with a group of his friends. He also began composing songs to the poetry of some of his favorite poets. At eighteen he enrolled at the University of Leipzig to study law. He lacked interest in the subject, however, and concentrated on musical studies, mostly with Friedrich Wieck, a well-known piano teacher and the father of Clara, Schumann's future wife. After only a year in Leipzig he transferred to the University of Heidelberg, hoping to find inspiration for law studies there. But, as he heard the songs of Schubert, piano pieces of Chopin, oratorios of Handel, and motets of Palestrina and Victoria, his interest in music only increased. He returned to Leipzig and resumed his musical studies with Wieck in earnest, aspiring to become a concert pianist but developing severe muscle problems in the fingers of his right hand.

At about this time Schumann also began to suffer periods of depression and began to question his sanity. Nonetheless, he continued to pursue his musical studies and literary interests. He founded the *Neue Leipziger Zeitschrift für Musik* (later to become the *Neue Zeitschrift für Musik*), a periodical that reviewed and presented related articles about contemporary compositions; he became acquainted with Felix Mendelssohn, who was appointed conductor of the Leipzig Gewandhaus orchestra; and he received a doctorate from the University of Jena in order to improve his standing with Wieck, who did not want his daughter to marry Schumann. He also continued to compose. In 1840, the year he finally married Clara, he composed more than 140 songs, including the cycles *Liederkreis* op.39, *Frauenliebe und -leben* op.42, and *Dichterliebe* op.48. In 1843 he began teaching composition, score reading, and piano at Mendelssohn's new Leipzig conservatory, and in 1847 he began conducting the Dresden *Liedertafel*. In 1848 he founded the Dresden *Verein für Chorgesang*, and in 1850 he became the municipal music director for the city of Düsseldorf, with responsibilities that included conducting an orchestra and chorus in ten subscription concerts per year, presenting two to three major concerts in the church, and managing the Lower Rhine Music Festival. Each of Schumann's appointments inspired him to compose music in specific genres, and, as with songs in 1840, he generally concentrated on one genre at a time. Many of his oratorio-like works were composed in 1843, most of his part songs for male voices were composed during the two years from 1847 to 1849, the vocal chamber works (which include some of his most beautiful music for multiple voices) were composed in 1849, and his church music was composed in 1852. During the 1840s and 1850s he also traveled extensively throughout Europe and Russia with Clara, who had become a successful and sought-after concert pianist, and he continued to have bouts of depression and poor mental health. In early February 1854 he began to complain about "strong and painful" auditory sounds, and in late February he attempted suicide by jumping from a bridge into the Rhine. He was sent to an asylum near Bonn, where his friend Johannes Brahms visited him frequently and where he remained until his death two years later at age forty-six.

Schumann composed nineteen choral/orchestral works, four opuses of vocal chamber music, thirty-six part songs for mixed voices, twenty-seven part songs for men's voices, and twelve part songs for women's voices. Most of the choral/orchestral works, especially those before Schumann's last compositional years, are secular and inspired by literary works that deal with the subject of spiritual redemption. These include *Das Paradies und die Peri, Scenen aus Goethes Faust, Manfred, Requiem für Mignon,* and *Der Rose Pilgerfahrt.* Although each of these works is unique in some respects, all are characterized by fluid, through-composed structures and melodies. At the end of his career Schumann composed two large-scale sacred works—a *Mass* and a *Requiem.* Both of these are characterized by traditional forms and structures, no doubt inspired by the Handel oratorios and Bach Passions that Schumann conducted in his position as municipal music director for the city of Düsseldorf.

Schumann called *Das Paradies und die Peri* "a new genre for the concert hall." In actuality it is not a new genre but rather a new form of an existing genre—oratorio. In place of the set recitatives, arias, and choruses, as Mendelssohn and other previous composers had structured their oratorios, Schumann composed what he called "Rezitativischer Gesang" (recitative-like song), which is a type of melody between recitative and aria. The text of *Das Paradies und die Peri,* a translation of the second tale of *Lalla Rookh* by the Irish poet Thomas Moore, relates the trials of the fairy Peri, who must say what gift heaven desires above all others before she is admitted to heaven herself. After two incorrect replies, "a warrior's blood" and "sighs of love," she answers correctly, "a tear of remorse." There is little dialogue and no recitative in the oratorio. The text is relayed through narrative sung by soloists and chorus, and the music reflects Schumann's desire for "a continuous succession of musical numbers." The premiere on December 4, 1843, sponsored by Mendelssohn and conducted by Schumann, was so enthusiastically received that another performance was given on December 11.

Scenen aus Goethes Faust was begun in 1844 with a scene from Goethe's *Faust* that was to be developed into an opera. Schumann later contemplated an oratorio and composed more music during 1849 and 1850, and in 1853 the work was completed with the composition of an overture. The original music of 1844, which became part three of the oratorio, was performed in three separate locations on August 29, 1849, to celebrate the 100th anniversary of Goethe's birth (the Weimar performance was conducted by Franz Liszt, while the Dresden performance was conducted by Schumann). The complete oratorio was not performed until 1862, after Schumann's death. It is unique in that it has no continuous narrative. As the title states, it is a collection of scenes from Goethe's epic poem, divided into three parts. The first two parts deal with Faust and Gretchen, and the third part deals with the general subject of transfiguration or salvation. All but scene one is headed by descriptive commentary. For example, scene two is preceded by the phrases "A pleasing landscape. Faust reclining on flowery turf, weary, restless, trying to sleep. Twilight. Spirits, charming little figures forming a circle, hovering above." The titles of the oratorio's seven scenes are "Szene im Garten" (Garden scene), "Gretchen vor dem Bild der Mater Dolorosa" (Gretchen in front of a picture of the sad mother), "Szene im Dom" (Cathedral scene), "Ariel. Sonnenaufgang" (Ariel. Sunrise), "Mitternacht" (Midnight), "Fausts Tod" (Faust's death), and "Fausts Verklärung" (Faust's transfiguration).

Manfred, composed in 1848, is even more unusual in that it has no specific genre title or description. It is like Mendelssohn's *Sommernachtstraum* in being scored for speakers, soloists, chorus, and orchestra, although it is not incidental music to a play. Instead, it is, as Schumann notes in the subtitle of the work, a "Dramatisches Gedicht von Lord Byron" (Dramatic Poem by Lord Byron). Schumann took Byron's poem, which he had first read in 1829, reduced its 1,336 lines to 975, divided it into fourteen sections that follow a long overture, and scored it mainly for speaker (Manfred) and orchestra; the parts for soloists and chorus are minor. With its main focus on speech, it is the work that most exemplifies Schumann's ideals for literary expression in music.

Requiem für Mignon, composed in 1849, is based on poetry from the eighth book of Goethe's novel *Wilhelm Meisters Lehrjahre.* Schumann quoted lines of Goethe's poetry as a preface to the music: "That evening was held the funeral service for Mignon. The company entered the Hall of the Past . . . and when seated, two choirs gently began to sing and ask, 'Whom do you bring to us in silent company?'" This question then becomes the first line of the music, sung by the chorus. What follows is a tableau of the funeral that describes the various elegiac qualities of Mignon and her lost youth.

Der Rose Pilgerfahrt (The Pilgrimage of a Rose) was composed in 1851, shortly after Schumann became municipal music director for the city of Düsseldorf. The work was originally scored for two soloists, chorus, and piano and was presented in the Schumanns' home. Soon after this performance, at the insistence of friends, the piano part was rescored for orchestra. However, Schumann preferred the piano version and felt that the orchestration was "unnecessary and uninteresting." The work is oratorio-like in that it relates a story by means of soloists and chorus and is divided into two large parts. Moreover, its text by Moritz Horn is similar to that of *Das Paradies und die Peri* in that both deal with the subject of fairies. In *Der Rose Pilger-fahrt* a rose asks to be transformed by elves into a maiden so that it might experience love. Franz Liszt characterized the music as "images which one might call visions of poetic mysticism. Clouds are metamorphosed into scents, waves into swelling tones; everything is a transparent allegory of an unutterable feeling."

The *Mass* op.147 and *Requiem* op.148 are unlike Schumann's other choral/orchestral works. Instead of being characterized by fluid forms and a focus on narrative expression, they are in traditional set-piece structures, with a focus on imitative choral textures. The only unique features are a movement (Offertorium) for solo soprano and solo cello in the *Mass*, and a free division of the text into nine untitled movements in the *Requiem*.

Since many of Schumann's songs and piano pieces are recognized as being among his most notable compositions, it is not surprising that the vocal chamber music would also be artistically superior. The three opuses of 1849—*Spanisches Liederspiel* op.74, *Minnespiel* op.101, and *Spanische Liebeslieder* op.138—are especially noteworthy. Each opus was composed for the Dresden *Verein für Chorgesang* that Schumann had founded in 1848, and each consists of a variety of solos, duets, and quartets accompanied by piano. The texts of op.74 and op.138 are translations of Spanish love songs that were popular in Germany during the mid-nineteenth century. *Spanisches Liederspiel* contains ten pieces—three solos, five duets, and two quartets. The first two duets ("Erste Begegnung" for SA and "Intermezzo" for TB) are models of lyricism and charm, and the fourth duet ("In der Nacht" for ST) is one of the most beautifully wrought and engaging vocal pieces of the Romantic era. The two quartets ("Es ist verraten" and "Ich bin geliebt") are also winsome, especially "Ich bin geliebt," the text of which is a testimony to the power of love over evil gossipers and slanderers. *Minnespiel* contains eight pieces—three solos, three duets, and two quartets. The tenor solo "Mein schöner Stern" is often extracted and performed alone. The alto and bass duet "Ich bin dein Baum" is, like "In der Nacht" from op.74, one of the great vocal pieces of the Romantic era; it is extraordinary in its appeal and compelling in its expressiveness. The first of the two quartets ("Schön ist das Fest des Lenzes") is an exuberant tribute to spring, and the second quartet ("So wahr die Sonne scheinet") is a gentle homage to love. *Spanische Liebeslieder*, with piano accompaniment for four hands, contains ten pieces—five solos, two duets, one quartet, and two movements for piano alone. The quartet ("Dunkler Lichtglanz") is another highly expressive love song.

A fourth opus of vocal chamber music, *Drei Gedichte* op.29, composed in 1840, contains one of Schumann's most popular mixed voice pieces, "Zigeunerleben." Inspired by the Roma (gypsy) music that was popular in Germany at the time, it is scored for SATB vocal quartet, piano, and optional triangle and tambourine.

With few exceptions, the part songs were composed between 1846 and 1853. Most of them are a cappella, strophic, basically homophonic, combined into opuses like the vocal chamber music, and written expressly for one of the ensembles Schumann was conducting. The genre was important to Schumann; he wanted to advance it as an art form, and he strove to make it artistically meritorious. His treatment of repeated strophes, for example, is novel and interesting. Instead of simply repeating the same music for different verses of text, he often adjusted rhythms, altered voicings, changed keys and tempos, introduced solos into the choral texture, and varied expressive markings (especially *messa di voce*). Of the seven opuses for mixed voices, four are titled *Romanzen und Balladen,* and all are scored for SATB chorus except *Vier doppelchörige Gesänge* op.141, which is scored for double chorus. The part songs for women's voices are grouped into two opuses (69 and 91), and those for men's voices are grouped into five opuses (33, 62, 65, 93, and 137). Op.137, titled *Fünf Gesänge aus H. Laubes Jagdbrevier* (generally referred to as simply *Jagdlieder*), is scored for four-part men's voices and four horns. The seven pieces in op.65, collectively entitled *Ritornelle,* are all canonic. Some are traditional in construction and are scored for equal voices, typically BBB. Some, however, are unique and ingenious. The first piece in the opus, "Die Rose stand im Tau," which was composed the day after Mendelssohn died, is structured as a canon at the fourth between the first tenor and first bass parts, with the other parts (TBB) accompanimental. The third piece, "Blüt' oder Schnee," is scored for three solo tenors in canon, with the addition of a chorus of TTBB at cadence points. In the final piece, subtitled "Canon infinitus," Schumann modulates each period of canonic writing to a new key so that the piece could, in theory, continue indefinitely. Schumann was especially fond of op.33 no.5, "Rastlose Liebe," which he printed in an edition of the *Neue Zeitschrift für Musik.*

CHORAL/ORCHESTRAL WORKS
SELECTED AND LISTED ACCORDING TO FAMILIARITY

Das Paradies und die Peri op.50 – 1843 – SSATTB solos, SATB chorus, and orchestra (including piccolo, tuba, cymbals, and bass drum) – 96 minutes. (1) Solo roles are for Peri (S), Die Jungfrau (S), Der Engel (A), Der Jüngling (T), and Gazna (B), with additional solos for an unnamed tenor; (2) there are also parts for SATB solo quartet; (3) the choral parts occasionally divide into SSAATTBB.

Requiem für Mignon op.98b – 1849 – SSAATB solos, SATB chorus, and orchestra (including harp ad lib.) – 12 minutes. (1) The work is in six short movements—one for chorus alone, one for SA duet, and the remainder for chorus and various solos; (2) the chorus briefly divides into SSAATTBB.

Requiem op.148 – 1852 – SATB solos, SATB chorus, and orchestra – 40 minutes. Except for brief melodic passages, solo scoring is for quartet.

Der Rose Pilgerfahrt op.112 – 1851 – SAATB solos, SATB chorus, and piano – 55 minutes. (1) Major solo roles are for the Rose (S) and an unnamed person (T); (2) minor solos are for AAB; (3) Schumann later scored the piano part for orchestra.

Szenen aus Goethes Faust (without opus number) – 1844–1853 – SSSSSS-AAAAATTBBBBBB solos, SATB chorus, and orchestra – 115 minutes. (1) Major solo roles are for Faust (B), Gretchen (S), and Mephistopheles (B); (2) minor solo roles are for Martha (S), an Evil Spirit (B), Ariel (T), Want (A), Guilt (A), Worry (S), Distress (S), Pater Ecstaticus (T), Pater Profundis (B), Pater Seraphicus (B), Doctor Marianus (B), Magna Peccatrix (S), Mulier Samaritana (A), Maria Aegyptiaca (A), Una Poenitentium (S), and Mater Gloriosa (A); (3) performances today usually combine roles so that the number of soloists is limited to approximately ten; (4) the choral parts divide frequently.

VOCAL CHAMBER WORKS
SELECTED AND LISTED ACCORDING TO FAMILIARITY

Zigeunerleben (from *Drei Gedichte* op.29) – 1840 – SATB solo quartet, piano, and optional triangle and tambourine – 3:30 minutes. (1) Except for very brief melodic passages, the scoring is for quartet; (2) two short phrases are marked for SS and TT duet, respectively, although they can easily be performed by SA and TB; (3) there is no part indicated for either triangle or tambourine.

So wahr die Sonne scheinet (from *Minnespiel* op.101) – 1849 – SATB solo quartet and piano – 3:30 minutes.

Ich bin geliebt (from *Spanisches Liederspiel* op.74) – 1849 – SATB solo quartet and piano – 3:45 minutes.

Schön ist das Fest des Lenzes (from *Minnespiel* op.101) – 1849 – SATB solo quartet and piano – 3:30 minutes.

Dunkler Lichtglanz (from *Spanische Liebeslieder* op.138) – 1849 – SATB solo quartet and piano four hands – 2:30 minutes.

PART SONGS
SELECTED AND LISTED ACCORDING TO FAMILIARITY

Gute Nacht (from *Vier Gesänge* op.59) – 1846 – SATB chorus a cappella – 1 minute. There are brief passages for solo soprano.

Am Bodensee (from *Vier Gesänge* op.59) – 1846 – SATB chorus a cappella – 3 minutes.

Romanze vom Gänsebuben (from *Romanzen und Balladen* op.145) – 1849–1850 – SATB chorus a cappella – 3 minutes. Passages for solo quartet alternate with passages for chorus.

Die Lotusblume (from *Sechs Lieder* op.33) – 1840 – TTBB chorus a cappella – 2:30 minutes.

Bei der Flasche (from *Jagdlieder* op.137) – 1849 – TTBB chorus and four horns (optional) – 2 minutes.

Die Rose stand im Tau (from *Ritornelle* op.65) – 1847 – TTBBB chorus a cappella – 2:45 minutes.

FRANZ LISZT 1811–1886

Liszt was born in Doborján, Hungary (now Raiding, Austria), into a musical family. His father, Adam, was an amateur singer, pianist, and cellist, who had served as a clerk at the Esterházy court and played under Joseph Haydn. Franz studied piano with his father, and by age eight he was playing works by Bach, Mozart, Clementi, and Hummel; at nine he gave his first public concert, the *Concerto* in E-flat major by Ferdinand Ries. When Liszt was eleven the family moved to Vienna, and the young prodigy began studying theory with Antonio Salieri and piano with Carl

Czerny, who said of Liszt, "Never before had I a student so eager, talented, or industrious." Liszt also played concerts that were attended by such notable composers as Beethoven and Schubert, and at about the time of his twelfth birthday he embarked on a tour with his father to Munich, Augsburg, Strasbourg, Stuttgart, and Paris, settling with his family in Paris, where he was denied admittance to the Conservatoire because he was not French. For the next several years Liszt played concerts in London and Manchester as well as in Paris and selected German cities, dazzling audiences with his virtuosity and gaining a reputation as the most accomplished living pianist (a December 1822 review in the *Allgemeine Zeitung* called him "a little Hercules"). He also was recognized as a capable composer; his opera *Don Sanche* was premiered in Paris in October 1825, just before his fourteenth birthday. With the death of his father in 1827, he began teaching piano privately, and he became intensely attracted to the Catholic Church, seriously contemplating becoming a priest. He continued to perform and compose works for the piano, however, and became especially known for his transcriptions and paraphrases of operas and orchestral works. His improvisations of themes from Mozart's *Don Giovanni* were extremely popular, and his transcription of Berlioz's *Symphonie fantastique* was published in 1830, before the appearance of the orchestral score. In addition, during the 1830s Liszt composed some of his most technically challenging solo piano works, including the six *Etudes d'exécution transcendante d'après Paganini*.

In 1835 he eloped to Switzerland with his lover Marie d'Agoult and taught piano at the newly formed Geneva Conservatoire, and during the next several years the couple had three children, one of whom was Cosima (born on Christmas Day 1837), who would first marry the pianist, conductor, and music critic Hans von Bülow, and then Richard Wagner. While continuing to maintain his permanent residence in Switzerland during the late 1830s and early 1840s, Liszt traveled widely, spending several months in 1837 at the home of French novelist George Sand in Nohant-Vic and performing six concerts in Vienna to support the effort to build a monument to Beethoven. Other performances during these years were in Spain, Portugal, Ireland, Romania, Turkey, and Russia, in addition to France, Germany, Austria, and England. In 1840 he began his conducting career with performances of Mozart's *Die Zauberflöte* and Beethoven's *Fantasie für Klavier, Chor und Orchester c-moll* (Choral Fantasy) op.80, and in 1848, having separated from Marie four years earlier, he moved to Weimar, Germany, where he was appointed *Kapellmeister* at the ducal court. While in Weimar, which was the home and center of the New German School of composition, he conducted Wagner's *Tannhäuser* and *Lohengrin,* Schumann's *Genoveva* and *Manfred,* and Berlioz's *Benvenuto Cellini.* He also conducted music of the past, including Friedrich Schneider's *Das Weltgericht* and Handel's *Messiah, Israel in Egypt,* and *Judas Maccabaeus.* In addition, he composed his first orchestral works, including *Les préludes* and the *Faust-Symphonie,* and his two large-scale organ works, the *Fantasie und Fuge über den Choral Ad nos ad salutarem* and the *Präludium und Fuge über den Namen BACH.* Furthermore, he attracted numerous visitors (e.g., Berlioz, Wagner, and Brahms), wrote essays on important works such as Wagner's *Lohengrin* and Berlioz's *Harold en Italie,* and furthered his ideas about the future direction of music, writing his essay "Über die zukünftige Kirchenmusik," in which he expressed his desire that religious music should "unite the theater and the church on a colossal scale."

In hopes of marrying Princess Carolyne Sayn-Wittgenstein, whom he had met in 1847 and who had been attempting to obtain an annulment from marriage to a Russian prince, Liszt and Carolyne moved to Rome in 1861. The annulment was granted, although the couple never married and they eventually separated. Liszt frequently visited St Peter's and the Sistine Chapel, where he was drawn to the sounds of Gregorian chant and the polyphony of Palestrina and other Renaissance composers. He was also drawn to the Cäcilien movement, which had as its mission the return of church music to the ideals of the Council of Trent and the Counter-Reformation. More important, Liszt composed most of his significant choral works and renewed his attraction to the religious precepts of the church: he took minor orders, resided in a monastery for two years and then in an apartment at the Vatican, and became known as "Abbé Liszt." He even became friends with Pope Pius IX.

His reputation as a performer and the subsequent desire of people all over Europe to either hear or meet him drew him away from the secluded monastic life. He returned to Weimar in 1869 to conduct and give master classes; he visited his homeland Hungary in 1870 and in 1875 was appointed president of the newly formed National Hungarian Royal Academy of Music (now named the Liszt Academy of Music); and in 1886 he attended celebrations in London in honor of his upcoming seventy-fifth birthday. In early July of that year he went to Bayreuth to visit his daughter Cosima and to attend the wedding of his granddaughter Daniela. While there he became ill with pneumonia and died on July 31, several months before his seventy-fifth birthday.

Liszt's choral output consists of five masses (including one Requiem), three oratorios, numerous motets, and varied settings of miscellaneous sacred and secular texts. Two masses, the first and last, are scored for men's voices with organ accompaniment. The *Messe für Männerchor*, composed in 1848 shortly after Liszt had arrived in Rome and experienced the Renaissance polyphony that was so prevalent at St Peter's and other churches, is, as related by Liszt, a reflection of "religious absorption, Catholic devotion, and exaltation." The work includes the traditional portions of the Ordinary, with the Benedictus set separately and entitled "Post elevationem." In addition, the Gloria and Credo are divided into various sections. The choral writing is mainly homophonic, with only occasional imitative passages, and the organ part basically provides harmonic support for the chorus. The *Requiem*, composed in 1867 and 1868 at the end of Liszt's residence in Italy, is divided into six movements—Requiem aeternam, Dies irae, Offertorium, Sanctus, Agnus Dei, and Libera me. The style of the music is like that of the earlier mass, although the solo writing is more extensive and the organ part is independent, especially in the Sanctus and Libera me. Also, the *Requiem* is scored for brass instruments and timpani ad lib. in the Tuba mirum and Judex ergo portions of the Dies irae, and in the Sanctus.

Two other masses are scored for soloists, mixed chorus, and orchestra. *Missa solennis zu Einweihung der Basilika in Gran* (called the "Graner Festmesse") was composed in 1855 for the dedication of the Basilica of Esztergom, the largest church in Hungary. It is in the style of Beethoven's *Missa* in C major op.86 of 1807—a quartet of soloists is often in dialogue with the chorus, and brief sections of independent orchestral passages are interjected into the vocal/choral texture. Liszt's writing is dramatic and expressive, reflective of that in Berlioz's *L'enfance du Christ*. The *Missa coronationalis* was composed for the coronation of Franz Joseph I and premiered on June 8, 1867, at the Mathias Church in Buda. At that time it contained only the traditional portions of the Ordinary. However, the following year Liszt added a Gradual motet to the Latin text "Laudate Dominum omnes gentes" (Psalm 117) and an instrumental Offertory. The style of the mass is like that of his earlier choral/orchestral work.

The fifth mass, *Missa choralis* for mixed voices and organ accompaniment, was composed in 1865 and is in the conservative Renaissance style of Liszt's mass and Requiem for men's voices. The *Missa choralis* is more reflective of past compositional techniques, however. For example, the Kyrie begins with an extended passage of imitative polyphony that is purely a cappella (the organ does not enter for two dozen measures); scoring for solo voices is minimal and does not occur until the Credo; the choral writing is limited in both tessitura and dramatic impact; and the organ part doubles the voices except for a brief passage in the Sanctus.

The first oratorio, *Die Legende von der heiligen Elizabeth*, was begun in 1857 before Liszt's move to Rome and completed in 1862. Its premiere (in Hungarian translation) was in Pest, Hungary, in 1865. The libretto relates events in the life of St Elizabeth (ca.1207–1231), who was of Hungarian birth and who married Ludwig, son of Landgrave Hermann I of Thuringia. The couple lived at the Wartburg Castle on the outskirts of Eisenach, and through a miracle related to Elizabeth's devotion to helping the poor, her husband was converted to Christianity and subsequently died in 1227 during a crusade. Forced to leave the castle by her mother-in-law Landgravine Sophie, Elizabeth built a hospice in Marburg, continued helping the poor, and was canonized in 1235. The castle, where Martin Luther began his translation of the New Testament, was restored in 1838 with the addition of six frescos depicting the life of St Elizabeth. Liszt's oratorio, in six scenes, is based on these frescos—"Ankunft der Elisabeth auf Wartburg" (Arrival of Elizabeth at the Wartburg), "Ludwig," "Die Kreuzritter" (The Crusaders), "Landgräfin Sophie," "Elisabeth," and "Feierliche Bestattung der Elisabeth" (Solemn burial of Elizabeth). The music reflects the New German School's emphasis on continuous musical flow and motivic organization. Liszt used five motifs (leitmotifs) throughout the oratorio—a Gregorian chant normally sung on the feast day of St Elizabeth, a hymn to St Elizabeth, a popular Hungarian folk song, an ancient pilgrim song of the Crusades, and a motif referred to as "the cross." The oratorio was popular during its day, with performances in Munich and Prague in 1866, the Wartburg Castle in 1867, St Petersburg in 1869, New York City in 1885, and Paris, Boston, and London in 1886.

Christus was begun immediately after the completion of *Elizabeth* and finished in 1868. It is in three distinct parts—Christmas Oratorio, After Epiphany, and Passion and Resurrection—and these parts are further divided into distinct sections, each with its own title. The first part has five sections, including "Stabat mater speciosa" and "The Three Holy Kings." The second part also has five sections, each of which relates a scene in the life of Christ—"The Beatitudes," "The Lord's Prayer," "The Foundation of the Church," "The Miracle" (related in Matthew 8), and "The Entry into Jerusalem." The third part has four sections—"Tristis est anima mea" (Matthew 26:38–39), "Stabat mater dolorosa," "O filii et filiae" (an Easter hymn), and "Resurrexit." The parts and sections were composed in random order, and some of them were performed before the entire oratorio was completed. "The Beatitudes" section of part two was performed in 1859, the "Stabat mater speciosa" was performed in Rome in 1866, and all of part one was performed in Vienna in 1871. The entire oratorio had its premiere in Weimar in May 1873. More than three hours in duration and scored for an especially large number of instruments and choral forces (including an offstage female choir), Liszt intended the work to be "colossal" and he referred to it as his "musical will and testament." It has no unifying musical motifs, although it has a unifying textual message. At the beginning of the score Liszt quotes from Ephesians 4:15, "Rather are we to practice the truth in love, and so grow up in all things in him who is the head, Christ."

Die Legende vom heiligen Stanislaus, often called simply *St Stanislaus*, tells the story of the martyrdom of Poland's patron saint in 1079. According to Liszt, it also tells of "the eternal conflict between the Church and the State." Liszt planned to divide the oratorio into four scenes.

Scene one (the people of Krakow complaining to Bishop Stanislaus of the cruelty of King Boleslaw II) was composed in 1874, and scene four (Boleslaw's anguish at having killed Stanislaus and the exaltation of his subjects for their ruler's new compassion) was composed in 1886 just before Liszt's death. Scenes two and three (Stanislaus rebuking the king, the king falsely accusing Stanislaus of theft, and the murder of Stanislaus) were never composed. Both completed scenes begin with extended orchestral preludes, the end of the second based on the Polish national anthem, and the majority of this scene is accompanied only by organ. The text of the first scene is in German, while the text of the second scene (Psalm 130 and "Salve Polonia") is in Latin.

Miscellaneous choral works include *Inno a Maria vergine* (Hymn to the Virgin Mary) for mixed chorus, harp, and organ (or piano four hands) composed in 1869; *Die Seligkeiten* (The Beatitudes) for baritone solo, mixed chorus, and organ ad lib. composed between 1855 and 1859 and later incorporated into the oratorio *Christus; Via cruces* (The way of the cross), subtitled "les 14 stations de la croix" (the fourteen stations of the cross) composed in 1878 and 1879 for mixed soloists and chorus with organ or piano accompaniment; *Es war einmal ein König* (There once was a king), also known as "The song of the flea," composed in 1844 to Mephistopheles' song in the first part of Goethe's *Faust* and scored for baritone solo, male chorus, and piano; and *Eine Faust-Symphonie* (A Faust symphony), composed in 1854 and revised in 1860, and scored for tenor solo, mixed chorus, and orchestra.

MASSES
COMPLETE AND LISTED IN CHRONOLOGICAL ORDER
ACCORDING TO DATE OF COMPOSITION

Messe für Männerchor – 1848 (revised in 1859 and 1869) – TTBB chorus and organ – 13 minutes. There are brief solo and quartet passages.

Missa solennis zur Einweihung der Basilika in Gran (called the "Graner Festmesse") – 1855 (revised in 1857–1858) – SATB solos, SATB chorus, and orchestra (including three flutes, cymbals, bass drum, harp, and organ) – 57 minutes. (1) The soloists mostly sing together as a quartet; (2) the choral parts occasionally divide into SSAATTBB; (3) the organ is not used as a basso continuo instrument to support the chorus but is used independently as an orchestral instrument.

Missa choralis – 1859–1865 – SATB chorus and organ – 38 minutes. (1) There are brief solo and quartet passages; (2) the choral parts occasionally divide into SSAATTBB; (3) the organ part is minimal and is used to support the chorus.

Missa coronationalis (called the "Krönungsmesse" or "Coronation Mass") – 1867 – SATB solos, SATB chorus, and orchestra (including organ) – 44 minutes. (1) The mass contains a Gradual motet, scored for SATB/TTBB chorus; (2) the choral parts occasionally divide in other movements.

Requiem – 1867–1868 – TTBB solos, TTBB chorus, and organ – 51 minutes. (1) There is scoring for two trumpets, two trombones, and timpani ad lib. in the Dies irae and Sanctus; (2) the organ part is independent and occasionally figural.

ORATORIOS
COMPLETE AND LISTED IN CHRONOLOGICAL ORDER
ACCORDING TO DATE OF COMPOSITION

Die Legende von der heiligen Elizabeth – 1857–1862 – SABBBBB solos, SATB
chorus, and orchestra (including piccolo, English horn, two harps, harmonium, and organ) – 150 minutes. (1) Solo roles are for St Elizabeth
(S), Landgravine Sophie (A), Landgrave Hermann (B), Landgrave Ludwig
(B), a Hungarian Magnate (B), the Seneschal (B), and Emperor Frederick
II (B); (2) the parts of Ludwig, the Magnate, the Seneschal, and Frederick
can be sung by the same singer; (3) the SATB chorus divides into eight
parts; (4) there is indication for a children's chorus ad lib.

Christus – 1862–1868 – SAATBB solos, SATB chorus, and orchestra similar
to that of St Elizabeth – 210 minutes. (1) The major solo role is for
Christ (B); (2) the SATB chorus divides into eight parts; (3) there is a
brief section of music in movement eleven for an offstage female choir.

Die Legende vom heiligen Stanislaus – 1874 and 1886 – SSSABBBB solos,
SATB chorus, and orchestra (including organ) – 60 minutes. (1) Major
solo roles are for Bishop Stanislaus (B), the Bishop's Mother (A), and
King Boleslaw (B); (2) minor solo roles are for Three Voices (SSS), an
Old Man (B), and a Knight (B).

RICHARD WAGNER 1813–1883

Wagner was born in Leipzig and first educated at the Kreuzschule in Dresden, where his family had moved in 1822. In 1828 the family moved back to Leipzig and Wagner continued his
education at the Nikolaischule, and after graduation in 1831 he enrolled at the University of
Leipzig and also began studies with the *Kantor* of the Thomaskirche. The following year he was
appointed chorusmaster of a small theater in Würzburg, and during the next decade he held
other minor appointments and spent three years in Paris earning a living by making piano
arrangements of operatic scenes and by writing music reviews. In 1843 he had his first operatic
success with the premiere of *Der fliegende Holländer* (The Flying Dutchman), and in that same
year he was appointed *Vice-Kapellmeister* at the court in Dresden, a position he retained for six
years and one that allowed him opportunities to compose choral works and conduct masterpieces such as Beethoven's *Symphony #9*. He fled to Zürich in 1849 to avoid imprisonment for
his outspoken political views, missing the premiere of *Lohengrin* in Weimar under Franz Liszt
in 1850, and for the next fourteen years he moved about to evade payment of debts. In 1864,
with the support of eighteen-year-old Ludwig II, King of Bavaria, Wagner settled in Munich, saw
the premiere of *Tristan und Isolde* in 1865 and *Die Meistersinger von Nürnberg* in 1868, and began
composition of his four operas collectively entitled *Der Ring des Nibelungen*. His Festspielhaus
in Bayreuth was built between 1872 and 1876, and his last opera, *Parsifal*, was premiered there
in 1882. He suffered his first heart attack also in 1882 and moved to Venice, where he suffered
another heart attack and died on February 13, 1883, at age sixty-nine.

Wagner composed twelve choral works, including three a cappella ceremonial cantatas for male chorus—*Der Tag erscheint* in 1843 for a memorial celebration of King Friedrich August I of Saxony; *Gruss seiner Treuen an Friedrich August den Geliebten* in 1844 for King Friedrich August II; and *Hebt an den Sang* ("An Webers Grabe") in 1844 for the move of Carl Maria von Weber's remains to Dresden. A fourth work for male chorus, *Das Liebesmahl der Apostel* (The feast of Pentecost), with orchestral accompaniment, was composed in 1843 for a festival performance of all the male-voice choruses in Saxony. The festival was sponsored by the Dresden Choral Society, and Wagner's work was premiered at the Dresden Frauenkirche on July 6, 1843, with twelve hundred singers and an orchestra of almost one hundred. Wagner wrote the text himself and scored the voices for a group of twelve soloists who represent the twelve apostles and who always sing together (mostly in unison), and a chorus of disciples that is divided into three separate ensembles. The work is mostly a cappella. The orchestra, which joins the chorus as they are singing, does not enter until the final fourth of the work (i.e., the chorus sings a cappella for approximately three-quarters of the work, or twenty-four out of thirty-three and a half minutes).

Other choral works include incidental music composed in 1835 for the play *Beim Antritt des neuen Jahres* and scored for mixed voices and orchestra; *Volks-Hymne,* an anthem composed in 1837 for the birthday of Tsar Nicholas; and three pieces for children's chorus composed in the 1870s. In addition, there are choral movements from operas that are occasionally extracted and performed separately. These include "The Procession to the Cathedral" from *Lohengrin,* the "Tournament Song" from *Tannhäuser,* and the opening and closing scenes as well as the "Homage to Hans Sachs" (act three, scene five) from *Die Meistersinger von Nürnberg.*

CLARA SCHUMANN 1819–1896

Clara Schumann was born in Leipzig, the daughter of Friedrich Wieck, who was a music and piano merchant as well as a distinguished piano teacher and master technician. Clara's mother, the granddaughter of flutist Johann George Tromlitz, was also a well-known musician, who performed as both singer and pianist at concerts in the Leipzig Gewandhaus. Clara studied with her father and many of the most renowned musicians in Leipzig, and she became familiar with the repertoire of the day by attending concerts in Leipzig and in other cities in Europe where her father was on tour. She herself played in the Gewandhaus at age nine and composed her first work, four polonaises for piano, at eleven. During her teenage years she performed in cities such as Paris and Vienna and was recognized as one of the finest virtuoso pianists of her time. In 1840, at age twenty-one, she married Robert Schumann and lived with him in Leipzig, Dresden, and Düsseldorf until his untimely death in 1856. For the remainder of her life she concertized throughout Europe and promoted her husband's music—playing his piano works on recital programs, making piano scores of his orchestral works, and editing his complete works for publication. From 1878 until her death she taught piano at the Hoch Conservatory in Frankfurt.

Schumann composed twenty-five solo lieder and three part songs in addition to approximately fifty piano works. The part songs, entitled collectively *Drei gemischte Chöre,* were composed for her husband as a birthday present and sung for him on his thirty-eighth birthday by members of the Dresden *Verein für Chorgesang,* which he had founded earlier that year. The three pieces are settings of poems by Emanuel Geibel (1815–1884), a popular poet of the time. The first, "Abendfeier in Venedig" (Evening celebration in Venice), lauds an Ave Maria sung during the ringing of bells from the many towers in Venice; the second, "Vorwärts" (Forward), chides the artist to stop dreaming and wavering and to press onward in art; and the third, "Gondoliera" (The gondolier), paints a picture of lovers on a gondola in Venice under the moonlight. All three pieces are scored for SATB voices a cappella.

PETER CORNELIUS 1824–1874

Cornelius was born in Mainz to parents who were both actors. As a child Peter became immersed in the theatrical world and also studied violin and music theory, and at age sixteen he joined the second violin section of the Mainz opera company, which toured to London shortly after he joined the ensemble. To further his education and professional opportunities, he moved to Berlin in 1844, living there with his uncle, the painter Peter von Cornelius (1783–1869), meeting the poets Joseph von Eichendorff and Paul Heyse, writing his own poetry, and becoming acquainted with Felix Mendelssohn and the conductor Hans von Bülow. In 1852 Cornelius moved to Weimar to be at the center of the New German School of composition and to serve as secretary to Franz Liszt. While in Weimar, Cornelius also wrote articles for the *Neue Zeitschrift für Musik* and other periodicals. Feeling that he had very little artistic independence in Weimar, however, in 1859 he moved to Vienna, where he met Brahms and where he worked with Wagner. In 1864 he followed Wagner to Munich, serving as Wagner's personal assistant as well as teaching at the Royal School of Music, and he became acquainted with the Leipzig choral conductor Carl Riedel, president of the Allgemeiner Deutscher Musikverein at that time. Cornelius developed an interest in sacred choral music, and in an 1871 letter to his brother, he wrote, "There will no doubt come a time for sacred music to return, and when it does, the overwhelming enthusiasm for it will deliver us from the terror and tyranny of our present academic situation, where in concerts we are subjected to the mummified heartbeat of an earlier time rather than hearing that of our own." He had little time to make an impact, however. His health declined as a result of diabetes, and he died in 1874, two months before his fiftieth birthday.

Cornelius's choral output consists of a few multimovement sacred works and approximately thirty smaller-scale a cappella pieces. The larger works include the *Stabat mater* for soloists, chorus, and orchestra, and the *Messe* in D minor for SATB chorus and organ ad lib. This latter work is based on the Gregorian Offertory chant *Tu es Petrus* and is written in a neo-Renaissance polyphonic style. Most of the smaller-scale works, which are the best known of Cornelius's repertoire, are settings of spiritual texts—poetry that alludes to God or that expresses transcendental feelings. *Liebe* op.18, for instance, consists of three pieces set to poetry of the seventeenth-century mystic poet Angelus Silesius, and *Requiem*, subtitled "Seele, vergiss sie nicht," is a setting of a poem by Friedrich Hebbel (1813–1863), composed by Cornelius in the year of Hebbel's death as a commemoration. In the *Requiem*, Cornelius repeats the first line of the poem, "Seele, vergiss sie nicht, vergiss nicht die Toten" (Soul, forget them not, forget not the dead), with similar music at each repetition to create an ABACA form. The *Drei Chorgesänge* op.11 are settings of poems by the popular German Romantic poets Heinrich Heine (1797–1856) and Friedrich Rückert (1788–1866) that deal with release from death's anguish.

Other pieces are elaborations of liturgical texts (chorales and Psalms). "Ach wie nichtig, ach wie flüchtig" op.9 no.1 (Oh how void, oh how elusive) is a reworking of the chorale text by Michael Franck (1609–1667), and "Mitten wir im Leben sind" op.9 no.3 (Though in the midst of life we are) is an arrangement of Martin Luther's chorale. The *Drei Psalmlieder nach Klaviersätzen von Johann Sebastian Bach* op.13 are settings of three Psalms to music arranged from Bach's keyboard works. Number one of the opus, "Warum verbirgst du vor mir dein Antlitz" (from Psalm 88), is based on Bach's first sarabande from the French Suite BWV812; number two, "Stromflut dahinrauscht durch Babels Gefilde" (from Psalm 137), is based on the third sarabande from the English Suite BWV808; and number three, "Heil und Freude ward mir verheißen" (from Psalm 122), is based on the second minuet from the Partita number one in B-flat major BWV825.

Cornelius's most famous choral piece, *Die Könige*, was originally composed in 1856 as one of the solo songs in *Weihnachtslieder* op.8. It was revised in 1870 for solo and chorus, with the soloist singing a text by Cornelius about the three kings visiting the manger in Bethlehem, and with the chorus singing the chorale "Wie schön leuchtet der Morgenstern" (How brightly shines the morning star). Two other notable pieces were composed at the end of Cornelius's life—*Die Vätergruft* op.19 to a poem by Ludwig Uhland (1787–1862) about the death of an anonymous Medieval hero, and *So weich und warm* about the loneliness of death.

A CAPPELLA WORKS
SELECTED AND LISTED ACCORDING TO FAMILIARITY

Die Könige (from *Weihnachtslieder* op.8) – 1856 (revised in 1870) – B solo and SATB chorus – 2:30 minutes.

Requiem ("Seele, vergiss sie nicht") – 1863 – SSATBB chorus – 8:30 minutes.

So weich und warm – 1874 – SATB chorus – 3:30 minutes.

Die Vätergruft op.19 – 1874 – B solo and SATB chorus – 3 minutes.

Liebe op.18 – 1872 – mixed chorus – "Liebe, dir ergeb' ich mich" for SSAATTBB chorus, 6:30 minutes; "Ich will dich lieben, meine Krone" for SSAA/TTBB chorus, 4:30 minutes; and "Thron der Liebe, Stern der Güte" for SSAA/TTBB chorus, 5:30 minutes.

Drei Psalmlieder nach Klaviersätzen von Johann Sebastian Bach op.13 – 1872 – SATB chorus – 6:30 minutes. The three numbers, identified and discussed above, are 2:30, 2:30, and 1:30 minutes in duration, respectively.

Drei Chorgesänge op.11 – 1871 – mixed chorus – "Der Tod, das ist die kühle Nacht" for T solo and SATB/SATB chorus, 5:30 minutes; "An den Sturmwind" for SATB/SATB chorus, 3 minutes; and "Die drei Frühlingstage" for SSATTB chorus, 2:30 minutes.

Trauerchöre op.9 – 1870 – TTBB chorus – "Ach wie nichtig" 5:30 minutes; "Nicht die Träne kann es sagen" 2:30 minutes; "Mitten wir im Leben sind" 6:30 minutes; "Grablied" 1:30 minutes; and "Von dem Dome" 4 minutes.

Absolve Domine – 1852 – TTBB chorus – 2:30 minutes.

ANTON BRUCKNER 1824–1896

Bruckner was born in the small town of Ansfelden, Austria, near the city of Linz—an area of strict and conservative Catholicism that was to influence him for his entire life. He began musical studies with his father, a schoolteacher and church organist, and at age ten he played his first church services. At eleven he studied with his godfather, also an organist, and at thirteen he was accepted as a chorister at the Augustinian monastery of St Florian. He sang masses there by Mozart and both Joseph and Michael Haydn, and he heard performances of oratorios, including Haydn's *Die Schöpfung* and *Die Jahreszeiten,* and Mendelssohn's *Paulus.* At age sixteen Bruckner left St Florian and enrolled in a teacher's training college in Linz, and at seventeen he wrote his first compositions—a mass for alto solo, two horns, and organ, as well as several motets, including *Pange lingua.* At twenty-one he became an assistant teacher at St Florian, at twenty-four he was appointed organist and composed his first large-scale work (a Requiem in memory of his friend and supporter Franz Sailer), and at thirty-one he returned to Linz as principal organist at the cathedral. In addition to his cathedral duties, he sang in and later directed a local male chorus (*Liedertafel*) named *Frohsinn.* He also composed numerous secular works for *Frohsinn* and other male vocal ensembles, including *Germanenzug* for male chorus and brass, which he considered his "first real composition." Lacking confidence in his work, however, and desiring academic credentials, he continued his musical studies in both Linz and Vienna and received a diploma from the Vienna Conservatory in 1861 (at age thirty-seven). Bruckner's desire for achievement, mixed with his self-doubt, led to a nervous breakdown in 1867 and a four-month confinement in a sanatorium. He apparently recovered completely, for he spent the remainder of his life engaged in successful professional activity: he composed many of his most artistically accredited works—including the *Messe in F-Moll* (Mass in F minor), *Te Deum, Psalm 150, Christus factus est, Os justi,* and *Locus iste*—and he experienced considerable acclaim with his improvisations at organ concerts in major venues throughout Europe, including Notre Dame in Paris and Royal Albert Hall and the Crystal Palace in London. Furthermore, he achieved his desire for academic recognition by being appointed professor of organ and composition at Vienna University (which awarded him an honorary doctorate in 1891) and by being honored with the Order of Franz Joseph. He died of natural causes while working on his ninth symphony, and he was buried in the crypt below the great organ at the monastery of St Florian.

As a result of Bruckner's self-doubt and lack of confidence, and also as a result of his focus on details (his nervous breakdown in 1867 was officially termed numeromania—a compulsive urge to count objects for no apparent reason), he was constantly revising his works. These revisions were generally minor, consisting of small changes in orchestration and the addition or excision of a few measures of music. However, they are of practical importance to performers, who may unwittingly be using different editions of a particular score (i.e., the conductor may be using a full score different from those of the choral singers and also different from the parts for the orchestral musicians).

Bruckner composed eight masses (including two Requiems), one Te Deum, five large-scale Psalm settings, thirty-two motets, nineteen large-scale secular works, and twenty-six shorter secular pieces. The masses are of two types—those neo-Renaissance works that are a cappella in spirit and those Romantic works that are expansive and fully orchestrated. The Renaissance-like works include all the masses except three (in B-flat minor, D minor, and F minor). Because of this concentration on Renaissance styles, it might be assumed that Bruckner was a proponent or member of the Cäcilienverein, a popular society of composers in the latter part of the nineteenth century whose mission was to return Catholic church music to the "Palestrinian style." This assumption is logical, especially since all of Bruckner's motets are reflective of Renaissance a cappella idioms. However, Bruckner was definitely not a supporter of the Cäcilien movement. His music composed on Renaissance models reflects only his experiences and employment in conservative environments. This is especially so for the early masses (including the Requiems) and the motets, which are limited in scope and duration. The *Messe in E-Moll* (Mass in E minor), for instance, was composed for the dedication of the Votive Chapel of the new Linz Cathedral, which could not accommodate an orchestra. In addition, the Bishop of Linz was particularly fond of the Palestrinian style. Three of the mass's six movements (Kyrie, Sanctus, and Agnus Dei) are in a Renaissance point-of-imitation texture, with minimal wind and brass accompaniment that is basically *colla parte* with the voices; the texture of the movements is therefore essentially a cappella. The other three movements (Gloria, Credo, and Benedictus), however, have instrumental participation that is independent and thematically prominent.

The masses in B-flat minor, D minor, and F minor all combine scoring and structural elements of the late Classical-era works by Joseph Haydn and Beethoven with expressive and textural elements of Romantic-era orchestral works by Liszt. The D minor and F minor masses, for instance, are like older, traditional masses in that they are scored for a quartet of soloists, the Glorias and Credos are in one movement divided into multiple sections delineated by varying tempos, and the music of the opening Kyrie returns in the Agnus Dei. Newer structural and musical elements include motifs that occur in multiple movements and thus unify the entire mass (e.g., ascending scalar passages in the Gloria, Sanctus, Benedictus, and Agnus Dei movements of the D minor mass), orchestral transitions that bind sections of music together in a fluid manner, and word painting devices such as descending chromatic lines to characterize the word "mortuorum" in the Credo (identical in both the D minor and F minor masses).

The *Messe in D-Moll* (Mass in D minor) was composed during the spring and summer of 1864 and first performed at the Linz Cathedral in November under Bruckner's direction. It was well received, a review of the premiere performance noting, "According to some of our most renowned musical experts, Anton Bruckner's mass . . . is the best of its kind that has been created in many years." Further performances took place at the Redoutensaal in Linz (December 1864) and at the Hofburgkapelle in Vienna (February 1867). Bruckner revised the mass in 1876 and also in 1881. The *Messe in F-Moll* (Mass in F minor) was composed in 1867 and 1868 as Bruckner's thanksgiving for his return to good health after his nervous breakdown. However, it was not performed until June 1872 at the Augustiner Church in Vienna—an event that caused considerable negative criticism by the Cäcilien supporters. Nevertheless, the mass was received well by the general population and there were numerous performances throughout the following decade, including those at the Hofburgkapelle in 1873, 1877, 1882, 1883, and 1884. Bruckner revised the mass in 1890 and 1893.

The other large-scale sacred works include *Psalm 114* (1852), *Psalm 112* (1863), *Te Deum* (1881–1884), and *Psalm 150* (1892). As with the masses, the earlier two works are based on Renaissance models: *Psalm 114* is basically a cappella, and *Psalm 112* is in a Venetian polychoral style. The latter two works are thoroughly Romantic and symphonic. Indeed, both the *Te Deum* and *Psalm 150*, with their expansive sonorities and broad harmonic palettes, are Bruckner's most symphonic choral works (i.e., they are the choral works that are most like his symphonies). This similarity is no doubt due to the fact that they were composed at a time when Bruckner was writing little else but symphonies; the *Te Deum* was composed between the completion of the fifth and seventh symphonies, and *Psalm 150*—Bruckner's final sacred work—was composed while he was writing the ninth symphony. Bruckner was especially fond of the *Te Deum,* which he called "the pride of [my] life." The first performance was with two pianos in the small Musikvereinsaal in Vienna in May 1885, and the first performance with orchestra was given by the Gesellschaft der Musikfreunde in January 1886.

Most of the motets were composed when Bruckner was employed at St Florian and Linz, and most were therefore composed for actual liturgical use. They are all in the Renaissance style: texts are in Latin, textures are basically a cappella (the few motets that are accompanied are scored for trombones that basically support the voices *colla parte*), and the voice parts are generally composed in a point-of-imitation manner. The most popular of the motets, which have been staples of choral performance in Europe and America for the many decades since their composition, are listed and annotated below.

The secular works, which represent almost half of Bruckner's choral output, are not as well known as the sacred works. Only one composition, *Helgoland,* is recognized as artistically meritorious and performed with any degree of frequency today. Furthermore, it is the only secular composition that Bruckner deemed of value, the only secular composition that he included in the scores he bequeathed to the Vienna Court Library, and the final work he completed in any medium. Written for the fiftieth anniversary of the Vienna Männergesangverein, it was premiered in October 1893 at the Winter Riding School of the Imperial Palace in Vienna. The text, by the Austrian author August Silberstein (1827–1900), is about the Saxon victory over the Romans on the island of Helgoland (formerly Heligoland), which is approximately thirty miles off the German coast, near the Elbe estuary. Another work to the poetry of Silberstein, *Germanenzug,* was composed in 1863 and premiered at the Oberösterreichisch-Salzburgischen Sängerbundes. It was a popular work during the latter part of the nineteenth century, so much so that its middle movement was performed at Bruckner's funeral.

MASSES

SELECTED AND LISTED IN CHRONOLOGICAL ORDER
ACCORDING TO DATE OF COMPOSITION

Requiem in D-Moll (Requiem in D minor) – 1849 – SATB solos, SATB chorus, three trombones, and strings – 36 minutes. (1) The text is in Latin; (2) the solo writing consists of short melodic passages and sections for quartet; (3) the chorus expands to SSATB in the Sanctus and TTBB in the Hostias; (4) a French horn is substituted for one of the trombones in the Benedictus.

Messe in D-Moll (Mass in D minor) – 1864 – SATB solos, SATB chorus, and orchestra (including organ) – 47 minutes. (1) The text is in Latin; (2) the solo writing, which is minimal, is mostly for quartet; (3) the choral parts occasionally divide; (4) the organ part, which is brief, is scored for instruments ad lib. in case there is no organ available for performance.

Messe in E-Moll (Mass in E minor) – 1866 – SSAATTBB chorus, two oboes, two clarinets, two bassoons, four horns, two trumpets, and three trombones – 35 minutes. (1) The text is in Latin; (2) Bruckner specified that the oboe, clarinet, and bassoon parts should be doubled; (3) Bruckner also expected an organ to be used in performance, although no part is scored.

Messe in F-Moll (Mass in F minor) – 1867–1868 – SATB solos, SATB chorus, and orchestra – 60 minutes. (1) The text is in Latin; (2) the solo writing, which is minimal, is mostly for quartet; (3) the chorus parts occasionally divide; (4) Bruckner expected an organ to be used in performance, although no part is scored; (5) the music of the Kyrie returns in the Agnus Dei; (6) there is a violin solo in the Benedictus.

OTHER LARGE-SCALE SACRED WORKS
SELECTED AND LISTED ACCORDING TO FAMILIARITY

Te Deum – 1881–1884 – SATB solos, SATB chorus, and orchestra (including three trumpets, tuba, and organ) – 23 minutes. (1) The text is in Latin; (2) except for brief melodic passages, the solo writing is for quartet; (3) the chorus parts divide occasionally into SSAATTBB.

Psalm 150 – 1892 – S solo, SATB chorus, and orchestra – 8 minutes. (1) The text is in German and begins "Hallelujah, Lobet den Herrn in seinem Heiligtum"; (2) the solo part is brief; (3) the chorus divides into eight parts.

Psalm 112 – 1863 – SATB/SATB chorus and orchestra – 10 minutes. (1) The text is in German and begins "Hallelujah, Lobet den Herrn, ihr Diener"; (2) the chorus parts are combined into one SATB ensemble for portions of the work.

Psalm 114 – 1852 – SSATB chorus and three trombones – 9 minutes. (1) Most of the work is a cappella; (2) the trombones basically accompany the voices *colla parte.*

LARGE-SCALE SECULAR WORKS
SELECTED AND LISTED ACCORDING TO FAMILIARITY

Helgoland – 1893 – TTBB chorus and orchestra (including three trumpets, tuba, and cymbals) – 14 minutes. (1) The text is in German; (2) some of the choral parts divide briefly.

Germanenzug – 1864 – TTBB chorus, three cornets, euphonium, four horns, four trumpets, three trombones, and tuba – 9 minutes.

MOTETS
SELECTED AND LISTED ACCORDING TO FAMILIARITY

Ave Maria – 1861 – SAATTBB chorus a cappella – 2:30 minutes.

Locus iste – 1869 – SATB chorus a cappella – 3:30 minutes.

Christus factus est – 1884 – SATB chorus a cappella – 5:30 minutes.

Os justi – 1879 – SSAATTBB chorus a cappella – 5 minutes.

Virga Jesse floruit – 1885 – SATB chorus a cappella – 4:30 minutes. The tenor and bass parts divide briefly.

Pange lingua – 1868 – SATB chorus a cappella – 4:30 minutes.

Ecce sacerdos – 1885 – SSAATTBB chorus, three trombones, and organ – 5 minutes.

JOHANNES BRAHMS 1833–1897

Brahms was born in Hamburg, where he began musical studies with his father, who was a string bass player in the Hamburg Philharmonie and who also played in dance halls and taverns. At age seven the young Brahms began piano lessons with a local teacher, at ten he gave his first public performance, and during his teenage years he played the piano in area theaters and made arrangements of popular symphonic compositions for local chamber ensembles. He also made arrangements of German folk songs for a local men's choral ensemble and became attracted to the Roma (gypsy) music that he heard from the many Hungarian refugees who had come to Germany beginning in 1848. Serious music interested him as well, especially that of the Renaissance and Baroque eras, and he spent considerable amounts of time studying compositions of Heinrich Schütz and J. S. Bach at the Hamburg library. At age seventeen Brahms heard the Hungarian violinist Ede Reményi (a.k.a. Eduard Hoffmann), whom he later accompanied on a tour throughout Europe, and at twenty he met and became close friends with Robert Schumann, who was a mentor to Brahms and provided him access to his extensive library of music and literature.

Throughout his twenties and early thirties, Brahms held several positions with choral ensembles: at twenty-four he was appointed conductor of the court choir in Detmold, at twenty-six he founded a women's chorus in his hometown of Hamburg, and at thirty he was appointed conductor of the Vienna Singakademie. While in Detmold, he began his *Requiem* and became acquainted with Arthur Schopenhauer, the pessimist philosopher who believed that life gives more pain than pleasure; while in Hamburg, Brahms composed much of his music for women's voices; and while in Vienna, he conducted numerous works of Bach, including the cantata *Ich hatte viel Bekümmernis* BWV21 and the Christmas oratorio *Weihnachtsoratorium* BWV248. Brahms left his position with the Singakademie after only a year, and throughout most of his thirties he accompanied recitals by the violinist Joseph Joachim and the singer Julius Stockhausen. During this time Brahms also composed a number of choral works with orchestral accompaniment, including the *Requiem, Rinaldo, Rhapsodie, Schicksalslied,* and *Triumphlied,* and between 1872 and 1875 he held his fourth choral position—conductor of the Vienna Gesellschaft der Musikfreunde—with which he conducted more works of Bach and also works of Handel. In the following years Brahms concentrated on purely symphonic music (his first symphony was not composed until 1874, when he was forty-one), although he continued to compose choral music as well, including the motets op.74 and op.110, *Nänie* op.82, the vocal quartets op.92, *Zigeunerlieder* op.103, and *Fest- und Gedenksprüche* op.109. His fame grew steadily, and among his many awards and accolades he was twice offered an honorary doctorate from Cambridge University (which he declined to accept), he was offered an honorary doctorate from the University of Breslau (which he did accept), he was given the honorary title "Commander of the Order of Leopold" by Kaiser Wilhelm, and—of great significance to Brahms—he was made a free citizen of the city of Hamburg. He composed no choral music after 1889, and during the last several years of his life he suffered from liver cancer, the cause of his death in March 1897 at age sixty-three.

Brahms's choral music is unique in a number of ways. Most important, it reflects a deep-felt personal despondency about life. Almost all of the sacred compositions, and many of the large-scale secular works as well, have texts that express Schopenhauer's philosophy of life pain—that existence is a task to be endured and that the only hope of joy is after death. This sentiment is expressed in passages from Brahms's first choral composition in 1856—*Geistliches Lied* op.30, "Laß dich nur nichts nicht dauren mit Trauren, sei stille" (Do not allow yourself to tarry in mourning and weeping, be calm)—to his last choral composition in 1889—*Wenn wir in höchsten Nöten sein* op.110 no.3, "Ob wir gleich sorgen früh und spat, so . . . wir zusammen ingemein dich rufen an . . . um Rettung aus der Angst und Not" (Although we are troubled morning until night, so . . . we all together call you . . . to deliver us from fear and sorrow). The many choral works between these framing compositions also express the sentiment of anguish in life, including: *Begräbnisgesang* op.13 (1858), "Hier ist er in Angst gewesen, dort aber wird er genesen" (Here [on earth] it [the body] suffered fear, but there [in heaven] it will find healing); *O Heiland, reiß die Himmel auf* op.74 no.2 (ca.1863), "Hie leiden wir die größte Not" (We suffer here in great distress); *Rhapsodie* op.53 (1869), "Ach, wer heilet die Schmerzen des, dem Balsam zu Gift ward?" (Ah, who will heal the sorrows of him for whom balsam turned to poison?); *Schicksalslied* op.54 (1868–1871), "Ihr wandelt droben im Licht auf weichem Boden, selige Genien. . . . Doch uns ist gegeben, auf keiner Stätte zu ruhn" (You wander above in the light on soft ground, blessed spirits. . . . But to us is not given any place to rest); *Warum ist das Licht gegeben* op.74 no.1 (1877), "Siehe, wir preisen selig, die erduldet haben" (See, we count them blessed, those who endure); *Ich aber bin elend* op.110 no.1 (1889), "Ich aber bin elend, und mir ist wehe" (But I am in misery and I suffer); and *Ach, arme Welt* op.110 no.2 (1889), "Ach, arme Welt, du trügest mich" (Ah, poor world, you deceive me). Only the few occasional works, such as *Triumphlied* op.55 and the part songs and vocal chamber works, which often have folk texts, deal with happiness on earth.

Another unique characteristic of Brahms's music, one that appears with almost as much consistency as the character of text, is a formal structuring of compositions based on canon or close imitation. The fascination with canons no doubt came from the Renaissance and Baroque compositions he studied, but also from the numerous canons he would have observed in Schumann's music. The canonic writing pervaded Brahms's compositions from the beginning of his career, whereas the strictness of canons gave way to close imitation in the later music. Some striking examples of strict complete canons are a double canon at the interval of the ninth in

Geistliches Lied op.30 (1856); a pair of contrary motion canons in *O bone Jesu* op.37 no.1 (ca.1859); a mirror canon for two solo voices in *Regina coeli laetare* op.37 no. 3 (ca.1863); and a canon in augmentation (appearing twice in the soprano voice simultaneously with once in the second bass voice) at the beginning of *Schaffe in mir, Gott, ein rein Herz* op. 29 no.2. Examples of canonic technique in short phrases abound throughout the music. Some exceptional instances are the baritone cantus firmus augmentation of the chorale melody in *Es ist das Heil uns kommen her* op.29 no.1; the inverted melodies in the fugal development of *Schaffe in mir, Gott, ein rein Herz* op.29 no.2; and the augmentation used in movements two and five of the *Requiem*. One further example serves to show the ingenuity of Brahms's writing: at the beginning of movement four of the *Requiem*—perhaps the most familiar of all of Brahms's music—the opening soprano melody is an exact inversion of the orchestral melody that precedes it.

Brahms composed one Requiem, six large-scale works to secular texts with orchestral accompaniment, six works with chamber accompaniment, eighteen a cappella sacred pieces, thirty-eight a cappella secular pieces, sixty vocal chamber pieces with piano accompaniment, and twenty canons. All these works were given opus numbers and published during Brahms's lifetime. Brahms also composed other works that were not given opus numbers and that were not published as a part of his general oeuvre. These include a mass and twenty-six folk song arrangements. The mass, sometimes referred to as the "Missa Canonica," was composed in 1856 and 1857 but was presumed lost and was not published or performed until 1984. It consists of four movements (Kyrie, Sanctus, Benedictus, and Agnus Dei) and is in the imitative polyphonic and canonic style of the works from the Renaissance and Baroque that Brahms studied during his youth.

The Requiem, entitled *Ein deutsches Requiem* (A German requiem), is undoubtedly the best-known sacred work of the Romantic era. It was begun in 1857, the year after Brahms's close friend Robert Schumann died, and was given by Brahms the exact same title as that of a work Schumann had noted in his diary and had hoped to compose one day. In 1864 Brahms sent Schumann's wife, Clara, a copy of what later became the fourth movement, "Wie lieblich sind deine Wohnungen" (How lovely are thy dwellings), with apologies for its presumed weakness. In 1867 the first three movements were composed and performed in memory of Franz Schubert by the Vienna Gesellschaft der Musikfreunde, and in 1868 two other movements, now numbers six and seven, were added, and all six movements were performed in the Bremen Cathedral. This performance, which was conducted by Brahms and which included excerpts from Bach's *Passio secundum Mattaeum* (St Matthew Passion) and Handel's *Messiah,* involved two hundred singers and an orchestra with forty-eight violins. Brahms added the fifth movement to his *Requiem* in 1869 and conducted this final version in February of that year at the Leipzig Gewandhaus. The theory that Brahms composed the fifth movement because of his mother's death is probably untrue, since his mother had died in 1865, before movements six and seven had been composed. The text of the Requiem consists of passages generally about peace and comfort that Brahms assembled himself from the Luther translation of the Bible, and the title, *Ein deutsches Requiem,* alludes to the fact that the work has German texts and to the indication that Schumann had made in his diary. The title has no reference to German nationalism. On the contrary, Brahms commented that he would have preferred to replace the word "German" in the title with "Human," thus changing the title of the work to *A Human Requiem* or *A Requiem for Humanity.*

The structure of the work has mirror characteristics similar to those found in a number of compositions by Bach. Movements one and seven share musical material and have ABABA and ABBA formal structures, respectively. In addition, they are in tripart mirror key relationships—movement one in F major, a major third lower in D-flat major, and in F major again, and movement seven in F major, a major third higher in A major, and in F major again. Movements two and six close with fugues, begin in minor keys, and have internal repeat structures; movements three and five have solos; and movement four, which stands in the middle of the *Requiem,* has the mirror formal structure of ABACA. In addition, the *Requiem* contains numerous instances of a motif derived from movement nine (the Lutheran chorale "Was helfen uns die Schweren Sorgen") of Bach's cantata *Ich hatte viel Bekümmernis* BWV21.

The most frequently performed and esteemed of Brahms's other choral works with orchestral accompaniment are *Rhapsodie* (called the "Alto Rhapsody"), *Schicksalslied,* and *Nänie.* All three are set to secular texts by renowned poets that seem to express Brahms's view of life, and perhaps because of the close personal relationship to the texts, the music is especially moving. *Rhapsodie* op.53, composed in 1869, is set to the central portion of Goethe's poem *Harzreise im Winter*—an account of the poet's journey to the Harz Mountains in 1777 to see a friend who had withdrawn from the world into the solitude of nature. It is curious that the lines of the poem Brahms set express the dismay of one who is destined to lead a solitary life, for Brahms composed the work for Julie Schumann, one of the daughters of Robert and Clara, as a wedding gift. Clara commented, "Johannes brought me a wonderful piece, which he calls his bridal song. It seems to me, however, to be the expression of his own heart's anguish." *Schicksalslied* op.54, composed between 1868 and 1871, is set to the poem *Hyperions Schicksalslied* (Hyperion's Song of Destiny) by Friedrich Hölderlin, a popular lyric poet of the early nineteenth century. Hölderlin's poem, which describes the struggle of ancient Greek people to liberate themselves from Turkish rule, presents a picture of idealized life struggling against the realistic suffering of humanity. *Nänie* op.82 was composed to a poem by Friedrich Schiller as a memorial to Brahms's friend Anselm Feuerbach, a painter who had died in 1880. The central expression of the poem is that all life is transitory—"Auch das Schöne muß sterben" (even beauty must die).

The other three choral works with orchestral accompaniment are not unified in their textual expressions or popular in appeal. *Rinaldo* op.50, which was begun in 1863 and intended as a competition piece for the Aachen Liedertafel, is a setting of Goethe's *Torquato Tasso.* Brahms's only example of a dramatic text, it was not well received at its premiere in February 1869. *Triumphlied* op.55 is a setting of portions of Revelation 19 and was composed as an occasional work to celebrate Germany's victory in the Franco-Prussian War at Sedan. It was dedicated to Kaiser Wilhelm I and performed frequently during the several years after its composition in 1870 and 1871. *Gesang der Parzen* (Song of the Parcae, or Fates) op.89, composed in 1882, is set to portions of act four of Goethe's *Iphigenie auf Tauris,* which expresses a theme similar to that of *Schicksalslied*—the gap between the idealized utopia of the gods and the suffering of humanity.

Two of the pieces with chamber accompaniment warrant discussion—*Geistliches Lied* op.30 and the *Vier Gesänge* op.17. Despite its opus number, which reflects its year of first performance and publication, *Geistliches Lied* was Brahms's first choral composition—composed in 1856 when Brahms was twenty-two and, therefore, before he had any association with a choral ensemble. It is an extraordinary first work—a masterful fusion of canonic technique, flowing melodies, and expressive harmonies. The *Vier Gesänge* were composed in 1860 for the Hamburg women's choir that Brahms had founded that year. The strophic construction of the four pieces reflects the folk music that fascinated Brahms during his youth, and the scoring for women's voices reflects the "bright, silvery sound" that Brahms found especially attractive.

The sacred a cappella works include the early mass without opus number described above, seven pieces in *Marienlieder* op.22, three Latin pieces in *Drei geistliche Chöre* op.37, the ceremonial motet *Fest- und Gedenksprüche* op.109, and seven German motets—two in op.29, two in op.74, and three in op.110. The *Marienlieder*, composed between 1859 and 1860, are, according to Brahms, "somewhat in the manner of old German church chorales and folk songs." They all have texts about the Virgin Mary, and they are all strophic, syllabic, basically homophonic, and infused with a modal quality. The three pieces in op.37, numbers one and two of which were probably written in 1859 for the Hamburg women's chorus, all include or are constructed of strict canons (described earlier). The other sacred a cappella works are motets with structures that are similar to those used by Schütz and Bach. *Es ist das Heil uns kommen her* op.29 no.1 is a chorale motet: a simple setting of the traditional Lutheran chorale is followed by a point-of-imitation development of each of the chorale's phrases. A striking part of the imitation is a cantus firmus statement of the chorale phrase in the first bass part at the end of each imitative point. *Schaffe in mir, Gott, ein rein Herz* op.29 no.2 is canonic and fugal; the motet's two sections are each divided into two parts—a canon followed by a fugue. Noteworthy features are the canon between the soprano and second bass at the opening of the motet (as has been mentioned) and the inverted melodies in the first fugue. *Warum ist das Licht gegeben* op.74 no.1, dedicated to the Bach scholar and biographer Philipp Spitta, is similar to Bach's motets *Der Geist hilft unser Schwachheit auf* BWV226 and *Komm, Jesu, komm* BWV229: multiple imitative sections are followed by a simple chorale setting. Brahms's motet has three intricately imitative movements and a fourth movement that is a traditional Lutheran chorale. *O Heiland, reiß die Himmel auf* op.74 no.2 is in chorale variation form: the motet is divided into five sections, each devoted to a verse of the text and each containing the chorale-like melody in one of the voice parts. Especially expressive is verse three, which characterizes the ebullient growth in spring, and verse four, which relates the suffering of humanity. *Ich aber bin elend* op.110 no.1 and *Wenn wir in höchsten Nöten sein* op.110 no.3 are both double chorus motets in the Venetian dialogue style. *Ach, arme Welt* op.110 no.2 is the simplest of the motets; it is homophonic and strophic, with three verses.

Fest- und Gedenksprüche (Festal and Commemorative Sentences) op.109 was dedicated to the mayor of Hamburg and composed for the ceremony that granted Brahms the status of freeman of the city. The premiere, in September 1889, was performed by the Cäcilienverein of Hamburg, which was augmented to more than four hundred voices. The work, Brahms's magnus opus, is the epitome of imitative technique and the equivalent of the *Deutsches Magnificat* SWV494 by Schütz or *Singet dem Herrn* BWV225 by Bach.

The secular a cappella works are all part songs. Two of the opuses—41 and 42—are for men's and women's voices, respectively; two of the opuses—62 and 93a—are folk-like in character, with melodies predominantly in the soprano voice, textures that are basically homophonic, and structures that are strophic; and two of the opuses—42 and 104—are more elaborate, with vocal parts that are independent and equal in melodic prominence, and with a degree of imitative writing. Two of the opuses—42 and 44—have piano parts ad lib. (the piano part is a basic reduction of the vocal parts). The most popular pieces in the folk-like opuses are "Waldesnacht" and "All meine Herzgedanken" from op. 62, and "Der bucklichte Fiedler," "Das Mädchen," and "O süßer Mai" from op.93a. All the pieces from op.42 and op.104 are popular.

The vocal chamber works include many of Brahms's most beloved and frequently performed pieces, including the *Liebeslieder Walzer* op.52, the three quartets of op.31, "O schöne Nacht" of op.92, and the *Zigeunerlieder* op.103. Since the music was composed for performers who were professional or musically skilled, the writing is advanced and all the parts are treated with a degree of equality.

Given the importance of Brahms as a choral composer, and given the popularity of his music, all of his choral compositions are listed below except for the canons and folk song arrangements, which have selected listings.

CHORAL WORKS WITH ORCHESTRAL ACCOMPANIMENT
COMPLETE AND LISTED IN CHRONOLOGICAL ORDER
ACCORDING TO DATE OF COMPOSITION

Ein deutsches Requiem op.45 – 1857–1868 – SB solos, SATB chorus, and orchestra (including piccolo, contrabassoon ad lib., tuba, harp, and organ ad lib.) – 70 minutes. (1) The text is in German and consists of passages from the Old and New Testaments; (2) the soprano solo is only in movement five and the bass solo only in movements three and six; (3) the chorus sings almost entirely throughout the work; (4) Brahms specified that two harps should play from the harp part; (5) the parts for contrabassoon and organ are scored.

Rinaldo op.50 – 1863–1868 – T solo, TTBB chorus, and orchestra – 60 minutes. (1) The text, by Goethe, is in German; (2) the tenor solo, which represents Rinaldo, appears throughout the work; (3) the chorus is scored for four parts (TTBB) until the end of the work, when there are also brief solo passages for TTBB.

Rhapsodie op.53 – 1869 – A solo, TTBB chorus, and orchestra of two flutes, two oboes, two clarinets, two bassoons, two horns, and strings – 14 minutes. (1) The text, by Goethe, is in German; (2) the work is referred to as the "Alto Rhapsody"; (3) the alto sings with the orchestra in the first half of the work and with the chorus and orchestra in the second half.

Schicksalslied op.54 – 1868–1871 – SATB chorus and orchestra – 17 minutes. (1) The text, by Hölderlin, is in German; (2) the choral parts divide briefly into SATTBB near the end of the work.

Triumphlied op.55 – 1870–1871 – B solo, SATB/SATB chorus, and orchestra (including contrabassoon, tuba, and organ ad lib.) – 20 minutes. (1) The text, from Revelation 19, is in German; (2) the baritone solo is brief and confined to the third movement of the work.

Nänie op.82 – 1880–1881 – SATB chorus and orchestra (including harp) – 12:30 minutes. (1) The text, by Schiller, is in German; (2) Brahms specified that two harps should play from the harp part.

Gesang der Parzen op.89 – 1882 – SAATBB chorus and orchestra (including contrabassoon and tuba) – 11:30 minutes. (1) The text, by Goethe, is in German; (2) the work is in one movement and is choral throughout.

CHORAL WORKS WITH CHAMBER ACCOMPANIMENT
COMPLETE AND LISTED IN CHRONOLOGICAL ORDER
ACCORDING TO DATE OF COMPOSITION

Geistliches Lied op.30 – 1856 – SATB chorus and organ – 5:30 minutes. (1) The
text, from the seventeenth century, is in German; (2) the first line of text
is "Lass dich nur nichts nicht dauern" (Let nothing ever grieve you).

Ave Maria op.12 – 1858 – SSAA chorus and organ or instrumental ensemble
of two flutes, two oboes, two clarinets, two bassoons, two horns, and
strings – 4:30 minutes. (1) The text is in Latin; (2) Brahms scored the
piece for organ or orchestra.

Begräbnisgesang op.13 – 1858 – SATB chorus and instrumental ensemble of
two oboes, two clarinets, two bassoons, two horns, three trombones,
tuba, and timpani – 8 minutes. (1) The text, from the sixteenth century,
is in German; (2) the bass part divides at the end of the piece.

Der 13. Psalm op.27 – 1859 – SSA chorus and organ – 5:30 minutes. (1) The
text, from the Bible, is in German; (2) Brahms later scored the organ part
for strings.

Vier Gesänge op.17 – 1860 – SSA chorus and instrumental ensemble of two
horns and harp – 14 minutes. (1) The texts, by Ruperti, Shakespeare,
Eichendorff, and Ossian, are in German; (2) the chorus divides into
SSAA in the fourth piece; (3) the titles of the four pieces are "Es tönt ein
voller Harfenklang," "Lied von Shakespeare," "Der Gärtner," and
"Gesang aus Fingal."

Tafellied op.93b – 1884 – SAATBB chorus and piano – 3 minutes. (1) The
text, by Eichendorff, is in German; (2) the chorus parts consist of dialogue between the men and women until the end of the piece.

SACRED A CAPPELLA WORKS
COMPLETE AND LISTED IN CHRONOLOGICAL ORDER OF OPUS NUMBERS

Messe (no opus number) – 1856–1857 – SSATB chorus a cappella and organ –
10 minutes. The Kyrie is scored for SATB chorus and basso continuo,
while the Sanctus, Benedictus, and Agnus Dei are scored for SSATB
chorus a cappella.

Marienlieder op.22 – 1859–1860 – SATB chorus a cappella – 17 minutes.
(1) The collection contains seven pieces: "Der englische Gruß," "Marias
Kirchgang," "Marias Wallfahrt," "Der Jäger," "Ruf zur Maria," "Magdalena," and "Marias Lob"; (2) all the pieces are strophic (most with five
or six verses) and basically homophonic.

Es ist das Heil uns kommen her op.29 no.1 – 1860 – SATBB chorus a cappella –
5 minutes. (1) The text is from the traditional Lutheran chorale; (2) the
first bass part is reserved for only single cantus firmus statements of the
chorale melody.

Schaffe in mir, Gott, ein rein Herz op.29 no.2 – 1856–1860 – SAATBB chorus a cappella – 6:45 minutes. (1) The text is from Psalm 51:12–14; (2) the scoring includes combinations for SATTB, SATB, and SAATBB.

Drei geistliche Chöre op.37 – ca.1859–1863 – SSAA chorus a cappella – 6 minutes. (1) The texts are in Latin; (2) the titles of the three pieces are "O bone Jesu," "Adoramus te," and "Regina coeli laetare."

Warum ist das Licht gegeben op.74 no.1 – 1877 – SSATBB chorus a cappella – 11 minutes. (1) The motet is in four movements; (2) the texts of the first three movements are from Job 3:20–23, Lamentations 3:41, and James 5:11; (3) the text of movement four is the Lutheran chorale "Mit Fried und Freud ich fahr dahin" by Martin Luther; (4) the scoring varies from SATB (movements one and four) to SSATBB (movements two and three).

O Heiland, reiß die Himmel auf op.74 no.2 – 1863–1864 – SATB chorus a cappella – 5:15 minutes. (1) The text authorship is unknown; (2) the motet consists of five movements (called "Versus" by Brahms).

Fest- und Gedenksprüche op.109 – 1888–1889 – SATB/SATB chorus a cappella – 9 minutes. (1) The work consists of three motets—"Unsere Väter hofften auf dich" (Psalm 22:4, 5–6, and 29:11), "Wenn ein starker Gewappneter" (Luke 11:21), and "Wo ist ein so herrlich Volk" (Deuteronomy 4:7, 9).

Ich aber bin elend op.110 no.1 – 1889 – SATB/SATB a cappella – 3 minutes. The text is from Psalm 69:30 and Exodus 34:6–7.

Ach, arme Welt op.110 no.2 – 1889 – SATB a cappella – 2 minutes. The text authorship is unknown.

Wenn wir in höchsten Nöten sein op.110 no.3 – 1889 – SATB/SATB a cappella – 3:30 minutes. The text is from the sixteenth century.

SECULAR A CAPPELLA WORKS
COMPLETE AND LISTED IN CHRONOLOGICAL ORDER OF OPUS NUMBERS

Fünf Lieder op.41 – 1861–1862 – TTBB voices a cappella – "Ich schwing mein Horn ins Jammertal" 45 seconds, "Freiwillige her" 1 minute, "Geleit" 1 minute, "Marschieren" 1 minute, and "Gebt Acht" 1:30 minutes.

Drei Gesänge op.42 – 1859–1861 – SAATBB voices a cappella and piano ad lib. – "Abendständchen" 2 minutes, "Vineta" 3:15 minutes, and "Darthulas Grabesgesang" 4 minutes.

Zwölf Lieder und Romanzen op.44 – 1859–1860 – SSAA voices and piano ad lib. – "Minnelied" 1 minute, "Der Bräutigam" 1 minute, "Barcarole" 1:15 minutes, "Fragen" 30 seconds, "Die Müllerin" 1 minute, "Die Nonne" 1:30 minutes, "Nun stehn die Rosen in Blüte" 1:15 minutes, "Die Berge sind spitz" 45 seconds, "Am Wildbach die Weiden" 45 seconds, "Und gehst du über den Kirchhof" 1 minute, "Die Braut" 1:30 minutes, and "Märznacht" 1 minute. The seventh through tenth pieces were composed in 1859 as *Vier Lieder aus dem Jungbrunnen* and combined with the other numbers for publication in 1866.

Sieben Lieder op.62 – 1873–1874 – SATB voices a cappella – "Rosmarin" 2 minutes, "Von alten Liebesliedern" 2:15 minutes, "Waldesnacht" 5 minutes, "Dein Herzlein mild" 1:30 minutes, "All meine Herzgedanken" 3 minutes, "Es geht ein Wehen" 2:30 minutes, and "Vergangen ist mir Glück und Heil" 2:45 minutes. All the pieces are scored for SATB except "All meine Herzgedanken," which is SAATBB.

Lieder und Romanzen op.93a – 1883 – SATB voices a cappella – "Der bucklichte Fiedler" 2 minutes, "Das Mädchen" 2:30 minutes, "O süßer Mai" 2 minutes, "Fahr wohl" 2:30 minutes, "Der Falke" 2 minutes, and "Beherzigung" 1 minute. All the pieces are scored for SATB except "Das Mädchen," which adds a soprano solo, and "O süßer Mai," which has a divided bass part.

Fünf Gesänge op.104 – 1888 – SAATBB voices a cappella – "Nachtwache I" 2:30 minutes, "Nachtwache II" 1:15 minutes, "Letztes Glück" 2:30 minutes, "Verlorene Jugend" 2 minutes, and "Im Herbst" 4 minutes. All the pieces are scored for SAATBB except the final one, which is scored for SATB.

VOCAL CHAMBER WORKS WITH PIANO ACCOMPANIMENT
COMPLETE AND LISTED IN CHRONOLOGICAL ORDER OF OPUS NUMBERS

Drei Quartette op.31 – 1859–1863 – SATB quartet and piano – "Wechselied zum Tanz" 6:15 minutes, "Neckereien" 2:15 minutes, and "Der Gang zum Liebchen" 4 minutes.

Liebeslieder Walzer op.52 – 1868–1869 – SATB quartet and piano four hands – 22 minutes. (1) The collection contains eighteen pieces—one T solo, two SA duets, two TB duets, and thirteen quartets; (2) most of the individual pieces are approximately one minute in duration.

Drei Quartette op.64 – 1862–1874 – SATB quartet and piano – "An die Heimat" 6 minutes, "Der Abend" 4:30 minutes, and "Fragen" 3:30 minutes.

Neue Liebeslieder Walzer op.65 – 1869–1874 – SATB quartet and piano four hands – 20 minutes. (1) The collection contains fifteen pieces—four S solos, one A solo, one T solo, one B solo, one SA duet, and seven quartets; (2) most pieces are approximately one minute in duration.

Vier Quartette op.92 – 1877–1884 – SATB quartet and piano – "O schöne Nacht" 3:15 minutes, "Spätherbst" 2 minutes, "Abendlied" 2:30 minutes, and "Warum" 2 minutes.

Zigeunerlieder op.103 – 1887–1888 – SATB quartet and piano – 17:30 minutes. (1) The collection contains eleven pieces—one featuring a soprano solo, five featuring a tenor solo, and five without solos; (2) many of the pieces have two sections, each of which repeats; (3) several of the pieces are strophic.

Sehnsucht op.112 no.1 – 1888 – SATB quartet and piano – 3:15 minutes.

Nächtens op.112 no.2 – 1888 – SATB quartet and piano – 1:30 minutes.

CANONS
SELECTED FROM OP.113

Göttlicher Morpheus op.113 no.1 – ca.1860–1863 – four equal voices a cappella – 1 minute.

So lange Schönheit wird bestehn op.113 no.6 – ca.1860–1863 – SSAA a cappella – 1:30 minutes. This is a double canon, one for the two soprano voices and the other for the two alto voices.

Einförmig ist der Liebe Gram op.113 no.13 – ca.1860–1863 – SSSSAA voices a cappella – 2 minutes. This is a double canon, one for the four soprano voices and the other for the two alto voices.

FOLK SONG ARRANGEMENTS
SELECTED FROM THE NINETEEN PIECES IN BOOK TWO

In stiller Nacht – published 1864 – SATB chorus a cappella – 1:30 minutes.

Abschiedslied – published 1864 – SATB chorus a cappella – 1:30 minutes.

Der tote Knabe – published 1864 – SATB chorus a cappella – 2 minutes.

Die Wollust in den Maien – published 1864 – SATB chorus a cappella – 1:30 minutes.

MAX BRUCH 1838–1920

Bruch was born in Cologne and began his musical studies with his mother, a well-known singer. He composed his first piece at age nine, and at fourteen won the Frankfurt Mozart-Stiftung award for the composition of a string quartet. His first opera, *Scherz, List und Rache*, was composed when he was twenty, and his second and most famous opera, *Die Loreley*, when he was twenty-five. He visited Leipzig in 1858, becoming acquainted with and admiring the compositional styles of Mendelssohn and Schumann, and in 1862 he settled in Mannheim. From 1865 to 1867 he was music director at the court in Koblenz, and from 1867 to 1870 he held a similar position in Sondershausen. Thereafter, he held various short-term conducting positions, including director of the Philharmonic Society in Liverpool from 1880 to 1883, and in the 1890s he taught at the Hochschule für Musik in Berlin, where two of his students were Ottorino Respighi and Ralph Vaughan Williams. While in Berlin, Bruch also conducted the choral society Sternscher Gesangverein. He remained an advocate of the musical style of Mendelssohn and Schumann his entire life, openly criticizing the New German School of composition and the music of Liszt and his followers.

Bruch composed five oratorios, ten miscellaneous choral/orchestral works set to sacred texts, seven small-scale sacred works with keyboard accompaniment, twelve secular cantatas, and sixty-six part songs. The earliest of the oratorios—*Odysseus* of 1872 and *Arminius* of 1875—were the two most popular of his large-scale choral works during his lifetime. The text of *Odysseus* relates eight scenes from Homer's poem of the same name (e.g., Odysseus on the island of Calypso, Odysseus in the Underworld, and Odysseus and the Sirens), and the music is highly dramatic and through-composed, with minimal use of unifying motivic material. *Arminius* is based on the life of Hermann, chief of the Cherusci tribe, who stopped the Roman advancement in Germany in AD 9. After the oratorio's premiere in Berlin, it was performed by the Brooklyn Academy of Music in March 1883 and by the Handel and Haydn Society of Boston two months later. Bruch's most popular oratorio after his death, *Moses,* was composed in 1895. It relates four episodes in the life of Moses, entitled "On Mount Sinai," "The Golden Calf," "The Return of the Spies from Canaan," and "The Promised Land." Bruch said of the text, "The story begins where Handel's *Israel in Egypt* ends." The work is scored for three soloists—the Angel of the Lord (S), Aaron (T), and Moses (B)—SATB chorus, and orchestra. The other two oratorios, *Achilleus* of 1885 and *Gustav Adolf* of 1898, never became popular and have rarely been performed.

    The miscellaneous choral/orchestral sacred works include the early *Jubilate-Amen* composed in 1858 and the late *Das Wessobrunner Gebet* of 1910; the sacred works for keyboard accompaniment include *Sei getreu bis in den Tod* of 1896 for SSATB chorus and organ and the six *Christkindlieder* of about 1917 for SSAA voices and piano; and the secular cantatas include *Das Feuerkreuz* of 1899 and *Trauerfeier für Mignon* of 1919. Approximately one-third of the part songs are scored for chorus and orchestra (e.g., the three *Hebräische Gesänge* and the three *Neue Männerchöre*), while the others are scored for a cappella chorus. These latter pieces include the nine *Lieder* op.60, number three of which—"Der Mutter Klage" (The mother's lament)—is based on an Irish folk song, and the six *Lieder* op.86, number two of which—"Kleine Maria" (Little Maria)—is a strophic setting of an ancient legend. Number four of opus 86, "Geh, wo Ruhm dir winket" (Go, where your fame beckons), is scored for SATB/SATB chorus and is one of Bruch's most popular part songs today. Twenty-two of the part songs, including the four *Männerchöre* of about 1863 and the six *Volkslieder* of about 1908, are for male voices.

JOSEPH (JOSEF GABRIEL) RHEINBERGER 1839–1901

Rheinberger was born in Vaduz, Liechtenstein, where his father was treasurer of the royal court. At age five the young Rheinberger began studying organ, and at seven he became the organist at the main church in Vaduz. During the following several years his musical education included harmony and piano, and at age twelve he was sent to Munich, where his studies continued at the Staatliche Hochschule für Musik and where he served as assistant organist at the church of St Ludwig. At eighteen he was appointed *Königlich Bairischer Hoforganist* (Royal Bavarian court organist) at the church of St Kajetan, at twenty he began teaching piano at the Hochschule, at twenty-four he took over the position of organist at the court church of St Michaels, and at twenty-five he was appointed director of the Munich Oratorienverein, with which he conducted large-scale choral/orchestral works of Bach, Handel, Mozart, Joseph and Michael Haydn, Beethoven, and Mendelssohn. Rheinberger resigned from the oratorio society in 1877 when he was named court *Hofkapellmeister* by King Ludwig II of Bavaria and was promoted to professor of music at the Hochschule, and for the remainder of his life he concentrated on the composition of accessible music for the church and amateur choral societies. He was made a Knight of the Order of St Gregory by Pope Leo XIII in 1880, and in 1899 he was granted an honorary doctorate from the University of Munich.

Throughout his adult life Rheinberger expressed disapproval of the New German School of composition and the music of Wagner and Liszt. Rheinberger also criticized the limiting restrictions of those composers adhering to the principles of the Cäcilien movement, although he was conservative and modeled much of his music on the works of past-era composers he frequently performed in his various church positions. He felt that Baroque composers were especially important, stating, "The modern contrapuntist must [emulate] the school of Bach, because only that schooling fashions and tempers the possibilities of musical combination in such a way that the strength of counterpoint makes every idea, every norm free and unconstrained." In spite of this philosophy, Rheinberger's music does not contain any of Bach's contrapuntal complexities. Instead, the textures are frequently homophonic. Furthermore, Rheinberger's music contains few instances of word painting, for according to him, "To understand the meanings of particular words, one should not pay attention to their specific interpretation. . . . The purpose of composition is to express the language of feeling, which an attention to specific words can disrupt and turn to conflict."

Rheinberger composed twenty-two masses (including four Requiems), five sacred oratorios and cantatas, two Stabat maters, two sets of music for Vespers services, eighty-one motets and hymns, and approximately fifty secular part songs. The masses range from simple works in a neo-Renaissance imitative style for equal voices a cappella to large-scale choral/orchestral works in the style of Mozart and Joseph Haydn. In a catalogue of his works compiled at the end of his life, Rheinberger listed six masses he felt were significant—four for a cappella chorus, one for male chorus and wind ensemble, and one for soloists, mixed chorus, and orchestra. Of the a cappella masses—*Missa brevis* in D minor op. 83, *Missa brevis* in F major op.117 ("Sanctissimae Trinitatis"), *Missa brevis* in G major op.151 ("St Crucis"), and *Missa* in E-flat major op.109 ("Cantus Missae")—opus 109 is considered to be the most significant today. It was composed in five days during January 1878 and was first performed at the Royal Bavarian court church, the Allerheiligen Hofkirche, on January 1, 1879. Dedicated to Pope Leo XIII, who was so taken with the work that he bestowed on Rheinberger the Order of St Gregory, it is in the Venetian double chorus style, with occasional passages of imitative polyphony and with themes based on Gregorian chant. The instrumental-accompanied masses identified by Rheinberger as significant are the *Missa* in B-flat major op.172 and the *Missa* in C major op.169 (the performing forces of both are listed below).

The two Requiems and the two Stabat maters are also large-scale works with instrumental accompaniment. The *Requiem* in D minor op.194 is modest in scoring and length, consisting of only three movements—Introit and Kyrie, Gradual ("Absolve, Domine, animas omnium fidelium"), and Agnus Dei and Communion. The *Requiem* in B-flat minor op.60 is much larger in scope, with five large sections (Introit and Kyrie, Dies irae, Offertory, Sanctus, and Agnus Dei and Communion), all but one of which are subdivided into two or three separate movements. The *Stabat mater* in C minor op.16 is scored for STB solos, SATB chorus, and orchestra, while the *Stabat mater* op.138 is scored for SATB chorus, organ, and strings ad lib. This latter work, divided into four movements, was composed in 1884 as an offering of thanks for the healing of an abscessed wound that had been on Rheinberger's hand since the early 1870s. One further choral/orchestral work merits mention—the Christmas cantata *Der Stern von Bethlehem*, composed in 1890 and scored for B solo, SATB chorus, and orchestra (including English horn, harp, and organ).

Other sacred repertoire includes Latin and German motets—the Latin works being the more plentiful, but the German works being the better known. The most notable of the Latin motets are the nine pieces in opus 176, composed in 1893 as a complete cycle of music for the four Sundays in Advent (numbers one and two for the first Sunday, numbers three and four for the second Sunday, numbers five and six for the third Sunday, and numbers seven through nine for the fourth Sunday). The most notable of the German motets and undoubtedly the best-known work by Rheinberger is *Abendlied* op.69 no.3 composed in 1855. It is in an ABA form, with text from Luke 24:29—"Bleib bei uns, denn es will Abend werden; und der Tag hat sich geneiget" (Stay with us, for it is becoming evening; and the day is coming to an end). All the motets and hymns, whether set to Latin or German texts, are in a neo-Renaissance style, with passages of imitative polyphony alternating with passages of homophony.

Rheinberger's secular music includes several significant collections of pieces. *Vom Goldenen Horn* op.182, composed in 1895, contains nine pieces that relate a story of two Turkish lovers—Assim (sung variously by solo T and B) and Assaïdy (sung by solo S and A). The title of the collection refers to the Bay of Bosphorus, the locale of the story, and the text is from *Rosenblätter, Lieder und Sprüche des Volkssängers und Improvisators Assim Agha Gül-hanendé*, an adaptation of original Turkish poetry published in Leipzig in 1893. The music, subtitled "Türkisches Liederspiel," was modeled after Schumann's *Spanisches Liederspiel* op.74 of 1849—similarly a collection of solos and choruses with piano accompaniment. *Liebesgarten* op.80 is a collection of five pieces composed in 1874. Poetry by Robert Reinick (1805–1852) and Rheinberger's wife, Fanny, reflect on love and its various states of happiness and sadness. *In Sturm und Frieden* op.170 consists of eight pieces set to the poetry of Julius Sturm (1816–1896), a theologian from Köstritz. Composed in 1892, the cycle reflects its title, "Sturm und Frieden" (Storm, or storminess, and peace, or calmness).

MASSES
SELECTED AND LISTED ACCORDING TO FAMILIARITY

Missa in E-flat major op.109 ("Cantus Missae") – SATB/SATB chorus a cappella – 24 minutes.

Requiem in B-flat minor op.60 – SATB solos, SSATTB chorus, and orchestra – 54 minutes.

Requiem in D minor op.194 – SATB chorus and organ – 23 minutes.

Missa brevis in G major op.151 ("St Crucis") – SATB chorus a cappella – 17 minutes.

Missa in A major op.126 – SSA solos, SSA chorus, and organ – 20 minutes. Rheinberger added a flute and string quintet to the organ part, although he most frequently performed the mass with accompaniment of organ alone.

Missa in F major op.190 – TTBB chorus and organ – 22 minutes.

Missa in C major op.169 – SATB solos, SATB chorus, and orchestra – 25 minutes.

Missa brevis in F major op.117 ("Sanctissimae Trinitatis") – SATB chorus a cappella – 19 minutes.

Missa brevis in D minor op.83 – SATB chorus a cappella – 15 minutes.

Missa in B-flat major op.172 – TTBB chorus, two flutes, two oboes, two clarinets, two bassoons, two horns, two trumpets, timpani, and string bass – 23 minutes.

GERMAN MOTETS AND HYMNS
SELECTED AND LISTED ACCORDING TO FAMILIARITY

Abendlied op.69 no.3 (Luke 24:29) – SSATTB chorus a cappella – 3:30 minutes.

Hymne nach dem 84. Psalm ("Wie lieblich sind deine Wohnungen") – SSAA chorus, harp, and organ – 5:30 minutes.

Es spricht der Tor in seinem Herzen (from Psalm 53) – SATB chorus a cappella – 2:30 minutes.

Ich liebe, weil erhöret der Herr (from Psalm 116) – SATB chorus a cappella – 2:15 minutes.

Warum toben die Heiden (Psalm 2:1–4, 11–12) – SATB chorus a cappella – 3:15 minutes.

Passionsgesang op.46 – SATB chorus and organ – 14 minutes.

LATIN MOTETS AND HYMNS
SELECTED AND LISTED ACCORDING TO FAMILIARITY

Neun Advent-Motetten op.176 – SATB chorus a cappella – "Ad te levavi" (Psalm 25:1–3) 2 minutes, "Universi qui te exspectant" (Psalm 25:34 and 85:8) 1:45 minutes, "Ex Sion species decoris ejus" (Psalm 50:2–5 and 122:1) 1:30 minutes, "Deus tu convertens vivificabis nos" (Psalm 85:7–8) 2:45 minutes, "Qui sedes, Domine, super Cherubim" (Psalm 80:2–3) 1:30 minutes, "Benedixisti, Domine, terram tuam" (Psalm 85:2–3) 2:15 minutes, "Rorate coeli desuper" (Isaiah 45:8) 2:15 minutes, "Prope est Dominus" (Psalm 145:18) 2:15 minutes, and "Ave Maria, gratia plena" (Luke 1:28) 21 minutes.

Christus factus est op.107 no.5 – SATB chorus a cappella – 4 minutes.

Meditabor op.133 no.2 – SSATTB chorus a cappella – 4 minutes.

Jesu, dulcis memoria op.58 no.4 – SATB chorus a cappella – 2 minutes.

Media vita in morte sumus – op.24 no.3 – SATB chorus a cappella – 1:45 minutes.

Omnes de Saba op.58 no.1 – SATB chorus a cappella – 2 minutes.

Salve regina op.107 no.4 – SATB chorus a cappella – 2:30 minutes.

Angelus suis op.140 no.5 – B solo, SATB chorus, and organ – 3:15 minutes.

Ave Maria op.172 no.3 – TTBB chorus a cappella – 3 minutes.

SECULAR PART SONGS
SELECTED AND LISTED ACCORDING TO FAMILIARITY

Vom Goldenen Horn op.182 – SATB solos, SATB chorus, and piano – 30:30 minutes. Of the nine pieces in the collection, two are for chorus alone and two for soloist and chorus.

Liebesgarten op.80 – SATB chorus a cappella – 14 minutes.

In Sturm und Frieden op.170 – SATB chorus a cappella – 23 minutes.

ANTONÍN DVOŘÁK 1841–1904

Dvořák was born near Kralupy, Bohemia (now the Czech Republic), and studied singing and the violin at a local school. In 1853 he was sent to the nearby town of Zlonice to continue his education (which included German, music theory, organ, and piano), and in 1857 he moved to Prague, where he attended the Prague Organ School and played the viola in the Cecilia Society orchestra. The society performed choral works by such Austrian and German composers as Beethoven, Mendelssohn, and Schumann, and other ensembles in Prague at the time performed works by New German School composers such as Liszt and Wagner. In 1862 Dvořák became principal violist of the Provisional Theatre, which presented numerous Italian operas by Mozart, Rossini, Donizetti, and Verdi, and during the late 1860s he began composing string quartets, symphonies, and song cycles—many of which he later destroyed. In 1874 he was appointed organist at the church of St Vojtěch, and upon the recommendation of Brahms, his works composed in the late 1870s began to be published. His symphonic compositions were then performed in major cities throughout the world, including Dresden, Hamburg, Berlin, London, and New York City, and in 1883 he was invited to conduct the Philharmonic Society of London and to compose a major choral/orchestral work for the 1885 Birmingham Festival. The Philharmonic Society's performances included his *Stabat mater* at Royal Albert Hall in March 1884 and his cantata *Svatebni košile* (The spectre's bride) in 1885. Other English performances over the next several years included his oratorio *Svatá Ludmila* (St Ludmilla) in 1886 and his *Requiem* in 1890.

Dvořák also conducted his works in other European capitals and received awards for his accomplishments. He was given the Austrian Order of the Iron Crown in 1889 and honorary doctorates from the Czech University of Prague and Cambridge University in 1890 and 1891, respectively; in 1891 he was named professor of composition at the Prague Conservatory; and in 1892 he accepted an invitation to become artistic director and professor of composition at the newly founded National Conservatory of Music in New York City. While in New York, he composed *The American Flag* and *Symphony #9* ("From the New World") and conducted these works and many others in performances at Carnegie Hall. He returned to his homeland in 1895 because the National Conservatory experienced financial difficulties and could no longer pay his salary, and he resumed teaching at the Prague Conservatory. His compositional activity at this time was focused on stage works, including his most successful opera, *Rusalka,* which was completed in 1900, and in 1901 he was appointed director of the Conservatory.

Dvořák's choral output includes two surviving masses (including a Requiem), one oratorio, two cantatas, a setting of the Stabat mater and Te Deum, several hymns and Psalms, and approximately twenty part songs. In chronological order, the most significant of the large-scale works are *Stabat mater, Svatebni košile* (The spectre's bride), *Svatá Ludmila, Mass* in D major, *Requiem, Te Deum,* and *The American Flag.*

The *Stabat mater* was composed in the spring of 1876 and orchestrated in the fall of 1877, with the first performance taking place in Prague on December 23, 1880. The work was well received and helped establish Dvořák as one of the most respected composers of his time. Following the premiere, performances took place in Budapest in 1882, in London in 1883, in London again (with Dvořák conducting) in 1884, and in Worcester in 1884 to celebrate the 800th anniversary of the founding of the cathedral. The music is structured in ten sections, with each section devoted to the particular dramatic expression of its textual content.

The cantata *Svatebni košile* was composed in 1884 and first performed in Pilsen in March 1885. As with the *Stabat mater,* the public reception to *Svatebni košile* was extremely positive, and numerous subsequent performances took place within a short span of time—in Olmütz and Prague in May; in Birmingham in August (with a chorus of four hundred singers and an orchestra of 150 instrumentalists); in Manchester in November; in Milwaukee, Wisconsin, in December; and in London and Glasgow in February 1886. The text of the cantata, which comes from a folk ballad by Karel Jaromír Erben (1811–1870), is about the nightmare of a bride taken by a ghost on a terrifying journey to a graveyard, where her wedding dress or petticoat (the literal translation of *Svatebni košile*) is strewn over tombstones. The poetic dialogue is divided into eighteen movements, most of which are connected to produce a continuous flow of music.

The oratorio *Svatá Ludmila* was composed in 1885 and 1886 and premiered in English translation in Leeds, England, on October 15, 1886. The publication the following year was in the original Czech as well as in English. The text of the oratorio is about Ludmilla (ca. 860–921), grandmother of St Wenceslas and later patron saint of Bohemia, who with her husband Prince Bořivoj is converted to Christianity. The music is in the mold of Handel and Mendelssohn works familiar to English audiences, with recitatives, arias, solo ensembles, and numerous choruses, all divided into three large parts or acts (like Handel oratorios), and with conservative nineteenth-century harmonies, a few remembrance motifs, and a chorale (as in Mendelssohn oratorios). Dvořák's chorale is "Hospdine, pomiluj ny" (Lord, have mercy on us), which is used at the baptism of Ludmilla and Bořivoj.

The *Mass* in D major was composed in 1887 for the consecration of a private chapel at Luzany, near Pilsen. It was originally scored for chorus and organ. However, at the insistence of his English publisher, Vincent Novello, Dvořák rescored it in 1892 for soloists (or small chamber chorus), chorus, and orchestra. The music is in the tradition of late masses by Joseph Haydn and all the masses of Schubert, with choral textures that are alternately imitative and homophonic, traditional harmonies without unifying motivic material, Gloria and Credo movements divided into connecting sections, and minimal writing for soloists.

The *Requiem* was composed in 1890 and premiered in Birmingham, England, in October 1891. It is in two large parts, the first divided into eight movements (consisting of the Introit and

Dies irae) and the second into five movements (Offertorium, Hostias, Sanctus, Pie Jesu, and Agnus Dei). Musically, it is more advanced than the *Mass*. For example, a four-note chromatic motif appears in most movements, vocal and choral textures are dramatically expressive of the text, and the writing for soloists consists of extended melodic passages (although not in the form of arias).

The *Te Deum* was composed in 1892, shortly before Dvořák arrived in America, and was premiered at Carnegie Hall on October 21 in a concert celebrating the 400th anniversary of Columbus's discovery of America. The work is divided into four sections, comparable to the four traditional movements of a symphony, with each section, like those in the *Stabat mater*, taking advantage of the dramatic implications of textual phrases.

The *American Flag* was begun immediately after Dvořák arrived in New York City and was completed two days before he began work on his *Symphony #9* (which was inspired by spirituals and folk songs sung to him by one of his African-American students at the National Conservatory). The *American Flag* was commissioned by Mrs. Jeannette Thurber, president of the National Conservatory, and premiered by the New York Musical Society on May 4, 1895. The text was written by Joseph Rodman Drake, the American poet who became famous for his satirical verses published in the *New York Evening Post,* and who died in 1820 at the age of twenty-five. Dvořák subtitled his work "For the United States of North America" and set Drake's poetry about the importance of the American flag in the war against the British in 1812 in four movements—"The Colors of the Flag," "The First and Second Apostrophes to the Eagle," "Interlude – March," and "Finale – Prophetic."

Most of the part songs were composed between 1875 and 1885 and issued in collections—for example, four pieces for mixed voices a cappella op.29, three pieces for male voices a cappella op.43, and five pieces for mixed voices a cappella op.63. This latter collection is Dvořák's most famous and is the only one with an overall title—*V přírodě* (In nature's realm or Songs of nature). The five pieces are all basically homophonic and in some sort of repeated structure. "Napadly písně v duši mou" (Melodies descended on my soul) is in an ABB form, with the A consisting of two similar phrases; "Večerní les rozvázal zvonky" (Bells ring at dusk) is ABAB, with each A consisting of four similar phrases; "Žitné pole" (The rye field) is strophic, with two verses; "Vyběhla bříza bělička" (The silver birch) is ABA, with the first A consisting of four similar phrases; and "Dnes do skoku a do písničky" (With dance and song) is ABCB, with each B comprising eight similar phrases (four major and four minor).

CHORAL/ORCHESTRAL WORKS
SELECTED AND LISTED IN CHRONOLOGICAL ORDER
ACCORDING TO DATE OF COMPOSITION

Stabat mater – 1876–1877 – SATB solos, SATB chorus, and orchestra –
80 minutes. (1) The solo writing consists of an aria for alto and a duet
for soprano and bass, plus movements for bass and chorus, tenor and
chorus, quartet alone, and quartet and chorus; (2) the choral parts occasionally divide into SSAA and TTBB.

Svatebni košile (The spectre's bride) – 1884 – STB solos, SATB chorus, and
orchestra – 76 minutes. The solo roles are for the Bride (S), Bridegroom
(T), and Narrator (B).

Svatá Ludmila (St Ludmilla) – 1885–1886 – SATB solos, SATB chorus, and orchestra – 200 minutes. The choral parts occasionally divide into SSAATTBB and SATB/SATB.

Mass in D major – 1887 – SATB solos or small chamber chorus, SATB chorus, and organ or orchestra of two oboes, two bassoons, three horns, two trumpets, three trombones, strings, and organ – 35 minutes. The solo or chamber chorus parts occasionally divide into SSAATTBB.

Requiem – 1890 – SATB solos, SATB chorus, and orchestra (including English horn) – 60 minutes. The choral parts frequently divide into SSAATTBB, although not for extended passages of music.

Te Deum – 1892 – SB solos, SATB chorus, and orchestra – 21 minutes. The choral parts occasionally divide into SSAA and TTBB.

The American Flag – 1892–1893 – ATB solos, chorus, and orchestra – 20 minutes. The choral parts occasionally divide into SSAATTBB.

PART SONGS
SELECTED AND LISTED ACCORDING TO FAMILIARITY

V přírodě (In nature's realm) op.63 – 1882 – SATB chorus a cappella – "Napadly písně v duši mou" 2:15 minutes, "Večerní les rozvázal zvonky" 4:15 minutes, "Žitné pole" 1:45 minutes, "Vyběhla bříza bělička" 2 minutes, and "Dnes do skoku a do písničky" 2:30 minutes. The second piece divides frequently into SSAATTBB.

Čtyři sbory (Four Choruses) op.29 – ca.1876 – SATB chorus a cappella – "Misto klekáni" (Evening's blessing) 2 minutes, "Ukolébavka" (Cradle song) 2:45 minutes, "Nepovím" (I won't tell) 2 minutes, and "Opuštěný" (The forsaken one) 2:30 minutes.

Z kytice národních písní slovanských (From a bouquet of Slavonic folk songs) op.43 – TTBB chorus and piano four hands – "Žal" (Sorrow) 3:45 minutes, "Divná voda" (Wondrous water) 3:30 minutes, and "Děvče v háji" (The maiden in the wood) 3:30 minutes.

HEINRICH VON HERZOGENBERG 1843–1900

Herzogenberg was born in Graz, Austria, where he received a classical education. From 1862 to 1865 he studied law at the University of Vienna and also attended music classes at the Vienna Conservatory. He returned to Graz in 1868, determined to devote his life to composition, and in 1872 he moved to Leipzig. While in Leipzig he developed a keen interest in the music of Bach, and in 1874 he founded the Bach-Verein with the Bach biographer Philipp Spitta (1841–1894). Herzogenberg became director of the Bach-Verein in 1875, and for the next decade he conducted numerous Bach cantatas and oratorios and composed a large number of sacred motets based on Lutheran models of the Baroque era. He also composed secular vocal chamber music modeled after the works of Schumann and Brahms. In 1885 Herzogenberg moved to Berlin to become professor of composition at the Hochschule für Musik, and during the final years of his life he concentrated on the composition of large-scale sacred works.

Herzogenberg's compositional output includes two masses (one of which is a Requiem), three oratorios, three cantatas (two sacred and one secular), ten opuses of motets, and six opuses of secular part songs and vocal chamber music. The *Requiem* in C minor op.72 and *Missa* in E minor op.87 were composed in 1891 and 1895, respectively. Both works are in Latin, with commonplace scoring for soloists, chorus, and orchestra, and with traditional structures (i.e., the mass consists of the five portions of the Ordinary, and the Requiem contains an Introit, Dies irae, Offertory, Sanctus, Agnus Dei, and Communion). The oratorios were also composed in the 1890s—*Die Geburt Christi* op.90 in 1895, *Die Passion* op.93 in 1896, and *Erntefeier* op.104 in 1899. All three works are settings of texts by the Protestant theologian Friedrich Spitta (1852–1924), older brother of Philipp, and all three are in the mold of Protestant German works of the late eighteenth century. *Die Geburt Christi* (The birth of Christ), for instance, is structured of recitatives, arias, choruses, and chorales, and its story is relayed without specific characters (i.e., the soloists and chorus portray no specific roles). Interestingly, however, the text is entirely biblical; there is no pietistic poetry as in the typical late-eighteenth-century oratorio. According to Spitta, "Free poetry had to be excluded, and only songs [chorales] that are true to the expressions of the Christmas spirit were used with biblical texts in order to create a genuine artistic work." The oratorio is in three parts—"Die Verheissung" (The promise), which presents texts dealing with prophesies and Advent; "Die Erfüllung" (The fulfillment), which tells of the birth of Jesus; and "Die Anbetung" (The Adoration), which consists of biblical passages of praise in addition to passages about the worship of Jesus by shepherds. Framing the entire work is an organ prelude and postlude based on the chorale "Vom Himmel hoch." Both Herzogenberg and Spitta desired to create a work that could be performed in churches by amateur musicians, and, as a consequence, the oratorio was modestly scored and limited in musical demands. The premiere performance was on the third Sunday of Advent in 1894 at the church of St Thomas in Strasbourg, with the librettist's Academic Church Choir.

The two sacred cantatas—*Totenfeier* op.80 of 1893 and *Gott ist gegenwärtig* op.106 of 1900—and all of the motets were also modeled on Lutheran works of the past. For example, the four motets in opus 102 are all based on Lutheran chorales: *Kommt her zu mir, spricht Gottes Sohn* uses the chorale as a cantus firmus in long notes in the tenor voice while the other voices participate in points of imitation derived from chorale phrases; *Soll ich denn auch des Todes Weg* embellishes the chorale and uses it as material for imitative phrases in all voice parts; *O Traurigkeit, O Herzeleid* uses the chorale melody as a cantus firmus in long notes in the soprano voice; and *Mitten wir im Leben sind* uses the chorale alternately as a cantus firmus in the soprano voice and as material for imitative phrases in all voices.

The secular works include *Deutsches Liederspiel* op.14 for mixed solo voices and piano four hands, *Vier Notturnos* op.22 for SATB voices and piano, *Lieder und Romanzen* op.26 for SSAA voices and piano ad lib., *Zwölf deutsche Volkslieder* op.35 for mixed voices a cappella, *Sechs Gesänge* op.57 for mixed voices a cappella, and *Sechs Mädchenlieder* op.98 for SSA voices and piano. The four nocturnes of opus 22—*Die Einsame* (The lonely one), *Die Nacht* (The night), *Zwei Musikanten* (Two musicians), and *Wie schön, hier zu verträumen* (How lovely, here to be dreaming)—all set to poetry of Joseph von Eichendorff (1788–1857), are considered to be comparable in artistic merit to vocal chamber works of Schumann and Brahms.

HUGO WOLF 1860–1903

Wolf was born in Windischgrätz, Styria (now Slovenj Gradec, Yugoslavia), where his father, an amateur musician, worked in the leather trade. Beginning at age four or five, Hugo studied violin and piano with his father, and for the next several years he played second violin in a small family chamber orchestra (Wolf's father played first violin, his older brother Max played cello, and close friends played other instruments). At eleven Wolf was sent to the Benedictine abbey of St Paul in Lavanttal, Carinthia, and while there he played organ for church services and made piano arrangements of scenes from Bellini, Rossini, Donizetti, and Gounod operas. At thirteen, Wolf transferred to the grammar school in Marburg (now Maribor), and at fifteen he began studies at the Vienna Conservatory, where one of his classmates was Gustav Mahler and where he was strongly attracted to opera and other vocal genres. During his early twenties he earned a living by teaching a few students and accompanying occasional recitals, and he briefly served as *Vice-Kapellmeister* at the Salzburg court. Wolf composed a small number of lieder, choruses, and instrumental chamber works during this time but was not successful in establishing himself as a composer. During his mid-twenties he served as a critic for the Vienna *Salonblatt,* becoming known for his criticisms of Brahms and for his support for Wagner and Liszt, and during his late twenties he entered into a period of compositional frenzy, sometimes writing several songs in one day. He continued writing lieder throughout his thirties, but his health declined at the end of this period as a result of syphilis most likely contracted when he was a teenager. He was insane during the final year of his life and died just several weeks before his forty-third birthday.

Wolf composed five accompanied and fifteen unaccompanied choral works. The accompanied repertoire includes the extended part songs *Die Stimme des Kindes* (seven minutes) and *Im stillen Friedhof* (four and one-half minutes) for SATB chorus and piano, and the cantata *Christnacht* for soprano (the angel of the annunciation), tenor (a shepherd), mixed chorus (representing shepherds, seraphim, and believers), and orchestra. The unaccompanied repertoire includes Wolf's most famous choral works, *Sechs geistliche Lieder,* composed in 1881 to poetry of Joseph von Eichendorff (1788–1857), one of the most popular German poets of the nineteenth century. The six pieces in the collection, each given a title by Wolf, are "Aufblick" (Upward look), "Einklang" (Concord), "Resignation," "Letzte Bitte" (Final prayer), "Ergebung" (Submission), and "Erhebung" (Exaltation). All are short homophonic pieces in a conservative harmonic language, with occasional chromatic passages. The final piece, "Erhebung," was sung at Wolf's funeral service on February 24, 1903, by the Wiener Chorverein. Other a cappella part songs include *Grablied* for SSATTB chorus and *Gottvertrauen* for SATB chorus.

GUSTAV MAHLER 1860–1911

Mahler was born near Iglau, Bohemia (now Jihlava, Czech Republic), where he received a classical education at the Iglau Gymnasium. He learned to play piano on his own, performing in public at age ten, and at fifteen he enrolled at the Vienna Conservatory. Hugo Wolf was also enrolled at the conservatory at that time, and the two students were strongly attracted to Wagner operas. Mahler attended lectures at the University of Vienna in 1877 and 1878, including those delivered by Anton Bruckner, and in the summer of 1880 he took a position as conductor of a small theater in Bod Hall, south of Linz, Austria. Other minor conducting positions followed, including *Kapellmeister* of the Landestheater in Laibach (now Ljubljana) in 1881 and *Kapellmeister* of the Stadttheater in Olmütz (now Olomouc) in 1883. In 1885 he became the interim director of the Neues Deutsches Theater in Prague, and in 1886 he was appointed director of the Neues Stadttheater in Leipzig. In all of these positions he conducted mostly operas (e.g., Mozart's *Don Giovanni* and Wagner's *Das Rheingold* and *Die Walküre*), although he occasionally also conducted oratorios. For instance, in 1885 he led performances of Mendelssohn's *Paulus* and Haydn's *Die Jahreszeiten*. Mahler became known as one of the finest conductors in Europe, and he steadily ascended to higher and higher positions. In 1888 he was appointed director of the Royal Hungarian Opera in Budapest, in 1891 he directed the Stadttheater in Hamburg, and in 1897 he moved to Vienna as director of the Hofoper. While in Vienna, he also conducted numerous concerts of the Philharmonic, including performances of Beethoven's *Symphony #9*. In 1907 Mahler moved to the United States to conduct operas at the Metropolitan Opera in New York City and orchestral performances the following year with the New York Symphony Orchestra. In 1909 he was appointed musical director of the orchestra, by that time named the New York Philharmonic. However, he became ill with bacterial endocarditis during the 1910–1911 season and returned to Vienna, where he died May 18, 1911, at age fifty.

Although Mahler's conducting activity was mainly with opera, he composed no works in that genre. Instead, he focused on large-scale symphonies and songs with orchestral accompaniment, completing nine major symphonies plus a movement of another and three song cycles plus a number of other separate songs. His first symphony, originally called a symphonic poem and later subtitled "The Titan," was composed between 1884 and 1888 (revised between 1893 and 1896), and his ninth symphony, a purely orchestral work with no extramusical program or title, was composed in 1908 and 1909. The works for soloists and orchestra include *Das Lied von der Erde* (The Song of the Earth) and the famous cycles *Lieder eines fahrenden Gesellen* (Songs of a Wayfarer), *Kindertotenlieder* (Songs on the Death of Children), and a collection of five songs on poems of Friedrich Rückert, generally referred to as the "Rückert-Lieder." Of Mahler's compositional output, four works are scored for chorus—the second, third, and eighth symphonies, and a cantata.

The cantata *Das klagende Lied* (Song of lament) was composed in 1880 shortly after Mahler graduated from the Vienna Conservatory. The work, with a text adapted by Mahler from a folk legend, is in three movements. In the first, "Waldmärchen" (Forest tale), a queen promises to marry one of two brothers—the one who finds a red rose in the forest. The younger, more handsome brother finds the rose, puts it in his hat, and falls asleep. The older, less attractive brother finds his sibling sleeping, kills him, and steals the rose. In the second movement, "Der Spielman" (The minstrel), a piper finds a bone of the dead brother and makes a flute from it, which, when played, relates the story of the murder. In the third movement, "Hochzeitsstück" (Wedding piece), the minstrel plays the flute at the wedding feast of the queen and older brother. When the queen hears the tale of murder, she faints, and the castle walls crumble. Mahler reduced the cantata to two movements and rescored it for smaller forces for its premiere with the Vienna Philharmonic in 1901, although performances today are usually of the original three-movement work.

The *Symphony #2* was begun in the summer of 1888, when Mahler composed an orchestral movement called "Totenfeier" (Funeral rite) as a sequel to *Symphony #1* (i.e., "Totenfeier" describes the funeral of the hero portrayed in the first symphony). Late in 1888 Mahler began work on another orchestral movement, a memory of the hero. However, this was not completed until 1893. Two other movements—a scherzo and vocal piece for alto solo called "Urlicht" (Primal light), with a text from *Des Knaben Wunderhorn*—were also composed in 1893, and the fifth and final movement—for soloists, chorus, and orchestra—was composed in the spring of 1894 after Mahler had heard a choral setting of Friedrich Klopstock's ode "Die Auferstehung" (The resurrection) at the memorial service for the conductor Hans von Bülow (who had died February 12, 1894). The first three movements were premiered in Berlin in March 1895, and the entire symphony was premiered by the Berlin Philharmonic in December 1895. The work was immediately popular and subsequently performed many times throughout the early years of the twentieth century. Mahler considered it his favorite symphony, and he conducted it for his farewell performance in Vienna, his first orchestral performance in New York City, and his first appearance in Paris.

The five movements of the symphony are labeled Totenfeier, Andante, Scherzo, Urlicht, and Aufersteh'n. The first and last movements, serving as large architectonic pillars, are more than twice the length of the others, and Mahler specified a pause of at least five minutes after the first movement. For most of the early performances of the symphony, Mahler provided program notes that described the symphony's message of a hero's death and resurrection. For movement one he wrote in part, "We stand by the coffin of a person well loved. His whole life, his struggles, his passions, his sufferings, and his accomplishments on earth pass before us for the last time"; for movement two, "A memory, a ray of sunlight, pure and cloudless, out of the departed's life"; for movement three, "A surge of life ceaselessly in motion, never ending. . . . The world looks distorted and crazy"; for movement four, "The moving voice of naïve faith sounds in our ears 'I am from God and will return to God'"; and for movement five, "The last judgment is at hand, and the horror of the day of days has come upon us. . . . The apocalypse rings out. . . . After all have left their empty graves . . . the gentle sound of a chorus of saints and heavenly hosts is heard, 'Rise again, yes rise again thou wilt.' A feeling of love fills us and illuminates our existence."

Symphony #3 was composed between 1893 and 1896 and premiered in 1902 at the Allgemeiner deutscher Musikverein festival in Krefeld. It is similar to *Symphony #2* in having an overall extramusical program, in the scoring of one of its movements for alto solo, and in employing chorus. The symphony's programmatic message is the creation of the world, which Mahler described in the form of titles—movement one, "Pan awakes, summer marches in (Bacchic procession)"; movement two, "What the wild flowers tell me"; movement three, "What the animals in the woods tell me"; movement four, "What man tells me"; movement five, "What the angels tell me"; and movement six, "What love tells me," with a motto from *Des Knaben Wunderhorn*, "Father, look on these wounds of mine – let no creature be lost." The alto solo in movement four is "Zarathustras Mitternachtslied" (Zarathustra's midnight song) from Friedrich von Nietzsche's *Also sprach Zarathustra*, with the opening phrase, "O Mensch, gib acht, was spricht die tiefe Mitternacht" (O man, take heed, what does the deep midnight say). Movement five is subtitled "Es sungen drei Engel" (Three angels sang) and opens with the phrase from *Des Knaben Wunderhorn*, "Es sungen drei Engel einen süßen Gesang mit Freuden es selig in den Himmel klang" (Three angels sang a sweet song that set heaven ringing with joy).

Symphony #8 was composed in eight weeks during the summer of 1906, orchestrated the following year, and premiered in September 1910 (Mahler's final European appearance as a conductor). It was nicknamed the "Symphony of a Thousand" by the organizer of the premiere because the performance was to include a little over a thousand performers (in actuality, it had only a little over seven hundred). The symphony is divided into two movements, both of which are extensively scored for chorus. The first movement is a setting of the ninth-century Latin hymn "Veni creator spiritus" (Come, creator spirit), which, with Mahler's emphasis of the texts "Veni, creator spiritus, mentes tuorum visita" (Come, creator spirit, visit the minds of your people) and "Accende lumen sensibus" (Kindle with light our senses), serves as a universal appeal for divine inspiration. The second movement, treated as the attainment of divine inspiration and the idealization of mankind's creative abilities, is a setting (in German) of the final scene of Goethe's *Faust,* in which Faust's soul ascends to heaven, where his beloved Gretchen has secured him a place of honor. The central message of Goethe's text is expressed in the final stanza, entitled "Chorus Mysticus" and beginning with the phrases, "Alles Vergängliche ist nur ein Gleichnis; das Unzulängliche hier wird's Ereignis" (All that is transitory is but an image; the insufficient here becomes fulfillment). The music of the symphony is unified by several motifs that appear in both movements. Of particular significance is the motif that begins and ends the symphony: in the first movement it is centered around the interval of a minor seventh (representing mankind's confinement within the octave to earth); at the end of the second movement it is centered around the interval of a major ninth (representing mankind's transcendence and ascent beyond the boundaries of earth to heaven).

CHORAL/ORCHESTRAL WORKS
COMPLETE AND LISTED IN CHRONOLOGICAL ORDER
ACCORDING TO DATE OF COMPOSITION

Das klagende Lied – 1880 (revised in 1892–1893 and 1898–1899) – SATB solos, SAATTBB chorus, and orchestra (including piccolo, English horn, bass clarinet, triangle, bass drum, cymbals, and two harps) – 65 minutes (original version).

Symphony #2 ("Resurrection") – 1888–1894 (revised in 1903) – SA solos, SSAATTBB chorus, and orchestra (including four flutes, four piccolos, four oboes, two English horns, five clarinets, bass clarinet, four bassoons, contrabassoon, ten horns, six trumpets, four trombones, tuba, two sets of timpani, bass drum, two military drums, triangle, cymbals, two tam-tams, ruth, two harps, and organ) – 85 minutes. (1) The ruth is a bundle of twigs or a birch broom; (2) in addition to the instruments specified above, Mahler calls for an offstage ensemble ("in the far distance") of four horns, four trumpets, timpani, bass drum, cymbals, and triangle.

Symphony #3 – 1893–1896 (revised in 1906) – A solo, SSAA chorus, unison children's chorus, and orchestra (including four flutes, four oboes, three clarinets, bass clarinet, four bassoons, eight horns, four trumpets, four trombones, two sets of timpani, two glockenspiels, tambourine, tam-tam, triangle, bass drum, ruth, and two harps) – 106 minutes.

Symphony #8 (Symphony of a thousand) – 1906 – SSAATBB solos, SATB/SATB chorus, unison children's chorus, and orchestra (similar to that for *Symphony #3*) – 85 minutes. (1) Solos represent no specific roles in the first movement, but in the second movement roles are Magna Peccatrix (S), Una Poenitentium (S), Mulier Samaritana (A), Maria Ae- gyptiaca (A), Doctor Marianus (T), Pater Ecstaticus (B), and Pater Pro- fundis (B); (2) an additional soprano solo at the end of the second move- ment, representing the role of Mater Gloriosa, is often sung by a chorus member; (3) Mahler calls for an extra four trumpets and three trom- bones that play at the end of the symphony.

RICHARD STRAUSS 1864–1949

Strauss was born in Munich, where his father was the principal hornist of the Munich court or- chestra and professor at the Königliche Musikschule. The young Strauss began studying piano at age four and violin at eight, attended many concerts by the Munich orchestra during his youth, and played violin in an amateur ensemble when he was eighteen. He also entered the University of Munich at eighteen but studied there only a year before traveling to Dresden and Berlin. At twenty-one he became Hans von Bülow's assistant with the Meiningen Orchestra and also began conducting the Meiningen Choral Society. Within a year of his appointments in Meiningen, von Bülow resigned and Strauss was appointed *Hofmusikdirecktor*. However, he was not treated well and the orchestra was reduced, so the following year he moved back to Munich to be the third conductor at the Munich Hofoper. He remained in Munich for three years, con- ducting such operas as Mozart's *Così fan tutte* and Verdi's *Un ballo in maschera,* and in 1889 he was appointed assistant conductor of the Weimar Opera. While in Weimar, he conducted Wag- ner's *Tristan und Isolde* as well as his own *Guntram,* and he gained fame with performances of his tone poems *Don Juan* and *Tod und Verklärung,* both composed in 1888 and 1889. He was in- vited back to the Munich Hofoper in 1894 as assistant to the ailing director Hermann Levi, and with the retirement of Levi in 1896 Strauss was promoted to director. He continued to conduct Wagner operas, including *Die Meistersinger,* and to compose and conduct his next four tone poems, *Till Eulenspiegels lustige Streiche* (1894–1895), *Also sprach Zarathustra* (1895–1896), *Don Quixote* (1896–1897), and *Ein Heldenleben* (1897–1898).

By the end of the nineteenth century Strauss was one of the most famous composers and conductors in Europe (Gustav Mahler was another), and he was named to more and more pres- tigious positions. In 1898 he was appointed director of the Berlin Hofoper, in 1901 he became president of the Allgemeiner Deutscher Musikverein and conductor of the Berlin Tonkünst- lerverein, and in 1919 he codirected the Vienna Staatsoper. Meanwhile, his opera *Salome* pre- miered in 1905 and was followed by *Elektra* in 1909, *Der Rosenkavalier* in 1911, *Ariadne auf Naxos* in 1912, and *Die Frau ohne Schatten* in 1919. He continued to conduct and compose for another three decades, finishing his career with the *Vier letzte Lieder* (Four last songs) in 1948. He had a heart attack on August 15, 1949, and died September 8 at age eighty-five.

Strauss composed ten works for chorus with orchestral accompaniment and thirty-six pieces for a cappella chorus. The accompanied works include *Wandrers Sturmlied,* inspired by Brahms's *Gesang der Parzen* and composed in 1884 to a text by Goethe; *Taillefer,* composed in 1903 for STB solos, eight-part mixed choir, and orchestra; *Bardengesang,* composed in 1905 for twelve-part male chorus and orchestra; *Die Tageszeiten,* composed in 1928 for TTBB chorus and orchestra; and *Olympische Hymn,* composed in 1934 for SATB chorus and orchestra and premiered at the 1936 Summer Olympics in Berlin.

The most famous of the a cappella choral works are large-scale compositions scored for eight to twenty voice parts, with thick and complicated rhythmic textures in an advanced harmonic language. The *Zwei Gesänge* op.34 were composed in 1897 for sixteen vocal parts and were premiered by the Cologne Hochschule Chorus in 1898 (number one of the opus) and 1899 (number two). The first of the two pieces, *Der Abend* (The Evening), is a mainly homophonic composition set to a poem by Friedrich Schiller that describes a sunset: Phoebus, the god of the sun, sinks into the arms of Thetis, one of the goddesses of the sea. The second piece, *Hymne* (Hymn), is a more polyphonic setting of a poem by Friedrich Rückert that compares the biblical story of the return of Joseph's favorite son to the return of spring after winter, calmness after a storm, and happiness after sadness. The *Deutsche Motette* was composed in 1913 to a poem by Rückert entitled "Die Schöpfung ist zur Ruh gegangen" (All creation is at rest). Strauss divided the work into two parts—an opening homophonic section that includes most of the poem and that accounts for approximately one-third of the music, and a lengthy point-of-imitation section that includes the final lines of the poem and that accounts for the remaining two-thirds of the music. *An den Baum Daphne* (To the tree Daphne) was composed in 1943 and premiered by the Vienna State Opera Chorus and the Vienna Boys' Choir in 1947. The work is a meditation on or epilogue to Strauss's opera *Daphne,* which was composed in 1936 and 1937 and premiered in 1938, and which was originally planned to have a choral ending. At the conclusion of the opera, Daphne is transformed by the god Zeus into a laurel tree so that his son Apollo may worship her in nature, and she sings a wordless melody offstage that is echoed by a solo oboe. In the choral work, this melody, again wordless, is sung by a solo soprano echoed by a solo treble (child) accompanied by the wordless chorus.

Other a cappella choral works are smaller in scale and less musically and vocally challenging. *Die Göttin im Putzzimmer* (The goddess in the boudoir) is yet another setting of a Rückert poem, composed in 1935 and premiered by the Vienna State Opera Chorus in 1952. The music is divided into two parts—a chaotic beginning that portrays the disorder of the boudoir, and a stately and cohesive ending that characterizes the goddess, who symbolizes love and creativity and who, when entering the boudoir, brings harmony and order into life. The *Drei Männerchöre* op.45 were composed in 1899 and premiered by the Schubertbund of Vienna. The texts of the three pieces are taken from a collection of folk songs, *Stimmen der Völker in Liedern,* compiled by Johann Gottfried Herder (1744–1803). "Schlachtgesang" (Song of battle) praises death on the battlefield; "Lied der Freundschaft" (Song of friendship) praises true and faithful friendship; and "Der Brauttanz" (Bethrothal dance) extols the happiness of couples as they dance at their wedding feasts.

A CAPPELLA CHORAL WORKS
SELECTED AND LISTED ACCORDING TO FAMILIARITY

Der Abend op.34 no.1 – 1897 – SSSSAAAATTTTBBBB chorus – 10 minutes.

Hymne op.34 no.2 – 1897 – SATB solos and SSSAAATTTBBB chorus –
11 minutes.

Deutsche Motette op.62 – 1913 – SATB solos and SSSSAAAATTTTBBBB chorus – 20 minutes.

Die Göttin im Putzzimmer – 1935 – SSAATTBB chorus – 6 minutes.

An den Baum Daphne – 1943 – S and treble solos and SATB/SATB chorus – 15 minutes.

Drei Männerchöre op.45 – 1899 – TTBB chorus – "Schlachtgesang" 3 minutes, "Lied der Freundschaft" 4:30 minutes, and "Der Brauttanz" 2:30 minutes.

GEORG SCHUMANN 1866–1952

Schumann was born in Königstein, Saxony, where his father was a violinist and his grandfather an organist. The young Schumann studied with both his father and grandfather, and at age nine he began playing the violin in the Königstein orchestra. At twelve he became the town organist, and at sixteen he entered the Leipzig Conservatory to study piano and composition. He held two minor conducting positions during his twenties and early thirties—director of the Danzig Gesangverein between 1890 and 1896, and director of the Bremen Philharmonische Gesellschaft between 1896 and 1899. In 1900 he was appointed director of the Berlin Sing-Akademie, one of the most prestigious choral positions in Europe and one that he held for fifty years.

Schumann composed six choral/orchestral works, six opuses of a cappella motets, and two opuses of part songs. The choral/orchestral works include the oratorio *Ruth* op.50, based on old Hebraic melodies, and the cantatas *Amor und Psyche* op.3 and *Totenklage* op.33. The most famous of the motets are *Drei geistliche Gesänge* op.31 and *Drei Motteten* op.52. The first of these opuses contains three Psalm settings—"Und ob ich schon wanderte im finstren Tal" (Psalm 23:4), "Siehe, wie fein und lieblich ist es" (Psalm 133:1, 3), and "Herr, wie lang" (Psalm 13:1–3). All are scored for SATB chorus, with occasional divisions, and are in a neo-Renaissance style, with alternating passages of imitative polyphony and homophony. The three motets in opus 52 are settings of varied texts: "Komm, heil'ger Geist" begins with the first verse of Martin Luther's chorale and ends with two verses of unknown origin; "Das ist ein köstliches Ding" is from Psalm 92:1–5; and "Herr, erhöre meine Worte" uses paraphrases of verses from Psalms 5 and 6. Numbers one and two of opus 52 are scored for eight-part chorus, while number two is for four voices. Two other opuses of motets are noteworthy—*Gesänge Hiobs* op.60, which contains three settings of verses from Job for mixed voices and organ, and *Drei Motetten* op.75, which contains three eight-voiced settings of chorale texts, including "Jerusalem, du hochgebaute Stadt" and "Mit Fried und Freud ich fahr dahin." The secular opuses are *Vier Lieder* op. 41 for men's voices and *Drei Altdeutscher Lieder* op.63 for mixed voices.

MAX REGER 1873–1916

Reger was born in Brand, near Bayreuth, where his father was a schoolteacher, amateur musician (proficient on the oboe, clarinet, and string bass), and author of a harmony textbook. Max studied piano and violin with his father and organ with a local church musician, and from ages thirteen to sixteen he often played the organ for church services and town functions. At seventeen he began studying with the musicologist and Bach scholar Hugo Riemann at the Wiesbaden Conservatory, and for the next decade he composed numerous organ works based on Lutheran chorale tunes. In 1901 Reger moved to Munich, accompanying the violinist Henri Marteau and the singer Josef Loritz and teaching a few students privately. He wrote a treatise on modern harmony, *Beiträge zur Modulationslehre,* in 1903; in 1904 he began teaching organ, theory, and composition at the Munich Akademie der Tonkunst; and beginning in 1905 he conducted the Porge Choir, performing Bach cantatas and works by Wolf and Liszt. In 1907 he was appointed professor of composition, conductor of the academic choir, and director of music at the University of Leipzig, and in 1911 he became conductor of the famous court orchestra in Meiningen, founded by Hans von Bülow. Reger resigned from this position in 1913 and moved to Jena, concentrating on composition and concert appearances. On his way home from a concert tour to the Netherlands, he stopped in Leipzig, where he had a heart attack and died approximately two months after his forty-third birthday. He had just completed the motet op.138 no.1, "Der Mensch lebt und bestehet nur eine kleine Zeit" (Man lives and exists only a short time).

Reger composed approximately twenty-five sacred choral works and twenty secular part songs. The sacred repertoire consists of several early Latin motets, five opuses of German motets, five Lutheran cantatas, and a few choral/orchestral works. The best known and artistically finest of his choral output are the German motets and cantatas—a logical result of Reger's involvement with the works of Bach. However, it is odd in that Reger was also a practicing Catholic his entire life. The three motets in opus 110 were composed separately between 1909 and 1912, when Reger was employed in Leipzig. *Mein Odem ist schwach* (My breath is weak) was dedicated to Gustav Schreck, *Kantor* of the Thomaskirche, where Bach had served the last decades of his life; *Ach, Herr, strafe mich nicht* (Oh Lord, rebuke me not) was dedicated to the conductor of the Dortmund Music Society; and *O Tod, wie bitter bist du* (Oh death, how bitter you are) was dedicated to the memory of Felix Mendelssohn's daughter Lili. The three motets are reminiscent of Baroque models only in occasional imitative textures and chorale-like passages. Otherwise, they are wholly Romantic, with solo lines (sung by an entire vocal section), liberal use of expressive tempo changes, and a highly chromatic harmonic vocabulary (Reger's chief compositional characteristic).

The cantatas are more reflective of Baroque models in that they are structured of variations of original Lutheran chorales, although Reger adorns the chorales with newly composed chromatic melodies and often harmonizes them in a chromatic language. *O Haupt voll Blut und Wunden,* for instance, is structured of ten variations, corresponding to ten verses of the original Lutheran chorale, and *Vom Himmel hoch, da komm ich her* is structured of fifteen varied statements of the original Lutheran chorale. The *Acht geistliche Gesänge* (Eight sacred songs) op.138 are short a cappella settings of texts from the poetic collection *Der deutscher Psalter* (The German Psalter), edited by Will Vesper (1882–1962) and published in 1913. Number one, "Der Mensch lebt und bestehet nur eine kleine Zeit," mentioned earlier, is scored for SATB/SATB chorus; number two, "Morgengesang" (Morning song), is for SSATBB chorus; number three, "Nachtlied" (Night song), is for SATBB; number four, "Unser lieben Frauen Traum" (Our blessed lady's dream), is for SSATBB; number five, "Kreuzfahrerlied" (Crusaders' song), is for SSATB; number six, "Das Agnus Dei" (The Lamb of God), is for SATTB; number seven, "Schlachtgesang" (Battle song), is for SATBB; and number eight, "Wir glauben an einen Gott" (We believe in one God), is for SSATB. All the pieces are homophonic and chorale-like.

Der 100. Psalm was composed for the 350th anniversary of the founding of the University of Jena and dedicated to its faculty, who bestowed on Reger an honorary doctorate. The work—usually performed today from an edition by Paul Hindemith in the 1950s in which the orchestral texture is thinned and twelve measures are deleted from the fugue—is divided into two movements, the second of which ends in a lengthy double fugue.

The most popular of the part songs are the *Drei Sechsstimmige Chöre* op.39, each dedicated to a different choral society—"Schweigen" (Silence) to the Leipzig Riedel Society, "Abendlied" (Evening song) to the Berlin Philharmonic Choir, and "Frühlingsblick" (Glimpse of spring) to the Kotzolt Choral Society. The textures of these part songs are mostly homophonic, and the harmonic language is more tonal than that in the motets and cantatas. The *Drei Chöre* op.6—"Trost" (Consolation), "Zur Nacht" (To the night), and "Abendlied" (Evening song)—are settings by minor poets in the style of Brahms, and the *Drei Gesänge* op.111b—"Im Himmelreich ein Haus steht" (A house stands in the kingdom of heaven), "Abendgang im Lenz" (Evening walk in spring), and "Er ist's" (It is)—are simple, tonal pieces and Reger's only settings for female voices.

SACRED CHORAL WORKS
SELECTED AND LISTED ACCORDING TO FAMILIARITY

O Tod, wie bitter bist du op.110 no. 3 (from Ecclesiastes 41) – 1912 – SSAATTBB chorus a cappella – 9:30 minutes.

Mein Odem ist schwach op.110 no.1 (from Job 17, 19, and 26) – 1909 – SSAATTBB chorus a cappella – 15 minutes.

Ach, Herr, strafe mich nicht op.110 no.2 (from Psalms 4, 6, 7, 16, and 18) – 1911 – SSAATTBB chorus a cappella – 16:30 minutes.

Der 100. Psalm op.106 – 1908–1909 – SATB chorus and orchestra (including organ) – 40 minutes. The choral parts occasionally divide into SSAATTBB, with one brief passage for SSSAAATTB.

Acht geistliche Gesänge op.138 – 1914 – SATB to SATB/SATB chorus a cappella (see above for specific titles and scorings) – 1:30–2 minutes per piece or about 14 minutes total.

Vom Himmel hoch da komm ich her – ca.1903 – SATB solos, SSAA children's chorus, two violins, and organ – 17 minutes.

O Haupt voll Blut und Wunden – ca.1905 – AT or AS solos, SATB chorus, violin, oboe, and organ – 18 minutes. The chorus divides into two SATB ensembles for the ending of the cantata.

O wie selig seid ihr doch, ihr Frommen – ca.1904 – S solo, SATB chorus, string quintet, and organ – 13:30 minutes.

Meinen Jesum lass ich nicht – ca.1904 – S solo, SATB chorus, violin, viola, and organ – 8 minutes.

Auferstanden, auferstanden – ca.1904 – A solo, SATB chorus, and organ – 9 minutes.

SECULAR CHORAL WORKS
SELECTED AND LISTED ACCORDING TO FAMILIARITY

Drei Sechsstimmige Chöre op.39 – 1899 – SAATBB chorus a cappella (see above for specific titles) – 4, 4:30, and 4:15 minutes.

Drei Chöre op.6 – 1892 – SATB chorus and piano (see above for specific titles) – 6, 2, and 4 minutes.

Drei Gesänge op.111b – 1909 – SSAA chorus a cappella (see above for specific titles) – 2, 2:15, and 2:30 minutes.

❦ RUSSIA ❦

All the significant Russian choral composers of the Romantic era studied or worked in St Petersburg or Moscow, with St Petersburg being the greater center of activity during the early part of the era and Moscow being more important, especially for choral musicians, during the latter part. The two earliest composers—Dmytro Bortnyans'ky and Mikhail Glinka—worked at the Imperial Court Cappella in St Petersburg, and seven composers—Grigory Lvovsky, Pyotr Tchaikovsky, Mikhail Ippolitov-Ivanov, Anton Arensky, Aleksandr Grechaninov, Aleksandr Glazunov, and Serge Rachmaninoff—studied at the St Petersburg Conservatory. In addition, César Cui and Nikolay Rimsky-Korsakov studied in St Petersburg, although not at the conservatory, and Rimsky-Korsakov was on the conservatory's faculty (teaching Ippolitov-Ivanov, Arensky, Grechaninov, and Glazunov). The other notable composers during the era either studied or taught at the Moscow Conservatory, which was not founded until 1866. Sergey Taneyev, Aleksandr Kastal'sky, and Pavel Chesnokov studied there and then became professors, and Viktor Kalinnikov served on the faculty. Several of the composers already mentioned were associated with both the St Petersburg and Moscow conservatories: Grechaninov and Rachmaninoff studied at the two institutions, and Tchaikovsky, Ippolitov-Ivanov, and Arensky studied in St Petersburg and taught in Moscow. The Moscow Synodal School of Church Singing, which developed a famous choir during the latter part of the nineteenth century, was also an important center of education. Chesnokov studied there as well as at the Moscow Conservatory, and Kastal'sky and Kalinnikov were Synodal School faculty members.

With such concentration of activity in limited geographical areas and with such appreciable contact among the composers, it is not surprising that the Russian music of the Romantic era exhibited a consistency of compositional style. What is surprising, however, is that this style began during the Classical era and extended well into the twentieth century. Bortnyans'ky, who lived almost completely during the Classical era and was familiar with its style (conducting such works as Haydn's *Die Schöpfung* and Mozart's *Requiem*), composed in a discernibly different manner. None of his works were accompanied by instruments, he employed no symphonic forms that involved development of motivic material, the textures of his music contained no figural motifs as were common in the orchestral music of the European Classical-era composers, and his harmonic progressions and tonal designs were unique and advanced for his time. Bortnyans'ky's a cappella and homophonic textures, wide tessituras, and completely choral scorings were indicative of Romantic-era compositions. Furthermore, while there were notable modifications to these characteristics during the Romantic era (e.g., expanded tessituras and more luxuriant harmonies), Bortnyans'ky's basic qualities of composition remained the same for composers such as Chesnokov and Rachmaninoff, who lived during the time of the twentieth century when many composers were experimenting with avant-garde techniques. The Russian qualities described here were, of course, most specific to Russian Orthodox church music—the genre of composition that was most popular during the Romantic era and the genre represented by every composer discussed here. Secular part songs were a cappella and basically homophonic, although with limited tessituras, and cantatas and patriotic hymns were often scored for chorus and orchestra.

The Russian Orthodox music consists of anthem-like pieces that are part of the Divine Liturgy or All-Night Vigil or that coincide with special liturgical events. The Divine Liturgy—officially named *Liturgiia Sv. Ioanna Zlatousta* (Liturgy of St John Chrysostom) after the patriarch of Constantinople who lived from 347 to 407—is the regular liturgical structure of the Russian Orthodox Church that equates to the Roman Catholic Mass Ordinary. The Russian Divine Liturgy is more complex, however, with a greater number of constituent parts and with a greater variance in those parts set to newly composed music. For instance, the Roman liturgy has only five parts that have traditionally been set to music (Kyrie, Gloria, Credo, Sanctus, and Agnus Dei), while the Roman liturgy has sixteen: *Velikaya Ekteniya* (the Great Litany), set to the text "Ghospodi, pomiluy" (Lord, have mercy on us); *Blagoslovi, dushe moya, Ghospoda* (Bless the Lord, O my soul), Psalm 103:1–6; *Slava otsu i yedinorodnï* (Glory to the father and only begotten son); *Vo tsarstvii tvoyem* (In your kingdom), with text from the Beatitudes (Matthew 5:3–12); *Priiditye, poklonimsya* (Come, let us worship); the Trisagion Hymn *Svyatï Bozhe* (Holy God); *Izhe heruvimï* or *Heruvimskaya pesn* (Cherubic Hymn); *Vyeruyu* (Creed); *Milost' mira* (Grace of peace); *Tebe poyem* (We sing to you); the hymn to the Virgin Mary, *Dostoyno yest* (It is truly fitting); the Lord's Prayer, *Otche nash* (Our father); *Hvalitye Ghospoda s nyebyes* (O praise the Lord from the heavens); *Blagoslovyen gryadï vo imya Ghospodnye* (Blessed is he who comes in the name of the Lord); *Vidyekhom svyet istinnï* (We have seen the true light); and *Da ispolnyatsya usta nasha khvalyeniya* (May our mouths be filled with your glory).

The *Vsenoshchnoye bdeniye* (All-Night Vigil) is the service that is celebrated before major feasts or on Saturday evenings. Its constituent parts, set frequently by Russian composers, are *Priiditye, poklonimsya* (Come, let us worship); *Blagoslovi, dushe moya, Ghospoda* (Bless the Lord, O my soul), Psalm 104:1–6; *Blazhen muzh* (Blessed is the man), Psalm 1:1; *Svete tihiy* (Gladsome light); *Nïne otpushchayeshï raba tvoyego, vladïko* (Lord, now let your servant depart in peace); *Bogoroditse devo* (Rejoice, O virgin); *Slava v vïshnih Bogu* (Glory to God in the highest); *Hvalite imia Ghospodne* (Praise the name of the Lord); *Blagosloven yesi, Ghospodi* (Blessed are you, O Lord); *Voskreseniye Hristovo videvshe* (Having beheld the resurrection of Christ); *Velichit dushe moya Ghospoda* (My soul magnifies the Lord); and *Vzbrannoy voyevode* (To you, victorious leader).

Only a few composers set complete or near-complete cycles of the Divine Liturgy and All-Night Vigil. Tchaikovsky, Ippolitov-Ivanov, and Rachmaninoff wrote one each, Grechaninov wrote four cycles of the Divine Liturgy and one of the All-Night Vigil, and Chesnokov wrote three cycles of the Divine Liturgy and two of the All-Night Vigil. Rimsky-Korsakov wrote a partial cycle of the Divine Liturgy, Kastal'sky wrote a complete Divine Liturgy and a partial All-Night Vigil, and Arensky wrote a partial Divine Liturgy. Most of the other composers wrote numerous pieces from both services but did not organize the pieces into cycles. In addition, almost all the composers wrote multiple settings of certain popular texts from the cycles.

Secular genres included opera, which was generally second in importance to church music with most of the Russian Romantic composers, and given the importance of choral music in Russia at the time, it is not surprising that the operas contain significant choruses and that several of these choruses are occasionally excerpted and performed separately on concert programs. These include the Sailor's Chorus for men's chorus from Rimsky-Korsakov's *Sadko,* the Polovetzian Patrol for men's chorus and Polovetzian Dances for mixed chorus from Borodin's *Prince Igor,* the Coronation Chorus for mixed chorus from Musorgsky's *Boris Godunov,* and the Chorus and Dance of Peasants for mixed chorus from Tchaikovsky's *Eugen Onegin.* In addition, it should be noted that many famous orchestral works (i.e., works considered purely orchestral today) were originally scored for chorus as well as orchestra. These works include Tchaikovsky's festival overture *1812* and the Polonaise from Rimsky-Korsakov's *Christmas Night.*

The major composers of the era in terms of significant choral repertoire are Bortnyans'ky, Tchaikovsky, Rimsky-Korsakov, Grechaninov, Kalinnikov, Chesnokov, and Rachmaninoff. The composers considered of less significance are Glinka, Lvovsky, Cui, Taneyev, Kastal'sky, Ippolitov-Ivanov, Arensky, and Glazunov. Other composers who contributed significant or frequently performed repertoire include Mily Balakirev (1837–1910), a renowned pianist, conductor, and composer of songs and also one of the first Russian nationalists, whose *Svïshe prorotsï* (From heaven the prophets) was frequently performed on tours by Russian choirs; Aleksandr Arkhangel'sky (1846–1924), a famous conductor who toured with his choir throughout Russia and Europe and whose *Hvalite imia Ghospodne* (Praise the name of the Lord) was well known during his time; Nikolai Kedroff (1871–1940), who composed a popular setting of *Otche nash;* Nikolay Tcherepnin (1873–1945), father of Alexander Tcherepnin (1899–1977), who composed two large-scale works—the cantata *Pesn' Safo* (Song of Sappho) and oratorio *Khozhdeniye Bogoroditse po mukam* (The descent of the Virgin Mary into hell); Aleksandr Nikol'sky (1874–1943), who is known for several compositions, including *Ghospod' votsarisia* (The Lord reigns) op.45 no.7 and *Milost' mira* (Grace of peace) op.3 no.3; and Nikolay Golovanov (1891–1953), who composed twenty-three choral works, two of which are scored for male voices and are relatively well known—*Dostoyno yest* op.1 no.4 and *Milost' mira* op.1 no.2.

DMYTRO (DMITRY) BORTNYANS'KY (BORTNIANSKY)
1751–1825

Bortnyans'ky was born in Glukhov (now Hlukhiv), Ukraine, near Kiev, where at age six he began singing at the Choristers' School. At seven he transferred to the Imperial Court Cappella in St Petersburg, and at ten he began studying with Baldassare Galuppi, court composer to Catherine the Great from 1765 to 1768. In 1769 Bortnyans'ky accompanied Galuppi to Venice, and during the following decade he composed three Italian operas and several Latin motets, including *Ave Maria* for soprano and alto duet in 1775 and *Salve regina* for alto solo in 1776. In 1779 he returned to Russia as assistant director of the Imperial Court Cappella and teacher of keyboard instruments to the royal family, and in 1783 he was appointed *Kapellmeister* to Catherine's son, Paul. With Catherine's death in 1796, Bortnyans'ky became director of the court cappella (the first native Russian to hold this position), and for most of the next two decades he expanded the court's repertoire by performing large-scale European choral/orchestral works such as Haydn's *Die Schöpfung* in 1802, Mozart's *Requiem* in 1805, Handel's *Messiah* in 1806, and Beethoven's *Christus am Oelberge* in 1813. Bortnyans'ky focused his attention on Russian church music in 1814, and in an effort to unify liturgical repertoire in Russia, he published a collection of liturgical chants (*prostoye penie*) in 1815. The following year he was given control of all church music and granted an exclusive license to print music in Russia. Tsar Aleksandr's edict sanctioning this monopoly read in part, "Everything sung in our churches must be printed and must consist of works composed by the director of the court cappella or other celebrated composers – these latter compositions printed with the approval of Mr. Bortnyans'ky."

Bortnyans'ky composed forty-five sacred concertos (thirty-five for SATB and ten for SATB/SATB), nine Cherubic hymns (seven for SATB and two for SATB/SATB), fourteen Te Deums, and approximately fifty other small-scale sacred pieces for the Russian Orthodox Church. The sacred concertos are generally three- or four-movement a cappella works that were sung at the conclusion of liturgical services during the reign of Catherine. The texts are mostly from the Psalms and the textures are mainly homophonic, with occasional imitative passages and phrases sung in dialogue between high and low voices. Paul I prohibited the genre for a period of time because he thought the concertos were too secular in style. However, they continued to be popular, and several circulated in copies throughout Europe. Berlioz praised their freedom of form, and Tchaikovsky was especially fond of *Skazhi mi, Ghospodi, konchinu moyu* (Concerto #32). Four of the Te Deums, all entitled *Tebye Boha khvalim* (We praise you, O God), are scored for SATB chorus a cappella, and ten others are scored for SATB/SATB chorus a cappella. The other sacred music is similar in texture and scoring, although shorter in duration and confined to one movement.

SACRED WORKS
SELECTED AND LISTED ACCORDING TO FAMILIARITY

Slava vo vyshnikh Bohu (Luke 2:14) Concerto #6 – SATB chorus a cappella – 5:30 minutes. The choral parts divide into SSAATTBB.

Izhe heruvimï (Cherubic Hymn #7) – SATB chorus a cappella – 4 minutes.

Skazhi mi, Ghospodi, konchinu moyu (from Psalm 39) Concerto #32 – SATB chorus a cappella – 13 minutes.

Vsi iazytsy vospleshchite rukami (from Psalm 47) Concerto #31 – SATB chorus a cappella – 6:30 minutes.

Voskliknite Ghospodevi, vsya zemlya (from Psalm 66) Concerto #4 – SATB chorus a cappella – 9:15 minutes.

Blazhen muzh, boyaysya Ghospoda (from Psalm 112) Concerto #28 – SATB chorus a cappella – 10:30 minutes.

MIKHAIL GLINKA 1804–1857

Glinka was born in Novospasskoye, near Smolensk, southwest of Moscow. During his youth he was fond of folk songs that were sung by household servants, and he learned to play the piano and violin from area teachers. At age eleven he began playing the violin in local orchestras, and at fourteen he entered the Noble Boarding School of the Pedagogical College in St Petersburg, furthering his study of piano and violin. After graduation in 1822 he returned to his hometown and rejoined the local orchestras, becoming acquainted with the works of such European composers as Haydn, Mozart, Beethoven, and Cherubini, and in 1824 he took a position as a civil servant in St Petersburg. In order to be in a warmer climate for his health, Glinka left Russia in 1828 for Italy, settling in Milan, where he heard the premieres of Donizetti's *Anna Bolena* and Bellini's *La sonnambula* and became friends with the two composers. After brief visits to Rome and Naples, he traveled in 1833 to Vienna and Berlin, returning to Novospasskoye in 1834 and St Petersburg in 1835. By this time he had composed his third opera, *Zhizn' za tsarya* (A life for the tsar), which premiered to critical acclaim in 1836. In 1837 he became a teacher of singing at the Imperial Court Cappella and also began composing church music. His fourth opera, *Ruslan i Lyudmila* (Ruslan and Ludmilla), was premiered in 1842, and for the remainder of his life he traveled throughout Europe. He took a keen interest in the music of J. S. Bach and Handel after 1851, particularly Bach's *B minor Mass,* which he heard in Berlin.

Glinka composed approximately twelve choral works, including *Velik nash Bog* (Our God is great) for SATB chorus a cappella, *Heruvimskaya pesn* (Cherubic Hymn) for SSATTB chorus a cappella, *Molitva* (Prayer) for SATB chorus and piano, *Yekteniya pervaya* (First Litany) for SATB chorus a cappella, and *Da ispravitsaya* (Let my prayer arise) for TTB chorus a cappella.

GRIGORY LVOVSKY 1830–1894

Lvovsky was born in Kishinev, Moldova, where in his youth he studied at the Kishinev Theological Seminary and conducted the seminary chorus and also the local Catholic cathedral choir. He later studied violin and composition at the St Petersburg Conservatory, and in 1856 he was appointed precentor at the church of St Alexander Nevsky Lavra. In 1858 he also became precentor at St Isaac Cathedral, and for the reminder of his life he served in both positions.

Lvovsky composed approximately one hundred sacred works based on Slavic chant and approximately twelve other sacred works that are freely composed. His most famous composition is *Ghospodi, pomiluy* (Lord, have mercy), a setting of the traditional text sung for the office of the Elevation of the Cross on the feast of the Universal Exaltation (or Elevation) of the Cross, which takes place every September 14. The text is also sung on the third Sunday of Lent. According to the rubrics of the liturgy, the text, which consists only of the phrase "Ghospodi, pomiluy," is to be repeated from one hundred to four hundred times—the cleric facing east, south, west, and then north during certain multiples of the repetitions. Lvovsky's setting contains seventy-eight statements. Three are sung slowly to a four-chord phrase, seventy-two are sung very fast (three times each per chord), and the final three are again sung slowly to the same chords as at the beginning of the piece.

CÉSAR CUI 1835–1918

Cui was born in Vilnius, where he received a classical education at the local gymnasium (the same school where his father taught French). The young Cui studied piano privately but did not consider music a career option. In 1851 he entered an engineering school in St Petersburg, and in 1855 he enrolled at the Academy of Military Engineering. His aptitude for engineering was apparently acute, for in 1857 he was appointed lecturer at the academy and in 1879 a professor. Along with his engineering work he maintained an interest in music, and he was drawn to composition after meeting the pianist, composer, and conductor Mily Balakirev in 1857. Between 1864 and 1877 Cui served as a music critic for the *Sanktpeterburgskiye vedomosti,* and in 1857 he composed his first opera, *Kavkazskiy plennik* (A prisoner in the Caucasus). Other operas followed, including *Vil'yam Ratklif* (William Ratcliff) composed between 1861 and 1868, and *Kapitanskaya dochka* (The captain's daughter) composed between 1907 and 1909. He also continued to serve as critic, writing for such newspapers and periodicals as the *Novoye vremya* (1876–1880 and 1917), *Nedelya* (1884–1889 and 1895), *Novosti i birzhevaya gazeta* (1896–1900), and *Revue et gazette musicale de Paris* (1878–1880).

Cui composed a collection of three sacred concertos, one Magnificat, and approximately fifty secular pieces. The sacred concertos, composed in 1910 and scored for SATB a cappella chorus, are entitled *Ghospodi, da ne yarostiyu* (Lord, in thy wrath), *Bozhe, Bozhe moy vonmi mi* (O God, my God, attend to me), and *Raduytesia, pravednii* (Rejoice in the Lord). The Magnificat, a setting of Luke 1:46–55 entitled variously *Pesn' presvyatïya Bogoroditsï* (Song of the most holy mother of God) or *Velichit dushe moya Ghospoda* (My soul magnifies the Lord), was composed in 1914 for the All-Night Vigil liturgical service. It is scored for solo soprano and SSAATTBB a cappella chorus.

The secular pieces include five collections of part songs for mixed voices a cappella, one set of part songs for mixed voices and orchestra, thirteen pieces for female and children's voices (plus seven duets for female and children), and two cantatas for mixed voices and orchestra.

PYOTR (PETER) TCHAIKOVSKY 1840–1893

Tchaikovsky (also spelled Chaikovsky and listed under *C* in many libraries) was born in a small town near Moscow, where his father was a mining engineer. Pyotr exhibited an early interest in literature and a talent for languages—at age six he read in French and German as well as Russian—and at seven he began writing essays and poems. He also loved listening to music and was especially fond of Mozart's *Don Giovanni.* At twelve he enrolled at the School of Jurisprudence in St Petersburg, where his family had moved, and for the next seven years he sang in the school chorus, studied voice and piano, and attended numerous concerts. He took a job with the Ministry of Justice at nineteen, and at twenty-one he was sent to various cities in western Europe as a translator for Russian dignitaries. At this time he began to take a serious interest in music, and in 1862, at age twenty-two, he enrolled at the St Petersburg Conservatory. He studied piano, flute, organ, theory, and composition, and in three years he had developed sufficient skills not only to compose, but to teach as well. He wrote his first symphony, subtitled "Winter

Daydreams," in 1866, and that same year he was also appointed to the faculty of the new Moscow Conservatory. He continued to teach and compose, writing the first version of the fantasy overture *Romeo i Dzul'etta* (Romeo and Juliet) in 1869. In addition, he served as a music critic for two Moscow newspapers from 1871 to 1875, and in 1873 he authored a series of articles on the music and life of Beethoven. During the next several years Tchaikovsky composed some of his most famous works, including the ballet *Lebedinoe ozero* (Swan Lake) between 1875 and 1876 and the opera *Yevgeny Onegin* (Eugene Onegin) and *Symphony #4* between 1877 and 1878.

He resigned from the faculty of the conservatory in 1877, and for the next decade he was supported by a devoted patron and friend, Nadezhda von Meck. Tchaikovsky was recognized throughout Russia and Europe as one of the great composers of the time, and from contemporary evidence he seems to have enjoyed his success. There is no evidence that he was an outcast from society, as is sometimes postulated, or that he was despondent about his life. To the contrary, he was a frequent participant in social events, and despite his unsuccessful marriage in 1877 and his program notes for *Symphony #4* about fate preventing eventual happiness, he had close friends and intimate relationships that were apparently satisfying. Throughout the late 1870s, 1880s, and early 1890s he continued to experience success with premieres of his compositions, including the opera *Orleanskaya deva* (The maid of Orléans) in 1878, the festival overture *1812* in 1882, the *Symphony #5* in 1888, and the ballet *Spyashchaya krasavitsa* (The Sleeping Beauty) in 1890. In 1889 he was appointed director of the Moscow branch of the Russian Musical Society, and for the next several years he maintained an active composing and conducting schedule, with the premieres of his opera *Pikovaya dama* (The Queen of Spades) in 1890, his ballet *Shchelkunchik* (The Nutcracker) in 1892, and his *Symphony #6* ("Pathétique") in 1893. Conducting engagements took him to cities such as Paris, Warsaw, Philadelphia, Baltimore, and New York, and he traveled to England in 1892 to receive an honorary doctorate from Cambridge University. On October 21, 1893, five days after conducting the premiere of *Symphony #6* in St Petersburg, Tchaikovsky became ill; four days later, the cause of his illness unknown, he died at age fifty-three. His brother Modest claimed that he drank unboiled water and contracted cholera, while others have suggested that he committed suicide.

Tchaikovsky composed two Services for the Russian Orthodox Church, ten separate sacred pieces, incidental music entitled *Snegurochka* (The Snow Maiden), four cantatas and occasional works for chorus and orchestra, and fifteen secular pieces for a cappella chorus. The Services—*Liturgiia Sv. Ioanna Zlatousta* (Liturgy of St John Chrysostom) op.41 and *Vsenoshchnoye bdeniye* (All-Night Vigil) op.52—were composed in 1878 and 1881 to 1882, respectively, for no particular occasion, commission, or condition of employment. Tchaikovsky was merely interested in church music. In a letter to Madame von Meck he wrote, "I very often go to mass. The Liturgy of St John Chrysostom is, in my view, one of the great works of art. . . . If one follows it closely, going carefully into the significance of the rites, it is impossible not to be spiritually moved." Both Services contain most of the constituent parts of their liturgies (see the introduction to this section of the Romantic era for a listing), and the All-Night Vigil is based on traditional Orthodox chants. Tchaikovsky subtitled the work "An essay at harmonizing ecclesiastical chants" and stated, "I want to preserve the ancient ecclesiastical chants, even though they are constructed on scales of a very special type and do not easily lend themselves to modern harmonizations."

Tchaikovsky's Liturgy of St John Chrysostom, which was the first unified musical cycle of the liturgy in history, was not completely well received at the time of its composition. Nikolai

Bakhmetev, the director of the Imperial Court Cappella, attempted to block publication of the work on the grounds that he had not approved it for church worship (i.e., Tchaikovsky had not adhered to the long-standing edict, made by Tsar Aleksandr in 1816, that approval of church music must be granted by the director of the Imperial Court Cappella). Tchaikovsky had submitted the work only to the Moscow Office of Sacred Censorship. A legal battle ensued, and the Russian Senate ruled that Tchaikovsky's work could be published, a ruling that basically eliminated future censorship by the Imperial Court Cappella and opened the doors for future Liturgy settings by other composers.

Nine of the separate sacred pieces were composed in 1885 and issued in a collection generally referred to as "Nine Sacred Pieces." Three of the pieces are settings of *Heruvimskaya pesn* (Cherubic Hymn); one is in F major, one in D major, and the third in C major. The other titles, some of which are from the Liturgy, are *Tebe poyem* (We sing to you), *Dostoyno yest* (It is truly fitting), *Otche nash* (Our father), *Blazhenni yazhe izbral* (Blessed are they whom you have chosen), *Da ispravitsya* (Let my prayer arise), and *Nïne silï nebesnïye* (Now the powers of heaven). The tenth piece is *Angel vopiyashe* (The angel cried out).

Snegurochka is incidental music to a play by Alexander Ostrovsky (1823–1886) based on a folk tale about a snow maiden who is the daughter of Frost and Spring and who can live in the mortal world as long as she does not fall in love. She does fall in love, however, and is commanded by the tsar to marry and remain on earth forever. The sun god Yarillo intervenes and shines his rays on her, thus causing her to melt and be released from her earthly obligation. The music, which is based on twelve folk tunes and which Tchaikovsky called "one of my favorite offspring," was composed and premiered in the spring of 1873. The chorus is scored in six of the work's nineteen movements, including "Tanets i khor ptits" (The birds' chorus), "Provody Maslenitsy" (Chorus for the procession on Shrove Tuesday), "Khorovod devushek" (Girls' round dance), "Marsh Tsaria Berendeia i khor" (March of Tsar Berendey and chorus), and "Final" (Finale).

The secular pieces include an arrangement of *Legenda* (Legend) from *Sixteen Songs for Children* op. 54 composed in 1881 and 1883. This song, about garlands of flowers Jesus supposedly put around the necks of his playmates, was so popular that Tchaikovsky transcribed it for tenor solo and chamber orchestra in 1884 and for a cappella chorus in 1889. Anton Arensky later used the song for his *Variations on a theme of Tchaikovsky* op.35a.

SACRED WORKS
SELECTED AND LISTED ACCORDING TO FAMILIARITY

Liturgiia Sv. Ioanna Zlatousta (Liturgy of St John Chrysostom) op.41 – 1878 –
   SATB chorus – 78 minutes total. (1) All the choral parts frequently divide; (2) concert performances today usually include approximately ten of the fifteen numbers or movements of the service, with a total time of approximately 54 minutes.

Heruvimskaya pesn (Cherubic Hymn) in C major – 1885 – SSAATTBB chorus a cappella – 5:30 minutes.

Blazhenni yazhe izbral (Blessed are they whom you have chosen) – 1885 –
   SSAATTBB chorus a cappella – 3 minutes.

Angel vopiyashe (The angel cried out) – 1887 – SATB chorus a cappella – 3:30 minutes. The parts briefly divide into SSAATTBB.

Vsenoshchnoye bdeniye (All-Night Vigil) op.52 – 1881–1882 – SATB chorus – 60 minutes total. All the parts frequently divide.

SECULAR WORKS
SELECTED AND LISTED ACCORDING TO FAMILIARITY

Snegurochka (The Snow Maiden) – 1873 – AT solos, SATB chorus, and orchestra – 80 minutes.

Legenda (Legend) – 1889 – SATB chorus a cappella – 3 minutes.

Bez pori, da bez vremeni (Much too soon in the season) – ca.1891 – SSAA chorus and piano – 3 minutes.

Vecher (Evening) – ca.1881 – TTB chorus a cappella – 3 minutes.

NIKOLAY (NIKOLAI) RIMSKY-KORSAKOV 1844–1908

Rimsky-Korsakov was born in Tikhvin, a short distance east of St Petersburg. He was educated at home under the guidance of his brother Voin, twenty-two years his elder, and although he showed an early interest in music and began playing the piano at age five, Nikolay followed in his brother's footsteps and in 1856 entered the Naval College in St Petersburg. He maintained his interest in music, however, attending numerous opera productions and studying piano. He especially liked Glinka's *Zhizn' za tsarya* (A life for the tsar), and he enjoyed playing the piano works of Bach, Beethoven, and Schumann. In 1861 he began studying composition with Mily Balakirev, teacher of César Cui, and became friends with both Cui and Modest Musorgsky. Rimsky-Korsakov's studies were interrupted by a three-year tour of military duty between 1862 and 1865, although he found pianos on which to practice when his ship was docked at ports, and while on board he studied Berlioz's treatise on orchestration and scores of Beethoven symphonies and quartets as well as works by Mendelssohn. After returning to St Petersburg he composed whenever he found time away from his duties as a clerk for the navy. His first symphony was premiered in 1865, and the initial version of his opera *Pskovityanka* (The Maid of Pskov) was finished in 1868. In 1871 he began teaching at the St Petersburg Conservatory, and in 1873, while maintaining his position at the conservatory, he was appointed Inspector of Naval Bands.

For the next several years Rimsky-Korsakov focused on the collection and harmonization of Russian folk songs, and he also began editing the operas of Glinka. In 1881 he expanded his editorial work, completing the orchestration of Musorgsky's opera *Khovanshchina* and tone poem *Ivanova noch' na Lïsoy gore* (St John's Night on Bald Mountain), and he also worked on the completion and orchestration of Borodin's opera *Knyaz' Igor'* (Prince Igor). In 1883 Rimsky-Korsakov was appointed assistant director of the Imperial Court Cappella under Balakirev, and for the next decade he composed a number of sacred works, many based on Russian znamenny and other chants. He also continued to compose operas and orchestral works, including his famous tone poems *Sheherazade* and *Svetlïy prazdnik* (Russian Easter Festival Overture). He resigned from the cappella in 1894, and during the remainder of his life he composed eleven more operas, including *Tsarskaya nevesta* (The Tsar's bride) in 1898 and *Zolotoy petushok* (The Golden Cockerel) between 1906 and 1907. In addition, he conducted his operas in European capitals and wrote a chronicle of his musical life. He died in March 1908 at age sixty-four and was buried at the Aleksandr-Nevsky monastery in St Petersburg next to Glinka, Musorgsky, and Borodin.

Rimsky-Korsakov composed forty works for the Russian Orthodox Church, four secular choral/orchestral cantatas, and thirty-two small-scale secular pieces. All of the sacred works are scored for a cappella SATB chorus with divisions, and a number are in a polyphonic, point-of-imitation texture. In addition, almost all were issued in collections, and, as was already mentioned, many are based on traditional chants. One of the first collections, *8 nomerov iz 'Liturgiia Sv. Ioanna Zlatousta'* (Eight numbers from the Liturgy of St John Chrysostom) op. 22, was composed in 1883 and contains two settings of *Heruvimskaya pesn* (Cherubic Hymn) and single settings of *Veruyu* (I believe), *Milost' mira* (Grace of peace), *Tebe poyem* (We sing to you), *Dostoyno yest* (It is truly fitting), *Otche nash* (Our father), and *Voskresnïy prichastïny stikh* (Sunday Communion Hymn). Opus 22b, composed in 1884, contains six pieces, including *Da molchit vsyakaya plot' chelovecha* (Let all mortal flesh keep silent) that is meant to be sung on Great and Holy Saturday in place of the Cherubic Hymn. The final collection of sacred pieces, without opus number, also composed in 1883 and 1884, contains twenty-three pieces (some in two parts), including three more settings of *Heruvimskaya pesn* (for a total of six settings of this text) and four more settings of *Tebe poyem* (also for a total of six).

The first cantata, *Stikh ob Alexeye Bozh'yem cheloveke* (Poem about Alexis, Man of God) op.20, was composed in 1878, directly after Rimsky-Korsakov finished his opera *Pskovityanka*, and premiered in January 1894. The text recounts the birth, marriage, and godly devotion of Saint Alexis, son of Euphemian. The second cantata, *Switezianka* (loosely translated as and subtitled "The Girl in the Lake") op.44, was composed in 1897 and premiered to an enthusiastic audience in March 1898. The text is about a young hunter who meets a beautiful girl on the banks of lake Svitez and promises her love and fidelity. She vanishes, and another girl appears in the lake and makes the hunter forget his promise. The lake girl then turns into the girl on the bank, chastises the hunter for breaking his promise, and draws him into the water, where both are seen as ghosts for years to come. The music is based on and uses Rimsky-Korsakov's song of the same name op.7 no.3. The third cantata, *Pesn' o veshchem Olege* (Song of Oleg the Wise) op.58, was composed in 1888 and 1889 and premiered in December 1889. The text is based on a Pushkin account of the warrior Oleg, who is told by a soothsayer that he will be victorious in battle but will be slain by his horse. The horse dies first and Oleg is perplexed. However, while visiting the grave of the horse, one of its bones is transformed into a snake that bites Oleg and poisons him. The final cantata, *Iz Gomera* op.60, was composed in 1901 and premiered in 1905. The work, subtitled a "prelude-cantata," consists mostly of a long and highly pictorial orchestral overture that depicts the sea voyage from Homer's *Odyssey*: Ulysses, thrown by Poseidon into the sea, is protected by the veil of the goddess Leucothea, daughter of Cadmus.

Most of the secular pieces were published in collections (two in opus 13, six in opus 16, two in opus 18, fifteen in opus 19, and four in opus 23). The pieces in opus 16, all of which alternate imitative and homophonic passages, are representative. Number one, *Na severe dikom* (Alone in the north), is scored for SATB chorus; number two, *Vakkhicheskaya pesn'* (Bacchanalian Song), is for TTBB chorus; number three, *Staraya pesnya: Iz lesov dremuchikh severmïkh* (Old Song:

From the dense northern forests), consists of a series of variations followed by a coda—the opening scored for SSAATTBB chorus, the first variation for SATB, the second variation for SATTB and SAATB, the third variation for SAT, the fourth variation for SATB, and the coda for SSAATTBB; number four, *Mesyats plïvyot i tikh i spokoyen* (The moon floats quietly and peacefully), is scored for SATB; number five, *Poslednyaya tucha rasseyannoy buri* (The last cloud of the scattered storm), is for SSAA; and number six, *Molitva: Vladïka dney moikh* (Prayer: master of my days), is for SATB, with occasional division into SSAATTBB. The fifteen pieces in opus 19 are all settings of Russian folk songs.

SACRED WORKS
SELECTED AND LISTED ACCORDING TO FAMILIARITY

Otche nash (Our father) op.22 no.7 – 1883 – SATB chorus a cappella – 3:30 minutes.

Da molchit vsyakaya plot' chelovecha (Let all mortal flesh keep silent) op.22b no.2 – 1884 – SATB chorus a cappella – 3:30 minutes. There are several brief passages scored for solo quartet.

Tebe poyem (We sing to you) #2 in F major – SATB chorus a cappella – 1:15 minutes.

Tebe poyem (We sing to you) #4 in G major – SATB chorus a cappella – 1 minute.

SECULAR WORKS
SELECTED AND LISTED ACCORDING TO FAMILIARITY

Stikh ob Alexeye Bozh'yem cheloveke (Poem about Alexis, man of God) op.20 – 1878 – ATB chorus and orchestra – 5:30 minutes.

Switezianka op.44 – 1897 – ST solos, SATB chorus, and orchestra – 16:30 minutes.

Pesn' o veshchem Olege (Song of Oleg the Wise) op.58 – 1888–1889 – TB solos, TB chorus, and orchestra – 17 minutes. The tenor soloist represents the soothsayer, while the bass soloist represents the warrior Oleg.

Iz Gomera op.60 – 1901 – SSA solos, SA chorus, and orchestra – 11:30 minutes.

SERGEY TANEYEV 1856–1915

Sergey Taneyev, nephew of Aleksandr Taneyev (1850–1918), was born in Vladimir-na-Klyaz'me in central Russia and began piano lessons when he was five. At nine he entered the Moscow Conservatory and at twelve began composition lessons with Tchaikovsky. Taneyev excelled as a pianist and when he was nineteen played the Brahms *Piano Concerto* in D minor as well as the first Moscow performance of the Tchaikovsky *Piano Concerto #1* in B-flat major; when he was twenty he toured throughout Russia as a recitalist. In 1878 Taneyev succeeded Tchaikovsky as teacher of harmony and orchestration at the Moscow Conservatory, adding classes in piano in 1881 and composition in 1883, and in 1885 he was appointed director. He resigned his positions at the conservatory in 1905, wrote a text on counterpoint—*Podvizhnoy kontrapunkt strogogo pis'ma* (Invertible counterpoint in the strict style) in 1906 (published in 1909)—and for the next several years combined composition with concertizing. He died of a heart attack at age fifty-eight.

Taneyev composed six choral works with instrumental accompaniment (including three cantatas) and sixty-six pieces for a cappella chorus (the majority of which are settings of secular texts). The cantatas are *Ya pamyatnik sebe vozdvig nerokotvorniy* (I have built myself a monument not made by hands) for the unveiling of the Pushkin Memorial in Moscow in 1880, *Ioann Damaskin* (John of Damascus) of 1883 to 1884, and Taneyev's most celebrated work, *Po prochtenii psalma* (At the reading of a Psalm) of 1912 to 1915. The a cappella sacred pieces include a setting of *Heruvimskaya pesn* (Cherubic Hymn) for SSATBB, and the secular pieces include *Na mogile* (Upon the grave) op.27 no.1 and *Razvalinu bashni* (The ruins of the tower) op.27 no.3.

ALEKSANDR KASTAL'SKY 1856–1926

Kastal'sky was born in Moscow, the son of a Russian Orthodox priest. He received a classical education during his youth, and at age twenty he enrolled at the Moscow Conservatory, where he studied piano, theory, and composition with Tchaikovsky and Sergey Taneyev. In 1887 Kastal'sky began teaching piano at the Moscow Synodal School of Church Singing, in 1891 he became assistant precentor of the Synodal choir, and in 1903 he was promoted to precentor. He served as director of the school from 1910 to 1918 and, changing his musical focus from sacred to secular music, conducted folk choirs in Moscow and Petrograd from 1918 to 1923. He wrote several treatises on folk music, and from 1923 until his death in 1926 he was professor of composition at the Moscow Conservatory. Kastal'sky was considerably influential to both church and folk music during his lifetime, and many composers of the early twentieth century—including Aleksandr Grechaninov, Viktor Kalinnikov, Pavel Chesnokov, and Serge Rachmaninoff—based their works on his precepts and compositional ideals. His books *Osobennosti narodno-russkoy muzïkal'noy sistemï* (Peculiarities of the Russian folk music system) and *Osnovï narodnogo mnogogolosiya* (Principles of folk polyphony) are considered to be important studies in ethnomusicology.

Kastal'sky composed approximately 130 works for the Russian Orthodox Church, twelve secular cantatas and hymns, and several collections of folk song arrangements. His sacred works include a setting of the *Liturgiia Sv. Ioanna Zlatousta* (Liturgy of St John Chrysostom), excerpts from the *Vsenoshchnoye bdeniye* (All-Night Vigil), and numerous other miscellaneous pieces. The liturgy, composed in 1905 and scored for SSAA chorus a cappella, was most likely written for a training choir of boys at the Synodal school. The textures are almost entirely homophonic and syllabic, producing a hymn or chorale effect, and there is very little text repetition. Kastal'sky's setting contains eleven movements—"Velikaya Ekteniya" (The Great Litany), "Yedinorodniy sïne" (The only begotten son), "Vo tsarstvii tvoyem" (In your kingdom), "Svyatï Bozhe" (Holy God), "Sugubaya yekteniya" (Augmented Litany), "Heruvimskaya pesn" (Cherubic Hymn), "Yekteniya prostelnaya" (The Litany of supplication), "Milost' mira" (Grace of peace), "Dostoyno yest" (It is truly fitting), "Otche nash" (Our father), and Miloserdiya dveri" (The doors of mercy).

Excerpts from the All-Night Vigil, all scored for SATB chorus with divisions, include two settings of *Blazhen muzh* (Blessed is the man), four settings of *Svete tihiy* (Gladsome light), three settings of *Nïne otpushchayeshï raba tvoyego, vladïko* (Lord, now let your servant depart in peace), two settings of *Slava v vïshnih Bogu* (Glory to God in the highest), and three settings of *Hvalite imia Ghospodne* (Praise the name of the Lord). Other sacred pieces include three settings of *Deva dnes* (Today the virgin) op.7b, each based on the traditional znamenny chant. In the first setting, scored for SSATTB chorus a cappella, the chant serves as a cantus firmus that migrates through several voice parts, beginning with the first sopranos and first tenors (the scoring of the tenor part an octave below the soprano was common with Kastal'sky and many composers in the generation following him). The second setting, scored for the same voice parts but designated "dlia bolshovo hora" (for large chorus), is more expansive, and the third setting, scored only for SATB chorus, is designated "dlia malovo hora" (for small chorus).

The secular cantatas and hymns, mainly devoted to patriotic and folk-oriented subjects, include *Pesni k rodinye* (Songs to the motherland) of 1901 to 1903, *K zarubezhnïm bratyam* (To our brothers overseas) of 1921, *Gimn truda* (Labor anthem) of 1923, *Derevenskaya simfoniya* (The village symphony) of 1923, *Sel'skiye rabotï v narodnïkh pesnyakh* (Rural work in folk songs) of 1924, and *V. I. Leninu: u groba* (To Lenin: at his graveside) of 1924.

MIKHAIL IPPOLITOV-IVANOV 1859–1935

Ippolitov-Ivanov was born in Gatchina, near St Petersburg, and received his initial musical training as a chorister at the church of St Isaac in St Petersburg. At age sixteen he enrolled at the St Petersburg Conservatory, studying string bass and taking orchestration classes with Rimsky-Korsakov, and after graduation he became acquainted with Mily Balakirev and a number of his followers. At twenty-three Ippolitov-Ivanov moved to Tbilisi, Georgia, where he directed the Academy of Music and the local branch of the Russian Music Society as well as the Tbilisi opera company. While in Georgia, he became interested in native folks songs and wrote a book—*Gruzinskaya narodnaya pesnya i yeyo sovremennoye sostoyaniye* (The Georgian folk song and its present state)—similar to the ethnomusicology writings of Kastal'sky. In 1893 Ippolitov-Ivanov was appointed professor of composition at the Moscow Conservatory, and in 1895, while continuing to teach at the conservatory, he became conductor of the Russian Choral Society. He was director of the conservatory from 1905 until 1922, and from 1925 until his death at age seventy-five he was musical director of the Bol'shoy Theater.

Ippolitov-Ivanov composed eight opuses of choral music, including four that are particularly noteworthy. Opus 29 consists of *2 zaprichastnïkh stikha* (Two verses for the Eucharist), the second of which—*Se nïne blagoslovite Ghospoda* (Behold, now bless the Lord)—is unusual in that it is completely homophonic, syllabic, and unmetered, thus giving it a chant-like quality (although it is not based on chant). Opus 37 is a setting of the *Liturgiia Sv Ioanna Zlatousta* (Liturgy of St John Chrysostom). Two of its movements are often extracted and performed separately—*Heruvimskaya pesn* (Cherubic Hymn) and *Blagoslovi, dushe moya, Ghospoda* (Bless the Lord, O my soul). Opus 38 contains five separate settings of the Cherubic Hymn, numbers three and five of which, both scored for SSAA chorus and in the key of E-flat major, are well known. Finally, opus 43 is a collection entitled *Izbrannïye molitvosloviya iz vsenoshchnogo bdeniye* (Selected prayers from the All-Night Vigil Service). As with the liturgy opus 37, two movements are often extracted and performed separately—*Svete tihiy* (Gladsome light) and *Blazhen muzh* (Blessed is the man).

ANTON ARENSKY 1861–1906

Arensky was born in Novgorod, south of St Petersburg, where his father was a doctor and amateur cellist and his mother a professional pianist. The young Arensky studied with his mother and advanced rapidly, composing songs and piano pieces at age nine. At seventeen he enrolled at the St Petersburg Conservatory, studying composition with Rimsky-Korsakov and winning awards for his work, and upon graduation at twenty-one he was immediately hired to teach courses in harmony and counterpoint at the Moscow Conservatory. His students there included Rachmaninoff and Aleksandr Skryabin. Arensky conducted the Russian Choral Society between 1888 and 1895, and from 1889 to 1893 he was also on the faculty of the Moscow Synodal School of Church Singing. He returned to St Petersburg in 1895, succeeding Mily Balakirev as director of the Imperial Court Cappella, and from 1901 (when he left the cappella) until his death of tuberculosis at age forty-four, he freelanced as a composer, conductor, and concert pianist.

Arensky composed five secular cantatas, ten secular part songs, and four sacred choruses. The cantatas—all for soloists, chorus, and orchestra, and in the style of Rimsky-Korsakov—include *Lesnoy tsar'* (The wood king), *Gimn iskusstvu* (Hymn to art), and *Kubok* (The goblet). The part songs were composed in four sets—two choruses for male voices a cappella, three choruses for mixed voices a cappella, two quartets for mixed voices a cappella, and three quartets for mixed voices and obbligato instruments. The last-mentioned set contains the well-known *Serenada* for SATB voices and cello.

The sacred choruses are all scored for SATB chorus a cappella and all set to liturgical texts from the *Liturgiia Sv Ioanna Zlatousta* (Liturgy of St John Chrysostom)—*Heruvimskaya pesn* (Cherubic Hymn), *Tebe poyem* (We sing to you), *Otche nash* (Our father), and *Hvalitye Ghospoda s nyebyes* (O praise the Lord from the heavens).

ALEKSANDR GRECHANINOV (GRETCHANINOFF) 1864–1956

Grechaninov was born in Moscow and began studying piano privately at age fourteen. At seventeen he entered the Moscow Conservatory, where for the next nine years he studied counterpoint and theory with Anton Arensky, and at twenty-six he transferred to the St Petersburg Conservatory, where he studied with Rimsky-Korsakov. During the late 1890s he taught piano in both St Petersburg and Moscow and experienced successes with his chamber and orchestral compositions. In 1903 he began working with the ethnographic society of Moscow University, and during the next several years he made a number of folk song arrangements for children. He also taught children at several schools during the first decade of the twentieth century. After the Russian Revolution in 1917 he traveled throughout Europe, spending time in London and Prague and living for several years in Paris, and in 1939 he moved to America, becoming a naturalized citizen in 1946. He is considered to be the leading composer of the New Russian Choral School, and his music for the Russian Orthodox Church was popular and frequently performed in the United States throughout the twentieth century.

Grechaninov composed four settings of the Liturgy of St John Chrysostom (op.13, op.29, op.79, and op.177), one setting of the All-Night Vigil (op.59), a cycle of hymns for Passion Week services (op.58), approximately twenty other miscellaneous liturgical and para-liturgical pieces for the Russian Orthodox Church, four Latin masses for the Catholic Church, and several Latin motets. The first of the Divine Liturgy settings (op.13) was composed in 1897 and is one of the earliest of Grechaninov's choral works. Modeled after Tchaikovsky's setting, the individual pieces are confined in scope and texture. Grechaninov's second setting of the Divine Liturgy (op.29), composed in 1902, is his best known of the four settings. The individual pieces are like those by Kastal'sky and Ippolitov-Ivanov in that numerous phrases are scored for the soprano (or first soprano) and tenor (or first tenor) in octaves and in that the textures are mainly homophonic. However, Grechaninov's music is more diversified, with some imitation between the soprano and tenor voices, occasional dialogue between the upper and lower voices, and variations in the rhythmic content of all the voices. In addition, the vocal ranges are expansive, the textures are dense, and the harmonies are luxuriant. The third setting of the liturgy (op.79) is unique in that it is scored for soloists, chorus, and instruments (strings, harp, and organ). Premiered in 1912 and then not performed again until the 1990s, this was the first and is the only setting of the liturgy to use instruments. The fourth liturgy (op.177) is scored for small choral forces.

The All-Night Vigil contains some of Grechaninov's most expansive and popular individual pieces. Several in the set are scored for double SSAATTBB chorus, and many of the pieces are published and performed separately, including *Blagoslovi, dushe moya, Ghospoda* (Bless the Lord, O my soul), *Blazhen muzh* (Blessed is the man), *Svete tihiy* (Gladsome light), and *Bogoroditse devo* (Rejoice, O virgin). Grechaninov also composed additional separate settings of *Blagoslovi, dushe moya, Ghospoda* and *Svete tihiy* (his most famous setting of this text).

The cycle of hymns for Passion Week, composed between 1911 and 1912, includes thirteen settings of texts that are drawn from various liturgical services throughout the week. Numbers one and two—*Se zhenih griadet* (Behold, the bridegroom comes) and *Chertog tvoy vizhdu* (I see your bridal chamber)—are sung at Matins services on Monday, Tuesday, and Wednesday; numbers three, four, five, and six—*Vo tsarstvii tvoyem* (In your kingdom), *Svete tihiy* (Gladsome light), *Da ispravitsia molitva moya* (Let my prayer arise), and *Nīne silï nebesnïye* (Now the powers of heaven)—are from the liturgy of the Pre-Sanctified Gifts, also celebrated on the first three days of Holy Week; number seven, *Vecheri tvoyeya taynïya dnes* (Of your mystical supper), is sung during the liturgy of Holy Thursday; number eight, *Razboynika blagorazumnago* (The wise thief), is a hymn for the Service of the Twelve Gospels that speaks of Jesus' promise of redemption for the repentant thief; number nine, *Tebe odeyushchagosia svetom* (You who clothe yourself with light), is sung at Vespers on Friday; number ten, *Bog Ghospod* (The Lord is God), is from the Matins Service on Holy Saturday; number eleven, *Ne rïday mene, mati* (Do not lament me, O mother), is also sung at the Nocturns before the Paschal Matins Service as well as the Matins Service on Holy Saturday; and numbers twelve and thirteen—*Yelitsï vo Hrista krestistesia* (As many as have been baptized) and *Da molchit vsyakaya plot' chelovecha* (Let all mortal flesh keep silent)—are from the Service for Great and Holy Saturday, called the Great Sabbath. The style of the music is similar to that employed in the All-Night Vigil, with several pieces scored for double

SSAATTBB chorus and a few of the pieces extracted and performed separately. Especially popular are *Vecheri tvoyeya taynïya dnes* and *Nïne silï nebesnïye*.

Of the well-known miscellaneous pieces, *Voskliknite Ghospodevi* (O be joyful in the Lord) op.19 no.2 is a sacred concerto modeled after those by Bortnyans'ky, with a text taken from several Psalms (66, 77, 97, and 47). *Svete tihiy* from op.23 is also popular and frequently performed.

SACRED WORKS
SELECTED AND LISTED ACCORDING TO FAMILIARITY

Svete tihiy (Gladsome light) op.23 no.2 – SSAATTBB chorus a cappella – 4 minutes. The bass part occasionally divides into BBB.

Heruvimskaya pesn (Cherubic Hymn) op.29 no.6 – SSAATTBB chorus a cappella – 3:30 minutes.

Nïne otpushchayeshï raba tvoyego, vladïko (Lord, now let your servant depart in peace) op.34 no.1 – TTBB chorus a cappella – 3 minutes.

Hvalite imia Ghospodne (Praise the name of the Lord) op.34 no.2 – SATB chorus (with divisions) a cappella – 3: 30 minutes.

Vecheri tvoyeya taynïya dnes (Of your mystical supper) op.58 no.7 – SSAA-TTBB/SSAATTBB chorus a cappella – 4:30 minutes. The two choruses join into one for the second half of the piece.

Nïne silï nebesnïye (Now the powers of heaven) op.58 no.6 – SSAATTBB/SSAATTBB chorus a cappella – 3:30 minutes. (1) The bass parts of both choruses occasionally divide into BBB; (2) the two choruses join into one for the second half of the piece.

Se zhenih griadet (Behold, the bridegroom comes) op.58 no.1 – SSAATTBB chorus a cappella – 3 minutes. The bass part occasionally divides into BBB.

Voskliknite Ghospodevi (O be joyful in the Lord) op.19 no.2 – SSAATTBB chorus a cappella – 3 minutes.

Bogoroditse devo (Rejoice, O virgin) op.59 no.4 – SSAATTBB chorus a cappella – 2:15 minutes.

ALEKSANDR GLAZUNOV 1865–1936

Glazunov was born in St Petersburg, where his father was a book publisher and his mother a pianist. The young Glazunov showed considerable musical talent at an early age, studying piano at nine, composing at eleven, and during his teenage years able to completely transcribe complex compositions after hearing them only once. At fourteen he began composition lessons with Rimsky-Korsakov, at sixteen he completed his first symphony and string quartet, and at nineteen he traveled to numerous cities in western Europe, including Weimar, where he met Franz Liszt and where his first symphony was performed. Throughout his twenties Glazunov concentrated on the composition of symphonic works, and in 1889 he began teaching composition at the St Petersburg Conservatory, remaining there for thirty years and serving as director from 1905 to 1930. He was highly respected as a composer throughout Russia and Europe, being granted honorary doctoral degrees from both Oxford and Cambridge universities in 1907, representing Russia at the Schubert centenary celebrations in Vienna in 1928, and conducting concerts of his music between 1929 and 1931 in Spain, France, England, and the United States.

Glazunov's instrumental output, which is extensive, includes eight completed symphonies and approximately forty overtures, suites, and tone poems. His choral output is limited, however, and consists of one piece for the Russian Orthodox Church, five cantatas and hymns, and several part songs and folk song arrangements. The large-scale secular works include a coronation cantata (op.56 of 1896), a cantata in memory of Pushkin's 100th birthday (op.65 of 1899), and a cantata celebrating the fiftieth anniversary of St Petersburg Conservatory (1912).

VIKTOR KALINNIKOV 1870–1927

Viktor Kalinnikov, younger brother of Vasily Kalinnikov (with whom he is occasionally confused), was born in the Mtsensk district of Russia, south of Moscow, and received his musical education at the Moscow Philharmonic Society's College for Music and Drama. After graduation he remained at the college and taught theory and oboe (one of his majors as a student), and from 1897 to 1923 he taught at the Moscow Synodal School of Church Singing. From 1899 to 1901 he also served as conductor and director of the music department at the Moscow Arts Theater, and in 1906 he was one of the founders of the People's Conservatory of Moscow. From 1922 until the end of his life he taught at the Moscow Conservatory, and, like Grechaninov, he was involved in the ethnographic society.

Kalinnikov composed twenty-four sacred pieces for the Russian Orthodox Church, fifteen secular part songs, and numerous arrangements of Russian folk songs. The church compositions are generally settings of the main texts from the Liturgy of St John Chrysostom and All-Night Vigil, although all of the pieces were written separately (i.e., not as part of a collection). The style of the compositions is similar to that of Grechaninov and Chesnokov, with expansive a cappella textures, occasional doubling of the soprano one and tenor one voice parts, alternating homophonic and imitative phrases, and melodies that are chant-like but generally not based on traditional znamenny chants.

The secular part songs, many of which are settings of texts by the leading Russian poets of the nineteenth century (e.g., Pushkin), are small-scale works. The scoring is not as expansive as in the church music, the textures are generally more homophonic, and there is more repetition of motivic material.

SACRED WORKS
SELECTED AND LISTED ACCORDING TO FAMILIARITY

Svete tihiy (Gladsome light) – SSAATTBB chorus a cappella – 2:30 minutes.

Heruvimskaya pesn (Cherubic Hymn) no.1– SSAATTBB chorus a cappella – 3:30 minutes. Most of the piece is scored for SATTBB.

Tebe poyem (We sing to you) no.1 – SSAATTBB chorus a cappella – 3 minutes.

Bogoroditse devo (Rejoice, O virgin) – SSAATTBB chorus a cappella – 3:15 minutes.

Nïne otpushchayeshï raba tvoyego, vladïko (Lord, now let your servant depart in peace) – SSAATTBB chorus a cappella – 3 minutes.

SECULAR WORKS
SELECTED AND LISTED ACCORDING TO FAMILIARITY

Vniz po matushke po Volge (Down the mother-river Volga) – TTBB chorus a cappella – 3:30 minutes.

Elegiya (Elegy) – SATB chorus a cappella – 4 minutes.

Na starom kurgane (On the ancient burial mound) – SATB chorus a cappella – 3 minutes.

Nam zviozdï krotkiye siyali (The gentle stars shone down on us) – SATB chorus a cappella – 3:30 minutes.

PAVEL CHESNOKOV 1877–1944

Chesnokov was born near Voskresensk, southeast of Moscow, and received his musical education as a chorister (from ages seven to seventeen) at the Moscow Synodal School of Church Singing. He remained at the school as a teacher of chant but continued his education by studying composition with Taneyev and Ippolitov-Ivanov at the Moscow Conservatory. From 1915 to 1917 he was the director of the Russian Choral Society, from 1917 to 1922 he was the principal conductor of the Moscow State Choir, and from 1922 to 1928 he was director of the Moscow Academic Choir. Meanwhile, he had been appointed professor of composition at the Moscow Conservatory in 1920 (a position he held until his death twenty-four years later), and in the 1930s he also served as the chorusmaster of the Bol'shoy Theater. Chesnokov was the first Russian musician (composer and performer) to achieve fame principally as a choral conductor and to be known almost exclusively for his choral compositions. Several of his sacred works circulated widely throughout Russia, Europe, and North America and became the works that introduced many twentieth-century non-Russians to Russian church music.

Chesnokov composed approximately four hundred sacred and one hundred secular works. In addition, he arranged many of his mixed chorus works and the mixed chorus works of Ippolitov-Ivanov and Grechaninov for male chorus, and he wrote the book *Khor i upravleniye im* (The choir and its direction). The sacred music consists of three settings of the Divine Liturgy, two settings of the All-Night Vigil, two settings of the Memorial (Funeral) Service, one setting of the Liturgy of Pre-Sanctified Gifts, and numerous miscellaneous liturgical and para-liturgical pieces. The texture of his music is generally homophonic (more so than that of the composers who preceded or followed him), and while the vocal ranges are expansive, with the first tenor and first soprano parts occasionally doubling each other for dramatic effect, the scoring is not particularly dense and the overall character of the music is transparent. Also, formal structures that are characterized by repeated sections of music provide clarity and accessibility. An example is *Spaseniye sodelal* (Salvation is created), undoubtedly Chesnokov's most popular piece and the most frequently performed Russian church composition outside Russia. It is part of a cycle of ten communion hymns op.25 and uses a Kievan chant as a cantus firmus, the first phrase of which is stated four times within the structure AABCAABC. The two AABC sections of the piece are virtually identical, except that the first cadences in a minor key (B minor), whereas the second cadences in the relative major (D major). Also, the second AABC is sung to the text "Alil-luiya." Another popular piece, *Duh tvoy blagiy* (Let your good spirit) op.25 no.10, is in an ABA structure, the A portions featuring short homophonic phrases in dialogue between the upper and lower voice parts, and the B section an imitative duet between the soprano and alto voice parts. In each of the A and B sections the phrases frequently repeat melodic material.

Several of the sacred pieces were composed for soloist and a cappella chorus, including the hymns in opus 40, which were written for celebrated opera singers at the time and for concert as opposed to church performance. *Blazhen muzh* (Blessed is the man) from the All-Night Vigil op.44 is also scored for soloist and chorus. The text is from Psalms 1:1, 6, 2:11, 12, and 3:9. *Pani-hida* op.39 (sometimes referred to as Chesnokov's Requiem or Memorial Service) combines original chant that alternates with homophonic phrases for chorus and newly composed music for soloists that is integrated into the choral texture. *Panihida* also contains many repetitive sections of music.

SACRED WORKS

SELECTED AND LISTED ACCORDING TO FAMILIARITY

Spaseniye sodelal (Salvation is created) op.25 no.2 – SATTBB chorus
a cappella – 3 minutes.

Blazhen muzh (Blessed is the man) op.44 no.2 – B solo and SATBB chorus
a cappella – 4:15 minutes. The choral parts divide briefly into SSATTBB.

Duh tvoy blagiy (Let your good spirit) op.25 no.10 – SSATTBB chorus a cappella – 2:15 minutes.

Velichit dushe moya Ghospoda (My soul magnifies the Lord) op.40 no.1 –
S solo and SATTBB chorus a cappella – 3 minutes. The choral parts
briefly divide into SSATTBB.

S nami Bog (The Lord is with us) op.40 no.6 – T solo and SSATTB chorus
a cappella – 4 minutes.

O tebe raduyetsia (All creation rejoices) op.15 no.11 – SSATTBB chorus a cappella – 3 minutes.

Hvalitye Ghospoda s nyebyes (O praise the Lord from the heavens) op.9 no.14 –
SATB chorus a cappella – 3 minutes.

Panihida (Requiem or Memorial Service) op.39 – ST solos and SATB chorus
a cappella – 54 minutes. Chesnokov made an arrangement of the work,
op.39a, for TB solos and TTBB chorus.

SERGE (SERGEY) RACHMANINOFF (RACHMANINOV)
1873–1943

Rachmaninoff was born near Novgorod, south of St Petersburg, and began piano lessons with his mother and a local teacher. When he was nine his family moved to St Petersburg and he enrolled at the conservatory, but three years later, not successful in his studies, he transferred to the Moscow Conservatory. He studied with Taneyev and Arensky and met Tchaikovsky, and at age fourteen he composed a few piano pieces and made sketches for an opera. At seventeen he composed his first choral work, a Latin motet entitled *Deus meus,* and the following year he completed his first piano concerto. He graduated with honors in piano at eighteen, and at nineteen, with the completion of his one-act opera *Aleko,* he graduated with the Great Gold Medal in composition. During the next three years he experienced success with the premieres of his piano prelude in C-sharp minor and *Aleko.* However, with a negative response to his first symphony in 1895, he entered a period of self-doubt and ceased compositional activity. In 1897 he was appointed conductor of the Moscow Private Russian Opera Company, and for the next several years he received positive reviews for his leadership of such operas as *Zhizn' za tsarya* (A life for the Tsar) by Glinka, *Samson et Dalila* by Saint-Saëns, *Carmen* by Bizet, and *Pikovaya dama* (The Queen of Spades) by Tchaikovsky. These successes led to invitations to conduct in London and New York City as well as incentives to return to composition. He wrote his second piano concerto between 1900 and 1901, his second symphony between 1906 and 1907, his first piano sonata in 1907, and his third piano concerto in 1909. In the meantime, he continued to conduct, leading the Bol'shoy Theater between 1904 and 1906 and touring the United States in 1909. His three most important choral works were composed during the next five years—the *Liturgiia Sv Ioanna Zlatousta* (Liturgy of St John Chrysostom) in 1910, *Kolokola* (The Bells) in 1913, and *Vsenoshchnoye bdeniye* (All-Night Vigil) in 1915. He fled Russia after the Russian Revolution in 1917 and moved to Stockholm, Copenhagen, and then New York City, and during the 1920s he toured throughout Europe and the United States as a concert pianist. During the 1930s he lived most of the time in a villa on Lake Lucerne in Switzerland, where he composed his *Rhapsody on a Theme of Paganini* and *Symphony #3,* and in 1939 he returned to the United States, where he died of cancer on March 28, 1943, at age seventy. He had hoped to be buried in either Switzerland or Russia, but because of the war his body remained in the United States, and he was buried in a cemetery outside New York City.

Rachmaninoff composed three sacred works to Church Slavonic texts, two secular choral/orchestral works, two collections of part songs, two a cappella cantatas, and one Latin motet. The Russian sacred works reflect Rachmaninoff's interest in traditional Russian Orthodox chant and in the singing he heard during his youth. In his *Recollections as Told to Oskar von Riesemann,* a collection of reminiscences by the composer about his life and work, he stated that he and his grandmother "spent hours standing in the beautiful churches of St Petersburg, where I took great interest in the singing, which was of unrivaled beauty. . . . [When I returned home] I sat at the piano and played all that I had heard." *V molitvakh neusïpayushchuyu Bogoroditsu* (The mother of God, ever vigilant in prayer) was composed during the summer of 1893 and premiered that same year by the famous choir from the Moscow Synodal School of Church Singing. The work, subtitled "Choral Concerto in G minor," is set to the *Kontakion,* the hymn for the feast celebrating the death (dormition) of the Virgin Mary. An English translation of the first line of text reads, "The tomb and death have not been able to hold the birth-giver of God, who is constant in supplications, and in intercessions an unfailing hope." The musical texture is mainly syllabic and homophonic, with three brief phrases of imitation.

The Divine Liturgy was composed in July 1910 and premiered in Moscow that fall. Church authorities at the time objected to the work's "spirit of modernism" and discouraged its use in church services. However, it became popular in concert halls throughout Europe and the United States, with portions of it performed in New York City and Cambridge, Massachusetts, in January and February 1914. The entire work consists of twenty movements in the style of Tchaikovsky, whose Divine Liturgy op.41 of 1878 served as a model for Rachmaninoff.

The All-Night Vigil, frequently referred to in the United States as Rachmaninoff's Vespers, was composed in two weeks during January and February 1915. The premiere performance was on March 10, 1915, by the Moscow Synodal Choir and was received enthusiastically. Kastal'sky wrote, "Rachmaninoff's new composition is undoubtedly a contribution of great importance to the church's musical literature. . . . One must hear for oneself how simple, artless chants can be transformed in the hands of a great artist." Nine of the work's fifteen movements are based on chants—some znamenny and some Kievan. Movement five, *Nïne otpushchayeshï raba tvoyego, vladïko* (generally referred to as the Nunc dimittis) was one of Rachmaninoff's favorite compositions; he hoped that it would be performed at his funeral. Movement six, *Bogoroditse devo* (Rejoice, O virgin), became the most popular of Rachmaninoff's compositions during the twentieth century, often extracted and performed separately.

The two secular choral/orchestral works were composed during the early 1900s, the period when Rachmaninoff had regained his confidence as a composer. The cantata *Vesna* (Spring) was written in 1902 to the poem *Zelyonïy shum* (Green rustle) by Nikolay Alexeyevich Nekrasov (1821–1878), one of Rachmaninoff's favorite poets. The story relates the tale of a husband's fury over his wife's infidelity. Confined with her throughout the winter, he has thoughts of killing her. But when the "green-rushing tides of spring . . . chant and sing" he has a change of heart and forgives her. The choral symphony *Kolokola* (The Bells) was composed in 1913 to a Russian translation of Edgar Allan Poe's famous poem *The Bells*. Rachmaninoff, like many musicians in Russia, was fascinated by the sounds of bells he heard from the many church steeples across the country, and the translation of Poe's poem by the Russian symbolist poet Konstantin Dmitrievich Balmont (1867–1943) was popular throughout the country. Rachmaninoff divided the poem into four movements—the first, an allegro; the second, a lento beginning with "Hear the mellow wedding bells, golden bells"; the third, a presto to "Hear them, hear the brazen bells, hear the loud alarum bells"; and the fourth, to changing tempos beginning with the lines, "Hear the tolling of the bells, mournful bells."

The earlier of the part song collections, *Six Choruses for Women's or Children's Voices with piano accompaniment* op.15, was composed between 1895 and 1896. The texts for five of the part songs (numbers two through six) came from poems that appeared in the magazine *Dyetskoe chteniye* (Children's reader). Number two, *Nochka* (Night), compares night to a mournful song that is chased away by the refreshing sunrise; number three, *Sosna* (Pine tree), is about a lonely pine tree that dreams of a far-off kingdom; number four, *Zadremali volnï* (Now the waves are sleeping), talks of the calm night sea under a radiant full moon; number five, *Nevolya* (Captivity), depicts the plight of a caged nightingale that does not sing until released; and number six,

Angel, is the song of an angel who cares for a sad and oppressed youth. The first of the part songs, *Slava narodu* (All glory to our people), is a setting of a patriotic text in honor of Tsar Nicholas II. The *Three Russian Folk Songs* op.41 were completed in 1926 and premiered by the Philadelphia Orchestra and Chorus on March 18, 1927, under the direction of Leopold Stokowski. The individual titles are *Cherez rechku* (Across the river), *Akh tï, Van'ka* (Oh, Ivan), and *Belolitsï, rumyanitsï vï moyi* (My fair-skinned, rosy-cheeked beauties).

SACRED WORKS
SELECTED AND LISTED ACCORDING TO FAMILIARITY

Vsenoshchnoye bdeniye (All-Night Vigil) op.37 – 1915 – AT solos and SSAATT-BB chorus a cappella – 67 minutes. (1) The alto solo, which is occasionally sung by the entire alto section (though not indicated to be done so by Rachmaninoff), occurs only in movement two; (2) tenor solos occur in movements four, five, and nine (Rachmaninoff indicates that those in movements four and nine may be sung by the first tenors); (3) each of the choral parts occasionally divides into three vocal sections.

V molitvakh neusïpayushchuyu Bogoroditsu (The mother of God, ever vigilant in prayer) – 1893 – SATB chorus a cappella – 6 minutes. (1) The choral parts occasionally divide into SSAATTB; (2) several brief phrases are marked for solo voice.

Liturgiia Sv Ioanna Zlatousta (Liturgy of St John Chrysostom) op.31 – 1910 – TB solos and SSAATTBB chorus a cappella – 95 minutes with liturgical chants (not composed by Rachmaninoff) and related choral responses (composed by Rachmaninoff), or approximately 75 minutes without the liturgical chants and responses. (1) The solos are intended for liturgical performance; (2) approximately half the work is scored for SATB chorus, there are several very brief passages for SSSAAATTTBB, and two movements ("Otche nash" and "Budi imya Ghospodnye") are scored for double chorus.

SECULAR WORKS
SELECTED AND LISTED ACCORDING TO FAMILIARITY

Kolokola (The Bells) op.35 – 1913 – STB solos, SATB chorus, and orchestra (including three flutes, English horn, bass clarinet, six horns, triangle, tambourine, cymbals, glockenspiel, celesta, harp, and piano) – 40 minutes. The chorus parts divide occasionally into SSAATTBB and once briefly into SSSAAATTTBBBB.

Vesna (Spring) op.20 – 1902 – B solo, SATB chorus, and orchestra – 17 minutes.

Three Russian Folk Songs op.41 – 1926 – AB chorus and orchestra – 12 minutes. Rachmaninoff recommended approximately twenty altos and twenty basses for the choral parts.

Six Choruses op.15 – 1894–1896 – SA chorus and piano – 12 minutes. The choral parts briefly divide into SSAA.

❧ ENGLAND ❧

With the development of schools and methods for the improvement of musical literacy, especially sight-singing, and with the widespread proliferation of music festivals, choral music flourished in England during the Romantic era. Music educators such as John Hullah (1812–1884) and John Curwen (1816–1880) began programs that reached and trained thousands of singers. Hullah, for instance, founded the Singing School of Schoolmasters and Schoolmistresses in 1841, and Curwen began publishing the *Tonic Sol-fa Reporter* in 1851 and a sight-reading course in the *Popular Educator* in 1852. Four hundred teachers (who taught approximately fifty thousand children) were enrolled in Hullah's school during its first year of operation, and in 1856 Curwen had twenty thousand people enrolled in his sight-singing course. The interest in these schools and courses, with the resultant training of so many singers, stimulated the composition of new choral works by such major composers as Sir Hubert Parry, Sir Charles Villiers Stanford, and Sir Edward Elgar as well as less well-known composers such as Samuel Sebastian Wesley, Sir George Macfarren, Sir William Sterndale Bennett, Sir Joseph Barnby, Sir John Stainer, Sir Arthur Sullivan, Charles Wood, and Samuel Coleridge-Taylor.

The creation and development of choral ensembles and festivals also initiated interest in the commissioning of new repertoire by both English and foreign composers. As a sampling, the Three Choirs Festival (established at the beginning of the eighteenth century and alternately held in Worcester, Hereford, and Gloucester) commissioned works by Parry and Elgar; the Birmingham Festival (founded in 1843) gave the premieres of Mendelssohn's *Elijah*, Sullivan's *The Light of the World*, Dvořák's *Requiem*, and Elgar's *The Dream of Gerontius;* and the Leeds Musical Festival commissioned Dvořák's *Svatá Ludmila*, Elgar's *Caractacus*, and seven works by Stanford. In addition, commissions came from choral ensembles such as the Royal Albert Hall Choral Society (later renamed the Royal Choral Society).

Not all the festivals and ensembles were devoted to new compositions, however. Oratorios by Handel continued to dominate the programs of many festival organizations, in particular those of the Handel Festival in London's Crystal Palace, and large-scale Bach choral/orchestral works became the focus of a movement whose mission was to revive music of the past. As stated in an article by Joseph Bennett about the Crystal Palace festival of 1877, Handel had become a national icon and the representation of England's nationalistic pride: "The affinity between Handel's music and our national character is strong enough to explain the phenomenon of the master's position. When he came to England, he came to his own, and his own received him." At about the same time, George Bernard Shaw wrote, "Handel is not a mere composer in England: he is an institution. What is more, he is a sacred institution." Bach works were regularly performed by the Bach Choir of London, founded in 1876 by Otto Goldschmidt (husband of the famous soprano Jenny Lind) and conducted by Stanford beginning in 1885, and works by both Handel and Bach were frequently performed by Mr Joseph Barnby's Choir, formed by the Novello publishing company to promote choral works in their catalogue. Bach and Handel works were also the focus of the Royal Albert Hall Choral Society, which was conducted by Barnby after Gounod's departure in 1871.

Most English composers of the Romantic era, including all those who lived into the twentieth century, composed works for the festivals; the composers early in the era—William Crotch, Robert Lucas Pearsall, and Sir John Goss—composed mainly for universities and cathedrals. In addition, most of the composers of the era achieved significant fame and were knighted. Furthermore, most of the composers were associated with Oxford or Cambridge universities and also with the Royal Academy of Music or the Royal College of Music. Only four composers (Pearsall, Wesley, Barnby, and Elgar) had no connection with Oxford or Cambridge, and only five composers (Goss, Pearsall, Wesley, Stainer, and Elgar) neither studied nor taught at the royal institutions. It is interesting to note that Elgar, England's most famous composer of the Romantic era, had no formal musical training or appointment as a teacher.

The main genres of composition were oratorios, odes, cantatas, and miscellaneous choral/orchestral works for the festivals; Anglican Services, anthems, motets, and hymn tunes for the church; and madrigals, part songs, and glees for choral competitions and small amateur choral ensembles. The choral/orchestral works composed early in the era, especially the oratorios, were generally in the mold of Handel and Mendelssohn, with set pieces, numerous choral movements, and conservative harmonies. The works in the later years of the era were fluid, through-composed works that were unified by leitmotifs. The church music remained in conventional styles of the recent past, whereas the small-scale secular pieces followed the patterns of German Romantic composers, with homophonic textures and careful attention to text declamation.

WILLIAM CROTCH 1775–1847

Crotch, who was born in Norwich, developed musical talents early in his youth. At two he could play familiar tunes such as "God save the king" on the family organ, and at three he was so skilled that he played concerts in Cambridge, Oxford, and London, including a performance for King George III at Buckingham Palace. By the time he was ten, he apparently could read any of Handel's organ concertos at sight and could also transpose them into any key. Between the ages of eleven and thirteen Crotch studied at Cambridge University and played for services at King's and Trinity colleges, and when he was fifteen he was appointed organist at Christ Church, Oxford. He began conducting orchestral concerts at Oxford when he was eighteen, at nineteen he received a bachelor's degree, at twenty-two he was admitted to the faculty and was named organist at St John's College, and at twenty-four he was granted a doctorate. He remained at Oxford for the next nine years, becoming known for an annual series of lectures on aspects of music history and aesthetics, and in 1806 he moved to London to freelance as a composer, performer, and lecturer. While in London, he gave periodic organ concerts to support local charities, conducted numerous concerts of the Philharmonic Society, and taught courses in harmony, counterpoint, and composition at the Royal Academy of Music. He also served as the first principal of the academy, wrote several books and articles (including *Elements of Musical Composition*), edited anthologies of music (e.g., *Specimens of Various Styles of Music*), and made piano duet arrangements of Handel oratorios, Haydn quartets, and Mozart concertos. Although he has not been recognized for his compositional skills, he has been acknowledged for his commitment to musical scholarship and for his establishment of compositional ideals that influenced composers throughout the beginning of the Romantic era. His orchestrations, which were scored for expanded wind and brass sections, were especially forward-looking in England at the time.

Crotch composed three oratorios, five odes, one cantata, twenty-two anthems, and one hundred glees, madrigals, rounds, and canons. The first oratorio, *The Captivity of Judah,* was composed between 1786 and 1789 and premiered at Cambridge University in 1789 (when Crotch was fourteen). The second oratorio, *Palestine,* was composed between 1805 and 1811 and premiered to critical acclaim in London in April 1812. Its libretto relates various events in the history of Israel, including Joshua's battle in Jericho, Moses on Mount Sinai, David and Goliath, the Nativity, the Crucifixion, and visions of Revelation. The musical structure and writing for chorus are very similar to Handel's *Messiah;* the oratorio even begins with a French overture. The third oratorio, composed between 1812 and 1828, is a complete resetting, with identical title, of the same text used for Crotch's first oratorio.

Most of the odes were composed for ceremonial occasions (e.g., the installation of Lord Greenville as Chancellor of Oxford University in 1810, the accession of King George IV in 1820, and the installation of the Duke of Wellington as Chancellor of Oxford University in 1834). The anthems are generally conservative in style and modeled on compositions of the Baroque. For instance, *The Lord is king* is based on a Purcellian ground bass, and *The joy of our heart is ceased* quotes the Dead March from Handel's oratorio *Saul.* Crotch's two most popular anthems during the nineteenth century are extractions from or arrangements of other works: *Lo, star-led chiefs* was originally a solo quartet in *Palestine,* and *Methinks I hear the full celestial choir* was originally published as a glee. Other anthems that were performed with some frequency are *Be peace on earth, How dear are thy counsels,* and *Comfort, O Lord, the soul of thy servant.* The only small-scale secular piece that is considered important is the glee for SATB voices, *Ring out ye crystal spheres.*

ROBERT LUCAS PEARSALL 1795–1856

Pearsall was born in Clifton, near Bristol, where his father was an army officer and amateur musician who played the violin and sang. Robert was educated privately in studies that prepared him for a career in law, and between 1821 and 1825 he worked in the legal profession. However, after a slight stroke in 1825, he gave up his law practice and devoted his time to antiquarian interests, painting, and music. In 1825 he also moved to Mainz, Germany, and became involved in the Cäcilien movement—following its precepts by composing Latin motets in the style of Palestrina. In 1830 Pearsall relocated to Karlsruhe, northwest of Stuttgart, and for the next decade he traveled frequently throughout Germany and England pursuing his antiquarian avocations. His final residence, beginning in about 1843, was on Lake Constance, close to the abbeys of St Gall and Einsiedeln, for which he composed a number of his sacred Latin pieces. Pearsall's interest in old musical styles was broad, encompassing sacred Lutheran music from the Baroque era as well as sacred Catholic music from the Renaissance. He also maintained a significant interest in Renaissance English madrigals, founding the Bristol Madrigal Society in 1837 and composing numerous madrigals and part songs for performance by its members.

Pearsall's choral output consists of approximately fifty Latin motets and related works, seven Anglican Services, twelve English anthems, three Lutheran chorale settings, twenty-three madrigals, and seventy part songs. The sacred music in Latin, which is characterized by conservative harmonies and textures of alternating imitative polyphony and homophony, includes a

Requiem, Te Deum, and the motets *Ecce quam bonum* and *Pange lingua.* The Anglican church music includes four Morning Services, two Evening Services, and one Burial Service—the *Evening Service* in G minor being the best known. The titles of the Lutheran works are *Christus ist erstanden, Ich stand in All,* and *In dulci jubilo.*

The secular repertoire is better known than the sacred, and a few of the madrigals have become staples on programs of English music from the Romantic era. The most famous madrigal, *Lay a garland* (set by Pearsall to the same music as his Latin motet, *Tu es Petrus*) is scored for SSAATTBB voices a cappella and is in the style of William Byrd: phrases are loosely imitative and several of the vocal parts participate in voice exchange (i.e., the two parts of each voice category—soprano, for instance—cross each other in melodic ascent and descent and have the same basic range). Other notable madrigals are *Great god of love* for SSAATTBB and *O ye roses* and *Light of my soul* for SSATTB.

The secular repertoire also includes a number of English balletts in the style of Morley—for example, two settings of *Sing we and chaunt it* and *No, no, Nigella* (one setting of each for SATB and one each for SSAATTBB). The other secular repertoire is represented by the homophonic part songs *Purple glow the forest mountains* and *O who will o'er the downs so free,* both scored for SATB voices. In addition, there are two relatively well-known pieces that Pearsall gave specific genre classifications—the "ante-madrigal" (in the style of music during the time of Henry VII, when the madrigal had not yet been developed in England) *Who shall have my lady fair,* which is a strophic piece for SATB voices with imitation of short motifs, and the "ballad-narrative" *Sir Patrick Spens,* which is scored for SATTB/SATTB.

SIR JOHN GOSS 1800–1880

Goss was born near Southampton in southern England, where his father, Joseph, was an organist. At age eleven John became a chorister at the Chapel Royal, and when his voice changed, he studied with Thomas Attwood and sang in the chorus of Covent Garden. He was appointed organist at Stockwell Chapel in 1821 and at St Luke's, Chelsea, in 1824, and in 1838 he succeeded Attwood as organist at St Paul's Cathedral. Goss became one of the composers of the Chapel Royal in 1856, he was knighted in 1872, and in 1876 he was granted a doctorate from Cambridge University.

His choral output consists of six Anglican Services plus several separate Service parts, forty-five anthems, a Requiem motet, and numerous secular glees. Of the Services, the only one known and performed today is the *Evening Service in E.* The anthems are better known and include the homophonic setting *These are they which follow the lamb* for SATB chorus a cappella, and the imitative motet-like setting *If we believe that Jesus died* for SATB chorus and organ (with a brief passage scored for SSATB). *Almighty and merciful God* and *O saviour of the world* are both scored for SATB chorus, with an organ accompaniment that basically doubles the choral parts. Other anthems that have entered the performing repertory include *God so loved the world; O taste and see; Praise the Lord, O my soul; Come, and let us return unto the Lord; I heard a voice from heaven; Lord, let me know mine end;* and *The wilderness.* The glees are represented by *List, for the breeze*—a setting for ATTB voices, with an AAB structure and numerous repetitions of a motif that paints the word "warble."

SAMUEL SEBASTIAN WESLEY 1810–1876

Wesley was born in London, the son of organist and composer Samuel Wesley (1766–1837) and grandson of Methodist minister and hymn writer Charles Wesley (1707–1788). Samuel Sebastian, whose middle name refers to Johann Sebastian Bach, began his musical education as a chorister in the Chapel Royal at age eight. During the following eight years he also sang frequently for special services at St Paul's Cathedral and for performances by the Concert of Ancient Music. At sixteen he became organist at St James Chapel and also pianist for the English Opera House, and for the remainder of his life he served as organist at some of the most important cathedrals in England, including Hereford, Exeter, Winchester, and Gloucester. While in Hereford and Gloucester he conducted performances of the Three Choirs Festival, including Bach's *St Matthew Passion* in 1871, and while in Winchester he wrote two important pamphlets in support of church music reform—*A Few Words on Cathedral Music* in 1849 and *Reply to the Inquiries of the Cathedral Commissioners relative to the Improvement in the Music of Divine Worship in Cathedrals* in 1854. In addition to his church positions he served as professor of organ at the Royal Academy of Music and was granted a doctorate in music from Oxford University.

Wesley composed six Anglican Services plus thirteen separate Service pieces (some in English and some in Latin), thirty-eight anthems, approximately two hundred hymn tunes, five glees, two part songs, and three secular cantatas. The Services include only one that is considered full and complete—a Morning and Evening Service in E major consisting of a Te Deum, Jubilate, Sanctus, Creed, Magnificat, Nunc dimittis, and two Kyries. The anthems include some of Wesley's best-known works—*Thou wilt keep him in perfect peace* for SATTB chorus and organ, *Cast me not away from thy presence* for SSATTB chorus and organ, and *Wash me throughly from my wickedness* for brief soprano solo, SATB chorus, and organ. The organ part basically doubles the choral parts in each of these anthems, and in *Cast me not away . . .* the text phrase "that the bones which thou hast broken may rejoice," with a dissonant chord accompanying the word "broken," apparently refers to an accident that had fractured Wesley's leg. His most famous anthem during the nineteenth century, *The wilderness and the solitary place,* was composed in 1832 for the opening of the rebuilt Hereford Cathedral and revised with orchestral accompaniment for a performance in Birmingham in 1852. Other anthems include *The face of the Lord; Blessed be the God and father; Ascribe unto the Lord;* and *O Lord, thou art my God.* Of the hymns, *Aurelia,* generally sung to the text "The church's one foundation is Jesus Christ her Lord," is well known and included in most modern-day Protestant hymnals. Other, lesser-known hymns include *Cornwall* ("We sing of God, the mighty source"), *Wetherby* ("O thou, who through this holy week"), and *Alleluia* ("Joyful, joyful, we adore thee, God of glory, god of love").

SIR GEORGE MACFARREN 1813–1887

Macfarren was born in London and received his first musical education from his father (also named George), who was a dancer, dramatist, and amateur musician. At sixteen the younger George entered the Royal Academy of Music, at twenty-one he was instrumental in founding the Society of British Musicians, and at twenty-four he was appointed a professor at the Royal Academy. During his twenties he also composed a number of operas and operettas, and during his thirties he became conductor at Covent Garden and also helped found the Handel Society. He had been slowly losing his eyesight since age ten, and at forty-seven he went totally blind. However, he continued to compose and teach. He succeeded William Sterndale Bennett in 1875 as professor of music at Cambridge University and also as principal of the Royal Academy of Music. He received honorary degrees from Cambridge, Oxford, and Dublin universities and was knighted in 1883.

Macfarren composed four oratorios, eight cantatas, two Anglican Services, a collection of *Introits for Holy Days and Seasons of the English Church,* twenty-five anthems, sixty part songs, and six glees. As with many of his colleagues, his oratorios were composed for the primary festivals of England—*St John the Baptist* for the Bristol Festival in 1873, *The Resurrection* for the Birmingham Festival in 1876, *Joseph* for the Leeds Festival in 1877, and *King David* for the Leeds Festival in 1883. *St John the Baptist* became quite popular; a review of an 1874 performance at the Leeds Festival included the comment, "Of all the works produced since [Mendelssohn's] 'Elijah,' it is thought none [but Macfarren's *St John the Baptist*] is likely to enjoy enduring popularity." Like the oratorios composed by Crotch, it is conservative and in a Handelian mold, although Macfarren makes use of recurring motifs. Two of the most notable cantatas were also composed for festivals—*Outward Bound* for Norwich in 1872 and *The Lady of the Lake* for Glasgow in 1876.

The Services and anthems have failed to achieve a degree of popularity, although a few of the part songs have been published in collections and have been performed with some frequency. The most popular is *Orpheus, with his lute,* which is set to text from act three, scene one of Shakespeare's *Henry VIII* ("Orpheus, with his lute made trees, and the mountain tops that freeze bow themselves when he did sing"). Another Shakespeare setting, *When daisies pied,* comes from act five, scene two of *Love's Labours Lost* ("When daisies pied, and violets blue, and lady-smocks all silver-white, and cuckoo-buds of yellow hue do paint the meadows with delight"). The well-known part song *You stole my love,* which is traditionally performed three times in quick succession (fast, faster, and as fast as possible), was composed not by George Macfarren but by his brother Walter.

SIR WILLIAM STERNDALE BENNETT 1816–1875

Bennett was born in Sheffield, near Manchester. His grandfather, John Bennett (1754–1837), was a singer in the choirs of King's, Trinity, and St John's colleges, Cambridge, and his father, Robert Bennett (1788–1819), was a chorister at King's College, organist at Trinity and St John's colleges, and also organist at the parish church of Sheffield. William became a chorister at King's College when he was eight years old (and his grandfather was still singing there), and two years later, being considered a child prodigy, he transferred to the Royal Academy of Music. While at the academy, he studied violin and piano as well as composition with William Crotch, and he became known for his exceptional performing abilities (at age twelve he played a piano concerto by Jan Ladislav Dussek, and at fourteen he sang the part of Cherubino in a student production of Mozart's *Le nozze di Figaro*). At sixteen Bennett composed his first symphony and piano concerto, the latter of which was played for King William IV and Felix Mendelssohn, and for the next six years he composed two or three major orchestral works per year—most received by critics and the public with considerable acclaim. Mendelssohn invited Bennett to visit Düsseldorf and hear the premiere of *Paulus,* and after reviewing a few of Bennett's works, he wrote to Thomas Attwood, "I think him the most promising young musician I know, not only in your country, but also here." The following year Bennett visited Mendelssohn in Leipzig and met Robert Schumann, who wrote in the *Neue Zeitschrift für Musik,* "Were there many artists like Sterndale Bennett, all fears for the future progress of our art would be silenced." At age twenty-one, Bennett began teaching at the Royal Academy, and for the remainder of his life he concentrated on teaching and performing; his compositional activity greatly diminished. In 1849 he founded the Bach Society, in 1854 he conducted the first English performance of Bach's *St Matthew Passion,* and in 1856 he was appointed director of the Philharmonic Society and professor of music at Cambridge University. Esteemed as one of England's most important musicians, he became principal of the Royal Academy of Music in 1866, and he was knighted in 1871. Finally, he was given the honor of a burial in Westminster Abbey.

Bennett composed one cantata, two odes, one oratorio, seven anthems, eleven hymn tunes, and three part songs. The cantata, odes, and oratorio were all written at approximately the same time. The cantata, *The May Queen* op.39, was commissioned by the Leeds Festival for its inaugural year (1858); the two odes—one for the opening of the International Exhibition (op.40) and one for Bennett's installation at Cambridge University (op.41)—were both composed in 1862; and the oratorio, *The Woman of Samaria* op.44, was composed for the 1867 Birmingham Festival. This latter work borrows two choruses ("Abide with me" and "God is a spirit") from an earlier incomplete oratorio, *Zion,* which Bennett worked on between 1839 and 1844 and which was inspired by Mendelssohn's *Elias.* The anthems, generally unknown today, include *Remember now thy creator; In thee, O Lord;* and *Oh that I knew where I might find him.*

Although Bennett composed only three part songs, all are considered to be fine examples of the genre as it existed in England during the Romantic era, and one has become a staple of programming. The two lesser-known pieces are entitled *Sweet stream that winds* and *Of all the arts;* the well-known part song, *Come live with me,* is a setting of text by Christopher Marlowe that is basically homophonic and strophic. Each of the two verses, virtually identical, is constructed of an overall ABA structure, with numerous repetitions of a triadic motif throughout both A sections.

SIR JOSEPH BARNBY 1838–1896

Barnby was born in York, where his father, Thomas, was an organist. At age seven Joseph began his musical education as a chorister at York Minster, and at sixteen he entered the Royal Academy of Music in London. He became the musical advisor to the publishing firm Novello and Company at age twenty-three, and at twenty-six he was appointed organist at St Andrew's, Wells Street, where he developed a large and active music program that included performances of such works as Gounod's *Messe solennelle.* Four years later, while maintaining his position at St Andrew's, Barnby began conducting a choral ensemble—Mr Joseph Barnby's Choir—formed by Novello to promote choral works in their catalogue. Compositions performed over the next several years included Handel's *Jephthe,* Beethoven's *Missa solemnis,* and Bach's *St Matthew Passion.* In 1871, at age thirty-three, Barnby succeeded Gounod as conductor of the Royal Albert Hall Choral Society and also moved from St Andrew's to St Anne's, Soho; four years later he added the position of precentor at Eton College. For the following decade Barnby conducted numerous large-scale works, including annual performances of Bach's *St John Passion* beginning in 1873, Dvořák's *Stabat mater* in 1883, and a concert presentation of Wagner's *Parsifal* in 1884. In 1892 he was knighted and appointed principal of Guildhall School of Music.

Barnby composed one oratorio, one cantata, twenty-one Anglican Services, forty-six anthems, over two hundred hymn tunes, and thirty-two part songs. The oratorio, entitled *Rebekah* and subtitled "A Sacred Idyll in Two Scenes," was composed in 1870; the cantata *The Lord is King* is a setting of Psalm 97; the Services include *The Canticles* (Te Deum, Benedictus, Jubilate, Magnificat, Nunc dimittis, Cantate Domino, and Deus miseratur), a cycle of hymns entitled *The Offertory Sentences,* and a Magnificat and Nunc dimittis in E-flat major; and the anthems are represented by *Sing and rejoice, O how amiable are thy dwellings,* and *I will give thanks unto thee, O Lord.* None of these works are well known today. However, approximately ten hymns appear in many of today's mainstream Protestant hymnals, and a few of the part songs have become popular. Of the hymns, *Laudes Domini* ("When morning gilds the skies, my heart awaking cries, may Jesus Christ be praised") and *O Perfect Love* ("O perfect love, all human thought transcending") are perhaps the most familiar. Others include *Nightfall* ("Now God be with us, for the night is closing"), *Burleigh* ("Lead us, O father, in the paths of peace"), and *All Saints* ("For all the saints, who from their labors rest"). The most popular part song and one of the most familiar part songs of the Romantic era, *Sweet and low,* is a homophonic and strophic setting of Tennyson's poem "Sweet and low, sweet and low, wind of the western sea." Barnby's other familiar part song is *Sleep, the bird is in its nest.*

Sir John Stainer 1840–1901

Stainer was born in London and as a young child studied organ with his father, William, a parish schoolteacher at St Thomas's, Southwark. At age nine John became a chorister at St Paul's Cathedral, and at fourteen he was appointed organist at St Benet, Paul's Wharf. At sixteen he served as organist at St Michael's College, Tenbury Wells, at nineteen he enrolled at Christ Church, Oxford, and during the next several years he held the positions of organist at Magdalen College and university organist. In addition, he received four degrees from Oxford, including a master's of arts and a doctorate in music, and he also founded the Oxford Philharmonic Society (in 1866, when he was twenty-six). In 1872 he succeeded John Goss as organist at St Paul's Cathedral, and in 1876, while maintaining his position at St Paul's, he became organist at the National Training School of Music. He was appointed principal of the National Training School in 1881, in 1888 he was knighted, and in 1889 he was given a professorship in music at Oxford. He was best known during his life as a scholar and teacher: he edited the collection *Early Bodleian Music,* which was one of the first carefully researched editions of pre-Renaissance music, and he authored several books on harmony, including *A Theory of Harmony, Founded on the Tempered Scale* in 1871 and *A Treatise on Harmony and the Classification of Chords* in about 1895.

Stainer composed two oratorios, three cantatas, twenty-two Anglican Services, approximately 150 hymns and canticles, more than twenty anthems, and several madrigals and part songs. The oratorios are *Gideon,* composed in 1865 as an exercise for his doctoral degree at Oxford University, and *The Crucifixion*, composed in 1887 and first performed at the parish church of St Marylebone. This latter work became one of the most popular oratorios during the first half of the twentieth century, being regularly performed during Holy Week in churches throughout England, Canada, and the United States. One of its choral movements, "God so loved the world," was extracted and published separately and became an even more popular anthem. Stainer called the oratorio "A Meditation on the Sacred Passion of the Holy Redeemer," and modeled it on the Passions of J. S. Bach, with reflective choruses, solos, and hymns (in place of chorales) that were to be sung by the chorus and congregation. The work is scored for TB solos, SATB chorus, and organ. The cantatas are *The Daughter of Jairus*, composed in 1878 for the Worcester Festival; *St Mary Magdalen*, composed in 1883 for the Gloucester Festival; and *The Story of the Cross*, composed in 1893 for no specific occasion.

None of the Services and few of the anthems are known today. *I saw the Lord* and the imitative, motet-like "How beautiful upon the mountains" from *Awake, awake, put on thy strength, O Zion* have been published and are contained in collections of English church music as representatives of Stainer's anthems. Similarly, a few of the hymns and canticles are included in modern-day Protestant hymnals. Examples are *Cross of Jesus* ("Cross of Jesus, cross of sorrow, where the blood of Christ was shed"), *Evening Prayer* ("Jesus, tender shepherd, hear me, bless thy little lamb tonight"), and the choral chant response *Sebaste* ("Hail, gladdening light"). In addition, Stainer composed a sevenfold Amen that was popular. The secular music is perhaps even less known than the Services and anthems. Only the eight madrigals of 1864, composed while Stainer was a student at Oxford, are occasionally cited as examples of English secular music from the Romantic era.

SIR ARTHUR SULLIVAN 1842–1900

Sullivan was born in London and began his musical education under the tutelage of his father, Thomas, the bandmaster at the Royal Military College in Sandhurst. Arthur learned to play the piano and showed an early interest in composition, and at age twelve he entered the Chapel Royal as a chorister. At fifteen he enrolled at the Royal Academy of Music, where he studied piano with William Sterndale Bennett and composition with John Goss, and at sixteen he continued his education in Europe at the Leipzig Conservatory. He returned to England in 1861, and during the next several years he conducted the Civil Service Musical Society (an amateur chorus in London) and served as organist at Covent Garden, at St Michaels in Chester Square, and at St Peter's in Cranley Gardens. During this time he also composed, and works such as the masque *Kenilworth*, which premiered at the Birmingham Festival in 1864, received positive reviews. In 1875 he became conductor of the Glasgow Choral and Orchestral Union, and his first successful dramatic stage collaboration with librettist William Schwenck Gilbert, *Trial by Jury*, was premiered at the Royalty Theatre. The following year Sullivan was named principal of the National Training School for Music (a position he held until John Stainer assumed it in 1881), and in 1878 he and Gilbert received acclaim for the production of *HMS Pinafore, or The Lass that Loved a Sailor*. The next theatrical collaboration between Gilbert and Sullivan, *The Pirates of Penzance, or The Slave of Duty*, was premiered in 1879, and in 1880 Sullivan was appointed conductor of the Leeds Triennial Musical Festival—for which he composed the sacred music drama *The*

Martyr of Antioch (1880) and the cantata *The Golden Legend* (1886). He also conducted the Leeds forces in a highly praised performance of Bach's *B minor Mass* (1883). Meanwhile, Gilbert and Sullivan continued to collaborate on more stage works, including *Patience, or Bunthorne's Bride* in 1881, *Iolanthe, or The Peer and the Peri* in 1882, *Princess Ida, or Castle Adamant* in 1884, and *The Mikado, or The Town of Titipu* in 1885. In 1885 Sullivan was named conductor of the Philharmonic Society of London, and for the next three years he and Gilbert wrote *Ruddigore, or The Witch's Curse* (1887), *The Yeoman of the Guard, or The Merryman and his Maid* (1888), and *The Gondoliers, or The King of Barataria* (1889).

Sullivan was held in high esteem during his life. He was given honorary doctorates in music from Cambridge University in 1876 and Oxford University in 1879, he received the Chevalier of the Légion d'Honneur in 1878 and was knighted by Queen Victoria in 1883, and he was given the Royal Victorian Order in 1897. After a long decline in health, followed by bronchitis in the fall of 1900, he died on St Cecilia's Day, November 22, and was buried at St Paul's Cathedral.

His choral output consists of three oratorios, two cantatas, two odes, three Te Deums, seventeen anthems, approximately sixty hymns, and twenty part songs. In addition, he composed numerous solo songs, including the famous ballad *The Lost Chord*. The oratorio *The Prodigal Son* was composed for and premiered at the 1869 Worcester Festival. The text is drawn from a variety of biblical sources and, according to Sullivan in the preface of the score, portrays the prodigal son "as a buoyant, restless youth, tired of the monotony of home, and anxious to see what lay beyond the narrow confines of his father's farm, going forth in the confidence of his own simplicity and ardor." Scoring is for SATB soloists, SATB chorus, and orchestra. Solo roles are not clearly defined, although the tenor soloist represents the son and the bass soloist the father. All soloists sing portions of narration, and the soprano and alto also sing passages of commentary on the story. The structure of the choral movements is reminiscent of the writing of Handel and Mendelssohn, with many sections of imitative counterpoint and occasional passages of chorale-like homophony. The second oratorio, *The Light of the World,* was composed for and premiered at the Birmingham Festival in 1873. Its text, like that of Handel's *Messiah,* is drawn from various biblical verses that relate the life of Christ. Its musical style, also like that of Handel, was considered too derivative to be artistically worthwhile, although the chorus "Yea, though I walk through the valley of the shadow of death" was extracted and published as an anthem. *The Martyr of Antioch,* called by Sullivan a "sacred music drama," is a setting of text about the martyrdom of St Margaret of Antioch in the third century, composed, as was already mentioned, for the 1880 Leeds Festival.

The cantata *On Shore and Sea* was composed for the opening of Royal Albert Hall in 1871. Subtitled by Sullivan a "dramatic cantata," it is based on the conflict between Christians and Moors, with focus on a sailor and his bride who are separated by war and then reunited. The final chorus, "Sink and scatter, clouds of war," was renamed "The Song of Peace" and performed frequently as a separate composition during the late nineteenth century. *The Golden Legend* was Sullivan's most successful choral/orchestral work (apart from the stage works written in conjunction with Gilbert). It was well received by audiences and critics alike and was considered by commentators of the time to be an artistically superior work. Stanford wrote, "It deserves a place on the shelves of the classics." Its text is based on the poem by Longfellow about a prince who suffers from an illness that can be cured only by a maiden's pure and willing sacrifice.

The odes and Te Deums were all occasional pieces—the odes composed for the opening of the Colonial and Indian Exhibition in 1886 and the laying of the Imperial Institute foundation stone in 1887, and the orchestral Te Deums to celebrate the British presumed victory in the Boer War and the Prince of Wales' return to good health in 1872 after having typhoid fever. The first of the Te Deums, entitled *Festival Te Deum*, is scored for soprano solo, mixed chorus, orchestra, organ, and military band and was performed in the Crystal Palace with more than one thousand musicians. The other, *Thanksgiving Te Deum*, was not performed until eighteen months after Sullivan's death.

The anthems are unknown today except for *We have heard with our ears, O God*, which is scored for SATB solos, SSATB chorus, and organ and is in the style of the verse anthems of Maurice Greene and William Croft. Approximately ten Sullivan hymns appear in today's mainstream Protestant hymnals, although only one of the hymns, *St Gertrude* ("Onward, Christian soldiers, marching as to war"), has achieved a degree of popularity.

The part songs include two collections—seven secular pieces composed in 1868 and five sacred pieces composed in 1871. Within the first set are *Echoes* and Sullivan's most popular part song, *The long day closes*, which was originally scored for male voices but has become known in an arrangement (not by Sullivan) for mixed voices SATB. Other popular separate pieces are *O hush thee, my babie* and *When love and beauty to be married are*, a madrigal from Sullivan's opera *The Sapphire Necklace, or The False Witness.*

The collaborative works with Gilbert contain many choral movements and scenes with choral passages, a majority of which are scored for soloists and male or female chorus. The most famous of these are "Brightly dawns our wedding day," "Behold the lord high executioner," "With aspect stern and gloomy stride," and "For he's gone and married Yum-Yum" from *The Mikado;* "Poor wandering one," "I am the very model of a modern major-general," and "When a felon's not engaged in his employment" from *The Pirates of Penzance;* and "We sail the ocean blue" and "Oh joy, oh rapture unforeseen" from *HMS Pinafore*. Choral portions in other operettas, while perhaps not so well known, are generally of equal effectiveness, charm, and wit.

SIR HUBERT PARRY 1848–1918

Parry was born in Bournemouth and educated at Twyford School, near Winchester, and at Eton College, near London. While at Twyford he attended services at Winchester Cathedral under the musical leadership of Samuel Sebastian Wesley, and while at Eton he studied music with George Elvey, choirmaster of St George's Chapel. Parry continued his education at Exeter College, Oxford, where he studied law and modern history. After graduation he worked as an underwriter at Lloyd's of London and studied music privately with William Sterndale Bennett and Edward Dannreuther, who introduced Parry to the music of Richard Wagner. Parry was strongly attracted to Wagner's music and principles of composition, and he traveled to Bayreuth to hear several operas, including the entire Ring cycle in 1876 and *Parsifal* in 1882. Feeling strongly that he should make music his career, Parry left Lloyd's in 1877 and worked as a sub-editor for George Grove, who at the time was preparing the first edition of the *Dictionary of Music and Musicians.* Parry became noted for his scholarly work (he wrote more than one hundred articles for the dictionary), and in 1883 he was named professor of musical history at the newly formed

Royal College of Music in London. He was also granted an honorary doctorate from Cambridge University in 1883 and from Oxford University in 1884. For the next several years he achieved minimal success with symphonic compositions. However, in 1887 he won widespread recognition for his first major choral work, *Blest Pair of Sirens,* and for the remainder of his life he concentrated on choral composition and scholarly writings. The choral works include numerous odes and oratorio-like works, and the writings include such books as *Studies of Great Composers* (1886), *The Music of the Seventeenth Century* (1902), *Johann Sebastian Bach: the Story of the Development of a Great Personality* (1909), and *Style in Musical Art* (1911). Parry succeeded Grove as director of the Royal College of Music in 1895, he was knighted in 1898, and in 1900 he was appointed to the faculty of Oxford University.

Parry composed three traditional oratorios, thirty miscellaneous choral/orchestral works of various genres (odes, cantatas, Psalm settings, and oratorio-like works), ten anthems, ten hymns, and approximately fifty part songs. The oratorios were all composed for English choral festivals—*Judith* for the Birmingham Festival in 1888, *Job* for the Three Choirs Festival in Gloucester in 1892, and *King Saul* for the Birmingham Festival in 1894. All the works have characteristics of Wagner's music, especially in the use of leitmotifs. For instance, *Job* is structured in four scenes, each through-composed, and the entire work is to be performed without a pause. Two leitmotifs pervade the music, one that begins and ends the oratorio and also appears in each scene, and another that almost always appears in the orchestra while Job is singing. Other characters have motifs as well, including God and Satan. The oratorio was well received; a review of the premiere noted its unconventionality and went on to note, "Dr. Parry takes a step towards what is known as 'advanced' music, departing . . . from the solid and dignified classical style."

Many of the miscellaneous choral/orchestral works were also composed for and premiered at English festivals. For example, *Ode on St Cecilia's Day* was written for Leeds in 1889, *L'Allegro ed il Pensieroso* for Norwich in 1890, *The Lotos-Eaters* for Cambridge in 1892, *Invocation to Music* for Leeds in 1895 (a festival celebrating the bicentenary of Henry Purcell's death), and *The Vision of Life* for Cardiff in 1907. Other choral/orchestral works were composed for special occasions (e.g., the *Te Deum* in D major for the coronation of George V in 1911) or for notable people and ensembles (e.g., *Blest Pair of Sirens*—Parry's best-known choral/orchestral work—in 1887 for Stanford and the Bach Choir of London).

Parry's most famous anthem, and one of the most famous anthems of the Romantic era, is *I was glad.* Composed for the coronation of Edward VII in 1902, it is noted for its treatment of text and appropriateness of occasion, including the stately introduction for organ, grand choral entrance to the text "I was glad when they said unto me, we will go into the house of the Lord," subdued and meditative setting of "O pray for the peace of Jerusalem," and climactic intensification of "and plenteousness within thy palaces." Other anthems include *Hear my words, ye people,* composed for the festival of the Salisbury Diocesan Choral Association in 1894.

The hymns are represented by *Repton* ("Dear Lord and father of mankind, forgive our foolish ways"), *Jerusalem* ("O day of peace that dimly shines through all our hopes and prayers and dreams"), and *Laudate Dominum* ("O praise ye the Lord, praise him in the height").

Most of the part songs were published in collections—*Six lyrics from an Elizabethan Song Book* in 1897, *Six modern lyrics* also in 1897, *Eight four-part songs* in 1898, *Six part songs* in 1909, and *Songs of Farewell* between 1916 and 1918. The latter collection, the individual pieces of which are often called English motets because of the sacred or spiritual qualities of their texts about death and afterlife, is considered to be one of the finest contributions to the a cappella part song repertory of the Romantic era. The first piece, *My soul, there is a country*, is a setting of poetry by the metaphysical author Henry Vaughan (1622–1695) scored for four mixed voices; *I know my soul hath power*, also for four voices, is from the poem *Nosce Teipsum* by Sir John Davies (1569–1626); *Never weather-beaten sail* is to text by Thomas Campion (1567–1620) and is scored for five voices; *There is an old belief*, which was sung at Parry's funeral, is set to a poem by John Gibson Lockhart (1794–1854) and is scored for six voices; *At the round earth's imagined corners*, scored for seven voices, is a setting of the famous poem about the Last Judgment by John Donne (1572–1631); and *Lord, let me know mine end* is a setting of Psalm 39 for double chorus. The first five pieces of the collection were premiered by the Bach Choir at the Royal College of Music on May 22, 1916. The complete set was performed at a memorial service for Parry at Exeter College, Oxford, on February 23, 1919, four months after the composer's death.

SACRED AND SECULAR WORKS
SELECTED AND LISTED ACCORDING TO FAMILIARITY

I was glad (from Psalm 122) – SSAATTBB chorus and organ – 6:30 minutes. (1) The first part of the anthem is scored for SSATTB, the middle part for SATB/SATB, and the ending for SSATB; (2) the anthem contains a short section of music set to the text "Vivat regina," supposedly to be sung only in the presence of the Queen of England.

My soul, there is a country (from *Songs of Farewell*) – SATB chorus a cappella – 4 minutes.

There is an old belief (from *Songs of Farewell*) – SSATTB chorus a cappella – 4:30 minutes.

At the round earth's imagined corners (from *Songs of Farewell*) – SSAATBB chorus a cappella – 7 minutes.

Music, when soft voices die – SATB chorus a cappella – 2 minutes.

There rolls the deep – SATB chorus a cappella – 2:30 minutes.

O love, they wrong thee much – SATB chorus a cappella – 3:15 minutes.

My delight and thy delight – SATB chorus a cappella – 3:30 minutes.

Hear my words, ye people – ST solos, SATB semichorus or quartet, SATB chorus, and organ – 8:30 minutes. (1) The semichorus/quartet and full chorus are scored in double chorus dialogue format for a portion of the anthem; (2) the full chorus briefly divides into SAATTBB.

Blest Pair of Sirens – SATB chorus and orchestra – 12 minutes.

Invocation to music – STB solos, SATB chorus, and orchestra (including bass clarinet, double bassoon, harp, and organ) – 55 minutes.

Job – STBB solos, SATB chorus, and orchestra – 69 minutes.

SIR CHARLES VILLIERS STANFORD 1852–1924

Stanford was born in Dublin and received a classical education that included study of the violin, piano, and organ. His father, John James, was a prominent lawyer and an amateur musician, and with frequent musical guests and concerts in the family home, Charles became acquainted with music of Bach, Handel, Mendelssohn, Schumann, and Brahms. At age eighteen Stanford enrolled at Cambridge University, becoming assistant conductor of the Cambridge Musical Society and conductor of the Cambridge Amateur Vocal Guild the following year, and at twenty-one he was appointed organist at Trinity College. After extended study trips to Leipzig and Berlin—which were a part of his university education and which gave him further knowledge of Mendelssohn, Schumann, and Brahms—he became conductor of the Cambridge Musical Society, performing with them works of Brahms (e.g., the *Rhapsodie* op. 53 and *Neue Liebeslieder Walzer* op.65) as well as some of his own compositions (such as his extended Psalm setting *God is our hope and strength* op.8). Stanford also composed Anglican Services and anthems for the Trinity College Chapel Choir. His reputation and stature in England grew, and in 1883 he was granted an honorary doctorate from Oxford University and he became the composition professor and orchestral conductor at the Royal College of Music in London. Between 1886 and 1902 he was conductor of the Bach Choir of London, between 1897 and 1909 he was conductor of the Leeds Philharmonic Society, and from 1901 to 1910 he was musical director of the Leeds Triennial Festival. In addition, he emulated his colleague Hubert Parry and wrote scholarly discourses. Articles such as "On musical criticism in England" and "Government and Music" appeared in music periodicals, and the book *Brahms and his music* was published in 1912. Meanwhile, he was granted honorary doctorates from Cambridge University in 1888, Durham University in 1894, and Leeds University in 1904, and he was knighted in 1902.

Stanford composed two oratorios, thirty-two miscellaneous choral/orchestral works, twelve publications of Anglican Service music, forty anthems and motets, numerous hymns and carols, and approximately one hundred part songs and folk song arrangements. The two oratorios—*The Three Holy Children* op.22 of 1885 and *Eden* op.40 of 1891—were both composed for and premiered at the Birmingham Festival. The first is in the conservative style of Mendelssohn. However, the second is in a modern style, characterized by chromatic harmonic language, leitmotifs, and through-composed scenes. A reviewer of the premiere commented, "Among oratorios it must be given a place by itself. . . . The whole differs so widely from all known standards of oratorio that we may not judge it by reference to them." It is curious, therefore, that it is known today only for its a cappella chorus "Flames of pure love are we," which Stanford called a "madrigale spirituale" and which is in a Palestrinian imitative style.

Like Parry, Stanford composed a majority of his choral/orchestral works for the festivals that were so popular throughout England. Seven were written for Leeds, including Stanford's first successful large-scale work, *The Revenge* op.24. Subtitled "A Ballad of the Fleet," it is a narrative setting of Tennyson's well-known poem scored for SATB chorus (with divisions) and orchestra. *Songs of the Sea* op.91 of 1904 and *Songs of the Fleet* op.117 of 1910 were also popular works written for Leeds, as was *Stabat mater* op.96, which was composed during 1905 and 1906 and premiered at Leeds Town Hall in October 1907. This latter work, Stanford's last for Leeds, is subtitled "Symphonic Cantata," no doubt reflecting the long and descriptive orchestral (i.e., symphonic) prelude that precedes four movements for soloists and chorus. Typical of all late Stanford works, the music is characterized by recurring motifs. Notable choral/orchestral works composed for other festivals include *Elegiac Ode* op.2 for Norwich in 1884, *The Battle of the Baltic* op.41 for Hereford in 1891, and *Requiem* op.63 for Birmingham in 1897.

The best known of the Anglican liturgical works are the Morning, Communion, and Evening Services in B-flat major composed in 1879 and collectively published as opus 10. Also popular are the Evening Service from the Morning, Communion, and Evening Services in A major op.12 composed in 1880; the Magnificat from the Morning, Communion, and Evening Services in G major op.81 composed in 1904; and the Morning, Communion, and Evening Services in C major op.115 composed in 1910. Most of the choral writing in the Services is scored for *decani* and *cantoris* divisions, the earlier two opuses are scored with orchestral accompaniment, and the later two opuses are accompanied only by organ. In addition, most of the individual portions of the Services, for example the *Te Deum* from opus 10, are unified by recurring musical motifs. The separate *Magnificat* in B-flat major op. 164, scored for double chorus a cappella, was composed for and dedicated to Parry. The dedication inscription reads, "Huic operi quod mors vetuit ne Carolo Huberto Hastings Parry vivo traderem nomen moerens praescribo" (This work, which his death prevented me from handing Charles Hubert Hastings Parry in life, I dedicate to his name in grief). The music, especially in the opening section, is very much in the style of double chorus dialogue motets by German composers of the Baroque era.

Most of the anthems (composed to English texts) and motets (composed to Latin texts) were written for performance in collegiate chapels. As such, they are generally more complex and lengthier than the sacred pieces written for metropolitan cathedrals or parish churches. *Eternal father* op.135 no.2, *And I saw another angel* op.37 no.1, and *For lo, I raise up* op.145, for instance, are all generally beyond the scale and scope of most anthems of the time. The three Latin motets op.38, Stanford's most famous sacred pieces, are further examples. Number two of the set, composed to the opening phrase "Coelos ascendit hodie, Jesus Christus rex gloriae, sedet ad patris dexteram, alleluia" (Ascended to the heavens today, Jesus Christ, king of glory, sits at the father's right hand, alleluia), is in double chorus dialogue style. Number three, the entire text of which is "Beati quorum via integra est, qui ambulant in lege Domini" (Blessed are the undefiled in the way, who walk in the law of the Lord), has aspects of Renaissance imitative polyphony.

The hymn *Engelberg*, occasionally set to the opening text phrase "We know that Christ is raised and dies no more," but more recently and frequently set to "When in our music God is glorified," has often served as music's hymn (i.e., the hymn that extols the importance of music in the church). The music is similar to and as effective as *Sine nomine* ("For all the saints, who from their labors rest") by Vaughan Williams. The six hymns op.113 published in 1910 are actually hymn-anthems; each is scored as a solo song accompanied by organ followed by an SATB elaboration of the hymn tune. The most popular piece from this set, *O for a closer walk with God*, is based on a chorale melody from the Scottish Psalter of 1635.

The part songs are mainly homophonic and strophic. However, the homophonic textures are offset by occasional rhythmic variances between the soprano and lower voice parts, and the different strophes or verses are changed rhythmically to conform to word declamation and dramatic effect. These characteristics can be seen in *Heraclitus* and *The blue bird*, Stanford's two most popular part songs. In the first of these there are rhythmic changes and differences in expressive markings between the two strophes, and in *The blue bird* the two strophes for the alto, tenor, and bass voices are almost identical. However, in the soprano voice, which is distinctly separate from the other voices, the two strophes are rhythmically varied. Uniquely, the soprano voice ends the part song alone, and on a note not part of the tonic chord.

SACRED WORKS
SELECTED AND LISTED ACCORDING TO FAMILIARITY

Beati quorum via (Psalm 119:1) op.38 no.3 – SSATBB chorus a cappella – 3:30 minutes.

Justorum animae op.38 no.1 – SATB chorus a cappella – 3:30 minutes.

Coelos ascendit hodie op.38 no.2 – SATB/SATB chorus a cappella – 2 minutes.

Eternal father op.135 no.2 – SSATBB chorus a cappella – 6:30 minutes.

And I saw another angel op.37 no.1 – T solo, SATB chorus, and organ – 5 minutes.

Magnificat in B-flat major op.164 – SATB/SATB chorus a cappella – 11:30 minutes.

SECULAR WORKS
SELECTED AND LISTED ACCORDING TO FAMILIARITY

The blue bird op.119 no.3 – SAATB chorus a cappella – 4 minutes.

Heraclitus op.110 no.4 – SATB chorus a cappella – 2 minutes.

Diaphenia – SATB chorus a cappella – 3 minutes.

Corydon, arise – SATB chorus a cappella – 3 minutes.

Quick, we have but a second – SATB chorus a cappella – 30 seconds.

The Revenge op.24 – SATB chorus (with divisions) and orchestra – 15 minutes.

SIR EDWARD ELGAR 1857–1934

Elgar was born in Broadheath, near Worcester, and educated at local schools. His father, William Henry, was a piano technician and owner of a music shop and also organist at St George's Roman Catholic Church in Worcester. Edward did not study music formally but learned to play the violin, organ, and piano after only a few private lessons. Additionally, he acquired skills as a composer from perusing scores in his father's shop. At age fifteen he began working for a solicitor, and in his early twenties he served as concertmaster of both the Worcester Amateur Instrumental Society and the Worcester Philharmonic. During his twenties he also played violin in the orchestras of the Three Choirs Festival (in Worcester in 1878, Hereford in 1881, and Gloucester in 1884). At twenty-five he was appointed conductor of the Worcester Amateur Instrumental Society, and at twenty-eight he succeeded his father as organist at St George's. Having achieved success with several performances of his instrumental works and desiring to be in a more active musical environment, he moved to London in 1890, where, except for teaching a few private students, he devoted his time to composition. His first cantata, *The Black Knight* op.25, premiered in 1893, and his first oratorio, *The Light of Life* op.29, premiered in 1896. His three most famous works—the orchestral *Variations on an Original Theme* (The Enigma Variations) op.36, the oratorio *The Dream of Gerontius* op.38, and the *Military March* (Pomp and Circumstance) op.39 no.1 in D major—premiered in 1899, 1900, and 1901, respectively. Meanwhile, he began conducting the Worcestershire Philharmonic Society in 1897. During the early 1890s he took summer vacations to Germany, where he heard Wagner's *Parsifal* (twice), *Tristan,* and *Die Meistersinger* in Bayreuth in 1892 and the complete Ring cycle in Munich in 1893. Elgar was particularly drawn to the leitmotif manner of musical construction and to Wagner's expanded harmonic vocabulary, both of which he had already employed in *The Dream of Gerontius* and would use further in later works. By the beginning of the twentieth century Elgar had achieved considerable fame. He was granted an honorary doctorate from Cambridge University in 1900, he was knighted by King Edward VII in 1904, and in 1905 he accepted an endowed professorship in his name at Birmingham University. His fame continued to increase during the 1920s (he was named Master of the King's Music in 1924), and during the 1930s he concentrated on recording many of his works. While composing his third symphony, a commission from the British Broadcasting Corporation, he developed cancer and died at the age of seventy-six.

Elgar composed four oratorios, eight cantatas and related choral/orchestral works, fifteen Latin motets, five anthems, and thirty-five part songs. The first oratorio, *The Light of Life,* was written in 1895 and 1896 and premiered at the Three Choirs Festival in Worcester Cathedral (for an encore performance three years later, the solo parts were revised extensively). The oratorio was originally titled "Lux Christi," but the publishing firm Novello and Company asked for an English title so as not to preclude performances by Anglican cathedral choirs. Elgar suggested "The Light that Shineth" but agreed to Novello's recommendation of "The Light of Life." The text is based on the biblical story of Christ restoring sight to a blind beggar, and the music is based on several leitmotifs that are introduced in an orchestral prelude Elgar called a "meditation." The major leitmotif, that representing Jesus as the giver of light to the world, also appears in the oratorio *The Apostles* op.49.

The Dream of Gerontius—considered to be Elgar's choral masterpiece and the greatest English oratorio of the Romantic era—was commissioned and premiered by the Birmingham Triennial Festival. The oratorio's libretto is from an 1865 poem by English theologian Cardinal John Henry Newman (1801–1890) that relates an old man's dream of his death and afterlife (*gerontius* means "old man" in Latin). In the dream, Gerontius accepts the inevitability of his death and asks his friends to pray for him. He then encounters a helpful priest, is joined by an angel who serves as his protector and guide, passes by menacing disposed souls (sung by the chorus), and is greeted by the Angel of the Agony, who served Jesus during his final hours on earth and who grants all deserving souls passage to eternal bliss. The music of the oratorio, like that of *The Light of Life,* is based on leitmotifs, most of which are introduced in a lengthy orchestral prelude and also sung by Gerontius in his first solo passage. Elgar was worried about the libretto's Catholic text, feeling that "the strong Catholic flavour of the poem and its insistence on the doctrine of purgatory would be prejudicial to success in a Protestant community." The Catholic libretto and highly chromatic music no doubt contributed to a flawed premiere performance, which as one observer noted, was "hideous. It was evident that the chorus did not know the parts they were trying to sing, and as the music became more chromatic, they slipped hideously out of tune. It was appalling—far worse than one had thought possible." The critics, however, recognized the greatness of Elgar's music, and highly acclaimed performances were soon presented in Düsseldorf (1901), Worcester (1901 and 1902), Chicago and New York City (1902), and London (1903).

Elgar's third and fourth oratorios, *The Apostles* and *The Kingdom* op.51, were also commissioned and premiered by the Birmingham Triennial Festival. They were intended to be the first two parts of an oratorio trilogy, with a projected oratorio (never composed) to be called "The Last Judgment" as the final part of the trilogy and with *The Light of Life* as a prologue. The text of *The Apostles,* from New Testament and Apocrypha passages compiled by Elgar himself, is divided into a prologue followed by seven scenes, each of which takes place in a different geographical location—"In the Mountain" (also entitled "The Calling of the Apostles"), "By the Wayside," "By the Sea of Galilee," "The Betrayal" (which takes place in Gethsemane, the palace of the high priest, and the temple), "Golgotha," "At the Sepulchre," and "The Ascension" (which takes place in heaven and on earth). The text of *The Kingdom,* similarly assembled by Elgar, is in five scenes that relate the beginnings of the Christian Church—the meeting of the disciples "In the Upper Room," reminiscences of the two Marys "At the Beautiful Gate," the descent of the Holy Spirit in "Pentecost," the healing of the lame man by Peter and John in "The Sign of Healing," and a communion by the disciples in another movement entitled "The Upper Room." Both oratorios share leitmotifs and both were well received by critics and the public. A review of *The Apostles* stated, "At the conclusion [of the performance] the audience remained for a few moments as if spell-bound. . . . Then the enthusiasm was not to be restrained."

The most famous of the cantatas and other miscellaneous choral/orchestral works—*The Music Makers* op.69—began with sketches in 1903 and was completed in 1912 for performance that year at the Birmingham Festival. The text, from an ode in the collection *Music and Moonlight* by British poet Arthur O'Shaughnessy (1844–1881), begins with lines that express Elgar's feelings about the loneliness of the creative artist—"We are the music makers, and we are the dreamers of dreams, wandering by lone sea-breakers, and sitting by desolate streams." Elgar's music for the ode is built on numerous motifs from his previous and most important compositions, including *The Dream of Gerontius,* the *Enigma Variations,* the first and second symphonies, and the *Violin Concerto.*

Other choral/orchestral works include *Scenes from the Bavarian Highlands* op.27, a setting of six poems by Elgar's wife, Alice, about her favorite geographical locations near Garmisch, Bavaria; *Scenes from the Saga of King Olaf* op.30, a cantata premiered by the North Staffordshire Music Festival in 1896, with text from Longfellow's famous poem about the life, battles, and death of the Norse crusader Olaf; and *Caractacus* op.35, a cantata commissioned by the Leeds Festival on the subject of the British chieftain who fought Roman invaders in the early years of Christianity.

The motets and anthems include pieces such as *Pie Jesu* op.2 no.1 (later changed to *Ave verum corpus*), *Ave Maria* op.2 no.2, and *Ave maris stella* op.2 no.3, all three composed for St George's Church while Elgar was organist there in the late 1880s; *O hearken thou* op.64, a setting of verses from Psalm 5 composed as an offertory motet for the coronation of George V; and *They are at rest* (without opus number), an "elegy for unaccompanied chorus" composed in 1909 for a service at the Royal Mausoleum commemorating the anniversary of Queen Victoria's death. Several choral movements from Elgar's oratorios have been extracted and published as anthems. These include "Light of the world, we know thy praise" from *The Light of Life* and "The Spirit of the Lord is upon me" from *The Apostles*.

Elgar downplayed the artistic value of his part songs, calling them "rot" and saying that they were composed in order to pay household bills. However, many of them are considered to be of high artistic stature. *Go, song of mine* op.57 was composed while Elgar was vacationing near Florence in 1909. Its text, a translation of a medieval poem by the English pre-Raphaelite painter and poet Dante Gabriel Rossetti (1828–1882), is dedicated to Alfred Littleton, one of Elgar's greatest supporters. After a five-measure introduction, the music is in ABA format, with a passage marked by Elgar "quasi recitative" sung by the tenors framing the A sections. The "Four Choral Songs" op.53 were composed in February 1907 while Elgar was visiting Rome. Number one of the set, *There is sweet music*, is a setting of the first verse of Tennyson's famous poem *The Lotos-Eaters*, the opening lines of which are, "There is sweet music here that softer falls than petals from blown roses on the grass, or night-dews on still waters between walls of shadowy granite, in a gleaming pass; music that gentlier on the spirit lies, than tired eyelids upon tired eyes; music that brings sweet sleep down from the blissful skies." The music is composed in two keys—the soprano and alto parts are in A-flat major, while the tenor and bass parts are in G major. For the beginning of the piece the parts (and keys) alternate. However, for the latter half of the piece the two keys operate simultaneously. Of striking effect is the alternation of A-flat major and G major chords that end the part song. The second and third numbers of opus 53—*Deep in my soul* and *O wild west wind*—are settings of poetry by Byron and Shelley, respectively.

A number of Elgar's part songs were composed as test pieces for choral competitions in England. That is, all choral ensembles in a competition were required to sing a single test piece. Two of Elgar's pieces in this category are *As torrents in summer* and *Evening Scene* (a particular favorite of the composer).

SACRED WORKS
SELECTED AND LISTED ACCORDING TO FAMILIARITY

The Dream of Gerontius op.38 – STBB solos, SATB chorus, and orchestra (including English horn, bass clarinet, contrabassoon, and organ) – 95 minutes. (1) Solo roles are for an Angel (S), Gerontius (T), a Priest (B), and the Angel of the Agony (B); (2) the soprano solo is in the mezzo-soprano range, and the two solo bass parts are usually sung by the same person; (3) the choral parts occasionally divide into SSSA and SATB/SATB, and in addition, the oratorio closes with choral forces—all singing simultaneously—for a semichorus of Angelicals (SSAA), chorus of Angelicals (SSA), and chorus of Souls (ATTBB).

The Apostles op.49 – SSATTBBB solos, SATB chorus, and orchestra – 126 minutes. (1) Solo roles are for Mary the Blessed Virgin (S), the Angel Gabriel (S), Mary Magdalene (A), a Narrator (T), St John (T), St Peter (B), Judas (B), and Jesus (B); (2) the parts of the narrator and St John are often sung by the same person; (3) the choral parts occasionally divide into SSAATTBB.

The Kingdom op.51 – SATB solos, SATB chorus, and orchestra – 100 minutes. (1) Solo roles are for the Blessed Virgin (S), Mary Magdalene (A), St John (T), and St Peter (B); (2) the choral parts divide into SATB/SATB, with scoring for a semichorus as well.

The Light of Life op.29 – SATB solos, SATB chorus, and orchestra – 63 minutes. (1) Solo roles are for the Mother of the Blind Man (S), a Narrator (A), the Blind Man (T), and Jesus (B); (2) the choral parts occasionally divide into SSAATTBB.

They are at rest – SATB chorus a cappella – 3 minutes. The choral parts occasionally divide into SAATTB.

Ave verum op.2 no.3 – S solo, SATB chorus, and organ – 2:30 minutes.

SECULAR WORKS
SELECTED AND LISTED ACCORDING TO FAMILIARITY

As torrents in summer (from the cantata *Scenes from the Saga of King Olaf* op.30) – SATB chorus a cappella – 2:30 minutes.

Go, song of mine op.57 – SAATTB chorus a cappella – 5 minutes.

There is sweet music op.53 no.1 – SSAA/TTBB chorus a cappella – 5 minutes.

My love dwelt in a northern land op.18 no.3 – SSAATTBB chorus a cappella – 4:30 minutes.

The shower op.71 no.1 – SATB chorus a cappella – 2:30 minutes.

Spanish Serenade ("Stars of the summer night") op.73 no.2 – SATB chorus, two violins, and piano (or chamber orchestra) – 1:45 minutes.

Deep in my soul op.53 no.2 – SAATTBB chorus a cappella – 5 minutes.

O wild west wind op.53 no.3 – SSAATTBB chorus a cappella – 3:30 minutes.

The Music Makers op.69 – A solo, chorus, and orchestra – 39 minutes. The choral parts occasionally divide into SSAATTBB.

Scenes from the Bavarian Highlands op.27 – SATB chorus and piano (original version of 1895) or orchestra (revised version of 1896) – 25 minutes.

Caractacus op.35 – STBBB solos, chorus, and orchestra – 100 minutes.

CHARLES WOOD 1866–1926

Wood was born in Armagh, Ireland, where he received his musical education as a chorister at the Armagh Cathedral. At age seventeen he entered the Royal College of Music in London, and after studying there for five years, chiefly with Stanford and Parry, he was appointed professor of harmony. In the same year as this appointment, he enrolled at Selwyn College, Cambridge, and became assistant to Stanford as conductor of the Cambridge University Musical Society as well as organist at Selwyn College. Wood received a bachelor's degree from Cambridge at twenty-four and both master's and doctoral degrees four years later. He became recognized for several choral/orchestral works, including *Dirge for Two Veterans* composed for the Leeds Festival of 1901 and *Song of the Tempest* composed for the Hovingham Festival of 1902, and in 1904 he was granted an honorary doctorate from Leeds University. An honorary doctorate from Oxford University followed in 1924, the same year that he succeeded Stanford as professor of music at Cambridge University.

Wood composed one mass, one Passion, twelve odes and cantatas, and approximately fifty anthems, motets, and canticles for Anglican Services. The mass and Passion, both composed in the early 1920s, are in a conservative polyphonic style, popular at the time in academic circles. The mass is scored for SATB voices and organ, and the Passion (*St Mark Passion*), which incorporates Gregorian chants and psalter melodies, is scored for STBB solos, chorus, and organ. The important choral/orchestral works were composed mainly during the two decades beginning in 1890 and ending in 1910. In addition to the two odes already mentioned, these include *Ode to the West Wind* of 1890, *Ode on Music* of 1892 to 1893, *Ode on Time* of 1898, and *A Ballad of Dundee* of 1904.

The liturgical music, for which Wood is best known, includes four Communion Services, twenty pairs of the Magnificat and Nunc dimittis, two sets of the Te Deum and Benedictus, and twenty-five anthems and motets. The most popular of these are the *Communion Service in the Phrygian mode* of 1923, the *Magnificat* and *Nunc dimittis* in F major of 1915 for double chorus (called the "Collegium Regale"), and two settings of the Magnificat and Nunc dimittis in E-flat major (referred to as set one and set two). The most famous anthem and one of the most popular anthems of the Romantic era in England—*Hail, gladdening light*—is scored for SATB/SATB chorus a cappella. Other popular anthems are *O king most high, Tis the day of resurrection,* and *O thou, the central orb.*

SAMUEL COLERIDGE-TAYLOR 1875–1912

Coleridge-Taylor was born in London and received his early musical education as a chorister at St George's Presbyterian Church, Croydon. He also learned to play the violin as a child. After his voice changed, he sang in the choir of St Mary Magdalene, Addiscombe, and at age fifteen he entered the Royal College of Music, where he studied composition with Stanford and where his fellow students included Ralph Vaughan Williams, Gustav Holst, John Ireland, and Frank Bridge. At twenty-three Coleridge-Taylor experienced his first success as a composer with the premiere of the cantata *Hiawatha's Wedding Feast,* which was considered to be on an artistic par with Mendelssohn's *Elijah,* and for the next decade he received numerous commissions from major festivals across England. From 1901 to 1904 he was conductor of the Westmorland Festival, in 1903 he was appointed professor of composition at Trinity College of Music in London, from 1904 until his death he was conductor of the Handel Society, and in 1910 he joined the faculty of the Guildhall School of Music. During the first decade of the twentieth century he made several trips to the United States to conduct the Coleridge-Taylor Choral Society—an ensemble based in Washington, D.C., and composed of African-American singers. As a person of African descent himself (his father was from Sierra Leone), he worked throughout his life to increase the stature of black musicians.

Coleridge-Taylor composed twelve cantatas and odes, a Morning and Evening Service plus a separate Te Deum, eight anthems, and twenty-six part songs. The most important of the choral/ orchestral works are three cantatas, published together as opus 30 and set to text from Henry Wadsworth Longfellow's epic 1855 poem *The Song of Hiawatha*. The first cantata, *Hiawatha's Wedding Feast* (1898), is scored for T solo, SATB chorus, and orchestra; the second, *The Death of Minnehaha* (1899), is scored for SB solos, chorus, and orchestra; and the third, *Hiawatha's De- parture* (1900), is scored for STB solos, chorus, and orchestra. Other choral/orchestral works in- clude *Five Choral Ballads* op.54, also set to poetry of Longfellow; *Kubla Kahn* op.61 to texts of the English poet Samuel Taylor Coleridge (1772–1834); and *A Tale of Old Japan* op.76 to poetry of Alfred Noyes (1880–1958).

The anthems include *Break forth into joy* (1892) and *By the waters of Babylon* (1899), and the part songs include *We strew these opiate flowers* and *How they so softly rest* for SSA chorus, and *All my stars forsake me, Dead on the Sierras,* and *The fair Almachara* for SATB chorus. In addi- tion, Coleridge-Taylor composed *Sea Drift* (subtitled a "choral rhapsody") for SSAATTBB chorus a cappella.

❧ THE UNITED STATES ❧

Most of the musical activity in the United States during the Romantic era was in Boston and New York City. All the composers mentioned in this section of the era worked in one or both of the cities, and furthermore, all the composers were born in the northeastern region of the country. Lowell Mason, Arthur Foote, George Whitefield Chadwick, and Horatio Parker were born in Massachusetts; George Frederick Bristow and Edward MacDowell were born in New York; John Knowles Paine was born in Maine; Dudley Buck was born in Connecticut; and Mrs. H. H. A. Beach was born in New Hampshire. The musical education of these composers was not confined to this limited geographical area, however. Five of the nine composers studied in Europe—Paine in Berlin; Buck in Leipzig, Dresden, and Paris; Chadwick in Leipzig and Mu- nich; MacDowell in Paris, Frankfurt, and Munich; and Parker in Munich—and Mrs. Beach lived and concertized in Germany for three years.

The draw of Europe and the veneration of European composers were pervasive phenomena that influenced almost all musical composition in the United States during the Romantic era. Most of the important published collections of music consisted of repertoire by European com- posers, choral societies and festivals were modeled after European organizations, and genres were basic replications of European counterparts in character, scoring, and structural design. For example, the collections of music, such as those published by Mason in the 1820s and Buck in the 1860s and 1870s, featured works or arrangements of works by Haydn, Mozart, and Bee- thoven, and the many choral societies that developed during the nineteenth century gave promi- nence to the performance of oratorios by Handel, Haydn, and Mendelssohn.

The most important and one of the earliest of the American choral societies—the Handel and Haydn Society of Boston—was founded in 1815 to improve "the style of performing sacred music" and to introduce "into more general use the works of Handel and Haydn and other em- inent composers." Notable American premieres of the society included Handel's *Messiah* in

1818, Haydn's *The Creation* in 1819, and Bach's *B minor Mass* in 1887. Similar societies in New York City include the New York Handel and Haydn Society (founded in 1817), the New York Choral Society and the New York Sacred Music Society (both founded in 1824), and the New York Oratorio Society (founded in 1873). Societies in other cities include the Musical Fund Society (1820) and the Philadelphia Choral Society (1897) in Philadelphia, the Sacred Music Society (1840) and the Cecilia Society (1856) in Cincinnati, and the Oratorio Society (1869) and Apollo Club (1872) in Chicago. The most popular works with all the societies were Handel's *Messiah, Judas Maccabaeus,* and *Israel in Egypt;* Haydn's *The Creation;* and Mendelssohn's *Elijah.* Other somewhat popular works were Bach's *St Matthew Passion* (performed in English translation), Schumann's *Paradise and the Peri* (also performed in English translation), and Liszt's *Christus.* The effect of these choral societies to the American cultural fabric was profound. As was reported in the *Musical Record* of 1879, "The knowledge and love of music have prodigiously increased within the last few years. . . . Thousands now assist in choral societies and go to concerts and operas who a few years ago could only have been tempted to hear the simplest ballads and most commonplace pianoforte pieces."

The consequence of so much focus on the music of Bach, Handel, Haydn, and Mendelssohn was also profound, for most of the American composers patterned their compositions on the works of these composers. For example, Bristow's two most important works—the oratorio *Daniel* and symphony *Niagara*—are closely related to Mendelssohn's *Elijah* and *Lobgesang,* Paine's *Mass* in D major and oratorio *St Peter* are based on German Baroque models, Buck's cantata *Legend of Don Munio* replicates the structure of Handel and Mendelssohn oratorios, and Mrs. Beach's *Mass in E-flat* has structural components of Haydn's late masses and melodic elements of Bach's *B minor Mass.* All the American composers of the Romantic era wrote in a conservative style, reflective of the past. None of the composers of the era subscribed to the precepts of Richard Wagner or other composers who forsook traditional forms and structures and who created new fluid, through-composed compositions.

Secular cantatas and odes were the primary genres of composition for the choral societies. Only three composers (Bristow, Paine, and Parker) wrote oratorios, while seven composers (all but Mason and MacDowell) wrote cantatas and odes. The texts for these works were often on American themes (e.g., Bristow's *The Pioneer* and *The Great Republic,* Paine's *Song of Promise,* and Foote's *The Farewell of Hiawatha*), and the American poet Henry Wadsworth Longfellow was a favorite source of textual material.

Anthems and Anglican Services (i.e., liturgical music for the Episcopal Church in America) were the main genres of composition for the church. Only Mason composed hymns, including the popular *Bethany* ("Nearer, my God to thee, nearer to thee") and *Hamburg* ("When I survey the wondrous cross on which the prince of glory died"). However, seven composers (all but Paine and MacDowell) wrote anthems, and four composers (Bristow, Buck, Parker, and Beach) wrote Services.

LOWELL MASON 1792–1872

Mason was born in Medfield, Massachusetts, and received his musical education at a local singing school. During his early teenage years he conducted area church and school choirs, and at eighteen he moved to Savannah, Georgia, where he worked first in a dry goods store and then in a bank. At twenty-three he became the choir director of Savannah's Independent Presbyterian Church and also the superintendent of the church's Sunday School program, and at twenty-eight he added the position of organist. Dedicated to both religious and musical public education for all people, he initiated the first Sunday School program for black children in America, which was begun at the Savannah Independent Presbyterian Church in 1826, and he compiled a hymnal with arrangements of music by "Haydn, Mozart, Beethoven, and Other Eminent Modern Composers Calculated for Public Worship or Private Devotion." To emphasize Mason's commitment to education, the hymnal, published in 1822 as *The Boston Handel and Haydn Society Collection of Church Music,* begins with an "Introduction to the Art of Singing" that is divided into three sections—a brief dictionary of musical terms, a primer on notation and the reading of music, and a collection of vocal exercises. Mason moved to Boston in 1827 to become president and music director of the Handel and Haydn Society (positions he kept until 1832), and in 1829 and 1831, respectively, he published two collections of music for children to use in Sunday School classes—*The Juvenile Psalmist* and *The Juvenile Lyre.* In 1831 he began serving as the choir director at Bowdoin Street Church (built for the famous Presbyterian clergyman Lyman Beecher), and in 1833 he helped found the Boston Academy of Music, which instructed three thousand students in its second year of operation. Between 1837 and 1845 he was superintendent of music for the Boston public school system, and from 1844 to 1851 he served as choir director at Boston's Central Church. Because of his high public profile and contributions to the cultural life of America, New York University granted him an honorary doctorate in 1855, and for much of the 1850s and 1860s many educational and church institutions throughout Europe and the United States invited him to lecture about music education.

Mason's known choral output is small, consisting of approximately thirty original hymns and hymn arrangements and several anthems. Many of the hymns have been consistently published in mainstream Protestant hymnals, and some have become quite popular. These include *Bethany* ("Nearer, my God to thee, nearer to thee"), *Hamburg* ("When I survey the wondrous cross on which the prince of glory died"), *Olivet* ("My faith looks up to thee, thou lamb of Calvary"), and *Malvern* ("Jesus, where'er thy people meet, there they behold thy mercy seat"). The most popular hymn arrangements are *Antioch* ("Joy to the world, the Lord is come, let earth receive her king"), the tune of which is attributed to Handel, and *Azmon* ("O for a thousand tongues to sing my great redeemer's praise") to a tune by Carl G. Gläser (1784–1829). The anthems are represented by *I will extol thee, my God, O king* and *O praise God in his holiness,* both scored for SATB chorus and keyboard accompaniment.

GEORGE FREDERICK BRISTOW 1825–1898

Bristow was born in Brooklyn, New York, the son of conductor and clarinetist William Richard Bristow (1803–1867). George studied piano with his father and violin and harmony with local teachers, and at age thirteen he began playing violin in the Olympic Theatre Orchestra. At eighteen he joined the violin section of the New York Philharmonic, and for the next several decades he played in other area orchestras as well. He remained with the New York Philharmonic until 1879 (thirty-six years), and for a number of these years he also held several conducting positions: from 1851 to 1863 he was conductor of the New York Harmonic Society (with which he directed Handel's *Messiah* and *Israel in Egypt,* Haydn's *The Creation* and *The Seasons,* and Mendelssohn's

Elijah), and from 1851 to 1863 he was conductor of the New York Mendelssohn Union. In addition, he served as choral director at St George's Chapel between 1854 and 1860, and he taught in the New York City public school system from 1854 until his death.

Bristow composed one oratorio, one choral symphony, one mass, five choral/orchestral odes and cantatas, five Anglican Services, and eighteen anthems. The oratorio (*Daniel* op.42) and symphony (*Niagara* op.62) are modeled on works by Mendelssohn: *Daniel* is constructed of recitatives, arias, and choruses and has occasional motivic repetitions as in *Elijah,* and *Niagara* is constructed of three orchestral movements followed by a multisectioned choral finale as in *Lobgesang (Symphony #2).* Further, the translation of *Lobgesang,* "Hymn of Praise," is similar to Bristow's subtitle for *Niagara,* "Hymn to Nature." *Daniel* was composed between 1865 and 1867 and premiered to an enthusiastic audience by the Mendelssohn Union at Steinway Hall in December 1867. Scoring is for two Angels (S and A), Azarrah (T), Meshach (T), Daniel (B), Nebuchadnezzar (B), Arioch (B), a Herald (B), SATB chorus that occasionally divides into SSAATTBB, and orchestra that includes triangle, cymbals, and organ. The work begins with an orchestral overture entitled "The Captivity of Israel," which is followed by a choral movement to verses from Psalm 137:1-6 ("By the waters of Babylon, there we sat down and wept"). The remainder of the oratorio relates the story of Daniel's interpretations of Nebuchadnezzar's dreams. The choral movement in *Niagara* is divided into five sections and scored for T and B solos, SA duet, and SATB chorus. The final section of music quotes portions of the "Hallelujah" chorus from Handel's *Messiah.* Bristow's *Mass in C major* op.57 is similar in construction and style to the D minor and F minor masses of Bruckner.

Three of the odes and cantatas warrant mention—*Gloria Patri, Praise to God* op.31, *The Pioneer* op.49, and *The Great Republic* op.47. The first of these works is scored for SATB solos, SATB chorus, and orchestra and consists of nineteen movements divided into two large parts. The first part is based on the Te Deum text and the second part on the Benedictus. *The Pioneer,* subtitled "A Grand Cantata," is scored for soloists, SATB chorus, and orchestra and relates the struggles of an early American family crossing the frontier. *The Great Republic,* subtitled "Ode to the American Union," is scored for speaker, SATB solos, SATB chorus, and orchestra. The work begins with an overture based on "Hail Columbia" and ends with an elaboration of the "Star-Spangled Banner."

The Anglican liturgical music is best represented by the *Morning Service* op.19, *Morning Service* op.51, *Evening Service* op.36, and *Evening Service* op.56, and the anthems include *Christ our Passover* ("Easter Anthem") op.39, *Light flashing into the darkness* ("Christmas Anthem") op.73, and two works published in the periodical *Tonic Sol-Fa Advocate*—*There is joy today* in 1882 and *O bells of Easter morning* in 1887.

JOHN KNOWLES PAINE 1839–1906

Paine was born in Portland, Maine, where his father owned a music shop and where he studied organ, piano, harmony, and counterpoint with a local musician from Germany. From ages nineteen to twenty-two Paine furthered his studies in Berlin at the Hochschule für Musik and also toured throughout Germany as a concert pianist and organist. When he returned to the United States in 1861, he settled in Boston and was immediately appointed organist at West Church (now known as Old West Church); within six months he also accepted a teaching position at Harvard University. During the following decade he gave organ concerts around Boston and lectures at the New England Conservatory and Boston University, and from 1866 to 1867 he revisited Germany, conducting several of his works, including the *Mass* in D major op.10. In 1875 he was appointed professor of music at Harvard, the first native-born American to hold such a post, and in 1896 he helped found the American Guild of Organists. His music curriculum at Harvard became the model for many other university courses of study in music, and his critically acclaimed performances of European choral works set a standard of excellence that helped elevate the cultural life of America.

Paine composed one mass, one oratorio, nine ceremonial and other occasional works for Harvard, four choral/orchestral works for national expositions, and four cantatas. The *Mass* in D major was composed while Paine was a student in Germany, and it premiered at the Berlin Singakademie during his return visit in 1867. Four movements had been performed previously at Harvard in 1865, and the first complete American performance was at the Music Hall in Boston in 1868. The work is modeled on the cantata masses of the Baroque and Classical eras, with the Gloria and Credo divided into separate movements and with several of those movements scored for solo voices. For instance, the "Quoniam tu solus sanctus" in the Gloria is for tenor solo, the "Et incarnatus est" in the Credo is for soprano solo, and the "Et in spiritum sanctum Dominum" in the Credo is for bass solo. Also Baroque and Classical are the fugues that end the final movements of the Gloria and Credo.

The oratorio *St Peter* op.20 was composed between 1870 and 1872 and was premiered by the Haydn Association of Portland in 1873; the Handel and Haydn Society of Boston performed it the following year. It is modeled on the Bach Passions, with recitatives, arias, choruses, and Lutheran chorales (including "How lovely shines the morning star" and "Praise to the father, the glorious king of creation"). In addition, it is structured in two parts, each with two scenes—"The Divine Call" and "The Denial and Repentance" in part one and "The Ascension" and "Pentecost" in part two. Similarities to Bach works were noted in a review: "One must be very much in love with Bach and very little influenced by the modern taste for lyric forms not to find a certain dryness in *St Peter*." However, as with the Bristow oratorio that preceded it, public and critical responses were generally positive. A review of the first performance projected that *St Peter* would likely take "its place among works of the masters."

The ceremonial works for Harvard, which are all scored for male voices, include *Domine salvum fac* op.8, composed in 1863 for the inauguration of the university's president, and the *Funeral Hymn for a Soldier* op.14 no.1, probably composed in 1863 as well. The most noteworthy of the works for expositions is the *Centennial Hymn* op.27, one of three compositions commissioned for the opening ceremonies of the Philadelphia exposition of 1876 (the other works are *The Centennial Meditation of Columbia* by Dudley Buck and *America Centennial March* by Richard Wagner). Paine's work is a short strophic hymn set to six verses of a poem by John Greenleaf Whittier. Other compositions for expositions include *Columbus March and Hymn* and *Freedom, our Queen* for the World's Columbian Exposition in Chicago in 1893, and *Hymn of the West* for the Louisiana Purchase Exposition in St Louis in 1904.

The well-known cantatas are *The Nativity* op.38 and *Song of Promise* op.43. The first of these, set to verses from John Milton's *On the Morning of Christ's Nativity* of 1629, was composed for and premiered at the sixth triennial festival of the Boston Handel and Haydn Society in 1883. It was well received (one review noted that the work would "add substantially to the reputation of the man who is now recognized as, beyond all rivalry, the first composer of America"), and subsequent performances were given by the Handel and Haydn Society of Pittsburgh and the People's Choral Union of Boston. *Song of Promise,* an ode in three movements, was commissioned by the Cincinnati May Festival and premiered in May 1888. The text is from George E. Woodberry's ode *My Country,* about America's beauty and the ideals of its people, published in the July 1887 issue of *Atlantic Monthly.*

SACRED WORKS
SELECTED AND LISTED ACCORDING TO FAMILIARITY

Mass in D major op.10 – SATB solos, SATB chorus, and orchestra (including organ) – 100 minutes. The choral parts occasionally divide into SSAATTBB.

St Peter op.20 – SATB solos, SATB chorus, and orchestra – 134 minutes. (1) Solo roles are for Peter (B) and unnamed S, A, and T (who serve as narrators and commentators); (2) there is also scoring for twelve male voices who portray "The Twelve Disciples" and for brief passages sung by a Maid Servant (S) and a Man Servant (T); (3) the chorus includes a "Chorus of Angels" (SSAA).

The Nativity op.38 – SATB solos, SATB chorus, and orchestra (including harp and organ) – 150 minutes.

Song of Promise op.43 – S solo, SATB chorus, and orchestra (including organ) – 30 minutes.

DUDLEY BUCK 1839–1909

Buck was born in Hartford, Connecticut, where he began studying music at Trinity College when he was sixteen. At eighteen he went to Europe, furthering his education in Leipzig for three years and then spending a year each in Dresden and Paris. He returned to Hartford in 1862 and was appointed organist at North Congregational Church, and in 1864 he published *Buck's Motette Collection: Containing a Variety of Pieces Suited to the Opening and Close of Divine Worship.* Most of the pieces were by European composers—either original compositions or arrangements. However, a few of them were composed by Buck himself. During the next several years he became increasingly known for his organ concerts, which were presented throughout New York and the New England states and which featured music of Bach and Mendelssohn, and in 1869 he moved to Chicago to serve as organist at St James' Church. After the Great Fire of 1871, which destroyed his home and all his musical scores, he returned to the East Coast, settling in Boston and taking the post of organist for the Music Hall Association. The *Second Motette Collection* was published in 1871, the same year he began teaching at the New England Conservatory and serving as organist at St Paul's Church. In 1875 he relocated to New York City, where he was appointed assistant conductor of the Theodore Thomas Orchestra and organist at St Ann's Episcopal Church in Brooklyn. In 1877 he moved from St Ann's to Holy Trinity in New York City and also became director of the newly founded Apollo Club. He left Holy Trinity in

1901, took over the music program at Plymouth Congregational Church in 1902, and in 1903 he retired from all positions and subsequently made several trips back to Europe.

Buck composed one large-scale sacred work, eleven secular cantatas (five for mixed voices and six for men's voices), two Anglican Services, fifty-five anthems, and several part songs. The large-scale sacred work, *The Forty-Sixth Psalm* op.57, was composed in the early 1870s and performed in 1874 by several prominent choral groups, including the Handel and Haydn Society of Boston and the Philharmonic Society of Rhode Island. The work is scored for SATB soloists, SATB chorus, and orchestra and is divided into seven movements—three for chorus, two for soloists (T and B), one for SATB quartet, and one for S solo and SSAATTBB quartet.

In chronological order, the secular cantatas for mixed voices are *Festival Hymn, The Legend of Don Munio, The Centennial Meditation of Columbia, Scenes from The Golden Legend,* and *Light of Asia.* The first of these is a short strophic work for chorus and orchestra, commissioned for the World Peace Jubilee in 1872. *The Legend of Don Munio* is an expansive work in twenty-three movements, premiered by the Harvard Musical Association in 1874. The text, from *The Spanish Papers* by Washington Irving (1783–1859), is about conflicts between Christians and Muslims in Spain and the Holy Land. The music is structurally similar to the oratorios of Handel and Mendelssohn, with recitatives, arias, and choruses. *The Centennial Meditation of Columbia* was commissioned for the 1876 Centennial Exhibition in Philadelphia. The text, specifically written by Sidney Lanier (1842–1881) for Buck and the exhibition, is about the journey of the Pilgrims in the Mayflower, the trials they faced in the American settlements, and their triumph over adversity and thanks to God. The music is scored for brief B solo, SATB chorus (with parts for SSAATTBB semichorus), and orchestra (including military drum, bass drum, and cymbals). *Scenes from The Golden Legend* was composed as a competition piece for the Cincinnati May Festival of 1880. The text is from Henry Wadsworth Longfellow's famous poem about a prince who suffers from an illness that can be cured only by a maiden's pure and willing sacrifice. *Light of Asia* is an oratorio-like work that was popular during the final decades of the nineteenth century. It was premiered by the New York Philharmonic and Newark Harmonic Society in 1887, performed at St James' Hall in London in 1889 (at which time it was declared to be the first performance of an American cantata in Europe), and later performed in New York City, Detroit, and Hartford. The text, from *the Light of Asia, or, the Great Renunciation* by Sir Edwin Arnold (1832–1904), is about Siddartha Gautama, who renounces life as an earthly prince, seeks enlightenment for six years, and then becomes the Buddha. The music is modeled after Mendelssohn's *Elijah.*

The secular cantatas for men were all composed for the Apollo Club of New York City and scored with accompaniment of string quintet, flute, piano, and organ (the chamber orchestration no doubt reflects Buck's desire to balance the twenty-three voices in the Apollo Club). The first two cantatas, *The Nun of Nidaros* and *King Olaf's Christmas,* are both settings of ballads from Longfellow's *The Musician's Tale - The Saga of King Olaf.* The third cantata, *The Chorus of Spirits and Hours,* is from Percy Shelley's *Prometheus Unbound,* and the fourth, *The Voyage of Columbus,* is to a text in both German and English by Buck himself based on Washington Irving's *The Life and Voyages of Christopher Columbus,* book three. The fifth cantata, *Bugle Song,* is set to a poem by Sidney Lanier, and the sixth, *Paul Revere's Ride,* is a setting of Longfellow's famous poem from *The Landlord's Tale.* This last cantata is based on the "Star-Spangled Banner," which is employed as a leitmotif.

The Services, both scored for chorus and organ, are the *Midnight Service for New Year's Eve* of 1880 and the *Communion Service in C major* of 1892. The anthems, also scored for chorus and organ, include *I will lift up mine eyes, Sing alleluia forth, He shall come down like rain, Darkly rose the guilty morning,* and *O how amiable.* The part songs, scored for SATB chorus a cappella, include *Break, break, break* from *Six Part Songs* op.10.

ARTHUR FOOTE 1853–1937

Foote was born in Salem, Massachusetts, where at age twelve he began piano lessons with a local teacher. At fourteen he enrolled at the New England Conservatory and at seventeen began studying with John Knowles Paine at Harvard University. Foote conducted the Harvard Glee Club from 1872 to 1874 and received a bachelor's degree in 1874 and a master's degree in 1875. In 1876 he was appointed organist at the Church of the Disciples in Boston, and two years later he became organist at Boston's First Unitarian Church. While maintaining his work at the church, he gave piano recitals and taught piano lessons and he took several trips to Europe. He helped found the American Guild of Organists in 1896, serving as its president from 1909 to 1912, and he was also active in the Music Teachers National Association. Meanwhile, he resigned his position at the Unitarian church in 1910, served as a guest lecturer at the University of California, Berkeley, in 1911, and from 1921 until his death he taught piano at the New England Conservatory. He is best known for his textbook *Modern Harmony in Its Theory and Practice* of 1905, which he coauthored with Walter R. Spalding.

Foote composed four choral/orchestral cantatas, thirty-five anthems, and fifty-two part songs. Three of the cantatas are settings of poetry by Henry Wadsworth Longfellow—*The Farewell of Hiawatha,* composed in 1885 and scored for men's chorus and orchestra; *The Wreck of the Hesperus,* composed between 1887 and 1888 and scored for mixed chorus and orchestra; and *The Skeleton in Armor,* composed in 1891 and scored for mixed chorus and orchestra. The fourth cantata, *Lygeia,* is a setting of text by G. Rogers, composed in 1906 and scored for women's voices and orchestra. Most of the anthems—including *Does the road wind uphill all the way* for alto solo, SATB quartet or chorus, and organ—were composed for the First Unitarian Church of Boston. None of the part songs are known today.

GEORGE WHITEFIELD CHADWICK 1854–1931

Chadwick was born in Lowell, Massachusetts, where he studied music with an older brother and began playing the organ publicly at age fifteen. At seventeen he began studying organ with Dudley Buck at the New England Conservatory, and at twenty-two he joined the faculty of Olivet College in Olivet, Michigan. The following year he went to Europe, studying first at the University of Leipzig and then at the Hochschule für Musik in Munich with Joseph Rheinberger, and while in Germany he experienced success with his first two string quartets and concert overture *Rip Van Winkle.* He returned to Boston in 1880, and during the next several years he taught privately and conducted a number of ensembles, including the Arlington Club men's chorus. In 1882 he joined the faculty of the New England Conservatory, in 1883 he was appointed organist at South Congregational Church (a position he held until 1893), and during the 1890s he also directed several festival organizations, including the Springfield Festival from 1890 to 1899 and the Worcester Festival from 1897 to 1901. He became the director of the New England Conservatory in 1897, and for most of the remainder of his life he concentrated on teaching and administrative duties and composing stage works (e.g., *The Padrone*).

Chadwick composed nine odes and cantatas, thirty-seven anthems, and thirty-nine part songs (nineteen for male chorus and twenty for female chorus). The odes and cantatas include *Ode for the Opening of the Chicago World's Fair*, composed in 1892 and scored for ST solos, SATB chorus, orchestra, and three separate woodwind ensembles; *Ecce jam noctis*, composed in 1897 for men's chorus, organ, and orchestra; and the Christmas cantata *Noël*, composed in 1907 and 1908 and scored for solo voices, chorus, and orchestra.

EDWARD MACDOWELL 1860–1908

MacDowell was born in New York City and began piano lessons when he was eight years old. At sixteen he went to Europe and studied at the Paris Conservatoire, at eighteen he moved to Stuttgart and then Wiesbaden, and at nineteen he enrolled at the Hoch Konservatorium in Frankfurt. After a year there he established a studio and taught privately, and for the 1881–1882 academic year he joined the faculty of the Städtische Akademie für Tonkunst in Darmstadt. During the next several years he experienced successes with a few of his compositions for piano, and in 1888 he returned to the United States—opening a studio in Boston, giving piano recitals, and composing. In 1896 he was appointed the first professor of music at Columbia University in New York City and also the conductor of the Mendelssohn Glee Club. He left the glee club after only two years and resigned from Columbia in 1904, and for the final years of his life, suffering from severe mental illness, he engaged in little musical activity. In 1907, however, he and his wife, Marian Nevins MacDowell, established the MacDowell Colony at their home in Peterborough, New Hampshire. This colony, which is still in existence today, is a retreat for composers, artists, authors, playwrights, filmmakers, and architects, and has supported the careers of noteworthy composers such as Leonard Bernstein, Aaron Copland, Michael Hennagin, Norman Dello Joio, and Lukas Foss.

MacDowell composed twenty-four part songs—eighteen for male chorus, three for female chorus, and three for mixed chorus. The most significant of the male chorus pieces—the *Drei Lieder für vierstimmigen Männerchor* (Three songs for four-voiced men's chorus) op.27—were composed in 1887 while MacDowell was in Germany. Dedicated to the conductor of the Zurich Gesangvereins Harmonie, the three pieces were set to both German and English texts (i.e., MacDowell translated the original German, with the intention that the part songs be sung in either language). Number one of the set, *Oben wo die Sterne glühen* (In the starry sky above), is a setting of poetry by Heine; the text of number two, *Schweizerlied* (Springtime), is by Goethe; and number three, *Der Fischerknabe* (The fisherboy) is set to a poem by Schiller. The textures of all three part songs are homophonic, and the scoring is for TTBB a cappella except for number two, which is for TTBBB. The part songs for female chorus are *Two College Songs* ("Alma mater" and "At Parting") and *Summer Wind*.

Perhaps the best-known American part songs of the Romantic era are the *Two Northern Songs* op.43, composed between 1890 and 1891 and set to poetry by MacDowell himself. Number one, *The Brook,* has a strophic quality in that the second half of the piece is similar to the first in melodic and rhythmic design. Number two, *Slumber Song,* is unified by several repetitions of the opening melodic material. Both pieces are scored for SATB voices a cappella, with occasional divisions for SATBB.

HORATIO PARKER 1863–1919

Parker was born in Auburndale, Massachusetts, near Boston, and began taking piano and organ lessons from his mother at age fourteen. He later studied composition with George Chadwick in Boston, and at nineteen he went to Europe to study composition with Joseph Rheinberger at the Hochschule für Musik in Munich. While in Europe, Parker also made frequent trips to England to attend choral festival performances. Upon returning to the United States in 1885, he served as organist and choirmaster at St Luke's Church in Boston until 1887, at St Andrew's Church in New York City (Harlem) in 1887 and 1888, and at Holy Trinity Church in New York City from 1888 to 1893. He also taught at the cathedral schools of St Paul and St Mary in Garden City, Long Island, from 1886 to 1890; at the General Theological Seminary of the Episcopal Church in 1892; and at the National Conservatory of Music in 1892 and 1893. In 1893 he went back to Boston to become organist and choirmaster at the historic Trinity Church on Copley Square, and the following year he was appointed professor of music at Yale University (a position he kept for the remainder of his life, adding that of dean of the School of Music in 1904). While teaching at Yale, he formed the New Haven Symphony Orchestra and conducted it from 1895 to 1918, and from 1903 until 1914 he also conducted the New Haven Choral Society. He traveled to England several times between 1899 and 1902 for performances of his cantatas, and in 1902 he was given an honorary doctorate from Cambridge University. That same year he resigned his position at Trinity Church and became organist and choirmaster at the Dutch Reformed Collegiate Church of St Nicholas in New York City. He suffered from poor health after 1910 (the year he left St Nicholas), and died of pneumonia at age fifty-six.

Parker's choral output consists of fourteen cantatas and oratorios, ten miscellaneous choral/orchestral odes and occasional works, three Anglican Services, twenty-four anthems, one motet, and thirty-one part songs. The most famous of his cantatas and oratorios, and without a doubt the most famous large-scale choral/orchestral American work of the Romantic era, is *Hora novissima* op.30, composed for the Church Choral Society of New York (whose president at the time was J. Pierpont Morgan) and premiered under Parker's direction at Holy Trinity Church on May 3, 1893. The work was immediately popular and was performed by the Boston Handel and Haydn Society and the Cincinnati Festival Chorus in 1894; at the Three Choirs Festival in Worcester, England, in 1899; and at the Chester Festival in 1900. Subtitled "The Rhythm of Bernard De Morlaix on the Celestial Country," its text is taken from the first part ("A vision of paradise") of the medieval poem *De contemptu mundi* by Bernard of Cluny. The music is scored for SATB solos, SATB chorus, and orchestra (including harp and organ), with each of the soloists assigned a substantial aria plus sections for quartet in three movements, and with the choral parts divided into SATB/SATB in one movement. The work is often referred to as an oratorio, although Parker did not call it that, and the term did not appear in the work's publication or in the program of the premiere performance. Furthermore, the text does not convey a dramatic story and the music does not have recitatives as were typical in oratorios of the day. With its structure of arias and choruses, it is better classified as a cantata.

Other important choral/orchestral works include the cantata *Dream-King and His Love* op.31, composed in 1891 and scored for T solo, SATB chorus, and orchestra; the oratorio *The Legend of St Christopher* op.43, composed for the New York Oratorio Society and premiered in 1898; and *A Wanderer's Psalm* op.50, composed for the Three Choirs Festival in Hereford, England, in 1900. The a cappella chorus "Jam sol recedit" (Now sinks the sun) from *The Legend of St Christopher* is often extracted from the oratorio and performed separately.

The cantatas include two works for Christmas—*The Holy Child* op.37 for STB solos, SATB chorus, and organ or piano, and *The Shepherd's Vision* op.63 for SATB solos, SATB chorus, and organ (with parts for oboe, strings, and harp ad lib.). Two of Parker's late choral/orchestral works are the oratorio *Morven and the Grail* op.79, commissioned by the Handel and Haydn Society of Boston for its centennial celebration in 1915, and the cantata *A.D. 1919* op.84, composed in 1919 to commemorate Yale graduates killed in World War I.

The Services consist of *Morning, Evening, and Communion* in E major of 1890, *Magnificat and Nunc dimittis* in E-flat major of 1893, and *Communion* in B-flat major of 1904. The best-known anthems are *Light's glittering morn* for B solo, chorus, and organ, and *God that makest earth and heaven* for SATB chorus and keyboard accompaniment. The motet is *Adstant angelorum chori*, composed in 1899 for SSAATTBB chorus a cappella.

Most of the part songs were composed for male chorus, including *Mountain Shepherd's Song* op.1 of 1883; *Blow, blow thou winter wind* op.14 of 1888; Three Choruses op.33 of 1893 (*My love, Three words,* and *Valentine*); and Three Part Songs op.48 (*Awake, my lady sweetlips, The lamp in the west,* and *The night has a thousand eyes*).

AMY (MRS. H. H. A.) BEACH 1867–1944

Amy Cheney (her maiden name) was born in Henniker, New Hampshire, the daughter of paper manufacturer Charles Abbott Cheney. At age two she improvised melodies on the piano with her mother, an amateur singer and pianist, and at four she could recall and play tunes from memory. She started piano lessons with her mother at six, and at seven she played works by Handel, Beethoven, Chopin, and others in public. Gaining fame as a concert pianist, she made her debut at seventeen with the Boston Symphony Orchestra, playing Chopin's *Piano Concerto in F minor* op.21. She curtailed her public performances the following year, however, when she married Dr. Henry Harris Aubrey Beach, a physician and lecturer on anatomy at Harvard University, who was twenty-four years her senior. For the remainder of her life she preferred to be called and listed her name as Mrs. H. H. A. Beach. She taught herself harmony, counterpoint, fugue, and orchestration and composed many of her best-known works during her twenties and thirties. Her most popular song, *Ecstasy* op.19 no.2, was composed in 1893; the *Gaelic Symphony* in E minor op.32, acknowledged to be the first symphony composed by an American woman, was premiered to critical acclaim in 1896; and the *Piano Concerto* in C-sharp minor op.45 was first performed in 1899. Other notable works include the song "The Year's at the Spring" op.44 no.1 from *Three Browning Songs* of 1900, and the *Piano Quintet* op.67 of 1907.

With the death of her husband in 1910, Mrs. Beach moved to Europe and resumed her concert career, receiving rave reviews for performances of her *Piano Concerto* in Berlin, Hamburg, and Leipzig. She returned to the United States in 1914, and for the next sixteen years she kept active as a concert recitalist and composer. After 1921 she spent the summers at the MacDowell Colony, and in 1925 she cofounded and served as the first president of the Society of American Women Composers. Throughout her career she maintained a late-Romantic style of composition, a style that was continuously popular with audiences but regarded by critics as old-fashioned by the third and fourth decades of the twentieth century. One of Mrs. Beach's early biographers wrote in 1940, "By most musicians of today, though not at all by the large public, this late nineteenth-century post-romantic music is regarded with scant respect and as of no interest."

Mrs. Beach composed one mass, one Anglican Service, approximately ten canticles and related Service music, twenty-four anthems and motets, and thirty-four secular works (twenty for female chorus, four for children, four for male chorus, and six for mixed voices). The *Mass in E-flat* op.5 was composed in 1890 and premiered by the Handel and Haydn Society of Boston with members of the Boston Symphony Orchestra on February 2, 1892. A review in *The Boston Herald* the following day commented that the work showed "genius in the line of composition, melodious ideas, and skill in the development and elaboration of themes." The work contains many elements of the late masses by Joseph Haydn, including choral textures that are alternately imitative and homophonic, writing for soloists that alternates between melodic and quartet passages, and Gloria and Credo movements that are divided into separate sections delineated by varying tempos. As another tribute to the past, the second Kyrie and the "Dona nobis pacem" portion of the Agnus Dei are based on melodic material from the beginning of the "Gratias agimus tibi" and "Dona nobis pacem" of Bach's *B minor Mass*.

The three most important sacred works are the *Service in A* op.63, *Festival Jubilate* op.17, and *The Canticle of the Sun* op.123. The *Service in A*, which contains music for both the Morning and Evening Services of the Episcopal Church, was composed between 1904 and 1905. The Te Deum and Benedictus portions of the Service were first performed at Emmanuel Church in Boston in the spring of 1906, and thereafter, all the portions of the Service were regularly performed at St Bartholomew's Episcopal Church in New York City. The Te Deum is distinctive in opening with a unison choral statement of the Te Deum chant from John Merbecke's *Book of Common Praier Noted* of 1550. *Festival Jubilate* was Mrs. Beach's first commissioned work and presumably the first work commissioned of an American woman composer. It was composed at the behest of the Board of Lady Managers of the Chicago World's Columbian Exposition of 1893 and performed for the dedication ceremonies of the Women's Building. The work is a setting of Psalm 100 with the addition of the Gloria Patri, and it is structured in an ABA format. *The Canticle of the Sun* was composed in five days at the MacDowell Colony during the summer of 1924. The first performance, at New York City's St Bartholomew's Episcopal Church in December 1928, was with organ accompaniment. The first orchestral performance was by the Toledo Choral Society and the Chicago Symphony in May 1930. Subsequent performances took place at Riverside Church in New York City and at several annual meetings of the American Guild of Organists. The text is a translation by Matthew Arnold (1822–1888) of St Francis of Assisi's *Canticum Solis*. The music is in ABA form, with numerous statements and manipulations of two primary motifs that pervade the work.

Mrs. Beach's most important secular work, *The Sea-Fairies* op.59, is a setting of Alfred, Lord Tennyson's revised poem of the same name based on book twelve of Homer's *The Odyssey* and published in 1853. The music was composed for the Thursday Morning Musical Club of Boston, a concert society founded in 1887, and it premiered at a club's meeting in February 1905 with piano accompaniment. The orchestral version was first performed the following April by the Eurydice Chorus and orchestra in Philadelphia, conducted by Walter Damrosch. Like many of Mrs. Beach's other works, *The Sea-Fairies* is in a traditional ABA format.

SACRED WORKS
SELECTED AND LISTED ACCORDING TO FAMILIARITY

Mass in E-flat major op.5 – SATB solos, SATB chorus, and orchestra (including organ) – 64 minutes.

The Canticle of the Sun op.123 – SATB solos, SATB chorus, and orchestra – 22 minutes.

Festival Jubilate op.17 – SSAATTB chorus and orchestra (including harp) – 20 minutes.

Service in A op.63 – SATB solos, SATB chorus, and organ – Te Deum (9 minutes), Benedictus (7 minutes), Jubilate Deo (6:15 minutes), Magnificat (8:30 minutes), and Nunc dimittis (5:30 minutes).

Help us, O God op.50 – SSATB chorus a cappella – 11:30 minutes.

Lord of all being op.146 – SATB chorus and organ – 7:15 minutes.

SECULAR WORKS
SELECTED AND LISTED ACCORDING TO FAMILIARITY

The Sea-Fairies op.59 – SSA solos, SSAA chorus, and orchestra of two flutes, two clarinets, two horns, harp, and strings – 20 minutes.

The Chambered Nautilus op.66 – SA solos, SSAA chorus, and orchestra (including organ) – 18 minutes.

Three Shakespeare Choruses op.39 – SSAA chorus and piano – "Over hill, over dale" (3 minutes), "Come unto these yellow sands" (3:30 minutes), and "Through the house give glimmering light" (3 minutes).

6

THE MODERN ERA

The Modern era began during the early years of the twentieth century when composers felt that the genres, tonalities, scorings, and notational symbols of the Romantic era could no longer satisfy their creative needs. Traditional genres were too confining for new ideas of expression, harmonic language based on functional tonality seemed to be exhausted, additional and unique colors were needed in scoring, and innovative elements of notation were required to manifest revolutionary concepts of communication. Consequently, dramatic changes affected virtually every element of music making. New genres ranged from stage productions that incorporated dance (e.g., Claude Debussy's *Le martyre de St Sébastien*) to vocal chamber music scored for a large ensemble of highly skilled soloists (e.g., Olivier Messiaen's *Cinq rechants* for twelve singers); experiments in new tonalities resulted in the dodecaphonic (twelve-tone) technique, pandiatonicism, bitonality, atonality, and divisions of the traditional chromatic scale into smaller units than half steps; scorings for uncommon colors included wordless chorus as an orchestral instrument, sprechstimme, numerous percussion instruments, and electronic sounds and instruments; and new notation consisted of a wide range of symbols to indicate such performance elements as variations in vibrato, speaking, singing in falsetto, producing the highest or lowest notes possible, and yelling, hissing, whispering, and so on. In addition, aleatoric performance became a feature of a number of Modern-era compositions; it is especially evident in passages of indeterminate rhythm within traditionally metered music.

New concepts of musical expression and new sounds, rhythms, and textures also resulted from exposure of twentieth- and twenty-first-century composers to a vast array of music from across the world. Beginning with the Universal Exposition in Paris in 1889 and continuing with the cultural exchanges that resulted from ease and frequency of international travel, composers heard unfamiliar popular idioms and music from non-Western cultures. As an outcome of this opportunity, Asian elements became particularly evident in music of the early modern French composers, and jazz styles were incorporated into the textures of twentieth-century German works.

The music of the Modern era has not, however, all been the result of desires to break with the past and create something new. On the contrary, many Modern-era composers have been committed to the revitalization of traditional genres and the restoration of older styles. This trend has occurred, in large part, because a wide range and prodigious amount of music from past centuries has been published, performed, made available in libraries, and studied in educational curricula, with the result that Modern-era composers have recognized the artistic value of these older compositions and have desired to contribute to long-standing traditions. Notable examples include neo-Medieval masses by Igor Stravinsky; neo-Renaissance a cappella masses by Ralph Vaughan Williams, Francis Poulenc, Vincent Persichetti, and Paul Hindemith; neo-Renaissance chansons by Debussy, Maurice Ravel, Messiaen, Hindemith, and Morten Lauridsen; neo-Renaissance madrigals by Hindemith, Elliott Carter, Jacob Druckman, and Lauridsen; neo-Baroque cantatas and Passions by Hugo Distler and Ernst Pepping; neo-Classical Psalm settings by Stravinsky; neo-Romantic oratorios by William Walton, Vaughan Williams, and Daniel Pinkham; and neo-Romantic part songs by Benjamin Britten and Samuel Barber.

Interest in folk music also contributed to the propagation of older genres and styles. Nationalistic pride spurred Hungarian composers such as Zoltán Kodály and Béla Bartók, British composers such as Gustav Holst and Vaughan Williams, and Estonian composers such as Veljo Tormis to research traditional folk songs of their countries, promote these songs through relatively unaltered transcriptions, and also incorporate elements of the folk music into their original compositions.

As a result of the divergence between creating new modes of expression and emulating old practices, and also as a result of the many disparate characteristics of composition, the Modern era, unlike all the previous historical eras, does not have a unifying stylistic characteristic or a combination of attributes that define it with relative clarity. A highly diversified and eclectic amalgam of compositional techniques has been exhibited throughout the era and in most of the countries of the Western Hemisphere. France was the first country to produce composers who broke away from Romantic-era styles and who created new modes of expression; especially significant were the harmonic innovations of Debussy and Ravel. Other European countries followed, with composers who created different new modes of musical expression—Austria and Germany with twelve-tone techniques, Italy and Spain with atonality and scoring for electronics, and the Eastern European countries with tone clusters and techniques such as aleatoric rhythms. The Scandinavian countries added to the array of avant-garde techniques (e.g., graphic notation), Russia and Estonia have been eclectic, and England and the United States have been mainly conservative in scoring and harmonic language. South America and Canada, also mainly conservative, have not produced a large number of composers and therefore have not made a significant impact on the development of choral music. Nevertheless, there are a number of composers from both countries who should be mentioned—Heitor Villa-Lobos, Alberto Ginastera, Antonio Estévez, Juan Orrego-Salas, Ariel Ramírez, and Osvaldo Golijov from South America, and Healey Willan, Godfrey Ridout, R. Murray Schafer, Imant Raminsh, and Eleanor Daley from Canada.

Villa-Lobos (1887–1959) was born in Rio de Janeiro, Brazil, and in his youth learned to play the clarinet, cello, and guitar. His father was an amateur musician who encouraged his son's musical development. However, Heitor did not study music formally. Instead, he learned compositional techniques from transcribing folk songs he collected from around the country, studying scores of European masters (especially J. S. Bach), and conversing with composers such as Darius Milhaud, who lived in Rio de Janeiro in 1917 and 1918. In 1923 Villa-Lobos went to Paris, where he met Ravel, d'Indy, Stravinsky, and Prokofiev and where he gained a degree of fame with his compositions based on South American folk material. After returning to Rio de Janeiro in 1923, Villa-Lobos devoted himself to music education, serving as superintendent of musical and artistic education for the city and promoting a cappella singing throughout Brazil. He became director of the newly established National Conservatory of Orpheonic (a cappella) Singing in 1942, and in 1945 he founded the Brazilian Academy of Music. In addition, he served as a musical ambassador for Brazil by touring the United States and conducting orchestras such as the Los Angeles Philharmonic, Boston Symphony, and New York Philharmonic. His most famous compositions were the series of nine suites called *Bachianas Brasileiras* (Tributes to Bach in a Brazilian style), each scored for a different combination of instruments or instruments and voices. The fifth suite, the best known, is for soprano solo and eight cellos, and the ninth suite is for wordless chorus or string orchestra or both together. Another series of suites for varied scoring, entitled *Chôros* (Brazilian street musicians), also involves chorus—number three for men's voices, clarinet, saxophone, bassoon, and three horns; number ten for SSAATTBB chorus and orchestra; and number fourteen for mixed chorus and band or orchestra. Other noteworthy choral works include *Missa São Sebastião* for three-part chorus, *Ave Maria* for SAATBB chorus a cappella, and *Magnificat-alleluia* for S solo, SATB chorus, and orchestra.

Ginastera (1916–1983) was born in Buenos Aires, Argentina, and was educated there at the Williams Conservatory and National Conservatory of Music. As a young man he became known for his ballet scores, and in 1941 he joined the faculties of the National Conservatory and San Martín National Military Academy. Between 1945 and 1947 he lived in the United States, where he studied at the Berkshire Music Center with Aaron Copland and visited prominent music schools, including Juilliard, Eastman, and Yale, and in 1948, upon returning to Argentina, he began teaching at the National University of La Plata. During the 1950s Ginastera traveled frequently to Europe to conduct his works, in 1958 he was appointed dean of the Catholic University of Argentina, and in 1963 he became director of the Latin American Centre for Advanced Musical Studies at the Instituto Torcuato di Tella. In 1966 his opera *Don Rodrigo* was presented by the New York City Opera at the opening of the New York State Theatre at Lincoln Center, and for the remaining years of his life he worked to complete numerous commissions. Ginastera's compositional output includes only three choral works—*Psalm 150*, a setting in Latin written as his graduation exercise from the National Conservatory, with scoring for SATB chorus (with divisions), unison boys' chorus, and orchestra; *Hieremiae prophetae lamentationes* (Lamentations of Jeremiah) for SATB chorus (with divisions) a cappella; and *Turbae ad passionem gregorianam* for TBB solos, SATB chorus (with divisions), boys' chorus, and orchestra. In an expanded tonal idiom, all the music is characterized by high tessituras and strong expressive demands.

Estévez (1916–1988) was born in Calabozo, Venezuela, and educated at the Escuela de Música y Declamación. Further studies were at Columbia University and the Berkshire Music Center. Between 1934 and 1945 he was an oboist in the Venezuela Symphony Orchestra, and from 1940 to 1948 he taught at the National School of Music in Caracas. He is known for his *Cantata criolla* of 1954 (sometimes called *Florentino, el que cantó con el diablo*), a work based on the legend about the devil challenging a folk singer to a duel and set to music that combines traditional folk elements and early modern styles of Debussy and Stravinsky.

Orrego-Salas (b.1919) was born in Santiago, Chile, where he studied music privately. In his early twenties he taught at the Santiago Conservatory and conducted the Catholic University choir, and between 1944 and 1946 he continued his education with Randall Thompson and Aaron Copland in the United States. From 1947 until 1961 he held several positions in Chile— professor of composition at the University of Chile, director of the Instituto de Extensión Musical, and dean of the music department at Catholic University—and in 1961 he returned to the United States to serve as director of the Latin American Music Center at Indiana University. His choral works, all in a neo-Classical idiom with expanded tonal harmonies characterized by chromatic melodies, include *Missa in tempore discordiae* (Mass in time of discord) of 1968 to 1969 for T solo, SATB chorus, four flutes, four clarinets, four trombones, percussion, piano, and strings; the oratorio *The Days of God,* set to biblical passages and poetry by Pablo Neruda and Dylan Thomas and scored for SATB solos, SATB chorus, and orchestra; and *Three madrigals* of 1967 and *Villancico* of 1969 for SATB chorus a cappella.

Ramírez (b.1921) was born in Santa Fe, Argentina, and in his youth became interested in the folk music of local gauchos and creoles. He studied music formally at the National Conservatory in Buenos Aires, with additional studies in Madrid, Rome, and Vienna, but he retained his interest in folk music and eventually collected and transcribed more than four hundred melodies. He founded the Compañía de Folklore Ariel Ramírez and became president of the Society of Authors and Composers of the Republic of Argentina (SADAIC). He is best known for his *Misa Criolla* of 1964, a liturgical setting of the five portions of the Roman Mass Ordinary plus the Ite missa est, set in the vernacular (Castilian) and based on the music of native folk dances. Scoring is for T solo, SATB chorus, percussion (including native Andean instruments), and keyboard. Other popular choral works include *Navidad Nuestra* of 1964, *Cantata Sudamericana* of 1972, and *Misa por la paz y la justicia* of 1980.

Golijov (b.1960) was born in La Plata, Argentina, to Eastern European Jewish parents who surrounded their son with Jewish liturgical and klezmer music as well as Argentinian tangos. In 1983 Osvaldo began studies in Israel at the Jerusalem Rubin Academy, and in 1986 he moved to the United States, where he studied with George Crumb at the University of Pennsylvania. Golijov became known for *La Pasión según San Marcos* (St Mark Passion), commissioned by the Internationale Bachakademie to commemorate the 250th anniversary of J. S. Bach's death and premiered in Stuttgart in September 2000. The text of the oratorio, mostly in Spanish, includes passages from St Mark's account of the Passion story, Jeremiah's lamentations, several Psalms, and the Kaddish. Scoring is for major female and male solos plus a number of other incidental solos that are to be sung by chorus members, large SATB chorus (divided into three ensembles at times), four percussionists, accordion, guitar, piano, two trumpets, two trombones, twelve violins, eight cellos, and four string basses. In addition, the score calls for Afro-Cuban and Capoeira dancers. The musical style is intentionally eclectic, with a wide array of popular Latin idioms that, in the composer's words, would "cover everything."

Other Modern-era Spanish-speaking composers include Gilberto Mendes (b.1922) from Brazil, Mario Lavista (b.1943) from Mexico, and Roberto Sierra (b.1953) from Puerto Rico. All these composers studied in their homelands as well as in Europe at modernist centers such as Darmstadt and Utrecht, and all incorporate avant-garde techniques or Medieval and Renaissance structures in their choral music. Mendes' *Motet em Ré Menor* (Motet in D minor) for SATB chorus a cappella, subtitled "Beba Coca-Cola," features repeated notes that form tone clusters and aleatoric rhythmic passages; Lavista's *Missa Brevis ad consolationis Dominam nostram* for SATB chorus a cappella is characterized by neo-Medieval usage of canons and hocket in a dissonant tonal idiom; and Sierra's *Missa Latina* for SB solos, SATB chorus, and orchestra is in a style that contrasts Renaissance imitative textures with modern sonorities.

Willan (1880–1968) was born in the Balham area of London, and in his youth he studied at St Saviour's Choir School, Eastbourne. In 1903 he was appointed organist and choirmaster at the church of St John the Baptist in Kensington, and in 1913 he moved to Toronto, Canada, to join the faculty of the Toronto Conservatory (now the Royal Conservatory of Music) and to serve as organist at St Paul's Anglican Church, Bloor Street. The following year he accepted an appointment at the University of Toronto and also began serving as precentor at St Mary Magdalene (where he remained until his death). His choral output, almost entirely sacred, consists of five Anglican Communion Services, nineteen masses, seventy motets and anthems, plus numerous carols, hymns, and large-scale liturgical works. Apart from his anthem *O Lord, our Governor*, composed for the coronation of Queen Elizabeth I, he is best known for his collection of *Liturgical Motets* written between 1928 and 1937 in a neo-Renaissance style without bar lines and scored for SATB chorus a cappella. Of the motets, the most popular are *I beheld her beautiful as a dove* for celebrations of the Blessed Virgin Mary (BVM), *Rise up, my love, my fair one* for Easter, *Lo, in the time appointed* for Advent, and *Hodie, Christus natus est* for Christmas. Willan's most acclaimed choral work, *An Apostrophe to the Heavenly Hosts*, is set to a variety of passages from Eastern liturgies and scored for SATB/SATB full chorus and SATB/ATB chamber chorus (called "Mystic Chorus I and II") a cappella. All the music is ultraconservative in its harmonic language.

Ridout (1918–1984) was born in Toronto, Canada, where he studied at the Toronto Conservatory with Healey Willan. In 1938 he gained fame for his *Ballade* for viola and string orchestra, in 1940 he joined the faculty of the Toronto Conservatory as a teacher of music history and theory, and in 1948 he was appointed professor of composition at the University of Toronto. Most of his choral works are in a conservative tonal idiom and scored with orchestral accompaniment. Examples include the dramatic symphony *Esther* of 1952, the motet *Pange lingua* of 1960, and the secular cantatas *The Dance* of 1960 and *When age and youth unite* of 1966.

Schafer (b.1933) was born in Sarnia, Ontario, Canada (near Detroit, Michigan). He studied briefly at the Royal Conservatory of Music in Toronto and the University of Toronto. However, he was basically self-taught. He has also been self-employed for most of his career (his appointments at Memorial University in Newfoundland and Simon Fraser University in British Columbia were both short-term). Considered to be the most noteworthy Canadian individualist of the Modern era, he has written seven books that explore contemporary music philosophies and phenomena (including *The Tuning of the World* of 1977, *On Canadian Music* of 1984, and *The Thinking Ear: On Music Education* of 1986) and has composed more than thirty choral works that expand traditional techniques of notation and parameters of scoring. *Epitaph for Moonlight* of 1968 is a setting of invented words by children (e.g., sloopfulp, neshmoor, and malooma) scored in graphic notation for SATB chorus and optional bells; *Threnody* of 1966 is a setting of accounts by children who witnessed the bombing of Nagasaki in 1945, scored for five child speakers, youth chorus, youth orchestra, and electronic tape; *Gamelan* of 1979 is a setting of five words (dong, deng, dung, dang, and ding) that imitate the sounds of a Balinese gamelan orchestra and that are scored in five pitches for SATB, SASA, or TBTB chorus a cappella; and *Apocalypsis Part One: John's Vision* (set to text about the end of the world as envisioned by John of Patmos) and *Apocalypsis Part Two: Credo* (set to text by the sixteenth-century Italian philosopher and astronomer Giordano Bruno), is scored for actors, dancers, vocal soloists, multiple choruses, wind and brass ensemble, and taped sounds of bells.

Raminsh (b.1943) was born in Ventspils, Latvia, but raised in Canada, where he moved with his family in 1948. His musical studies were at the Royal Conservatory in Toronto and University of Toronto and also at the Mozarteum in Salzburg and the University of British Columbia. His professional activities have included conducting the NOVA Children's Choir and AURA Chamber Choir, both of which he founded. He has composed more than sixty choral works, including *Ave, verum corpus* scored for SATB chorus (with divisions) a cappella, SATB chorus and strings, or SSAA chorus and piano or organ; *Magnificat* for A solo, SATB chorus, and piano (later orchestrated); and *Stabat Mater* for A solos and SATB/SATB chorus. All the music is in an expanded tonal idiom, often characterized by modal harmonies.

Daley (b.1955) was born in Parry Sound, Ontario, and educated at Queen's University in Kingston, Ontario, and the Royal Conservatory of Music in Toronto. She is known as a pianist and organist as well as a composer, and since 1982 she has served as director of music at Fairlawn Avenue United Church in Toronto. Her compositional output includes more than one hundred choral works, including commissions from the Elmer Iseler Singers, Toronto Children's Chorus, Vancouver Men's Chorus, the American Choral Directors Association, and the Texas Choral Directors Association. In addition, several of her compositions have received notable Canadian awards (e.g., the National Choral Award for Outstanding Choral Compositions for *Requiem* in 1994 and *Rose Trilogy* in 2004). Most of the repertoire is scored for SATB or SSAA voices a cappella or with piano or organ accompaniment and set to traditional and conservative diatonic harmonies. Sample pieces, those that have become especially popular, are *In Remembrance* (from the *Requiem*), originally scored for SATB chorus a cappella and later arranged for SSAA chorus a cappella; *Balulalow* for SATB chorus a cappella; *What sweeter music* for SSA chorus and piano or harp; *Ubi caritas* (Where there is love) for SSAA chorus a cappella; and *Angels will guide you home* for SSA chorus and piano.

❧ FRANCE AND SWITZERLAND ❧

As in the nineteenth century, most twentieth-century French composers studied at the Paris Conservatoire. These include the major composers Claude Debussy, Maurice Ravel, Arthur Honegger, Darius Milhaud, Maurice Duruflé, and Olivier Messiaen, as well as the minor choral composers Jean Langlais and Jehan Alain, plus eight of the nine other composers mentioned below in this introduction. Yet another composer, Lili Boulanger, was not officially enrolled at the Conservatoire, although she won its coveted award, the Prix de Rome. Four composers who were not Conservatoire students—Ernest Bloch, Frank Martin, Willy Burkhard, and Carl Rütti—

were born and trained in Switzerland, and Henk Badings was from and received his education in the Netherlands. The only Parisians with no connection to the Conservatoire were Francis Poulenc and André Jolivet.

The French composers in the twentieth century were, however, not unified in musical styles as they had been during earlier times. There were too many diverse influences in Paris at the approach of and during the early decades of the twentieth century. The Universal Exposition in Paris in 1889 exposed composers to eastern music, Wagner operas were frequently presented at the Opéra during the 1890s, Serge Diaghilev and the Ballets Russes had a long residency in Paris, Ida Rubinstein created a new type of musical stage genre, and Nadia Boulanger attracted numerous American composers (who brought works in a variety of popular American styles, from jazz to ragtime) to the Paris Conservatoire and American Conservatory in Fontainebleu. In addition, French composers were influenced by the Impressionist painters and Symbolist poets of the late nineteenth century, and authors such as Jean Cocteau (1889–1963) were instigators of new and modern aesthetic concepts.

It is not surprising that with exposure to such divergent cultural works and concepts, modern French composers either created new genres or modified older genres in ways that gave them new identities. Most notable was the development of staged theater works that originally included speaking roles and dancing but that later were arranged for concert performance and took on the form of an oratorio. Examples are Debussy's *Le martyre de St Sébastien* and Honegger's *Le roi David* and *Jeanne d'Arc au bûcher*. Symphonic works with scoring for wordless chorus were also new; the chorus was used as a new orchestral color in works such as Debussy's *Nocturnes* and Ravel's *Daphnis et Chloé*. In addition, cantatas (e.g., Poulenc's *Figure humaine* and *Un soir de neige*) and miscellaneous choral works with no genre designation (e.g., Martin's *Songs of Ariel*, Poulenc's *Litanies à la vierge noire*, and Jolivet's *Epithalame*) became more and more frequent as the twentieth century progressed.

Standard genres in traditional forms also continued to have a presence in France. This was especially so with sacred repertoire (masses, Latin motets, and extended Psalm settings) written for the Catholic Church by the late-twentieth-century composers Duruflé, Langlais, Messiaen, Alain, and Rütti, all of whom were/are organists with significant church positions. Furthermore, some composers (most notably Debussy, Ravel, Badings, and Messiaen) modeled works after Renaissance chansons.

Composers who are not mentioned above or discussed at length below but who made an impact on the direction of choral music or who composed choral works that are acclaimed and/or have entered the performing repertory are Joseph Guy Ropartz, Charles Koechlin, Florent Schmitt, Jean Roger-Ducasse, Joseph Cantaloube, Edgard Varèse, Marcel Dupré, Pierre Boulez, and Pierre Villette.

Ropartz (1864–1955) studied at the Paris Conservatoire under Dubois, Massenet, and Franck and later became director of the conservatoires in Nancy and Strasbourg. He composed two masses for chorus and organ—*Messe en l'honneur de Ste Anne* and *Messe en l'honneur de Ste Odile*—and a *Requiem* and two Psalm settings—*Psaume cxxxvi* (Psalm 136) and *Psaume cxxix* (Psalm 129)—for solos, chorus, and orchestra. Other choral works include *Salve regina* for mixed chorus and organ and *Six chansons populaires du Bourbonnais* for chorus a cappella.

Koechlin (1867–1950) studied at the Paris Conservatoire under Massenet and Fauré, and together with Maurice Ravel and Florent Schmitt founded the Société Musicale Indépendante in

1909. A noted lecturer and proponent of the music of J. S. Bach, Koechlin composed twenty-three choral works, including *Trois poèmes du "Livre de la Jungle"* op.18 for soloists, chorus, and piano or orchestra; *Quelques choeurs réligieux a cappella, de style modal* op.150; *Requiem des pauvres bougres* op.161 for chorus, piano, organ, and ondes martenot; and *Quinze motets de style archaïque* op.225 for chorus and woodwind quartet.

Schmitt (1870–1958) studied at the conservatoires in both Nancy and Paris, and in 1900 he won the Prix de Rome for his cantata *Sémiramis*. Called a revolutionary anarchist, he was known for his independent and eclectic style, and he became famous for his 1907 ballet *La tragédie de Salomé,* which was arranged as a symphonic poem in 1910. He composed five cantatas plus nine other choral/orchestral works and twenty miscellaneous pieces for varied scorings. His most famous choral work, *Psaume xlvii* (Psalm 47), was composed in 1903 as a requirement of the Prix de Rome and scored for S solo, mixed chorus, and orchestra (including organ). Its premiere in Paris in 1906 featured Nadia Boulanger playing the solo organ part. Other choral works include *Trois liturgies joyeuses* ("Veni creator," "Adjiciat Dominus," and "Magnificat") for SATB chorus and organ and *Chansons à quatre voix* for SATB chorus and orchestra or piano four hands.

Roger-Ducasse (1873–1954) studied at the Paris Conservatoire under Fauré and won the Prix de Rome in 1902 for his cantata *Alcyone*. In 1910 he became the inspector general for vocal instruction in the public schools of Paris, and in 1935 he succeeded Dukas as professor of composition at the Conservatoire. Roger-Ducasse composed twelve choral works, including three popular motets—*Regina coeli laetare, Crux fidelis,* and *Alma redemptoris mater*—each composed in 1911 and scored for S solo, SATB chorus, and organ.

Cantaloube (1879–1957) studied under d'Indy at the Schola Cantorum in Paris and became known for his collections and arrangements of French folk songs. His first published collection, *Chants paysans de Haute-Auvergne,* is his most famous and contains the popular and frequently performed "Baïlèro" and "L'amour de moi," both for mixed voices a cappella. Other collections include *Le chansonnier alsacien* and *Le chansonnier français* for three equal voices, and *Anthologie des chants populaires Franco-Canadiens* and *Noëls d'Europe,* both for four voices a cappella.

Varèse (1883–1965) studied at both the Schola Cantorum and Paris Conservatoire and also privately in Berlin. He moved to the United States in 1915 and established himself as a conductor and teacher (he conducted the Berlioz *Requiem* in New York City in 1917 and lectured at Columbia University in the 1940s), and he became known for his avant-garde chamber works employing numerous percussion instruments. His compositional output includes three choral works—*Ecuatorial* ("Prayer from Popol Vuh of Maya Quiché") for soloist or unison chorus, eight brass and six percussion instruments, piano, organ, and two ondes martenots; *Etude pour Espace* for chorus, two pianos, and percussion; and the unfinished *Nocturnal* for S solo, unison chorus, and chamber orchestra.

Dupré (1886–1971) studied at the Paris Conservatoire and won the Prix de Rome in 1914 with his cantata *Psyché.* He succeeded Gigout as professor of organ and was director of the Conservatoire from 1954 to 1956, and he followed Widor as organist at St Sulpice. Dupré was known for his performance cycles of the complete organ works of J. S. Bach and for his improvisations during tours throughout Europe and the United States. He composed twelve choral works, including his most famous, *De profundis* ("pour les soldats morts pour Patrie"), scored for STB solos, SATB (divided) chorus, and orchestra (including organ) or organ alone.

The Modern Era   567

Boulez (b.1925) studied at the Paris Conservatoire and later became known as a prominent conductor, spokesperson for science in music, and composer of electronic works. Highlights of his career include conducting operas at the Paris Opéra and Bayreuth Festspielhaus, serving as music director of the New York Philharmonic and BBC Symphony Orchestra, and directing the IRCAM (Institut de Recherche et Coordination Acoustique/Musique) at the Centre Pompidou. Like Varèse, he composed only three choral works—*Le soleil des eaux,* originally written in 1950 for soloists and revised in 1965 for mixed chorus and orchestra; *Le visage nuptial* of 1951 to 1952 (revised between 1986 and 1989) and scored for SA soloists, women's chorus, and orchestra; and *cummings ist der Dichter* of 1970 (revised in 1986) for sixteen solo voices or mixed chorus and chamber orchestra.

Villette (1926–1998) studied at the Paris Conservatoire and later became director of the Aix-en-Provence Academy and the Besançon Conservatory in northeast France. He composed two masses for S soloist, mixed chorus, two organs, and orchestra—*Missa da pacem* op.38 and *Messe en français* op.44—and fourteen Latin motets for SATB chorus a cappella, including *Ave verum* op.3, *Salve regina* op.5, *O quam amabilis* op.71, *Jesu dulcis memoria* op.78, and *Panis angelicus* op.80. Other popular motets are *O sacrum convivium* op.27 for SSAATTBB chorus a cappella and *Attende Domine* op.45 for SSATBB chorus a cappella.

CLAUDE DEBUSSY 1862–1918

Debussy was born in St Germain-en-Laye, close to Paris, and was educated at home by his mother. He began piano lessons with a pupil of Chopin at age eight, and at eleven he entered the Paris Conservatoire, where for the next several years he enjoyed playing the piano pieces of Chopin and Schumann and where he became attracted to the works of Berlioz. At seventeen Debussy composed his first mélodies (songs), and at eighteen he began teaching piano to the children of Nadezhda von Meck, the wealthy Russian widow who at the time was supporting and championing the music of Tchaikovsky. Debussy spent several months with Madame von Meck and her children in Russia during 1861 and then again in 1862, and he also accompanied the family to Vienna in 1862. In 1863 he became the accompanist for the Concordia choral society in Paris, then led by Charles-François Gounod, and in 1884 he won the Prix de Rome with the composition of his cantata *L'enfant prodigue,* which is scored for three soloists and orchestra. During his mandatory two-year study in Rome he became acquainted with the works of Renaissance composers, including Lasso and Palestrina, and he met Verdi and Liszt. Debussy was not interested in the music of these composers, however, and when he returned to Paris in 1887 he became associated with the Symbolist poets Paul Verlaine (1844–1896) and Stéphane Mallarmé (1842–1898) and formulated his aesthetic ideas based on their views of textual colors. Debussy was also influenced by the Impressionist movement in painting and by the nonwestern music he heard at the Universal Exposition in Paris in 1889.

Debussy's major works composed and performed at the end of the century—the cantata *La damoiselle élue* (1887–1888) and orchestral tone poems *Prélude à l'après-midi d'un faune* (1891–1894) and *Nocturnes* (1897–1899)—did not attract much public attention. However, beginning with the 1902 premiere of his opera *Pelléas et Melisande,* Debussy's music was critically acclaimed (as well as criticized), and during the first decade of the twentieth century performances took place throughout the world. *Prélude à l'après d'un faune* was performed in Boston in 1902, Berlin in 1903, London in 1904, Turin in 1906, and Rio de Janeiro in 1908; the first two *Nocturnes* were performed in Berlin and Boston in 1904, Oslo in 1906, and Milan in 1907; and *La mer* was performed in New York City and Boston in 1907 and in Budapest in 1910. Debussy often attended or took part in performances of his music, and he was especially popular in St Petersburg, Moscow, Amsterdam, and London. He curtailed his activities in 1915 when he developed colon cancer, and for the next three years he composed few works and was often confined to his home.

Debussy composed only five choral works that are complete and published. Another work, the mainly orchestral *Nocturnes,* has additional scoring in the third of its three movements for wordless female chorus. *Le printemps,* a setting of a short poem about the natural beauty of springtime, was composed in 1882 and scored for soprano solo, female chorus, and orchestra. It became popular after the 1928 publication of a vocal score, when it was renamed *Salut printemps* (the first words of text) and scored for piano accompaniment. *Invocation,* for male chorus and orchestra, was composed in 1883 and also was issued in an arrangement for piano in 1928. *La damoiselle élue,* subtitled "poème lyrique," was composed in 1887 and 1888 as a requirement of the Prix de Rome. It is a setting of a poem by Dante Gabriel Rossetti, in French translation, about a blessed young woman (damsel) in heaven who yearns for her earthly lover. *Le martyre de St Sébastien,* subtitled "mystère," was composed in 1910 and 1911 to fulfill a commission by the dancer Ida Rubinstein, who had become famous in 1909 for her nude "Dance of the Seven Veils" in a production of Oscar Wilde's *Salomé.* The libretto of *Le martyre de St Sébastien* was written by Gabriele D'Annunzio (the infamous Italian poet and novelist who fled to Paris in 1910 to escape creditors), and is based on the life of St Sebastian, the young and handsome Praetorian officer of the third century, who was martyred because of his sympathy for the Christians. The music is in five scenes (called "mansions") that recount various incidents in the life of the saint and that are related by a so-called "cross" motif that pervades the entire work. The original production, in which Rubinstein portrayed the role of St Sebastian, was a theater work approximately five hours in duration. For subsequent performances, the narration was reduced to short links between the musical numbers, and the presentation was in concert form (i.e., without costumes or staging). The work was popular in this oratorio-like form, and it influenced the oratorios by French composers throughout the twentieth century.

The *Trois Chansons de Charles d'Orléans* was composed over a period of time. The first and third chansons, "Dieu! qu'il la fait bon regarder" and "Yver, vous n'estes qu'un villain," were composed in 1898 and are similar in structure to the Parisian chansons of the Renaissance, with passages of imitative polyphony that alternate with passages of homophony. The second chanson, "Quand j'ai ouy le tabourin," was composed in 1908 and is in the style of an accompanied song, with a texted vocal solo in one part and guitar- and tambourine-like patterns to a *la la la* text in the other parts. The texts of all three pieces are by the Medieval French poet Charles d'Orléans (1391–1465), and the music is characteristic of Debussy's Impressionistic style: harmonies are juxtaposed in nontraditional ways to produce effects of color, chords move in parallel motion, and phrases consist of short motifs that are varied to express the specific content of textual phrases.

CHORAL WORKS
SELECTED AND LISTED ACCORDING TO FAMILIARITY

Trois Chansons de Charles d'Orléans – SATB chorus a cappella – "Dieu! qu'il la fait bon regarder" 2:30 minutes, "Quand j'ai ouy le tabourin" 2 minutes, and "Yver, vous n'estes qu'un villain" 2 minutes. (1) The second chanson is scored for A solo and AATTBB chorus, the choral parts normally sung by SATTBB; (2) the third chanson has brief passages scored for SATB solo quartet.

Nocturnes – "Sirènes" – SSAA chorus – 9:30 minutes. (1) The score calls for eight sopranos and eight altos, although performances today usually employ an entire female chorus of from twenty to forty voices; (2) the vocal writing is an integral part of the orchestral fabric and is pervasive throughout the movement; (3) the vocal parts are wordless (no vowels or consonants are indicated in the score).

Salut printemps – S solo, SSA chorus, and piano – 4:30 minutes.

La damoiselle élue – SA solos, SSAA chorus, and orchestra (including three flutes, English horn, bass clarinet, and two harps) – 20 minutes.

Le martyre de St Sébastien – speaker, SSSSAA solos, SATB chorus, and orchestra – 66 minutes. (1) The speaker portrays St Sebastian; (2) sung roles are for The Soul of Sebastian (S), the Twin Brothers Mark and Marcellian (AA), the Virgin Erigone (S), a Solo Voice (S), and a Voice from Heaven (S).

MAURICE RAVEL 1875–1937

Ravel was born in Ciboure, on the southwest tip of France near the town of St Jean-de-Luz, but grew up in Paris, where his family had moved shortly after his birth. He began piano lessons at age seven and studies in composition at twelve, and at fourteen he entered the Paris Conservatoire and also attended the Universal Exposition in Paris. He was fascinated by the nonwestern music he heard at the Exposition, especially the Javanese gamelan music and the Russian works conducted by Rimsky-Korsakov, and throughout the next several years he was attracted to the music of Emmanuel Chabrier and Erik Satie. In addition, he was drawn to the writings of the Symbolist poets Charles Baudelaire (1821–1867) and Stéphane Mallarmé (1842–1898). Ravel left the Conservatoire at age twenty but returned two years later and began composition lessons with Fauré. During the next several years Ravel composed a number of works that would bring him fame, including the orchestral overture *Shéhérazade* in 1898, the original piano version of *Pavane pour une infante défunte* in 1899 (the orchestral version appeared in 1910), and the piano piece *Jeux d'eau* in 1901. He attempted, unsuccessfully, to win the Prix de Rome with three cantatas in three successive years—*Myrrha* in 1901, *Alcyone* in 1902, and *Alyssa* in 1903—each, like Debussy's *L'enfant prodigue,* scored for three solo voices and orchestra. In spite of these failures, the *Pavane pour une infante défunte* and *Jeux d'eau* gained in popularity and were performed throughout Europe, and numerous works composed in the second and third decades of the twentieth century received critical and popular acclaim. These include the ballet *Daphnis et Chloé*, commissioned by Sergei Diaghilev (the Russian founder and director of the Ballets Russes) and premiered in 1912; the songs *Trois poèmes de Stéphane Mallarmé*, composed in 1913 and dedicated to Igor Stravinsky; the French Baroque dance forms in *Le tombeau de Couperin*, composed for solo piano between 1914 and 1917 and orchestrated in 1919; and the ballet *Boléro*, commissioned by Ida Rubinstein and composed in 1928. Ravel's orchestration of Musorgsky's *Tableaux d'une exposition* (Pictures from an exhibition) in 1922 also became extremely popular. Meanwhile, Ravel was given the Légion d'honneur in 1920, although he refused to accept it, and he was granted an honorary doctorate from Oxford University in 1928. In 1932 he began suffering from a rare brain disease, and after an unsuccessful operation in 1937 he died at the age of sixty-two.

Ravel composed two works that involve chorus—*Daphnis et Chloé* and *Trois chansons*. The ballet is like Debussy's "Sirènes" from *Nocturnes* in being scored for orchestra and wordless chorus. Unlike "Sirènes," however, the chorus does not sing throughout *Daphnis et Chloé*, although the choral parts are featured prominently at the beginning, in the middle, and at the end of the work—the middle portion consisting of an extended passage for a cappella chorus. Ravel arranged two suites from the ballet, one in 1911 that includes the movements "Nocturne," "Interlude," and "Danse guerrière," and one in 1913 that includes the movements "Lever du jour," "Pantomime," and "Danse générale." The chorus is scored only in the first and third movements of the second suite. The *Trois chansons*, composed in 1914 and 1915, are also like Debussy's chansons— the first and third pieces are modeled on Parisian chansons of the Renaissance, and the second piece is an accompanied song. "Nicolette" has elements of the programmatic works of Janequin, including onomatopoeic sounds; "Trois beaux oiseaux du paradis" is scored for soprano and tenor solos, with accompaniment by chorus set only to the word "Ah"; and "Ronde" resembles the humorous chansons of Pierre Certon.

CHORAL WORKS
COMPLETE AND LISTED ACCORDING TO FAMILIARITY

Trois chansons – SATB chorus a cappella – "Nicolette" 1:30 minutes, "Trois beaux oiseaux du paradis" 2:30 minutes, and "Ronde" 1:45 minutes. The second chanson is scored for S and T solos and SATB chorus.

Daphnis et Chloé – Suite #2 – SATB chorus and orchestra – 16 minutes. (1) The chorus is scored at the beginning ("Lever du jour") and end ("Danse générale") of the suite; (2) the vocal parts are wordless (no vowels or consonants are indicated in the score).

ERNEST BLOCH 1880–1959

Bloch was born in Geneva, Switzerland, where he studied violin with Louis Rey and solfège and composition with Emile Jaques-Dalcroze. Between 1896 and 1904 Bloch furthered his education in Brussels, Frankfurt, Munich, and Paris, and in 1904 he returned to Geneva, working there for the next several years as a bookkeeper and salesman. In 1911 he began lecturing on aesthetics at the Geneva Conservatory, and during the next several years he composed works, such as *Trois poems juifs* (Three Jewish poems) and *Schelomo*, that established him as a so-called Jewish composer. In 1916 he served as the conductor of a dance company touring the United States, the following year he began teaching theory and composition at the newly founded Mannes College of Music in New York City, and during the 1920s he was the director of two music schools—the Cleveland Institute of Music between 1920 and 1925, and the San Francisco Conservatory of Music between 1925 and 1930. He became a citizen of the United States in 1924. However, he returned to Switzerland in 1930 and for the next decade focused on composition and conducting. To evade the anti-Semitic climate in Europe during World War II, he went back to the United States in 1940 and taught composition at the University of California at Berkeley until his retirement in 1952.

Bloch composed two choral works—*America: an Epic Rhapsody* and *Avodath Hakodesh* (Sacred Service). The first of these, composed in 1926, is scored for chorus and orchestra and incorporates Native American tunes, English sea shanties, civil war songs, and African-American spirituals into a three-movement orchestral texture. *Avodath Hakodesh* was composed between 1930 and 1933 to texts from the Reform Jewish prayer book. Scoring is for speaker, baritone soloist, SATB chorus (with divisions), and orchestra (including three flutes, English horn, contrabassoon, celesta, two harps, triangle, cymbals, tambourine, snare drum, bass drum, and tam-tam). The text is in Hebrew except for the part of the speaker, which is in English, and the music is characterized by modal inflections based on traditional Jewish chants.

FRANK MARTIN 1890–1974

Martin was born in Geneva, Switzerland, and studied piano and harmony privately as a child. He became interested in composition at a very early age and at twelve was particularly moved by a performance of the J. S. Bach *Passio secundum Mattaeum* BWV244. Martin decided against a career in music and studied mathematics and physics. However, after extensive travels to Zurich, Rome, and Paris, he returned to Geneva and began studies in rhythmic music education (eurythmics) with Émile Jaques-Dalcroze. In 1928 Martin became a teacher at the Jaques-Dalcroze Institute, and at the same time he began lecturing at the Geneva Conservatory of Music and serving as director of the Technicum Moderne de Musique. From 1943 to 1946 he was president of the Swiss Musicians' Union, and from 1950 to 1957 he taught composition at the Cologne Hochschule für Musik. For the remainder of his life he traveled widely, playing recitals on the harpsichord and piano and conducting his works.

Martin composed two masses (one of which is a Requiem), five oratorios, four cantatas, and nineteen miscellaneous choral/orchestral works and chansons. The *Mass* consists of the traditional five portions of the Roman Mass Ordinary. The Kyrie, Gloria, Credo, and Sanctus were composed in 1922, and the Agnus Dei was added in 1926. The completed work was not released for performance or publication, however, until 1963, when it was premiered by the Bugenhagen Kantorei of Hamburg. Explaining the delay of release, Martin wrote (at the time of the premiere): "I considered [the mass to be] between God and myself. I felt then that an expression of religious feelings should remain secret and removed from public opinion." The music, while conservative in terms of harmonic vocabulary and traditional in terms of imitative textures, is not based on models of the past. The Agnus Dei is particularly inventive (and effective): the second chorus chants the text in a steady cortège-like succession of unchanging rhythmic values, while the first chorus sings a melody, mostly in unison, that is frequently in syncopation against the second chorus rhythms. The *Requiem*, which was inspired by sacred architecture in Venice and Monreal and composed in 1971 and 1972, consists of eight movements—Introitus, Kyrie, Dies irae, Offertorium, Sanctus, Agnus Dei, In paradisum, and Lux aeterna.

The five oratorios are *Le vin herbé* (1938–1941), *In terra pax* (1944), *Golgotha* (1945–1948), *Le mystère de la nativité* (1957–1959), and *Pilate* (1964). The first work, Martin's only oratorio to use a secular text, is based on the Tristan and Isolde legend. It is in three parts (the drinking of a magic potion, the lovers in the forest of Morois, and their death) and is scored for twelve solo voices and eight instruments (seven strings plus piano). The musical style is tonal and includes a quote of the famous leitmotif from Wagner's opera, although Martin uses a twelve-tone row for some of the melodic construction. The oratorio was well received and thus, as was probable with Honegger's *Le roi David*, its success no doubt provided encouragement for further works in the genre. *In terra pax* was commissioned by Radio Geneva for the celebration of Armistice Day and premiered in May 1945. It is in four parts (the sorrow of war, the joy of peace, the forgiveness of mankind, and divine peace). *Golgotha* was inspired by Rembrandt's etching "Three Crosses" and utilizes a text that alternates between Gospel passages and contemplative writings by St Augustine. *Le mystère de la nativité* is based on a fifteenth-century mystery play and was called a "scenic oratorio" by Martin—to be either staged or unstaged. *Pilate* is also based on a fifteenth-century mystery play and was designed for either stage or concert performance. It is divided into three levels of dramatic portrayal (Hell at the bottom, Earth in the middle, and Heaven at the top), each with corresponding musical depiction (atonal for Hell, eclectic for Earth, and tonally simple for Heaven).

The cantatas are *Les dithyrambs* (1915–1918), *Cantate pour le temps de Noël* (1929–1930), *Cantate pour le 1er août* (1941), and *Et la vie l'emporta* (1974). Each work calls for successively fewer resources—the first scored for soloists, mixed and children's choruses, and orchestra; the second for soloists, mixed and boys' choruses, strings, and keyboard; the third for soloists, mixed chorus, and organ or piano; and the fourth for two soloists, mixed chorus, and small instrumental ensemble of two flutes, oboe, oboe d'amore, harpsichord, organ, and strings. *Cantate pour le 1er août*, composed to celebrate the 650th anniversary of the Swiss Confederation, is a short hymn of praise. *Et la vie l'emporta*, Martin's final composition, is about the victory of life over death.

The miscellaneous compositions include a collection of four chansons for female voices composed in 1931 ("Sonnet," "Le coucou," "Ode," and "Le petit village"); a collection of three chansons for male voices composed in 1943 and 1944 ("Janeton," "Petite église," and "Si Charlotte avait voulu"); *Ode à la musique*, a setting of Guillaume de Machaut's poem composed for the Congrès de la Sociètè Pédagogique de la Suisse Romande in 1961; and the *Songs of Ariel*, composed in 1950 for the Nederlands Kamerkoor and premiered by the ensemble in 1953. About this latter work Martin wrote, "Long before deciding to write an opera on Shakespeare's *The Tempest*, which had been haunting my mind for many years, I chose to set for this choir [the Nederlands Kamerkoor] the *Songs of Ariel*, the fairy incarnating the Spirit of the Air in this play." The set of songs consists of "Come unto these yellow sands" and "Full fathom five" from act one, scene two; "Before you can say" from act four, scene one; "You are three men of sin" from act three, scene three; and "Where the bee sucks" from act five, scene one. The music of all five settings is reminiscent of English Renaissance madrigals, with numerous instances of word painting.

CHORAL WORKS
SELECTED AND LISTED ACCORDING TO FAMILIARITY

Mass – SATB/SATB chorus a cappella – 26 minutes. The choral parts occasionally divide into SSATBB/SSAATTBB.

Requiem – SATB solos, SATB chorus, and orchestra (including organ) – 46 minutes.

Songs of Ariel – SSAATTBB chorus a cappella – 12 minutes.

Golgotha – SATBB solos, SATB chorus, and orchestra (including organ) – 94 minutes. The only named solo role is Jesus (B); the other soloists are unnamed.

Ode à la musique – B solo, SATB chorus, trumpet, two horns, three trombones, string bass, and piano – 8:30 minutes.

ARTHUR HONEGGER 1892–1955

Honegger was born in Le Havre, on the northwest coast of France, where as a child he studied violin and harmony privately. He was strongly attracted to J. S. Bach cantatas he heard at the local Protestant church, and at age seventeen he enrolled at the conservatory in Zurich, Switzerland. At nineteen he transferred to the Paris Conservatoire, studying there with Charles-Marie Widor and Vincent d'Indy and working alongside fellow students Germaine Tailleferre, Georges Auric, and Darius Milhaud. These students were later joined by Louis Durey, Francis Poulenc, and Honegger himself in the group of composers referred to as "Les Six," although Honegger did not share the same aesthetic values as the other composers and developed a distinctive style, one related more to German than to French trends. An example of this Germanic style can be seen in the Lutheran chorales used in works such as *La roi David* and *Une cantate de Noël*. During World War II Honegger taught at the Ecole Normale de Musique in Paris and served as a critic for the weekly magazine *Comoedia*. However, his professional activities revolved mainly around touring across Europe and the United States as a conductor, lecturer, and accompanist and also supervising recordings of his works. He received numerous awards, including election to the Institut de France in 1938 and an honorary doctorate from the University of Zurich in 1948. During the last eight years of his life he suffered from heart disease, from which he died at age sixty-three.

Honegger composed six oratorios that are extant, three cantatas, and three miscellaneous choral works. The oratorios are *Le Calvaire* (1908), *Le roi David* (1921), *Judith* (1927), *Cris du monde* (1930–1931), *Jeanne d'Arc au bûcher* (1935), and *Nicolas de Flue* (1938–1939). Of these, *Le roi David* (King David) and *Jeanne d'Arc au bûcher* (Joan of Arc at the stake) are the most famous. *Le roi David*, like Debussy's *Le martyre de Saint Sébastien*, was composed as incidental music to a play and was originally staged. It was also immediately revised after its premiere: the genre subtitle was changed from "drama biblique" (biblical drama) to "psaume symphonique" (symphonic Psalm), spoken dialogue was reduced to short links between musical numbers, and the work was presented in concert form. These first two versions of the work were scored for solo voices, chorus, and seventeen wind and percussion instruments, while a further revision in 1923 was scored for full orchestra, including strings. The oratorio, which is divided into twenty-seven numbers that are grouped into three parts (David's Youth, David as King, and David's Old Age), was a huge success, performed more than seventy-five times within several years. *Jeanne d'Arc au bûcher,* subtitled an "oratorio dramatique," was commissioned by Ida Rubinstein, who played the title role and to whom the work is dedicated. The premiere took place in her home in 1935, and the first public performance was in Basil in May 1938. The libretto, by Paul Claudel, relates the accusations against and sufferings of Joan of Arc in the form of a book about her life, presented to her from heaven by the founder of the Dominican order, Brother Dominic. As events of her impending death unfold, earthly voices call her a heretic and demand her death, a judge and jury of animals (a pig, sheep, and an ass) declare her guilty, a group of kings and queens decide her fate through a ballet pantomime game of cards, and Joan is burned at the stake as she expresses her faith and as voices from heaven welcome her. The story is also a general exposé on suffering and humiliation and a commentary on contemporary French life. The prologue, for instance, begins with the text "Ténèbres! Ténèbres! Et la France était inane et vide" (Darkness! Darkness! And France was desolate and void).

The cantatas are *Les milles et une nuits* (The thousand and one nights), based on the medieval collection of Arabic stories, composed in 1936 and 1937, and scored for ST solos, four ondes martenots, and orchestra; *La danse des morts* (The dance of death), set to a poem by Claudel and composed in 1938; and *Une cantate de Noël* (A Christmas Cantata), composed in 1952 and 1953. This last work, which relates events surrounding the birth of Jesus, is framed by two Latin Psalms—"De profundis" (Psalm 130) and "Laudate Dominum omnes gentes" (Psalm 117)—and contains several carols, each in its original language (German, English, and French).

The miscellaneous choral works include *Cantique de Pâques,* composed in 1918, orchestrated in 1922, and scored for women's chorus, and *Chanson de Fagus,* composed in 1923 and 1924 and scored for S solo, SATB chorus, and piano.

CHORAL WORKS
SELECTED AND LISTED ACCORDING TO FAMILIARITY

Le roi David – two speakers, SAT solos, SATB chorus, and original scoring for chamber ensemble of two flutes (one of which doubles piccolo), oboe (doubling English horn), two clarinets (one of which doubles bass clarinet), bassoon, two trumpets, horn, trombone, celesta, piano, harmonium, string bass, timpani, and five percussion instruments necessitating two players – 68 minutes. (1) The speakers portray the roles of Le Récitant (Narrator) and La pythonisse (Witch of Endor); (2) the second movement of the work, "Cantique du berger David" (Song of the shepherd David), is often sung by a child.

Une cantate de Noël – B solo, unison children's chorus, SATB chorus, and orchestra (including harp and organ) – 25 minutes. The chorus divides occasionally into SSAATTBB.

Jeanne d'Arc au bûcher – five speakers, SSATB solos, children's chorus, SATB chorus, and orchestra (including bass clarinet, three saxophones, contrabassoon, two pianos, celesta, and ondes martenot) – 80 minutes. (1) Major speaking roles are for Joan of Arc and Brother Dominic; (2) minor speaking roles are for twelve characters divided among the remaining three speakers; (3) singing roles are for the Virgin Mary (S), the angels Marguerite and Catherine (S and A), and seven miscellaneous characters divided among T and B; (4) an additional brief solo is to be sung by a child from the children's chorus; (5) the chorus divides briefly into SATTBB and SSAATTBB.

Cris du monde – SAB solos, children's chorus, SATB chorus, and orchestra – 47 minutes.

La danse des morts – speaker, SAB solos, SATB chorus, and orchestra – 31 minutes.

DARIUS MILHAUD 1892–1974

Milhaud was born in Marseilles but grew up in nearby Aix-en-Provence, where his parents were members of the Comtat Venaissin sect of Jews. His father was an accomplished amateur pianist and his mother a singer, and at age three the young Milhaud was noted for both his keyboard and singing abilities. At seven he began violin lessons, at ten he played second violin in a local string quartet, and at thirteen he decided on a career as a composer and began studying harmony. He entered the Paris Conservatoire at seventeen and took classes with Paul Dukas and Charles-Marie Widor, and at twenty he met the poet Paul Claudel (1868–1955), whom he called "the great stroke of luck in my life." After working for the French foreign ministry during the early years of World War I, Milhaud followed Claudel to Brazil (Claudel was the French minister to Brazil and Milhaud was an attaché for propaganda), although he returned to Paris in 1919, and during the next decade he produced a prodigious amount of repertoire in a wide variety of genres, including opera, ballet, and incidental music for the theater, as well as orchestral, choral, solo vocal, and piano works. He was also a critic and author for the *Courrier* and an active recitalist and conductor. Some of his most recognized works were premiered in the 1930s, including the opera *Christophe Colomb* in 1930 and the piano piece *Scaramouche* in 1937, and during the 1940s his professional activities were focused on teaching—at Mills College in Oakland, California; at the Summer Institute in Aspen, Colorado; and at the Music Academy of the West in Santa Barbara, California. He also commuted to France to teach composition at the Paris Conservatoire beginning in 1947. In 1948 he was confined to a wheelchair as a result of severe rheumatoid arthritis. However, he continued to travel regularly between California and France until 1971, when he retired to Geneva, Switzerland.

Milhaud composed twelve sacred and secular cantatas in French, four sacred works in Hebrew, and twenty-seven miscellaneous choral works. The cantatas include *Cantate de la paix* op.166 of 1937, *Cantate de la guerre* op.213 of 1940, *Cantate des proverbes* op.310 of 1950, and Milhaud's most popular cantatas—*Cantate de la croix de charité* op.381 of 1959 and 1960, *Cantate sur des texts de Chaucer* op.386 of 1960, and *Cantata from Job* op.413 of 1965. The *Cantate de la croix de charité* was composed for the French Red Cross (Croix-Rouge) and is divided into three movements—heaven, earth, and charity; the *Cantate sur des texts de Chaucer* was composed for the University of Iowa and consists of three poems by Chaucer, set in both English and French, each preceded by an extended orchestral prelude; and the *Cantata from Job* was composed for the dedication of Temple Beth Zion in Buffalo, New York, and is divided into two sections, the first a setting of Job 37:1–13 and the second a setting in three sections of Job: 38:4–7, 8–11, and 16–21.

The compositions set to Hebrew texts include three works for Jewish services—*Kaddisch* ("Prière pour les morts") op.250, composed in 1945 and scored for T solo, SATB chorus ad lib., and organ; *Service sacré pour le samedi matin avec prières additionnelles pour le vendredi soir* (Sacred Service for Saturday morning with additional prayers for Friday evening) op.279, composed in 1947 and scored for speaker, B solo, SATB chorus, and orchestra (including organ); and *Cantate de l'initiation* ("Bar Mitzvah Israël") op.388, composed between 1948 and 1961 and scored for SATB chorus and chamber orchestra. The miscellaneous works include Milhaud's most famous choral composition, *Les deux cités* op.170, composed in 1937 and divided into three movements (Babylon, Elegy, and Jerusalem), and *Cantique du Rhône* op.155, composed in 1936 to a text by Claudel and divided into four untitled movements.

CHORAL WORKS
SELECTED AND LISTED ACCORDING TO FAMILIARITY

Les deux cités op.170 – SATB chorus a cappella – 13:30 minutes. (1) The choral parts divide into SAATTBB in the first movement; (2) the scoring calls for occasional solo SATB quartet.

Cantate de la croix de charité op.381 – STB solos, unison children's chorus, SATB chorus, and orchestra – 22 minutes. Solo roles are for the Woman (S), the Man (T), and the Voice of God (B).

Cantate sur des textes de Chaucer op.386 – SATB chorus and orchestra – 15 minutes.

Cantata from Job op.413 – B solo, SATB chorus, and organ – 20 minutes. (1) The text is in both English and Hebrew; (2) the choral parts divide occasionally into SSAATTBB.

Cantique du Rhône op.155 – SATB chorus a cappella – 10 minutes.

Naissance de Vénus op.292 – SATB chorus a cappella – 4:30 minutes.

Devant sa main nue op.122 – SSAA chorus or soloists a cappella – 3:30 minutes.

Promesse de Dieu op.438 – SATB chorus a cappella – 12 minutes.

Cantate de la guerre op.213 – SA solos and SATB chorus a cappella – 9 minutes.

Cantate de la paix op.166 – SAAT solos and SSAATTBB chorus a cappella – 5:30 minutes.

LILI BOULANGER 1893–1918

Boulanger was born in Paris into a musical family. Her father, Ernest Boulanger (1815–1900), was the winner of the Prix de Rome in 1836 and later became a teacher of singing at the Paris Conservatoire, her mother was an accomplished singer, and her older sister Nadia (1887–1979) was a famous teacher and conductor. Lili contracted bronchial pneumonia at the age of two and as a result had a weakened immune system that caused her activities to be limited. She studied music at home with her parents and sister and at twenty won the Prix de Rome (the first woman in history to win the prize) with her cantata *Faust et Hélène*. Her sojourn to Rome, as a stipulation of the prize, was interrupted by the outset of World War I. However, she returned in 1916, only to leave the following year because of declining health brought on by intestinal cancer, from which she died at age twenty-four.

Boulanger composed fifteen choral works—eight for chorus and orchestra, three for chorus and orchestra or piano, and four for chorus and piano. The most substantial and best known of the choral/orchestral works are three Psalm settings and the Buddhist prayer *Vieille prière bouddhique*. *Psalm cxxx* (Psalm 130), sometimes referred to by its Latin title "De profundis," was composed between 1910 and 1917. Beginning with an extended prelude and containing several instrumental interludes, it is the most orchestral of Boulanger's choral works. It is also the most rhythmically complex and tonally impressionistic. *Psalm cxxix* (Psalm 129) and *Psalm xxiv* (Psalm 24) were composed during the same years—1910 to 1916 and 1916, respectively. *Vieille prière bouddhique*, with a text from the Buddhist *Visuddhimagga* and with the subtitle "Prière quotidienne pour tout l'Univers" (Daily prayer for the entire universe), was composed between 1914 and 1917.

CHORAL WORKS
SELECTED AND LISTED ACCORDING TO FAMILIARITY

Psalm cxxx ("Du fond de l'abîme") – AT solos, SATB chorus, and orchestra (including organ) – 23:30 minutes. The chorus bass part divides frequently and the other parts divide occasionally.

Psalm xxiv ("La terre appartient à l'Eternel") – T solo, SATB chorus, and orchestra (including organ) – 3 minutes.

Psalm cxxix ("Ils m'ont assez opprimé") – B solo or unison male chorus and orchestra – 6 minutes.

Vieille prière bouddhique – T solo, SATB chorus, and orchestra – 7 minutes.

Les sirènes – A solo, SATB chorus, and piano – 5:30 minutes.

Hymne au soleil – A solo, SATB chorus, and orchestra or piano – 4 minutes.

Pour les funérailles d'un soldat – B solo, SATB chorus, and orchestra – 8 minutes.

FRANCIS POULENC 1899–1963

Poulenc was born in Paris and began playing the piano at age five. He did not study music formally, however, but received a classical education at the Lycée Condorcet. During his teenage years he became interested in music as a career, and between the ages of fifteen and nineteen he took music lessons privately with the Spanish pianist Ricardo Viñes, who introduced him to composers such as Georges Auric, Erik Satie, and Manuel de Falla and to the poets Guillaume Apollinaire (1880–1918), Paul Éluard (1895–1952), André Gide (1869–1951), and Paul Claudel

(1868–1955). Poulenc wrote several compositions while studying with Viñes, including the song cycle *Rapsodie nègre* for solo baritone and chamber ensemble, which was praised by critics and was also immediately popular with audiences. After service in the military between 1918 and 1921 and during studies with Charles Koechlin from 1921 to 1924, Poulenc composed the ballet *Les biches* for Sergei Diaghilev and the Ballets Russes, and in 1932 and 1938, he fulfilled two commissions from Princess Edmond de Polignac—the *Concerto* in D minor for two pianos and orchestra, and the *Concerto* in G minor for organ, strings, and timpani. The melodrama *L'histoire de Babar* (often called *Babar the Elephant*) was composed between 1940 and 1945, and the opera *Dialogues des Carmélites*, commissioned by La Scala, was composed between 1953 and 1956. During the 1930s, 1940s, and 1950s, Poulenc also toured extensively throughout Europe and the United States, often accompanying baritone Pierre Bernac, and during the early 1960s, having achieved celebrity status, he frequently attended major performances of his works. In January 1961, for instance, he attended the premiere of his *Gloria*, which was commissioned by the Serge Koussevitzky Music Foundation and performed by the Boston Symphony Orchestra and Chorus Pro Music at Boston's Symphony Hall under the direction of Charles Munch. In 1961 Poulenc composed the *Sept répons des ténèbres*, a commission by the New York Philharmonic for its opening season at the Lincoln Center for the Performing Arts, and in January 1963 he suffered a heart attack and died in his apartment in Paris, approximately three weeks after his sixty-fourth birthday.

Poulenc composed twelve sacred works (or twenty-four separate sacred pieces) and seven secular works (or twenty-four separate secular pieces). The sacred works were written after Poulenc experienced a religious reawakening during a pilgrimage to the chapel of the Black Virgin of Rocamadour. This pilgrimage closely followed the death in 1936 of his friend, the composer and critic Pierre-Octave Ferroud, and resulted in *Litanies à la vierge noire*. As Poulenc later wrote, "In this work I tried to depict the mood of 'country devotion' that so deeply struck me in that mountain locale." The *Messe en sol Majeur* (Mass in G major), composed the following year and dedicated to the memory of Poulenc's father, consists of the traditional portions of the Roman Mass Ordinary except the Credo and is reflective of the "unadorned architecture of a Romanesque church." The work's angular melodic lines and metric stresses of unaccented syllables set the musical style that would characterize much of Poulenc's choral music in later years. Other well-known and frequently performed sacred works include the *Quatre motets pour un temps de pénitence* (Four Lenten motets), which Poulenc said "are as realistic and tragic as a painting of Montegna"; *Quatre motets pour le temps de Noël* (Four Christmas motets), which are "more serene and less dramatic than the Lenten motets"; and the *Gloria*, which was Poulenc's favorite choral composition. Composed to counter the sad character of his most recently composed sacred choral works, the *Gloria* was written with a deliberate humorous character—like "those frescoes by [Benozzo] Gozzoli [ca.1421–1497] where the angels stick our their tongues," or like "some serious Benedictine monks I had once seen reveling in a game of football." The *Gloria* also best illustrates Poulenc's pointillistic manner of composition, in which a few short motifs are clearly delineated and arranged in various combinations. For instance, in the first movement, "Gloria in excelsis Deo," the initial motif appears twenty-two times—nine as a complete two-measure unit, eleven as the motif's first half in a one-measure unit, and two as the motif's second half, also in a one-measure unit. The second movement, "Laudamus te," consists of six motifs, each attached to a short fragment of text and most of them abbreviated as in the "Gloria in excelsis Deo."

The well-known secular works include two collections of chansons and two cantatas. The *Sept chansons*—Poulenc's first major secular work for chorus, composed in 1936 after Poulenc heard a performance of Monteverdi madrigals conducted by Nadia Boulanger—are settings of five poems by Éluard and two poems by Apollinaire. The music is somewhat Monteverdian, with rhythms that reflect natural speech inflection, but it is more in the style of the Parisian chanson of the Renaissance, with alternating passages of homophony and imitative polyphony. The *Huit chansons françaises,* a collection of eight settings of folk texts, was Poulenc's final secular work. The musical rhythms are simpler and the textures are more Renaissance-like than the earlier collection of chansons. *Figure humaine* (The face of man) is a setting of eight poems from Éluard's famous wartime collection, entitled *Poésie et Vérité 42,* about the silent anger of a suffering people and their faith in liberty. Poulenc set the poems during the summer of 1943, scoring six of them for double chorus and two for single chorus (number four of the set is for the first chorus alone, and number six is for the second chorus). The music is demanding and virtuosic, especially in the final movement, "Liberté," which is substantially longer than the others and which ends with solo sopranos in both choruses singing Es above high C. Poulenc recognized the artistic stature of his work, writing to his friend Marie-Blanche in July 1944, "There is one work . . . that reassures me that I have the right to compose: that is my Cantata on the poems by Éluard. . . . Its integrity and conviction conquer my most somber moods and my sharpest self-criticism." *Un soir de neige* (An evening of snow) was composed between December 24 and 26, 1944, and is a setting of four other poems by Éluard—"De grandes cuillers de neige" (Great lumps of snow), "La bonne neige" (The beautiful snow), "Bois meutri" (Scarred woods), and "La nuit le froid la solitude" (The night the cold the loneliness). Poulenc's serene and delicate writing in this "Petite Cantate de chamber" (Little chamber cantata), as Poulenc subtitled it, is almost completely in contrast to the writing in *Figure humaine.*

SACRED WORKS
COMPLETE AND LISTED IN CHRONOLOGICAL ORDER
ACCORDING TO DATE OF COMPOSITION

Litanies à la vierge noire – 1936 – SSA chorus of children or women and organ (arranged for strings and timpani in 1947) – 8 minutes. Three solo voices are occasionally specified for each choral part.

Messe en sol Majeur – 1937 – SATB chorus (with divisions) a cappella – 20 minutes. Three solo voices are occasionally specified for each choral part, including those that are divided.

Quatre motets pour un temps de pénitence – 1938–1939 – SATB chorus (with divisions) a cappella – "Timor et tremor" 3:15 minutes, "Vinea mea electa" 3:45 minutes, "Tenebrae factae sunt" 4 minutes, and "Tristis est anima mea" 3:15 minutes.

Exultate Deo – 1941 – SATB chorus a cappella – 2:30 minutes.

Salve regina – 1941 – SATB chorus a cappella – 5 minutes.

Quatre petites prières de Saint François d'Assise – 1948 – TBBB chorus a cappella – 7:30 minutes.

Stabat mater – 1950–1951 – S solo, SATBB chorus, and orchestra (including piccolo, English horn, bass clarinet, and two harps) – 32 minutes.

Quatre motets pour le temps de Noël – 1951–1952 – SATB chorus (with divisions) a cappella – "O magnum mysterium" 3 minutes, "Quem vidistis pastores" 2:30 minutes, "Videntes stellam" 3 minutes, and "Hodie Christus natus est" 2 minutes.

Ave verum corpus – 1952 – SSA chorus a cappella – 2:15 minutes.

Laudes de Saint Antoine de Padoue – 1957–1959 – TBB chorus (with divisions) a cappella – "O Jésu perpetua lux" 2 minutes, "O proles hispaniae" 45 seconds, "Laus regi plena gaudio" 2:15 minutes, and "Si quaeris" 2 minutes.

Gloria – 1959–1960 – S solo, SATB chorus (with divisions), and orchestra (including piccolo, English horn, bass clarinet, contrabassoon, and harp) – 25 minutes.

Sept répons des ténèbres – 1961–1962 – child solo, SATB chorus (SA sung by boys and TB sung by men), and orchestra – 24 minutes. (1) Poulenc states at the beginning of the score that "one may replace the boys' choral voices with women's choral voices, but *on no account* by girls' voices"; (2) the choral parts divide occasionally.

SECULAR WORKS
COMPLETE AND LISTED IN CHRONOLOGICAL ORDER
ACCORDING TO DATE OF COMPOSITION

Chanson à boire – 1922 – TTBB chorus a cappella – 3:30 minutes.

Sept chansons – 1936 – SATB chorus (with divisions) a cappella – "La blanche neige" 1 minute, "A peine défigurée" 1:15 minutes, "Par une nuit nouvelle" 1:15 minutes, "Tous les droits" 2:15 minutes, "Belle et ressemblante" 1:45 minutes, "Marie" 2 minutes, and "Luire" 1:45 minutes. Solos from one to three voices per part are occasionally specified.

Petites voix – 1936 – SSA children's or women's chorus a cappella – "La petite fille sage" 1:30 minutes, "Le chien perdu" 1 minute, "En rentrant de l'école" 30 seconds, "Le petit garçon malade" 2 minutes, and "Le hérisson" 45 seconds.

Sécheresses – 1937 – SATB chorus and orchestra – 17 minutes.

Figure humaine – 1943 – SSATBB/SSATBB chorus a cappella – 18 minutes.

Un soir de neige – 1944 – SSATBB chorus a cappella – 6 minutes.

Huit chansons françaises – 1945–1946 – SATB, SATBB, and TBB chorus a cappella – "Margoton va t'a l'iau" (SATB) 2 minutes, "La belle se siet au pied de la tour" (SATBB) 1:30 minutes, "Pilons l'orgue" (SATBB) 45 seconds, "Clic, clac, dansez sabots" (TBB) 2 minutes, "C'est la petit' fill' du prince" (SATBB) 5:30 minutes, "La belle si nous étions" (TBB) 1 minute, "Ah! mon beau laboureur" (SATB) 3:45 minutes, and "Les tisserands" (SATBB) 1:45 minutes.

WILLY BURKHARD 1900–1955

Burkhard was born near Bern, Switzerland, and received his musical education at the Bern Conservatory. He further studied in Leipzig, Munich, and Paris and became attracted to the music of the late Renaissance and early Baroque eras. He returned to Bern in 1924, teaching at the conservatory beginning in 1928, and in 1942 he joined the faculty of the Zurich Conservatory.

He composed two oratorios, eight cantatas, one mass, seven miscellaneous choral works accompanied by instruments, and twenty-three opuses of works for a cappella chorus. The most important compositions are the oratorio *Das Gesicht Jesajas* op.41 of 1933 to 1935 and the *Mass* op.85 of 1951 (both scored for soloists, chorus, and orchestra) and the cantata *Die Sintflut* op.97 of 1954 scored for SSAATTBB chorus a cappella. Other works include *Psalm xciii* (Psalm 93) op.49 of 1937 for unison chorus and organ; *Genug ist genug* op.53 of 1938 to 1939 for chorus, two trumpets, timpani, and strings; *Cantate Domino* op.61 no.2 of 1940 for soprano solo, mixed chorus, strings, and timpani; and *Frühlingsglaube* (without opus number) of 1950 for male chorus a cappella. All of these works are characterized by imitative polyphonic textures and traditional, although advanced, harmonies.

MAURICE DURUFLÉ 1902–1986

Duruflé was born in Louviers, south of Rouen, and received his musical education as a chorister at the Rouen Cathedral choir school. In his early teens he served as substitute organist at the school, in his mid-teens he studied organ with Louis Vierne and Charles Tournemire in Paris, and at eighteen he became substitute organist for Tournemire at the church of Ste Clotilde. At eighteen Duruflé also entered the Paris Conservatoire, where he studied organ with Eugéne Gigout and composition with Paul Dukas. Duruflé became assistant to Vierne at Notre Dame Cathedral when he was twenty-five, and he was appointed organist at St Etienne-du-Mont when he was twenty-eight. He remained at St Etienne-du-Mont for the next forty-five years, while also teaching harmony at the Conservatoire from 1943 to 1970. In addition, he was a noted performer, playing in the premiere of Poulenc's organ concerto in 1941 and touring frequently throughout Europe, Russia, and the United States with his wife, Marie-Madeleine (referred to as Madame Duruflé). His performing and teaching ended after an automobile accident in 1975, and for the remaining years of his life he was frequently confined to his home.

Duruflé's compositional output consists of only fourteen works—six for chorus, four for organ, and four for piano, orchestra, or chamber ensemble. The organ works, which include the famous *Prélude, adagio et choral varié sur le "Veni Creator"* op.4 and *Prélude et fugue sur le nom d'Alain* op.7, were composed early in his career, while the choral works were composed later. The *Requiem* op.9, which is considered to be one of the great masterpieces of twentieth-century choral repertoire, began as a series of organ pieces based on Gregorian chants. Duruflé remolded his sketches and incorporated them into the *Requiem* when he received a commission for a choral work from his publisher, Durand. The Gregorian chants are sometimes used prominently as a cantus firmus and sometimes woven discreetly into the fabric of the vocal and instrumental lines. For example, the first movement of the work begins with the tenors and basses singing an exact statement of the "Requiem aeternam" chant from the Mass for the Dead (found on page 1807 in the *Liber usualis*), the sopranos sing the "Te decet" in the middle of the movement, and the "Requiem aeternam" returns at the end of the movement as the principal melodic material of the orchestration. At the beginning and end of the second movement, the "Kyrie" chant (on pages 1807 and 1808 in the *Liber usualis*) is featured in long notes as a cantus firmus in the orchestra, and in the third movement, fragments of the "Domine Jesu Christe" chant (on pages 1813 and 1814) are heard in the orchestral, choral, and solo baritone parts. The overall structure and scoring of the work are based on Fauré's *Requiem:* Duruflé chose exactly the same movements and put them in the same order except for the addition of Lux aeterna between the Agnus Dei and Libera me; the scoring is for soprano and baritone soloists, the baritone singing in the Offertory and Libera me and the soprano singing in the Pie Jesu; and a number of the movements are in an ABA format.

The *Quatre motets sur des themes Grégoriens* op.10 are also based on Gregorian chants. In "Ubi caritas," which is from the Antiphon found on page 664 in the *Liber usualis,* the chant is mainly in the alto voice part and is accompanied by the other voices in a homophonic texture; in "Tota pulchra es," from the Antiphon on page 1320, the chant is in the soprano voice part and is accompanied by independent rhythms in the other voices; in "Tu es Petrus," from the antiphon found on pages 1515 and 1516, the chant is treated imitatively in all voice parts; and in "Tantum ergo," from the fifth verse of the hymn "Pange lingua" found on page 958, the chant appears as a canon between the soprano and tenor voice parts. The *Messe* ("Cum jubilo") op.11 and *Notre père* (Pater noster) also incorporate Gregorian chants.

CHORAL WORKS
COMPLETE AND LISTED IN CHRONOLOGICAL ORDER
ACCORDING TO DATE OF COMPOSITION

Requiem op.9 – 1947 – SB solos, SATB chorus, and orchestra (including piccolo, English horn, bass clarinet, cymbals, bass drum, tam-tam, celesta, harp, and organ) – 38 minutes. (1) The solos are specified for mezzo-soprano and baritone; (2) the solos may also be sung by choral sections, a performance option approved by Duruflé at the end of his life; (3) the soprano choral parts divide occasionally; (4) Duruflé made an arrangement of the orchestral accompaniment for organ in 1948.

Quatre motets sur des themes Grégoriens op.10 – 1960 – SATB and SSA chorus a cappella – "Ubi caritas" (SATTBB) 2:30 minutes, "Tota pulchra es" (SSA) 2:15 minutes, "Tu es Petrus" (SATB) 1 minute, and "Tantum ergo" (SATB) 3 minutes. The second soprano and alto parts divide in "Tota pulchra es."

Messe ("Cum jubilo") op.11 – 1966 – B solo, unison B chorus, and orchestra (including organ) – 18 minutes. The solo and choral parts are specified for baritone.

Notre père – 1977 – SATB chorus a cappella – 1:30 minutes.

ANDRÉ JOLIVET 1905–1974

Jolivet was born in Paris and developed an interest in music during his teenage years. At thirteen he began composing, at fourteen he began studying cello, and at fifteen he entered the choir school at the church of Notre Dame de Clignancourt. During his early twenties he was attracted to the music and wrote in the Impressionistic style of Debussy, Dukas, and Ravel. However, during his late twenties he became interested in the atonal music of Schoenberg and the percussion works of Edgar Varèse, with whom he studied. Jolivet later became friends with Messiaen and joined him in founding the group La jeune France, whose objectives were to compose music that had spiritual or human qualities and that dealt with mystical and erotic subjects. The four composers of La jeune France (Jolivet, Messiaen, Daniel-Lesur, and Yves Baudrier) were frequently referred to as the "quatre petits frères spiritualistes" (four little spiritual brothers). From 1945 to 1959 Jolivet was musical director of the Comédie Française, for which he wrote music to fourteen plays, and throughout the latter years of his life he made frequent trips to the Middle East, East Asia, and Africa in search of literature and music that related to his mystical ideals.

Jolivet composed seven choral works, including the vocal chamber piece *Epithalame* in 1953, the oratorio *La vérité de Jeanne* in 1956, and the mass *Messe "Uxor tua"* in 1962. *Epithalame* was commissioned by Marcel Couraud, conductor of the Chorale Nationale de Radio France (often referred to as the ORTF) and the Ensemble Vocal Marcel Couraud, and was dedicated to Jolivet's wife on the occasion of their twentieth wedding anniversary (an epithalamium is a wedding piece). The work is scored for twelve solo voices, which Jolivet called "a vocal orchestra" and is a setting of varied sacred Egyptian, Hindu, Chinese, Hebrew, and Greek texts. The music is also in a variety of styles—from onomatopoeic sounds of bells to jazz sounds reflective of American big bands. *La vérité de Jeanne* was commissioned by the Abbé Carl de Nys for the 500th anniversary of the process for the rehabilitation of Joan of Arc and was performed at the Festival de Domrémy. It is based on a fifteenth-century text and is scored for speaker, SSATBB solos, chorus, and large orchestra. The musical style is characterized by percussive sounds, soundscapes, and structures of melody and rhythm based on number ratios. The part of the narrator follows the tradition of earlier twentieth-century French oratorios in being scored for actress and dancer. The *Messe "Uxor tua"* is a setting of the traditional portions of the Roman Mass Ordinary scored for SSATB solos, SSATB chorus, flute, oboe (doubling English horn), bassoon, trombone, and organ.

HENK BADINGS 1907–1987

Badings was born in Bandung, Java, of Dutch parents, who moved to the Netherlands when Henk was eight years old. He prepared for a nonmusical career by studying at the Technical University in Delft, and in 1931 he began teaching paleontology and historical geology there. He also maintained a keen interest in music, and taught himself theory, harmony, and the rudiments of composition. In the early 1930s he was recognized for his symphonic compositions, and in 1934 he was appointed lecturer of composition and theory at Rotterdam Conservatory. He became codirector of the Amsterdam Muzieklyceum in 1937, from 1941 to 1945 he was director of the State Conservatory in The Hague, and during the 1960–1961 academic year he served as director of the electronic studio at the University of Utrecht. From 1961 to 1972 he taught acoustics at the university, and from 1962 to 1972 he was also professor of composition at the Staatliche Hochschule für Musik in Stuttgart. In addition, he frequently lectured in the United States and South Africa during the 1970s. Although much of his career was spent in the Netherlands, Badings is discussed here because his most famous choral compositions are settings of French texts and are similar in style to the works of early-twentieth-century French composers.

Badings composed fifteen choral/orchestral works, thirty a cappella and piano-accompanied works for mixed chorus, twenty-two works for male chorus, and thirteen works for female chorus. The choral/orchestral compositions, which are not well known, include nine cantatas—from *Kantate I* in 1936 to *Kantate IX* in 1987—and three oratorios—*Apocalypse* of 1948, *Jonah* of 1963, and *St Mark Passion* of 1970. The best-known and most frequently performed work is *Trois chansons bretonnes* of 1946. It is in the Impressionistic style of Debussy and Ravel and consists of "La nuit en mer" scored for SSAATTBB chorus and piano, "La complainte des âmes" scored for SSATBB chorus a cappella, and "Soir d'été" scored for SAATTBB and piano. Other popular works include the *Trois chants populaires* of 1953 and *Cinq poèmes chinois* of 1973. The first of these compositions consists of three popular *noëls* (Christmas carols) arranged for female chorus—"Noël nouvelet" and "Les anges dans nos campagnes" for S solo and SSAA chorus a cappella and "A la venue de Noël" for SSAA chorus a cappella. The second work, subtitled "Five choral songs on old Chinese poems," is in a more modern style. Glissandos and sprechstimme are featured in numbers one and five ("Le destin de l'homme" and "La danse des dieux"), and a tuning system based on a thirty-one-note scale is employed in number three ("Le pavillon de porcelaine"). Number two ("Evocation") is characterized by soundscapes, and number four ("La mort") is highly dissonant. All the pieces are scored for SSAATTBB chorus a cappella. Other works by Badings in a modern style include *Aus tiefer Not schrei ich zu Dir*, *Requiem*, and *Vocalizzo burlesco*. All three pieces were composed in 1978, and all feature avant-garde characteristics such as tone clusters, new notational symbols, and aleatoric performance.

JEAN LANGLAIS 1907–1991

Langlais was born in Fontenelle, a small town in the Brittany area of France. Blind from birth, he received his primary education at the Paris Institut des Jeunes Aveugles (Institute for the Young Blind), and while there he learned to play the organ and piano. At age twenty he enrolled at the Paris Conservatoire, where he studied organ with Marcel Dupré and composition with Paul Dukas, and during the next several years he also studied organ with Charles Tournemire, organist at the church of Ste Clotilde. In 1932 Langlais was appointed organist at St Pierre-de-Montrouge, and in 1933 he began teaching organ and composition and conducting the chorus at his alma mater, the Institut des Jeunes Aveugles. He was appointed organist at Ste Clotilde in 1945, a position he retained until 1987, and during those years he also toured extensively as an organ recitalist throughout the United States.

Langlais composed six masses and sixteen motets and Psalm settings. The two well-known masses are the *Messe solennelle*, composed in 1951 for liturgical services at Ste Clotilde and scored for SATB chorus and organ, and *Missa Salve regina*, composed in 1954, first performed at Notre Dame Cathedral in Paris, and scored for three solo voices (sung by either three tenors or unison child choristers), TTBB chorus, two organs (Grand Orgue and Orgue de Choeur), and two brass ensembles (two trumpets and two trombones with the Grand Orgue and one trumpet and three trombones with the Orgue de Choeur). The first of the masses is relatively subdued in quality, whereas the second mass, based on the "Salve regina" Gregorian chant, is festive and grandiose. Both masses consist of Kyrie, Gloria, Sanctus, and Agnus Dei movements; the Credo was sung as a Gregorian chant. The other masses are *Mass in Ancient Style* of 1952 for chorus and organ, *Missa in simplicitate* of 1953 for chorus and organ, *Missa Misericordiae Domini* of 1958 for double chorus and organ, and *Solemn Mass "Orbis factor"* of 1969 for chorus and organ. The motets and Psalm settings include the *Festival Alleluia* of 1971 for SATB chorus (with occasional divisions) and organ; *Te Deum* of 1973 for SATB chorus, trumpet, timpani, and organ; and *Three Marion Antiphons* ("Regina coeli," "Ave, regina coelorum," and "Salve regina") of 1974 for solo voice or unison chorus and organ.

OLIVIER MESSIAEN 1908–1992

Messiaen was born in Avignon, in southern France, and began playing the piano and composing at age seven. During the following several years he studied piano and harmony privately, and at eleven he enrolled at the Paris Conservatoire, studying organ with Marcel Dupré and composition with Paul Dukas. Messiaen's first composition, *Le Banquet céleste* for organ, was composed in 1928 (revised in 1960), and his first major work, *L'Ascension* ("Four Symphonic Meditations"), was composed in 1933 and 1934. Meanwhile, he was appointed organist at the church of La Trinité in 1931, a position he would retain for more than sixty years. In 1936 he and three other composers (one of whom was André Jolivet, his classmate at the Conservatoire) founded the group *La jeune France,* whose objectives were to compose music that had spiritual or human qualities and that dealt with mystical and erotic subjects. From 1939 to 1941, at the beginning of World War II, he served in the French army, spending the second year of his service as a prisoner of war, and while captive he composed the famous *Quatuor pour la fin du temps* (Quartet for the end of time) for clarinet, piano, violin, and cello. Upon his release in 1941 he began teaching harmony at the Conservatoire, and during the next decade he received acclaim for his large-scale *Turangalîla-Symphonie,* commissioned by the Boston Symphony Orchestra, composed between 1946 and 1948, and premiered under the direction of Leonard Bernstein. Messiaen's other large-scale works, the oratorio *La Transfiguration de Notre Seigneur Jésus-Christ* and opera *Saint François d'Assise,* were composed in the 1960s and 1970s. The music of these works is characterized by modal harmonies based on original modes, Hindu-like rhythmic patterns, and qualities of sensuality and primitivism—in the composer's words, "an iridescent music, music that will delight the auditory senses with delicate, voluptuous pleasures." The writing is also heavily influenced by birdcalls, which "produce an extremely sophisticated interlocking of rhythmic pedalpoints."

Messiaen composed five choral works. *O sacrum convivium,* subtitled "motet au Saint-Sacrement" (motet for Holy Communion) and composed in 1937, is in the Impressionistic style of Debussy and Ravel. It was one of the most popular and frequently performed sacred pieces of the twentieth century. *Trois petites liturgies de la Présence Divine,* characterized by Impressionistic vocal melodies and harmonies accompanied by instrumental birdcall effects and other rhyth-

mically complex patterns, was composed in 1943 and 1944 and consists of three movements—
Antienne de la conversation intérieure, with opening text "Dieu present en nous" (God present
in us); Séquence du verbe, cantique divin, with opening text "Dieu present en lui-même" (God
present in himself); and Psalmodie de l'ubiquité par Amour, with opening text "Dieu present
en toutes choses" (God present in all things). *Chant des déportés,* the least known of Messiaen's
choral works, was commissioned by Radio France to celebrate the liberation of prisoners from
concentration camps and premiered by the Orchestre Nationale de France in 1945. The text is
by Messiaen and begins, "En marchant, vers la mort, plus haut, soleil qui gémit, je trouverai
mon ciel et ma nuit" (Walking toward death, higher, groaning sun, I shall find my sky and my
night).

   Cinq rechants was composed in 1948 and dedicated to the Ensemble Vocal Marcel Couraud,
which gave the premiere. The work consists of five movements, each modeled after the verse/
refrain Renaissance chansons composed in the *musique mesurée* style and exemplified by Claude
Le Jeune. For instance, the first movement begins with a solo and is followed by a refrain
(rechant), duet, refrain, trio, and refrain. Movement three manifests the rhythmic organization
of *musique mesurée* with serialized expansions of note values. The text, which is by Messiaen and
which combines phrases in French with phrases in a newly created Hindu-like language, conveys sequences of a love relationship—from courtship to lovemaking and conflict to separation
and death. In keeping with the objectives of *La jeune France* to compose music about erotic subjects, the music in the *Cinq rechants* is often explicit. Notable are the depictions of copulation,
ejaculation, and pleasurable aftermath in movement four. According to Messiaen, the final measures of the movement, which are the only measures in a recognizable Impressionistic style,
portray "the lovers smoking cigarettes after having made love." Messiaen also said, "I consider
the *Cinq rechants* as one of my best works, and I am very fond of it."

   La Transfiguration de Notre Seigneur Jésus-Christ, composed between 1965 and 1969, was
commissioned by the Gulbenkian Foundation and premiered in June 1969 at the thirteenth
Gulbenkian Music Festival in Lisbon, Portugal. The text—assembled by Messiaen from the
Bible, Roman Missal, and the theological writings of Saint Thomas Aquinas—describes different aspects of Christ's Transfiguration. According to Messiaen, these texts are "divided into two
septenaries or groups of seven pieces. Each fragment of the Gospel narrative of the Transfiguration is followed by two pieces developing its basic ideas, and a chorale closes each of the two
septenaries." The music is characterized by frequent unison singing accompanied by rhythmically complex and colorful orchestrations.

CHORAL WORKS
COMPLETE AND LISTED ACCORDING TO FAMILIARITY

O sacrum convivium – SATB chorus or soloists a cappella (with a *colla parte*
   organ part marked ad lib.) – 5 minutes.

Trois petites liturgies de la Présence Divine – SSAA chorus, piano, ondes
   martenot, strings, celesta, vibraphone, and several percussion instruments – 34 minutes.

Cinq rechants – SSSAAATTTBBB solo ensemble a cappella – 21 minutes.

La Transfiguration de Notre Seigneur Jésus-Christ – TB solos, SATB chorus, solo piano, cello, flute, clarinet, marimba, xylophone, vibraphone, and orchestra – 90 minutes. According to Messiaen, the chorus should number at least one hundred, and the orchestra should contain sixty-eight strings and forty-one other instruments.

Chant des déportés – ST chorus and orchestra (including bass clarinet, piano, and cymbals) – 5 minutes. The ST choral parts are in octaves.

JEHAN ALAIN 1911–1940

Alain was born in Saint Germain-en-Laye, one of the suburbs of Paris, where his father, Albert (1880–1971), was organist at the parish church. Jehan studied with his father before entering the Paris Conservatoire at age seventeen and continuing studies with Marcel Dupré, Paul Dukas, and Jean Roger-Ducasse. At twenty-two Alain interrupted his studies to serve in the military, and at twenty-four he was appointed organist at the church of St Nicolas de Maisons-Laffitte and also at the synagogue on Rue Notre-Dame de Nazareth. He reentered military service in 1939 and was killed in action the following year; he was twenty-nine. His sacred choral music is frequently based on Gregorian chant or on melodies and flexible rhythms that are suggestive of chant, and his organ and secular choral music has modal and rhythmic elements of folk music from Morocco and India. Alain's younger sister, Marie-Claire (born 1926), became one of the most renowned organists of the twentieth century, playing hundreds of recitals throughout Europe and the United States, recording the complete works of J. S. Bach three times, and championing the organ works of her brother.

Jehan Alain composed 120 vocal and instrumental works during the decade between 1929 and 1939, including three masses, seven Latin motets, and eight sacred and secular works in French. The three masses were all composed in 1938—*Messe modale en septuor* (Modal mass in seven parts) for SA soloists or chorus, flute, and string quartet; *Messe grégorienne de marriage* (Gregorian mass of marriage) for T solo or unison voices and string quartet; and *Messe de Requiem* for SATB chorus and organ ad lib. The first two masses contain Kyrie, Gloria, Sanctus, and Agnus Dei movements, while the third mass has only a Kyrie, Sanctus, and Agnus Dei. The Latin motets include *Tu es Petrus* for SAB chorus and organ, *O salutaris hostia de Dugay* for SATB chorus a cappella, and *Tantum ergo* for TTBB chorus a cappella (another setting of *Tantum ergo* is scored for SS voices and organ). The works in French include *Prière pour nous autres charnels* for TB voices and organ.

CARL RÜTTI B.1949

Rütti was born in Zug, Switzerland, and received his musical education as a chorister at nearby Engelberg Monastery. He later studied piano and organ at the Zurich Conservatory, graduating in 1975, and in 1976 he went to London, where he was impressed by the singing of British choirs. He was especially moved by the singing at Brompton Oratory (the Church of the Immaculate Heart of Mary in South Kensington) and by a performance of Domenico Scarlatti's ten-part *Stabat mater* sung by the BBC Singers. These experiences inspired Rütti to compose choral music, and during the next several years (1976–1978) he wrote seven motets on poems by Rainer Maria Rilke, collectively entitled *Buch der Bilder.* In 1980 he received commissions from the Freiburg Cathedral Choir and Radio de la Suisse Romande, which resulted in the *Missa brevis* and *Magnificat,* and thereafter he composed numerous works for the BBC Singers and BBC Symphony Orchestra Chorus, Cambridge Voices, and choral ensembles in the United States.

Rütti has composed sixty-five choral works—twenty-two works for a cappella chorus and forty-three works for chorus and instruments. The a cappella works are the best known and most widely performed. *Nunc dimittis* begins with two tenor voices imitating the sounds of a wild dove and a pigeon, thus characterizing Luke 2:24, "and to oeer a sacrifice according to that which is said in the law of the Lord, a pair of turtledoves or two young pigeons." This verse precedes the text of the Nunc dimittis in verses 29–31, which are sung by the tenor soloist, and verse 32, "Lumen ad revelationem gentium, et gloriam plebes tuae Israel" (A light as revelation to the Gentiles, and the glory of thy people Israel), which is sung by the main choir. The *Missa Angelorum* began as the four-movement *Missa brevis* mentioned above. Rütti describes these movements as "a very sad sorrowful Kyrie, a Sanctus out in the evening landscape when the last light in the sky is colored with little clouds, a Benedictus as an invented Alpenhorn tune, and an Agnus Dei in the way we can see the Lamb in the Book of Revelation: huge and great." A Gloria and Ite missa est were added in 1993, and at that time Rütti renamed the mass for the German word *englisch* (angelorum), which means both English and angelic, and which conveys the thought that "the angels in heaven must sound like English choirs."

O magnum mysterium is in three connecting sections—a slow-moving soundscape to the opening text that expresses great mystery, a lively dance to the text that mentions the birth of Jesus, and an exuberant and fast-moving Amen. *Alpha et Omega* combines passages from John and Revelation, the title of the work coming from Revelation 21:6. As the text unfolds, John the Baptist tells two disciples that Jesus is the Lamb of God, the disciples ask Jesus where he lives, Jesus replies that he lives in the holy city of Jerusalem, and the chorus enumerates the many manifestations of Jesus, from the way, the truth, and the life, to alpha and omega. *Veni creator spiritus* was inspired by Thomas Tallis's forty-part motet *Spem in alium,* which Rütti heard in performances by the Cambridge Voices in 1994 and 1996. In composing his forty-part work, Rütti "chose the same casting as in the Tallis: 8 x SATBB standing in an octagon and surrounding the audience like a group of eight trees." However, Rütti moves the positions of some of these choruses to create the effect of sound from a distance.

CHORAL WORKS

SELECTED AND LISTED ACCORDING TO FAMILIARITY

Nunc dimittis – 1984 (revised in 1992) – T solo, SAB distant chorus, and
    SSSAATTBBB main chorus a cappella – 9:30 minutes. Rütti notes that
    the "main choir and distant choir should blend to a colorful, mysterious
    sound, as if light from heaven flew into our natural light (the distant
    choir could sing in the sacristy or from the gallery)."

Missa angelorum – 1982 – ST/SATB/SATBB chorus a cappella – 21 minutes.

O magnum mysterium – 1991 – SSSSAATTTBBBB chorus a cappella – 5 minutes.

Buch der Bilder – 1976–1978 – solos as specified below and SSSAATTBB chorus a cappella – "Bangnis" (SAA solos) 6:30 minutes, "Einsamkeit" (SAT solos) 6 minutes, "Herbst" (SSAAT solos) 6 minutes, "Gebet" (T solo) 8:30 minutes, "Fortschritt" (no solos) 3:15 minutes, "Abend" (ST solos) 6 minutes, and "Strophen" (SSAATTB solos) 8 minutes.

Alpha et Omega – 1994 – SATB solos and SSSAATTBBB chorus a cappella – 13:30 minutes. The solos represent John the Baptist (T), Jesus (B), and two disciples (S and A).

Ave Maria – 1993 – SATB chorus and organ – 4:30 minutes.

Ave maris stella – 1996 – SSAATTBB chorus a cappella – 6 minutes.

Veni creator spiritus – 1997 – eight SATBB choruses a cappella – 29 minutes.

Aus tiefer Not – 2006 – SSAATTBB chorus a cappella – 8 minutes.

An die Musik – 2003 – SATB/SATB chorus a cappella – 10 minutes.

Requiem – 2007 – SB solos, SATB/SATB chorus, strings, harp, and organ – 60 minutes. The solo soprano part may be sung by an adult or a child.

❦ AUSTRIA AND GERMANY ❦

Austria and Germany have been of relative equality in terms of the number of Modern-era composers born, educated, and employed in each country. Alexander Zemlinsky, Arnold Schoenberg, Anton Webern, Johann Nepomuk David, and Ernst Krenek were/are from Austria, while Paul Hindemith, Carl Orff, Hanns Eisler, Ernst Pepping, Franz Biebl, Hugo Distler, and Hans Werner Henze were/are from Germany. The two countries have not, however, been equal in world impact. The Austrian composers, especially Schoenberg, took the lead in developing new techniques of musical expression and in influencing composers throughout Europe, while the German composers looked back in history for inspiration and wrote in conservative musical languages. In particular, Schoenberg, Webern, and Krenek were pioneers in the development of the twelve-tone technique and other aspects of serialization, and their music was composed for highly skilled performers. On the other hand, Pepping and Distler were proponents of the Lutheran reform movement, which sought to return composition to styles of the late Renaissance and early Baroque, and Hindemith and Eisler wrote music that was of practical value to amateurs. In addition, Orff also looked back to past eras for compositional models.

A significant number of both Austrian and German composers were negatively affected by the Nazi regime and emigrated to the United States. Three of these composers—Zemlinsky, Schoenberg, and Krenek—were Jewish and took refuge in the United States to avoid persecution. Two other composers—Hindemith and Eisler (who eventually returned to Germany)—moved to the United States in order to express their craft freely.

Other composers, who have contributed in a less significant manner or who have written only a few works that have entered the general performing repertoire, are Hans Pfitzner, Franz Schmidt, Ernst Toch, Wolfgang Fortner, Kurt Hessenburg, and Heinz Werner Zimmermann. Alban Berg (1885–1935), who was a notable composer famous for his songs, chamber music, and operas *Wozzeck* and *Lulu,* wrote no choral music. His sometimes-cited *Die Nachtigall* for sixteen-voiced chorus is an arrangement of his solo song made by Clytus Gottwald in 1982.

Pfitzner (1869–1949) was born in Moscow but raised in Frankfurt, Germany, where his father became leader (concertmaster) of the Stadttheater orchestra in 1872. Hans studied at the Hoch Conservatory in Frankfurt between 1886 and 1890, and between 1897 and 1907 he taught at the Stern Conservatory in Berlin. In 1907 he was appointed director of the Strasbourg Conservatory in France and also conductor of the Strasbourg orchestra, and in 1920 he returned to Berlin to teach at the Prussian Academy of Arts. During the following decade he received several awards for his work, including the Bavarian Order of Maximilian, and during the 1930s and 1940s he served as a conductor and accompanist for various Nazi enterprises. He is most recognized for his opera *Palestrina,* composed between 1911 and 1915, and for his cantata *Von deutscher Seele,* composed in 1922 to German nationalistic poetry by Joseph Eichendorff (1788–1857). Other Pfitzner works include seven part songs, all scored for male chorus a cappella.

Schmidt (1874–1939) was born in Pressburg, Hungary (now Bratislava, Slovakia), and developed advanced keyboard skills as a young child. At fifteen he entered the conservatory of the Gesellschaft der Musikfreunde in Vienna, where he learned to play the cello, and from 1896 to 1911 he was a cellist in the Vienna Philharmonic. During this time he also played in the Vienna Hofoper orchestra, and beginning in 1901 he taught cello, piano, counterpoint, and composition at the conservatory. He is known for his oratorio *Das Buch mit sieben Siegeln,* composed between 1935 and 1937 for the 125th anniversary of the founding of the Vienna Gesellschaft der Musikfreunde and premiered there in July 1938. The text is from, and utilizes almost all of, the biblical book of Revelation. Schmidt organized this material into two parts, the first of which describes the first of the seven seals (sieben Siegeln) and the second of which describes the seventh seal and the ensuing silence in heaven. Schmidt also added texts to relate the apocalypse to contemporary life. The red horse, for instance, symbolizes the famine caused by World War I. The oratorio is scored for six soloists (a tenor representing John, a bass representing the Voice of the Lord, and an unnamed quartet), mixed chorus, and large orchestra (including organ). The musical texture is post-Romantic, with expanded tertian harmonies and thematic transformations of motifs.

Toch (1887–1964) was born in Vienna and studied at conservatories in both Vienna and Frankfurt. He taught at the Mannheim Hochschule für Musik beginning in 1913, and during the 1920s achieved success with his operas *Die Prinzessin* and *Egon und Emilie,* He emigrated to the United States in 1935, became a citizen in 1940, and for the next two decades composed sixteen film scores, three of which were nominated for Academy Awards. For the last years of his life he taught at the University of Southern California. Toch composed two cantatas for mixed chorus and orchestra—*Das Wasser* op.53 in 1930 and *Cantata of Bitter Herbs* op.65 in 1938—and two a cappella pieces for speaking chorus—*Fuge aus der Geographie* (Geographical Fugue) in 1930 and *Valse* in 1961. Both these latter pieces are examples of Gebrauchsmusik: the first, for SATB, is a strict fugue to a text that is a listing of cities, countries, lakes, rivers, and other geographical features of the world; the second, for SSAATTBB and percussion, is a waltz set to a nonsense text characterized by frequent alliterations.

Fortner (1907–1987) was born in Leipzig and studied piano and organ privately as a young child. In 1931 he became a lecturer at the Evangelisches Kirchmusikalisches Institut (Institute of Church Music) in Heidelberg, in 1946 he began teaching summer courses in Darmstadt, and from 1957 to 1973 he taught at the Musikhochschule in Freiburg. His choral output consists of eleven works plus an additional six part songs (three for male chorus and three for mixed chorus). Of significance is *Der 100. Psalm,* a twelve-tone work composed in 1962 and scored for SSATB chorus, three horns, two trumpets, and two trombones. Other recognized works include *Eine deutsche Liedmesse* of 1934 for mixed chorus a cappella; the cantata *An die Nachgeborenen* of 1948 for speaker, T solo, chorus, and orchestra; and *Gladbacher Te Deum* of 1973 for B solo, mixed chorus, orchestra, and electronic tape.

Hessenburg (1908–1994) was born in Frankfurt, studied in Leipzig, and spent the majority of his career teaching composition at the Musikhochschule in Frankfurt. He composed a large number of works in a variety of genres and was honored with several significant awards, including the Düsseldorf Schumann Prize in 1951. His choral output consists mostly of sacred works in a conservative idiom, constructed according to the principles of the Lutheran reform movement prevalent in Germany during the mid-twentieth century and popular with composers such as Pepping and Distler. Significant works include the motet *O Herr, mache mich zum Werkzeug deines Friedens* (O Lord, make me an instrument of your peace) op.37 no.1, composed in 1946, loosely based on the famous prayer of St Francis of Assisi, and scored for SSATBB chorus a cappella; the cantata *Vom Wesen und Vergehen* (On being and passing away) op.45, composed in 1948, set to a text by the German poet Matthias Claudius (1740–1815), and scored for SB solos, SATB chorus, two flutes, two oboes, two clarinets, two bassoons, and strings; and *Messe* op.113, composed in 1981 and 1982, set to the traditional Latin Roman Mass Ordinary texts, and scored for SATB solos, SATB chorus, and orchestra. Other works include the *Weihnachtskantate* op.27 of 1942 to 1943, *Weihnachtsgeschichte* op.54 of 1950 to 1951, and *Passionmusik nach dem Evangelisten Lukas* op.103 of 1977.

Zimmermann (b.1930) was born in Freiburg, Germany, and received his musical education at the Evangelisches Kirchmusikalisches Institut in Heidelberg. He returned there in the late 1950s to succeed Wolfgang Fortner as teacher of composition, in 1963 he became director of the Berliner-Spandau Kirchenmusikschule, and from 1975 until 1999 he taught composition at the Hochschule für Musik und Darstellende Kunst in Frankfurt. The majority of his choral works are settings of Psalm or other common sacred texts in a jazz idiom that Zimmermann referred to as "international folklore." Perhaps the best known of the works in this style is *Psalmkonzert,* composed in 1956 and 1957 and scored for B solo, unison children's chorus, SSATB chorus, three trumpets, vibraphone, and string bass. The work is divided into five movements—the first to Psalm 96:1–3, the second to Psalm 40:1–5, the third to Psalm 103:8–11, the fourth to Psalm 107:1–22, and the fifth a repeat of movement one. The children's chorus sings the Lutheran chorale "Now thank we all our God" as a cantus firmus in the first and fifth movements. Other works in the same style include *Psalm 67* of 1973 for SATB chorus, glockenspiel ad lib., and string bass; *Missa profana* of 1962 to 1977 for SSATB solos, mixed chorus, jazz group, and orchestra; *My help comes from the Lord* of 1974 for SATB chorus, organ, and string bass; and the four motets in *Weihnacht*—"Mache dich auf, werde licht" (Isaiah 60:1–2), "Und das Wort ward Fleisch" (John 1:14), "Fürchtet euch nicht" (Luke 2:10–11), and "Ehre sei Gott in der Höhe" (Luke 2:14)—composed in 1957 and 1958 and scored for SATB chorus (with divisions) and string bass.

ALEXANDER ZEMLINSKY 1871–1942

Zemlinsky was born in Vienna, where his father had converted from Catholicism to Judaism the year before Alexander was born. He began studying piano at age four, and at fifteen he entered the Vienna Conservatory. At twenty-two he was recognized for several of his chamber works, which were performed locally; at twenty-three he was appointed *Kapellmeister* at the Carltheater; and at twenty-four he served as conductor of an amateur orchestra, called Polyhymnia, in which Arnold Schoenberg played cello. The two composers became friends, and in 1902 Schoenberg married Zemlinsky's sister Mathilde. In 1903 Zemlinsky became a teacher of orchestration at the Schwarzwald School, where his pupils included Alban Berg and Anton Webern, and in 1904 he became the main conductor of the Volksoper. Also in 1904 he and Schoenberg founded the Vereinignung Schaffender Tonkünstler, a society for the promotion of new music in Vienna. Zemlinsky was one of the conductors with Gustav Mahler at the Hofoper beginning in 1907, and in 1911 he moved to Prague, where he became the director of the Neues Deutsches Theater. In 1923 he began serving as guest conductor of the Prague Philharmonic Orchestra, with which he led the music of Mahler, Smetana, Janáček, Schoenberg, Berg, and Hindemith, and in 1927 he moved to Berlin, first as assistant director at the Kroll Opera and then as teacher at the Musikhochschule. To avoid religious persecution, he moved to Vienna in 1933 and New York City in 1938. He suffered a stroke in 1939 and was essentially incapacitated for the remainder of his life.

Zemlinsky composed nine choral works—three Psalm settings, one work for the Jewish liturgy, and five miscellaneous secular cantatas and part songs. *Psalm lxxxiii* (Psalm 83), subtitled "Klage und Vertrauen in grosser Not" (Lament and trust at a time of great need), was composed in 1900, shortly after Zemlinsky's father died; *Psalm xxiii* (Psalm 23), subtitled "Der gute Hirt" (The good shepherd), was composed in 1910 when Zemlinsky was at the peak of his professional career; and *Psalm xiii* (Psalm 13), subtitled "Eine Bitte um Hilfe gegen Feinde des Volkes" (A prayer for help against enemies of the people), was composed in 1935 when Jews were being persecuted throughout Austria and Germany. The work for the Jewish liturgy, *Hochzeitsgesang* (Wedding Song), was composed in 1896 to texts in Hebrew from Psalm 118 for the wedding of two friends.

The secular works include two pieces for chorus and string orchestra—*Frühlingsglaube* (Belief in Spring) and *Geheimnis* (Secret)—composed in 1896 for performance by Polyhymnia and a choral society conducted by Schoenberg; *Minnelied,* composed for the Döblinger Männergesangverein in about 1895 and scored for TTBB chorus two flutes, two horns, and harp; and the seven-movement cantata *Frühlingsbegräbnis* (The Burial of Spring), composed in 1896 (revised ca.1903) to a text by the German poet and dramatist Paul Heyse (1830–1914).

CHORAL WORKS

SELECTED AND LISTED ACCORDING TO FAMILIARITY

Psalm xiii (Psalm 13) – SATB chorus and orchestra – 13 minutes.

Psalm xxiii (Psalm 23) – SATB chorus and orchestra (including celesta, glockenspiel, and two harps) – 10 minutes.

Psalm lxxxiii (Psalm 83) – SATB solos, SATB chorus, and orchestra – 14 minutes.

Frühlingsbegräbnis – SB solos, SATB chorus, and orchestra – 24 minutes.

Frühlingsglaube and *Geheimnis* – SATB chorus and strings – 4:30 and 1:30 minutes.

Hochzeitsgesang – T solo, SATB chorus, and organ – 3:30 minutes.

ARNOLD SCHOENBERG 1874–1951

Schoenberg was born in Vienna to parents who were Orthodox Jews of Hungarian descent. At age eight he began violin lessons, and, because his family was poor and could not afford further music studies, he taught himself to play the cello. He did not study music seriously until his twenties, when he met Alexander Zemlinsky and began playing in the amateur orchestra Polyhymnia. Zemlinsky was influential both personally and musically—introducing Schoenberg to his sister Mathilde, whom he married in 1902, teaching Schoenberg the basics of composition, and evaluating his early compositions. Some of these works, such as the *String Quartet* in D major of 1897, were received well by the public. Other works, beginning with *Verklärte Nacht* in 1899, were, however, unpopular and misunderstood. In 1902 he moved to Berlin to teach at the Stern Conservatory, and in 1903 he returned to Vienna and taught along with Zemlinsky at the Schwarzwald School, where their students included Alban Berg and Anton Webern. In 1904 Schoenberg and Zemlinsky founded the Vereinignung Schaffender Tonkünstler, a society for the promotion of new music in Vienna, and during the next several years Schoenberg wrote some of his most controversial works, including *Das Buch der hängenden Gärten*. During this time he also became known as a painter and exhibited canvases with Wassily Kandinsky and other members of *Der Blaue Reiter*. In 1910 Schoenberg taught at the Kaiserlich-Königliche Akademie für Musik und Darstellende Kunst in Vienna, and in 1911 he went back to teach at the Stern Conservatory in Berlin. By this time a number of his works, including *Pierrot lunaire*, were receiving performances and acclaim throughout Europe, and Schoenberg was in demand as a conductor. In 1925 he succeeded Ferruccio Busoni as professor of composition at the Akademie der Künste in Berlin. However, he was released from this position in 1933 because of his Jewish ancestry and religious beliefs, and he moved first to France and then to the United States to avoid persecution. He taught for one year at the Malkin Conservatory in Boston and then relocated to Los Angeles to better cope with his increasing asthmatic condition. During the 1935–1936 academic year he lectured at the University of Southern California, and in 1936 he was appointed professor of composition at the University of California in Los Angeles. He became a citizen of the United States in 1941, and in 1944 his asthma worsened and he also developed diabetes. He had a heart attack in 1946, which confined him to his home, although he continued to compose until his death in 1951 at age seventy-six.

Schoenberg composed five choral/orchestral works, three a cappella sacred pieces, five collections of part and folk songs, and several other miscellaneous secular pieces. The early works, those composed before 1923, are in an expanded Romantic-era style, with traditional harmonies and textures. Most of the later works are constructed of twelve-tone rows, the basis of which came from what Schoenberg called a "Grundgestalt" (earth or basic shape), and which he described as "the first creative thought of a composition, the basis from which all else is derived." These twelve-tone works are also considered to be atonal, although Schoenberg preferred the term *pantonal,* meaning "all tonal."

The major choral/orchestral works are *Gurre-Lieder* (Songs of Gurre), *Die Jakobsleiter* (Jacob's Ladder), *Kol nidre* (All vows), and *A Survivor from Warsaw. Gurre-Lieder* was composed mostly between 1901 and 1903 but not finished until 1911. It is an oratorio-like work in that it tells a dramatic story and is scored for soloists, chorus, and orchestra. However, Schoenberg did not call it an oratorio, and it is not referred to as one today. The text, from a nineteenth-century Danish account (in German translation) of the legend of King Waldemar and his love for Tove, is divided into three parts, the first and third of which are further divided into separate movements or songs. Part one, which presents the first ten songs, describes the love of Waldemar and Tove and Tove's death. Part two relates Waldemar's sorrow, and part three depicts a wild hunt in the form of a nightmarish dream. The musical style is characterized by wide intervallic leaps, chromatic harmonies, and leitmotifs that are used in transformational ways. *Die Jakobsleiter,* which was called an oratorio by Schoenberg, was begun in 1917 but never completed. Schoenberg finished (without orchestration) only the first of the work's projected two parts. His student Winfried Zillig finished the orchestration for the premiere performance in June 1961. The text of the completed portion, about earthly beings at various levels of spiritual evolution on Jacob's Ladder, is drawn mainly from Genesis 28, August Strindberg's *Jakob ringt,* and Honoré de Balzac's *Seraphita.* The musical style is characterized by sprechstimme, expressionistic harmonies, and twelve-tone melodic construction. *Kol nidre* was composed in 1938 to a rearrangement of the traditional Hebrew text for the Yom Kippur or Day of Atonement service. The work is scored for speaker, SATB chorus, and chamber orchestra and is in a conservative tonal language that is not twelve-tone. *A Survivor from Warsaw,* composed in 1947 and scored for speaker, male chorus, and orchestra, is a twelve-tone work of moderate difficulty. The text, by Schoenberg, portrays a typical roll call in a concentration camp during World War II.

The three sacred a cappella works are *Friede auf Erden* (Peace on Earth), *Dreimal tausend Jahre* (Three thousand years), and *De profundis* (Psalm 130). *Friede auf Erden,* which Schoenberg called "an illusion for mixed choir," was composed in 1907 to a poem by the Austrian novelist Conrad Ferdinand Meyer (1825–1898) about the birth of Jesus and resulting peace on earth. The music, in an expanded tonal idiom, is constructed around a musical motif attached to the words "Friede auf Erden" that occurs somewhat as a ritornello throughout the composition. *Dreimal tausend Jahre,* a short twelve-tone work only thirty-five measures long, was composed in 1949 to celebrate the establishment of the state of Israel and to commemorate the 3,000th anniversary of the Temple of Jerusalem. *De profundis* was commissioned by Serge Koussevitzky, music director of the Boston Symphony Orchestra from 1924 to 1949, for the first King David Festival in Jerusalem. Schoenberg completed the work on July 2, 1950, just eleven days before his death. The music combines sprechstimme (from whispers to shouts) and twelve-tone writing into a highly dramatic and evocative setting of the De profundis text.

The remaining choral music includes *Vier Stücke* (Four pieces) of 1925; *Drei Satiren* (Three satires), also of 1925, the first piece of which begins with the text question "Tonal oder atonal?"

(Tonal or atonal?); *Sechs Stücke für Männerchor* (Six pieces for male chorus) of 1929 and 1930, all of which are in a twelve-tone construction; and two tonal sets of folk song arrangements—*Drei Volksliedsätze* of 1929 and *Drei deutsche Volkslieder* of 1948.

CHORAL WORKS
SELECTED AND LISTED ACCORDING TO FAMILIARITY

Friede auf Erden op.13 – SSAATTBB chorus a cappella (or with instruments *colla parte* ad lib.) – 9 minutes.

De profundis (Psalm 130) op.50b – SSATBB chorus a cappella – 5 minutes.

Gurre-Lieder (without opus number) – speaker, SATTB solos, TTBB/TTBB/TTBB chorus, SSAATTBB chorus, and orchestra (including eight flutes, ten horns, and seven trombones) – 100 minutes. (1) Solo roles are for Waldemar (T), Tove (S), the Voice of the Wood-Dove (A), a Peasant (B), and Klaus the Jester (T); (2) the choral writing is minimal: the male choruses sing a total of about ten minutes in part three of the work, and the mixed chorus sings about 4:30 minutes at the very end of the work.

Die Jakobsleiter (without opus number) – SATTTBBB solos, SSSAAATTT-BBB chorus, and orchestra (projected to consist of 270 players, including eight harps, but later revised for regular large scoring) – 45 minutes. Solo roles are for Gabriel (B), One who is called into service (T), One who is rebellious (T), One who is struggling (B), One who is dying (S), the Chosen One (B), the Monk (T), and the Soul (S).

Vier Stücke op.27 – SATB chorus a cappella (the first three pieces) and SATB chorus, mandolin, clarinet, violin, and cello (the final piece only) – "Unentrinnbar" 1:30 minutes, "Du sollst nicht, du musst" 1:30 minutes, "Mond und Menschen" 3:15 minutes, and "Der Wunsch des Liebhabers" 4:30 minutes.

Sechs Stücke für Männerchor op.35 – TTBB chorus (with occasional divisions) a cappella – "Hemmung" 1:45 minutes, "Das Gesetz" 2:45 minutes, "Ausdrucksweise" 2:45 minutes, "Glück" 1:15 minutes, "Landsknechte" 4 minutes, and "Verbundenheit" 2:15 minutes.

Drei Satiren op.28 – SATB chorus a cappella (the first two pieces) and SATB chorus, viola, cello, and piano (the third piece) – "Am Scheideweg" 1 minute, "Vielseitigkeit" 45 seconds, and "Der neue Klassizismus" 9:30 minutes.

Drei deutsche Volkslieder op.49 – SATB chorus a cappella – "Es gingen zwei Gespielen gut" 3:30 minutes, "Der Mai tritt ein mit Freuden" 2:30 minutes, and "Mein Herz in steten Treuen" 4:15 minutes.

Drei Volksliedsätze (without opus number) – SATB chorus a cappella – "Schein uns, du liebe Sonne" 4 minutes, "Es gingen zwei Gespielen gut" 4 minutes, and "Herzlieblich Lieb, durch Scheiden" 1:45 minutes.

ANTON WEBERN 1883–1945

Webern was born in Vienna and learned to play the piano and cello while he attended schools in Graz and Klagenfurt, as well as Vienna. In 1902 he entered the University of Vienna, where he studied musicology, harmony, and counterpoint and where he received a doctorate in musicology in 1906 (his dissertation was an edition of the second volume of Heinrich Isaac's *Choralis constantinus*). During the time of his university studies he had private piano and cello lessons, and he also began to study with Arnold Schoenberg. Between 1908 and 1920 Webern had numerous short-term conducting positions in theaters in Bad Ischl, Innsbruck, Bad Teplitz, Danzig, Stettin, and Prague, and during the 1920s he served as director of several choral ensembles, including the Schubertbund, Mödlinger Männergesang, David Josef Bach's Singverein, and Chor Freie Typographia. He also conducted concerts of the Arbeiter-Symphonie and taught briefly at the Israelisches Blindeninstitut. His early compositions, like those of his mentor Schoenberg and fellow Schoenberg disciple Alban Berg, followed the post-Romantic principles of expressionism. However, his later compositions embraced the twelve-tone technique and took on a characteristic of sparseness (i.e., the musical textures were uncluttered and often contained numerous rests). In 1938 his music was labeled as "degenerate art" and was banned in Austria and Germany.

Webern composed five choral works. *Entflieht auf leichten Kähnen* (Take flight in light boats), to a text by the German poet Stefan George (1868–1933), is a double canon with tonal although highly chromatic harmonies; *Zwei Lieder* (Two songs), one of Webern's first compositions using the twelve-tone technique of melodic construction, is a setting of the second and third poems from Goethe's *Chinesisch-deutsche Jahres- und Tageszeiten,* the subject of which compares the process of aging to the passing of the seasons; and *Das Augenlicht* (The eye's radiance or Sparkle in the eye), *I Kantate* (Cantata #1), and *II Kantate* (Cantata #2) are all set to the poetry of Hildegard Jone (1891–1963), the German poetess, painter, and sculptor who was close friends with Webern. All three of these latter works are twelve-tone and pointillistic in texture.

CHORAL WORKS
COMPLETE AND LISTED IN CHRONOLOGICAL ORDER
ACCORDING TO DATE OF COMPOSITION

Entflieht auf leichten Kähnen op.2 – 1908 – SATB chorus a cappella – 2:30 minutes.

Zwei Lieder op.19 – 1925–1926 – SATB chorus, clarinet, bass clarinet, celesta, guitar, and violin – 2:30 minutes.

Das Augenlicht op.26 – 1935 – SATB chorus and chamber orchestra of flute, oboe, clarinet, saxophone, horn, trumpet, trombone, timpani, xylophone, glockenspiel, cymbals, harp, celesta, mandolin, eight violins, two violas, and four cellos – 5:30 minutes.

I Kantate op.29 – 1938–1939 – S solo, SATB chorus, and chamber orchestra of flute, oboe, clarinet, bass clarinet, horn, trumpet, trombone, harp, celesta, timpani, trap set, mandolin, and strings – 8:30 minutes.

II Kantate op.31 – 1941–1943 – SB solos, SATB chorus, and orchestra (including a bell and glockenspiel) – 15:30 minutes.

PAUL HINDEMITH 1895–1963

Hindemith was born near Frankfurt, where he began violin lessons at age twelve and entered the Frankfurt Conservatory at age fifteen. At nineteen he joined the first violin section of the Frankfurt Opera orchestra, and at twenty-two he became the orchestra's leader (concertmaster). While with the orchestra, he served as soloist in concertos by such composers as Mozart, Haydn, and Beethoven, and he played in German premieres of works by Debussy, Dukas, and Bartók. In 1923 he began playing viola instead of violin and became a member of the Amar Quartet, and in 1927 he moved to Berlin to be a teacher of composition at the Musikhochschule. At about this time he developed his ideas of practicality in composition, stating, "The composer today should write only if he knows for what purpose he is writing. The days of composition only for the sake of composition are perhaps gone for ever." As a manifestation of this philosophy, he composed several pieces for amateurs under the general title of *Sing- und Spielmusik* (Music for singing and playing), which he described in the preface to one of these pieces, *Frau Musica*, as music "not written for the concert hall or for professional musicians, [but for] those who like to sing and play for their own pleasure. . . . In keeping with this intention, no very great technical demands are made on the singers and players." Further explanation of this philosophy, which resulted in music referred to as "Gebrauchsmusik" (Workaday music, Music for use, or Functional music) and which resulted in the compositional process of using all twelve notes of the chromatic scale in a diatonic manner (a process usually called pandiatonic), was given in Hindemith's book *Unterweisung im Tonsatz* (The Craft of Musical Composition), written between 1935 and 1937.

In 1937 Hindemith left the Berlin Musikhochschule, in 1938 he moved to Switzerland to avoid the political turmoil in Germany and to concentrate on composition, and in 1940 he emigrated to the United States, serving as visiting professor at Yale University during that year and accepting a full professorship the following year. During the remainder of the 1940s he authored more books, including *Elementary Training for Musicians* in 1946, and he also founded the Yale Collegium Musicum for the performance of music from the Renaissance and Baroque eras. In 1946 he became a citizen of the United States, and in 1947 he gave a lecture tour through Italy, England, the Netherlands, Austria, and Switzerland. During the fall semester of 1949 he held the Charles Eliot Norton Chair of Poetry at Harvard University—giving a series of lectures that was published in 1952 as *A Composer's World*. He taught at both Yale and the University of Zurich from 1949 to 1953, when he resigned the position at Yale, and from 1957 to his sudden death in 1963 he toured as a conductor throughout England, Austria, Germany, South America, and Japan.

Hindemith's choral output includes four choral/orchestral works, several sets of pieces for chorus and chamber ensemble, and fourteen publications of a cappella pieces. Three of the choral/orchestral works merit discussion—the oratorio *Das Unaufhörliche*, the Requiem *When lilacs last in the door-yard bloom'd*, and *Apparebit repentina dies*. The oratorio was composed in 1931 to a text by the German essayist, novelist, and poet Gottfried Benn (1886–1956) that is neither narrative nor dramatic but that relates philosophical issues about permanence or change in the world—the basic premise being that mankind should follow the unceasing (*unaufhörlich*) natural law of constant transformation. The music, in the Gebrauchsmusik style, is divided into three parts, each further divided into separate movements. Scoring is for STBB soloists, mixed chorus, children's chorus, and orchestra (including organ). *When lilacs last in the door-yard bloom'd,* subtitled "A Requiem for those we love," was composed in 1946 to Walt Whitman's ode mourning the death of Abraham Lincoln. Hindemith sought to extend Whitman's message and memorialize Franklin Delano Roosevelt and the Americans who fought and died in World War II. The music, in an advanced pandiatonic style, is divided into eleven movements, one of which is the "Death Carol" for chorus to the text that begins "Come, lovely and soothing death." *Apparebit repentina dies* was composed for the 1947 Symposium of Music Criticism at Harvard University. The text, an anonymous Latin medieval poem about the Day of Judgment structured as an acrostic (i.e., each verse of the poem begins with successive letters of the alphabet except for J, V, and W), is comparable in content to the Dies irae.

The sets of pieces for chorus and chamber ensemble include several multimovement compositions in the collection entitled *Sing- und Spielmusiken für Liebhaber und Musikfreunde*. The first, *Frau Musica* (subtitled "In Praise of Music"), was composed in 1928 for two soloists (female and male), with accompaniment of strings and woodwind instruments ad lib. Hindemith revised the work in 1943 for female and male chorus and any combination of four instruments. *Wer sich die Musik erkiest* (Who himself chooses music) consists of several canons specifically composed for children.

The publications of a cappella repertoire include fourteen pieces for male chorus, a mass, and six chansons and twelve madrigals for mixed chorus. Most of the male chorus pieces are contained in two collections, *Lieder nach alten Texten* op.33 composed in 1923 and dedicated to the Stuttgart Madrigal Society, and *Five Songs on Old Texts* of 1937 and 1938. This latter collection consists of reworkings and new settings of four texts from the 1923 set plus a new composition. The *Messe für gemischten Chor a cappella* was composed in 1963 for the Wiener Kammerchor and conducted by Hindemith six weeks before his death. It is one of the masterful contributions to the twentieth-century neo-Renaissance settings of the Roman Mass Ordinary, begun with Ralph Vaughan Williams's *Mass in G minor* composed in 1920 and 1921. Hindemith's most popular compositions, the *Six Chansons* of 1939, were composed to poetry in French by Rainer Maria Rilke (1875–1926). All the pieces are indicative of the pandiatonic manner of composition. In "En hiver" (In winter), for example, Hindemith uses every note of the scale except one, within the span of four measures, and while doing so he maintains a feeling of diatonic tonality. In "Puisque tout passe" (Since all is passing), a brief setting of text about the brevity of love and art, Hindemith uses every note of the scale except two while maintaining almost a complete feeling of G major. Other a cappella works include the *Zwölf Madrigale* (Twelve madrigals), composed in 1958 after Hindemith had taught a course at Yale on the music of the late-Italian Renaissance madrigalist Carlo Gesualdo. The texts of all the madrigals are by Josef Weinheber (1892–1945), a civil servant with the Austrian postal service, who became known for his pessimistic commentary on social life of the mid-twentieth century. Hindemith's music emulates Gesualdo in rhythmic variety and also in harmonic complexity.

CHORAL WORKS

SELECTED AND LISTED ACCORDING TO FAMILIARITY

Six Chansons – SATB chorus a cappella – "La biche" 1:15 minutes, "Un cygne" 2 minutes, "Puisque tout passe" 30 seconds, "Printemps" 1:30 minutes, "En hiver" 1:15 minutes, and "Verger" 1 minute.

When lilacs last in the door-yard bloom'd – AB solos, SATB chorus, and orchestra (including bass clarinet and organ) – 63 minutes.

Apparebit repentina dies – SATB chorus, four horns, two trumpets, three trombones, and tuba – 23 minutes.

Zwölf Madrigale – SSATB chorus a cappella – "Mitwelt" 1 minute, "Eines Narren, eines Künstlers Leben" 2 minutes, "Tauche deine Furcht" 3 minutes, "Trink aus" 1:30 minutes, "An eine Tote" 6:30 minutes, "Frühling" 1 minute, "An einen Schmetterling" 2 minutes, "Judaskuss" 2:45 minutes, "Magisches Rezept" 3:15 minutes, "Es bleibt wohl" 2:15 minutes, "Kraft fand zu Form" 3:15 minutes, and "Du Zweifel" 2:30 minutes.

Mass – SATB chorus a cappella – 25 minutes.

JOHANN NEPOMUK DAVID 1895–1977

David was born in Eferding, Austria, west of Linz, and received his musical education as a chorister at the Augustinian monastery of St Florian, where Anton Bruckner had been a chorister in the late 1840s and early 1850s. David entered the Vienna Conservatory of Music in 1920, in 1934 he began teaching at the Leipzig Landeskonservatorium (later named the Hochschule für Musik), and in 1942 he was appointed the school's director. From 1945 to 1947 he taught composition at the Mozarteum in Salzburg, and from 1948 until 1963 he was professor of composition at the Hochschule für Musik in Stuttgart.

In addition to thirty orchestral works and twenty-one volumes of music for organ, David composed forty-five sacred and thirty-seven secular choral works. The sacred works are mostly based on Lutheran chorales and composed in a neo-Renaissance or neo-Baroque style. For instance, the *Stabat mater* of 1927 begins and ends with the upper (SSA) and lower voices (TBB) scored in a double chorus dialogue manner, with intermittent phrases of polyphonic imitation. In addition, the middle of the work combines homophony with brief imitative passages. The Kyrie and Credo of the 1952 *Deutsche Messe* are motet-like in their imitative textures; *Veni creator spiritus* of 1957 is based on the Gregorian chant; and *O Heiland, reiss die Himmel auf* of 1959 uses the Lutheran chorale tune as a cantus firmus. The secular works are also imitative but less complex and more madrigalistic. "Bienensegen" (Blessing of the bees) from *Drei Tierleider* (Three animal songs) of 1945, for example, has onomatopoeic sounds that imitate the buzzing of bees.

CHORAL WORKS
SELECTED AND LISTED ACCORDING TO FAMILIARITY

Drei Evangelien-Motetten (Three Gospel Motets) – 1972 – SATB chorus (with occasional divisions) a cappella – "Der Pharisäer und der Zöllner" (Luke 18:10–14) 2 minutes, "Lasset die Kindlein zu mir kommen" (Mark 10:13–16) 3:30 minutes, and "Die Ehebrecherin" (John 8:3–11) 3:30 minutes.

O Heiland, reiss die Himmel auf – 1959 – SAB chorus (with occasional division into SSSAAAB) a cappella – 6 minutes.

Veni creator spiritus – 1957 – SATB chorus (with occasional divisions) a cappella – 6 minutes.

Victimae paschali laudes – 1948 – SATB chorus – 6:15 minutes.

Deutsche Messe – 1952 – SATB chorus (with occasional divisions) a cappella – 12:30 minutes.

Stabat mater – 1927 – SSATBB chorus a cappella – 8 minutes.

Drei Tierlieder – 1945 – SSS solos and SATB chorus a cappella – "Bienensegen" (Blessing of the bees) 1:30 minutes, "Das Käuzchen" (The little owl) 2:30 minutes, and "Der Kater" (The tom cat) 2:30 minutes.

CARL ORFF 1895–1982

Orff was born in Munich, where he spent his entire life. At age five he began studying the piano, organ, and cello privately, and at ten he entered the Ludwigsgymnasium. At twelve he transferred to the Wittelsbacher Gymnasium, and at seventeen he enrolled at the Akademie der Tonkunst, where he developed a keen interest in music of the sixteenth and seventeenth centuries, especially the stage works of Monteverdi. Orff was appointed *Kapellmeister* of the Munich Kammerspiele when he was twenty-two, and at twenty-nine he cofounded the Güntherschule— a music education program for children that was based on dance and musical improvisation and that made use of recorders and numerous percussion instruments. The program was expanded during the 1920s and formalized as the *Orff-Schulwerk: elementare Musikübung*, which became the name of a publication issued in the 1930s. As a conductor, he led a number of Baroque-era works during the 1930s, including several Monteverdi operas and the *Historia der frölichen und siegreichen Aufferstehung . . . Jesu Christi* (Easter Oratorio) by Heinrich Schütz (which was staged), and during the 1930s he also became interested in ancient Greek and Roman drama. Between 1950 and 1960 he served as director of the Munich Hochschule für Musik, and during the latter years of his life he was given numerous awards, including honorary doctorates from the University of Tübingen in 1959 and the University of Munich in 1972.

Orff composed twenty-seven choral works, the majority of which were for stage (as opposed to concert) presentation. The most popular of these stage works, and undoubtedly the most frequently performed large-scale choral work of the twentieth century, is *Carmina Burana* (Songs of Beuern). Subtitled "Cantiones profanae" (profane songs), it was composed in 1936 and premiered with scenery and dance in Frankfurt in 1937. The text comes from a medieval manuscript in Latin and low German housed at the monastery of Benediktbeuern, located about forty miles from Munich. Orff set twenty-five poems from the manuscript and divided them into five sections—"Fortuna imperatrix mundi" (Fortune, empress of the world), which serves as a prologue and epilogue to the work; "Primo vere" (Spring), which is sung mainly by the women of the chorus and represents the blossoming of love; "Uf dem Anger" (On the green), which depicts springtime celebrations; "In taberna" (In the tavern), which is sung by the tenor and baritone soloists and the men of the chorus and which represents lustful yearnings; and "Cour d'amours" (The court of love), which represents the union of two lovers. The music is neo-

Medieval in sound, with chant-like passages and repetitive rhythmic motifs, and it is often referred to as primitive in character.

Orff followed *Carmina Burana* with *Catulli Carmina* (Songs of Catullus), composed between 1941 and 1943, and *Trionfo di Afrodite* (The triumph of Aphrodite), composed between 1949 and 1951. *Catulli Carmina,* subtitled "Ludi scaenici" (Scenic games), is a setting of twelve poems by the classical Roman poet Gaius Valerius Catullus (ca.84–54 B.C.), arranged in three acts framed by a *praeludio* (prelude) and *exodium* (epilogue) to portray the poet's love, betrayal, and disillusionment. *Trionfo di Afrodite,* subtitled "Concerto scenico" (a scenic concert piece), is a setting of poems by Catullus, Sappho (ca.630–612 to 570 B.C.), and Euripides (ca.480–406 B.C.), which are divided into seven scenes that represent ancient marriage rites.

CHORAL WORKS
SELECTED AND LISTED ACCORDING TO FAMILIARITY

Carmina Burana – 1936 – STB solos, SATB chorus (with divisions), children's chorus, and orchestra (including three flutes, English horn, contrabassoon, two pianos, celesta, five timpani, three glockenspiels, six cymbals, xylophone, ratchet, triangle, gong, castanets, rattles, bells, chimes, and a variety of drums) – 62 minutes. (1) The solos are demanding (the soprano has exceptionally long phrases plus a high *D*, the tenor part is in a very high range, and the baritone part includes passages in falsetto); (2) the choral divisions include SSAATTBB, TTTBBB, and SSATTB/SSATTB; (3) the orchestration has been arranged for two pianos and percussion.

Catulli Carmina – 1941–1943 – ST solos, SATB chorus (with divisions), four pianos, and a large battery of percussion instruments – 37 minutes.

Trionfo di Afrodite – 1949–1951 – SSATBB solos, SATB chorus (with divisions), and orchestra (including triple winds, extra brass, three pianos, three guitars, and numerous percussion instruments) – 42 minutes.

HANNS EISLER 1898–1962

Eisler was born in Leipzig and learned music on his own by reading theory books and studying scores. He also developed musical skills by playing when he could on borrowed or rented pianos. In 1908 he enrolled at the Staatsgymnasium in Vienna, where his family had moved in 1901, and in 1918 he began studies at the New Vienna Conservatory. Between 1919 and 1923 he studied privately with Arnold Schoenberg, and in 1925 he became a teacher at the Klindworth-Scharwenka Conservatory. During the next several years he involved himself with Marxist choral organizations, including the Karl Liebknecht Gesangverein and the Stahlklang Chorvereinigung, and in 1926 he joined the German Communist party. His most important choral works were composed in the 1930s, even though much of his music was banned during that time by the Hitler regime, and in 1937 he emigrated to the United States, teaching first at the New School of Social Research in New York City and then at the University of Southern California in

Los Angeles. Eisler returned to Vienna in 1948 and shortly after his arrival composed *Aufer-standen aus Ruinen,* which was adopted by the Deutsche Demokratische Republik (DDR) as its national anthem, and in 1949 he was appointed professor of composition at the Hochschule für Musik in Berlin. The final years of his life were devoted to what he termed "Angewandte Musik" (Applied music)—works in a conservative harmonic idiom that were accessible to the general public and that were written for film, theater, cabaret, dance, and plays.

Eisler composed eight choral/orchestral works and twenty-five a cappella pieces (eleven of which are for men's chorus), plus twenty songs for three-part children's chorus and nine canons. The choral/orchestral works include *Die Massnahme* of 1930 for three speakers, tenor solo, male chorus, mixed chorus, and chamber orchestra; *Die Mutter* of 1931 for mixed chorus and orchestra; and Eisler's most important work, the antifascist cantata *Deutsche Sinfonie,* composed between 1935 and 1939 and scored for two speakers, SABB solos, mixed chorus, and orchestra.

ERNST KRENEK 1900–1991

Krenek was born in Vienna, where he began playing the piano at age six and where he studied at the State Academy of Music from sixteen to twenty. During his twenties he continued his education in Berlin and also composed a number of works that were acknowledged to be artistically meritorious. These include the *String Quartet* op.6 of 1921 and the operas *Die Zwingburg* of 1922, *Orpheus und Eurydike* of 1923, and *Jonny spielt auf* of 1925. In the 1920s he also became associated with the International Society for Contemporary Music (ISCM), and in 1929 he received a commission from the Vienna Staatsoper for his tenth opera, *Karl V,* which was completed in 1933 and which was his first large-scale work constructed according to the twelve-tone technique. From 1930 until 1933 Krenek wrote articles for the *Frankfurter Zeitung,* and in 1938 he emigrated to the United States, teaching at Malkin Conservatory in Boston during the 1938–1939 academic year and at Vassar College in Poughkeepsie, New York, from 1939 to 1942. From 1942 to 1947 he served as dean of the School of Fine Arts at Hamline University in St Paul, Minnesota, in 1945 he became a citizen of the United States, and in 1947 he moved to Los Angeles to concentrate on composition. For a short period during the late 1960s and early 1970s he was associated with the University of California in San Diego. However, most of the time during the final forty years of his life was spent composing and traveling throughout Europe, lecturing, and conducting his works.

Krenek composed thirty-nine opuses of choral music. The early opuses include several works in a late-Romantic harmonic idiom scored for a cappella chorus and set to texts by Romantic-era poets—*Drei gemischte Chöre* op.22 of 1923 set to three poems by Matthias Claudius (1740–1815), *Die Jahreszeiten* (The Seasons) op.35 of 1925 set to four metaphysical poems by Friedrich Hölderlin (1770–1843), and *Vier Chöre* op.47 of 1924 set to four poems by Goethe (1749–1832). The opuses of the 1930s and 1940s, all in an advanced harmonic idiom characterized by twelve-tone construction, include some of Krenek's most important and critically acclaimed works. *Kantate von der Vergänglichkeit des Irdischen* (Cantata on the transitory nature of earthly things) op.72 was composed in 1932 to a variety of seventeenth-century poems on the subject of the cantata's title; the oratorio *Symeon der Stylit* (without opus, but catalogued as W84) was written between 1935 and 1937 (revised in 1987) to texts in Latin from the Psalms; and *Lamentatio Jeremiae Prophetae* op.93, one of Krenek's most challenging works, was composed in 1941 and 1942 after he had discovered and studied scores of the late-Medieval composer Jean de Ockeghem in the library of Vassar College. The texts of *Lamentatio Jeremiae Prophetae* correspond to three days of Holy Week—"In coena Domini" (Maundy Thursday), "In parascere" (Good Friday), and "In Sabbato Sancto" (Easter Sunday)—and each of these three sections of the work is further divided into three other sections, called "lessons." In addition to being dodecaphonic, the music is scored without bar lines, thus imposing rhythmic and metrical control on the conductor. Furthermore, the tonalities are based on the equal-tempered tuning system.

The works from Krenek's final period of composition include the motet *O Holy Ghost* op.186a, written in 1964 for the International Heinrich Schütz Society and set to the poem "O Holy Ghost, whose temple I Am" from John Donne's *The Litanie III,* and the oratorio *Opus sine nomine* op.238, composed between 1980 and 1988 to a text primarily written by the composer. The subject of the oratorio is autobiographical and is intended to convey a feeling of pessimism and resignation about the world. According to Krenek, "The text of the first part of the oratorio is from the book of Genesis—the story of the creation of the world and the early fate of Adam and Eve. The second part is the story of Orpheus and Eurydice. The third part is the story of Pandora and Prometheus—the Box is opened and all the knowledge of good and evil flies away; only Hope remains. The last part of the oratorio is a personal monologue and a dialogue with Hope, which remains forever but which is never answered." The oratorio is scored for two speakers, SSAATTTBB soloists, chorus, and large orchestra, and it was premiered in the Grosser Musikvereinsaal as part of the "Ernst Krenek Festwochenkonzerte," a series of concerts sponsored by the Gesellschaft der Musikfreunde to celebrate the composer's ninetieth birthday. The musical style is, again according to Krenek, "atonal and to an extent based on twelve-tone organization. It's a very advanced style and not easy to perform."

CHORAL WORKS
SELECTED AND LISTED ACCORDING TO FAMILIARITY

Lamentatio Jeremiae Prophetae op.93 – 1941–1942 – SSAATTBB chorus a cappella – 70 minutes.

O Holy Ghost op.186a – 1964 – SATB chorus (with divisions) a cappella – 2:30 minutes.

Kantate von der Vergänglichkeit des Irdischen op.72 – 1932 – S solo, SATB chorus (with divisions), and piano – 20 minutes.

Die Jahreszeiten op.35 – 1925 – SATB chorus (with occasional divisions) a cappella – 12 minutes.

Symeon der Stylit (W84) – 1935–1937 – SATB solos, SATB chorus (with divisions), and chamber orchestra of flute, oboe, clarinet, bassoon, horn, trumpet, trombone, piano, timpani, percussion, and strings – 100 minutes.

Drei gemischte Chöre op.22 – 1923 – SSAATTBB chorus a cappella – 6:30 minutes.

Vier Chöre op.47 – 1924 – SATB chorus a cappella – 4:30 minutes.

Cantata for Wartime op.95 – 1943 – SSAA chorus and orchestra – 12 minutes.

Santa Fe Timetable op.102 – 1945 – SSAATB chorus a cappella – 15 minutes.

Deutsche Messe op.204 – 1968 – SATB chorus, clarinet, trumpet, two trombones, timpani, and percussion – 20 minutes.

ERNST PEPPING 1901–1981

Pepping was born in Duisburg, Germany, north of Düsseldorf, and studied at the Hochschule für Musik in Berlin. During his twenties he received several awards for his compositions, including the Mendelssohn Prize in 1926, and his works were performed at important European venues, including the Donaueschingen Festival in 1927 and the Baden-Baden Festival in 1928. In 1934 he was appointed professor of music theory and composition at the Protestant Kirchenmusikschule of the Johannes-Stift in Berlin-Spandau, a position he kept for the remainder of his life, and between 1953 and 1968 he also taught at his alma mater, the Hochschule für Musik. He was lauded with honorary doctorates from Berlin's Freie Universität (1961) and Theologische Hochschule (1971), and his many awards include the Lübeck Buxtehude Prize in 1951 and the Düsseldorf Schumann Prize in 1956.

Pepping composed thirty-four sacred choral works plus an additional four sacred collections that contain approximately one hundred sacred pieces, and five secular works plus four collections of secular pieces. Most of the works, as well as the pieces in the collections, are scored for a cappella chorus and are in textures that emulate the motet style of the late Renaissance. Many of the works also incorporate Lutheran chorales. For instance, the *Deutsche Choralmesse* of 1928 is based on the chorale "Allein Gott in der Höh sei Ehr" (All glory be to God on high) and the *Spandauer Chorbuch* of 1934 to 1938 includes numerous chorale arrangements.

The large-scale a cappella works are considered to be Pepping's most noteworthy compositions. *Die Weihnachtsgeschichte des Lukas* (The Christmas Story as told by St Luke) and *Passionsbericht des Matthäus* (Passion story according to St Matthew) are both modeled after pre-Baroque German oratorios and historiae in motet fashion: they are completely polyphonic, without solos representing specific characters, and also without reflective poetry added to the biblical texts. The Matthew Passion, for instance, is very similar to the historiae of Heinrich Schütz. Most notably, the biblical story is framed by an introduction that serves as an announcement of the story—"Höre die Passion unseres Herrn Jesu Christi, wie sie geschrieben steht bei dem Evangelisten Matthäus" (Hear the Passion of our Lord Jesus Christ, as it is written in the Gospel according to St Matthew)—and a conclusion that begins "Herr Christe, erbarme dich unser, der du für uns gelitten, gekreuzigt wurdest für uns, gestorben für uns" (Lord Christ, have mercy on us, who for us has suffered, crucified for us, died for us). The *Missa Dona nobis pacem*, which is a setting of all five portions of the Roman Mass Ordinary, alternates passages of homophony with imitative polyphony, and *Heut und Ewig* (Now and forever), subtitled "Liederkreis für Chor nach Gedichten von Goethe" (Song cycle for chorus on poems by Goethe), is a series of twenty-five interconnected part songs.

CHORAL WORKS
SELECTED AND LISTED ACCORDING TO FAMILIARITY

Passionsbericht des Matthäus – 1950 – SATB/SATB chorus (with divisions)
a cappella – 77 minutes.

Die Weihnachtsgeschichte des Lukas – 1959 – SATB chorus (with divisions)
a cappella – 42 minutes.

Missa Dona nobis pacem – 1948 – SSAATTBB chorus a cappella – 20 minutes.

Heut und Ewig – 1948–1949 – SATB chorus (with divisions) a cappella –
63 minutes.

Kleine Messe – 1929 – SAB chorus a cappella – 7 minutes.

FRANZ BIEBL 1906–2001

Biebl was born in Pursruck, Germany, near Nuremberg, and studied music at the Musik-hochschule in Munich. In 1932 he was appointed *Kapellmeister* at the church of St Maria in München-Thalkirchen, and in 1939 he joined the faculty at the Mozarteum in Salzburg. He served in the military beginning in 1943, was captured by the Americans in Italy in 1944, and for the next year he was interned at Fort Custer, near Battle Creek, Michigan. While in the United States, he became familiar with American folk songs and African-American spirituals, many of which he arranged for chorus when he returned to Austria after the war. From 1948 until 1959 he served as *Kapellmeister* of the Stadtpfarrkirche in Fürstenfeldbruck, near Munich, and thereafter until his retirement at age sixty-five he headed the choral music division of the Bayerischen Rundfunk (Bavarian State Radio Broadcasting Company). He remained an active composer throughout the last several decades of his life, continuing to write choral works until several months before his death at age ninety-five.

Although Biebl composed approximately two thousand original choral works and arrange-ments of folk songs from the Americas and Europe, only one work, *Ave Maria* ("Angelus Do-mini"), is known. It was composed in 1964 for a chorus of firemen in Germany and scored for TTB/TTBB. After it became popular with performances and a recording by the American cham-ber ensemble Chanticleer, Biebl arranged it for various combinations of voices—from SSA/SSAA to SAT/SATB.

HUGO DISTLER 1908–1942

Distler was born in Nuremberg, where during his youth he attended the Realgymnasium and studied piano, music theory, and music history. At age nineteen he entered the Leipzig Conser-vatory, studying organ and choral conducting as well as piano and composition, and while in Leipzig, he was attracted to the sixteenth- and seventeenth-century music sung by the Thoman-erchor. In addition, he was exposed to the *Berneucher Kreis*, the liturgical reform movement in the Lutheran Church, and to the *Orgelbewegung*, the movement in organ building that desired a return to construction designs and tonal characteristics of Baroque instruments. In 1931 Distler was appointed organist at the Jakobikirche in Lübeck, and in 1933 he became head of the chamber music department at the newly founded Lübeck Staatsconservatorium und Hochschule für Musik. During the early 1930s he also taught at the Schule für Kirchenmusik in Berlin-Spandau. In 1937 he moved to Stuttgart to teach at the Würtemburgische Hochschule für Musik and to direct the Hochschule choir and Esslingen Singakademie, with which he conducted the Bach *Passio secundum Johannen* BWV245 and Monteverdi *L'Orfeo,* and in 1940, after highly acclaimed performances of his *Mörike Chorliederbuch* at the 1939 Festival für deutsche Chormusik in Graz, Austria, he succeeded Kurt Thomas as professor of composition, organ, and choral conducting at the Staatliche Akademische Hochschule für Musik in Berlin-Charlottenburg. The position of director of the Berlin Staats- und Dom-Chor was added in 1941, and in September 1942 Distler began rehearsals with the cathedral choir for a performance of the Schütz *Musicalische Exequien.* In October he received his third call to military duty (the two previous calls, in 1940 and 1941, were withdrawn by a high-ranking German official). However, fearing that he would not be excused a third time and demoralized by the political circumstances in Germany, he committed suicide on November 1 at age thirty-four.

Distler composed three large-scale sacred works plus three collections of sacred music and sixteen sacred pieces, and three collections of secular music plus an additional eight separate secular works. Much of the music is scored in mixed meters, with intricately rhythmic melodic lines that emulate the careful text declamation that was so prevalent in the music of Heinrich Schütz. The large-scale sacred works include two oratorios—the *Choral-Passion* op.7 and *Die Weihnachtsgeschichte* op.10. The first of these was composed in 1932 shortly after Distler had become organist at the Jakobikirche in Lübeck, and it premiered in 1933 at the Marienkirche. It is modeled on the *Passio secundum Matthaeum* by Schütz, which Distler performed several times in Lübeck, with soloists relating the words of the evangelist, Jesus, and other characters in unaccompanied recitative, and with the chorus singing the words of the crowd in addition to verses of the chorale "Jesu, deine Passion." Distler did not, however, limit himself to the Passion story as told by Matthew but rather assembled verses from all four Gospels. *Die Weihnachtsgeschichte,* composed in 1933 as a companion work to the *Choral-Passion,* is similarly constructed of unaccompanied recitatives, *turba* choruses, and chorale verses (seven variations of "Es ist ein Ros entsprungen"), although, like the historiae of Schütz, it has framing choruses as well—an *Eingangschor* (Introductory chorus) and a *Schlusschor* (Closing chorus).

The sacred collections include two sets of pieces designated for certain days of the liturgical year—*Der Jahrkreis* (The year's cycle) op.5, a set of fifty-two motets for children's chorus composed between 1932 and 1933, and *Geistliche Chormusik* (Sacred choral music) op.12, a publication of nine works (out of a proposed fifty-two), most of which were composed between 1934 and 1936. Based on Schütz's publication of the same name, this latter collection includes some of Distler's best-known and most important motets (e.g., *Singet dem Herrn ein neues Lied* for the fourth Sunday after Easter and *Wachet auf, ruft uns die Stimme* for the last Sunday after Trinity). The collection also includes *Totentanz,* a church drama in which a character portraying death and its inevitability confronts mortals such as an emperor, bishop, nobleman, physician, merchant, knight, sailor, hermit, peasant, old man, and child.

The secular collections include two sets of part songs—*Neues Chorliederbuch* op.16 of 1936 to 1938, which is divided into eight volumes (peasant songs in volume one, love songs in volumes two and three, calendar songs in volumes four through seven, and happy songs in volume eight), and *Mörike-Chorliederbuch* op.19 of 1938 and 1939, which contains forty-eight settings of poetry by Eduard Friedrich Mörike (1804–1875)—twenty-four for mixed chorus and twelve each for men's and women's choruses.

SACRED WORKS
SELECTED AND LISTED ACCORDING TO FAMILIARITY

Es ist ein Ros entsprungen (Lo, how a rose e'er blooming) from *Die Weihnachtsgeschichte* op.10 – SATB chorus a cappella – 3:15 minutes.

Singet dem Herrn ein neues Lied (Psalm 98) op.12 no.1 – SSATB chorus a cappella – 5:30 minutes.

Kleine Adventsmusik (A little Advent music) op.4 – speaker, SAB chorus, flute, oboe, violin, cello ad lib., and organ or piano – 30 minutes.

Totentanz (Dance of Death) op.12 no.2 – speaker and SATB chorus a cappella – 31 minutes.

Die Weihnachtsgeschichte (The Christmas Story) op.10 – SSTB solos and SATB chorus a cappella – 32 minutes.

Choral-Passion op.7 – TTBBB solos and SSATB chorus a cappella – 45 minutes. (1) Major solo roles are for an Evangelist (T), Jesus (B), and Pilate (B); (2) minor solo roles are for a High Priest (T) and Judas (B).

Wachet auf, ruft uns die Stimme op.12 no.6 – SS solos and SSATB chorus a cappella – 11 minutes.

Nun danket all und bringet Ehr op.11 no.2 – ST solos, SATB chorus, strings, and organ – 9 minutes.

O Heiland, reiss die Himmel auf op.21 no.3 – SATB chorus a cappella – 3:15 minutes.

Singet Frisch und wohlgemut op.12 no. 4 – SATB chorus (with occasional divisions) a cappella – 10 minutes.

Es ist das Heil uns kommen her op.6 no.2 – SATB chorus a cappella – 3:30 minutes.

SECULAR WORKS
SELECTED AND LISTED ACCORDING TO FAMILIARITY

Vorspruch (Preamble) op.19 no.1 – SATBB chorus (with divisions for SSATBB) a cappella – 1:45 minutes.

Ein Stündlein wohl vor Tag (An hour before dawn) op.19 no.2 – SATB chorus a cappella – 2:45 minutes.

Jedem das Seine (To each his own) op.19 no.3 – SATB chorus a cappella – 2:30 minutes.

Um Mitternacht (At midnight) op.19 no.10 – SAB chorus (with occasional divisions) a cappella – 2:30 minutes.

Der Feuerreiter (The Fire-crier) op.19 no.13 – SSAATTBB chorus a cappella – 3:45 minutes.

Nimmersatte Liebe (Insatiable love) op.19 no.19 – SSATB chorus a cappella – 3:15 minutes.

Denk es, o Seele (Be mindful, oh soul) op.19 no.21 – SATB chorus a cappella – 1:45 minutes.

Lebewohl (Farewell) op.19 no.23 – SSATB (with divisions to SSSSAATTBB) a cappella – 2 minutes.

HANS WERNER HENZE 1926–2012

Henze was born in Gütersloh, Germany, southwest of Hanover, and began music lessons with his father, an amateur musician who conducted a workers' chorus and brass ensemble and also played viola in local orchestras. In 1942 the young Henze attended the Brunswick State Music School, where he played timpani in the school orchestra, and in 1943 and 1944 his studies were interrupted while he served in the military. After the war he continued his education under Wolfgang Fortner at the Heidelberg Evangelisches Kirchmusikalisches Institut, and beginning in 1946 he also took summer courses in Darmstadt. His first symphony, opera, and ballet were composed in 1947, 1948, and 1949, respectively, and for the next fifty years he concentrated on those three genres, completing ten symphonies, eighteen operas, and fourteen ballets by the beginning of the twenty-first century. In addition to composing, he held several teaching positions, including professor of composition at the Staatliche Hochschule für Musik in Cologne between 1980 and 1991. He was also the artistic director of the Munich Biennale festival for new music theater beginning in 1988.

Henze's choral output consists of thirteen works, including two oratorios—*Das Floss der Medusa* of 1968 (revised in 1990) and *Jephte* of 1976. The first of these was commissioned by the North German Radio and premiered in Hamburg in December 1968. Subtitled "Oratorio volgare e militare," it is dedicated to Che Guevara, the Cuban revolutionary leader killed by the Bolivian government in October 1967. The story is introduced by one of the main characters in the oratorio's opening prologue: "You are about to hear an account of the Frigate 'Medusa,' which was shipwrecked on a voyage to Africa." As the ship sank, the captain, officers, and other dignitaries filled lifeboats while the remaining passengers were left to drift for thirteen days on a raft (Floss). Reports of this incident—the abandonment of the lower class by the upper class—circulated all over Europe and caused a sensation. As the prologue relates, "The story of betrayal and steadfastness and of nature's blind enforcement of fate's verdict did not change the world, but it lent support to the questions that must be asked; it aroused mistrust of a regime which later collapsed." The oratorio is in two parts and is scored for speaker, SB solos, three choruses, and large orchestra. The two soloists represent Jean-Charles (one of the survivors on the raft who relates the events) and La Mort (death). The choruses represent the living, the dying, and the dead. The soloists and choruses are to be placed on the stage as follows: the chorus of the living and Jean-Charles are to the left of the orchestra, the chorus of the dead with La Mort are on the right, and the speaker, Charon (based on the mythological figure who ferries the dead across the river Styx), is on the apron of the stage. The final line of the oratorio, spoken by Charon, makes the political intent of the oratorio clear: "The men who survived, having been taught by reality, returned to the world eager to overthrow it." Henze's other oratorio, *Jephte*, is not so much an original composition as it is a recomposition of Giacomo Carissimi's famous oratorio *Jephte* from the early seventeenth century. Henze's *Jephte* is scored for SSSATBB solos, six-part chorus, and instrumental ensemble consisting of four flutes, harp, guitar, mandolin, banjo, and percussion.

Other important Henze choral works include *Fünf Madrigäle* of 1947 for chamber chorus and chamber orchestra; *Chor gefangener Trojer*, a setting of passages from Goethe's *Faust* composed in 1948; *Muzen Siziliens* (The Muses of Sicily), a "choral concerto" set to text from Virgil's *Eclogues* for mixed chorus, two pianos, wind instruments, and timpani and composed in 1966; and *Orpheus Behind the Wire* ("Orpheus hinter dem Stacheldraht") scored for SSAATTBB chorus (with divisions) between 1981 and 1983.

❧ ITALY AND SPAIN ❧

Italian composers of the Modern era have continued the three-hundred-year tradition of writing operas. However, opera has no longer been the focus of compositional activity as it had been since the beginning of the Baroque era and as it had dominated Italian repertoire with the works of Donizetti, Verdi, and Puccini during the Romantic era. Modern-era Italian composers have been recognized for works in other genres, no new operas have entered the general performing repertory, and none of the new composers studied with or emulated the style of their older compatriots. Likewise, the operas composed by most Spanish composers of the Modern era are of minor significance in comparison to their works in other genres, and Spanish composers have sought influence by composers from France and Germany, not Italy or their homeland.

The most recognized Italian and Spanish composers of the Modern era—Pablo Casals, Ottorino Respighi, Luigi Dallapiccola, Goffredo Petrassi, Carlos Surinach, Luigi Nono, and Luciano Berio—all wrote in a variety of vocal and instrumental genres, although Respighi is known primarily for his orchestral works and Casals for his performance career. Manuel de Falla is also an important Spanish composer of the Modern era. However, he wrote very little choral music. Other, lesser-known but important Italian and Spanish composers are Ildebrando Pizzetti, Mario Castelnuovo-Tedesco, and Javier Busto. Additional composers who made a relatively minor impact on choral music and who, along with Falla will be discussed briefly in this section of the era, include Ferruccio Busoni, Lorenzo Perosi, Ermanno Wolf-Ferrari, and Gian Francesco Malipiero.

The composers early in the era (Busoni, Perosi, Falla, Wolf-Ferrari, Casals, Respighi, Pizzetti, Malipiero, and Castelnuovo-Tedesco) were limited in their exposure to new trends in France and Germany and thus wrote in traditional genres with conservative harmonies and textures. Later composers such as Dallapiccola, Petrassi, and Surinach were influenced by the music of Debussy and Schoenberg, which was performed and studied in the Italian conservatories during the early years of the twentieth century, and thus they embraced atonalism and twelve-tone techniques. The composers born in the 1920s (Nono and Berio) were of the generation of musicians who were interested in unexplored modes of musical expression and who embraced new technologies, especially electronics. Finally, the composers born after World War II (e.g., Busto), those who studied works of earlier historical eras, were or have been interested in a return to older genres and to compositions with conservative, neo-Romantic melodies and harmonies.

Busoni (1866–1924) was born in Empoli, Italy, near Florence, and exhibited virtuoso piano skills at age seven. At nine he performed the Mozart *Piano Concerto* in C minor K491 in public and also entered the Vienna Conservatory. During his adult years Busoni was known mostly as a performer, although he composed numerous works in a variety of genres, including the well-known opera *Doktor Faust*. His choral output includes three masses (one of which is the *Requiem* of 1881), three cantatas, three part songs for male chorus ("Frühlingslied," "Der Wirtin Töchterlein," and "Guten Abend, gute Nacht"), and the *Piano Concerto* in C major op.39. This last-named work, an expansive composition of approximately seventy minutes completed in 1904, concludes with a movement entitled "Cantico"—a setting for male chorus, piano, and orchestra of verses from *Aladdin* by the Danish poet and dramatist Adam Gottlob Oehlenschläger (1779–1850).

Perosi (1872–1956) was born in Tortona, Italy, south of Milan, and studied at the conservatories in both Milan and Rome. In 1894 he was appointed *maestro di cappella* at St Mark's Basilica in Venice, and in 1898 he assumed the same position at the Cappella Sistina in Rome. He composed thirty-nine masses (including six Requiems), twelve oratorios, thirteen Magnificats, and approximately three hundred motets. None of these works are well known today except the oratorios *La passione di Cristo secondo San Marco* of 1897, *La trasfigurazione di Cristo* of 1898, and *Mosè* of 1900.

Falla (1876–1946) was born in Cádiz, Spain, and first studied piano with his mother. He later studied at the Madrid Conservatory, and in the early years of the twentieth century he earned a living by composing zarzuelas (popular stage works that combined spoken dialogue with singing). In his early thirties he lived in Paris, where he was attracted to the music of Debussy and Ravel, and in his late thirties he returned to Spain and began writing stage works based on Spanish folk subjects. The most famous of these were subsequently remolded into the tone poems *El amor brujo* (Spell-bound love), *Noches en los jardines des España* (Nights in the gardens of Spain), and *El sombrero de tres picos* (The three-cornered hat). Falla's choral output consists of only four complete works, including *Balada de Mallorca* for SATB chorus (with divisions) a cappella. Set in 1933 to a text by the Catalan poet Jacinto Verdaguer (1845–1902) and composed for the Capella Classica in Majorca, it is an arrangement of Chopin's *Ballade* in F major. (The island of Majorca is where Chopin lived with George Sand and composed the *Ballade* in 1839.)

Wolf-Ferrari (1876–1948) was born in Venice and studied painting at the Accademia di Belle Arti in Rome. After moving to Munich in 1892 to continue his art studies, he became interested in music and enrolled at the Akademie der Tonkunst, studying composition under Joseph Rheinberger. Between 1903 and 1909 Wolf-Ferrari served as director of the Liceo Musicale in Venice, and in 1939 he was appointed professor of composition at the Salzburg Mozarteum. He composed fifteen operas (including *Cenerentola* between 1897 and 1900), one oratorio (*Talitha Kumi* in 1900), two cantatas (*La sulamite* in 1898 and *La vita nuova* in 1901), and eight miscellaneous small-scale pieces.

Malipiero (1882–1973) was born in Venice, the grandson of the opera composer Francesco Malipiero (1824–1887). Gian Francesco studied at the Liceo Musicale in Venice and in Bologna, and after serving as professor of composition at the Parma Conservatory, he returned to the Liceo Musicale in Venice as professor of composition and then director of the school. He is known not so much for his compositions, which include thirty-five operas, but for his editorship of the complete works of both Monteverdi and Vivaldi. Malipiero's choral compositions include three oratorios (*La cena* of 1927, *La Passione* of 1935, and *S Eufrosina* of 1942), one Requiem (*Missa pro mortuis* of 1938), and approximately ten cantatas.

PABLO CASALS 1876–1973

Casals was born in Vendrell, Spain, south of Barcelona, and learned to play the piano, organ, and violin as a child. At age eleven he entered the Escuela Municipal de Música in Barcelona and began cello lessons, and at seventeen he furthered his musical studies at the Madrid Conservatory. At nineteen he traveled to Paris, where he played in the orchestra of the Follies Marigny Theater, and at twenty he returned to Barcelona, where he was appointed principal cellist at the Gran Teatro de Liceo as well as professor of music at his alma mater, the Escuela Municipal de Música. During his late twenties he began touring throughout Europe, Russia, South America, and the United States, performing solo recitals and also playing in chamber ensembles devoted to the string trios and quartets of such standard European composers as Haydn, Beethoven, and Mendelssohn, and during his thirties, forties, and fifties he gave numerous master classes as well. Casals was known for his strong stance against political oppression and refused to play in Germany, Italy, or Spain under the dictatorships of Hitler, Mussolini, and Franco. In 1955 he moved to Puerto Rico, where he organized the Puerto Rico Symphony Orchestra in 1958 and the Puerto Rico Conservatory of Music in 1959. Meanwhile, in 1958 he gave a famous recital for the General Assembly of the United Nations, which at the time was celebrating its thirteenth anniversary, and he played at the White House for President John F. Kennedy in 1961. Beginning in 1962 Casals toured across the world promoting peace and conducting his oratorio *El Pessebre,* and in October 1971, just two months before his ninety-fifth birthday, he conducted his *Himno a las Naciones Unidas* (Hymn to the United Nations). In 1976, three years after his death, he was honored by King Juan Carlos I with a postage stamp commemorating his 100th birthday.

Casals composed twelve choral works, the majority of which are Latin motets. The most famous of these are *O vos omnes* and *Nigra sum,* both settings of traditional Latin texts in textures of conservative and highly effective and aesthetically satisfying tonal harmonies. Other motets include *Tota pulchra es* and *Recordare, virgo mater.*

El Pessebre, composed between 1943 and 1960 and premiered in Acapulco, Mexico, in December 1960 (Casals refused to allow the premiere to take place in Spain), is a setting of text by the Spanish poet Joan Alavedra (1896–1981) about the birth of Jesus. The work, from the award-winning poem "Poema del Pessebre" in Catalan, is divided into two main parts preceded by a prologue. Part one is entitled "On the Way to Bethlehem," and the three sections of part two are entitled "The Caravan of the Three Kings," "The Manger" (El Pessebre), and "The Adoration."

CHORAL WORKS
SELECTED AND LISTED ACCORDING TO FAMILIARITY

O vos omnes – ca.1932 – SATB chorus (with frequent divisions) a cappella – 3:30 minutes.

Nigra sum – 1942 – SSA chorus and piano or organ – 5:30 minutes. The SSA parts may be sung by TTB.

Tota pulchra es – 1942 – T solo ad lib. and SATB chorus (with occasional divisions) a cappella – 3 minutes. The T solo consists of an a cappella ten-measure passage that may be sung by the entire tenor section.

Cançó a la verge – 1942 – SA chorus and organ or piano – 3 minutes.

El Pessebre – 1943–1960 – SATBB solos, SATB chorus (with occasional divisions), and orchestra – 90 minutes.

OTTORINO RESPIGHI 1879–1936

Respighi was born in Bologna and learned to play both the piano and violin from his father, a piano teacher. Between the ages of twelve and twenty the young Respighi studied at the Liceo Musicale in Bologna, and during two extended trips to Russia between 1901 and 1903 he had composition lessons with Nikolay Rimsky-Korsakov. In 1902 and again in 1908 Respighi met occasionally with Max Bruch in Berlin. However, during most of the years between 1903 and 1912 he learned music by playing in orchestras in Bologna and by transcribing scores of the Baroque era for local performances. In 1913 he moved to Rome, where he became professor of composition at the Liceo Musicale di S Cecilia, and in 1915 and 1916 he composed his first successful orchestral work, *Fontane di Roma* (Fountains of Rome). In 1923 he was appointed director of the Liceo Musicale, at this time named the Conservatorio di S Cecilia, and in 1923 and 1924 he composed *Pini di Roma* (Pines of Rome). *Feste romane* (Roman festivals) followed in 1928, and for the next several years Respighi traveled throughout Europe accompanying vocal recitals and conducting his works. He developed a heart condition during the last several years of his life, and he died at the age of fifty-six.

Respighi composed four published choral works (another five works remain unpublished), all in a conservative style, characterized by traditional harmonies and colorful orchestrations. The cantata *Christus* op.24, composed between 1898 and 1899, is scored for TB solos, male chorus, and orchestra; the cantata *I persiani* op.60, composed in 1900 and revised in 1906, is scored for ATB solos, male chorus, and orchestra; *La primavera* op.136, composed between 1918 and 1922, is scored for STBB solos, mixed chorus, and orchestra; and Respighi's best-known and most frequently performed choral work, *Lauda per la natività del Signore* (Laud to the Nativity), was composed between 1928 and 1930 and is scored for SAT solos, SATB chorus (with divisions), and instrumental chamber ensemble of flute (doubling piccolo), oboe, English horn, two bassoons, triangle, and piano four hands. The text of this popular cantata is about the announcement and birth of Jesus, with the vocal solos portraying the roles of the Angel who appeared to the shepherds (S), Mary (A), and a Shepherd (T).

ILDEBRANDO PIZZETTI 1880–1968

Pizzetti was born in Parma and, like Respighi, studied with his father, who was a piano teacher. The young Pizzetti furthered his studies at the Parma Conservatory between 1895 and 1901, and while there he developed a love for the theater and for music from the Renaissance. Between 1902 and 1904 he was assistant conductor of the Teatro Regio di Parma, and in 1907 he returned to the Parma Conservatory to teach harmony and counterpoint. He moved to Florence in 1908 to teach at the Istituto Musicale (by then named the Florence Conservatory), becoming its director in 1917, and during the following years he became a frequent writer of articles for the periodical *La voce* and for the newspapers *Il secolo* in Milan and *La nazione* in Florence. In 1924 he was appointed director of the Milan Conservatory, in 1936 he moved to Rome to become professor of composition at the Accademia di S Cecilia, and between 1947 and 1952 he served as the academy's president. For the remaining years of his life he toured throughout Europe and the United States, conducting and lecturing.

Pizzetti composed six choral/orchestral works and seven a cappella choral opuses. The orchestral works include the wedding cantata *Epithalamium* of 1939 and *Cantico di Gloria "Attollite portas"* of 1948, this latter work scored for three choruses, twenty-two wind instruments, two pianos, and percussion. The a cappella opuses include the *Messa di Requiem* of 1922, *De profundis* of 1937, *Tre composizioni corali* of 1942 to 1943, and *Due composizioni corali* of 1961. The set of three pieces (*Tre composizioni corali*) is Pizzetti's most frequently performed choral work. Dedicated to Pius XII on the occasion of his twenty-fifth anniversary as pope, it is scored for SATBB chorus and consists of the separate pieces entitled "Cade la sera," "Ululate, quia prope est dies Domini," and "Recordare Domine."

MARIO CASTELNUOVO-TEDESCO 1895–1968

Castelnuovo-Tedesco was born in Florence, where he attended the Istituto Musicale Cherubini from ages fourteen to nineteen. From nineteen to twenty-three he attended the Liceo Musicale in Bologna, and during this time he also traveled to Florence to take composition lessons with Ildebrando Pizzetti. During his late twenties and thirties he earned a living by playing piano concerts and accompanying vocal recitals and by writing for several musical periodicals, including *La critica musicale, Il pianoforte,* and *La rassegna musicale.* He moved to Larchmont, New York, in 1939 and then to Los Angeles, California, in 1940, and in 1945 he became a citizen of the United States. During the 1940s and 1950s he composed numerous film scores and also taught at the Los Angeles Conservatory of Music, later renamed the California Institute of the Arts, where his students included Jerry Goldsmith, Henry Mancini, André Previn, and John Williams.

Castelnuovo-Tedesco composed four oratorios, six works for Jewish services, three sacred cantatas, several motets and Christmas carols, and thirteen opuses of part songs. The oratorios are *Il libro di Ruth* op.140 of 1949, *Il libro di Giona* op.151 of 1951, *The Book of Esther* op.200 of 1962, and *Tobias and the Angel* op.204 of 1964 to 1965. The works for Jewish services include the *Sacred Service* op.122 of 1943 (revised in 1950), *Kol nidrei* (no opus number) of 1944, *Songs and Processionals for a Jewish Wedding* op.150 of 1950, and *Memorial Service for the Departed* op.192 of 1960. The cantatas are *Naomi and Ruth* op.137 of 1947, *The Queen of Sheba* op.161 of 1953, and *The Fiery Furnace* op.183 of 1958. This latter work, although subtitled "a small cantata," is an oratorio-like composition with dramatic biblical dialogue related in frequent passages of recitative by a narrator and a trio of children's or women's voices portraying Shadrach, Meshach, and Abednego. Accompaniment is for organ and percussion.

The part songs include several opuses of pieces scored for chorus and piano and devoted to and titled after famous poets (e.g., *Keats' Songs* op. 113 of 1942 to 1951, *Two Longfellow Songs* op.149 of 1950, and *Four Christina Rossetti Songs* op.153 of 1951). Castelnuovo-Tedesco's most famous opus of part songs, *Romancero gitano* op.152 of 1951, consists of seven settings of poems by Federico García Lorca scored for SATB solos, SATB chorus, and guitar. The individual pieces are "Baladilla de los tres rios" (Little ballad of the three rivers), "La guitarra" (The guitar), "Puñal" (The dagger), "Procesión" (Procession), "Memento" (Memory), "Baile" (Dance), and "Crótalo" (Rattlebox).

Luigi Dallapiccola 1904–1975

Dallapiccola was born in what is now Pazin, Croatia, south of Trieste in northeast Italy. He began studying piano locally at age eight, and at twelve he studied in Graz, Austria, where his family had been relocated because the Austrian government, which controlled the area of northeastern Italy at the time, suspected that the Dallapiccolas were Italian nationalists. At fifteen Luigi commuted to Trieste for lessons in piano and harmony, and for the next several years he took trips to Bologna and Florence to expand his musical horizons. Of particular importance to the young musician were the operas of Mozart and Wagner and the piano and orchestral works of Debussy. At nineteen Dallapiccola enrolled at the conservatory in Florence, where he was exposed to the music of Schoenberg, whose *Pierrot lunaire* made a significant impact on the young and impressionable student, and after graduation he taught piano privately and gained a reputation as an excellent piano recitalist. In 1930 he taught piano at the conservatory, substituting for his teacher Ernesto Consolo, and in 1934 he was officially appointed professor of piano. During the 1940s he was active as a music critic for such publications as *Il mondo*, and during the 1950s he traveled throughout Europe and the United States giving lectures (e.g., at the Berkshire Music Center in 1951) and holding visiting teaching appointments (e.g., at Queens College of the City University of New York during the 1956–1957 academic year). His early works are in a relatively conservative style, with diatonic and chromatic harmonies, whereas his late works are all dodecaphonic, either completely so or in combination with modal and chromatic melodies and harmonies.

Dallapiccola composed eleven choral works, including six that are recognized as artistically meritorious or that have become relatively well known through frequent performance. The early works are represented by *Sei cori di Michelangelo Buonarotti il giovane*. The first two pieces of this collection, "Il coro delle malmaritate" (Chorus of the unhappily married wives) and "Il coro dei malammogliati" (Chorus of the unhappily married husbands), were composed in 1933 and are madrigalistic in style, with alternating passages of homophony and imitative polyphony and with varied rhythms for expressive effect. The second two pieces, "I balconi della rosa" and "Il papavero," were composed in 1934 and 1935 and are scored for boys' or female chorus and seventeen instruments. The third two pieces, "Il coro degli Zitti" and "Il coro dei Lanzi briachi," were composed in 1935 and 1936 and are scored for mixed chorus and orchestra.

The middle-period works include the oratorio *Job* and the two collections *Canti di prigionia* (Songs of captivity) and *Canti di liberazione* (Songs of liberation). *Job* was composed in 1950 and premiered at the Teatro Eliseo in Rome. Subtitled "sacra rappresentazione" and with text in Italian, it is divided into seven movements. *Canti di prigionia,* Dallapiccola's most famous choral work, was composed between 1938 and 1941 as a statement about the oppressive political actions of Mussolini. According to Dallapiccola, "I should have liked to protest, but I was not so ingenuous as to disregard the fact that in a totalitarian regime the individual is powerless. Only by means of music would I be able to express my indignation." The work is in three movements, each of which deals with the final statements of historical figures who have been condemned to death—"Preghiera di Maria Stuarda" (Mary Stuart's prayer), "Invocazione di Boezio" (The invocation of Boethius), and "Congedo di Girolamo Savonarola" (Girolamo Savonarola's farewell). The music combines twelve-tone rows with modal and chromatic writing, and fragments of the Gregorian chant "Dies irae" are incorporated into the texture. *Canti di liberazione,* composed between 1951 and 1955, is similarly based on three expressions of freedom from political oppression—a letter from the French theologian Sebastian Castellio in 1555, passages from Exodus 15, and excerpts from St Augustine's *Confessionum.*

The late works are represented by *Requiescant* and *Tempus destruendi – Tempus aedificandi* (A time to destroy – A time to build up). The first of these was composed in 1957 and 1958 as a commission by Radio Hamburg. The three texts of the work, all in English, are from Matthew 11:28 ("Come unto me, all ye that labor and are heavy laden, and I will give you rest"), Oscar Wilde's *Requiescant* ("Tread lightly, she is near"), and James Joyce's *A portrait of the artist as a young man* ("Dingdong! The castle bell!"). The music is divided into five movements, two of which are for orchestra alone and which serve as interludes between the texted settings. *Tempus destruendi – Tempus aedificandi* was composed in 1970 and 1971 as a commission for the Testimonium concert in Tel Aviv, Israel, in 1971. The work is a setting of two Medieval Latin texts—"Ploratus" (Lamenting) and "Exhortatio" (Urging)—that deal with the destruction and rebuilding of Jerusalem. By extension, Dallapiccola wrote that "the work takes on a wider significance: the building of a new civilization, with new or renewed values, on the ruins of an old, outmoded one." The music, entirely dodecaphonic, is characterized by wide melodic leaps and dissonant harmonies.

CHORAL WORKS
SELECTED AND LISTED ACCORDING TO FAMILIARITY

Canti di prigionia – 1938–1941 – SATB chorus (with divisions), two pianos, two harps, and percussion instruments (including vibraphone, xylophone, timpani, bells, cymbals, tam-tams, and triangle) – 24 minutes. The second movement is scored for women's chorus and instruments.

Canti di liberazione – 1951–1955 – SATB chorus (with divisions) and orchestra – 30 minutes.

Sei cori di Michelangelo Buonarroti il giovane – "Il coro delle malmaritate" and "Il coro dei malammogliati" (both of 1933) – SAATBB chorus a cappella – 10 minutes.

Requiescant – 1957–1958 – SA children's chorus, SATB chorus, and orchestra (including piccolo, English horn, bass clarinet, saxophone, contrabassoon, harp, celesta, xylophone, vibraphone, glockenspiel, and numerous other percussion instruments) – 18 minutes.

Tempus destruendi – Tempus aedificandi – 1970–1971 – S solo and SSAATT-BB chorus a cappella – 11 minutes. There are also brief solo parts for another S plus AATTBB.

Job – 1950 – speaker, SATB solos, SATB chorus, and orchestra (including celesta, piano, xylophone, vibraphone, and organ) – 33 minutes. (1) Major solo roles are for a Narrator (speaker), Job (B), and friends of Job (S, A, and T); (2) minor solos are for four messengers (SATB); (3) the choral parts divide briefly into two SATB speaking choruses.

GOFFREDO PETRASSI 1904–2003

Petrassi was born in Zagarolo, near Palestrina, on the outskirts of Rome, and at age seven, his family moved to Rome, where the young Petrassi entered the Scuola Cantorum di S Salvatore in Lauro as a chorister. When his voice changed at age fifteen he took a job in a music shop and thus had the opportunity to study scores, at twenty-one he took harmony lessons privately, and at twenty-four he enrolled at the Conservatorio di S Cecilia. Four years later he was recognized for two compositions—his graduation exercise *Tre cori* (which was never published) and his *Partita* for orchestra (which became one of his most praised works). From 1934 to 1936 he taught counterpoint, harmony, and choral composition at the Accademia di S Celilia in Rome, and in 1939 he was appointed the main professor of composition at the Conservatorio di S Celilia. He was also general director of the opera house La Fenice in Venice from 1937 to 1940. During the 1950s, as his fame increased, Petrassi was invited to the United States and Austria to lecture and hold workshops, and in 1959 he returned to the Accademia di S Celilia to teach advanced composition courses. He remained at the Accademia until his retirement in 1974, holding a position also at the Accademia Chigiana in Siena in 1966 and 1967 and continuing to travel and teach privately until the early 1990s, when he became almost totally blind. He was one of the most long-lived composers in history, dying of natural causes at the age of ninety-eight.

Petrassi composed six choral/orchestral and four a cappella choral works. It is interesting to note that he also composed music for ten Italian movies—six features and four shorts. The choral/orchestral works include *Salmo IX* (Psalm 9), composed between 1934 and 1936, set in Latin in two large parts and characterized by sections of recitative (for both chorus and single vocal sections alone), melismatic word paintings, and tonal harmonies; *Coro dei morti*, composed in 1940 and 1941 and subtitled a "dramatic madrigal"; and his most important large-scale work, *Noche oscura,* composed in 1950 and 1951, set to text by the Spanish mystic St John of the Cross (1542–1591) and structured on a four-note musical cell similar to that used by Stravinsky in his *Symphony of Psalms.*

The earliest of the published a cappella works is *Nonsense,* composed in 1952 to five whimsical texts by Edward Lear, set in Italian translation—"C'era una signorina" (There was a young lady), "C'era un vecchio musicale" (There was an old musician), "C'era un vecchio di Rovigo" (There was an old man from Rovigo), "C'era una signorina di Pozzillo" (There was a young lady from Pozzillo), and "C'era una vecchia di Polla" (There was an old lady from Polla). A sixth setting of a Lear limerick, *Sesto, non-senso,* was composed separately in 1964. Other a cappella works include *Motetti per la Passione* composed in 1965 and *Tre cori sacri* composed between 1980 and 1983. This latter set of pieces consists of three extracts from the Credo—"Et incarnatus," "Crucifixus," and "Resurrexit"— representing Christ's birth, death, and resurrection.

CHORAL WORKS
SELECTED AND LISTED ACCORDING TO FAMILIARITY

Nonsense – 1952 – SATB chorus (with frequent divisions) a cappella –
10 minutes.

Tre cori sacri – 1980–1983 – SATB chorus a cappella – 10 minutes.

Salmo IX (Psalm 9) – 1934–1936 – SATB chorus (with occasional divisions), strings, two pianos, and brass and percussion instruments – 35 minutes.

Noche oscura – 1950–1951 – SATB chorus (with occasional divisions) and orchestra – 24 minutes.

Motetti per la Passione – 1965 – SSATTBB chorus a cappella – 12 minutes.
Comment: The first, third, and fourth motets are scored for SSTBB, and the second motet is for SATTB.

Coro dei morti – 1940–1941 – TTBB chorus, brass instruments, three pianos, percussion, and five string basses – 16 minutes.

CARLOS SURINACH 1915–1997

Surinach was born in Barcelona and learned to play the piano as a child by taking lessons from his mother. Between the ages of twenty-one and twenty-four he studied at the Barcelona Conservatory, at twenty-five his studies continued at the Hochschule in Düsseldorf, and at twenty-six he transferred to the Preussische Akademie der Künste in Berlin. He returned to Spain in 1942 to serve as conductor of the Barcelona Philharmonic Orchestra and also director of the Gran Teatro del Liceo, and between 1947 and 1950 he lived in France, spending most of his time there composing ballet music. In 1951 he moved to the United States, becoming a citizen in 1959 and composing ballets for notable companies, including the Martha Graham Company and Joffrey Ballet. He also taught at Carnegie Mellon University and gave lectures at other universities, including Yale. He is best known for his use of Spanish dance forms, especially flamenco, and for his colorful orchestrations.

Surinach composed four choral works. *Cantata de San Juan* was commissioned by CBS television in 1963 and, according to the composer, was "written in homage to the island of Puerto Rico and dedicated to the city of San Juan." The text, set in both English and Spanish translation, is divided into three movements—"Annunciation," which presents the story of Zacharias and Elizabeth and the birth of their son John; "Baptism," which is about John's baptism and prophecy; and "Death," which relates John's murder as ordered by Herod's daughter Salome. *Canciones del alma* (Songs of the Soul) was composed in 1964 and consists of settings of four poems by the Spanish mystic St John of the Cross (1542–1591). These poems, set in four corresponding movements are, "Noche oscura del alma" (Dark night of the soul), "Llama de amor viva" (Living flame of love), "Delirio del alma por ver a Dios" (The soul longing to see God), and "Gozo a la fe" (Joy in the faith). *The Missions of San Antonio* was composed in 1969 and scored for male chorus and orchestra, and *Via cruces*, subtitled "A cycle of fifteen saetas [short songs sung in religious ceremonies] for chorus and guitar" was composed in 1972.

CHORAL WORKS
SELECTED AND LISTED ACCORDING TO FAMILIARITY

Cantata de San Juan – 1963 – SATB chorus and percussion ensemble consisting of four timpani, cymbals (orchestral, suspended, and antique), triangle, xylophone, and tam-tam – 17 minutes.

Canciones del alma (Songs of the Soul) – 1964 – SATB chorus a cappella – 20 minutes.

LUIGI NONO 1924–1990

Nono was born in Venice into a family of artists and amateur musicians. Between 1943 and 1945 he studied under Malipiero at the Venice Conservatory, and during the several years that followed he studied law at the University of Padua. Between 1950 and 1957 he was a student at the Internationale Ferienkurse für Neue Musik (International Summer Courses for New Music) in Darmstadt, where he particularly valued the instruction of Edgard Varèse, and from 1957 to 1959 he became a lecturer and teacher there. Two famous speeches from these years are noteworthy—"Die Entwicklung der Reihentechnik" (The evolution of serial technique), delivered in 1958, in which he named himself as well as Pierre Boulez, Bruno Maderna, Karlheinz Stockhausen, and others as members of the "Darmstadt School," and "Presenza storica nella musica d'oggi" (Historical presence in music of today), in which he decried the avant-garde music of John Cage. During the 1960s Nono was associated with the electronic Studio di Fonologia (RAI) in Milan and became known for his political messages in works such as *Canti di vita e d'amore – sul ponte di Hiroshima, La Fabrica Illuminata,* and *Ricorda cosi ti hanno fatto in Auschwitz.* During the 1980s he worked at the Experimentalstudio der Heinrich-Strobel-Stiftung in Freiburg and composed a number of works that included live electronics.

Nono composed sixteen works for chorus. The most celebrated of these, *Il canto sospeso,* was composed in 1955 and 1956 to fragments of letters by European Resistance fighters. It is a twelve-tone work divided into nine movements—three for orchestra alone, three for soloists and orchestra (one of which is also scored for the women of the chorus), and three for chorus (one a cappella, one for chorus and orchestra, and one for chorus and timpani). The texture of the music corresponds to the fragmentation of text in the letters, although there are also passages of Renaissance-like polyphony and madrigalistic word painting. A review of the work credited it with achieving "a synthesis—to a degree hardly thought possible—between an uncompromisingly avant-garde style of composition and emotional, moral expression." Another important work, *Prometeo,* was composed between 1981 and 1984 as an opera and revised in

1985 as a concert piece. Subtitled "Traggedia dell'ascolto" (A tragedy of listening), it combines ancient and modern texts (e.g., by Aeschylus and Friedrich Hölderlin) as an exercise in the various acoustical and spatial effects of sound.

CHORAL WORKS
SELECTED AND LISTED ACCORDING TO FAMILIARITY

Il canto sospeso – 1955–1956 – SAT solos, SATB chorus, and orchestra – 28 minutes.

Prometeo – 1981–1984 (revised in 1985) – two speakers, SSAAT solos, SATB chorus (with divisions), orchestra, and electronics – 134 minutes.

La terra e la compagna – 1957–1958 – ST solos, SATB chorus (with divisions), four flutes, four trumpets, four trombones, percussion, and strings – 8 minutes.

Liebeslied – 1954 – SATB chorus, timpani, vibraphone, glockenspiel, cymbals, and harp – 6 minutes.

Cori di Didone – 1958 – SATB chorus (with divisions) and percussion (six players) – 10 minutes.

Das atmende Klarsein – 1981 – SATB chorus (with divisions), flute, and electronics – 36 minutes.

LUCIANO BERIO 1925–2003

Berio was born in Oneglia, southwest of Genoa, on the Ligurian Sea. He received his first musical instruction from his father and grandfather, who were both organists and composers, and at age nine he played piano in family chamber music gatherings. At twenty he entered the Milan Conservatory, where he was exposed to the music of Milhaud, Bartók, Stravinsky, Hindemith, and Schoenberg, and at twenty-seven he went to the United States, where he took courses at the Berkshire Music Center in Tanglewood and studied composition with Luigi Dallapiccola. While in the United States, Berio also attended a concert of electronic music held in October 1952 at the Museum of Modern Art in New York City. In 1953 he met Karlheinz Stockhausen (1928–2007) at a conference on electronic music in Basle, Switzerland, and in 1955 he cofounded the Studio di Fonologia Musicale (RAI) in Milan. Berio returned to the United States in 1960, teaching at Tanglewood during that summer; substituting for Darius Milhaud at Mills College in Oakland, California, during the spring of 1962 and then again for the 1963–1964 academic year; and serving on the faculty of the Juilliard School of Music from 1965 to 1971. In 1974 he was appointed director of the electro-acoustic studio of the IRCAM (Institut de Recherche et Coordination Acoustique/Musique) at the Centre Pompidou in Paris, and during the late 1970s he served as artistic director for two performing ensembles—the Israel Chamber Orchestra and the Accademia Filarmonica Romana. He continued his conducting activities during the 1980s, leading the Orchestra Regionale Toscana beginning in 1982 and guest conducting the Maggio Musicale Fiorentino in 1984, and in 1987 he founded and became director of the electronic studio Tempo Reale in Florence. During the final decade of his life Berio received numerous awards, including honorary doctorates from the University of Siena in 1995, University of Turin and University of Edinburgh in 1999, and University of Bologna in 2000. He was also the featured composer in numerous festivals across Europe.

Berio composed twelve choral works that are published, the most famous of which is *Coro*, written in 1975 and 1976 (revised in 1977) for West German Radio, Cologne. The work is structured in thirty-one movements or "episodes" that juxtapose poetry of Pablo Neruda with folk song texts from a variety of countries and in a variety of languages. According to Berio, "There are no quotations or transformations of actual folk songs (with the exception of Episode VI, where a Yugoslav melody is used, and Episode XVI, where I quote a melody from my *Cries of London*); rather, there is a development of folk techniques and modes which are combined without reference to specific songs." The scoring stipulates that in performance, pairs of the forty singers are to be placed in close proximity to instruments of corresponding range. Thus, for instance, the ten sopranos are to stand next to the upper wind, brass, and stringed instruments.

Other notable choral works include *Magnificat,* composed in 1949, set to the traditional Latin text, and divided into eight interconnecting sections; *Cries of London,* composed in 1973 and 1974 for the King's Singers, revised in 1975 for eight-part mixed chorus, and set to phrases shouted by London street vendors; and Berio's final composition, *Stanze,* composed in 2003 and premiered by the Orchestre de Paris in January 2004. This last-named work is set to the poetry of Berio's five favorite poets (Paul Celan, Giorgio Caproni, Edoardo Sanguineti, Alfred Brendel, and Dan Pagis) and is divided into five chambers or rooms (called *stanze* in Italian).

CHORAL WORKS
SELECTED AND LISTED ACCORDING TO FAMILIARITY

Coro – 1975–1976 (revised in 1977) – SATB chorus and orchestra – 56 minutes. The chorus is to consist of forty voices (ten sopranos, ten altos, ten tenors, and ten basses) and the orchestra of forty instruments.

Magnificat – 1949 – SS solos, SSAATB chorus, and chamber ensemble of flute, oboe, two clarinets, two horns, two trumpets, two trombones, string bass, two pianos, vibraphone, timpani, snare drum, cymbal, and three tam-tams – 14 minutes.

Stanze – 2003 – B solo, three male choruses, and orchestra – 28 minutes.

Cries of London – 1973–1974 (revised in 1975) – AATTBB solo voices a cappella (revised in 1975 for SSAATTBB chorus a cappella) – 16 minutes.

JAVIER BUSTO B.1949

Busto was born in Hondarribia, in northern Spain, on the Bay of Biscay. He studied medicine and received a medical degree from the University of Valladolid. However, he developed an interest in music, which he studied on his own, and has spent the majority of his professional career conducting choral ensembles. He directed the Coro Ederki in Valladolid between 1971 and

1976; he founded Coro Eskifaia in Hondarribia, which he conducted between 1978 and 1994; and in 1995 he founded the Cantemus Koroa ladies' choir in San Sebastián. This latter ensemble has won numerous competitions, including those held in Ejea de los Caballeros, Avilés, and Tours, and Busto has become recognized as one of Europe's leading choral conductors. He was featured at the Fourth World Symposium on Choral Music in Sydney, Australia, in 1996, and at the Tokyo Cantat in 2000.

Busto has composed fifteen choral pieces, including the popular *Ave Maria* for SATB chorus and optional organ accompaniment, and *Ave maris stella* for solo voice and SATB chorus a cappella. Both of these pieces exhibit traits of Busto's general musical style. In *Ave Maria* (and also *O sacrum convivium*), for example, trio passages in parallel motion alternate between the upper (soprano and alto) and lower (tenor and bass) voices, primary phrases consist of repeated chordal motifs, and chant-like choral recitation passages underscore and accompany other melodic phrases. In *Ave maris stella* (and also *Laudate pueri* and *Pater noster*) solo chant-like phrases are combined with homophonic choral sections of music. In addition, these latter motets consist of occasional aleatoric rhythmic passages.

∝ HUNGARY, POLAND, AND THE CZECH REPUBLIC ∝

The Eastern European composers in Hungary, Poland, and the Czech Republic had a high degree of interest in folk music during the early years of the Modern era. All the significant choral composers from these countries born in the final decades of the nineteenth century collected native folk melodies and set them as vocal solos with piano accompaniment or as arrangements for a cappella chorus. These composers also wrote new compositions based on the original tunes. Leoš Janáček, Béla Bartók, and Zoltán Kodály were noted worldwide for their dedication to the collection and preservation of folk songs, and Karol Szymanowski, Bohuslav Martinů, and Lajos Bárdos employed folk songs as a basis for many of their compositions. A majority of these composers were also interested in music education and worked to establish music programs for the youth of their countries and to provide the youth with new compositions.

The Eastern European composers born during the first two decades of the twentieth century maintained an interest in folk music, especially during their early careers. However, most of these composers, as well as most of those born in the 1930s, developed interests in modern compositional techniques. György Ligeti is known for tone clusters, Witold Lutoslawski for aleatoric passages of music, Henryk Mikołaj Górecki for minimalistic development of motivic material, and Krzysztof Penderecki for the creation of new notational symbols and other avant-garde modes of performance. The composers born later in the era—Zdeněk Lukáš, Petr Eben, and György Orbán—plus Mátyás Seiber, who was born at the beginning of the twentieth century, emulated the textures and forms of Renaissance and Baroque genres while writing in modern, pantonal harmonies.

Six of the composers mentioned above were born and worked in Hungary, four were from Poland, and four were from the Czech Republic. Three additional Czech Republic composers (Josef Bohuslav Foerster, Alois Hába, and Jan Hanuš) and one Hungarian (György Kurtág) also wrote significant choral music.

Foerster (1859–1951) was born in Prague, where his father Josef (1833–1907) was an organist and choirmaster at several well-known churches, professor at the Prague Organ School, and teacher of theory at the Prague Conservatory. The young Foerster studied at the Organ School between 1879 and 1882 and then succeeded Dvořák as organist at the church of St Vojtech. In 1893 Foerster moved to Hamburg, Germany, working there as a music critic for the *Neue Hamburger Zeitung* and other newspapers and teaching at the Hamburg Conservatory beginning in 1901, and in 1903 he relocated to Vienna, where he wrote for *Die Zeit* and taught at the New Conservatory. He returned to Prague in 1919, and for the next two decades he taught at both the conservatory and university. His choral output consists of four masses scored for mixed chorus and organ, including *Glagolská mše* (Glagolitic Mass) op.123 and *Missa in honorem S Francisci Assisiensis* op.131; seven cantatas scored for soloists, chorus, and orchestra, including his most famous work, *Mrtvým bratřím* (To the Dead Brothers) op.108; and forty-four part songs, most of which are settings of Czech folk texts.

Hába (1893–1973) was born in Vizovice, in the Zlin region of the Czech Republic, where he played violin and string bass in his father's folk ensemble. He studied at the Prague Conservatory beginning in 1914, and shortly thereafter he composed his first piece in quarter tones. His education continued at the Berlin Hochschule für Musik, and in 1923 he returned to Prague and established the department of microtonal music at the conservatory. For the remainder of his life he devoted himself to the construction of musical instruments capable of producing, and the composition of works utilizing, quarter tones. The instruments consist of a piano, harmonium, clarinet, trumpet, and guitar, and the compositions include the opera *Matka* (the Mother), the choral *Suite* op.13 (Hába's first choral quarter-tone work), and several opuses of pieces for children (e.g., *5 Children's Choruses* op.42).

Hanuš (1915–2004) was born in Prague and studied at the Prague Conservatory. After graduation he worked in the music publishing business, becoming editor of several companies and overseeing the complete editions of Dvořák and Janáček. Hanuš was a prolific composer, whose output includes seven symphonies, five operas, and three ballets as well as eight masses (including a Requiem), four oratorios (including two Passions), and several motets. A number of these works plus others were written for children (Hába served as chairman of the Czech Company for Music Education), including a collection of ten disparate compositions composed between 1969 and 1977 and entitled *Opus spirituale pro juventute* op.65. Works for mixed chorus include the avant-garde oratorio *Ecce homo* op.97, the mass *Mše Hlaholska* (Glagolitic Mass) op.106, the Requiem *Messa da Requiem* op.121, and the cantata *The Earth is Speaking* op.8.

Kurtág (b.1926) was born in Lugoj in western Romania, and at age five he began studying piano with his mother. His formal music education was at the Liszt Academy of Music in Budapest, where a fellow student and friend was György Ligeti. In 1957 Kurtág furthered his education in Paris, working with Olivier Messiaen and Darius Milhaud and copying many of the works of Anton Webern, and in 1958 he returned to Budapest. He taught at the Bartók Music School from 1958 until 1963, in 1967 he began teaching piano at the Liszt Academy, and in 1969 he began teaching chamber music as well. He moved to Berlin, Germany, in the 1990s and served as composer-in-residence for the Berlin Philharmonic from 1993 to 1995 and as a member of the Akademie der Künste from 1998 to 1999. Notable among his six choral works, all of which are in a synthesis of Medieval, Baroque, and Modern styles, are *Omaggio a Luigi Nono* op.16 of 1979 (revised in 1985), *8 Choruses* op.23 of 1981 and 1982 (revised in 1984), and *Pesni unīniya i pechali* (Songs of Despair and Sorrow) op.18 of 1980 to 1994.

LEOŠ JANÁČEK 1854–1928

Janáček was born in the Moravian region of the Czech Republic, where his grandfather and father were choral directors and educators. At age eleven Leoš entered the Augustinian monastery in Brno as a chorister, several years later he moved to the German Realschule, and at fifteen he enrolled at the Czech Teachers' Institute. After graduation in 1872 he began leading the Augustinian monastery chorus, performing music of Palestrina, Lasso, and Joseph Haydn, and in 1873 he was appointed choirmaster of the male choral society Svatopluk. In 1876 he became conductor of the Czech Beseda Choral Society, conducting such works as the Mozart *Requiem* and the Beethoven *Missa solemnis,* and in 1879, desiring to further his education, he matriculated at the Leipzig Conservatory. He continued his education at the Vienna Conservatory in 1880, and in 1881 he founded the Brno Organ School. During the next several years he became interested in folk music and collected Moravian songs, and between 1894 and 1903 he composed his first successful opera, *Jenufa.* After the turn of the century he was recognized for his choral compositions *Kantor Halfar* (Halfar the Schoolmaster), *Na Soláni Čarták* (Čarták on the Soláň), and *Amarus,* and between 1916 and 1926 he composed some of his most significant works, including the operas *Příhody lišky Bystroušky* (The Cunning Little Vixen) and *Več Makropulos* (The Makropulos Affair), the orchestral *Sinfonietta,* and the mass *Glagolská mše* (sometimes listed as *Mša glagolskaja* or *Misa slavonija*). He was elected to the Prussian Academy of Arts in 1927 and died of pneumonia the following year at age seventy-four.

Janáček composed nine choral/orchestral works, eleven Latin motets and a Latin mass, ten Czech hymns, approximately twenty part songs and folk song arrangements, and several miscellaneous patriotic and ceremonial works with piano or instrumental chamber accompaniment. The most famous of the choral/orchestral works is *Glagolská mše,* which was composed in the fall of 1926, revised and simplified in the spring of 1927, and published in its revised format in 1929. The original version existed only in manuscript fragments. However, it was reconstructed by Paul Wingfield after Janáček's death, and it is this reconstructed original version, which contains an opening and closing "Intrada" not in the revised version, that has become standard today. The name of the mass, *Glagolská* (Glagolitic), refers to the script used in the ancient Church Slavonic language and to the Slavonic language of the mass text. The work contains the traditional five portions of the Roman Mass Ordinary, each of which is given a Slavonic title—"Ghospodi pomiluj" (Kyrie), "Slava" (Gloria), "Věruju" (Credo), "Svet" (Sanctus), and "Agneče Božij" (Agnus Dei)—and instrumental movements both frame the mass and demarcate its center (i.e., an interlude for organ solo stands in the middle of the Credo).

Other important choral/orchestral works include the cantatas *Amarus* and *Věčné evangelium* (Eternal Gospel). *Amarus,* composed in 1896 and 1897, is about a young, lonely man who forsakes his daily ritual of filling the altar lamp with oil and follows two lovers to a cemetery, where he finds his mother's grave and dies. *Věčné evangelium,* composed in the spring of 1914 and premiered in February 1917 by the Pražský Hlahol, is based on a poem about universal love by Janáček's favorite poet, Jaroslav Vrchlický (1853–1912). The composition is divided into four movements: in the first, the medieval Sicilian mystic Joachim da Fiore preaches the gospel of love; in the second, passages about the vanity of the world alternate with an angel's message that the salvation of the world is forthcoming; in the third, Joachim reinforces the angel's message, stating that the "eternal gospel shines forth in gladness"; and in the fourth, an epilogue, the chorus closes with proclamations about love's empire and eternal salvation.

The Latin mass, subtitled "After the Messe pour Orgue by Franz Liszt," was composed in 1901 and contains the traditional five portions of the Roman Mass Ordinary, with the Sanctus divided into two movements (Sanctus and Benedictus). An additional mass in E-flat major was begun in 1907 and 1908 but never completed; only the Kyrie, Gloria, and Agnus Dei movements were finished by Janáček.

The part songs include *Píseň v jeseni* (Autumn song), composed in 1880 to commemorate the twentieth anniversary of the Beseda Brněnská (Brno Artists' Union), and *Kačena divoká* (The Wild Duck), composed in about 1885 for schoolchildren. The part songs also include arrangements for chorus and piano of six Moravian duets (Moravské dvojzpevy) composed by Antonín Dvořák.

CHORAL WORKS
SELECTED AND LISTED ACCORDING TO FAMILIARITY

Glagolská mše (Glagolitic Mass) – 1926–1927 – SATB solos, SATB chorus (with divisions), and orchestra (including organ) – 40 minutes. (1) The T solo depicts a priest, the S solo an angel, and the chorus the people of the Czech Republic; (2) the organ is featured as a solo instrument in the middle portion of the Credo and in a toccata after the Agnus Dei.

Věčné evangelium (The Eternal Gospel) – 1914 – ST solos, SATB chorus (with occasional divisions), and orchestra (including three flutes, English horn, contrabassoon, harp, and organ) – 21 minutes. The T solo portrays the role of Joachim da Fiore and the S solo portrays an angel.

Amarus – 1896–1897 (revised in 1901) – STB solos, SATBB chorus, and orchestra – 30 minutes.

Na Soláni Čarták (Čarták on the Soláň) – 1911 (revised in 1920) – T solo, TTBB chorus, and orchestra – 8 minutes.

Píseň v jeseni (Autumn song) – 1880 – SATB chorus (with divisions to SSAATTBB) a cappella – 4 minutes.

Kačena divoká (The Wild Duck) – 1885 – SATB chorus (with divisions) a cappella – 2:30 minutes.

Mass in B-flat major – 1901 – SATB chorus and organ – 12 minutes.

Otče náš (Our father) – 1901 – T solo, SATB chorus, and piano or harmonium (revised in 1906 for harp and organ) – 15:30 minutes.

BÉLA BARTÓK 1881–1945

Bartók was born in Nagyszentmiklós, Hungary (now, Sînnicolau Mare, Romania), to parents who were amateur musicians. At age five Béla began studying piano with his mother, and at ten he began composing. The family moved frequently during his childhood, spending from one to several years each in the Ukraine, Romania, and Slovakia, and in the 1890s they settled in Pozsony, Hungary (now in western Slovakia), where Béla played the organ at the Catholic gymnasium. In 1899 he enrolled at the Budapest Academy of Music, and during the next several years he developed into an accomplished pianist. He became known for his transcriptions of orchestral works, especially Richard Strauss's *Ein Heldenleben* and Franz Liszt's *Rhapsodie espagnole,* and for his performances of Liszt's *Piano Sonata* in B minor. In 1904 Bartók began what would be a lifelong interest in folk music, writing to his sister in December of that year that he planned "to collect the finest Hungarian folk songs and to raise them (adding the best possible piano accompaniments) to the level of art song." In 1905 he met Zoltán Kodály, and in 1906 the two composers began publishing their folk song transcriptions and arrangements. In 1906 Bartók was also appointed professor of piano at the Budapest Academy of Music (a position he kept until 1934, at which time the Academy had been renamed the Liszt Academy of Music), and for the next several years he composed numerous piano pieces based on folk melodies. Many of these pieces use pentatonic scales and are characterized by spare textures and frequent ostinatos—styles that would also define the later orchestral works.

Throughout the early decades of the twentieth century Bartók continued collecting folk songs, eventually gathering ten thousand melodies, and he also was in demand as a concert pianist. In about 1920 he worked in the ethnographic department of the Hungarian National Museum, in 1924 he published a collection of 320 Hungarian folk song transcriptions entitled *A Magyar népdal* (Hungarian Folk Music), and at the end of the 1920s he achieved fame for his orchestral work *A csodálatos mandarin* (The Miraculous Mandarin)—composed in 1918 and 1919, orchestrated in 1924, and premiered in 1928. In the 1930s he worked as an ethnomusicologist at the Hungarian Academy of Sciences and also composed one of his most popular orchestral works, *Music for Strings, Percussion, and Celesta* (1936), and in 1940 he moved to New York City, where he resided until his death. During the 1941–1942 academic year he held a research appointment at Columbia University (which had granted him an honorary doctorate in 1940), and during the spring semester of 1943 he held a visiting faculty appointment at Harvard University. His *Concerto for Orchestra,* commissioned by the Koussevitzky Music Foundation, was composed in 1943 and premiered in 1944 by the Boston Symphony Orchestra. Also in 1944 he was diagnosed with leukemia, from which he died in September 1945 at the age of sixty-four.

Bartók composed two large-scale choral works with instrumental accompaniment, approximately twenty-five folk song arrangements for mixed chorus, and nine volumes of folk song arrangements for two- and three-part children's chorus. The most famous of the choral/orchestral works is *Cantata Profana,* subtitled "A kilenc csodaszarvas" (The nine enchanted stags or The giant stags) and composed in 1930. The text is from a Romanian folk ballad about nine brothers who spent so much time in the depths of the forest that they were transformed into the stags they hunted. The music is based on the Lydian and Mixolydian modes, with frequent augmented fourth and minor seventh melodic intervals. The other choral/orchestral work, *Falun* or

Tri dedinské scény (Three Village Scenes) of 1926, is a rescoring and recomposition of three Slovak folk song arrangements—"Svatba" (Wedding), "Ukoliebarka" (Lullaby), and "Tance mládencov" (Lad's Dance)—for solo voice and piano that Bartók had made in 1924.

Two sets of folk song arrangements, both characterized by modal melodies, are well known and frequently performed. *Štyri slovenské piesne* (Four Slovak Folk Songs) for SATB chorus with piano accompaniment consists of "Zadala mamka" (published in English as Wedding Song), "Na holi, na holi" (published as Song of the Hay-Harvesters), "Rada pila, rada jedla" (Song from Medzibrod), and "Gajdujte, gajdence" (Dancing Song). The *Magyar népdalok* (Hungarian Folk Songs) for SATB chorus a cappella consists of "A rab" (The prisoner), "A bujdosó" (The Wanderer), "Az eladó lány" (Finding a husband), and "Dal" (Lovesong). A third well-known set, published in English as *Three Hungarian Folk Songs,* is a choral transcription of three Bartók folk song arrangements made by Benjamin Suchoff in the late 1950s.

CHORAL WORKS
SELECTED AND LISTED ACCORDING TO FAMILIARITY

Cantata Profana – 1930 – TB solos, SATB/SATB chorus, and orchestra (including triple winds, several drums, and harp) – 20 minutes.

Štyri slovenské piesne (Four Slovak Folk Songs) – ca.1916 – SATB chorus and piano – 5 minutes.

Magyar népdalok (Hungarian Folk Songs) – 1930 – SATB chorus a cappella – 11 minutes.

Tri dedinské scény (Three Village Scenes) – 1926 – SSAA chorus and chamber orchestra – 11:30 minutes.

ZOLTÁN KODÁLY 1882–1967

Kodály was born in Kecskemét, Hungary, south of Budapest, and received his first musical instruction from his father, who was an amateur violinist, and his mother, who was a singer and pianist. Zoltán attended elementary school in Galánta (now Galanta, Slovakia), where he was introduced to folk music, and his grammar school education was in Nagyszombat (now Trnava, Slovakia), where he learned to play the piano, violin, viola, and cello. In 1900 he began a degree program in languages (Hungarian and German) at Budapest University and also enrolled in music classes at the Academy of Music, and in 1905 he met Béla Bartók and began collecting folk songs. The first collection of these songs, *Magyar népdalok* (Hungarian Folk Songs), was published in 1906, the same year Kodály went to Berlin and Paris to further his education and also the same year he completed his doctoral dissertation, "A Magyar népdal strófaszerkezete" (The stanzaic structure of Hungarian folk song). He was appointed to the Academy of Music faculty in 1907, teaching composition over the next several years to Lajos Bárdos and Mátyás Seiber, and between 1917 and 1919 he also wrote numerous articles on folk music for the magazine *Nyugat* and the newspaper *Pesti napló.* During the 1920s he achieved fame as a composer with such works as *Psalmus hungaricus* and his opera *Háry János* as well as the orchestral suite drawn from it, and during the 1930s he became known for his involvement in the Singing Youth movement, an educational initiative that created music education courses in the Hungarian school system. In 1940 Kodály joined the faculty of the Hungarian Academy of Sciences, teaching courses in ethnomusicology, and throughout the latter part of the 1940s he traveled throughout Europe, the United States, England, and Russia, conducting his works and lecturing on folk music and music education. He received honorary doctorates from Budapest University in 1957, Oxford University in 1960, and the University of Toronto in 1966, and he was named president of the International Folk Music Council in 1961 and honorary president of the International Society of Music Education in 1964.

Kodály composed twenty choral works with instrumental accompaniment and approximately 150 pieces for a cappella chorus. The accompanied works include his most famous choral composition, *Psalmus hungaricus,* a setting of a sixteenth-century paraphrase of Psalm 55 composed in 1923 for the fiftieth anniversary of the union of Pest, Buda, and Óbuda into Budapest. Other notable accompanied choral works are the *Budavári Te Deum,* composed in 1936 for the 250th anniversary of the recapture of Buda from the Turks, and *Missa brevis,* originally composed as an organ mass but transcribed for chorus in 1948, with all five portions of the Roman Mass Ordinary plus opening and closing instrumental movements entitled, respectively, "Introitus" and "Ite, missa est." All these works have modal harmonies and imitative textures that reflect Kodály's devotion to Hungarian music of past centuries.

The a cappella pieces are similarly reflective of past styles. The settings of sacred texts—such as the motet *Jézus és a kufárok* (Jesus and the traders) and the Psalm settings *A 114. genfi zsoltár* (Geneva Psalm 114) and *A 121. genfi zsoltár* (Geneva Psalm 121)—are characterized by traditional harmonies and textures, while the secular pieces are based on folk songs or folk idioms. Examples include *Mátrai képek* (Matra pictures), a setting of five folks songs from the Matra region of Hungary, and *Lengyel László* (King László's Men or Magyars and Germans), which incorporates fragments of a number of Hungarian folk melodies. The a cappella pieces are also reflective of Kodály's commitment to music education for both children and adults. As a consequence, he wrote approximately sixty pieces for young voices (scored specifically for children or for high voices in general), and approximately twenty pieces for adult male chorus.

CHORAL WORKS
SELECTED AND LISTED ACCORDING TO FAMILIARITY

Psalmus hungaricus (adapted from Psalm 55) – 1923 – T solo, SATB chorus
   (with divisions), and orchestra (including harp and organ ad lib.) –
   23 minutes. (1) The T solo is extensive and pervades the entire work;
   (2) Kodály recommended a children's chorus to augment the women's
   voices.

Missa brevis – 1948 – SATB chorus (with divisions) and orchestra or organ –
   33 minutes. The choral divisions include a brief passage for SSSAATB.

Budavári Te Deum – 1936 – ST solos, SATB chorus (with divisions), and orchestra (including organ) – 21 minutes. (1) The S and T solos are brief;
   (2) a few passages are marked for SATB solos ad lib.

Jézus és a kufárok (Jesus and the traders) – 1934 – SATB chorus (with occasional divisions) a cappella – 6:30 minutes.

Mátrai képek (Mátra pictures) – 1931 – SATB chorus (with divisions) a cappella – 11 minutes.

Sik Sándor Te Deuma (The Te Deum of Sándor Sik) – 1961 – SATB chorus (with a brief passage for divided sopranos) a cappella – 5:15 minutes.

Adventi ének (Advent song) – 1943 – SAB chorus (with a brief passage for SABB) a cappella – 5 minutes. The title is at times listed as "Veni, veni Emmanuel."

A 114. genfi zsoltár (Geneva Psalm 114) – 1952 – SATB chorus and organ – 3:30 minutes.

A 121. genfi zsoltár (Geneva Psalm 121) – 1943 – SATB chorus (with occasional divisions) a cappella – 3 minutes.

An Ode for Music – 1963 – SATB chorus (with frequent division for TTBB) a cappella – 5 minutes.

I will go look for death – 1959 – SATB chorus a cappella – 2 minutes.

Este (Evening) – 1904 – S solo and SSATB chorus (with occasional divisions for SSSAATTBB) a cappella – 4 minutes.

Esti dal (Evening song) – 1938 – SATB chorus a cappella – 3 minutes.

Ave Maria – 1935 – SSA chorus a cappella – 3 minutes.

Angyalok és pásztorok (The angels and the shepherds) – 1935 – SA/SSA chorus a cappella – 5:30 minutes. The SA chorus represents the angels and the SSA chorus represents the shepherds.

KAROL SZYMANOWSKI 1882–1937

Szymanowski was born in the Ukraine and attended music school from ages fourteen to nineteen in Elisavetgrad (now Kirowograd). In 1901 he moved to Warsaw, where he studied harmony, counterpoint, and composition privately and where he became interested in modern compositional trends, and during the next several years he traveled to Italy, Austria, and France to hear the music of such composers as Debussy and Ravel. Like many other composers from Eastern European countries, he also developed an interest in folk music. In 1927 he was appointed director of the Warsaw Conservatory, and in 1930 he became rector of the Warsaw Music Institute. His health began to fail in the ensuing years (he had contracted tuberculosis in 1929), and after an extended confinement to a sanatorium, he died in March 1937 at the age of fifty-four.

Szymanowski is best known for his operas and orchestral works, especially the opera *Król Roger* (King Roger) composed between 1920 and 1924, ballet *Harnasie* composed between 1923 and 1931, and *Symphony #2* composed in 1909 and 1910. His choral output consists of seven works, the most famous of which is *Stabat mater*, composed in 1925 and 1926 and scored for SAB solos, SATB chorus (with divisions), and orchestra (including harp and organ). The text is a Polish translation of the traditional Latin poem, and the music reflects Szymanowski's interest in ancient Polish folk music. Other important choral works include the cantata *Agave*, composed in 1917 and scored for A solo, SSAA chorus, and orchestra, and *Symphony #3*, composed between 1914 and 1916 and scored for T or S solo, mixed chorus, and orchestra. This latter work, subtitled "Pieśń o nocy" (The Song of the Night), is in an expanded Impressionistic style.

BOHUSLAV MARTINŮ 1890–1959

Martinů was born in Polička, Bohemia (now in northern Czech Republic), and studied violin when he was a child. By the time he was fifteen he was a member of the Polička String Quartet and a soloist in public recitals, and at sixteen he entered the Prague Conservatory. During his twenties he taught violin privately and played occasionally in the Czech Philharmonic, and in his early thirties he was a permanent member of the orchestra. When he was thirty-three he went to Paris, where he composed his first opera, *Voják a tanečnice* (The Soldier and the Dancer), and when he was forty he developed an interest in folk music. In 1941, when he was fifty-one, he moved to the United States, and during the next decade he held temporary positions at the Berkshire Music Center, Princeton University, and the Mannes School of Music. He returned to Paris in 1953, taught at the American Academy of Music in Rome in 1956, and in 1957 he moved to Switzerland, where he died of stomach cancer at age sixty-eight.

Martinů was a prolific composer, whose output includes sixteen operas, fifteen ballets, six symphonies, and twenty-eight choral works (sixteen accompanied by instruments and twelve a cappella). Most of the instrumentally accompanied choral works are classified as cantatas, including *Polní mše* (Field Mass), which was composed in 1939 and dedicated to the Free Czech Army Band and which is set to a text by the Czech novelist Jiří Mucha (1915–1991) that combines Psalm verses and passages from Matthew 6:9–12 with poetry by Mucha himself. Other cantatas include four works composed between 1955 and 1959 to texts by Miloslav Bures and collectively entitled "Songs of the Highland." The first work, *Otvírání studánek* (The Opening of the Wells), is a salute to spring as children ritually clean town wells; the second, *Legenda z dýmu bramborové nati* (Legend of the Smoke from Potato Tops), tells the story of the Virgin Mary, whose image on an altar piece is transformed into a living person; the third, *Romance z pampelišek* (Romance of the Dandelions), relates simple summer pleasures experienced by peasants; and the fourth, *Mikeš z hor* (Mikeš from the Mountains), is a winter tale about a shepherd tending his flock in the snowy cold mountains. An additional important cantata, *The Prophecy of Isaiah*, was commissioned by the state of Israel and is in Hebrew.

The a cappella compositions include Martinů's most popular pieces, *5 českých madrigalů* (Five Czech Madrigals). They are similar to the folk song arrangements of Bartók, with traditional texts and melodies and with modal harmonizations.

CHORAL WORKS
SELECTED AND LISTED ACCORDING TO FAMILIARITY

Polní mše (Field Mass) – 1939 – B solo, TTBB chorus, wind ensemble (two piccolos, two clarinets, three trumpets, and two trombones), piano, harmonium, and percussion – 25 minutes.

5 českých madrigalů (Five Czech Madrigals) – 1948 – SATB chorus a cappella – 5:30 minutes.

Otvírání studánek (The Opening of the Wells) – 1955 – speaker, AB solos, SSAA chorus, two violins, viola, and piano – 20 minutes.

Legenda z dýmu bramborové nati (Legend of the Smoke from Potato Tops) – 1956 – SAB solos, SATB chorus, flute, clarinet, French horn, accordion, and piano – 21 minutes.

Romance z pampelišek (Romance of the Dandelions) – 1957 – ST solos and
SATB chorus (with divisions) a cappella – 13 minutes.

Mikeš z hor (Mikeš from the Mountains) – 1959 – ST solos, SATB chorus,
two violins, viola, and piano – 22 minutes.

Gilgameš (also called *The Epic of Gilgamesh*) – 1955 – speaker, STBB solos,
SATB chorus, and orchestra – 54 minutes.

The Prophecy of Isaiah – SAB solos, TTBB chorus, trumpet, viola, timpani,
and piano – 20 minutes.

LAJOS BÁRDOS 1899–1986

Bárdos was born in Budapest, Hungary, where as a child he studied the violin and viola. In 1919 he enrolled at the Budapest Academy of Music, studying composition with Zoltán Kodály between 1921 and 1925, and in 1928 he joined the faculty of the Academy, teaching theory, choral conducting, and church music history until 1967. Meanwhile, during the 1920s, 1930s, and 1940s he conducted several prominent Hungarian choirs, including the Cecilia Kórus between 1926 and 1941, the Palestrina Kórus from 1929 to 1933, and the Budapesti Kórus from 1941 to 1947. In addition, he organized the Enekio lfúsag (Singing Youth) movement in 1938, which helped establish choirs in villages throughout Hungary, and from 1942 until 1962 he conducted the choir at the church of St Mátyás.

Bárdos composed seven masses, numerous motets, twenty-five part songs for mixed voices, approximately sixty part songs for equal voices, and four volumes of folk song settings. The specific number of motets and part songs is difficult to assess because Bárdos revised and altered many of his smaller-scale compositions, and most of these exist in multiple manuscripts. The sacred repertoire includes *Magyar Népmise* (Hungarian Folk Mass) composed in 1985, and the motets *Alleluja, dicsérjétek* (Psalm 148) for SATB chorus (with divisions) a cappella and *Az úr énnékem örizö pásztorum* (Psalm 23) for SATB chorus and organ. Other motets include the Latin settings *Dixit Dominus Domino meo* for SATB chorus and organ, and *Libera me* (which incorporates statements of the Gregorian Dies irae chant), *Sacerdotes Domini,* and *Sperent in te* for SATB chorus a cappella.

The secular repertoire includes the popular *Régi Táncdal,* a setting of a Hungarian folk song for SATB chorus a cappella, published in English as *Tambur.*

MÁTYÁS SEIBER 1905–1960

Seiber was born in Budapest, Hungary, and learned to play the cello during his youth. In 1919 he entered the Budapest Academy of Music, furthering his study of cello and taking composition classes taught by Zoltán Kodály, and in 1924 he took a minor teaching position in Frankfurt, Germany. In 1927 Seiber began teaching theory and jazz at the Hoch Conservatory in Frankfurt and also began playing cello in the Lenzewski Quartet, and in 1935 he moved to England, where he composed a number of film scores and gave frequent lectures on jazz. He joined the faculty of Morley College in 1942 (teaching there with Michael Tippett), and during the following years he made several trips back to Budapest; in 1948 he attended the International Bartók Festival, and in 1956 he met György Ligeti, whose *Atmosphères* is dedicated to Seiber's memory. He gave a series of lectures at several universities in South Africa in 1960, and while there he was killed in an automobile accident at age fifty-five.

Seiber composed ten choral works, the most famous of which are *Three Hungarian Folk Songs* and *Ulysses*. The folk songs, composed in 1931, are published in English as "The Handsome Butcher," "Apple, Apple," and "The Old Woman." All consist of repeated melodic phrases arranged in varying textures and for varying voices, and all are tonal (i.e., they do not have the modal characteristics of Bartók and Martinů folk song settings). The cantata *Ulysses*—composed in 1946 and 1947 and scored for T solo, SATB chorus, and orchestra—is a setting of the James Joyce text about the contemplation of the universe. Other Seiber works include *Missa brevis* and *Three Fragments*. The mass is a setting of the Kyrie, Sanctus, Benedictus, and Agnus Dei, composed in 1924 and scored for SATB chorus a cappella. The style is neo-Renaissance, with alternating passages of imitative polyphony and homophony and with the Benedictus set as a "canon in diapente" (canon at the interval of a fifth). *Three Fragments,* composed in 1957, is a chamber cantata set to passages from James Joyce's *A Portrait of the Artist as a Young Man* and scored for speaker, wordless SATB chorus (with occasional divisions), and instrumental ensemble consisting of flute, clarinet, bass clarinet, violin, viola, cello, piano, and eight percussion instruments. The musical vocabulary of this work is atonal.

WITOLD LUTOSLAWSKI 1913–1994

Lutoslawski was born in a small town northeast of Warsaw, Poland, and began studying piano at age six with his father, an amateur pianist. At eleven he continued piano lessons with professional teachers, at thirteen he began violin lessons, and at fourteen he entered the Warsaw Conservatory. During the 1940s he earned a living by playing in cabarets and making arrangements of popular orchestral works for piano duet, and he also became involved in Polish musical politics, serving as secretary and treasurer of the Polish Composers' Union and as director of music for Polish Radio. He achieved recognition as a composer during the 1950s for his *Concerto for Orchestra,* written between 1950 and 1954, and *Muzyka żałobna* (Musique funèbre or Funeral Music), written between 1954 and 1958, and in the 1960s he was noted for his aleatoric compositions such as *Jeux vénitiens,* written for chamber orchestra. He was honored with the Polish Solidarity Prize in 1983 and the Order of the White Eagle in 1994, one month before he died at age eighty-one.

Lutoslawski composed only one choral work, *Trois poèmes d'Henri Michaux*. Written between 1961 and 1963, this set of three pieces ("Pensées," "Le grand combat," and "Repos dans le Malheur") is scored for twenty-part chorus and instrumental ensemble consisting of two flutes, two oboes, three clarinets, two bassoons, two trumpets, two trombones, several percussion instruments, harp, and two pianos. The musical style is advanced and includes aleatoric performance of both pitch and rhythm, and extensive passages that call for vocal production ranging from whispering and moaning to shouting. Lutoslawski also published a collection of Christmas carol arrangements entitled *Twenty Polish Carols*. Originally written in 1946 for unison children's chorus or S solo and piano, they were transcribed between 1984 and 1989 for S solo, SATB chorus, and orchestra.

GYÖRGY LIGETI 1923–2006

Ligeti was born in Transylvania (now Romania) and studied at the Klausenberg Conservatory between 1941 and 1943. In 1945 he took courses at the Liszt Academy of Music in Budapest, Hungary, and in 1950 he joined the faculty there as a teacher of harmony and counterpoint. In 1956 he moved to Vienna and then Cologne, where he became interested in electronic music, and for the next several years he taught at the Darmstadt summer program and at the Academy of Music in Stockholm. During the 1972–1973 academic year he was composer-in-residence at Stanford University in California, in the summer of 1973 he taught at the Berkshire Music Center in Tanglewood, Massachusetts, and in the fall of 1973 he was appointed professor of composition at the Musikhochschule in Hamburg, Germany, a position he retained until 1989. Thereafter, Ligeti concentrated on composition and served on several notable arts councils, including the Österreichischer Kunstsenat (Austrian Art Senate), Széchenyi Irodalmi és Muvészsti Akadémia (Hungarian Academy of Literature and Art), and the Academia Scientiarum et Artium Europaea (European Academy of Sciences and Arts).

Ligeti composed three works for multiple voices and instruments and twenty works for a cappella chorus. Most of the early works are a cappella settings of folk texts in a modal harmonic language that was typical during the first half of the twentieth century in Eastern European countries. The works composed in the 1950s and 1960s feature tone clusters in textures of slow-moving harmonies that are often referred to as soundscapes. The best-known example of this style is *Lux aeterna*, which became famous when it was used in the 1968 movie *2001: A Space Odyssey.* Other works containing passages of tone clusters are the set of two part songs *Éjszaka* (Night) and *Reggel* (Morning), and the *Requiem.* Later works, such as the *3 Phantasien,* are in a harmonic language that combines elements of traditional folk music with expanded tonal harmonies.

Two other works merit comment—*Aventures* of 1962 and *Nouvelles aventures* of 1962 to 1965. Both are scored for three voices (coloratura soprano, alto, and baritone) and seven instruments (flute, French horn, percussion, harpsichord, piano/celesta, cello, and string bass). The vocal parts are set to an invented language (written in phonetic lettering) that, according to Ligeti, expresses "all the ritualized human emotions . . . in a kind of opera, with the unfolding adventures of imaginary characters on an imaginary stage."

CHORAL WORKS
SELECTED AND LISTED ACCORDING TO FAMILIARITY

Lux aeterna – 1966 – SSSSAAAATTTTBBBB chorus a cappella – 8:30 minutes.

Éjszaka (Night) and *Reggel* (Morning) – 1955 – SSAATTBB chorus a cappella – 5 minutes.

3 Phantasien – 1983 – SSSSAAAATTTTBBBB chorus a cappella – 11 minutes.

Magyar etüdök (Hungarian etudes) – 1983 – SSSSAAAATTTTBBBB chorus a cappella – 6 minutes.

Requiem – 1963–1965 – SA solos, SATBB/SATBB chorus, and orchestra (including triple winds, celesta, harp, harpsichord, and numerous percussion instruments) – 27 minutes.

ZDENĚK LUKÁŠ 1928–2007

Lukáš was born in Prague, Czech Republic, and studied there at the Theater Institute. From 1953 until 1964 he directed the Česká Píseň, the choir of the Czech Radio in Píseň, and in 1964 he returned to Prague, where he taught at the Conservatory and later directed the women's chorus of the Czech State Ensemble of Songs and Dances. In addition to five operas and numerous instrumental works, he composed twelve choral works plus a number of folk song arrangements. The most significant of the choral works is the *Requiem,* composed in 1992 and scored for SSATB chorus a cappella. Dedicated to and premiered by the Cékád'áci, the choir of the CKD metal works company in Prague, it is divided into seven movements—Requiem aeternam, Dies irae, Lacrymosa, Offertorium, Hostias, Sanctus, and Agnus Dei. The musical style is tonal in that Lukáš rarely uses notes outside the diatonic scale. However, the combination of notes in chords often produces striking dissonances. Other notable works are *Magna est vis veritatis* (Great is the power of truth) and *Missa Brevis* (Kyrie, shortened text of the Gloria, Sanctus, Benedictus, and Agnus Dei), both composed in the 1990s and scored for SATB chorus a cappella.

PETR EBEN 1929–2007

Eben was born in Žamberk, Czech Republic, and in his youth learned to play the violin, cello, and organ. His musical training was furthered at the Prague Academy of Music, which he entered in 1948. Between 1955 and 1990 he taught at the University of Prague, and between 1990 and 1994 he was professor of composition at his alma mater, the Prague Academy of Music. During the 1990s he also toured extensively through Europe, Australia, and the United States as a pianist in chamber ensembles, and in addition, he was an active organ recitalist. He was named an Honorary Fellow of the Royal College of Organists and has received honorary doctorates from the Royal Northern College of Music in Manchester, England (where he taught during the 1978–1979 academic year), and from the University of Prague.

Eben being principally a composer of sacred music for the Catholic Church, his choral output includes three masses, four oratorios, and numerous cantatas and motets. The masses are *Missa adventus et quadragesimae,* composed in 1951 and 1952 and scored for unison chorus and organ; *Truvérská mše* (Trouvère Mass), composed in 1968 and 1969 and scored for unison chorus or congregation, optional descant, two recorders, and guitars; and *Missa cum populo,* composed in 1981 and 1982 and scored for mixed chorus, congregation, brass, and organ. Three of the oratorios—*Apologia Sokratus* of 1967, *Posvátná znamení* (Sacred Symbols) of 1992 to 1993, and *Anno Domino* of 1998 to 1999—include scoring for children's chorus. The remaining oratorio, *Iacobus* of 2002, is scored for B solo, mixed chorus, and orchestra.

Other significant repertoire includes the *Prazske Te Deum* (Prague Te Deum) of 1989 to 1990, scored for mixed chorus, brass and percussion instruments, and organ, and the motets *Salve regina* and *De circuitu aeterno* (From the eternal cycle), both composed in the 1990s and scored for SATB chorus a cappella. This latter motet, set to verses from Ecclesiastes 1:4–9, is known for its complex and active rhythmic structure. Most of Eben's a cappella music is neo-Renaissance in style, often based on Gregorian chant (e.g., the motet *Salve regina*), and with a pandiatonic harmonic language.

HENRYK MIKOŁAJ GÓRECKI 1933–2010

Górecki was born in Czernica, Poland, near Rybnik, and received his musical education at the State Higher School of Music in Katowice. After several years in Paris, he returned to his alma mater to teach and eventually become rector. He left the school in 1979 to concentrate solely on composition, and during the 1990s he achieved worldwide fame for his third symphony, *Symfonia pieśni żałosnych* (Symphony of Sorrowful Songs) op.36, scored for soprano solo and orchestra. He has received numerous awards for his work, including the UNESCO International Composers Rostrum award in 1973 for his cantata *Do matki* (Ad Matrem) and an honorary doctorate in 1994 from the University of Warsaw. His compositions of the 1950s and 1960s demonstrate extremes of style, from the very modern *Symphony #1* and *Epitafium*, which employ serial techniques and are characterized by pointillistic textures, to the conservative *Trzy utwory w dawnym stylu* (Three Pieces in Old Style) for strings of 1963, which is based on Polish folk music idioms and characterized by modal harmonies. His compositions of the 1970s and later are in the style that has made him famous—tonal harmonies in slow-moving harmonic rhythms, with sparse textures and a continuous repetition of short motifs.

Górecki has composed twenty-two opuses of choral music, eight of which are collections (mostly of folk song settings). Several of the works were composed for significant Polish events. For instance, the second symphony, *Kopernikowska* (Copernican) op.31, was written for the 500th anniversary of the birth of the Polish astronomer Copernicus, and *Beatus vir* op.38 was commissioned by Karol Wojtyła, Cardinal of Kraków (later Pope John Paul II), for the 900th anniversary of the martyrdom of Saint Stanislaw and premiered in June 1979 during the pope's first visit to Poland. In addition, *Miserere* op.44 was composed in reaction to the government's handling of a protest by the Rural Solidarity Trade Union in March 1981, and *Totus tuus* was composed for Pope John Paul II's third visit to Poland. Several works are distinctively set to only a few words of text. The 6:15-minute *Amen* has just the one word, the 32:30-minute *Miserere* has only the five words "Domine Deus noster, miserere nobis" (Lord our God, have mercy on us), and the 10-minute *Totus tuus* is limited to the text "Totus tuus sum, Maria, mater nostri redemptoris, virgo Dei, virgo pia, mater mundi salvatoris" (I dedicate myself to you, Mary, mother of our redeemer, virgin of God, virgin holy, mother of the world's savior).

CHORAL WORKS
SELECTED AND LISTED ACCORDING TO FAMILIARITY

Totus tuus op.60 – 1987 – SATB chorus (with divisions) a cappella – 10 minutes.

Szeroka woda (Broad waters) op.39 – 1979 – SATB chorus a cappella – "A ta nasza Narew" (On our river Narew) 4:30 minutes, "Oj, kiedy na Powiślu" (Oh, when in Powiśle) 1 minute, "Oj, Janie, Janie" (Oh, Johnny, Johnny)

3:30 minutes, "Polne róze rwala" (She picked wild roses) 2 minutes, and "Szeroka woda" (Broad waters) 4 minutes.

Euntes ibant et flebant (Psalm 125:6 and 94:6) op.32 – 1972 – SSSAAATTTBBB chorus a cappella – 9 minutes.

Wislo moja, wislo szara (My vistula, grey vistula) op.46 – 1981 – SATTB chorus a cappella – 4:30 minutes.

Miserere (Psalm 50) op.44 – 1981 (revised in 1987) – SATB chorus (with divisions) a cappella – 32:30 minutes.

Amen op.35 – 1975 – SATB chorus a cappella – 6:15 minutes.

Beatus vir (Psalm 112) op.38 – 1979 – B solo, SATB chorus, and orchestra – 32 minutes.

Pięć, pieśni Kurpiowskich (Five Songs from Kurpie) op.75 – 1999 – SATB chorus a cappella – "Hej, z gory, z gory" (Hey, down, down) 4 minutes, "Ciamna nocka" (Dark is the night) 3 minutes, "Wcoraj, dziwcyno, nie dzisiaj" (It was yesterday, my lass, not today) 5 minutes, "Z Torunia ja parobecek" (From Turun I come to see you) 2:30 minutes, and "Wysla burzycka, bandzie desc" (A storm is coming, there will be rain) 9 minutes.

Kopernikowska (Copernican) op.31 – 1972 – SB solos, SATB chorus, and orchestra – 37 minutes.

KRZYSZTOF PENDERECKI B.1933

Penderecki was born in Dębica, Poland, and studied music at the State Higher School of Music (now the Academy of Music) in Kraków. Immediately upon graduation he joined the faculty as a teacher of composition, and in his twenties he won awards for his *Psalmy Dawida* (Psalms of David) and *Strofy* (Strophes). From 1966 to 1968 he taught composition at the Volkwäng Hochschule für Musik in Essen, Germany, and from 1972 until 1987 he was rector of his alma mater. He also held a visiting faculty appointment at Yale University from 1973 to 1978. During the 1980s and 1990s he became popular as a conductor in Europe and the United States, conducting his works with many of the world's leading orchestras, serving as music director of the Kraków Philharmonic from 1987 to 1990, and being appointed principal guest conductor of the NDR Symphony Orchestra in Hamburg in 1988. His musical style before the 1980s is avant-garde, with newly created notational symbols, aleatoric passages of music, use of quarter tones, and sprechstimme. His later music is more traditional and tonal, although dissonant, and several compositions (e.g., *Te Deum* of 1979 to 1980, *Polskie requiem* of 1980 to 1984, and *Credo* of 1998) incorporate old Polish hymns.

Penderecki's total compositional output includes the operas *The Devils of Loudun* (1968) and *Paradise Lost* (1975–1978), *Tren* (subtitled "Threnody to the Victims of Hiroshima") of 1960 for fifty-two strings, and *Symphony #2* ("The Christmas Symphony") of 1979 to 1980. The choral output consists of twenty-five works, including five oratorios and ten Latin canticles, motets, and mass movements. The oratorios are *Passio et mors domini nostri Jesu Christi secundum Lucam* (1963–1966), *Dies Irae* (1967), *Utrenia* (1969–1971), *Kosmogonia* (1970), and *The Seven Gates of Jerusalem* (1996–1997).

Passio et mors domini nostri Jesu Christi secundum Lucam, generally referred to as the *St Luke Passion,* was commissioned by the West German Radio to commemorate the 700th anniversary of the founding of Münster Cathedral. According to Penderecki, the choice of St Luke for his Passion oratorio was "not only for literary reasons, on account of the especially beautiful language, but rather because there had already been two unusually good Passion compositions based on Matthew and John." These two Passions were by J. S. Bach and were used by Penderecki as models. For instance, the *St Luke Passion* is divided into two movements, with reflective texts interspersed between the biblical passages. In addition, Penderecki paid homage to Bach by using his name as a musical motif (B-flat, A, C, B-natural) more than one hundred times throughout the score. Penderecki's Passion has become one of the composer's best-known works and has been performed frequently across Europe to communicate the composer's view that "the *Passion* is the suffering and death of Christ, but also the suffering and death of Auschwitz, the tragic experience of mankind of the first half of the twentieth century."

Dies Irae, the full title of which is *Dies Irae: Oratorium ob memoriam in Perniciei castris in Oswiecim necatorum inexstinguibilem reddendam* (Oratorio in memory of those murdered at Auschwitz), made the connection to Auschwitz more direct. It was commissioned for the unveiling of an international monument at the Auschwitz-Birkenau concentration camp and was premiered there by the Kraków Philharmonic Orchestra and Choir in April 1967. Penderecki combined texts from the Bible, "Eumenides" by Aeschylus, and modern Polish and French poems (translated into Latin), and divided the work into three parts (Lamentatio, Apocalypse, and Apotheosis). The oratorio is scored for STB solos, chorus (which divides into twenty-four parts), and orchestra (which has no violins or violas), and it utilizes stylistic elements similar to those of the *St Luke Passion.* Most striking in the *Dies Irae* are the sounds of a siren, chains, and a thunder sheet.

Utrenia is actually a diptych of two oratorios— *Utrenia I: The Entombment of Christ,* composed in 1969 and 1970 and premiered in April 1970 at the Altenberg Cathedral, and *Utrenia II: The Resurrection,* composed in 1970 and 1971 and premiered in May 1971 at the Münster Cathedral. *Utrenia I,* which uses Russian Orthodox liturgical texts for Great Friday and Saturday, is divided into five movements (two of which are a cappella) and is scored for SATBB solos, two mixed choirs, and orchestra. *Utrenia II,* which uses Slavic Passover texts, is divided into six movements and has a similar scoring. The two oratorios differ considerably in their moods and textures: *Utrenia I* is dark and somber while *Utrenia II* is bright and joyful.

Kosmogonia (Cosmogony) was composed in 1970 for the twenty-fifth anniversary of the United Nations. It is an avant-garde work, the text of which presents views on the origin of the world (e.g., "The form of the earth is excellent and spherical; its movement circular") and the infinite nature of the universe (e.g., "Man is needed: the rising sun shines forth, the darkness has vanished"). Scoring is for STB solos, SATB chorus (with divisions), and orchestra (including quadruple winds, a large battery of percussion instruments, harp, celesta, piano, harmonium, and organ).

The Seven Gates of Jerusalem was conceived as an oratorio. However, after its premiere, Penderecki called it his Seventh Symphony. It was commissioned by the city of Jerusalem to commemorate its 3,000th anniversary and was premiered there in January 1997. Performances in Warsaw followed two months later. The dedication of the score reads, "Ad majorem Dei gloriam et eius sanctae civitatis laudem aeternam" (To the greater glory of God and to the eternal praise of his holy city) and is meant to commemorate the triumphs of ancient peoples and the Jews who survived the Holocaust. The text of the oratorio consists of biblical passages from the books of Psalms, Isaiah, Jeremiah, Daniel, and Ezekiel, divided into seven movements. All texts are in Latin except for that used in movement six, a passage from Ezekiel describing God's miracle in the valley of bones, which is to be sung in the vernacular (in Warsaw it would be Polish, while in England and the United States it would be English). The number *seven* pervades the work. In addition to its title (both seven gates and seventh symphony), Penderecki uses seven notes for the themes of movements two and four, seven loud chords to end the final movement, and seven quarter notes on a single pitch repeated throughout the oratorio. The orchestration is especially large—SSATB solos, three mixed choirs, and two orchestras (a large orchestra onstage that includes four percussion groups, and an offstage ensemble of winds).

Of the other choral works, the *Psalmy Dawida* (Psalms of David) were composed to fragments of four Psalms (28, 30, 43, and 143), each scored for different forces and each producing a different effect: "Ad te, Domine, clamabo" (Unto you, Lord, I cry), for SATB/SATB chorus and instruments, is dramatic; "Exaltabo te, Domino" (I will extol you, Lord), for SATB a cappella chorus, is contemplative; "Quia tu es Deus, fortitudo mea" (For you are God, my strength), for SSAATTBB chorus and instruments, is pleading; and "Domine, exaudi orationem meam" (Lord, hear my prayer), for alternating a cappella chorus and instruments, is prayerful.

The constituent parts of the *Polskie requiem* (Polish Requiem) were composed and performed over a period of time: "Lacrimosa" (later incorporated into the Dies irae) was written in 1980 to celebrate the unveiling of a monument to the Solidarity Movement in Gdansk; "Agnus Dei" was written for the funeral of Cardinal Wysznski in 1981; and the beginning portions of the Dies irae were written in 1984 for the fortieth anniversary of the Warsaw Uprising. The complete Requiem was premiered in Stuttgart in September 1984 and was conducted by Mstislav Rostropovich.

CHORAL WORKS
SELECTED AND LISTED ACCORDING TO FAMILIARITY

Stabat mater – 1962 – SATB/SATB/SATB chorus a cappella – 8:30 minutes. This work was later incorporated into the *Passio et mors domini nostri Jesu Christi secundum Lucam*.

Passio et mors domini nostri Jesu Christi secundum Lucam (Passion and death of our Lord Jesus Christ according to St Luke) – 1963–1966 – SB solos, children's chorus, SATB/SATB/SATB chorus, and orchestra (including four flutes, bass clarinet, two saxophones, contrabassoon, six horns, numerous percussion instruments, vibraphone, harp, piano, harmonium, and organ) – 85 minutes.

Dies Irae – 1967 – STB solos, SATB chorus (with divisions), and orchestra (including triple winds, piano, harp, and numerous percussion instruments) – 22 minutes.

Psalmy Dawida (Psalms of David) – 1958 – SATB chorus (with divisions for SSAATTBB and SATB/SATB), numerous percussion instruments (requiring from six to eight players), celesta, two pianos, harp, and four string basses – 10 minutes.

Agnus Dei – 1981 (revised in 1984) – SSAATTBB chorus a cappella – 7:15 minutes.

Veni Creator – 1987 – SSAATTBB chorus a cappella – 8:30 minutes.

Benedicamus Domino – 1992 – TTTBB chorus a cappella – 3:15 minutes.

Benedictus – 1993 – SATB chorus a cappella – 3 minutes.

Pieśń Cherubinów (Song of the Cherubim) – 1986 – SSAATTBB chorus a cappella – 7 minutes.

Polskie requiem (Polish Requiem) – 1980–1984 (revised in 1993) – SATB solos, SATB/SATB chorus (with divisions to twenty-two parts), and large orchestra – 90 minutes.

Wymiary czasu i ciszy (Dimensions of Time and Silence) – 1960 – forty-part chorus, forty-two percussion instruments (requiring three players), harp, celesta, piano, and strings – 15 minutes.

Credo – 1998 – SAATB solos, children's chorus, SATB chorus (with divisions), and large orchestra – 51 minutes.

GYÖRGY ORBÁN B.1947

Orbán was born in the northcentral region of Romania and studied at the Academy of Music in nearby Cluj-Napoca. In 1973 he began teaching theory and counterpoint there, and in 1979 he became editor of the publishing firm Editio Musica Budapest. In 1982, while continuing his editorial work, he was appointed professor of theory and composition at the Liszt Academy of Music. Although his choral output is somewhat large (nine masses, four oratorios, and several publications of motets and part songs), only a few of the motets have achieved recognition. These include *Ave Maria* in D major, *Cor mundum crea in me, Deus* (Create in me a clean heart, O God), and the popular *Daemon irrepit callidus allicit cor honoribus* (The demon sneaks expertly, tempting the honorable heart). All are scored for SATB chorus a cappella.

❧ RUSSIA AND ESTONIA ❧

There is very little that unifies the compositional preferences of the Russian and Estonian composers during the Modern era. All of the composers in the first half of the era except for Aleksandr Skryabin (i.e., Igor Stravinsky, Cyrillus Kreek, Sergey Prokofiev, Dmitry Kabalevsky, Dmitry Shostakovich, and Georgy Sviridov) were interested in folk music, native legends, or subjects related to national pride. For instance, all of Stravinsky's early works deal with folk material, Kreek was devoted to Estonian folk music (both sacred and secular), and Prokofiev, Kabalevsky, Shostakovich, and Sviridov wrote a considerable number of works that either praised or criticized the state of Russia during the Soviet regime. The composers later in the era—Rodion Shchedrin, Alfred Schnittke, and Arvo Pärt (and Sviridov as well)—have devoted a large part of their choral output to sacred or spiritual subjects, while Veljo Tormis has set secular Estonian folk texts almost exclusively. Two composers, Prokofiev and Kabalevsky, composed a number of works about or for children.

The styles of the composers also vary, not only from the beginning to the end of the era and from country to country, but also from composer to composer of the same general time frame. For example, Stravinsky and Prokofiev, both from Russia and of the same generation (only nine years apart in age), wrote in completely different styles, and Shostakovich, only fifteen years younger than Prokofiev, also composed in a unique manner. In addition, Stravinsky's style changed radically through the course of his development. Of the four composers born between 1930 and 1935, Tormis's folk-based style is characterized by sharp dissonances, Shchedrin's music is reminiscent of Rachmaninoff's harmonic language, Schnittke's approach was deliberately eclectic, and Pärt's textures are minimalistic.

Of the eight Russian and three Estonian composers discussed in this section of the Modern era, all but one were trained in major conservatories—five in Moscow (including the Estonian Tormis), four in St Petersburg (including the Estonian Kreek), and one in Tallinn (Pärt). Stravinsky, who is one of the most major composers of the entire Modern era, had no formal music education.

ALEKSANDR SKRYABIN 1872–1915

Skryabin was born in Moscow, the son of a famous concert pianist who died shortly after Aleksandr's birth. The young Skryabin began playing the piano at age five, at eleven he began private lessons, and at sixteen he entered the Moscow Conservatory. He became a virtuoso pianist, who toured throughout Europe, Russia, and the United States, and he also became famous for his colorful piano and symphonic compositions and for his flamboyant personality. His death from blood poisoning at age forty-three was a highly publicized event in Russia. Skryabin composed one work scored for chorus, the *Symphony #1* op.26. Written in 1899 and 1900, it is divided into six movements, the last of which has parts for ST solos and SSATBB chorus set to text by Skryabin himself in praise of art. The brief choral conclusion to the symphony is sung to the phrase "Slava iskusstvo, vovyeki slava" (Glory to art, forever glory).

IGOR STRAVINSKY 1882–1971

Stravinsky was born near St Petersburg into an aristocratic and musical family. His mother was an amateur singer and pianist and his father, Fyodor Stravinsky (1843–1902), was a famous operatic bass-baritone. In his youth Igor learned languages and other nonmusical subjects from his governesses, and his knowledge of music came from perusing his father's many musical scores, attending concerts, and meeting composers who visited the Stravinsky home. He received a classical gymnasium education during his early teenage years, and in 1901 he entered St Petersburg University as a student of law. He studied harmony, counterpoint, and composition privately, first with students of Rimsky-Korsakov, then with Rimsky-Korsakov's son Vladimir, and finally with Rimsky-Korsakov himself. After minor successes with a few compositions, Stravinsky was commissioned by Serge Diaghilev to compose a ballet. The result was *Zhar'-ptitsa*, also called *L'oiseau de feu* (The Firebird), which premiered to considerable critical acclaim in Paris in 1910 and which brought the composer immediate fame. Another successful ballet, *Petrushka*, followed in 1911, and *Vesna svyashchennaye*, also called *Le sacre du printemps* (The Rite of Spring), premiered to a famous riot in 1913. In 1914 Stravinsky moved to Switzerland, composing *Histoire du soldat* (The Soldier's Tale) in 1918, and in 1920 he moved to France, where for the next decade he worked on new commissions and revisions of his previously composed works. He also was active conducting his works on tours throughout Europe, and during the 1930s he made several extensive tours in the United States. In 1935 and 1936 he supervised the writing of his two-volume autobiography, *Chroniques de ma vie* (Chronicles of my life), and in 1939 he established his primary residence in California, but spent time at Harvard University giving a series of lectures that resulted in the book *La poétique musicale* (Poetics of Music). During the 1940s and 1950s he maintained an active schedule of composing and conducting, writing his neo-Classical opera *The Rake's Progress* between 1947 and 1951 and his first serial works, *Cantata* and *Septet*, between 1951 and 1953. After his first stroke in 1955 and a diagnosis of polycythemia (a rare blood disease), he gradually reduced his activities. His final appearance as a conductor was the 1966 premiere of his *Requiem Canticles* in Princeton, New Jersey. In 1969 he moved to New York City, where he died two years later at age eighty-eight; he was buried in San Michele, near Venice, Italy, close to the grave of Diaghilev.

Stravinsky composed fifteen choral works plus four stage compositions that have considerable scoring for chorus and two choral works that are arrangements of pieces by other composers. All the original compositions are typically divided into three stylistic periods—Russian, neo-Classical, and serial. The Russian period is identified by the choral works composed during the early part of the twentieth century and set to folk-based or Church Slavonic texts. Representative compositions include the *Four Russian Peasant Songs*, collectively entitled *Podblyudnïye* (In the Presence of the Dish or Saucer) because the words and syllables that Stravinsky chose to set resemble divination songs that were traditionally sung at Christmas while peasant women told fortunes from tea leaves spilled in dishes or saucers, and *Svadebka*, called *Les noces* (The Wedding), which was first conceived as a cantata depicting peasant nuptials but was finally realized as choreographic scenes with dancers. The scenes, which Stravinsky called tableaux and which convey no story, depict the preparation of the bride in her house, the preparation of the bridegroom in his house, the bride departing her house, and the wedding feast. The premiere of the work in Paris in 1923 was choreographed by Bronislaya Nijinska. Three years later Diaghilev produced *Les noces* in London, with Georges Auric and Francis Poulenc playing two of the four piano parts. The music is characterized by motifs that are repeated in a motoristic manner and by modal melodies, some of which are derived from folk songs and liturgical chants.

The neo-Classical period is characterized by works based on traditional formal structures, with frequent scoring for an orchestral ensemble consisting mainly of wind instruments and with sparse textures of pandiatonic harmonies. Representative compositions, written in the 1930s and 1940s, include Stravinsky's two most popular works—*Symphonie de psaumes* (Symphony of Psalms) and *Mass*. The first of these, commissioned by the Boston Symphony Orchestra for its fiftieth anniversary celebration, is divided into three movements, called "Prayer" (Psalm 38:13, 14), "Thanksgiving" (Psalm 39:2–4), and "Hymn of Praise" (Psalm 150). The first movement is in an ABA form, the second is a double fugue, and the third reflects a rondo or ritornello form. The *Mass* was begun in 1944 after Stravinsky had purchased a few scores of Mozart masses and commented, "As I played through these rococo-operatic sweets of sin, I knew I had to write a mass of my own, but a real one, that is, a liturgical mass." The Mozart masses were in fact liturgical, but they were not in a style that appealed to Stravinsky, who wanted to write "very cold music . . . that will appeal directly to the spirit . . . and for use in the church." He also specified that the soprano and altos parts should be sung by children. Regardless of this statement, the premiere performance was sung by a mixed choir of adults at La Scala opera theater in Milan, and many performances since then have been in concert halls. The five movements of the *Mass* are in arch or mirror form—the Kyrie and Agnus Dei are entirely choral and in three sections, the Gloria and Sanctus are melismatic in nature and feature soloists, and the Credo, Stravinsky's "statement of faith," stands at the center of the work.

Another important composition from the neo-Classical period, *Oedipus rex,* was originally intended as an opera to celebrate the twentieth anniversary of the Ballet Russes, but it premiered in concert form at the Théâtre Sarah-Bernhardt in May 1927 and was called by Stravinsky an opera-oratorio. The staging was minimal, with static characters in masks who moved only their arms and heads and thus, according to Stravinsky, gave "the impression of living statues." The libretto, in Latin, is based on the Sophocles tragedy of Oedipus, who, forsaken by his parents as a child, unwittingly kills his father and marries his mother. When he learns the truth of his relationship, he blinds himself.

The choral works composed in the 1950s combine melodic and rhythmic serial techniques with other modes of construction, whereas the works composed in the 1960s are generally completely twelve-tone. *Cantata,* a setting of anonymous fifteenth- and sixteenth-century English lyrics, is constructed of rhythmically complex movements (called by Stravinsky "ricercars") that alternate with a rhythmically simple refrain. As in the *Mass,* the movements are organized in arch form, with a central movement for tenor solo subtitled "cantus cancrizans" (song in retrograde). Similarly, *Canticum sacrum*—subtitled "ad honorem Sancti Marci nominis" and dedicated "to the city of Venice, in praise of its Patron Saint, the Blessed Mark, Apostle"—is in arch form, with the final movement an almost exact retrograde of the first movement and with a central movement that is fugal. The second and fourth movements feature solos, the central three movements represent the three virtues (charity, hope, and faith), and all five movements of the work are organized to reflect the architecture of the five cupolas of St Mark's Basilica. The final five choral works are all twelve-tone. *Threni: id est Lamentationes Jeremiae prophetae,* set to an Old Testament text, and *A Sermon, a Narrative, and a Prayer,* set to passages from the New Testament and a poem by the Elizabethan dramatist Thomas Dekker (ca.1572–1632), are companion works. *Anthem* is a setting of the final poem of the *Four Quartets* from T. S. Eliot's "Little Gidding," and *Introitus* is a setting of the Introitus portion of the Roman Requiem Mass, composed after the death and in memory of Eliot. The text of *Requiem Canticles* also uses portions of the Requiem Mass (verses of the Dies irae and Libera me) and, like many of Stravinsky's other works from his final stylistic period, is in arch form—movements one, five, and nine are orchestral while movements two through four and six through eight are variously scored for solo voices and chorus.

CHORAL WORKS
COMPLETE AND LISTED IN CHRONOLOGICAL ORDER
ACCORDING TO DATE OF COMPOSITION

Zvezdolikiy (Star-Face or Star-Faced One), also called *Le roi des étoiles* (The King of the Stars) – 1911–1912 – TTBB chorus and orchestra – 4:30 minutes.

Podblyudnïye (In the Presence of the Dish or Saucer), called *Four Russian Peasant Songs* – 1914–1917 (revised in 1954) – SSAA a cappella (original version) or equal voices and four horns (revised version) – 4 minutes.

Otche nash' (Our father) – 1926 (revised in 1949) – SATB chorus a cappella – 2 minutes. The original version is in Church Slavonic, while the revision, entitled *Pater noster,* is in Latin.

Symphonie de psaumes (Symphony of Psalms) – 1930 – SATB chorus and large orchestra (including harp and two pianos) – 21 minutes. The orchestra contains no violins or violas.

Simvol verï (Symbol of faith) – 1932 (revised in 1949) – SATB chorus a cappella – 2:30 minutes. The original version is in Church Slavonic, while the revision, entitled *Credo,* is in Latin.

Bogoroditse devo (Blessed virgin) – 1934 – SATB chorus a cappella – 1:30 minutes. The original version is in Church Slavonic, while the revision, entitled *Ave Maria,* is in Latin.

Babel (Genesis 11:1–9) – 1944 – speaker, TB chorus, and large orchestra – 6 minutes.

Mass – 1944–1948 – SATTB solos, SATB chorus, and double woodwind quintet (two oboes, English horn, two bassoons, two trumpets, and three trombones) – 18 minutes.

Cantata – 1951–1952 – ST solos, SSAA chorus, and chamber ensemble (two flutes, two oboes, English horn, and cello) – 25 minutes.

Canticum sacrum – 1955 – TB solos, SATB chorus, and orchestra (including harp and organ, but excluding violins) – 20 minutes.

Threni: id est Lamentationes Jeremiae prophetae – 1957–1958 – SATTBB solos, SATB chorus, and orchestra (including sarrusophone, flugelhorn, piano, celesta, and harp) – 35 minutes.

A Sermon, a Narrative, and a Prayer – 1960–1961 – speaker, AT solos, SATB chorus (with occasional divisions), and large orchestra (including three tam-tams, piano, and harp) – 16 minutes.

Anthem ("The dove descending breaks the air") – 1962 – SATB chorus a cappella – 2:15 minutes.

Introitus ("T. S. Eliot in memoriam") – 1965 – TB chorus, piano, harp, two timpani, two tam-tams, solo viola, and solo string bass – 5 minutes.

Requiem Canticles – 1965–1966 – AB solos, SATB chorus, and large orchestra (including xylophone, vibraphone, tubular chimes, harp, piano, and celesta) – 15 minutes.

STAGE WORKS
SELECTED AND LISTED IN CHRONOLOGICAL ORDER
ACCORDING TO DATE OF COMPOSITION

Svadebka, also called *Les noces* (The Wedding) – 1914–1923 – SATB solos, SATB chorus (with divisions), four pianos, and percussion – 23 minutes.

Oedipus rex – 1926–1927 – speaker, ATTBBB solos, male chorus, and orchestra – 52 minutes. Solo roles are for Jocasta (A), King Oedipus (T), a Shepherd (T), Creon (B), Tiresius (B), and a Messenger (B).

Perséphone – 1933–1934 – female speaker, T solo, children's chorus, SATB chorus, and large orchestra (including two harps and piano) – 50 minutes.

The Flood – 1961–1962 – speakers, TBB solos, SAT chorus, and large orchestra (including celesta, piano, and harp) – 23 minutes. (1) Speaking roles are for a Narrator, Noah, Noah's Wife, a Caller, and Noah's Sons; (2) solo roles are for Satan (T) and two unnamed basses.

ARRANGEMENTS
COMPLETE AND LISTED IN CHRONOLOGICAL ORDER
ACCORDING TO DATE OF COMPOSITION

J. S. Bach: Choral-Variationen über das Weihnachtslied "Vom Himmel hoch da komm' ich her" – 1955–1956 – SATB chorus and orchestra – 10 minutes.

C. Gesualdo di Venosa: Tres sacrae cantiones –1957–1959 – SATTBB chorus a cappella – "Da pacem Domine" 2 minutes, "Assumpta est Maria" 2 minutes, and "Illumina nos" 2:30 minutes.

CYRILLUS KREEK 1889–1962

Kreek was born in Ridala, Estonia, and studied at the St Petersburg Conservatory in Russia. While a student, he developed an interest in Estonian folk music, collecting and transcribing numerous melodies and, beginning in 1914, recording many of them on a phonograph. In 1917 he took a teaching position in Haapsalu, Estonia, where, except for temporary appointments at the conservatory in Tallinn during the 1940s, he remained for much of his life. His interest in folk material extended to sacred as well as secular music, and he is known for a collection of Psalm settings, called *Taaveti laulud* (Psalms of David), which he composed between 1914 and 1944. Popular among these are the 1923 settings *Kiida, mu hing, Issandat* (Bless the Lord, O my soul—Psalm 104), *Onnis on inimene* (Happy is the man—Psalms 1, 2, and 3), *Issand, ma hüüan su poole* (O Lord, I call to you—Psalm 141), and *Päeval ei pea päikene sind vaevama* (The sun will not strike you by day—Psalm 121). Kreek's most famous choral composition, however, is his *Requiem* of 1927, set to an Estonian translation of the text used in the Mozart *Requiem* and scored for T solo, SATB chorus, and orchestra (including organ). The secular music includes *Talvine ohtu* (A Winter's Evening) of 1915 and *Maga, maga, Matsikene* (Sleep, sleep, Little Mats) of

1922—both scored for SATB chorus a cappella. The style of all the music reflects the modal characteristics of the original folk material.

SERGEY PROKOFIEV 1891–1953

Prokofiev was born in the Yekaterinoslav district of the Ukraine and was given a broad classical education as a child: his father taught him science, his mother piano, and his governesses foreign languages. He attended opera performances in Moscow when he was eight and in St Petersburg when he was ten, and in between those years he composed his first opera, *Velikan* (The Giant), which was performed in his home by family members and friends. During the summers of 1902 and 1903 he studied theory, orchestration, and composition privately, and in 1904, at age thirteen, he entered the St Petersburg Conservatory. Student works during the next decade consisted of several piano sonatas and concertos, a substantial number of songs, and a few choral works, and in 1914 and 1915 he composed his first major work, *Skifskaya syuita* (Scythian Suite) op.20. Modeled on Stravinsky's *The Rite of Spring*, it featured dissonant harmonies and motoristic textures meant to elicit the shocking audience response that the Stravinsky work received at its controversial premiere on May 29, 1913. The work was also intended to draw attention to Prokofiev, which it did. Demonstrating his versatility, however, he modeled his next orchestral work—the *Classical Symphony* op.25 of 1916 and 1917—on the symphonies of Joseph Haydn, and in 1917 and 1918 he expanded his musical vocabulary further by notating avant-garde techniques such as choral whispers and glissandos in his cantata *Semero ikh* (They are Seven) op.30, a setting of a text by the symbolist poet Konstantin Bal'mont (1867–1942) about seven giants who destroy the world.

Feeling limited by the culture of Russia after the Revolution of 1917, Prokofiev moved to the United States in 1918, touring as a pianist and conductor for the next several years. In 1919 he received a commission from the Chicago Opera, which resulted in his most famous opera, *Lyubov'k tryom apel'sinam* (The Love for Three Oranges) op.33, and in December 1921 his third piano concerto was premiered by the Chicago Symphony Orchestra. Meanwhile, he had spent the summers of 1920 and 1921 touring throughout Europe, and in 1922 he moved to a home near the Ettal monastery in southern Germany. He returned to Russia for several concert tours between 1927 and 1932, composed the ballet *Romeo i Dzhuletta* (Romeo and Juliet) op.64 for the Bol'shoy in 1935 and 1936, and returned to Russia permanently in 1936. For the next several years he composed primarily works for children, including *Petya i volk* (Peter and the Wolf) op.67 (the text of which he wrote himself) and patriotic works such as his famous cantata *Aleksandr Nevskiy* op.78. In 1941 to 1943 he composed his monumental opera *Voyna i mir* (War and Peace) op.91, and for the next decade he was frequently challenged by the artistic leaders of the Soviet Union, and a number of his works were banned. He died at age sixty-one, the same day as Joseph Stalin—March 5, 1953.

Prokofiev composed ten choral/orchestral works and five opuses of small-scale pieces. Several of the choral/orchestral works are known, whereas none of the smaller-scale pieces have entered the performing repertoire. *Aleksandr Nevskiy* (Alexander Nevsky) op.78 was originally composed in 1938 as music for the film by Sergei Eisenstein about Nevsky's defeat of Teutonic invaders at the 1242 Battle on the Ice at Lake Chudskoye. The film and its music were so successful that Prokofiev took parts of the film score and fashioned them in 1939 into a cantata-like work divided into seven movements—"Russia under Mongolian Yoke," "Song about Alexander Nevsky," "The Crusaders in Pskov," "Arise, ye Russian People," "The Battle on the Ice," "The Field of the Dead," and "Alexander's Entry into Pskov."

Ballada o malchike, ostavshemsya neizvestnïm (Ballad of an Unknown Boy or Ballad of the Boy who Remained Unknown) op.93 was composed in the summer of 1942, orchestrated the following year, and premiered in February 1944. The text, by the political activist poet Pavel Antokolsky (1896–1978), has direct reference to events of the time: A young man, whose mother and sister were murdered by fascists when he was a boy, kills a fascist commander by blowing up his car with a grenade. Although the young man remains anonymous, his action is seen as heroic by the Russians.

The oratorio *Na strazhe mira* (On Guard for Peace) op.124 was commissioned by the Children's Radio Division of the Moscow Youth Orchestra and was premiered in Moscow in December 1950. The circumstances of the commission are reflected in the text, which is about the protection of youth from the ravages of war. The work is divided into three parts, each of which is further divided into three or four movements. Part one speaks of the ravages of war; the first two movements are titled "Scarcely Had the Earth Recovered from War's Thunder" and "To Those Who Are Ten Years Old." Part two describes the peaceful life of Soviet children, with movements entitled "We Do Not Want War," "Dove of Peace," and "Lullaby." Part three celebrates those who fight for peace, the closing movement of which is "The Whole World is Poised to Wage War on War." Prokofiev, who was awarded the Stalin Prize for the oratorio, said, "In this oratorio I have tried to express my feelings about war and peace, and also my firm belief that there will be no more wars, that all the nations of the world will safeguard peace and save civilization, our children, and our future."

CHORAL WORKS
SELECTED AND LISTED ACCORDING TO FAMILIARITY

Aleksandr Nevskiy (Alexander Nevsky) op.78 – 1939 – A solo, SATB chorus, and orchestra (including piccolo, English horn, bass clarinet, saxophone, contrabassoon, bells and other percussion instruments, and harp) – 35 minutes.

Na strazhe mira (On Guard for Peace) op.124 – 1950 – two speakers, A and boy solos, boys' chorus, mixed chorus, and large orchestra – 36 minutes.

Ballada o malchike, ostavshemsya neizvestnïm (Ballad of an Unknown Boy) op.93 – 1942–1943 – ST solos, mixed chorus, and large orchestra – 22 minutes.

DMITRY KABALEVSKY 1904–1987

Kabalevsky was born in St Petersburg and received a classical education from his father, who was a noted mathematician. In 1916 the family moved to Moscow, where Dmitry studied and then taught at the Conservatory, and during his thirties, while maintaining his teaching position at the Conservatory, he served as music critic and editor of the Soviet music magazine *Sovetskaya muzïka*. From 1949 to 1952 he was head of the music department of the Moscow Art Institute, and from 1952 until his retirement in the 1980s he was secretary of the Composers' Union of the Russian Federation. He developed a keen interest in music education, which was manifested in numerous compositions for children's voices and a program of public education that was based on listening, singing, and marching (no instruments were involved). In addition, he wrote two books about the musical training of youth—*Vospitaniye uma i serdtsa* (Educating the mind and the heart) and *Prekrasnoye probuzhdayet dobroye* (Beautiful things evoke goodness). As a loyal Communist, who wrote consistently in a conservative musical language, he was appreciated by the Soviet administration and awarded some of its highest honors, including the Lenin Prize in 1972 and Hero of Socialist Labor in 1974.

In addition to six operas, four symphonies, and several concertos and sonatas, Kabalevsky composed nine choral/orchestral works and numerous small-scale vocal pieces. His first important work, *Poèma bor'bï* (Poem of Struggle) op.12 of 1930, is scored for mixed chorus and orchestra. Most of the other major compositions involve children's chorus, including *Parad molodosti* (Parade of Youth) op.31 of 1941, *Pesnya utra, vesnï i mira* (The Song of Morning, Spring, and Peace) op.57 of 1957 to 1958, *Lenintsï* (Leninists) op.63 of 1959, and *Rekviyem* (Requiem) op.72 of 1962, which is dedicated to the victims of World War II.

DMITRY SHOSTAKOVICH 1906–1975

Shostakovich was born in St Petersburg and began his formal education at the Mariya Shidlovskaya Commercial School. At age nine he entered the St Petersburg Conservatory, where he excelled as a pianist, and by eleven he was able to play the entire Bach *Das wohltemperierte Clavier*. He transferred to the Petrograd Conservatory at thirteen, and during the next several years he was exposed to contemporary music of Hindemith, Bartók, and Krenek as well as to traditional works by such European composers as Beethoven, Schumann, and Liszt. Throughout his student years Shostakovich composed a variety of small-scale instrumental and vocal works that attracted little attention. However, the successful premiere of his first symphony by the Leningrad Philharmonic in 1926 (a performance that was broadcast on radio) brought him considerable attention, and for the next decade he composed a steady stream of important works, including the second symphony in 1927, the third symphony in 1929, and the opera *Lèdi Makbet Mtsenskogo uyezda* (Lady Macbeth of the Mtsensk District) between 1930 and 1932. This opera, which premiered in 1934, was so successful that it was performed almost one hundred times in both Leningrad and Moscow within the span of two years. In 1937 Shostakovich began teaching at the St Petersburg Conservatory (then named the Leningrad Conservatory), in 1939 he was named professor of composition, and in 1943 he was appointed professor of composition at the Moscow Conservatory. For the next ten years—until the death of Stalin in 1953— Shostakovich served as a spokesperson for Soviet artistic views and mandates, traveling throughout Europe and the United States at the behest of the government, and in the late 1950s he assumed the role of Russia's most celebrated composer. He was named president of the first Tchaikovsky International Competition in 1958, and in 1966, in honor of his sixtieth birthday, he was awarded the Order of Lenin and the Gold Medal of the Hammer and Sickle. His health declined as a result of polio, which he had contracted in the 1950s, and two heart attacks (1966 and 1971), and he died six weeks before his sixty-ninth birthday.

Shostakovich composed eighteen choral works in addition to thirty part songs and folk song arrangements. The large-scale works include two symphonies that have scoring for chorus in their final movements. *Symphony #2*, subtitled "Oktyabryu" (To October) and composed in 1927, was commissioned by the Propaganda Department of the State Music Publishing House for the tenth anniversary of the October Revolution, and *Symphony #3*, subtitled "Pervomay-skaya" (The First of May), was composed in 1929. An additional symphony, *Symphony #13*, sub-titled "Babiy Yar," was composed in 1962 and contains vocal solo and choral writing throughout set to a text by the Russian poet Yevgeny Yevtushenko (b.1933) that criticizes the Stalinist regime by making reference to Babi Yar, a ravine outside Kiev where thousands of men, women, and children (mostly Jews) were massacred in 1941. The five movements of the symphony are enti-tled "Babiy Yar," "Yumor" (Humor), "V magazinye" (In the Store), "Strakhi" (Fears), and "Kary-era" (A Career).

Other choral/orchestral works include the cantata *Kazn' Stepana Razina* (The Execution of Stepan Razin) and the oratorio *Pesn' o lesakh* (Song of the Forests). The cantata was composed in 1964 to a poem by Yevtushenko about the Cossack hero Stepan Razin (1630–1671), who revolted against the tsar in 1670 but was captured and beheaded the following year. The oratorio, for which Shostakovich won the Stalin Prize, was composed in 1949. The text by Yevgeni Dolma-tovsky praises the Soviet government's postwar reforestation efforts, with references to Stalin as the "great gardener."

The part songs and folk song settings include two sets of pieces composed in 1951—*Ten Choruses on Texts by Revolutionary Poets*, which, according to Shostakovich, "are centered around a single theme: the 1905 Revolution," and *Ten Russian Folk Songs*, which are arrangements of folk songs published in Russia between 1896 and 1943.

CHORAL WORKS
SELECTED AND ARRANGED ACCORDING TO FAMILIARITY

Symphony #13 ("Babiy Yar") op.113 – 1962 – B solos, unison male chorus, and large orchestra – 64 minutes.

Kazn' Stepana Razina (The Execution of Stepan Razin) op.119 – 1964 – B solo, mixed chorus, and large orchestra (including two harps and celesta) – 30 minutes.

Pesn' o lesakh (Song of the Forests) op.81 – 1949 – TB solos, boys' chorus, mixed chorus, and large orchestra – 37 minutes.

Ten Choruses on Texts by Revolutionary Poets op.88 – 1951 – SATB chorus (with divisions) a cappella – 35 minutes.

Ten Russian Folk Songs (no opus number) – 1951 – SATB chorus (with divi-sions) and piano – 27 minutes.

GEORGY SVIRIDOV 1915–1998

Sviridov was born near Kursk, Russia, south of Moscow, where he attended music school begin-ning in 1929. In 1932 he enrolled at the Central Music Tekhnikum in St Petersburg (Leningrad at the time), and between 1936 and 1941 he was a student of Shostakovich at the St Petersburg

(Leningrad) Conservatory. Sviridov became known as a concert pianist and composer of vocal works set to the writings of Russia's two most famous early-twentieth-century poets—Sergey Yesenin (1895–1925), who was known for his poems criticizing the Bolshevik government and for his self-destructive behavior that eventually led to his suicide, and Vladimir Mayakovsky (1893–1930), who was the leading poet of the Russian Revolution era and of the Russian Futurism movement and whose behavior also resulted in suicide. Throughout the latter part of the twentieth century many famous vocalists included Sviridov's songs on their recital programs. The noted Russian baritone Dmitry Hvorostovsky, for instance, sang a special concert in honor of Sviridov's eightieth birthday that was attended by many Russian dignitaries and that was broadcast on national television.

His compositional output includes more than a dozen choral/orchestral works, one large-scale collection of a cappella pieces, and approximately twenty part songs. The works with orchestral accompaniment include three oratorios—*Dekabristï* (The Decembrists), *Dvenadtsat* (The Twelve), and *Pateticheskaya oratoriya* (Pathetic Oratorio). This third work, also called *Oratorio Pathetique,* uses fragments of Mayakovsky's poems to form a narration in seven movements. The first three movements are about years of battle and civil war, while the final four movements address revolution, peace, and reconstruction. The premiere of the oratorio at the Moscow Conservatory was triumphant. Shostakovich called it "a work of genius," and performances were soon mounted all over Russia. In addition, the oratorio won the Lenin Prize in 1960. Other important choral/orchestral works include *Poèma pamyati Sergeya Yesenina* (Poem in memory of Sergey Yesenin); *Kurskiye pesni* (Kursk Songs), which won the USSR State Prize in 1968; *Derevyannaya Rus'* (Wooden Russia); and *Sneg idyot* (The Snow Is Falling).

The large-scale collection of a cappella pieces, *Pesnopeniya i molitvï* (Canticles and Prayers), composed at the end of Sviridov's life, is a work of twenty-six motets set to a variety of liturgical poems. The music, which is supposedly incomplete (i.e., more motets were planned but not composed), has been compared to Rachmaninoff's *Vsenoshchnoye bdeniye* (All-Night Vigil) op.37.

VELJO TORMIS B.1930

Tormis was born near Tallinn, Estonia, the son of a church choirmaster and amateur violinist. The young Tormis sang in his father's choir and began music studies at age twelve. At thirteen he took organ lessons at the Tallinn Conservatory, and at twenty-one he enrolled at the Moscow Conservatory. From 1955 to 1966 he taught at schools in Tallinn—the Music School and the Music High School—and during much of the same time he was also a consultant to the Estonian Union of Composers. He is known for settings of ancient runic folk songs (*regisvärsid*), which became an interest of his after he attended a traditional wedding ceremony on the island of Kihnu in 1959, and he is compared to Bartók and Kodály as an important collector of folk melodies and as a composer who masterfully sets the folk material in effective and critically acclaimed compositions.

Tormis has composed more than two hundred choral works, many of which are collections or sets of pieces. A number of these collections are extensive and contain numerous pieces that are grouped into parts or separate cycles. For instance, *Eesti kalendrilaulud* (Estonian Calendar Songs) consists of five parts, one of which (the final part) is the popular *Jaanilaulud* (St John's

Day Songs). *Unustatud rahvad* (Forgotten Peoples) consists of fifty-one pieces divided into six parts—*Liivlaste Pärandus* (Livonian Heritage) of 1970 (five pieces); *Vadja Pulmalaulud* (Votic Wedding Songs) of 1971 (seven pieces); *Isuri Eepos* (Izhorian Epic) of 1975 (ten pieces); *Ingeri-maa Õhtud* (Ingrian Evenings) of 1979 (nine pieces); *Vepsa Rajad* (Vespian Paths) of 1983 (fifteen pieces); and *Karjala Saatus* (Karelian Destina) of 1989 (five pieces). A number of Tormis's works are also in multiple languages. *Laulusild* (Bridge of Song), for example, includes both Finnish and Estonian folk songs (first separate and then together). *Piispa ja pakana* (The Bishop and the Pagan), which was commissioned by the King's Singers, is in Finnish, Latin, and English: the murder of the British Christian missionary Bishop Henry by the Finnish peasant Lalli in 1158 is related simultaneously in Finnish (from folk songs) and Latin (a setting of a Gregorian chant sequence), with commentary sung in English.

While Tormis often incorporates folk songs into his compositions, he also composes original works that only use folk texts or legends. Such is the case with *Raua needmine* (Curse Upon Iron), which is based on the ninth rune of the Finnish Kalevala. According to Tormis, "The idea of the composition derives from shamanism: in order to acquire power over a material or immaterial thing, one communicates knowledge to the object. Thus the describing and explaining of the birth of iron to iron itself forms a part of the shamanic process." In other words, as is stated in the preface to the score, "Everything created by man may turn against man himself if he starts using his creation without attention to ethics. The evil hidden in iron will turn against man through the man himself." The music combines repetitive and motoristic phrases that produce the effect of an incantation with vocal glissandos and sprechstimme, and to further the dramatic effect of the text, Tormis asks the chorus to assume different postures (e.g., "bend suddenly at the knees and then straighten up slowly," "cower," and "stand to attention, heads held high").

CHORAL WORKS
SELECTED AND LISTED ACCORDING TO FAMILIARITY

Laulusild (Bridge of Song) – 1981 – SATB chorus (with divisions) a cappella – 5 minutes. Tormis later made arrangements of the piece for children's, women's, and men's chorus.

Raua needmine (Curse Upon Iron) – 1972 (revised in 1991) – TB solos, SSSSAAAATTTTBBBB chorus, and shaman drum – 10 minutes. The choral parts are almost entirely homophonic.

Laulud laulust ja laulikust (Songs about Song and the Singer) – 1966–1971 – SSAA and optional solos a cappella – 12 minutes.

Lauliku lapsepõli (The Singer's Childhood) – 1966 – S solo and SSSAA chorus a cappella – 3 minutes.

Laivassa lauletaan (Singing Aboard Ship) – 1983 – A solo and SATB chorus a cappella – 5:30 minutes.

Jaanilaulud (St John's Day Songs) – 1967 – AA solos and SSSSAAAATTTTBBBB chorus a cappella – 14 minutes. This collection of seven pieces is the fifth part of *Eesti kalendrilaulud* (Estonian Calendar Songs).

Sügismaastikud (Autumn Landscapes) – 1964 – SATB chorus (with divisions) a cappella – 9 minutes. This collection of seven pieces is the third part of *Looduspildid* (Nature Pictures).

Karajala Saatus (Karelian Destiny) – 1989 – SATB chorus (with divisions) a cappella – 25 minutes. This collection of five pieces is the sixth and final part of *Unustatud rahvad* (Forgotten Peoples).

Piispa ja pakana (The Bishop and the Pagan) – 1992 (revised in 1995) – ATB solos and TTBB chorus a cappella – 10 minutes. The A solo is for male countertenor.

Pikse litaania (Litany to Thunder) – 1974 – TB solos, TTBB chorus, and bass drum – 5 minutes.

RODION SHCHEDRIN B.1932

Shchedrin was born in Moscow, where his father was a composer, violinist, and teacher at the Moscow Conservatory. Rodion studied at the Moscow Choir School beginning in 1945 and at the Moscow Conservatory between 1950 and 1955, and he returned to teach at the Conservatory from 1965 until 1969. In 1973 he succeeded Shostakovich as Chairman of the Composers' Union of the Russian Federation, and in 1989 he became a member of the Berlin Academy of Arts. He has been recognized as a virtuoso piano recitalist as well as a respected composer, and he has won numerous awards for his work, including the USSR State Prize in 1972, the State Prize of Russia in 1992, and an honorary professorship at the Moscow Conservatory in 1997. His compositional output includes four operas, five ballets, and twelve concertos, as well as five choral/orchestral works and approximately twelve part songs and small cantata-like pieces.

His most famous choral work, *Zapechatlyonnïy angel* (The Sealed Angel), is a large-scale composition of about sixty minutes duration composed in 1988. It is set to text in Church Slavonic and is based on a story by the Russian novelist Nikolai Leskov (1831–1895) about a miraculous icon. According to Shchedrin, "The tale is a parable about the imperishable nature of beauty, the futility of power, and the immortality and power of art. As such, it recalls Dostoyevsky's prophetic words: 'The world will be saved by beauty.'" The music is divided into nine interconnecting movements and is scored for SATB chorus (with divisions) and svirel, an ancient Russian shepherd's flute. The texture of the scoring is mainly a cappella; the shepherd's flute (or traditional flute, a substitute approved by Shchedrin) plays only intermittently throughout the score, mostly as interludes. The harmonic language is completely tonal and is reminiscent of liturgical works by Chesnokov and Rachmaninoff.

ALFRED SCHNITTKE 1934–1998

Schnittke was born in Engels, Russia, southeast of Moscow, and received his initial musical education in Vienna, where his family had moved during the late 1940s. In 1949, having returned to Russia, he enrolled in the Choirmasters' Department of the October Revolution Music College in Moscow, and in 1953 he began studying at the Moscow Conservatory. Between 1962 and

1972 he taught instrumentation at the Conservatory, and during this time he became known for his many film scores. His serious instrumental and vocal works were often challenged by the Soviet government, and thus in 1990 he moved to Hamburg, Germany, where he taught composition at the Hochschule für Musik. His health declined as the result of a series of strokes. However, he composed actively until his death at age sixty-three.

Schnittke's choral output is limited to ten large-scale works, including two symphonies. *Symphony #2*, subtitled "St Florian," is a tribute to Anton Bruckner and is divided into six movements that correspond to the portions of the Roman Mass Ordinary (Kyrie, Gloria, Credo, Sanctus, Benedictus, and Agnus Dei); soloists and chorus are set to Latin phrases, while the orchestra provides meditations on the text. *Symphony #4* combines znamenny and Gregorian chants with Lutheran chorales and Hebrew cantillations. Other important works include *Requiem* of 1975, which is set to the traditional portions of the Latin Mass for the Dead plus the Credo from the Mass Ordinary, and *Stikhi pokayannïye* (Poems of Penitence) of 1987, which is a setting for a cappella chorus of eleven poems from ancient Russia by unknown monks.

ARVO PÄRT B.1935

Pärt was born in Paide, Estonia, and began his formal music education in 1954 at the Tallinn Music Middle School. In 1957 he entered the Tallinn Conservatory, and after graduation in 1963 he worked as a recording engineer for Estonian Radio. During the 1960s he also composed a number of film scores. By 1970 he became recognized as a composer of serious works, and in 1980 he moved to Vienna and then Berlin, where he has written the majority of his compositions. Many of his early works use serial techniques of melodic construction and either are based on works by J. S. Bach (e.g., *Credo* of 1968, which is a transformation of the C major Prelude from book one of *Das wohltemperierte Clavier*) or incorporate the motif based on Bach's name—B-flat, A, C, and B-natural (e.g., the 1964 *Collage über B-A-C-H*). Later works, those composed after 1976, are in a minimalistic style characterized by the blending of diatonic scales and triadic arpeggios. Pärt calls this style "tintinnabuli" (from the effect of sound lingering after a bell has been struck) and describes it as "music of essentials, music of few notes, but of great strength and purity."

Pärt's choral output consists of approximately forty works, the indefinite number resulting from the withdrawal of several compositions. The large-scale works include the *Passio domini nostri Christi secundum Joannem* (St John Passion) of 1982, *Miserere* of 1989 (revised in 1992), *Berliner Messe* of 1990 to 1991, and *Kanon Pokajanen* (Canon of Repentance) of 1997. The first of these works is reflective of the historiae by Heinrich Schütz, with an opening chorus (*exordium*) that announces the story ("The Passion of our Lord Jesus Christ according to St. John") and a closing chorus (*conclusio*) that reflects on the Passion ("You who have suffered for us, have mercy upon us. Amen"). *Miserere* alternates verses of Psalm 51 with verses of the Medieval-era Dies irae poem (i.e., verses 1–3 of the Psalm are followed by verses 1–7 of Dies irae, 4–19 of the Psalm, and 8 of Dies irae). The *Berliner Messe* consists of the traditional five portions of the Latin Mass Ordinary plus two alleluia verses—"Emitte spiritum tuum" (Send forth your spirit) and "Veni sancte spiritus reple tuorum corda fidelium" (Come holy spirit, fill the hearts of your faithful people)—and the motet "Veni sancte spiritus, et emitte coelitus lucis tuae radium" (Come holy spirit and send forth a ray of your heavenly light). *Kanon Pokajanen* is a setting in Church Slavonic based on the Canon of Repentance, which is a part of the Russian Orthodox morning office. Reflecting on the work, Pärt comments, "In this composition, as in many of my vocal works, I tried to use language as a point of departure. I wanted the word to be able to find its own sound, to draw its own melodic line."

The large-scale compositions were generally not written as the result of a commission, while many of the small-scale compositions were written for specific occasions. For instance, *I am the true vine* was composed for the 900th anniversary of Norwich Cathedral, and *The woman with the alabaster box* and *Tribute to Caesar* were commissioned for the 350th anniversary of the establishment of the Karlstad Diocese in Sweden.

CHORAL WORKS
SELECTED AND LISTED IN CHRONOLOGICAL ORDER
ACCORDING TO INITIAL DATE OF COMPOSITION

An den Wassern zu Babel sassen wir und weinten (Psalm 137) – 1976–1984 (revised in 1994) – SATB chorus and chamber orchestra of piccolo, oboe, clarinet, bassoon, horn, and strings – 6:30 minutes.

Summa – 1977 – SATB chorus a cappella – 5:30 minutes.

Cantate Domino canticum novum (Psalm 95) – SATB chorus (or soloists) and organ – 1977 (revised in 1996) – 3 minutes.

De profundis (Psalm 130) – 1977–1980 – TTBB chorus, organ, and percussion ad lib. – 6:30 minutes.

Passio domini nostri Christi secundum Joannem (St John Passion) – 1982 – TB solos, SATB solo quartet, SATB chorus, oboe, bassoon, violin, cello, and organ – 70 minutes. (1) Solo roles are for Pilate (T), Jesus (B), and the Evangelist (SATB quartet); (2) the chorus sings mostly *turba* passages.

Te Deum – 1984–1985 (revised in 1992) – SATB/SATB/SATB chorus, piano, strings, and tape – 29 minutes.

Sieben Magnificat-antiphonen (Seven Magnificat Antiphons) – 1988 (revised in 1991) – SATB chorus (with divisions) a cappella – 9 minutes.

Magnificat (Luke 1:46–55) – 1989 – S solo and SSATTBB chorus a cappella – 7 minutes.

Miserere (Psalm 51 and Dies irae) – 1989 (revised in 1992) – SATTB solos, SATB chorus, and chamber orchestra of oboe, clarinet, bass clarinet, bassoon, trumpet, trombone, electric guitar, bass guitar, percussion, and organ – 35 minutes.

The Beatitudes (Matthew 5) – 1990 (revised in 1991) – SATB solos or SATB chorus and organ – 6 minutes.

Berliner Messe – 1990–1991 (revised in 1991–1992 and 1997) – SATB chorus and organ – 24 minutes. The 1991–1992 revision is a recomposition of the organ accompaniment for strings, and the 1997 revision is an arrangement of the string accompaniment for organ.

I am the true vine (John 15:1–14) – 1996 – SATB chorus (with occasional divisions) a cappella – 8 minutes.

Kanon Pokajanen (Canon of Repentance) – 1997 – SATB chorus (with divisions) a cappella – 83 minutes. There are brief SAT solo passages.

The woman with the alabaster box (Matthew 26:6–13) – 1997 – SATB chorus (with frequent divisions) a cappella – 6:30 minutes.

Tribute to Caesar (Matthew 22:15–22) – 1997 – SATB chorus (with occasional divisions) a cappella – 7:15 minutes.

Peace upon you, Jerusalem (Psalm 122) – 2002 – SSAA chorus (with divisions) a cappella – 5 minutes. There is a brief passage for two solo sopranos.

❧ SWEDEN, NORWAY, DENMARK, AND FINLAND ❧

Virtually all the Scandinavian composers of the Modern era have worked in and have been committed to the musical development of the country of their birth—Wilhelm Stenhammar, Hugo Alfvén, Sven-Erik Bäck, Ingvar Lidholm, Lars Edlund, Lars Johan Werle, Arne Mellnäs, and Sven-David Sandström from Sweden; Edvard Grieg, Knut Nystedt, Egil Hovland, and Trond Kverno from Norway; Carl Nielsen, Per Nørgård, Niels La Cour, and Bo Holten from Denmark; and Jean Sibelius, Einojuhani Rautavaara, and Jaakko Mäntyjärvi from Finland. Grieg, who lived and composed during the Romantic era, is included with the Modern composers for convenience; as the single significant nineteenth-century Scandinavian composer, it is more logical to discuss his work with later composers than to isolate him or combine him with his European contemporaries. Moreover, his interest in folk music and in establishing a nationalistic musical identity relates him to the many Scandinavian composers who followed him and shared his values.

Folk and nationalistic texts were important to most of the composers early in the era. Grieg based two significant collections of a cappella pieces (one sacred and one secular) on Norwegian folk melodies, Nielsen's most noteworthy choral/orchestral works are set to texts about Danish life, Sibelius used the Finnish national epic poem *Kalevala* as a source for many of his compositions, and Stenhammar composed an important Swedish patriotic work and Alfvén made Swedish folk song arrangements. Other text sources were prominent later in the era. For instance, the composers born during the decade beginning in 1915 (Nystedt, Bäck, Lidholm, Edlund, and Hovland) concentrated on sacred texts, whereas the more recent composers (especially Werle, Rautavaara, Nørgård, Mellnäs, Holten, and Mäntyjärvi) have been eclectic in their choice of subject matter.

Genres, textures, and styles also changed. During the early years of the era, choral/orchestral works, homophonic textures, and neo-Romantic sonorities predominated; during the later years, the compositions were for the most part a cappella, textures were polyphonic, and styles were either avant-garde or neo-Renaissance. Avant-garde techniques (e.g., sprechstimme, choral glissandos, aleatoric rhythms, and fragmented melodies) were particularly important to the composers between Nystedt and Sandström, so much so that Scandinavian choral music of the twentieth century is often equated with these innovative styles of composition. However, beginning with La Cour and continuing with Kverno and Holten, the styles have returned to more conservative approaches. On the other hand, interest in polyphonic a cappella neo-Renaissance textures, especially of motets composed for the Lutheran and Roman Catholic churches, began with Nielsen and continued with most composers thereafter.

EDVARD GRIEG 1843–1907

Grieg was born in Bergen, on the southwestern coast of Norway, and began piano lessons at age six with his mother, an accomplished pianist. At fifteen he enrolled at the conservatory in Leipzig, Germany, and for the next several years he heard many works by composers such as Johannes Brahms and Robert Schumann at the Gewandhaus. At nineteen Grieg returned to Bergen, at twenty he furthered his education with private studies in Copenhagen, and at twenty-one, becoming interested in folk music, he cofounded Euterpe, a society for the promotion of Scandinavian music. He was appointed conductor of the Bergen Philharmonic Society in 1866, and the following year he helped establish the Norwegian Academy of Music. His most famous composition, the incidental music to Henrik Ibsen's 1867 play *Peer Gynt,* was composed in 1874 and 1875, and between 1880 and 1882 he conducted the Bergen Harmonic Society. For the remainder of his life he made frequent tours throughout Germany and the Netherlands as pianist and conductor of his works.

Grieg composed three choral/orchestral works and thirty-eight a cappella or piano-accompanied pieces, sixteen of which are contained in two collections. Two of the choral/orchestral works were popular during Grieg's lifetime—*Foran sydens kloster* (Before a Southern Convent) op.20 of 1871 for SA solos, SSAA chorus, and orchestra, and *Landkjending* (Land-Sighting) op.31 of 1872 (revised in 1873 and 1881) for B solo, TTBB chorus, and orchestra (with organ ad lib.). The two collections are Grieg's most famous works—*Album for mandssang, fritt efter norske folkeviser* (Album for male voices, freely arranged from Norwegian folk songs) op.30, and *Fire salmer* (Four Psalms) op.74. This latter collection, based on texts and melodies from *Aeldre og nyere norske fjeldmelodier* (Older and Newer Mountain Melodies) of 1853 to 1867, contains Grieg's final compositions.

CHORAL WORKS
SELECTED AND LISTED ACCORDING TO FAMILIARITY

Fire salmer (Four Psalms) op.74 – 1906 – B solo and SATB chorus a cappella – "Hvad est du dog skjøn" (How fair is your face) 5:30 minutes, "Guds søn har gjort mig fri" (God's son has set me free) 6 minutes, "Jesus Kristus er opfaren" (Jesus Christ our Lord is risen) 7:30 minutes, and "I Himmelen" (In heaven above) 5:15 minutes.

Album for mandssang, fritt efter norske folkeviser (Album for male voices, freely
arranged from Norwegian folk songs) op.30 – 1877–1878 – B solo, incidental TTBB solo quartet, and TTBB chorus a cappella – 28 minutes.
The twelve pieces in the collection are "Jeg lagde mig så sildig" (I lay down
so late), "Bådn-låt" (Children's Song), "Torø liti" (Little Toro), "Kvålins
halling," "Dae ae den største dårleheit" (It is the greatest foolishness),
"Springdans" (Spring Dance), "Han Ole" (Young Ole), "Halling," "Dejligst
blandt kvinder" (Fairest among women), "Den store, hvide flok" (The
great white host), "Fantegutten" (The gypsy lad), and "Røtnams-Knut."

CARL NIELSEN 1865–1931

Nielsen was born near Odense on the island of Funen (now Fyn), Denmark, into a family of amateur musicians. He was drawn to music in his youth, attending performances by a local orchestra, and at age fourteen he began playing horn and trombone in a military orchestra. He also
learned to play the violin during his teenage years, and between 1884 and 1886 he studied at the
Copenhagen Conservatory. In 1889 he joined the violin section of the Royal Theater Orchestra,
the following year he took a leave of absence to travel in France and Italy, and during the 1890s
he occasionally conducted the Odense Music Society and Royal Theater orchestras. During
these years he experienced successes with his first symphonic compositions, and in 1915 he was
appointed head of the Copenhagen Musikforening (Music Society). Between 1916 and 1919 he
taught theory and composition at the Copenhagen Conservatory, and for the remainder of his
life he grew in stature as more and more of his works were performed to critical acclaim.

Nielsen's compositional output includes sixteen choral/orchestral cantatas, seventeen
a cappella part songs, a set of three motets, and incidental music to eighteen plays. Three of the
choral/orchestral works are noteworthy. *Fynsk foraar* (Springtime on Funen) op.42 is autobiographical in nature and reflects the composer's love for his native land. Composed specifically
for the Danish Choral Society as a work about Danish history and life, it was premiered by nine
hundred singers to an audience that included King Christian X. *Hymnus amoris* op.12 was
Nielsen's first major choral composition and a work he favored throughout his life. The text,
written by Danish folklorist Axel Olrik (1864–1917) specifically for Nielsen (who had it translated from Danish into Latin), is about four stages of love in a man's life—"Barndom" (Childhood), "Ungdom" (Youth), "Mandom" (Manhood), and "Alderdom" (Old Age). The texts of the
four stages begin, respectively, "Amor mihi vitam donat" (Love gives me life), "Amor est votum
meum et desiderium" (Love is my craving and my desire), "Amor est fons meus" (Love is my
fountain), and "Amor est pax meus" (Love is my peace). *Søvnen* (Sleep) op.18 is a work in ABA
form that is noted for its dissonant writing in the B section, which represents a nightmare.
Nielsen was particularly fond of the effect of the music, although critical response was generally
negative. One reviewer called it "the wildest chase of the falsest notes."

The part songs are divided between eight pieces scored for men's chorus, five scored for
mixed chorus, and four scored for women's chorus. Representative compositions include *Fredlys
din jord* (Preserve your earth) and *Til min fødeø* (To the island of my birth) for TTBB, *Foraarssang*
(Spring song) for SATB, *Sjølunds sangere* (The Singers of Sjølund) for SATTB, and *Edderkoppens
sang* (The Spider's Song) for SSA.

The *Tre Motetter* (Three Motets) op.55, composed at the end of Nielsen's life, are in a neo-Renaissance style. Clearly modeled on the works of Palestrina, each motet is constructed of successive points of imitation, with occasional and brief phrases of homophony that interrupt the texture of long polyphonic phrases.

The most famous of the works scored as incidental music for plays, *Aladdin* op.34, was commissioned in 1917 by the Royal Theater in Copenhagen and composed in 1918 and 1919 for performances of *Aladdin, eller Den forunderlige Lampe* (Aladdin, or the Wonderful Lamp) by the Danish poet Adam Oehlenschläger (1779–1850). Nielsen's music is scored in thirty movements for AB solos, SATB chorus, and orchestra.

CHORAL WORKS
SELECTED AND LISTED ACCORDING TO FAMILIARITY

Tre Motetter (Three Motets) op.55 – 1929 – mixed chorus a cappella – "Afflictus sum" (Psalm 37:9) for ATTB chorus, 7:15 minutes; "Dominus regit me" (Psalm 22:1–2) for SATB chorus, 4 minutes; and "Benedictus Dominus" (Psalm 30:22) for SSATB chorus, 5 minutes.

Fynsk foraar (Springtime on Funen) op.42 – 1921 – STB solos, SATB chorus, and orchestra – 18 minutes.

Hymnus amoris op.12 – 1896–1897 – STBB solos, SATB chorus, and orchestra – 21:30 minutes.

Søvnen (Sleep) op.18 – 1903–1904 – SATB chorus and orchestra – 19 minutes.

JEAN SIBELIUS 1865–1957

Sibelius was born in Hämeenlinna, a small town north of Helsinki, Finland, and began taking piano lessons from an aunt when he was seven. At fifteen he studied violin with a local band director, and for the remainder of his teenage years he improved his ability by playing violin in a local string quartet and family trio (his brother played cello and his sister piano). In 1885, at age twenty, he enrolled at both the University of Helsinki (as a law student) and at the Helsinki Institute of Music. He remained at the University for only a year but continued at the Institute of Music for four years, studying piano with Ferruccio Busoni in 1888 and the beginning of 1889. In the fall of 1889 Sibelius was awarded a government scholarship to study in Berlin, and from October 1890 until June 1891 he was in Vienna. The experiences in these European cities not only created interest in such composers as Wagner and Bruckner but also created in Sibelius a desire to learn about native Finnish music and literature. Once back in Finland, he studied the *Kalevala* (the Finnish epic folk poem about ancient lands called Kaleva) and traveled throughout the country to hear folk songs. Also at this time he composed the cantata *Kullervo*, which premiered in April 1892 to considerable critical acclaim, and he began teaching theory and violin at the Helsinki Institute of Music and Kajanus's Philharmonic Orchestra School. In 1896 he gave a highly publicized lecture at the University of Helsinki entitled "Some perspectives on folk music and its influence on art music," and in 1897 he received a pension from the government, which allowed him to concentrate exclusively on composition for the remainder of his life.

During the years at the turn of the century when Russia was in control of Finland, Sibelius became a spokesperson for Finnish independence and composed several works of a political nature. These include *Atenarnes sång* (Song of the Athenians), *Isånmaalle* (To the Fatherland), and his most famous work, *Suomi herää* (Finland Awakens), which was later renamed *Finlandia*. During the early years of the twentieth century he traveled to European capitals, where his works were receiving frequent performances, and in 1914 he visited the United States, where he not only was greeted enthusiastically but also was awarded an honorary doctorate from Yale University. His celebrity gradually replaced his creative inspiration, and although he lived until age ninety-one, his last major composition, the tone poem *Tapiola* op.112, was composed in 1926, thirty-one years before his death.

In addition to seven renowned symphonies and numerous chamber music compositions, Sibelius composed eighteen choral/orchestral concert works, twelve choral pieces with piano accompaniment, forty a cappella part songs, several a cappella pieces to sacred texts, and ten works of incidental music for plays, including *Stormen* (The Tempest) op.109 for SATBB soloists, SATB chorus, and orchestra. *Finlandia* was composed in 1899 as an orchestral tone poem for a political rally in support of free speech. In 1927 Sibelius extracted the final portion of the work and published it as the last section of his Masonic ritual music op.113, with text by the opera singer Väinö Sola. In 1937 he replaced those words with others by the popular Finnish poet and essayist Veikko Antero Koskenniemi (1886–1962). It is this latter text, with the opening phrase "Oi, Suomi, katso, sinum päiväs koittaa" (O Finland, look, your dawn approaches), that subsequently became famous around the world. The music was first published as a hymn in twentieth-century Protestant hymnals with text beginning "Be still, my soul, the Lord is on thy side."

Kullervo op.7 was Sibelius's first major instrumental work and also the first of the composer's works to be based on Finnish folklore. The text, which comes from runes 31 through 36 of the *Kalevala*, is about Kullervo (which means pearl of combat), nephew of the warrior Untamo, and is set by Sibelius in five movements: the "Introduction" is an orchestral portrait of Kullervo as a tragic hero; "Kullervo's youth," also orchestral, depicts Kullervo's unhappy childhood with his uncle; "Kullervo and his sister," for soloists, chorus, and orchestra, relates the hero's encounter with his long-lost sister; the orchestral "Kullervo goes to war" represents the killing of Untamo; and the vocal/choral/orchestral finale, "Kullervo's death," tells of Kullervo's suicide from the sword given to him by the god Ukko. The music is characterized by ostinatos, pedal points, folk-like melodies, woodwind sonorities, and motoristic repetition of short motifs.

Two other important Sibelius works are also settings of texts from the *Kalevala*. The cantata *Tulen synty* (The Origin of Fire) op.32 is the story from rune 47 of darkness and light in the lands of Kaleva: in part one of the cantata the lands are dark because princess Louhi has stolen the sun and moon and also the fires from people's homes; in part two the god Ukko restores light by creating new fire with a strike of his sword. *Väinön virsi* (Väinö's Song) op.110, one of Sibelius's final compositions, is from rune 43 about the druid Väinämöinen, who rebuilt the Sampo (a magic mill that produces vast quantities of food and metal) and who prayed to the god Jumala for protection and blessing.

Several popular cantatas set to texts meant to promote nationalistic pride include *Sandels* op.28, named after Swedish general Johan August Sandels (1764–1831), who led troops to victory against Russian forces at the Battle at Virta Bridge; *Snöfrid* op.29, about the hero Gunnar, who was guided in life by the beautiful siren Snöfrid and by the precept that blessings will come to "the man who lifts his shield to protect the small and weak of the world"; and *Oma maa* (Our Native Land) op.92, a paean to the lights of Finland (northern lights and endless summer days), that begins with the text "Truly blessed is he who in youth is not exiled from his country, torn from happiness and from the graves of his heroes."

The majority of the part songs mirror the larger works in textual content and emphasis, with numerous settings of texts from the *Kalevala* and its companion volume the *Kanteletar*. Representative examples are the early *Venematka* (The Boat Journey) op.18 no.3 of 1893, the cycle *Rakastava* (The Lover) op.14 of 1894, and *Sortunut ääni* (The broken or silenced voice) of 1898. A substantial number of other part songs are settings of texts by poets who wrote about subjects of national pride. These include *Työkansan* marssi (Workers' March) of 1896, *Aamusumussa* (In morning mist) of 1896, *Isänmaalle* (To the Fatherland) of 1900 (revised in 1908), and *Uusmaalaisten laulu* (Song of the Uusimaa people) of 1912. Most of the part songs were originally scored for male voices, although a number of them (e.g., *Rakastava*) were later arranged for mixed or women's choruses.

The a cappella pieces with sacred texts include *Suur' olet, Herra* (The lofty heaven) op.113 no.11, *Soi kiitokseski Luojan* (We praise you, our creator) op.23 no.6, and *Joululaulu* (Christmas Song) of 1929. The piece known in English as "Onward, ye peoples" was composed in 1927 as the sixth part of the Masonic ritual music (*Musique Religieuse* op.113) and scored for male chorus and harmonium with the text "Onward, ye brethren." Sibelius later arranged the piece for mixed chorus with piano accompaniment and altered the text to be more universal.

CHORAL WORKS
SELECTED AND LISTED ACCORDING TO FAMILIARITY

Finlandia op.26 – 1899 – SATB chorus and orchestra – 9 minutes. Sibelius also arranged the choral parts for men's voices.

Kullervo op.7 – 1891–1892 – SB solos, TB chorus, and orchestra – 70 minutes.

Tulen synty (The Origin of Fire) op.32 – 1902 – B solo, TTBB chorus, and orchestra – 10 minutes.

Väinön virsi (Väinö's Song) op.110 – 1926 – SATB chorus and orchestra – 7:30 minutes.

Sandels op.28 – 1898 (revised in 1915) – TB chorus and orchestra – 9 minutes.

Snöfrid op.29 – 1900 – speaker, SATB chorus, and orchestra – 11 minutes.

Oma maa (Our Native Land) op.92 – 1918 – SATB chorus and orchestra – 12 minutes.

Rakastava (The Lover) op.14 – 1894 – TTBB chorus a cappella – "Missä armahani" (Where is my beloved) 1:30 minutes, "Armahan kulku" (The path of my beloved) 1:30 minutes, and "Hyvää iltaa, lintuseni" (Good night, my little bird) 3:30 minutes. Sibelius arranged the complete opus in 1898 for SB solos and SATB chorus.

Sydämeni laulu (Song of my heart) – no opus number – 1898 – TTBB chorus a cappella – 2 minutes.

Laulun mahti (The power of song) – no opus number – 1895 – TTBB chorus
a cappella – 3:15 minutes.

Aamusumussa (In morning mist) – no opus number – 1896 – TTBB chorus
a cappella – 1:30 minutes.

WILHELM STENHAMMAR 1871–1927

Stenhammar was born in Stockholm, Sweden, where his father Per Ulrik Stenhammar (1828–
1875) was an architect and composer and an aunt and uncle were professional singers. Wilhelm
sang in a family vocal ensemble as a child, read books on music, and studied several instruments privately. He did not have a formal music education but excelled nevertheless as a concert pianist, conductor, and composer. He was noted for his performances of the Brahms first
piano concerto and for his participation with the Aulin Quartet, and between 1897 and 1925 he
held conducting posts with several important orchestras, including the Stockholm Philharmonic Society (1897–1900), New Philharmonic Society (1904–1906), Göteborg Orchestral Society (1906–1922), and Royal Opera (1924–1925).

Stenhammar composed seven choral/orchestral works and one set of three a cappella
choral pieces; two additional a cappella pieces—"Norrland" and the well-known "Sverige"—are
extractions from other works. Two cantatas are notable: *Ett folk* op.22, which contains the patriotic a cappella movement "Sverige," was composed in 1904 and 1905 and is scored for B solo,
mixed chorus, and orchestra; and *Sången* op.44, composed in 1921 for the 150th anniversary of
the Swedish Royal Academy of Music, is scored for SATB solos, children's chorus, mixed chorus,
and orchestra. The text of this latter cantata, by the composer Ture Rangström (1884–1947), is
about the power of nature to right the wrongs of mankind. The a cappella set, composed in 1890,
is entitled *3 Körvisor till dikter av J. P. Jacobsen* (Three choral ballads to poems by J. P. Jacobsen),
also called *Tre a cappella korsange* (Three a cappella choruses)—"September," "I seraillets have"
(In the harem garden), and "Havde jeg, o havde jeg en datterson, o ja!" (If I had, oh if I had a
grandson, oh). All the music is in a conservative musical language, with textures in the
choral/orchestral works that are modeled after Haydn and Beethoven.

HUGO ALFVÉN 1872–1960

Alfvén was born in Stockholm, Sweden, and attended the Stockholm Conservatory between
1887 and 1891. He was a violinist in the Hovkapellet opera orchestra from 1890 to 1892, and
thereafter he conducted choral ensembles—a group of church and regional choruses called the
Siljan Choir from 1904 to 1957, the Musices of Uppsala University from 1910 to 1939, and the
famous male ensemble Orphei Dränger (also from Uppsala University) from 1910 to 1947. His
choral output is extensive, consisting of fifty-seven works in addition to numerous folk song
arrangements. Notable or popular compositions include the oratorio *Herrans bön* (The Lord's
Prayer), the patriotic cantata *Sveriges flagga* (Sweden's flag), the part song *Aftonen* (Evenings) for

SATB chorus and piano (also arranged for male chorus and solo voice with instrumental ensemble), and the folk song arrangement *Och jungfrun hon går i ringen* (A maiden joins the ring) for SATB chorus a cappella.

KNUT NYSTEDT B.1915

Nystedt was born in Oslo, Norway, and studied music privately with a number of notable composers and performers, including Aaron Copland and Robert Shaw. Between 1946 and 1982 he was organist and choirmaster at the Torshov church in Oslo, and in 1950 he founded the Det norske solistkor (Norwegian Soloists Choir), with which he toured extensively until 1990 (performing in Germany, France, Israel, the United States, Japan, Korea, and China as well as throughout the Scandinavian countries). He also was professor of choral conducting at the University of Oslo and conductor of the university's Schola Cantorum from 1964 until 1985. In 1966 he was made a Knight of the Royal Order of St Olav by the king of Norway; in 1975 he was given a Distinguished Service Citation by Augsburg College in Minneapolis, Minnesota; and in 1980 he was awarded the Norwegian Arts Council Music Prize. His compositional output totals almost two hundred opuses of instrumental and vocal music, including numerous anthems in English and the commissions *Apocalypsis Joannis* op.155 of 1998 for the Oslo Philharmonic Orchestra, *The Word Became Flesh* op.162 of 2001 for the Augsburg College Choir, and *Reach Out for Peace* op.164a of 2001 for the Norwegian Ceciliaforeningen (Cecilian Chorus). Much of Nystedt's music is characterized by tone clusters and frequent changers of meter, with occasional use of sprechstimme and new notational devices.

CHORAL WORKS
SELECTED AND LISTED ACCORDING TO FAMILIARITY

O crux op.79 – 1977 – SSAATTBB chorus a cappella – 6:30 minutes.

Lucis creator optime op.58 – 1968 – SB solos, SATB chorus (with divisions to sixteen parts), and orchestra – 25 minutes.

The Burnt Sacrifice op.36 – 1954 – speaker, SATB chorus, and orchestra – 20 minutes.

Veni op.81a – 1978 – SSAATTBB chorus a cappella – 5 minutes.

De profundis op.54 – 1964 – SATB chorus (with divisions) a cappella – 7:30 minutes.

The Path of the Just op.61 – 1968 – SATB chorus (with divisions) a cappella – 4 minutes.

Peace I leave with you op.43 no.2 – 1957 – SATB chorus a cappella – 2:30 minutes.

Suoni op.62 – 1970 – SSAA chorus, flute, and marimba – 8 minutes.

Missa brevis op.102 – 1984 – SATB chorus a cappella – 15 minutes.

Shells op.70a – 1973 – SSAA chorus a cappella – 4 minutes.

Stabat mater op.111 – 1986 – SATB chorus and cello – 15:30 minutes.

SVEN-ERIK BÄCK 1919–1994

Bäck was born in Stockholm, Sweden, and received his first musical instruction there at the Music High School, where his main instrument was violin. He continued his education at the Royal College of Music in Stockholm and the Schola Cantorum Basilienis and Accademia di Santa Cecilia in Rome. Between 1940 and 1953 he played professionally in two ensembles—the Kyndel Quartet and the Barkel Quartet—and from 1953 to 1958 he was leader of the chamber ensemble of the Swedish Radio Orchestra. In 1958 he was appointed principal of the Edsberg Music School and also director of the Swedish Radio Music School.

His compositional output includes three operas, five ballets, numerous instrumental concert works, and approximately one hundred choral publications (including sixty hymns). The best known of the choral works are a series of motets composed between 1959 and 1963 for the Roman Catholic liturgical year. Examples include *Nox praecessit* (Romans 13:12, Matthew 21:5, and Luke 4:19) for the first Sunday in Advent, *Domine memento mei* (Luke 23:42–43) for Good Friday, *Ego sum panis vitae* (John 6:35–36) for the middle Sunday of Lent, and *Et verbum caro factum est* (from the Responsory to the eighth lesson of second vespers of the Nativity) for Christmas Day. The harmonic language of all the motets is dissonant, although the textures are neo-Renaissance, with successive phrases of imitative polyphony alternating with brief passages of homophony.

INGVAR LIDHOLM B.1921

Lidholm was born in Jönköping, between Malmö and Stockholm, Sweden, and studied at the Royal Academy of Music beginning in 1940. In 1943 he became a member of the viola section of the Royal Swedish Opera Orchestra, and between 1947 and 1956 he conducted the Örebro Orchestra. During these years he also traveled throughout Europe, taking summer courses in Darmstadt and studying with Mátyás Sieber in England. From 1956 to 1965 he was director of chamber music programs for Swedish Radio, and between 1965 and 1975 he was professor of composition at the Royal Academy of Music, serving as director of planning for the radio music department from 1974 to 1979.

Lidholm has composed numerous choral works, six of which have become well known. The first four are extended a cappella motet-like compositions: *Laudi,* with text in Latin, is a setting in three movements of Old Testament passages—"Homo natus de muliere" (Man born of woman) from Job 14:1–2, "Haec dicit Dominum" (Thus says the Lord) from Joel 2:12–13, and "Laudate Dominum omnes gentes" (Praise the Lord all people) from Psalm 116; *Canto LXXXI* is a setting in English of Ezra Pound's poem that begins "What thou lovest well remains, the rest is dross"; . . . *a riveder le stelle* (to behold again the stars), with opening text "Ma la notte risurge, e oramai é da partir" (But night again is rising, time is now that we depart), is a setting of the final verse from Canto 34 of the Inferno portion of Dante's *Divine Comedy;* and *De profundis* combines passages from Psalm 130 with phrases from texts by the famous Swedish playwright August Strindberg (1849–1912). It should be noted that *De profundis* as well as another choral work, *Vindarnas klagan* (Lament of the Winds) of 1981, were incorporated by Lidholm into his opera *Ett drömspel* (A Dream Play), begun in 1978 and completed in 1989. The textures of the motet-like works are basically imitative, while the harmonic language contains whole tone scales, tone clusters, and passages of polytonality. In addition, there are instances of choral glissandos. The remaining important works, listed and annotated below, represent Lidholm's contributions to the part song and choral/orchestral repertoire.

CHORAL WORKS
SELECTED AND LISTED ACCORDING TO FAMILIARITY

Laudi – 1947 – SATB chorus a cappella – 10:30 minutes.

Canto LXXXI – 1956 – SATB chorus (with divisions) a cappella – 9 minutes.

. . . a riveder le stelle – 1971–1973 – S solo and SATB chorus (with divisions) a cappella – 13 minutes. Lidholm recommends a chorus of sixty-four voices, divided into sixteen voices per part.

De profundis – 1983 – SATB chorus (with divisions) a cappella – 8 minutes.

Three Strindberg Songs – 1964 – SATB chorus (with divisions) a cappella – "Valkommen ater snalla sol" (Welcome back sweet sun) 1 minute, "Ballad" 2:30 minutes, and "Sommarafton" (Summer's evening) 3:15 minutes.

Skaldens natt (The Poet's Night) – 1957–1958 – S solo, SATB chorus (with divisions), and orchestra – 40 minutes.

LARS EDLUND B.1922

Edlund was born in Karlstad, Sweden, west of Stockholm, and received his musical training at the Ingesund Music School, Stockholm Musikhögskolan, and Basle Schola Cantorum. He sang in Eric Ericson's Chamber Choir in the 1940s and founded the vocal chamber ensemble Camerata Holmiae in the 1960s. In addition, he taught aural skills at the Stockholm Musikhögskolan and published two important ear-training books—*Modus novus* in 1963 and *Modus vetus* in 1967. Both books contain original compositions as well as musical examples.

His popular choral compositions include three a cappella pieces for SATB chorus (with divisions) and three works for chorus and orchestra. *Elegi,* composed in 1971 and revised in 1972, is a setting of text about nature (clouds over the ocean, birds over the waves, volcanoes in the distance) by the Swedish surrealistic poet Gunnar Ekelöf (1907–1968). The music features choral glissandos, soundscapes, and phrases broken into isolated syllables. *Gloria,* composed in 1969 to the traditional Latin mass text, is scored for tenor solo that occurs at the beginning of the work as an extended and vocally demanding incipit, and SATB chorus that has occasional passages of speech. *Nenia,* of 1975, is based on both the text and music of Monteverdi's madrigal *Lasciatemi morire:* Edlund fractures the text and melodic material into small fragments, which are expanded into soundscapes and developed to be only reminiscent of Monteverdi's original music. The choral/orchestral works include *Missa Sancti Nicolai* of 1979 for SATB solos, SATB chorus, and percussion instruments; *Maria*, a cantata based on the Passions of Heinrich Schütz and scored for TB solos and SATB chorus; and *Saligprisningarna* (The Beatitudes) of 1971, scored for children's chorus, SATB chorus, flute, electric guitar, cello, string bass, and organ.

EGIL HOVLAND 1924–2013

Hovland was born in Fredrikstad, south of Oslo, Norway, and received his musical education at the Oslo Conservatory. Further studies were with Aaron Copland at the Berkshire Music Center in Tanglewood, Massachusetts, and with Luigi Dallapiccola in Florence. From 1949 until 1994 Hovland served as organist and choirmaster at Glemmen Church in Fredrikstad and in 1983, as one of several citations for his contributions to the cultural life of Norway, he was made Knight of the Royal Order of St Olav. Hovland has composed approximately two hundred choral works, including seven masses, fifty motets, and one hundred hymns. The masses are represented by *Missa vigilate* of 1967 and *Missa misericordiae* and *Missa verbi*, both of 1973. The motets include the well-known *Saul*, which is characterized by tone clusters, twelve-tone melodies (often sung in unison by the chorus), and aleatoric distribution of rhythms.

CHORAL WORKS
SELECTED AND LISTED ACCORDING TO FAMILIARITY

Saul (Acts 8:1–4, 9:1–4) – 1972 – speaker, SATB chorus (with divisions), and organ – 6 minutes.

How long, O Lord (Psalm 13) – 1968 – SSAATTBB chorus a cappella – 5:30 minutes.

Missa misericordiae (Mass of Mercy) – 1973 – SATB chorus a cappella – 14 minutes. (1) The text is in English; (2) the work is divided into four movements—Kyrie, Gloria, Sanctus, and Agnus Dei.

Laudate Dominum (Praise the Lord) – 1976 – SSA chorus a cappella – 3 minutes. The text consists only of the words "Laudate Dominum."

Return, my soul (Psalm 116:7, 5, 8, 3, 4) – 1986 – S solo and SSAATTBB chorus a cappella – 6 minutes.

LARS JOHAN WERLE 1926–2001

Werle was born in Gävle, north of Stockholm, Sweden, and as a child taught himself to play the piano. He studied at Uppsala University and also independently with Sven-Erik Bäck. During his student years his interest in choral music and jazz led him to sing in the Bel Canto Choir and to play in a jazz ensemble. In 1958 he became a producer for Swedish radio, and during the

1960s he achieved fame for the first of his fifteen operas, *Drömmen om Thérèse* (Dream about Thérèse), which was scored for accompaniment of instrumental chamber ensemble and tape and which was presented on an arena stage. His choral compositions include several extended a cappella works modeled after Monteverdi madrigals and set to canzonas and sonnets by the early-Renaissance humanist poet Francesco Petrarca (1304–1374)—*Canzone 126 di Francesco Petrarca* of 1967, *Sonetto di Petrarca 292* of 1979, *Sonetto trentacinque* of 1989, and *Sonetto 292* of 1993. Other important choral works include the jazz-influenced *trees*, composed in 1982 and set to a poem by e. e. cummings, and *Nautical Preludes*, composed in 1970 to the composer's own poetry.

EINOJUHANI RAUTAVAARA B.1928

Rautavaara was born in Helsinki, Finland, and studied at the University of Helsinki (graduating with a degree in musicology in 1952) and the Sibelius Academy (graduating with a diploma in 1957). Further studies were with Aaron Copland and Roger Sessions in 1955 at the Berkshire Music Center in Tanglewood, Massachusetts, and with Vincent Persichetti at the Juilliard School of Music in New York City during the 1955–1956 academic year. Between 1966 and 1991 Rautavaara held several teaching positions at the Sibelius Academy—lecturer from 1966 to 1976, artist professor from 1971 to 1976, and professor of composition between 1976 and 1991.

He has composed ten dramatic stage works, eight symphonies (the last of which, subtitled "The Journey," was commissioned by the Philadelphia Orchestra in 1999), numerous concertos and other instrumental compositions, and fifty choral works. The significant secular choral works are scored for a cappella chorus and set to the poetry of major European writers of the early twentieth century. *Suite de Lorca,* for example, employs four poems by Federico García Lorca (1898–1936)—"Canción de jinete" (The rider's song), "El grito" (The scream), "La luna asoma" (The moon rises), and "Malagueña." The music is basically tonal, with rhythmic characteristics of Spanish popular songs, and each of the four pieces has a different textural or harmonic feature—ostinatos in "Canción de jinete," glissandos in "El grito," a Phrygian scale in "La luna asoma," and guitar-like effects in "Malagueña." Rautavaara chose the poetry of Lorca again in 1993 when he was commissioned by the Tokyo Philharmonic Chorus for a work "whose text and music were to have a relationship to the world of today." The resulting composition, *Canción de nuestro tiempo* (Song of our time), utilizes the poems "Oda a Walt Whitman" (Ode to Walt Whitman), "Meditación primera y última" (First and last meditation), and "Ciudad sin sueño" (Sleepless City). According to Rautavaara, the first poem, which is set in a movement subtitled "Fragmentos de agonía" (Fragments of agony), "shows the harsh, inhuman world of industrial society and war"; the music for the second poem "symbolizes the enigma of time, with dense pentatonic fields and harmonic clusters that suddenly change into completely different harmonies"; and in the third poem, set in a movement subtitled "Nocturno del Sarajevo" (Nocturne of Sarajevo), Lorca's imagery "seemed to associate strongly with the world [of Sarajevo] in 1993." *Die erste Elegie* is a setting of the first poem from *Duino Elegies* by Rainer Maria Rilke (1875–1926), with the opening lines, "Wer, wenn ich schriee, hörte mich denn aus der Engle Ordnungen" (Who among the host of angels would hear me, were I to cry out). Rautavaara associated these lines with the "mysticism surrounding the ruins of postwar Vienna." Commissioned by the Europa Cantat, the expansive work is constructed of a twelve-tone row based on four triads.

Two other large-scale secular choral works are settings of poetry by Scandinavian writers. *Katedralen* (The Cathedral) combines several poems by Edith Södergran (1892–1923)—"Vid Nietzsches grav" (At Nietzsche's grave), "Stjärnorna" (The stars), "Vanvettets virvel" (The whirlpool of madness), and "Är jag lögnare" (Am I a liar). The music is characterized by polyphonic textural masses (tone clusters and soundscapes) that represent cathedral arches reaching for the stars, with the countering effects of aleatoric rhythms, sprechstimme, and glissandos. The poetry of the famous Romantic-era Finnish novelist Aleksis Kivi (1834–1872) is used for *Halavan himmeän alla* (In the shade of the willow), an adaptation of three songs from Rautavaara's opera *Aleksis Kivi*—"Ikävyys" (Melancholy), "Laulu oravasta" (The squirrel), and "Sydämeni laulu" (Song of my heart). The music is based on a twelve-tone row that is derived from a changing series of minor triads.

A further major secular work, *True and False Unicorn,* is a setting of poetry by the American avant-garde writer and filmmaker James Broughton (1913–1999). Rautavaara describes the poetry and his music as "a Tapestry of Voices, where the characters and mythical animals in a tapestry each speak one by one on the Unicorn, the personification of the artist." The work is divided into four sections—"Before the Arras," "Horn and Hounds," "Snare and Delusion," and "Mon seul désir." The music is mainly tonal, with frequent parallel triads sung by the upper voices, occasional quotation of familiar melodies such as "America" (My country, 'tis of thee, sweet land of liberty, of thee I sing), and original melodies in jazz and popular styles. For dramatic effect Rautavaara scores several of the work's twenty movements for solo speakers and sprechstimme chorus.

The sacred choral music is represented by a number of works set to Latin texts: *Canticum Mariae Virginis* combines the Vespers hymn "Ave maris stella" with the canticle of the Virgin Mary "Gaude Maria virgo"; *Magnificat,* an extensive work in five movements, and *Credo,* a series of variations characterized by parallel fourths sung by the upper voices over pedal point figures sung by the lower voices, are settings of the traditional Roman texts; and *Missa Duodecanonica,* a twelve-tone work featuring canons in every movement, is a setting of the Kyrie, Sanctus, and Agnus Dei. Other sacred works include Finnish settings of Psalm 23, Psalm 130, and the Lord's Prayer (*Herran rukous*).

CHORAL WORKS
SELECTED AND LISTED ACCORDING TO FAMILIARITY

Suite de Lorca – 1973 – SATB chorus (with divisions) a cappella – 6:15 minutes. There are brief incidental solos in the first and third pieces.

Sommarnatten (Summer night) – 1975 – SSA solo trio and SATB chorus (with divisions) a cappella – 3 minutes.

Och glädjen den dansar (With joy we go dancing) – 1993 – S solo and SATB chorus (with divisions) a cappella – 2:30 minutes.

Die erste Elegie (The First Elegy) – 1993 – SS solos and SATB chorus (with divisions) a cappella – 9:30 minutes.

Katedralen (The Cathedral) – 1983 – thirty-two part chorus (8S, 8A, 8T, and 8B) a cappella – 16:30 minutes. There are brief incidental soprano and bass solos.

Canticum Mariae Virginis (Song of the Virgin Mary) – 1978 – SATB chorus (with divisions) a cappella – 7:30 minutes.

Magnificat – 1979 – SSA solos and SSAATTBB chorus (with divisions) a cappella – 16 minutes.

Credo – 1972 – SATB chorus (with divisions) a cappella – 4:15 minutes.

Kaksipsalmia (Two Psalms) – 1968 (revised in 1971) – SATB or TTBB chorus a cappella – "Psalm 23" 2 minutes and "Psalm 130" 1:30 minutes.

True and False Unicorn – 1971 (revised in 2000) – male and female speakers, SATB chorus (with divisions), and electronic tape (original version) or orchestra (revised version) – 46:30 minutes.

Canción de nuestro tiempo (Song of our time) – 1993 – SATB chorus (with divisions) a cappella – 14:30 minutes.

PER NØRGÅRD B.1932

Nørgård was born in Gentofte, north of Copenhagen, Denmark, and studied at the Royal Danish Conservatory. Further studies were in Paris with Nadia Boulanger and at the ISCM (International Society for Contemporary Music) festival in Cologne, where he was exposed to the music of Stockhausen, Boulez, and Berio. In 1958 Nørgård began teaching at the conservatory in Odense, on the island of Fyn, and in 1960 he returned to the Royal Danish Conservatory to teach composition. From 1965 until his retirement in 1994 he was professor of composition at the conservatory in Århus, Denmark. His compositional output includes five operas, six symphonies and numerous instrumental works, and approximately one hundred choral compositions (half of them scored for chorus and instruments and half scored for chorus a cappella).

The choral repertoire with instrumental accompaniment is chamber in nature (i.e., the scoring is for a small complement of instruments, not for orchestral forces), and almost all of the works include percussion. In addition, the large-scale oratorio-like works are diverse in their scoring: the Christmas oratorio *Det skete i de dage* (It happened in those days) has parts for actors and speakers as well as children's and mixed adult choruses, trumpet, strings, and percussion; *Dommen* (The Judgment) requires ATBBB soloists, three choruses (children's, women's, and mixed), plus wind instruments, strings, piano, tape, and percussion; and *Babel* is scored for soloists, mixed chorus, dancers, and instruments. The smaller-scale accompanied work *Singe die Gärten mein Herz, die du nicht kennst* (Sing of the gardens, my heart, that you do not know) exists in two versions—one for five instruments plus two percussion players and one for piano alone. Composed to the twenty-first poem of *Sonette an Orpheus* by Rainer Maria Rilke (1875–1926), it incorporates a phrase of music from Schubert's song *Du bist die Ruh'*. It was also used by Nørgård as the final section of his *Symphony #3*. Several works have scoring for percussion ad lib. *Drømmesange* (Dream Songs) and "Halleluja – vor Gud er forrykt" (Hallelujah – our God is mad) from *To Adolf Wölfli-Lieder*, for instance, can be performed with or without the scored parts for three drums.

The a cappella repertoire includes Nørgård's most noteworthy choral work, *Wie ein Kind*, which combines the poetry of Rilke and the Swiss artist Adolf Wölfli (1864–1930), who spent most of his adult life in a psychiatric hospital. In the notes to the score, Nørgård explains that the first movement of the work, "Wiigen-Lied" (Lullaby), "is punctuated by strange, distant calls, reminiscent of those of a street vendor or those of a mother calling from way up in a tower block to her child way down in a narrow courtyard"; the second movement, "Frühlings-Lied" (Spring Song), "is the song of the happy child, the child in vital harmony—open, playful, sensually aware"; and the third movement, "Trauermarsch mit einem Unglücksfall" (Funeral March with attendant minor accident), "repeats the musical themes of the first movement, but a male soloist, who does his best to sing after the fashion of his fellow singers, suffers some embarrassing frustrations."

Jeg hører regnen (I hear the rain) was inspired by the sound of the ocean and the overtones that the waves seemed to produce. The music begins with whispered and sibilant sounds, with changing vowels performed independently by the singers, and also the aleatoric execution of finger snaps, claves, or drums. During the remainder of the piece, the sopranos, altos, and basses are scored in a melodically tonal texture while the tenor part is punctuated by the terse recitation of a few words. *Frostsalme* (Frost Psalm) is an intermingling of two poems by the popular Danish poet Ole Sarvig (1921–1981)—"Aret" (The Year) and "Korsalme" (Choral Hymn). The ambiguity created by the amalgamation of the two poems is furthered by the distribution of the choral forces into four choral ensembles and the disposition of the singers into varying formations during performance. In addition, the sounds of whistling and crotales (which the singers play ad lib.) add to the dramatic effect. *Maya danser* (Maya dances) is an extraction from Nørgård's opera *Siddharta*, in which children sing of the barren Queen Maya's longing for a child of her own. *Tre motetter til Agnus Dei* (Three Agnus Dei motets) consists of the text from the Latin Mass Ordinary divided into three segments: in the first, "Agnus Dei" (Lamb of God), the harmonies are diatonic; in the second, "qui tollis peccata mundi" (who takes away the sins of the world), the writing is modulatory; and in the third, "dona nobis pacem" (give us peace), the music is dissonant and chromatic.

CHORAL WORKS
SELECTED AND LISTED ACCORDING TO FAMILIARITY

Wie ein Kind (Like a child) – 1979–1980 – ST solos and SATBB chorus a cappella – 13 minutes.

To Adolf Wölfli-Lieder (Two Adolf Wölfli Songs) – 1979–1982 (revised in 1992) – SATB chorus and percussion ad lib. – "Aftensang" (Evening Song) 4 minutes and "Halleluja – vor Gud er forrykt" (Hallelujah – our God is mad) 6 minutes. The first piece is a cappella and the second piece has scoring for three drums (each of a different size and timbre).

Drømmesange (Dream Songs) – 1981 – SATB chorus and percussion ad lib. –
13:30 minutes. Percussion parts are scored for three drums.

Jeg hører regnen (I hear the rain) – 1992 – SATB chorus (with divisions)
a cappella – 5:30 minutes.

Singe die Gärten mein Herz, die du nicht kennst (Sing of the gardens, my heart,
that you do not know) – 1974 – SSAATTBB chorus and flute, clarinet,
horn, harp, piano, and percussion (version A) or piano (version B) –
11 minutes.

Frostsalme (Frost Psalm) – 1975–1976 – SSSSAAAATTTTBBBB chorus
a cappella - 13:30 minutes.

Maya danser (Maya dances) – 1979 (revised in 1992) – SATBB chorus (with
divisions) a cappella – 3:30 minutes.

Tre motetter til Agnus Dei (Three Agnus Dei motets) – 1983 – SATB chorus
a cappella – 7 minutes.

Tre hymniske ansatser (Three hymnic dispositions) – 1985–1986 – SATB chorus (with divisions) a cappella – 10 minutes.

ARNE MELLNÄS 1933–2002

Mellnäs was born in Stockholm, Sweden, where he received his musical education at the Musikhögskolan. He also studied privately with György Ligeti in Vienna and with several teachers at
the Gaudeamus Foundation and Contemporary Music Center in the Netherlands. Between 1963
and 1986 he taught at his alma mater, the Musikhögskolan, and during the 1980s and 1990s
he held positions with the ISCM (International Society for Contemporary Music)—chair of the
Swedish section beginning in 1983 and president of the ISCM council beginning in 1997. His
compositional output includes five operas, twelve orchestral works, numerous instrumental
chamber and solo vocal pieces, and twenty choral compositions.

Four of the choral works are set to poems by the prolific American poet e. e. cummings
(1894–1962)—*dream* of 1970, *seeker of truth* and *a wind has blown the rain away* of 1973, and
sweet spring of 1994. These pieces as well as most of Mellnäs's other compositions are avant-
garde in notational language. *Aglepta*, for instance, is almost completely aleatoric, with whispers
and screams, sprechstimme, and a variety of symbols for nontraditional performance. The text is
based on an ancient untranslatable incantation from Smaland in southern Sweden, "Aglaria pid-
hol garia ananus qepta," which is stated twice in the composition—first divided into phonetic fragments and then whispered as a complete phrase. Mellnäs states that "the composition is like a be-
witched tree. The notes and chords in the score are like a trunk, while the other sounds are the
branches and leaves." *Succsim* is set to a variety of disjunct vowel and consonant sounds in a manner that Mellnäs describes as "a succession of simultaneous tonal events." The title of the piece is
derived from the first letters of the words "succession" and "simultaneous," and the music combines traditional and avant-garde techniques. *Bossa buffa* is based on the phrase ascribed to Cicero,
"Nemo saltat sobrius, nisi forte insanity" (No one dances sober unless he is mad). The music incorporates bossa nova rhythms with clicking sounds, finger snaps, and other unusual noises.

CHORAL WORKS
SELECTED AND LISTED ACCORDING TO FAMILIARITY

Aglepta – 1969 – SSA chorus a cappella – 4:30 minutes.

dream – 1970 – SATB chorus a cappella – 8 minutes.

a wind has blown the rain away – 1973 – SATB chorus a cappella – 5 minutes.

Succsim – 1964 (revised in 1967) – SATB chorus (divided into 4S, 4A, 4T, and 8B) a cappella – 6:30 minutes.

Bossa buffa – 1973 – SATB chorus a cappella – 6 minutes.

10 ordspråk (Ten Proverbs) – 1981 – SATB chorus a cappella – 16 minutes.

SVEN-DAVID SANDSTRÖM B.1942

Sandström was born in Borensberg, in southcentral Sweden, and between 1963 and 1967 he studied art and musicology at the University of Stockholm. From 1968 to 1972 he studied composition with Ingvar Lidholm, György Ligeti, and Per Nørgård at the Royal College of Music, and during the next two decades he became acquainted with a large amount of choral repertoire by singing in the Hägersten Motet Choir. Sandström achieved fame with the 1982 premiere of his Requiem, *De ur alla minnen fallna* (To those totally forgotten), and in 1985 he returned to the Royal College as a professor of composition. His choral output consists of approximately fifty works, most set to sacred texts and written in an advanced harmonic idiom, with twelve-tone melodic construction and aleatoric rhythms. Several motets are set to traditional Latin texts, such as *Ave Maria,* which was commissioned by the Association of Swedish Choirs for the Hägersten Motet Choir. Several others are in English: *A Cradle Song / The Tyger* is a setting of poems from William Blake's *Songs of Innocence and Experience,* and *Hear my prayer, O Lord* uses the passage from Psalm 102 that Henry Purcell set in his famous anthem. Sandström also quotes Purcell's music—first in its entirety without alteration and then in part as fragments of melody.

CHORAL WORKS
SELECTED AND LISTED ACCORDING TO FAMILIARITY

Ave Maria – 1994 – SATB/SATB chorus a cappella – 8:30 minutes.

Agnus Dei – 1980 – SSAATTBB chorus a cappella – 5 minutes.

A Cradle Song / The Tyger – 1978 – SSSSAAAATTTTBBBB chorus a cappella – 15 minutes.

Hear my prayer, O Lord – 1986 – SSAATTBB chorus a cappella – 4 minutes.

En ny Himmel och en ny jord (A new heaven and a new earth) – SAATBB chorus a cappella – 8 minutes.

De ur alla minnen fallna – 1979 – SATB solos, girls' chorus, mixed chorus, and orchestra – 100 minutes. The work is also called *Requiem tilegnet de ud af mindet Faldne* (Requiem dedicated to those fallen from memory).

High Mass – 1993–1994 – SSSAA solos, SATB chorus, and orchestra (including organ) – 94 minutes.

NIELS LA COUR B.1944

La Cour studied at the Royal Danish Conservatory between 1964 and 1969 and at the Conservatorio de S Cecilia in Rome in 1975. In 1978 he returned to the Royal Danish Conservatory to teach theory, and from 1968 to 1977 he taught the same subject at the Carl Nielsen Academy of Music in Odense. He is known for composing Latin church music in a conservative harmonic language based on Gregorian chant. Examples, all scored for SATB chorus a cappella, include *3 Motetti Latini 1982* ("Hodie Christus natus est," "Ave Maria," and "Laudate Dominum"), *3 Motetti Latini 1988* ("Petite et accipietis," "Tu es Petrus," and "Magnificat"), *4 Salmi per coro* of 1985 ("Sicut cervus," "Nonne Deo," "Exultent et laetentur," and "Dominus custodit te"), and *Missa brevis* of 1989.

TROND KVERNO B.1945

Kverno was born in Oslo, Norway, and studied music at the conservatory there. In 1967 he received a degree in church music, and the following year he was granted degrees in both theory and choral conducting. In 1971 he returned to the conservatory to teach theory, and between 1973 and 1994 he held several positions at the Norwegian State Academy of Music—teacher of theory in 1973, senior lecturer in church music and composition in 1978, and professor of church music in 1994. During these years he also served as organist and choirmaster at several Oslo churches and was involved in reforms of the Scandinavian Lutheran Church. His choral output consists mostly of a cappella works set to sacred texts, composed in a tonal harmonic language, and scored in textures of neo-Renaissance polyphony. Notable compositions include twenty-three hymns for the Norwegian Hymn Book (Norsk Salmebok) and several Latin motets that have become well known—*Ave maris stella*, *Stabat mater dolorosa*, and *Ave verum corpus*. His most acclaimed work is the *Passio Domini Nostri Jesu Christi secundum Mattheum* (St Matthew Passion), which, with its a cappella scoring and structure of polyphonic movements, is reminiscent of Pepping's *Passionsbericht des Matthäus* and therefore reflective of the Lutheran reform movement during the middle years of the twentieth century. According to Kverno, "The modern age needs to erect the Romanesque crucifix again [and to show] the Lamb of God . . . here in the madhouse of our time and for all eternity."

CHORAL WORKS
SELECTED AND LISTED ACCORDING TO FAMILIARITY

Ave maris stella – 1976 – SSA/TBB chorus a cappella – 4:30 minutes.

Corpus Christi Carol – SATB chorus a cappella – 3:30 minutes.

Stabat mater dolorosa – SATB chorus (with divisions) a cappella – 9 minutes.

Passio Domini Nostri Jesu Christi secundum Mattheum (St Matthew Passion) –
1986 – SAATTTTBBB solos and SATB/SATB chorus a cappella –
95 minutes.

BO HOLTEN B.1948

Holten studied musicology at the University of Copenhagen and bassoon at the Royal Danish
Academy of Music. Between 1976 and 1979 he served as editor of *Dansk Musiktidsskrift,* and in
1979 he founded the professional vocal ensemble Ars Nova, with which he subsequently toured
throughout Scandinavia and other countries in Europe and produced twenty recordings. In
1991 he began a series of guest conducting concerts with the BBC Singers in London, and in
1996 he founded a new ensemble, Musica Ficta. He has composed both instrumental and
choral genres and has been acclaimed for rejecting avant-garde techniques and writing in a substantial, well-crafted, and accessible tonal style. Describing his philosophy, he has said that
"modernism has provided an alibi for amateurism. The framework for a given experiment
comes to set the agenda for artistic expression, so craftsmanship takes a back seat."

His best-known work, *Regn og Rusk og Rosenbusk* (Rain and Rush and Rosebush), is a setting
of passages from the fairy tale *De Viises Steen* (The Stone of the Wise Man) by the famous Danish
author and poet Hans Christian Andersen (1805–1875). The music is scored for either twelve solo
voices (SSSAAATTTBBB) or four soloists (SSAT) and eight-part chorus (SAATTBBB); Holten
provides a diagram in the score as to the preferred standing arrangements of the singers. Other
notable works include *In nomine* of 1999 for twenty-four solo voices, commissioned by the BBC
Singers for their seventy-fifth anniversary and based on the Renaissance "In nomine" tune; *First
Snow* of 1996 for eight-part chorus, commissioned by the Canadian professional choral ensemble Pro Coro and set to two poems (in English translation) by the Icelandic poet Stephan G.
Stephansson (1853–1927) — "First Snow" and "Hermit Peak"; *Alt har sin tid* (A Time for Everything) of 1990 for eight-part chorus, commissioned by the Jutland Chamber Choir and set to
the familiar passages from Ecclesiastes; and *The Marriage of Heaven and Hell* of 1992 to 1995
for twelve soloists or twelve-part chorus, commissioned by the BBC Singers for their seventieth
anniversary and set to eight poems from *Songs of Innocence and of Experience* by William Blake.
In addition, Holten has composed two sets of motets in a neo-Renaissance style for SATB
chorus — 5 *Grundtvig-Motets* of 1983, composed to celebrate the 200th anniversary of the birth
of the poet N. F. S. Grundtvig (1783–1872), and *Three Latin Motets* of 1985 — "Aut quomodo"
(Matthew 7:3), "Fulcite me floribus" (from Song of Songs), and "Haec dies" (Psalm 118).

JAAKKO MÄNTYJÄRVI B.1963

Mäntyjärvi was born in Turku, Finland, and educated at the University of Helsinki, where he
studied English and linguistics, and the Sibelius Academy, where he studied music theory and
choral conducting. He has served as a professional translator and computer system manager at
the English Centre Helsinki and also as translator for the Finnish Music Information Centre

and the Ondine record label. In addition, he has been involved with a number of choral ensembles, most notably the Tapiola Chamber Choir, for which he has been composer-in-residence.

He has composed approximately forty choral works, including *Psalm 150 in Kent Treble Bob Minor,* a vocal adaptation of a change-ringing bell pattern commissioned by the Cork International Choral Festival in 1999, *The Ballad of the Oysterman* commissioned by Chanticleer in 2001, and *Armahda meidän päällem'* (Have mercy upon us) commissioned by the King's Singers in 2002. Other significant repertoire includes *Four Shakespeare Songs* of 1984, *Dagen svalnar* (Day is cooling) of 1991 (revised in 1993), *Pseudo-Yoik* of 1994, and *O magnum mysterium* of 2007. His most acclaimed work is *Canticum calamitatis maritimae.* Composed in 1997 and subtitled "In memoriam naufragii Estoniae 28.ix.1994," it is a lengthy setting (13:30 minutes) in ten movements for SB solos and SSAATTBB chorus. The text consists of excerpts from the Latin Mass for the Dead, Psalm 107:23–30, and a Finnish Broadcasting Company report of the sinking of the ferry Estonia during a storm in the Baltic Sea on September 28, 1994. Mäntyjärvi describes the piece as "a meditation involving three distinct elements—individual [based on a folk song-like melody reminiscent of "Nearer, my God, to thee"], objective [the broadcast report], and collective [the Psalm text "They that go down to the sea in ships"]." The music is basically neo-Medieval in texture, with chant-like effects and parallel motion chords, but it also has modern elements such as whispers and other nonvocal sounds.

❧ ENGLAND ❧

The majority of the English composers, both early and late in the Modern era, have written in a conservative style, with conventional rhythms, diatonic melodies, and tonal harmonies characterized by a native predilection for consonances—called *contenance angloise* (English countenance)—that had begun in the latter years of the Medieval era. Also conservative have been the genres (e.g., mass, motet, oratorio, cantata, anthem, Magnificat and Nunc dimittis, and part song). A few composers late in the era wrote in pandiatonic harmonies, and composers beginning with the generation of Michael Tippett expanded the mainstream harmonic and rhythmic language by employing avant-garde techniques such as sprechstimme and aleatoric rhythms. However, the instances of modern harmonies and avant-garde techniques have been occasional, and their applications moderate. The majority of English composers during the era also continued the tradition of insular education and exposure to repertoire. Only Frederick Delius traveled widely and composed in a cosmopolitan idiom. Other early composers such as Ralph Vaughan Williams, William Walton, and Percy Grainger studied briefly in cities on the European continent, and later composers such as Lennox Berkeley, Elisabeth Lutyens, Kenneth Leighton, Peter Maxwell Davies, and Giles Swayne spent longer periods of study away from England. None of these composers, however, absorbed or represented the music they heard abroad.

English composers early in the era were like their counterparts in Eastern European and Scandinavian countries in that they were intensely interested in native folk songs. Vaughan Williams and Gustav Holst, for instance, collected hundreds of folk melodies and set many of them in choral arrangements. English composers throughout the era have had an interest in combining secular texts with traditional sacred liturgical or biblical passages in order to create a contemporary and more universal message. Sample works include *Dona nobis pacem* by Vaughan Williams, *Hymnus Paradisi* and *Requiem* by Herbert Howells, *War Requiem* by Benjamin Britten, and *Requiem* by John Rutter. In other works such as *Hodie* by Vaughan Williams and *A Child of Our Time* by Tippett, contemporary poetry is interpolated into the fabric of oratorio texts in emulation of German Baroque compositions.

The vast majority of composers discussed in this section of the Modern era were born and employed in England. However, a few composers were born elsewhere (Australia, South Africa, Scotland, and Wales) but professionally active in England. One composer, Alun Hoddinott, had no significant presence in England (he was born and employed for most of his life in Wales), although his music has English characteristics. Of the thirty-five representative English composers, those who have achieved the highest stature are Delius, Vaughan Williams, Holst, Howells, Walton, Tippett, Britten, and John Tavener. Those who have achieved lesser stature and have not been given separate entries below are briefly discussed here.

Sir Granville Bantock (1868–1946) was born in London and studied at the Royal Academy of Music. Between 1892 and 1896 he was editor of the *New Quarterly Musical Review*, in 1900 he was appointed principal of the Midland Institute School of Music in Birmingham, and in 1908 he succeeded Edward Elgar as professor of composition at Birmingham University. His choral output consists of nine choral/orchestral cantatas and several a cappella choral symphonies, all in a conservative harmonic idiom. The cantatas include *Sea Wanderers* of 1906, *Omar Khayyám* of 1906 to 1909, *Song of Liberty* of 1914, and *The Pilgrim's Progress* of 1928. The choral symphonies are *Atlanta in Calydon* of 1911, *Vanity of Vanities* of 1913, and *A Pageant of Human Life,* also of 1913.

E. J. Moeran (1894–1950) was born near London and received his musical education at the Royal College of Music and privately with John Ireland. During the 1920s Moeran composed mainly chamber music works in the chromatic style of Frederick Delius, and during the 1930s his focus changed to larger-scale symphonic works. His choral compositions, limited in number, include the collection *Songs of Springtime.* Written in 1930 and scored for SATB chorus a cappella, the seven part songs in the collection are entitled "Under the Greenwood Tree," "The River-God's Song," "Spring, the Sweet Spring," "Love Is a Sickness," "Sigh No More Ladies," "Good Wine," and "To Daffodils." Another single part song, *Phyllida and Corydon,* is also significant.

Eric Thiman (1900–1975) was born in Ashford, Kent, and studied at Trinity College of Music in London and the University of London. In 1932 he was appointed to the faculty of the Royal Academy of Music, and for the remainder of his life he held several administrative positions, including examiner to the Royal Schools of Music and examiner to the Faculty of Music and dean of the faculty at the University of London. He was also organist and choirmaster at City Temple Congregational Church. His numerous choral works include the large-scale cantatas *The Last Supper* of 1930, *The Parables* of 1931, and *The Temptations of Christ* of 1952; the anthems *A Morning Prayer, I will lay me down in peace, O for a closer walk with God,* and *Immortal, invisible, king of glory;* and the part songs and folk song arrangements *Go lovely rose* for mixed voices, *Morning Song* for female voices, and *False Phillis* and *The Gentle Maiden* for male voices.

Peter Racine Fricker (1920–1990) was born in London and educated at the Royal College of Music. He also studied at Morley College, where he worked with Michael Tippett and served as an assistant to Mátyás Seiber. In 1952 Fricker succeeded Tippett as music director at Morley College, in 1955 he joined the faculty of the Royal College of Music, and in 1964 he moved to the United States to teach at the University of California, Santa Barbara. His nineteen choral works include five motets, two sets of madrigals, two sets of carols, the neo-Classical oratorio *The Vision of Judgement,* and the part song collection *Seven Little Songs* for SATB chorus a cappella.

David Bedford (b.1937) was born in London and studied composition at the Royal Academy of Music with Lennox Berkeley. Further studies were in Milan at the RAI (Radio Audizioni Italiane) electronic studio and in Venice with Luigi Nono. Between 1968 and 1980 Bedford taught at Queen's College, London, and from 1983 to 1987 he was on the faculty at Gordonstoun School in Scotland. Since then he has served as director of youth music and composer-in-residence for the English Sinfonia. He was first recognized in 1963 for his thirty-voiced choral work *Two Poems,* in which durational values, called by Bedford "space-time," were measured in seconds. Other notable choral works include *Star Clusters, Nebulae and Places in Devon* of 1971 for two eight-voiced choruses and brass instruments, *Twelve Hours of Sunset* of 1974 for twelve-voiced chorus and large orchestra, and *The Golden Wine Is Drunk* of 1974 for sixteen-part chorus a cappella.

FREDERICK DELIUS 1862–1934

Delius was born in Bradford, near Leeds, into a musically cultured family of German heritage. He had piano and violin lessons as a child but did not study music formally. Instead, he attended the Bradford Grammar School and then the International College in Isleworth, near London. After graduation he traveled to France, Germany, Sweden, and Norway as part of his work in the family wool business, and in 1884 he moved to the United States, where he was employed at an orange plantation in Florida. While in Florida, he studied composition privately with a local musician named Thomas F. Ward (1856–1912), and from 1885 to 1886 he studied at Danville College in Virginia. In 1886 he returned to Europe, studying at the Leipzig Conservatory for two years, and in 1895 he moved to Paris and joined the circle of musicians that included Gabriel Fauré, Maurice Ravel, and Florent Schmitt. During the next fifteen years Delius composed several operas, including *A Village Romeo and Juliet* between 1899 and 1901. He did not receive public recognition, however, until the premiere of *A Mass of Life* in 1909. By the 1920s his health began to deteriorate from syphilis he had contracted in 1895, and for the next decade he was assisted by Peter Warlock, who served as a copyist, and Eric Fenby, who took dictation when Delius could no longer see and who helped compose Delius's final major work, *Songs of Farewell.*

Delius composed ten choral/orchestral works and eleven part songs. Most of this music, no doubt stemming from a lack of formal training and study of traditional repertoire, is unconventional and idiosyncratic in formal design and harmonic language. *Sea Drift,* for instance, which is generally assumed to be his greatest work, is a seeming fantasy for solo baritone with choral commentary. Sections of Walt Whitman's poem "Out of the Cradle Endlessly Rocking" from *Sea Drift* unfold seamlessly in a continuous narrative, French impressionistic-like harmonies rarely come to a cadence, and orchestrations are atmospheric without explicitly depicting specific words or phrases. Similar in style are *Songs of Sunset* (originally titled *Songs of Twilight and Sadness*), which interconnects eight poems by Ernest Dowson (1867–1900), and *Songs of Farewell,* a setting of five poems from Whitman's *Leaves of Grass*. The two choral/orchestral works with sacred titles are even more unorthodox. *A Mass of Life* is a setting of text from *Also sprach Zarathustra* by Friedrich Nietzsche, which Delius called "a choral celebration of the Will to say Yea to life in the joy of the eternal recurrence of all things." *Requiem*, subtitled "To the memory of all young artists fallen in the war," is a setting of poetry loosely based on biblical passages assembled by Delius that deal with the brevity and meaninglessness of life.

The a cappella pieces are also characterized by formal ambiguity and nonfunctional Impressionistic harmonies. *To be sung of a Summer Night on the Water*, particularly atmospheric, is set in two movements for wordless chorus; the chorus is alone in the slow first movement, and a tenor soloist to a *la, la* text joins the chorus in the fast dance-like second movement.

CHORAL/ORCHESTRAL WORKS
SELECTED AND LISTED IN CHRONOLOGICAL ORDER
ACCORDING TO DATE OF COMPOSITION

Sea Drift – 1903–1904 – B solo, SATB chorus (with occasional divisions), and large orchestra – 25 minutes.

A Mass of Life – 1904–1905 – SATB solos, SATB/SATB chorus, and large orchestra – 85 minutes.

Songs of Sunset – 1906–1907 – AB solos, SATB chorus (with divisions), and large orchestra – 33 minutes.

Requiem – 1913–1914 – SB solos, SATB chorus (with divisions), and large orchestra – 30 minutes.

Songs of Farewell – 1930 – SSAATTBB chorus and large orchestra – 18 minutes.

A CAPPELLA WORKS
SELECTED AND LISTED ACCORDING TO FAMILIARITY

On Craig Ddu (also called *Mountain Silence*) – 1907 – SATTBB chorus a cappella – 3:30 minutes.

To be sung of a Summer Night on the Water – 1917 – SATTBB chorus a cappella – 4 minutes.

The splendour falls on castle walls – 1923 – SATB chorus a cappella – 3:15 minutes.

Midsummer Song – 1908 – SSAATTBB chorus a cappella – 1:30 minutes.

RALPH VAUGHAN WILLIAMS 1872–1958

Vaughan Williams was born in Down Ampney, Gloucestershire, but during most of his childhood he lived in a family home near London. He studied piano and harmony in his youth with an aunt and also had violin and organ lessons. His formal music studies began in 1890, when he entered the Royal College of Music, and continued in 1892 at Trinity College, Cambridge.

Further studies were with Max Bruch in Berlin in 1897 and Maurice Ravel in Paris in 1908. Meanwhile, Vaughan Williams had met Gustav Holst in 1895, and the two young composers began developing an interest in English folk music. At about the same time Vaughan Williams also gained an appreciation for Elizabethan and Jacobean music and for the work of Béla Bartók and Zoltán Kodály, both of whom were devoted to gathering folk songs from Hungary. During the early years of the twentieth century Vaughan Williams collected more than eight hundred English folk melodies and composed several important works based on British music of the past, including a number of folk song arrangements and *Fantasia on a Theme by Thomas Tallis* for string orchestra. He also conducted masterpieces of the past (e.g., Bach's *St Matthew Passion*) in his position as conductor of the Leith Hill Musical Festival from 1905 to 1953, and he selected and composed hymns for *The English Hymnal*. In 1919 he was appointed professor of composition at the Royal College of Music, and from 1920 to 1928 he was conductor of the Bach Choir. For the remainder of his life he combined composition and teaching with conducting his works throughout Europe and the United States. Among his many honors and awards were an honorary doctorate from Oxford University in 1919 (he had already earned a doctorate from Cambridge in 1901) and the Order of Merit in 1935. (Knighthood was offered in 1935 but he refused to accept it.) He died of natural causes at age eighty-five and was buried in Westminster Abbey close to the graves of Henry Purcell and Charles Villiers Stanford.

In addition to ten stage works and more than thirty orchestral compositions (including nine symphonies, two of which employ chorus), Vaughan Williams composed thirty-nine choral/orchestral works, thirty-two choral pieces scored a cappella or with keyboard accompaniment, fourteen hymns, thirty-five carols, and twenty-nine folk song arrangements. The choral/orchestral works include three major compositions set to texts by Walt Whitman, whose poetry was so meaningful to Vaughan Williams that he carried a pocket edition of *Leaves of Grass* with him for most of his life. *A Sea Symphony* is set in four movements to poems from *Sea Drift* ("Song for all Seas, all Ships" and "Song of the Exposition" in movement one, "On the Beach at Night alone" in movement two, and "After the Sea-Ship" in movement three) and from *Passage to India* (in movement four); *Toward the Unknown Region* is set to "Darest Thou Now O Soul" from *Whispers of Heavenly Death* (the first line of poetry is "Darest thou now O soul, walk out with me toward the unknown region"); and *Dona nobis pacem* combines biblical and other texts with Whitman's "Beat! Beat! Drums," "Reconciliation," and "Dirge for Two Veterans" from *Drum Taps*. The subject matter of all these texts expresses themes that were common to Vaughan Williams and that are seen in many works throughout his life—the journey of one's soul in *A Sea Symphony* and *Toward the Unknown Region,* and the unassailable nature of humankind's spirit in *Dona nobis pacem.* This last-named work is especially important in the development of choral music in the Modern era in that it combines traditional Latin liturgical texts with accordant secular poetry.

The three most notable choral/orchestral works set to sacred or semisacred texts by other authors also express themes of an uplifting nature and make reference to circumstances of secular modern life. In *Five Mystical Songs,* a setting of poems by the Welsh metaphysical poet and priest George Herbert (1593–1633), comparisons are made between sacred and secular tenets; in the oratorio *Sancta civitas* (The Holy City), the spirit's triumph over adversity is related through verses from the biblical book of Revelation that describe the fall of Babylon and St John's vision of a new heaven; and in the Christmas cantata *Hodie* (This Day), Vaughan Williams relates the circumstances of modern life to the birth of Jesus by combining biblical passages with poetry by John Milton, Miles Coverdale, Thomas Hardy, George Herbert, and Ursula Vaughan Williams (his wife). In Milton's "Hymn on the Morning of Christ's Nativity," for instance, there is the phrase "And waving wide her myrtle wand, she [nature] strikes a universal peace through sea and land. No war, or battle's sound, was heard the world around."

Two other choral/orchestral works are significant both for their beauty of music and for their textual messages. *Serenade to Music,* a paean to the charm of music, is set to the text that begins "How sweet the moonlight sleeps upon this bank! Here will we sit and let the sound of music creep in our ears" from act five, scene one of Shakespeare's *The Merchant of Venice.* Scoring was originally for sixteen specific soloists, whom Vaughan Williams identified by their initials in the score (i.e., each vocal part was marked with the soloist's initials). The cantata *In Windsor Forest,* adapted from music in Vaughan Williams's opera *Sir John in Love,* concludes with Thomas Campion's air that ends with the phrases, "All our pride is but a jest, none are worse and none are best; grief and joy and hope and fear, play their pageants everywhere; vain opinion all doth sway, and the world is but a play."

The early compositions, including a cappella and keyboard accompanied works, are in a conservative harmonic language and are frequently based on music of past eras. For example, the *Mass*—with imitative textures, chant-like melodies, double chorus dialogues, and meters such as 4/2, 3/2, and 2/2—is modeled after masses of the Renaissance. In addition, most of the folk song arrangements were composed before the 1930s. The later compositions, while still harmonically conservative, are characterized by modal melodies and ambiguous tonalities. An example is the part song *Silence and Music,* composed for the collection *A Garland for the Queen* honoring the coronation of Elizabeth II in 1953. The *Three Shakespeare Songs* of 1951 include some of Vaughan Williams's most advanced and colorful harmonies, including tone clusters, parallel motion chords, and concluding sonorities that are not in the tonic key.

CHORAL/ORCHESTRAL WORKS
SELECTED AND LISTED IN CHRONOLOGICAL ORDER
ACCORDING TO DATE OF COMPOSITION

A Sea Symphony – 1903–1909 (revised in 1923) – SB solos, SATB chorus (with divisions), SSAA semichorus, and large orchestra (including organ) – 66 minutes. The semichorus is limited to two passages in the fourth movement.

Toward the Unknown Region – 1904–1906 – SATB chorus and orchestra – 13 minutes.

Five Mystical Songs – 1911 – B solo, SATB chorus (with divisions), and orchestra – 20 minutes.

Fantasia on Christmas Carols – 1912 – B solo, SATB chorus, and orchestra (including organ and bells) – 12 minutes.

Sancta civitas (The Holy City) – 1923–1925 – TB solos, SATB chorus (with divisions), SATB semichorus (with divisions), SSA distant chorus, and orchestra – 31 minutes. According to Vaughan Williams, "The semichorus should sit behind the full chorus and consist of about twenty singers (6,6,4,4,). The distant choir, consisting of boys' voices if possible, should be out of sight and must have a special conductor."

Flos campi – 1925 – solo viola, SATB wordless chamber chorus (with divisions), and chamber orchestra – 22 minutes.

Magnificat – 1932 – A solo, SSAA chorus, and orchestra (including extensive flute solo) – 13 minutes.

Five Tudor Portraits – 1935 – AB solos, SATB chorus (with divisions), and orchestra – 45 minutes.

Dona nobis pacem – 1936 – SB solos, SATB chorus (with divisions), and large orchestra (including bells and organ) – 36 minutes.

Serenade to Music – 1938 – SSSSAAAATTTTBBBB solos and orchestra – 14 minutes.

Hodie (This Day) – 1953–1954 – STB solos, SATB chorus (with divisions), a small unison children's ensemble (preferably boys), and orchestra (including celesta and piano) – 70 minutes. (1) The opening and closing movements, "Prologue" and "Epilogue," serve as framing choruses similar to those in Lutheran historiae; (2) the children relate the biblical narrative; (3) two a cappella "chorals" (i.e., chorales), "The blessed son of God" and "No sad thought his soul affrights," are often extracted and performed separately.

SACRED WORKS – A CAPPELLA OR WITH ORGAN ACCOMPANIMENT
SELECTED AND LISTED IN CHRONOLOGICAL ORDER
ACCORDING TO DATE OF COMPOSITION

Salve festa dies ("Hail thee, festival day") – ca.1905 – SATB hymn – 2:30 minutes.

Sine nomine ("For all the saints, who from their labors rest") – ca.1905 – SATB hymn – 2:30 minutes.

Down Ampney ("Come down, O love divine") – ca.1905 – SATB hymn – 2:30 minutes.

O clap your hands (Psalm 47) – 1920 – SATB chorus (with divisions), brass, and organ – 3:15 minutes.

Mass – 1920–1921 – SATB solos and SATB/SATB chorus a cappella – 24 minutes.

O vos omnes – 1922 – A solo and SSAATTBB chorus a cappella – 5:30 minutes.

King's Weston ("At the name of Jesus ev'ry knee shall bow") – 1925 – SATB hymn – 2:30 minutes.

O how amiable (Psalms 84 and 90) – 1934 – SATB chorus and organ – 3 minutes. The anthem ends with a unison chorus setting of the Doxology ("O God, our help in ages past").

O taste and see – 1952 – SATB chorus and organ – 1:30 minutes.

A Vision of Aeroplanes (Ezekiel 1) – 1956 – SATB chorus (with divisions) and organ – 9:30 minutes.

SECULAR PART SONGS AND FOLK SONG ARRANGEMENTS
SELECTED AND LISTED IN CHRONOLOGICAL ORDER
ACCORDING TO DATE OF COMPOSITION

Three Elizabethan Songs – 1891–1896 – SATB chorus a cappella – "Sweet day" 2 minutes, "The willow song" 1:15 minutes, and "O mistress mine" 2 minutes.

Come away death – 1896–1902 – SSATB chorus a cappella – 3:30 minutes.

Rest – 1902 – SSATB chorus a cappella – 3:15 minutes.

Bushes and Briars – 1908 – SATB or TTBB chorus a cappella – 2:30 minutes.

Down among the dead men – 1912 – TTBB chorus a cappella – 2 minutes.

Five English Folksongs – 1913 – SATB chorus a cappella – "The dark-eyed sailor" 2:15 minutes, "The spring time of the year" 3 minutes, "Just as the tide was flowing" 2 minutes, "The lover's ghost" 4 minutes, and "Wassail Song" 2:30 minutes.

The Turtle Dove – ca.1924 – B solo and SSATB chorus a cappella – 3:30 minutes.

Greensleeves – ca.1945 – SATB chorus (with divisions) a cappella – 6 minutes.

Three Shakespeare Songs – 1951 – SATB chorus (with divisions) a cappella – "Full fathom five" 3 minutes, "The cloud-capp'd towers" 3 minutes, and "Over hill, over dale" 1 minute.

Silence and Music – 1953 – SATB chorus a cappella – 4:15 minutes.

GUSTAV HOLST 1874–1934

Holst was born in Cheltenham, northeast of Bristol, into a family that had been musicians for generations. His great-grandfather, Matthias (1769–1854), had been a composer, pianist, and harpist at the Imperial Russian court in St Petersburg before moving to England in 1799; his grandfather, Gustavus Valentine, had also been a pianist and harpist; and his father, Adolph (1846–1901), was a church musician and teacher of piano and organ. Gustav studied these instruments with his father, as well as violin and trombone with other teachers, and in 1893 he entered the Royal College of Music, where he studied with Charles Villiers Stanford and Sir Hubert Parry. In 1895 Holst met Ralph Vaughan Williams, who was to become his lifelong friend and fellow collector of English folk songs, and in 1896 he followed in his friend's footsteps by conducting a choral ensemble (the Hammersmith Socialist Choir). At this time he also developed an interest in Hindu literature and philosophy and studied Sanskrit at University College in London. For the next several years he played trombone in the Queen's Hall and Scottish orchestras, and in 1903 he was appointed to the faculty of James Allen's Girls' School in Dulwich. In 1905 he became director of music at St Paul's Girls' School, Hammersmith, and while maintaining this position he also taught at Morley College between 1907 and 1924. Holst came to fame in 1918 with the premiere of *The Planets,* which became one of the most popular compositions of the twentieth century. However, being of frail health since his childhood, he maintained a low public profile and concentrated on his compositional and teaching activities. He died of heart failure at age fifty-nine and was buried at Chichester Cathedral.

Holst's total compositional output consists of fifty-two choral works in addition to fifteen stage works, thirty-four orchestral compositions, and thirty-three solo songs. Other than *The Planets,* the most important of the choral/orchestral works is *The Hymn of Jesus,* composed during the latter half of 1917 and dedicated to Vaughan Williams. The text is taken from two Gregorian chants—"Vexilla Regis" and "Pange lingua"—and the Apocryphal Acts of St John. The main theme of this last-named text, which Holst translated into English from the original Greek, is of religious ecstasy—in particular the ecstasy caused by dancing (e.g., "Divine grace is dancing" and "The Holy Twelve dance with us, all things join in the dance"). The harmonic language is tonal, and the expressive elements of the text are heightened by a brief passage of sprechstimme and a lengthy melisma on the word "Ah."

Other important choral/orchestral works include *A Choral Fantasia,* set to the poem *Ode to Music* by the British poet laureate Robert Bridges (1844–1930), and *Christmas Day,* subtitled a "Choral Fantasy on Old Carols" and based on "Good Christian men, rejoice," "God rest you merry, gentlemen," "Come, ye lofty, come, ye lowly," and "The first Nowell." The most popular of the a cappella pieces are the Christmas carols *In the bleak midwinter,* set to poetry of Christina Rossetti (1830–1894), and *Lullay my liking,* set to an old English Medieval poem. The anthem *Turn back, O man* for SATB chorus and organ is also popular.

CHORAL WORKS WITH INSTRUMENTAL ENSEMBLE ACCOMPANIMENT
SELECTED AND LISTED IN CHRONOLOGICAL ORDER
ACCORDING TO H CATALOGUE NUMBER

Choral Hymns from the Rig Veda – group one H97 – 1908–1910 – "Battle Hymn," "To the Unknown God," and "Funeral Hymn" for SATB chorus and orchestra – 20 minutes; group two H98 – 1909 – "To Varuna," "To Agni," and "Funeral Chant" for SSAA chorus and orchestra – 13 minutes; group three H99 – 1910 – "Hymn to the Dawn," "Hymn to the Waters," "Hymn to Vena," and "Hymn of the Travelers" for SSAA chorus, solo harp, and orchestra – 12 minutes; and group four H100 – 1912 – "Hymn to Agni," "Hymn to Soma," "Hymn to Manas," and "Hymn to Indra" for TTBB chorus, strings, brass, and percussion – 15 minutes.

Christmas Day H109 – 1910 – SATB solos, SATB chorus, and orchestra – 5 minutes.

The Cloud Messenger H111 – 1909–1910 – SATB chorus (with divisions) and orchestra – 43 minutes.

Two Psalms H117 (Psalm 86 "To my humble supplication" and Psalm 148 "Lord, who hast made us for thine own") – 1912 – T solo (Psalm 86 only), SATB chorus (with divisions), strings, and organ – 12 minutes.

A Dirge for Two Veterans H121 – 1914 – TTBB chorus with brass and percussion – 6:30 minutes.

The Planets H125 – 1914–1916 – SAA/SAA wordless chorus and orchestra – 50 minutes. The chorus sings only in the final movement, "Neptune, the Mystic."

The Hymn of Jesus H140 – 1917 – SATB/SATB chorus, SSA semichorus, and large orchestra (including celesta, piano, and organ) – 22 minutes.

Ode to Death H144 – 1919 – SATB chorus (with divisions) and orchestra (including optional celesta and organ) – 12:30 minutes.

First Choral Symphony H155 – 1923–1924 – S solo, SATB chorus (with occasional divisions), SATB half-chorus (drawn from the full chorus), and large orchestra (including celesta and organ) – 50 minutes.

Seven Partsongs H162 – 1925–1926 – S solo, SSAA chorus, and strings – 23 minutes.

A Choral Fantasia H177 – 1930 – SB solos, SATB chorus (with divisions), brass, strings, organ, and percussion – 16:30 minutes. (1) The S solo may be sung by a semichorus of sopranos; (2) both solos are brief.

A CAPPELLA AND KEYBOARD ACCOMPANIED WORKS
SELECTED AND LISTED IN CHRONOLOGICAL ORDER
ACCORDING TO H CATALOGUE NUMBER

Ave Maria H49 – 1900 – SSSSAAAA chorus a cappella – 3:30 minutes.

In the bleak midwinter H73 no.1 – 1904–1905 – SATB chorus a cappella – 3 minutes.

Four Partsongs for Children H110 – 1910 – SSAA chorus and piano – "Song of the Ship-builders" 2:30 minutes, "Song of the Shoemakers" 1 minute, "Song of the Fisherman" 2 minutes, and "Song of the Drovers" 1:30 minutes.

Nunc dimittis H127 – 1915 – SSAATTBB chorus a cappella – 3:30 minutes.

This have I done for my true love H128 – 1916 – SATB chorus a cappella – 5:30 minutes.

Lullay my liking H129 – 1916 – S solo and SATB chorus a cappella – 3 minutes.

The Evening-watch H159 – 1924 – SSAATTBB chorus a cappella – 4:30 minutes.

SIR EDWARD BAIRSTOW 1874–1946

Bairstow was born in Huddersfield, near Manchester, and received his formal education at Balliol College, Oxford. He also studied organ at Westminster Abbey. In 1893 he was appointed organist at All Saints, Norfolk Square; in 1899 he moved to Wigan parish church (where he also conducted the Wigan Philharmonic Society); and in 1907 he became organist at the parish church in

Leeds. He remained associated with the city of Leeds, serving as organist for the Leeds Festival and as conductor of the Leeds Philharmonic Society beginning in 1917. However, he resigned the position at the parish church in 1913 and became organist at nearby York Minster. In 1939 he also became conductor of the York Musical Society. He was knighted by King George V in 1932 and received honorary doctorates from Leeds University in 1936 and Oxford University in 1945.

Bairstow is known mainly for his anthems and Anglican Service music composed in a traditional and conservative harmonic language. Most popular of the anthems are three introits or short anthems—*I sat down under his shadow; Jesu, the very thought of thee;* and *I will wash my hands in innocency*—all scored for SATB chorus and organ. Other anthems, also scored for SATB chorus and organ, include *Let all mortal flesh keep silence* and *Save us, O Lord*. The liturgical music includes two complete sets for Morning, Communion, and Evening Services—one set in D major and one in E-flat major.

JOHN IRELAND 1879–1962

Ireland was born in a small town near Manchester and at age fourteen was admitted to the Royal College of Music. He also studied at the Royal College of Organists, becoming a Fellow at age sixteen, and at Durham University, receiving a bachelor's degree in 1905. Between 1904 and 1926 he was organist at St Luke's Church in Chelsea, and from 1920 to 1939 he taught composition at the Royal College of Music, where one of his students was Benjamin Britten. Ireland is known primarily for *Greater love hath no man,* which became one of the most frequently performed anthems in mainstream Protestant churches during the latter part of the twentieth century. It is set to the text from Song of Solomon 8:7 that begins "Many waters cannot quench love, neither can the floods drown it" and is scored for brief SB solos, SATB chorus, and organ. Other sacred works include *Vexilla Regis* for SATB solos, SATB chorus, brass, and organ; *Te Deum* in F major for SATB chorus and organ; and *These things shall be,* a commission from the BBC for the coronation of George VI, scored for baritone or tenor solo, SATB chorus, and orchestra.

EDGAR BAINTON 1880–1956

Bainton was born in London and excelled as a pianist during his youth. He made his first public performance as a soloist at age nine, and at sixteen he entered the Royal College of Music. He began studying composition with Charles Villiers Stanford three years later, and at twenty-one he was appointed teacher of piano and composition at Newcastle upon Tyne Conservatory of Music. Bainton became principal of the conservatory in 1912. In 1933 he moved to Australia, serving there as director of the New South Wales State Conservatorium of Music in Sydney and as founder and conductor of the New South Wales Symphony Orchestra (later named the Sydney Symphony). While in Australia, he became known for his performances of British repertoire, including Edward Elgar's *The Dream of Gerontius.*

Bainton's compositional output includes ten choral/orchestral works and approximately the same number of anthems. The large-scale works include *The Blessed Damozel,* set to the famous poem by the pre-Raphaelite painter and poet Dante Gabriel Rossetti (1828–1882), and *To the name above every name*, set to verses by the metaphysical poet Richard Crashaw (1613–1649). Bainton's most famous anthem, and one of the most admired anthems of the early twentieth century, is *And I saw a new heaven*. A setting of Revelation 21:1–4 scored for SATB chorus and organ, it epitomizes the expansive and euphonious post-Romantic style favored by English composers of the time. Other anthems include *Open thy gates, Christ in the wilderness*, and *The heavens declare thy glory*.

PERCY GRAINGER 1882–1961

Grainger was born in southern Australia, and spent his youth in Melbourne, where his home schooling included piano lessons. Demonstrating considerable musical ability (he gave his first public piano recital at age twelve), he was sent at thirteen to the Hoch Conservatory in Frankfurt, Germany. At nineteen he moved to London to establish himself as a concert pianist and teacher, and while there he was drawn to the writings of Rudyard Kipling (1865–1936) and also to English folk songs. Like Ralph Vaughan Williams and Gustav Holst, Grainger traveled across the country collecting folk songs, recording them on a phonograph beginning in 1906 and arranging many of them for chorus. In 1914, at the beginning of World War I, he relocated to the United States, and in 1917 he joined the army and spent the next two years playing in and composing for one of the army bands. During the 1920s he toured extensively as a concert pianist throughout Australia, Europe, and Denmark, and during the 1930s and beyond he concentrated his efforts on writing for and lecturing at educational institutions. He maintained an active schedule until his death of cancer in 1961 at age seventy-eight.

Grainger's choral output includes an extended cycle of part songs set to texts extracted from Kipling's *The Jungle Book* of 1894 and numerous folk song arrangements—some from Danish and others from Scottish sources but most from England. It is because this choral output is predominantly English that Grainger is discussed here rather than with American or Australian composers. The *Jungle Book* cycle includes the two popular part songs *Morning-Song in the Jungle* and *The Peora Hunt*. The best-known folk song arrangements are *Brigg Fair* and *Irish Tune from County Derry*. This latter piece, scored for wordless a cappella chorus, is better known as *Danny Boy*. Other folk song arrangements include *I'm seventeen come Sunday, Danny Deever, Shallow Brown*, and *The lost lady found*.

SIR ARNOLD BAX 1883–1953

Bax was born on the outskirts of London and entered the Royal Academy of Music when he was seventeen. He took no professional teaching appointments after his studies, nor did he pursue a conducting or performing career, even though he was an accomplished pianist. Instead, he devoted his professional energies to composition and to the writing of poetry. He also traveled extensively and spent lengthy periods of time in Ireland, Dresden, and Russia. His compositional focus was on instrumental genres, and he became well known for his ballets, incidental music for plays, film scores, tone poems, and symphonies. He was knighted in 1937 and made Master of the King's Music in 1942, and in 1943 he wrote an autobiography entitled *Farewell, My Youth*.

His choral output consists of twenty works, most of which are choral/orchestral secular cantatas. Popular among these are *Fatherland*, composed in 1907 (revised in 1934) to an English translation of the Swedish poem "Vaart Land" (Our Land) from *Fänrik Staal's Saagner* (Ensign Staal's Tales) by Finland's national poet Johan Ludvig Runeberg (1804–1877); *Enchanted Summer*, composed in 1910 to passages from act two, scene two of *Prometheus Unbound* by the English lyric poet Percy Shelley (1792–1822); and *Walsinghame*, composed in 1926 to the poem of the same name by the English writer and explorer Sir Walter Raleigh (ca.1552–1618). Of the several works set to sacred texts is Bax's most acclaimed choral composition, the Latin motet *Mater ora filium*, composed in 1921 and scored for SSAATTBB chorus a cappella. Other works set to sacred texts include *Gloria, Nunc dimittis*, and *Te Deum*, all composed in 1945 and scored for SATB chorus and organ.

SIR WILLIAM H. HARRIS 1883–1973

Harris was born in London and became a Fellow of the Royal College of Organists when he was fifteen. At sixteen he entered the Royal College of Music, where he studied composition with Charles Wood, and during the next several years he served as assistant organist at both Temple Church and Lichfield Cathedral. In 1919 he became organist at New College, Oxford, and in 1921 he was appointed professor of organ and composition at the Royal College of Music, retaining this position until 1953 while also serving as organist at Christ Church Cathedral beginning in 1929 and at St George's Chapel, Windsor, beginning in 1933. In addition, he was conductor of the Bach Choir from 1926 until 1933 and president of the Royal College of Organists between 1946 and 1948. He was knighted in 1954, and from 1956 until 1961 he was director of musical studies at the Royal School of Church Music.

Harris is best known for his double chorus a cappella motet *Faire is the heaven* set to text by the English poet laureate Edmund Spenser (1552–1599). The texture of the music is reminiscent of Renaissance motets, with a section of imitative polyphony framed by passages of double chorus dialogue, and its harmonic language is characterized by expansive traditional tonalities. Similar scoring, textures, and tonalities are found in other motets, including *Bring us, O Lord God* set to text by John Donne (1572–1631).

REBECCA CLARKE 1886–1979

Clarke was born near London and educated at the Royal Academy of Music beginning in 1903 and at the Royal College of Music beginning in 1907. In 1912 she joined the viola section of the Queen's Hall Orchestra—the first female to be admitted to a professional orchestra in England—and in 1916 she moved to the United States to pursue a concert career. She achieved success with her viola sonata composed in 1919 and her piano trio composed in 1921. However, in 1924 she returned to London, where she felt that she would receive more substantial recognition as a performer and composer. She played in a professional piano quartet during the late 1920s and 1930s, but with little advancement in her compositional and concert career, she returned to the United States at the beginning of World War II, remaining there in relative obscurity until her death at age ninety-three.

In addition to numerous solo songs and sonatas for violin and viola, Clarke composed eight secular part songs and three pieces set to sacred texts, all in a conservative harmonic idiom. The part songs include *Music, when soft voices die* to a poem by Shelley, *A Lover's Dirge* to verses from Shakespeare's *Twelfth Night,* and *The Owl* to Tennyson's poem of the same name. The sacred repertoire is represented by the anthem *He that dwelleth in the secret place* (Psalm 91) for SATB solos and SATB chorus, the Christmas carol *There is no rose of such virtue* for B solo and ATBB chorus, and the Latin motet *Ave Maria* for SSA chorus.

SIR ARTHUR BLISS 1891–1975

Bliss was born in London and was educated at Pembroke College, Cambridge, and the Royal College of Music. In 1921 he was appointed conductor of the Portsmouth Philharmonic Society, and in 1923 he moved to Santa Barbara, California, where he conducted local groups and played piano in chamber ensembles. He returned to London in 1925 and received recognition for several of his compositions, including his choral symphony *Morning Heroes,* and after a brief period back in the United States on the faculty of the University of California at Berkeley, he served as director of music for the BBC. He was knighted in 1950 and named Master of the Queen's Music in 1953.

While recognized mainly for his stage works (film scores, ballets, and incidental music to plays), Bliss was particularly fond of his choral compositions, especially *Morning Heroes.* Composed in 1930 and dedicated "to the memory of my brother Francis Kennard Bliss and all other comrades killed in battle," it is a large-scale work (approximately one hour in duration) scored for speaker (called "orator"), SATB/SATB chorus, and large orchestra. The text is drawn from a wide variety of sources, including "Hector's farewell to Andromache" from book six and "Achilles goes forth to battle" from book nineteen of the *Iliad,* "The City Arming" and "Bivouac's Flame" from Walt Whitman's *Drum Taps,* and "Spring Offensive" by Wilfred Owen. The music is traditional in all respects. Two other notable choral/orchestral works are similar in style and content. *The Beatitudes,* a cantata composed in 1962 that begins with an orchestral prelude subtitled "A troubled world," alternates the nine beatitudes from the Sermon on the Mount with complementary poetry by Henry Vaughan, George Herbert, Dylan Thomas, and Jeremy Taylor. Scoring is for ST solos, SATB chorus (with occasional divisions), SATB semichorus (drawn from the full chorus), and orchestra (including two harps and organ). *Pastoral,* subtitled "Lie strewn the white flocks" and dedicated to Edward Elgar, was composed in 1928 to the poetry of Ben Jonson, John Fletcher, Angelo Ambrogini (better known as Poliziano), and Robert Nichols. Scoring is for A solo, SATB chorus, and orchestra.

Smaller-scale works include seven anthems, the most familiar of which are *Seek the Lord* (1956) for SATB chorus and organ; *Stand up and bless the Lord your God* of 1960 for SB solos, SATB chorus, and organ; *O give thanks unto the Lord* of 1965 for SATB chorus and organ; and *Lord, who shall abide in thy tabernacle* of 1968 for SATB chorus and organ.

HERBERT HOWELLS 1892–1983

Howells was born in a small town in southwestern England and at age eighteen began studying with the organist at Gloucester Cathedral. At twenty he enrolled at the Royal College of Music, where he became Charles Villiers Stanford's most prized composition student (Stanford called him his "son in music"). In 1916 Howells worked as an assistant organist at Salisbury Cathedral and as an editor of Tudor church music, and in 1917 he was appointed to the faculty of the Royal College of Music. He remained at the college until shortly before his death, although he held several other positions as well. In 1936 he succeeded Gustav Holst as director of music at St Paul's Girls' School, Hammersmith; between 1941 and 1945 he was the substitute organist at St John's College, Cambridge; and in 1950 he was appointed professor of music at the University of London. Meanwhile, he received honorary doctorates from Oxford University in 1937 and Cambridge University in 1961, and in 1966 he was named an Honorary Fellow at St John's College, Cambridge.

His choral output consists of ten choral/orchestral works; one hundred anthems, motets, canticles, and hymns; and approximately fifty part songs. His two most acclaimed works were composed shortly after the death, in 1935, of his nine-year-old son Michael but were not released for performance or publication until many years later. *Hymnus Paradisi* was written between 1936 and 1938 and revised for its first performance in 1950 at the Three Choirs Festival in Gloucester. The text, set in five movements after an orchestral Preludio, consists of "Requiem aeternam" from the Latin Requiem Mass, "The Lord is my shepherd" (Psalm 23), "Sanctus – I will lift up mine eyes" from the Latin Mass Ordinary and Psalm 121, "I heard a voice from heaven" from the Anglican Burial Service, and "Holy is the true light" from the Salisbury Diurnal. Relating the composition to the death of his son, Howells wrote that such a loss "might naturally impel a composer . . . to seek release and consolation in language and terms most personal to him. Music may have the power beyond any other medium to offer that relief and comfort. It did so in my case." The other work, *Requiem,* was composed in 1936 from sketches begun in 1932 but not made available for performance until 1980. Its six movements, which include repeats of texts used in *Hymnus Paradisi,* are "Salvator mundi" from the Anglican Burial Service (sung to the English text beginning "O Saviour of the world"), "Psalm 23," "Requiem aeternam," "Psalm 121," "Requiem aeternam" (a different musical setting than that in movement three), and "I heard a voice from heaven."

The music in *Hymnus Paradisi* and *Requiem* is restrained both in tonality and expression (i.e., the harmonies are conservative and the dynamic range is limited). In *Stabat mater* and *Missa Sabrinensis,* two other notable large-scale works, the harmonies are more dissonant and the expressive range more varied; this is especially evident in the mass (the title of which refers to the River Severn in Gloucester).

Other sacred repertoire includes numerous settings of the Magnificat and Nunc dimittis, many composed for specific cathedrals and chapels. The most famous pairing of these two canticles, subtitled "Collegium Regale," was written for King's College, Cambridge, in 1945. Additional noteworthy pairs were for Gloucester Cathedral in 1946; St Paul's Cathedral in 1951; Worcester Cathedral in 1951; St George's Chapel, Windsor, in 1952; and St Luke's church in Dallas, Texas, in 1975. The anthem *Like as the hart* and the Christmas carol/anthem *A spotless rose* are frequently performed and are considered to be exemplars of their genres. The motet *Take him, earth, for cherishing*, composed in 1964 and dedicated "to the honoured memory of John Fitzgerald Kennedy, President of the United States of America," is also highly acclaimed. Its text is from *Hymnus circa Exsequias Defuncti* by Prudentius (348–413).

The secular repertoire is of less interest and popular appeal, although there are several compositions that are performed with some frequency. These include the extended part song *Inheritance* scored for SSAATTBB chorus a cappella, and the two madrigal-like pieces *In youth is pleasure* and *Before me careless, lying*, both scored for SSATB chorus a cappella.

SACRED CHORAL WORKS
SELECTED AND LISTED ACCORDING TO FAMILIARITY

Like as the hart (from Four Anthems of 1941) – SATB chorus and organ – 5:15 minutes. (1) The piece ends with a brief S solo ad lib. that can be sung by the choral first sopranos; (2) most of the anthem is scored for unison and two-part chorus.

Requiem – 1932 – SATB solos and SATB/SATB chorus a cappella – 20 minutes.

A spotless rose – 1919 – B solo and SATB chorus a cappella – 3 minutes.

Magnificat and Nunc dimittis (Collegium Regale) – 1945 – SATB chorus and organ – 9 minutes.

Take him, earth, for cherishing – 1964 – SATB chorus (with divisions) a cappella – 9 minutes.

Hymnus Paradisi – 1936–1938 (revised in 1950) – ST solos, SATB chorus (with divisions), and orchestra – 45 minutes.

Missa Sabrinensis – 1954 – SATB solos, SATB chorus (with divisions), and orchestra – 75 minutes.

Stabat Mater – 1963–1965 – T solo, SATB chorus (with divisions), and orchestra – 52 minutes.

O pray for the peace of Jerusalem (from Four Anthems of 1941) – SATB chorus and organ – 6:30 minutes.

My eyes for beauty pine – 1925 – unison chorus (except for one brief SATB passage) a cappella – 3 minutes.

Here is the little door – 1918 – SATB chorus a cappella – 3:30 minutes.

Mass in the Dorian Mode (also called *Missa Sine Nomine*) – 1912 – SATB chorus a cappella – 22 minutes.

An English Mass – 1955 – SATB chorus and orchestra – 35 minutes.

Magnificat and Nunc dimittis (St Paul's) – 1951 – SATB chorus and organ – 12 minutes.

Magnificat and Nunc dimittis (Gloucester) – 1946 – SATB chorus and organ – 10 minutes.

Haec Dies – 1918 – SSATB chorus a cappella – 3 minutes.

PETER WARLOCK 1894–1930

Warlock, whose name was Philip Heseltine during his youth, was born in London and educated at Eton. In 1913 he entered Oxford University to study classics but, dissatisfied with this choice of school and subject material, he transferred to the University of London the following year. Becoming interested in a musical career, however, he left his studies in 1915 and took a job editing early music at the British Museum. In 1916 he published the first of what would be many articles under the pseudonym Peter Warlock, and during the 1920s he worked for Frederick Delius, whose music he was attracted to beginning in 1909. During the 1920s he also composed numerous songs and wrote several books, including *Thomas Whythorne: An Unknown Elizabethan Composer* and *Carlo Gesualdo: Prince of Venosa: Musician and Murderer.* Warlock had suffered from fits of depression throughout his life, and suicide was suspected when he was found dead in his home of gas poisoning at age thirty-six.

His compositional output consists of twenty-four small-scale choral pieces, the best known of which are settings of texts for Christmas. These include *Benedicamus Domino* and *Cornish Christmas Carol* of 1918 for SSAATTBB chorus a cappella; *Bethlehem Down* and *What Cheer? Good Cheer!* of 1927 for SATB chorus a cappella; *Tyrley Tyrlow* and *The Sycamore Tree* of 1923 for SATB chorus and orchestra; and *Balulalow,* also of 1923, for S solo, SATB chorus, and strings. The motet *Corpus Christi* of 1919 for SSAATB chorus a cappella has also achieved a degree of popularity. All the music is characterized by conservative harmonies, with mild dissonances and occasional chromaticism in the style of Delius.

EDMUND RUBBRA 1901–1986

Rubbra was born in Northampton and began piano lessons at age eight. In 1920 he enrolled at Reading University and the following year at the Royal College of Music, where he studied with Gustav Holst, and in 1925 he began teaching privately. During the 1930s he worked mainly as a music critic and reviewer for several magazines; between 1947 and 1968 he was a lecturer at Worcester College, Oxford; and from 1961 to 1974 he was a professor of composition at Guildhall School of Music and Drama. He received several distinguished awards for his work, including honorary doctorates from Durham University in 1949, Leicester University in 1959, and Reading University in 1960. He was also named Commander of the Order of the British Empire in 1960.

Rubbra composed fifty-nine opuses of choral music, including five masses, twenty-two motets, several cantatas and canticles for Anglican Services, and also several part songs. Best known are the five a cappella motets of opus 37, composed in 1934 and set to texts by the notable British metaphysical poets of the sixteenth and seventeenth centuries—Robert Herrick, Henry Vaughan, John Donne, and Richard Crashaw. For another important work, *Inscape,* Rubbra chose spiritual poems by the nineteenth-century Jesuit priest Gerard Manley Hopkins and divided the poems into five movements—"Pied Beauty," "The Lantern out of Doors," "Spring," "God's Grandeur," and "Epilogue." Other sacred repertoire includes Rubbra's largest choral work, *Lauda Sion,* which is set in three parts to the twenty-four-versed hymn by St Thomas Aquinas; *Missa in honorem Sancti Dominici,* composed in a neo-Renaissance style at the time of

Rubbra's conversion to Catholicism; and *Mass in honour of St Teresa of Avila,* a late work composed in memory of the sixteenth-century Spanish mystic St Teresa.

The secular repertoire is represented by two sets of madrigals (op.51 and op.52) to texts by the English Renaissance poet and composer of lute songs, Thomas Campion. The musical textures, with instances of word painting, are reminiscent of balletts and madrigals by Thomas Weelkes and John Wilbye.

CHORAL WORKS
SELECTED AND LISTED ACCORDING TO FAMILIARITY

Five Motets op.37 – 1934 – mixed chorus a cappella – "Eternitie" (SSAATT-BB) 2:30 minutes, "Vain wits and eyes" (SATB/SATB) 1:30 minutes, "A Hymn to God the Father" (SSAATB) 3 minutes, "The Search" (SATB) 2:30 minutes, and "A Song" (SAB) 2:30 minutes.

Lauda Sion op.110 – 1960 – SB solos and SSATTBB chorus a cappella – 12 minutes.

Missa in honorem Sancti Dominici op.66 – 1948 – SATB chorus a cappella – 15 minutes.

Mass in honour of St Teresa of Avila op.157 – 1981 – SATB chorus a cappella – 8:30 minutes.

Five Madrigals op.51 – 1940 – SATB chorus a cappella – "When to her lute Corinna sings" 2 minutes, "I care not for these ladies" 1:45 minutes, "Beauty is but a painted hell" 2:15 minutes, "It fell on a summer's day" 1 minute, and "Though you are young" 2:30 minutes.

Two Madrigals op.52 – 1941 – SATB chorus a cappella – "Leave prolonging thy distress" 1:45 minutes, and "So sweet is thy discourse" 2 minutes.

Inscape op.122 – 1964–1965 – SATB chorus, strings, and harp or piano – 20 minutes.

GERALD FINZI 1901–1956

Finzi was born in London and studied privately with Edward Bairstow in 1917 and with Reginald Owen Morris in 1925. Between 1930 and 1933 Finzi taught at the Royal Academy of Music, and in 1940 he experienced his first major success with *Dies natalis,* a cantata for high voice and strings. During the 1940s he gained further recognition as a composer, and he also assembled one of the finest and largest personal libraries of English poetry and literature in England. In addition, he collected, edited, and catalogued the manuscripts of Sir Hubert Parry. His activity was reduced during the 1950s as a result of Hodgkin's Disease, and he died in 1956 at age fifty-five.

Finzi composed twenty-five choral works, divided almost equally between settings of sacred and secular texts. Well-known sacred works are represented by the cantata *In terra pax* op.39, the canticle *Magnificat* op.36, and the three anthems of op.27. *In terra pax,* subtitled "A Christmas Scene," is a setting of the Christmas story from Luke 2:8–14 framed with two poems by England's poet laureate Robert Bridges (1844–1930)—"A frosty Christmas Eve" and "But to me heard afar." The work is in an arch or mirror form, with the framing poems scored for baritone soloist, two inner sections of biblical verse scored for chorus, and the center section, the words of the angel to the shepherds, scored for soprano solo. *Magnificat,* set in English without the final Gloria Patri passage, was composed for the choirs of Smith and Amherst colleges in Massachusetts and premiered during the Christmas season of 1952. The first of the anthems, to text by the American poet and minister Edward Taylor (ca.1642–1729), was composed for the marriage of Finzi's sister-in-law; the second anthem, also to a text by Taylor, was composed for St Cecilia's Day services at the church of St Sepulchre, Holborn, and premiered there by the combined choirs of the Chapel Royal, St Paul's Cathedral, Westminster Abbey, and Canterbury Cathedral; the third anthem, to a text by Henry Vaughan (1622–1695), was commissioned by the BBC and premiered during a BBC Evensong broadcast in October 1953.

The secular repertoire includes Finzi's most popular pieces—the *Seven Unaccompanied Partsongs* op.17. Composed to poetry of Robert Bridges and set in a musical style characterized by careful attention to word declamation, the cycle was premiered by the BBC Singers during a broadcast in December 1938. *For St Cecilia* op.30, subtitled "Ceremonial Ode," was commissioned by the St Cecilia's Day Festival Committee for a performance at Royal Albert Hall on November 22, 1947. The text, a part of the commission, is by Edmund Blunden (1896–1974) and makes reference to past English composers who wrote odes to St Cecilia—John Merbecke, William Byrd, John Dowland, Henry Purcell, and George Frideric Handel.

CHORAL WORKS
SELECTED AND LISTED ACCORDING TO FAMILIARITY

Seven Unaccompanied Partsongs op.17 – 1934–1937 – mixed chorus a cappella – "I praise the tender flower" (SATB) 2 minutes, "I have loved flowers that fade" (SAT) 2:15 minutes, "My spirit sang all day" (SATB) 1:30 minutes, "Clear and gentle stream" (SATB) 4 minutes, "Nightingales" (SSATB) 3 minutes, "Haste on, my joys" (SSATB) 2 minutes, and "Wherefore tonight so full of care" (SATB) 3 minutes.

In terra pax op.39 – 1951–1954 – SB solos, SATB chorus (with divisions), strings, harp, and cymbal (arranged for orchestra in 1956) – 17 minutes.

Intimations of Immortality op.29 – 1949–1950 – T solo, SATB chorus, and orchestra – 40 minutes.

For St Cecilia op.30 – 1947 – T solo, SATB chorus (with divisions), and orchestra – 17 minutes.

Magnificat op.36 – 1952 – SATB chorus (with divisions) and organ (arranged for orchestra in 1956) – 9:15 minutes.

Let us now praise famous men op.35 – 1951 – SA or TB chorus and piano – 2:30 minutes.

Three Anthems op.27 – SATB chorus and organ – "My lovely one" (1948) 2:15 minutes, "God is gone up" (1951) 4:15 minutes, and "Welcome sweet and sacred feast" (1953) 7:15 minutes.

SIR WILLIAM WALTON 1902–1983

Walton was born in Oldham, near Manchester, where his father was a local choirmaster and his mother a singer. At age ten the young Walton became a chorister at Christ Church Cathedral, Oxford, and at sixteen he entered the university as a student. He had a keen interest in the music of continental composers and studied scores of Debussy, Ravel, Prokofiev, and Stravinsky on his own, and after leaving the university in 1920 (without a degree), he traveled to Italy. He received public recognition in 1929 for *Façade*, "an Entertainment for reciter and six instruments," characterized by an eclectic mixture of styles, including jazz and popular idioms, and the premiere of his oratorio *Belshazzar's Feast* in 1931 brought him national fame. He composed a number of film scores during the 1930s, and during much of the 1940s he dedicated himself to writing the opera *Troilus and Cressida*. Thereafter, he focused on smaller-scale works and on conducting his compositions throughout Europe. He was awarded seven honorary doctorates, including one from Oxford University in 1942, and he was knighted in 1951.

Walton's choral output is limited, consisting of only twenty works. However, many of these are well known and highly acclaimed—especially the oratorio *Belshazzar's Feast*, which is one of the most famed large-scale choral/orchestral works of the twentieth century. It was initiated by a commission in 1929 from the BBC for a modest work (one soloist, small chorus, and fifteen-piece instrumental ensemble). Walton did not wish to be limited by these specifications, however, and arranged for his yet uncomposed work to be premiered at the Leeds Festival in October 1931. Knowing that the festival was to perform the Berlioz *Requiem* and thus had extra brass instrumentalists, conductor Sir Thomas Beecham told Walton, "You might as well use everything available. You'll never hear the piece again." Walton took the advice and scored *Belshazzar's Feast* for two brass bands (each consisting of three trumpets, three trombones, and tuba) in addition to an already large orchestra and a very large double chorus. The work is divided into three parts, each part in an ABA format and each part separated by an a cappella solo baritone recitative. The first part—with the text from Psalm 137, "By the waters of Babylon"—is the lament of the Israelites in captivity. The second part—with colorfully scored praises to the gods of gold, silver, iron, wood, stone, and brass—is a depiction of Belshazzar's lavish court. The third part—with text, "Then sing aloud to God our strength. Make a joyful noise unto the God of Jacob"—is a hymn of praise to God. Similar extensive scoring occurs in the *Coronation Te Deum*, composed for the investiture ceremony of Queen Elizabeth II in 1953, and in the *Gloria*, composed "for the 125th anniversary of the Huddersfield Choral Society and the 30th year of Sir Malcolm Sargent as its conductor."

Significant small-scale works include the wedding anthem *Set me as a seal upon thine heart*, with text from Song of Solomon; the motet *Where does the uttered music go*, set to a poem by the English poet laureate John Masefield (1878–1967) for the unveiling of the Memorial Window in the church of St Sepulchre, Holborn, and premiered by the BBC singers; *The Twelve*, subtitled "an anthem for the feast of any apostle," set to a poem by W. H. Auden (1907–1973) and premiered by the choir of Christ Church, Oxford, in 1965; *Missa Brevis*, a setting of the Kyrie, Sanctus and Benedictus, Agnus Dei, and Gloria commissioned by the Friends of Coventry Cathedral; and *Cantico del sole*, a motet for the 1974 Cork International Choral Festival set to text in Italian by St Francis of Assisi. In addition, it should be noted that Walton composed four a cappella Christmas carols—*Make we joy in this fest*, *What Cheer*, *King Herod and the Cock*, and *All this time*.

CHORAL WORKS
SELECTED AND LISTED IN CHRONOLOGICAL ORDER
ACCORDING TO DATE OF COMPOSITION

Belshazzar's Feast – 1930–1931 (revised in 1948 and 1957) – B solo, SATB/ SATB chorus, and large orchestra (including saxophone, percussion instruments requiring four players, two harps, organ, and piano ad lib.) – 37 minutes. (1) The choral writing includes several a cappella passages as well as extensive passages for double chorus; (2) the orchestration calls for two additional brass ensembles, each consisting of three trumpets, three trombones, and tuba.

Set me as a seal upon thine heart – 1938 – T solo and SATB chorus a cappella – 3:15 minutes.

Where does the uttered music go – 1945–1946 – SSAATTBB chorus (divided further into six-part S and six-part A) a cappella – 6 minutes.

Coronation Te Deum – 1952–1953 – SATB/SATB chorus and large orchestra (including organ and optional extra brass ensemble of four trumpets, three trombones, and side drums) – 10 minutes. The choral parts call for three separate semichoruses—ATB (all male), SSA *decani* (boys), and SSA *cantoris* (boys).

Gloria – 1960–1961 – ATB solo trio, SSAATTBB chorus, and large orchestra (including optional organ) – 19 minutes.

The Twelve – 1964–1965 – SATB/SATB chorus and orchestra – 11 minutes.

Missa Brevis – 1965–1966 – SSSAATTB solos, SATB/SATB chorus, and organ – 8:30 minutes. The solo writing is for a brief SSS trio and AATTB quintet.

Jubilate Deo – 1971–1972 – SSAATTBB chorus and organ – 3:15 minutes.

Cantico del sole – 1973–1974 – SATB chorus (with divisions) a cappella – 7:30 minutes.

Magnificat and Nunc dimittis – 1974 – SATB chorus and organ – 6 minutes.

SIR LENNOX BERKELEY 1903–1989

Berkeley was born on the outskirts of Oxford and was educated in several distinguished private institutions, including Dragon School, Oxford. In the mid-1920s he studied at Merton College, Oxford, and in 1927 he went to Paris, where he studied with Nadia Boulanger for five years. While in Paris he converted to Catholicism and became interested in sacred Latin genres, and after returning to England in 1932 he worked for the BBC and became friends with Benjamin Britten, to whom he dedicated his *Stabat Mater*. From 1946 to 1968 Berkeley taught composition at the Royal Academy of Music—teaching William Mathias, Peter Maxwell Davies, David Bedford, and John Tavener—and during the 1970s his professional activity decreased as a result of Alzheimer's disease. He was recognized with several notable awards, including an honorary doctorate from Oxford University in 1970, the Papal Knighthood of St Gregory in 1973, and British knighthood in 1974.

His choral output consists of thirty-nine compositions—nine choral/orchestral works and thirty masses, motets, anthems, canticles, and hymns. The choral/orchestral works include the oratorio *Jonah* op.3 of 1935 and the cantata *Domini est terra* op.10 of 1937. The Latin church music is best represented by the a cappella *Mass for Five Voices* (SSATB) op.64, composed for the choir of Westminster Cathedral. Written in a neo-Renaissance point-of-imitation style, with examples of thematic inversion, the work consists of the traditional portions of the Roman Mass Ordinary except the Credo. Other Latin repertoire includes the SATB a cappella motets *Crux fidelis* op.43 no.1 of 1955, *Justorum animae* op.60 no.2 of 1963, and *Ubi caritas et amor* op.96 no.2 of 1980.

Representative examples of the works set to English texts are the anthems *Thou hast made me* op.55 no.1 of 1960 to a text by John Donne, and *Lord, when the sense of thy sweet grace* op.21 no.1 of 1944 to text by Richard Crashaw, both pieces scored for SATB chorus and organ. Also representative is the Christmas carol *I sing of a maiden* scored for SATB chorus a cappella or unison chorus with organ accompaniment.

SIR MICHAEL TIPPETT 1905–1998

Tippett was born in London, where during his youth he attended public schools and studied piano. In 1923 he entered the Royal College of Music; in 1928 he moved to Oxted, Surrey, and conduced local amateur ensembles there for two years; and in 1930 he returned to the Royal College of Music for further studies. During the following several years he conducted the South London Orchestra, and in 1940 he was appointed music director of Morley College. The premiere in 1944 of his oratorio *A Child of our Time* brought him recognition with British audiences and critics, and he also became known for his talks on BBC radio, many of which were published as essays in the collections *Moving into Aquarius, Music of the Angels,* and *Tippett on Music.* In the 1960s he began to travel throughout Europe and other countries (his first visit to the United States was to the Aspen Summer Festival in 1965), and he remained active until his death six days after his ninety-third birthday.

In addition to five operas, including *The Midsummer Marriage* and *The Knot Garden,* he composed nineteen choral works, fifteen of which are published. The most notable of these are his three oratorios—*A Child of Our Time, The Vision of Saint Augustine,* and *The Mask of Time. A Child of Our Time* is based on two occurrences in Tippett's life during 1938. The first was the reading of the novel *Ein Kind unserer Zeit* (in English translation) about the life of Herschel Grynspan, a youth who had killed a German diplomat because of the Nazi treatment of Jews in Germany and who, by this action, had set off the "Kristallnacht," the large-scale harassment and torture of Jews throughout Germany and Austria on November 9 and 10, 1938. Tippett said that he had found Grynspan "another of the many scapegoats I wished to commemorate: the unnamed, deranged, soldier/murderer." The other occurrence in Tippett's life was a course in Jungian psychology, which inspired the composer's ideas about light and darkness, expressed in the motto that heads the oratorio, "The darkness declares the glory of light." The music, which according to Tippett is "direct and simple," is divided into three parts, each further divided into multiple, connected movements. The first part is about the state of oppression in the world, the second part relates the story of Grynspan (although he is not identified), and the third part is a message about salvation: "I would know my shadow and my light, so shall I at last be whole."

The content and arrangement of the movements are based on the Passions of J. S. Bach, with recitatives, arias, choruses, and chorales. For the chorales, which are reflective commentaries, Tippett chose five African-American spirituals—"Steal away," "Nobody knows the trouble I see," "Go down, Moses," "O, by and by," and "Deep river." The oratorio was first performed by the Morley College choirs and the London Philharmonic Orchestra in March 1944.

The Vision of St Augustine was commissioned by the BBC and premiered by the BBC Symphony Orchestra and Chorus in Royal Festival Hall in January 1966. The text, in Latin and Greek, is based on Augustine's "Confessions" and is in three parts—the conversation between the saint and his dying mother, his vision, and his invocation to silence of mind and soul. The musical style is complex, with numerous virtuosic wordless vocalizations that Tippett calls "glossolalia."

The Mask of Time was commissioned by the Boston Symphony Orchestra to celebrate its 100th anniversary. The score was completed in December 1982 and performed in April 1984 by the Tanglewood Festival Chorus and the Boston Symphony Orchestra at Symphony Hall in Boston. The text, assembled by Tippett from a wide variety of sources, "is explicitly concerned with the transcendental. It deals with those fundamental matters that bear upon man, his relationship with Time, his place in the world as we know it and in the mysterious universe at large." The work is in two parts, each with five movements and each with a programmatic description. The first part gives an account of the creation, with strong references to music, including, "The supposed beginning of the cosmos," the "Creation of the World by Music," and a "Dream of the Paradise Garden." The second part describes life on earth, including, "The Triumph of Life," "Hiroshima, mon amour," and "The Singing Will Never Be Done." The musical style is advanced, with tone clusters and complex chords and rhythms, and Tippett includes quotations from some of his previously composed works and from other sources (e.g., the Gregorian chant "Veni Creator Spiritus" and excerpts from Haydn's *The Creation*, Handel's *Messiah*, and Monteverdi's *Ecco mormorar l'onde*).

The smaller-scale sacred works include the double chorus Latin motet *Plebs Angelica* (Angelic host) composed for the choir of Canterbury Cathedral, and the canticle set *Magnificat and Nunc dimittis*, subtitled "Collegium Sancti Johannis Cantabrigiense" and composed for the 450th anniversary of the founding of St John's College, Cambridge. The small-scale secular works are represented by the madrigal *Dance, Clarion Air*, composed for and included in the madrigal collection *A Garland for the Queen* (modeled after the Renaissance collection *The Triumphes of Oriana*), and the folk song arrangements in *Four Songs from the British Isles*, each of which is from a different locale ("Early one morning" from England, "Lilliburlero" from Ireland, "Poortith Cauld" from Scotland, and "Gwenllian" from Wales).

CHORAL WORKS
SELECTED AND LISTED IN CHRONOLOGICAL ORDER
ACCORDING TO DATE OF COMPOSITION

A Child of Our Time – 1939–1941 – SATB solos, SATB chorus (with occasional divisions), and orchestra – 70 minutes.

Two Madrigals – 1942 – SATB chorus a cappella – "The Source" and "The Windhover," both 2:15 minutes.

Plebs Angelica – 1943–1944 – SATB/SATB chorus a cappella – 3 minutes.

The Weeping Babe – 1944 – S solo and SATB chorus a cappella – 4:30 minutes.

Dance, Clarion Air – 1952 – SSATB chorus a cappella – 4 minutes.

Four Songs from the British Isles – 1956 – SATB chorus a cappella – "Early one morning" 3 minutes, "Lilliburlero" 1:30 minutes, "Poortith Cauld" 5:30 minutes, and "Gwenllian" 2:30 minutes.

Crown of the Year – 1958 – SSA solos, SSA chorus, recorders, strings, percussion, and piano – 23 minutes.

Magnificat and Nunc dimittis – 1961 – SATB chorus (with occasional divisions) and organ – 7 minutes. The Nunc dimittis ends with a brief S solo ad lib.

The Vision of Saint Augustine – 1963–1965 – B solo, SATB chorus (with occasional divisions), and large orchestra (including celesta, piano, marimba, and numerous other percussion instruments) – 35 minutes. Much of the choral writing is for two parts.

The Mask of Time – 1980–1982 – SATB solos, SATB chorus (with occasional divisions), and orchestra – 90 minutes.

ELISABETH LUTYENS 1906–1983

Lutyens was born in London, where her father, Sir Edwin Lutyens, was a prominent architect. In 1922 she attended the Ecole Normale in Paris, and several years later the Royal College of Music in London. She excelled as a violist. However, she did not pursue a concert career, nor did she actively promote her compositions, which during the 1930s and 1940s were dodecaphonic and in a chromatic harmonic language. Examples include the *Chamber Concerto #1* of 1939 and the cantata *O saisons, o châteaux* for solo soprano, mandolin, guitar, harp, and strings of 1946. Her work in the 1950s and 1960s combined elements of serial technique with traditional harmonies, as seen in her two most important choral works—*Cantata De amore* for ST solos, mixed chorus, and orchestra of 1957, and *The Essence of our Happinesses* for T solo, mixed chorus, and orchestra of 1968. Other notable works from her total of thirteen choral compositions include the motets *Excerpta Tractatus logicophilosophici* for mixed chorus a cappella of 1953, *The Country of the Stars* for mixed chorus a cappella of 1963, and *The Hymn of Man* for male chorus a cappella of 1965 (arranged for mixed chorus in 1970).

BENJAMIN BRITTEN 1913–1976

Britten was born on St Cecilia's Day (November 22) in Lowestoft, southeast of Norwich. His father was a dentist and his mother a singer and pianist, who declared when Britten was only a child that he would become the fourth famous *B* (i.e., he would achieve the fame and be in the company of Bach, Beethoven, and Brahms). Britten studied the piano and viola during his youth, and by the age of fourteen had composed more than one hundred pieces. At eighteen he began studying composition privately with Frank Bridge, and after two years at a public school in the small town of Holt he enrolled at the Royal College of Music, studying composition there with John Ireland. Britten was attracted to the a cappella choral medium during his student years and, among other works, composed *A Hymn to the Virgin* in 1930 and *A Boy Was Born* between 1932 and 1933. This latter work received its premiere on BBC radio in February 1934. During the 1930s he worked for the BBC and composed a number of film scores, and he also met the poet W. H. Auden, with whom he would collaborate for the remainder of his life, and the singer Peter Pears, who would become his life partner.

Britten achieved his first major recognition as a composer with his orchestral *Variations on a Theme of Frank Bridge,* performed in 1937 at the Salzburg Festival, and his *Piano Concerto,* dedicated to Lennox Berkeley and premiered at a BBC Promenade Concert in 1938. In 1939 Britten and Pears sailed to North America, visiting Canada first and then spending approximately a year each in New York and California, and while in the United States the two gave numerous recitals and Britten composed two important works for Pears—*Les Illuminations* in 1939 and *Seven Sonnets of Michelangelo* in 1940. During the return journey to England in 1942 Britten composed two important choral works—*Hymn to St Cecilia* and *A Ceremony of Carols.* Once back in England, he focused on composing operas, and in 1945 he received critical acclaim for *Peter Grimes,* premiered at Sadler's Wells. Other operas followed in quick succession, including *The Rape of Lucretia,* which premiered at Glyndebourne in 1946; *Billy Budd,* which premiered at Covent Garden in 1951; and *Gloriana,* composed for the coronation celebrations of Queen Elizabeth II in 1953. Britten also continued to compose works for Pears (e.g., the *Serenade* for tenor, horn, and strings in 1943 and the *Holy Sonnets of John Donne* for high voice and piano in 1945) and to tour with him throughout Europe, Asia, India, and Russia. In addition, Britten fulfilled important commissions such as the *War Requiem* for the newly built Coventry Cathedral, and he continued to compose operas (his last being *Death in Venice* from 1971 to 1973). In April 1973 he suffered a stroke during an operation to replace a weak heart valve, and until his death in 1976 at age sixty-three his health declined and his mobility was impaired. In recognition of his extraordinary contributions to the musical life of England, he was given the country's highest honor—Life Peer, with the title Baron Britten of Aldeburgh.

Britten's choral output is extensive, consisting of forty works that range from large-scale choral/orchestral compositions to a cappella and piano-accompanied part songs, and liturgical pieces and anthems for the Anglican Church to concert cantatas set to sacred and secular texts. The most important of the choral/orchestral works and one of the most acclaimed works of the twentieth century is the *War Requiem,* which has been compared in artistic stature to the Bach Passions, Beethoven *Missa solemnis,* and Brahms *Ein deutsches Requiem* and which thus ranks Britten with these composers as predicted by his mother. Britten's work is scored for three distinct ensembles—mixed chorus and orchestra with soprano soloist, tenor and baritone soloiosts with chamber orchestra, and boys' chorus with organ—that ideally should be separated spatially in performance. The text of the traditional Latin Mass of the Dead (Requiem aeternam, Dies irae, Offertorium, Sanctus, Agnus Dei, and Libera me) is sung by the mixed chorus, soprano soloist, and boys' chorus, while the tenor and baritone soloiosts sing textually compatible poems by Wilfred Owen (1893–1918), the British poet and soldier who was killed in action one week before World War I ended. The music for the Latin and English texts alternates throughout the work until the end of the final movement, when "Let us sleep now" and "In paradisum dedu-

cant te Angeli" (May the angels lead you into paradise) are sung simultaneously by all performing forces. The solos were written for specific singers, each representing a different country
engaged in war—soprano Galina Vishnevskaya (wife of cellist and conductor Mstislav Rostropovich) from Russia, baritone Dietrich Fischer-Dieskau from Germany, and tenor Peter Pears
from England. To further emphasize the war aspect of the Requiem, Britten dedicated it "in loving memory" to four British soldiers who died during World War II, and he also headed the work
with the motto by Owen, "My subject is War, and the pity of War. The Poetry is in the pity . . . All
a poet can do today is warn." The music is characterized by the tritone interval (augmented
fourth) and scalar passages that ascend in one tonal area and descend in another. As examples,
the tritone is prominently played by bells at the beginning, in the middle, and at the end of the
work, and scalar passages are the main compositional element of the Agnus Dei. In addition,
movements of the Requiem often begin with large sections of music that alternate between performing forces and end with fragmented sections that alternate frequently and in close proximity.

Several of the cantata-like works are, like the *War Requiem,* highly acclaimed for their artistic stature. In addition, they are frequently performed in both churches and concert halls. *A Ceremony of Carols* is a setting of nine Medieval and Renaissance Christmas poems framed by the
Gregorian chant "Hodie Christus natus est" (Today Christ is born). The music is characterized
by canonic and echo vocal effects and colorful harp sonorities. *Rejoice in the Lamb,* subtitled a
"Festival Cantata," is set to passages from *Jubilate Agno* by Christopher Smart (1722–1771), who
wrote the poem while confined to an insane asylum. Smart's text used by Britten begins with
the naming of selected characters from the Old Testament (e.g., Nimrod, Ishmael, and Daniel)
who are identified with animals (e.g., a leopard, tiger, and lion) in praising God; the end text lists
musical instruments with clever and random associated rhymes. The poem for *A Hymn to St
Cecilia,* which has as its focus the thrice-stated verse that begins "Blessed Cecilia, appear in visions to all musicians, appear and inspire," was written for and dedicated to Britten by Auden.
Britten set the poem in three comparable sections—the first featuring *fauxbourdon*-like passages over a slower-moving cantus firmus, the second featuring fast-moving imitative phrases
above a slower-moving cantus firmus, and the third constructed of imitative phrases over a
ground bass.

Three additional cantatas are significant, although less frequently performed. *Saint Nicolas*
combines text about the life of the Bishop of Myra (patron saint of children, seamen, and travelers) with two well-known hymns—"All people that on earth do dwell" and "God moves in a
mysterious way"; *Cantata Misericordium,* composed for the centenary of the Red Cross in 1963,
is set to a text in Latin about compassion based on the parable of the Good Samaritan; and *Cantata Academica Carmen Basiliense,* composed for the 500th anniversary of the founding of the
University of Basle, is set to a text in Latin in praise of the city of Basle and its university, with
passages from the university's charter.

The most popular of the small-scale sacred works are *A Hymn to the Virgin,* set to Medieval-
era texts in both English and Latin (chorus one is in English, while chorus two is in Latin); *Festival Te Deum,* set in three sections, the first and third of which are chant-like and impart an
ABA' form; *Jubilate Deo,* which is also in an ABA' form—the A sections characterized by dialogue between the high and low voices and the slower B section reminiscent of the treble solo
in *Rejoice in the Lamb;* and two Christmas works—*A Shepherd's Carol* and *Chorale*—composed
to texts by W. H. Auden for a December 1944 BBC radio broadcast entitled *A Poet's Christmas.*

A Shepherd's Carol is in verse/refrain format, the verses written for solo voices as recitatives and the refrain set to the text "O lift your little pinkie and touch the winter sky, love's all over the mountains where the beautiful go to die." *Chorale*, subtitled "After an old French Carol," is in three verses, the first and third of which are homophonic (like a chorale) and the second of which is imitative.

The part songs include three significant collections—*Five Flower Songs*, set to poetry of Robert Herrick (1591–1674), George Crabbe (1754–1832), and John Clare (1793–1864), plus an anonymous folk text; *A. M. D. G.*, set to seven poems by Gerard Manley Hopkins (1844–1889); and *Sacred and Profane*, subtitled "Eight Medieval Lyrics." Similarly, the music composed for the Anglican Church includes three famous and frequently performed pieces—*A Hymn to the Virgin*, *Festival Te Deum*, and *Jubilate Deo*.

CHORAL WORKS
SELECTED AND LISTED IN CHRONOLOGICAL ORDER
ACCORDING DATE OF COMPOSITION

A Hymn to the Virgin – 1930 – SATB/SATB chorus a cappella – 3:15 minutes. The second chorus is to be sung either by a semichorus or by a solo quartet.

Two Part Songs – 1932 (revised in 1933) – SATB chorus and piano – "I Lov'd a Lass" 3:30 minutes and "Lift Boy" 4:30 minutes.

A Boy Was Born – 1932–1933 – boy solo, unison boys' chorus, and SSAATTBB chorus a cappella (or with organ accompaniment ad lib.) – 32 minutes.

A. M. D. G. – 1939 – SATB chorus a cappella – "Prayer I" 1:45 minutes, "Rosa Mystica" 3:30 minutes, "God's Grandeur" 2:45 minutes, "Prayer II" 4 minutes, "O Deus, ego amo te" 1:45 minutes, "The Soldier" 2 minutes, and "Heaven-Haven" 1:15 minutes. The title of the work is the motto of the Jesuit order of priests that stands for *Ad majorem Dei gloriam* (To the greater glory of God).

Hymn to St Cecilia – 1941–1942 – SATB solos and SSATB chorus a cappella – 12 minutes. The solo writing consists of one brief phrase for each of the soloists.

A Ceremony of Carols – 1942 – boy solo, SSA chorus of trebles (boys), and harp – 22 minutes. The work exists in an SATB arrangement not made or approved by Britten.

Rejoice in the Lamb – 1943 – SATB solos, SATB chorus, and organ – 18 minutes.

The Ballad of Little Musgrave and Lady Barnard – 1943 – TBB chorus and piano – 9 minutes.

Festival Te Deum – 1944 – S solo, SATB chorus, and organ – 7 minutes. The solo consists of two brief passages.

A Shepherd's Carol – 1944 – SATB solos and SATB chorus a cappella – 4 minutes.

Chorale – 1944 – SSAATTBB chorus a cappella – 4:30 minutes.

Saint Nicolas – 1947–1948 – boy and T solos, SATB chorus, SA semichorus, congregation, piano duet, strings, percussion, and organ – 50 minutes. (1) The boy solo portrays the young Saint Nicolas in three brief passages, all identical and sung from a balcony accompanied by organ; (2) scoring is for three additional solo boys singing a brief passage in unison, also sung from a balcony and accompanied by organ; (3) the SA semichorus is to be placed away from the main chorus, preferably in a balcony other than that used by the boy soloists; (4) the congregation joins the other forces in two hymns.

Spring Symphony – 1948–1949 – SAT solos, SATB chorus, boys' chorus, and large orchestra (including two harps) – 42 minutes.

Five Flower Songs – 1950 – SATB chorus a cappella – "To Daffodils" 2 minutes, "The Succession of the Four Sweet Months" 1:45 minutes, "Marsh Flowers" 2:15 minutes, "The Evening Primrose" 2:30 minutes, and "The Ballad of Green Broom" 2:30 minutes.

Choral Dances from Gloriana – 1954 – SATB chorus a cappella – "Time" 1:30 minutes, "Concord" 2:15 minutes, "Time and Concord" 1:30 minutes, "Country Girls" (SA chorus) 1 minute, "Rustics and Fishermen" (TTBB chorus) 1 minute, and "Final Dance of Homage" 2:15 minutes.

Hymn to Saint Peter – 1955 – S solo or S semichorus, SATB chorus, and organ – 6 minutes.

Antiphon – 1956 – SSS solos or semichorus, SATB chorus, and organ – 5:30 minutes.

Cantata Academica Carmen Basiliense – 1959 – SATB solos, SATB chorus, and orchestra (including celesta ad lib. and piano) – 20 minutes.

Missa Brevis – 1959 – SSA treble solos, SSA treble chorus, and organ – 10 minutes.

Jubilate Deo – 1961 – SATB chorus and organ – 2:30 minutes.

War Requiem – 1960–1961 – STB solos, SATB chorus (with occasional divisions), SA boys' chorus, chamber orchestra requiring twelve players, and large orchestra (including piano, organ, and percussion instruments requiring four players) – 82 minutes. The performers are divided into three distinct groups—S solo, SATB chorus, and large orchestra in one group; TB solos and chamber orchestra in another group; and boys' chorus and organ in a third group—each group to be spatially separated in performance and each requiring its own conductor.

A Hymn of St Columba (Regis regum rectissimi) – 1962 – SATB chorus and organ – 2 minutes.

Cantata Misericordium – 1963 – TB solos, SATB chorus, piano, harp, timpani, and strings – 20 minutes. The strings are scored for solo string quartet plus an additional ensemble of strings.

Sacred and Profane – 1974–1975 – SSATB chorus a cappella – "St Godric's Hymn" 1:30 minutes, "I mon waxe wod" 30 seconds, "Lenten is come" 2:30 minutes, "The long night" 1:15 minutes, "Yif ic of luve can" 2:30 minutes, "Carol" 1:30 minutes, "Ye that pasen by" 2:15 minutes, and "A death" 3 minutes.

JOHN JOUBERT B.1927

Joubert was born in Cape Town, South Africa, where he attended the South African College of Music. He continued his musical studies at the Royal Academy of Music in London beginning in 1946, between 1950 and 1962 he served on the faculty of the University of Hull, and from 1969 to 1986 he taught at the University of Birmingham. He was recognized throughout his career for his many choral works, and in 1991 he was awarded an honorary doctorate from Durham University.

His choral output consists of eleven choral/orchestral works and thirty-eight smaller-scale compositions. The larger works include the cantata *The Martyrdom of St Alban* op.59, the oratorio *The Raising of Lazarus* op.67, and two choral symphonies—*Gong-Tormented Sea* op.96 and *The Choir Invisible* op.54. The smaller-scale pieces, the most popular of Joubert's compositions, include the Christmas carols *Torches* op.7a and *There is no rose* op.14, the award-winning anthem *O Lorde, the Maker of Al Thing* op.7b, and the cycle of four motets for Advent *Rorate coeli* op.107. The harmonic language of the early works is traditional, with instances of mild dissonance; the language of the later music is tonal, although expanded in dissonance and harmonic coloration.

CHORAL WORKS
SELECTED AND LISTED ACCORDING TO FAMILIARITY

Torches op.7a – 1952 – SATB chorus and organ – 1:30 minutes.

O Lorde, the Maker of Al Thing op.7b – 1952 – SATB chorus and organ –
5:15 minutes.

There is no Rose op.14 – 1954 – SATB chorus a cappella – 2:30 minutes.

Rorate coeli op.107 – 1985 – SATB solos and SATB chorus (with divisions)
a cappella – 15 minutes. The solo writing consists of a brief S solo, brief
passages for SATB and SSA with chorus, and an extended ST duet with
chorus.

Gong-Tormented Sea op.96 – 1982 – B solo, SATB chorus (with divisions),
and large orchestra – 38 minutes.

South of the Line op.109 – 1985 – SB solos, SATB chorus (with divisions),
two pianos, and percussion (requiring five players) – 28 minutes.

THEA MUSGRAVE B.1928

Musgrave was born in Midlothian County, Scotland, and received her initial musical education at the University of Edinburgh. Further studies were with Nadia Boulanger at the Paris Conservatoire and with Aaron Copland at the Berkshire Music Center in Tanglewood, Massachusetts. Musgrave moved to London in 1954 and that year was recognized for her *Cantata for a Summer's Day* scored for speaker, SATB solos, flute, clarinet, string quartet, and string bass. Her *Clarinet Concerto* of 1968 and *Horn Concerto* of 1971 brought additional recognition, and in 1972 she moved to the United States, where since 1970 she had been serving as a visiting professor at the University of California, Santa Barbara. While in the United States she composed a number of operas, including *Mary, Queen of Scots* (1975–1977), *A Christmas Carol* (1978–1979), *Harriet, the Woman Called*

Moses (1984), *Simón Bolívar* (1989–1992), and *Pontalba, a Louisiana Legacy* (2003). She also taught at Queens College of the City University of New York (1987–2002) and conducted her works with the Philadelphia Orchestra, San Francisco Symphony, Hong Kong Philharmonic, and Jerusalem Symphony. Tributes to her have included honorary doctorates from Old Dominion University in Virginia, New England Conservatory, Smith College, and the University of Glasgow, and she was also named Commander of the Order of the British Empire.

Musgrave's choral output consists of twenty works, most of which are scored for a cappella chorus. The early compositions, such as the *Four Madrigals* set to poems by Sir Thomas Wyatt (1503–1542), are traditional in harmonic language and texture. The later compositions are more modern and incorporate avant-garde techniques. In *Rorate coeli,* for example, which is a setting of two intertwined poems ("Rorate coeli desuper" and "Done is a battle on the dragon black") by the Scottish poet William Dunbar (ca.1460–ca.1520), there are passages of aleatoric rhythm, indeterminate pitch, sprechstimme, tone clusters, and choral glissandos. The three sets of *On the Underground* make use of minimal avant-garde techniques, although they are written in an advanced tonal idiom. The title of the sets comes from a public arts program initiated in 1986 that displays poems on the cars of the British subway system. Musgrave's selections of poetry are random, with no intended continuity. For instance, Set one, subtitled "On gratitude, love and madness," contains the poems "Benediction" by James Berry (b.1924), "Her Anxiety" by W. B. Yeats (1865–1939), "Lady 'Rogue' Singleton" by Stevie Smith (1902–1971), "Much Madness is divinest Sense" by Emily Dickinson (1830–1886), "Aunt Jennifer's Tigers" by Adrienne Rich (b.1929), and "Sometimes" by Sheenagh Pugh (b.1950).

CHORAL WORKS
SELECTED AND LISTED ACCORDING TO FAMILIARITY

Four Madrigals – 1953 – SATB chorus a cappella – 6 minutes.

Rorate coeli – 1974 (revised in 1976) – SSAATTBB solos and SSAATTBB chorus a cappella – 12 minutes.

O caro mé sonno – 1978 – SATB chorus (with divisions) a cappella – 2 minutes.

On the Underground – 1994–1995 – Set 1, SSAATTBB chorus a cappella, 9:30 minutes; Set 2, SATB chorus a cappella, 5 minutes; and Set 3, ST solos and SSAATTBB chorus a cappella, 12 minutes. There are also brief solo passages for SSA in Set 3.

For the Time Being: Advent – 1986 – speaker and SATB chorus (with divisions) a cappella – 26 minutes.

KENNETH LEIGHTON 1929–1988

Leighton was born in Wakefield, northeast of Manchester, and sang as a chorister at Wakefield Cathedral. He studied both classics and music at Queen's College, Oxford, and in 1951 worked with Goffredo Petrassi in Rome. Between 1953 and 1955 Leighton taught at Leeds University, from 1955 until 1968 he was on the faculty of the University of Edinburgh, and in 1968 he returned to Oxford as professor of music at Worcester College. Throughout his career he was awarded numerous prizes, including the Cobbett Medal in 1968, and in 1977 he received an honorary doctorate from the University of St Andrews.

While his orchestral compositions employ modern harmonic elements, the choral music is tonal and only mildly dissonant. Much of his extensive choral output is devoted to a cappella or organ-accompanied works set to sacred texts. Included are several well-known motets and anthems as well as seven masses—*Missa Sancti Thomae* of 1962, *Mass* of 1964, *Missa Brevis* of 1967, *Sarum Mass* of 1972, *Missa Cornelia* and *Missa Sancti Petri* of 1979, and *Missa Christi* of 1988. Notable exceptions to the sacred repertoire are the *Six Elizabethan Lyrics* of 1972 for S solo and SSAA chorus a cappella, and the *Symphony #2* of 1974, subtitled "Sinfonia mistica," for S solo, mixed chorus, and orchestra.

CHORAL WORKS
SELECTED AND LISTED ACCORDING TO FAMILIARITY

Drop, drop, slow tears – 1961 – SATB chorus (with divisions) a cappella – 3:15 minutes. This anthem, published separately, is the fourth movement of *Crucifixus pro nobis*.

Lord, when the sense of thy sweet grace – 1978 – S solo and SATB chorus (with divisions) a cappella – 5 minutes.

Quam dilecta (Psalm 84:1–9, 12, 13) – 1966–1967 – S solo and SSATB chorus a cappella – 7 minutes.

Let all the world in every corner sing – 1965 – SATB chorus and organ – 3:30 minutes.

Lully, lulla, thou little tiny child – 1948 – S solo and SATB chorus a cappella – 3 minutes.

Give me the wings of faith – 1962 – SB solos, SATB chorus, and organ – 4 minutes.

Missa Brevis – 1967 – SATB chorus a cappella – 13 minutes. (1) The mass is a setting in English of the Kyrie, Sanctus, Benedictus, Agnus Dei, and Gloria plus two responses to the commandments; (2) the soprano choral parts occasionally divide into *decani* and *cantoris* ensembles.

Mass – 1964 – SATB solos, SATB/SATB chorus, and organ – 25 minutes. The mass is a cappella except for the Credo.

ALUN HODDINOTT 1929–2008

Hoddinot was born in southern Wales and during his youth studied violin and viola. In 1946 he joined the viola section of the newly founded National Youth Orchestra of Wales, and several years later he enrolled at University College, Cardiff. He joined the faculty of the Welsh College of Music and Drama in 1951, and in 1959 he returned to University College, Cardiff, as a faculty member—first as a lecturer in music and in 1967 as professor of composition. His professional accomplishments include cofounding the Cardiff Festival of Twentieth Century Music, and his honors include being named Commander of the Order of the British Empire.

In addition to five operas, ten symphonies, and numerous concertos and sonatas, Hoddinott has composed sixty-four opuses of choral music, or approximately one hundred individual works. Most of these are divided between oratorios and cantatas scored for chorus and orchestra, and motets and anthems scored for a cappella chorus or chorus with keyboard accompaniment; his choral output also includes several collections of Welsh folk song arrangements and a few secular part songs. The most noteworthy of the large-scale works is the cantata *Sinfonia fidei*, commissioned by the Llandaff Festival in association with the Welsh Arts Council and set in three movements to three Medieval texts—"Sequentia de Sancto Michaele" (A Sequence for St Michael), "Ave maris stella" (Hail, star of the sea), and "Vexilla regis prodeunt" (The banners of the king advance). An important collection of part songs commissioned by the Cardiff Festival of Choirs in 1978, *Dulcia iuventutis* is also a setting of three Medieval texts in three movements—"Nunc est bibendum" (Now is the time for drinking), "Novus amor" (New love), and "Tenera iuventa" (Tender youth). Other significant works include two settings of Welsh folk legends—*An apple tree and a pig*, about the warrior poet Myrddin (Merlin), and *Black Bart*, about the sea captain Barti Ddu, who was victorious in battle against Spanish sailors. The musical style of all the works is rhythmically and harmonically conservative, with a prevalence of pantonal sonorities.

CHORAL WORKS
SELECTED AND LISTED ACCORDING TO FAMILIARITY

Puer natus – 1972 – SATB chorus (with divisions) and organ – 2:30 minutes.

Sinfonia fidei – 1977 – ST solos, SSAATTBB chorus, and large orchestra – 22 minutes.

Dives and Lazarus – 1965 – SB solos, SATB chorus (with occasional divisions), and chamber ensemble of two flutes, oboe, two clarinets, bassoon, two trumpets, trombone, timpani, piano duet, and strings – 16 minutes. The instrumentation is also arranged for organ, piano duet, and strings.

Dulcia iuventutis (The joys of youth) – 1978 – SATB chorus (with divisions) and piano duet – 10 minutes.

Out of the deep – 1970 – SATB chorus (with divisions to SSSAATTTBB) a cappella – 12 minutes.

An apple tree and a pig – 1968 – SATB chorus (with divisions) a cappella – 10 minutes.

Black Bart (Barti Ddu) – 1968 – SATB chorus (with occasional divisions) and orchestra – 18 minutes.

WILLIAM MATHIAS 1934–1992

Mathias was born in southwestern Wales and attended the University College of Wales in Aberystwyth and the Royal Academy of Music in London. Between 1959 and 1968 he served on the faculty of University College of North Wales in Bangor, in 1968 he taught at the University of Edinburgh, and in 1970 he returned to University College of North Wales in Bangor as professor of composition. Meanwhile, he became a Fellow of the Royal Academy of Music in 1965 and he earned a doctorate in music from the University of Wales in 1966. In 1972 he founded the North Wales Music Festival at St Asaph Cathedral, and during the following years until his untimely death at age fifty-seven, he was active filling commissions from institutions throughout the British Isles and the United States. For his accomplishments he was named Commander of the Order of the British Empire in 1985 and was awarded an honorary doctorate from Westminster Choir College in Princeton, New Jersey, in 1987.

Mathias composed in excess of ninety opuses of choral music in addition to several hymn tunes. Most of these works are settings of sacred texts accompanied by organ and characterized by traditional diatonic harmonies and uncomplicated rhythmic textures. The most popular of the settings in English is *Let the people praise thee, O God*, composed for the marriage of Prince Charles and Princess Diana in 1981. The popular Latin works include two sets of motets—*Ave Rex*, subtitled "A Carol Sequence" and consisting of the Medieval-era poems "Ave rex," "Alleluya, a new work is come on hand," "There is no rose of such virtue," and "Sir Christèmas"; and *Rex Gloriae*, the four individual pieces of which are identified below. The *Missa Aedis Christi*, dedicated to the memory of Sir William Walton, is a setting of the Kyrie, Gloria, Sanctus, Benedictus, and Agnus Dei.

CHORAL WORKS
SELECTED AND LISTED ACCORDING TO FAMILIARITY

Let the people praise thee, O God op.87 (Psalm 67) – 1981 – SATB chorus (with divisions) and organ – 5 minutes.

Ave Rex op.45 – 1969 – SATB chorus (with divisions) and organ – 12 minutes. The work is also scored for orchestra (including organ).

Lux aeterna op.88 – 1982 – SAA solos, boys' chorus, SATB chorus (with divisions), and orchestra (including harp, piano, and organ) – 58 minutes.

Rex Gloriae op.83 – 1980 – SATB chorus (with divisions) a cappella – "Laetentur coeli" 3 minutes, "Victimae paschali" 3 minutes, "O nata lux" 1 minute, and "O rex gloriae" 2 minutes.

Salve regina op.96 no.5 – 1986 – TTBB or SATB chorus – 3 minutes.

Nativity Carol op.77 no.3 – 1978 – SATB chorus and organ – 3 minutes.

Missa Aedis Christi op.92 – 1983 – SATB chorus (with divisions) and organ – 15 minutes.

SIR PETER MAXWELL DAVIES B.1934

Davies was born in the vicinity of Manchester and attended both the Royal Manchester College of Music and the University of Manchester. Further studies were in Rome with Goffredo Petrassi. From 1959 to 1962 he was director of music at the Cirencester Grammar School, and between 1962 and 1965 he worked in the United States with Roger Sessions and Milton Babbitt at Princeton University. Upon returning to England, he wrote music for and participated with the

Pierrot Players and the Fires of London—both of which were instrumental ensembles devoted to modern music. He also taught at the Darlington Summer School and became its artistic director in 1979. He founded the St Magnus Festival in Orkney, where he had moved in 1971, and between 1985 and 1994 he was associate conductor and composer-in-residence of the Scottish Chamber Orchestra. He was named Commander of the Order of the British Empire in 1981 and was knighted in 1987.

His compositional output is extensive, consisting of twenty-eight stage works (including the opera *Taverner*), eight symphonies, several tone poems and concertos, numerous chamber works, and twenty-two publications of choral music. Most of the early works are motets set to medieval Latin texts and characterized by sharp dissonances and pointillistic textures. The later works include large-scale cantatas such as *Solstice of Light* of 1979 and *Corpus Christi, with Cat and Mouse* of 1993.

CHORAL WORKS
SELECTED AND LISTED ACCORDING TO FAMILIARITY

Ave Maria – Hail, blessed flower – 1961 – SATB chorus a cappella – 2 minutes.

Five Motets – 1959 – SATB solos, SATB/SATB chorus, and chamber orchestra (revised in 1962 for sixteen instruments) – "Spes, via, vita" 3:30 minutes, "Alma redemptoris mater" 4 minutes, "O lux quam non videt alia lux" 6 minutes, "Nec mora, carnifices Gemini" 2 minutes, and "Attollite portas principes" 2:30 minutes.

Veni sancte spiritus – 1963 – SAB solos, SATB chorus (with divisions), and chamber orchestra – 20 minutes.

Four Carols from "O Magnum Mysterium" – 1960 – SATB chorus a cappella – "O magnum mysterium" 1:30 minutes, "Haylle, comly and clene" 1:15 minutes, "Alleluia, pro virgine Maria" 2:15 minutes, and "The fader of heven" 1:30 minutes.

SIR JOHN TAVENER B.1944

Tavener was born in London, where his father was organist at St Andrew's Presbyterian Church in Frognal, Hampstead, and where he attended Highgate School along with fellow classmate John Rutter. In 1961 Tavener became organist at St John's Presbyterian Church in Kensington, and in 1962 he entered the Royal Academy of Music, studying composition there with Sir Lennox Berkeley. During the next several years Tavener was recognized for his opera *The Cappemakers*, song cycle *Three Holy Sonnets of John Donne*, and cantatas *Cain and Abel* and *The Whale*, the latter work calling for a wide variety of nontraditional vocal sounds. With the composition of the *Celtic Requiem* in 1969 he began to compose in block chords with static rhythmic textures, and after his conversion to the Greek Orthodox faith in 1977 this musical style became fixed and characteristic of all his later works. He has received numerous commissions and has become one of the most recognized composers in modern times; for his contributions to the musical life of England he was knighted in 2000.

Tavener's choral output numbers more than one hundred works, the vast majority of which are settings of sacred texts. Several of the large-scale compositions are massive in terms of scoring and length. For instance, *Ultimos ritos* of 1972, which is based on the Crucifixus of Bach's *B minor Mass,* calls for five male speakers in addition to soloists, mixed chorus, orchestra, and electronic tape, and *The Veil of the Temple* of 2003 requires four mixed choruses and multiple orchestral ensembles and lasts approximately seven hours. Other large-scale compositions are more standard in terms of performing forces and duration. The *Celtic Requiem* is scored for S solo, children's chorus, mixed chorus, and orchestra, and the oratorio *We shall see him as he is* calls for STT solos, mixed chorus, two trumpets, two timpani, organ, and strings. According to Tavener, this latter work, which was commissioned by the Cheshire County Council for the 900th anniversary of Chester Cathedral, is "constructed as a series of ikons with a refrain ('We shall see him as he is'). . . . Each ikon depicts a different event in the life of Christ, as seen through the eyes of His beloved apostle, John."

Many of the smaller-scale works are a cappella, the best known being *The Lamb* and *Song for Athene.* The first of these pieces, to text by William Blake (1757–1827), is a Christmas carol/anthem that was premiered by the choir of King's College, Cambridge, during its Festival of Nine Lessons and Carols on December 24, 1982. *Song for Athene,* subtitled "Alleluia, may flights of angels sing thee to thy rest," was commissioned by the BBC and premiered by the BBC Singers in 1994. It was made famous, however, when it was performed at the funeral service for Princess Diana in Westminster Abbey on September 6, 1997. *Two Hymns to the Mother of God* was written in memory of Tavener's mother and was premiered by the choir of Winchester Cathedral in December 1985, and *A Village Wedding* was commissioned by the Vale of Glamorgan Festival and was premiered by the Hilliard Ensemble in August 1992. Set to a text that describes a traditional wedding in Greece, this latter work was made popular by the American chamber ensemble Chanticleer.

CHORAL WORKS
SELECTED AND LISTED ACCORDING TO FAMILIARITY

The Lamb – 1982 – SATB chorus a cappella – 3:30 minutes.

Song for Athene – 1993 – SATB chorus (with divisions to SSAATTTBBBB) a cappella – 7 minutes.

Two Hymns to the Mother of God – 1985 – "A Hymn to the Mother of God" for SATB/SATB chorus (with divisions to SAAATBBB/SAAATBBB) a cappella, 3:30 minutes, and "Hymn for the Dormition of the Mother of God" for SSATBBB chorus a cappella, 3 minutes.

A Village Wedding – 1992 – ATTB voices a cappella – 9:30 minutes.

Ikon of Light – 1984 – SATB/SATB chorus and string trio – 42 minutes.

JOHN RUTTER B.1945

Rutter was born in London and educated at Highgate School, where one of his classmates was John Tavener, and at Clare College, Cambridge. He taught for a short period of time at the University of Southampton, in 1975 he returned to Clare College as director of music, and in 1979 he left the college and founded the Cambridge Singers, with which he toured and made numerous recordings of English repertoire. Most notable among the recordings, many of which are on the Collegium label that Rutter founded in 1984, are retrospectives of the English madrigal (*Flora gave me fairest flowers*) and part song (*There is sweet music*) as well as music of the English Church (*Faire is the heaven* and *Hail, gladdening light*). In addition to his work with the Cambridge Singers and his many guest conducting appearances with choral ensembles in England and the United States, he has served as editor of a number of choral collections published by Oxford University Press, including *Carols for Choirs* and *100 Carols for Choirs* (shared with Sir David Willcocks) and *European Sacred Music* (shared with Clifford Bartlett). His numerous choral compositions, written in a tonal musical style accessible to amateur singers, have made Rutter one of the most performed composers of modern times.

Of the larger-scale popular works, *Gloria* is a setting of the traditional Latin text from the Roman Mass Ordinary divided into three movements; *Requiem* combines portions of the Latin Mass for the Dead (Requiem aeternam, Pie Jesu, Sanctus, Agnus Dei, and Lux aeterna) with Psalms 130 (Out of the deep) and 23 (The Lord is my shepherd); *Magnificat* interpolates a fifteenth-century English carol (Of a rose, a lovely rose) and the Sanctus into the standard Latin text; and *Te Deum* uses an English translation of the traditional Latin text. The popular smaller-scale works include several Christmas carol/anthems (e.g., *Candlelight Carol, What sweeter music, Shepherd's Pipe Carol, Nativity Carol,* and *Star Carol*) and a large number of anthems—all of equal quality and appeal. Also popular are several works set to secular texts—*When Icicles Hang* (especially the movements "Good ale" and "Blow, blow, thou winter wind") for mixed chorus and orchestra, *Fancies* for mixed chorus and chamber orchestra, and *Five Childhood Lyrics* for mixed chorus a cappella.

LARGER-SCALE CHORAL WORKS
SELECTED AND LISTED ACCORDING TO FAMILIARITY

Gloria – 1974 – SATB chorus (with divisions), brass ensemble (four trumpets, three trombones, and tuba), timpani and percussion (two or three players), and organ – 18 minutes. The second movement contains a brief S solo, SA duet, and SSA trio.

Requiem – 1985 – S solo, SATB chorus (with divisions), and chamber orchestra (two flutes, oboe, two clarinets, bassoon, two horns, timpani, percussion, harp, and strings) or small instrumental ensemble (flute, oboe, cello, timpani, glockenspiel, harp, and organ) – 38 minutes.

Magnificat – 1990 – S solo, SATB chorus (with divisions), and orchestra or chamber ensemble (flute, oboe, clarinet, bassoon, horn, timpani, percussion, organ, harp, and strings) – 37 minutes.

Te Deum – 1988 – SATB chorus (with divisions) and orchestra or instrumental ensemble (three trumpets, three trombones, tuba, timpani, percussion, and organ) – 7 minutes.

SMALLER-SCALE CHORAL WORKS
SELECTED AND LISTED ACCORDING TO FAMILIARITY

Candlelight Carol – SATB chorus and organ – 4 minutes.

What sweeter music – SATB chorus and organ – 4:15 minutes.

Shepherd's Pipe Carol – SATB chorus and organ – 3 minutes.

For the beauty of the earth – SATB chorus and piano – 3:30 minutes.

A Gaelic Blessing – SATB chorus and organ or guitar – 1:45 minutes.

GILES SWAYNE B.1946

Swayne was born in Hitchin, north of London, and studied at the Royal Academy of Music and Ampleforth College, Cambridge. Further studies were at the Conservatoire in Paris and Accademia Musicale Chigiana in Siena, and also in Africa, where he became acquainted with indigenous folk music. He was recognized in 1979 for his a cappella choral tone poem *CRY* op.27, which incorporates elements of African folk music, and in 1984 for his emulation of Classical textures in the chamber opera *Le nozze di Cherubino*. His best-known choral works—*Magnificat* op.33, *Nunc dimittis* op.44, and *Missa Tiburtina* op.40—are characterized by pervasive pointillistic textures. Other works, such as *Three Shakespeare Songs* op.4 and *The Tiger* op.68, have sections of aleatoric rhythm, sprechstimme, and choral glissandos, and scoring for a variety of nontraditional vocal sounds.

BOB CHILCOTT B.1955

Chilcott was born in Plymouth and was a chorister and choral scholar at King's College, Cambridge. Between 1985 and 1997 he sang with the professional vocal ensemble the King's Singers, and since then he has devoted his time to composition and conducting. Throughout his career he has conducted many of the world's most renowned choral ensembles, including the RIAS-Kammerchor of Berlin, Jauna Musika of Lithuania, Taipei Chamber Singers, Tower New Zealand Youth Choir, and Orphei Dranger of Uppsala, Sweden. He has also been director of the chorus at the Royal College of Music and principal guest conductor of the BBC Singers. His work with youth choirs has been the focus of his professional activity, and he has composed upwards of thirty works especially for treble voices. The most famous of these compositions is *Can you hear me* for SS chorus and piano. Other popular pieces for children include *Be simple little children* for SSA and piano, and *A Little Jazz Mass* for SSA chorus (arranged for SATB chorus), piano, and optional bass drum kit. Noteworthy repertoire for adult mixed chorus includes several multimovement works—*Canticles of Light* for SATB chorus, treble voice chorus, and orchestra or organ and chimes; *The Making of the Drum* for SATB chorus and percussion; and *The Modern Man I Sing* and *Fragments from His Dish* for SATB chorus (with divisions) a cappella.

JAMES MACMILLAN B.1959

MacMillan was born southwest of Glasgow, Scotland, in the small town of Kilwinning. He studied music at the universities of Edinburgh and Durham, and served for a short period of time as a faculty member at the University of Manchester. He then went on to hold a number of professional positions, including composer-in-residence for the Scottish Chamber Orchestra, Artistic Director of the *Music of Today* series of contemporary music for the Philharmonia Orchestra in London, and composer/conductor of the BBC Philharmonic. In recognition of his work he was named Commander of the Order of the British Empire in 2004.

His choral output consists of nine large-scale works scored for orchestra or sizeable instrumental ensemble and fifty-five smaller-scale pieces scored a cappella, with keyboard accompaniment (usually organ), or small instrumental ensemble. Most of the repertoire focuses on political issues or traditional Roman Catholic texts, and the musical style is characterized by tonal harmonies in the choral parts (purposefully written for amateur singers) and highly dissonant and complex instrumental parts. In addition, MacMillan frequently uses rhythms that are reflective of the Medieval era.

The large-scale works include four notable compositions—*Cantos sagrados,* composed in 1989, premiered in 1990 by the Scottish Chamber Choir at Old St Paul's Church in Edinburgh, and set to traditional Latin liturgical texts and the poetry (in English translation) by the Latin American poets Ariel Dorfman (movement one, "Identity," and three, "Sun stone") and Ana Maria Mendoza (movement two, "Virgin of Guadalupe"); the cantata *Seven Last Words from the Cross,* commissioned by BBC television, composed in 1993, and premiered in 1994 by Cappella Nova and the Scottish Ensemble, with text in Latin and English assembled from the four Gospels; *Quickening,* a cocommission from the BBC Proms and Philadelphia Orchestra, composed in 1998 and premiered at Royal Albert Hall in 1999 by the Hilliard Ensemble, BBC Symphony Orchestra and Chorus and the Westminster Cathedral Boys' Choir, and set to poetry by the British poet Michael Symmons Roberts (b. 1963); and *St John Passion,* composed in 2007 and premiered in Barbicon Hall, London, by the London Symphony Orchestra and Chorus, and set to text in Latin and English from the Bible.

The smaller-scale pieces include the motet *Divo Aloysio sacrum,* composed in 1991 for the Jesuit church of St Aloysius, Garnethill, in Glasgow, where the text (which translates as "Saint Aloysius, pray for us") is inscribed over the church's main door; *Christus vincit,* written for the 1994 St Cecilia's Day service at St Paul's Cathedral, London, and set to the seven words, "Christus vincit, Christus regnat, Christus imperat, Alleluia" (Christ conquers, Christ is king, Christ is lord of all, Alleluia); and *Seinte Mari moder milde,* commissioned by King's College, Cambridge, for its annual Festival of Nine Lessons and Carols, composed in 1995, and set to a thirteenth-century anonymous text.

CHORAL WORKS
SELECTED AND LISTED IN CHRONOLOGICAL ORDER
ACCORDING TO DATE OF COMPOSITION

Cantos sagrados – 1989 – SATB chorus and organ (orchestrated in 1997) – 22 minutes. The orchestration calls for a large percussion section in addition to piano and celesta.

Divo Aloysio sacrum – 1991 – SATB chorus and optional organ – 6 minutes.

Seven Last Words from the Cross – 1993 – SSAATTBB chorus and strings – 45 minutes.

Christus vincit – 1994 – S solo and SSAATTBB chorus a cappella – 7 minutes.

Seinte Mari moder milde – 1995 – SATB chorus and organ – 6 minutes.

Quickening – 1998 – ATTB soloists, children's chorus, mixed chorus, and large orchestra (including numerous percussion instruments, chamber organ, and grand organ) – 50 minutes. The A solo is for countertenor and the B solo is for baritone.

St John Passion – 2007 – baritone soloist, chamber chorus, standard mixed chorus, and large orchestra (including numerous percussion instruments and organ) – 85 minutes. The baritone soloist represents Christ and the chamber chorus portrays the role of the narrator.

TARIK O'REGAN B.1978

O'Regan was born in London and educated at Oxford and Cambridge universities. He also attended Columbia University, where he held a Fulbright Fellowship, and Harvard University, where he held a Radcliffe Institute Fellowship. Professional appointments have included composer-in-residence at Corpus Christi College, Cambridge; Research Affiliate at the Yale Institute of Sacred Music; and Fellow Commoner in Creative Arts at Trinity College, Cambridge.

His choral output totals forty works, most composed in an expanded tonal idiom and scored for soloists and a cappella chorus. Two of the works are based on music by the Medieval-era composer Guillaume de Machaut. *Scattered Rhymes* of 2006 is a companion work to and employs motivic fragments from Machaut's *Messe de nostre dame;* the text uses three poems from Petrarch's *Canzoniere* and an anonymous fourteenth-century English poem, and scoring is for ATTB soloists (who sing the Petrarch poetry) and SATB chorus. *Douce dame jolie* of 2007 utilizes melodic material from Machaut's virelai of the same name; scoring is for ATTB solo quartet. Three other works are part of a cycle of motets entitled *Sequence for St Wulfstan.* The texts, drawn from the medieval *Portiforium of St Wulfstan* housed in the Parker Library at Corpus Christi College, Cambridge, are settings in Latin and English meant for different seasons of the liturgical year. *Beatus auctor saeculi* (Blest author of this earthly frame) is for Christmas, *Tu claustra stripe regia* (O thou from regal ancestors) is for Candlemas, and *O vera digna hostia* (O thou from whom hell's monarch flies) is for Easter. All three works were composed in 2003 and are scored for SATB chorus a cappella. Other notable works include *Magnificat and Nunc Dimittis* (subtitled "Variations for Choir") of 2001 for SATB solos (four or eight singers, called the "concertante choir"), SSAATTBB chorus (called the "ripieno choir"), and soprano saxophone or cello; *Dorchester Canticles,* consisting of "Cantate Domino" (O sing unto the Lord a new song) and "Deus misereatur" (God be merciful unto us), composed in 2004 and scored for T solo, SATB chorus, organ, and percussion and harp ad lib.; and *The Ecstasies Above* of 2006, set to a poem by Edgar Allan Poe (1809–1849) and scored for SSAATTBB solos, SATB chorus, and strings.

⊗ THE UNITED STATES ⊗

The United States during the Modern era, while subject to a vast array of influences from around the world and while exposed to the many styles of writing from innovative and progressive currents in Europe, has been by and large the most conservative of all the countries in the Western Hemisphere. Only nine of the significant composers discussed below have written in styles that equate with new developments: Charles Ives experimented with polytonalities and textures, Henry Cowell was one of the first initiators of tone clusters (although these were not used extensively in his choral works), Louise Talma incorporated serial techniques into her writing, Lukas Foss employed aleatoric rhythms, Pauline Oliveros created new notational symbols, Pozzi Escot and Charles Wuorinen utilized mathematical principles in their organizational structures, John Harbison wrote in a highly dissonant tonal idiom, and John Adams embraced minimalism. All the other composers have written in styles that are traditional, especially in terms of tonality. The most forward-looking of the composers—Elliott Carter, Leonard Bernstein, Lukas Foss, Daniel Pinkham, Dominick Argento, and Eric Whitacre—have employed pantonality to some degree; their harmonies, while basically tonal, include chords consisting of nondiatonic notes. On the other end of the spectrum, the most conservative of the composers—Nathaniel Dett, Leo Sowerby, Howard Hanson, Virgil Thomson, Roy Harris, Randall Thompson, Aaron Copland, Jean Berger, Samuel Barber, Ulysses Kay, Dave Brubeck, and Karel Husa—have been predominantly tonal and diatonic in their writing. The remaining twenty-three composers— Ross Lee Finney, Halsey Stevens, William Schuman, Alan Hovhaness, Gian-Carlo Menotti, Norman Dello Joio, Irving Fine, Vincent Persichetti, Ned Rorem, Kirke Mechem, Jacob Druckman, Samuel Adler, Michael Hennagin, John Corigliano, Paul Chihara, Morten Lauridsen, Carol Barnett, Stephen Paulus, Libby Larsen, René Clausen, David Conte, Matthew Harris, and Aaron Jay Kernis—have written in a pandiatonic harmonic language (i.e., their harmonies are basically limited to notes within the diatonic scale).

One-fourth of the composers listed above, including those both conservative and progressive and those from both early and late in the era, studied in France with Nadia Boulanger (1887–1979). Sister of composer Lili Boulanger (discussed in the French section of this chapter), Nadia studied at the Paris Conservatoire beginning at age ten. She developed into an accomplished pianist and organist and gave numerous recitals throughout Europe and the United States (during a tour in 1925 she played the organ in the premiere of Copland's *Symphony for Organ and Orchestra*). In addition, she was in demand as a conductor and led performances with the Boston Symphony Orchestra, Philadelphia Orchestra, and New York Philharmonic. Her main claim to fame, however, was as a teacher—first of her sister, whose frail health confined her to her home, and then as an instructor at the Ecole Normale de Musique and the Conservatoire in Paris and at the American Conservatory in Fontainebleau. She also gave private lessons and in total taught approximately 150 American composers, including Dett, Thomson, Roy Harris, Copland, Talma, Finney, Carter, Fine, Husa, Pinkham, Chihara, Conte, and Matthew Harris.

Many composers who did not study with Boulanger (and some who did) were attracted to such institutions and musical centers as the Institute of Musical Art and the Juilliard School of Music in New York City; the Berkshire Music Center at Tanglewood in Massachusetts; the Curtis Institute in Philadelphia; the Eastman School of Music in Rochester, New York; Harvard and Yale universities; and the University of California, Berkeley. A sizable number of composers were supported by Serge Koussevitzky (music director of the Boston Symphony Orchestra from 1924 to 1949, who championed contemporary music and commissioned numerous works) and by the Koussevitzky Foundations established in 1942. In addition, an extensive list of composers won Pulitzer Prizes.

The best known of the composers in terms of recognition for their choral output (i.e., composers other than Copland, Carter, Menotti, Bernstein, Rorem, Corigliano, and Adams, who are known mostly for their compositions in other genres) represent the conservative and tonal styles of composition. Thompson, Pinkham, Lauridsen, and Whitacre are the most popular, published, and performed composers, and Hanson, Talma, Barber, Dello Joio, Fine, Persichetti, Foss, Argento, Hennagin, Adams, Paulus, Clausen, and Conte are all recognized either for their breadth of acclaimed choral repertoire or for their contributions to the development of the choral art. Composers who have been recognized for their choral writing but who are not discussed in depth in this chapter include Normand Lockwood, Cecil Effinger, David Diamond, Lou Harrison, Vaclav Nelhybel, Jacob Avshalomov, William Bolcom, Frank Ferko, and Z. Randall Stroope.

Lockwood (1906–2002), who was born in New York City and who studied with Ottorino Respighi in Rome and Nadia Boulanger in Paris, taught at Oberlin College Conservatory from 1932 until 1943 and at Union Theological Seminary in New York City from 1945 to 1953. Thereafter he held brief appointments at Trinity University in San Antonio, Texas, and at the University of Hawaii, Manoa, before joining the faculty of the University of Denver in 1961 (where he remained until 1974). His choral output of more than 150 compositions includes several settings of Walt Whitman poems, the best known of which is *Out of the Cradle Endlessly Rocking* of 1938 for SATB chorus a cappella. Other Whitman settings include *Dirge for Two Veterans* of 1936, *Elegy for a Hero* of about 1951, and *I Hear America Singing* of 1953. The musical style of these pieces, as well as most of his others, is characterized by tonal harmonies and rhythmic textures that adhere closely to natural text declamation.

Effinger (1914–1990) was born in Colorado Springs, Colorado, and educated at Colorado College, where he studied both music and mathematics. He also studied with Nadia Boulanger at the American Conservatory in Fontainebleau, France. In the late 1930s and early 1940s he played oboe in the Colorado and Denver symphony orchestras, and he also served on the faculty of Colorado College. From 1948 until 1981 he taught at the University of Colorado in Boulder. In addition to establishing himself as a prolific composer (his output totals 168 compositions), he invented the Musicwriter (a notational typewriter) and Tempowatch (a metronome that measures the tempo of live performances). His one hundred choral works include several large-scale oratorios—*St Luke Christmas Story* of 1953, *The Invisible Fire* of 1957, and *Paul of Tarsus* of 1968—and two popular sets of part songs—*Four Pastorales* ("No Mark," "Noon," "Basket," and "Wood") of 1962 for SATB chorus and oboe, and *Set of Three* ("Trail by Time," "This Trail," and "Inner Song while Watching a Square Dance") of 1961 for SATB chorus and brass ensemble or piano.

Diamond (1915–2005) was born in Rochester, New York, and educated at the Cleveland Institute of Music, Eastman School of Music, and New Music School in New York City. He also studied with Nadia Boulanger in Paris. After living in Italy for fourteen years in the 1950s and early 1960s, he returned to the United States and taught at the Manhattan and Juilliard schools of music (1966–1967 and 1973–1997, respectively). Of his sixteen published choral works, several are settings of texts for Jewish services, including *Mizmor L'David* of 1951 for T solo, SATB chorus, and organ. Secular works include *This Sacred Ground,* a setting of Abraham Lincoln's "Gettysburg Address" for B solo, children's chorus, SATB chorus, and orchestra, and *To Music,* a setting of the poems "Invocation to Music" by John Masefield and "Dedication" by Henry Wadsworth Longfellow for TB solos, SATB chorus, and orchestra. All the music is in a conservative, tonal idiom.

Harrison (1917–2003) was born in Portland, Oregon, and educated at several schools in San Francisco, where he studied horn and clarinet, played the harpsichord and recorder in early music ensembles, and became interested in world music. He also developed an interest in the music of Charles Ives and edited a number of his manuscripts, including the *Symphony #3,* which he conducted in New York City and which won for Ives a Pulitzer Prize (shared with Harrison). After experiments with twelve-tone techniques, he made several trips to Asia and settled on a style of music based on just intonation and scored for percussion instruments. With his partner William Colvig he constructed a set of metallophones modeled after Javanese gamelans, and he composed several choral works set to texts in Esperanto. These include *Novo odo* of 1961 to 1968 and *La koro sutro* (Heart sutra) of 1972. Compositions set to other texts include *Mass to Saint Anthony* of 1939 to 1952 (a setting of the Latin Mass Ordinary beginning with a cry of anguish that reflects the terror of Hitler's invasion of Poland) and *A Joyous Procession and a Solemn Procession* of 1962 (scored for high and low voices, two trombones, and percussion, and printed on a long, scroll-like score that includes calligraphy and drawings by Harrison).

Nelhybel (1919–1996) was born in the Czech Republic and educated in Prague at the conservatory and university there. Further studies were at the University of Fribourg in Switzerland. Between 1939 and 1957 he worked for Radio Prague, Swiss Radio, and Radio Free Europe, and he also conducted the Czech Philharmonic Orchestra. In 1957 he emigrated to the United States, becoming a citizen in 1962 and teaching at the University of Massachusetts Lowell from 1978 to 1979 and at the University of Scranton in Pennsylvania between 1994 and 1996. He is best known for his compositions scored for band and wind ensemble. However, several choral works have become popular, including *Estampie natalis* (a Christmas work scored for SAT solos, SSAATTBB chorus, and chamber ensemble), *Cantus* (a setting of five texts in Latin that express concern for the future, scored for SATB chorus and band), and *Caroli antiqui varii* (a setting of seven ancient Christmas carols for SSATTBB chorus a cappella).

Avshalomov (b.1919) was born in China, where his father, Aaron Avshalomov, (1894–1965), was a composer and conductor of the Shanghai Symphony Orchestra from 1943 to 1946. Jacob emigrated to the United States in 1937 and studied at the Eastman School of Music and the Berkshire Music Center. Between 1946 and 1954 he served on the faculty of Columbia University, conducting the university orchestra and chorus in the American premieres of Bruckner's *Messe in D-Moll* (Mass in D minor) and Tippett's *A Child of Our Time,* and from 1954 to 1995 he was conductor of the Portland, Oregon, Junior Symphony Orchestra (now the Portland Youth Philharmonic). Avshalomov's most popular choral works are *Tom o' Bedlam,* a setting of an anonymous seventeenth-century verse about a beggar released from an insane asylum, scored for SATB chorus (with divisions), oboe, tabor, and jingles, and winner of the New York Music Critics' Circle Award in 1953; *The Most Triumphant Bird,* a setting of poems by Emily Dickinson, scored for SATB chorus (with divisions), viola, and piano; *I Saw a Stranger Yestere'en,* a setting of an ancient Gaelic rune, for SATB chorus and violin; and *Wonders,* a setting of poems by William Blake, for SATB chorus (with divisions) a cappella.

Bolcom (b.1938) was born in Seattle, Washington, and studied with Darius Milhaud at Mills College and with Olivier Messiaen in Paris. During the 1965–1966 academic year he served on the faculty of the University of Washington, between 1966 and 1968 he taught at Queens College of the City University of New York, and from 1968 until 1970 he was composer-in-residence at the Yale School of Drama and the New York University School of the Arts. In 1973 he joined the faculty of the University of Michigan, becoming chair of the composition department there in 1988. He is known for his work in reviving ragtime and for composing original rag pieces, and also for performing nineteenth-century popular American songs with his wife, Joan Morris. His compositional output includes fourteen works with scoring for chorus. Most acclaimed of these is *Songs of Innocence and of Experience,* composed between 1956 and 1981 and scored for SSATBB solos, boy solo, a wide variety of vocal ensembles (including mixed chorus, children's chorus, madrigal ensemble, and country, rock, and folk singers), and large orchestra (including two saxophones, organ, piano, guitar, electric guitar, and bass guitar). Subtitled "A musical illumination of the poems of William Blake," it is a multidimensional and stylistically eclectic work that is most often performed in stage productions. Other smaller-scale works include *Chorale on St Anne's Hymn* of 1988 for S solo, SATB chorus, and organ; *The Mask* of 1990, a cycle of five pieces for mixed chorus and piano in an advanced and atonal idiom; and *Alleluia* of 1992 for SATB chorus a cappella.

Ferko (b.1950) was born in Barberton, Ohio, and in his youth he became involved in church music; at age fourteen he took a position as an organist and at sixteen as a choirmaster. After formal musical education at Valparaiso, Syracuse, and Northwestern universities, where he earned bachelor's, master's, and doctoral degrees, respectively, he returned to church work, which has continued to be the focus of his professional activity. Of his twenty-six published choral works, most are sacred settings in Latin, including a large number of motets. Significant among these are *The Hildegard Motets* of 1992 and 1993, commissioned by His Majestie's Clerkes of Chicago and scored overall for SATB chorus (with divisions) and incidental countertenor and alto solos in the first motet. The music, based on chants by Hildegard von Bingen, is characterized by sharp dissonances that frequently occur in tone clusters (e.g., the beginning and end of "O verbum Patris" and the middle of "Hodie aperuit"). *Hildegard Triptych* of 1997 and 1998, a second work based on Hildegard chants, was commissioned by the Dale Warland Singers, for which Ferko served as composer-in-residence between 2001 and 2003. Scoring is for SATB/SATB chorus a cappella.

Stroope (b.1953) was born in Albuquerque, New Mexico, and received degrees in music from the University of Colorado and Arizona State University. He has served as director of choral activities at the University of Nebraska, Omaha, and Rowan University in Glassboro, New Jersey, and he has led summer festivals in Somerset, England, and Rome, Italy. In addition, he has been a frequent conductor of festival choruses in the United States, and he has toured with his choirs to many countries around the world, including Australia, Russia, South Africa, Canada, and Japan. His choral output numbers more than eighty compositions, most of which are characterized by traditional diatonic harmonies, with occasional use of modern techniques such as sprechstimme. Representative large-scale works are *An American Te Deum,* scored for SSA chorus, solo violin and cello, percussion, and piano, and *Cantus Natalis,* scored for SATB chorus, treble chorus, brass, percussion, and organ. Popular smaller-scale works include *Amor de mi alma* (You are the love of my soul), *The Conversion of Saul,* and *I am not yours*—all scored for SATB divided chorus a cappella.

Mention should also be made of Alice Parker (b.1925), who is basically known for her arrangements of folk songs, hymns, and spirituals but who also composed four operas and more than 250 original choral works. Born in Boston, Massachusetts, she was educated at Smith College and the Juilliard School of Music, where she studied choral conducting with Robert Shaw and began making choral arrangements that were performed and recorded by the Robert Shaw Chorale. Many of these arrangements and others from later years became staples of programming with high school and collegiate choral ensembles. In 1985 Parker founded Melodious Accord, which she has conducted in numerous performances since then, and she has been active as a lecturer and author. Her videos (including *Shall We Gather – Singing Hymns with Alice Parker* and *The Reason Why We Sing – Community Song*) have become popular educational tools, and her books (including *The Anatomy of Melody*) provide insights into her success as a leader of American choral music during the twentieth century. Her original choral compositions include eleven large-scale choral/orchestral works (including *Commentaries* of 1978 set to a combination of folk texts and poems by Emily Dickinson, and *Earth, Sky, Spirit* of 1986 set to Native American texts), twenty-six cantatas for chorus and chamber orchestra (including *An Easter Rejoicing* of 1972 set to a variety of hymn texts, spiritual poems, and biblical passages, and *A Sermon from the Mountain: Martin Luther King* of 1969 set to texts by King with the addition of spirituals), thirty-three choral suites (including *A Garland of Carols* of 1968, *Back-Woods Ballads* of 1983, *Wesley Madrigals* of 1989, and *Six Hymns to Dr. Watts* of 1975), and more than one hundred individual small-scale pieces.

CHARLES IVES 1874–1954

Ives was born in Danbury, Connecticut, into a musical family. His father played the flute, violin, piano, and cornet and was a bandmaster as well as conductor of choral and orchestral ensembles. The young Ives studied piano, organ, harmony, and counterpoint with his father and began composing at age thirteen. At fourteen he was employed as organist at a local church, and at nineteen he became organist at St Thomas's Episcopal Church in New Haven, where he had enrolled at Hopkins Grammar School in order to prepare for entry into Yale University. Between ages twenty and twenty-four he studied at Yale, taking music courses with Horatio Parker and also serving as organist at Center Church on-the-Green, and upon graduation in 1898 he entered the insurance business in New York City. From 1900 to 1902 he was also choirmaster at Central Presbyterian Church, during which time he presumably composed most of his ten Psalm settings. After 1902 he held no further music positions, and in 1927 he ceased compositional activity, stating that he had no more inspiration for music.

Ives composed the majority of his forty-six choral works (twenty-six sacred and twenty secular) during the six-year period from approximately 1896 to 1902. The earlier works, written during his student years at Yale and shortly thereafter, emulated nineteenth-century genres and styles of European composers such as Mendelssohn, Dvořák, and Tchaikovsky. *The Celestial*

Country, for example, is a cantata divided into seven movements, with solo arias, solo quartets, choruses, and instrumental interludes characterized by traditional harmonies and rhythmic textures. The later works, composed during his time at Central Presbyterian Church, were experimental and nontraditional in melodic and harmonic construction. For instance, the phrases in *Psalm 24* are built of successively expanding and contracting melodic intervals, from the minor second to the perfect fifth and returning to the minor second, with the soprano voice part of each phrase ascending a chromatic scale (often with intervallic leaps of a minor or major ninth) and the bass voice part of the same phrase descending in mirror form; the harmonic texture of *Psalm 67* is polytonal, with the soprano and alto parts in C major and the tenor and bass parts in G minor; and the chordal structures in *Psalm 90* are frequently outside the overall C major tonality of the piece, and there is an instance of serial rhythmic construction. Also, a lengthy section in *Three Harvest Home Chorales* is constructed of three different meters that occur simultaneously—4/4 per measure in the soprano and alto parts, 3/2 per measure in the tenor part, and 9/2 over the space of two measures in the bass part.

CHORAL WORKS
SELECTED AND LISTED ACCORDING TO FAMILIARITY

Psalm 67 – ca.1898–1899 – SSAATTBB chorus a cappella – 2:30 minutes.

Psalm 90 – 1923–1924 – SSAATTBB chorus, bells (requiring four players), and organ – 10 minutes.

Psalm 24 – ca.1902 (revised ca.1912–1913) – SSAATTBB chorus a cappella – 3:15 minutes.

Psalm 54 – ca.1902 – SATB chorus (with divisions) a cappella – 3:30 minutes.

Psalm 150 – ca.1898–1899 – SATB chorus (with divisions), SSAA boys' chorus, and optional organ – 2:30 minutes.

Three Harvest Home Chorales – ca.1902 (revised ca.1912–1913) – SATB chorus, four trumpets, three trombones, tuba, and organ – 7 minutes.

Turn ye, turn ye – ca.1896 – SATB chorus and organ – 2:30 minutes.

Easter Carol – ca.1896 (revised ca.1901) – SATB solos, SATB chorus, and organ – 6 minutes.

The Celestial Country – 1898–1902 (revised in 1912–1913) – TB solos, SATB/SATB solo quartet, SATB chorus (with divisions), string quartet or string orchestra, trumpet, euphonium, timpani, and organ – 35 minutes.

For you and me – ca.1895–1896 – TTBB chorus (arranged for SATB chorus) a cappella – 1 minute.

NATHANIEL DETT 1882–1943

Dett was born in Drummondsville (later named Niagara Falls), Ontario, Canada, and began studying piano at age five. When he was eleven his family moved to Niagara Falls, New York, and between sixteen and twenty-one he served as organist at the British Methodist Episcopal

Church, now named for him. In 1908 he became the first African-American to receive a bachelor's degree from Oberlin College Conservatory, and in 1932 he received a master's degree from Eastman School of Music. Meanwhile, between 1908 and 1933 he held teaching positions in four institutions—Lane College in Tennessee (1908–1911), Lincoln Institute in Missouri (1911–1913), Hampton Institute in Virginia (1913–1932), and Bennett College in North Carolina (1937–1942). While at the Lincoln Institute, he served as chair of the music department and toured across the United States with the Institute choir, and in 1930 the choir also presented concerts in Europe. Dett authored the popular book *The Emancipation of Negro Music,* and throughout his career he presented numerous lectures across the United States. For his accomplishments he was awarded honorary doctorates from Howard University in 1924 and Oberlin College Conservatory in 1926.

Of Dett's approximately seventy choral works, several are original compositions based on African-American spirituals and many others are arrangements of spirituals. The original works include the cantata *The Chariot Jubilee,* based on "Swing low sweet chariot," and the oratorio *The Ordering of Moses,* based on "Go down Moses," with the incorporation of additional spirituals such as "And when Moses smote the water" and "He is king of kings." *The Chariot Jubilee*—scored for T solo, mixed chorus, and orchestra—was premiered by the St Cecilia Society of Boston in 1920. *The Ordering of Moses*—composed in 1937 and scored for SATBB solos, mixed chorus, and orchestra (including organ)—was premiered in 1939 at the Cincinnati Festival. The most popular of the spiritual arrangements is *Listen to the Lambs.* Also popular is the motet *Ave Maria* for S solo and SATB chorus a cappella.

LEO SOWERBY 1895–1968

Sowerby was born in Grand Rapids, Michigan, and studied piano, organ, and theory privately in Chicago. In 1918 he graduated with a master's degree from the American Conservatory in Chicago, and in 1921 he won the Prix de Rome from the American Academy in Rome, which enabled him to study in Italy for the next three years. He served on the faculty of the American Conservatory in Chicago between 1925 and 1962, and from 1927 to 1962 he was organist and choirmaster at the Episcopal Cathedral of St James. He was the first church musician to win a Pulitzer Prize (for his 1944 cantata *Canticle of the Sun*), and he was also the first American to be named a Fellow of the Royal School of Church Music in London. His approximately 150 choral works are exclusively devoted to sacred cantatas, anthems, Communion Services, and canticles. The cantatas include *Canticle of the Sun,* mentioned above, *Great Is the Lord* of 1933, *Forsaken of Man* of 1939, and *Christ Reborn* of 1950. The anthems include *The Righteous live for evermore,* subtitled "Anthem for All Saints" and scored for SATB chorus and organ.

HOWARD HANSON 1896–1981

Hanson was born in Wahoo, Nebraska, a short distance west of Omaha, where he attended Luther College. Further studies were at Northwestern University, at the Institute of Musical Art in New York City, and in Rome (where he did not study with Respighi, as is sometimes stated). Between 1916 and 1919 he taught at the College of the Pacific (now the University of the Pacific) in northern California, and from 1924 until his retirement in 1964 he was director of the East-man School of Music in Rochester, New York. He achieved widespread public attention with the 1930 premiere of his *Symphony #2,* subtitled the "Romantic," and his *Symphony #4* of 1943, sub-titled "The Requiem," which won a Pulitzer Prize. In addition to his work as an administrator and composer, he was an active conductor who led performances with the New York Symphony Orchestra and the Boston Symphony Orchestra as well as with the Eastman-Rochester Sym-phony Orchestra, which he founded and with which he made numerous recordings.

His choral output includes several choral/orchestral settings of texts by Walt Whitman and several smaller-scale works set to Psalm texts. Of the Whitman settings, *Songs from Drum Taps* is a three-movement work ("Beat! Beat! drums," "By the bivouac's fitful flame," and "To thee old cause") dedicated to the composer's parents; *Song of Democracy* (to the poem "An Old Man's Thought of School" from *Leaves of Grass*) was composed for the 100th anniversary of the Na-tional Education Association and the fiftieth anniversary of the Music Educators National Con-ference; *The Mystic Trumpeter* was commissioned by the University of Missouri in Kansas City; and *Symphony #7,* subtitled "A Sea Symphony" and divided into three movements (taken from the poems "The Ship Starting," "The Untold Want," and "Joy, Shipmate, Joy"), was composed for the fiftieth anniversary of the National Music Camp at Interlochen in Michigan. The Psalm settings include *The One Hundred Twenty-first Psalm* for baritone or contralto solo, SATB chorus (with divisions), and organ or piano; *The One Hundred Fiftieth Psalm* for SATB chorus (with di-visions) and organ or piano; and Hanson's best-known choral composition, *How excellent thy name* (from Psalm 8). The musical language of all the compositions is neo-Romantic, with tonal harmonies, uncomplicated rhythms, and homophonic textures.

CHORAL WORKS
SELECTED AND LISTED ACCORDING TO FAMILIARITY

How excellent thy name (Psalm 8:1, 3–6) – 1952 – SSAA chorus and piano or SATB chorus and organ – 5 minutes.

The Lament for Beowulf – 1925 – SATB chorus and orchestra – 20 minutes.

The Cherubic Hymn – 1949 – SATB chorus and orchestra – 12 minutes.

Song of Democracy – 1957 – SATB chorus and orchestra – 12 minutes.

Songs from Drum Taps – 1935 – B solo, SATB chorus (with divisions), and orchestra – 18 minutes. The B solo occurs only in the work's second movement.

The Mystic Trumpeter – 1970 – speaker, SATB chorus, and orchestra – 14:30 minutes.

VIRGIL THOMSON 1896–1989

Thomson was born in Kansas City, Missouri, and studied piano and organ in his youth. He en-tered Harvard University in 1919 and for the next several years served as accompanist and as-sistant conductor of the Harvard Glee Club. In 1921 he went to Paris, where he studied with

Nadia Boulanger at the Ecole Normale de Musique. Upon returning to the United States the following year, he was appointed organist and choirmaster of Boston's King's Chapel, and in 1925 he returned to Paris, where he remained until 1940. While in Paris, he was influenced by Erik Satie and Igor Stravinsky, and he collaborated with Gertrude Stein on his first opera, *Four Saints in Three Acts* (a later opera, *The Mother of Us All,* also has a libretto by Stein). Thomson became famous for his reviews and articles published between 1940 and 1954 in the *New York Herald Tribune* and later collected in four anthologies—*The Musical Scene, The Art of Judging Music, Music Right and Left,* and *Music Reviewed, 1940–1954*—and for the remainder of his career he traveled across the United States giving lectures and conducting his works.

His choral output includes two relatively well-known cantatas and several anthems and hymns—all composed in a conservative musical idiom, with diatonic harmonies and traditional rhythmic textures. Of the cantatas, *The Nativity as Sung by the Shepherds,* a setting of poetry by the English metaphysical poet Richard Crashaw (1613–1649), was composed between 1966 and 1967 and is scored for ATB solos, SATB chorus, and orchestra, and *Cantata on Poems of Edward Lear* ("The Owl and the Pussycat," "The Jumblies," "The Pelican Chorus," "Half an Alphabet," and "The Akond of Swat") was composed in 1973 (revised in 1974) and is scored for SBB solos, SATB chorus, and piano. Of the anthems, two works are settings of Psalms—*De profundis* (Psalm 30) composed in 1920 (revised in 1951) and scored for SATB chorus a cappella, and *Three Antiphonal Psalms* (Psalms 123, 133, and 136) composed between 1922 and 1924 and scored for SA/TB chorus a cappella. The hymn *My shepherd will supply my need* of 1937 for SATB chorus a cappella is Thomson's most famous composition.

HENRY COWELL 1897–1965

Cowell was born in Menlo Park, California, and was home schooled during his youth. Most of his formal musical education was at the University of California, Berkeley, although he also studied briefly at the Institute of Musical Art in New York City. He became known for his modernist compositional techniques, which included tone clusters, and beginning in the 1920s he toured the United States and Europe playing recitals of his piano music. In 1924 he founded both the New Music Society of California and the publication series *New Music,* and during the 1940s and 1950s he taught at the New School for Social Research in New York City, Columbia University, and the Peabody Conservatory of Music. During the last decade of his life, having developed an interest in world music, he traveled to such locales as India, China, Japan, and Tahiti.

Cowell's prolific compositional output numbers almost one thousand works, including twenty-one symphonies, more than one hundred songs, and forty-five choral pieces. The cantata . . . *if He please* of 1955 (scored for boys' or children's chorus, mixed chorus, and orchestra or piano) is representative of his modern style, with numerous instances of tone clusters, and *Zapados sonidos* of 1964 for SSAATTBB chorus and tap dancer is also progressive. Other works, composed for amateur singers, are more traditional. Examples include *The Morning Cometh* of 1937 and *To a White Birch* of 1950 for SATB chorus a cappella, *Fire and Ice* of 1943 for male chorus and band, and *With Choirs Divine* of 1952 for SSA chorus and optional piano.

ROY HARRIS 1898–1979

Harris was born near Chandler, Oklahoma, and took piano and clarinet lessons during his youth. His college education was at two campuses of the University of California—Los Angeles and Berkeley—and further studies were at the MacDowell Colony in Peterborough, New Hampshire, and in Paris with Nadia Boulanger. Between 1933 and 1976 he taught at numerous colleges and universities, including Mills College (1933), Westminster Choir College (1934–1938), Cornell University (1941–1943), Indiana University (1957–1960), and California State University at Los Angeles (1970–1976). He is known primarily for his symphonic and choral works based on American folk songs or set to texts by American poets. His best-known composition, *Symphony #4*, subtitled "Folk-Song Symphony," incorporates the tunes "The girl I left behind," "Western Cowboy," and "Johnny comes marching home," in addition to several other folk melodies; *Freedom's Land* (which Harris originally composed for B solo, SATB chorus, and orchestra, and later arranged for both women's and men's chorus with various accompanimental forces) is a setting of a patriotic text by Archibald MacLeish; and *Symphony for Voices* is a three-movement work set to "Song for all seas, all ships," "Tears," and "Inscription" by Walt Whitman. Other Whitman settings include *Walt Whitman Suite* for SATB chorus, string quartet, and piano, and the part songs *To thee, old cause; Year that trembled;* and *Freedom, toleration*—all scored for SATB chorus a cappella. Additional part songs for SATB chorus are arrangements of American folk songs (e.g., *Work Song* and *The Bird's Courting Song*) or African-American spirituals (e.g., *Li'l Boy Named David*).

RANDALL THOMPSON 1899–1984

Thompson was born in New York City and attended private school in New Jersey (the Lawrenceville School, where his father was an English teacher). In 1916 he entered Harvard University, and between 1922 and 1925 he studied at the American Academy in Rome. In 1927 he was appointed organist and lecturer at Wellesley College, from 1931 to 1934 he traveled across the United States observing music education programs as part of a Guggenheim Foundation fellowship, and for the remainder of his career he held positions at a number of prestigious institutions: in 1937 he taught at the University of California at Berkeley; in 1939 he was appointed director of the Curtis Institute of Music in Philadelphia (where one of his students was Leonard Bernstein); in 1941 he became head of the music department at the University of Virginia in Charlottesville; in 1946 he taught at Princeton University; and in 1948 he joined the faculty of Harvard University. He was known during the latter half of his life as the "Dean of American Choral Composers," and several of his choral compositions (e.g., *Alleluia* and selections from *Frostiana*) were among the most widely published and performed of all choral works composed in the twentieth century. His musical language is melodically and harmonically diatonic, characterized by parallel motion chords in first or second inversion.

Thompson's choral output consists of twenty-seven works and sets of pieces, the most popular of which are small-scale compositions scored for mixed chorus a cappella or chorus with piano accompaniment. *Alleluia*, a setting of the single word that reflects on the biblical passage from Job 1:21, ("The Lord giveth and the Lord taketh away. Blessed be the name of the Lord"), was commissioned for the opening of the Boston Symphony Orchestra Berkshire Music Center at Tanglewood. *Frostiana*, a setting of poems by Robert Frost collectively subtitled "Seven Country Songs," was composed for the 200th anniversary of the incorporation of the town of Amherst, Massachusetts. *The Last Words of David,* performed most frequently in its arrangement for mixed chorus and piano, was commissioned by the Boston Symphony Orchestra in honor of the twenty-fifth anniversary of Serge Koussevitzky as music director.

The well-known larger-scale works include *The Peaceable Kingdom,* a setting of numerous passages from Isaiah divided into eight movements and inspired by the painting "The Peaceable Kingdom" by Edward Hicks, and *The Testament of Freedom,* a setting of passages from the writings of Thomas Jefferson divided into four movements—"The God who gave us life gave us liberty at the same time" from *A Summary View of the Rights of British America* (1774), "We have counted the cost of this contest" and "We fight not for glory or for conquest" from *Declaration of the Causes and Necessity of Taking up Arms* (1775), and "I shall not die without a hope that life and liberty are no steady advance" from a letter to John Adams (1821).

Other large-scale works include two oratorios and a Requiem. *The Nativity According to Saint Luke,* composed for the 200th anniversary of Christ Church, Cambridge, is divided into seven scenes (Zacharias and the Angel, The Annunciation, The Visitation, The Naming of Jesus, The Apparition, The Adoration, and The Song of Simeon) and is scored for eight soloists plus four small roles for shepherds, SATB choir, and small orchestra (flute, oboe, clarinet, bassoon, horn, trumpet, percussion, organ, string quartet, string bass, and church bells). *The Passion According to Saint Luke,* commissioned by the Handel and Haydn Society of Boston for its 150th anniversary, is a sequel to *The Nativity* and is divided into two main sections, each with five scenes (The Entry into Jerusalem, The Passover, The Institution of the Lord's Supper, The Agony in the Garden, Peter's Denial, The Mocking of Jesus, The Trial, The March to Calvary, The Crucifixion, and The Entombment). Scoring is for nine solo roles (although some of the minor roles can be sung by the same person or by members of the chorus), SATB choir, and orchestra. The *Requiem,* subtitled a "Dramatic Dialogue for Double Chorus," consists of a wide variety of sacred texts on the general subject of the triumph of faith over death and is set in five movements, each of which is further divided into multiple sections.

CHORAL WORKS

SELECTED AND LISTED ACCORDING TO FAMILIARITY

Alleluia – 1940 – SATB (also arranged for SSAA and TTBB) chorus a cappella – 5 minutes.

Frostiana – 1959 – various voicings and piano or orchestra – "The Road Not Taken," SATB, 5 minutes; "The Pasture," TBB, 2:15 minutes; "Come In," SAA, 3:30 minutes; "The Telephone," SAA/TTBB, 4 minutes; "A Girl's Garden," SAA, 3 minutes; "Stopping by Woods on a Snowy Evening," TBB, 3:15 minutes; and "Choose Something Like a Star," SATB, 5:30 minutes. The first and last pieces are the most popular of the set.

The Last Words of David (2 Samuel 23:3–4) – 1949 – SATB chorus and orchestra, band, or piano – 4 minutes.

The Peaceable Kingdom – 1936 – SATB/SATB chorus a cappella – 18 minutes.

The Testament of Freedom – 1943 – TTBB chorus and orchestra, band, or piano – 11:30 minutes.

Glory to God in the Highest – 1958 – SATB chorus a cappella – 1:30 minutes.

The Best of Rooms – 1963 – SATB chorus a cappella – 3:30 minutes.

AARON COPLAND 1900–1990

Copland, whose parents were Jewish immigrants, was born in Brooklyn, New York. He began to play the piano at age seven and compose at twelve, and between thirteen and twenty he studied piano, theory, and composition privately. In 1921 he went to France, where for the next several years he studied with Nadia Boulanger at the American Conservatory in Fontainebleau and privately in Paris, and where he became acquainted with Stravinsky, Milhaud, and other composers living in France at the time. During the 1930s and 1940s Copland composed most of his significant instrumental works, including the ballets *Billy the Kid* in 1938, *Rodeo* in 1942, and *Appalachian Spring* in 1943 and 1944; the film score *The Red Pony* in 1948; *Fanfare for the Common Man* for brass and percussion instruments in 1942; and *Lincoln Portrait* for speaker and orchestra, also in 1942. During the 1940s he also served as assistant director of the Berkshire Music Center at Tanglewood and taught William Schuman, Eliott Carter, Leonard Bernstein, Irving Fine, Lukas Foss, Jacob Druckman, and many other students who would become significant composers. By the 1950s Copland was hailed as the greatest living American composer (*Appalachian Spring* had won a Pulitzer Prize and the New York Music Critics' Circle Award), and throughout the next several decades he was active as a conductor and lecturer (he was the first American composer to hold the Harvard University Norton Professor of Poetry Chair). He received a number of distinguished citations for his work, including a Presidential Medal of Freedom in 1964, a Kennedy Center Honors Award in 1979, and a Congressional Gold Medal in 1986. He suffered from Alzheimer's disease during the latter part of his life and died of heart failure at the age of ninety.

Copland composed twelve choral works, including two pieces (*Stomp your foot* and *The promise of living*) that were extracted from his opera *The Tender Land*. The popular part songs such as *Simple Gifts*, *Long Time Ago*, *I Bought Me a Cat*, *Ching-a-Ring Chaw*, and *The Little Horses* were set by Copland as solo songs and arranged for chorus by Irving Fine. These songs, the pieces from *The Tender Land*, and *What do we plant* represent Copland's Americana style, with melodies either based on folk songs or emulating folk styles. *In the Beginning*, an extended motet-like work set to Genesis 1:1–2, 7, features solo recitatives (indicated by Copland to be sung "in a gentle, narrative manner, like reading a familiar and oft-told story") that alternate with sections of imitative writing and parlando effects for chorus. *Las Agachadas*, subtitled "The Shake-Down Song," is based on a melody found in the collection *Folk Music and Poetry of Spain and Portugal* edited by Kurt Schindler.

CHORAL WORKS
SELECTED AND LISTED ACCORDING TO FAMILIARITY

Stomp your foot – 1954 – SATB chorus (with occasional divisions) and piano four hands or orchestra – 3 minutes.

The promise of living – 1954 – SATBB chorus and piano four hands or orchestra – 5 minutes.

In the Beginning – 1947 – A solo and SATB chorus (with occasional divisions) a cappella – 16:30 minutes.

Lark – 1938 – B solo and SATB chorus (with divisions) a cappella – 4 minutes.

Las Agachadas – 1942 – SATB solo quartet and SSAATTBB chorus a cappella – 3:30 minutes.

What do we plant – 1935 – SSA chorus and piano – 3 minutes.

LOUISE TALMA 1906–1996

Talma was born in Arachon, France, but raised and educated mostly in the United States. In the early 1920s she attended the Institute of Musical Art in New York City, and in the later 1920s she was a student of Nadia Boulanger at the American Conservatory in Fontainebleau, France. Further studies were at New York and Columbia universities. Between 1928 and 1979 she taught at Hunter College of the City University of New York, and beginning in 1943 she became a Fellow of the MacDowell Colony in Peterborough, New Hampshire, where most of her music over the following decades was written.

She composed seventeen choral works, many of which are cycles or collections of pieces set to related poetry. *Let's Touch the Sky*, her most recognized choral work, is a setting of three poems by e. e. cummings—"anyone lived in a pretty how town," "love is more thicker than forget," and "if up's the word"; *La Corona* is a setting in seven movements of the "Corona" sonnets by John Donne—"Holy Sonnets," "Resurrection," "Annunciation," "Ascension," "Nativitie," "Temple," and "Crucifying"; *Voices of Peace* combines texts from a variety of sources—the Roman Mass Ordinary ("Agnus Dei"), St Francis of Assisi ("Lord, make me an instrument of thy peace"), Gerard Manley Hopkins ("When will you ever, peace"), and the Hebrew Sabbath Service and Roman Latin Missal ("Shalom! Pax et bonum"); and *A Wreath of Blessings* brings together prayers by William Cartwright, George Herbert, Lucy Larcom, and anonymous Irish and Hebridean sources. Other compositions include two Psalm settings (*Psalm 84* of 1978 and *Psalm 115* of 1992), two masses (*Mass for the Sundays of the Year* and *Mass in English*, both of 1984), and two cantata-like works (*A Time to Remember*, set to excerpts of speeches by John F. Kennedy in 1966 and 1967, and *The Leaden Echo and the Golden Echo*, set to poetry of Gerard Manley Hopkins in 1950 and 1951). All the works are in an advanced tonal idiom except *La Corona*, which is twelve-tone.

CHORAL WORKS
SELECTED AND LISTED IN CHRONOLOGICAL ORDER
ACCORDING TO DATE OF COMPOSITION

Let's Touch the Sky – 1952 – SATB chorus, flute, oboe, and bassoon – 10:30 minutes.

La Corona – 1954–1955 – SATB chorus a cappella – 20 minutes.

Voices of Peace – 1973 – SATB chorus and strings – 25 minutes.

A Wreath of Blessings – 1985 – SATB chorus a cappella – 7:30 minutes.

ROSS LEE FINNEY 1906–1997

Finney was born in Wells, Minnesota, and studied at the University of Minnesota and Carleton College. Further studies were in Paris with Nadia Boulanger and in Vienna with Alban Berg. Between 1929 and 1948 he served on the faculty at Smith College in Northampton, Massachusetts, and in 1949 he was appointed professor of composition at the University of Michigan. His early choral works are tonal: the *Pilgrim Psalms* of 1945, a collection of fifteen Psalm settings for SATB chorus and either piano or organ accompaniment (also arranged for orchestra), is based on American hymnody, and *Spherical Madrigals* of 1947 for SATB chorus a cappella is in a pandiatonic idiom. This latter work, a collection of pieces set to poems on the subject of circles and globes (e.g., "All-circling point" from Richard Crashaw's *In the Glorious Epiphany of Our Lord God*, "His body was an orb" from John Dryden's *Upon the Death of the Lord Hastings*, and "On a round ball" from John Donne's *A Valediction: of weeping*), is one of the important examples of the revival of Renaissance genres and styles in the twentieth century. Finney's later compositions employ twelve-tone techniques and modern modes of rhythmic organization. For example, the cantata *Edge of Shadow*, composed in 1959 and scored for SATB chorus and percussion, is based on a tone row that is varied and that incorporates instances of sprechstimme, and the trilogy of cantatas *Earthrise* (*Still Are New Worlds* of 1962, *The Martyr's Elegy* of 1967, and *Earthrise* of 1978), scored for soloists, mixed chorus, tape, and orchestra, combines serial techniques with fluid manipulation of rhythms and motifs that Finney called "memory as a musical phenomenon."

HALSEY STEVENS 1908–1989

Stevens was born in Scott, New York, south of Syracuse, and studied at Syracuse University and the University of California at Berkeley. Between 1935 and 1937 he taught at Syracuse University, from 1937 to 1944 he served on the faculty at Dakota Wesleyan University, and in 1948 he was appointed professor of composition at the University of Southern California. While remaining at the University of Southern California, where one of his students was Morten Lauridsen, he held visiting appointments at Yale University (1960–1961) and Williams College (1970). Stevens is noted for his tonal part songs for SATB chorus a cappella (e.g., *Go, lovely rose* of 1942, *Like as the culver on the bared bough* of 1954, *Lady, as thy fair swan* of 1966, and *An Epitaph for Sara and Roland Cotton* of 1971) and anthems and motets (e.g., *Venite, exultemus* of 1957 for SATB chorus and brass quintet or keyboard, and *In te, Domine, speravi* of 1964 for SATB chorus and organ). Also popular are *A New Year Carol* of 1960 for SATB chorus a cappella, and *Four Carols* ("All this night," "What sweeter music," "As I out rode," and "A virgin most pure") of 1952 for TTB chorus a cappella. Larger-scale works include *Songs from the Paiute* composed in 1976 and scored for T solo, SATB chorus (with divisions), four flutes, and timpani; *A Testament of Life* of 1959 for TB solos, SATB chorus, and orchestra; and *Magnificat* of 1962 for SATB chorus, trumpet, and strings or keyboard.

ELLIOTT CARTER 1908–2012

Carter was born in New York City and raised there and in Europe, where his family had business enterprises. He studied piano in his youth, and after studies at the Horace Mann School in New York City he enrolled at Harvard University (studying English literature and Greek philosophy) and consecutively at the Longy School (studying piano, oboe, and solfège). Further studies in music were at the Ecole Normale de Musique in Paris with Nadia Boulanger. During the 1940s and 1950s Carter held several short-term teaching appointments at the Peabody Conservatory of Music (1946–1948), Columbia University (1948–1950), Queens College of the City University of New York (1955–1956), and Yale University (1960–1962), and between 1964 and 1984 he served on the faculty of the Juilliard School of Music. He became famous in the 1950s for his *String Quartet #1* and *Variations for Orchestra,* and his reputation was secured with such works as the *String Quartet #2* in 1959, *Oboe Concerto* in 1987, *Violin Concerto* in 1990, and *Clarinet Concerto* in 1996. His numerous accolades include two Pulitzer Prizes (1960 and 1973) and the United States National Medal of Arts (the first composer to receive this award).

Carter's nine published choral works were all written in the 1930s and 1940s and are in a conservative and tonal harmonic idiom. Especially popular are three a cappella pieces that emulate the style of Renaissance English madrigals—*To Music* of 1937 for S solo and SATB chorus, *Heart not so heavy as mine* of 1938 for SATB chorus, and *Musicians wrestle everywhere* of 1945 for SSATB chorus. This last-named work, to a poem by Emily Dickinson, features imitative phrases that alternate with brief homophonic passages, and melodic and textural fabrics that characterize the poetry in the form of word painting.

JEAN BERGER 1909–2002

Berger was born in Hamm, Germany, and raised in Alsace-Lorraine. He studied at the universities of Heidelberg and Vienna, receiving a doctorate in musicology in 1931, and in 1932 he began his professional career as assistant conductor of the Darmstadt Opera Company. Because of his Jewish ancestry, he fled Germany in 1933 and moved to Paris, where for the next several years he worked as a professional accompanist, mainly for vocalists. While in Paris he also conducted the choral ensemble Les Compagnons de la Marjolaine and became recognized for his choral work *Le sang des autres.* In 1939 he relocated to Rio de Janeiro and became assistant conductor of the Teatro Municipal and a faculty member at the Conservatorio Brasileiro de Musica, and in 1941 he emigrated to the United States, serving in the army in 1942 and becoming a citizen in 1943. After his service in the army, he lived in New York City and worked as an arranger, accompanist, and coach for the CBS and NBC radio networks. Between 1948 and 1968 he held faculty appointments at Middlebury College in Vermont (1948–1959), the University of Illinois, Urbana (1959–1961), the University of Colorado, Boulder (1961–1966), and Colorado Women's College in Denver (1968–1971), and for the remainder of his life he held visiting professor appointments at several universities in Great Britain (including Cambridge, Oxford, and Glasgow); he also lectured throughout England, South America, and the United States.

Most of Berger's compositions are traditional in texture and scoring and conservative in harmonic language—an idiom accessible to the amateur performer and general public but counter to the European style of composition prevalent at the time. According to Berger, "The living composer in Germany—probably in all of Western Europe—is not expected to write music that can please." However, Berger felt that a new direction in choral performance was needed. As he explained, "My studies of history make me feel that we are gradually seeing the end of the traditional concert as the main event of our musical life, since the circumstances which created it are so totally different from our own." As a consequence of this belief, he composed a number of works for staged chorus, with librettos "organized so that the chorus is the chief protagonist of a stage action." Representative works, all scored for SATB chorus and a small "combo" of instruments, are *Yiphtah and His Daughter* of 1972, *Birds of a Feather* of 1969, and *Stone Soup* of 1975.

Works in the traditional and conservative unstaged style include several pieces that were well known and frequently performed by collegiate, high school, and church ensembles during the latter half of the twentieth century. Most popular were the short anthem *The eyes of all wait upon thee* (Psalm 145:15–16) scored for SATB chorus a cappella, and the extended motet *Brazilian Psalm* (also called *Psalmo Brasileiro*) for SSAATTBB chorus a cappella. Other popular works are *Magnificat* for S solo, SATB chorus, flute, and triangle (performed occasionally with dancers); *Psalm 57* for SATB chorus and organ; and *Six Madrigals* ("My true love hath my heart," "I find no peace," "Art thou that she," "To Mistress Isabel," "Lost is my quiet," and "Harvester's Song") for SATB chorus a cappella.

SAMUEL BARBER 1910–1981

Barber was born in West Chester, Pennsylvania, and in his youth was tutored by his aunt (a singer) and uncle (a composer), Louise and Sidney Homer. Barber was precocious in his development, composing an operetta *(The Rose Tree)* at age ten and entering the Curtis Institute at fourteen, and when he was eighteen he was given an award for a violin sonata (now lost). At twenty-one he received widespread recognition for his orchestral overture *The School for Scandal,* and when he was twenty-eight his reputation was further enhanced with performances of his first *Essay for Orchestra* and *Adagio for Strings* by Arturo Toscanini and the NBC Symphony Orchestra. Meanwhile, while at the Curtis Institute he met and became close friends with Gian Carlo Menotti, and between 1935 and 1937 the two lived in Italy while Barber was studying at the American Academy in Rome. Between 1939 and 1942 he taught at the Curtis Institute, and for the remainder of his life he focused almost entirely on filling high-profile commissions. The ballet *Medea* was composed in 1946 for Martha Graham, the *Piano Sonata* of 1949 was commissioned by Irving Berlin and Richard Rogers for the twenty-fifth anniversary of the League of Composers, the opera *Vanessa* (which won a Pulitzer Prize) was written between 1956 and 1957 and premiered at the Metropolitan Opera in 1958, the *Piano Concerto* was commissioned by the New York Philharmonic for the opening of the Lincoln Center for the Performing Arts in 1962, and the opera *Antony and Cleopatra* was similarly commissioned for the first season (1966) of the Metropolitan Opera at Lincoln Center. Barber composed few works in the 1970s and died of cancer at age seventy.

Of his twenty choral works, all in a tonal idiom with diatonic melodies and harmonies, the most popular are adaptations of songs or orchestral compositions. *Agnus Dei* is a setting of his *Adagio for Strings,* which itself is an orchestral transcription of the second movement of his 1936 *String Quartet;* the part songs *Heaven-Haven* and *Sure on this shining night* are choral arrangements of his solo songs from opus 13; *Under the Willow Tree* is an extraction from his opera *Vanessa;* and *The monk and his cat* is a choral arrangement of his solo song from *Hermit Songs* op.29. Other popular part songs—*To be sung on the water* and the three pieces of *Reincarnations* ("Mary Hynes," "Anthony O Daly," and "The Coolin")—are newly composed.

Only two of the choral works are large-scale compositions scored for chorus and orchestra. *Prayers of Kierkegaard,* commissioned by Serge Koussevitzky and premiered by the Boston Symphony Orchestra, is a setting of prayers taken from the writings of the Danish philosopher and theologian Søren Kierkegaard (1813–1855), and *The Lovers,* commissioned by the Girard Bank of Philadelphia and premiered by the Philadelphia Orchestra, is a setting of eleven poems from *Twenty Poems of Love and a Song of Despair* by the Chilean writer and politician Pablo Neruda (1904–1973).

CHORAL WORKS
SELECTED AND LISTED IN CHRONOLOGICAL ORDER
ACCORDING TO DATE OF COMPOSITION

Let down the bars, O death (from *The Virgin Martyrs*) – 1936 – SATB chorus a cappella – 2 minutes.

Reincarnations – 1937–1940 – SATB chorus a cappella – 10 minutes.

A Stopwatch and an Ordnance Map – 1940 – TTBB chorus and timpani – 5:30 minutes.

Prayers of Kierkegaard – 1954 – S solo, SATB/SATB chorus, and orchestra or chamber orchestra – 19 minutes. The work also calls for T and A solos ad lib.

Under the Willow Tree – 1957 – male or female solo, SATB chorus, and piano – 3:30 minutes.

Sure on this shining night – 1961 – SATB chorus and piano – 2:30 minutes.

Heaven-Haven (subtitled "A nun takes the veil") – 1961 – SATB chorus a cappella – 2 minutes.

The monk and his cat – 1967 – SATB chorus and piano – 2:30 minutes.

Agnus Dei – 1967 – SSAATTBB chorus a cappella – 8 minutes.

To be sung on the water – 1968 – SATB chorus a cappella – 3 minutes.

The Lovers – 1971 – B solo, SATB chorus (with divisions), and orchestra – 32 minutes.

WILLIAM SCHUMAN 1910–1992

Schuman was born in New York City, and during his teenage years he wrote popular songs and played in jazz bands. In his early twenties he studied harmony and counterpoint privately and also took summer music courses at the Juilliard School of Music, and between 1935 and 1937 he was enrolled at Columbia University Teachers College. During the course of his studies he also taught at Sarah Lawrence College, where he conducted the college chorus between 1939 and 1945. He was recognized as a noteworthy composer after a performance of his *Symphony #2* by Serge Koussevitzky and the Boston Symphony Orchestra in 1939, his *Symphony #3* won a New York Music Critics' Circle Award in 1941, and the cantata *A Free Song* won a Pulitzer Prize in 1943. Between 1945 and 1948 he was director of publications for G. Schirmer, and from 1948 until 1962 he was president of Juilliard School of Music. Continuing his prestigious appointments, he served as president of the Lincoln Center for the Performing Arts between 1962 and 1969, and for several years during the 1970s and also several years during the 1980s he was chairman of the MacDowell Colony. For his accomplishments and contributions to the cultural life of the United States, he was awarded numerous honorary degrees, a National Medal of Arts (1987), and a Kennedy Center Honors Award (1989).

Schuman composed twenty-five choral works, five of which are settings of texts by Walt Whitman. Included are *Carols of Death,* Schuman's best-known choral composition, which is a cycle of three part songs, the first set to Whitman's "The Last Invocation," the second to "Darest Thou Now O Soul" (titled "The Unknown Region" by Schuman), and the third to the verse "Come lovely and soothing death" (titled by Schuman "To all, to each") from "When Lilacs Last in the Dooryard Bloom'd"; *A Free Song,* subtitled "Secular Cantata #2," which is a two-movement work, the first a setting of Whitman's "Long, too long, America" and "Look down, fair moon," and the second a setting of "Song of the Banner at Daybreak"; and *Perceptions,* which is a cycle of eight part songs (six scored for SATB chorus a cappella, one for SSA, and the other for TTBB) set to passages from a variety of Whitman poems.

Schuman's other popular choral works include *Mail Order Madrigals,* a cycle of four part songs set to texts from the 1897 Sears Roebuck catalogue; *Five Rounds on Famous Words* (Health, Thrift, Caution, Beauty, and Haste); and *Casey at the Bat,* a cantata arranged from Schuman's opera *The Mighty Casey.* All the works are tonal, with pandiatonic harmonies and occasional unresolved dissonances.

ALAN HOVHANESS 1911–2000

Hovhaness was born in Somerville, Massachusetts, and educated at the New England Conservatory. Further studies were at the Berkshire Music Center with Aaron Copland and Leonard Bernstein. During his student days, Hovhaness became exposed to the music of India, and throughout the remainder of his life he traveled widely and composed in a variety of styles. He was recognized for his *Symphony #2* op.132 of 1955, subtitled "Mysterious Mountain," and he received accolades for two works composed in 1970—the orchestral tone poem *And God Created Great Whales* op.229 no.1 for orchestra and taped sounds of whale vocalizations, and the *Symphony #21* op.234, subtitled "Etchmiadzin." His compositional output is large, consisting of twelve operas, sixty-seven symphonies, a number of instrumental chamber pieces and songs, and over fifty choral works. The vast majority of the choral works are sacred, including several masses—the early *Missa brevis* op.4 of 1935 scored for SATB chorus, organ, and strings (written in a neo-Renaissance modal style); *The Way of Jesus* op.278 of 1974 (a folk mass scored for SATB chorus, unison chorus or congregation, three guitars, and orchestra); and *A Simple Mass* op.282 of 1975 scored for soloists, SATB chorus, and organ. Other choral works that have entered the performing repertory are the anthem *Make a joyful noise* op.105 of 1967 for SATB chorus, brass, and organ, and *Magnificat* op.157 of 1958 scored for soloists, SATB chorus, and orchestra and characterized by aleatoric sections of music.

GIAN CARLO MENOTTI 1911–2007

Menotti was born in Cadegliano, Italy, a small town on Lake Lugano. He demonstrated an early interest in music by composing an opera, *The Death of Pierrot*, at age seven, and at twelve he enrolled at the Verdi Conservatory in Milan. At seventeen he moved to the United States to attend the Curtis Institute in Philadelphia, and while there he met and became close friends with Samuel Barber, one of his fellow students. At twenty-two Menotti began the composition of his opera *Amelia al ballo*, which was premiered in English translation as *Amelia goes to the Ball* in 1937 and performed at the Metropolitan Opera in New York City the following year, and in 1939 he received a commission from NBC radio for the opera *The Old Maid and the Thief*. During the 1940s he composed *The Medium* and *The Consul*, the latter of which won both a Pulitzer Prize and the New York Drama Critics' Circle Award for the best musical play of 1954, and in 1951 he composed *Amahl and the Night Visitors*, a commission from NBC television (the first such commission in history), which premiered on Christmas Eve 1951. In 1958 Menotti founded the Spoleto Festival of Two Worlds, and in 1977 he added Charleston, South Carolina, as a second festival site. Meanwhile, operas continued to be the focus of his compositional activity, with *Goya* being composed in 1986 for the singer Plácido Domingo and the Washington National Opera. During the final decade of his life he composed little music, although he remained active until his death at age ninety-five.

Menotti's choral output includes two masses, five cantatas, and eight miscellaneous choral works—all basically tonal. Of the masses, *Missa "O pulchritudo"* was commissioned by the Bel Canto Chorus of Milwaukee and premiered in 1979. It consists of the traditional Latin Mass Ordinary except the Credo, which is replaced by a setting of text by St Augustine, "O pulchritudo, tam antiqua et tam nova, sero te amavi" (O beauty, ever old and ever new, too late have I loved you). *Mass for the Contemporary English Liturgy* was composed in 1985 and is scored for congregation, SATB chorus, and organ.

The first of Menotti's cantatas, *The Death of the Bishop of Brindisi*, is considered to be one of his most effective compositions. Commissioned by the Cincinnati Musical Festival Association and premiered at the May Festival in 1963, it is a setting of text by the composer based on the Children's Crusade of 1212: at the end of his life, the Bishop of Brindisi, in dialogue with a nun, expresses his remorse for letting children sail to their deaths. Other cantatas include *Muero porque no muero* composed in 1982 and set to a Spanish text based on words by Teresa of Avila (1515–1582), *For the Death of Orpheus* composed in 1990 and premiered by the Atlanta Symphony Orchestra under the direction of Robert Shaw, and *Llama de Amor Viva* composed in 1991 and set to a text based on the writings of St John of the Cross.

The miscellaneous works include Menotti's most popular and best-known choral work, *The Unicorn, the Gorgon, and the Manticore*. Subtitled "The Three Sundays of a Poet," which represent the three stages of an artist's life and development, it was composed in 1956 as a theater piece for chorus, chamber ensemble, and ten dancers. The chorus relates the drama in fourteen movements (an introduction, march, and twelve madrigals, most of which are a cappella), while the instrumental chamber ensemble accompanies the dancers, who depict the action of the story in seven interludes. The text, written by Menotti, is about an anonymous man in a castle who defies societal expectations by having unusual pets—a unicorn, gorgon, and manticore—that he parades around town. Of the remaining miscellaneous works, *Moans, Groans, Cries, and Sighs*, subtitled "A Composer at Work," was commissioned in 1981 by the King's Singers; *Gloria*, scored for T solo, mixed chorus, and orchestra, was commissioned in 1995 by the American Choral Directors Association; and Menotti's final composition, an a cappella motet for SATB chorus (with divisions) entitled *Regina caeli*, was written in 1999.

CHORAL WORKS
SELECTED AND LISTED ACCORDING TO FAMILIARITY

The Unicorn, the Gorgon, and the Manticore – 1956 – SSAATTBB chorus and instrumental ensemble of flute, oboe, clarinet, bassoon, trumpet, cello, string bass, harp, and percussion – 42 minutes. (1) Most of the choral writing is a cappella; (2) the instruments play mainly in separate interludes.

The Death of the Bishop of Brindisi – 1963 – SB solos, children's chorus, SATB chorus, and orchestra (including bass clarinet, two pianos, and harp) – 30 minutes. (1) Solo roles are for the Bishop (B) and the Nun (S); (2) the children's chorus is generally in two parts but has a brief passage in three parts.

Muero porque no muero – 1982 – S solo, SSATTBB chorus, and orchestra – 11 minutes. The choral writing is brief and occurs only at the end of the cantata.

For the Death of Orpheus – 1990 – T solo, SATB chorus (with divisions), and orchestra (including piccolo, bass clarinet, contrabassoon, and harp) – 12 minutes.

Llama de Amor Viva – 1991 – B solo, SATB chorus (with divisions), and orchestra (including piccolo and harp) – 9:15 minutes.

Missa "O pulchritudo" – 1979 – SATB solos, SATB chorus (with divisions), and orchestra – 43 minutes.

NORMAN DELLO JOIO 1913–2008

Dello Joio was born in New York City and began his musical education with his father and godfather, both of whom were organists. At fourteen, while he was enrolled at All Hallows Institute, the young Dello Joio began playing the organ at Star of the Sea Church. Between 1932 and 1934 he studied at the College of the City of New York, in 1936 he began taking courses at the Institute of Musical Art, and from 1939 to 1941 he studied at Juilliard Graduate School. Further studies were at Yale University with Paul Hindemith. In 1945 Dello Joio joined the faculty of Sarah Lawrence College, and in 1948 he was recognized for his *Variations, Chaconne and Finale,* which was performed by the New York Philharmonic under Bruno Walter and which won the New York Music Critics' Circle Award. Dello Joio was appointed professor of composition at Mannes College in 1956, and in 1972 he became dean of the Fine and Applied Arts School at Boston University. Meanwhile, he won a Pulitzer Prize in 1957 for his *Meditations on Ecclesiastes* for string orchestra, and his score for the television production *The Louvre* won an Emmy in 1965.

One-fourth of Dello Joio's thirty-two choral works are settings of texts by Walt Whitman. These include his most popular compositions—*The Mystic Trumpeter, A Jubilant Song,* and *Song of the Open Road*—all written within a ten-year span beginning in 1943. In each of the works Dello Joio treats the poetry freely, adapting it by deleting verses and rearranging lines to increase dramatic impact, and also, like William Schuman, by giving some of the poems new titles. Such is the case with *A Jubilant Song* and *As of a Dream.* Other Whitman settings, with titles matching the poetry, are *Vigil Strange, Proud Music of the Storm,* and *Years of the Modern.* Dello Joio's longest Whitman setting, *Songs of Walt Whitman,* is to a cycle of the poems "I Sit and Look Out," "The Dalliance of Eagles," and "Tears," plus a montage entitled by the composer "Take our hand, Walt Whitman." Popular compositions set to other poetry include *To Saint Cecilia,* an adaptation of John Dryden's poem "A Song for St Cecilia's Day"; *Come to me, my love,* a selection of lines from "Echo" by Christina Rossetti; *The Poet's Song,* from poetry by Alfred Lord Tennyson; and *Of Crows and Clusters,* based on "Two Old Crows" by Vachel Lindsay.

Approximately one-fourth of Dello Joio's choral output is set to sacred texts, including three liturgical masses—*Mass of 1969, Mass in Honor of the Eucharist* of 1975, and *Mass in Honor of the Blessed Virgin Mary* of 1984. The vocal forces of the first work are exclusively for mixed chorus, while the latter two works include scoring for cantor and congregation. Additional sacred works include the two Psalm settings annotated below, *Prayers of Cardinal Newman* of 1960 for SATB chorus and organ, and *The Holy Infant's Lullaby* of 1961 variously scored for SATB chorus and piano, SSAA and piano, and unison chorus and piano or organ.

SECULAR CHORAL WORKS
SELECTED AND LISTED IN CHRONOLOGICAL ORDER
ACCORDING TO DATE OF COMPOSITION

The Mystic Trumpeter – 1943 – STB solos, SATB/SATB chorus, and horn –
8 minutes.

A Jubilant Song – 1945 – SATB chorus (with divisions) and piano –
6:30 minutes. The scoring includes a brief S solo.

Song of the Open Road – 1952 – SATB chorus, trumpet, and piano –
9:30 minutes.

To Saint Cecilia – 1958 – SATB chorus (with occasional divisions) and brass
ensemble or piano – 15 minutes. The scoring includes a brief B solo.

Come to me, my love – 1972 – SATB or SSA chorus and piano – 3 minutes.

The Poet's Song – 1973 – SATB chorus and piano – 4 minutes.

SACRED CHORAL WORKS
SELECTED AND LISTED IN CHRONOLOGICAL ORDER
ACCORDING TO DATE OF COMPOSITION

Mass – 1969 – SATB chorus, brass ensemble, and organ or piano – 20 minutes. The scoring includes a brief B solo.

A Psalm of David – 1950 – SATB chorus, strings, brass ensemble, and percussion – 25 minutes.

Psalm of Peace – 1972 – SATB chorus, trumpet, horn, and organ or piano – 16 minutes.

IRVING FINE 1914–1962

Fine was born in Boston, Massachusetts, and was educated at Harvard University. Further musical studies were at the American Conservatory in Fontainebleau with Nadia Boulanger. Between 1939 and 1950 Fine taught theory at Harvard and also conducted the Harvard Glee Club, and from 1950 until his death he was on the faculty of Brandeis School of Creative Arts. In addition, he taught composition at the Berkshire Music Center, served as the pianist of the Boston Symphony Orchestra, and wrote articles for such publications as *Musical America* and *The New York Times*. His choral output includes nine original works and a number of arrangements of songs by Aaron Copland. The most popular of the original works, *The Hour-Glass,* is a cycle of six part songs set to poetry of Ben Jonson, scored for SSAATTBB or SATB chorus with divisions and occasional brief solo passages, and characterized by tonal, diatonic harmonies that are distributed in tall chords (i.e., chords that range from low bass notes to high soprano notes). Fine also composed four additional cycles of part songs—*The Choral New Yorker, McCord's Menagerie,* and two series of *Three Choruses from Alice in Wonderland* (the first series scored for SATB chorus and piano and the second for SSA chorus and piano). The choral arrangements of Copland's solo songs are popular with public school and amateur choral ensembles.

CHORAL WORKS AND ARRANGEMENTS
SELECTED AND LISTED ACCORDING TO FAMILIARITY

The Hour-Glass – 1949 – SATB chorus (with divisions) a cappella – "O know to end as to begin" 3 minutes, "Have you seen the white lily grow" 2 minutes, "O do not wanton with those eyes" 1:30 minutes, "Against jealousy" 3 minutes, "Lament" 2:45 minutes, and "The Hour-glass" 2 minutes.

Three Choruses from Alice in Wonderland – 1942 – SATB chorus and piano (orchestrated 1949) – "The Lobster Quadrille" 3 minutes, "Lullaby of the Duchess" 3:30 minutes, and "Father William" 3 minutes.

Simple Gifts ("Shaker Song") – SA (or TB) chorus and piano – 2 minutes.

Ching-a-Ring Chaw – SSAA chorus and piano – 1:45 minutes.

I Bought Me a Cat – ST solos, SSA chorus, and piano – 3 minutes.

Long Time Ago – SATB chorus and piano – 2:30 minutes.

VINCENT PERSICHETTI 1915–1987

Persichetti was born in Philadelphia, Pennsylvania, and was enrolled at the Combs Conservatory of Music at age five. He remained there for fifteen years, studying piano, organ, and string bass, and graduating in 1935 with a bachelor's degree. He continued his studies at the Philadelphia Conservatory, receiving a master's degree in 1941 and a doctorate in 1945, and he also studied at the Curtis Institute. Meanwhile, he taught theory and composition at the Philadelphia Conservatory beginning in 1941, and in 1947 he joined the faculty of the Juilliard School of Music, becoming chair of the composition department in 1963. In addition, he served as director of publications for Elkan-Vogel beginning in 1952, and he published the text *Twentieth Century Harmony* in 1961.

His twenty choral works, all in a conservative pandiatonic harmonic idiom, include several cantatas and part songs that were staples of programming for high school and collegiate choral ensembles during the latter decades of the twentieth century. Six of the works are settings of poetry by e. e. cummings—two sets of part songs (*Two Cummings Choruses* op.33 and *Four Cummings Choruses* op.98) for two voices and piano, two compositions for women's voices (*Two Cummings Choruses* op.46 for SSAA chorus a cappella and *Spring Cantata* op.94 for SSAA chorus and piano), *Glad and Very* op.129 for two voices, and *Flower Songs* op.157 for SATB chorus and strings. The pieces in the earliest and latest of these opuses are the most popular—"sam was a man" and "Jimmie's got a goil" in opus 33, and "Flowers of Stone," "Spouting Violets," "Early Flowers," "Is There a Flower," "A Yellow Flower," "The Rose Is Dying," and "Lily Has a Rose" in opus 157. Other popular secular works include the *Winter Cantata* op.97—a setting of eleven Japanese haiku.

The well-known sacred works include the *Mass* op.84 and *Te Deum*, commissioned separately by New York City's Collegiate Chorale; *Te Deum* op.93, commissioned by the Pennsylvania Music Educators Association; and *The Creation* op.111, commissioned by the Juilliard School of Music. The *Mass* is one of the most noteworthy examples of neo-Renaissance writing in the twentieth century. Unmetered phrases and chant-like melodies, with repetition of motifs and alternating textures of imitative polyphony and homophony, reflect on the writing of the late sixteenth century. The oratorio *The Creation*, which Persichetti considered his most significant composition, is set to texts, all in English, taken from more than two dozen diverse sources, including Asian and Western myths, religious and secular poetry, and excerpts from scientific manuals.

CHORAL WORKS
SELECTED AND LISTED IN CHRONOLOGICAL ORDER
ACCORDING TO DATE OF COMPOSITION

Mass op.84 – 1960 – SATB chorus (with occasional divisions) a cappella – 20 minutes.

Stabat Mater op.92 – 1963 – SATB chorus (with divisions) and orchestra – 28 minutes.

Te Deum op.93 – 1963 – SATB chorus (with divisions) and orchestra – 12 minutes.

Winter Cantata op.97 – 1964 – SSAA chorus, flute, and marimba – 18 minutes.

The Creation op.111 – 1969 – SATB solos, SATB chorus (with divisions to twelve parts), and large orchestra – 60 minutes.

Flower Songs op.157 – 1983 – SATB chorus (with occasional divisions) and strings – 20 minutes.

ULYSSES KAY 1917–1995

Kay was born in Tucson, Arizona, and in his youth learned to play the piano, violin, and saxophone. His formal musical education was at the University of Arizona and Eastman School of Music, with further studies at the Berkshire Music Center and Yale and Columbia universities. From 1953 to 1968 he served as editorial advisor and music consultant for Broadcast Music, Inc., and between 1968 and 1988 he taught at Herbert H. Lehman College of the City University of New York. He also had brief appointments as a visiting professor at Boston University and the University of California at Los Angeles. His thirty choral works, all in a tonal idiom characterized by chromatic harmonies, include five cantatas and several noteworthy a cappella pieces. Of the cantatas, *Song of Jeremiah* was composed in 1945 (revised in 1947) and scored for B solo, mixed chorus, and orchestra; *Choral Tryptich* of 1962, based on Psalms 5 and 13 plus other biblical texts, is scored for mixed chorus and strings or organ; *Stephen Crane Set* of 1967 is for mixed chorus and thirteen instruments; and *Parables* of 1969, a setting of two anonymous Western American tales, is scored for mixed chorus and nine instruments. The a cappella pieces include *Christmas Carol* of 1943 for SSA chorus, *Come Away, Come Away Death* of 1944 for TTB chorus, *Lincoln Letter* of 1953 for B solo and SATB chorus, and *A Wreath of Waits* of 1954 for SATB chorus.

LEONARD BERNSTEIN 1918–1990

Bernstein was born in Lawrence, Massachusetts, and began piano lessons when he was ten. His formal education was at Harvard University, where he met and became friends with Aaron Copland, and also at the Curtis Institute, where he studied orchestration with Randall Thompson and conducting with Fritz Reiner. Further studies were at Tanglewood, where he studied conducting with Serge Koussevitzky and became his assistant in 1942. In 1943 Bernstein was appointed assistant conductor of the New York Philharmonic and came into the public eye in November of that year when he substituted on national radio for an ailing Bruno Walter. In 1944 he was recognized for several compositions—the *Symphony #1*, subtitled "Jeremiah," which was premiered by the Pittsburgh Symphony Orchestra and was the winner of the New York Music Critics' Circle Award; the ballet *Fancy Free,* which premiered at the Metropolitan Opera House; and the musical *On the Town,* which premiered on Broadway. Several other acclaimed musicals appeared on Broadway during the 1950s, including *On the Waterfront* in 1954, *Candide* in 1956, and *West Side Story* in 1957. During the 1950s Bernstein was also appointed music director of the New York Philharmonic (the first American-born person to hold this position). His conducting activities expanded throughout the 1960s, and his many acclaimed performances, including the Mahler symphonies with the Vienna Philharmonic and broadcasts of the *Young People's*

Concerts with the New York Philharmonic, elevated him to the status of America's most celebrated and famous conductor. His recordings earned eleven Grammy awards, and in addition, he was given a Lifetime Achievement Grammy and a Kennedy Center Honors Award.

Of his ten choral works, approximately half are set to Hebrew texts. These works include several small-scale liturgical and folk pieces and the *Chichester Psalms* and *Symphony #3*, subtitled "Kaddish." Commissioned by the Southern Cathedrals Festival in England for a performance by the combined choirs of Chichester, Winchester, and Salisbury cathedrals, *Chichester Psalms* is a work in three movements—Psalms 108:2 and 100 representing praise in movement one, Psalms 23 and 2:1–4 representing peace and war in movement two, and Psalms 131 and 133:1 representing the struggle for and achievement of peace in movement three. All three movements are characterized by repeat structures (ABCBA in movement one, AAB and A and B simultaneously in movement two, and ABA in movement three), and movements one and three are unified by a five-note motif. Of notable poignancy is the transformation of the motif from its octave form symbolizing praise at the beginning and end of movement one, its dissonant setting exemplifying struggle at the beginning of movement two, and its tonal manifestation as a chorale set to the text "Hineh mah tov umah nayim, shevet ahim gam yahad" (Behold how good and how pleasant it is for brethren to dwell together in unity) at the conclusion of movement three. *Symphony #3* was commissioned by the Koussevitzky Music Foundation and the Boston Symphony Orchestra for the orchestra's seventy-fifth anniversary in 1955. However, it was not completed or performed until December 1963 (by the Israel Philharmonic in Tel Aviv) and January 1964 (by the Boston Symphony Orchestra), at which time it was dedicated "to the beloved memory of John F. Kennedy," President of the United States, who was assassinated November 22, 1963. The work, which is based on the Hebrew prayer often spoken by mourners at funerals and memorials, is like the Lutheran Passions of the Baroque era in combining traditional sacred texts with contemporary poetry or dialogue.

The compositions with texts other than Hebrew include *Choruses from The Lark* and *Missa Brevis*. The first of these works consists of two sets of pieces extracted from incidental music composed for the play *The Lark,* about the life of Joan of Arc. The first set, entitled *French Choruses,* consists of three pieces, the first of which, "Spring Song," is an adaptation of Claude Le Jeune's *Revoici venir du printemps* (spelled "Revecy venir le printemps" by Bernstein). The second set of pieces, entitled *Latin Choruses,* consists of several texts from the Roman Mass Ordinary, including the Benedictus, Sanctus, and Gloria. Bernstein later adapted and rearranged the music from the Lark choruses for *Missa Brevis,* which he dedicated to Robert Shaw on the occasion of his retirement as Music Director of the Atlanta Symphony Orchestra. Mention should also be made of *Mass,* "a theatre piece for singers, players, and dancers" that was composed for the opening in September 1971 of the John F. Kennedy Center for the Performing Arts in Washington, D.C., and scored for both boys' and mixed chorus.

CHORAL WORKS
SELECTED AND LISTED ACCORDING TO FAMILIARITY

Chichester Psalms – 1965 – boy solo, SATB chorus, and instrumental ensemble of three trumpets, three trombones, two harps, percussion, and strings – 18 minutes. (1) The scoring also calls for a brief SATB solo quartet, which is usually performed by members of the chorus; (2) according to the composer, "[While] the soprano and alto [choral] parts are written with boys' voices in mind, it is possible, though not preferable, to substitute women's voices"; (3) the boy solo "must not be sung by a woman, but either by a boy or by a counter tenor"; (4) the text of the work is in Hebrew.

Choruses from The Lark – 1955 – SSATTBB chorus and percussion – *French Choruses* with drum, 3:30 minutes, and *Latin Choruses* with bells, 6 minutes.

Missa Brevis – 1988 – countertenor solo, SSAATTBB chorus, and percussion – 11:30 minutes.

Symphony #3 ("Kaddish") – 1963 – speaker, S solo, boys' chorus, SATB chorus (with divisions), and orchestra – 42 minutes. (1) The boys' chorus is divided into a brief five-part canon; (2) the speaker's texts are in English while the sung texts are in Hebrew.

DAVE BRUBECK 1920–2012

Brubeck was born in Concord, California, and in his youth took piano lessons from his mother, a piano teacher. He later studied music formally at the College of the Pacific in Stockton, California, and at Mills College with Darius Milhaud. Brubeck had had an interest in jazz since age thirteen, when he began playing professionally in a jazz ensemble, and in 1949 he founded the Dave Brubeck Trio, which by 1958 evolved into the Dave Brubeck Quartet and which subsequently became one of the most long-lived and successful jazz ensembles of the twentieth century. Although most of his professional activity has centered around jazz performance, he has composed a number of classically oriented instrumental and choral works, including three oratorios and three cantatas—all containing passages that are to be improvised. *The Light in the Wilderness* of 1968, Brubeck's best-known and most frequently performed choral work, was inspired by the composer's service as an infantryman in World War II and composed for the Cincinnati Ecumenical Council. Its text is drawn from a variety of biblical passages that relate the teachings of Jesus, and its music is characterized by a mixture of conservative styles and modern techniques such as aleatoric rhythms and twelve-tone melodies. Scoring is for B solo, SATB chorus, and either organ with string bass and optional percussion or traditional orchestra, and a separate guide is published to aid the keyboardist in seven passages that are to be improvised. *Beloved Son,* subtitled an "Easter Oratorio," was composed for the American Lutheran Women's Convention. Its text, by the Lutheran poet Herbert Brokering, is divided into three sections—Abba Father (the scene in the Garden of Gethsemane), Eli (the walk to Calvary and the Crucifixion), and Rabboni (the Resurrection)—and its musical style combines jazz and classical idioms, with quotes from the music of J. S. Bach. Scoring is for SB solos, children's choir, SATB chorus, jazz quartet, and standard orchestra. *Voice of the Holy Spirit,* subtitled "Tongues of Fire," relates the story of Pentecost, which according to Brubeck depicts "the confusion and separateness imposed at the Tower of Babel." It is scored for B solo, SATB chorus, and various combinations of instruments.

The three cantatas—*The Gates of Justice* of 1969, *Truth Is Fallen* of 1971, and *La Fiesta de la Posada* of 1975—are similar in scoring and musical style. Additional choral works include the mass *To Hope* of 1980 for SATB solos, SATB chorus, piano, and optional handbells and celesta, and *Pange Lingua Variations* of 1983 for SATB chorus, brass ensemble, organ, strings, and percussion. This latter work, commissioned by the Cathedral of the Blessed Sacrament in Sacramento, California, is in an *alternatim* style: phrases of the Gregorian chant alternate with newly composed music. Text is in both Latin and English, and scoring is for mixed chorus and orchestra.

KAREL HUSA B.1921

Husa was born in Prague and in his youth learned to play the piano and violin. His formal musical education was first at the Prague Conservatory and then at the Ecole Normal de Musique in Paris, where he studied composition with Arthur Honegger, and at the Paris Conservatoire, where he studied with Nadia Boulanger. In 1954 he moved to the United States to teach at Cornell University, and in 1959 he became an American citizen. He remained at Cornell until his retirement in 1992, and during the latter years of the twentieth century he fulfilled important commissions (e.g., the *Concerto for Orchestra* in 1986 from the New York Philharmonic) and garnered significant awards (e.g., a Pulitzer Prize in 1969). His most significant choral work, *An American Te Deum*, was composed in 1976 to a variety of texts in Latin and English that, according to the composer, "express the feelings and aspirations of immigrants, mostly in the Midwest." Scoring is for B solo, SATB chorus, and band (arranged for orchestra in 1977). Other important choral works include *Apotheosis of this Earth*, composed in 1972 and scored for SATB chorus (singing random syllables of text) and orchestra, and *Three Moravian Songs* ("The Sun," "The Night," and "Aspen Leaves") composed in 1981 and scored for SATB chorus a cappella.

LUKAS FOSS 1922–2009

Foss was born in Berlin, Germany, and in his youth became a proficient pianist. In 1933 he continued his piano studies in Paris (and also studied flute, composition, and orchestration), and in 1937 he furthered his education in the United States at the Curtis Institute, studying composition with Randall Thompson and conducting with Fritz Reiner. Additional studies were with Serge Koussevitzky between 1939 and 1943 at the Berkshire Music Center and with Paul Hindemith in 1939 and 1940 at Yale University. In 1944, at age twenty-two, Foss was acknowledged for his cantata *The Prairie*, which was premiered by the Collegiate Chorale under the direction of Robert Shaw and which won a New York Music Critics' Circle Award, and in 1951 his reputation as a composer was further enhanced with the premiere of his *Piano Concerto #2*. In 1953 he was appointed professor of composition at the University of California in Los Angeles, and during the 1960s, 1970s, and 1980s he served as music director of several orchestras, including the Buffalo Philharmonic (1963–1970), Brooklyn Philharmonic (1971–1980), Kol Israel Orchestra in Jerusalem (1972–1976), and Milwaukee Symphony (1981–1986).

His thirteen choral works are divided between early compositions that are tonal and conservative in their harmonic language and later compositions that are nontraditional, experimental, and in some cases avant-garde. The early harmonically conservative works include *The Prairie* of 1944 set to poetry by Carl Sandburg; *Behold, I build an house,* a brief "biblical cantata" composed for the dedication of the Marsh Chapel at Boston University in 1950; *A Parable of Death* commissioned in 1952 by the Louisville Philharmonic Society and set in seven movements to poetry by Rainer Maria Rilke; and *Psalms,* a setting of Psalms 121, 95, 98, and 23 composed in 1955 and 1956.

The later, more modern works include *Fragments of Archilochos*, a cycle of twelve phrases by the ancient Greek satirist, each repeated three times in random order by groups of singers and instrumentalists; *Lamdeni mi* (Teach me), a work based on three twelfth-century Hebrew chants (the music of which is fragmented and transformed) for chorus and six instrumentalists, who create plucked and beaten sounds; and *American Cantata,* a setting of text phrases taken from American historical documents and poems that Foss calls "a drama, a tragedy: Whitman-like innocence (solo tenor) ignored by an indifferent environment (a world of pollution, money, pseudo-science), challenged in a trial situation, and finally destroyed." The music contains quotations from several American folk songs and nursery tunes, and it combines tonal, atonal, and popular harmonic idioms.

CHORAL WORKS
SELECTED AND LISTED IN CHRONOLOGICAL ORDER
ACCORDING TO DATE OF COMPOSITION

The Prairie – 1944 – SATB solos, SATB chorus, and chamber orchestra – 45 minutes.

Behold, I build an house – 1950 – SATB chorus and piano or organ – 10 minutes.

A Parable of Death – 1952 – female speaker, T solo, SATB chorus, and either large or chamber orchestra – 32 minutes.

Psalms – 1955–1956 – T solo, SATB chorus (with occasional divisions), and chamber orchestra or two pianos – 13 minutes.

Fragments of Archilochos – 1965 – male speaker, countertenor solo, four SATB chamber choruses, large mixed chorus ad lib., mandolin, guitar, and percussion – 10 minutes.

Lamdeni mi – 1973 – SATB chorus and percussion – 9 minutes.

American Cantata – 1976 – male and female speakers, T solo, SATB/SATB chorus, and chamber orchestra (including celesta, two electric guitars, piano, and electric organ) – 36 minutes.

DANIEL PINKHAM 1923–2006

Pinkham was born in Lynn, Massachusetts, and began playing the piano and composing at age five. Between 1937 and 1940 he attended Phillips Academy, where he studied harmony and served as the school's carillonneur, and from 1940 to 1944 he continued his education at Harvard University. Further studies were with Arthur Honegger and Nadia Boulanger in Paris, and with Paul Hindemith, Samuel Barber, and Aaron Copland at the Berkshire Music Center. During the 1940s and 1950s Pinkham held faculty appointments at Boston Conservatory and Boston and Harvard universities, and in 1958 he was appointed music director at Boston's historic King's Chapel (a position he retained for forty-two years). He also served on the faculty of the New England Conservatory beginning in 1959. In addition to working as a composer, teacher, and conductor, he was a noted harpsichordist and champion of early music (he founded the department of early music at the New England Conservatory), and for his many accomplishments he was awarded six honorary degrees, including doctorates from Westminster Choir College in 1979, New England Conservatory in 1993, and Boston Conservatory in 1998.

Pinkham's compositional output includes four symphonies, several concertos and sonatas, numerous organ pieces and songs, and more than two hundred choral works. Approximately one-third of the choral works are extended multimovement compositions set to sacred texts. Of these, the most popular and best known are several early cantatas—the *Wedding Cantata* set in four movements to passages from the Song of Songs ("Rise up, my love," "Many waters cannot quench love," "Awake, O north wind," and "Set me as a seal upon thine heart"); the *Christmas Cantata,* subtitled "Sinfonia Sacra," set in three movements to the traditional Latin texts "Quem vidistis pastores," "O magnum mysterium," and "Gloria in excelsis Deo"; and the *Easter Cantata* in three movements (plus an opening prelude) to passages from John 20:13, Matthew 28:5–7, and Psalms 118:24 and 68:18, 32–34.

Other extended compositions include five oratorios, three of which were written as semitheater works. *Daniel in the Lions' Den,* commissioned and premiered by the Pro Arte Chorale of Boston, with a subsequent performance by the Handel and Haydn Society of Boston, was, according to Pinkham, "conceived as a theater piece and consequently lends itself to a variety of multimedia production possibilities." *The Passion of Judas,* premiered in concert form by the National Presbyterian Church of Washington, D.C., was later given a semistaged performance in Boston's King's Chapel (stage directions and costume suggestions are identified in the score). The text and scoring are modeled on the Passions of J. S. Bach, with a combination of biblical passages and contemporary poetry. Pinkham describes the juxtaposition of old and new texts as "levels of time. The chorus, representing the *timelessness* of the Old Testament, sings only in three Psalms; the Narrator reads the New Testament scripture in his role of reporter; and the three modern texts are played by the five soloists . . . and serve to show . . . the human qualities of quite ordinary folk." *The Descent into Hell,* commissioned and premiered by West Virginia Wesleyan College, is a setting of text by Pinkham based on a Greek description of the Harrowing of Hell as found in the Apocryphal New Testament. Like the historiae of Schütz, the oratorio begins with a chorus that introduces the story and ends with a chorus of praise. Although no staging is indicated, costumes for the soloists are recommended.

The extended works set to secular texts include *To Troubled Friends,* a setting of four poems ("To a troubled friend," "Father," "A fit against the country," and "Evening") by the American Pulitzer Prize winner James Wright, and *Four Elegies,* a setting of poems by the British poets Robert Herrick ("To his dying brother, Master William Herrick"), Richard Crashaw ("Upon the death of a friend"), Henry Vaughan ("Silence, and stealth of days"), and John Donne ("At the round earths imagin'd corners"). Both works, indicative of Pinkham's style of writing in the 1970s and 1980s, are in a pantonal idiom, with highly dissonant harmonies.

The majority of the smaller-scale repertoire is set to sacred texts and, generally composed or intended for church choirs, is more harmonically conservative than the extended sacred and secular music. Representative sacred pieces include several Christmas carols and anthems and a collection of Psalm motets (examples of which are identified below). The small-scale secular repertoire is parallel in style to the extended works: early pieces (e.g., *Five Canzonets*) are tonal, while later pieces (e.g., *Love can be still*) are more advanced harmonically.

EXTENDED CHORAL WORKS
SELECTED AND LISTED IN CHRONOLOGICAL ORDER
ACCORDING TO DATE OF COMPOSITION

Wedding Cantata – 1956 – SATB chorus and piano or organ (later arranged for two horns, celesta, and strings) – 10 minutes.

Christmas Cantata – 1957 – S solo or S semichorus, SATB chorus, and double brass choir – 9:30 minutes.

Easter Cantata – 1961 – SATB chorus, brass ensemble, timpani, percussion, and celesta – 11:30 minutes.

Requiem – 1963 – AT solos, SATB chorus, brass ensemble, and string bass – 15 minutes.

Stabat Mater – 1964 – S solo, SATB chorus, and chamber orchestra (including harp) – 16 minutes.

St Mark Passion – 1965 – STBB solos, SATB chorus, brass ensemble, string bass, timpani, percussion, harp, and organ – 32 minutes.

Jonah – 1967 – speaker, ATB solos, SATB chorus, and orchestra – 26 minutes.

Ascension Cantata – 1970 – SATB chorus and orchestra – 12 minutes.

To Troubled Friends – 1972 – SATB chorus, strings, and electronic tape – 18 minutes.

Daniel in the Lions' Den – 1972 – speaker, TBB solos, SATB chorus, two pianos, percussion, and electronic tape – 20 minutes.

Fanfares – 1975 – T solo, SATB chorus (with divisions), two trumpets, two trombones, timpani, percussion, organ, and electronic tape – 12 minutes.

The Passion of Judas – 1976 – SATBB solos, SATB chorus, clarinet, viola, string bass, harp, and organ – 32 minutes.

The Descent into Hell – 1979 – STB solos, SATB semichorus (twelve singers), SATB chorus, brass ensemble, timpani, percussion, organ, and electronic tape – 20 minutes.

Four Elegies – 1979 – T solo, SATB chorus, chamber orchestra, and electronic tape – 13:30 minutes.

SMALL-SCALE WORKS
SELECTED AND LISTED ACCORDING TO FAMILIARITY

The Sheepheards Song ("A Caroll or Himme for Christmas") – 1971 – S solo, SATB chorus, and electronic tape – 3:30 minutes.

Evergreen ("A Christmas Carol for Unison Voices") – 1974 – unison chorus and chord-producing instrument (e.g., organ, piano, harp, harpsichord, or guitar) and percussion instruments ad lib. – 2 minutes.

Love can be still – SSATB chorus a cappella – 8 minutes.

Farewell, vain world – 1964 – SATB chorus a cappella – 2 minutes.

Five Canzonets – 1960 – SA chorus a cappella – 3:30 minutes.

Psalm Motets – SATB chorus a cappella (organ ad lib.) – "Open to me the
gates of righteousness" 1 minute, "Thou has loved righteousness" 3 minutes, "Behold, how good and how pleasant" 2 minutes, and "Thou hast
turned my laments into dancing" 1 minute.

Three Lenten Poems of Richard Crashaw – 1965 – SSA (or SATB chorus),
string quartet (or string orchestra), and handbells (or celesta or harp) –
5 minutes.

When God Arose – 1979 – SSATB solos, SATB chorus, organ, harpsichord,
and percussion – 7 minutes.

NED ROREM B.1923

Rorem was born in Richmond, Indiana, but raised in Chicago, where he studied music theory
at the American Conservatory with Leo Sowerby. After brief periods of additional study at Northwestern University (1940–1942) and the Curtis Institute (1942), Rorem worked in New York
City as secretary and music copyist for Virgil Thomson. He then continued his education in
1946 at the Berkshire Music Center with Aaron Copland, at the Juilliard School of Music in 1947
with Bernard Wagenaar, and at the Ecole Normal de Musique in Paris with Arthur Honegger.
Rorem remained in Paris for six years, composing numerous songs and socializing with the literary and musical elite of the time (including Francis Poulenc), and in 1958 when he returned
to the United States, he joined the faculty of the Curtis Institute. During the 1960s and 1970s
he became recognized for his song cycle *War Scenes* (premiered in 1969) and orchestral suite
Air Music, which won a Pulitzer Prize in 1976, and he also became known for his several published diaries, especially *The Paris Diary* (1966) and *The New York Diary* (1967). In 1980 he returned to the Curtis Institute as professor of composition, and in the following years he received
numerous commissions from organizations such as the Santa Fe Chamber Music Festival and
Atlanta, Pittsburgh, and Chicago symphony orchestras.

Rorem's compositional output includes more than four hundred songs and approximately
seventy choral compositions. Two of the earliest choral works, both for a cappella chorus, are
among his most popular—*Four Madrigals,* a setting of poems in English translation by Sappho,
and *From an Unknown Past,* a setting of seven old English poems by unknown authors arranged
from solo songs. The madrigals are noteworthy examples of twentieth-century pieces in a neo-
Renaissance style: the texts are set syllabically, with careful attention to speech declamation, and
the textures are characterized by alternating passages of homophony and imitative polyphony
(the third madrigal begins with a phrase immediately imitated in inversion). The pieces in *From
an Unknown Past,* being arrangements of solo songs, are, like the famous part songs by Samuel
Barber, excellent representatives of the part song genre in the twentieth century. Two other popular neo-Renaissance works, both composed in 1973, are the *Three Motets* ("O Deus, ego amo
te," "Oratorio Patris Condren: O Jesu vivens in Maria," and "Thee, God, I come from, to thee
go"), composed to poems by Gerard Manley Hopkins, and *Missa Brevis,* a setting in Latin of the
Kyrie, Gloria, Sanctus, Benedictus, and Agnus Dei portions of the Roman Mass Ordinary. All
the works are in a tonal idiom, with occasional chromatic melodies and pandiatonic harmonies.

Works in a more advanced tonal and harmonic idiom include *In Time of Pestilence,* a collection of six short madrigals on verses of Thomas Nashe (1567–1601), each ending with the phrase "Lord, have mercy on us," and *Truth in the Night Season,* a setting of Psalm 92 based on a partial tone row (four notes). Rorem's several large-scale works include the twelve-movement *An American Oratorio,* which was commissioned and premiered by the Mendelssohn Choir of Pittsburgh for the celebration of its seventy-fifth anniversary. The text combines the writings of eight American authors (Emma Lazarus, Edgar Allan Poe, Henry Wadsworth Longfellow, Mark Twain, Sidney Lanier, Herman Melville, Stephen Crane, and Walt Whitman), all of which deal with the subject of withdrawal from the world. As a motto for the oratorio, Rorem quotes "Where is the world we roved, Ned Bunn? Hollows thereof lay rich in shade" from Melville's "To Ned."

CHORAL WORKS
SELECTED AND LISTED IN CHRONOLOGICAL ORDER
ACCORDING TO DATE OF COMPOSITION

Four Madrigals – 1947 – SATB chorus a cappella – 6:30 minutes.

From an Unknown Past – 1951 – SATB chorus a cappella – 10 minutes.

Two Psalms and a Proverb – 1962 – SATB chorus and string quintet – 10 minutes.

Truth in the Night Season – 1966 – SATB chorus (with divisions) and organ – 5 minutes.

In Time of Pestilence – 1973 – SATB chorus (with occasional divisions) a cappella – 8 minutes.

Three Motets – 1973 – SATB chorus and organ – 7 minutes.

Missa Brevis – 1973 – STB solos and SATB chorus (with occasional divisions) – 15 minutes.

Little Prayers – 1973 – SB solos, SATB chorus, and orchestra – 22 minutes.

Surge, Illuminare – 1977 – SATB chorus and organ – 4 minutes.

O Magnum Mysterium – 1978 – SATB chorus (divided into SATTB) a cappella – 3 minutes.

An American Oratorio – 1983 – T solo, SATB chorus (with occasional divisions), and orchestra – 40 minutes.

What Is Pink – 1987 – SA chorus and piano – 12 minutes.

KIRKE MECHEM B.1925

Mechem was born in Wichita, Kansas, and educated at Stanford and Harvard universities, with further studies in Vienna. His principal teachers in the United States were Walter Piston and Randall Thompson, and his principal supporter in Vienna was Josef Krips, who became conductor of the San Francisco Symphony Orchestra and programmed a number of Mechem's symphonies. After brief appointments teaching at Stanford University and serving as composer-in-residence at San Francisco University, he devoted his time and energies to composing full time. His prolific compositional output includes numerous operas, for which he is best known (*Tartuffe* has been performed worldwide), and songs and song cycles (e.g., *Songs of the Slave*). He has also composed a large number of choral works, including several popular cycles. Of these, *Winging Wildly,* scored for SSATB chorus (with occasional divisions) a cappella, is a set of three pieces to poetry about or that mentions birds—"Birds at Dusk" by Sara Teasdale, "The Caged Bird" by Paul Dunbar, and "Everyone Sang" by Siegfried Sassoon. *Songs of Wisdom,* scored for SATB chorus (with divisions and incidental SATB solos) a cappella, is a set of five motets—"The Song of Moses," "A Love Song," "The Protest of Job," "A Song of Comfort," and "A Song of Praise." Distinctively, each motet begins with a solo a cappella recitative. *Five Centuries of Spring,* scored for SATB chorus a cappella, is a setting of the poems "Spring" by Thomas Nashe, "From You I Have Been Absent" by William Shakespeare, "Laughing Song" by William Blake, "Loveliest of Trees" by A. E. Housman, and "Spring" by Edna St Vincent Millay. *American Madrigals,* scored for SATB or SSAA chorus and chamber ensemble, is a cycle of five pieces based on American folk songs—"Kind Miss," "He's Gone Away," "Kansas Boys," "Adam's Bride," and "New York Girls." The single-movement choral works are represented by *Professor Nontroppo's Music Dictionary* (a setting of Italian tempo and other musical terms), *Time* (a setting of lines found on an antique bell, with the inclusion of numerous onomatopoeic bell sounds), and *Island in Space* (a setting of text adapted from words spoken by the American astronaut Russell Schweickart). All the music is in a tonal idiom, with only occasional dissonances.

DOMINICK ARGENTO B.1927

Argento was born in York, Pennsylvania, and educated at the Peabody Conservatory of Music and Eastman School of Music. Additional studies were with Luigi Dallapiccola at the Cherubini Conservatory in Florence, Italy. In 1958 Argento was appointed to the faculty of the University of Minnesota, and in 1963 he cofounded the Center Opera Company (now named Minnesota Opera). During the 1970s and 1980s he composed several notable operas, including *Postcard from Morocco* in 1971, and also several notable song cycles for specific singers, including *From the Diary of Virginia Woolf* for mezzo-soprano Janet Baker in 1974 (which won a Pulitzer Prize), *The Andrée Expedition* for baritone Håkan Hagegård in 1982, and *Casa Guidi* for mezzo-soprano Frederica von Stade in 1983 (a recording of which won an Emmy in 2004). In recent years Argento has received numerous commissions from renowned organizations, including the New York City Opera, Washington National Opera, and Baltimore and St Louis symphonies.

Argento has composed more than twenty choral works in addition to fourteen operas, eighteen miscellaneous orchestral works, and seven song cycles. The early choral works include *A Nation of Cowslips* (a cycle of part songs set to doggerel verses by John Keats about his travels through England), *The Revelation of Saint John the Divine* (a "Rhapsody" in three movements—"Prologue and Adoration," "The Seven Seals and Seven Trumpets," and "Jubilation and Epilogue"), and *Jonah and the Whale* (an oratorio based on the fourteenth-century poem "Patience, or Jonah and the Whale" and a variety of other texts, including biblical passages, the Kyrie from the Roman Mass Ordinary, a sea shanty, and an original verse by Argento). The oratorio's musical style is equally diverse, with traditional forms such as fugue and chorale presented in tonalities that range from traditional to twelve-tone, and the oratorio's structure is bound together by threes: the tone row is based on ascending and descending diminished thirds, the instrumentation is in groups of threes (three trombones, three percussionists, and three keyboards), and there is extensive use of triple meter and the key of E-flat major.

The middle-period works include several of Argento's most celebrated compositions. *Peter Quince at the Clavier* is a setting of the complete poem of the same name by the American poet Wallace Stevens (1879–1955); according to Argento, "Stevens' poem takes [the story of Susanna and the Elders from an apocryphal chapter in the Book of Daniel] for a metaphor of the emotive power of beauty on the human spirit (in particular, the beauty of music), its use and abuse in stirring our feelings, and its lingering strength in memory." Argento subtitled the work "Sonatina for Mixed Chorus and Piano Concertante" and divided the music into four traditional movements—expository, slow and rhapsodic, fast and virtuosic, and conclusionary, with repeats of melodies from previous movements. *I Hate and I Love,* subtitled "Odi et amo," is a setting of six poems by the ancient Roman poet Gaius Valerius Catullus (ca.84 B.C.–ca.54 B.C.) about his love and hate for Clodia—"a married woman ten years his senior, beautiful, cultured, elegant, and incurably dissolute." *A Toccata of Galuppi's* is a setting of the poem by the British Victorian poet Robert Browning (1812–1889) about "human frailty" as it relates to "the decline of grandeur in eighteenth-century Venice." All three works are constructed of twelve-tone elements presented in a pantonal manner; melodies are frequently lyrical, and harmonies, except for those used to create harsh effects, often consist of major and minor tonalities. In *A Toccata of Galuppi's,* Argento overlays phrases of the *Toccata #11* in B-flat major by the eighteenth-century Italian Baldassare Galuppi with a set of variations on a twelve-tone theme.

Of Argento's other popular choral works, *Gloria* is a setting of the beginning of the traditional Latin text (from "Gloria in excelsis Deo" through "Glorificamus te") that Argento incorporated into his opera *The Masque of Angels,* and *Te Deum,* subtitled "Verba Domini cum verbis populi" (Words of the Lord with popular words), is a setting of six anonymous Middle English lyrics that correspond to six sections of the traditional Latin text. As is stated by Argento in the preface to the score, "Each English lyric either treats the theology of the original text in vivid and popular language or is almost a vernacular paraphrase of the Latin itself." Describing the music, Argento states, "To avoid the potential monotony of an all-pervading solemnity, the Middle English out-of-doors music provides, as it were, a sometimes lusty and humorous, sometimes pastoral and contemplative commentary."

CHORAL WORKS
SELECTED AND LISTED IN CHRONOLOGICAL ORDER
ACCORDING TO DATE OF COMPOSITION

Gloria (from *The Masque of Angels*) – 1963 – SATB chorus (with divisions) and piano (later arranged for organ, percussion, harp, and strings) – 3:30 minutes.

The Revelation of St John the Divine – 1966 – T solo, TTBB solo quartet, TTBB chorus (with occasional divisions), brass ensemble, percussion, piano, and harp – 35 minutes.

A Nation of Cowslips – 1968 – SATB chorus a cappella – "The Devon Maid"

1:30 minutes, "On Visiting Oxford" 2:30 minutes, "Sharing Eve's Apple" 2:30 minutes, "There Was a Naughty Boy" 2:30 minutes, "A Party of Lovers at Tea" 3:30 minutes, "Two or Three Posies" 1:30 minutes, and "In Praise of Apollo" 3:30 minutes.

Jonah and the Whale – 1973 – speaker (invisible to the audience), STB solos, SATB chorus, and small instrumental ensemble – 53 minutes.

Peter Quince at the Clavier – 1980 – SATB chorus and piano – 20 minutes.

I Hate and I Love – 1982 – SATB chorus (with occasional divisions) and percussion – 15:30 minutes.

Te Deum – 1987 – SATB chorus and orchestra (including harp and celesta) – 42 minutes.

A Toccata of Galuppi's – 1989 – SATB chorus, harpsichord, and string quartet – 20 minutes.

Spirituals and Swedish Chorales – 1994 – SATB chorus a cappella – "So, I'll sing with my voice" 2:30 minutes, "Vi lofve dig, o store Gud" 1 minute, "There's singing up in heaven" 1:15 minutes, "En dag skall uppgå för vår syn" 1:30 minutes, and "What can that shadow be" 1:30 minutes. The first piece includes scoring for ST solos.

Walden Pond – 1996 – SATB chorus, three cellos, and harp – 22:30 minutes.

JACOB DRUCKMAN 1928–1996

Druckman was born in Philadelphia, Pennsylvania, and in his youth learned to play the violin and piano. He studied with Aaron Copland at the Berkshire Music Center and with Vincent Persichetti and Bernard Wagenaar at the Juilliard School of Music, and in addition, he attended the Ecole Normale de Musique in Paris. Between 1957 and 1972 he taught at Juilliard, and during some of this time he also worked at the Columbia-Princeton Electronic Music Center and the electronic music studio at Yale University. From 1972 to 1976 he taught composition at Brooklyn College of the City University of New York, in 1976 he was appointed chair of the composition department and director of the electronic music studio at Yale, and from 1982 to 1986 he was composer-in-residence for the New York Philharmonic. Throughout his career he received numerous commissions from some of the most renowned symphony orchestras in the United States, including Boston, Chicago, Cleveland, New York, and Philadelphia.

Druckman's choral output consists of only several published works, two of which are noteworthy. The *Four Madrigals* of 1958—set to the poetry of the late Renaissance English poets Francis Beaumont ("Shake off your heavy trance"), Ben Jonson ("The faery beam upon you"), John Donne ("Death, be not proud"), and Robert Herrick ("Corrina's going a-maying") and scored for SATB chorus a cappella—are considered to be masterful contributions to the genre and artful representations of the neo-Renaissance style of writing in the twentieth century. Especially effective is the imitative writing in the fourth madrigal. *Antiphones,* to three poems by Gerard Manley Hopkins, is scored for SATB/SATB chorus a cappella and is characterized by sprechstimme, aleatoric performance of rhythms, nontraditional vocal sounds, and other avant-garde techniques.

SAMUEL ADLER B.1928

Adler was born in Mannheim, Germany, but raised primarily in the United States, where his family had emigrated in 1939. His formal education was at Boston and Harvard universities as well as at the Berkshire Music Center, and his teachers included Randall Thompson, Paul Hindemith, and Aaron Copland. From the early 1950s to the late 1970s Adler held various positions in Texas—music director at Temple Emanu-El in Dallas (1953–1966), music director of the Dallas Lyric Theater and the Dallas Chorale (1954–1958), instructor of fine arts at the Hockaday School in Dallas (1955–1966), and professor of composition at the University of North Texas (1957–1977). Between 1966 and 1995 he was professor of composition at the Eastman School of Music, and in 1997 he joined the faculty of the Juilliard School of Music. As an outgrowth of and commitment to his teaching, he wrote three textbooks—*Choral Conducting* in 1971, *Sight Singing* in 1979, and *A Study of Orchestration* in 1982—and in addition to his university appointments he has given master classes and workshops and has conducted at festivals in countries throughout the world. He has received commissions from the Cleveland Orchestra and National, Dallas, Pittsburgh, and Houston symphony orchestras, and in recognition of his work he has been awarded honorary doctorates from Southern Methodist and Wake Forest universities and St Louis Conservatory.

In addition to five operas, six symphonies, twelve concertos, and eight string quartets, Adler's compositional output consists of more than one hundred choral works, including seven Services and Service pieces for the Jewish liturgy and twelve Psalm settings. Of the liturgical repertoire, *B'shaaray Tefilah* of 1963 is a setting of the Sabbath Service scored for cantor, SATB chorus, and organ, and *Shir Chadash* of 1960 is a setting of the Friday Evening Service scored for cantor, unison chorus, and organ. The Psalm settings include *Psalm 124* and *Psalm 24* of 2003, *Psalm 146* of 1985, and *Two Psalm Motets* ("O Lord, open thou my lips" from Psalm 51 and "The Lord reigneth" from Psalm 99). The secular repertoire is represented by *Five Choral Poems* ("Autumn Rain," "Strings in the Earth," "Nothing Is Enough," "Some One," and "A Kiss"), composed in 1954 in the style of the Hindemith *Six Chansons* and scored for SATB chorus a cappella; *Five Choral Pictures* ("The Immortals," "Snow," "Marriage," "Owl," and "People Glow"), a setting of poems by Robert Sward (b.1933), composed in 1964, characterized by canons and ostinatos, and scored for SATB chorus a cappella; *Two Shelley Songs* ("To-" and "The Fugitives"), composed in 1980 in contrasting neo-Romantic and modern idioms (with some tone clusters) and scored for SATB chorus and piano; and *The Way They Are*, a set of eight humorous madrigals ("Cynthia," "Lucille-Ann," "Betsy," "Sue," "Archibald," "Jeff," "Allen," and "Timothy"), composed in 1983 to poems by Hollis Summers (b.1916) and scored for SATB chorus a cappella.

PAULINE OLIVEROS B.1932

Oliveros was born in Houston, Texas, and educated at the University of Houston and San Francisco State College. In the late 1950s she cofounded the San Francisco Tape Music Center, and in 1967 she joined the faculty of the University of California, San Diego. She resigned her teaching position in 1981 to devote herself entirely to composition, although she subsequently served as composer-in-residence at Northwestern University (1996) and Mills College in Oakland, California (1999). She is considered one of the leading pioneers of avant-garde music in the United States, with most of her music containing improvisation and meditation along with electronic tape sounds drawn from environmental phenomena. Her acclaimed "ceremonial opera" *Crow Two* of 1974 calls for performers to communicate telepathically with the audience and for members of the audience to participate with the performers on stage. Her most popular choral work, *Sound Patterns* of 1961, calls for an SATB choral ensemble to produce a wide variety of nontraditional vocal sounds.

POZZI ESCOT B.1933

Escot was born in New York City and educated at the Juilliard School of Music, where she studied with William Bergsma and Vincent Persichetti, and between 1957 and 1961 she studied at the Staatliche Hochschule für Musik in Hamburg, Germany. In 1964 she joined the faculty of the New England Conservatory of Music, later becoming a professor of graduate theoretical studies and composition, and in 1972 she also joined the faculty of Wheaton College. In addition to her teaching duties she has served as editor of the music journal *Sonus* and as president of the International Society of Hildegard von Bingen Studies, and she has lectured in numerous universities across the United States and Europe, including Columbia, Stanford, Princeton, Harvard, and Chicago. She also has written two books—*Sonic Design: The Nature of Sound and Music* (coauthored with Robert Cogan) and *Sonic Design: Practice and Problems*—both published in 1981 and both written about the relationship between music and mathematics. Escot first received attention as a composer with her fifth symphony, *Sands...,* premiered by the New York Philharmonic in 1975, and she has since received accolades for her *Fourth String Quartet* and *Piano Concerto*. Her most notable choral work—*Missa Triste* of 1981—is a setting of the Agnus Dei, Credo, Kyrie eleison, and Gloria as a representation of peace, belief, mercy, and glory. Scoring is for women's chorus and three optional treble instruments that double the vocal parts *colla parte*. Other choral works include *Visione 97* for SSTTBBBB chorus or solo singers a cappella, *Ainu I* for mixed chorus a cappella, and *Symphony #4* for A solo, mixed chorus, and orchestra.

MICHAEL HENNAGIN 1936–1993

Hennagin was born in The Dalles, Oregon, but spent most of his youth in Los Angeles, California, where his family had moved when he was eight. He received his formal education at Los Angeles City College and the Curtis Institute, with further musical instruction from Darius Milhaud at the Aspen Summer Music Festival (1961) and from Aaron Copland at the Berkshire Music Center (1963). From 1963 to 1965 he worked as a film and television composer in Los Angeles, and from 1966 to 1972 he taught at Kansas State Teachers College in Emporia, Kansas. In 1972 he joined the faculty of the University of Oklahoma, where he served as composer-in-residence and professor of theory and composition until his retirement in 1992. Throughout his career he received numerous commissions and awards, including grants from the National Endowment for the Arts and the MacDowell Colony.

The majority of his best-known choral works are cycles of part songs set to the poetry of

American authors—Emily Dickinson (*Three Emily Dickinson Songs*), Edwin Arlington Robinson (*The House on the Hill*), and Walt Whitman (*By the Roadside* and *Give Me the Splendid Silent Sun*). Each cycle contains pieces that exhibit Hennagin's two most common styles of writing—lyrical melodies harmonized by sonorous tonalities and fast-paced repetitive rhythmic motifs in a pantonal harmonic idiom. This juxtaposition is especially evident in *Give Me the Splendid Silent Sun*: the first piece, "Take me away," consists entirely of whispered, spoken, and shouted rhythmic patterns over a repetitive instrumental texture, and the second piece, "Sunrise," is characterized by long, flowing melodies. Similar textures are exhibited in *Psalm 136* (rhythmic) and *Psalm 133* (melodic). In *Prayer of St Francis*, both textures occur simultaneously (the piano part consists of repetitive undulating rhythms, whereas the choral parts are slower-moving and melodic). Hennagin's most popular pieces, the a cappella part songs *Walking on the green grass* and *Under the Greenwood Tree*, are similar in tonality although not defined in rhythmic texture.

CHORAL WORKS
SELECTED AND LISTED IN CHRONOLOGICAL ORDER
ACCORDING TO DATE OF COMPOSITION

Walking on the green grass – 1958 – SATB chorus a cappella – 2 minutes.

The House on the Hill – 1960 – B solo and SATB chorus a cappella – 11 minutes.

Under the Greenwood Tree – 1964 – SATB chorus a cappella – 5 minutes.

Three Emily Dickinson Songs – 1971 – SA chorus and piano – "Heart we will forget him" 3 minutes, "Going to heaven" 7 minutes, and "The world feels dusty" 4 minutes.

By the Roadside – 1976 – SATB chorus (with divisions) a cappella – "Hast never come to thee an hour" 4:30 minutes, "Gods" 5 minutes, and "Gliding o'er all" 4 minutes.

Psalm 133 – 1986 – SATB chorus and organ – 4:30 minutes.

Psalm 136 – 1986 – SATB chorus (with divisions) and organ – 4 minutes.

My, My, Mother Goose – 1987 – SATB chorus (with occasional divisions) and large percussion ensemble – 17 minutes.

Give Me the Splendid Silent Sun – 1989 – SATB chorus (with divisions), piano, and percussion – "Take me away" 8 minutes and "Sunrise" 6 minutes.

Prayer of St Francis – 1990 – SATB chorus (with occasional divisions) and piano – 7 minutes.

JOHN CORIGLIANO B.1938

Corigliano was born in New York City and educated at Columbia University. During the 1960s he worked as a music programmer for radio station WQXR and as an assistant to Leonard Bernstein in the production of the Young People's Concerts television series, and during the early

1970s he worked as a producer for Columbia Masterworks recordings. Between 1971 and 1986 he taught at the Manhattan School of Music, and beginning in 1973 he also taught at Lehman College of the City University of New York. From 1987 to 1990 he was composer-in-residence for the Chicago Symphony Orchestra, and in 1992 he joined the faculty of the Juilliard School of Music. His orchestral works have been performed by many of the renowned orchestras in the United States, and several of his compositions have won significant awards—the score to the film *The Red Violin* won an Academy Award in 1999, and his *Symphony #2* won a Pulitzer Prize in 2000.

Corigliano's most noteworthy vocal composition, *A Dylan Thomas Trilogy*, was composed between 1960 and 1976. The first and final works in the trilogy, *Fern Hill* and *Poem on His Birthday*, include scoring for chorus; the middle work, *Poem in October*, has scoring only for T solo and instruments. The music of *Fern Hill* is reminiscent of the tonal "Americana" writing of Aaron Copland and Samuel Barber, while the writing in *Poem on His Birthday* is more modern and dissonant, with instances of aleatoric rhythms, tone clusters, and choral glissandos. Of Corigliano's other choral works, *L'invitation au voyage*, to an English translation of the poem by the French poet Charles Baudelaire (1821–1867), is characterized by French Impressionist harmonies, and *What I Expected Was...*, to poetry of the English poet Stephen Spender (1909–1995), is highly dissonant.

CHORAL WORKS
SELECTED AND LISTED ACCORDING TO FAMILIARITY

Fern Hill – A solo, SATB chorus, and orchestra or strings, piano, and harp – 18 minutes.

Poem on His Birthday – B solo, SATB chorus (with divisions), and orchestra – 30 minutes.

What I Expected Was... – SATB chorus, brass, and percussion – 7 minutes.

L'invitation au voyage – SATB chorus a cappella – 7 minutes.

CHARLES WUORINEN B.1938

Wuorinen was born in New York City and in his youth distinguished himself as both a virtuoso pianist and a serious composer (he won the New York Philharmonic's Young Composers' Award at age sixteen). His academic studies were at Columbia University, where he received a bachelor's degree in 1961 and a master's degree in 1963, and between these years he founded the Group for Contemporary Music. He joined the faculty of Columbia University in 1964, the Manhattan School of Music in 1971, and Rutgers University in 1984, and in addition, he held visiting appointments at Princeton and Yale universities as well as at the New England Conservatory. In 1985 he began a residency with the San Francisco Symphony, and since then he has received commissions from the Boston Symphony, Cleveland Orchestra, New York City Ballet, and New York City Opera. He first came to the attention of critics and the public with his electronic composition *Time's Encomium,* which won a Pulitzer Prize in 1970 and which is based on many aspects of serialism and fractal geometry.

Wuorinen's choral works include two masses—*Mass for the Restoration of St Luke in the Fields* of 1982 for S solo, SATB chorus, violin, three trombones, and organ, and *Missa Renovata* of 1992 for SATB chorus, flute, three trombones, timpani, and strings—and two oratorios— *The Celestial Sphere* of 1980 and *Genesis* of 1989. The first of the oratorios, commissioned by Augustana College in observance of the 100th anniversary of the Handel Oratorio Society, is divided into four parts, each beginning with an orchestral "symphony." The first part, entitled "Symphony About the Empyrean," is based on the text "Lord, What Is Man" by William Fuller; the second part, entitled "Symphony About the Ascension," is from the book of Acts; the third part, "Symphony About the Holy Ghost," describes aspects of the Pentecost; and the fourth part, "Second Symphony About the Empyrean," is again from Fuller's "Lord, What Is Man." The second oratorio, composed as part of Wuorinen's appointment as composer-in-residence for the San Francisco Symphony Orchestra, relates the story of Creation, with the incorporation of Gregorian chants. Scoring is for S solo, SATB chorus, and orchestra.

PAUL CHIHARA B.1938

Chihara was born in Seattle, Washington, and educated at the University of Washington and Cornell University. Further studies were in Fontainebleau with Nadia Boulanger, in Berlin with Ernst Pepping, and at the Berkshire Music Center with Gunther Schuller. Chihara held faculty appointments at the University of California in Los Angeles, California Institute of Technology, and California Institute of the Arts, and he also served as composer-in-residence for the Los Angeles Chamber Orchestra and the San Francisco Ballet. His compositional output includes more than fifteen film scores plus commissions from the Boston Symphony Orchestra (*Saxophone Concerto* in 1981), Los Angeles Philharmonic (*Symphony #2,* also in 1981), Cleveland Orchestra (*Viola Concerto* in 1989), and Chamber Society of Lincoln Center (*Minidoka* of 1996). Four of his choral works are notable—two that are essentially tonal and based on folk songs in the manner of Renaissance masses (e.g., those utilizing the L'homme armé tune), and two that are highly dissonant and employ modern compositional techniques. *Ave Maria – Scarborough Fair,* for TTBBBB chorus a cappella, uses the folk tune as a cantus firmus in the baritone voice parts (set to the Latin text "Ave Maria"), and *Missa Carminum,* subtitled "Folk Song Mass" and scored for SATB/SATB chorus a cappella, similarly incorporates folk tunes into the fabric of music set to the traditional Latin Mass Ordinary and based on the Gregorian chant *Deus genitor alme.* For example, "Sally Gardens," "I wonder as I wander," "Willow Song," the "Houlihan," and "I once loved a boy" (all in English) appear in the Kyrie, Gloria, Sanctus, Benedictus, and Agnus Dei movements, respectively, and the Gregorian chant, according to Chihara, runs "like sinews through the body of the work." The Benedictus is further enhanced with passages in Hebrew. *Magnificat* for SSSAAA chorus a cappella is structured of chant tones that are to be performed randomly and that create tone clusters, and *The 90th Psalm,* for SSSAAATTTBBB chorus, organ, and optional brass quartet, is based on a twelve-tone row, with scoring for choral glissandos, sprechstimme (mainly whispers), and polyrhythms. Other choral works, such as the part song *A Slumber did my spirit seal* of 1969 for SATB chorus a cappella, have an oriental sound—

melodies are based on five-note scales, and harmonies shift dramatically between major and minor sonorities.

JOHN HARBISON B.1938

Harbison was born in Orange, New Jersey, and educated at Harvard and Princeton universities as well as at the Musikhochschule in Berlin. In 1969 he joined the faculty of the Massachusetts Institute of Technology, becoming an institute professor in 1996, and between 1969 and 1973 and from 1980 to 1982 he was also music director of the Cantata Singers. In addition, he was composer-in-residence for the Pittsburgh Symphony Orchestra between 1981 and 1983 and for the Los Angeles Philharmonic from 1985 to 1988. He has received commissions from the Boston and San Francisco symphony orchestras, and his instrumental compositions have been performed by many renowned orchestras in the United States and Europe. His most significant choral work, *The Flight into Egypt* set to text from Matthew 3:13–23, received a Pulitzer Prize. Composed in 1986 and scored for SB solos, SATB chorus, and orchestra (including organ), the cantata is fugal in texture (reflecting the "sacred ricercar" subtitle), angular in melodic structure, and dissonant in harmonic vocabulary. Other works similar in style, though scored for a cappella chorus, include *Two Emmanuel Motets* of 1990—"Wherefore I put thee in remembrance" (2 Timothy 1:6–9) and "Beloved, let us love one another" (1 John 4:7–11)—for SATB chorus; *Ave Verum Corpus* of 1990 for SSATB chorus and optional string quintet or string orchestra; and *Concerning them which are asleep* (1 Thessalonians 4:13–18) of 1993 for SSATBB chorus a cappella. Harbison's early (1959) setting of *Ave Maria* for SSAA chorus a cappella is more conjunct in melodic design and less dissonant in harmonic vocabulary.

MORTEN LAURIDSEN B.1943

Lauridsen was born in Colfax, Washington, and raised in Portland, Oregon. His music studies were at Whitman College and the University of Southern California, and he joined the faculty of the University of Southern California in the mid-1970s. He has composed for many professional and collegiate choral ensembles in the United States, including the Los Angeles Master Chorale (for which he was composer-in-residence between 1994 and 2001) and the Harvard Glee Club, and his music has been performed by a wide array and vast number of ensembles across the world. With several works having sold well over 100,000 copies, Lauridsen is the most published and performed American choral composer of modern times. His best-known works are secular cycles of individual pieces. *Mid-Winter Songs* is a setting of five poems by the English author Robert Graves (1895–1985) that, in the words of Lauridsen, "relate insights regarding the human condition . . . rich in symbolism of dying and rejuvenation, light and darkness." *Madrigali,* subtitled "Six 'Fire Songs' on Italian Renaissance Poems," was inspired by the madrigals of Monteverdi and Gesualdo and set to texts used by these composers and other late-Renaissance madrigalists. The musical textures are replete with Renaissance techniques, including word painting and eye music (e.g., the phrase "Luci serene e chiare" begins with two whole notes that depict "eyes serene and clear"), and the harmonies are unified by what the composer terms the "fire chord" (a minor triad with an added major second). *Les Chansons des Roses* is set to five French poems by the German poet Rainer Maria Rilke (1875–1926). The musical language reflects the lyrical and elegant language of the texts, with distinct melodic and harmonic materials recurring throughout the cycle.

Other popular works include the motet *O Magnum Mysterium,* composed with mellifluous harmonies in an AABA form (a form that Lauridsen favors), and the cantata-like *Lux Aeterna,* set in five interconnected movements to traditional Latin texts that deal with the subject of light—the "Introitus" from the Requiem Mass for the Dead, the ending of the Te Deum "In te, Domine, speravi," the hymn "O nata lux," the Sequence "Veni, sancte spiritus," and the "Agnus Dei" and "Lux aeterna" from the Requiem Mass.

CHORAL WORKS
SELECTED AND LISTED IN CHRONOLOGICAL ORDER
ACCORDING TO DATE OF COMPOSITION

Mid-Winter Songs – 1980 – SATB chorus and piano (original scoring) or orchestra – "Lament for Pasiphaë" 5:15 minutes, "Like Snow" 1:30 minutes, "She Tells Her Love While Half Asleep" 3:45 minutes, "Mid-Winter Waking" 1:30 minutes, and "Intercession in Late October" 6:30 minutes.

Madrigali – 1987 – SATB chorus (with occasional divisions) a cappella – "Ov' è, lass', il bel viso" 2:30 minutes, "Quando son più lontan" 4 minutes, "Amor, io sento l'alma" 1:30 minutes, "Io piango" 3:15 minutes, "Luci serene e chiare" 2:30 minutes, and "Se per havervi, oime" 4:30 minutes.

Les Chansons des Roses – 1993 – SATB chorus (with occasional divisions) a cappella (except for "Dirait-on," which is with piano) – "En une seule fleur" 2:30 minutes, "Contre qui, rose" 3:30 minutes, "De ton rêve trop plein" 2 minutes, "La rose complète" 4 minutes, and "Dirait-on" 4:15 minutes.

O Magnum Mysterium – 1994 – SATB chorus (with divisions) a cappella – 6:30 minutes.

Lux Aeterna – 1997 – SATB chorus (with divisions) and chamber orchestra or organ – 27 minutes. The central movement of the work, "O nata lux," is a cappella and published separately.

JOHN ADAMS B.1947

Adams was born in Worcester, Massachusetts, and in his youth became an accomplished clarinetist. At age ten he began theory and composition lessons, and at fourteen he began composing. After receiving two degrees from Harvard University, he moved to California, where in 1972 he joined the faculty of the San Francisco Conservatory. In 1978 he became an advisor for the San Francisco Symphony Orchestra, between 1982 and 1985 he was the orchestra's composer-in-residence, and during the late 1980s he was the creative chair and conductor of the St Paul Chamber Orchestra. His first opera, *Nixon in China,* was premiered in 1987, and his second opera, *The Death of Klinghoffer,* premiered in 1991. Since then he has composed other stage works, including *El Niño* in 1999 and 2000, *Doctor Atomic* in 2004 and 2005, and *A Flowering Tree* in 2006. Two of these works are oratorio-like in conception and have been premiered with minimal staging in concert halls. *El Niño,* subtitled "A Nativity Oratorio," is a setting of a wide variety of texts, including passages from the Old and New Testaments, the Wakefield Mystery Play, and poetry of the Mexican poet Rosario Castellanos; scoring is for SAT plus three countertenor solos, SATB chorus, children's chorus, and orchestra. *A Flowering Tree,* subtitled "An Opera in Two Acts," is a setting of text, in English translation, from ancient Indian folklore; scoring is for STB solos, SATB chorus, and orchestra (including recorders and celesta). In addition to his work as a composer, Adams has been an active conductor, appearing with such ensembles as the London Symphony Orchestra, Halle Orchestra, Oslo Philharmonic Orchestra, and Royal Concertgebouw Orchestra.

His choral output—all in the minimalism style of Philip Glass (b.1937) and Steve Reich (b.1936), characterized by extensive repetitions of short motifs—consists of several large-scale choral/orchestral works (e.g., *Harmonium* and *On the Transmigration of Souls*) and excerpts from his operas (e.g., *Choruses from The Death of Klinghoffer*). *Harmonium,* composed in 1980 and 1981 for the San Francisco Symphony Orchestra and Chorus, is a setting of "Negative Love or The Nothing" by John Donne and "Because I could not stop for Death" and "Wild Nights" by Emily Dickinson. The text of Donne's poem, which, according to Adams "examines the qualities of various forms of love . . . from the carnal to the divine," is preceded by "a single, pulsating note [sung on the syllable "no"] that, by the process of accretion, becomes a tone cluster, then a chord, and eventually a huge, calmly rippling current of sound that takes on energy and mass until it eventually crests on an immense cataract of sound"; the second poem is set as a slow "pastoral elegy" with sudden shifts of harmony; and the third poem, "violent and sexual," is in the minimalistic style of repetitive motifs that characterized the work's beginning. *On the Transmigration of Souls* was composed for the New York Philharmonic in commemoration of the first anniversary of the World Trade Center attacks on September 11, 2001. Called by Adams "a memory space," the work begins with prerecorded street sounds and the reading of victims' names by friends and family members. This is followed by fragments of text sung by the chorus and then sentences about the victims drawn from newspaper remembrances ("Portraits of Grief" from *The New York Times*) sung by both choruses. The *Choruses from The Death of Klinghoffer* are extractions from Adams's opera about the 1984 hijacking of the Italian cruise ship *Achille Lauro* and the subsequent killing of Leon Klinghoffer, one of its passengers. In the opera, the "choruses stand apart from the action and are devoted to the voice of nations (the Jews and the Palestinians) or to the natural world (the ocean, the desert, night and day, creation and decay)."

CHORAL WORKS

SELECTED AND LISTED IN CHRONOLOGICAL ORDER
ACCORDING TO DATE OF COMPOSITION

Harmonium – 1980–1981 – SATB chorus (with divisions) and large orchestra (including four flutes, harp, piano, and synthesizer) – 33 minutes.

Choruses from The Death of Klinghoffer – 1990 – SATB chorus (with divisions) and orchestra – "Chorus of the Exiled Palestinians" 8:30 minutes, "Chorus of the Exiled Jews" 8:30 minutes, "Ocean Chorus" 5:45 minutes, "Night Chorus" 3:30 minutes, "Chorus of Hagar and the Angel" 5:15 minutes, "Desert Chorus" 5 minutes, and "Day Chorus" 4:30 minutes.

On the Transmigration of Souls – 2002 – SATB chorus (with divisions), children's chorus, electronic tape, computer-controlled sound system, acoustic piano (tuned one-fourth above the orchestral pitch), and orchestra – 25 minutes.

CAROL BARNETT B.1949

Barnett was born in Dubuque, Iowa, and in her youth she learned to play the flute, violin, and piano. She studied composition with Dominick Argento at the University of Minnesota, receiving a bachelor's degree in 1972 and a master's degree in 1976, and, becoming known for her choral works, she was appointed composer-in-residence for the Dale Warland Singers in 1992. She has received commissions for orchestral works from the Minnesota Orchestra and St Paul Chamber Orchestra, and she has composed for numerous choral ensembles, including the Westminster Abbey Choir and Harvard Glee Club. Her well-known choral works include *Cinco poemas de Bécquer* of 1979, a setting of five poems ("Del salón en el ángulo oscuro," "Besa, besa," "Como la brisa que la sangre orea," "Yo so ardiente," and "Voy contra mi interés") by Gustavo Adolfo Bécquer (1836–1870) scored for SATB chorus (with divisions), recorder, guitar, and wind chimes; *Epigrams, Epitaphs* of 1986, a setting of five poems ("The Lady Who Offers Her Looking-Glass to Venus" by Matthew Prior, "My Own Epitaph" by John Gay, "On Setting Up of Mr. Butler's Monument in Westminster Abbey" by Samuel Wesley, "Epitaph on Two Piping-Bullfinches of Lady Ossory's" by Horace Walpole, and "On My First Son" by Ben Jonson) scored for SATB chorus (with occasional divisions) and piano four hands; and *The Last Invocation,* a setting of the poem by Walt Whitman scored for SATB chorus (with divisions) a cappella. Other choral works include *Requiem* of 1981 for SSA chorus a cappella, and *Valediction* of 1989 for TTBB chorus, cello, and piano. While much of Barnett's writing is dissonant, most of her choral music is tonal, with diatonic melodies and triadic harmonies.

STEPHEN PAULUS B.1949

Paulus was born in Summit, New Jersey, and educated at the University of Minnesota, where he studied composition with Dominick Argento and received a bachelor's degree in 1971, a master's degree in 1974, and a doctorate in 1978. Throughout the late 1970s and early 1980s he was involved with the Minnesota Composers Forum, which he cofounded in 1973, and in the 1980s he was composer-in-residence for the Minnesota Orchestra (1983) and Atlanta Symphony Orchestra (1988). He has received commissions for orchestral works from many of the major orchestras in the United States, including the New York Philharmonic, Cleveland Orchestra, Dallas Symphony Orchestra, and Houston Symphony, and he has composed operas for several companies, including his most famous work, *The Postman Always Rings Twice,* for Opera Theatre of St Louis.

A prolific composer, Paulus has written more than three hundred works, approximately half of which are choral and all of which are in a neo-Romantic idiom characterized by lyric melodies and triadic harmonies. The most popular of the choral works, and one of the most frequently performed a cappella works in modern times, is *Pilgrims' Hymn*. Structured in two strophes (i.e., two verses of text set to the same music), it is the closing music of Paulus's opera *The Three Hermits*, the libretto of which, based on an 1885 folk story by Leo Tolstoy, relates the encounter of a bishop and three hermits, who, unable to learn the Lord's Prayer, teach the bishop that their own form of praying is well loved by God. Other popular and frequently performed works include *Jesu Carols*, a setting of four Medieval and Renaissance-era anonymous carols ("Jesu's Lyfelyne," "The Ship Carol," "Waye Not His Cribb," and "The Neighbors of Bethlehem") in French and English; *Madrigali di Michelangelo*, a setting of poems and letters by the Renaissance painter, sculptor, architect, and poet Michelangelo; and *MusiQuotes*, a setting of six quotations from a variety of seventeenth- and eighteenth-century sources about the generally positive qualities of music (e.g., "The man that hath no music in himself, nor is not moved with concord of sweet sounds" from Shakespeare's *The Merchant of Venice*, and "I think I should have no other mortal wants, if I could always have plenty of music" from George Eliot's *The Mill on the Floss*).

CHORAL WORKS
SELECTED AND LISTED ACCORDING TO FAMILIARITY

Pilgrims' Hymn – SSAATTBB chorus a cappella – 3 minutes.

Jesu Carols – SATB chorus (with divisions) and harp – 10 minutes.

Madrigali di Michelangelo – S solo and SATB chorus (with divisions) a cappella – 17 minutes.

MusiQuotes – SSATB chorus and piano – 13 minutes.

Arise, my love – SSAATTBB chorus a cappella – 6:30 minutes.

Splendid Jewel – SSAATTBB chorus a cappella – 3:30 minutes.

Alleluia – SATB chorus a cappella – 5:15 minutes.

LIBBY LARSEN B.1950

Larsen was born in Wilmington, Delaware, and educated at the University of Minnesota, studying composition with Dominick Argento and receiving a bachelor's degree in 1971, a master's degree in 1975, and a doctorate in 1978. During her studies she cofounded, along with Stephen Paulus, the Minnesota Composers Forum, now called the American Composers Forum. Between 1983 and 1987 she was composer-in-residence for the Minnesota Orchestra, and subsequently she served in the same capacity for the Charlotte (North Carolina) and Colorado symphony orchestras. In addition, she has held residencies in several educational institutions, including the California Institute of the Arts, the Arnold Schoenberg Institute, and Cincinnati Conservatory. Her more than one hundred choral works exhibit a variety of textures and styles, all tonally oriented.

Larsen's large-scale works include *The Settling Years* of 1988, a setting of pioneer texts in three movements for SATB chorus, woodwind quintet, and piano; *A Creeley Collection* of 1984, a setting of five poems by the American poet Robert Creeley (1926–2005) for SATB chorus, flute, percussion, and piano; *Dance Set* of 1980, a three-movement work based on early American dances (two step, waltz, and polka) set to scat syllables and scored for SATB chorus, clarinet, drum set, piano, and cello; and *Ringeltanze* (Circle Dance) of 1983, a five-movement Christmas work based on medieval French dance carols, scored for SATB or TTBB chorus, handbells, and strings, with optional timpani. Smaller-scale works are represented by *Everyone Sang* of 1983 for SATB chorus, harp, and percussion, and *I Just Lightning* of 1994 for SSAA chorus and percussion.

RENÉ CLAUSEN B.1953

Clausen was born in Wilton, Iowa, and educated at St Olaf College and the University of Illinois. After brief teaching appointments in the early 1980s at West Texas State and Wichita State universities, he joined the faculty of Concordia College in 1986. He has conducted the Concordia Choir in numerous concerts across the United States and Europe and also in a number of recordings, and in addition, he has conducted a large number of All-State and other festival choruses. His more than seventy choral compositions—many of which have been commissioned by collegiate, church, and high school ensembles—range from expansive motets with pandiatonic harmonies to simple homophonic anthems and part songs in a traditional and triadic harmonic language. The former category is represented by three noteworthy works, all in the late-Renaissance style of music performed frequently during the twentieth century at St Olaf and other midwestern Lutheran colleges. *Magnificat,* commissioned by the Texas Choral Directors Association in 1988 and set to a combination of the opening lines of the traditional Magnificat text in both Latin and English, is reminiscent of motets by Heinrich Schütz, with alternating point-of-imitation phrases and short fragments of texts in dialogue between the upper and lower voice parts; *In Pace,* commissioned by the University of Miami Chorale in 1996 and written in memory of the victims of the Holocaust, is a point-of-imitation motet set to a text from a composition by the Renaissance English composer John Sheppard that begins "In pace, in idipsum dormiam et requiescam" (In peace, I will lie down and rest); and *O Vos Omnes,* a noncommissioned work composed in 1986, emulates sixteenth-century Lutheran motets by incorporating a chorale ("O sacred head now wounded") into the texture of newly composed music. Clausen also combines languages (Latin, English, and Hebrew) and scores a central imitative section of the work for aleatoric performance. The simpler works are represented by the anthem-like piece *All that hath life and breath praise ye the Lord,* a setting of phrases adapted from Psalms 96 and 22 composed in 1981 for the Wichita State University A Cappella Choir, and the part song *Tonight, Eternity Alone* of 1991 set to a passage of *Dusk at Sea* by the American poet Thomas S. Jones, Jr. (1882–1932). Clausen's most popular composition, *Set me as a seal,* is a movement from his cantata *A New Creation* composed in 1989. The cantata, scored overall for chorus and chamber ensemble, is a setting of various biblical and liturgical passages (excerpts from the Latin Mass Ordinary) and a poem by George Herbert (1593–1633)—all of which, according to Clausen, express "various aspects of the human/God, God/human relationship."

CHORAL WORKS
SELECTED AND LISTED ACCORDING TO FAMILIARITY

Set me as a seal – SATB chorus a cappella – 3 minutes.

All that hath life and breath praise ye the Lord – S solo and SATB chorus (with divisions) a cappella – 3 minutes.

Tonight, Eternity Alone – SATB chorus (with divisions) a cappella – 3:30 minutes.

Magnificat – S solo and SSAATTBB chorus a cappella – 6:45 minutes.

In Pace – SSAATTBB chorus a cappella – 8 minutes.

O Vos Omnes – S solo and SATB/SATB chorus a cappella – 9 minutes.

DAVID CONTE B.1955

Conte was born in Denver, Colorado, but raised outside Cleveland, Ohio, where his mother was a singer in the Cleveland Symphony Orchestra Chorus under the direction of Robert Shaw. In his youth Conte learned to play the piano, cello, and guitar, and he became acquainted with choral repertoire by attending rehearsals of the symphony chorus. His formal musical education was at Bowling Green State University (bachelor's degree in 1978) and Cornell University (master's degree in 1981 and a doctorate in 1983), with further studies at the Ecole Normale de Musique in Paris and with Nadia Boulanger in Paris and Fontainebleau. After brief appointments at Cornell and Colgate universities and the American Conservatory at Fontainebleau, Conte joined the faculty of the San Francisco Conservatory of Music as professor of composition and conductor of the conservatory chorus.

In addition to six operas, two film scores, and sixteen instrumental pieces, he has composed approximately forty choral works, many of which have been commissioned by professional ensembles such as Chanticleer and the San Francisco Symphony Orchestra Chorus. His music for voices is characterized by careful attention to text declamation and interpretation of textual expression, structures that highlight and unify contextual relationships, and harmonic textures reflective of the so-called "Americana" sound created by Aaron Copland and furthered by John Corigliano.

The Chanticleer commissions include two of Conte's most popular works—*Ave Maria,* composed in a neo-Renaissance motet style, and *Charm me asleep,* a part song set to the poem "To Music – To Becalm His Fever" by Robert Herrick. Of other important commissions, *Invocation and Dance* (composed for the San Francisco Gay Men's Chorus) is a setting of poetry from Walt Whitman's *When Lilacs Last in the Dooryard Bloom'd,* and *Elegy for Matthew* (composed for the New York City Gay Men's Chorus), *September Sun* (composed for St Bartholomew's Episcopal Church in New York City), and *The Nine Muses* (composed for the American Choral Directors Association) are settings of poetry by John Stirling Walker. The poem for *Elegy for Matthew* was written in memory of Matthew Shepherd (a student at the University of Wyoming who was fatally attacked in a hate crime in October 1998) as an acrostic, with the first letters of the poem's initial stanza spelling MATTHEW S; the poem for *September Sun,* written in memory of the vic-

tims of the terrorist attack on September 11, 2001, is a similar acrostic that spells GOD DWELLS
IN JOY IN THE MIDST OF SORROW; and the poem for *The Nine Muses,* entitled *We Sing the
Muses,* is about the transfiguring power of art and is divided into the verses "Music," "Dance,"
"History," "Astronomy and Astrology," "Tragedy," "Sacred Poetry," "Comedy," "Epic Poetry," and
"Lyric Poetry."

CHORAL WORKS
SELECTED AND LISTED ACCORDING TO FAMILIARITY

Ave Maria – 1991 – SATB chorus a cappella – 2 minutes.

Charm me asleep – 1994 – SATB chorus (with occasional divisions) a cappella – 4:30 minutes.

Invocation and Dance – 1986 – TTBB chorus (arranged for SATB chorus in
1989), harp, piano four hands, percussion, and strings, or piano four
hands and percussion – 13 minutes.

September Sun – 2002 – SATB chorus (with divisions) and strings – 17 minutes.

The Waking – 1985 – SATB chorus and piano – 5 minutes.

O magnum mysterium – 2003 – SSATBB chorus a cappella – 3 minutes.

MATTHEW HARRIS B.1956

Harris was born in Sleepy Hollow, New York, and attended the Aspen Music Festival for three
summers during his teenage years. After graduation from high school he enrolled at the New
England Conservatory for a year and then Juilliard School of Music, where he studied with Elliott Carter, Milton Babbitt, and Roger Sessions and received bachelor's, master's, and doctoral
degrees. Further studies were at Harvard University, the Berkshire Music Center, and the American Conservatory in Fontainebleau, France, where he and his fellow student David Conte were
the last American pupils of Nadia Boulanger. Harris held brief faculty appointments at Fordham
University and Kingsborough College of the City University of New York and was also composer-in-residence at the Aspen Music Festival. Scenes from his opera *Tess* have been presented
by the New York City Opera, and his choral works have been performed by numerous professional ensembles, including the Dale Warland Singers, Phoenix Bach Choir, Los Angeles Chamber Singers, Western Wind, and Santa Fe Desert Chorale.

　　One of his earliest choral works and also one of his most popular is book one of *Shakespeare
Songs,* which contains settings of "Hark, hark, the lark," "Full fathom five," and "Who Is
Silvia"—all scored for SATB chorus a cappella. Further books, each containing three or four
Shakespeare settings, were composed in 1990 (book two), 1992 (book three), 1995 (book four),
and 2002 (book five). Other early popular works include three compositions set to poetry of
renowned twentieth-century Hispanic poets—Octavio Paz (1914–1998), Federico García Lorca
(1898–1936), and Pablo Neruda (1904–1973). *Object Lesson* is a setting of three sections from
Paz's poem *Lección de cosas* about decorative objects on a bookcase (the first section, "Xochip-

illi," describes a fruit tree carved from jade; the second section, "Niño y Trompo," is about a toy top; and the third section, "Objetos," ruminates about our relative awareness of objects that live alongside us all); *Two Lorca Songs* is a setting of poems from Lorca's *Poema del Cante Jondo*— "Las seis cuerdas" (The six strings) and "Crótalo" (Castanet); and *Oceanic Eyes* is a setting of four Neruda poems identified below. In all the works, Harris captures essences of the poetry and conveys them in engaging and expressive pandiatonic harmonies and characteristic rhythms. Of the later works, *Innocence & Experience* is a setting of three poems by William Blake, *A Child's Christmas in Wales* is a setting of seven passages from Dylan Thomas's narrative, and *Three Plums* is a setting of poems by William Carlos Williams.

CHORAL WORKS
SELECTED AND LISTED IN CHRONOLOGICAL ORDER
ACCORDING TO DATE OF COMPOSITION

O Sacrum Convivium – 1993 – SATB chorus (with divisions to SAATTBBB) a cappella – 2 minutes.

Object Lesson – 1994 – SSAA chorus a cappella – 6 minutes.

Two Lorca Songs – 1994 – mixed chorus a cappella – "Las seis cuerdas" (SATB) 3:30 minutes and "Crótalo" (SSATB) 3 minutes.

Oceanic Eyes – 1997 – SATB chorus, guitar, and string quartet – "Leaning into the afternoons" 4 minutes, "Girl lithe and tawny" 3 minutes, "Tonight I can write" 10 minutes, and "In my sky at twilight" 3 minutes.

Innocence & Experience – 2000 – SATB chorus a cappella – "The Sick Rose" 1 minute, "The Lamb" 3 minutes, and "The Tiger" 2 minutes.

A Child's Christmas in Wales – 2002 – SATB chorus and chamber ensemble – 28 minutes.

AARON JAY KERNIS B.1960

Kernis was born in Philadelphia, Pennsylvania, and educated at the San Francisco Conservatory of Music, Manhattan School of Music, and Yale University. His teachers have included John Adams, Jacob Druckman, and Charles Wuorinen. Soon after the completion of his studies he was recognized for his orchestral work *Dream of the Morning Sky*, premiered by the New York Philharmonic in 1983. In 1998 his *String Quartet #2*, subtitled "musica instrumentalis," received a Pulitzer Prize. While his choral repertoire represents only a small portion of his total compositional output, his several choral works are noteworthy. Most effective is a setting in 1998 of three texts by the medieval mystic nun Mechthild of Magdeburg (1210–ca.1285). Entitled *Ecstatic Meditations*, the three texts, set as three separate pieces ("Effortlessly love flows," "How the soul speaks to God," and "I cannot dance, O Lord"), are scored for SATB chorus (frequently expanded to SSAATTBB) a cappella, with S and T solos in the second piece. A fourth setting of the same author, "How God answers the soul" scored for SSTT solos and SATB/SATB chorus, was composed in 1996 and is published as the fourth piece in the *Ecstatic Meditations* cycle. The three 1998 pieces are unified in musical style and characterized by pandiatonic harmonies, shifting meters, active and complex rhythms, and textures that word-paint textual phrases. In "Effortlessly love flows," for instance, the phrase "The Holy Spirit is our harpist" is represented by a chromatic scale that results in a sound cluster; in "How the soul speaks to God," melismatic passages indicate the words "longing" and "flowing"; and in "I cannot dance, O Lord," melodic fragments are designed to portray "whirling" in the phrase "There will I stay with you whirling." The writing in all three pieces is virtuosic, and the cycle is considered to be one of the significant choral works of the late twentieth century. Other choral works by Kernis include *Stein Times Seven* of 1980 for SSATB chorus and piano; *Dorma, Ador* of 2000 for A solo, SATB chorus, and optional handbells; and *Garden of Light,* a choral symphony commissioned by the Disney Corporation for its millennium celebrations scored for boy and SATB solos, SATB and children's choruses, and orchestra. Several movements of the symphony (e.g., "In search of hope," "Is there a place," and "Light of heaven") are extracted and arranged for SATB chorus and piano.

ERIC WHITACRE B.1970

Whitacre was born in Reno, Nevada, and educated at the University of Nevada, Las Vegas, where he sang in university choral ensembles, and at the Juilliard School of Music, where he studied composition with John Corigliano. The successes of Whitacre's first works, composed when he was in his early twenties (*Go, lovely rose, Cloudburst,* and *Water Night* for chorus, and *Ghost Train* and *Godzilla Eats Las Vegas* for wind ensemble), brought him widespread recognition and status as one of the leading composers of the late twentieth century. In the years since his twenties, he has received numerous commissions from collegiate and professional choral and instrumental ensembles, and in addition, he has been invited to hold residencies in colleges and universities across the United States and to conduct his works in countries throughout the world, including Canada, Japan, Australia, and China.

His first choral composition, *Go, lovely rose,* was written when he was twenty-one and a student at the University of Las Vegas. Set to a poem by Edmund Waller (1606–1687) and dedicated to the conductor of the university's Chamber Chorale, David B. Weiller, the music exhibits characteristics of style—most notably pandiatonic chord clusters—that would become a trademark of Whitacre's later music. Two other part songs—*With a lily in your hand* set to a poem by Federico García Lorca (1898–1936) and *I hide myself* set to a poem by Emily Dickinson (1830–1886)—were added the year after the composition of *Go, lovely rose,* and all were combined into a cycle entitled *Three Flower Songs.* The ensuing two choral works, Whitacre's most famous and popular, were also composed during his student days and dedicated to choral conductors whose influence he desired to acknowledge. *Cloudburst,* to a setting in Spanish adapted from a poem by Octavio Paz (1914–1998), is dedicated to Dr. Jocelyn K. Jensen, conductor of the Eldorado High School Concert Choir. The music is characterized by dramatic and effective atmospheric sounds, including phrases of aleatoric whispers, finger snaps, a brief passage for speaker, and writing for windchimes and a thunder sheet. *Water Night,* to an English translation of a Paz poem, is dedicated to Dr. Bruce Mayhall, then director of choral activities at the University of Nevada, Reno. The musical texture of pandiatonic chord clusters, incorporating up to fourteen notes, is Whitacre's most effective use of this technique.

Compositions of the late 1990s include two commissions, both set to the poetry of e. e. cummings—*little tree* for the San Francisco Symphony Chorus, Vance George, director, and the three pieces in the cycle *Three Songs of Faith* (sometimes printed as *Three Songs of Praise*) for Northern Arizona University in celebration of its centennial. While each of the pieces incorporates choral clusters, the harmonies and textures are varied to create a more diversified expressive effect. Diversity of writing also characterizes *Leonardo Dreams of His Flying Machine,* commissioned by the American Choral Directors Association, although the chord cluster technique and basic homophonic writing returns and is effectively demonstrated in *Lux Aurumque* (a Christmas piece set in Latin to a poem that translates as "Light, warm and heavy as pure as gold, and the angels sing softly to the new-born baby") and *Sleep* (set to an adaptation of Robert Frost's poem "Stopping by woods on a snowy evening").

CHORAL WORKS
SELECTED AND LISTED IN CHRONOLOGICAL ORDER
ACCORDING TO DATE OF COMPOSITION

Three Flower Songs – 1990–1992 – SATB chorus (with divisions) a cappella – "I hide myself" 3 minutes, "With a lily in your hand" 2:30 minutes, and "Go, lovely rose" 4 minutes.

Cloudburst – 1992 – SATB chorus (with divisions), handbells, percussion, and piano – 8:30 minutes. The work includes brief passages for a speaker and S solo.

Water Night – 1995 – SATB chorus (with divisions to 5S, 4A, 3T, and 3B) a cappella – 5:15 minutes.

little tree – 1997 – SATB chorus (with divisions) and piano – 5 minutes.

Three Songs of Faith – 1999 – SATB chorus (with divisions) a cappella – "i will wade out" 2:45 minutes, "hope, faith, life, love" 3:30 minutes, and "i thank You God for most this amazing day" 6:45 minutes.

Lux Aurumque – 2000 – SATB chorus (with divisions) a cappella – 4 minutes.

Sleep – 2000 – SATB chorus a cappella – 5:30 minutes.

Leonardo Dreams of His Flying Machine – 2001 – SATB chorus and percussion – 8:30 minutes.

A Boy and a Girl – 2004 – SATB chorus (with divisions) a cappella – 4:30 minutes.

GLOSSARY

A

A cappella – performance by voices without instrumental accompaniment.

Aleatoric – performance that is governed by the chance decisions of performers, not by notational strictures.

Alt-Bachisches Archiv – a collection of music composed by the ancestral predecessors of J. S. Bach.

Alternatim – alternation of polyphony and Gregorian chant, usually in sections of music set to verses of Biblical text; a compositional technique seen in settings of many Magnificats during the early decades of the Renaissance era.

Anthem – a genre of composition with a sacred text in English, generally used in Protestant worship services; the Protestant equivalent of a Catholic motet. There were two types of anthem in England during the late Renaissance and Baroque eras, *full* and *verse*. The *full* anthems were scored for chorus without soloists; the *verse* anthems were scored for soloists, chorus, and accompaniment of either organ or consort of viols.

B

Ballett (pronounced *bal*-et) or Balletto – secular musical genre of the Renaissance era in England and Italy, characterized by homophony, repeated sections of music, dance qualities, and *fa la la* refrains.

Basso continuo (also called *thoroughbass* and *figured bass*) – an independent melodic bass line in vocal compositions of the Baroque era, generally with figures underneath. The bass line is to be played by instruments such as the cello, violone, and bassoon, and the figures are to be realized by chord producing instruments such as the harpsichord, organ, theorbo, and lute. Participation of multiple instruments—one or more to play the melodic bass line and one or more to play the harmonies—is assumed.

Basso seguente – a melodic bass line that is not independent but instead that follows the lowest sounding voice part of a composition; predecessor of the *basso continuo*. Performance by only one melodic bass instrument is standard.

C

Cantata – a genre of composition begun in the Baroque era, generally secular and scored for solo voices and basso continuo during the early part of the era, and sacred and scored for solos, chorus, and instruments during the latter part of the era and beyond. The sacred works are frequently divided into multiple movements.

Cantoris – the portion of a choral ensemble in an Anglican church that is on the left side (facing the high altar) of the chancel area—the cantor's side. The *cantoris* faces the *decani*.

Cantus firmus – one part of a vocal texture, usually the tenor voice part, that is set in longer note values than the other parts; most often a preexistent melody (i.e., a Gregorian chant, hymn or chorale melody, or popular tune).

Canzonet or **Canzonetta** – secular musical genre of the Renaissance era in England and Italy, characterized by a predominant melody in the top-most part of a vocal texture.

Catch – a type of English round set to a humorous or ribald text and scored for three male voices.

Cecilian – a reference to St Cecilia, patron saint of music, and to societies of composers in Germany and Austria during the Romantic era who desired a return of church music to the motet style of Palestrina.

Chalumeau – a woodwind instrument similar to a recorder, used mainly in the French Baroque.

Chanson – small-scale secular vocal composition set to a French text and meant for performance by soloists in ensemble during the Medieval and Renaissance eras; counterpart to the Italian madrigal.

Chantre ordinaire – normal singer in chapels and courts of the French Renaissance and Baroque.

Chorale – the German term for a hymn used in the Lutheran Church.

Colla parte – Italian term meaning *with the parts;* used to designate instruments that should play from and with vocal parts.

Collegium musicum – a society of amateur musicians, usually in a college or university, that presents regular concerts.

Color – see *isorhythm*.

Concert spirituel – the first public concert society in France; begun in 1725.

Concertato – a style of composition during the Baroque era that employed contrasts of smaller and larger performing forces, usually soloists and a few instruments for the smaller forces (generally called *concertino*), and chorus and full orchestration for the larger forces (called *concerto grosso*).

Concerto delle donne – an ensemble of women in the court of Ferrara in the mid- and late-sixteenth century; famous for virtuosic performances of madrigals.

Contrafactum – a vocal work in which a new text, generally sacred, has been substituted for the original one, generally secular.

Contratenor – the male alto part in music of the Renaissance era in England.

Cori spezzati – Italian for *divided (broken) choirs,* used to specify compositions for two or more choirs that are to be separated spatially in performance; also called *polychoral, cori spezzati* compositions were popular at St Mark's Basilica in Venice during the mid- to late-sixteenth century.

Counterpoint (Contrapuntal) – term used in the latter part of the Baroque era and beyond to describe the combination of multiple melodic lines, usually in a fugal arrangement.

Countertenor – general term for a male alto.

D

Da capo – an indication generally used in arias that are ABA in structure (the second A is a repeat or *da capo* of the first A).

Decani – the portion of a choral ensemble in an Anglican church that is on the right side (facing the high altar) of the chancel area—the dean's side. The *decani* faces the *cantoris*.

Discant – a style of composition during the Medieval era in which all parts of a composition move at the same speed. During the Renaissance, *discant* referred to a similar style, but with a melodically prominent upper voice part, sometimes called *treble dominated.*

Dodecaphonic – a style of music popular during the first half of the twentieth century in which the twelve tones of the chromatic scale were organized in series to create a basis for the melodic and choral construction of a composition.

E

Élévation – French term generally used for a motet sung during the portion of the Roman Catholic mass in which the elements of communion are lifted.

F

Fauxbourdon – a technique of composition during the fifteenth century employing sonorities that move in parallel motion.

Figured bass – the bass line of a basso continuo part with numbers indicating chords that are to be realized by keyboard players.

Fioritura – highly ornamental passages.

Formes fixes (singular, Forme fixe) – French term for fixed forms, referring to compositional structures characterized by repeated verse/refrain schemes used in secular music of the Medieval and early Renaissance eras; the typical *formes fixes* are the ballade, rondeau, and virelai.

Frottola – secular vocal genre of the Renaissance era generally set to a humorous or ribald Italian text; the musical style is mainly homophonic, and scoring is for SATB solo voices.

G

Galant – a pre-Classical style of music in the latter half of the eighteenth century, generally homophonic and light in texture.

Gebrauchsmusik – German for *practical* or *useful music,* used to describe compositions in the first half of the twentieth century that were harmonically accessible and technically unchallenging and that could be performed by amateurs.

Gentleman of the Chapel Royal – an adult male singer in the English royal chapel during the Renaissance and Baroque eras.

Grand motet – French term for a large, multimovement motet composed during the Baroque era in France.

H

Haute-contre – French term for a male alto or the alto part of a composition to be sung by an adult male.

Head motif – a group of notes, usually from four to six, used as a motto or compositional unifying device at the beginning of the Kyrie, Gloria, Credo, Sanctus, and Agnus Dei portions of masses during the Renaissance era.

Historia (plural, Historiae) – Latin for *history* or a *narrative of past events,* used to indicate a genre of German settings of the nativity and passion/resurrection stories during the Medieval, Renaissance, and early Baroque eras.

Historicus – the evangelist or narrator in an oratorio.

Hocket – a compositional device of the thirteenth and fourteenth centuries characterized by the quick alternation of single notes or a short group of notes between two voices; as one note or group of notes sounds in one voice, the other voice is silent.

Homophony (Homophonic) – vertical and chordal texture of music; opposed to *polyphony* (polyphonic) or *counterpoint* (contrapuntal).

I

Incipit – Latin term for *beginning;* used to indicate the short chant fragment that begins the Gloria and Credo portions of a liturgical mass setting or that stands before portions of other compositions.

Ingressus – the Ambrosian chant that corresponds to the Roman introit, generally occurring in settings for Vespers services.

Intermedii – musical interludes for soloists and chorus; performed between acts of spoken plays during the sixteenth century in Italy.

Isorhythm (Isometric) – a construction technique utilized during the Medieval era that involved repetition of phrases. The term *talea* was given to phrases that were repeated with identical rhythms but different melodies; the term *color* was given to phrases that were repeated with identical rhythms and melodies.

K

Kantorei – the singers and instrumentalists in a German chapel, court, or cathedral.

Kapellmeister – German for *chapel master;* the highest musical position in German cathedrals, chapels, and courts.

Konzertmeister – German for *concertmaster.*

L

Lai (plural, Lais) – monophonic secular song of the Medieval era.

Lamentations – Renaissance era musical settings of verses from the Lamentations of Jeremiah, each verse always beginning with Hebrew letters (Aleph, Beth, Ghimel, etc.); an important part of Holy Week services.

Lauda (plural, Laude) – a nonliturgical monophonic sacred composition of the thirteenth and fourteenth centuries, generally syllabic and set in verse/refrain format to an Italian text.

Leitmotif – German for *leading motif.* The term refers to motifs of a composition during the Romantic era that were associated with dramatic events, characters, or emotions, and that recurred throughout a composition as an organizing or structural device.

Liber usualis – book of the common or ordinary chants used in Roman Catholic liturgies of the Mass and the most important Offices.

Lied (plural, Lieder) – German for *song.* In choral music the *lied* is characterized by homophony, with a predominant melody in the top voice and accompanimental textures in the lower voices.

M

Madrigal – a genre of composition begun in Italy during the Renaissance era; generally a small-scale work set to a serious secular Italian text and scored for solo voices in ensemble. During the Baroque era it was scored for single solo voices and basso continuo.

Madrigalism – a form of word painting in which textual images are matched by musical patterns; particularly evident in madrigals of the Renaissance era.

Maestro della musica – Italian musical master of a court.

Maestro di cappella – Italian musical master of a chapel or cathedral.

Magnificat – a musical setting of the text from Luke 1:46–55 beginning "Magnificat anima mea Dominum" (My soul magnifies the Lord); also called the *Canticle of the Virgin,* it is performed in Roman Catholic services at Vespers and in Anglican Services at Evening Prayer.

Maître de chapelle – French term for *master of the chapel,* the highest musical position in a French chapel.

Maître de musique – French term for *master of music,* the highest musical position in a French court or cathedral.

Maître des enfants – French term for *master of the children* (or *master of the choristers*).

Masque – a type of work popular in the seventeenth and early eighteenth centuries in England that combines vocal and instrumental music, dance, elaborate stage scenery, and poetry.

Mass – a musical setting of the Ordinary portions (Kyrie, Gloria, Credo, Sanctus, and Agnus Dei) of the Roman Catholic liturgical service.

Mean – a soprano voice part in music of the Renaissance era in England of medium range; lower than the treble voice part.

Melisma (Melismatic) – a long group of notes, generally six or more, set to a single syllable of text; seen in festive chants of the Medieval era and most music of the Baroque.

Messa di voce – the performance practice during the Baroque, Classical, and Romantic eras of slightly swelling and decreasing the volume of single notes.

Messe basse solennelle – French term for *solemn low mass.*

Monody (Monophonic) – a single melodic line, usually accompanied by basso continuo and generally associated with vocal genres of the early seventeenth century.

Monophony – a single unaccompanied melodic line, as in Gregorian chant.

Motet – a genre of composition generally set to a sacred Latin text and scored for chorus in an imitative style.

Musica ficta – term used to describe the process of raising notated pitches by a half step (semitone) in music of the Medieval and Renaissance eras; used to avoid melodic motion by a tritone or to ensure that cadences are approached by a half step. The related term *musica recta* is used to describe the process of lowering notated pitches by a half step to make them melodically more convincing.

Musica reservata – term used during the Renaissance era to describe compositions that set texts in an expressive manner without overt word painting.

Musique mesurée (also called Vers mesurée) – French term for *measured music* or *measured verse;* prominent in chansons of the latter half of the sixteenth century and characterized by long and short rhythmic values that correspond to accented and unaccented syllables of text.

N

Neume – a name for a note in Gregorian chant.

Note nere – a style of composition in the Renaissance era characterized by black notes (i.e., quarter and eighth notes), as opposed to white notes (i.e., half and whole notes); usually seen in Italian madrigals of the latter half of the sixteenth century.

O

Oboe da caccia – oboe in the tenor range used during the Baroque era.

Oboe d'amore – oboe in the alto range used during the Baroque era.

Ode – a genre of composition set to a secular poem and scored for soloists, chorus, and instruments; popular during the Baroque era and used to celebrate special occasions such as royal ceremonies, political victories, or observances of saints' days, most notably St Cecilia.

Ondes martenot – an electronic instrument used by French composers during the twentieth century that produces a sliding or glissando effect.

Oratorio – a genre of composition begun in Italy during the Baroque era; generally a multisectional or multimovement setting of a sacred dramatic or moral allegorical text scored for soloists, chorus, and instruments.

Oratory – Baroque-era building or part of a church where prayer services were held and oratorios were presented.

Ordinary – those portions of the Roman Catholic mass (Kyrie, Gloria, Credo, Sanctus, and Agnus Dei) that do not vary during the liturgical year and that generally constitute a musical setting of the mass. During the Medieval and early Renaissance eras, a setting of the five portions of the Ordinary was referred to as a *mass cycle.*

Organum – a type of composition during the Medieval era in which an improvised voice followed an existing liturgical chant melody at a fixed interval.

Ostinato – a pattern of notes that is repeated consecutively at least several times.

P

Pandiatonic – a composition of the twentieth century characterized by the use of all eight notes of the diatonic scale in a tonal manner.

Pantonal – a composition of the twentieth century characterized by the use of all or most of the twelve notes of the chromatic scale used in a tonal or diatonic manner.

Paraphrase – a freely composed melody based upon and closely resembling a preexisting melody, usually a chant; seen in mass compositions of the Renaissance era.

Parody – a type of mass composition common during the Renaissance era based upon all the voice parts of a previously composed piece of music, usually a motet, madrigal, or chanson.

Passaggio (plural, Passaggi) – melismas in compositions of the late Renaissance and Baroque eras, fast in tempo and necessitating virtuosic technical skills from performers.

Passion – an oratorio based on the crucifixion story.

Pastorale – a play that incorporates songs and choruses.

Petit motet – French term for a small-scale motet of the Baroque era in France scored for soloists and basso continuo.

Point of imitation – a section of music set to one text phrase in which all parts of a vocal texture imitate each other in both melody and rhythm; one of the most common compositional devices of the late Renaissance. A composition in *point-of-imitation* style generally contains from four to eight imitated textual phrases and thus contains four to eight *points of imitation.*

Polychoral – compositions for multiple choirs (see *cori spezzati*).

Polyphonic lied – German secular genre of the mid-sixteenth century, characterized by a predominant melody in the top voice and polyphonic textures in the lower voices.

Polyphony (Polyphonic) – Renaissance era texture of multiple lines of music, each of which generally maintains independence; contrasted with *monody* (monophonic) and with *counterpoint* (contrapuntal).

Polytextual – two or more different texts, often in different languages, occurring simultaneously; usually found in compositions of the Medieval era.

Precentor – the staff member of an Anglican church who is responsible for leading the singing during liturgical services.

Prima prattica – Italian for *first practice,* used to refer to music of the Renaissance era in which polyphony was supposedly more important than text; *prima prattica* compositions are characterized by imitative polyphony scored for voices a cappella or for voices with nonindependent basso continuo accompaniment.

Q

Quodlibet – a composition in which multiple preexisting melodies are presented either successively or simultaneously.

R

Recitative (Italian, Recitativo) – a style of composition for solo voice that began in the early years of the Baroque era to emulate natural speech; *recitativo secco* (dry recitative) was accompanied by basso continuo alone, *recitativo accompagnato* (accompanied recitative) was accompanied by basso continuo and other instruments, usually strings.

Requiem – a mass for the dead; also called *Missa pro defunctis.*

Responsorial – the alternation of a soloist (or soloists) and chorus.

Ritornello – a short passage of music, usually instrumental, that occurs more than once as an interlude.

S

Sackbut – the predecessor of the trombone; used in consorts during the Renaissance era to accompany choral music *colla parte.*

Sarum chant – chant used in England, especially at Salisbury Cathedral between the thirteenth and the sixteenth centuries.

Seconda prattica – Italian for *second practice,* used to refer to music of the Baroque era in which melody and rhythm were subordinate to text; *seconda prattica* compositions are characterized by vertically conceived textures and scoring for soloists and chorus with independent basso continuo accompaniment.

Sepolcra (plural, Sepolcri) – a type of Passion oratorio, generally performed on Maundy Thursday and Good Friday during the Baroque era, with costumes, some acting, and stage scenery consisting of a replica of the holy sepulchre.

Sequence – a type of *trope* inserted between phrases of liturgical chant during the Medieval era; also the repetition of a short group of notes at ascending or descending pitch levels.

Sine nomine – Latin for *without name;* given to a mass composed in the Renaissance era that has no identified source of compositional material.

Si placet – Latin for *as you please;* used to indicate vocal and instrumental scoring during the late Renaissance and early Baroque eras according to resources at hand or personal preferences; refers to the addition or deletion of voices or instruments to a composer's scoring.

Soggetto cavato – Italian for *carved from the words;* a cantus firmus constructed of pitches that correspond to vowels of a name.

Sous-maître – French term for one of the musical leaders of the royal chapel in France during the Baroque era. King Louis XIV employed four *sous-maîtres* simultaneously, each being responsible for music during a quarter of the year.

Sprechstimme – German for *speaking voice.* A style of composition during the twentieth century in which melodies are rhythmically (and occasionally melodically) notated and performed halfway between singing and speaking.

Stile antico – Italian for *ancient style;* used to refer to compositions of the Baroque era in the Renaissance *prima prattica* style.

Stile concertato – Italian for *concerted style;* used to refer to compositions of the Baroque era that employ contrasts of smaller and larger performing forces; see *concertato.*

Stile moderno – Italian for *modern style;* used to refer to compositions of the Baroque era in the *seconda prattica* style.

Stile rappresentativo – Italian for *representative style;* used to refer to compositions of the early Baroque era that employ freedom of rhythm, as in recitative, to emulate natural speech patterns.

Strophic – multiple verses of text set to the same music, as in hymns, chorales, or part songs.

Succentor – the assistant to or deputy of the precentor in Anglican churches.

Symphonie – French term for an orchestral prelude or introductory movement.

T

Taille – French term for *tenor,* generally referring to the tenor voice part in a composition.

Talea – see *isorhythm.*

Te Deum – a musical setting of the sacred text "Te Deum laudamus, te Dominum confitemur" (We praise thee, O God, we acknowledge thee to be the Lord); usually set in Latin or English for services of thanksgiving, consecration, and other celebratory events.

Tenor lied – a German composition, generally homophonic, in which a preexisting melody is used as a cantus firmus in the tenor voice part.

Tessitura – the range of a vocal or instrumental part.

Theorbo – a large bass lute, used as a basso continuo instrument in the Baroque era.

Through-composed – the style of composition characterized by a continuous flow of new music, without sectional repeats.

Treble – highest voice part in the soprano range; term used to designate a boy soprano in England.

Trope – new music inserted between phrases of liturgical chant during the Medieval era.

Turba (plural, Turbae) – Latin term meaning *turmoil* or *uproar,* used in Passion settings to indicate passages of music for chorus sung by a crowd of people.

Tutti – performance by all the vocal or vocal and instrumental forces of a composition.

V

Villancico – a Spanish poetic and musical genre characterized by verses or stanzas (*coplas*) and a refrain (*estribillo*); generally secular, strophic, homophonic, and rustic in the late-fifteenth and early-sixteenth centuries, and sacred, with texts related to Christmas, in the late-sixteenth century; a popular form in Latin America during the seventeenth century.

Villanella – Italian form of secular music from the mid- to late-sixteenth century, generally strophic, of rustic character, and for three voices with a prominent melody in the top voice; similar to the canzonet.

Viol – any member of the family of fretted and bowed stringed instruments of the sixteenth and seventeenth centuries.

Viola da gamba – a specific type of viol played on or between the legs.

Viola d'amore – a viol with the range of a modern viola, played on the shoulder.

Violone – the lowest-pitched stringed instrument of the Baroque era; predecessor of the modern stringed bass.

Voice exchange (in German, Stimmtausch) – the scoring of two voices of the same vocal range (generally soprano or tenor) that exchange melodic passages during the course of a composition.

W

Word painting – effect created by musical figures that illustrate textual words or phrases; related to *madrigalism.*

Z

Zink – an early form of trumpet, made of wood and used during the Renaissance era.

COMPOSER INDEX

Page numbers in boldface represent primary entries. All other page numbers represent secondary entries, namely the composer, era, or section given in parentheses.

Casals, Pablo, **611–612**, 609 (Modern Italy and
Spain)
Castelnuovo-Tedesco, Mario, **613–614**, 609 (Mod-
ern Italy and Spain)
Cavalli, Francesco, **197–198**, 191 (Baroque Italy),
202 (Strozzi), 232 (Lully)
Cavendish, Michael, **166**, 138 (Renaissance
England), 160 (Morley), 169 (Vautor)
Certon, Pierre, **41–42**, 19, 20, 21 (Renaissance
France), 37 (Sermisy), 42 (Goudimel), 113
(Lasso), 570 (Ravel)
Chadwick, George Whitefield, **552–553**, 545
(Romantic United States), 554 (H. Parker)
Charpentier, Marc-Antoine, **234–240**, 198
(Carissimi), 230 (Baroque France), 243
(Bernier)
Cherubini, Luigi, **392–393**, 387 & 388 (Classical
Italy and France), 410 (Le Sueur), 506 (Glinka),
613 (Castelnuovo-Tedesco)
Chesnokov, Pavel, **519–520**, 502, 503, 504 (Roman-
tic Russia), 513 (Kastal'sky), 518 (Kalinnikov),
650 (Shchedrin)
Chihara, Paul, **750–751**, 711 (Modern United States)
Chilcott, Bob, **708**
Child, William, **316**, 313 (Baroque England), 318
(Wise), 318 (Blow)
Ciconia, Johannes, **12–13**, 6 (Medieval Introduc-
tion), 21 & 22 (Dufay)
Cimarosa, Domenico, **391–392**, 387 & 388 (Classi-
cal Italy and France)
Clarke, Jeremiah, **325**, 313 (Baroque England), 318
(Wise), 325 (Croft), 342 (Greene)
Clarke, Rebecca, **684–685**
Clausen, René, **756–757**, 711 & 712 (Modern
United States)
Clemens non Papa, Jacobus, **39–40**, 19 & 20
(Renaissance France), 38 (Gombert), 112 (Vaet),
112 & 113 (Lasso), 120 (Handl)
Clérambault, Louis-Nicolas, **245–246**, 231
(Baroque France)
Coleridge-Taylor, Samuel, **544–545**, 524 (Romantic
England)
Comes, Juan Bautista, **347**, 346 (Baroque Spain
and the New World)
Compère, Loyset, **27**, 17 (Renaissance Introduc-
tion), 19, 20, 21 (Renaissance France), 25 (Ock-
eghem), 26 (Busnois), 29 (Desprez), 35 (Mou-
ton), 38 (Gombert)
Conte, David, **757–758**, 711 & 712 (Modern United
States), 758 (M. Harris)
Copland, Aaron, **722–723**, 553 (MacDowell), 561
(Ginastera), 562 (Orrego-Salas), 660 (Nystedt),
663 (Hovland), 664 (Rautavaara), 700 (Mus-
grave), 711 & 712 (Modern United States), 728
(Hovhaness), 732 (Fine), 734 (Bernstein), 738
(Pinkham), 741 (Rorem), 745 (Druckman), 746

(Adler), 747 (Hennagin), 749 (Corigliano), 757
(Conte)
Corigliano, John, **748–749**, 711 & 712 (Modern
United States), 757 (Conte), 760 (Whitacre)
Cornelius, Peter, **468–469**, 441 & 442 (Romantic
Austria and Germany)
Cornysh, William, **140–141**, 135 & 138 (Renais-
sance England), 143 (Taverner), 144 (Johnson),
148 (Tallis)
Costeley, Guillaume, **44–45**, 19 & 21 (Renaissance
France)
Couperin, François, **244–245**, 230 (Baroque
France), 243 (Bernier), 570 (Ravel)
Cowell, Henry, **719**, 711 (Modern United States)
Croce, Giovanni, **80**, 49 & 51 (Renaissance Italy),
137 (Renaissance England), 160 & 161 (Morley),
164 (Dowland), 166 (Cavendish), 167 (Kirbye),
179 (Dering)
Croft, William, **325–326**, 313 (Baroque England),
325 (J. Clarke), 534 (Sullivan)
Crotch, William, **525–526**, 525 (Romantic
England), 529 (Macfarren), 529 (Bennett)
Crüger, Johannes, **267**, 125 (Hassler), 251 (Baroque
Germany)
Cui, César, **507**, 502 & 504 (Romantic Russia), 510
(Rimsky-Korsakov)

D

D'India, Sigismondo, **86**, 49 (Renaissance Italy)
D'Indy, Vincent, **434–435**, 409 (Romantic France),
422 (C. Franck), 431 (Fauré), 561 (Villa-Lobos),
566 (Canteloube), 573 (Honegger)
Daley, Eleanor, **564**, 560 (Modern Introduction)
Dallapiccola, Luigi, **614–616**, 609 & 610 (Modern
Italy and Spain), 619 (Berio), 663 (Hovland),
743 (Argento)
David, Johann Nepomuk, **599–600**, 589 (Modern
Austria and Germany)
Davies, Sir Peter Maxwell, **704–705**, 672 (Modern
England), 692 (Berkeley)
Debussy, Claude, **567–569**, 559 & 560 (Modern
Introduction), 562 (Estévez), 564 & 565 (Mod-
ern France and Switzerland), 569 & 570 (Ravel),
573 (Honegger), 583 (Jolivet), 584 (Badings), 585
(Messiaen), 597 (Hindemith), 610 (Modern Italy
and Spain), 610 (Falla), 614 (Dallapiccola), 628
(Szymanowski), 691 (Walton)
Delibes, Léo, **426–427**, 409 (Romantic France)
Delius, Frederick, **674–675**, 672 & 673 (Modern
England), 673 (Moeran), 688 (Warlock)
Della Valle, Pietro, **197**, 191 (Baroque Italy)
Dello Joio, Norman, **730–732**, 553 (MacDowell),
711 & 712 (Modern United States)
Demantius, Christoph, **127–128**, 100 (Renaissance
Germany and Austria), 129 (Vulpius), 132

Marenzio, Luca, **75–77**, 45 (Philips), 49, 50, 51
(Renaissance Italy), 74 (Vecchi), 83 (Gesualdo),
86 (d'India), 121 (Lechner), 125 (Hassler), 137
(Renaissance England), 158 (Byrd), 164 (Dow-
land), 192 (Monteverdi), 209 (A. Scarlatti), 213
(Lotti), 215 (Caldara)

Martin, Frank, **571–573**, 564 & 565 (Modern France
and Switzerland)

Martini, Padre Giovanni Battista, **224–225**,
190–191 (Baroque Italy), 229 (Gasparini), 310 &
311 (J. Christian Bach), 353 (Soler), 361 (Gassmann), 362 (Adlgasser), 376 (W. A. Mozart),
388 (Jommelli), 393 (Rossini), 440 (Puccini)

Martinů, Bohuslav, **629–630**, 621 (Modern Hungary, Poland, and the Czech Republic), 631
(Seiber)

Mason, Lowell, **546–547**, 545 & 546 (Romantic
United States)

Massenet, Jules, **428–430**, 409 (Romantic France),
431 (Fauré), 434 (d'Indy), 565 (Ropartz), 565
(Koechlin)

Mathias, William, **703–704**, 692 (Berkeley)

Mattheson, Johann, **286**, 222 (Marcello), 243
(Gilles), 251 (Baroque Germany), 288 (Telemann), 302 (Graun), 326 (Handel)

Mechem, Kirke, **742–743**, 711 (Modern United
States)

Mellnäs, Arne, **668–669**, 653 (Modern Sweden,
Norway, Denmark, and Finland)

Mendelssohn, Felix, **450–456**, 87 (Allegri), 398
(Attwood), 399 (S. Wesley), 408 (Romantic
Introduction), 412 (Berlioz), 418 (Gounod),
429 (Massenet), 441 & 442 (Romantic Austria
and Germany), 449 (Hensel), 457, 458, 460
(R. Schumann), 468 (Cornelius), 470 (Bruckner), 483 (Bruch), 484 (Rheinberger), 488 &
489 (Dvořák), 494 (Mahler), 500 (Reger), 510
(Rimsky-Korsakov), 524 & 525 (Romantic England), 529 (Macfarren), 529 & 530 (Bennett),
533 (Sullivan), 537 (Stanford), 544 (Coleridge-
Taylor), 545 & 546 (Romantic United States),
547 & 548 (Bristow), 550 & 551 (Buck), 611
(Casals), 715 (Ives)

Mendes, Gilberto, 562 & 563 (Modern Introduction)

Menotti, Gian Carlo, **729–730**, 711 & 712 (Modern
United States), 726 (Barber)

Merulo, Claudio, **68**, 49 (Renaissance Italy), 65
(Porta), 73 (Vecchi), 78 (G. Gabrieli), 124 (Hassler)

Messiaen, Olivier, **585–587**, 559 & 560 (Modern
Introduction), 564 & 565 (Modern France and
Switzerland), 583 (Jolivet), 622 (Kurtág), 714
(Bolcom)

Milhaud, Darius, **575–576**, 430 (Widor), 561 (Villa-
Lobos), 564 (Modern France and Switzerland),

573 (Honegger), 619 (Berio), 622 (Kurtág), 714
(Bolcom), 722 (Copland), 736 (Brubeck), 747
(Hennagin)

Moeran, E. J., **673**

Mondonville, Jean-Joseph Cassanéa de, **247–248**,
231 (Baroque France)

Monte, Philippe de, **60–61**, 48, 49, 50, 51 (Renaissance Italy), 71 (Striggio), 112 & 113 (Lasso), 119
(Regnart), 119 (Handl)

Monteverdi, Claudio, **191–196**, 38 (Gombert), 50
(Renaissance Italy), 69 (Wert), 70 (Ingegneri),
70 (Striggio), 128 (Demantius), 132 (M. Praetorius), 135 (Renaissance England), 179 (Dering),
190 & 191 (Baroque Italy), 197 (Grandi), 197 &
198 (Cavalli), 198 (Carissimi), 202 (Strozzi), 214
(Caldara), 252 & 255 (Schütz), 267 (Crüger), 270
(Buxtehude), 276 (J. M. Bach), 579 (Poulenc),
600 (Orff), 606 (Distler), 611 (Malipiero), 662
& 663 (Edlund), 664 (Werle), 694 (Tippett), 751
(Lauridsen)

Morales, Cristóbal de, **90–92**, 38 (Gombert), 52
(Verdelot), 52 (C. Festa), 62 (Palestrina), 87 &
88 (Renaissance Spain and the New World), 92
(Guerrero), 96 (Victoria), 346 (Baroque Spain
and the New World)

Morley, Thomas, **160–163**, 18 (Renaissance Introduction), 71 (A. Ferrabosco), 80 (Croce), 137 &
138 (Renaissance England), 156 (Byrd), 166 (Farnaby), 166 (Cavendish), 168 (Jones), 171 (Pilkington), 175 (Wilbye), 177 (Weelkes), 527 (Pearsall)

Mosto, Giovanni Battista, **51**

Mouton, Jean, **34–35**, 19, 20, 21 (Renaissance
France), 37 (Sermisy), 53 & 54 (Willaert), 55 (Arcadelt), 90 (Morales), 112 (Vaet)

Mozart, Leopold, **360–361**, 311 (J. Christian Bach),
357 & 358 (Classical Austria and Germany), 375
(W. A. Mozart)

Mozart, Wolfgang Amadeus, **375–381**, 87 (Allegri),
224 (Martini), 229 (Gasparini), 251 (Baroque
Germany), 307 (C. P. E. Bach), 311 (J. Christian
Bach), 321 (Purcell), 356 (Classical Introduction), 357 (Classical Austria and Germany), 360
(Eberlin), 360 (L. Mozart), 362 (Adlgasser), 363
(J. Haydn), 370 (Albrechtsberger), 371 & 372 (M.
Haydn), 381 & 382 (Hummel), 382 (Schubert),
392 (Cherubini), 393 (Rossini), 398 (Attwood),
399 (S. Wesley), 407 & 408 (Romantic Introduction), 424 (Saint-Saëns), 428 (Massenet),
442 (Romantic Austria and Germany), 445 (Beethoven), 450 (Mendelssohn), 461 & 462 (Liszt),
470 (Bruckner), 483 (Bruch), 484 & 485 (Rheinberger), 488 (Dvořák), 494 (Mahler), 497
(Strauss), 502 (Romantic Russia), 505 (Bortnyans'ky), 506 (Glinka), 507 (Tchaikovsky), 525
(Crotch), 529 (Bennett), 545 (Romantic United
States), 547 (Mason), 597 (Hindemith), 610

(Busoni), 614 (Dallapiccola), 623 (Janáček), 641 (Stravinsky), 643 (Kreek)

Mundy, William, **153–154**, 138 (Renaissance England), 155 (White)

Musgrave, Thea, **700–701**

N

Nanino, Giovanni Bernardino, 72 (G. M. Nanino)

Nanino, Giovanni Maria, **72**, 45 (Philips), 49 & 50 (Renaissance Italy), 80 (F. Anerio), 86 (Allegri)

Nelhybel, Vaclav, **713**, 712 (Modern United States)

Nenna, Pomponio, 84 (Gesualdo)

Nicolai, Philipp, **123**, 99 & 100 (Renaissance Germany and Austria), 297 & 298 (J. S. Bach), 310 (J. C. F. Bach)

Nielsen, Carl, **655–656**, 653 & 654 (Modern Sweden, Norway, Denmark, and Finland)

Nikol'sky, Aleksandr, 504 (Romantic Russia)

Nivers, Guillaume-Gabriel, **233–234**, 231 (Baroque France), 243 (Bernier), 245 (Clérambault)

Nono, Luigi, **618–619**, 609 & 610 (Modern Italy and Spain), 623 (Kurtág), 674 (Bedford)

Nørgård, Per, **666–668**, 653 (Modern Sweden, Norway, Denmark, and Finland), 669 (Sandström)

Nystedt, Knut, **660–661**, 653 & 654 (Modern Sweden, Norway, Denmark, and Finland)

O

Obrecht, Jacob, **33–34**, 19, 20, 21 (Renaissance France), 26 (Busnois), 28 (Agricola), 35 (Brumel), 38 (Gombert), 102 & 103 (Isaac)

Ockeghem, Jean de, **24–26**, 6 (Medieval Introduction), 17 (Renaissance Introduction), 19, 20, 21 (Renaissance France), 22 (Dufay), 26 (Busnois), 27 (Compère), 28 (Agricola), 29 & 30 (Desprez), 33 (La Rue), 34 (Obrecht), 36 (Brumel), 41 (Certon), 603 (Krenek)

Oliveros, Pauline, **746–747**, 711 (Modern United States)

Orbán, György, **638**, 621 (Modern Hungary, Poland, and the Czech Republic)

Orff, Carl, **600–601**, 589 (Modern Austria and Germany)

O'Regan, Tarik, **710**

Orrego-Salas, Juan, **562**, 560 (Modern Introduction)

Othmayr, Caspar, **110–111**, 100 (Renaissance Germany and Austria)

P

Pachelbel, Johann, **277–279**, 251 (Baroque Germany)

Padilla, Juan Gutiérrez de, **348–349**, 346 (Baroque

Spain and the New World), 347 (Fernandes), 349 (Capillas)

Paine, John Knowles, **548–550**, 545 & 546 (Romantic United States), 552 (Foote)

Palestrina, Giovanni Pierluigi da, **61–65**, 18 & 19 (Renaissance Introduction), 35 (Brumel), 46 (Philips), 49, 50, 51 (Renaissance Italy), 52 (Verdelot), 54 (Willaert), 58 (D. M. Ferrabosco), 60 (Monte), 65 (Porta), 67 (A. Gabrieli), 72 (G. M. Nanino), 80 & 81 (F. Anerio), 81 (G. F. Anerio), 88 (Renaissance Spain and the New World), 90 (Morales), 95 & 96 (Victoria), 113, 114, 115 (Lasso), 124 & 125 (Hassler), 137 (Renaissance England), 167 (Kirbye), 172 (Tomkins), 181 (Gibbons), 207 (Pitoni), 209 (A. Scarlatti), 281 (Fux), 346 (Baroque Spain and the New World), 347 (Comes), 349 (Capillas), 392 (Cherubini), 399 (S. Wesley), 408 (Romantic Introduction), 418 (Gounod), 427 (Dubois), 442 (Romantic Austria and Germany), 448 (Loewe), 450 (Mendelssohn), 456 (R. Schumann), 463 (Liszt), 526 (Pearsall), 567 (Debussy), 623 (Janáček), 656 (Nielsen)

Parker, Alice, **715**

Parker, Horatio, **554–555**, 545 & 546 (Romantic United States), 715 (Ives)

Parry, Sir Hubert, **534–536**, 524 (Romantic England), 537 & 538 (Stanford), 543 (Wood), 679 (Holst), 689 (Finzi)

Parsons, Robert, **154**, 138 (Renaissance England), 155 (Byrd)

Pärt, Arvo, **651–653**, 639 (Modern Russia and Estonia)

Pascual, Francisco, **352**, 346 (Baroque Spain and the New World)

Passereau, Pierre, **36**, 19 & 21 (Renaissance France), 37 (Janequin)

Paulus, Stephen, **754–755**, 711 & 712 (Modern United States), 755 (Larsen)

Pearsall, Robert Lucas, **526–527**, 525 (Romantic England)

Peñalosa, Francisco de, **90**, 27 (Compère), 87 & 88 (Renaissance Spain and the New World), 89 (Escobar)

Penderecki, Krzysztof, **635–638**, 621 (Modern Hungary, Poland, and the Czech Republic)

Pepping, Ernst, **604–605**, 560 (Modern Introduction), 589 (Modern Austria and Germany), 591 (Hessenburg), 670 (Kverno), 750 (Chihara)

Pergolesi, Giovanni Battista, **227–229**, 191 (Baroque Italy), 221 (Durante), 392 (Cherubini)

Perosi, Lorenzo, **610**, 609 (Modern Italy and Spain)

Pérotin, 5 (Medieval Introduction)

Persichetti, Vincent, **733–734**, 560 (Modern Introduction), 664 (Rautavaara), 711 & 712 (Modern United States), 745 (Druckman), 747 (Escot)

S